1,000,000 Books
are available to read at

Forgotten Books

www.ForgottenBooks.com

Read online
Download PDF
Purchase in print

ISBN 978-1-5279-2913-5
PIBN 10944001

This book is a reproduction of an important historical work. Forgotten Books uses state-of-the-art technology to digitally reconstruct the work, preserving the original format whilst repairing imperfections present in the aged copy. In rare cases, an imperfection in the original, such as a blemish or missing page, may be replicated in our edition. We do, however, repair the vast majority of imperfections successfully; any imperfections that remain are intentionally left to preserve the state of such historical works.

Forgotten Books is a registered trademark of FB &c Ltd.
Copyright © 2018 FB &c Ltd.
FB &c Ltd, Dalton House, 60 Windsor Avenue, London, SW19 2RR.
Company number 08720141. Registered in England and Wales.

For support please visit www.forgottenbooks.com

1 MONTH OF FREE READING

at

www.ForgottenBooks.com

By purchasing this book you are eligible for one month membership to ForgottenBooks.com, giving you unlimited access to our entire collection of over 1,000,000 titles via our web site and mobile apps.

To claim your free month visit:

www.forgottenbooks.com/free944001

* Offer is valid for 45 days from date of purchase. Terms and conditions apply.

English
Français
Deutsche
Italiano
Español
Português

www.forgottenbooks.com

Mythology Photography **Fiction** Fishing Christianity **Art** Cooking Essays Buddhism Freemasonry Medicine **Biology** Music **Ancient Egypt** Evolution Carpentry Physics Dance Geology **Mathematics** Fitness Shakespeare **Folklore** Yoga Marketing **Confidence** Immortality Biographies Poetry **Psychology** Witchcraft Electronics Chemistry History **Law** Accounting **Philosophy** Anthropology Alchemy Drama Quantum Mechanics Atheism Sexual Health **Ancient History Entrepreneurship** Languages Sport Paleontology Needlework Islam **Metaphysics** Investment Archaeology Parenting Statistics Criminology **Motivational**

THE WESTERN
JOURNAL OF EDUCATION

ESTABLISHED 1852.

OLD SERIES: GOLDEN ERA, VOL. XLVI.   SAN FRANCISCO, JANUARY, 1903.   NEW SERIES: VOL. VIII NUMBER 1

State Aid to Secondary Schools

DAVID RHYS JONES

[NOTE.—In view of the recent adoption of a constitutional amendment in this state, empowering the legislature to raise money by general tax for the maintenance of high schools, there is very general interest in the question, how the proceeds of such tax, if it shall be imposed, may best be distributed. In order to an intelligent determination of this question, it is very desirable that the experience of other states in dealing with a similar question should be consulted. The paper which follows will offer much of information relative to the history of state aid to secondary education in some of the most progressive of our sister states. The writer, Mr. David Rhys Jones, a graduate of the University of Wisconsin, who has had experience as teacher and principal in the high schools of Wisconsin and in the elementary schools of California, has recently been appointed Reader in Education in the University of California. This paper is a preliminary draft of his thesis for the Master's degree in our University.—ELMER E. BROWN.]

Good governments, like good citizens, possess certain well-defined virtues. The history of state and federal aid to education furnishes one of the best examples of governmental virtue in effective operation. Realizing that in no better way could the general welfare be promoted and the larger blessings of liberty be secured to the people than by their enlightenment, the national government has given to the states for educational purposes more than two hundred and fifty thousand square miles of land, or more than the combined areas of the states of New Hampshire, Massachusetts, New York, New Jersey, Pennsylvania, Ohio, Indiana, and Illinois. The proceeds of the sales of these lands constitutes about eighty per cent of the permanent school funds of the states. Referring to the increased provision for education, W. T. Harris says*: "The national government bases itself on the ability of the people as people to govern themselves thru the ballot-box. The history of education shows how it has seemed fit to make provision for the enlightenment of those citizens. It has grown clear in the process of ages that the only help which may be safely given to individuals or communities is the help that aids and increases self-help. All other help dwarfs the individual and weakens the state. Now, the only infallible aid to self-help that has been found up to this time is education which produces intellectual enlightenment and training in moral habits. This alone is help that is good

* Editor's Preface, "Education in the United States," by Richard G. Boone.

alike for sound and perverse. It improves the former and corrects the latter. This view of education has been seen by the fathers of the republic and preached by the religious founders of our colonies. The conviction has become so generally prevalent that it has produced the joint action—private, national, state, and municipal—looking toward the foundation and encouragement of schools and supplementary institutions."

In this paper a brief review of the attitude of the several states towards the encouragement of secondary education, as seen in the granting of special aid to such schools, will be followed by a more detailed account of the present systems in a few of the most progressive states.

COLONIAL PERIOD

At the outbreak of the Revolutionary War but four of the present states had well-defined systems of public schools, viz: Massachusetts, New Hampshire, Connecticut, and Maryland. Other colonies, however, had at various times taken action toward the encouragement of schools, including schools of a secondary grade. Their establishment was often brought about by the action of legislative bodies in the colonies, and grants of land ranging from six hundred acres to five thousand acres each were made to the various schools. Massachusetts made an appropriation of a thousand acres each to several of her schools; while Connecticut required a school to be maintained in every county and granted to the support of each of these schools six hundred acres of land. Various revenues accruing to the colonies were given to the support of schools of this class; and in some colonies a stated sum was annually appropriated for their support. The promotion of learning was regarded not only as a moral and religious duty; but also as a civic responsibility.

THE ACADEMY PERIOD

The period of the academies may be regarded as extending from the Revolutionary War to the close of the Civil War. These institutions were founded by private initiative or were ecclesiastical undertakings in response to religious enthusiasm. They relieved the impoverished communities of the necessity of maintaining at public expense schools of an intermediate character. Recognizing their service for the promotion of education, the newly-formed states, with but little else to give, gave liberally of their lands for the support of these schools, and when better able made liberal appropriations of money also. Several of the states found it necessary to adopt some definite system of granting aid to these schools. In some states they were given one-half of a township of land; in others they received their respective portions of an annual appropriation of money; while the most of the states aided them according to their needs, with but little of uniformity in the amounts granted. In Tennessee and Kentucky these schools were supported by extensive land grants, ranging from six thousand acres to twelve thousand acres to each school. Pennsylvania, in 1843, had over one hundred academies and seminaries that had together received nearly half a million dollars from the treasury of the state; while the total amounts expended for this purpose exceeded two millions of dollars in New York and also in Louisiana. In Louisiana each school was required to admit without fees a certain number of indigent pupils; and in some states these schools received aid from the state in recognition of their services in the training of teachers for the common schools. No other conditions than these two seem to have been imposed upon the state-aided schools. Their service in the education of the youth of the land seemed to justify the states in their policy of liberal support

THE HIGH SCHOOL PERIOD

The academies in many states were not accessible to the large majority of qualified pupils. Only in exceptional cases were these schools free to those in attendance, and many miles of travel and long absences from home were necessary to enjoy the advantages offered by them. The rise of the public high school is part of a widespread movement toward organizing under public control a complete system of educational institutions. By the close of the Civil War the public high school had become an established factor in education, although it was not until twenty years later that it overtook the academies in the enrollment of students. In the most of these states these schools were a part of the common school system of the state and maintained in the same manner as the elementary schools; while in a few states they were entirely independent of them. In either case the burden of their support generally rests upon the district in which they are located. Where they are a part of the common school system of the state, the apportioned public school money is usually much less than the cost of maintaining the elementary schools; and the cost of maintaining a high school becomes an additional burden upon the local community. With but few possible exceptions, such schools have been established by voluntary action of the various communities in which they are found. No better proof of this can be had than the experience of states having laws requiring their establishment. At least fifty-four towns in Massachusetts, not obliged by law to maintain a high school, are at present supporting such schools. Wherever they are found they have appeared in response to a public demand and are a worthy testimony to the spirit of the American people in educational matters. Every city points with just pride to its public high school, while villages and rural communities have equal, if not greater cause to be proud of the excellent schools which a progressive spirit has provided. Possibly no other single feature of our smaller cities and villages is more frequently used than this as a criterion for judging the character of the community. Changes in the social, industrial, and commercial world have brought with them a demand for a better preparation for the duties of life. The public high schools have grown up in response to these demands. Their number in the United States increased from 2,526 in 1890 to 6,005 in 1900, and the number of students from 202,963 to 519,251 in the same period; and the income from tuition fees in these schools increased from $404,973 in

1890 to $537,576 in 1900. While the burden of their support is comparatively easy upon the larger cities, their maintenance is a heavy drain upon the resources of the smaller cities and villages, and many communities are unable to provide such means of educating their children. As a result of this condition many of the most deserving pupils are obliged to discontinue their studies at the end of the elementary course; while others are obliged to accept the work of a very inferior but somewhat advanced school in lieu of a good high school education.

RECENT LEGISLATION

The modern movement in legislation affecting high schools aims to extend to all qualified pupils the opportunity of obtaining a free secondary education in well-equipped and properly classified public high schools. To this end all taxable property within the state is made to contribute to the support of high schools, as well as to the support of elementary schools and universities. There is an unmistakable effort to extend to pupils in rural sections the advantages that have hitherto been available only to those residing in the more populous centers. Experience has shown that when the educational forces of a state are agreed as to what is for the best interests of the children of the state, the people are generally willing and ready to provide it.

In at least eleven of the most progressive states recent legislation has been enacted relative to the granting of state aid to high schools, or for the purpose of making such schools free to all qualified pupils of the state. In Maine the high schools and academies receive state aid, ranging from two hundred and fifty dollars to one thousand dollars each annually, with the proviso that they admit all qualified students without the payment of fees; in New Hampshire, towns not maintaining high schools are obliged to pay the tuition fees of their residents who may attend such schools elsewhere. Five thousand dollars is annually raised by the state to reimburse the weaker towns for this expenditure; and all schools classified as high schools or approved academies must maintain a four-year course preparatory to college or technical school or normal school, and be approved by the superintendent of public instruction. When a pupil has completed the full course in any school of New Jersey, and is obliged to go elsewhere for more advanced work, the district in which such pupil is a resident must pay the amount of tuition fees agreed upon between the boards of the two schools concerned. The provision in Ohio is similar to this, with the exception that in Ohio the boards of two adjoining districts may enter into an agreement by which all pupils of a district not maintaining a high school are to be instructed in a neighboring high school for an amount agreed upon by the two boards. Under such circumstances the pupil is expected to attend the school selected. In Massachusetts, the duty of providing the means of obtaining a secondary education rests upon each community, and where the community is not able to provide the means, it has been required to pay the tuition fees of its residents attending high schools in other towns. The recent modifications of this law will be presented more fully in the discussion of the system of that state in another part of this paper. Wisconsin, after extending aid to the free high schools of the state for twenty-five years, has recently provided that where a town, part of a town, or city is not included within a high school district, the amount of tuition fees for residents of such communities shall be entered upon the tax roll of the town, part of the town or city not within a free high school district, and be paid by the town or city treasurer to the treasurer of the school furnishing such instruction. A more detailed account of the system of this state will follow, as will also an account of the Minnesota system. In Minnesota, each regularly organized state high school receives from the state one thousand dollars annually, and must instruct all qualified pupils without payment of fees. The high schools of North Dakota are classified as four-year, three-year, and two-year schools, and the various schools of each class receive annually from the state the sum of one hundred and seventy-five dollars, one hundred and forty dollars, and one hundred dollars respectively. Nebraska, in her second attempt to extend to all qualified pupils a free secondary education, requires the careful estimate of the actual cost per pupil in such high schools as have been declared by the boards to be open to non-resident pupils, and the county, or part of the county, not included within a high school district, in which any given child is a resident, is obliged to pay the actual cost of the instruction of such child, when he shall have attended such public high school. When this amount exceeds seventy-five cents per week for each pupil, the excess is paid from the funds of the state. All such high schools must be approved by the state superintendent of public instruction and by him declared "to be properly equipped as to teachers, appliances and course of study." An earlier law fixing the amount of tuition fees at three dollars per month was declared unconstitutional, as that amount was not in all cases the actual cost of services rendered.

Where the state is able to extend but a limited amount of aid to the high schools, the granting of this aid on the condition that all charges for the instruction of non-resident students be discontinued, would not be of material advantage to some of the schools in the smaller cities and villages, which are now enabled to carry on the work of a high school by their revenue from tuition fees; while other schools having but few such pupils would receive a much larger additional revenue. The large amount given to each school in Minnesota makes the elimination of all tuition fees possible. This might be effected without material injustice to any school, by distributing a part of the appropriation on the basis of the number of non-resident students enrolled in the schools.

The provisions for manual training departments and for industrial education must be passed with mention of but three. In Massachusetts, every community of twenty thousand inhabitants is required to maintain a manual training department in connection with the high school and also in connection with the grades. New Jersey duplicates from the state funds all amounts between two hundred and fifty dollars and five thousand dollars raised by taxation or subscription or both for the establishment of manual training departments in connection with the public schools, or for the establishment of a manual training school. It is provided that no school shall receive more than five thousand dollars for this purpose in any one year. In Wisconsin, each school maintaining a manual training department receives two hundred and fifty dollars annually. A special appropriation of five thousand dollars is made for this purpose.

The development of the high school system of four of the states, Massachusetts, New York, Wisconsin, and Minnesota, will be reviewed in the following pages as representing the growth of the movement toward systematic aid to high schools, and embodying the customary provisions for the granting of such aid.

MASSACHUSETTS

The first legal provision for secondary education in Massachusetts dates back to 1647, when every town of one hundred families was obliged to maintain a grammar school that would prepare its students for entrance to the university. This was but enacting into law what the more populous sections of the colony had already done of their own accord. This law was frequently modified to conform to the varying vicissitudes thru which the colony was forced to pass until 1826, when a law was enacted requiring every town of five hundred families to maintain a high school. This law, with but occasional deviations, has remained to the present time. Under its provisions one hundred and eighty-five of the three hundred and fifty-three towns in the state would not be required to maintain a high school, while at present at least fifty-four of these towns are supporting such schools.

In 1891, a law was passed requiring every town not supporting a high school to pay for the tuition of its qualified pupils in the high schools of other towns or cities, and should it see fit, for their conveyance also. In 1895, the state began to reimburse towns whose valuation was less than $500,000, for amounts expended by them for the tuition of high school pupils. This law was considerably modified in 1902, to keep pace with public sentiment. The present law requires towns of more than five hundred families to support public high schools without receiving aid from the state; while towns of less than this number are grouped into five classes:

1. Towns whose valuation averages a larger sum for each pupil in the average membership of their puplic schools than the corresponding average for the commonwealth. These are not entitled to state aid if maintaining a high school, nor to reimbursements for amounts expended for the tuition of pupils attending high school elsewhere.

2. Towns without high schools of their own and with a valuation of less than $750,000 each. These are entitled to the full amount expended for the tuition of qualified pupils attending any of the approved high schools in the state.

3. Towns without high schools of their own and with a valuation of more

than $750,000 each. These are reimbursed for one-half the amount expended for such tuition.

4. Towns that maintain high schools of their own with two or more teachers each. Such towns are entitled to receive annually from the treasury of the commonwealth toward the support of such high school the sum of three hundred dollars.

5. Towns that maintain high schools of their own with only one teacher each. These receive no aid from the state.

There are at present twenty-four towns of the first class, eighty-nine of the second class, eighteen of the third class, thirty-three of the fourth class, and twenty-one of the fifth class. The act continues, "and no expenditure shall be made by the commonwealth on account of high school instruction under the provisions of this section unless the high school in which such instruction is furnished has been approved by the [state] board of education."

It is the evident intent of this law to secure to each child the opportunities of obtaining a secondary education, and at the same time to protect the child against the injustice of having to accept under the name of high school education that which does not come up to the high school standard. In this respect the schools are following the lead of the business world, which demands laws to protect it against adulterated goods bearing labels that would lead the consumer to suppose them genuine. It is provided that if the towns now attempting to carry on high school work in schools of but one teacher will give up the attempt and send their pupils to neighboring high schools, or if they will build up an approved school of two or more teachers, they will be entitled to state aid in the same manner as other schools.

All approved high schools must meet the following requirements: *

1. That it shall be "adequately equipped" and be "kept by a principal and such assistants as may be needed, of competent ability and good morals."

2. That it shall give instruction in designated subjects, "as the school committee consider expedient to be taught in the high school, and in such additional subjects as may be required for the general purpose of training and culture, as well as for the purpose of preparing pupils for admission to state and normal schools, technical schools and colleges."

3. That it shall maintain "one or more courses of study, at least four years in length."

4. And that it "shall be kept open for the benefit of all the inhabitants of the city or town for at least forty weeks, exclusive of vacations, in each year."

The method of distributing the proceeds of the general fund of the state is deserving of careful study. The permanent school fund is now considerably in excess of four millions of dollars, and an annual addition of one hundred thousand dollars is made to it until the fund shall amount to five millions, at which figure it is to remain.

*Massachusetts School Document, No. 8, 1902.

Section 4. One-half of the annual income of said school fund shall, without a specific appropriation, be apportioned and distributed for the support of public schools in the following manner: every town which complies with all laws relative to the distribution of said income and whose valuation of real and personal property, as shown by the last preceding assessors' valuation thereof does not exceed one-half million dollars shall annually receive three hundred dollars; but if its rate of taxation for any year shall be eighteen dollare or more on a thousand dollars, it shall receive fifty dollars additional; every such town whose valuation is more than one-half million dollars and does not exceed one million dollars shall receive two hundred dollars; and every such town whose valuation is more than one million dollars and does not exceed two million dollars shall receive one hundred dollars; and every such town whose valuation is more than two million dollars and does not exceed three million dollars shall receive fifty dollars. The remainder of said half shall be distributed to towns whose valuation does not exceed three million dollars and whose annual tax for the support of the public schools is not less than one-sixth of their whole tax for the year, as follows: every town whose school tax is not less than one-third of its whole tax shall receive a proportion of said remainder expressed by one-third; every town whose school tax is not less than one-fourth of its whole tax shall receive a proportion expressed by one-fourth; every such town whose school tax is not less than one-fifth of its whole tax shall receive a proportion expressed by one-fifth; and every such town whose school tax is not less than one-sixth of its whole tax shall receive a proportion expressed by one-sixth. All money appropriated for other educational purposes, unless otherwise provided, shall be paid from the other half of said income. If the income in any year exceeds such appropriations, the surplus shall be added to the principal of such fund.

It will be noted that no town whose valuation exceeds three millions of dollars is made to share in this distribution, and that one-half the annual income is reserved for the general school expenses of the commonwealth. In another section, it is provided that no town failing to comply with the requirements of the law in regard to high schools shall share in this distribution. The law evidently aims to help those who most need help, and who are most willing to help themselves.

NEW YORK

Having aided in the support of the early Latin grammar schools, New York contributed liberally to the promotion of secondary education after the turbulent wars of the second half of the eighteenth century had passed and academies had begun to be established by private and religious enterprise. Regarding it as the duty of the state to "promote the gospel and the public school," the legislatures made liberal grants for the maintenance of these early schools, which otherwise could not have carried on their work. When the revenues from land grants proved insufficient, a money appropriation was added.

In 1784, the University of the State of New York was established, and its organization was made to include all secondary schools in the state, whether public or private. In 1813, a plan for permanent and systematic aid to such schools was provided by the establishment of a "Literature Fund," whose income was set apart for the support of the various academies, as was deemed "just and equitable." This fund at first amounted to a little over ten thousand dollars, and has been constantly increasing. In 1893 it amounted to over two hundred and eighty thousand dollars. Up to 1900, more than two million dollars had been apportioned to the secondary schools of New York; and more than sixty special grants of land and money in addition had been made to various academies in immediate need of assistance. The annual appropriations increased from ten thousand dollars in 1830 to one hundred thousand dollars in 1887, and to three hundred and fifty thousand dollars in 1902. Of this twenty-eight thousand dollars is income from the United States deposit of 1836, a considerable portion is income from the Literature Fund, and the rest comes from the general fund of the state. Thirty thousand dollars is annually appropriated from the income of the deposit of 1836 for the maintenance of normal classes in the various academies. These classes are limited to twenty-five students each, and the academy receives from the state one dollar per week for the instruction of each scholar.

The general school law of 1864 provided for the establishment of academical departments in any of the union free school districts where such grade of instruction was demanded. These departments were subject to the control of the regents, and shared like the regular academies in the distribution of state moneys. This was a part of the movement to provide secondary education by means of public high schools. A provision was at this time made whereby the property of private institutions might be transferred to public control.

Up to 1886 there was no well-organized plan of distribution of the state subsidy that seemed satisfactory. There seems, however, to have been a decided tendency toward the apportioning of at least a part of the money upon the basis of certain specified conditions pertaining to the school—such as the number of students pursuing certain studies, or according to the number of students enrolled in the schools. A fixed amount to each school, irrespective of the work or of the needs of the school seems never to have been a common practice. In this particular, the policy of the state has been maintained to the present time, and stands in marked contrast to that of other states which aid in the maintenance of secondary schools. In 1866 a plan was put in force for determining the amount to be apportioned to each school. Examinations were instituted, certificates were issued and reports to the regents were made accordingly. In 1870 the answer papers in these examinations were made returnable to the office of the regents and were there subject to review and revision. At one time, thirty-four per cent of all appropriations were made upon the basis of these returns. The remaining sixty-six per cent were distributed as follows: Each school received annually one hundred dollars, besides one cent for each day's attendance as shown by the school register, and an amount equal to that raised by the school for general equipment, not to exceed five hundred dollars in one year. In 1898, the secretary of the high school department of the university recommended that further distribution on the basis of examination returns be discontinued.

In accordance with this recommendation the method of payment by results has been discontinued and apportionments are now made as follows: (a) one hundred dollars is allowed to each school approved by the regents without regard to its size or special attainments; (b) a sum not exceeding two hundred and fifty dollars for the purchase of approved books and apparatus is allowed each school raising for the same purpose an equal amount from local sources; (c) the balance of the fund is distributed on the basis of total attendance of academic students, provided that each student whose attendance is so counted must hold a "regents' preliminary certificate" for admission to the school, or the school must have been approved by two university inspectors, as having a higher entrance requirement than the minimum prescribed for the preliminary certificate. Of the three hundred and fifty thousand dollars appropriated for this purpose under the present laws, about twenty per cent will be distributed under item (a), about fifteen per cent under item (b), and about sixty-five per cent under item (c).

Regents' examinations are held in January and June in seventy-three subjects, covering all the courses in the high school curriculum, and in March in twenty-six subjects only. In 1901, these examinations were taken by six hundred and ninety nine of the seven hundred and forty-one secondary schools in the university. Each diploma issued by the regents to a graduate of a secondary school shows on its face the subjects in which its holder has passed regents' examinations. These diplomas are accepted in lieu of entrance examinations in the subjects which they cover by institutions of higher education not only in New York state but also generally thruout the United States. As the regents' preliminary examinations furnish the standard for admission to the secondary schools, their influence extends to all the lower grades, and large numbers of pupils from the ungraded rural schools take these tests in the neighboring high schools and academies. *

To carry on this work efficiently, a large staff of examiners is required and nine school inspectors, one of whom is an inspector of apparatus.

MINNESOTA.†

To Minnesota belongs the distinction of being the first state in the union to provide free secondary instruction in public high schools for all qualified pupils of the state. The constitutional convention of 1857 declared it the "duty of the legislature * * * * to cherish the interests of education * * * and to establish a general system of public schools * * * and to adopt all means which they may deem necessary and proper to secure to the people the advantages and opportunities of education." The successive legislatures have been earnest in the endeavor to perform this duty; and it is but just to say that they have discharged so important a trust with much credit to themselves as well as with inestimable benefits to the people of the state.

The early secondary schools of the state were little more than advanced

---

*From advance sheets of "The Making of Our Middle Schools," by Elmer E. Brown. Published by Longmans, Green, & Co., New York.

†Copies of recent reports relative to the high schools of Minnesota were received from J. W. Olson, state superintendent of public instruction.

elementary schools, and the few students completing the work of these schools found their preparation so deficient that they were not prepared to take up the work of the state university. The instruction offered in the academies was so much superior to that of the public high schools that nearly all students desiring to continue their studies beyond the secondary schools were obliged to attend these private institutions. In 1869 William W. Folwell was appointed president of the University of Minnesota, and in his first report he urged the necessity of a better organization of the public school system of the state. Referring to the secondary schools, he said: "Our system of public instruction will not be an organized whole until the 'secondary' schools are graded not merely with reference to the primary schools below but to the university above. This can be done not only without detriment, but with advantage to that great class of students who will choose to content themselves with academic education only." This was the beginning of the movement that has finally resulted in the establishment of "a complete, continuous, and efficient system of schools which should offer to every child in Minnesota a liberal education."

This suggestion, however, was not acted upon immediately. The need was beginning to be felt, but the plan to be followed was not altogether evident. In 1872, the state superintendent of schools appointed a committee consisting of the city superintendent of Winona, Minneapolis, and Red Wing to suggest some plan for securing a course of study in the high schools that would be preparatory to the State University. In the fall of the same year, President Folwell appeared before the convention of the city and county superintendents and invited them "to join in an endeavor to bring about a vital, organic connection between the university and the high schools." At that time no state had organized or provided for an adequate system of schools between the elementary schools and the state university; nor was there at that time any well-defined relation between the then existing high schools and the universities, with the possible exception of the newly-established accrediting system of Michigan. President Folwell then advocated the organization of a comprehensive system embracing all grades, in which the state university "may form the 'roof and crown' of a noble structure of high schools based firmly on the broad foundation of the common schools of the state."

Two years later, 1875, State Superintendent Burt referred to the conditions that then existed in these words:

It is a fact that the best material for colleges and universities is scattered thro the agricultural parts of our state. It is not urban but rustic, while the high schools are not in the country, but in the city. This fact suggests the strongest form in which the question of state patronage for some of our high schools can be put. Should not the principal school of a county be open, free of charge for tuition, to the aspiring and worthy youth in the rural part of the county? Should such persons, partly at the expense of the state, be induced to enter upon a higher course of learning? Would it not conduce to the public welfare for the state to say to boards of education in our leading high schools,

Open your doors to all scholars in the rural districts prepared to enter your regular classes and willing to graduate and pass on to the courses of study in higher institutions, and you shall be compensated for the cost of furnishing instruction?

In August, 1877, the State Teachers' Association recommended that boards of education in the cities and larger villages make all possible effort to provide a course of instruction that would prepare for admission to the university, and that whenever possible, they admit outside students to those courses on liberal terms. Their resolution with reference to legislation upon this provision is worthy of note. It is the keynote to the purpose that is fast being realized in this state:

Resolved, That the legislature be requested to make suitable appropriation for paying the tuition of country students in the high schools of the state, so that a free education from ABC to the master of arts may be the birthright of every child in the state.

It might also be noted that here again the service of the able president of the university is evident, for the resolutions were written by President Folwell. The state was also favored in having about this time such men as Cushman K. Davis and John S. Pillsbury as governors, both of whom had in their annual messages urged such action upon the legislature.

The first high-school law was passed in 1878, but through omission of the word "annually" in the section providing an appropriation for these schools, the law became inoperative after one year. Its provisions were similar to those of the law of 1881, which is the foundation of the present high school system of the state.

The annual appropriation for the state high schools has been increased from twenty thousand dollars in 1881 to one hundred and fifteen thousand dollars in 1901, and the amount annually apportioned to each school has been increased from four hundred dollars to one thousand dollars in the same period. Four classes of schools are entitled to special state aid, as follows, viz.: 1. State high schools receive one thousand dollars each. The schools of this class are all four-year schools with courses of study adequate to prepare for admission to the collegiate department of the University of Minnesota. 2. State graded schools receive four hundred dollars each. These schools must have at least four departments in charge of a principal and teachers having such qualifications as may be required under the rules established by the state high school board. They are required to have "suitable school buildings, a substantial library and such other apparatus as is necessary for doing efficient work." 3. Semi-graded schools, or schools of two departments, are entitled to two hundred dollars each. 4. State rural schools of a single teacher are entitled to one hundred dollars each. The following annual appropriations are made: For aid to the state high schools, the sum of one hundred and fifteen thousand dollars; for aid to the graded schools, fifty-two thousand dollars; for aid to semi-graded schools, twenty-five thousand dollars; and sixty thousand dollars for aid to rural schools—a total of two hundred and fifty-two thousand dollars, "to be paid out of any moneys in the state treasury not otherwise appropriated." In 1902, one hundred and twenty graded schools and one hundred and forty-one state high schools were entitled to a share of this subsidy. An additional sum of five hundred dollars is given to each state high school giving instruction in the common branches "in a manner which shall be most helpful to persons intending to teach said branches." Ten thousand dollars is annually appropriated for this purpose.

Under the provisions of an act of 1901 the state superintendent of public instruction, the president of the University of Minnesota, ex-officio, and a superintendent or principal of any high school in the state of Minnesota, to be appointed by the governor, subject to confirmation by the senate, constitute a "state high school board." The members of this board serve without compensation, but are entitled to their actual and necessary expenses. They appoint a high school inspector and a graded school inspector, and make all rules and regulations relating to examinations, reports, acceptances of schools, courses of study and other proceedings in connection with high and graded schools claiming state aid. But an optional English or business course of study must be offered and maintained in addition to the course or courses of study required to be taken for admission to the state university.

Since 1885 a system of state examinations has been in operation. While the taking of this examination is ordinarily optional with the school, the state board may, however, require a school to take the examination as a part of the annual inspection. No grants of money are based on examination results. Their main purpose "is not to test the students, but to promote the general efficiency of the schools." All state high schools are "accredited" to the university on becoming established as approved schools.

The following laws relating to state high schools, and the rules and regulations of the high school board will aid in determining the standard set for approval of state high schools:

REQUISITES.—In order to be entitled to state aid as a state high school, such school shall have first fully complied with the following conditions, viz.:

First—It shall have maintained for the school year next preceding that for which aid is granted at least nine (9) months school.

Second—It shall admit students of either sex from any part of the state without charge for tuition, but no such school shall be required to admit nonresidents unless they shall pass an examination in all the common school branches pursued and completed in the eighth (8th) grade of the graded schools of this state, viz.: Arithmetic, English grammar, geography and United States history.

Third—It shall have regular and orderly courses of study, embracing all the branches prescribed by the state high school board, as prerequisite for admission to the collegiate department of the University of Minnesota.

Fourth—It shall be subject to such rules and regulations, not inconsistent with this act, as may be prescribed by the state high school board, and such school shall be open to visitation by any member of said board or the high school inspector at all times.

INSPECTIONS AND REPORTS.—The state high school board shall cause each high school receiving aid under this act to be visited at least once in each school year by the high school inspector or such assistant as it may appoint, who shall carefully inspect the instruction and discipline of the classes and make a written report on the same immediately, and no money shall be paid in any case until such report shall have been received and examined by the board, and the work of such school approved by a vote of said board.

DISCRETIONARY POWER OF BOARD.—The high school board shall have full discretionary power to consider and act upon applications of high schools for state aid, and, subject to the provisions of this act, may prescribe the conditions upon which such aid will be granted; and it shall be its duty to accept and aid such high schools only as will, in its opinion, if aided, efficiently perform the services contemplated by law; but not more than seven (7) schools shall be added in each county in any one year.

Any school accepted and continuing to comply with the law and regulations of the board made in pursuance thereof shall be aided not less than two (2) years.

In case any state graded school, as hereinafter provided, shall have attained such a degree of proficiency as to entitle it to promotion to a high school, and the state high schools in the county shall have already reached the number of seven (7), such graded school, in the discretion of the board, may be so promoted, and take the place of the high school in the county first receiving state aid for the period of at least two (2) years; that any state high school so deprived of state aid shall continue under the supervision of the board, with all the privileges, except state aid, of a preparatory school for the University of Minnesota.

RULES AND REGULATIONS OF THE STATE HIGH SCHOOL BOARD RELATING TO HIGH SCHOOLS

APPLICATIONS FOR STATE AID TO HIGH SCHOOLS

1. All applications for state aid shall be made to the secretary of the board on the official blank prepared for that purpose, and shall be made not later than October 1, during the school year for which aid is requested.

2. All applications shall be considered by the board, and schools considered worthy shall be accepted for supervision. Applications shall be considered at special meetings only in cases where delay in making application appears to have a valid reason.

3. The applications of schools accepted for supervision shall be referred to the high school inspector, whose duty it shall be to visit such schools during the ensuing school year and to submit a special report to the high school board at the next annual meeting.

4. At the annual meeting following the year during which a school has been under supervision, the high school board, taking into consideration the report of the inspector, the report of the examiner, and such other information as may be at hand, shall grant state aid to schools whose work and organization may appear to be satisfactory and to give promise of permanency.

5. A state high school is defined as a school which has received state aid to high schools, and which is under the supervision of the high school board.

The acceptance of a school for supervision shall not confer a right to the name before the state aid shall have been granted.

6. Schools whose terms of state aid have expired and which have made re-application for aid, may be replaced on the list unconditionally, or if unfavorable conditions come to the knowledge of the board, such as a change of local policy or the employment of a superintendent and instructors whose qualifications are not well known, the school may be accepted merely for supervision, and the question of a place on the list may be deferred until the next annual meeting.

CONDITIONS REQUISITE TO ACCEPTANCE

The following requirements are in accord with the past experience of the board and are made with a view to secure conditions which render efficient work practicable and give promise of permanence. The increase of state aid to one thousand dollars justifies great care in admitting schools to the list.

1. A comfortable building providing not less than four grade rooms below the high school, and high school quarters consisting of at least a main room, a large recitation room, a laboratory, and an office.
2. A well organized graded school, having not less than four distinct departments below the high school, and including not less than eight years of elementary and grammar school instruction.
3. A well chosen geographical library for the sixth and seventh grades.
4. An adequate library of American history of eighth grade work.
5. Suitable wall maps, a globe and an unabridged dictionary for each of the upper grades.
6. A liberal supply of reading matter in sets for each grade.
7. A well qualified superintendent having general charge of grading, instruction, discipline and of the care of the building.
8. A liberal schedule of salaries. It is not the policy of the high school board to prescribe salaries, but in the light of experience the board expresses a want of confidence in the ability of a school to earn the state grant of one thousand dollars without salaries liberal enough to secure the services of a competent superintendent and instructors of approved experience. Experience also demonstrates that towns having a population of less than one thousand people, and an assessed valuation of less than two hundred thousand dollars are seldom justified in undertaking the expense of supporting a state high school.
9. Scholarly classes, well started in at least the first two years of high school work, with a good prospect of classes to follow in regular succession, to maintain a full four years' course.

CONDUCT OF THE SCHOOL

1. Students admitted to the high school shall have satisfactorily completed the common school branches.
2. Permanent records shall be kept to show where each grade pupil belongs, and what subjects each high school student has completed.
3. The school shall hold sessions of not less than nine months each year.
4. The high school shall be open, free of tuition, to all non-resident pupils, upon passing the examination required by law.
5. The high school department (including grammar school students, if necessary) shall be placed in charge of a well qualified assistant.
6. The superintendent of the school shall be provided with an ample reci-

tation room and office, and shall have reasonable time in school hours for general supervision.

7. Boards of education shall adopt a liberal policy in making provision to supply the following library facilities and scientific equipment as rapidly as classes come forward to need them. The amounts named represent the cost of respectable beginnings for small classes.

a. Material in sets for four years' course in high school reading, fifty dollars.

b. A botanical or zoological outfit of tables, inexpensive dissecting microscopes, one compound microscope, dissecting instruments, glass jars and alcohol or formalin for preserving material, etc., eighty dollars.

c. Apparatus and equipments adequate to carry on a year's work in physics as outlined in manual, two hundred dollars.

d. Suitable desks, chemicals and glassware for a year's work in chemistry, ninety dollars.

e. A working school library for the use of students in the preparation of their daily work. The amounts named below are sufficient, if expended with judgment, to equip the various classes fairly well. It is understood that none of these books are required until classes are formed that need them. It is better to equip the classes one or more at a time, and equip each thoroly, than to scatter a small appropriation. The principal subjects which require assistance from a working library are: English literature, one hundred dollars; general history, one hundred dollars; civics, forty dollars; political economy, sixty dollars; senior American history, seventy-five dollars; senior geography, seventy-five dollars; physiography, fifty dollars; chemistry, thirty dollars; physics, forty dollars; zoology, fifty dollars; botany, seventy-five dollars; foreign languages, twenty-five dollars each.

8. The board of education of each school shall issue diplomas to those students who shall be certified by the superintendent to have satisfactorily completed the preliminary subjects and the work covered by twelve high school credits and a four years' course in reading. A year's work in a subject is called a credit.

The plan of extending aid to schools that are not yet sufficiently advanced to assume the work of a well-organized high school, aims to promote the efficiency of these schools, and encourage them in the effort to reach such a standard of excellence that they may become high schools, or if only elementary schools, that their graduates may be entitled to admission to the neighboring high schools.

"TRUSTEES MAY APPLY TO HAVE GRADED SCHOOL ADVANCED TO HIGH SCHOOL.—When any state graded school shall have attained such a degree of proficiency as to satisfy the trustees thereof that it has the qualifications necessary to entitle it to be advanced to the class of state high schools and to receive aid as such, said trustees may make application to the state high school board to have such graded school raised to the class of state high school, and if upon an examination into the records and standing of such school, the board is satisfied that it has attained a standard of curriculum, teachers and daily work, complying with all the requirements necessary to entitle it to a promotion, the said board may raise such state graded school to a state high school, entitling it to state aid as such."

' The act of 1881, providing for aid to state high schools, was entitled, "An Act for the encouragement of higher education." In its interpretation of this statement, the high school board has required the schools receiving this aid to expend it in improving the quality of its instruction and in providing additional equipment. The amounts annually expended by the schools for general equipment may be gathered from the following table. The amounts expended by the schools given are fairly representative of that expended by schools of like enrollment:

SCHOOLS	Enrollment	Chemistry	Physics	Botany and Zoology	History	English Literature	General Library	Supplementary Reading	Tot. 1 for 1901-02	Averaging for Preceding Five Years
Red Wing	218	160	120	20	..	..	36	100	436	475
Wabasha	76	90	25	15	25	10	40	..	205	251
Wadena	55	25	20	..	20	10	75	15	165	159
Warren	42	86	27	15	10	8	54	58	258	242
Waseca	96	150	100	50	60	40	150	75	625	465
Hopkins	55	300	600	100	80	50	450	275	1855	..*
Pipestone	124	12	150	60	20	10	70	38	360	218
Plainview	50	107	..	5	..	32	6	20	170	120
Preston	76	95	35	20	30	..	75	60	315	196
Princetown	43	75	75	..	25	25	40	..	240	170
Red Lake Falls	65	..	75	10	25	..	55	..	165	121
Duluth	623	239	279	269	..	..	550	..	1337	2088

*Added this year.

SUMMARY OF EXPENDITURES DURING THE YEAR

Chemistry	$9,181 00
Physics	9,912 00
Biological Science	3,272 00
Special Historical Libraries	4,091 00
Special Literature Libraries	3,430 00
General Libraries	11,026 00
*Grade Reading in Sets	6,826 00
Total	$47,738 00

*Excluding the large cities.

SUMMARY OF EXPENDITURES DURING THE PAST NINE YEARS

	1893-4	1894-5	1895-6	1896-7	1897-8	1898-9	1899-00	1900-01	1901-02
Library	$2,383	$8,675	$9,336	$10,795	$9,917	$8,651	$9,800	$13,570	$18,547
Science	5,436	12,602	10,453	9,647	11,202	9,009	14,961	16,997	22,365
Grade Reading in Sets	1,500	2,167	3,078	3,077	5,017	4,930	5,721	7,836	6,826
Total	$9,319	$23,444	$22,867	$24,219	$26,136	$22,590	$30,482	$38,503	$47,738

WISCONSIN[1]

At the time of the admission of Wisconsin as a state, but three villages supported anything like an advanced school at public expense. The early colleges and academies received annual grants from the state for their services in training teachers for the common schools.

To encourage the establishment of public high schools, an annual appropriation of $25,000 was voted by the legislature of 1875, and three courses of study were prepared by the state superintendent, two of which were adapted to the four-year schools of the larger cities and the other, a three-year course, was designed to cover the needs of smaller places. At this time there were in the state twenty-seven advanced schools, many of which were carrying on high school work. During the year, eighteen new schools were established, and in all twenty schools shared in the first apportionment. Of these, thirteen were newly-formed high schools that had been created after the passage of the measure providing for aid to high schools. By the provisions of the bill, each approved free high school[2] was to receive annually an amount equal to one-half the actual amount it expended for instruction, but not to exceed five hundred dollars.[3] Less than one-third of the appropriation was apportioned at the close of the first year, as the cost of instruction was less than eighteen thousand dollars. But during the following year, 1877, thirty-two new schools were added, and by the close of the school year of 1879–80, ninety-one free high schools were entitled to receive aid from the state, and the total appropriation of $25,000 was apportioned among them.

As might naturally be expected, this aid went to the schools of the cities and larger villages, and together with the tuition fees received from non-resident students, was of considerable help in the maintenance of these schools.

To encourage the establishment of high schools in communities not supporting a graded system of schools, the legislature of 1885 appropriated an additional sum of $25,000 expressly for free high schools in towns having no graded schools. The plan seems to have aimed to encourage the estab-

---

[1] I am indebted to Mr. L. D. Harvey, state superintendent of public instruction, for copies of the latest reports on the high schools of the state, including advance sheets of his forthcoming report containing an historical sketch of the early provisions for secondary education in Wisconsin.

[2] The term "free" high schools is used to distinguish the public high schools of the state from the thirteen "independent" high schools in nine of the large cities. The latter are not included in the provisions relating to high schools, and do not share in the various appropriations.

[3] A similar law had been passed by the legislature of Main in 1873.

lishment of township or union high schools, but owing to the independent district system, the formation of such schools was prevented. To further encourage their establishment, the next legislature provided that township high schools should receive as special aid from the state one-half of the whole amount expended by them for instruction, and that the remainder of the $25,000 appropriated for this purpose should be merged with the other high school fund. The provisions of this act are in force at the present time. The ordinary three-year and four-year high schools share pro rata, and none may receive more than five hundred dollars per annum, while the township high schools receive one-half the amount actually expended for instruction. Yet after fifteen years of such inducement, but nine such schools have been organized. Under the provisions of this act, six schools received at the last distribution of revenues, November, 1902, amounts ranging from five hundred and sixty-two dollars and fifty cents to one thousand and eighty-five dollars each, while the other schools not affected by this provision received four hundred and fifty-eight dollars and five cents each. The attempt to organize rural high schools has been repeatedly pronounced a failure, so far as the experience of Wisconsin in this matter is concerned.

As the number of free high schools in the state increased, it was found necessary to increase the annual appropriation, until at present it is one hundred thousand dollars. In his next report, State Superintendent L. D. Harvey will recommend that the sum be increased to one hundred and fifty thousand dollars. The provisions of the law apply to the three-year schools in the same manner as to the four-year schools. One hundred and seventy-six four-year schools, and forty-six three-year schools shared this year in the distribution of the one hundred thousand dollars. Of the four-year schools, one hundred and seventy received four hundred and fifty-eight dollars and five cents each, and six received amounts somewhat less. Four of the forty-six three-year high schools received the maximum amount of four hundred and fifty-eight dollars and five cents each, while some received as low as two hundred and forty-seven dollars and thirty-two cents.

To be eligible to a share in the benefits of this distribution, each school must comply with the following requirements:

1. The qualifications of all teachers employed in the high school must be approved by the state superintendent of schools.

2. The course of study offered by the school must have the approval of the state superintendent of schools; as must also the number of teachers needed to efficiently carry on the work as outlined in the course of study.

3. Each state-aided school must submit to inspection by the state superintendent, or by an inspector appointed by him.

4. The school is obliged to make such reports to the office of the state superintendent of schools as may be required by that office.

The standard set for admission to the high school teaching force of the state requires that all candidates pass an examination given by the state board of examiners, or hold a countersigned diploma from an approved university·

college, or normal school. Diplomas issued by State Normal Schools, and by the State University to graduates having completed the prescribed amount o` work in pedagogy, are accepted as high school credentials for a period, of one year, upon the approval of the state superintendent of schools. Upon certified testimony of good moral character and of successful teaching for a period of eight months, the diploma may be countersigned by the superintendent of public instruction, and thus becomes a permanent state certificate. In accordance with legal requirements, the state superintendent of schools prepares "; course or courses of study suitable to be pursued in free high schools," and these are made the courses of all such schools. These courses are prepared with much care, and it is seldom that a school is permitted to deviate far from the work as outlined in them. In this way uniformity of work is maintained thru out the state. The state inspector of high schools aims to visit every school once in each year. During these visits he plans to inspect not only the character and quality of the actual work of both teacher and pupil, but also the general condition of all school property; the work of the grammar grades; the standards set for admission into the high school; the general equipment of the school, including reading libraries, reference libraries, apparatus for the scien tific laboratories, etc. He aims to meet and confer with members of the schoo` board, and feels perfectly free in calling their attention to needed improve ments, as well as in commending them for improvements made. During intermission or after the close of school, he meets with the teachers and is ready to offer suggestions or be of assistance to them in their work. His visit is usually of much benefit to the school; but in this particular much depends upon the person selected for this important office. The appropriations are made in accordance with the report of the results of this inspection.

The university accrediting system is entirely independent of the syster of state inspection. Any high school wishing to be placed upon the "accredited list" of the university is required to make application to a university committee on accredited schools, in order that its work may be inspected with such end: in view. The university inspector visits the school, which is accredited or rejected upon his report of its work and general equipment. This report in nc way affects the apportionment of the annual appropriation for high schools The university employs as high school inspector an experienced high schoc principal, who devotes his entire time to the inspection of high schools. H is assisted in this work by other members of the faculty, those in the department of education in particular. Experience has proved that the two systems of inspection can be carried on in perfect harmony, and with increased benefit t the schools. Instead of resulting, as might be supposed, in two forces pulling in somewhat different directions, each has been found to contribute to the other

The legislature of 1901 provided for the admission of all qualified pupil into any of the high schools of the state whose accommodations are such as will permit of increased attendance, and required the town, nart of a town, or city of which the pupil is a resident, and which is not included within a high school district, to pay the cost of instruction. The maximum amount that any school may charge for such service is placed at two dollars per month. A noticeable increase in the number of non-resident pupils enrolled in the public high schools has followed the passage of this act. The town or city treasurer receives from the treasurer of the high school a certified statement of the amount due for instructing pupils residing in such town or city. If no part of the town or city is included within a high school district, the amount is added to the general tax of the town; but if any part of the town or city is included within a high school district, the amount due for instruction of high school pupils residing outside of such district is added to the tax levied upon that portion of the town or city not included within such district.

The same legislature, 1901, appropriated sixty thousand dollars for the support of graded schools in villages not maintaining a high school. These schools were designated as schools of the "first class," and schools of the "second class" respectively. One hundred and thirty-four schools of the first class received three hundred dollars each, and one hundred and eighty-eight schools of the second class received one hundred dollars each at the recent distribution of this appropriation. These schools are similar to the graded and semi-graded schools of Minnesota, and the conditions upon which they are entitled to a share in the apportionment resemble those specified in the discussion of the system of that state.*

The sum of five thousand dollars is annually appropriated for the support of manual training departments in connection with the high schools. Each school maintaining a department of manual training is entitled to receive two hundred and fifty dollars from this appropriation; but owing to the difficulty of securing well-trained teachers for these departments, not more than ten schools have received aid from this fund in any one year, and but seven schools were aided in 1902, although the provision for state aid to such departments has been in force for seven years. Provision has been recently made for the establishment of county schools of agriculture and domestic economy, and an annual appropriation of five thousand dollars is made for their support. Whenever a county maintains a county training school for teachers it is reimbursed by the state to the extent of one-half the amount expended for instruction. Six such schools are at present maintained. The generous policy of the state in the support of its public schools has more than offset the seeming disadvantage of having so large a proportion of foreign-born citizens.

In conclusion: All recent legislation affecting hig schools aims to accomplish two important ends, viz.: First, TO EXTEND TO ALL QUALIFIED PUPILS THE OPPORTUNITY OF OBTAINING A FREE SECONDARY EDUCATION. Secondly, TO PROVIDE SUCH MEANS OF EDUCATION IN WELL-EQUIPPED AND PROPERLY CLASSIFIED PUBLIC HIGH SCHOOLS.

---

*In Wisconsin the current school funds are apportioned to the districts in proportion to the number of persons between the ages of four and twenty years residing in each; in Minnesota, in proportion to the number of scholars between the ages of five and twenty-one years who have been enrolled and have been in attendance forty days in the public schools.

A Review of Education in California for the Past Year

FREDERIC BURK

In the effort to put down the events of educational progress of the past year, which I have undertaken at the request of the editor of the WESTERN JOURNAL OF EDUCATION, I have discovered that the really important events are frequently events of spirit and of the tendency rather than of historic deed. I have not hesitated, therefore, to express this spirit of things. I have grouped the subjects of discussion under four topics: the preparation of teachers, the field of administration, new legislative measures, and the high school situation.

PREPARATION OF TEACHERS.

The new certification law, abolishing two grades of elementary certificate, and authorizing only certificates entitling the teacher to teach in any grade o the elementary schools, has gone into operation apparently to the satisfaction of all persons concerned. Teachers, administrative officers, and the public generally have accepted its provisions as a simple matter of course, which proves the wisdom of the measure. The corollaries to the change indicate, however, that the measure is of more far-reaching importance than even its promoters conceived. During an operation of eighteen months it is manifest that without further legislation practically all teachers of the future will be professionally and specially trained.

Trained Teachers in the Future

Previously, graduates of grammar schools would take a year in a cramming school and then obtain a primary certificate by county board examination. After teaching a primary school a few years or so, they would again submit themselves to the cramming process in book definitions of the few subjects additional necessary for a grammar grade certificate. They would then be content. This system led as a rule to a mere superficial memory-cram as a basis of the preparation of teachers. It was easy for the teachers, but hard upon the pupils. Above all it omitted two of the chief essentials in preparing a teacher—a thoro building up of real knowledge and a thoughtful intelligence such as high schools aim to give; and, secondly, professional training in the technique and in meaning of education. It is one thing to know a fact, but quite another thing to be able to teach this fact rightly and with the least expenditure of the pupil's time and effort. The old system omitted both, and indirectly fostered superficial book memorizing, for this was the method by which the teacher herself learned, and unconsciously she used the same method of instructing her pupils. The spirit of the new law is such that few prospective teachers are now attempting to make use of the superficial short-cut to a teachers' license. During the past year the number of persons taking county board examinations has fallen away more than one-half, and in many counties no certificates have been issued by examinations. Nearly all of the private cramming schools have been closed. The old system enabled applicants to gain the grammar grade certificate by easy stages, but now that it is to be obtained only by a single leap, the requirement is too strenuous upon the memory. The trustees, and the public generally, by the discussion prior to the passage of the bill, have been awakened to the fact that the old system gave very shallow results, and a general prejudice against the old system seems established. Persons preparing to be teachers are now ready and eager to take the high school course with the view of taking two years more in a normal school, or four years in a university, to obtain culture, general education and professional training special to teaching. These facts indisputably promise that within a few years the professional training and the cultivated general intelligence possessed by teachers in the public schools will be immensely improved The problem of preparing efficient teachers is now clearly landed upon the doorsteps of the normal schools and universities with increased responsibility in the matter, in that they will here after be exclusively accountable for the thoroness of the work.

In the light of this decided turn of affairs, a second and most important movement toward improving the quality of the teaching force was inaugurated at the meeting of the Joint Board of Normal School Trustees, held in Los Angeles in April of the past year. A resolution was adopted declaring that after July, 1906, the admission requirement of all California State normal schools should be high school graduation, and that such schools as chose to should establish this standard before this time might do so. This resolution represents, after a struggle of three years, a victory for those in favor of a sharp separation between academic and professional training, with the result that students should enter normal schools with thoro high school training, and that normal schools should confine themselves strictly to the professional training of teachers. The measure was first brought up in the Joint Board meeting in 1899 and was defeated, the representatives of the San Francisco Normal alone voting for it. However, upon a very questionable legal bridge, this school decided nevertheless to insist upon the requirement for high school graduation as a basis of admission and has since maintained it. The following year no attempt was made to force the measure, but in 1901, at Chico, President Dailey, of the San Jose Normal School, introduced the measure a second time. It was however, defeated, San Jose and San Francisco representatives alone supporting it. Nevertheless, the San Jose school in 1901 enforced the new standard for itself. At the meeting in 1902, the Chico school unexpectedly joined the forces of San Jose and San Francisco. President Van Liew admitted, that while at present his school, by reason of the present paucity of high schools as feeders would be injured by such a requirement, nevertheless the measure was for the best interests of the schools of the state. The resolution as stated was carried by the votes of San Francisco, San Jose and Chico. The representatives of San Diego and Los Angeles, except President Pierce of the latter school, voted against the measure. There can be little doubt, however, that in 1906 this

Raising the Normal School Standard of Admission

new standard will become universal. President Van Liew of Chico is earnestly fostering the establishment of high schools in the north, and in the town of Chico itself, which heretofore has been without a high school, a new high school opened in August, earnestly encouraged by the normal school officials In 1906, if not before, Chico will be fully ready to adopt the high school standard of admission. There is far less reason in the south for the normal schools competing in academic studies with the high schools, for the high schools are more numerous. At any rate the competition of quality of the teaching product is one against which a minority cannot well hold out. Graduates of the schools of high school admission represent four years' academic study in general knowledge with two years' exclusively professional training, making six years preparation in all, while the graduates of schools which rest upon a grammar school basis have only four years to show for both general knowledge and professional training combined and condensed. The distinction is one too obvious to permit public approval of the latter schools. The schools which admit only high school graduates, now give no academic work, but devote their entire attention to special pedagogic instruction and actual training in their training schools. The cost to the state will be much less, and students will not be obliged to leave their homes for four years and, further, their general knowledge, as well as their professional training, will be much more thoro. This step of progress on the part of the normal schools fits in most neatly with the new certification law, and enhances the promise of an immensely better equipped teaching force for the state's schools in a few years. The amendment to the constitution permitting the legislature to extend state aid to high schools will in a short time relieve tension in the matter by producing a larger number of high schools from which the normal schools may draw.

In the matter of the university preparation of teachers, the State Board of Education has taken a significant action by the passage of a resolution providing that after July, 1906, graduates of the universities will not be entitled to teach unless they present evidence of teaching experience in well equipped training schools. The significance of this resolution is to compel the universities properly to equip training schools. About one-third of the university graduates apply for certificates as teachers but, as an exception to all other applicants for certificates upon credentials, no experience in teaching has been required of them. There has been a peculiar confusion in the public mind regarding two essentials of an efficient teacher—theory and experience in teaching. The product of theory is perspective and pedagogic judgment, and the product of teaching is technique. We cannot get pedagogic judgment of any depth or breadth from teaching, nor can we get technique from theory. The common error is to consider these two essentials substitutes one for the other Both instruments are essential. The universities have been dilatory in providing well equipped training schools. Their pedagogic departments have now been established for ten years, yet have only been half equipped, and the missing half is the one of pressing need; for, while educational theory more or less floats in the atmosphere, technique is only to be gained by actual life in the schoolroom. Moreover, for ten years the universities have been content to reap for their graduates the same emoluments, as tho they were completely fitted to enter the public schoolroom, and they have been slow about fulfilling their manifest duty in the matter. There has been a lethargy in the administrative departments of the universities and a seeming callousness to the needs of the schools for well trained university graduates as teachers. There has been in the past a disposition on the part of the universities in this matter to ask the pupils of the state to wait the convenience of the internal adjustment of university affairs, which so far as can be learned, depends upon some sort of private feuds among the various university departments inimical to the pedagogical department. Whatever it is, it manifestly requires some personal assurance to ask the schools of the state teeming with young destinies to put up with teachers untrained in practical technique, until these trifling domestic imbroglios can be healed with due courtesy to the personal feelings of the handful of quarreling dominies concerned—hence the action of the State Board.

Hopeful University Outlook

However, during the past year there have been other hopeful signs. Professors Brown and Cubberley have returned, after a year's travel and study, with renewed energy and determination. President Wheeler has within the past few months given public utterances to his conviction that the chief necessity of the university is now a teachers' training school, and Professor Brown is planning, at least upon paper, a training school, which, when realized, will put California in advance of any state in the union. It is proposed that, practically under the same roof, a child may enter the kindergarten and be emitted finally a Ph. D. There will be the provision all along the line for the training of teachers in every department from the kindergarten to the university. At Stanford, President Jordan, with equal clearness of conviction, realizes the necessities, but plans are not yet so definite. Both Professors Brown and Cubberley came back from their eastern visit with views strengthened favorably toward the practical side of training. Present courses in the universities' pedagogical departments are being modified in the light of this conviction, so far as possible, and at least the present year closes more hopefully for the soundness of what the universities will attempt to do with the problem of preparing teachers, than any of the past ten.

ADMINISTRATION OF SCHOOLS

The topic of the preparation of teachers leads us to the problem of the selection of teachers and the administration of their work. There are three large factors upon which the final efficiency of the instruction of pupils depends: the efficiency of the teachers, the efficiency of the administrative department, and the people who make the laws and determine the conditions under which the school system operates. Popular judgment has been prone to regard the efficiency of the teachers as the chief, if not exclusive factor, but a little reflection shows that this factor only becomes important when the administration and supervision are upon a high plane of efficiency. In California at present this favorable condition does not exist. Efficient teachers, by mere virtue of their capabilities and efficiency, are rarely able to gain positions, and if by fortuitous chance they are appointed, the crude and inadequate systems of supervisions hamper and discourages the exercise of their best abilities. As the governing rule, the factor which determines the appointment of teachers is influence of friends upon the administrative officers, and efficiency, at best, serves to justify appointments previously made upon grounds of influence. Manifestly, teachers with that elasticity of character which permits them to go to the most questionable extremes in securing influence are the most likely to be appointed, and a premium is thus set upon a low plane of professional ideals. The appointing officers are few who take the initiative, and go forth to search for the most efficient teachers, but, as the most exclusive rule, they elect from those who are out of positions for various reasons, illegitimate as well as legitimate. Certainly, we cannot expect efficiency to grow and flower in an atmosphere which continually tends to dwarf and minimize its importance. To improve the efficiency, under this state of affairs, requires reform, not so much of the teachers directly, but of the administrative system. Reform of the administrative system means, not reform of the officers who happen at any time to be holding office, but, if the reform is to be permanent, of laws and public sentiment, which makes the character of the office. Here, in the laws and in public sentiment, we find the real African of the woodpile. There is no provision of law nor controlling public sentiment which requires any qualification of trustees and boards of education special to the highly responsible duties they are called upon to exercise. In this essential particular of possessing that probity of character to resist personal influence, the method of their own election generally makes necessary the selection of men most susceptible to illegitimate influence. In large cities the condition is aggravated by the machine system of politics.

The Cause of Inefficiency in Teaching

Necessity for Reform in Administration

The value of efficient teachers is still further handicapped by the crudities and incompetency of the prevailing supervision system. Even with efficient teachers, good schools are beyond our reach, unless we are provided with supervisors of the highest grade of technical expertness in the management of schools and in methods of instruction. We must have expert superintendents, courses of study framed by expert judgment, and regulations of management which call for efficiency of teachers and use it wisely. But, again, there is no provision of law setting any special qualifications for supervising officers, nor guarding in any way the highly technical nature of these duties. County superintendents are elected by popular vote, county boards of education by the county supervisors, city superintendents by the same officials who elect the teachers and under the same wretched conditions. It is inevitable, therefore, that efficiency must, by the force of the defective law, again be discounted. Personal influence, not professional ability, must constitute the controlling factor. The existing supervising systems, as a rule, are not framed to harvest the results of efficiency, nor to enable efficient teachers to work under the best conditions, but have for their purpose the prevention of the shirking of formal duties, and to provide a kind of work for which incompetent teachers can be held accountable. In doing this, the real fruits of efficient teaching are too often lost, and efficient teachers are compelled to follow the same beaten path of perfunctory school-keeping laid down for incompetents. There are

Crudities of Supervision

some exceptions to this rule, both in supervising officers and in schools, but these are the products of accident, not the product of the necessities of the school system, and, as such, we must regard them merely as happy mitigating circumstances without permanency. What we need are provisions of law which make these chance exceptions the rule.

Thus we have brought forcibly home to us that there cannot be any real guarantee of an efficient school system without the construction of new school laws, which shall protect efficiency of teachers and of administrative systems.

New School Law and Public Sentiment a Necessity

But laws are only framed by public sentiment and intelligence, and the problem of real improvement of the schools is the problem of raising public sentiment. Therefore, it is very manifest that the true and successful point of attack upon weaknesses of the school system is the school law and public sentiment.

The teaching efficiency is already better than the present administrative and supervision system are capable of using; and if the quality of teaching is to be greatly improved we can expect no proportional improvement of the schools, because it cannot be used effectively. Yet as wretched as is the system of supervision it is really better than the provisions of law and public demand, because individuals generally try to do the right thing when not prevented. The chief point of attack is, therefore, the public intelligence concerning good laws.

I have made this statement of existing conditions in order that the meaning of several movements and tendencies of the past year should be significant. The problem of the improvement of the administration has been attacked from two or three standpoints. An internal line of attack is that of the movement to establish a code of professional ethics, to prevent the use of political influence by teachers, by the force of regulations within the teaching body. In the latter part of 1901-2, an effort was made in the state board of education to define unprofessional conduct (stated in the political code as an offense by which a teacher's certificate could be revoked) so as to include the securing of a position by personal or political influence. But this effort was defeated in committee discussion. At the meeting of the State Teachers' Association, in December, 1902, John Swett, chairman of a committee on professional ethics of the council of education, introduced at the council meeting resolutions as follows, together with a report setting forth the reasons for their adoption:

The Code of Professional Ethics

First—It shall constitute unprofessional conduct for any one holding a teacher's certificate to submit any argument or plea in obtaining or retaining a position, other than those constituting evidences of professional competency; or knowledge to permit any other person, in behalf of the applicant, to do that which is defined above as unprofessional conduct on the part of the applicant.

Second—It shall constitute unprofessional conduct for any one holding a teacher's certificate to seek a position which is not either legally vacant, or definitely known to become vacant at a special time, unless requested to do so by the properly constituted authority."

The resolutions were adopted by the council and also by the association. with the instructions that the secretary should ask the State Board of Education, and all county boards of education to notify all institutional and local boards employing teachers of this code, and also that the state and county boards should adopt these resolutions in defining the term "unprofessional conduct," as used in the political code. Further, all teachers' organizations wer to be requested to adopt these resolutions as qualification of membership i the organization. President Van Liew, in the state board, in November, brought up the resolutions and moved their adoption, but at the suggestion of Professor Brown, the resolutions were deferred until the next meeting, in order to enable members to consider them. The movement is a growing one, as shown by the fact that another committee on professional ethics in the Teachers' Association, headed by H. M. Bland, of San Jose, reported a series of resolutions. The California Schoolmasters' Club, in April, appointed a committee, under the chairmanship of Mr. D. S. Snedden, and an important report has been printed and will come up for adoption at the January meeting. The real purpose of this movement, it appears, is not a sentimental one, **Practical Purpose of the Code** but grows out of the realization that no occupation has gained the dignity of a profession without a code of ethics governing its members, and that the key of success in making school work what it should be, both for the pupils and the teachers, lies in the ability to remove the school from the influences of personal or political favoritism. Any effort of the teachers, acting internally, will help, but clearly the essential change must come from public intelligence, which shall frame rigorous protective laws and sentiment.

A revolutionary step was also taken by the Board of Education of San Francisco, in July, by holding competitive examination for the appointment of teachers to vacancies in the San Francisco school department. The examination consisted of a written and an oral test, each counting **Civil Service in San Francisco** one-half. The highest thirty were appointed to the substitute list. The written examination was upon pedagogical questions, and the system was such that there was no opportunity for favoritism. The oral examination, by the members of the board, of course, made influence possible, but the results showed that with almost no exceptions, none except those who obtained a high marking in the impersonal written test, were successful. Consequently, the system proved that it had landed a powerful blow against personal influence in the selection of teachers. There can be no question, however, that such a system is far from ideal in obtaining the most efficient teachers, for an examination in mere book knowledge and theory will fail as a sure means of obtaining the most practical teachers. But the board of education has made a most courageous beginning. It is significant to observe, however, that public sentiment has not risen to commend the board for the stand taken, and without this the measure is certainly doomed to repeal, and can be considered only temporary. Any permanent system must come from the people and be formulated into a legal provision supported by public sentiment. A year previous the board had requested a commission composed of the presidents and the heads of the educational departments of the two universities, the state superintendent, and the principal of the San Francisco Normal School, to prepare a plan for the appointment of teachers which should free the department from personal influence. This commisssion's report, delivered last year, held that under existing laws there could be no guarantee of the selection of the most efficient, unless the absolute courage to resist influences, and the sound judgment of the board of education were assumed. Upon this basis, a plan of appointment was recommended, providing that the board should take the initiative in discovering the most efficient teachers by visiting, personally, the schools of other cities and picking off the best teachers; further, the competitive examination was recommended for a small minority of those who should be appointed. This report was severely attacked, however, by public opinion, which held that the local teachers should be given the preference in San Francisco. This argument, so frequently offered, shows the weakness of present public judgment to govern its school system, for efficiency, not residence, must be the chief qualification. A new movement is now on foot looking to an organization of the leading citizens, and finding mass support in all the club organizations of the city, which shall act to compel the appointment of efficient administrative officers and teachers, unaffected by personal influences, but the organization at this writing has not yet been effected. In Santa Barbara, also, a similar organization is being effected. The council of education, at its July meeting, appointed several committees to investigate and report upon projects to improve the administrative and advisory service and free it from its impediments. A committee under the chairmanship of Superintendent James Foshay, of Los Angeles, is to report a plan for the appointment of teachers in cities. Systems of supervision in cities are being considered by a committee headed by Superintendent McClymonds, of Oakland, and two other committees under the leadership of Robert Furlong and A. E. Shumate, respectively, will consider supervision of rural schools. In the California Schoolmasters' Club, a committee under the chairmanship of Superintendent James A. Barr, of Stockton, proposes to submit a plan of appointment of teachers. These reports may be expected during the ensuing year.

Weakness of Public Sentiment

Committees Upon Administration

There has been considerable discussion during the past year regarding some improvement of the county administrative system in the matter of the superintendent and county boards of education. Regarding the superintendent it is pointed out that there are no required qualifications for the office; that election by popular vote through the medium of a political convention may be a guarantee of the person with the largest personal influence, of social political, sectarian or class affiliations, but not necessarily any assurance of any expert fitness for the technical duties of school supervision; that the supervision, which amounts to one visit a year to each district, even if the superintendent is qualified, really is no supervision at all; that the superintendent, if qualified, thoroly honest and reliable, and protected from influence, should have more control of the selection of teachers in the various districts. With the beginning of 1903, about one-third of the county superintendents of the state go out of office. Some were defeated at the polls, some failed to be renominated, some declined to be considered. The majority of these, having reached the height of a local ambition, now drift into other occupations, and only a few return to teaching. A study of the elections fails to show that either the conventions or the people have shown any serious discrimination in the selections, in so far as educational competency is concerned. The better qualified candidates, from an educational standpoint, have been both elected and defeated indiscriminately. About ten of the most efficient superintendents, ranking with the best in the state, with the advantage of four to twelve or more years' experience in administration, have been retired, for reasons which had nothing whatever to do with their efficiency as officers.

County Boards and Superintendents

The Lessons From Popular Elections

Such a fact bears its own forcible lesson, and were the public interest in schools not asleep, would speedily lead to legislative reform. No business house could long retain public confidence if from one-sixth to one-third of its most efficient officers, representing the reserve capital of experience, were relieved in favor of wholly inexperinced administrative officers. Experience is the only qualification which is not mere chance in the selection of school officers, and to throw this away is manifestly suicidal folly. What are we to do about it? No one knows, but all should be thinking about it. Some suggest a state system of administration, which is being used in older states, with opportunity for transference and promotion of local superintendents, and with special requirements in the matter of qualifications of such officers. With regard to the county boards, it is generally agreed, outside of the circles of the county board officers themselves, and the majority of these also concur, that this form of school administration is necessarily inadequate, generally incompetent, and that the method of appointment has nothing to commend it. It is difficult to discuss the matter, for there are enough members of these boards who are so strenuously supporters of the patronage system, even in the schools, that they at once organize for common defense, and invoke the political powers for their personal protection. But certainly something should be done, but the past year records nothing except a growing conviction that radical reform of county supervision is absolutely necessary for any substantial progress in the rural schools.

Proposed Laws

Three movements looking toward legislative action may be expected to have some important reactionary effects, aside from their direct provisions, upon the efficiency of the schools. I refer to the proposed measure relative to the consolidation of school districts, and the transportation of pupils to school at public expense, compulsory education, and free text books.

Consolidation of School Districts

The immediate advantages of the consolidation of school districts, as shown by the experience in the large area of eastern states which have now adopted the plan, are economy, which enables more money to be expended for the development of the central school, the introduction of the graded school system, buildings as well equipped as in cities in hygienic and educational conditions, promptness and regularity of attendance. But the indirect advantages are even of greater importance. The consolidation of the small rural classes, frequently of not more than six to a dozen pupils, provides the saving of salaries, which can be used in procuring a higher grade of teachers. Also, several classes being in one building, the school can have a principal, and if the desire is such, the principal can be a man. The trouble with the male teacher at present is that the salaries paid in district schools, sixty or seventy dollars, is so small that, as a necessary rule, the man is either untrained and inefficient, and is only using the school as a stepping stone, or else he is a failure in life. Our school system offers small field for competent men, well trained in the expert problems of teaching and supervision, and who are making a life-profession of school work. . The consolidation plan would scatter over the rural sections a large number of principalships which might command salaries of eighteen hundred or two thousand dollars, and be capable of supporting competent men with families. If competent, these principals could offer the rural schools what is not possible at present—constant, adequate and skilled supervision. Further, the centralized school, being removed from local district influence, would, even under the existing system of trustee elections, be somewhat more removed from the petty interference of personal influence. Professor Cubberley, at the last legislature, drew up a bill permitting school districts to consolidate, but the public did not understand it, and it failed to become a law. Superintendent Hugh Baldwin, of San Diego, has been agitating and educating the people of his county during the past year, and brought the matter before the county superintendents' convention in May, with the result that a committee under the chairmanship of Miss Minnie Coulter, superintendent of Sonoma county, was appointed to bring the subject again before the legislature. The council of education has also appointed a committee, under the leadership of Miss E. M. Tilton, superintendent of San Mateo school, and she is most energetically at work upon a report.

The discussion of free-text books for California leads directly to important significance for better schools. And aside from the question of economy to patrons of the school, free texts will mean, under intelligent operation, the topical system of teaching history, geography, literature and science. The free-text system does not necessarily mean the gift to pupils of texts, but that the school may purchase sets of books in variety, and to these topical lessons may be assigned. The supplementary system of reading will thus become widely increased, and eventually, the memorizing of history, geography, and science texts, without comprehension of meaning, will receive a death blow. The system, thus interpreted, signifies incalculable improvement in the teaching of the subjects mentioned. Superintendent E. M. Cox, of Santa Rosa, has been appointed chairman of a committee of the council of education, which reports to the State Teachers' Association this month, and it is to be hoped that this report will be published and widely disseminated.

Free Texts and Better Teaching

Compulsory education, as a principle, has had an uphill struggle in California. A provision, tho defective, has been in our statutes for years, but has commanded no respect. A bill framed by Superintendent J. W. McClymonds, of Oakland, was presented to the last legislature, but failed to become a law. The superintendents' convention has appointed a committee to bring the matter again before the legislature. A committee from the council of education, under direction of Dr. E. C. Moore, has compiled an exhaustive report upon the conditions requiring some legal provision, and showing the experience in other states. Charitable and social organizations are alive to the situation and are urgent. Census reports show an alarming percentage of pupils who do not attend school. Still the movement encounters much public opposition. It is doubtful that even if a bill can be carried thru the legislature, it will not be operative unless the public intelligence regarding the functions of schools is radically changed. The current popular view of public schools is that they are institutions provided by the charity of the state to save parents the expense of giving their offsprings the benefits of an education. Therefore, whether or not the parent chooses to take advantage of this free offering is purely optional. Under this understanding of the purpose of schools, there is no justification of a compulsory school law, nor can argument for it from this standpoint, ever be deduced. But another viewpoint of the schools recognizes that the democratic system of American government by the people necessarily implies a people educated to be rulers. Universal education is a necessary essential to universal suffrage, and compulsory education is necessary to any conception of the American state. Children are given free education, not as charity to parents, but children must be

Change in Public Sentiment Necessary for Compulsory Education

educated as a matter of self protection on the part of the state. We are as vitally interested in the education of our neighbor's children as in our own, for our neighbor's children will be part of the future law-givers. Until the people of California are led to grasp this conception of the relation between the state and its schools, it will be useless to attempt compulsory education.

It was a surprise to schoolmen that the amendment to the constitution permitting the legislature to appropriate state funds for the support of high schools was carried at the November election. It is certainly to be hoped that no hasty action will be taken during the present session of the legislature. It would be much better for the school world and people to reflect and discuss the new situation presented, for two or four years, without taking any hasty action. The high school problem is in a muddle, and while there are few clear ideas, on the other hand it is very manifest that the solution involves action affecting essentials of the entire school system. It is questioned seriously whether the present form of high school, both in period and subjects of study should not be recognized radically. The present high school course is charged with lack of practical touch with the world, with being a junk shop of traditional material handed down from the colleges of a century or so ago, with being a mere feeder to the traditional culture courses in the colleges. The high school course of study is now a bone of contention among several masters. The universities demand its control as preparatory feeders to university courses; the mechanic and business man want to make of it trade schools in their lines; the pedagogue declares that the courses should lead not to any special preparation nor to any special occupation, but should prepare for citizenship and general intelligence; the forces of tradition insists that it shall continue along the line of the past. At present the universities and tradition, which agree very thoroughly, hold the fort, and serenely inform the others that in preparing pupils for colleges, the high school best prepares for life. Some personal feeling has been developed by the accrediting system in California by which the authorities, to control the high school courses, has been virtually vested in the college faculties. The high school principals and teachers, strangely enough, are not a significant factor in the contest. They are chiefly young men and women fresh from the universities bearing with them college prejudices, and as a rule they stand firmly for the traditional college entrance requirements. The educational departments, for reasons already stated, have not yet succeeded in making any pedagogical impression upon their graduates different from popular tradition. During the past year or so, the voice of the pedagogue has been heard crying in the wilderness. He takes up the studies of the course in the high school and is demanding to know what is the product of the teaching. What is the product of four years in Latin? What is the output of algebra? What is the value of the narrow and prescribed course in literature? Very manifestly the direct purpose of these courses is to lead up to certain university courses in the subjects, but the traditional reply comes that Latin gives culture, that algebra trains the reason, etc. But the pedagogue declares that this is traditional nonsense, that a power gained by exercise in one field cannot be transferred to another field, that the kind of reasoning power gained in algebra applies only to algebra, and unless algebra is for universal use, it can have no claim to universal treatment in the high school. This traditional view is so ingrained by tradition that the pedagogue is having uphill work of it. The Scholia Club, composed of school-men around San Francisco, for the past few months has been debating this question vigorously, and it is very manifest that the present high school course rests for its entire argument upon the assumption that certain formal drills, as Latin, algebra, laboratory science, build up a few general faculties which can be used for any purpose thereafter. The pedagogues maintain that this is not true and that any power is the result of special training. Consequently, from this point of view, the high school must determine what the useful information or powers are which are universally required, and special courses must be fitted to meet these ends. Mr. F. E. Thompson has been appointed by the Council to prepare a report upon this problem and it will soon be distributed.

The Use of Studies

At the State Association last year there was organized a State High School Association for the purpose of threshing out these questions. The organization has not been very vigorous, but a beginning has been made. Under the chairmanship of Mr. D. S. Snedden, a committee of ten has been organized to deal with pedagogical issues involved, and some profitable discussions have been held. However, no great progress is possible until a deeper pedagogical interest in the relative value of the studies is stirred among the high school teachers. At present they are depressed by an apathy as to what is the educational output of their work, and have devoted their energies only to the matter of how to meet university requirements, accepting these as articles of faith. In the meantime, the boys who leave the grammar school with no prospect of attending college, and the girls who have anything else to do, drift away from the high school. The system, except as a college preparatory school, is becoming ever more and more unpopular, and is out of joint with public demands. Intelligent preparation for the problems of civic, social and industrial citizenship are not included in its curriculum. General knowledge is not considered knowledge of worth. College ideals of research, intensive study, cultivation of the general faculties have crowded out the notion that the high school should fit its pupils to know, feel, and do that which the

The High School Association

average man or woman of general intelligence knows, feels and does. Very little progress is to be chronicled, except the fact that a number of people are thinking. Some have forcibly advocated that the present twelve years, apportioned to the elementry and high schools combined,

New Division of Elementary and Secondary Schools

be now divided into two six-year periods—an elementary school and a secondary school. The elementary school, under some views then should receive emphasis upon essential tool-getting, and the secondary school should then be modeled in a way quite different from the present high school, perhaps finding time in the last two years to give special preparation either for business occupation, profession, trade or for college. The Alameda County Teachers' Association has been the chief center of this discussion.

In conclusion, as perhaps the most optimistic sign of the times is to be noted the awakening of interest in organization of school men for discussion of the technical problems of the school and its administration. The Council of Education has appointed some

Activity of Organization

forty different committees upon all kinds of pressing problems, pedagogical, administrative and supervisory. It will probably meet monthly the coming year for the discussion of these reports, and it is hoped that means will be found for wide general distribution of these reports. The High School Association will probably get upon its feet, and an effort will be made to organize local high schools throughout the state for discussion and public agitation of school problems. The Southern Schoolmasters have long had an organization and the California Schoolmasters' Club which meets three times a year in San Francisco constantly has a large waiting list of nominees, altho during the past year its limitation has been advanced from 100 to 125. It has also appointed a number of important working committees upon general problems. There has also been organized in San Francisco under the leadership of Dr. E. C. Moore, the Scholia Club, limited in membership with the purpose of discussion of technical pedagogical questions. It meets monthly for a dinner and discussion.

Progress will come with agitation, internal and external.

Public Speaking of To-Day

J. A. Wians, University of California.

It may be, a later generation will look back to this period of awakening national consciousness as a time when oratory had a new birth. Many notable speeches have been made in recent years, and some of them have been gathered into such volumes as this.

But whether or not there is any real oratory to-day, there certainly is a surprising amount of public speaking, and especially in America. It is equally certain that the American people listen to a vast deal of distressingly poor speech-making. This is, in part, due to the fact that men without fitness and training are dragged upon the platform by the enormous demand for speakers;

but it is also due to certain false ideas in regard to what the platform of to-day demands.

And of these misconceptions, I should place first the idea that effective speaking requires little preparation. Because some Depew makes a telling speech with apparently little preparation, we all decide to shine in the same easy way, forgetting that we are not all Depews. We forget that the orator who speaks brilliantly on short notice is probably treating a subject in which he is a specialist, and on which he has been speaking and writing for years; so that, little matter what theme is suggested, he is soon on a familiar trail. And we forget, too, that it is one of the littlenesses of great men, that they like to give impression that their great efforts are extemporaneous. It is safe to say that nearly all the stories told of great speeches made "on the spur of the moment" are not true. The assertion that Webster's memorable "Reply to Hayne" was impromptu is given the lie by Webster's own statement, that it was based upon full notes made for another speech on the same general subject. Again, he said, "The materials of that speech had been lying in my mind for eighteen months." He might have added that they were the product of years of study. "No man," said Webster, "is inspired by the occasion; I never was." And again, "There is no such thing as extemporaneous acquisition." We are told that Lincoln delivered his masterpiece, the Gettysburg address, impromptu, but authentic history records that he prepared it with great care.

A speaker owes it to his audience to make all practicable preparation. It may not be possible or desirable to write out the speech. The actual language may be extemporized in many cases by the skillful; but no plea but that of necessity can excuse one from careful consideration and arrangement of subject-matter. Perhaps only one out of a dozen thoughts occuring to a speaker is really worth expressing. How often are we bored by speakers who go rambling on, hiding their tiny kernel in a bushel of chaff, hoping somewhere to make a point, and looking for a good place to stop. Loose expressions, wild assertions, puerile reasoning, pointless illustrations, unclinched arguments, distracting digressions, make up the speeches of those who do not first bring their ideas to the test of formulation, who prepare their speeches "while you wait." Those brilliant thoughts we think we think—how they disappear before the test of pen and paper! But too many speakers, having gained some little glibness, developed overmuch the dangerous American "gift of gab," confident of coming out somewhere, are too indolent to make the preparation they owe their audiences. It would be poetic justice to make them listen to their own speeches from a phonograph.

Another false idea, which is a cause of much poor speaking, arises from a misconception of the term "conversational style." There is such a multitude of witnesses testifying that this is the style best adapted to the present, that the statement commands respect. But what does this flexible term mean? It is often taken to mean careless, familiar, monotonous, weak talk, and to be inconsistent with good form, dignity, strength, and feeling.

Does it mean that I am to speak to five hundred people as to one person? Surely, I cannot use the same degree of strength and loudness. I should not be heard; and the first requirement is to be heard. But one may be conversational at the top of his voice. Suppose a man is shouting across a roaring torrent; so long as he is expressing thought to the man on the other side, he is conversational. So a speaker may be conversational, tho he throw his voice out over ten thousand people. And does conversational speaking demand that one have no more dignity of bearing or language than in conversation? But we have all degrees of dignity in conversation. It depends upon the hearers, the subject, and the occasion. Some take conversational style to be inconsistent with force. But do we never become forceful in conversation? Never enthusiastic? The mistaken ideas arise from the fact that poor conversation, such as we use in discussing the weather, is taken as the basis of comparison. The true conception is, that our public speech should be based upon our best conversation, enlarged and dignified as subject and occasion and subject are more dignified. It should be conversational in its elements.

It is undoubtedly true that public speech has been modified in the last fifty years in the direction of simplicity. As the heavy manners, the profound bows, of our grandfathers have passed, so the "grand manner" has, to a great extent, passed from the platform. The speaker no longer puts himself on a pedestal. This more self-conscious age will not bear so patiently the "highfalutin" and the grandiloquent.

But it is a serious mistake that many speakers make when, trying to obey the injunction, "Be conversational," they avoid grandiloquence, only to fall into over-familiarity. Frank, close relation with one's audience is perhaps the very essence of the conversational style; but genuine dignity should never be sacrificed. The average American audience of today approves of it as much as did the audiences of Demosthenes. Again, in avoiding the rolling oratund, which the old-school orator was too likely to use on all occasions, speakers often adopt a weak, slovenly enunciation. In seeking a conversational diction free from the heavy Latin words and constructions, they fall into vulgarity. Yet, any intelligent audience, educated or uneducated, in city or in county, knows that the platform demands good English. Rightly considered, the conversational style holds no speaker back from his best. It requires conformity to no set standards; it is as flexible as individuality. It is not inconsistent with dignity and elevation, though it is at war with bombast and grandiloquence.

Nor is it opposed to strength, earnestness, enthusiasm. We are sometimes told that the speech best adapted to this time has little emotion in its composition. The statement is almost absurd unless oratory is indeed dead. The most notable definitions of oratory, from Aristotle down, have made its most distinctive element, persuasion. But persuasion is conviction plus appeal to motives, feelings, that control the will. Oratory deals with living issues, personal truths "that come home to men's business and bosoms." It looks to action; and we never act until some emotion—love of self, of home, of friends, of country—moves the will. The public speech that has no emotional elements is only an essay vocalized.

Is not the truth right here—that this age is less tolerant of the insincere display of emotion? That it distinguishes more sharply between sentiment and sentimentality, between pathos and bathos, emotion and emotionalism? It is more inclined to demand facts, arguments, the appeal to reason, first. It likes less the open, direct appeal to feelings; it prefers being inspired to being exhorted. Yet there is nothing to which the present-day audience responds so quickly and so heartily as to a touch of sincere feeling. We still have hearts as well as heads. Yet many men, disgusted by some ranter, suppress the emotions they really feel, and reduce their speaking to dull indifference. To pass over ineffectiveness, in which the two are about equal, which is the more insincere—the man who feins emotion, or the man who suppresses the earnestness he really feels? When public speech dispenses with the emotional element, it loses its best excuse for being; for the message that is cold, that does not depend to some extent upon the warm energy of personality, were better intrusted to cold type.

It has not been my privilege to review the contents of his volume; bu I am willing to risk the testing of the above ideas by the speeches that follow. The fact that they have won success and have been remembered gives me confidence that here will be found no lack of careful preparation, of dignity of thought or expression, of lofty imagination, or of the glow of genuine human feelings.

Governor Geo. C. Pardee

In the December number of the JOURNAL appeared, Very appropriately, an excellent picture of State Superintendent Thomas J. Kirk, re-elected as head of the school department. With the new year comes a change of Executive of the state government, Governor Pardee succeeding Governor Gage. The January issue of the JOURNAL presents a good likeness of the new governor, and a sketch of his career to date by one who has known him well for more than a dozen years.

GoVernor Geo. C. Pardee was born in San Francisco, July 25, 1857. Three years later the family removed to Oakland. In the later 60's they lived for three years in San Diego, returning to Oakland where

GEORGE C. PARDEE
Governor-elect of California

their home has been ever since. The father, Dr. E. H. Pardee, was a skillful oculist and a man of great force of character. Politically, an original Fremont Republican, he served Oakland as its mayor and Alameda county as state senator; bold, independent, fearless in thought and action, he continued until his death a personality of force and influence in the community. George was the only child.

The son graduated from the Oakland High School at seventeen. Entering the State University, he received the degrees of A.M. and Ph.D. in 1879. He spent two years at Cooper Medical College, San Fran cisco, after which, upon the advice of its eminent founder, Dr. L. C. Lane, he went to Europe and entered the University of Leipsic in 1881, graduating there four years later, having taken special courses meanwhile in Berlin, Vienna and Paris. During his absence in Europe he wrote a series of letters for the San Francisco "Chronicle," some of which were published during the recent campaign as indicative of the character of the writer. He returned to Oakland and in 1887 married Miss Helen Penniman, a former schoolmate and a teacher in the Oakland schools.

He first appeared in public life in 1889 thru an appointment to the Board of Health by a reform mayor, after an exciting city campaign. A fight was on against the local water company which was furnishing a fluid "turged in winter time, in summer foul." The young doctor, as chairman of a committee, secured analysis of the water by State University experts, and never flagging, kept up a persistent agitation of the question, until relief came in the form of a filtering system finally introduced by the company.

At the next municipal election, he was nominated to beat a very popular Democrat who, as councilman, had not agreed with the doctor's views upon the question at issue. The doctor won easily and upon assuming office, immediately set to work to secure a reduction of water rates. In 1893 he was elected mayor as the municipal reform candidate. During his mayoralty, the great strike of the American Railway Union occurred. The Southern Pacific Mole was taken possession of by a force of U. S. marines. Soldiers guarded the trains leaving Oakland. Coxey's army came to Oakland from San Francisco, was provided with temporary quarters by the mayor; arrangements were made for transportation desired by it, and declining to move, it was made to go by a show of force by the determined official.

Much prejudice was raised against the doctor during the recent campaign because of his attitude in this crisis, but the citizens of Oakland who recall the situation commend him. Nor was this all he had to contend with during his term as mayor.

The Oakland Water Front Company had erected and long maintained a high board fence and toll gate at the foot of the main street of the city. The mayor, at the head of a battalion of police and street laborers, destroyed the fence and opened the street to the water channel. The Water Front Company then drove piles into the bay around the city front to show its ownership of the same. The mayor followed with another pile driver which removed the offending timbers. The company resorted to an injunction. The mayor interviewed the judge and after protracted argument, induced him to revoke the order. Whatever the property rights involved may have been, the company ceased driving its piles and has since been ready to divide up and sell its water front holdings. The city front is not barred, the mayor is governor, and the judge who reconsidered is on the supreme bench of the state.

After his term as mayor, the doctor for a number of years held no public office. His independence put him out of touch somewhat with the managers of the dominant political party. He had dared to oppose the organization and must pay the penalty. But since his entrance into public life in Oakland his hand was felt in every campaign. His personality had grown so strong it had to be reckoned with. His devotion to his party on state and national issues could not be questioned. Therefore he continued to grow. In 1898 he swept the county at the primaries, against an opponent distinguished alike for his affability and his eloquence, and went to the State Convention as the candidate of his county for governor. Withdrawing gracefully when he saw the result was inevitable, he heartily supported his successful opponent in the campaign and became, in all political fairness, the logical nominee in 1902.

That he did not receive a greater majority at the polls may be attributed to three causes, chiefly; namely: The opposition of enemies made in his brief, strenuous political career; a thoroly unfounded but vigorously asserted charge that he was not a friend to labor; and the conviction from a study of his past that he would prove obdurate and refractory under certain conditions. His campaign speeches revealed the man to those who had not followed his political career. He was courteous to his opponent, and all his utterances were simple, direct and dignified. He was never vulgar or frivolous. He played no part. He did not practice the demagogue. He could not assume the aristocrat. Though of dignified and manly carriage, he has the very spirit of comradarie. By his former schoolmates, the laborers and business men of Oakland, he is addressed familiarly as "Doc" or "George." They know he is one with them, without a trace of the snob in him.

He has promised to give the people of the state "a righteous administration." He will do his best to keep his word and it will not be an easy task; for old practices and abuses have the force of inertia. They are not easily stopped. The new administration will fall heir to whatever objectionable features may have been in the old. But if the governor cannot undo, he may fairly be held responsible for his own acts—his attitude toward the legislation submitted to him and his own exercise of the appointive power. In this his real self must show, and upon this his administration will be rated in the history of the state.

His relation to the school should be a happy one. A native of California, his enthusiasm and pride can be counted upon. Educated in the public schools, he is their staunch friend. A graduate of the State University at his age he knows its value as tested in the crucible of life. His children have attended a public school in a section of the city where families in very humble circumstances predominate, altho they might have had their choice of schools. Their mother, a former teacher, is a woman of great practical sense.

A successful professional man, he believes in high compensation for expert work—and teaching is expert work. He will be discriminating in his appointment to places of educational trust. Judging by his acts and utterances, he will not favor great interference with the natural development of the schools. He detests shams too much and is too sane to believe in educational incubators or elixirs. He will favor neither fogyism nor faddism. Mr. A. B. Nye, his executive secretary, is a man of sound sense and high ideals. His private secretary, Mr Arthur Elston is a lawyer, graduate of the State University, ex-principal of a grammar school and a member of the Alameda County Board of Education. So the teachers of the state may feel confident that they and the schools will receive intelligent and sympathetic treatment.

PHILIP M. FISHER, Oakland, Cal.

PUBLISHERS' NOTICE.

THE WESTERN JOURNAL OF EDUCATION succeeds to the subscription lists, advertising patronage, and good will of the Golden Era, established in San Francisco in 1852.

Subscription, $1.50 a year. Single copies, 15 cents.

Remit by check, Postoffice order, Wells, Fargo & Co., or by stamps.

ADVERTISEMENTS—Advertisements of an unobjectionable nature will be inserted at the rate of $3.00 a month per inch.

MSS.—Articles on methods, trials of new theories, actual experiences, and school news, reports of teachers' meetings, etc., urgently solicited.

Address all communications to THE WESTERN JOURNAL OF EDUCATION, 723 Market Street, San Francisco.

HARR WAGNER, Editor.

THE WHITAKER & RAY COMPANY PUBLISHERS.

Entered at the San Francisco Post-office as second-class matter.

The Official Organ of the Department of Public Instruction of the State of California.

The article which appeared in the last issue of THE JOURNAL on "Stanford University and its Relation to the Public School System" was written by W. C. Doub, at that time Superintendent of schools of Kern county.

***

The California Teachers' Association

(Editorial Review]

The meeting at Los Angeles, December 29 to January 3, 1903, was the largest in the history of the association. There were over 1900 badges given out. Booker T. Washington vitalized the last two days of the association. His lectures had an antiseptic effect on the colds caught in Hazard's Pavilion on the opening night. The section meetings were slightly interesting. The general sessions lagged. The program, both before and after its delivery, lacked "the conservation of intellectual activity" of the meeting at Sacramento, and the well-shot intelligence of the big guns at Monterey. The program, however, was decidedly respectable, and had many commendable features The President, A. E. Shumate, presided creditably. The address of welcome by Mayor Snyder was dignified, tactful and a model of its kind. Superintendent Foshay followed with a talk that almost warmed the pavilion. The response, by Mrs. J. E. Chope, was eloquent, poetical and in good taste. The address by Mrs. Ella F. Young, of the Department of Education of the University of Chicago, was an intelligent discussion of the subject of "Habit." Her power is not in a robust voice, but in her analysis, clear perceptions and fresh knowledge of her subject. Professor Hopkins, of the University of Kansas, gave several formal addresses. They were vigorous in thought, large of view and sound as to doctrine. The schoolmasters, however, will remember him for his bit in the after-banquet speech at the spread of the Schoolmasters' Club. It was a genial flow of humor, good for laughter and good for thought. The reception in the Cumnock School of Expression, a quaint, roomy, Shakespearian house, was a decidedly successful affair. It was the social event of the meeting.

The music, the dancing, the punch (orange juice and H$_2$O), were enjoyed by all.

Wednesday afternoon, Professor Cubberley discussed the "Rural School Problem," and Professor Young, "Social Progression of Childhood," and Professor Hopkins, "The Coming Oxford—American," to a large audience of good listeners. The election of officers resulted as follows: O. W. Erlewine, President; Mrs. J. E. Chope, First Vice President; Edward Hyatt, Second Vice President; Mrs. M. M.

FitzGerald, Secretary; C. C. Hughes, Assistant Secretary; Job Wood, Railroad Secretary; Philip Prior, Treasurer. San Francisco was selected as the next place of meeting.

Thursday, January 1st, the teachers visited Pasadena, Long Beach, Santa Monica, Spring Street, Mount Lowe, etc.

Thursday the Schoolmasters' Club gave a banquet. There were about one hundred guests. The toasts were by Dr. Elmer E. Brown, Professor E. M. Hopkins, Samuel T. Black and A. H. Suzzallo.

On Friday afternoon the teachers gave a warm greeting and close attention to Dr. Elmer E. Brown, who spoke on "Education and National Character." C. W. Mark also spoke on the election of teachers in San Francisco. Booker T. Washington spoke Friday afternoon and Friday evening to cheerful and enthusiastic audiences. He is great.

The editor was not able to be present at many of the department sections. It would require more than an amateur tourist and a kite-shaped track to be at Hazard's Pavilion, Blanchard's Hall, Cumnock School of Expression, High School Auditorium, Normal School Building, etc., during sessions. Supt. Hugh J. Baldwin arranged a great program and it was well carried out in the legislative section. The primary, grammar and high school sections were also well represented.

The Council of Education did perhaps the most serious work in its career at the Los Angeles meeting. It certainly outlined sufficient work to keep itself busy. The discussions on High Schools, Compulsory Education and Text Books were of great value. The reports are to be put in pamphlet form and circulated.

The Association made many valuable recommendations on text books, compulsory education, union of school districts, supervision of schools, etc. President Shumate appointed the following committee to take charge of the promotion of such legislation: Richard D. Faulkner, Thomas J. Kirk, Frederic Burk, Hugh J. Baldwin, Geo. A. Sackett, A. E. Shumate, Jas. A. Barr, E. C. Moore, D. S. Snedden, C. L. Biedenbach, P. M Fisher.

NOTES

The badges represented the beautiful poinsettia in burnt leather. They were unique and appropriate.

John Swett was the liveliest and most active and most cheerful member of the association.

The attendance from San Francisco and sections of the state north of Tehachipi was much larger than expected.

President Samuel T. Black's "Reminiscences" at the banquet were deliciously humorous, and his Scottish stories had the tang of heather to them.

The Los Angeles "Times" treated the association as an unwelcome guest, and its cynical reports were read, but were not considered courteous.

⁂

Supt. of Public Instruction Thomas J. Kirk has been so busily engaged on proposed legislation of interest to the schools, that the official department is omitted for this month.

**

The larger part of THE JOURNAL is devoted this month to a consideration of the high schools, and to the able and timely review of the educational problems of the year. School officials and teachers will find these articles well worth reading. They furnish an intelligent basis for the discussion of problems now at hand.

THE DEDICATION OF THE LOCKWOOD SCHOOL

LOCKWOOD SCHOOL—NEW BUILDING

The dedication of the new school building in the Lockwood district, Alameda county, Saturday, December 13, 1902, was an important event. Mr. C. H. Greenman, the principal, had worked very hard to make the event successful. Parents, teachers, trustees and children of Lockwood and the neighboring districts were present. The children sold and distributed a splendid illustrated edition of the *Elmhurst Review*, giving an interesting history of the school. Mr. Hazelton read a report of the building of the school. The school children, under the leadership of H. H Johnson, Miss Louise Toaspern, Prof. Paul Martin, Miss Grace Crane and others, furnished the music, Thomas J. Kirk, Superintendent of Public Instruction, delivered an eloquent and appropriate address, Supt. T. O. Crawford touched the hearts of all by his well-timed remarks, Harr Wagner gave a slightly humorous talk. The people enjoyed the program, and were delighted with the new and elegant school building, which is a model of its kind.

The news of Mr. E. F. Goodyear's death was lamented by his friends and received with sincere regret by the school people of the state. He was a native of California and a graduate of the State University. He taught in the high schools of the state for several years and was principal of the Kern County High School for two and one half years. He was the coast representative of the Macmillan Company during the past seven years and as such representative he was an illustration of what a bookman should be. He had the welfare of the schools at heart, as well as the interests of the company which he represented. The school people soon learned that his word could be relied on when discussing the value of books, because he employed none but straightforward and honest tactics. He had a host of friends, and it is said of him that he never lost one, because in him was combined extreme courtesy with a sterling character. We commend his life as an example to all.

⁂ WESTERN SCHOOL NEWS ⁂

MEETINGS

National Educational Association, President Charles W. Eliot. Boston, July 6–10, 1903.
National Superintendents' Convention, Cincinnati, Ohio. February 2, 24.

NOTES

Gertrude Rowell has been appointed as teacher of English in the San Jose Normal School.

Ex-Supt. P. W. Smith of Placer county has been elected principal of the Auburn schools.

A. F. Gunn, of the American Book Co., sent the first cablegram from Los Angeles to Honolulu.

The trustees of the Colusa High School will advertise for bids for a new building. The bids are to be opened January 24th.

Lawrence Walsh has been appointed by Mayor Schmitz a member of the San Francisco Board of Education, vice James Denman, term expired.

Ex-Supt. S. A. Crookshanks of Tulare county has returned to his fine ranch near Visalia, and expects to spend the rest of his days looking after his family interests.

The work of establishing the State Polytechnic school at San Luis Obispo is being carried forward by the Board of Trustees with considerable progress. Contracts have been let for two buildings.

Frank J. Browne, author of Browne's Series of Arithmetics, and formerly Superintendent of Public Instruction of State of Washington, has been appointed to the headmastership of Hoitt's School for Boys at Menlo Park.

Ex-Supt. J. A. Wagener of Stanislaus City has arranged to travel throughout the eastern states with a unique plan to promote immigration to California. He has secured an Hawaiian quartet, an exhibit wagon, and stereopticon views of the scenery, products, etc., of California.

There was an entire change in the Board of Education of Los Angeles city, with the exception of one member. This makes the task of the city superintendent extremely difficult, for it requires at least a year for the new board to become familiar with the ideals and the routine of the department, and it frequently happens that a majority of the board desire to inaugurate new and impractical methods in the transaction of business.

W. C. Doub, ex-superintendent of Kern county, has been appointed Pacific Coast Representative of the Macmillan Company to succeed E. F. Goodyear, deceased. The appointment of Mr. Doub will be well received by the school officials of California. He is a graduate of Stanford University, an industrious worker, and will present his books from the standpoint of merit. His integrity and experience as a teacher, superintendent and public spirited citizen, are splendid equipments for a useful career as a bookman.

The Girls' Industrial College of Texas, to the presidency of which Mr. Work has been called, is a new state institution located at Denton, North Texas. It is for the higher education of white girls in the arts and sciences, including literary courses, kindergarten instruction, telegraphy, stenography, photography, drawing, painting, designing and engraving in their industrial application, general needlework, including dressmaking, bookkeeping, the chemical study of food scientific and practical cooking, practical housekeeping, nursing and care of the sick, the care and culture of children, and such other subjects as may be deemed necessary from time to time in preparing girls for practical life. The students will be apportioned by counties, and admission determined by a system of competitive examinations or by appointment of county authorities. A fine building is now in process of construction, and the college will be opened in September, 1903. Mr. Work is to be there the first of January for the purpose of beginning the work of organization and the selection of teachers. It is with many regrets that he leaves San Francisco and the many friends and co-laborers with whom he has here been associated.

D. Appleton & Co., New York, has issued a handsomely illustrated edition of Lessing's "Minna von Barnhelm." Price 50 cts.

The Accrediting System of the University of California

University of California, December 27. — The relation of the high school to the University, the whole accrediting system, will be greatly bettered by an important change in the system of the examination of schools, which will be announced in President Wheeler's forthcoming Biennial Report as president of the University of California. This new system blends the system now in vogue, by which there is a special examiner for every subject, with the system in vogue in some of the states by which there is a single school examiner for all subjects.

A special examiner will be appointed who will spend from August to December of every year examining every school as a whole. He will be a man who is acquainted through practical experience and professional training with school management and organization. It will be his function to bring the University as a whole into relation with the school as a whole. He will be, moreover, a man competent in scholarship to hold a position as a University teacher. During the period from January to May of each year he will offer instruction in the University in the Department of Education.

It is important, however, that the relation of special departments of the University to special departments of the high schools should still be direct. During the second half year, therefore, representatives of the different specialties will make visits to such schools as may seem most to need their attention, either because they may not have been recently examined by a representative of the specialty in question, or because through the appointment of a new teacher, or through uncertainty in the judgment of the school examiner, the data may seem insufficient to guarantee the accrediting.

This new system of examining high schools in order to determine whether or not their graduates shall be admitted to the University, upon recommendation of the principal, without examination, will bring it to pass that the University will have some means of knowing the schools as wholes, and of estimating their organization and general management. At the same time, the individual teachers will not lose the inspiration and advice obtained through contact with University professors representing their various specialties.

Thus while the relation of a University specialty to the corresponding school department will be direct, yet it is as pupils of the school, rather than of the single teacher, that students will be judged as to their fitness for University life and work, for it is only on the basis of the school as a whole that a single department achieves success.

It is hoped by the new system to combine the merits of the Minnesota or Michigan system with the good points of the California system.

Literary Notes

"Masterpieces of Greek Literature," with biographical sketches and notes by John Henry Wright, Professor of Greek in Harvard University. Houghton, Mifflin & Co., Publishers. The author has collected in a book of nearly 500 pages much of the best there is in Greek prose and poetry. The translation has been very carefully done. The name of the translator in each case is given and such names as Hay, Moore, Rosetti, Browning and Arnold are among the list. It is a book that deserves a place in every library.

"Development of the Child in Later Infancy," by Com. payre, translated by Mary E. Wilson, a member of the Graduated Seminary in Child Study, University of California. D. Appleton & Co., Publishers. Price $1.20 net. Wm. T. Harris gives an excellent introduction. This is a very valuable contribution to the literature of Child Study. The chapters on "Learning to Speak," "Development of the Moral Sense" and "Morbid Tendencies" are interesting chapters.

"Emmy Lou, Her Book and Heart," by George Madden Marten. McClure, Phillips & Co., Publishers. Price $1.50. This is one of the most entertaining and natural books of child life in reference to public schools, yet written. The illustrations are fine, but it is Emmy Lou, copying digits, who interests and charms us from the beginning. It is no fairy story. Emmy Lou is a real girl. It should be in every school library in the state.

Edwin Herbert Lewis has written "A First Manual of Composition," Price 50 cts., and "A Text Book of Applied English Grammar," Price 60 cts. Macmillan Co. are the publishers. The author says in his introduction that instead of correcting faulty punctuation, if a student learns by heart forty typical sentences, with their punctuation, that he will ever after be able to apply the proper punctuation to other sentences.

POPULAR SONG

Mrs. Jennie L. Thorp was in receipt of a letter Thursday from the superintendent of schools of Placer County ordering two hundred copies of "California, Queen of Old Columbia." Mrs. Thorp states the song is already in use in many counties of the state, and an additional testimonial as to its popularity is the fact that so far over twelve hundred copies have been sold.

Above song is for sale by us. Price, 10 cents per copy. Special rate in quantities. THE WHITAKER & RAY CO. San Francisco.

Institutes

Madera County

The Tenth Annual Session of the Madera County Teachers' Institute convened at the Christian church. Dec. 16, 17 and 18, Miss Estella Bagnelle, the county superintendent, presiding.

The address of welcome was made by Miss Bagnelle, in which she complimented the teachers on their past work and expressed the hope that they would so continue to be earnest, faithful workers.

Mr. Job Wood of Sacramento was then introduced and made a few introductory remarks before taking up the discussion of the topic "Reading and Spelling," which be handled in an animated and instructive manner. In the afternoon the discussion of the subject by the Institute in general, added interest and force to the various points impressed by the morning lecture.

Mr. E. B. Williams, principal of the Madera High School, read an excellent paper upon the "High School in Relation to the Grammar School," introducing views and ideas which should awaken a new interest in the people of the commmnity.

Mr. Wood took up the discussion of "Geography," leading from home geography, our needs and wants, to the great commercial world, domestic and foreign commerce.

On Wednesday morning, Prof. Geo. R. Kleeberger spoke on "Nature Study."

In the afternoon Mr. Kleeberger lectured on "Written Expression," basing his theme on his morning work.

Mr. Wood followed by "Discipline that Fits for Life." He said that discipline should begin very early in life. Compel obedience, for he who learns to obey will some day be able to command. Train people to have some purpose in life. Give them some responsibility; it strengthens mind and character.

Thursday morning was delightfully spent in the discussion of "Arithmetic," led by Mr. Wood and assisted by a primary class from Madera schools. Much benefit was derived from the practical work thus given and interest was at its highest.

Miss Augusta M. Cole discussed the "Teachers' County Club" in the afternoon, advising teachers to be benefited by co-operation, and aid derived therefrom; demonstrating the value of study along a given line, and advocating *study* for every progressive teacher.

The Institute was entertained Tuesday evening by the teachers of Madera District, the program consisting of music, a farce, and progressive games.

On Wednesday eve the Knickerbocker Club of San Francisco, under the auspices of the Teachers' County Club, gave its Recital at Athletic Hall, inspiring all by its magnificent renditions.

The Institute was a decided success, each period lively, never lagging, and interest always at its keenest. Before each session some musical number was given, adding much to the program. Institute adjourned Thursday, p. m., and each teacher "if she did not look pleasantly forward to Institute, *did* look gratefully back to it.   C. W. E.

Ventura County.

Superintendent George Sackett called his institute for the week of December 16th—and struck a howling storm in the middle! It was a regular southeaster, one of those described by Dana in "Two Years Before the Mast," when the hide ships had to slip their cables and put to sea off the California coast. And this was a splendid specimen of its kind. The great waves dashed against the shore and splashed thirty or forty feet into the air; the rain came in torrents, and the teachers navigated the streets with great difficulty.

Mr. Sackett had planned his meeting with great care, so as to give his teachers opportunities in three directions—the *theoretical*, from the point of view of the Normal School and the University; the *practical*, from the standpoint of the working teacher and superintendent; and the *ethical*, as presented by cultured thinkers from abroad.

The first of these was held up by President Black of the San Diego Normal School and Miss Rodgers, one of his training teachers; and by Professor David Snedden of the Department of Education in Stanford University. Mr. Black talked about Number Work and the Monroe Doctrine; Miss Rodgers about the Ward method in reading and the Speer method in Arithmetic. Mr. Snedden was raised in this county, had long been a teacher and member of the Board of Education, so that his stay was an ovation and his work of peculiar interest and force.

On the practical side were many discussions of the every-day school problems, taking part in by the working teachers of the county and the working Superintendent of a neighboring county, Edward Hyatt of Riverside. These covered many phases of school work, such as institutes, decoration, book-keeping, nature study, discipline, grammar, arithmetic, etc. They were engaged in by Miss Crusoe, Miss Johnson, Mr. Kauffman, Mr. Haydock, Mr. Zahn, Mr. Owen, Miss Dwyer, Mr. Good, Mr. Beers, Superintendent Sackett, Mr. Potter, Mr. Guillon, Mr. Blackstock, Mr. Fox, Miss Burnette, Miss Bruere, and many others: In geography

Mr. Hyatt's experiences on the Colorado Desert were especially commended by President Black and by the local papers as being of peculiar interest and value to all teachers of children.

In the line of general culture were the lectures of Professor Dudley on "Color;" and one by Dr. Robert McIntyre of Los Angeles, although this was finally prevented by the storm. Superintendent Sackett's printed programs were a model of typographic art, and were said by good judges to be the best ever printed in the state.

After the storm the sun shone, and the teachers went home dry shod and at peace with the world.

Riverside Institute.

The Riverside Institute this year was a short and a merry one. It continued for two days, adjourning on the 3d to join the State Association at Los Angeles.

Job Wood Jr. of Sacramento gave his practical work on drill in arithmetic and a talk on "Discipline," all very helpful to the teachers. Elwood Cubberley of Stanford gave a description of schools and education in England, most interesting and useful.

Harr Wagner of San Francisco gave his breezy talk, "Why Some Teachers Succeed," greatly enjoyed and appreciated by the teachers who succeed, and by the others, too.

Helen Brooks, a Wellesley woman, gave a literary lecture on Browning, which carried her hearers back to the days of Professor Griggs.

A. L. Walker of Stockton described his experiences as a teacher in the Phillipines. This took well, as it was a genuine piece of life.

Professor Dudley of Wisconsin gave interesting lectures on "Color" and on "Wireless Telegraphy."

At the close of the institute the whole teaching force of the county packed up bag and baggage and embarked on their special train for Los Angeles, with a half-fare rate. The distance is some seventy miles. The teachers congregated in congenial groups of traveling companions and had a jolly journey. Superintendent Hyatt acted as train-boy and distributed sandwiches, olives and apples.

Arrived in Los Angeles, the city swallowed them for four days—Booker Washington, Mt. Lowe, pedagogy, Catalina, Council of Education, receptions, hotels, shop windows—all of this kept them busy till it was time to go home; and they went back to their schools, scattered far and wide, rested and refreshed by this dip into the full flowing tide of humanity.

Institute Notes

J. P. Greeley held the Orange county institute Dec. 22, 23, 24 at Santa Ana. Among the instructors were T. H. Kirk of Santa Barbara, Prof. W H. Dudley of Chicago and Frank J. Browne. The institute was a notable success. This institute practically closed Supt. Greeley's official work in Orange county. During the fourteen years he has served as superintendent, the schools made rapid progress. Supt. Greeley conducted the office in a most excellent manner. The teachers' library is an illustration of his work. Altho Orange county is one of the smaller counties and one of those most recently organized, yet Supt. Greeley built up the largest teachers' library in the state. There were many expressions of regret on the part of teachers and citizens, on account of the fact that the pleasant relations of superintendent and teachers were to close on Jan. 5, 1903.

Supt Hugh J. Baldwin held the institute at San Diego the week beginning Dec. 16 He secured as instructors Frank J. Browne, President G. A. Gates of Pomona, Dr. Edwards and several others. The week was a profitable one and the teachers expressed themselves as well pleased with the program furnished by Supt. Baldwin.

BOOK REVIEWS

"Palatial Tone-Placing, Articulation in Singing," by Louis Crepaux, member Paris Grand Opera and medalist from the Paris Conservatory of Music and Declamation. This scientific brochure is one of the most important contributions to the technique of tone-placing that has been published during recent years. Prof. Crepaux easily stands at the head of the teachers of Voice-culture of San Francisco. He is a scholar and a teacher of great ability. The first chapter in the book is palatal tone-placing; the second is on reflection; the third on discrimination in aiming tones. The latter part of the book is devoted to articulation in singing. The following extracts on how to use labial muscles is a good example of his style of treatment. For further particulars in reference to book address Louis Crepaux, Y. M. C. A. Bldg., S. F., Cal.

I must first call the attention of the English-speaking student to the relation of proper articulation to tone production. This question, not having heretofore been properly understood, has not received the attention it deserves, and consequently many a good tone is spoiled by improper articulation.

The Romanic languages—French, Italian and Spanish, and also the Provencal dialect of Southern France, which has been made famous by the poet Mistral in his masterpiece "Mireille" —all have their articulations as perfect in singing as in speech, and the singers of these countries can speak and sing on the same principle of articulation.

Supposing the singer to have had some good training in tone-placing, and that he has no special defect of speech, such as stammering or lisping; in a very short time he will acquire a good articulation which will not alter nor injure his tones, but will, on the contrary, assist in projecting and reflecting them. Furthermore, this singer, by simply strengthening his articulation, will be able to sing what is termed "parlamente,"—that is to say, to speak in the voice. This may be said of all European singers who sing in the Romanic languages, patois and dialects.

The principle of the "parlamente" cannot,

however, be practically taken up and applied to English-speaking singers.

Since beginning the study of the English language, and particularly since I have been teaching singing in this language, my observations have led me to the conclusion that some of the proper articulations of speech cannot be the proper ones in singing, and must therefore be altered.

Many English articulations being uttered on a very defective principle for singing, the following examples will assist the student in overcoming some of these difficulties. It will be observed that in these articulations the lower lip is improperly drawn downward, and sometimes backward and downward, a motion which is very injurious to tone production as it causes a downward muscular reflex action on the larynx.

I could quote many examples of English articulations where the tone is injured on account of the misuse of the lower lip, but a few will enable the student to find many others having similar misutterance.

Soft c, s, r, y, and the diagraph sw.

In the utterance of the articulations s and sw, as in the English words *set* and *swear*, the lower lip is depressed and drawn downward and backward with such a forcible motion that it causes a contracting muscular reflex action on the larynx.

The utterance of r in such English words as *large*, *charge*, *care*, *dare*, etc., also causes an improper downward and backward motion of the lower lip.

In the articulation of y in the words *yellow*, *yet*, *why*, etc., the lower lip is also misused.

D. C. Heath & Co., Boston, Mass., has published "Select Poems of Coleridge," edited by A. J. George, with introduction and notes. The notes cover over a hundred pages and are very complete.

L. Du Pont Syle of the University of California has edited Scott's "Lady of the Lake" for a Volume in Heath's English Classics. The illustrations are very fine and the introduction and notes are given with a keen literary appreciation of the great poem.

"Introduction to Botany" by William Chase Stevens of the University of Kansas has been published by D. C. Heath & Co. This book, in illustration, arrangement and method of presentation, represents the best there is in text-book making.

"German Daily Life," by R. Kron. Newson & Co., Publishers, New York. Price 75 cts. This is a recent addition to Newson's Modern Language Series. It is a worthy guide to German life and customs and is a most valuable reader for the class in German.

"Guide Right, Ethics for Young People," is a new book on an important subject by Emma L. Ballou, March Brós., Publishers, Lebanon, Ohio. Price, holiday edition, 75 cts; library edition, 40 cts. The book was written for use in the school room and is well adapted for such use. It is the author's aim to have the children see the beauty of goodness and to make their lives good and true.

"How to Study Literature" is an interesting guide to the intensive study of literary masterpieces, by B. A. Heydrick. Publishers, Hinds & Noble, New York. The discussions of the various kinds of Poetry and Prose and the specimen studies of Tennyson's "Bugle Song" and other masterpieces, will be helpful to the student and teacher.

**

"Notable Speeches by Notable Speakers of the Greater West," edited by Harr Wagner, has just been published by the Whitaker & Ray Co. It is bound in half morocco, printed on laid paper, portraits in double toned ink, and taken all together, is the handsomest book ever issued on the Pacific. It contains 432 pages. The speeches represent forty different orators, from Uncle George's G. T. Bromley's witty school speech to Samuel M. Shortridge's greatest masterpiece. The price of the book is $5.00 per volume.

A Bargain in Pianos—For sale, a fine new piano, never used, price $350, will sell for $250. Address Piano, care of WESTERN JOURNAL OF EDUCATION, 723 Market st., S. F., Cal.

For sale—A scholarship in leading business college, price $100, will sell for $50. Address Business, care of WESTERN JOURNAL OF EDUCATION, 723 Market st., S. F , Cal.

**

There is more Catarrh in this section of the country than all other diseases put together, and until the last few years was supposed to be incurable. For a great many years doctors pronounced it a local disease, and prescribed local remedies, and by constantly failing to cure with local treatment, pronounced it incurable. Science has proven catarrh to be a constitutional disease, and therefore requires constitutional treatment. Hall's Catarrh Cure, manufactued by F. J. Cheney & Co., Toledo, Ohio, is the only constitutional cure on the market. It is taken internally in doses from ten drops to a teaspoonful. It acts directly on the blood and mucous surfaces of the system. They offer one hundred dollars for any case it fails to cure. Send for circulars and testimonials. Address, F. J. CHENEY & CO., Toledo, O.

Sold by Druggists, 75c.

Hall's Family Pills are the best.

Special Announcement
IN PRESS

Stories of Our Western Birds

BY JOSEPH AND ELIZABETH GRINNELL

A Supplementary Book in the "Western Series of Readers" for the Middle Grades

Richly Illustrated, Price, net, 50 Cents

To be published by

The Whitaker & Ray Company

SAN FRANCISCO

TO THE CLERK:—This is the Official Journal of Education. The law requires that filed in the School Library before the close of each month.

THE WESTERN JOURNAL OF EDUCATION

FEBRUARY, 1903

Contents

Compulsory Education...Dr. E. C. Moore, University of California   65
    This is the complete report to the Council of Education on "The Need of a Compulsory Education Law in California."

The Practical of Manual Training ....Cree T. Work   77
    President of the Industrial Training School for Women, Denton, Texas.

Free Text-Books......................Supt. E. M. Cox, Santa Rosa   88
    This is a report of the committee appointed by the California Council of Education "To Compile a Report Upon the System of Free Text-Books and Its Adaptability to School Conditions in California."

Editorial...   98
    Increase Pay for Teachers. Editorial Review of Some Proposed Legislature

Book Reviews   101
    Liberty Documents. School Composition. Social Life of the Early Republic.

Western School News......................................   103

Miscellaneous..   105

HARR WAGNER, Editor

New Books for Nature Study

BARTLETT'S ANIMALS AT HOME   45 cents

For Third Reader Grade

This little book is intended to arouse the interest of children in certain individual animals, and by so doing to awaken an interest for Natural History in general. In each story one particular animal is described in such a way as to illustrate the life of a class.

PYLE'S STORIES OF HUMBLE FRIENDS   50 cents

For Third Reader Grade

The stories in this book are about animals and birds familiar to the children. They are simple in their manner of presentation and most sympathetic in treatment. The many pictures drawn by the author are vividly illustrative of the incidents described.

BRADISH'S STORIES OF COUNTRY LIFE   40 cents

For Third Reader Grade

These recollections of a childhood spent on a northwestern farm, aim to emphasize the attractiveness of life in the country, and to add to its charm by awakening an intelligent interest in its many activities.

KELLY'S SHORT STORIES OF OUR SHY NEIGHBORS   50 cents

For Third Reader Grade

Entertaining and instructive reading, telling about the birds, insects, and other living creatures around us, in such an interesting manner as to arouse in the child a desire to become better acquainted with the wonders of the animate world.

STOKES'S TEN COMMON TREES   40 cents

For Third Reader Grade

A series of simple nature lessons for young children familiarly treated and giving a few definite impressions of what trees are and how they live.

DANA'S PLANTS AND THEIR CHILDREN   65 cents

For Fourth Reader Grade

These charming readings are as interesting as stories and are not only instructive in themselves, but teach the most important lessons a child can learn — to see to think; to observe for himself, and thus to become an intelligent student of nature.

Popular Works in Botany and Zoölogy

Holder's Stories of Animal Life	$0.60
Needham's Outdoor Studies	.40
Cooper's Animal Life	1.25
Gray's How Plants Behave	.54
How Plants Grow, with a Popular Flora	.80
Herrick's Chapters on Plant Life	.60
Johonnot's Book of Cats and Dogs	.17
Friends in Feathers and Fur	.30
Neighbors with Wings and Fins	.40
Some Curious Flyers, Creepers, and Swimmers	.40
Some Neighbors with Claws and Hoofs	.54
Glimpses of the Animate World	1.00
Lockwood's Animal Memoirs—	
Part I. Mammals	.60
Part II. Birds	.60
McGuffey's Familiar Animals and Their Wild Kindred	$0.50
Living Creatures of Water, Land, and Air	.50
Monteith's Popular Science Reader	.72
Burnet's School Zoölogy	.75
Needham's Elementary Lessons in Zoölogy	.90
Steele's Popular Zoölogy	1.20
Apgars' New Plant Analysis	.50
Leavitt's Outlines of Botany	1.00
The same. With Gray's Field, Forest, and Garden Flora	1.80
Wood's New American Botanist and Florist—Lessons and Flora	1.72

AMERICAN BOOK COMPANY   PUBLISHERS

NEW YORK   CINCINNATI   CHICAGO   BOSTON   ATLANTA   DALLAS

THE WESTERN JOURNAL OF EDUCATION

Established 1852.

OLD SERIES: GOLDEN ERA, VOL. XLVI.   SAN FRANCISCO, FEBRUARY, 1903.   NEW SERIES: VOL. VIII NUMBER 2

Compulsory Education

Report to the Council of Education on the Need for a Compulsory Education Law in California

When the personified Laws of Athens appeared to Socrates in prison and persuaded him that it would be wrong for him to accept the means of escape from death which his friend Crito had provided, they began by asking if he had any complaint to make against them which justified him in attempting to destroy them and the state. "In the first place did we not bring you into existence? Your father married your mother by our aid and begot you. Say whether you have any objection to urge against those of us who regulate marriage?" "None," he replied. "Or against those of us who regulate the system of nurture and education of children in which you were trained? Were not the laws, who have charge of this, right in commanding your father to train you in music and gymnastics?" "Right, I should reply," said Socrates,[1] and this statement taken from the early literature of education is the first reference to compulsory education which we possess. Some years afterward when Plato wrote his Laws, having provided for the outer organization of the state, he turned to the means of its accomplishment and for this purpose established schools of various kinds, and decreed: "In these several schools let there be dwellings for teachers, who shall be brought from foreign parts by pay, and let them teach the frequenters of the school the art of war and the art of music, and they shall come, not only if their parents please, but if they do not please; and if their education is neglected, there shall be compulsory education of all and sundry, as the saying is, as far as this is possible; and the pupils shall be regarded as belonging to the state rather than to the parents."[2] The world waited for a long time for the coming of a lawmaker who would enforce these principles of state legislation, but at last he came in the person of learning loving Charles the Great, who, after a considerable attention to the revival of learning in

---
[1] Plato, Crito 50.
[2] Plato, Laws VII—804.

his kingdom, issued a capitulary in the year 802 enjoining upon his subjects that "every one should send his son to study letters, and that the child should remain at school with all diligence until he should become well instructed in learning."[1] Alfred the Great (873-901), who laid the foundations of England, regarded education as one of the chief instruments in the hands of a king for the improvement of his people, and so desired to extend its blessings to all his freeborn subjects, that he made a law requiring that every freeman possessed of two hides of land should keep his sons at school until they were fifteen years of age, "because," as he said, "a man born free, who is unlettered, is to be regarded no otherwise than as a beast, having like them no understanding."[2] Luther, in an address to the municipal councils of the German towns, exhorted them to establish Christian schools everywhere, both elementary and secondary, urging them to "forget not the poor youth. * * The strength of a town does not consist in its towers and buildings, but in counting a great number of learned, serious, honest, and well educated citizens."[3] While our own forefathers of New England in 1642 ordered that "the selectmen of every town in the several precincts and quarters where they shall dwell shall have a vigilant eye over their brethren and neighbors, to see first that none of them shall suffer so much barbarism in any of their families as not to endeavor to teach, by themselves or others, their children and apprentices so much learning as may enable them perfectly to read the English tongue and knowledge of the capital laws, upon penalty of twenty shillings for each neglect therein."[4]

These historical statements indicate the reasons which have led some thirty states, beginning with Massachusetts in the year 1852, to adopt compulsory school legislation. All such legislation is based upon the reasoning of Socrates that the laws which bring children into existence must also regulate the system of nurture and education in which they are trained; that their guardian responsibility requires them to command that the young shall be educated properly; that even if their parents do not please to send them to school, inasmuch as they belong to the state rather than to their parents, the interest of the state in them is paramount to that of their parents. It is sometimes said that compulsory education is not becoming in a free people, that it belongs to military paternalisms rather than to a democratic government, since it interfers with the liberty of the individual. Without a compulsory education law the penalty of non-attendance at school falls upon the child in every case. Compulsory legislation does sometimes interfere with parental negligence and coercion, but it does so to guarantee the liberty of the child. And every act to enforce it is an act to enforce the educational rights of children, which must be the more carefully guarded because of their inherent helplessness. "In our day," says Professor Nicholson, "the

---

[1] Pertz, Leges, 1-107.
[2] Drane, Christian Schools and Scholars, 200.
[3] Lindsay, Luther in Ency. Britt.
[4] Report of U. S. Commissioners of Education, 1899-1900—1-98.

economic value of various so-called moral forces is altogether underestimated. Parents ought to have seen that it would pay them in the long run to have their children properly educated."[1]

The more recent investigations of history, sociology and the biological sciences place a daily increasing emphasis upon the determining character of social surroundings. The keynote of all recent scientific discovery is that the individual plant, animal or man does not inherit its qualities, or get them by spontaneous variation, but does get them and is what it is because of the influences which play upon it—in the case of man, thru social tradition. This means that in our day the formative power of the school is infinitely more clearly recognized than ever before. In some form or other it is proven to be the indispensable agent in the making of men, and our warrant for urging its claims has been trebled and quadrupled in the last twenty years. On the other hand the standard of social survival has been raised alarmingly.

The weeding out process is applied more relentlessly than ever before. Ability of a much high order than heretofore is demanded in all forms of industry. Natural products decrease; machinery, more swift and complicated, is daily introduced, processes of production become more complex. All this means either that increasing care must be taken in equipping men for life or that increasing numbers of men must join the ranks of the unemployed. Incompetence and stupidity cannot anywhere find a place in the tide of progress. The economic, political, and moral well-being of the state demand that its process of education shall be closely fitted to its processes of growth; that the rear guard shall march with the vanguard. Choose on the one hand the school, on the other the almshouse and the penitentiary—is the dilemma which confronts every community in the United States.

Hence to the reasons which prompted the adoption of an ineffective compulsory education in California in the year 1874, very many more can be added which call for the adoption of an effective law at the present time. Advance sheets of the census of 1900, prepared by the United States census office to exhibit the working of the school systems of the various states, indicate that California has fallen from the fourteenth place among the states in 1890, as determined by the per cent of children between ten and fourteen years of age who are able to read and write, to the nineteenth place in 1900. Correspondence with the chief statistician for population reveals the following facts:

The total illiterate population of the State of California in 1900 from ten to fourteen years of age, both inclusive, classified as to sex, general nativity, and color, was:

		Males	Females
Native white—native parents	226	117	109
Native white—foreign parents	295	166	129
Foreign white	206	118	88
Colored, including Negroes, Chinese, Japanese and Indians	552	246	306
Totals	1279	647	632

[1] Nicholson, Strikes 51.

These figures indicate that a part of our population, as large as that of a town of 1000 people, is utterly without educational advantages. But these figures are no guide as to the number of school age in the state who do not attend school in any given year. The report of the state superintendent of education gives the number of children between five and seventeen years of age who attended no school at any time during the year 1900 as 71,054, 1901 as 74,691, 1902 as 59,656.

Owing to the inadequacy of available school statistics it is quite impossible to determine exactly what proportion of this number were of school age, and more difficult to determine how many would have been affected by a law requiring attendance at school between the ages of eight and fourteen years. It is to be hoped for many reasons that the time is not far off when distributed statistics of a more serviceable character will be gathered. . Superintendent Webster in a recent public utterance reported the number of census children who attended no school in the city of San Francisco for the year ending May 1, 1902, as 19,434. Of this number, said the superintendent, about 16,000 were of school age. More than 6000 of these it was estimated, would be affected by a compulsory education law. The principal of a large school in one of the poorer quarters of San Francisco said in my hearing a few days ago, that with an effective compulsory law he could gather 1,000 more children into school from his neighborhood alone.

The total number of census children in Los Angeles for the year 1901 was 32,003. The total enrollment for that year was 21,648, less 488 over seventeen years of age plus 2,764 in private schools in 1901, assumed for the argument to be all seventeen or under, though actually not, leaving 8,079 census children not attending school. Using the difference between the estimated number of children in Texas between the ages of five and eighteen years and the number of children enumerated in the school census between the ages of eight and seventeen years, as given in the Report of the United States Commissioner of Education for the year 1899-1900, as a rough basis for estimating what part of the total school population is under eight years of age, we get the following result:

Estimated number of children in Texas between 5 and 18.........1,070,000
Census children between 8 and 17 years of age................... 729,365

Approximate number of children in Texas between 5 and 8 and 17 and 18 years of age....................................... 340,635

Deducting one-sixth for seventeen to eighteen years of age leaves not more than 298,868 from five to eight, or 28 per cent of the whole number of children from five to seventeen years of age were from five to eight years of age. Using this proportion as a standard, we find approximately 8,961 children in Los Angeles between the ages of five and eight years. But 6,200 of these are in public school, and assuming that 28 per cent of the private school attendance is made up of children of this age (not an unfair assumption, because the number that attend private kindergartens, etc.), we have 6,973 of this age in school, leaving 6,091 from eight to seventeen years not in school. Our question becomes, how many of these were between the ages of eight and fourteen years and come within the intention of a compulsory education law? Assuming that the number of children from fourteen to seventeen years of age is but 500 less than the number from five to eight years of age, we get a total number of 16,422 children from five to eight and fourteen to seventeen years of age, leaving approximately 15,581 children from eight to fourteen years of age who should be in school. Of this number 12,772 are enrolled in the grades, 178 in the high school, and assuming that one-half of all who attend private schools are of this age (an unwarranted assumption, as the children in private schools are usually in private kindergartens and beginning schools or over fourteen years of age), we find that 1,249 children from eight to fourteen years of age, in the city of Los Angeles, should be in school and are not.

If it should be objected that these figures are very hypothetical, it may be said in reply that in every case they have been interpreted in favor of the number attending school, and a less liberal interpretation would show, not 1,249, but nearer 2,000 children between the ages of eight and fourteen who are not in school. Our figures show that over 15 per cent of the total number of census children not in school in Los Angeles are between eight and fourteen years of age. Assuming that this proportion holds for the state at large (by no means an unwarranted assumption), we get 10,658 children between the ages of eight and fourteen years who were not in school at all during the year 1900 in the State of California, 11,203 in 1901, and 8,948 in 1902.

Distributed statistics being indispensable to the value of this report, the chairman of your committee addressed a personal letter to each county superintendent in the state, begging him to report the estimated number of children of school age in his county who were not in school and the reasons which they would most likely give for such non-attendance. To this request twenty superintendents immediately replied. A second request was sent to the others, which brought nine more responses. Your committee regrets to report that twenty-eight superintendents took no interest in the matter. Of the twenty-nine that replied only six hazarded to guess in figures. Their estimates averaged indicate that, according to their judgment, 44 per cent of the census children non-attending in their counties were of school age. Two or three were so bold as to say that a compulsory education law would put 15 to 20 per cent more children in school. We beg, therefore, to report having exhaustively studied the data obtainable, that we believe that 15 per cent or more of the non-attending census children fall within the scope of a compulsory education law.

There is another and perhaps a more convincing way to show the need for such a law. If its limits were fixed at eight and fourteen years, it would in effect guarantee to each child in the State nearly six years of schooling, i. e., it would place almost all in the grammar schools for at least a part of the course. Statistics at hand indicate that while 47 per cent of the census children of the State are enrolled in primary schools, only 23 per cent attend grammar shools I submit that this proportion is not satisfactory.

Superintendent Furlong of Marin County has called my attention to the following facts. I quote from his letter: "A study of the official records of daily attendance at school in this county, for last year, shows another quite a different condition. The total enrollment for the year was 2,287 pupils, the average number belonging was 1,694, and the average daily attendance was only 1,588. This shows an average daily absence of 699. Over 30 per cent, or nearly one-third of the children enrolled at school, were absent daily during the year. This is wrong. A law compelling regular attendance would perhaps reduce absenteeism to 10 per cent or less, sickness alone being a valid excuse for it. Such a law is desirable in this State. Let me observe here that census statistics are very misleading as to the number of children that are not being educated. Such records show only the number failing to attend school at any time."

Applying this method to the state, we find a total enrollment in 1900, 1901 and 1902 of 257,557, 258,977, 264,038; in kindergartens, primary and grammar schools the average number belonging being 200,833, 202,148, 207,655, while the average daily attendance was 188,420, 188,730, 197,217, or 69,137, 71,247, 66,821, or 26.8 per cent, 27 per cent and 25.3 per cent of the children enrolled in the State were absent daily during these years.

Various reasons are assigned by the superintendents for this condition of affairs. Thirteen refer to the fact that children are kept at home to work by their parents; five refer to parents "too poor or too shiftless" to procure proper clothing for their children; twelve assign utter indifference or lack of appreciation of the value of education on the part of parents as a reason; five ascribe non-attendance to the fact that parents are foreigners and peculiarly indifferent to their children learning English; four declare that parents say, "If my children do not want to go to school they will not be compelled to do so"; four believe that lack of parental control, truancy in towns or villages resulting in practical vagrancy, is a cause—one of them, indeed, that it is the chief cause; seven speak of the fact that schools are too far distant; four, of sickness as a cause; one, of poor school conditions; one, of children that have no parents or guardians; one, of the absence of the stimulating influence of High Schools; one, of lack of a permanent home; and one, of neighborhood quarrels.

The menacing character of these conditions cannot be over-emphasized. Mr. Jacob Riis has said that "three fourths of all juvenile delinquency in New York is the result of truancy, the street life of children." Mr. W. Douglass Morrison, in his book on juvenile offenders, writes: "Seventeen in every hundred of the juveniles sent to reformatory schools in 1891 were unable to read or write, and seventy in every hundred could only read or write imperfectly. That is to say, only 13 per cent of the children sent to reformatories had received an ordinary school board education. The defective state of education among reformatory school inmates which these statistics reveal is in some measure to be attributed to the defective mental capacity of the children themselves. But deficiency in ordinary mental capacity is only a partial explanation of the facts. There can be no doubt that many of these children are wholly ignorant or badly educated owing to parental neglect. And in so far as neglect to bestow the element of education on the child is to be taken as a sign of moral obliquity in the parent, it is unquestionable that at least 50 per cent of the parents of juvenile offenders are in this condition."[1] And again: "The only way in which it seems possible to effect this improvement," i. e., in economic conditions of the most impoverished sections of the juvenile population, "is by raising the standard of industrial efficiency among the least favored members of the juvenile population. How this reform is to be accomplished is undoubtedly a most formidable problem. It will never be accomplished if left to the parents of such children, in cases where they have parents. It is a reform which must proceed from collective action on the part of the community. At present the community confines its operations to bestowing industrial training on children who have actually fallen ; it is probable that it would be a wiser, and in the end a more economic, policy to bestow a similar training on those who are likely to fall."[2] Nor should such community action be undertaken to better the condition of cities merely. It is no longer believed that virtue is synonymous with country life. Carelessness, indifference, idleness and loafing, as they exist in country villages, are perhaps more destructive to the young of the land than are the vices of city life, for those who succumb to them do not have to defy the same weight of social suggestion making for orderliness and labor. Very frequently the cry is thoughtlessly raised in our land that the schools make criminals. Yet more thorough investigations show that more than eight times as many criminals are made outside the schools as come into being after contact with them. We have spoken of the legal and economic value of general education. These are, indeed, its negative virtues. Its positive contributions in the making of citizens and moral men are its incomparable benefits.

"The greatest menace to the full success of our school system," writes one superintendent, "is the need of a compulsory education law." Another: "I am constrained to believe that in the majority of cases non-attendance is due to the indulgence and indiscretion of parents." Compulsory education is "a matter which I consider of the utmost importance," writes a third. "I feel that there is great necessity for a compulsory law that will prove operative," says a fourth. "There can be no doubt about the need for an effective law," says a fifth. "In this county the sentiment seems to be that all children ought to attend school, even if it is at a great sacrifice on

---

[1] Morrison, Juvenile Offenders, 109.
[2] Morrison, Juvenile Offenders, 177.

the part of the family, notwithstanding I believe we should have a compulsory law that is effective as possible, for all children of America should have at least a grammar school education," says a sixth. Such are some sample statements that have come to me in the last few days. Only one superintendent from whom I have heard expresses himself as opposed to such a law. "It would often bring dissension, and the district would be better without it," he writes. "Have taught in public schools thirty-five years. Most always found those who wished to enforce compulsory education occasionally preferred strife to friendship. The best in the community would not interfere. Compulsory education might do in cities. Think it, as a whole, quite an injury in rural districts.

Such is the need for an effective law in California. How may it best be met? The experience of older States may be of assistance to us. "Every child between seven and fourteen years of age," reads Section 1 of Chapter 44 of the Revised Laws of Massachusetts, enacted November 21, 1901, to take effect January 1, 1902, "shall attend some public school in the city or town in which he resides during the entire time the public day schools are in session." And the only exceptions are that the child may attend a private day school teaching thoroughly all the subjects of the legal course of study and approved by the School Committee, or be otherwise instructed in those branches, or if his physical or mental condition is such as to render such attendance inexpedient or impracticable. "Every person having under his control a child as described in this section shall cause him to attend school as herein required; and if he fails for five day sessions or ten half-day sessions within any period of six months, while under such control, to cause such child whose physical or mental condition is not such as to render his attendance at school harmful or impracticable, so to attend school, he shall, upon complaint of a truant officer and conviction thereof, be punished by a fine of not more than twenty dollars. Whoever induces or attempts to induce such a child to absent himself unlawfully from school, or employs or harbors a child who, while school is in session, is unlawfully absent from school, shall be punished by a fine of not more than fifty dollars." A child unlawfully excluded from school may recover damages from the city or town in an action of tort for such unlawful exclusion. Section 1, Chapter 46, declares: "The county commissioners of each county shall maintain, either separately or jointly, in a suitable place not at or near a penal institution, a truant school for the instruction and training of children committed thereto as habitual truants, absentees or school offenders." "A child between seven and fourteen years of age who willfully and habitually absents from school contrary to the above provisions shall be deemed an habitual truant." "A child between seven and sixteen years of age who may be found wandering about in the streets or public places of any city or town, having no lawful occupation, habitually not attending school and growing up in idleness and ignorance, shall be deemed to be an habitual absentee." "A child under fourteen years of age who persistently violates the reasonable regulations of the school which he attends, or otherwise persistently misbehaves therein, so as to render himself a fit subject for exclusion therefrom, shall be deemed to be an habitual school offender."

Chapter 671 of the Laws of 1894 of the State of New York: "Every child between eight and sixteen years of age, in proper physical and mental condition to attend school, shall regularly attend upon instruction at a school in which at least the common school branches * * * are taught, or upon equivalent instruction by a competent teacher elsewhere than at school, as follows: Every such child between fourteen and sixteen years of age, not regularly and lawfully engaged in any useful employment or service, and every such child between eight and twelve years of age, shall so attend upon instruction as many days annually during the period between the 1st days of October and the following June, as the public school of the city or district in which such child resides shall be in session during the same period." Every child between twelve and fourteen years of age shall attend upon instruction eighty consecutive days, except for holidays, vacations and detentions by sickness. Occasional absences not amounting to irregular attendance are permitted. Every person in parental relation to a child between eight and sixteen years old shall cause him so to attend or make affidavit that he is unable so to compel such a child to attend, or be subject to a fine not exceeding five dollars for the first offense, and for each subsequent offense not exceeding fifty dollars, or to imprisonment not exceeding thirty days, or to both fine and imprisonment. It shall be unlawful for any firm or corporation to employ any child between the ages of eight and twelve years in any business whatever during any part of the term in which the public schools are in session, the penalty being fifty dollars for each offense. The school authorities of each city or district shall appoint an attendance officer. The attendance officer may arrest without warrant any child between eight and sixteen years of age found away from his home and who then is a truant from instruction. The school authorities of any city or school district may establish schools or set apart separate rooms in public school buildings for children between eight and sixteen years of age who are habitual truants from instruction upon which they are lawfully required to attend, or who are insubordinate or disorderly during their attendance upon such instruction, or irregular in such attendance. Such schools or rooms shall be known as a truant school; but no person convicted of crimes or misdemeanors, other than truancy, shall be committed thereto.

On May 12, 1902, the Legislature of Ohio passed a Compulsory Education Act intended to cure the defects of previous laws, compelling all parents, guardians and others who have care of children to cause them to be instructed in reading, spelling, writing, English grammar, geography and arithmetic, and all such parents, guardians, etc., having charge of any child between the ages of eight and fourteen years, to send such child to a public, private or parochial school, for the full time that the school attended is in session, in no case to be less than twenty-four weeks. Such attendance to begin within the first week of the school term. Unless the child shall have been excused by the superintendent of schools, wherever there is such superintendent, or by the clerk of the board of education in other cases, or by the principal of the private or parochial school upon satisfactory showing, either that the child is being instructed at home by a qualified person, or that his bodily or mental condition does not permit such attendance at school. In case these officers refuse to grant such excuse, appeal may be taken to the probate judge of the county. Similarly, all the children between the ages of fourteen and sixteen years of age, not engaged in some regular employment, shall attend school for the full term unless likewise excused. Any parent or guardian failing to place such child in school within the time prescribed shall be subject to a fine of not less than five nor more than twenty dollars, and upon failure or refusal to pay such fine shall be imprisoned in the county jail not less than ten days nor more than thirty.

No child under fourteen years of age shall be employed or be in the employment of any person, company or corporation while the schools are in session, unless such child shall present a certificate issued by the Superintendent, or in case there be none, by the clerk of the board of education, showing that he has successfully completed the above course of study, or if between the ages of fourteen and sixteen, a knowledge of his or her ability to read and write legibly the English language, subject to a fine of not less than twenty-five or more than fifty dollars.

The law is equally drastic with regard to truants. Every child between the ages of eight and fourteen years, and every child between the ages of fourteen and sixteen years unable to read and write the English language, or not engaged in some regular employment, who is an habitual truant from school, or who absents himself habitually from school, or who while in attendance at any public, private or parochial school is incorrigible, vicious or immoral in conduct, or who habitually wanders about the streets and public places during school hours, having no business or lawful occupation, shall be deemed a juvenile disorderly person.

Truant officers shall be appointed in city districts and in special and township districts, vested with police powers. It shall be his duty first to notify the parent of the fact that his child does not attend school, and in case of continued failure to do so he shall make complaint against the parent. In case the parent prove inability to cause the child to attend school, the child shall be adjudged to be a juvenile disorderly person and committed, if under ten years of age, to a children's home, or if not eligible, then to a house of refuge if there be one in the county, or to the boys' industrial school or the girls' industrial home, or to some other juvenile reformatory.

When any truant officer is satisfied that any child, compelled to attend school by the provisions of this act, is unable to attend school because absolutely required to work, at home or elsewhere, in order to support itself or help support or care for others legally entitled to its services, who are unable to support or care for themselves, the truant officer shall report the case to the authorities charged with the relief of the poor, and it shall be the duty of such officers to afford such relief as will enable the child to attend school the time each year required under this act.

Any officer, principal, teacher or other person mentioned in this act neglecting to perform any duty imposed upon him by this act shall be fined not less than twenty-five or more than fifty dollars for each offense.

It is hereby made the duty of every board of education in this state to provide sufficient accommodations in the public schools for all children in their district compelled to attend the public schools under the provisions of this act. Authority to levy the tax and raise the money necessary for such purpose is hereby given the proper officers charged with such duty under the law.

Senate bill No. 110, passed by the Senate and Assembly of the last Legislature, but not signed by the Governor, reads as follows:

An Act to enforce the educational rights of children and providing penalties for the violation of the Act.

Section 1. Unless excused as hereinafter provided, each parent, guardian, or other person in the State of California having control or charge of any child between the ages of eight and fourteen years, shall be required to send such child to a public school, during each school year, for a period of at least five months of the time during which a public school shall be in session in the city or city and county or school district in which said child resides, and at least eighteen weeks of such attendance shall be consecutive; provided, that should it be shown to the satisfaction of the board of education in the city or city and county, or of the board of trustees of the district in which said child resides, that the child's bodily or mental condition is such as to prevent or render inadvisable attendance at school or *application to study*, a certificate from any reputable physician that the child is not able to attend school, or that its attendance is inadvisable, must be taken as satisfactory evidence by any such board; or proof being given that the parents or parent are extremely poor or sick, and that the services of the child are actually needed to support such parents or parent; or that such child is being taught in a private school, or by a private tutor or at home by any person capable of teaching, in such branches as are usually taught in the primary and grammar schools of this state; or that no public school is located within two miles, by the nearest traveled road, of the residence of the child; or that the child has completed the prescribed grammar school course; then it shall be the duty of such board of education or board of trustees, upon application of the parent or guardian or other person having the control or charge of such child, to excuse such child from attendance at school during the continuance of such defect or condition upon which such excuse is granted. And provided further, that circumstances rendering attendance impracticable or dangerous to health, owing to unusual storm or other sufficient cause, shall work an exemption from the penalties of this Act. If any parent or guardian or other person having control or charge of any such child presents proof to such board of education or board of trustees, by affidavit, that he is unable to compel such child to attend school said parent, guardian or other person shall be exempt-from the penalties of this Act, as regards the subsequent non-attendance at school of such child, and such child may, in the discretion of such board, be deemed a truant and subject to assignment to the parental school.

In the light of this legislation the provisions of senate bill No. 110 of 1901 are satisfactory as to age limits—eight to fourteen years—but somewhat deficient in period of attendance, five months being rather too brief a period. Yet the suggestive effect of the law may operate to extend this term in most cases. There are some objections to making boards of education and of trustees the determining authorities in making excuses, as their interest in such matters maybe somewhat indifferent, but as they stand midway between the careless parent and the frequently overzealous teacher or superintendent, they are perhaps the best available arbiters to whom to entrust the introduction of a new law. Sickness or poverty of parents is no reason for excusing a child from attendance at school. It is the very best of reasons why he should be insured at least that advantage. Specialists in these matters know that the number of parents in any community actually too poor to send their children to school is hardly worth considering. Most states have taken no account of this phase of the matter, and California cannot afford to reproach herself in this way. Besides, this is the very worst form of state economy. Switzerland has learned to pension all such children, in order that she may send them to school. And the action of Ohio in making each county provide the things most needful for its children is jeweled wisdom in comparison with this provision, which would prevent the natural order by making the infants provide for the adults. A compulsory education law will not compel attendance at school, nor even suggest it, if *may* is written for shall with regard to the action of the board concerning children whose parents confess inability to cause them to attend school.

There is crying need at the present time that boards of cities and counties should be required by law to appoint an attendance officer so that it should be the duty of some one person at least to inform himself and the public upon the actual conditions of school attendance in the state. This provision for several reasons should not be optional but mandatory. The provision for parental schools is highly satisfactory, being much superior to the Ohio law. But why not permit the attendance officer to make complaint in the proper court without having his apprehensions "approved by the aforesaid school authorities"? The point cannot be too strongly emphasized that a parental school is a school and not a penitentiary or reformatory. In this respect the law is strong, but in most others it is useless and doomed to carry not even the weight of suggestive legislation unless changed in several particulars, for it is overloaded with exceptions and has hardly a merit in it. No compulsory education can be in any great measure successful unless a child labor law fixing the same time limits for non-employment is also on the statute book. It is to be hoped that such a law will be passed and every man who has the real interest of the state at heart should urge its adoption. A very careful private census conducted by one of my classes in the university reveals the fact that about one hundred children under the age f fourteen are employed by firms in the city of Oakland alone, and this is hardly a tithe of the whole number so employed in California. Advance sheets of this forthcoming report kindly furnished me by the state commissioner of labor statistics, reporting the result of a very careful canvass of the city and county of San Francisco, show that twenty-five boys and one girl under twelve years of age are employed in manufacturing and mercantile establishments, and that 1042 boys and 288 girls under sixteen and over twelve years of age. are so employed there. This means that thousands who stay away from school in San Francisco are not kept out to work.

One of the chief features of a compulsory education should be a provision requiring boards of education to provide sufficient accommodations in the public schools for all children in their district, compelled to attend the public schools by the act. Another should pronounce severe penalties against anyone who hinders such children from so attending school, and the experience of older states is that legislation of too lax a character to secure the object for which it was undertaken is a pernicious hindrance to the accomplishment of its ends.

Respectfully submitted,
E. C. MOORE,
Chairman of Committee on Compulsory School Legislation.

The Practical Value of Manual Training

CREE T. WORK

[Read before the San Francisco Council of Jewish Women.]

Before attempting to assign a value to anything it is desirable that the thing to be appraised be clearly described. The manual training movement in education, like many other steps in human endeavor, has met with opposition in many quarters, even by some good people in San Francisco, because its purpose has not been understood. Some has assumed that the object of manual training is to produce craftsmen, "to make carpenters and draftsmen of the boys," to afford opportunity for boys to begin a trade before they leave school, and thus save time. The erroneous definitions of the subject found in the public mind might properly be named either "legion" or "et cetera," because they are so numerous. Without taking the time to criticise such definitions directly, I shall endeavor to point out some of the fundamental features of manual training as it is being viewed and planned by the leaders in the movement, and as it is being approved and fostered by the leading psychologists and pedagogues, philosophers, superintendents, university men, and practical thinkers of the country. I shall not attempt to tell you much that is new, but to recall to your minds some of your own observations and experiences, and to speak of certain of their educative possibilities. For, after all, if we can give correct and appropropriate setting to our own earlier experiences in the light of what has followed, I conceive that we are thereby approaching a valuable working theory for the training of our children. In what I have to say I shall use the masculine pronoun in the generic sense as a rule, because girls and boys alike need the kind of education I am talking about. As they get into the later grammar grades the actual work may properly be differentiated to correspond to the interests of the two sexes,— as domestic science for girls and tool work for boys,—but the educational principle is the same. For, be it understood, manual training, and the manual training idea includes a variety of work Manual training is the intelligent direction of the tendency and inherent power of a person to do things, to the end that the individual's all-round efficiency in life may thereby be increased. Manual training is a method of training the mind thru the hand and eye, or the training of the hand and eye in connection with the mind. Manual training is executive thinking. It is an opportunity for the mind to express itself in action,—in accomplishing something. The formal carrying out of the manual training method involves many problems. The question of the kind of work to be undertaken is one that is always interesting. The natural desire is to keep the work as economical as possible, so in the primary grades, as a rule, paper and cardboard work, modeling, sewing, weaving, basketry, and whittling are being introduced because they can be done with simple equipment in an ordinary schoolroom, directed by the regular grade teacher. In the grammar grades the enlarging interests and powers of the pupils necessitates other materials, more elaborate equipment, and special teachers at the present. The work here usually includes wood work, cooking, bent iron work, advanced basketry, carving, drafting, designing, home-keeping.

In talking of the practical value of this kind of work in education, I desire first to remind you of the fact of our great material and social progress and of the great change in the conditions of civilization in the past decades. Time is not far past when the world was a great planetary body, on which humanity seemed capable of being lost sight of. Now it is a little sphere suspended in space, around which hundreds travel every year. Our fathers before crossing the ocean bade their parents good-by with great weeping, hardly hoping to see them again, and certainly not to hear from them for many months. Now we visit our cousins in Europe during the summer vacation, and meanwhile exchange a half-dozen letters with friends in Manila. We say hello! to our Denver neighbors, or send a message to Australia in the morning before breakfast. Our intimate relationships have brought with them great obligations. An individual can no longer isolate himself from his fellows, and say, "I am not interested," "I am under no obligation to my neighbor," "I have no need of a better or different preparation for life than my ancestry had." Along with our material and social advancement has arisen a demand for progress in education, both in matter and method. Formerly the aim was chiefly the training of idealists in the higher institutions, or rather, I should perhaps say, the training of individuals for the accomplishment of certain ideals, which ideals came within what are generally known as "the professions." We are beginning to see that we must train for the realities of life. In the education of the common people it is not long since the three R's were deemed sufficient, and even yet they are fondly held to by some as "*the* essentials" in public school education. No one doubts the fact of these subjects being essential in the education of children, but modern educationists agree that they have no claim to be classed as *the* essentials. There are numerous subjects quite as essential to the well being of an individual as that he be able to read, write and cipher. I believe it will also be found true that these same devotees at the shrine of the three R essentials, in their ignorance of the nature of mind, regard knowledge and intellectual discipline as something that can be dealt out in pieces quite as a lumber dealer handles boards, or to be put up in doses after the custom of the apothecary.

Imagine the continuation of the stage coach from San Francisco to Portland—"Behind the times" you say—Why? Because we are progressing and have found better and speedier ways of reaching our desired destination. Even the horse cars on the lower end of Market street are incongruous, as compared with our electric systems of transit. In education, likewise, stage coach and horse car methods are being supplanted by more modern, up-to-date means of intellectual development. We have come to the point where it is recognized that the blending together of subjects fit for the child mind into an outline of thought—a unity—is the direction our efforts should take. This means that a child may learn to write, to read and to cipher to better advantage if he learns them in connection with other things. We must cease teaching unrelated and unnecessary facts, because that is not education in the modern sense.

Our definitions of education have always depended upon what we want to use it for. During the Renaissance (about the 16th century) education was understood to mean the proper study of books. They wanted to revive learning and regenerate the world by means of books. Next the Jesuits considered it most important to store the memory with facts and give ability to reproduce what was taught. They aimed at the perpetuity of a system of thought. Comenuis thought "that man should know all things." He would produce "walking encyclopedias." Education has recently been defined as "the preparation of the individual for social efficiency." A public school is a place for educating the public—largely the children—for social living. It behooves those who have charge of the public schools to study social conditions, and to frame the curriculum accordingly. It is said that the horse cars mentioned are run for the purpose of holding a valuable franchise. Just as, sooner or later, there will be a demand that this franchise be properly used or that it be surrendered to those who will use it to better public advantage, so likewise the times demand of the teachers who hold the right of way in public education that they apply up to date, practical methods along their thoroughfare.

It is held that manual training is a method suited to the end of education and to the nature to be educated. It is not a cure-all for educational ills. It will not create faculties. It is simply a method of aiding the development of powers already in existence. It is a method demanded by the nature of the child. Children do not, and cannot "sit still and study" books for long periods as they are often asked to do. Their physical and mental energies are so closely united that it is quite impossible for the mind to act very long at one time without bodily activity as well. Manual training simply utilizes these conditions. It endeavors to direct this complex activity in profitable lines. It uses the energy spent in such activity to the end of developing power—power to think and power to do. Manual training provides for the utilization of the doing tendency in children to promote their intellectual and physical development.

Who has not heard the child say a dozen times in a day or more, "What can we do now?" or "What can I make now?" It is his constant desire to be making things. He seldom says "What can I think about?" or "What can I study?" He is doing his best thinking, his most effective studying, while he is *doing* something. Give his doing careful direction and you both increase and direct his thinking. To be more specific as to what happens in manual training, let me illustrate. You all have what are known as senses—those of seeing, feeling and hearing being especially strong. You will all grant that these senses are capable of being trained. They were trained chiefly in your case, as in every case, when you were young—when you were growing. That is the time when sense training should be given—the time it will count for most. In young children the senses predominate over the intellect—we might almost say that they are the intellect of the little child. Now, nothing will train these senses better than the proper use of them. The senses carry impressions to the mind, which holds them for future use in thinking. This process of impression through the senses is going on every day in children. The impressions received from time to time are compared, classified, and elaborated in the mind, and thus the receptive process goes on. But meanwhile the results of the sense combinations are flowing out in expression, the hand being the chief agent of expression during the early years. Thus it is seen that the senses are being trained in expression in conjunction with their training by impression. But it is not the senses alone that are being affected by these processes. The intellect, by comparison, selection and elimination is meanwhile working over these facts of sense, and thus thought and the power of thought are being produced. Expression results in a kind of reactionary experience which confirms in the mind the thing expressed, thus leaving a new impression, as it were, which gives the feeling of something learned. In other words, when the result of sense impression and expression are worked over in the mind, or assimilated, we have sense knowledge as a result. Sense knowledge—knowledge gained through the senses—is the foundation of the so-called abstract thinking. Imagine, if you can, all of your sense knowledge as having left you. Now try to think without it. You may choose your own subject, but still you cannot think without drawing on sense knowledge to make it intelligible. The most abstract thought must depend upon sense knowledge for its meaning. Now, the larger the store of sense knowledge, the better will be the foundation that is laid for after intellectual operations. Manual training affords opportunity for adding largely to the child's knowledge of material things. Even if our children were to live in ease and luxury, their happiness and comfort would be enhanced by the knowledge that comes through doing. For example, they would get an appreciation of skilled arts by participation in the production of art. Likewise, industry and all that it means is best appreciated by those who have learned industry in the concrete.

Manual training will not teach itself; it cannot run haphazard. It requires proper equipment, materials and instruction as do other subjects. Then it becomes training (illustrate concretely with foot-stool and tea-pot stand).

Some of the items of intellectual power which are developed by manual training may be briefly touched upon. Not only does it train the child's senses to discriminate between things that appeal to them, but it developes an *intellectual* discrimination which lies at the basis of good judgment. The pupil in manual training has always before him the tangible proof of the rightness or the wrongness of his mental picture, his observation, his reasoning, his judgment. He has confirmed in his mind that which is correct, while the incorrect is eradicated by the concrete failure resulting from it. Manual training also brings about many acts of association of objects and ideas, and thus cultivates the power and habit of association, an important intellectual acquisition. Many valuable ideas are naturally correlated with the work. For example, numerous geometric terms, constructions and propositions receive practical demonstration in the course of the work. So likewise the interpretation of the material phenomena of hand work is a valuable disciplinary training.

There are also certain fundamental ideas which manual training does much to arouse and strengthen, and which have a very practical bearing not only on the further education of the child, but on all his after life. I shall refer to a few of these, the development of which it is not safe to postpone during the school life of the child. The first that I would mention is training in the accomplishment of a purpose. It has long been the custom to try to instil into young minds a high and noble purpose in life. This is good, but the child will be better helped to his high purpose, by *doing* something which requires a direct purpose to a definitely set and foreseen end. The intellectual purpose of too many people is worked out (or more likely defeated) more by a series of accidents or providences rather than by any power said persons exercise in the matter, simply because they have never learned what it is to work to an end, to strive for a purpose. The period of sense development, of concrete lessons, of the tendency to do things, of thought-action growth, is the time to give such training. Manual training would suggest to the child good and meaningful purposes, would encourage his effort by providing means of working, would train him in orderly and prompt decisions in working, and would reward him by a sense of having accomplished the thing aimed at. In manual training the concrete requirements are such that the purpose cannot fade or be forgotten. Only one thing satisfies in the case and that is complete accomplishment. One can almost see the tenacity of a child grow as he strives with his hands and his mind to overcome the resistance of the material world. The quality of stick-to-it-iveness is sadly lacking in hosts of people. Manual training will put more of it into the children. A lesson constantly emphasized by this work is that decision and tenacity of purpose are large elements of success.

Another fundamental idea which manual training is well calculated to develop is that of economy. Pupils are taught how to save by saving. They calculate the amount of material needed for their projects, they measure it out, and are taught to make it a part of their business to see how much can be gotten out of a certain amount of material, how materials can be divided to the best advantage, how remnants and odds and ends may be properly and profitably utilized. The children can be very easily and naturally led to see how this economy of material carries with it economy of time and energy in most cases. For example, if a pupil cuts off a piece of board a half larger than is needed for his purpose, the piece must be either re-cut or dressed down to the proper size, thereby involving an additional expenditure of both time and labor as well as a waste of material. His reward for care in cutting the material the right size at the beginning is the evident saving of his own time and energy.

The establishing in the mind of the complete idea of rightful ownership is greatly enhanced by manual training. It is a popular idea that we own that which in some way we have come to possess. And it is a humiliating fact that the means by which we come into possession is often lost sight of in the essential sense. Many people covet, without planning means whereby they might rightfully possess. Many others are so intent on possession that they will justify any means to attain their end. The covetous discontent of the former, and the lying, gambling, stealing methods of the latter promote anarchy. Many a young man and young woman in this city, drawing salary for half-hearted or nominal service will never be fit for anything else, and will always be liable to dishonest dealing because of a dearth of experience which demonstrates rightful possession or ownership. Hundreds of them, yes, even thousands of them, are investing in lottery tickets, with the vicious idea that anything they may win will be honorably gotten gain for them. They will sell their conscience, their honor, their manhood, their virtue for gain, and try to make themselves and others believe that it has been a right transaction. Even the school children are early inducted into a system of false moral and political economy by show-window and store-counter nickel-in-the-slot machines, wheels of fortune, and other devices which encourage the young to squander and gamble away what they have begged for at home, and which do much to inculcate false notions as to what constitutes legitimate business. To counteract such influences as these, we need to teach children very clearly what rightful ownership is. Manual training provides concrete lessons in this direction. In this work the child becomes a producer and comes into possession through production. He takes his piece of work home, his face beaming with pride and satisfaction, because the work represents his own thought, his own time, his own toil. In doing the work, he has become a contributor to society, he has made wealth in a degree, and has thereby ranged himself so far on the side of the productive class, the useful members of society. Every such lesson tends to clarify and strengthen his views of what it is to rightfully possess a thing. He is learning both the pleasure and the honesty of earning possessions. The children are daily taught the proper regard and their responsibility for the property of others, in the care they are required to take of the equipment with which they work.

We have heard and talked so much about capital and labor in these latter days that they have become personified out of all recognition. Two children are talking—Says Johnnie, "Say, Mary, are Capital and Labor two different men or are they the same man with one big name?" "I think," says Mary, "that it is a man and his wife; for I heard papa read something yesterday about Capital and Labor going to get divorced." There have already been too many cases of this kind of divorce. We want to so train our children to understand, to respect and to enjoy labor, that they may not become entangled in difficulty over the labor problem. Manual training work gives a solid foundation for thought relative to labor. It makes laborers of the rising generation. Rich and poor meet here together and work on the same footing. Because of this, they are not so likely to be separated in their views of the question of labor in after years. Henceforth there will be latent in their minds ideas which will do much to give a clear, mature view of the whole subject of economics. In the manual training work, lifes' experiences are anticipated, or rather begun, in fair degree. The complete idea of what it is to labor will hardly come to those who are not trained to do hand labor.

So far, I have been endeavoring to show the practical force of manual training in the process we call education. I wish to show in a stronger light, if possible, its practical value in the after life of the pupil. I would emphasize the fact that the school is not to prepare people for a life that lies in the future, but that it is a vital part of that life. The child in the first grade is, or should be, in just as real life, according to his comprehension, as are his parents. The education of the school should be such as to develop the life of the pupils. Child nature has always demanded something practical in education. For years educators feared to respond to this demand lest they sacrifice the intellectual development of children. For be it remembered that the classical scholars' idea of intellectual development has been the growth of intellect through a process of drill, memorizing, abstract mental gymnastics; said development being for the purpose of enabling its possessors to enter more fully into the ideal conditions of mind in the so-called higher realms of thought. This fallacy is falling into disrepute among educators now, and they are seeing that practical concrete thought has quite as great developing power as the abstract. The common people have generally been agreed on this matter. They wanted the school to give intellectual power, but what for? The power supposed to be developed by the three R's was, in the public mind, for practical living. "Read, write, cipher, or you cannot live aright," said they; "you cannot gain material prosperity and the happiness and station consequent upon it." But we have passed the age when reading, writing and arithmetic suffice for these ends. There are other things requisite for full living nowadays. As previously stated, the friends of education who constantly refer to the three R's as "the essentials" should awake to a realization of the fact that our educational interests, as well as our material affairs, have been making some mighty strides in recent years. Government by the people requires education of the common people for their work. Heretofore our colleges and universities have educated men largely for the professions and for leadership. We need to see to it that our public schools educate the mass of the people for social living, if we are to expect them to elect their own leaders and to make intelligent demands upon the professions.

Since education is to develop and to train for life, it is well to test our theories and our educational matter by asking, "What will our children do in life?" Let me ask you and all the parents of this city, what will your boy or your girl do in life after leaving school? Not what do you wish them to do, but what are they by the nature of conditions destined to do? The question carries the same term as its answer; namely, to *do* something, to work, to succeed perchance by laboring at something tangible, concrete, practical. I do not know exactly what it will be, you do not know, but history shows that some such demand will be laid upon the mass of the children passing thru our schools. The education we give should get the children ready for their duties. The spirit of the times demands ability to *do*. Manual training will do much toward this end. While it does not train for any particular trade, it gives such general ability to do things, to execute ideas in the concrete, that those who take it are, as a result, better able to take up the labor which falls to their lot without serious loss of time or great inconvenience. The common people cannot be either best satisfied or helped most by an education which goes over their heads, or rather, which goes off at a tangent to their interests.

Suppose we succeeded in our very common ambition to get our children all into the professions. There would be none left to be patrons and clients. Suppose we even succeeded in getting them all clerkships in stores and offices, starting at five dollars per week. They would soon lose their positions or have their salary cut because there would not be enough efficient men to work at the trades for five dollars or more per day to keep up the salaries of the five-dollar-per-week clerks; nor enough intelligent, thrifty, home keepers to provide a market for the goods the clerks want to handle. We must train the mass for definite purposes in life; else they will soon become dissatisfied, as is even now the case, and have bad feeling toward those who have been educated for definite ends. It is quite as much the function of the school to make good, intelligent home keepers out of the mass of girls as it is to prepare the exceptional ones for the so-called higher education. Likewise the nine boys who are to be the work-a-day men are certainly entitled to the same consideration in the preparation for their work as the one boy who is ambitious for a career in the college fraternities and later in a profession or the political arena.

We are a young nation, and yet at that, we have already been dominated too long by the old university ideals of Europe. The demands to be laid upon American youth during the next half century will be such as were not conceived by the founders of European universities. Ours is the home for all nations, and a large proportion of those who come to us are those for whom the university ideals did nothing and can do nothing because they are inadequate to daily need. They have come here to share the welfare of a free people who early began the solution of industrial and social problems on a basis unknown in Europe. The demanding is becoming more emphatic every day that we develop our system of education to correspond to our industrial and social needs.

If you were each to enumerate the shortcomings of yourself and your neighbors as regards pratical living, I doubt not such terms as these would occur in many of your lists: wasteful, lazy, purposeless, thriftless, careless, erratic, indecisive, changeable, clumsy, impractical. They are descriptive of common failings. They also indicate a weakness in our educational system. Our schools should endeavor to do more to reduce these evils by cultivating the opposite traits of those named. As previously shown, manual training methods have positive value in this respect. I believe our system of education has two bad tendencies which should be corrected: First, it tends to cultivate in many an ambition for promotion and distinction which is doomed to disappointment in most cases because the rewards are limited to small numbers. Second, it fails to cultivate the natural ambition which many children have for home life and practical labor, and which, if developed, would largely promote home-working and home-sustaining. Classical education has fostered both of these tendencies, not only in the colleges, but by controlling the public school curriculum to the same effect. The new education, including manual training, would correct such evils by preparing pupils for practical success in common life. In answering the question, "Why do boys not want to go into the grammar school?" Prof. Elmer E. Brown of the University of California recently said: "Because at the grammar school age boys are trying to think the thoughts of men, and there is as yet too little in the grammar school to satisfy manly thought. Reform is needed." The nature of the reform that is coming is largely characterized by the manual training idea. It is concisely described by an English writer in the *London Saturday Review* of September 13, 1902. He says: "To do things, to be observant and quick of eye, to be ingenious in contrivance, to be clever in manipulating all the kinds of material from early years in order that school life may by a graded process lead up to the actual business of life, is the system which American educationists are most intent on establishing for the budding American intellect. There are advocates of the old classical drill, but they are a diminishing quantity, and the universities are making wide their gates to admit the new classes of pupils who are being educated in the reformed secondary schools. * * * In America there is undoubtedly a more vivid interest in education through all classes of people than there is in England. It is seen to be related to personal and national success more clearly than it is here. More municipal interest is shown in it. * * * The Americans are in the full tide of theories of education which apparently reverse the older conceptions."

A proper step in public education was taken by the people of our own state at the recent election in the adoption of the constitutional amendment providing for special taxation in support of high schools and technical schools. These, and especially the technical schools, provide valuable supplementary instruction for pupils from the grammar grades. But still, most children cannot go so far in school; we need to make all the school life of the child to fit him for the common lot of men and women. The more general introduction of manual training will help to this end.

A common objection brought against the introduction of manual training into our primary and grammar schools is that the curriculum is already overcrowded, and we cannot afford the time for it. Teachers in this city, who otherwise seem very clear headed, have said to me that they did not see how their pupils were to be promoted at the end of the term if they had to take the time for manual training. There have been a half dozen or more important subjects added to the curriculum since such objections were first argued. Necessity requires that we teach more subjects now than formerly. If all subjects were taught now as the three R's were formerly taught, children would have to be in school 24 hours per day. The curriculum was very full then—just as crowded as it is now. And I am not denying that the curriculum is now overcrowded, but it is not by reason of too many subjects; it is overcrowded with irrelevant and superfluous matter in most of the subjects. In other words, the reorganization of the curriculum to meet the requirements of the new education and of modern psychology requires the reorganization of the subject matter, the casting out of large portions of it which are of no value, and the unifying or correlating of the educative features. It is generally conceded by our foremost educators that too much of the pupil's time is taken up in committing and drilling upon formulated and ancient divisions and problems of the different subjects of the ordinary school curriculum. It has been demonstrated that when the child's thinking is done in vital, realistic relations, it takes less of it in point of time to establish the proper habit of thought than when it is done abstractly or by the old classical methods. Especially is this true of young children, who do not possess the concrete data of sense experience on which to base and by which to ballast the abstract process. These vital relations of thought must be learned sometime; why not in their proper connection during the period of rapid development? I have seen many a child in the grammar grades struggle over the solution of little problems in simple fractions in the manual training class, who had been drilled thoroughly, according to the classical idea, in the arithmetic of the paper and pencil, the blackboard, the text book and the ordinary school desk. I have heard pupils in these grades repeat glibly statements from a geography relative to the value of our products exported to foreign ports, and from history dealing with the question of slavery as it was affected by labor saving machinery versus hand labor. Yet these same pupils had never been provided with opportunities to experience what it is to produce a thing, or what hand labor means. The concrete demonstration of thought gives it new bearing. Thought is enlarged and multiplied, ideas are completed by psycho-manual experiences. Teachers in San Francisco who two years ago told me they thought the manual training would interfere with the progress of their pupils have recently volunteered the statement that it has not hindered their work in the least, and that they are converted.

Time fails me to more than refer to a few other objections that are sometimes heard. "Manual training" says one, "is an extra, tacked on to the curriculum." It is not this when rightly understood and properly taught, any more than are arithmetic or grammar. "It costs too much," says another, "and we cannot afford embellishments now." It costs money, although not an excessive amount. We spare no expense in keeping up to the times in business affairs; why should we want to deprive our children of the best education for the sake of slightly enriching our estates? The taxes paid for the public schools are the best investment property owners are making nowadays. "I do not believe it belongs in the public schools," says another. To those who honestly hold this opinion after studying the subject carefully, time will bring more light. Twenty years ago only two or three educators of standing in our country had the courage to urge the claims of manual training. Today the pedagogue who objects to it is regarded somewhat in the light of a back number or an obstructionist by the educational forces of the land. If the real description of the unbelief of a certain class of teachers were recorded, it would probably run something like this: "I was educated without manual training; it is a fad; this is not the place to teach trades; I may have to learn something more; it might make me more work; I know nothing about it, and I don't want to know anything, so please keep it away and let me and my school slumber on in peace." We feel toward these people quite as we did toward the fond mother who wrote as follows to the teacher: "As I do not want Julia to know anything about her insides, you will please excuse her from the class in physiology and hygiene."

In brief conclusion I must say a word about manual training in the San Francisco public schools. Two years and a half ago seven manual training laboratories, well equipped with benches and tools for wood work, were opened for the boys of the seventh and eighth grades. All boys in these grades are required to take the work. Each boy receives a lesson of one hour and a half to two hours each week. The work is conducted according to system, that the boys may get full value for the time spent. It counts toward promotion, and has come to be considered as regular school work. To correspond to this work for the boys, the girls have had sewing and cooking, the latter having been well systematized by Miss Kate Whitaker. There are seven well equipped cooking laboratories for the girls in corresponding sections of the city with the manual training laboratories. The sewing is rather haphazard, and not looked after as it should be. During the past term a number of schools have introduced in the lower grammar and upper primary grades weaving, and raffia and reed work in an informal way, with very good results. This work has not been required by the Board of Education, and so shows a laudable spirit of progress, energy and enthusiasm on the part of the principals and teachers who have undertaken it. Certain of our primary schools have for some time given some paper folding and other advanced kindergarten work. So it is that a beginning in the working out the manual training idea in the San Francisco schools has been made. But it is only a beginning. The work should grow until hand work in some form is provided for every grade, from the first to the eighth, for girls and boys. In the primary grades, paper, card-board, modeling, raffia, weaving, reed, sewing, bent iron work and the like should be introduced. The work may very profitably be the same for boys and girls up to, and perhaps including, the fifth grade. All this can be done by regular teachers in the regular school room. In the sixth grade tool equipment should be provided, preferably for girls and boys both, and the instruction given by special teachers until such time as the regular teachers can prepare for it.

Fully as much time and more if possible, should be given to the work in the primary grades as is now being given in the seventh and eighth grades, but it should be divided into shorter periods. These recommendations are not an outburst of theoretic opinion. Similar things are being done by other cities where the conditions are no better than they are in San Francisco, where the curriculum is just as much crowded, where the course is the same length, and where the grade of work done in other subjects is fully as high and as good as that which is being done in San Francisco. The chief thing that stands in the way of our forging ahead in these matters is the lack of public sentiment, both in the school department and out of it. If the present Board of Education has not gone as far in the development of this feature of school work as they desire, it is because public sentiment has not shown itself ready to support further advances. Now that there is an awakened interest in education among the women of the city, including so many of mothers of the children for whom schools are conducted, it is safe to predict that ere long much more will be done to make the schools more efficient in training for daily living. And I take it that your honorable body here represented this afternoon, is in the front rank of those who purpose seeing to it that our schools measure up to their opportunity and their duty. I commend to you the manual training movement as one which is worthy of your best effort. Urge its enlargement upon the Board of Education, befriend it in the schools, agitate it before the public, let us have the benefit of your suggestions as to how it can be improved upon. Let no belated pedagogue, no public spiritless taxpayer, no hinderer of progress, stand in the way of your making the demand that the rising generation be taught how to do as well as how to think.

⁂

Books are the best things, well used; abused, among the worse.

Free Text-Books*

[Report of the committee appointed by the California Council of Education "To Compile a Report Upon the System of Free Text-Books and Its Adaptability to School Conditions in California."]

PREPARED BY SUPT. E. M. COX OF SANTA ROSA
Chairman of the Committee

Free text-books have been talked about and written about a great deal and used in some states for many years. They have been required by law in all the public schools of Massachusetts since 1884 and were permitted by law after 1873. Nebraska and Delaware have required them since 1891; New Hampshire since 1890; and Maine since 1889, tho they were used extensively in this state for many years preceding this time. Philadelphia has used them eighty-five years, New York City seventy years, and various other cities from forty to sixty years. More than twenty states either require or permit districts to furnish free text-books, the following named states requiring them, viz: Delaware, Idaho, Massachusetts, Maine, New Hampshire, Nebraska, New Jersey, Pennsylvania, Rhode Island, Vermont, and Maryland.

It is therefore not necessary to deal in opinions or speculations in "compiling a report" on this question. The reports of the state superintendents of schools in these various states contain extensive accounts of their experiences with this system. In addition to the contents of these annual reports, we have answers from fifteen state superintendents to certain questions which were sent to them in order that we might have very late, definite and comparative facts on some of the particularly vital points in connection with this subject. Replies were received from the superintendents of the states of Connecticut, Minnesota, Colorado, Nebraska, Delaware, New Hampshire, Iowa, Pennsylvania, Michigan, South Dakota, Maryland, Vermont, Maine, Wisconsin, and Massachusetts.

The questions asked were as follows:

1. What effect has the furnishing of text-books free to pupils had upon attendance?

2. Has the free text-book system had a tendency to introduce the newest and best books, or has the effect been the opposite?

3. Has the system caused pupils to be less careful with books than they were when the books were their own property?

4. Has the expense of free text-books been found objectionable? What has your experience shown to be the cost?

5. Does there seem to be ground for the objection that free text-books tent too much toward communism?

6. Please mention any other advantages or disadvantages of free text-books which you deem important.

*Read before the California Council of Education at Los Angeles, December 29, 1902.

QUESTION I

With the exception of Colorado, where the superintendent reports a well enforced compulsory education law in effect, all the states affirm that free text-books have benefited attendance. They emphasize that their statistics and observations show that attendance is both larger and more regular. The Connecticut report says that attendance was increased 20 per cent by this system. From reading various reports of the effects of free texts, it is certain that regularity of attendance is stimulated and no children are kept from school because of insufficient books.

QUESTION II

Excepting from South Dakota and Connecticut, the replies state that the newest and best books are introduced. South Dakota's law allows changes every five years, and, as the law is new, its effect in this regard has not been experienced. Connecticut reports that it brings "neither the best nor the worst." Some states report that where superintendents influence the selection of books the results have been especially good. Several reports emphasize that the ease with which exchanges can be effected, when this system is in force, has made it simple and economical to keep up with the newest and best. It is very evident that the adoption of free text-books has not introduced books cheap in quality.

QUESTION III

The free books are more carefully kept than those privately owned excepting in three states. Colorado reports pupils less careful with free books and Minnesota and Nebraska say that pupils "are no less careful with them than with their own." It is generally pointed out that greater care is taken because teachers are required to give more definite and immediate supervision to the care of the books. Pupils are instructed in the care of them. They are, in most cases, allowed to take them home by special permission.

QUESTION IV

In all cases free text-books cost less money. The following are extracts taken from the reports sent us:

South Dakota—Free text-books are much cheaper.

Connecticut—The expense is not an objection. It is less than a dollar per year per pupil.

New Hampshire—About $1.25 per pupil per year, including high schools and also including supplies.

Delaware—Expense is not objectionable.

Colorado—The cost is less.

Vermont—The cost is seventy-five cents per year.

Minnesota—This has not been raised as a serious objection. The average is about sixty cents per year.

Nebraska—It is cheaper, the average is about fifty-five cents.

Pennsylvania—Cheaper. In 1897 (we have no later data at hand) average was fifty-six cents.

Maine—Cheaper. The average is ninety-five cents.
Iowa—Cheaper.
Maryland—The expense is no objection. The plan is exceedingly popular. Expense (1900-1) fifty-two cents per pupil.
Michigan—The expense is from ten to fifty per cent less.
Wisconsin—About one-third the cost of the old plan.
Massachusetts—Very much cheaper—less than half. The average for five years (1895-1900) was $1.54 per pupil, including high schools and also including supplies.

Extensive figures have been and can be gathered on the question of cost. It would be possible for us to quote and compile extensive tables showing that school districts are now buying very desirable books at from twenty to 70 per cent cheaper than our children now pay for our state texts.

The last report of the secretary of the Maryland State Board of Education gives a list of books adopted and the prices paid by each of the counties in his state. The prices average from a fourth to a sixth less than the quoted wholesale prices given in the publishers' catalogs. These lists include a great variety of books published by leading book firms. We quote, in illustration, the prices paid for some books that are well known in California schools. The books quoted are not so much cheaper than list prices as many others that are in use.

Book	Publishers' Wholesale Price	Maryland Contract Price
Complete Geography. Frye	$1.25	$1.03
Cyr's Primer	.24	.19$\frac{1}{2}$
" First Reader	.28	.22$\frac{3}{4}$
" Second Reader	.36	.29$\frac{1}{4}$
" Third Reader	.50	.40$\frac{5}{8}$
" Fourth Reader	.60	.48$\frac{3}{4}$
" Fifth Reader	.70	.52$4/5$
Stepping Stones to Literature—		
First Reader	.30	.25
Second Reader	.40	.33
Third Reader	.50	.41
Fourth Reader	.60	.50
Fifth Reader	.60	.50

We could give long lists of contract prices from this and other states, but it must needs greatly extend this report. Since these figures are easily available, we shall leave the question of expense to the general statements above quoted from the various state superintendents.

QUESTION V

There is no more tendency toward communism than there is from free schools, free supplies, etc. This criticism does not hold where the system is in operation. It does not seem to be offered as an objection except by those who wish to conceal the true reason for their opposition.

In addition to the answers to these five questions and in response to the sixth, many other points were mentioned in favor of free text-books, and no objections or criticisms were offered from any states excepting Colorado and

Michigan. Most of the others say that there are no objections worth mentioning, and this is especially true of the states that have used the system longest.

The state superintendent of Colorado writes:

"The disadvantages are—fostering of a spirit of dependence on part of parents and an irresponsibility on part of children. In many cases the school books of a family form the only library, and in any case the books when preserved are valuable for reference; and form an always valued possession for the child. Unless extraordinary precautions are taken, the books are unwholesome and sometimes disease producing."

The state superintendent of Michigan says (after a very strong approval of the system):

"There are some disadvantages, one of which is in case of an outbreak of communicable disease it becomes necessary to have all books disinfected or destroyed. Under our laws . . . this has not proven to be a disadvantage or a very great expense . . . There are good arguments on both sides of the question, but the general impression in Michigan is that it is advantageous from nearly every standpoint to use free text-books."

Most of our reports emphasize that there is a considerable saving in time at the opening of terms of school, as all pupils can immediately be supplied with books. The old system often caused delay at the opening of a term and inconvenience at various times thru the slowness or inability of some parents to provide their children with necessary books. It is also reported by many that pupils can be more readily classified and re-classified when the book account of the parents does not have to be taken into consideration. Some superintendents point out that compulsory education should be accompanied by free text-books; that it is but fair to furnish pupils with tools to work with when the law compels their parents to send them to school.

So far as we could learn, and the literature on this subject has been gone over very carefully, there is not a case of the abandonment of the free text-book system by any state or large city. In nearly every case of state adoption, the system had been previously used in various communities of the state.

Another great saving which can't be expressed in figures but must be apparent to everyone is, that under this plan every book will be used until worn out. Experience with free text-books has shown that a book is serviceable for from three to seven years. Generally five to six years is reported. Under private ownership great numbers of books are used but a year or two. Considerably fewer books need to be purchased by districts than are now bought by individuals, and thus the expense to communities must be considerably less even on the basis of retail prices.

Several superintendents mention the fact that the law in their states has rapidly grown in favor and has become strongly intrenched in popular approval.

Another point that is made is that in the adoption of text-books under this system there should not be state uniformity; that the adoption, under necessary limitations by the state law, should be by counties or districts.

There are three objections offered to state adoption. The system offers very great temptations to corruption, whereas a division into county or district authority avoids much of this. The state adoption also does not give opportunity to the necessary competition which is as important a factor in text-books as in any commercial lines. Again, state adoption does not offer sufficient opportunity for the satisfaction of local needs and desires.

In the biennial reports of several states the arguments which have been advanced against free text-books are summarized and answered.

Inasmuch as the replies to our questions were so unanimously in favor of free text-books as to offer no opportunity to bring forward the opposing arguments we shall attempt to gather together the chief points and the replies. In various states the opposition have raised these points:

1. It prevents the children from owning the books they use and from preserving them at home, thus accumulating a small private library, oftentimes the only one in the home.

2. It cultivates dependence.

3. It tends to spread contageous diseases

4. It makes taxes higher.

5. Why should free text-books be furnished and not free food and clothing?

6. It will require too much time of teachers and boards of education in the management of the system.

These points have been practically answered in the replies sent us to our set of questions. However, there are answers given to *these* questions and we shall attempt to gather the essential points. The states which really ought to know, from a trial of the system, whether these objections are good or not, with the exceptions noted earlier in this report, claim they do not hold.

Free text-books need not prevent a pupil from owning his own books if he chooses. However, a library of worn school books is not a very precious thing, and in these days with so many school libraries and public town and city libraries, this objection must loose all of the small potency it once had. It may be added that in California this would be still further so on account of the liberal provision we have had and now have for the support of a library in every school district in the state.

If free books develop dependence, our free schools must do so, too. Our laws now require free schoolhouses, free supplies, free apparatus, free libraries, free teaching. Is it likely to create greater dependence to add to this list free books?

Some of the reports we have already quoted have dealt with the third objection. The reports from Michigan, Massachusetts, and Iowa are very explicit on this point. They pronounce ordinary care all that is necessary in this matter. Philadelphia with eighty-five years and New York with seventy years' use have not been depopulated or subject in an unusual degree to epidemics. Besides, is there more danger from free school books than from free public library books, which are far more likely to be placed in the hands of sick and convalescent persons than are school text-books?

The question of taxes and expense has already been pretty fully dealt with. It will probably add a little to the tax rate, but it requires little argument to show that it costs the community or the state less to furnish free school books. This will be more fully dealt with later.

The states do or should compel attendance at school. This necessitates the pupils having books. They are part of the equipment of the school. Hence the attempt to class free books with free food and clothing has no foundation.

Superintendent Barrett (Report 1900-1) summarizes the experience of Iowa and the arguments in favor of free text-books, and in substance the same facts appear in other reports, as follows:

1. It is the duty of the government to educate its future citizens so that they may be intelligent defendants of its rights and liberties. The state should see that all its school children are properly equipped for the work.

2. It makes the public schools free in fact as well as in name and removes a barrier that now prevents many poor children from attendance.

3. It secures uniformity of books in the district, and is much cheaper for the community, because the books are bought at the lowest wholesale prices and are used by more than one pupil.

4. It saves time at the beginning of each term of school because the pupils are supplied with books immediately and can go to work without the usual and sometimes annoying delay.

5. It secures better classification especially in rural schools and in all districts where there is a large floating population.

6. It develops and cultivates a careful use of public property on the part of the pupils, because they are held responsible for any unnecessary wear or damage of the books in their possession.

7. It gives opportunity to secure fresh and modern books, and prolongs the school life of many pupils who could not afford the expense for books in the higher grades.

8. It banishes unpleasant distinctions between those who can and those who cannot afford to buy their own books, such as often arise under a law providing free text-books for indigent children alone.

Superintendent Jackson (Report 1898) of Nebraska summarizes thus:

The advantages and arguments in favor of free text-books may be summed up in the following:

1. They increase school attendance.

2. They save time in the organization of the school.

3. They secure complete uniformity of text-books within the school.

4. They enable teachers to control better the organization and administration of the school.

5. They spread a richer course before pupils in the lower grades.

6. They will render more frequent changes possible.

7. They are much cheaper to the community.

The evidence gathered from the states where free text-books are used is overwhelming, almost unanimous, in their favor. The longer they have been used the more positive are the users that the system is a great boon. There does not seem to be any point raised in opposition which has not been repeatedly refuted by experience.

The school conditions in California, with the exception of our text-book system, are not greatly different from those in the states now using free text-books. It does not seem that it should be difficult, therefore, to apply this experience to our own state and to reach some conclusion on the second part of our topic — "Its adaptibility to school conditions in California."

In an earlier part of the report a further discussion of the expense question was postponed until it could be taken up in its relation to our own state. Already we are expending in this state large sums from our public treasuries for the purchase of supplemental books. The last report of our Superintendent of Public Instruction shows that we are expending an average of $70,000 per year on library books, a large portion of which is for supplementary text-books. In some counties all of the library fund and a considerable amount from the county fund are so expended. From the same report, the sale of text-books published by the state is shown to be such that parents pay $90,000 or more per year for them.

The expense to the state in support of the State Printing Office and other expenses in connection should be added to this. In addition to this, parents are required to buy text-books in some subjects in which there is no state text, and supplemental texts in various subjects where more elementary or more advanced work is desired than is given in the state texts.

Tho it is impossible to know just how much money is now spent for text-books in this state, it is very evident that it is considerably more than free text-books would cost us at the rate which other states are paying. The enrollment in our schools below high schools for the year 1899–1900, taken from the last report of our State Superintendent, was 188,420. At a rate of seventy-five cents per year per pupil, which is considerably above the amount required in most of the states where supplies and high school texts are not included, it would cost California $141,315 per year to furnish free text-books. The assessed valuation of the property of the state in the same year (1900) was $1,193,764,673. An additional tax rate of 1 1·5 cents on $100 assessment would supply the necessary funds in case none of the library fund which we now enjoy should be used for this purpose. Maryland enrolled 224,004 children in her schools during the year 1900–1. Her appropriation from 1896 until 1900 was $150,000 per year, at which time it was reported that a surplus had accumulated in several counties, and the tax was reduced. There is no question but that free text-books would prove to be a matter of economy in California, as they have done in every state where they are used.

Probably no state has ever suffered more seriously from out-of-date text-books than California. The history text our children are required to use was issued in *1888*. Our text says nothing about the great social and political events that have transpired since the beginning of Harrison's administration. There is nothing about the history of our nation for the last fifteen years, to which the best texts devote from fifteen to sixty pages. There has been no revision and there is no prospect of any such thing very soon. Even were the funds to do this placed in the hands of our State Board immediately, it would be sometime before the revision could be accomplished, the printing done, and the books distributed and introduced in the schools. Our Complete Geography is one of the latest books of our series. It was issued in 1893. All the statistical figures are from the census of 1890. Hawaii, Cuba, Porto Rico, the Philippines, and Alaska have so completely changed that that portion of the book treating of them is obsolete, and many other portions such as that on South Africa, are but slightly less so. About two years ago our State Board attempted to furnish us with an up-to-date history. The printing question became involved, and we are still using the old text, with no prospect of an early change. Free text-books would involve none of these difficulties. As books are worn out, they can be replaced with the newest and best, or exchange prices can be arranged with publishers. Free competition would make it possible for us to have the best texts produced by the best text-book writers and publishers.

It has become evident to school people that there is a variety of needs in California schools. No system of state uniformity is likely to be satisfactory to all. The reports of state superintendents of eastern states show that systems of state uniformity are often unsatisfactory and are being abandoned. But with private ownership of books there must be this uniformity or there will be very heavy expense upon parents who move from place to place. Free text-books can be as varied as are the communities and avoid this difficulty. It is also important that in each school there should be a variety of text-books. If bought by the district, there can be a sufficient variety with no additional expense. It does not make any difference in the expense to the district whether one hundred books of one kind are purchased or fifty of each of two kinds.

Our schools in California are now to a considerable degree furnished with free text-books In some counties probably half of the books are furnished by the district. It is a common practice thruout the state to furnish many sets of readers, drawing-books, song books, etc. In some counties all of the library funds are expended for supplementary text-books and some districts supply free text-books thruout.

In one of the large counties of this state there is a regulation of the county board of education that no other purchases shall be made from the library fund until in the judgment of the county superintendent the school is suitably supplied with the supplemental books mentioned in the course of study.

Another county advises trustees thus:

"First of all, see if your teacher needs any supplemental reading; furnish that before buying anything else."

Another county says:

"The county board strongly advises that the library fund be spent for books to supplement the regular text-books, and for a few standard reference books."

Still another says:

"All the books designated above (supplemental books named in the body of the course of study) for the use of teachers and pupils, are to be purchased with county and library funds"; and in another place, "When a teacher takes charge of a school she should at once secure, thru the trustees, as many of the books . . . as the pupils . . . require."

We might quote from many more, but it must be evident from this that free texts are not unknown in California and it will not require a change of principle to go still further in this line. Some attempt has been made to ascertain how many districts purchase *all* of their text-books from county and library funds, but it was not possible to obtain any definite results. It is certain, however, that there are many districts which now purchase with public funds all the state text-books, as well as others, that are used by their pupils.

It may be argued that as the law now provides that districts shall purchase books for all indigent children, that therefore no further provision need be made. Such a proceeding is charity, and it immediately must raise a distinction between the poverty-stricken and those who are not. All children in our public schools should be on an equal footing. No child wishes to carry with him a book bearing the stamp of the district unless all do so.

So far as experience of others can guide us, there is no reason why we should not adopt a free text-book system. So far as our needs go, there is no question but that we must soon find a way out of our present difficulties. Our present system is very expensive, and the books must be revised or changed.

Under the present constitution of the state, the State Board of Education must "compile . . . and adopt a uniform series of text-books for use in the common schools thruout the state." While this provision stands thus, no system but a uniform one is possible. Legislation is now being considered which will enable the State Board to secure better books. It should not be difficult to provide means by which the schools may be furnished with these books free of cost to the pupils and at the same time preserve to the counties and school districts their present freedom in meeting local needs thru supplementary books. This plan would not be so objectionable as one which requires absolute uniformity and it can be placed in operation in conformity with our present constitution. The State Board might be authorized to buy better copyrights, a fund provided for furnishing the books to the districts for the use of the pupils, and the work would be complete.

Plans, such as have proven so successful in Maryland, Nebraska, and most of the New England states, would require an amendment to the constitution as to uniformity. In these states the books are provided thru county or district adoptions. These adoptions are controlled by general laws which regulate time, price, manner of adoption, etc. Any of these successful plans could be readily utilized in this state. Our state and county boards already furnish all the necessary machinery. The work would be little different from the present adoption of supplementary books, texts in subjects not supplied by the state, and high school texts for county high schools. Most of these tried systems would easily and naturally adopt themselves to California conditions.

PUBLISHERS' NOTICE.

THE WESTERN JOURNAL OF EDUCATION succeeds to the subscription lists, adVertising patrouage, and good will of the Golden Era, established in San Francisco in 1852.
Subscription, $1.50 a year. Single copies, 15 cents.
Remit by check, Postoffice order, Wells, Fargo & Co., or by stamps.
ADVERTISEMENTS—Advertisements of an unobjectionable nature will be inserted at the rate of $3.00 a month per inch.
MSS.—Articles on methods, trials of new theories, actual experiences, and school news, reports of teachers' meetings, etc., urgently solicited.
Address all communications to THE WESTERN JOURNAL OF EDUCATION, 723 Market Street, San Francisco.
HARR WAGNER, Editor.
THE WHITAKER & RAY COMPANY PUBLISHERS.
Entered at the San Francisco Post-office as second-class matter.

The Official Organ of the Department of Public Instruction of the State of California.

Increase Pay for Teachers.—The Chicago Board of Education has increased the pay of all of the teachers in the school department. . Other cities have done likewise. The increased cost of living, the strenuous demand on the teachers as citizens, and additional requirements along the line of professional duties, make an increase of pay an act of simple justice. Los Angeles should not boast of its prosperity until it pays its teachers a living salary. San Francisco has over one hundred and fifty millions in the savings banks, and a tax roll that has increased much more rapidly per capita than the population. Yet there has been no effort made—it has not been even hinted in public places—that the teachers of the San Francisco School Department should be granted better pay. If a hundred dollars per year were added to each teacher's salary the addition would not much more than cover the increased cost of house rent.

It is therefore but an act of simple justice that now at a time when the taxpayer is getting additional revenue from his property, that the teachers should be paid more liberally. The time is opportune for the board of eduction of the city of San Francisco, for the boards of education of other incorporated cities to increase the teachers' pay, and for the boards of supervisors in the fifty-seven counties of California to increase the current school revenues.

The interests of the state demand that the teachers be paid more generously. The age limit at both ends borders nearer maturity than ever before. The earning years of a teacher's life are limited. The conditions are such that the strong young woman and the strong young man will not enter the professional training schools to become teachers. The result will be a mentally and physically weak generation of teachers.

The men whose red blood surges in strong veins are leaving the schoolroom. Why? Because, while there is some vacant room at the top, there is little else.

We have a generation of strong men and strong women in California in charge of the schools. But if the state when it enjoys prosperity, ignores the teachers' rights, the next generation of teachers will be runts.

Editorial

San Francisco has a superintendent who receives $4000. The assessor has just been voted $8000. The city has four deputies who receive the small salary of $1800, a salary fixed by a board of education of four members, three of whom were teachers. An elementary teacher must serve five years to get the salary of $62.50 per month, while the policemen who are able to measure up properly in physical examination, receive much more for carrying a club. The time is ripe for an insistent demand for an increase in pay for every member in the schoolroom. It is a demand that need not be made on the selfish ground of individual necessity. It is a demand that should be made in the interest of the welfare of the state.

* * *

A Review of Proposed Educational Legislature.—A large number of bills of an educational character are now pending before the legislature. The most important is the text-book bill, proposed by Supt. Thomas J. Kirk, and introduced into the Assembly by A. H. Drew, and into the Senate by Frank Leavitt. The vital element in this bill is contained in the clause which authorizes the State Board of Education, or a commission, to secure copyrights and plates of text-books in the open market. The passage of this bill will undoubtedly result in the state securing good books and having the same manufactured in this state. Senator Emmons has introduced a bill providing for free text-books. This bill is not likely to pass. An excellent discussion on free text-books, by Supt. E. M. Cox, will be found in this issue of the JOURNAL.

Senator Rowell has introduced a bill providing for an ad valorem tax of one and one-half cents on each one hundred dollars to support high schools. This money shall be apportioned as follows:

SEC. 5. The money in said state high school fund shall be apportioned to the high schools of the state by the superintendent of public instruction in the following manner: He shall apportion one-third of the annual amount among the county, district, city, union, or joint union high schools of the state, irrespective of the number of pupils enrolled or in average daily attendance therein, except as hereinafter provided; the remaining two-thirds of the annual amount he shall apportion among such schools pro rata upon the basis of average daily attendance as shown by the official reports of the county or city and county school superintendents for the last preceding school year; *provided*, that such high schools have been organized under the law of the state, or have been recognized as existing under the high school laws of the state and have maintained the grade of instruction required by law of the high schools; *and provided*, that no school shall be eligible to a share of said state high school fund that has not during the last preceding school year employed at least two regularly certificated high school teachers for a period of not less than one hundred and eighty days with not less than twenty pupils in average daily attendance for such length of time, except in newly established high schools wherein the minimum average daily attendance for the first year of one hundred and eighty days may be but twelve pupils, and the number of teachers but one; *and provided*, that before receiving State aid, each school shall furnish satisfactory evidence to the superintendent of public instruction of the possession of a reasonably good equipment of building, laboratory and library, and of having maintained, the preceding school year, proper high school instruction for a term of at least one hundred and eighty days; *provided further*, that the foregoing provisions relating to the average daily attendance, the number of teachers employed, and the length of term required shall not operate to disqualify any legally established high school from receiving a share of said state high school fund if in existence and maintaining a regular high school course on January first, nineteen hundred and three.

Senator Diggs has introduced an amendment to Section 1617, which practically gives life tenure to all teachers except in rural districts of one teacher, as follows:

To employ the teachers and, excepting in incorporated cities having boards of education, immediately notify the superintendent of schools, in writing, of such employment, naming the grade of certificate held by the teachers employed; also, to employ janitors and other employes of the schools; to fix and order paid their compensation, unless the same be otherwise prescribed by law; *provided*, that no board of trustees shall enter into any contract with such employes to extend beyond the thirtieth day of June next ensuing. (*Provided, however*, that in all school districts having graded schools in which two or more teachers are employed, the board of trustees shall employ and retain in the school department all teachers who have taught for five or more years consecutively in said school, until said teacher shall be removed on charges sustained for unfitness, violation of school law, or incompetency.)

There is also an amendment to Section 1593, which provides for the election of school trustees on the first Friday in April.

Senator Welsh has introduced a bill providing for the maintenance of a separate class for deaf children by the oral system, whenever five or more such children live in a district.

There are various appropriation bills for the support of schools, the most important are: $250,000 for a new building at the University of California, $200,000 for the San Francisco State Normal School, $90,000 to complete the building at San Diego, and an appropriation for buildings at the Chico State Normal.

There is also a bill to establish a girls' polytechnic school.

Senator O'Neal has introduced a bill which takes away the authority of the presidents of the normal schools to nominate teachers.

There is a compulsory education bill, and a juvenile court bill, which are surely in the line of progress. Assemblyman Lewis of Riverside County has introduced several bills to repeal the present institute laws. There are many other bills introduced, affecting the school laws in various ways, but they will probably die in committee if the proposed legislation is a radical departure from the present status. The temper of the present legislature does not seem to favor any revolutionary measures, so far as the public school system is concerned.

* * *

NOTES

Prof. Alex B. Coffey is writing a series of heart to heart talks for the "Northwest Journal of Education." The talks are bright, witty and inspiring.

* * *

Supt. C. B. Gilbert of Rochester, N. Y., has resigned to accept the management of the school text-book department of D. Appleton & Co., at a salary of $7000. Prof. E. R. Shaw has been elected his successor.

* * *

President Nicholas Murray Butler, in his annual report, states that there are one hundred and twenty-six teachers employed at Columbia University whose salary does not average $1000.

* * *

President E. Benjamin Andrews of Nebraska University was voted an increase of salary from $6000 to $8000. He addressed a letter to the board of regents declining to accept the raise in view of the fact that if the funds warranted, the underpaid professors should have the raise.

* * *

A group picture of the State Board of Education, the City and County Superintendents, printed on heavy plate paper, will be issued with the compliments of the WESTERN JOURNAL OF EDUCATION, February 15th. Any teacher or subscriber to the JOURNAL may have a copy free by sending 4 cents to prepay postage.

Book Reviews

"The Conduct of Composition Work in Grammar Schools." By Henry Lincoln Clapp and Katherine W. Huston, Boston, D. C. Heath & Co., 1902. Pages, 47. Price, 25 cents.

Multum in parvo. It consists of three brief chapters dealing respectively with "Choice and Arrangement of Material," "What to Guard Against," "The Correcting of Compositions," and a fourth, made up largely of sample compositions by pupils who have "proved the pudding." There is not a superfluous sentence in the book. The plan is evidently of one who is blessed with both liberal culture and pedagogical insight. Elementary school teachers can ill afford to be without this gem. W. S. *Small.*

* * *

"Social Life in the Early Republic." By Anne Hollingsworth Wharton. Philadelphia. J. B. Lippincott Co., 1902. Pages, 346. Price, $3.00.

This is a delightful addition to Miss Wharton's already significant list of restorations of society in colonial and early republican days. The society she writes of is "society in its best sense—the meeting of men and women for rational intercourse and enjoyment." Miss Wharton's essays are as valuable and charming in their field as Mr. Earle's restoration of colonial New England. She is *con amore* with her subject. Letter, diary, and traditional tale are skilfully woven into her vivacious narrative. Intimate personal touches reveal new aspects of men and events—significant side lights which are commonly lacking in our scientific histories. Apropos of the selection of the present Washington as the site of the National Capitol, Mr. Jefferson is shown to have appreciated the tenet of oriental diplomacy: better is speech when the belly is fed; for when he was approached by Mr. Hamilton upon the subject, he "pleaded ignorance, having just returned from abroad," but urged Mr. Hamilton to "dine with him the next day, meet a few Virginians, and discuss the matter calmly over Madeira and punch." Thus the "site of the Capitol, like many other important matters, was decided over a glass of wine." The chapter entitled, "A Ladies' Battle," gives an intimate insight into a phase of politics that never will be played out.

Such books as this are invaluable adjuncts to the school historical libraries. Historical teaching, even in the secondary—nay in the elementary—schools, is prone to concern itself over much with movements, tendencies, principles, at the expense of the imaginative reconstruction of men, times and customs.

Books of this kind in the school library will help preserve a wholesome balance.

The book is beautifully printed and bound and profusely illustrated. *W. S. Small.*

* * *

"Liberty Documents," with contemporary exposition and critical comments drawn from various writers. Selected and prepared by Mabel Hill. Edited with an introduction by Albert Bushnell Hart, Ph.D. New York. Longmans, Green & Co., 1901. Pages 448. XXVIII. Price $2.00.

This is a valuable addition to the constantly increasing number of historical source-books. The extracts from the original documents here presented make plain the path traveled by our forefathers in their long march towards personal and political liberty. Citations from contemporary exposition and from standard constitutional historians complete the material of the book. Twenty-four groups of documents are drawn upon, begining with the coronation oath and charter of Henry I (1101) and ending with President McKinley's messages for 1898 and 1899. In general, due respect for proportion is shown in the selections. The treatment of the slavery period might have been somewhat expanded.

It is well recognized by secondary as well as college teachers, that access to just such material as this is necessary in order to make political history interesting. For high schools, normal schools and colleges with limited library funds a supply of the Library Documents is invaluable. It might well be made a supplementary text in both English and American history, in connection with some comprehensive and comparatively inexpensive text-book.

Of the intrinsic worth of such historical study there is no question. The concluding sentence in Professor Hart's introduction expresses this perfectly: "Perhaps also in these days of storm and stress, of the creation of new political powers and influences, of undreamed of complications with the affairs of the rest of the civilized world, it may be worth while to bring to the minds of young people the truth that our personal liberty, our freedom to move about, to take up callings, and to make the most of ourselves, is not a privilege which defends itself; that it behooves a free people not to give up principles for which they and their forefathers have been contending during more than eight centuries."

The book is well made, clearly printed on good paper and substantially bound. It has a full table of contents and a satisfactory index. *W. S. Small*

* * *

"Pyle's Stories of Humble Friends." By Katherine Pyle. With pictures by the author. Cloth, 12mo, 197 pages. Price, 50 cents. American Book Company.

Miss Pyle is the sister of the well-known author and artist, Howard Pyle, and she has much of the latter's ability in writing and illustrating. The stories in this book, which is intended for the third reader grade, are about animals and birds familiar to children. They are simple in their style, attractive in their subject matter, and well suited to arouse the pupil's interest and to cultivate a feeling of sympathy for our "humble friends." The illustrations add to the interest of the stories.

* * *

"Pitman's Stories of Old France." By Leila Webster Pitman, author of "Another Girl's Experience." Cloth, 12mo, 312 pages. Illustrated. Price, 60 cents. American Book Company.

Well suited to serve as an introduction to French history, this book presents charming stories of the most salient characters and events of Old France, written with the utmost fidelity to truth and at the same time clothed with romantic interest.

* * *

"Merrill's Studies in Zoology." By James Merrill. Cloth, 12mo, 232 pages. Price, 75 cents. American Book Company.

The directions in this laboratory guide are simple and suggestive as well as comprehensive. The plan of the work was tested, before publication, with pupils of all grades in the high school.

* * *

"Wood's The Children's First Story Book." By May H. Wood. Cloth, 12mo, 80 pages. Illustrated. Price, 25 cents. American Book Company.

This book is designed to be used as a supplementary reader. The simplicity of its reading matter and the number and beauty of its illustrations adapt it admirably to the tastes and capabilities of children who are just beginning to read and have mastered the first lessons of some standard text-book.

⚐ WESTERN SCHOOL NEWS ⚐

MEETINGS

National Educational Association, President Charles W. Eliot, Boston, July 6-10, 1903.
National Superintendents' Convention, Cincinnati, Ohio, February 2, 24.

INSTITUTES.

San Luis Obispo County. April 22-23-24. Supt. Frederic P. Johnson.

El Dorado County, Feb. 12 to 16. Supt S. B. Wilson.
Kern County, the week of March 16th. Supt. R. S. Stockton.

OTHER INSTITUTES TO BE HELD THIS TERM.

Sonoma County, Minnie Coulter.
Marin County. Supt. J. B. Davidson.
Stanislaus County, Supt. Florence Boggs.
San Mateo County, Supt. Etta M. Tilton.
Nevada County, Supt. J. G. O'Neil.

NOTES

A. O. Burke has been elected principal of the Perris school.

The board of education of the city of Fresno has let contracts for three new school buildings.

President Dailey of the San Jose State Normal School, is arranging for a summer session.

Dr. E. Benjamin Andrews was the chief attraction at the Montana State Association this year.

Hon. Frank H. Short of Fresno was a recent speaker to the students of the University of California.

Howard L. Lunt, formerly of Riverside, has been elected to a position in the Los Angeles High School.

Supt. R. L. Stockton of Kern County has made a most excellent move in establishing an Arbor Day for his county.

Supt. Kate Ames of Napa County has issued a circular to those interested in education outlining her policy for the next four years.

The Supreme Court of Utah has finally settled that the adoption of the books made by the State Text-Book Convention last June was legal.

Montana is at the present time agitating a text-book law. It is very probable that a law creating a text-book commission will be passed.

Mr. Hamilton, formerly deputy superintendent of Los Angeles County, has been elected principal of the "B" Street School, San Diego.

President Halderman of the Tulane University, New Orleans, has been selected to deliver the address at Charter Day exercises, University of California.

President Pierce of Los Angeles State Normal School reports that there is a great demand for normal graduates this year. He had to send out five teachers before graduation.

Jesse D. Burks, formerly of San Diego State Normal, has been appointed acting principal of the Speyer Training School, an experimental school in connection with Teachers' College, Columbia University.

Dr. Albert J. Aitkens of the California Medical College, has announced a new discovery in reference to the effect of electricity on the blood. His experiments will require some radical changes in the text-books on physiology.

Prof. Walter Magee, teacher of physical culture in University of California, has been elected supervisor of physical culture in the San Francisco School Department. Robert Barth has been elected as the assistant teacher of physical culture.

Prof. Chas. E. Hutton, who has served faithfully as a teacher for over fifty years, has resigned from the chair of mathematics in the Los Angeles State Normal School. The members of the faculty presented him with a lounging chair.

Jacques W. Redway, the noted geographer, will be one of the lecturers at the King County Institute, Washington, in April. Prof. Redway's trip to Washington will undoubtedly lead to the correction of the mistake in his Natural Geography where he places Portland in the Puget Sound Valley.

Closing Days of the Confederacy

Scenes and incidents connected with the period covered by the month of April, 1865, until General Johnson's surrender, April 27th, especially the experiences of Jefferson Davis and his cabinet after their flight from Richmond, April 3rd, are graphically told in "Civil War Stories" (The Whitaker & Ray Company, San Francisco). The author has made a close study of the official war records, Union and Confederade, and, in this work, has grouped into conseputive form, many of the most interesting parts connected with the Civil War as detailed in the one hundred and thirty great volumes constituting those records the puplication of which was recently completed by the government at a cost of nearly $3,000,000. There is a demand on the part of schools and public libraries for a work of this character, and in this book are printed facts which, until recently, have been locked up in the archives of the War Department, inaccessible to the general public. As now printed in the government publication they are still of little service to the public on account of the great size and number of the books and the lack of arrangement in their presentation.

✦✦

The San Jose State Normal School graduated a large and efficient class in January. Dr. Elmer E. Brown of Berkeley was the principal speaker. His concluding remarks were: " 'The good is a great enemy of the best.' Do not go out to work for the things that are good simply, but for the things that are best." President Dailey made brief remarks before presenting the diplomas to the graduates. He spoke of his regret at having to lose the January class, but said he felt confident that its members would do their part, and reflect credit upon their school. In closing, he said: "I am certain you will do good work. Do your whole duty; be true to yourselves; be true to your God. I want to hear good reports of you. I shall be personally disappointed, the school will be disappointed, if we do hear such reports. This school is known, like the tree, by its fruits. The better the work each one of you do, the more your diploma is worth to you."

* * *

Supt. J. F. Saylor of Spokane, Wash., has resigned. It is reported that the board of education refused to give him the initiative in reference to the selection of a high school principal, and that he at once took down his law books and began the study of law.

Amador County Institute

Superintendent George A. Gordon called his institute to meet at Jackson, December 1, 2 and 3. He secured a list of notable instructors. Miss Jenne M. Long of the Dramatic School, 2152 Sutter street, San Francisco, spoke on common sense reading and gave an evening entertainment that was delightfully interesting and highly instructive.

Mr. F. F. Bunker of San Francisco State Normal School, gave practical talks on methodology. Professor W. H. Dudley of the University of Chicago, gave a talk on "Wireless Telegraphy," and also the lecture on "Color in Nature," illustrated with the stereopticon.

Dr. C. C. Van Liew, president of Chico State Normal School, gave several strong, interesting addresses.

Mr. A. L. Walker, who recently returned from the Philippines, spoke on his experiences in educational work on the islands.

A number of the local teachers also took part in the institute, and it was in all respects very successful.

***

There was held February 1, in the rooms of the Teachers' Annuity Association, San Francisco, a conference of the executive committee of the California High School Association, and the high school principals from around the bay; C. L. Breidenbach of Berkeley, is president. The principals discussed the changed system of high school examinations by the University, and the University entrance examination requirements. Those present were A. W. Scott, Alameda; M. C. James, Berkeley; F. H. Clark and Frank Morton, Lowell High School; Elisha Brooks, of the Girl's High School; Joseph O'Connor, Mission High School; Dr. John Gamble, Haywards; E. M. Cox, Santa Rosa; James Pond, Oakland; F. Liddeke, Centerville.

* * *

D. J. Sullivan, deputy superintendent of the schools of San Francisco, was asked to resign his position by Superintendent Langdon. Mr. Sullivan refused. He was then dismissed. It is understood that Mr. Sullivan will contest the right of the superintendent to dismiss him without cause. L. M. Shelly was selected as Mr. Sullivan's successor.

* * *

E. Howard, principal of the Kelseyville school, was elected recorder of Lake County at the last election.

Of Interest to All

Clerk of School Trustees—Have you selected your library books yet?

Teacher—I have; and we need them at once.

Clerk—Please give me the titles and publishers.

Teacher—They are all recent publications of Ginn & Co., and are as follows: "The Cyr Readers by Grades," books, 1-8; "Tarbell's Composition," "Kemp's History for Graded and District Schools," and Frye's new geographies—"The Elements" and "Grammar School."

Clerk—Why do you want Frye's geographies?

Teacher—Because they have the best maps that can be made, the most attractive and adequate illustrations, and are the most modern in methods and contents. We have sets of the Frye books which came out first, the "Primary" and "Complete," and like them very much, but this new set is an improvement even upon those excellent books. We shall need two dozen of each. The state book is so poor, you know.

Clerk—Very well, I'll get the geographies, but I thought I bought enough supplementary readers to last forever last year. Why do you ask for the Cyr?

Teacher—They are so well graded, and have such an excellent selection of material from a literary standpoint. I know, for I used them in the Normal before coming here, and our training teacher said the vocabulary in these readers supplements the state readers beautifully.

Clerk—All right, I'll order several sets of the "Cyr Readers"; but how about that new fangled history by Kemp? The state history looks good to me.

Teacher (a little bit disgusted)—You evidently never taught school. Kemp's history is the only book for the lower grades, written in accordance with the recommendation of the committee of seven, presenting history from ancient to modern times as a unit.

Clerk—That certainly is the correct thing to do even if the state history doesn't take up the subject that way. You shall have a set of Kemp's, but that will exhaust our library fund for the year.

Teacher—Never mind, I'll have my seventh and eighth grade pupils buy "Tarbell's Composition" themselves, for they are through with the state grammar, and really need a book of this kind in their hands. It correlates so well with the work in literature which they take up at this time. It is just the book I've wanted for a long time.

A WEEK LATER.

Clerk—The books have come and certainly are a great improvement on those you have been using. I sent direct to the publishers and made quite a saving in discounts and express charges. We shall be able to raise your salary next year because of this, and because of your good judgment in selecting these books. If you are looking for additional supplementary material in any line you had better write to Ginn & Co., 325 Sansome street, San Francisco, Cal.

S. C. Smith

is their California agent.

Teacher—Thanks, awfully. I'll do it.

* * *

H. M. Bland of the State Normal School, San Jose, has formed a teachers' union, and has asked to be recognized by other unions.

* * *

Hon. E. W. Davis, secretary of the board of regents of the University of California, and formerly superintendent of Sonoma County, died Saturday, February 7, 1903. Mr. Davis was a man of many noble traits of character, and his death is regretted by hundreds of warm personal friends.

POPULAR SONG

Mrs. Jennie L. Thorp was in receipt of a letter Thursday from the superintendent of schools of Placer County ordering two hundred copies of "California, Queen of Old Columbia." Mrs. Thorp states the song is already in use in many counties of the state, and an additional testimonial as to its popularity is the fact that so far over twelve hundred copies have been sold.

Above song is for sale by us. Price, 10 cents per copy. Special rate in quantities. THE WHITAKER & RAY CO., San Francisco.

The leading color pictures in the February Century—the most novel and curious in subject of any that magazine has yet published,—are from interesting and beautiful studies of the aurora borealis made by Frank Wilbert Stokes while in the Arctics in the fall of 1892 and are richly worthy the subject. They reproduce in tint for the first time in a popular magazine the wonderful effects of the aurora. Mr. Stokes, probably the first real colorist to visit the Arctic regions, was with the Peary and relief expeditions on the Kite when he was privileged to see some color displays worth all the dangers and privations of the trip. His word painting is as vivid and interesting as his color work.

* * *

"Civil War Stories," soon to be issued from the press of the Whitaker & Ray Company, San Francisco, details at length the earnest efforts made by President Lincoln, Andrew Johnson, and representative Maynard of Tennessee, backed by General McClellan, in the early stages of the war, to send a Union force into East Tennessee in aid of the thousands of loyalists of that portion of Tennessee. A characteristic letter written by "Parson Brownlow" while confined in the county jail of Knoxville is also included. It is evident that in refusing to comply with General McClellan's repeated orders to take possession of East Tennessee, General Buell failed to meet the exspectations of President Lincoln and the general-in-chief of the Union armies.

* * *

"The Teacher at Work."—A Manual of Suggestions and Directions for Public School Instruction. By Wilbur H. Bender, Ph.B. Chicago, A. Flanagan & Co., 1902.

This manual has grown out of the author's experience of six years as the head of the training department of the Iowa State Normal School. The author says modestly that "the Volume is hesitatingly given to the public with the hope that it may help some teacher occasionally to do more for the children under his care." This it is sure to do. It deals in a clear and positive way with a great many practical details of school management and instruction. The tone of the book is mellow and undogmatic for a treatise on formal pedagogy. The value of the book would be greater if it contained somewhat less in regard to the mechanics of teaching and somewhat more in regard to the hygienic principles which condition effective educational work. The selected list of pedagogical books recommended as especially valuable, illustrates this characteristic of the book, being especially full in the former aspect, and very meager in the latter.

* * *

J. S. Hunter has written and the Whitaker & Ray Co. published "The Business Man's Arithmetic." The book develops a rational principle to the solution of all business problems, independent of set rules and with fewer figures than are used in operating with other methods.

The American Book Co. has issued in Language Series the following excellent and useful books: "Nathan the Wise," by Dickhoff, Price 80 cts; "Advanced French Prose Composition," by Francois, Price 80 cts; Bruno's "Le Tourde La France," edited by L. C. Syms, Price 60 cts; Foncin's "Le Pays de France," edited by Muzzarelli, Price 60 cts., and "Mon Oncle et Mon Cure," edited by Elizabeth M. White, for school-use, Price 50 cts. These books are carefully edited with explanatory introduction and notes.

* * *

The Schoolmasters' Club gave a banquet at the California Hotel, Saturday evening, January 12th, Prof. E. P. Cubberley, presiding. Addresses were made by Dr. Elmer E. Brown, Prof. Julius Goebel, Dr. E. C. Moore, and a Japanese student of Stanford University.

* * *

A Bargain in Pianos—For sale, a fine new piano, never used, price $350, will sell for $250. Address Piano, care of WESTERN JOURNAL OF EDUCATION, 723 Market st., S. F., Cal.

* * *

For sale—A scholarship in leading business college, price $100, will sell for $50. Address Business, care of WESTERN JOURNAL OF EDUCATION, 723 Market st., S. F, Cal.

Augsburg's Drawing
AN ENTIRELY NEW SYSTEM

Special Features are

1. Directness and Simplicity
2. Usableness by the average teacher and pupil
3. A practical and not theoretical treatment of the subject

The system consists of Books I. II, III, each 75 cents, and Pupils' Practice Books. Price 15 cents each.

Each book contains an abundance of blank paper for practice purposes, and on each fifth leaf of the several books is an outline of the work for the following week. These outlines tell the pupil what to do, and by means of simple drawings show the pupil how the work is to be done.

Complete descriptive circular sent on request.

The Augsburg System is now officially used in seventeen counties in California.

Published by

EDUCATIONAL PUBLISHING COMPANY

809 Market Street, San Francisco, Cal.

Boston   New York   Chicago

THE WESTERN JOURNAL OF EDUCATION

MARCH, 1903

Contents

Judicial Consideration of Juvenile Offenders......Judge Clamroth	107
The Utility of Books..........................Mrs. E. L. Bigelow	114
What the Country Wants from the Universities...Arthur B. Hadley	117
President of Yale University.	
State High Schools..................................T. H. Kirk	118
Drawing the Universal Medium.........D. R. Augsburg	121
Current Educational Thought........................	123
Educational Expenditure; Educational Improvements in the Past Thirty Years; The Needs of American Public Education, President Eliot.	
President Eliot and the Public Schools............Ossian H. Lang,	12
In the January-March Forum.	
For the Trustees	128
Preventable Diseases in Rural Districts; Educational Possibilities of Country Life, Edwin Berwick; The County Superintendent, S. Y. Gillan; Farmers Favor Consolidation, I. D. Harvey.	
The State Flower of California....................	130
An Account of the Poppy: To the Eschscholtzia, Chas. H. Allen; Cops De Oro, Ina Coolbrith; God's Gold, Joaquin Miller; In Poppy Fields, Edwin Markham; The Flower of the West, Rose Hartwick Thorpe; The Poppies and the Clover, Madge Morris.	
A Simple Method in Frustums..............L. M. Hollingsworth	133
Superintendents....................................	135
Why Do Boys Leave Home?..................Job Wood Jr.	141
Official Department......................Thomas J. Kirk	144
Superintendent of Public Instruction.	
The New State High School Law...................	145
Editorial...	149
Book Reviews	150
Western School News.............................	153
Miscellaneous.....................................	155

HARR WAGNER, Editor

15 cents per copy — $1.50 per year

New Books for Nature Study

BARTLETT'S ANIMALS AT HOME 45 cents
For Third Reader Grade

This little book is intended to arouse the interest of children in certain individual animals, and by so doing to awaken an interest for Natural History in general. In each story one particular animal is described in such a way as to illustrate the life of a class.

PYLE'S STORIES OF HUMBLE FRIENDS 50 cents
For Third Reader Grade

The stories in this book are about animals and birds familiar to the children. They are simple in their manner of presentation and most sympathetic in treatment. The many pictures drawn by the author are vividly illustrative of the incidents described.

BRADISH'S STORIES OF COUNTRY LIFE 40 cents
For Third Reader Grade

These recollections of a childhood spent on a northwestern farm, aim to emphasize the attractiveness of life in the country, and to add to its charm by awakening an intelligent interest in its many activities.

KELLY'S SHORT STORIES OF OUR SHY NEIGHBORS 50 cen[ts]
For Third Reader Grade

Entertaining and instructive reading, telling abo[ut] the birds, insects, and other living creatures around [us] in such an interesting manner as to arouse in the chi[ld] a desire to become better acquainted with the wo[n]ders of the animate world.

STOKES'S TEN COMMON TREES 40 cen[ts]
For Third Reader Grade

A series of simple nature lessons for young childre[n] familiarly treated and giving a few definite impressio[ns] of what trees are and how they live.

DANA'S PLANTS AND THEIR CHILDREN 65 cen[ts]
For Fourth Reader Grade

These charming readings are as interesting as stori[es] and are not only instructive in themselves, but tea[ch] the most important lessons a child can learn — to s[ee,] to think, to observe for himself, and thus to become [an] intelligent student of nature.

Popular Works in Botany and Zoölogy

Holder's Stories of Animal Life	$0.60
Needham's Outdoor Studies	.40
Cooper's Animal Life	1.25
Gray's How Plants Behave	.54
How Plants Grow, with a Popular Flora	.80
Herrick's Chapters on Plant Life	.60
Johonnot's Book of Cats and Dogs	.17
Friends in Feathers and Fur	.30
Neighbors with Wings and Fins	.40
Some Curious Flyers, Creepers, and Swimmers	.40
Some Neighbors with Claws and Hoofs	.54
Glimpses of the Animate World	1.00
Lockwood's Animal Memoirs—	
Part I. Mammals	.60
Part II. Birds	.60

McGuffey's Familiar Animals and Their Wild Kindred	$0.[ ]
Living Creatures of Water, Land, and Air	
Monteith's Popular Science Reader	
Burnet's School Zoölogy	
Needham's Elementary Lessons in Zoölogy	
Steele's Popular Zoölogy	1.[ ]
Apgars' New Plant Analysis	
Leavitt's Outlines of Botany	1.[ ]
The same. With Gray's Field, Forest, and Garden Flora	1.[ ]
Wood's New American Botanist and Florist—Lessons and Flora	1.[ ]

AMERICAN BOOK COMPANY PUBLISHE[RS]

NEW YORK   CINCINNATI   CHICAGO   BOSTON   ATLANTA   DALLAS

204 PINE ST., SAN FRANCISCO

THE WESTERN JOURNAL OF EDUCATION

Established 1852.

Judicial Consideration of Juvenile Offenders*

JUDGE CLAMROTH.

In discussing the general subject, "Judicial Consideration of Juvenile Offenders," a large field presents itself to view, particularly to one who for some years has come in constant touch with the juvenile offender, whom I call by preference the juvenile delinquent, and one who has in his smal way, in the police court of a city of twelve thousand souls, tried to carry into effect his ideas, his principles and his conclusions, which are the result of interesting and instructive research into the why and wherefore of the deplorable state of affairs in the juvenile world.

Let us begin by dividing our subject:

First—What are the present conditions of the law in our state regarding juvenile delinquents?

Second—What can be done to remedy the defects of the present law?

Third—Causes of so much delinquency among juveniles.

First: The present conditions of the law regarding juvenile delinquents.

We are still suffering from the old idea, long since exploded, that criminals are normal persons, for some reason or other choosing to act as if they were not normal and our law deems it necessary to punish them in such a manner that would as nearly as possible fit each offence, taking no regard of the criminal's nature, his character, his environments, or root from which he sprung; in other words, parentage, home, physical or moral condition count for nothing; it is enough that a crime has been committed and that there should be some punishment therefor. The law makes the "punishment fit the crime," but it looses all sight of the criminal. Whereas, it is a fact, not quite generally accepted, that the criminal is a distorted person, who has fallen out of the social ranks, from weakness, disease or distortion or environments, and the treatment should be offered these unfortunates quite as much as to the leper, the idiot, or the lunatic, and their weak-

---

*Printed by request of the Legislative Department of the California Teachers' Association. A bill has passed both houses of the present legislature providing a court for juvenile delinquents.

ness and misery should not be exposed to the public gaze any more than the idiot, leper or lunatic.

The law of our state practically says, that if any person over a certain age is charged with committing a crime he must be tried before a competent tribunal and if found guilty, punished by either fine or imprisonment; or, if the court deem it wiser in the case of juveniles, to place the boy or girl in one or the other of certain homes for a limited period; and should a higher degree of crime be committed, or should he prove incorrigible, he may be sent to one of our reform schools. That is all.

One rule for all.

One rule for the clever, intelligent, learned and respected judge of the higher court, a man of sound judgment and wise discretion, who can read between the lines of the statute as it appears on the books, and the same rule for the justice of the peace, who may be anything but clever, anything but intelligent, or learned or respected.

One rule for the adult and practically the same for the juvenile.

One rule for the boy who has been reared in luxury, with every attendant privilege and advantage, but who may by some mischievous prank get into the law's clutches, the same rule for the boy brought up in crime, reared in the slums, associate of thieves and criminals.

One rule for the naturally vicious and degenerate, the same rule for the boy who, thru environment, has been brought low.

One rule for the strong, healthy lad, the same for the weak, puny lad.

Is it right, is it just; is it the best our civilization can boast of?

True, the law also provides for the separation of the juvenile from the adult criminal, but it does not separate the juvenile from the juvenile, which is the curse of institutional treatment for the juvenile delinquents.

Your boy, my boy, may some day get into the clutches of the law, and I beg of you in justice to yourselves and in justice to the boy, do you believe he should be judged in the same way and manner as the adult offender, and do you for a moment believe he should be punished by being shut up with such vicious characters as it has been my misfortune to meet among juvenile delinquents?

Our law thinks only of Punishment, Punishment, Punishment; it precludes all else; while its cry, and our cry, should be, Correction, Correction, Correction.

"It is an offence against society greater than any child can commit to subject it to the consequences of the criminal law as executed in most of the states of the Union."

Second: What can be done to remedy the defects of the present law?

A child should not under any condition be dealt with as an adult, for which reason an entirely separate code of laws should be established for the juvenile. Can you educate and correct a child by punishment alone, which is all the law provides for? Can you, oh teachers, with a book in one hand and a switch it the other, succeed in your work and task?

Juveniles who have offended should have the most jealous care of the state. Harshness cannot help them. But the idea must become implanted in their minds, that society is for their benefit and good, and not for their disgrace and degradation. Being in a formative state, they naturally are more sensitive to treatment than adults, and most of all must be dealt with kindly.

You know, that if your child is led to think that you dislike him or have a poor opinion of him, he is apt to become what you consider him. So with the delinquent, if he is led to think that society is against him, he is apt to become just what the world considers him.

The chances are almost a certainty, that if a child is convicted of a crime, and imprisoned and disgraced, he will become an outcast and habitual criminal; but if corrected in a charitable and reasonable manner, and as I have before suggested, is taught that Society and State are his friends, seeking to do him good, and not his enemy, a useful member is saved to society.

This brings us to the juvenile court, an institution which, if correctly established, would do more good for the delinquent children than all our charitable institutions put together.

New York, Chicago, Philadelphia, and many other cities have tried it with remarkable success.

The plan I favor is to establish a court in each county for the proper handling of the juvenile. Give to this court the power to take complete charge of all cases of crime or delinquency among children under sixteen years of age; put at the head of the court a lawyer, a man of family, who has thoroly studied the principles of criminal anthropology; a man not so old that he has forgotten his boyhood days, and above all, no politician. Make it the court of courts in one sense, for the children are the future citizens of our glorious Republic, and upon them depends its future welfare, and every one this court can save means so much for right, so much for country, so much for God.

Give this court the power to appoint in each community, responsible and intelligent persons, versed in criminology, whose duty it shall be to thoroly investigate and inquire into the nature and character of the culprit, his environment, his physical, moral and mental condition generally, so that the court may be thoroly advised and posted, thus being the better able to determine what course to pursue with the culprit. The offender should be put on probation under the surveillance of the court and probation officer, which latter should look after the offender's training, his social surroundings and influence; and should, best of all, should it be lacking, obtain a true home for him, where his plastic and formative nature may be changed and a good, useful and honored citizen be produced.

True, these conditions cannot always prevail, but when possible and practicable, a home should be found for him, and if he already have one, let him remain there under the surveillance of the proper officer, whose duty shall also extend to the betterment of his home conditions, and let him attend school, more particularly a day industrial school, to keep the mind and fingers from idleness.

A. Douglas Morrison, one of the most able and learned of criminologists, says in his "Juvenile Offenders": "It is, as a rule, inadvisable to commit children to corrective institutions, who are living under normal parental conditions, even if these children have become offenders against criminal law. The discipline of a somewhat inferior home is always better than the discipline of an institution, and the effects of parental solicitude are much more likely to be effectual in the ultimate reclamation of the wayward child, than any kind of state machinery."

The admonitary system as suggested, aided by industrial education in the day schools, should bring about the reform of the delinquent in almost any case, but if not, then let institutional correction be tried; commit the culprit to a reform school for an indefinite period, the time of his detention to depend upon his behavior and improvement. But be sure that this reform school be directed in the right way; let there be more attention paid to individuals and let the different classes of delinquents be separated as much as possible.

Should neither of these be effective, then we must resort to the punitive method, but only when it clearly appears that the delinquent is a hopeless congenital or born criminal. Such ones should be separated from society and not allowed to reproduce their kind.

The admonitary system of treatment of the juvenile delinquent, aided by compulsory attendance at the public schools, has been tried by me for the past four years, and out of possibly two hundred and fifty cases, I have the knowledge of but two failures. My method, if I may be permitted to call it so, altho I rather dislike to claim it owing to its many, many shortcomings, which, however, only exist thru necessity or rather lack of legal sanction, is to receive the culprit in my private office after a regular complaint has been sworn to and a warrant issued, and taking the consequences in my own hands, I question the boy and the witnesses until I am convinced of either of the boy's innocence or guilt.

In the event of his guilt, I proceed to have a quiet, simple talk with the youngster. I discover here and there little trails leading me to the inner recesses of the youngster's heart and soul, he becomes more and more confidential; I touch upon his home life, his mother, his father; ah! how loose that tongue becomes when well lubricated by the oil of kindness and gentleness, and how quickly that little tongue leads to the reason of it all. The boy is sent home, subject to the order of the court, his story, thru the aid of the police and others, investigated; if found true, and it usually is, the sentence is suspended pending good behavior, and he is required to report at regular intervals, in the meantime being under the watchful eye of the police, parent and court, and in certain cases, where particularly needed, under the supervision of some benevolently inclined individuals who visit the homes, and who, under the direction of the court, after full discussion, make suggestions to the parents, the better to help them rear the boy properly.

In some cases the probationary period has not exceeded a month; but in others, particularly in those where the reformation and education of the boy is retarded by antagonism of the parents, a longer period may be necessary.

This method of care of the juvenile delinquent, I have merely presented in outline, but my experience teaches me that some such method must be devised to stem the tide of juvenile delinquency, and it must be taken hold of by us all, who love right, who love our Country and who love our God.

Third: Causes of so much delinquency among juveniles.

"A man is shaped by the surroundings in which he has been born and is obliged to live," says a writer; and we naturally expect to find the majority of these juvenile delinquents spring from the lower classes where they have been born and reared in environments that are calculated to develop criminal tendencies, and there is no doubt that the best born, if reared in these environments, would go wrong. What but crime can develop in the formative period of a child's life, when constantly subject to cold and hunger, squalor and filth, and impure conditions generally; so, as I have said, we naturally expect this from the lower classes, but why so much delinquency among boys of the middle class, and to my mind it is due to improper home influence, either thru untruthfulness, bad example or over-indulgence.

Untruthfulness, to my mind, gleaned from experience with youthful unfortunates who have been brought before me, is the starting point of many a child's downfall; in fact, almost every case I have invested starts there, and I have followed up this pernicious trait thru many twists and turns and various gradations until it has become a strong habit, so strong as to be second nature, and the youthful culprit has been able to deceive for a long period of time, not only parents but those whose business it is to trace just such things and discover perpetrators of crime.

Fear of punishment is one of the most common causes for untruthfulness. How sad it is that so many, many parents govern their children solely thru fear and but seldom love, "that antidote for all ills, that slayer of sin," be the guide to their actions, and as a result, very early in life the child learns that a simple fib will save many a punishment, and soon this simple fib, nurtured and cultivated by the dread and fear of unrighteous punishment, grows into a well developed life, the branches of which are deceit, dishonesty, and disrespect, and later the fruitage. Ah, how beautiful and luscious that fruit, that enables him to do so many forbidden things, seems to the child; it grows and ripens, but oh, the bitterness, when it ripens into crime. God save them; and on whom the blame?

The question of discipline is a vital one, and I firmly believe all parents regard it as such; but how many have studied it thoroly or even looked into the matter? How many parents get together, for "in union there is strength," and discuss the matter of discipline calmly and thoughtfully, as they would, for instance, the purchase of a dwelling or any matter of financial importance. No. On the spur of the moment they chastise in anger. Why, the vast majority of them put more thought to the training of a horse or dog, or to the satisfying of some social or educational ambition, than they do the training of their offspring, and they seem to expect the training of the child to spring out of nothing, simply to grow, like "Topsy."

We find statistics galore as to the mental education of our children, but where the statistics as to their moral training? We find each family experimenting by itself, some successfully, but too often the reverse and no record kept.

Bad example does perhaps as much to bring the youth of this country low as anything else.

How often we make use of the so-called "white lies" to our children, and think by this petty deception we have satisfied the child. Yes, undoubtedly we have, but can we measure the damage to the little one's listening brother or sister, whose simple mind has not yet been sufficiently trained to distinguish the coloring matter that may be injected into the untruth. Ah! friends, these "white lies" are but embryo "black" ones, and by the use of them in the home, the child early in life becomes impregnated with that subtle and corrosive poison of deceitfulness, that miserable trait of character that is the very fountain spring of so much woe and misery, that trait that makes of us hypocrites, whom Christ condemns in stronger terms than any other kind of sinner.

A good example means more for a child's future than almost anything else.

But pray, how can we properly train a child if we daily and hourly forbid him to do the very things we are constantly doing, unless we explain to him the difference and the reason?

No, we seem to forget that children are reasonable beings, capable of reasoning or being reasoned with, or perhaps we are too busy with some favorite occupation or our book is too intensely interesting, and it is so much easier to simply say "Don't," and if the next day this very child answers you with a sharp, short "Won't" or "Don't," he is immediately punished, and why? For copying us! We can see ourselves in our children and we should use these human mirrors more, and study our characters in them, and thru and in our children help not only ourselves but them, and society generally.

A home where family quarrels are a common and usual thing is also a fruitful starting place for juvenile delinquents, for unkind and disrespectful words on the part of the elders of the family toward each other is but sowing the seeds of disrespect into the soil, rich and fertile, and the harvest is usually gathered in the slums of the police court.

Another fruitful cause of so much delinquency among the juveniles is the extreme laxity of home control. In this beautiful country of ours where we have so many sunshiny days, the youngsters are out and away, as they should be, but the old-fashioned notion that parents are entitled to know where their children are and with whom they associate and what they are doing, seems to have become a dead letter, and naturally these young colts, free from all restraints, with the animal passions of their budding manhood and womanhood given full play, are only too apt and and prone to fall when temptation presents itself. I believe in giving children the greatest amount of liberty possible, but the restraining touch of the loving hand of the parent must be ever ready to prevent the fall, for which reason parents should seek to promote a feeling of comraderie between themselves and their children, by entering into their every day affairs, by joining in their pleasures and studies, by mourning with them over childish troubles, and in this way making the home a harbor of safety rather than a haven of unrest. Crabidness, lack of sympathy, indifference, constant fault-finding on the part of the parents, is enough to drive any child to some extreme act, and constant scolding and threatening is such a puzzle to a child, who, too young to understand itself, is certainly unable to understand you. But the child can understand love and sympathy; he longs for that, aye, even as we older ones in our own troubles, tho for years motherless, still long for that same sympathy and love.

Another cause that has come prominently under my notice is the fact that too little entertainment is offered to the juveniles at home. Home may be a peaceful place—aye, perhaps too peaceful; father and mother may sit quietly around all evening studying the Bible or discussing Darwin or Huxley, occupations highly interesting to a young lad of twelve; and these good people, upon coming to an appropriate stopping place, pause and wonder what has become of Jim. I know where he is. He has become so thoroly imbued and saturated with the Darwinian theory of evolution that he is cutting up monkey shines somewhere in town to the edification of some one. Now, monkey shines, so-called, are all right, but when these same monkey shines are allowed to go beyond the limits of reason, they are apt to become unpleasant for the community and too often lead to an acquaintance with the police. It is the duty of the parents to make home life interesting and entertaining to their offspring in order to maintain the proper parental control over them.

We might keep on in this way forever, finding here a little, there a little, that may lead to delinquency among the juveniles, and perhaps you may say these things are all too small and unimportant, but believe me, our lives are mostly made up of little things and it is the strict and untiring attention to these same little things that makes us capable of great things, and I ask you how great, really great things, have gone to make up our individual lives.

The few matters I have called your attention to, as being causes leading to delinquency among juveniles, have not been couched in the most scientific terms, perhaps, but I assure you they are the result of painstaking and conscientious endeavor to ascertain the reason of it all, and I invariably found the beginning some trifling infraction of the rules of society.

So, if some method be found whereby the delinquent and also the home may be reached, we have the system that will solve the problem.

In addition to this, we should find a place in the curriculum of every school for the study of our girls of the commonplace duties of motherhood, and thereby counteract the growing inclination in the present generation, at any and every cost, to repudiate and belittle motherhood, that state which brings to us "God's noblest gift, woman perfected."

A greater willingness to bear the God-given, self-chosen burdens of life and a little less of love of ease and comfort, is what we should inculcate into the minds of both our girls and boys, the better to fit them for the responsibilities of their future life and for their ultimate welfare.

And after this addition to our school curriculum, the revision of our Penal Code, and the establishment of our juvenile court, let us ardently pray that the court may remain closed for want of business three hundred and sixty-five days in the year.

The Utility of Books

MRS. E. L. BIGELOW, BISHOP, CAL.

The historian Gibbon once made the assertion that he would not give up his love of reading for all the wealth of the Indies. He expressed *multum in parvum* in that phrase "love of reading." Who that possess that priceless gift would part with it for the wealth of the Indies and the wealth of all other countries combined? Wealth obtained at such a sacrifice would be like Midas' gold, and we, too, would cast it into the waters to be rid of its hateful presence!

When wearied with the cares and perplexities of the day the perusal of a magazine article or some recent novel acts as a restorative, and we seem to be borne away from the actual, the ideal takes possession, and we revel in its fantasies. It is not merely as a pastime that we desire to regard books, but of their utility.

The biographies of noble men and women inspire us to follow in their footsteps. Even the little ones are benefited by this class of literature, as they read in the handy classics the lives of Washington, Lincoln, Franklin. and many others of whom America is justly proud today. They are never too young to learn about these true heroes of our national life. When they attain to manhood and womanhood they will better comprehend *the more complete* biographies of these noted men. No one denies the utility of history, be it ancient, mediæval, or modern. It acquaints us with the customs, habits, and mode of living of the people of different ages. We delight to peruse the writing of Gibbon, Macaulay, Prescott, Fiske, Carlyle, and of other historians. What a blank the past would be if historians had not compiled facts of ancient times, and thus preserved for future generations the annals of the past.

Historical novels are more beneficial to the rising generation than the ponderous volumes of ancient lore. Scott thus familiarized the people of England and Scotland with the history of their own country as he probably could not have done had he simply written a history of England or Scotland. "Ivanhoe" and "Kenilworth" are as fascinating as the most romantic novel, and also convey so much historical knowledge. Cooper's historical tales bring the days of the French and Indian wars so vividly to mind, and impress its scenes upon the reader as no history of that time could have done. Mrs. Catherwood's "Romance of Dollard" revives interest in the Dauphlin of Louis XVI. We sympathize with him in his exile, and admire the nobleness of his character. The story is said to be high and pure in purpose and so full of all that is best in life. Sarah Orne Jewett's "Tory Loreo" (a serial from the "Atlantic" and recently published in book form), recalls the days of John Paul Jones. His reckless attacks upon the enemy's ships is depicted so vividly that we can see the old warrior as he strikes right and left. No school boy will ever forget his wonderful exploits after reading this vivid description. Many of the recently published historical novels should be in the school libraries, and they are descriptive of colonial times, and thus are supplemental to the school histories.

We might journey still further from the accustomed routes of travel, and venture to assert that novels *not* historical have their mission on this terrestrial sphere. Dickens' novels were written to exterminate the wrongs of the oppressed. No Little Dorrits are now in debtor's prisons in England, no Nicholas Nickelbys are now insulted by ignorant principals of private schools, and no poor Smikes are abused to the destruction of both mind and body. Dickens' "Little Folks" familiarize children with Little Nell, Paul Dombey, Dodo's Child Wife, Poor Smike, and many others, and when older they will become delighted to become better acquainted with these characters, and also with others not previously known to them. "Our Mutual Friend" will deter young people from becoming misers. His "Tale of Two Cities" will teach our boys and girls the cruelty of oppression that led to that terrible revolution in France, and in later years Carlyle's "French Revolution" will impress the same fact more deeply upon their receptive minds. "Don Quixote" may seem an absurdity to many, but the people of Spain were convinced of the foolishness of their actions by its perusal, as it was a true account of the Spanish customs of that day.

Charlotte Bronté showed that in "Jane Eyre" that "laws and principles are not for the times when there is no temptation," but when temptation comes in its most alluring form—when even conscience and reason seemed to turn traitors and charged her as a criminal. But when the angel form of her sainted mother spoke to her spirit, saying: "My daughter, flee temptation," she could firmly reply: "Mother, I will." Charlotte Yonge gives many useful facts in her "Book of Golden Deeds." The brave men women therein described should inspire one to noble deeds and higher impulses. She devoted *the entire proceeds* to the "Heir of Redcliffe" to equip a missionary ship, and "Daisy Chain" built a missionary college in New Zealand. Jules Verne's stories seemed utterly preposterous when first published, but recent newspaper accounts declare that his seemingly fantasies are becoming realities. The explorer Mansen avers that a submarine boat may be used to reach the North Pole, and one is already in construction for that purpose. It should be named the Nautilus in memory of *that* Nautilus that penetrated "Twenty Thousand Leagues Under the Sea"! Some *real* adventurers may yet make "A Trip to the Moon," and ascertain its present condition more accurately than the wisest astronomers have yet been able to discern with the most powerful telescopes. What would we have known of the Manx people if Hall Caine had not described them so minutely? His books read as tho they were weird tales of ancient story. We deeply sympathize with his heroes and heroines, and trust that their trials and tribulations were somewhat exaggerated. "Into each life some rain *must* fall," but surely the sunshine must *sometimes* penetrate the gloom. Caine evidently believes that truth is stranger than fiction, and depicts the Manx scenes in a realistic manner, even tho the sympathetic reader experiences a revulsion of feeling in the perusal of the sad denouement. Miss Muloch's "Woman's Kingdom" must convince its readers that woman has a higher mission than merely to gratify her selfish desires. Bret Harte depicts life in a mining camp so vividly that we know that his heroes and heroines are drawn from actual life. His stories are as real as a history of a mining camp would be.

Books of travel are most assuredly useful to us poor mortals, the contents of whose purses are too meager for the fulfillment of long-cherished plans. We can accompany noted travelers into foreign counties and almost discern the castles of ancient story, the grandeur of the Alps, the far-famed scenery of the Rhine, as they present it to the mind's eye. We cannot yet descend from the heights attained by the perusal of the writings of Robert Louis Stevenson, Rudyard Kipling, and J. Rider Haggard to discern their utility. They each have a purpose, but as yet we revel in their fantasies and fail to read between the lines.

Can we discover any utility in poetry? Whittier's anti-slavery poems aroused the American people to the terrible evils of slavery. Longfellow depicted the woes of the Acadians in so pathetic a manner that we can never forget the utter misery of it all. Bryant gives us a higher ideal of life in "Thanatopsis": "So live, that when thy summons comes to join the innumerable caravan, thou go, not as the galley slave scourged to his dungeon, but as one who wraps the drapery of his couch about him and lies down to pleasant dreams." Edwin Markham's "Man With the Hoe" caused people to reflect upon the hardships of the laborer, and to sympathize with him in his manifold deprivations. In "The Sower" and "The Angelus" he gives the reverse picture, showing the dignity of labor and the rewards that it brings in piece of mind, and consciousness of work well done. He thus continues to show his passionate sympathy with the toiling millions. In his fine tribute to Lincoln he thus concludes:

>   And so he came
> From prairie cabin up to capitol.
> One fair Ideal led our chieftain on.
> Forever more he lived to do his deed
> With that fine stroke and gesture of a King.
> He built the rail-pile as he built the state,
> Pouring his splendid strength thru every blow,
> The conscience of him testing every stroke,
> To make his deed the measure of a man.
>
> So came the chieftain with his mighty heart,
> And when the step of Earthquake shook the house,
> Wrenching the rafters from their ancient hold,
> He held the ridge-pole up, and spiked again
> The rafters of the home. He held his place—
> Held the long purpose like a growing tree—
> Held on thru blame and faltered not at praise,
> And when he fell in whirlwind, he went down
> As when a kingly cedar, green with boughs,
> Goes down with a great shout upon the hills,
> And leaves a lonesome place against the sky.

WHAT THE COUNTRY WANTS FROM THE UNIVERSITIES

ARTHUR B. HADLEY
President of Yale University

The country wants three things from the universities—first, they should furnish men who have the necessary training and habits to enable them successfully to pursue those callings in life which require book knowledge as their basis; second, they shall make discoveries which shall help in the international race for leadership and shall enable the business of the country to be conducted in a more intelligent manner in the future than it has been in the past; and, third, they shall give to their students a training in public spirit which shall make them not merely producers or discoverers, but good citizens.

**

Education is the only interest worthy the deed controlling anxiety of the thoughtful man.—Wendell Phillips.

**

If a man empties his purse into his head, no man can take it away from him.—Franklin.

State High Schools

T. H. KIRK

Now that an amendment to the constitution of California has carried, and the state legislature has provided state aid for local high schools, it would appear to be a fit time for California educators to look into the workings of secondary schools thus aided in other states.

One of the most noteworthy systems of this kind exists in the state of Minnesota. The ninth annual report of the state high school inspector, Professor George B. Aiton, is a most readable and suggestive contribution to the history of secondary schools. For the benefit of THE WESTERN JOURNAL OF EDUCATION reads, I offer this very brief review of Mr. Aiton's report:

The state high school board of Minnesota consists of three members. The president is always a superintendent of a city system; the secretary is the superintendent of public instruction; and the examiner is the president of the state university. The high school inspector is the regular visiting agent of the board. The inspectorship was established by legislation nine years ago, and it has been an important factor in maintaining state control of the schools.

Minnesota's growth in population has been very rapid during the last ten years; but the growth of the state high schools has more than kept pace with the increase of population. In 1893, there were about seventy schools; now there are one hundred and forty-one.

Each school in good standing formerly received four hundred dollars annually from the state. Later this amount was increased to eight hundred. Now it is one thousand. This is in addition to the money each school receives, as the lower schools do, from a state mill tax and the annually distributed proceeds of the permanent school funds.

It has been the policy of the high school board not to encourage the establishment of a school in a town of less than a thousand inhabitants or one having a taxable valuation of less than two hundred thousand dollars. Yet, so keen has been the desire of the people to secure such schools, many small communities have taxed themselves to the legal limit. In this connection Mr. Aiton says:

"Whatever criticism may be made, it cannot be said that state aid to high schools has a tendency to encourage communities to throw the burden of support on the shoulders of other people."

During the last eight years the enrollment of pupils has increased sixty per cent; and the number of graduates one hundred per cent, and that, too, from courses of four years. The true significance of these figures is shown when it is noted that the population of Minnesota has increased relatively but thirty-four per cent in the decade following the year 1890.

Many interesting statistics, covering the same period of eight years, are given in respect to subjects of study. It is evident from these that the demand for Greek is only one-third as great at the end of the period as it was at the beginning. For Latin it has increased two-fold; for German three-fold; for French a little less than two-fold; for rhetoric three-fold; for English classics three-fold; for mathematics two-fold; for history three-fold; for manual training less than two fold; while for science it has increased only eighteen per cent. In regard to manual training, it ought to be said that the demand at the beginning was small; therefore, the two-fold increase does not mean so much. On the other hand, at the beginning, the demand for science was comparatively large; consequently, the eighteen per cent increase means more of growth than is at first apparent.

Mr. Aiton has the following to say respecting superintendents, instructors, and the tendency of secondary education:

"The school is so nearly what the superintendent makes it; the kind of teachers employed, the quality of janitor's work, the care of the school grounds, the condition of the school library, the supply of reading for the grades, the neatness of the laboratories, in a word, the thrift and the unthrift of a school so nearly correspond to the general make-up and experience of the superintendent, that for several years I have striven earnestly for a general efficiency in the superintendency. * * * * * * * *

"In this particular class of towns (small country) financial management is frequently in the hands of retired farmers whose money has come by hard knocks. There is no better or more substantial class of citizens in the state, but they cannot believe that a young man's services are worth nine hundred dollars a year in cash. They know that an additional ten dollars an acre will buy a better farm; but the secretary has applications by the dozen, and when it comes to the employment of a superintendent they think they can get quite as good service for less money than other towns. They would just as lieve trim off a little style anyway, so they cut salaries, employ a cheaper man and as in any other business they get about what they pay for. Sometimes the new man is bright. If so, he soon learns that his ambition to be at the head of a state high school has led him to seek a position for which in justice to the cause he should have waited for a year or two. A man of this type usually takes care of the local situation. Sometimes, the new man proves so incompetent that public discontent causes a change of policy. But, in the majority of instances, the school comes under an unambitious, unenterprising kind of administration that steers clear of failure and yet never attains success. It would seem that a state tendering one thousand dollars annual aid over and above the proceeds of a state mill tax and the pro rata share of the income from our school fund ought to have some way of preventing boards of education from naming a salary so low as to invite inexperience or confessed mediocrity to take charge of a state high school. If the question be raised why so much about qualifications and compensation of the superintendent, reply may be made fairly that the efficient superintendent has a way of bringing about the other conditions requisite to successful school work. The local superintendent with natural judgment, education, tact, and at least some experience, is the agency by which public sentiment, I mean educational sentiment at large, becomes effective in each locality. An efficient superintendent is the surest and most practical guaranty the state can have for the proper and effective expenditure of state money —the surest guaranty of a creditable school.

"I have just spoken of the need of protecting school against the kind of service usually secured by ill-judged attempts to employ a superintendent for less than market value. Schools also need protection against the arbitrary action of board members who dismiss efficient superintendents and teachers for personal reasons. As our boards are constituted, four votes can throw out an employee, and, tho every other man, woman and child in town be favorable, there is no appeal, no redress. In case a teacher has offended an influential board member, whose business relations enable him to control the other votes, no matter how valuable his services may be or how blameless his life, there is no help for the teacher. He simply must pack his grip and seek employment elsewhere. I do not say that it would be well for the state to exercise inquisitorial or revisory functions; certainly the state high school board cannot be burdened with investigations of this character. The existence of a state school fund, the imposition of a state school tax, and the granting and acceptence of state aid, raise the management of a school rather above the ordinary status of a question relating to the location of a village pound, but I still believe in the policy of local control of school matters. In spite of the injustice done the children, the taxpayer and the state, I yet believe that the action of a local board should be final; but I am of the opinion that the enactment of a general law, providing, after a reasonable time of probation, for longer terms of service, would curtail the personal element in school elections and encourage businesslike methods of conducting public business. In former reports I have borne testimony to the faithful, unrewarded services of board members. They are the first to be blamed and the last to be rewarded. Whatever of excellence is found in a school is popularly ascribed to the superintendent and teachers; board members do not receive a tithe of the credit they merit, but, all said, some short cut is needed to shield schools from arbitrary and unexpected changes. A longer term appears to me to be the most practical measure in harmony with the theory of local authority. * * * * * * * *

"A few years since our poorest teaching proceeded from instructors whose knowledge of life was, perhaps, wide enough, but whose knowledge of subject-matter was deficient. As our system grows older, our instructors enter the school room more and more by regular channels, and bring with them a school and college education. The typical inefficient instructor of today is not illiterate, but is without worldly knowledge, and is unused to take the initiative. Eight years in the grades, four years in a high school, and four years in college, taken consecutively, even with such professional training as may be given before one has had experience, keep a young person too steadily with books and bookish people to develop the timber and twist requisite to deal with the children of people who are wrestling with facts for a living. If prospective teachers would break their courses for a year or so, and enter some competitive employment, they would be able to resume their studies greatly the gainers by a knowledge, not to be had from books, of what people think and of the way people earn a living. * * * * * * * *

"Secondary education, that is to say, the curriculum, is in a state of unrest the world over, and Minnesota schools are in the movement. As long as secondary education was maintained by tuition and was confined to preparation for college, as in the New England academy, it was quite possible to get on for a century with a traditional course of study. Its Spartan simplicity and rigo bred three generations of men whose superiors as law givers and founders of empire we shall not soon see. But this system, with all its virtues, was narrow and inexorable and individualistic. It took no note of the needs of the many. The student whose taste did not conform to the subject-matter taught was dismissed as a dunce. The student entered the academy that he might enter college, he entered college that he might enter a profession, he entered a profession that he might become distinguished. Even to this day the graduate of the old-time system recounts with pride the number of distinguished men his old academy and college have turned out, rather than the influence his alma mater has had in shaping our material welfare and public policy.

"When secondary education was established as part of the public school system it was natural that a diversity of views should arise, and that an effort should be made by means of business courses, industrial courses, and English courses to meen public wishes.

"I regard the present disposition to question our high school courses as an indication of a live public interest. Public interest may contain some destructive elements, but in the main it is constructive. The people may at times be shortsighted and mistaken in their measures, but there is no other public institution so near the firesides of the people, and so unhesitatingly supported as our public schools. Far from looking with rueful on the constant agitation of high school courses and instruction, I am in favor of making all promising ventures that, in the end, we may hold fast to the best. For my own part, I do not know what the high school course of the future must be; I do not know anyone who does know; but I do know that our high schools are multiplying and growing, that they are gathering strength and are storing up traditions and associations, and that they are gaining a large place in the social and intellectual life of our communities all over the state. I have every confidence that discussion and the exercise of local choice in its interplay with inherited preferences and state influences will evoke, if not the high school course of the future, certainly parallel courses adapted to the varied tastes and capabilities of the young people who are to profit by our mistakes and our efforts."

Drawing the Universal Medium

D. R. AUGSBURG, OAKLAND, CAL.

In all modes of expression, in all mediums of expression, the idea does not change, it is eternal. The mode and medium alone change. The idea is spiritual, the mode and medium are material. For example: a blacksmith hammers a horseshoe out of iron with a hammer, a draughtsman draws it on paper with a pencil. The mechanical process differs but the mental process is the same. A wood carver draws a design on paper with a pencil and then reproduces the design in wood with chisels. The mental part of the work is the same in both acts, the mechanical alone differs. If a blacksmith can draw beautiful designs on paper, he can hammer them out of iron; if a draughtsman can draw beautiful designs on paper, he can hammer them out of iron as soon as he has overcome the mechanical difficulties of working in iron. If any person can draw a design on paper (I do not mean copy), he can produce that design in any form, whether in metal, wood or stone, as soon as he has overcome the mechanical difficulties of working in each material. It would not be very much amiss to say that a blacksmith draws with his hammer, a stonecutter with mallet and chisel, a tailor with shears, a painter with brush and a carpenter with various tools.

There are many mediums of expression and many modes of expression. We may draw an idea on the blackboard with crayon, on paper with pen, pencil, brush or charcoal; we may paint it in water or oil colors; we can cut it from paper with scissors, from wood with a knife, model it in clay, carve it in wood or hammer it from metal; it may be made in the carpenter shop, in the paint shop, in the machine shop; it may be fashioned in the foundry or the forge, manufactured in the factory or cut in the quarry, and in all these different modes and mediums, the idea does not change—the change is alone in the material.

The drawing is the oldest, easiest, quickest, and most economical of perfecting and completing an idea with a view to its construction in any material, and its use is universal among all civilized nations. There is scarcely a manufactured article, a piece of woven fabric, a building of any kind that does not pass thru the hands of the designer or draughtsman before it is possible to become an article of sale or utility. If a machinist construct a machine, it is from a drawing. A builder is guided by his drawing, a stonecutter looks to his drawing, and all they contain are first drawn on paper. The battleship Wisconsin requires more than 1500 drawings to show all of her details. The sculptor makes the rough draft of his statue on paper. In all departments, in all professions, the drawing is universally used as a means of expressing the object to be constructed. No, not a steamer crosses the ocean, not a vessel sails the seas, not a bridge spans the river, not a railroad crosses the continent, not a temple points toward heaven without the aid of this art called drawing.

Then as the idea is without change and the drawing applicable to all modes of expression, then it follows if one can represent his ideas by means of a drawing, there is only one obstacle in the way to his expressing the same idea in any form of work whether it be in wood, metal or stone, and that obstacle is the mechanical difficulty of working in the different materials. For example, if a person has accurate knowledge of a human head to draw it on paper with a pencil, he can draw it with a pen, paint it in water or oil colors, model it in clay, cut it from paper with scissors, carve it from wood, cut it from stone, hammer it from metal, embroider, etch or engrave it *as soon as he has overcome the mechanical difficulies of working in each.*

The mechanical in all departments of work is easiest to teach, easiest to learn, and easiest in which to become proficient. The thought part, the spiritual part, is acquired by few. Such a person as acquires both is usually found at the head of the department as foreman, manager, director, superintendent, or president. He is the one who speaks with authority.

For these reasons, I have made bold to place this outline before you, not that drawing is the basis or foundation of these arts, but that it is common to them all. The idea worked out and made complete in drawing may be used in any of these departments of work:

Mechanical Arts	Reproductive Arts	Productive Arts	Plastic Arts	Decorative Arts
Trades	Printing	Original work in	Sculpture	Lettering
Engineering	Engraving	any department	Carving	Frescoing
Perspective	Etching		Modeling	Tapestry
Manual Training	Lithography		Moulding	Embroidery

Be good, my child, and let who will be clever;
Do noble deeds, not dream them, all day long;
And so make life, death, and that vast forever,
One grand, sweet song. —*Kingsley.*

Current Educational Thought

President Eliot has recently read three papers of great importance, which has caused much comment. The burden of all three is the importance of the public school in American life and the need of more money for their support. The substance of these papers is given here in logical order.

EDUCATIONAL EXPENDITURE.

The expenditure per pupil in the common schools of the United States is altogether insufficient. The average expenditure per pupil for the whole school year in the United States in 1900-1901 was $21.14; but this expenditure varies from $33.52 in the North Atlantic division to only $7.54 in the South Central division. The average daily expenditure per pupil for the whole United States in 1900-1901 was 14.7 cents. The Rocky Mountain and Pacific Coast divisions, 18.9 cents; the South Atlantic division, 8.6 cents, and the South Central but 7.8 cents.

Let us now compare the annual expenditure on the public-school child with what is paid by a well-to-do family on its child sent to an endowed or a private school. The private school charges a tuition fee of from $100 to $500 a year for day pupils. In the endowed secondary schools the total charge varies between $400 and $1,000. It is easy to provide lodging and food at a cost of $5 a week; so that the charge for tuition and general care at these institutions must be from $200 to $600 a year of forty weeks. If you ask on what these large tuition fees are expended, the answer is chiefly on teaching. A public school which has a teacher for every forty pupils is unusually fortunate; the private and endowed schools not infrequently provide a teacher for every eight or ten pupils. Moreover, they employ a more expensive kind of teacher, for they use a large proportion of men and a larger proportion of college graduates.

These figures show that the well-to-do Americans, who can afford to spend on the education of their children whatever seems advantageous, are ready to spend liberally for their children's education. Is it not plain that if the American people were all well-to-do, they would multiply by four or five the present average school expenditure per child and per pupil for the whole year in the United States from $80 to $100 for salaries and maintenance instead of $17.36 as now. Is it not obvious that instead of providing in the public schools a teacher for forty or fifty pupils, they would provide a teacher for every ten or fifteen pupils? Would there not be a play-ground around every school-house? If the American people thought they could afford it, would not a school-house be kept in as perfect sanitary condition as a hospital?

The American people cannot afford to persist in the present low school expenditure per pupil and per year. We ought to spend more public money on schools, because the present expenditures do not produce all the good results which were expected and may be reasonably aimed at.

Among the disappointments with popular education is the failure to discover a successful method of dealing with the barbarous vice of drunkenness. The accusation rests not against the moral disposition of the majority of the people, but against their reasoning power; and it is precisely that reasoning power which good schools ought to train. The persistence of gambling—an extraordinarily unintelligent form of pleasureable excitement; the crimes of violence committed in great number all over the United States, in the older States as well as in the new; the daily reading matter of the American public, ephemeral in nature and bad in form or substance; the quality of the popular theatres of to-day; the subjection of our people to medical delusions and their credulous patronage of medicine men and women; corruption in government, especially in large cities; industrial wars, involving pecuniary loss and physical and moral injury; the spoils or patronage system in the civil service of the United States—these are the evidences that the common schools have grappled unsuccessfully with the tremendous problem put before them. They have done what they ought toward developing the power to reason justly; the training supplied by them is inadequate, and the results obtained from popular education may, in view of these things, be said to be profoundly disappointing.

Lastly, the final test of the value of the education given to an individual or to a nation is continuous mental growth. If we include in this growth the development of character, this continuous enlargement and improvement is the supreme human felicity. Now, there are two common obstacles to the attainment of this felicity. The first is the untimely arrest of education in youth; the second is the dulling and contracting effect of many methods of earning a livelihood. Any comprehensive survey of the social and industrial conditions of the American people will bring an open-minded inquirer to the conclusion that these two obstacles to the continuous development of the human individual are both formidable to-day. For millions of American children systematic education stops far too soon; and for millions of adults the mode of earning a livelihood affords so little mental training, and becomes so automatic, that mental growth is seriously hindered, if not arrested. In such cases—and they occur by millions—it is in reading and in the play of the domestic affections and the social interests that lie all the possibilities of mental and spiritual growth. Shall we not agree that from this point of view the American schools have thus far been much less serviceable than they ought to have been, or, at least, than we want them to be?

What should be the effect on our minds to-day of these disappointments and of these unsurmounted difficulties? Surely a new and hearty resolution to do what we can to make the schools better and more effective to all righteous ends. But this greater effectiveness unqustionably means greater costliness. Could anybody imagine it to be unreasonable to spend for the mental and moral training of a child as much as is spent on his food? If that equality in expenditure could be established all over the Union there would result a prodigious improvement in the public schools.

EDUCATIONAL IMPROVEMENTS IN THE PAST THIRTY YEARS.

The first gain I mention is the kindergarten, from which schools and colleges of every grade have learned much about the importance of dealing with the individual child, rather than with large groups of children. The kindergarten also sets an excellent example to all schools in making it part of the teacher's function to know something personally of the families from which her pupils come.

In the selection of the studies of the first eight school years out of the twelve there has been substantial improvement within thirty years. Thus there are more observation studies on the programme; less arithmetic, and little more geography; less spelling and grammar, and more literature; wiser teaching of geography as a natural history subject, and not a list of names;

a better teaching of history as a story of discoveries, industries, commerce, peoples, and institutions, and not of battles and dynasties.

Important improvements in the programmes of secondary schools have also taken place. Fewer subjects are now required of the individual, although more subjects are taught in the schools. The attention of the pupil can be more concentrated on kindred subjects, and one or two subjects may be carried beyond the elements.

The continuous creation of new secondary schools for boys, placed agreeably in the country, has been a noticeable phenomenon during the past thirty years. There has been throughout the country a striking improvement in school buildings. These are much better heated and ventilated; they are also kept cleaner. Three new kinds of schools have been instituted—the manual training school, the mechanic arts high school, and the evening school.

The greatest educational success of the last thirty years is the complete adoption of the elective system in a few institutions, and its partial and progressive introduction in almost all. The elective system is more costly than the prescribed, but it has made real scholarship possible to thousands of young Americans by the time they are twenty-two years of age; it has raised very much the standard of labor for both teachers and taught in our colleges and universities, and it has made it possible for thousands of American students to win that joy or delight in study which accompanies the sense of mastery or of clear achievement. Accompanying this great administrative success another improvement of the utmost value is the raising of the standard of attainment for professors. This means a longer and more thorough preparation, and accordingly a higher salary.

In no department of education has greater improvement been made during the past generation than in professional education. The whole provision for training young men for the new scientific professions has been created in this country during the last fifty years, and America's success in the scientific industries is evidence that the new schools of science and technology have done good work. The changes, however, in education for the old professions of divinity, law, and medicine are quite as striking as the new creations for applied science.

The other costly developments of the past thirty years have had influence along the whole line of education from the primary school through the university. The first is the higher education of women, a development which has taken place within a single generation, involving a large increase of expenditure. The second is the increased attention given to the welfare of the body, and to athletic sports.

Every educational improvement of the past thirty years that I have mentioned has been costly; but every one has justified itself in the eyes of the tax-payers, or of those who voluntarily pay for it; not one would now be recalled; and the total result encourages the expectation that large additional expenditures would commend themselves to the people at the start, and in the end would prove to be both profitable in the material sense and civilizing in the humane sense.

* * *

THE NEEDS OF AMERICAN PUBLIC EDUCATION.

First among the objects for which increased expenditure should be made in the schools supported by taxation are the school-houses and school-yards.

In cities and large towns all school buildings should be fire-proof, and particularly all halls and stairways should be fire-proof. Wooden staircases should be absolutely prohibited in schools intended for children under fifteen years of age. The interior woodwork should be reduced to the lowest terms, and should be carefully constructed with reference to the facility of keeping it clean. The materials of walls should not be absorbent, but, on the contrary, should resist both moisture and gases, and should be capable of thorough cleansing. Again, whether in town or country, a large open space should surround every school building, and should be kept with neatness and decorated with shrubs and flowers. The space about the school should be so arranged that hundreds of children could occupy it without marring its decorative vegetation.

A skillful physician should be officially connected with every large school. It should be his duty to watch for contagious diseases, to prevent the too early return of children who have suffered from such diseases, to take thought for the eyes of the children, to give advice at the homes about the diet and sleep of the children whose nutrition is visibly defective, and, in short, to be the protector, counselor, and friend of the children and their parents with regard to health, normal growth, and the preservation of all the senses in good condition. Such medical supervision would be costly, but it would be the most rewarding expenditure that a community could make, even from the commercial point of view, since nothing impairs the well-being and productiveness of a community so much as sickness and premature disability or death.

Better teachers is the next object for additional expenditure. Every teacher should know the best methods of teaching his subjects. College professors heretofore have been apt to think that knowledge of the subject to be taught was the sufficient qualification of a teacher; but colleges, as well as all schools, have suffered immeasurable losses as a result of this delusion. Of course, it is better for a teacher to know his subject without knowing the right method of teaching it than to acquire a formal method without knowing the subject; but teachers who are acquainted at the start with both subject and method are what schools and colleges urgently need. With better teachers would come better teaching, as, for instance, better biological and geographical instruction, these natural history studies being pursued by the pupils in the open air as well as in the school-rooms. All public open spaces, whether country parks, forests, beaches, city squares, gardens or parkways, should be utilized for the instruction of the children by teachers capable of interesting them in the phenomena of plant and animal life. But this means quite a new kind of common school teachers.

Given better teachers, the next additional expenditure should be due to a large reduction in the number of pupils placed before a single teacher. Twenty to twenty-five pupils to a teacher are quite enough, if there is to be secured an adequate degree of attention to the individual pupil and a proper classification of each group of pupils. This very urgently needed improvement would not necessarily double the item of salaries, for one competent teacher, with an intelligent though less experienced assistant, could take care of forty pupils.

In order to keep good a large staff of teachers employed by a city or town, a system of retiring allowances for teachers is indispensable. The American practice of keeping in office superannuated teachers who have served long and well, though considerate toward the few veterans, is very inconsiderate toward the hundreds of children whose education is impaired. A proper pension system gives the managers of a school system the means of retiring such teachers, and of replacing them by fresh, well-selected appointees, without causing any hardships or wounding any feelings.

The universal employment of highly-trained superintendents in both urban and rural systems is a much needed improvement. Such superintendents should be entirely independent of political influences, and should enjoy a large measure of authority and freedom in their functions. They ought, as a rule, to be men of college education, who have had some experience themselves as teachers.

An urgently needed improvement in the public schools is the enrichment of the school programme for the years between nine and fourteen, and the introduction of selection among studies as early as ten years of age. An incidental effect of this would be the development of departmental instruction —that is, skillful teachers would teach one subject through several grades. The departmental method develops in both teachers and pupils a growing interest in their work, and increases greatly the personal influence of teachers, because the staying pupils work through several successive years under the same teacher.

Manual training schools, mechanical arts high schools, and trade schools ought to become habitual parts of the American school system; and normal schools and colleges ought to provide optional instruction in these subjects, since all public school teachers ought to understand them. Another additional expenditure which all public schools ought to incur as soon as possible is a development of instruction in drawing. Music ought to be made much more of in all American schools than it now is. The course of musical instruction is broken off too early, and the skill gained before fourteen years of age is lost later through disuse.

With these objects in view the expenditure in those parts of our country where it is now smallest ought to be raised as rapidly as possible to the level of those regions where it is now greatest; and in those regions where the expenditure is now most liberal it ought to be doubled as soon as possible.

* * *

PRESIDENT ELIOT AND THE PUBLIC SCHOOLS

Ossian H. Lang in the January-March Forum.

The particular shortcomings which President Eliot complains of, "our disappointments with popular education," are all selected from the panroama of public adult life in America. He very ingeniously fixes the whole responsibility for most of the causes of his moral and intellectual grievances upon a lack of reasoning power on the part of the majority of the people; thereby projecting the inference that, if the schools had exercised greater care in training this reasoning power, the state of American civilization would be more uniformly satisfactory. The first two "disappointments" which he thinks ought to be remedied by improvement in the training of the reasoning power are the unsuccessful struggle with "the barbarous vice of drunkenness" and the "persistence of gambling," which latter he considers "an extraordinarily unintelligent form of pleasurable excitement." Yet Dr. Eliot has been called pessimistic for expressing the optimistic belief in the efficacy of the cultivation of the intellect as the method for annihilating drunkenness. and gambling.

The reception of President Eliot's remarks by the newspaper world illustrated anew the readiness, amounting almost to recklessness, with which everything reprehensible in national life is charged to the schools. The prevalence of crime, indifference or hostility to the churches, irreverence to parents, gambling, increase of the liquor traffic, and what not—all these figure among the grievances for which the schools are held responsible. If these complaints could be accepted as evidence of a strong faith in the power of the schools and a sorrow that the expectations have not been fully realized, teachers might have reason to be regretfully proud of them. But, as a matter of fact, the charges represent frequently merely a human weakness in fixing the responsibility for the shortcomings of civilization at some place most convenient and at the same time defensible by reasonable argument. When it comes to a distribution of praise for the good there is in the world, the credit assigned to the schools is usually less liberal; though President Eliot, for one, took pains to enumerate a number of American achievements whose development he believed to have been due to the influence of the schools.

Rightly or wrongly, the schools, especially the common schools, are held to account for whatever is awry in civilization, whether this is due to a weak moral sense or to lack of intelligent reasoning in the mass of the people. Reformers are regarding the schools with growing faith in their power to shape the future of the nation. At the recent State convention of New York police chiefs, at Elmira, the spreading feeling expressed itself in the suggestion by Chief Moore to the effect that the criminal court of the State should be introduced as a study in the public schools.

**

FOR THE TRUSTEES

PREVENTABLE DISEASES IN RURAL SCHOOL DISTRICTS.

By Edwin Berwick.

Looking over the census of 1900 you will find recorded for that year to date of census, 524,000 deaths—262,000 of them from preventable diseases. Many of these deaths were due to unsanitary condition of school outbuildings, which are not infrequently breeding grounds of typhoid fever, diphtheria, and other zynotic diseases. These deadly diseases, asy ou know, grow like the yeast you put in bread from spores or germs which multiply with exceeding rapidity when placed in suitable conditions. The intelligent teacher knows that the free use of that cheapest of all disinfectants, dry earth, will render these places inoffensive and innocuous and remove all chance of mischief. Don't suppose because you live in country districts you are free to violate God's laws of cleanliness. The census proves that the percentage of deaths from typhoid was greater in the country than in cities. It was 17.02 per M in cities and 25.43 in rural districts.

School trustees, I believe, each and all would prefer seeing their children healthy to paying a doctor's or undertaker's bill. It is for you to know these laws to see to it that your scholars not only breathe fresh air, but that they understand those methods by which it is made poisonous; that as citizens they may take an intelligent interest in sanitation as applied to town and country life; for only in this way of applied science is your teaching of physiology of any practical use. It is the daily bearing of the facts you teach on the individual life that is the valuable—I might almost say the only valuable—result of your teaching. They should be part of the child's life capital. The old scholastic system of teaching things that had no such bearing is responsible for that tone of impatient contempt with which old farmers speak of "book-larnin." When your modern teaching of hygiene shall have reached its full development, it will be considered as discreditable to be sickly as is now to be drunk.

* * *

THE COUNTY SUPERINTENDENT.

The county superintendent's hand is very near the pulse of the public schools; he knows the needs of the common school as no one else can, for his knowledge is based upon actual observation. Doctrines, visions and ideals that emanate from the seclusion and isolation of the scholar's study are well enough in their way, but a practical man of affairs in daily contact not only with the teachers as they are and where they are at work, but also with the children who are taught, and with the people who support the schools; who is one of the people, chosen by the people who support the schools; who is going about among the people; who has the knowledge that comes from contact with the life habits of the communities in which the schools are—such a one has a rich fund of experimental pedagogy which makes his counsel of the greatest value in associations composed of those who would make a serious study of pedagogy. In the Western States the county superintendent is the only one engaged in school work who has opportunity to get a bird's-eye-view of the schools as they are. Yet in some quarters this officer receives scant consideration from professional teachers and leaders in education.

It is a safe estimate to say that at least five chances to one the great men of the future, those who supply the directive energy of the next generation, are now in the country and village schools. Therefore it behooves those who study educational problems to acquaint themselves with the work actually doing in those schools. Let us not take a pessimistic view because of some of the shortcomings and the necessary limitations of the country school. When there is manifest an earnest disposition and effort to bring about more efficient work in the country schools, and there is in many counties, every one who can in any way promote the spirt of helpfulness should do so. "The deplorable condition of the country schools" and the "lamentable inefficiency of the county superintendents" are strings that have been harped upon long enough. Let teachers in the higher ranks quit lamenting and deploring and turn their attention to helping and encouraging and progress toward better things will be more rapid.—*S. Y. Gillan in The Western Teacher.*

* * *

EDUCATIONAL POSSIBILITIES OF COUNTRY LIFE.

The country school and the country child at present are receiving considerable attention. Not more than they should it seems to me. The country school and the farm offer great possibilities in an educational way within the next few years. The great effort at present is to get the average farmer to realize the possibilities. Not only must the farmer let the dead past bury its dead and set his face toward the future, toward new methods and ideas but also the average country school teacher must see the necessity of a quickening in the daily work of the school. A smattering of reading, geography and arithmetic is not all that the country child needs. If so, why are so many farmers moving to the cities to educate their children and then complain that the training received there educates them away from the farm?

* * *

FARMERS FAVOR CONSOLIDATION.

We have been unable to find a single instance where, after trying both systems fairly, the farmers preferred the inferior district school to the superior central school, providing the conditions of transportation and the details had been properly attended to.—*State Supt. L D Harvey, Wisconsin.*

* * *

The State Flower of California

Hon. John A Bliss introduced into the Assembly and Senator Smith into the Senate a bill to make the Golden Poppy the State Flower of California. The bill passed both houses and was signed by Governor Pardee, March 2d. The daughter of Assemblyman Bliss was one of the original advocates of the Poppy as the State Flower. Miss Bliss did not live to see her wish gratified, but her father persisted in his efforts and the sentiment that clusters about the Poppy did not leave it even in the halls of the legislature.

Here is a brief account of the way the signing of the bill was celebrated in Sacramento:

The Governor has affixed his signature to Senate bill 251, which makes the golden poppy (eschscholtzia) the State flower. This bill was introduced in the Senate by Smith and in the Assembly by Bliss. Both gentlemen had it all arranged to have the signing of the bill celebrated by placing the State flower on the desk of every legislator; but owing to a train wreck the flowers did not arrive until last evening.

The Governor's message was read and then Senator Smith called upon Senator Shortridge to present the quill, taken from the wing of a California eagle, which the Governor used in signing the bill, to Mrs. Lemmon of Oakland. Shortridge delivered a graceful speech. He dwelt at length on the energetic work done by Mrs. Lemmon to have the Legislature designate the poppy as the State flower. Mrs. Lemmon made a short speech in reply, in which she explained that a similar bill had passed the Legislature two years ago, but had been pocketed by Governor Gage. Assemblyman Bliss was also accorded the privileges of the Senate. "God's Gold," he said, "was an inspired name for the beautiful flower that had been selected by the State as its floral emblem."—*S. F. Call.*

The teachers of the public schools should give a lesson on the State Flower. A part of a day could be made very instructive, suggestive and entertaining. It might be well to set aside some Friday afternoon for Poppy exercises. Let the schoolhouse, if possible, be decorated with poppies, and the recitations, essays, etc., be about the poppy. Plenty of material can be secured for such an afternoon from the book called "The Golden Poppy," published by Emory E. Smith of Palo Alto.

AN ACCOUNT OF THE POPPY.

The botanical name of the golden poppy is Eschscholtzia. The Spanish name is Copa de Oro, "Cup of Gold." It is also called Amopola. Two Russians, Chamisso, a botanist, aged 34, and Eschscholtz, a surgeon and naturalist, aged 22, explored the regions about San Francisco Bay and secured specimens of plants, among them the poppy, which was named Eschscholtzia in honor of Dr. Eschscholtz. The expedition to which these Russians belonged was fitted out by Count Romanzoff, a Russian nobleman in 1815, and was under the command of Captain Kotzebue. After exploring the west and south coast of Alaska, Kotzebue came down and entered what is now known as San Francisco Bay, October 1816. It was not until 1820, however, that the first printed description of the poppy appeared.

The golden poppy has figured conspicuously in the art and poetry of California.

TO THE ESCHSCHOLTZIA.
Chas. H. Allen.

Bright golden emblem of our Golden State,
    Flashing athwart our hills thy tongues of flame,
No flower more beauteous Flora can create,
    And none more worthy of thy lasting fame,
Thy fragile leaflets, nodding to the breeze,
    Drink in the sunshine of each daylight hour,
Treasure it up, and then with affluent ease
    Return it to us in a rich, resplendent flower.

Thy slender helmet pointed to the skies,
    Bathed in the dews of "incense-breathing morn,"
Leaps from his seat, then with a glad surprise
    Thy petals open and a flower is born.
The meadow-lark trills forth his matin lay,
The wild bee drones its drowsy cradle hum,
Glad nature welcomes in the perfect day,
    Rejoicing that the beauteous Queen of Flowers has come.

* * *

GOD'S GOLD.
Joaquin Miller.

This Golden Poppy is God's gold;
The gold that lifts, nor weights us down
The gold that knows no miser's hold,
The gold that banks not in the town,
But careless, laughing, freely spills
Its hoard far up the happy hills—
Far up, far down, at every turn—
What beggar hath not gold to burn?

—*From "The Golden Poppy," Published by Emory E. Smith.*

THE POPPIES AND THE CLOVER.
Madge Morris.

A California School Song:

A song for California's birth,
The golden land of all the earth.
Sing it over, over
The poppies and the clover.
Sing it over, over
The poppies and the clover.

Wide open stands our Golden Gate,
Wide welcome to our Golden State,
Sing it over, over
The poppies and the clover.

The golden of all golden lands
We hold its greatness in our hands,
Sing it over, over
The poppies and the clover.

The patriot's song of home we'll sing
And liberty shall ring and ring
Ever-over, over
The poppies and the clover.

* * *

THE FLOWER OF THE WEST.
Rose Hartwick Thorpe.

Flower of the Westland, with calyx of gold,
Swung in the breeze over lave-woven sod;
Filled to the brim with the glory of God,
All that its wax-petaled chalice can hold.

This was the birth of it: on the brown plain
The sun dropped a kiss in the footprint of rain.

* * *

IN POPPY FIELDS.
Edwin Markham.

Here the poppy hosts assemble,
How they startle, how they tremble;
All their royal hoods unpinned
Blow out lightly in the wind.

Men that in the cities grind
Come! before the heart is blind,
Here is gold to labor for;
Here is pillage worth a war.

COPA DE ORA.

Ina Coolbrith.

Thy satin vesture richer is than looms
  Of Orient weave for raiment of her kings;
  Not dyes of olden Tyre, not precious things
Regathered from the long-forgotten tombs
Of buried empires, not the Iris plumes
  That wave upon the tropic's myriad wings,
  Not all Sheba's queenly offerings,
Could match the golden marvel of thy blooms.
For thou are nurtured from the treasure veins
  Of this fair land; thy golden rootlets sup
    Her sands of gold—of gold thy petals spun.
Her golden glory thou; on hills and plains
  Lifting, exultant, every kingly cup
    Brimmed with the golden vintage of the sun.

* * *

A SIMPLE METHOD IN FRUSTUMS.

L. M. HOLLINGSWORTH.

The method found in the arithmetics for computing the volume of frustums is very objectionable. It is only suitable for classes well advanced in geometry. The following method is far simpler:

Rule for square pyramid: To the product of the upper and lower diameters, add $\frac{1}{3}$ of the square of their difference and multiply by the heigth; or

To the product of the upper and lower diameters and the height, add the square of difference between upper and lower diameters multiplied by $\frac{1}{3}$ the height.

Assuming a frustum to be 16 in. sq at the bottom, 10 in. sq. at the top, and 16 in. high, the following will illustrate:

If we cut away two opposite sides and then subdivide the side pieces by perpendicular cuts from upper corners, we will cut to the lines on the bottom as shown in Fig. 1, which represents the base of the frustum.

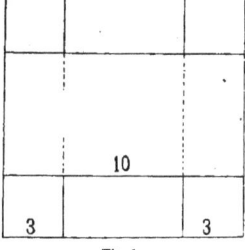

The central square represents the upper base. The central piece is filled out into a rectangular prism by placing a side piece, inverted, at each end, as shown in Fig. 2. The rectangular prism is computed by the first part of the second rule. The corner pieces are rearranged into a pyramid, as shown in Fig. 3.

This pyramid always measures, along each lower edge, the difference between the upper and lower diameters of the original frustum, and its volume is computed by the last half of the second rule.

The rectangular prism contains 2560 cu. in., and the pyramid contains 192 cu. in.; hence the frustum contains 2752 cu. in.

As the volume of a frustum of a cone is .7854 of that of a square frustum of same dimensions, it is only necessary to multiply answer obtained by either of the preceding rules by .7854.

Observation. All frustums of equal height, which are also parts of cones or pyramids of equal height, are to each other as the areas of their bases.

The foregoing is embodied in a copyrighted method, which is free to any teacher.

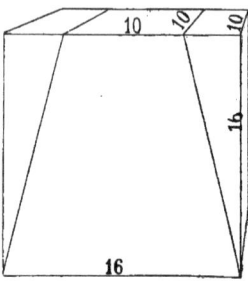

Fig. 2.

Advanced Work

To find the volume of hexagonal frustum of a pyramid. Multiply volume of frustum of same dimensions formed on the square B by .866 if the diameters are given. If the upper and lower edges of one side are given, assume them to be the upper and lower diameters of a frustum of the same height constructed on A, whose volume is to be multiplied by 2.598.

Using the same method, multiply frustum constructed on C by 5.82843, or one constructed on D by .82843 to find volume of octagonal frustum, or one constructed on E by .866 for pyramid of three equal sides.

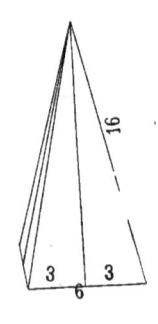

Fig. 3.

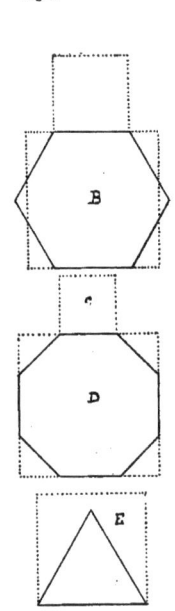

Interesting Notes About the County Superintendents of California

A group picture of the state board of education and the county and city superintendents has just been issued. It will be sent free to any subscriber of THE JOURNAL sending four cents to repay postage.

The following information in reference to the education, experience, and personality of the various county superintendents will be of interest. In a number of instances it was impossible to get reliable data. The notices are conclusive evidence that the superintendents are, as a rule, well prepared by education and experience for the office.

WILDA A. JORDAN, superintendent of Alpine County, was born in Alpine County, December 12, 1877. She is a daughter of Mrs. Grover, who served as superintendent of Alpine County for a number of years. She was educated at the Los Angeles High School and Normal.

T. O. CRAWFORD, superintendent of Alameda County, has been elected twice by large majorities on a minority ticket. He has been a practical teacher and principal for many years.

GEORGE A. GORDON, superintendent of Amador County, is a native Californian. He was graduated from the San Jose State Normal School in the spring of 1884, and had had fifteen years' experience as a successful teacher before his election to the office of superintendent in November, 1898. He is now serving his second term.

R. H. DUNN, superintendent of Butte County, is an experienced teacher. He was first elected to the office of superintendent in 1898, and served the people with such success that he was reëlected in 1902. He had no opposing candidate.

JOHN WATERS, superintendent of Calaveras County, is a Native Son and a practical teacher. He was elected superintendent in 1898, and reëlected in 1902.

A. A. BAILEY, superintendent of Contra Costa County, was born in Wisconsin. He located in Santa Cruz in 1874; was elected superintendent of Contra Costa County in 1879 and served till 1887. From 1893 to 1895 he was county clerk, and was principal of Concord schools until he again took the office of superintendent in January, 1903.

LILLIE LAUGENOUR, superintendent of Colusa County, is a native of North Carolina. She came to California when a child; was educated in the public schools of Colusa County and Pierce Christian College at College City; taught in the grammar schools of Colusa county for sixteen consecutive years; resigned school to enter the campaign for the county superintendency of schools in 1898.

MRS. M. A. LEISHMAN, superintendent of Del Norte, was elected in 1902. She is well-equipped both by education and personality for the position of superintendent.

S. B. WILSON, superintendent of El Dorado county, was born in Canada in 1861, and graduated from the Provincial Normal School and Toronto University. He came to California in 1887, and has taught school with success at Paso Robles, Placerville and Georgetown since that time

Former Supt. T. E. McCarty has filed a contest and the case is now in the supreme court.

G. N. FREMAN, superintendent of Fresno county, has been connected with the public schools of this state for about ten years. In this state he was a teacher in Hesperian College, Woodland, for years, and was twice elected county superintendent of Yolo county. He was appointed superintendent of Fresno county in January, 1892, and was elected for four years in November, 1902.

F. S. REAGER, superintendent of Glenn county, was born in Glenn (then Colusa) county in 1868; was educated in Playa district school and graduated in 1888 from a private normal school in Orland; began teaching in 1888 and taught in district town and high schools till elected superintendent in 1898; was reëlected in 1902.

GEORGE UNDERWOOD, superintendent of Humboldt county, was born in Ohio in 1855; educated in the common schools and the National Normal, Lebanon, Ohio; taught five years in Ohio and twenty years in California, the last fourteen as principal of the Rohnerville school; served several years as a member of the board of education of this county and elected county superintendent of schools November 4, 1902. Scores of successful young men and women in the various walks of life testify to the marked ability of George Underwood as an educator, and it was largely owing to the united efforts of these loyal and grateful pupils and their friends that he was elected to the county superintendency.

MRS. M. A. CLARKE, superintendent of Inyo county, was born in Gold Hill, Nev. After graduating from the high school, she entered the state normal at San Jose, finishing in December, 1887; taught sixteen months in Alameda county Came to Inyo in the fall of 1889, and has resided there since. She earned her life diploma on the old law of seventy months' experience. Most of her practical work has been as principal.

ROBT. L. STOCKTON, superintendent of Kern county, was born at Santa Rosa, Cal., October 25, 1863. His parents meeting with reverses, removed to Kern county in 1872. He recived his education there and in Los Angeles. He has been engaged in teaching mostly in Kern county since 1881, and has served several years as member of the board of education, where he made a record for himself by his stand on educational matters, which resulted in his being elected by a large majority.

MRS. NANNIE E. DAVIDSON, superintendent of Kings county, was born in the South, coming to California at the age of six years. Was educated in the public and normal schools of California. Her father, Dr. T. O. Ellis, was one of the early educators of this state, and elected to the office of superintendent of schools of Tulare, Merced and Fresno counties. In the last named county Mrs. Davidson was her father's assistant. Mrs. Davidson holds a normal certificate, an educational and life diploma; these credentials, her long experience as a teacher and previous training, eminently qualify her to perform the duties of the office to which she was elected by one of the largest majorities in the county.

MARK KEPPEL, superintendent-elect of Los Angeles county, is a native son, thirty-five years of age, and a graduate of San Joaquin Valley College, class of '92. His teaching experiences covers one year's work in San Joaquin county, one in Yolo country, and seven years in Los Angeles city.

C. W. HAYCOCK, superintentendent of Lake county, was born in Norwich county, Canada, August 16, 1871; came to California when twelve years old with his parents, and has resided here since then. Attended the grammar schools of Canada and California, the Lakeport Academy and California College. Mr. Haycock was admitted to practice law before the supreme court of this state in March, 1902. He taught in the grammar schools of Lake county for six years prior to entering the superintendent's office in 1899.

J. F. DIXON, superintendent of Lassen county, has been a successful teacher for a number of years. He was elected to succeed Otis M. Doyle in 1902.

School Superintendents

JAS. B. DAVIDSON, superintendent of Marin county, is an experienced teacher, having served a number of years as the successful principal of the Sausalito schools.

JULIA L. JONES, superintendent of Mariposa county, has served the county faithfully for eight years, and has been elected to serve the third time. She was elected in 1898 and 1902 without opposition.

ESTELLE BAGNELLE, superintendent of Madera county, was elected to succeed herself without any opposition. She is a graduate of the San Jose State Normal School.

J. F. BARBEE, superintendent of Mendocino county, was born thirty-five years ago in Missouri; came to California two years later; was reared on a farm at Willits, Mendocino county; educated in the common schools; passed the teachers' examination, and secured a position in a primary school, which he held three and a half years, resigning to accept the principalship of the public schools at Covelo, Cal. Held that position four years and resigned to take the principalship of the Fort Bragg schools. Held that position five years and was elected county superintendent of schools of Mendocino county. Re-elected superintendent November 4, 1902.

MISS CORDA HAYES, superintendent of Mono county, is a successful teacher. This is her first term as superintendent.

MRS. ANNA SILMAN, superintendent of Merced, is a native of Platteville, Wis., the daughter of Mr. and Mrs. M. Stewart. Her early education was received in the public schools of that place. Later, she took courses in Guernsey Academy, Platteville Normal School, and a years's training in the Oshkosh Normal School. She filled responsible positions in her native state with marked success and has not lowered her record in the thirteen years of active work she has done in the Merced public school, the appreciation of which is shown in the latter case by the large vote given her at the late election.

DUNCAN STIRLING, superintendent of Monterey county, is a graduate of the San Jose State Normal. He was principal of the Castroville schools for years, and for nine years principal of the Salinas grammar schools; for the past five years he has been a member of the county board of education.

MISS NELLIE FORREST, superintendent of Modoc county, is a daughter of Dr. J. M. Forrest; deceased was born in Mendocino county, Cal.; moved to Alturas, the county seat of Modoc county, when but one year old; then reared and educated in the public schools until she gained the position and honor of one of the most successful teachers in the county. While teaching five successful years in Alturas public school, with books at hand, and close application at her home, she fitted herself for, and on November 4, 1902, was elected superintendent.

MISS KATE AMES, superintendent of Napa county, was educated in the schools of California. She has been a student at the San Jose Normal School, Napa county, and is a graduate of Stanford University. She has taught for a number of years in Napa and has been superintendent for one term. She is also well known as an institute instructor, and an active worker in the various educational associations.

J. G. O'NEIL, superintendent of Nevada county, has been a successful teacher for many years in Nevada county, and in November, 1902, was elected as an independent candidate to the present position.

J. B. NICHOLS, superintendent of Orange county, was born and raised in Wisconsin. He is a graduate of the Central Normal College of Indiana, also of the Illinois State Normal University. He has had about twenty years' experience as a teacher in the public schools, and has held the position of principal or superintendent for a number of years.

TILLIE NAOMI KRUGER, superintendent of Plumas county, was born near

Crescent Mills, Cal.; graduated from Nevada State University in 1901 with B.A. degree; was principal for two terms of the Greenville school; elected superintendent in 1902.

CHAS. NELSON SHANE, superintendent of Placer county, was born in Muskingum county, Ohio. He was educated at the Northwestern Ohio Normal Univrsity. Came to California in 1886, and taught sixteen years in Placer county. Eight years ago he was tendered, and accepted, the principalship of the Auburn public school, which position he held until he was elected county superintendent of schools of Placer county, November 4, 1902. Mr. Shane is a progressive educator and will spare no pains to keep his schools in the front ranks.

EDWARD HYATT, superintendent of Riverside county, was born in Pennsylvania; educated in Ohio, and trained by some twenty years' experience in the schools of California. After a university course, he worked up thru ungraded country schools, village grammar schools, and high schools; and is now beginning his third term as county superintendent. He was first elected by the narrow margin of 171; next time by 750, and in the election just passed had a majority of more than 2500, receiving more ballots than any other officer ever voted for in the county.

B. F. HOWARD, superintendent of Sacramento county, has served as superintendent sixteen years, and is now entering on his fifth term.

JOHN GARNER, superintendent of San Benito county, is a thoro public school man, and has been elected three times without opposition.

A. S. McPHERON, superintendent of San Bernardino county, was born in Knox county, Tenn., in 1843. His parents moved to Iowa in 1851, where a public school education was received; served in the 15th Iowa Infantry during the war; completed classical course at Oberlin College, Ohio, in 1871; principal of high and grammar school, Akron, O., till 1873; principal of normal department of Tabor College, Iowa, for seven years; four years principal Albuquerque Academy, Albuquerque, N. M.; three years in schools of Los Angeles; last fourteen years a resident of Redlands, Cal, most of the time being a teacher in the public schools; the last four years previous to assuming the duties of the office of county superintendent of schools being a teacher in the Redlands High School; appointed to the office of county superintendent September 1, 1901, and elected to same office November 4, 1902.

HUGH J. BALDWIN, superintendent of San Diego county, was born in Massachusetts; taught in district schools in Nevada county; served as principal of the National City and Coronado schools for a number of years; was elected president of the State Teachers' Association in 1892, and county superintendent of schools of San Diego county in 1898 and again in 1902. He has served continuously on the county board of education since 1886.

WM. H. LANGDON, superintendent of San Francisco county, was born in Alameda county in 1873; educated in the public schools of Contra Costa county; graduated from San Jose State Normal School in 1892; was principal of schools in Fresno city in 1894; was principal of schools in San Leandro for eight years. His home has been in San Francisco for more than twelve years, and for the last five years he has been a teacher and principal in the San Francisco evening schools. In 1896 he was admitted to practice law and has kept an office in this city since his admission to the bar. During the last summer vacation he completed a course at the California Business College. Has taken an active interest in educational affairs; was first vice-president of the California Teachers' Association.

E. B. WRIGHT, superintendent of San Joaquin county, was formerly principal of Lodi school. He was elected in 1898 and reëlected in 1902. He is an experienced and successful public school man.

FREDERIC PERLEY JOHNSON, superintendent of San Luis Obispo county, was born in Ohio in 1865. He is a graduate of Boston Latin School, Amherst College and Andover Theological Seminary. He has done post-graduate work in Berlin. The University of California gave him B. A. in 1898. He taught four and a half years in the high schools.

MISS ETTA TILTON, superintendent of San Mateo county, is a native of San Mateo county; has a fine record as teacher and superintendent. She is now serving her third term.

W. S. EDWARDS, superintendent of Santa Barbara county, was born in Alfred, Allegany county, New York. He attended the public schools of that state; afterwards taught several terms of school during his college work, and graduated from Alfred University with the degree of A.B. in 1889. Later he engaged in school work as supervising principal of high school and grade work in Wisconsin and also in Kansas, where he became familiar with the school system of the different states. In Santa Barbara county his experience has been as principal of a grammar school, assistant and then principal of high school work.

D. T. BATEMAN, superintendent of Santa Clara county, is a native of Ohio. He is a graduate of Lebanon Normal School, and has been teaching in Santa Clara county since 1882. The last fourteen years, in San Jose Mr. Bateman has done much special work at the Stanford University. L. J. Chipman, the former county superintendent, has contested the election of Mr. Bateman.

J. W. LINSCOTT, superintendent of Santa Cruz county, was born in Jefferson, Lincoln county, Maine, May 7, 1848. Educated in the public schools and seminaries of native state. Taught school prior to coming to California. Arrived in California, April, 1869, and began teaching near Watsonville immediately after arrival. Principal of Watsonville schools from September, 1872, to December, 1890. Elected county superintendent of schools November, 1882, and has served continually since that time.

MRS. K. BRINCARD, superintendent of Shasta county, has a fine record as a teacher in the Redding schools. She entered upon her first term as superintendent January, 1903.

DAN H. WHITE, superintendent of schools of Solano county, was born in Petaluma, Sonoma county, December 29, 1865. Mr. White graduated from the high school of his native city in 1884 at the head of his class. In 1887 he took up the work of teaching, which has been his life work ever since. Mr. White taught school in his native county for two years, and in July, 1889, assumed the principalship of the Cordelia Grammar School. He continued in this capacity until January, 1899, when he began his duties as county superintendent of schools. He was appointed a member of the Solano county board of education in 1893, and served as president of the board for the three years previous to his election to the office which he now holds. At the recent election, Mr. White was re-elected, receiving the handsome majority of 1138 votes over his opponent. He was married to Miss Sarah E. Higgins of Green Valley, Solano county, December 14, 1892, and has a family consisting of one son and a daughter.

MISS GRACE ARDIS JOHNSON, superintendent of Siskiyou county, was born in Etna Mills, Siskiyou county, Cal. In 1898 she received the degree of B.A. from Stanford University, and returned to Siskiyou, where she taught in the public schools for two years. The two years succeeding she was engaged in European study and travel. On her return to Siskiyou, Miss Johnson was almost unanimously elected superintendent of schools of her native county.

MISS MINNIE COULTER, superintendent of Sonoma county, was born in Santa Rosa. She attended the public schools in Santa Rosa, also Mc Means' private normal school, and taught school eight years in Sonoma county, the last four years being in the Santa Rosa city schools. Miss Coulter spent four years at Stanford University, and graduated from the Pedagogic Department in May, 1898. She was elected superintendent of schools of Sonoma county, Nov. 4, 1898, with a majority of 1820 on the Democratic ticket, when the county went 600 Republican; reëlected by a majority of 2034 Nov. 4, 1902, when the county went 900 Republican. Miss Coulter was grand president of the Native Daughters in 1892-3.

MISS FLORENCE BOGGS, superintendent of Stanislaus county, is one of the youngest superintendents in the State, and has a most excellent record as a teacher.

C. W. WARD, superintendent of Sutter county, has a good record as a teacher, and is well prepared professionally for the important work of superintending.

MISS BELLE ALEXANDER, superintendent of Sierra county, has taught successfully for several years.

G. P. MORGAN, superintendent of Tuolumne county, was born at Columbia, Tuolumne county, June 1, 1859. Attended the public school at Columbia, Normal School at San Jose. Commenced teaching in 1877. Has been principal of the Columbia school since 1880, and has been elected superintendent five times.

MISS ELLEN LYNCH, superintendent of Tehama county, is a native daughter of the Golden West and of Tehama county. She is a graduate of the State Normal School of Chico, 1895 She has taught regularly since that time, and served on the County Board of Education for two years.

MISS LIZZIE H. FOX, superintendent of Trinity county, was born, reared and educated in Weaverville, Trinity county, Cal. Experience as teacher in the public schools of the county (three districts) extends over a period of ten years. She holds a grammar school life diploma. Prior to her election as superintendent of schools Miss Fox was vice-principal of the Weaverville public schools for three years. She was elected to the office of county superintendent of schools in 1894; reëlected to the same office in 1898, and again reëlected, without political opposition, in 1902.

C. J. WALKER, superintendent of Tulare county, is in the prime of life. He is a normal graduate; has a fine record as a teacher and principal; was elected, without any opposition, in November, 1902.

GEORGE L. SACKETT, superintendent of Ventura county, was born in Petaluma, Sonoma county, Cal., Jan. 3, 1865. Educated in the schools of California and at the Northwestern University, Evanston, Ill. Taught two years in Illinois, four years in Ventura county, and was principal of the Santa Paula schools of Ventura county at the time he was elected county superintendent of schools. Was elected as successor to Hon. S. T. Black, Nov. 6, 1894, reëlected Nov. 8, 1898, and reëlected for a third term Nov. 4, 1902. He is a member of the Delta Upsilon college fraternity, a Native Son, a Mason, an Odd Fellow and a Woodman of the World,

MRS. MINNIE DeVELBISS, superintendent of Yolo county, was born in New York; came to California when very young and made her home in Yolo county; educated in Woodland public schools and Hesperian college; has taught in the public schools of Yolo county for a period of twelve years; has been associated with the schools of Yolo county for twenty-five years.

JAS. A. SCOTT, superintendent, has a fine record as a superintenden and teacher, and was elected for the third time November, 1902.

Why Do the Boys Leave School?

JOB WOOD JR.

Column one (1) of the table below shows the enrollment of boys and girls by counties in the primary and grammar schools of the state for the year closing June 30, 1902; column two (2) shows the excess of boys or the excess of girls by counties; column three (3) shows the number of boys and the number of girls graduating from the grammar schools for the year closing June 30, 1903, and column four (4) shows the excess of boys or the excess of girls graduating.

PRIMARY AND GRAMMAR SCHOOLS

Table A

COUNTIES	Enrollment Boys	Enrollment Girls	Excess of Boys	Excess of Girls	Graduates Boys	Graduates Girls	Excess of Graduates Boys	Excess of Graduates Girls
Alameda	11,398	11,242	56	....	294	389	....	95
Alpine	20	40	....	20	....	1	....	1
Amador	1,107	1,096	11	....	44	77	....	33
Butte	1,689	1,687	2	....	40	46	....	6
Calaveras	1,171	1,090	81	....	16	24	....	8
Colusa	785	686	99	....	40	44	....	4
Contra Costa	1,832	1,682	150	....	53	53	....	....
Del Norte	281	256	....	25	5	9	....	4
El Dorado	811	769	42	....	9	21	....	12
Fresno	3,949	3,860	89	....	83	128	....	45
Glenn	535	492	43	....	26	25	1	....
Humboldt	2,925	2,929	....	4	49	76	....	27
Inyo	316	297	19	....	2	7	....	5
Kern	1,583	1,469	64	....	42	65	....	23
Kings	970	936	34	....	27	46	....	19
Lake	632	573	59	....	21	18	3	....
Lassen	468	486	....	82	6	7	....	1
Los Angeles	18,868	18,481	387	....	105	153	....	48
Madera	561	595	....	34	5	11	....	6
Marin	1,122	1,070	52	....	27	50	....	23
Mariposa	458	468	....	10	2	8	....	6
Mendocino	1,962	1,864	98	....	57	68	....	11
Merced	906	817	89	....	42	57	....	15
Modoc	590	619	....	29	5	14	....	9
Mono	145	144	1	....	3	1	2	....
Monterey	1,971	1,895	76	....	37	43	....	6
Napa	1,442	1,321	121	....	52	60	....	8
Nevada	1,453	1,385	68	....	10	13	....	3
Orange	2,421	2,225	196	....	73	109	....	36
Placer	1,283	1,316	....	33	42	62	....	20
Plumas	353	349	4	....	6	13	....	7
Riverside	1,948	1,827	121	....	82	113	....	31
Sacramento	3,878	3,627	251	....	79	164	....	85
San Benito	676	631	45	....	27	43	....	16
San Bernardino	2,888	2,746	142	....	101	140	....	39
San Diego	3,285	3,128	162	....	20	29	....	9
San Francisco	25,370	21,956	3,414	....	701	928	....	227
San Joaquin	2,809	2,820	....	11	35	73	....	38
San Luis Obispo	1,939	1,808	131	....	17	46	....	29
San Mateo	1,226	1,009	217	....	17	21	....	4
Santa Barbara	1,937	1,823	114	....	36	42	....	6
Santa Clara	4,972	4,810	162	....	50	51	....	1
Santa Cruz	1,861	1,894	....	33	71	104	....	33
Shasta	1,833	1,714	119	....	46	73	....	27
Sierra	308	382	....	74	9	5	4	....
Siskiyou	1,465	1,450	....	15	27	44	....	17
Solano	1,888	1,771	117	....	34	57	....	23
Sonoma	3,877	3,666	211	....	51	88	....	37
Stanislaus	961	917	44	....	33	33	....	....
Sutter	546	520	26	....	27	34	....	7
Tehama	1,040	1,053	....	13	32	52	....	20
Trinity	296	255	41	....	....	2	9	2
Tulare	2,269	2,228	41	....	98	89	9	....
Tuolumne	983	965	....	32	9	22	....	13
Ventura	1,559	1,443	116	....	57	69	....	12
Yolo	1,201	1,238	....	37	14	31	....	17
Yuba	713	658	55	....	20	36	....	16
Totals	135,585	128,453	7,502	370	2,916	4,087	19	1,190

Column one (1) of the table below shows the enrollment of boys and girls in the high schools of the state by counties for the year closing June 30, 1902; column two (2) shows the excess of boys or the excess of girls enrolled; column three (3) shows the number of boys and the number of girls graduating from the high schools; column four (4) shows the excess of boys or the excess of girls graduating from the high schools.

HIGH SCHOOLS

Table B	1		2		3		4	
COUNTIES	Enrollment		Excess of		Graduates		Excess of	
	Boys	Girls	Boys	Girls	Boys	Girls	Boys	Girls
Alameda	1015	1593	....	578	103	148	....	45
Alpine	....	....	....	....	....	....	....	....
Amador	....	....	....	....	....	....	....	....
Butte	29	45	....	16	8	6	2	....
Calaveras	....	....	....	....	....	....	....	....
Colusa	36	52	....	16	6	8	....	2
Contra Costa	20	51	....	31	....	....	....	....
Del Norte	15	24	....	9	....	....	....	....
El Dorado	....	....	....	....	....	....	....	....
Fresno	309	363	....	54	24	16	5	....
Glenn	34	35	....	1	4	4	....	....
Humboldt	51	93	....	42	7	23	....	16
Inyo	....	....	....	....	....	....	....	....
Kern	63	88	....	25	2	2	....	....
Kings	46	109	....	63	10	17	....	7
Lake	24	44	....	20	....	....	....	....
Lassen	....	....	....	....	....	....	....	....
Los Angeles	557	870	....	313	124	192	....	68
Madera	6	24	....	18	2	1	1	....
Marin	30	58	....	28	2	7	....	5
Mariposa	....	....	....	....	....	....	....	....
Mendocino	113	128	....	15	18	28	....	10
Merced	59	77	....	18	7	11	....	4
Modoc	....	....	....	....	....	....	....	....
Mono	....	....	....	....	....	....	....	....
Monterey	39	70	....	31	8	20	....	12
Napa	68	87	....	19	10	20	....	10
Nevada	15	17	....	2	1	2	....	1
Orange	126	148	....	22	20	28	....	8
Placer	33	44	....	11	1	1	....	....
Plumas	....	....	....	....	....	....	....	....
Riverside	187	218	....	31	16	29	....	13
Sacramento	123	229	....	106	18	19	....	1
San Benito	15	26	....	11	7	4	3	....
San Bernardino	172	286	....	114	26	44	....	18
San Diego	181	198	....	17	21	36	....	15
San Francisco	670	1094	....	424	77	131	....	54
San Joaquin	155	191	....	36	14	25	....	11
San Luis Obispo	88	100	....	12	8	11	....	3
San Mateo	31	47	....	16	4	6	....	2
Santa Barbara	167	210	....	43	21	32	....	11
Santa Clara	420	626	....	206	45	51	....	6
Santa Cruz	113	191	....	78	18	33	....	15
Shasta	24	61	....	37	11	13	....	2
Sierra	....	....	....	....	....	....	....	....
Siskiyou	44	61	....	17	1	5	....	4
Solano	136	182	....	46	31	24	7	....
Sonoma	145	239	....	94	21	45	....	24
Stanislaus	42	71	....	29	4	19	....	15
Sutter	15	12	3	....	3	7	....	4
Tehama	25	74	....	49	2	11	....	9
Trinity	....	....	....	....	....	....	....	....
Tulare	166	218	....	52	31	29	2	....
Tuolumne	....	....	....	....	....	....	....	....
Ventura	91	166	....	75	4	9	....	5
Yolo	81	93	....	12	9	23	....	14
Yuba	51	69	....	18	8	9	....	1
Totals	5830	8682	3	2855	757	1152	20	41

The school census of the State for the year closing June 30, 1902, shows that there were 189,585 boys and 184,414 girls between the ages of five and seventeen years, or 5171 more boys than girls. The enrollment of pupils in the primary and grammar schools of the State, as reported by the County Superintendents, for the year closing June 30, 1902, is given in table A, col.

1. From this table it will be seen that there were 7132 more boys enrolled than there were girls. Col. 4 of this table shows that 1171 more girls graduated from the grammar schools than boys, even with 7132 more boys enrolled.

Table (B) shows that 2852 more girls were enrolled in the high schools than there were boys, and that 395 more girls graduated from the high schools.

The percentage of boys graduating from the primary and grammar schools on the enrollment of boys is 2.1 plus. The percentage of girls graduating from the same schools on the enrollment of girls is 3.2.

The percentage of boys graduating from the high schools on the enrollment of boys is 13. The percentage of girls graduating from the same schools on the number of girls enrolled is 13.2.

These statistics seem to indicate a great many more boys than girls in the primary schools, and that there is a decided falling off of boys in the grammar schools. The boys who succeed in passing the grammar schools seem to about hold their own with the girls in the high school work.

The opinion is general that the boys drop out of the grammar schools owing to the demand for their labor on the part of the family. A careful investigation of the facts, it seems to me, will indicate that the boy himself is responsible in most instances for quitting school. His constant dissatisfaction and his lack of interest cause the parent to allow him to quit school and go into the labor market, where he underbids the man with a family to support and earns enough money to teach him bad habits. Fortunate, indeed, is the boy whose earnings must go towards the support of his father or mother, or towards the education of a brother or sister. This seems to develop real manhood.

The chief difficulty of the boy in the grammar schools arises from the fact that the girl of his own age is at least two years his senior in development and training for neat work. The law of the State considers the girl at eighteen as old as the boy at twenty-one. In comparison with the girl's papers the boy's papers, as a rule, are much less deserving of credits than those of the girl. He is measured in the school work by the girl's work. This work, being much neater, receives the credits and the praise of the teachers, while the boy's work is returned to him with red marks enough to discourage a stouter heart. The boy's courage fails him. He wishes to try something in which his efforts will be appreciated.

If the education of the children really makes stronger men and women, some means of holding the boys as well as the girls till the grammar schools, at least, are completed, should be developed. An investigation that will show the real cause for the boy's dropping out of school would be of interest. If the course of study is not calling for work that interests him, more practical subjects should be selected. If the examination methods are discouraging the boys by undue emphasis of their mistakes, a change to methods that will point out to the boy some, at least, of his capabilities, should be made.

Official : Department

STATE BOARD OF EDUCATION

GEORGE C. PARDEE, *President of the Board* .... Governor, Sacramento.
MORRIS ELMER DAILEY .... President State Normal School, San Jose.
E. T. PIERCE .... President State Normal School, Los Angeles.
C. C. VAN LIEW .... President State Normal School, Chico.
BENJAMIN IDE WHEELER .... President University of California, Berkeley.
ELMER E. BROWN .... Prof. of Theory and Practice of Education, University of Cal., Berkeley.
SAMUEL T. BLACK .... President State Normal School, San Diego.
FREDERIC BURK .... President State Normal School, San Francisco
THOMAS J. KIRK, *Secretary of the Board* ..... Superintendent Public Instruction, Sacramento.

The State Board of Education has been called to meet at Sacramento on Saturday, March 28, at 9:30 A.M.

* * *

Teaching in training classes while preparing at a State Normal School or at the University for the profession of teaching cannot in my opinion be counted as experience required by Sub. 4th Section 1521 of the Political Code for a life diploma. The experience therein alluded to and required is in my opinion that of an actual teacher in charge of a regular school or class for which wages are received.

* * *

Under the present law, the grades constituting the primary and grammar grades are determined by the course of study adopted by the respective county, city or city and county boards of education. There is no state uniformity in this matter. A bill is now before the legislature seeking to determine by general rule the point at which grammar grade work ends and high school work begins. Much difference of opinion exists on this question and I have not sought to urge at this time solution by the legislature. The educational forces of the State should take up this matter and endeavor to reach a wise conclusion before legislative action is taken.

* * *

In answer to the question, "Has the teacher the right to refuse request of a parent to permit a pupil to leave school an hour or more before close of daily session in order that such pupil may take music lesson?" I state that while strongly believing that the interest of the pupil and of the state demand that due consideration be given to the teacher and to the school trustees as to the hours of daily attendance at school, there is no authority in law for contravening the will of the parent on such questions. The parent is above all others in power to grant excuses for non-attendance at school. There is now before the legislature a measure for enforcing the educational rights of children which, if it should become law, would doubtless have a bearing on the foregoing question.

Official Department

Answering the questions, "Has a teacher or board of school trustees the right to demand a physician's certificate for the health of children that have recently had smallpox upon their return to school?" I would state that by Section 1662 of the Political Code, school trustees have authority "to exclude from school children suffering from contagious or infectious diseases," etc. This implies that the trustees must be satisfied by some means that children seeking admission to school are free from infectious diseases. I am therefore of the opinion that the trustees have the right to demand a physician's certificate in this matter.

* * *

Owing to the legislation just passed and approved respecting school census and other measures pending which will more or less effect the forms of blanks to be furnished by this office, county superintendents and other school authorities must anticipate some delay in receiving census marshal's blanks, teachers' reports, etc. These things will be supplied at the earliest possible date after knowing just what changes must be made.

THOMAS J. KIRK,
Supt. Pub. Inst.

THE NEW HIGH SCHOOL LAW

The following excerpt from the "Senate Daily History," showing the various steps taken to make the High School bill a law, will be of interest to students of civil government:

An Act creating a fund for the benefit and support of high schools and providing for its distribution.

Introduced by Senator Rowell.

Jan. 14—Read first time. To printer. Jan. 17—From printer.
Jan. 19—To committee.
Jan. 23—From committee, with recommendation to pass as amended.
Jan. 26—Amendment adopted. Read second time.
Jan. 26—Ordered to print, and to third reading. Feb 4—Engrossed.
Feb. 6—Read third time, amended, and to printer.
Feb. 9—Re-engrossed: Passed. To Assembly.
Feb. 10—In Assembly: Read first time. To Com. on Ed.
Feb. 16—Read third time, and passed.
Feb. 18—In Senate: Enrolled. To Governor.
Mar. 2—Approved by Governor.

An Act creating a fund for the benefit and support of High Schools and providing for its distribution.

The people of the State of California, represented in Senate and Assembly, do enact as follows:

Section 1. There is hereby levied annually for the fifty-fifth and fifty-sixth fiscal years, ending respectively June thirtieth, nineteen hundred and four, and June thirtieth, nineteen hundred and five, an ad valorem tax (one and one half cents) upon every hundred dollars of the value of the taxable property of the state, which tax shall be collected by the several officers charged with the collection of state taxes, in the same manner and at the same time as other state taxes are collected, upon all and any class of property, which tax is for the support of regularly established high schools of the state. And it is further enacted that, beginning with the fifty-seventh fiscal year, to wit: July first, nineteen hundred and six, it shall be the duty of the state controller, annually, between the tenth day of August and the first day of September, at the time that he is required to estimate the amount necessary for other school taxes, to estimate the amount necessary to be levied for the support of high schools. This amount he shall estimate by determining the amount at fifteen dolars per pupil in average daily attendance in all the duly established high schools of the state for the last preceding school year, as certified to him by the state superintendent of public instruction. This amount the state controller, between the dates above given, must certify to the state board of equalization.

Sec. 2 The state board of equalization at the time when it annually determines and fixes the rate of state taxes to be collected, must declare the levy and the rate of tax for the support of state high schools in conformity with the provisions of section one of this act.

Sec. 3. The money collected as provided in sections one and two hereof, after deducting the proportionate share of expenses of collecting the same to which other taxes are subject, must be paid into the state treasury, to be by the state treasurer converted into a separate fund, hereby created, to be called the "state high school fund."

Sec. 4. The money paid into the state high school fund is hereby appropriated without reference to fiscal years for the use and support of regularly established high schools and is exempt from the provisions of part three, title one, article eighteen, of an act entitled "An act to establish a Political Code," aproved March twelfth, eighteen hundred and seventy-two, relating to the state board of examiners.

Sec. 5. The money in said state high school fund shall be apportioned to the high schools of the state by the state superintendent of public instruction in the following manner: He shall apportion one third of the annual amount among the county, district, city, union, or joint union high schools of the state, irrespective of the number of pupils enrolled or in average daily attendance therein, except as hereinafter provided; the remaining two thirds of the annual amount he shall apportion among such schools pro rata upon the basis of average daily attendance as shown by the official reports of the county or city and county school superintendents for the last preceding school year; *provided,* that such high schools have been organi ed under the law of the state, or have been recognized as existing under the high school laws of the state and have maintained the grade instruction required by law of the high schools; *and provided,* that no school shall be eligible to a share of said state high school fund that has not during the last preceding school year employed at least two regularly certificated high school teachers for a period of not less than one hundred and eighty days with not less than twenty pupils in average daily attendance for such length of time, except in newly established high schools wherein the minimum average daily attendance for the first year of one hundred and eighty days may be but twelve pupils (and but one teacher); *and provided,* that before receiving state aid, each school shall furnish satisfactory evidence to the superintendent of public instruction of the possession of a reasonably good equipment of building, laboratory, and library, and of having maintained, the preceding school year, proper high school instruction for a term of at least one hundred and eighty days; *provided further,* that the foregoing provisions relating to the average daily attendance and the number of teachers employed shall not operate to disqualify any legally established high school existing at the date of the passage of this act from receiving a share of said state high school fund until July 1, 1904.

Sec. 6. The principal of every high school entitled to aid in accord with the foregoing provisions shall annually at the close of the term and prior to receiving his last month's salary and as a requisite for such salary make out under oath and deliver to the county superintendent of the county or city and county wherein such high school is situated a full and complete report to show the number of pupils enrolled, the average daily attendance, number of teachers regularly employed, the courses of instruction pursued, and such other information as may be required by the superintendent of public instruction and the county superintendent of · schools, the said report to be made upon blanks furnished by said superintendent of public instruction as other school report blanks are furnished; *provided,* that in the case of joint union high school districts the principals thereof shall report as above required to the county superintendents of each of the counties having territory within joint union high school districts, and in such reports the statistics of attendance and other data for each county separately and collectively shall be given.

Sec. 7. The county superintendent of every county, or city and county, wherein is located a high school, shall annually, at the time required for making reports for primary and grammar schools, make report under oath to the superintendent of public instruction, showing the number of pupils enrolled, average daily attendance, number of teachers regularly employed, and such other information regarding the high schools of his county, or city and county, as he may deem proper, or as may be required by the superintendent of public instruction; said report to be made upon blanks furnished by the superintendent of public instruction.

Sec. 8. It shall be the duty of the county or city and county superintendent of schools of every county, or city and county, wherein is located a high school, or the building or buildings of a joint union high school, on the order of the board of trustees of such high school, to draw his requisition upon the county auditor against the funds of such high school, but no requisition shall be drawn unless the money is in the fund to pay it, and no requisition shall be drawn upon the order of the board of high school trustees or board of education against the state high school fund, except for teachers' salaries, and the order shall state the monthly salary of the teacher, and name the month or months for which such salary is due. Upon the receipt of such requisition the auditor shall draw his warrant upon the county treasurer in favor of the parties for the amount stated in such requisition, and the county treasurer is hereby authorized to pay the same.

Sec. 9. High schools organized under the present law for the establishment of high schools and receiving state aid under this act shall within one year after first beginning to receive such state aid provide at least one course of study such as will prepare pupils for admission to one of the colleges of the University of California, and for that purpose said high schools shall be subject to inspection by a duly accredited representative of said university. High schools eligible to receive state aid as herein provided shall admit as students only such pupils as have completed the full course of instruction prescribed for the primary and grammar schools of the county or city and county wherein the high school is located, or an equivalent course, or such pupils as may show by thorough examination that their qualifications are equivalent to the requirements for graduation from said primary and grammar school course; *provided,* that pupils otherwise qualified to enter a high school and residing in territory wherein no high school exists shall have the right to attend any high school that receives state aid under the provisions of this act without the payment of tuition fee, if such schools have room or accommodations for them.

Sec. 10. The state controller must keep a separate account of the high school fund raised as provided in sections one and two of this act. He must on the first Monday in January and on the first Moday in July in every year report to the superintendent of public instruction a statement of all moneys belonging to the state high school fund. He must draw his warrant on the state treasurer in favor of any county or city and county treasurer whenever such treasurer presents, with his endorsement, an order drawn by the superintendent of public instruction against the state high school fund and the intendent of public instruction against the state high school fund, and the case of counties having joint union high school districts the order of the superintendent of public instruction and the warrant of the state controller shall be in favor of the county treasurer of that county wherein the high school building or buildings are located or wherein the high school is being conducted.

Sec. 11. It is hereby made the duty of the treasurer of every county, or city and county, that receives state money under the provisions of this act to place the same to the credit of the funds of the respective high schools of his county, or city and county, in accord with the apportionment made by the superintendent of public instruction, and to pay out the same according to the provisions of section eight of this act.

Sec. 12. This act shall take effect and be in force from and after its passage.

PUBLISHERS' NOTICE.

THE WESTERN JOURNAL OF EDUCATION succeeds to the subscription lists, advertising patronage, and good will of the Golden Era, established in San Francisco in 1852.

Subscription, $1.50 a year. Single copies, 15 cents. Remit by check, Postoffice order, Wells, Fargo & Co., or by stamps.

ADVERTISEMENTS—Advertisements of an unobjectionable nature will be inserted at the rate of $3.00 a month per inch.

MSS.—Articles on methods, trials of new theories, actual experiences, and school news, reports of teachers' meetings, etc., urgently solicited.

Address all communications to THE WESTERN JOURNAL OF EDUCATION, 723 Market Street, San Francisco.

HARR WAGNER, Editor.
THE WHITAKER & RAY COMPANY PUBLISHERS.
Entered at the San Francisco Post-office as second-class matter.

The Official Organ of the Department of Public Instruction of the State of California.

The Board of Education of San Francisco has asked for a bond issue of $4,000-000 to secure money for new buildings.

***

C. W. Childs, D. T. Bateman and A. E. Shumate of San Jose have issued an Arbor Day circular to the trustees and teachers of Santa Clara county.

***

The Summer School of the University of California will be held June 25th to August 5th. President Wheeler has secured Albert Bushnell Hart, professor of history, Harvard, as the principal lecturer in history.

***

Dr. Edwin R. Shaw died February 11th. He was recently elected superintendent of the schools of Rochester, N. Y. Dr. Shaw was dean of the first school of pedagogery in America. His life was wholly consecrated to educational work.

***

The death of Virna Woods, a teacher in the Sacramento school department, on March 6th, was of unusual sadness. She performed her labors as a teacher quietly, but in the larger field of literary endeavor her voice had in it a national note. Virna Woods as poet, novelist and dramatist, belonged to the gifted few.

***

It is time for a crusade in favor of larger salaries for county superintendents in small counties. The work is harder, the exposure greater, the need of wise leadership more necessary and the pay is often scandalously small. State Superintendent Olsen of Minnesota is leading off in the demand for justice and decency in this matter —*A. E. Winship, in New England Journal of Education.*

The crusade should be started in California also. It will be a surprise to the readers of the JOURNAL, no doubt, to learn that quite a number of the counties of Northern California do not pay over $600 per year salary to superintendents of schools. The amount is ridiculously small.

Why Boys Leave School.—Job Wood Jr., deputy superintendent of public instruction, presents a problem for serious consideration in this issue of the JOURNAL. Each school trustee, teacher, superintendent and parent can contribute more or less to the solution of the problem. The great good is in having the boys take advantage of the means of education offered by our excellent school system. The building of school-houses, the furnishing of text-books, the employment of strong teachers, are of no value to the boy who prefers to loaf about a saloon to securing an education. We are not so much concerned about our system of education as we are to have every boy secure all the advantages of the system. Trustees, teachers and superintendent should take special pride in the report of the school that shows a large enrollment and average daily attendance of boys in the upper grades.

**

THE MAKING OF OUR MIDDLE SCHOOLS
Editorial Review

"American institutions are an expression of American character,' is the strong sentence which opens chapter one of a book that the author does not venture to dignify with the high title of *History*. The book, however, will make history. The book is described on the title page as "An Account of the Development of Secondary Education in the United States. By Elmer Ellsworth Brown, Ph. D., Professor of Theory and Practice of Education in the University of California." The publishers and holders of the copyright are Longmans, Green & Co. The dedication is briefly inscribed as follows: "To My Wife." The preface is brief, and contains a definite, clear and complete statement of the volume from the author's prospective. The book is prepared for two classes of readers. First, the text-book class, second, the "general reader." Eleven pages of the book are devoted to the introduction, then comes a chapter on the "Grammar Schools of Old England," which treatment naturally leads to a consideration of the "Early Colonial Grammar Schools," in chapter III. It is not until chapter XIII is reached and half the book has been read, that you come to the part which treats of the real genius of our secondary institutions. It is the chapter on "The Movement Towards Public Control." This is followed by an historic account of "The First High Schools." The most thoughtful chapter in the book is the one on "The Outlook." There are many vital sentences in these latter pages. There are a number of them that would stand for axioms: "A Divorce of Manners from Morals is Bad for Both," "The Discovery of Teachers is as Important as the Making of Teachers," "It Can Hardly be Doubted that We are Moving Towards a Time When Our Country Will be the World." The closing paragraph of the book is typical of the fine spirit, the historical poise and scholarly consideration of the entire volume.

"It takes wisdom, and patience, and poise and unbounded good to discharge the responsibilities of an intermediary position such as is occupied by our middle schools. But if such graces shall abound in the teachers and managers of the schools, these will deserve well of their country; and even tho we are a democracy we shall not be wholly ungrateful."

The last hundred pages of the volume are devoted to Statistics of Secondary Schools, Courses of Study, Bibliography, Index, etc.

The book as a whole represents the centralized thought of Dr. Brown on secondary education. It is a digest of a vast amount of material that is not readily accessible to the average reader.

The book will have an important place in every teacher's library, in the pedagogical department of public libraries, in the class-room where the history of education is studied.

An additional review will appear in the April number by Dr. Willard S. Small of the State Normal School of Los Angeles.

* * *

POEM
Prof. Chas. H. Allen.

Lincoln Day was observed at the State Normal School, San Jose, with appropriate ceremonies. Prof. Chas. H. Allen read the following original poem:

>Washington, Father—Lincoln, Savior of our land,
> Names to revere—names that shall ever live;
>'Twined in their wreaths of laurel let them stand,
> With all of honor that the world can give.
>
>Each in his sphere a hero, truly great,
> Moved by a love of freedom, strong and pure;
>So long as heaven shall preserve our State
> Within our hearts their memory shall endure.
>
>One saved a people from a tyrant's power
> And built a nation fair and strong to see,
>The other guided through our darkest hour
> And by a pen-stroke made a people free.
>
>Then let us raise our voices in acclaim,
> Let every heart join in the joyful song,
>And this sound doctrine let each voice proclaim,
> "Our country—right or wrong—BUT RIGHT THE WRONG!"

WESTERN SCHOOL NEWS

MEETINGS

National Educational Association, President Charles W. Eliot, Boston, July 6-10, 1903.

INSTITUTES.

San Luis Obispo County, April 22-23-24. Supt. Frederic P. Johnson.
El Dorado County, Feb. 12 to 16. Supt S. B. Wilson.
Kern County, the week of March 16th. Supt. R. S. Stockton.
San Francisco, April 8, 9, 10. Supt. W. H. Langdon.

OTHER INSTITUTES TO BE HELD THIS TERM.

Sonoma County, Minnie Coulter.
Marin County. Supt. J. B. Davidson.
Stanislaus County, Supt. Florence Boggs.
San Mateo County, Supt. Etta M. Tilton.
Nevada County, Supt. J..G. O'Neil.

NOTES

Ex-Supt. J. B. Brown of Humboldt county has been elected principal of the Lafayette School of Eureka.

Ex-Supt. J. W. Graham of Kings county is on a visit to Texas, New Mexico and other states in search of land.

Ex-Supt. J. P. Greely of Orange, as Assistant Clerk of the Assembly, made an excellent record for faithful and efficient service.

Dr. Edward Starbuck of Stanford University returned recently from a trip to Chicago, where he delivered a course of six lectures.

Mrs. Katharine Ball, supervisor of drawing in the San Francisco School Department, will spend May, June and July of this year in Japan.

Caspar Hodgson, who has had charge of D. C. Heath & Co.'s interests in the Pacific States since 1894, has received a call to New York city, which is a decided promotion. He is to have charge of the Department of Publicity and General Promotion in the house of Silver, Burdett & Co,, whose business has been centralized in New York, and hereafter Mr. Hodgson's field will be the United States. This is the first time a bookman trained in the Pacific States has been called to so important a post. The honor is well merited by Mr. Hodgson, who has, during the last three years, secured more business in the state adoptions of the "Pacific West" than any other bookman. It will be but natural for Caspar Hodgson to ramble back occasionally to the land and the people he knows so well, and we expect the removal to be temporary only.

Supt. S. B. Wilson of Eldorado county held his institute at Placerville February 15 16, 17 and 18. The instructors were Robt. Furlong of Marin county, T. H. Kirk of Santa Barbara, and Miss Jenne M. Long, School of Dramatic Art, 2152 Sutter. A number of the local teachers took an active part in the program. The Eldorado teachers are very active in promoting good fellowship at an institute, and the instructors report a royal and successful week.

We desire to call the attention of our readers to the notice of Dr. G. S. Moore's Scientific Hair Restorer, office 32 O'Farrell Street. The treatments offered by Dr. Moore bring excellent results. The testimonials offered are from well-known people and convincing. The following is a sample of the testimonials:

G. S. MOORE.—Having had a very bad case of falling hair I used one bottle of your hair restorer, and to my surprise and satisfaction a few applications completely arrested its falling. I can highly endorse all that it is recommended for.
Respectfully yours,
W. H. NASH, 12 Crocker Bldg., S. F.
Jan. 3, 1901.

For sale—A scholarship in leading business college, price $100, will sell for $50. Address Business, care of WESTERN JOURNAL OF EDUCATION, 723 Market st., S. F , Cal.

cents per copy $1.50 per year

APRIL, 1903

CONTENTS

The World's Peace as Assured by Economic Tendencies........ John B. Clark, L. L. D.	155
An Appeal for the Next Step in Human Progress....... Mary H. Hunt	157
An Educational Exhibit...	160
The First Lyric ....Herbert Bashford	161
Current Educational Thought.......................................	162

Let Us Be Reminded; Meditations, Edward Howard Griggs; Angelo's Last Work; One Mood of the City; Duty; Technical Schools Needed; Two Races Live on the Soil of the South—Both Must be Educated; Call of the Twentieth Century, David Starr Jordan; Normal Schools, Dr. Charles De Garmo.

Official Department....................................Thomas J. Kirk	170

Superintendent of Public Instruction.

The School Text-Book Law; Compulsory Education; The Formation of Union School Districts; The Appointment of Members of County Boards of Education; The New High School Law; School Teachers' Annuity Fund; Levying County School Tax; The Election of School Boards; School Bonds; The Apportionment of School Funds; School Elections; Separate Classes for Deaf Children; The School District Library Funds; The Admission of Children in the Public Schools; The Formation of New School Districts; Investing of School Funds; Change of Name of School District; Duties of County Superintendent; In Reference to School Bonds. Charter Day Address, Gov. Geo. C. Pardee

The Meeting of the State Board of Education............................	207
The University of California, Summer Session.	210
Editorial...	213
Western School News..	214
Book Reviews..	215
Miscellaneous...	217

HARR WAGNER, Editor

THE WESTERN JOURNAL OF EDUCATION.
723 Market St.
San Francisco

Nature Study for Little Folks

BARTLETT'S ANIMALS AT HOME 45 cents

For Third Reader Grade

This little book is intended to arouse the interest of children in certain individual animals, and by so doing to awaken an interest for Natural History in general. In each story one particular animal is described in such a way as to illustrate the life of a class.

PYLE'S STORIES OF HUMBLE FRIENDS 50 cents

For Third Reader Grade

The stories in this book are about animals and birds familiar to the children. They are simple in their manner of presentation and most sympathetic in treatment. The many pictures drawn by the author are vividly illustrative of the incidents described.

BRADISH'S STORIES OF COUNTRY LIFE 40 cents

For Third Reader Grade

These recollections of a childhood spent on a north-western farm, aim to emphasize the attractiveness of life in the country, and to add to its charm by awakening an intelligent interest in its many activities.

ABBOTT'S A BOY ON A FARM 45 cents

For Third Reader Grade

This book presents two stories by Jacob Abbott new and attractive form. As revised, these are mirably suited to hold the interest of young read and to train youthful instincts naturally and healthfully. The illustrations are numerous and pleasing.

STOKES'S TEN COMMON TREES 40 cents

For Third Reader Grade

A series of simple nature lessons for young childre familiarly treated and giving a few definite impressio of what trees are and how they live.

DANA'S PLANTS AND THEIR CHILDREN 65 cents

For Fourth Reader Grade

These charming readings are as interesting as stori and are not only instructive in themselves, but tea the most important lessons a child can learn — to s to think, to observe for himself, and thus to become intelligent student of nature.

Best New Text-Books for Elementary Grades

BARNES'S NEW ELEMENTARY UNITED STATES HISTORY $0.60

This book is thoroughly modernized and entirely rewritten by the well-known writer for children, Dr. James Baldwin. It tells the story of the country in a series of biographies of important men, as recommended by the Committee of Fifteen. The incidents narrated show the manners of the time, and the stories are all intensely interesting. The numerous illustrations form an important aid to the understanding of the text.

NEW EDUCATION READERS

Book I, $0.35; Book II $0.35
Book III, .40; Book IV .45

Novel in plan and character, simple and teachable. Well graded, with frequent reviews. They correlate the leading features of the phonic, the synthetic, the word, and the sentence methods, but require no special preparation on the part of the teacher. They accomplish more than other systems attempt, and contain numerous illustrations.

BASKERVILL AND SEWELL'S LANGUAGE COURSE

LANGUAGE LESSONS $0.
SCHOOL GRAMMAR .

The Language Lessons are simple, presenting a gre Variety of material and introducing the element grammar in an easy and untechnical way. The Sch Grammar is scholarly as well as practical. The exe cises are numerous, and the illustrative sentences ca fully chosen.

WINSLOW'S NATURAL ARITHMETIC

Book I, $0.30; Book II, $0.
Book III .

Prepared on the popular and successful spiral pl of instruction. The work is easy and practical, t subject-matter varied and interesting. The proble are based upon facts gathered from different studies corresponding grade, thus correlating arithmetic wi other subjects. The books offer modern examples a modern methods.

AMERICAN BOOK COMPANY PUBLISHE

NEW YORK   CINCINNATI   CHICAGO   BOSTON   ATLANTA   DALLAS

204 PINE ST., SAN FRANCISCO

The Western Journal of Education

Established 1852.

Old Series: Golden Era, Vol. XLVI.　　San Francisco, April, 1903.　　New Series: Vol. VIII. Number 4.

The World's Peace as Assured by Economic Tendencies

By JOHN B. CLARK, LL.D.
Professor of Political Economy, Columbia University.

I rejoice in the limitation which makes this paper a short one: and I rejoice also in the freedom from limitation which permits me to discuss arbitration on a basis of broad theory. This, however, will not take us out of the realm of facts; for theories speak for tendencies, and tendencies mean facts of the future. If you wait for the future to become present you can bring theories to account. Some of the tendencies of which I have undertaken to write move with the slowness which is imputed to the mills of the gods, and the person who should try to test the correctness of them will have to wait a long and tedious time. They remind me of the tendencies to constitutional freedom in Russia, of which Stepniak used to be fond of saying: "It is perfectly safe to prophesy —only you must not set the date."

There are some things which we can prophesy with absolute confidence, without setting dates. There are other things that we can prophesy with reasonable confidence, setting a date which is not too remote; and still others that we can prophesy with some confidence as destined to come in the near future.

There are three very distinct types of movement now in progress, all three of which afford guarantees of peace between the nations. The three together constitute only a certain part of that very comprehensive thing that we call economic evolution, which means, in the end, the culmination of everything that the finest optimism ever sees in the future for mankind. I thoroughly believe that it is in the realm of economic law that we are to find the method whereby mankind is to perfect itself, and the hope of the future is to be realized on earth. The finest optimism needs to find a scientific basis for its confidence, and will find it easily, if it comprehends certain things that are written in economic law. Only a very small part of that grand culmination is involved in the mere establishment of a tribunal between nations that requires conscious effort and the immediate result is not satisfactory.

We are struggling for a great end and are now discouraged about it and now encouraged. It is an end the importance of which is not possible to measure in language; yet it is only a part of a much greater one. We are trying to put one broad, shapely stone, but one stone only, into a beautiful edifice, the completion of which is assured by the forces I refer to. The establishment of tribunals that shall guarantee peace on earth is the beginning of a long development.

There are some things which a theoretical economist sees in the future for mankind, in consequence of the particular forces with which it is his province to deal. Competition means much: it means a limitless progress in the accumulation of wealth. It means rising wages, and this does not mean altogether sordid gains for the laboring class, but rather means a steadily rising level of the life of humanity. There are moral survivors as well as material ones to be counted on; for character is to survive as well as wealth, and in ways that I have not time to describe, a wealth of culture and even of virtue is coming with the abundance of material goods. I want just to speak of something more limited and modest in scope, a part only of the general movement, and leading to a consummation which is a modest part of the whole.

We have heard very instructive things said upon the influence of commerce. It is impossible adequately to describe the importance of that influence. I consider that the commerce which is opening before the world is the first of three great influences, the culmination of which means the extension of the great inert, outlying sections of the world, of the benefits of civilization. It is the assimilating to that which is highest in humanity of that which has been left out in the competitive race. It is the extension to Asia, to Africa and to South America of the mode of living which prevails where civilization has done its best. Commerce is the beginning of this. With the quick establishment of lines of communication it is easy to exchange goods, and that means much. It means the cremation of ties which are of the utmost importance and tend to bind men together. They tend to make war easy, one would think; for they afford a myriad provocations to war. On the other hand, they tend to make the damages created by war so much in excess of any gains which are possible as, in time, to make war practically unknown.

But commerce is only the beginning. We are to see it in the outlaying regions of the earth, with which we are now coming into close connection, an assimilation to our own methods of life. We are to see Asia produce things as we produce them. It will have its mills. The Asiatic is imitative, and assimilative; and he will use machinery as we use it, and will become the competitor of ourselves in the producing and exporting of goods. Enormous changes will take place in the face of the commercial world; and the outcome of it all will be an assimilation of economic status, the extension to Asia of the benefits of our civilization.

This is not the end. This is only what will come in the middle period which is not immediately before us, but is not far off. Fifty years is nothing in history; and I should say that in fifty years one would see much of this consummated. There are other things that will not consummate themselves in five hundred years, and the comprehensive name for all of them is the attainment of a true economic equilibrium in the world as a whole—a condition of forces in which no further assimilation or transformation is necessary, and in which all the quarters of the world, producing things in the same way, standing on the same economic level, shall engage in a neck-and-neck race of civilization.

What does all this mean specifically, as bearing on the question we are discussing? It has very broad applications; but I will give it only a limited one. The specific application has reference to arbitration treaties. They are in line with the general evolution and are imperatively needed. We should make them efficient in form. Not long ago, in a conversation with my honored colleague, Professor Moore, I asked him how much gain he thought there would be if a tribunal of arbitration should be established, and if recourse to it should be absolutely voluntary. He thought it would be worth much even if the nations did nothing in the way of binding themselves to have recourse to it; but he thought it was of great importance that sooner or later, and sooner rather than later, the nations should bind themselves to use it. He thought it was of importance that we who were striving to secure such a treaty should aim in the end to get it in that form. In fact he converted me from the view which I confess I had held up to the time when he overwhelmed me with precedents, that the mere existence of a tribunal would be very nearly sufficient for the needs of mankind.

The importance of this contribution to the general evolution of which I have spoken seems to me to lie here, that it will tide humanity over a very critical interval—a "dead centre," as mechanics would call it. Having established even such a tribunal as is now in existence at The Hague, recourse to which is absolutely voluntary, we shall sooner or later reach a state in which we shall refer all disputes to its jurisdiction. The industrial development of the outlaying regions of the earth, particularly of Asia, which is immediately before us, is to thrust the nations of the world into a thousand commercial entanglements, and to create difference of interest of a pecuniary sort. It is to place them where, if they would quarrel over dollars, they would do it every day in the year, and where, if a quarrel over dollars would lead to war, they would be in a condition of perpetual warfare. I can think of no condition whatever so favorable to the growth of tribunals of arbitration as one in which there should be continually arising causes of dispute over which the nations would feel ashamed to resort to violence. That sentiment of honor which compels a man sometimes to fight another man—according to codes of honor which prevail in some countries —might range itself entirely against such a course, if the dispute were one of pecuniary interest, and that on a small scale. A man would be as thoroughly disgraced for striking another over a dispute about a few dollars as, according to the same code, he would be disgraced if he did not fight him for certain other causes. If every day in the year we are compelled to adjudicate interests of the minor sort in some other way than by warfare, we establish a precedent that sooner or later will compel us to refer all causes to such adjudication—a precedent which in time will be overwhelming in its coercive power. Apply to it a hundred times in small cases and you will find yourselves compelled to apply to it in large cases; and while you will not be in the millennium, nor particularly near it, you will have entered the portal of the long road that leads to it.

An Appeal for the Next Step in Human Progress
MARY H. HUNT.

The March number of the *Century Magazine* has three articles which show that the great ethnic changes now going on in this country are challenging attention. According to the census of 1890 the decendants of our English ancestors are still in the majority in the United States. But that majority is being rapidly diminished by the half a million people per year from the old world who are passing through the gateways of this nation to become American citizens. In commenting on this, one of the *Century* writers, Gustave Michaud, says: "What the new-comers are is, in large measure, what the nation will be."

Professor Giddings throws light on this prospect by reminding us that our English ancestors were the product of the admixture of the same three great racial types that are now coming to our shores, the achieving Baltic, the conservative, philosophical Alpine, and the artistic, "leisure-loving" Mediterranean or romance races. From that point of view, there is certainly reason to hope that the blending, amid the boundless resources of this new world, of the English, Teuton, Celt, Latin, and even the Slav, may result, "as intimated by Bayard Taylor, in his Centennial Ode" in "a people stronger, and yet more sensitive, nobler and yet more impressionable" than any whose story is told on the pages of history. That will depend on the development here of the best possibilities of those invading multitudes. To them "America spells opportunity," says Jacob A. Riis, one of the three *Century* writers referred to, and we have, he says, in "the schoolhouse, clean and bright as the flag that floats over it, the making of the tomorrow," which these people are bringing to us.

Dr. Frohlich, of the University of Vienna, Austria, recently said to the writer: "Three curses, militarism, ecclesiasticism and alcoholism, are weighing down southern Europe, from which you are now getting your largest immigration. If these immigrants bring you the blight of alcoholism for the civil and religious liberty you give them, it will be a disastrous exchange for you."

When he was shown the temperance education map of the United States all white with every black patch removed, because no State is now without a temperance education law, and the pen with which the Governor of Georgia signed the last law requiring the public school children of this land, home and foreign born, to be taught with other laws of health the physiological reasons for total abstinence from alcoholic drinks and other narcotics, he exclaimed, "Most wise, most wise. That will save you."

Cotemporaneous with this invasion from the lands of the vine has been the enactment of those laws which require the children of these invaders, as well as our own, to learn in our public schools the perilous character and effects of alcohol. Is not this one of the many providences which has provided the succor for the times of special need that it pleases the American to note in our national history.

Alcohol destroys capacity for self-government, which is the corner stone of our free institutions. Do the men and women engaged in public school education in this country realize that the lofty mission thus committed to them in this matter is nothing less than the perpetuity of this government by the people?

Dr. Harris, United States Commissioner of Education, attributes the disparagements of this study found in the reports of some school superintendents to the fact that they have not yet reduced it to what he terms "pedagogical form." Such form in the case of the study of other regular branches has been the result of centuries of study and education planning. In the latest manuals of the instruction in school physiology this subject has been so graded. Although the first temperance education law was enacted twenty years ago, the study is yet so comparatively new that there is still in some quarters lack of comprehension of the fact that it is a science, with a body of truth to be taught that must be adapted to the progressing capacities of pupils from year to year, as are the truths of such studies as arithmetic, geography, history, and grammar. The object of this study, as already implied, is to teach as a progressive branch all future Americans the physiological reasons for right physical habits, including especially those relating to alcoholic drinks and other narcotics, and to do so as these habits are being formed, new ones each year of the child's life, and thus intelligently to guide to the best physical and consequent mental and moral life.

Ability to make out a course of study that will secure this object or to recognize one when properly made out implies:

1. Knowledge of the subject of anatomy and physiology.

2. Knowledge of the laws of health, or general hygiene.

3. Knowledge of the nature of alcoholic drinks and other narcotics, and of their effect upon the various organs of the body and mind, and therefore upon the character.

4. The pedagogic sense that will select the simplest truths for the youngest classes, and so progressively develop the subject that new and interesting matter will be added each year from grade to grade, until the subject is covered, as it can be with a minimum of thirty or forty lessons per year, from the first primary through the five grammar years and the first year in the high school.

5. The pedagogic sense that will recognize that in this, as in every other study, the school furnishes to the child three sources of information—the *teacher*, the *book*, and *observation*, including experimental work. Where any one of these

sources is withheld, as the child progresses far enough to profit by it, there is a loss in results.

6· The pedagogic sense that applies the statistics of school attendance, which show that a very large proportion of pupils attend school only about five years of two hundred days each (see report of Commissioner of Education). To postpone this study until the sixth year, or later, is to withhold from large numbers, and those most needing it, especially the foreign born, even in States having the highest school attendance, knowledge of the physical reasons for the laws of health and total abstinence.

Lastly, to make our course of study in this subject, a conscience is needed that can appreciate and respond to the obligation to provide the utmost warning instruction that will guide all the children safely past the pitfalls which beset their paths, and a patriotism that will gladly prosecute the work committed by the nation to the teachers of its children, of saving, through education, the republic from corruption by alcoholic, narcotic, and other unhygenic habits.

As Dr. Harris implies, pedagogic criticism of the study reveals the pedagogic lack of the critic. The schoolman who says this study for all pupils is "an unnecessary repetition of the same matter year after year" has not in the selection of topics and manuals of instruction graded the subject to the progressive capacities of the pupils, taking care that new and important matter which the pupil can comprehend is added each year: Let him do that and the trouble he complains of will vanish. The doubter needs to read farther who thinks the indorsed school physiologies are not teaching the truth about alcohol and other narcotics. The critic who would have this study put into the higher, at the expense of the lower grades, should study the statistics of school attendance, which show how many of his pupils, and those who most need it, would thereby lose it. Can it be "an unimportant matter of mere pedagogics" whether fourth year pupils, who have books in other subjects, shall have them in this? If they do not, the school will never furnish the foreign born future American, who does not go to school beyond the fourth year, the written page as one source of information in behalf of that sobriety which is essential to his becoming a good citizen.

Every step of progress in human liberty in our land has been not for ourselves alone, but for the world as well. If we ask, at what cost? we find the answer in the story of the bleeding feet of our soldiers at Valley Forge, and told again in the graves in every cemetery over which are floating the weather-stained flags that on Memorial Days we change for fresh ones to mark the last resting places of those who gave their lives for liberty on this western hemisphere. At an untold cost of blood and treasure, religious and civil liberty has become our heritage that like the beacon in our greatest harbor, is beckoning the world to our gates. For these new comers, as for us, the next step in human progresss is liberty from alcohol slavery. Someone has said, "The edge of the sabre is finished, and that of the thinker has come," and that progress henceforth is not to be a blood-stained pathway. It will not be, my countrymen and women engaged in public education, if you, recognizing the supreme command of our times, rise to meet it with the thoughtful study and wise teachings that are both your legal and moral obligation.

The facts that the United States has the smallest per capita of consumption of alcohol of any of the great nations, that the better knowledge of hygiene which you have been teaching is one cause of the increase of four and one-tenth years in length of life reported by the last census, that the children have carried from school the story that alcohol injures working ability until abstinence is largely required of employees by the business of the country, and that where the study is pursued as herein outlined, cigarette smoking is decreasing—all show how large is the debt this country already owes to its teachers.

The countless heroes of the past pointing to the priceless sacrifice through which liberty has thus far come, the present with its perils, the future with its hopes, all appeal to you to be increasingly loyal to your magnificent opportunities to train the great army of future Americans to a sobriety that will dethrone alcohol.

An Educational Exhibit

Notes Concerning the Department of Education at the Universal Exposition, St. Louis, 1904.

The Department of Education at the Universal Exposition was organized in October, 1901, and has had nearly a year of preliminary work. The director of the department is Mr. Howard J. Rogers of Albany, New York, whose exposition experience was gained as superintendent of the New York state educational exhibit at the Chicago Exposition, 1893, and as Director of Education for the United States Commission at the Paris Exposition of 1900. As an advisory committee to support Mr. Rogers, the National Educational Association has selected the following men:

Dr. Wm. T. Harris, chairman, Washington, D. C.; Edwin A. Alderman, New Orleans, La.; Nicholas Murray Butler, New York City; W. T. Carrington, Jefferson City, Mo.; Newton C. Dougherty, Peoria, Ill.; Andrew S. Draper, Champaign, Ill.; Daniel S. Gilman, Baltimore, Md.; Aaron Gove, Denver, Colo.; James M. Greenwood, Kansas City, Mo.; Arthur T. Hadley, New Haven, Conn.; William R. Harper, Chicago, Ill.; Halsey C. Ives, St. Louis, Mo.; Lewis H. Jones, Cleveland, Ohio; Charles M. Jordan, Minneapolis, Minn.; David Starr Jordan, Stanford University, Cal.; James McAllister, Philadelphia, Pa.; William H. Maxwell, New York City; Carroll G. Pearse, Omaha, Neb.; Jacob Gould Schurman, Ithaca, N. Y.; F. Louis Soldan, St. Louis, Mo.; Calvin M. Woodward, St. Louis, Mo.

The field of education has been divided into eight general groups as follows:

Group 1, Elementary Education; Group 2, Secondary Education; Group 3, Higher Education; Group 4, Special Education in Fine Arts; Group 5, Special Education in Agriculture; Group 6, Special Education in Commerce and Industry; Group 7, Education of Defectives; Group 8, Special Forms of Education—Text Books, School Furniture, School Appliances.

Under these groups the subject is subdivided into twenty-six classes.

The object of the educational exhibit from the beginning has been to secure from the United States a thoroughly comprehensive and systematized exhibit of the educational resources of this country and to secure for comparison and for scientific study an exhibit from all foreign nations noted in any way for educational progress. The facilities placed at the disposal of the Chief of the Department of Education by the executive authorities in St. Louis have been such as to render possible the accomplishment of both these objects. There are at the present time about ten of our great commonwealths which are actively engaged in the preparation of a thorough exhibit. Others are waiting the action of the state legislatures which will meet in January, 1903, to provide the ways and means for the development of an exhibit. Three of the largest municipalities of the country, New York, Chicago and St. Louis, have taken the preliminary steps, and others are giving the matter favorable consideration. The great colleges and institutions of learning of the country have also responded most promptly, and exhibits are now being prepared from Yale, Columbia, Cornell, Chicago, Illinois, and many others. Other institutions of equal rank have the matter under consideration and favorable decisions are anticipated.

The American Library Association has

appointed a special committee for the preparation of an exhibit of library methods and resources. The agricultural and mechanical colleges and experiment stations of the country have united for a great collective exhibit for which they have asked from Congress an appropriation of $100,000, and which there seems every liklihood of their receiving. The four largest art schools in the country are applicants for space.

The industrial and technical institutions of the country have already responded generously to the invitation to exhibit.

The education of defectives will be an innovation in exposition methods, as the schools for the blind and the schools for the deaf and dumb in this country have both decided to maintain a model school in actual operation on the exposition grounds during the entire exposition period.

The exhibit of publishers, manufacturers of school furniture, school apparatus and school appliances will be larger than ever before, and the facilities which can be given them are superior to any heretofore granted.

The participation of foreign countries in the Department of Education is most satisfactory, inasmuch as four of the nations which are of the greatest interest to the United States, and which have exercised the greatest influence upon our own institutions, namely, England, France, Germany and Japan, have decided to make extensive educational exhibits. Many other nations have also applied for exhibit space. The value of an educational exhibit on the above lines is easily demonstrated to everybody, and the permanent benefit lies in the opportunities for comparison which it affords, the investigations which it inspires, and the acquaintances and friendships which it engenders. It should always be borne in mind that many of the most far-reaching results, both in the general education of the public and in the special processes of schools, are due to international expositions. The most notable instances are the development of industrial art as the result of the Crystal Palace Exposition in 1851; the spread of manual training and industrial drawing as a result of the Centennial Exposition in 1876;; the re-organization of primary instruction in France as a result of the Exposition of 1878; and the rapid growth in art education, in civic improvement and in art ideals in this country, as a result of the Columbian Exposition of 1893.

At no time in the history of the world have the great nations of the earth been so concerned in the industrial and commercial development of their resources, and at no previous time has it been so strongly impressed upon the minds of the cabinets of the nations that the industrial and commercial success of a nation is directly due to the training which its citizens receive. For this reason, if for no other, it will be considered of paramount importance that there shall be assembled at St. Louis an exposition of educational methods and educational systems which will repay careful investigation and study from the standpoint of the material as well as the intellectual development of the nation.

The First Lyric

Herbert Bashford in April Ainslee.

What keen, sweet rapture must have thrilled
The heart of Nature when she heard
The first glad lyric of a bird!
When that impassioned music spilled
From out the deeps of dawn — ah me,
'Twas then God fashioned Ecstacy!

Current Educational Thought

Let Us Be Reminded

Extracts from a discussion before the Teachers' Club of Alameda County.

A true teacher is a true man or a true woman.

Teachers should be as members of a great family, bearing toward one another a fraternal spirit.

Only by confidence in one another can the confidence of the community be gained.

Schools are most liberally supported where patrons and teachers work in sympathy.

It then becomes a duty to shield our brothers from harsh criticisms, and to be ready with timely words of commendation.

"Etiquette" is the synonym of a word that means "ticket." It is a sign of what the package contains, or is made up of. A person is mistaken in supposing that he may be one thing and appear to be somethnig different, for somewhere about him will be the "ticket" which marks his true worth.

Teachers are guides by example rather than by precept.

Professional spirit begins with the individual. Individuals make up conventions of teachers, impressing their purposes and sympathies upon those gatherings. In this atmosphere springs up the spirit of comradeship and devotion which controls the profession and places it upon a high plane.

Teaching will secure recognition as the noblest of professions when the bonds of fraternity have grown stronger.

* * *

Meditations*

By Edward Howard Griggs.

WISDOM.

[Rome, December 16, 1898]

How miserably life may deteriorate when it is lived habitually in narrow and mean things. It is not a question of poverty or wealth, though grinding poverty makes it more difficult to live constantly in great interests. But with a very slight command of money one may center one's life in the supreme realities. Personal love with its deep below deep of revelation may be ours if we do not degrade it by unworthiness or a cheap familiarity. The miracle of beauty which nature plays over daily before us may be ours, from the first glory of the dawn to the Venetian pageant of the sunset, and on to the sublime shining of the stars of night. The the thought of all seers and poets may speak to us.

And with this world of greatness yearning to unfold itself to us we can spend our energies in petty irritation, in spying upon the slight failures of others, in seeking to secure the best physical comforts for ourselves!

There must be a certain noble prodigality in great living. Some things are of such absolute value that one must spend time, money, life for them without thought or hesitation. If the virtue of common sense is a thrifty prudence in little things, the at least equally important uncommon sense consists in knowing the absolute when it comes to accepting it at its worth.

* * *

ANGELO'S LAST WORK

This work of Angelo's grows upon me. How different from the early Pieta, the master's first great achievement. There it is the Madonna upon whom the attention centers, and Angelo has given her the grave majesty and superb strength of a Greek goddess who has suffered and become human. Here the Christ is the center; he is made larger and more powerful, while the Madonna is more human and less mighty. Inexpressibly beautiful is the Christ face as it leans against the mother's. Not the divine Christ this, but the "man of sorrows and acquainted with grief," solemn, sad as the endless pain of life.

---
*Extracts from his book "Meditations."

ONE MOOD OF THE CITY

The night has come and from the silent bay
I see the myriad lights climb up the hill;
The ferry quietly moves on its way
Beneath God's stars which shine so far and still.
The city's peace is different from the day
Which garish light and troubled noises fill;
The buildings rising dimly outlined seem
The fair and peaceful city of a dream.
The night, the night has come, and with the night
The throng that filled the streets has sought its home;
The night, the night is here, and light on light
Seems soaring up to reach the heaven's dome;
A different throng of other aspect quite
Begins now through the lighted streets to roam;
The victims who in turn on error prey
Give night a meaning darker than the day.
The gaudy theatres attract their crowd,
Saloons and gambling dens are quickly filled
Coarse, painted women speak in accents loud,
The voice of vice at night is never stilled—
Belated girls from workshops hasten cowed,
As if escape from harm were what they willed;
Beneath the sidewalk in each filthy den,
What once were women dance to wrecks of men.

* * *

DUTY

[San Francisco, January 27, 1896]

Men frequently abandon their property when they no longer have use for it, and imagine they are very benevolent. So when a man finds his life a wreck he is apt to say he will live for others. Yet one can give to others only what one's life is worth to oneself.

To abandon a mean situation is not the path to a better one. Only when we are faithful to the little duty are we worthy to meet a larger one. It is often necessary to leave a situation that offers small chance for the realization of our lives, but it makes all the difference in the world whether we sneak meanly out from under the little duty or climb bravely through and over the top.

* * *

Technical Schools Needed

Southern Educational Bulletin.

If we would develop with the greatest profit to ourselves and the world any small part of the large and varied resources of this vast Southern empire of nearly a million square miles—as large as Austria, Germany, France, Spain, the British Isles, and the New England States combined, and much richer in natural resources—then we must not only educate all our people in a general way, but they must be given specific knowledge and skill to do particular kinds of work. We must have a few polytechnic schools, and many technical and trade schools for teaching the theory and practice of every industrial art, from the intense cultivation of the soil and the care of forests to engineering and the manufacture of the finest fabrics and the most delicate machniery. And there must be commercial schools, such as all the great commercial countries of the world are establishing and maintaining.

Germany, France, Switzerland, Denmark, England, the New England and Northern states have their hundreds of such schools, on which they lavish millions of dollars, every million returning its ten millions. It is these schools and the knowledge and skill gained in them that have made Denmark, with its few acres of sterile soil and its northern climate, the second country in the world in per capita wealth; enabled the Swiss peasants and mechanics to deposit in their savings banks $200,000,000—about $75 per capita for the entire population; helped the German people burdened with an immense army and a double system of royal governments, to wealth, power and industrial and commercial supremacy; enabled France to pay a war indemnity otherwise ruinous and leave her people unimpoverished; assisted England in regaining her place, which she was rapidly losing, at the head of European nations; and enabled our own manufacturing states to compete successfully with European countries within their own ports and territory. Brains, skill, the power to make and use machinery, and to control the forces of nature count for much in the production of wealth.

Nor is this kind of education valuable alone for the increased power of production it brings to the individual and the community. It gives real culture of mind and heart as well, increasing beyond measure the power to see straight and think to definite purpose, and giving a firm and sure foundation that resists the floods and storms. Froebel was not far wrong when he asserted that this working out with the hands the images of the soul. the thoughts of the mind, the desires of the heart—this busy, powerful activity—constitutes the real kingdom of God on earth. Mr. Page, in the *World's Work* for June, 1901, says the wonderfully rapid extension of manual and industrial training as a means of mind culture as well as hand culture are the most striking facts in present educational progress. "It seems to have been clearly demonstrated that pupils who are taught to do things with their hands do better work also with their minds than those who do not have manual training. The most noteworthy movement in educational work in the near future seems likely to be based on this fact. It is a movement straight towards common sense and toward the strengthening of democratic character." And again he says, "The race has found its development by doing things. By doing things it has learned its wisdom and built its institutions. Common sense expressed in action —that is the American character behind it for a thousand years."

**

Two Races Live on the Soil of the South—Both Must be Educated

From Southern Educational Bulletin

Two races live and work side by side on the soil of these states. In industrial and civil life they are inseparably united; in social life influencing each other at every point, but forever divided. "In all things purely social * * * separate as the fingers, yet one as the hand in all things essential to mutual progress." Both these races must be fully and freely educated, each race and each individual according to native ability and demands of life. The only solution of what we call "the race problem" is in the right education of all individuals of both races. One-third of the people are black. This third must do one-third of the work and produce one-third of the wealth, or it must be a burden to the other two-thirds, bringing down by so much the total production and the total wealth. It must represent one-third of the moral virtue and civic strength, or it must be a menace and constant source of weakness. We must also remember that light is sweet to the black child as well as to the white child, and that

"Without light, all life is sad."

Doubtless the schools of the white children are not quite the best kind of schools for the colored children at the present stage of the race's development. But this does not relieve us of the responsibility; it only makes it necessary that we study the problem more closely. In solving it we shall doubtless learn something for the good of our own race.

**

Call of the Twentieth Century

DAVID STARR JORDAN.

[Extract from an address delivered before the State Teachers' Association of Minnesota, December, 1902.]

A new century has come upon us and it is my part tonight to appear as its advance agent, self-appointed, to set before you the work it is to do and its need of men to do it.

In most regards one century is like another. Just as men are men, so times are times. In the twentieth century there will be the same joys, the same sorrows, the same marrying and giving in marriage, the same round of work and play, of wisdom and duty, of folly and distress, which other centuries have seen. Just as each individual man has the same organs, the same passions, the same functions as all the others, so it is with all the centuries.

But you know men not by their likenesses, which are many, but by their differences, which are few and subtile, but all important in determining our likes and dislikes, our friendships, loves and hates. So with the centuries; we remember those which are past, not by the mass of common traits in history and development, but by the few events or thoughts, unnoticed at the time, but which stand out like mountain peaks raised above "oblivion's sea," when the times are all gathered in and the century begins to blend with "the infinite azure of the past." Not wars and conquests mark a century. The hosts grow small in the vanishing perspective, but the thoughts of men, their attitude toward their environment, their struggles toward duty, these are the things which endure. Compared with the centuries that are past, the twentieth century in its broad outlines will be like the rest. It will be selfish, generous, careless, devoted, fatuous, efficient. But these traits, it seems to me, must stand out above all others, and in a higher degree than any other century will be strenuous, complex and democratic.

Thanks to Roosevelt

Strenuous it must be, as we can all see, and we have to thank the young man of the twentieth century who gave us the watchword of the strenuous life. Our century has a host of things to do, bold things, noble things, tedious things. It has only a hundred years to do them in, and two of these years are gone already. We must be up and bestir ourselves. If we are called to help in this work, there is no place for an idle mniute. Idle men and idle women no doubt will cumber our ways, for there are many who have never heard of the work to do, many who will never know that there has been a new century. These the century will pass by with the gentle tolerance she shows to clams and squirrels, but on those of us whose life she claims, she will lay heavy burdens of duty.

More than any of the others, the twentieth century will be democratic. The greatest discovery of the nineteenth century was that of the reality of external things. That of the twentieth century will be this axiom in geometry: "The straightest line is the shortest distance between two points." If some thing needs doing, do it. The more plainly, directly, honestly, the better.

Trusted to Heredity

The earlier centuries cared little for the life of a man. Hence they failed to discriminate. In masses and mobs they needed kings and rulers, but could not choose them. Hence the device of selecting as a ruler the eldest son of the last ruler, whatever his nature might be. A child, a lunatic, a monster, a sage—it was all the same to these unheeding centuries. The people could not follow those they understood or who understood them. They must trust all to the blind chance of heredity.

Tyrant or figurehead, the mob, which, from its own indifference, creates the pomp of royalty, threw up its caps for the king and blindly died for him, or because of his folly, with the same unquestioning loyalty. In like manner did the mob fashion lords and princes in its own image. Not the man who would do, or think, or help, but the eldest son of a former lord was chosen for its homage. The result of it all was no use was made of the forces of nature, for those who might have learned to control them were hunted to death. The men who could think or act for themselves were in no position to give their actions leverage.

When a people really means to do something, it must resort to democracy. It must value men as men, not as functions of a chain or heredity.

Democracy does not mean equality— just the reverse of this, it means individual responsibility, equality before the law, of course—equality of opportunity, but no other equality save that won by faithful service. That social system which bids men rise must also let them fall if they cannot maintain themselves. To choose the right man means the dismissal of the wrong.

No Use for the Incompetent

The weak, the incompetent, the untrained, the dissipated find no growing welcome in the century which is coming. It will have no place for the unskilled laborers. A bucket of water and a basket of coal will do all that the unskilled laborer can do if we have skilled men for their direction. He has no part in the conduct of democracy. He exists in spite of democracy. The children of the republic are entitled to something better.

A generous education, a well-directed education should be the birthright of each one of them. Democracy may even intensify natural inequalities. The man who cannot say no to cheap and vulgar temptations falls all the lower in the degree to which he is a free agent. In competition with men alert, loyal, trained and creative, the dullard is condemned to a life of hard labor, through no direct fault of his own. Keep the capable man down and you may level the incapable up. But this the twentieth century will not do, and this it is not now doing. Sir Henry Wayne describes the progress of civilization as the movement from status to contract. This means movement from the mass to the man, from tradition to democracy.

So in this strenuous and complex age, this age of "fierce democracy," what have we to do, and with what manner of men shall we do it? Young men of the twentieth century, will your times find place for you? Plenty to do in every direction and all the space I can take would be filled by a mere enumeration. In agriculture a whole great empire is yet to be won in the arid West, and the West that is not arid and the East that never was, must be turned into one vast market garden.

The twentieth century will treat a farm as a friend and it will yield returns for such friendship. In the twentieth century vast regions will be reclaimed to civilization, not by imperialism, but by permeation. The table lands of Mexico, the plains of Manchuria, the Pampas of Argentine, the moors of Northern Japan, all these regions in our temperate zone offer a welcome to the Anglo-Saxon farmer.

Science of Medicine Advancing

In medicine the field of action is growing infinitely broader, now that its training is securely based on science, and the divining-rod no longer classed among its implements of precision. Not long ago, it is said, a young medical student in New York committed suicide, leaving behind this touching phrase: "I die because there is room for no more doctors." And this is just now, when, for the first time, it is worth while to be a doctor. Room for no more doctors, no doubt, of the kind to which he belonged—men who know nothing and care nothing for science and its methods, who have no feeling for their patients and whose prescriptions are given with no more conscience than goes into the fabrication of an electric belt or the compounding of a patent medicine.

What is true in medicine applies also to the profession of law. The pettifogger must give place to the jurist. The law is not a device for getting around the statutes. It is the science and art of equity. The lawyers of the future will not be the pleaders before juries. They will save their clients from need of judge or jury. In every civilized nation the lawyers must be the law givers. The sword has given place to the green bag. The demand of the twentieth century will be that the statutes coincide with equity. This condition educated lawyers can bring about. To know equity is to be its defender.

Need Serious Politicians

In politics the demand for serious service must grow. As we have to do with wise men and clean men, statesmen, instead of vote manipulators, we shall feel more and more the need of them. We shall demand not only men who can lead in action, but men who can prevent unwise action. Often the policy which seems most attractive to the majority is full of danger for the future. We need men who can face popular opinion, and if need be, to face it down. The best citizen is not afraid to cast his vote away by voting with the minority.

The need of the teacher will not grow less as the century goes on. The history of the future is written in the schools of today, and the reform which gives us better schools is the greatest of reforms. It is said that the teacher's noblest work is to lead the child to his inheritance. This is the inheritance he would win; the truth that men have tested in the past and the means by which they were led to know that it was truth. "Free should the scholar be —free and brave," and to such as these the twentieth century will bring the reward of the scholar.

The twentieth century will mark an epoch in the history of religion. Some say, idly, that religion is losing her hold in these strenuous days. But she is not. She is simply changing her grip. The religion of this century will be more practical, more real. It will deal with the days of the week as well as with the Sabbath. It will be as patent in the marts of trade as in the walls of a cathedral, for man's religion is his working hypothesis of life, not of life in some future world, but of life right here today, the only day we have in which to build a life.

The man of the twentieth century will be a hopeful man. He will love the world and the world will love him. "There is no hope for you," Thoreau once said, "unless this bit of sod under your feet is the sweetest for you in this world—in any world." The effective man takes his reward as he goes along. Nowhere is the sky so blue, the grass so green, the opportunities so choice, as now, here, today, the time, the place where his work must be done.

The man who can trust is a man of character. It was said of Lincoln that he was "a man too simply great to scheme for his proper self." This man who schemes for his own advancement, who can lay pipes and pull wires may seem to succeed. "God censents, but only for a time." Sooner or later, if he lives long enough, the selfish man finds his end in utter failure.

The men who control the twentieth century will be religious men. They will not be religious in the fashion of monks, ascetics, mystic dreamers or emotional enthusiasts. Their religion will be their working hypothesis of life. And in the wise and helpful life it will find ample justification. It will deal with the world as it is in the service of the "God of things as they are." It will find God's world not a vale of tears, a sink of iniquity, but a world in which the rewards of right living are instant and constant. It will find that indeed his service is perfect freedom, for the great things of the world are done in His way and His way only.

**

Normal Schools

Dr. Charles De Garmo, Cornell University.

Half a century of experience with normal schools has demonstrated the fact that they can promote the cause of education in the preparation of elementary teachers, better than can any other agency. So far they have had to stand largely alone in securing the means of existence. The time for such isolated struggle for survival should now be a thing of the past, and all educational forces should unite for the adequate development of these schools. Their support should by no means depend either upon their importunity or upon their political influence, but upon their capacity to promote the cause of education; it should originate quite as much outside as inside the schools themselves.

The first reason why normal schools should be more liberally supported is that they have too few teachers to do their work in the most effective way. Is there any just reason why the students of a normal school should not have as many teachers as an equal number of college or university students? Yet the college or university has twice as many teachers for a given body of students as has the normal school. It is a fortunate normal school that has one teacher for every twenty students, yet almost every college and university in the country has a teacher for every ten students. Again, the work of the normal school is much more intensive than that of the university; for the one must do its training in two years, whereas the other has four. The normal school is therefore at a double disadvantage, since it has but half the teaching force and half the time enjoyed by the university and college.

There are two especially deplorable results that arise from an adequate number of teachers. They are, first, the passive, listening attitude of mind engenered by mass teaching; and second, the necessity of a fixed curriculum for all. The evils of mass teaching are too well known to need discussion. Not even in elementary education is it longer possible for every one to do everything. Besides the common branches, think of music, drawing, cooking, manual training for both boys and girls, decoration and design, nature study in all sciences for all grades, etc. Moreover, different persons have differing capacities, tastes and educational destinations. It must be evident from these and other considerations, that it is a wasteful public policy to compel the normal school longer to put up with half the teachers it ought to have.

The second reason why the normal schools should have better financial support is that they may be enabled more radidly to continue the improvement they have begun in the quality of their teaching force. Correspondence with some forty of the representative normal schools of the United States shows that in nearly all, the number of college and university-trained teachers has doubled, and in many cases quadrupled, within the last fifteen years. Indeed, it is rare to find a school in which for a man, at least, such training is not now required a requisite to appointment. If the best college and university-trained men are to be attracted to these schools and kept in them, better salaries must be paid. In such a country as ours, $1,000 a year will secure an unlimited number of $1000 candidates, but in the end they must prove to be inexperienced or in some important respect inefficient. The normal school ought to be able to secure the best educational talent to be found in the United States. It should be able to attract the Stanley Halls, the Deweys, and the Parkers to its principalship, and equally good men in the realm of teaching to its faculty. Nothing else would so rapidly improve the public school as to have its teachers taught by the best minds. But it is vain to expect a ten-thousand-dollar man to teach for the pittance that will barely support him in decency from day to day, leaving little or nothing for improvement or for the future. He must, in justice to his future family, turn to another profession, to business, to engineering, or even to the farm. The salaries of our normal school principals should be from four to six thousand dollars per year, and that of the professors from two to four thousand. These schools are doing all that now lies in their power to improve their teaching force, but they suffer the double affliction of their poverty, for the salaries they can offer are both low in amount and few in number.

The third reason why the normal school should be more liberally supported is that its present work should be multiplied. Where it now trains one teacher, it ought to train five. To attain this result more than the appropriation of more money is needed, for just as debased coin will displace good money, so cheap and inadequate training for teachers will, if given full credit, displace that which is more efficient, even if the better is only a little more expensive. In the training of teachers, there ought always to be a surplus of inducement on the side of the more thoro preparation. If a teacher can secure a permanent license by taking a training that is brief, cheap, easy, and inadequate, the economic motive alone will keep that teacher away from the normal school, where she would secure a professional education imparted not by one person alone, but by a faculty; not for a year only, but for two or more years. I do not deplore this cheap and inadequate local training as the beginning of a teacher's preparation, but if it is allowed to be her final preparation, the teaching force of the country will never attain half the efficiency of which it is capable. The state of New York has women enough to teach her schools who will prepare themselves in the best possible way, if required or induced to do so. The state is financially able to give them the finest training to be found in the world. All that is necessary is that money enough be appropriated and that the surplus of inducement be on the side of the better professional preparation.

The only other reason I shall now urge for more generous support of normal schools, is that these schools should be enabled greatly to extend the range of their work. Whatever concerns the welfare of the best elementary schools, whether in cities or elsewhere, is the legitimate field of the normal school. These institutions should be places where any person may find instruction in any subject that may properly be taught to children. This means that students should have the opportunity of preparing to teach manual training both to boys and to girls in all grades, to become experts in the elements of domestic science, to understand the art of adornment of person and dwelling, to become expert in drawing, designing, moulding, weaving, etc.; as well as to become able to teach the various aspects of nature work in the grades. Such work requires division of labor for the student and multiplication of teaching force in the faculty. Yet if our normal schools are to be the fertile source of new ideas, if they are to infuse the potent spirit of their unquenchable enthusiasm to successive generations of teachers, these things they must do, this support and extention they must have.—*American Education.*

* * *

Gov. Geo. C. Pardee's Address Charter Day—University of California.
[Extract]

The time will never come when the University of California can ever say that the present Governor of this State has been false to his Alma Mater; and I hope the time will never come when the finger of scorn can be pointed at him, or scorn and contumely heaped upon the name of a representative University man and graduate. I believe that there is work to do, work of the greatest importance to this State, and work of the greatest importance to the community, by you young people who sit here on the floor of Harmon Gymnasium today, and who, in a shorter or longer period, will go out into life and become integers in the community of this State and of this world. If you are false to this, if you are false to your University, then you are false to the State. You are ingrates in the deepest sense of the word and have done an injury to the institution which you will then have disgraced.

Therefore, I say to you again, young people, do not forget the debt you owe to yourselves, the debt that you owe to our Alma Mater, and the debt you owe to the people of this State, and when the opportunity is offered you to do the service of this State, be men and women and refuse it not.

Official Department

State Board of Education

GEORGE C. PARDEE, *President of the Board* .... Governor, Sacramento
MORRIS ELMER DAILEY....... ....President State Normal School, San Jose
E. T. PIERCE............................... ....President State Normal School, Los Angeles
C. C. VAN LIEW ....President State Normal School, Chico
BENJAMIN IDE WHEELER......... ....,......President University of California, Berkeley
ELMER E. BROWN .... Prof. of Theory and Practice of Education, University of Cal., Berkeley
SAMUEL T. BLACK ....President State Normal School, San Diego
FREDERIC BURK ....President State Normal School, San Francisco
THOMAS J. KIRK, *Secretary of the Board* ..... Superintendent Public Instruction, Sacramento

THE NEW SCHOOL LAWS

SACRAMENTO, March 27, 1903.

Editor Harr Wagner, San Francisco, Cal.:—If I can get the time I wish to review all the educational measures that have been passed by the legislature and approved by the Governor and have you print the article in the JOURNAL, but my time is closely occupied and I leave on the 2nd of April for a trip of about ten days on a visit to the state institutions in the south, beginning at San Jose. Calls for sundry measures that have been passed are made upon me every day, and I. cannot obtain bills to supply all that ask for them. I think that you could not do better than to publish a number of the measures in full, and I herewith hand you Assembly Bill 37 (Drew), the so-called text-book bill; Assembly Bill 27 (Foster), an act to enforce the educational rights of children; Assembly Bill 345 (Leininger), amending section 1763 by requiring a majority of all the appointive members of the County Board of Education to be experienced teachers holding not lower than grammar school certificates, and providing that in counties where there are high schools at least one of the members to be appointed on the county board of education shall hold a high school certificate; Assembly Bill 352 (Dougherty) is important to school superintendents in apportioning library funds. It increases the amount to be apportioned to districts having five or more teachers. Assembly Bill 532 (Black) is a measure now being much inquired about. It is a new section added to the Political Code, providing for the formation and maintenance of union school districts and. for transportation of pupils to a central school. I believe that no matter more important to the school interests of the state could be published in the April number of the JOURNAL than these bills which have now become law. Very truly yours,

THOMAS J. KIRK,
Superintendent of Public Instruction.

The School Text-Book Law

An act amending section 1874 of the Political Code, providing for the appointment of a standing committee of the state board of education on school text-books; authorizing said committee subject to approval of the state board of education to revise, compile, and manufacture school text-books; prescribing the duties of said committee relating to copyrights, engravings, plates, and other matters for printing and publishing school text-books; providing a royalty fund; authorizing the payment of royalties and the hire of plates of copyright matter, and for the performance of other acts necessary to procure a meritorious, uniform series of state school text-books; granting powers, subject to the approval of the state board. of education, to said committee to prescribe and enforce the use of such school text-books, and to adopt a list of books from which county and city and county boards of education must select books for supplementary use in the primary and grammar schools; prescribing books for use in various branches of study taught in the primary and grammar schools; providing the penalty for failure to use the state series of school text-books; authorizing such committee to appoint a secretary; prescribing the duties of such secretary and fixing his compensation; prescribing the duties of the superintendent of public instruction upon the publication or revision and adoption of a book or a number of books of the state series; providing that the superintendent of state printing shall have supervision over the mechanical work of printing such text-books; making an appropriation, to be known as the text-book appropriation, and specifying the uses to which it may be put; directing of what funds the state school book fund shall consist, and prescribing the use of the moneys in said fund and continuing the present law for the distribution of state school text-books.

The people of the State of California, represented in senate and assembly, do enact as follows:

SECTION 1. Section eighteen hundred and seventy four of the Political Code is hereby amended to read as follows:

1874. 1. In compiling or causing to be compiled and adopted a uniform series of school text-books for use in the common schools of the state, as required by section seven (7) of article nine (9) of the State Constitution, the state board of education shall, within thirty days after the passage of this act, meet and appoint three members of said board, to wit, the governor, the superintendent of public instruction and one other member of said state board of education as a standing committee on school text-books. The said committee shall be designated and known as the state text-book committee, and shall immediately organize and enter upon the discharge of its duties, and shall have power, subject to the approval of the state board of education, to revise in whole or in part and to manufacture such text books as are now in use; to compile or cause to be compiled under its direction, and to manufacture such other or additional text-book or books as it may deem necessary or proper for use in the primary and grammar schools (the common schools) of the state; to purchase or hire plates, maps, and engravings of copyright matter; to contract for, or lease copyrights, for the purpose of being used in compiling, printing and publishing such books; to provide for the payment of royalties or for the leasing of plates for the making of the whole or any part of a book or books, and to do any and all acts that may be necessary for the purpose of procuring a meritorious uniform series of text-books for use in all the primary and grammar schools of the State of California. Said committee shall have power, subject to the approval of the state board of education, to prescribe and enforce the use of a uniform series of text-books, and to adopt a list of books for supplementary use from which county and city and county boards of education shall select and adopt books for supplementary use in primary and grammar schools in their respective counties and cities and counties, as required by section seventeen hundred and twelve of the political code. As soon as any text-book shall have been compiled, printed, adopted, and is ready for distribution, it shall be the duty of every county and city and county superintendent of schools in the state to order a sufficient number thereof to give at least one copy of every such book to every public school district library in the county or city and county in which he is superintendent, and payment therefor shall be made by him by drawing his requisition without the order of the board of school trustees against the library funds of the respective districts in his county or city and county for the cost and remitting the same to the official who has charge of the sale of state school text-books. In cities where the city school superintendent or city board of education is accustomed to draw requisitions upon the library funds, it is hereby made the duty of such superintendents or boards of education to order and pay for copies of books of the state series for their school libraries as hereby provided in lieu of the county superintendents.

2. Instruction shall be given in the following subjects in the primary and grammar schools of the state in the several grades in which they may be required, viz: Reading, writing, orthography, language lessons, and English grammar, arithmetic, geography, history of the United States, elements of physiology and hygiene, vocal music, elementary bookkeeping, drawing, nature study, and civil government; and it shall be the duty of the said text-book committee to revise such of the books of the present state series or publish such new ones in any of the above-mentioned subjects as may be necessary for the proper study and teaching of them, and for the purposes of compilation and publication may make use of any copyright matter deemed suitable, and may purchase or hire plates, maps, or engravings of such copyright matter, may contract and arrange for the payment of royalties, and shall designate such book or books, when published, as belonging to and forming a part of the state series of school text-books, subject to the approval of the state board of education.

3. The said text-book committee shall elect a secretary, who shall be a person of recognized educational ability and experience, who shall be provided with an office at the state capitol in Sacramento in connection with that of the superintendent of public instruction, and who shall keep the books, accounts, and all records of the said committee and perform such other duties as may from time to time be required of said secretary by said committee. Said secretary shall hold office at the pleasure of the committee and shall receive a salary of one hundred and sixty-five dollars per month, payable monthly in the same manner and from the same fund as the salaries of state officers are paid.

4. The said text-book committee may secure copyrights, in the name of the people of the State of California, to any book that may be compiled under this act, and whenever any one or more of the state school text-books shall have been compiled, published, and adopted, the superintendent of public instruction shall issue an order to all county and city and county boards of education by sending notice by registered mail to the secretaries of all such boards requiring the uniform use of said book or books in all the primary and grammar schools of this state, and when said order shall have thus been given and published, the same shall remain in force and effect for a term of not less than four nor more than eight years; *provided*, that said order for the uniform use of said book or books shall not take effect until the expiration of at least one year from the time of the completion, purchase, or the leasing of the electrotype plates of said book or books; but nothing in this act shall be construed to prevent any county, city, or city and county from adopting any one or more of the state series of school text-books whenever said book or books shall have been published and is ready for distribution; *provided, further,* that whenever any plates, maps, or engravings of any publisher or author are adopted for use as hereinbefore provided, the state text-book committee shall enter into a contract for not less than four nor more than eight years for the use of the same, and shall require a good and suf-

ficient bond of the owner of such plates, maps or engravings, guaranteeing that the same shall be kept revised and up to date as may be required by the state board of education.

5. Any county, city and county, city or school district that refuses or neglects to use the state series of school textbooks in the grades and in the subjects for which they are intended and at the time as required in the foregoing subdivisions of this act must, upon satisfactory proof of such refusal or neglect, have the state money to which it is otherwise entitled, withheld from it by the superintendent of public instruction.

6. The superintendent of state printing shall have the supervision of all mechanical work connected with the printing and publishing of such books as may be compiled and adopted by said text book committee and approved by the state board of education, and all such printing and binding shall be done in the state printing office. The superintendent of state printing shall annually on the first day of July, and oftener, if requested, submit to the said text-book committee a detailed statement showing the number and name of books of the state series published by him during each year.

7. Whenever any book authorized to be published under this act is ready for sale or delivery to pupils, the state printer shall submit to the said text-book committee, and it in turn to the state board of education, an itemized statement, showing the exact cost of the material, printing, binding, and finishing of such book in editions of five thousand or more, and the state board of education shall thereupon determine and fix the price of such book as required by law, by adding to the cost of manufacturing, the price contracted to be paid as royalty, or for the use of the plates, maps or engravings of the copyright matter therein contained, and said price shall be deemed to be the whole cost of publication of such book at Sacramento. The amount fixed for royalty or cost of plates of copyright matter shall, as the books are sold, be kept separate from other proceeds from the sale of state school text-books, and deposited in the state treasury to the credit of a fund to be designated and known as the "Text-Book Royalty Fund," the same to be paid out quarterly or semi-annually, as may be agreed between the owners of copyright matter and said text-book committee, on the order of the said state text-book committee, in payment of royalties or hire of plates, maps or engravings of copyright matter in the same manner as other claims upon the state treasurer are paid.

8. The sum of twenty thousand dollars is hereby appropriated out of any money in the state treasury not otherwise appropriated, for the purpose of carrying out the provisions of this act. Said appropriation, which shall be known as the "text-book appropriation," shall be subject to the drafts of the said text-book committee for all the expenses incurred by it, except the salary of the secretary, which is otherwise provided for in this act; *provided*, that all claims shall be presented to the state board of examiners for their approval; said appropriation shall be subject to the drafts of the said committee for all moneys needed for the payment of royalties, for the purchase or hire of such plates, maps, or engravings that may be necessary but which can not be arranged to be paid for as provided in subdivision seventh hereof, for expert opinions as provided for in subdivision nine of this act, for printing, stationery, postage, and expressage that will be required by said commiteee, and for manufacturing any edition of any book of

the state series now in use or which may hereafter be adopted for use in the primary and grammar schools. It is provided that all moneys that have been received or that may hereafter be received from the sales of state series of school text-books, except that which is received in payment of royalties and provided in this act to be deposited to the credit of the text-book royalty fund, shall be kept by the state treasurer as a separate and distinct fund, to be known as the "state school book fund," which fund shall be subject to the drafts of the said text-book committee for all expenses incurred by the superintendent of state printing for all material, labor, and other expenses necessary in the mechanical work of printing and publishing state school text-books; all claims to be drawn after being certified to by the superintendent of state printing, as provided in subdivision four of section five hundred and twenty-six of the Political Code; *provided*, that all demands on the state school book fund shall be presented to the state board of examiners in itemized form for their approval; and upon the approval of the state board of examiners, the state controller is hereby authorized and directed to draw his warrant, and the state treasurer is hereby authorized and directed to pay the same, in conformity with the provision of this section.

9. Before selecting any text-book matter to be used in the compilation or revision of a state school text-book, the said committee may, subject to the approval of the state board of education, secure one or more educational experts to examine and give their opinions on the merits of any book or books or parts of a book that may be taken under consideration, and the claims for payment of such expert service shall be paid in like manner as other claims are paid out of the state text-book appropriation; *provided*, that the expense of such expert examination and opinion shall not exceed the sum of two hundred dollars ($200.00) for any one book that may be adopted and published as a book of the state series.

10. The existing law which provides the manner and the means for the distribution of state school text-books is hereby continued in force and effect.

SEC. 2. All acts and parts of acts in conflict with this act are hereby repealed.

SEC. 3. This act shall take effect immediately.

* * *

Compulsory Education

An act to enforce the educational rights of children and providing penalties for violation of the act.

The people of the State of California, represented in senate and assembly, do enact as follows:

SECTION 1. Unless excused as hereinafter provided, each parent, guardian, or other person, in the State of California, having control or charge of any child between the ages of eight and fourteen years, shall be required to send such child to a public school, during each school year, for a period of at least five months of the time during which a public school shall be in session, in the city or city and county or school district in which said child resides, and at least eighteen weeks of such attendance shall be consecutive; *provided*, that should it be shown to the satisfaction of the board of education of the city or city and county, or of the board of trustees of the school district, in which such child resides, that the child's bodily or mental condition is such as to prevent or render inadvisable attendance at school, or application to study, a certificate from any reputable physician that the child is not able to attend school, or that its attendance is inadvisable, must be taken as satisfactory evidence by any such board, or proof being given that the parents or parent are extremely poor or sick, and that the services of the child are actually needed to support such parents or parent; or that such child is being taught in a private school, or by a private tutor, or at home by any person capable of teaching, in such branches as are usually taught in the primary and grammar schools of this state; or that no public school is located within two miles, by the nearest traveled road, of the residence of the child; or that the child has completed the prescribed grammar school course; then it shall be the duty of such board of education or board of trustees, upon application of the parent, or guardian, or other person having the control or charge of such child, to excuse such child from attendance at school, during the continuance of such defect or condition upon which such excuse is granted; *and provided further*, that circumstances rendering attendance impracticable or dangerous to health, owing to unusual storm or other sufficient cause, shall work an exemption from the penalties of this act. If any parent or guardian or other person having control or charge of any such child presents proof to such board of education or board of trustees, by affidavit, that he is unable to compel such child to attend school, said parent, guardian or other person shall be exempt from the penalties of this act, as regards the subsequent non-attendance at school of such child, and said child may, in the discretion of such board, be deemed a truant and subject to assignment to the parental school.

SEC. 2. Any parent, guardian, or other person having control or charge of any such child, who shall fail to comply with the provisions of this act, shall, unless excused or exempted therefrom as hereinbefore provided, be deemed guilty of a misdemeanor, and upon conviction, shall be liable, for the first offense, to a fine of not more than ten dollars or to imprisonment for not more than five days, and for each subsequent offense he shall be liable to a fine of not less than ten nor more than fifty dollars, or to imprisonment for not less than five days nor more than twenty-five days, or to both such fine and imprisonment.

SEC. 3. The board of education of any city or city and county, or the board of trustees of any school district, shall, on the complaint of any person, make full and impartial investigation of all charges against parents or guardians or other persons having control or charge of any such child, for violation of any of the provisions of this act. If it shall appear upon such investigation that any such parent or guardian or other person has violated any of the provisions of this act, it is hereby made the duty of the secretary of such board of education, except as hereinafter provided, or the clerk of such board of trustees, to make and file in the proper court a criminal complaint against such parent, guardian or other person, charging such violation, and to see that such charge is prosecuted by the proper authorities; *provided*, that in cities, and cities and counties having an attendance officer or officers, such officer or officers shall, under the direction of the board of education, or the city superintendent of schools, make and file such complaint, and see that such charge is prosecuted by the proper authorities.

Sec. 4. The board of education of any city, or city and county, may appoint and remove at pleasure one or more attendance officers of such city, or city and county, and shall fix their compensation, not exceeding one thousand dollars per annum for any such officer, payable from the county or special school fund of such city or city and county, and shall prescribe their duties, not inconsistent with law, and make rules and regulations for the performance thereof; *provided*, that in any city, or city and county, containing less than twenty thousand school census children, not more than one attendance officer shall be appointed, and in any city, or city and county, containing more than twenty thousand school census children, not more than one attendance officer shall be appointed for each twenty thousand school census children, or fraction greater than one half thereof.

Sec. 5. It shall be the duty of the attendance officer to arrest during school hours, without warrant, any child between eight and fourteen years of age, found away from his home, and who has been reported to him by the teacher, the superintendent of schools, or other person connected with the school department as a truant from instruction upon which he is lawfully required to attend within the city, or city and county. He shall forthwith deliver the child so arrested either to the parent, guardian or other person having control or charge of such child, or to the teacher from whom said child is then a truant, or if such child shall have been declared an habitual truant, he shall bring such child before a magistrate for commitment by him to a parental school, as provided in this act. The attendance officer shall report promptly such arrest, and the disposition made by him of such child, to the school authorities of such city, or city and county. Any child may be reported, in the meaning of this act, who shall have been absent from school without valid excuse more than three days or tardy on more than three days, any absence for a part of a day being regarded as a tardiness. Any child who has once been reported as a truant and who is again absent from school, without valid excuse, one or more days, or tardy on one or more days, may again be reported as a truant. Any child may be deemed an habitual truant who shall have been reported as a truant three or more times. Any child who has once been declared an habitual truant and who, in a succeeding year, is reported as a truant from school one or more days or tardy on one or more days without valid excuse, may be again declared an habitual truant.

Sec. 6. The board of education of any city, or city and county, may establish schools in a manner hereinafter prescribed, or set apart rooms in public school buildings for children between eight and fourteen years of age, who are habitual truants from instruction upon which they are lawfully required to attend, or who are insubordinate or disorderly during their attendance upon such instruction, or irregular in such attendance. Such school or room shall be known as a parental school. A parental school, as herein designated and provided for, shall be one of the primary and grammar schools of the city, or city and county, and the teachers therein, shall have the same qualifications and be employed and paid in the same manner as in other primary and grammar schools; but such parental school shall be established and maintained specially for the instruction therein of such pupils, between the ages of eight and fourteen years, as shall be committed thereto as provided in this act, and no pupil shall be committed to, or required to, attend, such school, except as in this act provided. Said board of education may make such special rules and regulations for the government of a parental school as shall be consistent with the provisions and purposes of this act and not contrary to law. Such board may provide for the detention, maintenance and instruction of such children in such schools; and such board or the city superintendent of schools in any city, or city and county, may, after reasonable notice to any such child, and an opportunity for the child to be heard, and with the consent of the parent, guardian or other person having control or charge of such child, order such child to attend such school, or to be detained and maintained therein for such period and under such rules and regulations as such board may prescribe, not exceeding the remainder of the school year. If such parent, guardian, or person having control or charge of such child shall not consent to such order, such child may be proceeded against under this act. If any child, in any city, or city and county in which a parental school shall be established, shall be an habitual truant, or be irregular in attendance at school, within the meaning of these terms as defined in this act, or shall be insubordinate or disorderly during attendance at school, it shall be the duty of the attendance officer, or of the secretary of the board of education if there be no attendance officer, to make and file a complaint against such child, in the proper court, charging the fact, and to see that such charge is prosecuted by the proper authority; and if the court, upon the hearing of such complaint, shall find that such charge is sustained, the court shall render judgment that such child be committed to, and be detained and maintained in, a parental school in such city, or city and county, for a term not to exceed the remainder of the current school year; *provided,* that if the parent, guardian or other person having control or charge of such child shall, within three days after the rendition of such judgment, execute a good and sufficient bond to the board of education of the city or city and county in which said court is situated, with sufficient sureties, in the sum of two hundred dollars, conditioned that such child will, during the remainder of such current school year, regularly attend some public or private school in such city, or city and county, and not be insubordinate or disorderly during such attendance, such bond to be approved by the judge of said court and be filed with the secretary of the board of education, then such court shall make an order suspending the execution of such judgment so long as the condition of such bond shall be complied with. If the condition of such bond be violated, such court, upon receiving satisfactory evidence of the fact in any action brought therefor, shall make an order declaring such bond forfeited and directing such judgment to be thenceforth enforced. Such board of education may, at any time within one year after any such bond shall be declared forfeited, have execution issued against any or all of the parties to such bond, to collect the amount thereof; and all moneys paid or collected on such bond shall be paid over to the parental school fund of such city, or city and county. No fees shall be charged or received by any court or officer in any proceeding under this section. The confinement of any child in a parental school shall be conducted with a view to the improvement of the child and to its restoration, as soon as practicable, to the school which he would, if not so confined, be required to attend. The city superintendent of schools, or, if there be no city superintendent, the board of education of any city, or city and county, shall have authority, in their discretion, to parole at any time any child committed to, or ordered to attend, a parental school, except when such commitment shall be by judgment or order of a court; and when such commitment of any child shall be by judgment or order of a court, such court may, on the recommendation of the city superintendent of schools, or the board of education, make an order paroling such child, upon such terms and conditions as shall be specified in the order. The expense incurred by any city, or city and county, in purchasing or renting a school site, erecting or renting a building and equipping the same, for the maintenance of a parental school, shall be paid out of funds other than those collected for the maintenance of schools. The salaries of teachers and the expense for all school supplies in a parental school shall be paid out of the same funds from which similar salaries and expense are paid for primary and grammar schools, but all other expense incurred in the maintenance of such parental schools shall be paid out of the parental school fund.

SEC. 7. Whenever any board of education shall determine that it is necessary or expedient for the city or city and county to establish and maintain a parental school, said board shall furnish to the city council, or other governing body of such city or city and county, all necessary and required information and statistics, and if, after consideration, such city council or other governing body grants its consent for the establishment of such parental school, then the board of education shall furnish to the authorities whose duty it is to levy taxes in such city, or city and county, thirty days before the time specified by law for fixing the annual tax rate, an estimate of the cost of purchasing or renting a suitable site, and also an estimate of the cost of renting or erecting a suitable building and equipping the same for occupancy as a parental school, and the cost to the city or city and county, other than for salaries of teachers and for school supplies, of conducting the school for the remainder of the current school years. When, pursuant to such consent by such governing body, such estimates shall have been so made and furnished by the board of education of any city, or city and county, it is hereby made the duty of the authorities whose duty it shall be to levy taxes in such city, or city and county, at the time of levying the taxes, to levy a special tax upon all taxable property of said city, or city and county, sufficient in its judgment to provide for the facilities requested by the board of education, and from which such estimates shall have been furnished. It shall be the duty of the board of education, yearly, thereafter, to present to the authorities of the city, or city and county, whose duty it is to levy taxes, on or before the first Monday in July, an estimate of the moneys required for conducting the parental school for the school year, other than for the salaries of teachers and for school supplies. When such estimate shall have been so presented, it shall be the duty of said authorities to levy a special tax upon the taxable property of said city, or city and county, sufficient to maintain such school for the year, exclusive of salaries of teachers and expense of school supplies. All taxes in this act provided for shall be computed, entered upon the tax roll and collected, in the same manner as other taxes are computed, entered and collected, and when collected shall be placed in a separate fund, to be known as the "parental school fund," and shall be paid out on the order of the board of education for the purposes set forth in this act; *provided,* that all moneys so collected for the purchase of sites or buildings, or the erection or equipment of buildings for parental school purposes, shall be placed in a separate fund, to be known as the "parental school building fund," and shall be used solely for the purpose or purposes for which collected, except that after such purpose or purposes shall have been fully accomplished, the residue of such fund, if any, may be transferred to said parental school fund.

SEC. 8. Two or more school districts or cities may unite in the following manner, to form a joint district for the maintenance of a joint parental school. When any board of education or board of school trustees has secured, in the manner as set forth in section 7 of this act, the consent of the legislative body of the city or school district, in which said board of education or board of school trustees holds office, for the union of two or more districts to form a joint parental school district, said board of education or board of trustees shall transmit such information to the board of supervisors of the county of which said city or school district or districts forms a part, setting forth at the same time the cities or districts with which said city or district seeks to unite for the maintenance of a joint parental school. When such information has been received by the board of supervisors from all the cities or school districts seeking to be united, it is hereby made the duty of the board of supervisors, by resolution, to declare such cities or school districts united for the maintenance of a joint parental school, to be known as the joint parental school district of (give the names of the school districts uniting). When the districts have been so united, the boards of education or boards of trustees of the cities or school districts so uniting shall appoint a board of trustees for the joint parental school district, to consist of five members, (unless the number of cities or school districts uniting exceeds five), who shall be appointed from the membership of the boards of the several districts or cities uniting, by the respective boards in approximate proportion to the census children between five and seventeen years of age, in the districts uniting; *provided however,* that each district shall be represented by at least one member on the board of trustees of the joint parental school district. The members so appointed, to serve for the remainder of the term of office for which they were elected on their respective boards of education or boards of trustees, and when vacancies occur on said board of trustees of joint parental school districts, they shall be filled by the board making the original appointment. The superintendent of schools of each of the cities or school districts uniting, shall be ex-officio members of the board of trustees of the joint parental school district, without the right to vote. In the management of a parental school within a school district, city, or city and county, the right to transport pupils to and from school at public expense, when, in the judgment of the board of education, or board of school trustees, the interest of the pupil demands it, is hereby conferred upon such boards. All the powers and duties by any section of this act conferred or imposed upon the boards of school trustees or boards of education of any city, or city and county, in the management of, and the securing of, funds for a parental school within a city or school district, are hereby conferred upon and imposed upon the board of trustees of any joint parental school district in the management of and the securing of funds for the support of a joint parental school; *provided however,* that in estimating the expense of maintenance of a joint parental school the amount of money needed for the payment of teachers' salaries for the furnishing of school supplies, shall be included in the estimate of expenses; *and provided further,* that the estimates shall be transmitted to the board of supervisors of the county of which the joint parental school district forms a part. When such estimates shall have been so transmitted, it is hereby made the duty of the board of supervisors to levy a special tax upon the taxable property within the boundaries of the joint parental school district, sufficient to provide the facilities requested by the board of trustees of the joint parental school district, and for which such estimates shall have been furnished, and yearly thereafter when the estimates of the total expense of the maintenance of the joint parental school and increased facilities shall have been furnished the board of supervisors, it shall be the duty of said board to levy a special tax sufficient to maintain the school for the year. All taxes in this act provided shall be computed and entered upon the tax roll and collected in the manner prescribed for the collection of taxes in section 7 of this act; *provided,* that all moneys so collected shall be collected by the county tax collector and apportioned to the credit of the joint parental school district, and placed in the fund for which they were specially collected. If for sites or buildings, to be placed in a fund known as the joint parental school building fund, to be used exclusively for the purposes for which they were collected, the same as set forth in section 7 of this act. The board of trustees of joint parental school districts shall organize, by the election of one of their number as chairman, and by the election of a secretary who shall be the city superintendent of schools, or the secretary of a board of education or the clerk of one of the boards of education or boards of trustees of the cities, or school districts united, and such secretary shall serve without additional salary. All moneys in a joint parental school fund shall be paid out on the order of the board of trustees of the joint parental school district for the purposes herein set forth, and in the same manner that funds are paid from the ordinary school funds of a school district.

SEC. 9. All fines paid as penalties for the violation of any of the provisions of this act shall, when collected or received, be paid over by the justice or officer receiving the same to the treasurer of the city, or city and county, in which the offense was committed, to be placed to the credit of the parental school fund of such city, or city and county, if there be such a fund, otherwise to the credit of the general school fund of such city, or city and county, or to the county treasurer, to be placed to the credit of the school fund of the school district in which the offense was committed.

SEC. 10. Any parent or guardian of any deaf, dumb, or blind child, legally entitled to admission to said institution, shall send such child to said institution until such child shall have been therein for five years, or shall have reached the age of majority, unless such child shall be excused from such attendance by the board of education or board of trustees of the city, city and county, or school district in which such child resides, for the reason that the child's bodily or mental condition is such as to prevent or render inadvisable attendance at said institution, or for the reason that such child is receiving proper instruction at home or in some public or private school. Any parent or guardian failing to comply with the requirements of this section shall be guilty of a misdemeanor, and be punishable as provided in section two of this act.

SEC. 11. Any justice of the peace, or recorder of the city or city and county or any justice of the peace of the township in which the school district is located, or in which the offense is committed, shall have jurisdiction of all offenses committed under the provisions of this act.

SEC. 12. This act shall take effect and be in force from and after July 1st, nineteen hundred and three.

SEC. 13. An act entitled an act to enforce the educational rights of children, approved March 28th, eighteen hundred and seventy-four, and all acts and parts of acts in conflict with any of the provisions of this act are hereby repealed.

* * *

The Formation of Union School Districts

An act to add a new section to the Political Code of the State of California, to be known as section 1674, providing for the formation of union school districts and the maintenance therein of union schools.

The people of the State of California, represented in Senate and assembly, do enact as follows:

SECTION 1. A new section is hereby added to the Political Code, to be known as section sixteen hundred and seventy-four, to read as follows:

1674. Union school districts may be formed, and union schools may be maintained therein, as in this section provided.

First—When a majority in each district, as shown by the last preceding school census, of the head of families residing in two or more school districts in the same county, shall unite in a petition to the county superintendent of schools for the formation of a union school district, to comprise the districts so petitioning, he shall, within twenty days after receiving said petition, call an election for the determination of the question, and shall appoint three qualified electors in each of the districts petitioning to conduct the election therein: Said election shall be held separately and simultaneously at the public school house in each of the districts petitioning, and shall be called by posting notices thereof in three of the most public places in each district, one of which places shall be the public school house in each district, at least ten days before said election. Said election shall be conducted by the officers appointed for that purpose, in the manner prescribed by law for conducting school elections. The ballots at such election, in each district, shall contain the words, "For the Union School District," and the voter shall write or print after said words on his ballot the word "Yes" or the word "No." It shall be the duty of said election officers in each district to canvass the vote at said election, and report the result to the county superintendent of schools within five days subsequent to the holding of said election.

Second—If a majority of the vote cast

at such election, in each and every of such districts, shall be in favor of such union school district, the county superintendent shall (except in the case of the formation of a union district consisting of but two districts, and as hereinafter provided for in subdivision fourth of this section), within fifteen days after receiving the returns of the election held therein, direct the board of trustees in each of said districts to call a meeting of the qualified electors of their respective districts, in the manner provided in section sixteen hundred and seventeen of this code for calling district meetings. At said meeting the qualified electors shall in each district select one representative, whose powers and duties shall be as hereinafter specified. The representatives so chosen shall name the union school district, and shall have power to make temporary arrangements for the location of one or more union schools therein, and, if satisfactory apartments or buildings in a suitable location are offered or can be procured, for a consideration or at a rental which would make it advisable to accept the same, they shall have the power to secure an option of a lease on such apartment or building for a period not to exceed three years from the first day of July next ensuing. Within forty days after their selection they shall notify the county superintendent of schools that they desire to meet to locate one or more union schools in and for such union district. Thereafter the representatives so chosen shall meet in conjunction with the county superintendent of schools, at a time and place to be named by the superintendent, for the purpose of determining the location of such union school or schools. At such meeting the superintendent shall be the chairman, and shall be entitled to vote and participate in all its proceedings. Should said representatives fail to unanimously agree upon a location for such school or schools, they shall propose in writing to the county superintendent then present, or, if he is not present, they shall transmit to his office, within ten days, the names of the locations which they, or any of them, favor. Within twenty days after receiving such notice, the superintendent shall call an election as provided in subdivision one hereof, to determine the location of the union school or schools. At such election only such sites as have been named by the representatives and certified to the county superintendent shall be voted upon. Any form of ballot by which the voter signifies his choice of location or locations shall be allowed. The result of said election shall be determined and certified to the county superintendent, as provided in said subdivision one. The location or locations which receive the largest number of votes shall be chosen as the location or locations of the school or schools.

Third—A union school district, formed of school districts not all in the same county, is designated a joint union school district.

(1) When a majority in each district, as shown by the last preceding school census, of the heads of families residing in two or more districts, not all in the same county, shall unite in a petition to the county superintendents of their respective counties for the formation of a joint union school district, to comprise the districts so petitioning, it shall be the duty of each of said superintendents, within twenty days after receiving said petition, to call an election in the district or districts in his county petitioning, for the purpose of determining the question, and appoint three qualified electors in each of such petitioning districts, to conduct the election therein. Said election shall be called and conducted in all respects as specified in subdivision one of this section, except that the form of ballot shall be "For the joint union school district," and the result thereof shall be reported by the election officers in each district to the superintendent of the county in which such district is situated, within five days subsequent to the holding of said election.

(2) If a majority of the votes cast at such election, in each and every of such districts, shall be in favor of such joint union school district, the county superintendent in each county shall (except in the case of the formation of a joint union district consisting of but two districts, and as hereinafter provided for in subdi-

vision four of this section), within fifteen days after receiving the returns of the election, direct the board of trustees in the district, or districts, in his county, to call a meeting of the qualified electors, as provided in subdivision two of this section. At said meeting the qualified electors, in each district, shall elect a representative, as provided in said subdivision. The representatives so chosen shall meet at a time and place to be agreed upon among themselves, and name the joint union school district. The location of the joint union school, or schools, shall be determined by the joint action of the representatives chosen and the county superintendents of the counties, in manner and form as provided for the location of a union school, or schools.

Fourth—Proceedings for the formation of, or for admission to, a union or joint union school district may be begun at any time, but the schools in the district uniting to form, or that are admitted to, a union or joint union school district, shall remain under the control of their respective boards of trustees until the first day of July next succeeding the formation of the union or joint union district and the location of the union or joint union school, or schools, or of admission to a union or joint union district, on which first day of July the districts uniting to form the union or joint union school district, or the districts admitted to such union, shall cease to exist, except for purposes specified in this section, and the terms of office of the school trustees in said districts shall expire, and the district property of each district so uniting or admitted shall vest in such union or joint union district and pass to the control of the board of trustees of such district, to be held and disposed of by them, as provided in section sixteen hundred and seventeen of this code; *provided,* that in union or joint union school districts formed by the union of but two school districts, no selection of representatives, as provided for in subdivision two of this section, is necessary, and the two boards of trustees for the original school districts shall act as the representatives, and shall constitute the board of trustees for the new union or joint union school district, and each of such trustees shall continue in office for the term for which he was elected, except as hereinafter provided; *and provided further,* that the proceeds of any sale by the board of trustees of the union or joint union school district, of school property that originally belonged to any of the original districts, must first be applied to the discharge of any bonded indebtedness of such original district.

Fifth—In the formation of union or joint union school districts, the representatives selected according to the provisions of subdivision two of this section shall act as a board of trustees for such union or joint union school district, until the election or appointment and qualification of the regular board of trustees, as hereinafter provided.

Sixth—In union or joint union school districts, formed by the union of more than two school districts, the board of trustees shall be composed of one member elected from each district composing the union or joint union district, at the time and in the manner presented for the election of school trustees, except as otherwise provided in this section. The county school superintendent (or superintendents by concurrent action in joint union school districts) shall, in union or joint union school districts composed of three or more school districts, divide the districts composing the union or joint union school district into three classes, as nearly equal in number of school districts as possible, to be designated by him (or them) as class A, B, and C, respectively. At the first annual school election following the organization of the union or joint union school district and the location of the school or schools, the districts in class A, as so divided and designated, shall each elect a school trustee for one year; the districts in class B shall each elect a school trustee for two years; the districts in class C shall each elect a school trustee for three years; and all the trustees so elected shall constitute the board of trustees of the union or joint union school district. At each annual election thereafter, as terms of office expire, the school trustees shall be elected for three years, and, in case of expiration of term of appointment, for the unexpired term. Vacancies in the board of school trustees shall be filled by appointment by the county superintendent of schools (in case of joint union school districts by appointment by the county superintendent of the county in which the vacancy occurs), the appointee or appointees to hold until the first day of July next succeeding the appointment.

Seventh—In union or joint union school districts formed by the union of but two school districts, the board of trustees of the union or joint union district shall consist of the two boards of trustees of the districts so uniting, and each trustee shall continue to hold office for the term for which he was elected; *provided,* that should one or more additional districts at any time be admitted to such union or joint union district, the board of trustees shall then consist of one trustee from each of the original districts, as provided in subdivision six of this section, and the terms of the trustees in the two original districts and of the trustees in the district or districts admitted shall expire on the first day of July next ensuing after the admission of the third district.

Eighth—After the location of the union or joint union school, or schools, has been determined, as provided in subdivision two of this section, the representatives, acting as a board of trustees, or their successors, may erect or lease a suitable building, as they may deem most advisable. A lease shall not be made for a longer period than three years. A building may be erected under the provisions of sections eighteen hundred and thirty to eighteen hundred and thirty-nine, inclusive, of this code, relating to a district tax, or sections eighteen hundred and eighty to eighteen hundred and eighty-nine, inclusive, of this code, relating to the issuance of bonds. In all cases the plans must be approved by the county superintendent of schools of the county in which the school house is to be located.

Ninth—No change of location of any union or joint union school, when once established, shall be made, except upon a petition to the county superintendent of schools (or superintendents, in case of a joint union district), signed by two thirds of the heads of families residing in such district, as shown by the last preceding school census, and then only in accordance with all the provisions for the original location of the school, as contained in subdivisions two and three of this section.

Tenth—The powers and duties of boards of trustees in union or joint union school districts shall be such as are now, or may hereafter be, assigned by law to boards of school trustees, except as otherwise provided in this section.

Eleventh—Boards of trustees of union or joint union school districts shall hold regular meetings at the school building, at such time as may be provided in the rules and regulations adopted by them for their own government. Such meetings shall not be held less frequently than quarterly. Special meetings may be held at the call of the president of the board. Upon the request, in writing, signed by a majority of any board, the president of said board shall call a meeting thereof, pursuant to such request. Of all special meetings of any board the members thereof shall have at least two days' notice, issued and served by the clerk thereof. At special meetings no business shall be transacted other than as specified in the call therefor; *provided,* that in union and joint union districts formed by the union of more than three school districts the board may appoint an executive committee, consisting of the president and the clerk and one other member of the board, to attend to the routine business of the board, their action to be reported to the board for ratification at its first regular meeting ensuing.

Twelfth—The course of study shall be that prescribed by the proper authority, and shall embrace a period of not less than eight years, except as may be hereafter provided by law; and the text-books used shall be those adopted by the proper authorities. In joint union districts the provisions of section fifteen hundred and eighty-three of this code shall apply.

Thirteenth—The board of trustees of a union or joint union school district may contract, in such manner as they may deem best, for the transportation, to and from school, of such pupils as may seem to such board to be in need of such transportation, and shall pay for such transportation, in the usual manner, out of any funds available for the purpose; *provided,* that all such contracts for transportation shall be first approved by the county superintendent (or superintendents) of schools of the county (or counties) in which such district is situated.

Fourteenth—Whenever in their judgment it may be deemed advisable the board of trustees for any union or joint union school district may unite with the trustees of any other school district, single, union, or joint, in the employment of a supervising principal, who shall devote such time to the supervision of instruction in the several school districts and shall receive such compensation from each board of trustees as may be agreed upon by them.

Fifteenth—(1) On the first day of July next ensuing after the formation of a union or joint union school district, or the admission thereto of a school district, the county superintendent of schools (or superintendents in joint union school districts) shall transfer, by requisition upon the county auditor, all funds remaining to the credit of the different districts uniting to form the union or joint union district (or to the credit of the district admitted thereto) to the credit of such union or joint union district.

(2) For the purposes of school census enumeration and the apportionment of school moneys, the several school districts uniting to form a union or joint union school district shall be regarded as continuing their separate existence; *provided, that* but one census marshal shall be appointed to take the school census for all of such uniting districts, whose duty it shall be to take the census for each and all of such several districts and include the same, separately stated for each district, in one report; *and provided further, that* no moneys shall be apportioned directly to any of such several districts, while forming a part of an organized union or joint union school district, but there shall be apportioned to such union or joint union district the aggregate of moneys that would be apportioned to the several school districts composing it, if such several districts were not united.

Sixteenth—(1) Any school district may be admitted to a union or joint union school district by action of the board of supervisors of the county in which such school district is located, upon such terms as may be agreed upon between the board of trustees of the school district seeking admission and the board of trustees of the union or joint union school district, whenever a majority of the heads of families residing in such school district, as shown by the last preceding school census, shall present to said board of supervisors a petition for such annexation, accompanied by a petition for such annexation signed by a majority of the members composing the board of trustees of the union or joint union district to which admission is desired. The county superintendent of schools shall then classify the newly admitted district, in class A, B, or C, as provided in subdivision six of this section, for the election of a trustee thereby. If such petitioning school district and such union or joint union school district be not wholly situated in the same county, then said petitions shall be presented in duplicate to the board of supervisors of each and every county in which any part of either of such districts is situated, and such annexation shall be made only by the concurrent action of all of such boards of supervisors; and in that case the classification of the annexed district, for election of a trustee, shall be made by concurrent action of the county superintendents of each and all of such counties.

(2) A portion of a school district may be admitted to an adjacent union or joint union school district by action of the board of supervisors of the county in which such school district is situated, whenever a majority of the heads of families residing in such school district, as shown by the last preceding school census, shall present to said board of supervisors a petition for such annexation, accompanied by a petition for such annexation signed by a majority of the members com-

posing the board of trustees of the union or joint union district to which admission is desired. The board of supervisors shall attach such annexed portion of a school district to a contiguous original school district forming part of the union or joint union district, for voting and other purposes, and such annexed portion shall thereafter be a part of the original district to which it is so attached, and cannot subsequently withdraw from the union or joint union district, except as the district to which it is so attached withdraws. Such annexed portion shall have no representation on the board of trustees of the union or joint union school district, except as a part of the district to which it is attached. If such portion of a school district and such union or joint union school district be not wholly situated in the same county, then said petitions shall be presented in duplicate to the board of supervisors of each and every county in which any part of either of such districts is situated, and such annexation, and such attachment of annexed portion to one of the original districts, shall be made only by the concurrent action of all such boards of supervisors.

(3). Any school district contained in a union or joint union school district may, in like manner, withdraw from such union or joint union district by action of the board (or boards) of supervisors of the county (or counties) in which the union or joint union district is located, upon such terms as may be agreed upon between the trustee of the school district seeking to withdraw and a majority of the other members of the board of trustees of the union or joint union district, whenever a majority of the heads of families residing in the union or joint union district, including two thirds of the heads of families residing in the district seeking to withdraw, as shown by the last preceding school census, shall present to such board or boards of supervisors a petition for such withdrawal, accompanied by a written consent to such withdrawal signed by a majority of the members composing the board of trustees of such union or joint union district.

Seventeenth — Any union or joint union school district, formed under the provisions of this section, and which shall have been in existence three years or more, may be dissolved in the following manner: A petition signed by two-thirds of the heads of families residing in such district, as shown by the last preceding school census shall be presented to the county superintendent of schools of the county in which such district is situated, setting forth briefly the reasons for dissolution and praying that the question may be submitted to the voters in such district. Upon receiving such petition the superintendent shall, within twenty days, call an election in the district, submitting to the voters therein the question of dissolution of such district. If such petitioning district be not wholly situated within the same county, said petition shall be presented in duplicate to the superintendent of each county having territory within such district, and each superintendent so petitioned shall, within twenty days after receiving such petition, call an election in the territory situate within his county and forming part of such district, and appoint three electors resident within such territory to conduct such election therein. Notice of such election, which must be held throughout the district on the same day and during the same hours, shall be given by posting written or printed notice thereof in at least three of the most public places in such district for at least twelve days next before the day set for such election; and if such district be not wholly situated in the same county, said notice shall be posted for said time in three of the most public places in the portion of the district in each county. Said election shall be conducted in the manner provided by law for conducting school elections. The ballots shall have printed on them the words "for dissolution," and the voters shall write or print thereafter the word "yes" or the word "no." The election officers shall report the result of such election, within five days thereafter, to the county superintendent of schools of the county of which they are residents. If a majority of all the votes cast at such election be opposed to dissolution, no further petition shall be entertained or election ordered for a similar purpose within three years next following such election. If the district in which such election is held be wholly situated in one county, and if two thirds of all the votes cast at such election be in favor of dissolution, the county superintendent of such county shall forthwith certify the result of such election to the board of supervisors of such county, and such board shall, at its first regular meeting thereafter, make an order declaring such union district dissolved, such order to take effect at the end of the current school year, except as hereinafter provided. If the district in which such election is held be not wholly situated in one county, each of the county superintendents of the counties having territory therein shall immediately certify to the others the result of the election in his own county, and if two thirds of all the votes cast at such election be in favor of dissolution, all of such county superintendents shall, jointly, forthwith certify the result of such election to the board of supervisors of each of such counties, and said boards, and each of them, shall, at the first regular meeting thereafter, make an order declaring such union or joint union district dissolved, such order to take effect at the end of the current school year, except as hereinafter provided. When a union or joint union school district has been thus dissolved, the property thereof shall be sold by the board of supervisors of the county in which such property is situated, and the proceeds of such sale, together with any moneys in the treasury to the credit of such dissolved district, shall be apportioned to and placed to the credit of the school districts that composed such dissolved district in proportion to the value of property in each of such school districts, as determined by the last previous assessment therein for school purposes, and the board or boards of supervisors of the county or counties in which such dissolved district is situated shall make such orders, and such transfers from county to county, as may be necessary or proper to effect such apportionment. From and after the time of making of the order or orders hereinbefore provided for, declaring a union or joint union school district dissolved, the original school districts composing the same, with such additional territory as shall have been annexed to them, shall be considered to be in existence again, as separate districts, and subject to the provisions of sections fifteen hundred and ninety-three to sixteen hundred and two of this code, relating to elections for school trustees, the first of such elections in each of such districts to be held as in the case of a newly formed district; but such order or orders shall not affect the continuance of the union or joint union board of trustees, or the maintenance of the union or joint union school, until the end of the current year, at the expiration of which time such board and school shall cease to exist.

Sec. 2. This act shall take effect and be in force from and after its passage.

* * *

The Appointment of Members of County Boards of Education

An act to amend section 1768 of the Political Code of the State of California relating to county boards of education.

The people of the State of California, represented in senate and assembly, do enact as follows:

Section 1. Section 1768 of the Political Code is hereby amended to read as follows:

1768. First—Except in any city and county, there shall be a county board of education, which shall consist of the county superintendent of schools and of four other members, appointed by the board of supervisors of the county.

Second—A majority of the members appointed by the board of supervisors shall be experienced teachers, holding not lower than grammar school certificates in full force and effect.

Third—At their last regular meeting preceding the first day of July, in the year nineteen hundred and three, the board of supervisors shall appoint two persons to serve on said board of education for the period of two years; and thereafter, each and every year, the board of supervisors at the last regular meeting preceding the first day of July, shall appoint two persons to serve on said board of education for the period of two years; *provided,* that in all counties in which there are one or more high schools at least one of the appointive members of the board of education for such county or counties shall hold a certificate of the high school grade.

Fourth—If the board of supervisors of any county refuse or neglect to appoint members of the county board of education, as provided in subdivision three of this section, it shall be the duty of the county superintendent to appoint them. Should a vacancy occur at any time in the county board of education, it shall be the duty of the board of supervisors to appoint a party to fill such vacancy.

Fifth—The members of the county board of education, elected or appointed, shall qualify within ten days after receiving notice of their election or appointment.

Sixth—The county board of education shall organize on the first meeting subsequent to the first day of July in each year, by electing one of their number president of the board. The county superintendent shall be ex officio secretary of the board.

Seventh—For the transaction of business three members shall constitute a quorum; but no teacher's certificate shall be issued, renewed, or revoked, nor shall any books or apparatus be adopted, except by an affirmative vote of at least three members of the board. On the call of any member, the ayes and nays shall be taken upon any proposition, and the vote shall be recorded in the minutes of the board.

SEC. 2. All acts or parts of acts in conflict with this act are hereby repealed.

* * *

The New High School Law

An act creating a fund for the benefit and support of High Schools and providing for its distribution.

The people of the State of California, represented in senate and assembly, do enact as follows:

SECTION 1. There is hereby levied annually for the fifty-fifth and fifty-sixth fiscal years, ending respectively June thirtieth, nineteen hundred and four, and June thirtieth, nineteen hundred and five, an ad valorem tax (one and one half cents) upon every hundred dollars of the value of the taxable property of the state, which tax shall be collected by the several officers charged with the collection of state taxes, in the same manner and at the same time as other state taxes are collected, upon all and any class of property, which tax is for the support of regularly established high schools of the state. And it is further enacted that; beginning with the fifty-seventh fiscal year, to wit: July first, nineteen hundred and six, it shall be the duty of the state controller, annually, between the tenth day of August and the first day of September, at the time that he is required to estimate the amount necessary for other school taxes, to estimate the amount necessary to be levied for the support of high schools. This amount he shall estimate by determining the amount at fifteen dollars per pupil in average daily attendance in all the duly established high schools of the state for the last preceding school year, as certified to him by the state superintendent of public instruction. This amount the state controller, between the dates above given, must certify to the state board of equalization.

SEC. 2. The state board of equalization at the time when it annually determines and fixes the rate of state taxes to be collected, must declare the levy and the rate of tax for the support of state high schools in conformity with the provisions of section one of this act.

SEC. 3. The money collected as provided in sections one and two hereof, after deducting the proportionate share of expenses of collecting the same to which other taxes are subject, must be paid into the state treasury, to be by the state treasurer converted into a separate fund, hereby created, to be called the "state high school fund."

SEC. 4. The money paid into the state high school fund is hereby appropriated without reference to fiscal years for the use and support of regularly established high schools and is exempt from the provisions of part three, title one, article eighteen, of an act entitled "An act to establish a Political Code," approved March twelfth, eighteen hundred and seventy-two, relating to the state board of examiners.

SEC. 5. The money in said state high school fund shall be apportioned to the high schools of the state by the state superintendent of public instruction in the following manner: He shall apportion one third of the annual amount among the county, district, city, union, or joint union high schools of the state, irrespective of the number of pupils enrolled or in average daily attendance therein, except as hereinafter provided; the remaining two thirds of the annual amount he shall apportion among such schools pro rata upon the basis of average daily attendance as shown by the official reports of the county or city and county school superintendents for the last preceding school year; *provided*, that such high schools have been organized under the law of the state, or have been recognized as existing under the high school laws of the state and have maintained the grade instruction required by law of the high schools; *and provided*, that no school shall be eligible to a share of said state high school fund that has not during the last preceding school year employed at least two regularly certificated high school teachers for a period of not less than one hundred and eighty days with not less than twenty pupils in average daily attendance for such length of time, except in newly established high schools wherein the minimum average daily attendance for the first year of one hundred and eighty days may be but twelve pupils (and but one teacher); *and, provided*, that before receiving state aid, each school shall furnish satisfactory evidence to the superintendent of public instruction of the possession of a reasonably good equipment of building, laboratory, and library, and of having maintained, the preceding school year, proper high school instruction for a term of at least one hundred and eighty days; *provided further*, that the foregoing provisions relating to the average daily attendance and the number of teachers employed shall not operate to disqualify any legally established high school existing at the date of the passage of this act from receiving a share of said state high school fund until July 1, 1904.

SEC. 6. The principal of every high school entitled to aid in accord with the foregoing provisions shall annually at the close of the term and prior to receiving his last month's salary and as a requisite for such salary make out under oath and deliver to the county superintendent of the county or city and county wherein such high school is situated a full and complete report to show the number of pupils enrolled, the average daily attendance, number of teachers regularly employed, the courses of instruction pursued, and such other information as may be required by the superintendent of public instruction and the county superintendent of schools, the said report to be made upon blanks furnished by said superintendent of public instruction as other school report blanks are furnished; *provided*, that in the case of joint union high school districts the principals thereof shall report as above required to the county superintendents of each of the counties having territory within joint union high school districts, and in such reports the statistics of attendance and other data for each county separately and collectively shall be given.

SEC. 7. The county superintendent of every county, or city and county, wherein is located a high school, shall annually, at the time required for making reports for primary and grammar schools, make report under oath to the superintendent of public instruction, showing the number of pupils enrolled, average daily attendance, number of teachers regularly employed, and such other information regarding the high schools of his county, or city and county, as he may deem proper, or as may be required by the superintendent of public instruction; said report to be made upon blanks furnished by the superintendent of public instruction.

SEC. 8. It shall be the duty of the county or city and county superintendent of schools of every county, or city and county, wherein is located a high school, or the building or buildings of a joint union high school, on the order of the board of trustees of such high school, to draw his requisition upon the county auditor against the funds of such high school, but no requisition shall be drawn unless the money is in the fund to pay it, and no requisition shall be drawn upon the order of the board of high school trustees or board of education against the state high school fund, except for teachers' salaries, and the order shall state the monthly salary of the teacher, and name the month or months for which such salary is due. Upon the receipt of such requisition the auditor shall draw his warrant upon the county treasurer in favor of the parties for the amount stated in such requisition, and the county treasurer is hereby authorized to pay the same.

SEC. 9. High schools organized under the present law for the establishment of high schools and receiving state aid under this act shall within one year after first beginning to receive such state aid provide at least one course of study such as will prepare pupils for admission to one of the colleges of the University of California, and for that purpose said high schools shall be subject to inspection by a duly accredited representative of said university. High schools eligible to receive state aid as herein provided shall admit as students only such pupils as have completed the full course of instruction prescribed for the primary and grammar schools of the county or city and county wherein the high school is located, or an equivalent course, or such pupils as may show by thorough examination that their qualifications are equivalent to the requirements for graduation from said primary and grammar school course; *provided,* that pupils otherwise qualified to enter a high school and residing in territory wherein no high school exists shall have the right to attend any high school that receives state aid under the provisions of this act without the payment of tuition fee, if such schools have room or accommodations for them.

SEC. 10. The state controller must keep a separate account of the high school fund raised as provided in sections one and two of this act. He must on the first Monday in January and on the first Monday in July in every year report to the superintendent of public instruction a statement of all moneys belonging to the state high school fund. He must draw his warrant on the state treasurer in favor of any county or city and county treasurer whenever such treasurer presents, with his indorsement, an order drawn by the superintendent of public instruction against the state high school fund, and the case of counties having joint union high school districts the order of the superintendent of public instruction and the warrant of the state controller shall be in favor of the county treasurer of that county wherein the high school building or buildings are located or wherein the high school is being conducted.

SEC. 11. It is hereby made the duty of the treasurer of every county, or city and county, that receives state money under the provisions of this act to place the same to the credit of the funds of the respective high schools of his county, or city and county, in accord with the apportionment made by the superintendent of public instruction, and to pay out the same according to the provisions of section eight of this act.

SEC. 12. This act shall take effect and be in force from and after its passage.

School Teachers' Annuity Fund

An act authorizing any teacher or public officer who is now a contributor to a public school teachers' annuity and retirement fund in any county, or consolidated city and county, of this state, where there are no annuitants drawing annuities from the said fund of such county, or consolidated city and county, to cease to be a contributor to such fund within sixty days from the taking effect of this act and to have returned to him the amount contributed by him thereto, or such part thereof as may be available for that purpose.

The people of the State of California, represented in senate and assembly, do enact as follows:

SECTION 1. Within sixty days after the taking effect of this act, any teacher or public officer who is now a contributor to a public school teachers' annuity and retirement fund in any county or consolidated city and county in this state, created under the provisions of an act approved March 29, 1897, entitled "An act to amend an act approved March 26, 1895, entitled 'An act to create and administer a public school teachers' annuity and retirement fund in the several counties, and cities and counties in the state,'" as amended, may withdraw from such organization by complying with the provisions of this act; *provided, however,* that the provisions of this act shall not apply to any county or consolidated city and county, where there are, at the time of the taking effect of this act, any annuitants drawing annuities from the said fund of such county, or consolidated city and county.

SEC. 2. Any such teacher, or public officer, desiring to avail himself of the provisions of this act, shall within sixty (60) days after the taking effect of this act, sign and file with the board of public school teachers' retirement fund commissioners of the county, or consolidated city and county, where such teacher or public officer is then a contributor, a notice in writing to the effect that such teacher, or public officer, thereby withdraws from the said organization, and shall at the same time sign and file with the clerk, secretary, officer, or board, whose duty it is to issue the salary warrants of such teacher or public officer, a notice similar in substance to the said notice filed with the said board of commissioners.

SEC. 3. The said board of commissioners, shall, at its next regular meeting after the expiration of said sixty (60) days, pass a resolution directing that all money contributed to said public school teachers' annuity and retirement fund by such teachers or public officers so withdrawing, shall be immediately returned to such teachers or public officers. If the amount in the fund of said organization, after the payment of all legal demands, shall be insufficient to pay each withdrawal the full amount contributed by him, then the said board shall compute the pro rata amount that shall be paid to each, the same to be in proportion to their respective contributions, and shall specify in said resolution the amount to be returned to each.

SEC. 4. The president and secretary of said board shall thereupon issue warrants to the persons entitled thereto, in such amounts as shall have been so computed and specified by said board, and the treasurer of said fund shall pay the same to the person named in each respective warrant, or to his heirs or assigns.

SEC. 5. From and after filing the notices, specified in section two hereof, each teacher or public officer giving such notices shall be relieved from all burdens and liabilities imposed by the said act designated in section one hereof.

SEC. 6. The clerk, secretary, officer, or board, whose duty it is to issue the salary warrants of such teachers or public officers, shall, from and after the filing of the said notice with him or it, cease to note on the salary warrant of such teacher or public officer any amount to be deducted therefrom by the treasurer on account of said fund.

SEC. 7. This act shall take effect immediately.

School Teachers' Annuity Fund

An act to amend sections four (4), five (5), eight (8), nine (9), ten (10), eleven (11), twelve (12), and thirteen (13) of an act approved March 29, 1897, entitled "An act to amend an act approved March 26, 1895, entitled 'An act to create and administer a public school teachers' annuity and retirement fund in the several counties, and cities and counties in this state,'" as amended March 23, 1901.

The people of the State of California, represented in senate and assembly, do enact as follows:

SECTION 1. Section four (4) of an act approved March twenty-ninth, eighteen hundred and ninety-seven, entitled "An act to amend an act approved March twenty-sixth, eighteen hundred and ninety-five, entitled 'An act to create and administer a public school teachers' annuity and retirement fund in the several counties, and cities and counties in the state,'" is hereby amended to read as follows, viz:

Section 4. In addition to the powers hereinbefore granted to said board, it shall have the power, (1) to provide for the payment of its necessary expenses, such as printing, stationery, and postage stamps; and where the number of those subject to the burdens of this act is greater than one hundred, it may employ a clerk at a salary not to exceed fifty (50) dollars per annum; and (2) to make such needful rules and regulations for the transaction of its business, from time to time, as may be necessary; the said expenses and the said clerk's salary shall be paid from the annuity fund in such counties or consolidated cities and counties, wherein there shall be "annuity funds," but, wherever there shall be no "annuity fund," the said expenses shall be paid from the "distribution fund," and the said salary from the reserve fund.

SEC. 2. Section five (5) of the act designated in section one hereof is hereby amended to read as follows, viz:

Section 5. Those subject to the burdens of this act in each county, or in each consolidated city and county, at a meeting called for the purpose by the superintendent of public schools of such county or of such city and county, on the first Saturday in May following the creation of the fund hereinafter specified, shall elect by ballot five of their number, who shall constitute a committee on retirement; the members of said committee shall, immediately after their election, classify themselves by lot so that one shall serve for one year, two serve for two years, and two shall serve for three years; and, annually, at a meeting to be called in the same manner on the first Saturday in May of each year after the first meeting, the successor or successors of the member or members of said committee whose term of office is about to expire, shall be elected for a term of three years; provided, however, that said committee shall always consist of at least one class teacher from some primary school, one from some grammar school, and one from some high school in the county, or consolidated city and county, whenever such election is possible. In the event of a vacancy, the superintendent of schools shall appoint until the next annual election.

Within fifteen days after the taking effect of this amendatory act, the contributors to said fund in any county, or consolidated city and county, in this state, at a meeting called for that purpose, by the superintendent of public schools of such county, or consolidated city and county, (or if he neglects or refuses to call such meeting, then such meeting may be called by ten of such contributors,) may select and designate by resolution adopted by a majority vote of those present, which of the two alternatives presented in section 8 class two, in section 8 class six, in section 8 class seven, and in section 11, respectively, shall be followed in such county or consolidated city and county.

In the event that no such meeting is called or held for the purpose of making such selection and designation, the said contributors in such county, or consolidated city and county, wherein no such meeting shall be held, will be deemed to have selected the first (marked subdivision "A") of each of the above mentioned alternatives.

In counties and consolidated cities and counties where a public school teachers' annuity and retirement fund shall be hereafter created the said selection and designation shall be made at the said meeting to be held on the first Saturday in May following the creation of said fund. After any selection and designation shall have been made, pursuant to this section, no change shall ever be made thereafter in that connection. A certified copy of all resolutions adopted pursuant to this section shall be furnished by said meeting of said contributors to the board of public school teachers' retirement fund commissioners of such county or consolidated city and county.

SEC. 3. Section eight of the act designated in section one hereof is hereby amended to read as follows, viz:

Section 8. Any public school teacher or any occupant of one of the offices mentioned in subdivision four of section twelve of this act, who has been a contributor under the provisions of this act, and who has ceased teaching, for a time, or has ceased to occupy such office, may again become a contributor upon returning to teaching in the public schools of this state, or upon becoming an occupant of any one of the offices mentioned in said subdivision four of section twelve, and shall thereupon be credited with his said previous service and contribution; *provided*, that no person shall become a contributor to a public school teachers' annuity and retirement fund under this act who does not hold a valid certificate or diploma to teach in the public schools of this state.

The annuitants under this act are classed as follows:

ANNUITANTS.

Class One. Any teacher who shall have served in the public schools of this state for thirty years as a teacher, and who shall have been subject to the burdens imposed by this act for thirty years, shall be entitled to retire under the provisions of this act.

Any teacher who has served in the public schools of this state, and who has served in one or more of the offices mentioned in said subdivision four of section twelve, and the aggregate period of whose service in the said public schools and in said office or offices shall be thirty years, and who shall have been subject to the burdens imposed by this act during said thirty years, shall be entitled to retire under the provisions of this act; *provided, however,* such teacher shall have held a valid certificate or diploma to teach in the public schools of this state during all of said period. Annuitants of class one shall be entitled to receive from the said public school teachers' annuity and retirement fund the sum of thirty (30) dollars per month in counties, and fifty (50) dollars per month in consolidated cities and counties, payable quarterly.

Class Two. Any teacher who shall have served in the public schools of this state for thirty years, and who was unable to contribute to said public school teachers' annuity and retirement fund for thirty years, by reason of the non-establishment or non-existence of said fund, and any teacher who shall have served in the public schools of this state, and who shall have served in one or more of the offices mentioned in said subdivision four of section twelve, and the aggregate period of whose service in the said public schools, and in said office or offices, is thirty years, and who has held a valid certificate or diploma to teach in the public schools of this state during all of said period, and who was unable to contribute to said fund for thirty years by reason of the non-establishment or non-existence of said fund, shall be retired upon application to the said board under either subdivision A or subdivision B, hereof, as the contributors to said fund in such county, or consolidated city and county, shall have selected to follow, as provided in section five of this act.

A. Such applicant upon retirement shall receive from the public school teachers' annuity and retirement fund the sum of thirty (30) dollars per month in counties, and fifty (50) dollars per month in consolidated cities and counties, payable quarterly; *provided,* that such applicant for retirement is, at the date of the taking effect of this amendatory act, a contributor to the public school teachers' annuity and retirement fund in the county or consolidated city and county, where he is teaching or holding such office, or becomes a contributor thereto within ninety (90) days after he becomes such teacher or such office holder, and shall have paid into the said fund, at the time of such retirement, a sum aggregating what he would have paid into said fund in thirty (30) years, had he been a contributor thereto for that period; *provided, further,* that annuities under this class shall not begin until five (5) years after the retired teacher became a contributor.

B. Such applicant upon retirement shall receive from the public school teachers' annuity and retirement fund the sum of five (5) dollars per month, payable quarterly, for every two and one half (2 1-2) years or fraction thereof equal to or greater than one half of two and one half years) such teacher or office holder shall have contributed to said fund, until the maximum annuity of thirty (30) dollars per month in counties and fifty (50) dollars per month in consolidated cities and counties shall have been reached; *provided,* that such applicant for retirement is, at the date of the taking effect of this amendatory act, a contributor to the public school teachers' annuity and retirement fund in the county, or consolidated city and county where he is teaching or holding such office, or becomes a contributor within ninety (90) days after the taking effect of this amendatory act, or becomes a contributor thereto within ninety (90) days after he becomes such teacher or such office holder.

No person shall be retired under this subdivision unless he shall have paid into said fund, at the time of such retirement, a sum aggregating what he would have paid into said fund in thirty (30) years had he been a contributor thereto for that period.

No teacher or office holder shall be retired until he has been a contributor to the fund for five (5) years.

Class Three. Any public school teacher who shall have served for thirty years, twenty-five of which shall have been in the public school of this state or partly in the public schools of this state and partly in one or more of the offices mentioned in said subdivision four of section twelve, and who shall have been subject to the burdens imposed by this act for twenty-five years, shall receive upon retirement after thirty years of such service, the sum of thirty (30) dollars per month in counties, and fifty (50) dollars per month in consolidated cities and counties, payable quarterly; *provided,* he shall have paid into the said fund, at the time of such retirement, a sum aggregating what he would have paid into said fund in thirty (30) years, had he been a contributor thereto for that period.

Class Four. Any public school teacher or any officer mentioned in said subdivision four of section twelve, subject to the burdens of this act, who shall remove to another county in this state, may continue to be a contributor to the public school teachers' annuity and retirement fund in the county, or in the consolidated city and county, from which he removed, so long as he continues to be a public school teacher or the occupant of one of said offices; and it is hereby made the duty of the county treasurer of the county, or consolidated city and county, wherein such teacher or officer agreed to become subject to the burdens of this act, to receive such contributions of such non-residents, and to place such contributions to the credit of the public school teachers' annuity and retirement fund.

Class Five. Any teacher who ceases to serve in the public schools of any county, or of any consolidated city and county, or who ceases to serve in one of the offices mentioned in said subdivision four of section twelve, in the county or consolidated city and county, where he has been subject to the burdens imposed by this act, and who shall have served in the public schools of this state for thirty (30) years, or who shall have served partly in the public schools of this state and partly in one or more of the offices mentioned in said subdivision four of section twelve, for an aggregate period of thirty (30) years, shall be entitled to retire, and to receive from the public school teachers' annuity and retirement fund of the county, or consolidated city and county, to which he has contributed for at least five (5) years, an annuity equal to such proportion of the maximum annuity granted under this act as the time he has been subject to the burdens imposed by this act in such county, or consolidated city and county, bears to the period of thirty years.

Class Six. Contributors to said public school teachers' annuity and retirement fund retiring under this class, shall be retired either under subdivision A, or subdivision B hereof, as the contributors to said fund in such county, or consolidated city and county, shall have selected to follow, as provided in section five of this act.

A. If any teacher, or any office holder mentioned in said subdivision four of section twelve, after the expiration of fifteen (15) years, and before the expiration of thirty (30) years, of service in the public schools of this state or of service partly in the said public schools and partly in one or more of the offices mentioned in said subdivision four of section twelve, shall be compelled, by reason of incapacity, to retire from public school service, or from one of the offices mentioned in said subdivision four of section twelve, while holding a valid certificate or diploma to teach in the public schools of this state, such retiring teacher, or office holder, if a contributor to the said fund at the time of retirement, shall be entitled to receive, from the public school teachers'. annuity and retirement fund, as many thirtieths (30ths) of the full annuity as he has had years of said service, by paying into the public school teachers' annuity and retirement fund the contributions to said fund corresponding to those years of service rendered at a time when, or in a place where, it was impossible to make such contributions by reason of, the non-existence of a public school teachers' annuity and retirement fund; *provided,* that he shall have contributed to the said fund for five years before he becomes an annuitant.

B. If any teacher or any office holder mentioned in said subdivision four of section twelve, after the expiration of five years, and before the expiration of thirty years of service in the public schools of this state, or of service partly in the said public schools and partly in one or more of the offices mentioned in said subdivision four of section twelve, shall be compelled by reason of incapacity, to retire from public school service, or from one of the offices mentioned in said subdivision four of section twelve, while holding a valid certificate or diploma to teach in the public schools of this state, such retiring teacher or office holder, if a contributor to the said fund at the time of retirement, shall be entitled to receive from the public school teachers' annuity and retirement fund a sum in dollars equal to such proportion of the maximum annuity granted under this act as the time he shall have been subject to the burdens of this act bears to the period of thirty years; *provided, however,* that those who have served in the public schools of this state, or partly in the said public schools and partly in one or more of the offices mentioned in said subdivision four of section twelve, at a time when, or in a place where, it was impossible to make contributions to said fund, by reason of the non-existence of said fund, may receive in addition to the proportion of the maximum annuity last hereinabove specified, such an additional proportion of the full annuity as the number of years of said service, while not burdened with the provisions of this act, bears to thirty years; *provided, further,* that they shall have paid into the said fund, at the time of their retirement, an amount equal to what they would have paid into said fund had they been subject to the burdens imposed by this act for the full time of said service, not to exceed thirty years; *and provided, further,* that no person retired under this subdivision B shall ever receive a greater annuity than he would have received had he retired on account of years of service; *and provided, further,* that he shall have contributed to the said fund for five years before he becomes an annuitant.

Class Seven. Contributors to said public school teachers' annuity and retirement fund, retiring under this class, shall be retired under either subdivision A, or under subdivision B, hereof, as the said contributors to said fund in such county, or consolidated city and county, shall have selected to follow, as provided in section five of this act.

A. Any public school teacher who shall have been subject to the burdens imposed by this act, for a period of at least five years, and who shall have served in the public schools of this state for a period of fifteen (15) years, or partly in the said public schools and partly in one or more of the offices mentioned in said subdivision four of section twelve, for a period of fifteen years, and who has held a valid certificate or diploma to teach in the schools of this state during all said period, and who shall have been declared incapacitated, by the committee on retirement, to perform the duties of a public school teacher, or the duties of the office which he may be occupying, if he should be occupying one of the offices mentioned in said subdivision four of section twelve, shall be entitled to retire and to receive an annuity from the public school teachers' annuity and retirement fund, equal to such proportion of the maximum annuity granted under this act as the time he has been subject to the burdens imposed by this act bears to the period of thirty years.

B. Any public school teacher who shall have been subject to the burdens imposed by this act for a period of five years (5), and who shall have served in the public schools of this state for a period of five (5) years, or partly in the said public schools and partly in one or more of the offices mentioned in said subdivision four of section twelve, for a period of five years, and who has held a valid certificate to teach in the schools of this state during said period, and who shall have been declared incapacitated by the committee on retirement, to perform the duties of a public school teacher, or the duties of the office which he may be occupying, if he should be occupying one of the offices mentioned in said subdivision four of section twelve, shall be entitled to retire, if a contributor to the fund at the time of retirement, and to receive an annuity, from the public school teachers' annuity and retirement fund a sum in dollars equal to such proportion of the maximum annuity granted under this act, as the time he shall have been subject to the burdens imposed by this act bears to the period of thirty years.

Class Eight. Teachers of public evening schools receiving a salary of fifty (50) dollars or less per month, shall be subject to one half of the burdens, and shall be entitled to one half of the benefits, of this act; *provided*, that any public school teacher who is employed both in a day and an evening school shall be considered for the purposes of this act to be employed in a day school only; *provided, further*, that an evening public school teacher, who at any time before retirement under the provisions of this act shall become a day public school teacher, or an occupant of one of the offices mentioned in said subdivision four of section twelve, shall upon retirement as a day public school teacher, or as one of said officers, be credited with half time for his said evening school service, under the class in which he may be retired.

HIGH SCHOOL AND OTHER PUBLIC SCHOOL TEACHERS.

High school and other public school teachers in counties, or in consolidated cities and counties, in which the act of which this act is amendatory has been in force, who were unable by reason of any imperfection in the terms of said act, to become contributors, shall be allowed, upon admission under the terms of this act, and upon the payment of the amounts they would have paid had they been contributors, to date the time of their admission from the time of the organization of the public school teachers' annuity and retirement fund in their county or consolidated city and county. City treasurers are hereby directed to pay into the public school teachers' annuity and retirement fund of their respective counties the contributions of teachers and officers, whose salaries are paid by, or through, city treasurers, in the same manner as provided in the act of which this act is amendatory, to be paid by the treasurer of a county, or consolidated city and county.

Compliance with these provisions shall

render any public high school or other public school teacher eligible to the benefits provided in any one of the eight classes of annuitants in this act created to which such teacher may be qualified.

SUSPENSION OF ANNUITIES.

Any and all annuities shall be suspended if the recipient returns to the profession of teaching or becomes the occupant of one of the said offices mentioned in subdivision four of section twelve. Any annuity less than two-thirds of the maximum annuity shall cease at the expiration of one year from the time at which the committee on retirement, constituted in section five of this act, shall decide that the recipient has been restored to the capacity of performing the duties of a public school teacher.

All teachers now employed in the public schools of this state who filed the notice specified in the act of which this act is amendatory, within ninety days after the passage of this amendatory act in counties or in consolidated cities and counties where the provisions of any act or acts to which this act is amendatory are now applicable, and all other public school teachers in other counties or consolidated city and county who become contributors within ninety days after the establishment of a public school teachers' annuity and retirement fund therein and who shall have paid at the time of retirement an amount equal to what they would have paid had they been subject to the burdens imposed by the provisions of this act for thirty (30) years, shall not suffer any reduction of annuities; *provided, however,* that the provisions of this paragraph shall not apply to counties or consolidated cities and counties in which the contributors to said fund shall select to be governed by the provisions of subdivision B of classes two, six and seven respectively of section eight, and subdivision B of section eleven, as provided in section five.

SEC. 4. Section nine of the act designated in section one hereof is hereby amended to read as follows, viz:

Section 9. If at the end of any quarter year there shall not be a sufficient amount of money in the "annuity fund," or in the "distribution fund," as the case may be, to pay all warrants and demands of annuitants in full, then the money in that fund shall be divided pro rata among them, and the sum received by each annuitant shall be in full discharge of all claims against said fund to that date.

SEC. 5. Section ten of the act designated in section one hereof is hereby amended to read as follows, viz:

Section 10. The public school teachers' annuity and retirement fund herein provided for, shall consist of the following, with the income and interest thereof: (I) Twelve (12) dollars per school year, of the salaries paid to all those subject to the burdens imposed by this act, in each county or consolidated city and county, shall be deducted from the warrants for salary, and paid by the treasurer of the county, or consolidated city and county, to the public school teachers' retirement fund commissioners of said county, or consolidated city and county; and it shall be the duty of the secretary of the board of education in every incorporated city or town, or consolidated city and county, and the clerk of the board of trustees of every public school district outside of such city or town, or consolidated city and county, to note on each warrant the amount to be so deducted therefrom by the treasurer, and if classified, the class under this act to which the teacher belongs. (II) All moneys received from gifts, bequests and devises, or from any other source. (III) All moneys, pay, compensation, or salary forfeited, deducted or withheld from the warrant or demand for salary of any teacher or teachers for and on account of absence from duty from any cause, which the board of education of every incorporated city or town, or the board of trustees of every school district outside of such city or town, may appropriate and set apart for the aforesaid fund; and said board of education or board of trustees, are hereby empowered to appropriate such moneys, or any part thereof, for such fund; *provided,* that in consolidated cities and counties, after the establishment of an annuity fund therein, it is hereby made the duty of the boards of education to appropriate, monthly, at least one half of such moneys for such fund.

SEC. 6. Section eleven of the act designated in section one hereof is hereby amended to read as follows, viz:

Section 11. The said public school teachers' annuity and retirement fund shall be divided either as designated in subdivision A hereof, or as designated in subdivision B hereof, as the said contributors to said fund in such county, or consolidated city and county, shall have selected to follow pursuant to the provisions of section five (5) hereof.

A. The said public school teachers' annuity and retirement fund in each county, or consolidated city and county, shall be divided into two distinct funds, or accounts, (1) the permanent fund, and (2) the annuity fund.

(1) The permanent fund.

(a) The permanent fund shall consist of: (I) Twenty-five per cent of all contributions from those affected by this act; (II) Twenty-five per cent of all gifts, bequests, or devises, unless otherwise ordered by the donor or the testator; (III) Twenty-five per cent of all moneys deducted from the salaries of teachers because of absence from duty.

(b) When the permanent fund shall amount to the sum of fifty thousand (50,000) dollars, then all moneys thereafter received shall go into the annuity fund, except such gifts, devises, or bequests as may be specially directed by its donor or testator to be placed in the permanent fund.

(c) It shall be the duty of the public school teachers' retirement fund commissioners to invest the aforesaid permanent fund in interest-bearing bonds issued by the federal state, county, city and county, or municipal governments, and to apply the interest thereon as herein directed.

(2) The annuity fund.

(a) The annuity fund shall consist of: (I) The income derived from the permanent fund; (II) All other moneys belonging to the public school teachers' annuity and retirement fund, not hereinbefore directed to be placed in the permanent fund; (III) All moneys in the fund provided for in the act to which this is amendatory.

(b) The annuity fund shall be the only one from which annuitants shall be paid.

(c) If at the end of any fiscal year there remain any surplus in the annuity fund, said surplus shall be deposited by the public school teachers' retirement fund commissioners in any savings bank, or savings banks, designated by them.

B. The said public school teachers' annuity and retirement fund, in each county, or consolidated city and county, shall be divided into two distinct funds or accounts, (1) the reserve fund and (2) the distribution fund.

(1) The reserve fund.

The reserve fund shall consist of:

(a) All moneys collected from the unclassified contributors for the first five years after the creation of said fund.

(b) Sixty (60) per cent of all moneys collected from the unclassified contributors for the second five years after the creation of the fund.

(c) Fifty (50) per cent of all moneys collected from unclassified contributors for the third five years after the creation of the fund.

(d) Thirty (30) per cent of all moneys collected from the unclassified contributors for the fourth five years after the creation of the fund.

(e) One hundred per cent of all collections from the classified contributors during the first period of their classification, as hereinafter classified.

(f) Ninety per cent of all collections from the classified contributors during the second period of their classification, as hereinafter classified.

(g) Eighty per cent of all collections from the classified contributors during the third period of their classification, as hereinafter classified.

(h) Seventy per cent of all collections from the classified contributors during the fourth period of their classification, as hereinafter classified.

(i) All collections from sources other than said collections from contributors; all donations, and all interest accrued on such reserve fund for a period of twenty years from the creation of said fund.

It shall be the duty of the public school

teachers' retirement fund commissioners to place the reserve fund at interest, monthly, in a savings bank selected by the said commissioners. All original contributors to a public school teachers' annuity and retirement fund in any county or consolidated city and county, and all those who became contributors thereto within the first five years after the creation of said fund shall be known as unclassified contributors.

All who become contributors during the first decade after the fund shall have been in existence for five years shall be known as Class A, and those who become contributors to said fund during each decade thereafter shall be known as classes B, C, D, respectively; each of said classes shall exist for four periods, the first three being for ten years each and the fourth for five years.

When the term for which any class has been formed shall have elapsed, all contributors to such classes who continue to contribute, shall be considered as unclassified.

(2) The distribution fund.

The distribution fund shall not be formed in any county or consolidated city and county, until the said public school teachers' annuity and retirement fund shall have been in existence for five years. It shall then consist of

(a) The income not hereinbefore set aside and declared a part of the reserve fund.

(b) After the said fund shall have been in existence for twenty years, in addition to the income not heretofore set aside for the reserve fund, there shall be transferred quarterly, during the next five years, from the reserve fund to the distribution fund, sixty (60) dollars; *provided,* that the earnings of the reserve fund for that period shall be equal to, or shall exceed, two hundred and forty (240) dollars per annum. If the earnings of the reserve fund shall not equal two hundred and forty (240) dollars per annum, the amount transferred quarterly from the reserve fund to the distribution fund shall be equal to the quarterly interest of the reserve fund.

(c) After the said fund shall have been in existence for twenty-five (25) years, the distribution fund shall consist of the income not heretofore set aside for the reserve fund, and one hundred and sixty (160) dollars to be transferred quarterly, during the next five years from the reserve fund to the distribution fund; *provided, however,* that this amount does not exceed the quarterly earnings of the reserve fund for that period. Should the one hundred and sixty (160.00) dollars exceed the said quarterly earnings, then an amount equal to the quarterly earnings of the reserve fund shall be so transferred.

(d) After the said fund shall have been in existence for thirty years the distribution fund shall consist of the income not heretofore set aside for the reserve fund and all of the interest of the reserve fund during the next five years. And should the aforesaid fail to give sufficient funds to pay half of the annuities due, then there shall be transferred quarterly from the reserve fund, over and above the earnings of the reserve fund, thirty (30) dollars per quarter.

(e) After the said fund shall have been in existence for thirty-five years, the distribution fund shall consist of the income not heretofore set aside for the reserve fund. Also the interest on the reserve fund, distributed quarterly during the next five years, and should this not be sufficient to pay half of the annuity due, then there shall be transferred from the reserve fund, in addition to the interest, sixty (60) dollars quarterly.

(f) After the said fund shall have been in existence for forty years, the distribution fund shall consist of the income not heretofore set aside for the reserve fund, the interest on the reserve fund distributed quarterly, and a sum taken from the reserve fund in addition thereto, equal to twelve times the increase in contributors to the said public school teachers' annuity and retirement fund for the preceding year; that is, if the said contributors increase by 20 during the year 1934, then during the year 1935 there shall be taken from the reserve fund, in addition to the interest, two hundred and forty (240.00) dollars per annum.

All disbursements shall be from the distribution fund, except as otherwise provided in section four.

SEC. 7. Section twelve of the act designated in section one hereof is hereby amended to read as follows, viz:

Section 12. This act shall be binding upon such public school teachers, and such officers mentioned in said subdivision four of section twelve as shall sign and deliver to the public school teachers' retirement fund commissioners, and to the secretary of the board of education of the incorporated city or town, or consolidated city and county, or to the clerk of the board of trustees of the school district, in which they are employed, a notice in substantially the following form:

——— ———19—.

To the Public School Teachers' Retirement Fund Commissioners, of ——— county (or city and county):

You are hereby notified that I agree to be bound by, and desire to avail myself of the provisions of the act of the legislature of the State of California, approved March 29th, eighteen hundred and ninety-seven, entitled "An act to amend an act approved March twenty-sixth, eighteen hundred and ninety-five, entitled 'An act to create and administer a public school teachers' annuity and retirement fund in the several counties, and cities and counties in the state,'" as amended March 23, 1901, and ———, 1903.

Signed ———————.

provided, that at least thirty public school teachers within the county, or consolidated city and county, shall file the notice hereinbefore set forth; *provided, further,* that in all counties, or in consolidated cities and counties, where there is a less number of teachers than thirty, this act shall be binding on all those who so signify their intention of being bound thereby.

(2) In consolidated cities and counties it shall be binding upon all teachers elected or appointed to teach in the public schools of such consolidated cities and counties after the passage of this act.

(3) Annuities heretofore granted under the provisions of the act of which this act is amendatory shall be continued for the same amount as heretofore paid, subject, however, to the conditions imposed by sections nine (9) and eleven (11) of this act,

(4) Any county, consolidated city and county, or city superintendent of schools of this state, and any deputy superintendent of schools for any county, consolidated city and county, or city of this state, and any person engaged in any other educational work, required by law to have the qualifications of a teacher in the public schools of this state, may avail himself of the provisions of this act; and wherever the word "teacher" is used in this act it shall be deemed to include such officer or officers.

SEC. 8. Section thirteen of the act designated in section one hereof, is hereby amended to read as follows, viz:

Section 13. Every public officer who shall issue, or receive in his official capacity, any warrant, or who shall receive or pay out any money in any manner connected with, pursuant to, or dependent upon, the provisions of this act, shall keep a full, accurate and public record of all his transactions pertaining to the same.

SEC. 9. This act shall take effect immediately.

* * *

Levying County School Tax

An act to amend section 1818 of the Political Code, relating to the duties of boards of supervisors levying county school tax.

The people of the State of California, represented in senate and assembly, do enact as follows:

SECTION 1. Section eighteen hundred and eighteen of the Political Code is hereby amended to read as follows:

1818. The board of supervisors of every county having less than three hundred and forty thousand inhabitants must, annually, at the time of levying other county taxes, levy a tax, to be known as the county school tax, the maximum rate of which must not exceed fifty cents on each one hundred dollars of taxable property in the county, nor the minimum rate be less than sufficient to raise a minimum amount reported by the county superintendent, in accordance with the provisions of the preceding section. The supervisors must determine the minimum rate of the county school tax as follows: They must deduct fifteen per cent from the equalized value of the last general assessment roll and the amount required to be raised, divided by the remainder of the assessment roll, is the rate to be levied; but if any fraction of a cent occur, it must be taken as a full cent on each one hundred dollars.

(A) In every county, or city and county, constituting but one school district, a portion of the school funds for any fiscal year subsequent to the present fiscal year equal in amount to the sum total of teachers' salaries for the next preceding fiscal year payable out of the school fund in question, shall constitute a special fund, to be used only for the payment of teachers' salaries as hereinafter provided, and to be known as the teachers' salary fund; *provided,* that no portion of any school fund consisting of moneys which are applicable exclusively to some special purpose defined by statute other than the payment of teachers' salaries shall be deemed a part of such school fund for the purposes of this act. Out of the teachers' salary fund shall be paid the salaries of all teachers holding in the fiscal year positions which existed in the preceding fiscal year. No other demands whatsoever shall be paid out of such fund. If, by any increase in the rate of salaries, or for any other cause, such fund should be insufficient to pay all of the salaries which constitute demands against it such fund shall be divided pro rata among such demands, and the portion of such demands unpaid shall be payable out of any available money in the school fund of which said teachers' salary fund constitutes a part. If teachers' positions other than or in addition to those which existed in the preceding fiscal year are created, the salaries of teachers holding such different or additional positions shall not be paid out of the teachers' salary fund, but out of any other available moneys; but the amount of such salaries shall be included in determining the amount of the teachers' salary fund for the succeeding fiscal year. If there remain in any fiscal year any money in any teachers' salary fund after the payment of all legal demands for such year against such fund, such money so remaining shall be transferred to the general school fund of which said teachers' salary fund is a part, and shall become available for the payment of any unpaid lawful demands against such general fund. It shall be the duty of any officer whose duty it is to audit demands against the school fund of any such county, or city and county, in this state, on or before the first Monday of the fiscal year, to file with the board of supervisors of such county, or city and county, and with the officer whose duty it is to pay demands against the school fund of any such county, or city and county, a certified copy of the statement made by him of the amount of money used in such county, or city and county, for the payment of teachers' salaries for the next preceding fiscal year, and no demands against the school funds of such county, or city and county, shall be allowed, audited, or paid until said copies shall have been filed, as aforesaid. The allowance, audit, or payment of any demand out of a teachers' salary fund in violation of this act, may be enjoined by the suit of any teacher whose salary is payable from said fund. The members of the governing body of any such county, or city and county, in this state, who shall pass a demand against said teachers' salary fund in violation of the provisions of this act, and any officer whose duty it is to audit demands against such fund and who shall audit a demand against said teachers' salary fund in violation of the provisions of this act, and any officer whose duty it is to pay demands against such funds, and who shall pay a demand against said teachers' salary fund in violation of this act, shall each be jointly and severally liable therefor to any teacher whose salary is payable from said fund who shall have been damaged by the allowance, audit, and payment of such demand.

SEC. 2. This act shall take effect and be in force from and after its passage.

The Election of School Boards

An act to amend section 1882 of an act entitled "An act to establish a Political Code of the State of California, approved March 12, 1872, relating to the issue of bonds of school districts."

The people of the State of California. represented in senate and assembly, do enact as follows:

SECTION 1. Section eighteen hundred and eighty-two of an act entitled "An act to establish a Political Code in the State of California, approved March twelfth, eighteen hundred and seventy-two, relating to the issue of bonds of school districts," is hereby amended so as to read as follows:

1882. Such notice must contain:

1. Time and place of holding such election;

2. The names of inspectors and judges to conduct the same;

3. The hours during the day in which the polls will be open;

4. The amount and denomination of the bonds; the rate of interest and the number of years, not exceeding forty, the whole or any part of said bonds are to run.

SEC. 2. This act shall take effect immediately.

* *

School Bonds

An act to amend section 1885 of an act entitled "An act to establish a Political Code of the State of California," approved March 12, 1872, relating to the issue of bonds of school districts.

The people of the State of California, represented in senate and assembly, do enact as follows:

SECTION 1. Section eighteen hundred and eighty-five of an act entitled "An act to establish a Political Code of the State of California," approved March twelfth, eighteen hundred and seventy-two, is hereby amended to read as follows:

1885. The board of supervisors by an order entered upon its minutes shall prescribe the form of said bonds and of the interest coupons attached thereto, and must fix the time when the whole or any part of the principal of said bonds shall be payable, which shall not be more than forty years from the date thereof.

SEC. 2. This act shall take effect immediately.

* * *

The Apportionment of School Funds

An act to amend section 1858 of the Political Code of the State of California, relating to the apportionment of school funds.

The people of the State of California, represented in senate and assembly, do enact as follows:

SECTION 1. Section eighteen hundred and fifty-eight of the Political Code is hereby amended to read as follows:

1858. All state school moneys apportioned by the superintendent of public instruction must be apportioned to the several counties in proportion to the number of school census children, as shown by the returns of the school census marshals of the preceding school year; *provided,* that Indian children whose parents are on government reservations, or are living in the tribal relation, and Mongolian children not native born, shall not be included in the apportionment list. The superintendent of schools in each county must apportion all state and county school moneys as follows:

First—He must ascertain the number of teachers each district is entitled to by calculating one teacher for every seventy school census children, or fraction of such number not less than twenty school census children, as shown by the next preceding school census; and in cities or districts wherein separate classes are established for the instruction of the deaf, as provided in section 1618 of this code, an additional teacher for each nine deaf children, or fraction of such number, not less than five, actually attending such classes; *provided,* that all children in any asylum, and not attending the public schools, of whom the authorities of said asylum are the guardians, shall not be included in making the estimate of the number of teachers to which the district in which the asylum is located is entitled.

Second—He must ascertain the total number of teachers for the county, by adding together the number of teachers assigned to the several districts.

Third—Five hundred dollars shall be apportioned to each district for every teacher assigned to it; *provided,* that to districts having ten and less than twenty school census children, shall be apportioned four hundred dollars; *provided further,* that to districts having over seventy school census children and a fraction of less than twenty, there shall be apportioned twenty dollars for each census child in said fraction.

Fourth—All school money remaining on hand after apportioning to the districts the moneys provided for in subdivision three of this section, must be apportioned to the several districts in proportion to the average daily attendance in each district during the preceding school year. Census children, wherever mentioned in this chapter, shall be construed to mean those between the ages of five and seventeen years.

Fifth—Whenever in any school year, prior to the receipt by the counties, cities, or cities and counties of this state, of their state, county, or city school fund, the school districts or cities shall not have sufficient money to their credit to pay the lawful demands against them, the county, city, or city and county superintendent shall give the treasurer of said county, city, or city and county an estimate of the amount of school money that will next be paid into the county, city, or city and county treasury, stating the amount to be apportioned to each district. Upon the receipt of such estimate, it shall be the duty of the treasurer of said county, city, or city and county to transfer from any fund not immediately needed to pay claims against it, to the proper school fund, an amount not to exceed ninety per cent of the amount estimated by the superintendent, and he shall immediately notify the superintendent of the amount so transferred. The funds so transferred to the school fund shall be re-transferred by the treasurer to the fund from which they were taken, from the first money paid into the school fund after the transfer.

Sec. 2. All acts and parts of acts in conflict with the provisions of this act are hereby repealed.

Sec. 3. This act shall take effect and be in force from and after its passage.

* * *

School Elections

An act to amend section 1596 of an act entitled "An act to establish a Political Code of the State of California," approved March 12, 1872, relating to elections for school trustees.

The people of the State of California, represented in senate and assembly, do enact as follows:

Section 1. Section fifteen hundred and ninety-six of an act entitled "An act to establish a Political Code of the State of California," approved March twelfth, eighteen hundred and seventy-two, is hereby amended so as to read as follows:

1596. Trustees or board of education charged with the calling, conduct and carrying on of elections, may subdivide the district into election precincts for the holding of the election, and may change and alter such precints as often as occasion may require, and must appoint one inspector and two judges of election in each precinct; if none are so appointed, or, if those appointed are not present at the time for opening the polls, the electors present may appoint them, and they shall conduct the election.

Sec. 2. This act shall take effect immediately.

Separate Classes for Deaf Children

An act to add a new section to the Political Code, to be known as section 1618, providing for the establishment and maintenance of separate classes in the common schools for the instruction of the deaf.

The people of the State of California, represented in senate and assembly, do enact as follows:

SECTION 1. A new section is hereby added to the Political Code, to be known as sixteen hundred and eighteen, to read as follows:

1618. The board of education of every city or city and county, or board of school trustees of every school district in this state, containing five or more deaf children, or children who from deafness are unable to hear common conversation, between the ages of three and twenty-one years, may in their discretion establish and maintain separate classes in the primary and grammar grades of the public schools, wherein such pupils shall be taught by the pure oral system for teaching the deaf.

SEC. 2. This act shall take effect and be in force from and after its passage.

* * *

The School District Library Funds

An act to amend section 1713 of the Political Code of California in relation to district libraries.

The people of the State of California, represented in senate and assembly, do enact as follows:

SECTION 1. Section seventeen hundred and thirteen (1713) of the Political Code of California is hereby amended to read as follows:

1713. Except in cities not divided into school districts the library fund shall consist of not less than five nor more than ten per cent of the county school fund annually apportioned to the district; *provided,* that should ten per cent exceed fifty dollars, fifty dollars only shall be apportioned to the district; except that in districts having five or more teachers, there shall be apportioned a sum not less than ten dollars nor more than fifteen dollars for each teacher employed; *and provided further,* that the school trustees of each district in the county shall, in the month of July in each year, notify the superintendent of the county as to what amount they desire to be apportioned for their respective districts for the year.

SEC. 2. This act shall be in force and take effect from and after its passage.

* * *

The Admission of Children in the Public School

An act to amend section 1662 of the Political Code of the State of California, relating to the admission of children in the public schools of this State.

The people of the State of California, represented in senate and assembly, do enact as follows:

SECTION 1. Section sixteen hundred and sixty-two of the Political Code is hereby amended to read as follows:

1662. Every school, unless otherwise provided by law, must be open for the admission of all children between six and twenty-one years of age residing in the district, and the board of school trustees, or city board of education, have power to admit adults and children not residing in the district, whenever good reasons exist therefor. Trustees shall have the power to exclude children of filthy or vicious habits, or children suffering from contagious or infectious diseases, and also to establish separate schools for Indian children and for children of Mongolian or Chinese descent. When such separate schools are established, Indian, Chinese, or Mongolian children must not be admitted into any other school; *provided,* that in cities and towns in which the kindergarten has been adopted or may hereafter be adopted as part of the public primary schools, children may be admitted to such kindergarten classes at the age of four years; *and provided further*, that in cities or school districts in which separate classes have been or may hereafter be established, for the instruction of the deaf, children may be admitted to such classes at the age of three years.

SEC. 2. All acts and parts of acts in conflict with the provisions of this act are hereby repealed.

SEC. 3. This act shall take effect immediately.

* * *

The Formation of New School Districts

An act to amend section fifteen hundred and seventy-seven of the Political Code of California, relating to the formation of new school districts.

The people of the State of California, represented in senate and assembly, do enact as follows:

SECTION 1. Section fifteen hundred and seventy-seven of the Political Code is hereby amended to read as follows:

1577. First—No new school district shall be formed at any other time than between the first day of December and the fifth day of April, nor at that time unless the parents or guardians of at least fifteen census children, residents of such proposed new district, and residing at a greater distance than two miles by a traveled road from the public school house in the district in which said parents or guardians reside, present a petition to the superintendent of schools, setting forth the boundaries of the new district asked for; *provided*, that the provision requiring that the petitioners shall reside a distance of more than two miles by a traveled road from the said public school house may be dispensed with when the petition shall be signed by the parents or guardians of fifty or more census children residents of a district containing more than three hundred census children.

Second:—The boundaries of a school district, except as provided in section one thousand five hundred and fifty-one of the Political Code, shall be changed only between the first day of January and the fifth day of April in any year, and then only when at least ten heads of families residing in the districts affected by the proposed change of boundaries shall present to the superintendent of schools a petition setting forth the changes of boundaries desired, and the reasons for the same; *provided*, that two or more districts lying contiguous may at any time be united to constitute but one district, whenever a petition signed by a majority of the heads of families residing in each of said districts shall be presented to the superintendent of schools.

Third—Joint districts (that is, districts lying partly in one county and partly in another) may be formed at any time between the first day of December and the fifth day of April in any year, whenever a petition signed by the parents or guardians of at least fifteen census children, residents of such proposed joint district and residing at a greater distance than two miles by a traveled road from any public school house, shall be presented to the superintendent of each county affected by the proposed formation of the joint district; *and provided further*, that the provision requiring that the petitioners shall reside a distance of more than two miles by a traveled road from any public school house may be dispensed with when the petition shall be signed by the parents or guardians of fifty or more census children residents of districts any one of which contains more than three hundred census children. All the provisions relative to the formation of joint districts shall be by concurrent action of the superintendent and the board of supervisors of each county affected; *still further provided*, that by concurrent action of the boards of supervisors and the county school superintendents, contiguous school districts or parts of such school districts lying in different counties may, on proper petitions as above required, be united to form a joint school district, and the school property within the territory thus united shall become the property of the newly formed joint school district.

Fourth—The children residing in any newly formed district, in any district whose boundaries have been changed, or in any joint district, shall be permitted to attend the school in the district or districts from which the newly formed district was constituted until the first day of July next succeeding the formation or change.

Fifth—Whenever a district shall be united with a municipality or with another district, all funds belonging to said district shall be transferred, by requisition of the superintendent of the county upon the county auditor, to the municipality or district with which said district is united.

SEC. 2. This act shall take effect and be in force from and after its passage.

* * *

Investing of School Funds

An act to amend section 680 of the Political Code of the State of California, relating to investing school funds.

The people of the State of California, represented in senate and assembly, do enact as follows:

SECTION 1. Section six hundred and eighty of the Political Code of the State of California is hereby amended so as to read as follows:

680. Whenever and as often as there is in the state treasury the sum of ten thousand dollars as the proceeds of the sale of state school lands, the board must invest the same in the civil funded bonds of this state, or in the bonds of the United States, or in the bonds of the several counties, city and county, cities or towns, or school districts of this State; the investments to be made in such manner and on such terms as the board shall deem best for the fund; *provided,* that no bonds of any county, city and county, city or town or school districts, shall be purchased of which the debt, debts, or liabilities at the time exceed fifteen per cent of the assessed value of the taxable property of such county, city and county, city or town or school district.

SEC. 2. This act shall take effect immediately.

* * *

Change of Name of School District

An act to provide for the change of name of school districts and the manner of making such change.

The people of the State of California, represented in senate and assembly, do enact as follows:

SECTION 1. Whenever a petition shall be presented to the board of supervisors, signed by at least fifteen qualified electors of said district, asking that the name of any school district be changed, the said board of supervisors shall designate a day upon which they will act upon such petition, which day must not be less than ten days nor more than forty days after the receipt thereof. The clerk of the said board of supervisors must give notice to all parties interested, by sending by registered mail to each of the trustees of such school district, a notice of the time set for the hearing of said petition, which notice must be mailed at least ten days before the day set for hearing, whereupon the board shall by resolution either grant or deny the petition, and if granted, the clerk shall notify the county superintendent of the change of the name of said district.

SEC. 2. This act shall take effect immediately.

Duties of County Superintendents

An act to amend section 1817 of the Political Code, relating to the duties of county superintendents of schools.

The people of the State of California, represented in senate and assembly, do enact as follows:

SECTION 1. Section eighteen hundred and seventeen of the Political Code is hereby amended to read as follows:

1817. The county superintendent of every county having a population of less than three hundred and forty thousand inhabitants must, on or before the first regular meeting of the board of supervisors, in September in each year, furnish the supervisors and the auditor, respectively, an estimate, in writing, of the minimum amount of county school fund needed for the ensuing year. This amount he must compute as follows:

First—He must ascertain, in the manner provided for in subdivisions one and two of section eighteen hundred and fifty-eight, the total number of teachers for the county.

Second—He must calculate the amount required to be raised at five hundred dollars per teacher. From this amount he must deduct the total amount of state apportionment, and the remainder shall be the minimum amount of county school fund needed for the ensuing year; provided, that if this amount is less than sufficient to raise a sum equal to six dollars for each census child in the county, then the minimum amount shall be such a sum as will be equal to six dollars for each census child in the county.

SEC. 2. This act shall take effect and be in force from and after its passage.

* * *

In Reference to School Bonds

An act to re-enact section 681 of the Political Code, relating to the duties of clerks of boards of supervisors, trustees, common council, or other governing board or body of a county, city and county, city or town, or school district in this state, upon the issuance and sale of bonds for any purpose, and decreeing that the state shall not be required to file a certified check, bond or other assurance in law upon its application to purchase.

The people of the State of California, represented in senate and assembly, do enact as follows:

SECTION 1. Section six hundred and eighty-one of the Political Code is hereby re-enacted to read as follows:

681. Whenever the board of supervisors, trustees, common council, or other governing board or body of any county, city and county, city or town, or school district of this state shall vote bonds for any purpose, or shall refund any bonds already issued, and said bonds are ready to be sold, the clerk of such board, trustees, common council, or other governing board or body shall forthwith, by mail, postage prepaid, notify the state board of examiners and state treasurer, at the capitol, of such issuance and sale of bonds, and shall give the name by which the bonds are known, the amount of the issuance, the denomination of each bond, the rate of interest, and length of time bonds are to run. No certified check, bond, or other assurance in law shall be required from the state upon its application to purchase bonds.

SEC. 2. This act shall take effect immediately.

Meeting of the State Board of Education

The State Board of Education met at Sacramento Saturday, March 28, 1903, at 9:30 A. M. All the members were present: George C. Pardee (President of the Board), Morris Elmer Dailey, E. T. Pierce, C. C. Van Liew, Benjamin Ide Wheeler, Elmer E. Brown, Samuel T. Black, Frederic Burk, Thomas J. Kirk (Secretary of the Board).

Under the head of communications a letter was received from Edward Hyatt, Secretary of the County Board of Education of Riverside county, in reference to the case of T. C. Welsh. The County Board of Education asked that Mr. Welsh's life diploma be revoked for evident unfitness for teaching. It was decided by vote of the State Board that Mr. Welsh be requested to show cause why his life diploma should not be revoked.

A communication was received and read from the American Book Company in reference to the plates furnished for McMaster's History. This brought up a discussion of the new text-book law. The Board proceeded to elect the members of the permanent text-book committee. The election was by ballot, and resulted in the selection of Governor Pardee and Superintendent Kirk, two of the members recommended in the law. The third member chosen was Elmer Ellsworth Brown.

The State Board of Education then took a recess in order to give the text-book committee an opportunity to organize. Governor Pardee was elected chairman of the committee. The text-book committee decided to recommend to the Board for adoption the text and plates of McMaster's, with supplemental chapters on California history by K. C. Babcock, and to pay the American Book Company a royalty of thirty per cent of the net list price. The Board adopted the report of the committee. The State Printer, W. W. Shannon, was called upon to give an estimate on the cost of printing McMaster's History, and he estimated the price at fifty-five cents.

Dr. Brown reported on accredited universities in accordance with Circular No. 5, printed herewith.

Frederick Burk, Benjamin Ide Wheeler, and C. C. Van Liew were appointed a committee on the OFFICIAL JOURNAL OF EDUCATION.

A committee consisting of Elmer E. Brown, Morris E. Dailey, and Edward T. Pierce was appointed to report on professional ethics.

Dr. Fletcher B. Dresslar was given under seal of the Board authority as special commissioner to the schools of Germany, with a request that he report his observations to the Board.

The Board granted diplomas and documents to the following applicants:

UNIVERSITY DOCUMENTS.

Gertrude T. Berg, Solano; Sophia P. Comstock, Sacramento; Veronica Anita Dufficy, Marin; Elizabeth Hassard, Kings; Charlotte A. Henley, Alameda; Milo Azem Tucker, Los Angeles.

NORMAL DOCUMENTS.

Gertrude Allen, Chico; Juanita V. Austin, Los Angeles; Laura Bethell, San Jose; Cora B. Dam, San Jose; Bessie T. Doten, San Jose; Olivia Edmondson, San Jose; Ida Fisch, Los Angeles; Florence R. Gill, Chico; Dora Pankey Glines, Los Angeles; L. Alice Halsey, San Jose; Myrtle Luella Hamilton, Los Angeles; Iola M. Harris, San Jose; Ida M. Harmon, San Jose; Mandilla G. Hays, San Jose; Carmela M. Hughes, San Jose; Beatrice L. Jamison, San Jose; Henry Kerr, Los Angeles; Rose R. Linebaugh, San Jose; Jessie A. Lotspeich, Los Angeles; Catharine V. Manning, San Francisco; A. Selene Menihan, San Jose: Genevieve McGinness, Chico; Ida P. McMillin, San Jose; Melvin Neel, Los Angeles; Ida M. Nelson, San Jose; Joseph Netz, Los Angeles; Margaret G. O'Connell, San Diego; Mildred L. Overfelt, San Jose; Crilla D. Shonkurler, Chico; Lottie A. Simpson, San Jose; Susie M. B. Spooner, San Jose; Anna Sprague, Chico; Margaret Strouse, Chico; Frances E. Sullivan, San Jose; Elizabeth J. Taylor, San Jose; Mable A. Thompson, San Jose; Clara Vincey, San Jose; W. E. White, Los Angeles; Katheryn Jarman Williams, San Jose; Ella May Wright, Los Angeles; Harriet E. Quilty, San Jose.

HIGH SCHOOL DIPLOMAS.

Burnell Finley Bassett, Humboldt; Alice Josephine Bristol, San Mateo; Sophia P. Comstock, Sacramento; Henry Kerr, Los Angeles; Emma A. Lauff, Del Norte; Lydia D. Lawhead, Yolo; George Walter Monroe, Los Angeles; William Thomas Mooney, Siskiyou; Jennie L. Powers, San Francisco; Peter T. Riley, San Francisco; A. E. Shumate, Santa Clara; George E. Springer, Butte.

GRAMMAR SCHOOL DIPLOMAS.

Edna Aldersley, Napa; Belle Alexander, Sierra; Olive A. Alexander, Santa Clara; Amalia Anderson, Alameda; M. Elnora Arbuthnot, Los Angeles; S. Florence Baldwin, Humboldt; Leetta Barber, Los Angeles; Lucy A. Barker, Kings; Franklin K. Barthel, Santa Clara; Olive S. Bartlett, San Francisco; Kate

R. Beauvais, Alameda; Ruth Edith Benjamin, Napa; Mrs. Pollie Boettcher Berka, Sonoma; Dora Wertz Beswick, Orange; John A. Bevington, San Diego; Eva Kerr Blair, Fresno; Olive P. Blackmar, San Benito; Mary Eugenie Boyd, Marin; Laura Russell Brotherton, Marin; Malwine C. Bronson, Solano;. Annette R. Brandt, Contra Costa; Mary ___ Briggs, Ventura; Elizabeth Buckley, Yolo; Irene A. Burns, Placer; Minnie Burger, Mendocino; Mary M. Cain, Los Angeles; A. E. Camp, Butte; Mrs. A. E. Camp, Butte; Genevieve Carroll, San Francisco; Lydia A. Carroll, San Francisco; Luna Carter, Alameda; Nalilla A. Cass, Fresno; Mabel G. Chandler, Marin; Edith Cheney, Santa Clara; Sadie H. Chick, Humboldt; Birdie Anslyn Church, Kings; Clara A. Clarke, Humboldt; E. Anina Clausen, San Francisco; Annie Brewer Cliff, San Diego; Susan R. Codd, San Joaquin; Anna Louise Coddington, Sonoma; Lida Coddington, Alameda; Julia C. Coffey, San Francisco; Sarah Coleman, Fresno; Mary H. Collier, San Diego; Amy B. Cookson, San Francisco; Callie M. Coombs, Mendocino; Clara Cooper, Riverside; Louise M. Cox, San Francisco; W. P. Cramsie, Yuba; Martha A. Crooks, Alameda; Edson N. Cuddeback, Yuba; Laura E. Cuddeback, Humboldt; Kate J. Curley, Santa Clara; Ella R. Daniel, San Francisco; Bernice Gertrude Davis, Los Angeles; Florence Davis, San Francisco; Ala Cochran Dean, San Diego; M. Frances Delphy, San Diego; Minnie E. Dewar, Ventura; Jennie M. Deyo, Los Angeles; Caroline Dolman, Alameda; Jessie Donaldson, Sacramento; Charlotte C. Easton, Santa Clara; Mrs. Ida V. Cooley Edwards, Tehama; Emma Eisenhart, Riverside; Alice M. Ellenhorst, Contra Costa; Inez M. Elsmore, Humboldt; Emma A. Farnham, Santa Cruz; Jasper J. Finney, Solano; Mollie E. _anigan; Humboldt; Grace C. Fleck, Monterey; Ida M. Fleming, Sacramento; Amy V. Fletcher, San Benito; Mary T. Ford, Stanislaus; Charlotte K. Fortna, Sutter; Eva M. Frank, Los Angeles; Cora B. Freeman, Los Angeles; LaVerne L. Freeman, Sutter; Lutie M. Fuller, Shasta; Ruby A. Fuller, San Luis Obispo; Aura F. Gallup, Los Angeles; B. Lenore Gambitz, San Francisco; Lillian M. Gambitz, San Francisco; Anna Lena Gansner, Plumas; Maud V. Garvey, Yuba; James W. Grace, Butte; Lydia E. Grafe, San Francisco; Allan H. Grant, Yuba; Myrtle A. Green, San Joaquin; Alice Priscilla Haines, San Diego; Velma R. Hanson, Lake; Ollie E. Hargrave, Mendocino; Myrtle B. Haskin, Ventura; Susan Orpha Harris, Mendocino; Elizabeth F. Harvey, San Francisco; Mary Hawley, Los Angeles; Mandilla G. Hays, Sonoma; Ella M. Hazen, Stanislaus; Ethel L. Heanan, Marin; Anna W. Henderson, Ventura; Ruby M. Hickerson, Plumas; Mrs. Christine Hill, Santa Cruz; Lottie A. Howard, Sonoma; Ella V. Hulse, San Diego; Olive E. Hyde, Los Angeles; Helena A. Jackson, Napa; Edith May Johnson, Monterey; Alice E. Jones; Santa Clara; Eva V. Joseph, Monterey; James A. Joyce, Mendocino; Elizabeth Kesserling, Glenn; Stella Keys, Orange; Lydia D. Killefer, Orange; Grace Kimball, Fresno; Belle C. Kincaid, San Francisco; Alta Lane, Colusa; William H. Langdon, San Francisco; Martha A. Latham, San Francisco; Tillie Lewis, Stanislaus; Celia Lewison, San Francisco; Mabel Lincoln, Santa Cruz; Harriet Elizabeth Lingscheid, Tehama; Anna M. Livingston, San Diego; Mary E. Lloyd, Alpine; Janie Logan, Humboldt; Katherine G. Lyons, San Francisco; Ella M. Martin, Shasta; Ruth E. Bourns Marsan, Mendocino; Elva E. Marsh, Plumas; Tennie Matthews, San Luis Obispo; Emma Matzenbach, Sonoma; Georgia May, Humboldt, Fresno; Flora R. McIsaac, Marin; Katherine Reardon McQuaid, Yuba; Annie McWilliams, Yolo; Joseph E. Meadows, Kings; Lillian F. Merryman, Shasta; Carrie Belmer Miller, Sacramento; Frank J. Miller, Santa Barbara; Lou A. B. Milwain, Alameda; Effie M. Minor, Mendocino; Annie F. Zane Murray, Humboldt; Edith M. Myers, Santa Barbara; Katherine Nevius, Los Angeles; Alice C. Nilon, Nevada; Lucille O'Connell, San Francisco; Lulu O'Connor, Sonoma; Jennie F. O'Reilly, San Francisco; Mildred L. Overfelt, Santa Clara; Mabel E. Palmer, Alameda; Mary Paterson, San Benito; Edith M. Peirson, Butte; Jessie S. Peters, Marin; Nellie Mary Petray, Los Angeles; Laura M. Phelps, Stanislaus; Hattie B. Phoenix, San Luis Obispo; Ethel Poage, Mendocino; Sempronia Polhemus, Sonoma; Chas. T. Pool; Bessie Hoff Price, Mendocino; Emma T. Ransdell, Mendocino; Alice C. Reid, Monterey; Irma Rhodes, Santa Cruz; M. Enna Ringo, Santa Clara; Callie E. Robinson, Humboldt; Ivory Elmer Rollins, Shasta; A. C. Ross, Santa Clara; Clara Comegys Ross, Mendocino; Nellie Ross, Sonoma; Mary Ogden Ryan, Los Angeles; Margaret L. Sabin, Napa; Reward Salisbury, Glenn; Katie E. Crocker Schellhorn, Shasta; Eda H. Schlicher, Orange; Edwin S. Scott, Mendocino; H. Benton Scott, Mendocino; Rose H. Schubert, San Mateo; Margaret E. Smith, Yolo; Mrs. Nellie I, Smith, Lake; Helen E. Spafford, San Francisco; Terese F. Spencer, San Francisco; Minnie Sperling, Sacramento; Mrs. Sabra Spurgeon, Lake; Mrs. J. A. Starrett, Sonoma; Mattie L. Steele, Los Angeles, Leonard Stevens, Stanislaus; Cora A. Stone, San Joaquin; Charlotte E. Stubbs, Sacramento; Winifred Styles, Kings; Emma G. Sullivan, San Francisco; Mrs. Blanche Roddick Sullivan, Siskiyou; Sarah I. Sweet, Humboldt; Joseph I. Taylor, Fresno; Anna L. Thomas, Santa Cruz; May Thomas, Mendocino; F. Louise Therwachter, Santa Cruz; Emily L. Travis, Yuba; Joseph Perry Utter, Mendocino; Josie Peveler, Del Norte; Rose Valpey, Stanislaus; Gertrude Vasche, Merced; Ida M. Wallace, Sacramento; Lilly Walsh, Monterey; Helen Dibble Watson, Sonoma; Anne G. Wattles, Sonoma; Angie Hendrix Webster, Santa Clara; George M. Weems, Kings; Maude

. L. Welch, Santa Clara; .Effie West, Sacramento; Nettie Miller Wetmore, Madera; Charlotte Wheeler, Siskiyou; Charles Whited, Mendocino; W. H. Whited, Mendocino; Carrie A. Whiting, San Joaquin; Adorno A. Whitman, Los Angeles; Josie E. Wickham, Butte; Zora DeWitt Wilcox, Napa; Artie Williams, San Diego; Harriett L. Willis, Los Angeles; Lulu E. Wolf, San Francisco; Lottie B. Wood, Santa Cruz; Zella E. Wood, Los Angeles; Mary Woodward, Los Angeles; Anna H. Yates, Alameda.

KINDERGARTEN-PRIMARY.

Mary F. Ledyard, Los Angeles.

SPECIAL LIFE DIPLOMAS.

Ida Garbarino, San Francisco, bookkeeping and typewriting; Lena L. Ingraham, Orange, drawing and manual training; Harriet E. Rademaker, San Francisco, bookkeeping; Mary Leila Richards, San Francisco, stenography; Terese F. Spencer, San Francisco, stenography; Frank L. Thompson, Ventura, commercial branches, including shorthand and typewriting.

NEW ISSUE.

Mary I. Wheeler, San Francisco (Date of original April 1, 1882).

SPECIAL HIGH SCHOOL CREDENTIALS.

Miss Clara Edith Bailey, Mr. W. P. Boynton, Mr. J. O. Churchill, Miss Alice Freeman, Mrs. Emily U. Knape, Mr. A. A. Mackenzie, Miss Anna A. McNair, Mr. Clayton F. Palmer, Miss Inez Payton, Miss Mary Helen Post, Miss Dorothy Poppy, Mr. Allan Robertson, Mr. William H. A. Rutherford, Mr. Frank C. Schofield, Mr. Archibald C. Smith, Mr. James S. Snoddy, Mr. E. W. Stoddard, Miss Hannah Thomas, Mr. Henry C. Tillman, Mr. Bert X. Tucker.

CIRCULAR NO. 5

SACRAMENTO, Cal., April 1, 1903.

To County and City and County Boards of Education, and to County and City Superintendents of the State of California:

HIGH SCHOOL CERTIFICATES.

You will please take notice that at a meeting of the State Board of Education held on March 28, 1903, the institutions given herewith, belonging to the Association of American Universities, were designated as the accredited Universities and Colleges, the same to take the place of those heretofore designated, to go into effect July 1, 1903.

On and after said date, and until further notice, County and City and County Boards of Education are authorized to grant High School Certificates (according to law as provided in Sections 1521(2)(a) and 1775(1)(a) of the Political Code of California) to graduates of the following Universities:

University of California, Berkeley, California; Catholic University of America, Washington, D. C.; The University of Chicago, Chicago, Illinois; Clark University, Worcester, Massachusetts; Columbia University, New York City, New York; Cornell University, Ithaca, New York; Harvard University, Cambridge, Massachusetts; The Johns Hopkins University, Baltimore, Maryland; The Leland Stanford Junior University, Palo Alto, California; University of Michigan, Ann Arbor, Michigan; University of Pennsylvania, Philadelphia, Pennsylvania; Princeton University, Princeton, New Jersey; University of Wisconsin, Madison, Wisconsin; Yale University, New Haven, Connecticut.

Graduates of the above-mentioned colleges may be granted certificates upon presentation of a recommendation from the faculty of any one of these institutions; *provided,* that such recommendation shall show that the applicant has taken courses in the theory of education, or in the actual practice of teaching, under supervision of the pedagogical faculty, equivalent to twelve hours per week for one-half year; *provided,* that after July, 1906, at least one-third of the prescribed pedogogy shall consist of actual teaching in a well-equipped training school of secondary grade, directed by the Department of Education.

UNIVERSITY DOCUMENTS.

Graduates of the above-mentioned Universities may, upon recommendation of a County or City and County Board of Education of California, and by compliance with the rules of the State Board, be granted the University Document, as provided in Sub. 5th of Section 1775 of the Political Code.

NORMAL SCHOOLS.

The following-named State Normal Schools were placed on the accredited list, pursuant to the provisions of Section 1775 of the Political Code: State Normal School of New Hampshire, at Plymouth; State Normal School of Nebraska, at Peru.

The attention of the State Board was called to the report that some County Boards of Education have been granting grammar school certificates to gradutes of accredited Normal Schools holding only the elementary diploma of such schools. Such action is illegal and must not be continued. In all cases it is the *highest diploma* granted by the accredited institutions only that is designated by the State Board of Education to be the equivalent of a California State Normal School Diploma.

BOOKS FOR SUPPLEMENTARY USE.

By the passage and approval of the so-called text-book bill, the State Text-Book Committee, therein provided for, "shall have power, subject to the approval of the State Board of Education, * * * to adopt a list of books for supplementary use from which County and City and County Boards of Education shall select and adopt books for supplementary use in primary and grammar schools in their respective counties and cities, and counties, as required by section seventeen hundred and twelve of the Political Code." County and City and County Boards of Education will please take notice of this provision of the law and govern themselves accordingly. A list of supplementary books from which adoptions may be made will soon be prepared and published by this department.

In the April number of the WESTERN JOURNAL OF EDUCATION will be published the so-called text-book bill and sundry other laws relating to the public schools of the State.

STATE TEXT-BOOKS.

The State Text-Book Committee has under way the compilation of a new State series U. S. History, which it is hoped may be published in time for the opening of schools the coming school year. It is the purpose of this committee, and also of the State Board of Education, to proceed as rapidly as practicable with the revision of the present series of school text-books, but at this time no definite information as to when any of the books will be ready for use can be given.

Respectfully, THOMAS J. KIRK,
Superintendent of Public Instruction and ex-officio Secretary of State Board.

The University of California
Summer Session, June 25 to August 15, 1903

President Benjamin Ide Wheeler, in an open letter to the press, which accompanies advance sheets of the announcement of the summer session, writes as follows:

BERKELEY, April 1, 1903.

My Dear Sir: It is the custom of the University of California to offer for six weeks every summer courses particularly planned to meet the needs of teachers and of any who may wish the intellectual stimulation to be derived from contact with other students and from instruction from competent specialists, abreast of the times and really in control of their material. The summer session of the University of California has assumed a national character in teaching force and in student body. Its faculty includes scholars of the first rank from the chief universities of the country—men chosen as leaders in their specialties. The courses offered are of the most varied character, ranging from history to physiology, from forestry to methods of teaching. As this is the purely public enterprise of a State University, as the undertaking is absolutely without any tinge of personal pecuniary advantage for any individual, and as this work is one of far-reaching influence for the general good, I hope that you may feel it possible to aid in bringing to general attention some of the facts set forth in the enclosed announcement for the next summer session, from June 25th to August 5th.

Very sincerely yours,
BENJ. I. WHEELER.

THE SUMMER SESSION OF THE UNIVERSITY OF CALIFORNIA.

The six-weeks summer session of the University of California for this year—from June 25th to August 5th—has come to take on a national scope in teaching force and in student body. Last summer 830 students were enrolled, or more than in the summer session of any other American university.

From all the chief American universities scholars recognized as leaders in their specialties will come to California for the next summer session. Instruction will be offered in philosophy, education, history, political economy, Greek, Latin, English, German, French, Spanish, Italian, mathematics, physics, chemistry, botany, physiology, zoology, mineralogy, civil engineering, drawing, entomology, forestry, agriculture, and physical culture.

FACULTY OF THE SUMMER SESSION.

Benj. Ide Wheeler, Ph.D., LL.D., President of the University; Leon Josiah Richardson, A.B., Assistant Professor of Latin and Dean of the Summer Session; Charles Edwin Bennett, A.B., Professor of Latin in Cornell University; Benjamin Parsons Bourland, Ph.D., Professor of Romance Languages in Adelbert College of Western Reserve University; George Rice Carpenter, A.B., Professor of Rhetoric and English Composition in Columbia University; Albert Bushnell Hart, Ph.D., Professor of History in Harvard University; Paul Mon-

Official Department

roe, Ph.D, Adjunct Professor of the History of Education in Columbia University; George Herbert Palmer, LL.D., Litt. D., Alford Professor of Natural Religion, Moral Philosophy, and Civil Polity in Harvard University; Gifford Pinchot, M. A., Forester of the United States Department of Agriculture; William Emerson Ritter, Ph.D., Professor of Zoology; Hugo Karl Schilling, Ph.D., Professor of the German Language and Literature; Henry Morse Stephens, M.A., Professor of History, and Director of University Extension; Irving Stringham, Ph.D., Professor of Mathematics; Edward James Wickson, M.A., Professor of Agricultural Practice and Superintendent of University Extension in Agriculture; James Rowland Angell, M.A., Associate Professor of Experimental Psychology in the University of Chicago; Robert Herrick, A.B., Associate Professor of Rhetoric in the University of Chicago; Charles Atwood Kofoid, Ph.D., Assistant Professor of Histology and Embryology; Winthrop John Van Leuven Osterhout, Ph.D., Assistant Professor of Botany; Charles Palache, Ph.D., Assistant Professor of Mineralogy in Harvard University; William James Raymond, B.S., Assistant Professor of Physics; George Wright Shaw, Ph.D., Assistant Professor of Agricultural Chemistry; Chauncey Wetmore Wells, A.B., Assistant Professor of English Composition; Charles William Woodworth, M.S., Assistant Professor of Entomology; Frank Watts Bancroft, Ph.D., Instructor in Physiology; Edward Booth, Ph.B., Instructor in Chemistry; Carlos Bransby, M. A., Instructor in Spanish; Frederick Gardner Cottrell, Ph.D., Instructor in Chemistry; Ludwig Joseph Demeter, M.A., Instructor in German; John Henry Dye, B.S., Instructor in Civil Engineering; William Scott Ferguson, Ph.D., Instructor in Greek and Roman History; Thomas Lorenzo Heaton, B.L., LL.B., Instructor in Education; Lincoln Hutchinson, M.A., Instructor in Commercial Geography; Derrick Norman Lehmer, Ph.D., Instructor in Mathematics; Simon Litman, Dr.Jur., Instructor in Commercial Practice; Frederick William Henry Meyer, Instructor in Drawing; Charles Albert Noble, Ph.D., Instructor in Mathematics; Henry Washington Prescott, Ph.D., Instructor in Latin; George Frederick Reinhardt, B.S., M. D., Instructor in Physical Culture; Harry Beal Torrey, M.S., Instructor in Zoology; Beverly Sprague Allen, Reader in English; Eleanor Stow Bancroft, M.D., Assistant Clinician in the Medical Department; Milton Julius Blackman, Assistant in Chemistry; Garrick Mallory Borden, M.A., Secretary of University Extension and Staff Lecturer; Morris Hoyt Covert, B.S., Assistant in Physics; Calvin Olin Esterly, A.B., Assistant in Zoology; Charles Edmund Fryer, M.L., Reader in History; Nathaniel Lyon Gardner, B.S., Assistant in Botany; Charles Conklin Haines, A.B., Reader in English; Benjamin Richard Jacobs, Assistant in Chemistry; Conrad Loring, B.S., Assistant in Civil Engineering; Larrance Page, A.B., Assistant in Physics; Louisa Adelle Place, Assistant in Physical Culture; Owen Henry Robertson, Assistant in Chemistry; Albert Nelson Sheldon, Assistant in Physics; Frank Enos Smith, Assistant in Civil Engineering; Marius Joseph Spinello, M.A., Assistant in Italian; Leslie Morton Turner, Reader in English; Washington Wilson, Reader in Education.

LECTURERS.

Samuel T. Black, President of the San Diego State Normal School; James A. Foshay, M.A., Pd.D., Superintendent of Los Angeles City Schools; J. P. Greeley, Ex-County Superintendent of Orange County Schools; Thomas Jefferson Kirk, State Superintendent of Public Instruction; John W. Linscott, County Superintendent of Schools, Santa Cruz; John W. McClymonds, A.B., Superintendent of Oakland City Schools; James Sutton, Ph.B., Recorder of the Faculties.

Many of the courses will be specially planned to fit the needs of teachers who wish to learn modern pedagogical methods, and to bring themselves abreast of the times in point of view and in judgment of material. All the resources of library, laboratories, museums, and gymnasiums will be at the disposal of the summer students.

THE COURSE OF EDUCATION.

Paul Monroe, Ph.D., Adjunct Professor of the History of Education in Columbia University; Samuel T. Black, President of the State Normal School, San Diego; James A. Foshay, M.A., Pd.D., Superintendent of City Schools, Los Angeles; J. P. Greeley, Ex-County Superintendent of Orange County Schools; Thomas L. Heaton, B.L., LL.B., Instructor in Education; Thomas J. Kirk, State Superintendent of Public Instruction; John W. Linscott, County Superintendent of Schools, Santa Cruz; John W. McClymonds, A.B., Superintendent of City Schools, Oakland; Charles E. Bennett, A.B., Professor of Latin in Cornell University; George R. Carpenter, A.B., Professor of Rhetoric and English Composition in Columbia University; Hugo K. Schilling, Ph.D., Professor of the German Language and Literature; Irving Stringham, Ph.D., Professor of Mathematics; Robert Herrick, A.B., Associate Professor of Rhetoric in the University of Chicago; James R. Angell, M.A., Assistant Professor of Experimental Psychology in the University of Chicago; Winthrop J. V. Osterhout, Ph.D., Assistant Professor of Botany; Chauncey Wetmore Wells, A.B., Assistant Professor of English Composition; Henry Washington Prescott, Ph.D., Instructor in Latin; Nathaniel Lyon Gardner, B.S., Assistant in Botany;

For students graduating in and after 1904, not more than four of the (eight or twelve) units in Education required for the Teacher's certificate, may consist of courses taken in Summer Sessions. Only numbered courses of this department may be counted in satisfaction of this requirement.

Students in Education are advised to take one or more courses in Psychology, if they have not already done so. Beginning with the summer of 1904, Psychology will be made prerequisite to one or more of the courses in Education offered in summer sessions.

1. History of the Theory of Education during Modern Times.
Professor Monroe.
A study of educational ideas and practices from the Humanistic Renaissance of the fourteenth and fifteenth centuries to the present time. The aim of the course is to present the essential features of the educational thought of the past as a basis for the more detailed historic, philosophical, and methodic study of the principles of education as formulated in the present. 2 units.

2. Educational Conference.
Professor Monroe.
For the critical study of educational literature relating to the topics discussed in Course 1. Open to those taking Course 1. 2 units.

3. The practice of teaching.
Mr. Heaton, assisted by President Black and Superintendents Foshay, Greeley, Kirk, Linscott and McClymonds.

The course will consist of lectures and readings; application of educational principles to the daily work of the schools, to organization, discipline, and class-teaching. Special attention will be given to methods of teaching which have been successfully used in schools. The work will relate to both the Elementary and the High School, with special stress on the work of the Elementary School.

Each of the Superintendents will give three addresses, the remainder will be given by Mr. Heaton.

Topics: Superintendent Foshay, Examinations and Promotions, Discipline, Music; Superintendent Linscott, Advanced Arithmetic; Superintendent McClymonds, Primary Arithmetic; Superintendent Greeley, Teachers' Library, School Library, and the Teaching of History; President Black, Rural Schools, Problems of School Administration; Superintendent Kirk, School Law, School Records, School Funds and their Use. 2 units.

Open to teachers of experience.

4. Methods of teaching.
Mr. Heaton.
More detailed conference on the work of Course 3. Open to those taking Course 3. 2 units.

Elementary Psychology.

Introduction to Physiological Psychology.
Assistant Professor Angell.
Teachers' Course in Ancient History.
Dr. Ferguson.
The Odyssey of Homer.
Dr. Prescott.
The Teaching of Latin.
Professor Bennett.
Methods of Correcting Compositions.
Assistant Professor Wells.
The Basis of Correctness in English Usage.
Professor Carpenter.
A course specially adapted to the needs of teachers of Rhetoric and English Composition.
The Teaching of German.
Professor Schilling.
Logic of Mathematics.
Professor Stringham.
Plant Biology.
Assistant Professor Osterhout.
Plant Morphology.
Assistant Professor Osterhout.
Elementary Plant Physiology.
Mr. Gardner.

Among the notable features of the Summer Session will be the lectures on forestry by Mr. Gifford Pinchot, Forester of the United States Department of Agriculture; and practical talks on school affairs by six California school administrators—State Superintendent Thomas J. Kirk, Superintendents James A. Foshay, J. P. Greeley, John W. Linscott, and John W. McClymonds, and President Samuel T. Black of the San Diego State Normal School.

Berkeley has a delightful summer climate, cool and stimulating. The University is picturesquely situated on the slopes of the Berkeley hills, overlooking the Golden Gate. Berkeley is a town of 16,000 people, twenty minutes by electric car from Oakland, and near to the manifold opportunities of San Francisco, which can be reached in fifty minutes for a ten-cent fare. Special lectures and art exhibits, trips to points of interest, and provision for athletic and other recreations, all help to make the Summer Session a profitable and enjoyable way of spending a summer vacation. There are ample accommodations in Berkeley, with private families, at an expense of from $25 to $35 per month. The tuition fee of $12 entitles the student to all the privileges of the Summer Session. Special railroad rates are offered by the Southern Pacific and the Santa Fe. The Recorder of the Faculties will supply any tailed information requested.

PUBLISHERS' NOTICE.

THE WESTERN JOURNAL OF EDUCATION succeeds to the subscription lists, advertising patronage, and good will of the Golden Era, established in San Francisco in 1852.

Subscription, $1.50 a year. Single copies, 15 cents.
Remit by check, Postoffice order, Wells, Fargo & Co., or by stamps.

ADVERTISEMENTS—Advertisements of an unobjectionable nature will be inserted at the rate of $3.00 a month per inch.

MSS.—Articles on methods, trials of new theories, actual experiences, and school news, reports of teachers' meetings, etc., urgently solicited.

Address all communications to THE WESTERN JOURNAL OF EDUCATION, 723 Market Street, San Francisco.

HARR WAGNER, Editor.
THE WHITAKER & RAY COMPANY PUBLISHERS.
Entered at the San Francisco Post-office as second-class matter.

The Official Organ of the Department of Public Instruction of the State of California.

PRESIDENT ROOSEVELT in his tour of the country centers public interest in our colleges and universities. It is not the rich banker, the pork packer, or the astute political boss of the ward that attracts his personal attention. It is the college president, the university, the great body of earnest students everywhere. In this State, Pomona College, Stanford University, and the University of California are prominent centers of his itinerary.

* * *

SCHOOL LAWS.—This issue of the JOURNAL contains the important school laws passed by the recent legislature. A decided step in educational progress has been made. In fact it was an epoch-making legislature so far as the public schools were concerned. The Text-Book Law, the law in reference to the Educational Rights of Children, The Formation of Union School Districts, and the New High School Law are the four most important laws of the session. Public sentiment has been educated to such an intensity upon these problems, that immediate steps will be taken to carry out the provisions of the law on the part of the State Board of Education, the county superindendents, the trustees, and the teachers.

* * *

MANUAL TRAINING for the Filipinos. A great mistake has been made in not introducing more industrial education in public schools in the Philippines. The Commission and the Superintendent had no prejudice except their own to overcome. The opportunity was great. It has been partly lost. It is not, however, too late to teach the Filipino something else besides reading, writing and arithmetic. Dexterity with the hands, habits of thrift, ability to do things, and do them well is the white teacher's burden in the Philippines. The burden of education is a heavy one upon us. Booker T. Washington at Tuskegee has given us an object lesson in the education of the colored race. Is it possible that we shall not avail ourselves of it in the education of the native races of our Island Possessions?

* * *

WE NEED a Jacob Riis on our board of education—a man who will arouse the public to the necessity of providing playgrounds and suitable buildings for our children. The Lincoln School is provided with a rusty statue of Abraham Lincoln. Its playground for children should be improved. The children should have room to breathe, room, more room. Health, which is largely the result of fresh pure air, should be the primacy in education—not reading and arithmetic. We need more than new buildings, new text-books and compulsory education, In our large cities we need playgrounds, and air fresh and pure as modern sanitary conditions in a large city can make it.

⚐ WESTERN SCHOOL NEWS ⚐

MEETINGS

National Educational Association, President, Charles W. Eliot, Boston, July 6-10, 1903.

California Teachers' Association, O. W. Erlewine, president; Mrs. M. M. Fitz Gerald, secretary, 1627 Folsom Street, San Francisco; December 28 to 31, 1903.

Summer Normal School, State Normal School, San Jose; Morris E. Dailey, President. June 20, 12 weeks.

Summer Session, University of California, June 25 to August 5, Berkeley, Cal. Application should be sent to the Recorder of the Faculties, on or before June 15.

National Summer School of Music. 2014 Van Ness Ave., July 6 to July 18; Samuel C. Smith, 325 Sansome st., S. F.

Summer School of Drawing; Miss Horton, Oakland; D. R. Augsburg. July 20, two weeks.

NOTES

A. E. Winship, editor of the N. E. Journal of education, has been on an extended tour in the northwest.

Mrs. Dorothea Moore promoted the bill providing proper treatment for juvenile delinquents. It is now a law.

Mrs. Will S. Green of Colusa promoted a bill to establish an industrial school for girls. It was passed, but was not signed by the Governor.

A colored graduate of the State Normal School at Los Angeles has been selected by Booker T. Washington for an important place in the Tuskegee Institute.

President Benjamin Ide Wheeler delivered a series of lectures at different points in the San Joaquin Valley the week of April 1st on "The Characteristics of the Great Peoples."

A bill appropriating $100,000 for a new building for the San Francisco State Normal School failed to recieve the signature of the Governor. The normal school received $40,000 for its support.

Dr. Fletcher B. Dresslar of the department of the theory and practice of education of the University of California has been granted a year's leave of absence. He will study in Germany.

The charter day exercises at the University of California, March 23, was specially interesting this year. The addresses were made by President Jordan, Governor Pardee, and President Wheeler.

The Santa Barbara school teachers have asked for a raise of salary of twenty-five per cent. It is only fair and right that the school teachers should share in the prosperity of the trusts and other enterprises.

Edwin Ginn, of the well-known firm of book-publishers, with his family, is spending a few months in southern California, and in a recent interview as to whether Ginn & Co. was to join the trust, said, "Not so long as I am alive."

The Chico State Normal School received $28,500 for a new building. The San Diego State Normal, $61,000 for the completion of its building. The University of California received $250,000 for a new building. The Polytechnic school at San Luis Obispo also received liberal appropriations.

Miss Katherine M. Ball, supervisor of drawing in the San Francisco school department, gave a lecture to the patrons of the Franklin Grammar School on the evening of March 9th. Her subject was "French Art of the Nineteenth Century," the lecture being illustrated by seventy stereoptican views. The latter part of the month President Samuel T. Black of the San Diego State Normal School gave the children of the 7th and 8th grades an interesting talk on his travels in England, Scotland, and Ireland during the past summer.

The joint committee of the City of San Jose teachers and Santa Clara County teachers, H. M. Bland, chairman, has completed its work of organizing teachers' unions with the result that there are now in Santa Clara County two complete organizations, one having jurisdiction over the City of San Jose, the other having jurisdiction over the county. The city union is officered by A. E. Shumate. president; Jennie Cilker, and Susie Gallimore, secretary. The officers of the county union are W. R. Trace, president; D. T Bateman, county superintendent of schools, secretary, and H. N. Bullock, treasurer. Both unions have charters from the Federated Trades.

The May number of the JOURNAL will contain a large number of the most important papers and the proceedings of the California Teachers' Association. A copy of this issue will be mailed to each member of the association. Superintendents and teachers will find valuable materials in the reports of the council of education and other papers for discussion at teachers' meetings, local and county institutes The June number will be largely devoted to a consideration of the formation of union school districts.

Book Reviews

"The Bible for Children," arranged from the King James Version. By Mrs. J. B. Gilder. Preface by Rev. Francis Brown and introduction by Bishop Henry C. Potter. New York. The Century Company, 1902. Pages, XIII, 475. Price, $3.00.

In this book a much needed work is accomplished. There is slight room for disagreement with the author of the preface when he says that "the appeal of the Bible to children's minds is both natural and simple. Its narratives tell their own story. Its poetry chants its own beauty....Like words of genius generally, and more than most, the Bible makes its distinct impression on untutored minds. Nothing has yet been found to take the place of the Bible story and the mother's knee." At the knee of every wise mother in Christendom intelligent selection of material has been made from the great thesaurus. The dreary and unedifying have been ignored. But wisdom is of old a very rare and precious possession. The great majority of children either have had the Bible forced upon them indiscriminately (witness the pathetic account of Ruskin's experience) or they have failed of their birth-right on account of the parent's indifference. There has been urgent call for a book of Bible material selected with sympathetic appreciation at once of the needs of childhood and of the significance of the context of the Bible. This the compiler manifests in a marked degree. "Large portions of narrative" are chosen "as the basis of selection, with extracts of less extent, but still considerable, from the great lyrics and sermons and didactic verse and serious correspondence, to which we give the conventional names of psalm, prophecy, proverb and epistle." The conventional verse divisions have been disregarded, and a new grouping of chapters adopted, the guiding principle of which is unity of subject. Thus the old testament portions are grouped under thirteen books bearing such titles as "The Beginnings," "Abraham and Isaac," "Jacob and Joseph," "Solomon, the King," "The Captivity and the Return." Little is excluded, it seems to me, that is significant to children. The great epic figures and dramatic events and legitimate mystery are all there. Likewise little dead matter is included, tho if the compiler has erred it is on the side of inclusion.

The book is beautifully made and adorned with twenty-four full-page illustrations from the old masters. Remembering our own introduction to the Bible, we, children of a larger growth, may fairly envy the children of to-day their mode of entering into this great spiritual inheritance.   *W. S. Small.*

* * *

"Tarr & McMurry's Geography" supplementary volume. California. Harold W. Fairbanks. Macmillan & Co., publishers. Price 30 cents.

This volume on local geography has many attractive features. Mr. Fairbanks is especially strong on physiography; and so thruout the book you will find the physical features of the state emphasized. The maps are well made, and are fairly accurate. Of course, there are mistakes, like having the Nevada, California and Oregon railroad extend to Alturas, and California Northwestern stop at Ukiah. But these minor mistakes do not affect the teaching value of the book. The relief map, the province map, the map showing distribution of rainfall, are excellent. The chapters on "The History and Industrial Development," "The Coast Ranges," etc., are of special value. Mr. Fairbanks has traveled over the country gathering geographical material first hand, and has the facility to put it into first class shape for text-book work.

* * *

For those to whom the fiction of the magazines is always first the February Century has provided liberally. Lovey Mary visits Miss Viny and goes with Mrs. Wiggs and all the family on a picnic which proves decidedly Wiggesque. The second part of Abigail H. Fitch's "When the Consul Came to Peking" carries its characters to safety through some thrilling adventures. "The Yellow Van" continues in interest. There is wit in Virginia Frazer Boyle's "Her Freedom," and much pathos in Kate W. Hamilton's "The Baby From Ruggles's Dip." There is another Pa Gladden story, too, "Knights to the Rescue," in which Elizabeth Cherry Waltz takes her gentle, lovable hero on an unusual errand of mercy.

The American Book Company has issued Horace Moore's "Horace's Odes and Epodes and Carmen Saeculare," edited by Clifton Moore of Harvard University. Price, $1.50.

D. Appleton & Co. have issued a school grammar of "Attic Greek," edited by Thomas Dwight Goodell of Yale University. This is a book of 334 pages, well printed and carefully edited. The author has endeavored to simplify the study of Greek. * * *

G. P. Putnam & Sons, New York, have issued in the series "Heroes of the Nation," "Augustus Caesar and the Organization of the Empire of Rome," by John B. Firth. This treats of Caesar in all of his various relations as warrior, statesman, and as a social and religious reformer. Price, $1.35.

D. Appleton & Co. have issued in the Twentieth Century Text-Book "The Life of the Ancient Greeks," by Professor Gulick of Harvard University. This book will be invaluable to the student of the Greek language. The book aims to present the essential facts of daily life among the Greeks.

The Macmillan Company have published an "Ancient History for Beginners," by George Willis Botsford, of Columbia University. The work has numerous maps and illustrations, and is written in a very interesting manner. The author follows the report of the Committee of Seven and aims to present ancient history as a unit, comprising three closely related parts—the Orient, Greece, and Rome—which covers a year's work in the beginning classes in the high school. The style is to be particularly commended, also the full-page and double-page maps and the illustrations in the text. They are the best the editor has seen in any book of the kind.

Little, Brown & Co. have issued "The Struggle for a Continent," edited from the writings of Francis Parkman, by Pelham Edgar. The author, with the aid of connective notes, has presented in the historian's own language a series of brilliant and absorbing historical pictures, which scenes are laid in Florida, Massachusetts, in the Great West and in Canada, the whole forming a continued story of the conflict between England and France for the mastery of the New World. The volume includes 500 pages, with maps, portraits of historical personages, and other illustrations. Price, $1.50.

Macmillan & Co. have issued "Real Things in Nature," a reading book of science for American boys and girls, by Edward S. Holden, formerly President of the University of California, now Librarian of the United States Military Academy at West Point. The book is divided into several books. Book one is devoted to astronomy, book two to physic, book three to meteorology, book four to chemistry, book five to geology, book six to zoology, book seven to botany, book eight to the human body, and book nine to the early history of mankind.

The American Book Company has issued Kutner's "Commercial German," by Arnold Kutner of the High School of Commerce, New York City. There are 404 pages. Price, $1. This certainly is a very valuable book, and just the kind of a book that we need in our commercial courses in high schools.

Longmans, Green & Co. have issued "Interpreted Reading," by Cora Marshland, Professor of Elocution and Oratory in the Kansas State Normal School. This book treats of Interpretive Reading, breathing, voice culture, and gestures. The selections are made with considerable care. There is more of the strength of strong literature in this volume than is usually found in the modern text-book on reading.

The Macmillan Company have issued a book of special interest to teachers, "The Method of the Recitation," by Charles A. McMurry and Frank McMurry. The book is dedicated to John W. Cook, President of the Illinois Normal School. "The Method of Recitation" is based on schoolroom work, and it is designed to be a practical application of the principles of methods to the various problems of schoolroom instruction. It is based fundamentally upon the inductive and deductive movement of acquiring the use of knowledge. The inductive and deductive movement is certainly confusing, and it is fortunate that the body of the book is in clearer and more definite English than the preface. The book treats of such subjects as "Why General Notions or Concepts are the Glow of Instruction," "How Individual Notions Should be Presented," "How General Notions be Applied," "The Value of Types," "Laws Underlying Processes in Teaching," "Applications and Criticisms—Lesson Plans."

The Macmillan Company have issued a special method in the "Reading of Complete English Classics for the Course of the Common Schools," by Charles McMurry. The subjects treated are the "Educational Value of Literature," "The Use of Masterpieces as a Whole," "The Value of Classics to the Teachers," and "List of Books." The principal objection to the subject may be found in the very poor selection of books for reading. Practically, every myth or imaginative book that has ever been published is given in the list. If the children are fed on such material as offered in this book exclusively, it is no wonder that they grow up fond of the yellow stories in the newspapers. The time is come when those who are interested in the training of children know the line of reading must insist, on something better than fanciful tales. Of the nineteen books offered in the fourth grade for regular reading thirteen are fairy tales. The others are nature stories, and there is one good book, "The Four Great Americans." Price, 75 cents.

"History for Graded and District Schools" by E. W. Kemp, of the Indiana State Normal School at Terre Haute is a new departure in the making of history books. The idea has been to present the unity of history, and to lead the child to comprehend the unbroken stream of life from the beginning. The book is pedagogically correct. It will take years of the promotion of common sense before the book will be regularly adopted for use in the public schools. In the first place there are no beautiful pictures. The audacity of the author to write a book without pictures, and a history too. Does the author not know that pictures are a contribution to mental indolence, and make the book sell? The opening chapter is "Arza and His Seven Sons," the next is "How Kufu Lived," the next is "What the Hebrews Taught the World," and continuing in systematic order to "The Development of the Nation—the United States." The book is written in an interesting manner. The publishers are Ginn & Co., S. C. Smith, representative, 325 Sansome street, San Francisco, Cal.

* * *

Poster Exhibit—League of Cross Cadets.

The Poster Carnival, League of the Cross Cadets, will be held in Mechanics' Pavilion, April 13 to April 18, and will be of special interest to all artists, teachers, pupils and schools of drawing.

The Carnival will include an exhibition of original posters, executed by artists and pupils of the public and private schools and academies of the State. It will stimulate interest in poster work and be a valuable lesson to the school children of the city.

Already many schools have signified their intention to exhibit, and this promises to be one of the most interesting features of this novel entertainment, gotten for the very worthy object of raising funds for the proposed League of the Cross Building.

Valuable prizes are offered for the best specimens of poster, and keen rivalry has been aroused among the schools and academies. It will be the first general exhibit of posters given in San Francisco.

The general rules governing the exhibits and contests are as follows:

Prizes.

Class "A" (open to all)—For the best poster, $100; for the best collection, high schools, valuable trophy; for the best class exhibit, high schools, valuable trophy; for the best individual poster, high schools, $25.

Class "B"—For the best collection, grammar grade schools, valuable trophy; for the best class exhibit, grammar grade schools, valuable trophy; for the best individual poster, grammar grade schools, $25; for the best collection, primary grade schools, valuable trophy; for the best class exh bit, primary grade schools, valuable trophy; for the b st individual poster, primary grade schools, $25.

1.—The posters must bear the words "Poster Carnival, League of the Cross Cadets, Mechanics' Pavilion, April 13 to April 18, 1903."

2.—Sizes—For Class "A" the minimum length should be twenty-four inches.

3.—The posters of Class "A" should express any of these ideas: First, "Carnival"; second, "Temperance"; third, "Military." The League of the Cross Cadets is both a military and temperance organization.

4.—Posters may be executed in ink, crayon and colors.

5.—Posters are the property of exhibitors.

7.—All posters offered for exhibition must be ready for delivery on or before April 1, 1903.

Those desiring to enter contest may apply for further information to Martin W. Fleming, Secretary, 87 Flood Building.

NOTES

The article on "Juvenile Offenders" was written by Judge Henry H. Klamroth of Pasadena, not Clamroth, as printed in the March number.

Alexander B. Coffey has been writing a series of articles for the "Northwest Journal of Education." In a recent issue, in giving advice to the young lady teachers in reference to expenditures, said: "A young lady school teacher can dress on from $50 to $75 yer year." If Mr. Coffey should ever get up sufficient courage to marry one he would find out that he was somewhat wrong in his estimate of how much it costs per annum for a lady to dress.

* * *

Edward W. Davis.

Richard D. Faulkner.

A short time before the meeting of the California Teachers' Association at Santa Rosa in 1898 Edward W. Davis was compelled to lay down his work and seek rest and climate in the hope that he would regain his health and strength and be able to continue his work as Secretary of the Board of Regents of the University of California. We missed him at Santa Rosa, for he had long been a familiar figure at the Association. I was particularly impressed by his absence and moved that the Association extend him its greetings and hope for his speedy restoration to health.

It was my pleasure to know E. W. Davis since 1878. He presided over the first teachers' institute I attended in this state. He was a courageous man and admired courage in others. He gave and received blows without flinching. He was not only ambitious to succeed in his own undertakings but he was glad to see others succeed. In a letter to me, written less than two years ago, he said, "I like the men who *make* success. While *success* is not exactly a manufactured article, yet it can be made from grit, perseverance, intelligence, honesty and labor."

I present below a few brief facts of his life:

Edward W. Davis was born in Washington county, Iowa, September 5, 1848. He came with his parents, George W. and Ellen R. Davis, across the plains in 1854. The family settled in Santa Rosa in 1858, the intervening time having been spent in El Dorado, Solano and Sacramento counties.

As a boy Mr. Davis attended the public schools of Santa Rosa. In 1868 he went with his brother, William R. Davis, to Oakland, where both prepared in the Brayton College School for admission to the University of California. He entered the University in 1870 but was compelled to withdraw on account of his eyes in 1872. He afterwards passed the examination, taking his degree many years later.

In 1876 he was elected Superintendent of Schools of Sonoma county. At this time the superintendent of his county was ex-officio a member of the State Board of Education. In the early 80's he was editor and proprietor of the *Santa Rosa Republican*; later he and his father invested in improved vinticultural and agricultural properties near Santa Rosa, during which time he was president of the Santa Rosa National Bank. In 1892 he was a candidate for Congress but was defeated. In 1894 he was again elected Superintendent of Schools of Sonoma county, but resigned, before the expiration of his term, to become Secretary of the Board of Regents of the University of California. He was energetic in the discharge of his duties until his failing health compelled him to obtain a leave of absence. The Board granted him an indefinite leave. His office was never declared vacant. The Board clung to the hope that his life would be spared and that he could take up his work again; but he could not overcome the tuberculosis with which he was so long afflicted and which he fought so manfully. He died at his home in Santa Rosa February 8, 1903.

At the time of his funeral the courts and public schools were closed in respect of his memory. He leaves a widow, Margaret Young Davis, a daughter Mary, and a son William B. His estate is valued at about $45,000, his long sickness having reduced his property very materially.

In the death of E. W. Davis the University of California lost a loyal son and the Board of Regents an efficient secretary, for there never was an hour, from 1870, when he entered the University until his dying day, that his mind and heart were not concerned above all else with its maintainance and expansion, with its rightful power and influence.

It is sad that one so gifted and energetic, so brave and courageous, so honest and unswerving should have been compelled to wear out his life in inaction; but even these years of inactivity were an inspiration to every one who knew him.

Don't You Find Trouble

in keeping your pupils interested in

BOOKKEEPING?

If you will use the ELLIS SYSTEM you will have no further trouble. It was prepared by men who have had years of experience not only in the schoolroom but in the business world. This system teaches the kind of business and bookkeeping that business men want.

The Gregg System of Shorthand is particularly adapted to High School work on account of its simplicity, rapidity, and legibility.

We have made arrangements with the leading business college in San Francisco to give a special course in these subjects to teachers. Write us for full information.

ELLIS PUBLISHING COMPANY   1236 Market Street, San Francisco

THE WESTERN JOURNAL OF EDUCATION

MAY, 1903

Special Number Containing the Proceedings of
The California Teachers' Association

CONTENTS

PROGRAM 219
CONSTITUTION 228
COUNCIL OF EDUCATION 230
    Relation of Course of Study of Normal and High Schools—C. C. Van Liew; The Present High School Course in Reference to Average Intelligence—R. L. Sandwick; Promotion of Pupils in Rural Schools—Robert Furlong; County Boards of Education—A. B. Shumate; The Present High School Course in Latin in Accredited High Schools—Edward Hohfeld; Commercial Course for High Schools—J. H. Francis; Uniformity of the High School Course—S. D. Waterman; Algebra—J. D. Graham; Algebra—A. W. Stamper; The State Arithmetic—A. L. Mann; Supervision of Rural Schools—Kate Ames; Teachers' Institute—J. H. Strine.

GENERAL SESSIONS 268
    Address of Welcome—Mayor M. P. Snyder; Address of Welcome—James A. Foshay; Response—Mrs. J. B. Chope; Habit—Ella F. Young; Culture and Its Enemies—E. M. Hopkins; President's Address—A. B. Shumate; Our Country School Problem—E. P. Cubberley; Social Progression in Childhood—Ella F. Young; Address by Booker T. Washington on the Tuskegee Institute; The Race Problem—Extracts from an Address by Booker T. Washington; Education and National Character—Elmer E. Brown; The Ideal Normal School—H. M. Bland; The Child-Study Circles—Mrs. W. W. Murphy.

HIGH SCHOOL ASSOCIATION 297
    Review of the Year's Work—C. L. Biedenbach; Disciplinary Value of English; Gertrude Henderson; The Educational Value of Mathematics—Dr. A. W. Scott; The Educational Value of Modern Languages—Valentin Buehner; Latin as a Formal Discipline—Frank Morton; On Formal Discipline—Dr. E. C. Moore.

GRAMMAR SCHOOL GRADE 318
    Minutes; Literature in the Grammar Grades—Miss M. R. Duraind; Historical Chart Teaching—Miss Christine Hart; What the High School Demands of the Grammar School—Lewis B. Avery; The Course of Study in the Grammar Schools—Its Limitations—George S. Wells; The Scope and Duties of the Principal in Relation to the School—George Dudley Kierulff; Teaching of History in the Grammar Grades—Julia C. Coffey; The Elementary Course of Study—C. E. Keyes; The Grammar School Course as a Preparation for Life—F. A. Wagner.

PRIMARY SCHOOL SECTION 351
    Introductory Remarks—Rebecca P. English; Morals and Manners—Ellwood P. Cubberley; The Rational Method of Reading—Mrs. M. L. Westover; Primary Reading—Miss Julia Dwire; Correlation—Frances Cook Holden; Arithmetic Without a Pencil—Edith M. Joy.

KINDERGARTEN SECTION 356
    How to Overcome the Isolation of the Kindergarten—Cora A. Reavis.

SCHOOL LEGISLATION SECTION 358
    General School Legislation—James A. Foshay; Some Needed Legislation—Edward Hyatt; The Advantages and Disadvantages of a Free Text-Book System—S. D. Waterman.

MANUAL TRAINING SECTION 366
    Manual Training in Secondary Schools—Elmer E. Brown; Manual Work for the First Grade—Mary F. Ledyard; Experimentation by the Pupil in Domestic Science—Mary L. Gower.

PHYSICAL CULTURE SECTION 371
    In Relation to Physical Culture—Louis Fritz; The German System of Physical Culture—Fred Detmers.

MUSIC SECTION 376
    Minutes; Beginnings in Music—Miss Ida Fisher; Voice Quality—Estelle Carpenter.

Newest Secondary Text-Books

H LL'S BEGINNINGS OF RHETORIC AND COMPOSITION $1.25

By *Adams Sherman Hill*, Boylston Professor of Rhetoric and Oratory, Harvard University.

This book is intended to teach young writers to express themselves correctly; not by dry mechanical devices, but by stimulating them to put their natural selves into their compositions. It lays emphasis on correct rather than on incorrect forms, and on better rather than on worse methods of expression. Numerous practical exercises are given on every important point, sufficiently varied for the most painstaking teacher.

KUTNER'S COMMERCIAL GERMAN $1.00

By *Arnold Kutner*, High School of Commerce, New York City.

A complete course in German for commercial students, furnishing much information which will be useful in business life. It is the first attempt to introduce American students to a foreign language by means of its commercial vocabulary, and contains not only the elements of commercial German, but also reading lessons, grammatical tables, exercises on grammar, and reading selections dealing with German business customs and institutions. Special attention is given to the study of commercial correspondence, business forms, documents, newspaper articles, and advertisements.

WOLFSON'S ESSENTIALS IN ANCIENT HISTORY $1

By *Arthur Mayer Wolfson*, Ph.D., Assistant History, DeWitt Clinton High School, N York; in consultation with *Alfred Bush Hart*, LL.D., Harvard University.

Prepared on the plan recommended by the Commi of Seven, this book meets satisfactorily the most ex ing college entrance requirements in history, and c bines in one volume Greek and Roman history, that of the Eastern nations. The work covers school year. The illustrations, the list of topics fo search, and the bibliographies of parallel reading, serve special mention.

FRANÇOIS' ADVANCED FRENCH PROSE COMPOSITION $0

By *Victor E. François*, Instructor in Frenc the University of Michigan.

This book for the third and fourth years in schools or for the second year in colleges, can be with any complete grammar. Part I includes rul grammar for review, a list of verbs with the requ preposition, a variety of French texts, work in tran sition, etc. Part II, on the other hand, has an inter ing subject.—"A Stranger Visiting Paris," upon w are based numerous French and English passages translation, some of which are original, while ot have been borrowed from notable French writers.

NEW CATALOGUE FOR 1903

The American Book Company's new *Descriptive Catalogue of High School and College Text-Books* is now ready for distribution. For the convenience of teachers, separate Catalogues have been issued containing the newest and best books in the following branches of study: English, Mathematics, History and Political Science, Science, Modern Languages, Ancient Languages, and Philosophy and Education. If you are interested in any of these branches, the publishers will be very glad to send you on request the catalogue sections which you may wish to see.

In Press and in Preparation

THE GATEWAY SERIES OF ENGLISH TEXTS

For admission to colleges. Edited under the general supervision of Henry Van Dyke, Professor of English Literature, Princeton University.

MORRIS AND MORGAN'S LATIN SERIES

For schools and colleges. Prepared under the editorial supervision of Edward P. Morris, A. M., Professor of Latin, Yale University, and Morris H. Morgan, Ph.D., Professor of Classical Philology, Harvard University.

A GREEK SERIES FOR COLLEGES AND SCHOOLS

Edited under the supervision of Herbert Weir Smyth, Ph. D., Eliot, Professor of Greek Literature, Harvard University.

Modern Language Texts

The *Modern Language Texts* in French, Ge man, and Spanish, now issued by the American B Company, are noteworthy for their suitability for use both secondary schools and colleges. In addition grammars, lesson books, and reading books, there now published twenty-five different French texts forty German texts, nearly all of which are edited notes and vocabulary. For the most part they foll the lines laid down and recommended in the Repor the Committee of Twelve of the Modern Language A ciation of America. New volumes are constantly be added to this series.

AMERICAN BOOK COMPANY   PUBLISHE

NEW YORK   CINCINNATI   CHICAGO   BOSTON   ATLANTA   DALLAS

204 PINE ST., SAN FRANCISCO

THE WESTERN JOURNAL OF EDUCATION

ESTABLISHED 1852.

SAN FRANCISCO, MAY, 1903.

PROCEEDINGS
California Teachers' Association
THIRTY-SIXTH ANNUAL SESSION
Los Angeles, December 29, 1902, to January 3, 1903.

To the Teachers of California and the Friends of Education:

It costs but one dollar per year to belong to the California Teachers' Association, which needs your financial support. Every progressive teacher should feel it his duty to be a regularly contributing member even tho he be unable to attend all the annual sessions. His money is well spent in furthering the interests of education and of teachers in general. Membership carries with it the right to reduced rates upon railroads and steamships in making trips to annual meetings, and to a copy of the proceedings which alone is well worth the small fee. If you are not already a member, you can join by paying your dollar to any city or county superintendent of schools, or by sending it to the secretary, Mrs. M. M. FitzGerald, 1627 Folsom street, San Francisco.

PROGRAM

Officers for 1902.—A. E. Shumate, President, San Jose; J. B. Millard, Vice-President, Los Angeles; Mrs. J. E. Chope, Vice-President, Salinas; Mrs. M. M. Fitz Gerald, Secretary, 1627 Folsom street, San Francisco; Charles C. Hughes, Assistant Secretary, Alameda; Lewis B. Avery, Railroad Secretary, Redlands; Philip Prior, Treasurer, San Francisco.

Officers for 1903.—O. W. Erlewine, President; Mrs. J. E. Chope, First Vice-President; Edward Hyatt, Second Vice-President; Mrs. M. M. Fitz Gerald, Secretary; C. C. Hughes, Assistant Secretary; Job Wood, Railroad Secretary; Philip Prior, Treasurer.

Committees

Reception.—A. E. Baker, chairman; B. O. Kinney, Mrs. Laura I. Thompson, J. H. Francis, A. C. Brown, Mary F. Claypool, Margaret C. Downing, W. A. Ellis, Mrs. Clara M. Preston, Janet M. Henderson, Edith M. Joy, Mark Keppel, Nora H. Millspaugh, Vesta A. Olmstead, B. W. Reed, Olga H. Dorn.

Hotels.—A. W. Plummer, chairman; Ray G. VanCleve, M. C. Bettinger, George E. Larkey, R. B. Emery, Fidelia Anderson, Bertha C. Prentiss, E. R. Young, Jennie Bourne, Maude Boyle, Laura J. Campbell, Rose Hardenberg.

Badges.—Louisa A. Williams, chairman; Helen E. Hunt, Alice C. Cooper, M. Louise Hutchinson, Charles J. Fox.

Introduction. — Supt. J. A. Foshay, chairman; T. J. Kirk, S. T. Black, W. H. Housh, Lulu C. Bahr, Mrs. Theodore Coleman, E. T. Pierce, J. W. McClymonds, R. D. Faulkner, Geo. E. Larkey, J. H. Strine, Geo. L. Sackett, Rose H. Hardenberg, Mary F. Ledyard, Ednah A. Rich, J. P. Greeley, F. P. Davidson, Edward Hyatt, J. B. Millard.

Place of Meeting.—Melville Dozier, chairman; Charles E. Hutton, Everett Sheperdson.

Excursions.—T. J. Phillips, chairman; Charles A. Kunou, Byron J. Badham, J. W. Henry, W. A. Ellis.

Music. — Kathryn Stone, chairman; Mrs. Mary E. Dunster, Jennie Hogan.

School Books and Appliances.—B. W. Reed, chairman; J. P. Yoder, W. G. Tanner.

Ushers.—F. A: Bouelle, chairman; Mattie S. Tedford, Mary E. Le Van, Marion Washburn, N. Ellen Case, Grace J. Grey, Lillian D. Hazen, Florence Longley, Mabel M. Moody, Burney Porter, Jeannette Havemann, Emma V. Caleff, Cora Reavis, B. J. Badham, C. J. Fox, J. P. Yoder, Robert Lane, A. C. Brown, W. G. Tanner, W. A. Ellis, B. W. Reed, G. H. Prince, Edward Dolland, Claude Faithfull, and Charles A. Kunou.

Membership.—C. W. Mark, Chairman; J. W. McClymonds, W. S. Edwards, Hugh J. Baldwin, Edward Hyatt, J. P. Greeley, James A. Foshay, George L. Sackett, A. S. McPherron, J. H. Strine.

Resolutions.—O. W. Erlewine, chairman; T. J. Kirk, J. H. Strine, S. T. Black, C. L. McLane, Geo. L. Sackett, J. W. McClymonds, John Swett, Richard D. Faulkner, C. W. Mark, A. C. Barker, M. E. Dailey, W. D. Kingsbury, J. B. Millard, P. M. Fisher, H. M. Bland.

General Sessions

Tuesday, December 30, 1902, 7:30 P.M.

Hazard's Pavilion.

Music—"God Bless Thee, Love," (V. E. Nessler), Laurel Quintet, San Jose: Mrs. Hillman Smith, soprano; Nella Rogers, mezzo soprano; Carrie Foster McLellan, contralto; Milton L. Lawrence, tenor; J. M. Reynolds, baritone; Minnie Alice Tuck, accompanist.

Invocation, Rev. Warren F. Day.

Addresses of Welcome, Mayor M. P. Snyder, Los Angeles; Supt. J. A. Foshay, Los Angeles.

Responses, Mrs. J. E. Chope, Salinas; R. D. Faulkner, San Francisco.

Music—Scene de la Csarda (Hubay), Miss Ethel Kathryn Holladay, Violinist.

Address, "Habit," Mrs. Ella F. Young, Professor of Education, University of Chicago.

Address, "Culture and Its Enemies," E. M. Hopkins, Ph.D., Prof. of English and Rhetoric, University of Kansas.

Wednesday, December 31, 1902, 1:30 P.M.

Simpson's Auditorium.

Music—(a) "June" (Lowell), (b) Song (Franz), Los Angeles Normal Glee Club.

President's Address, A. E. Schumate, San Jose.

Address, "Our Rural School Problem," E. P. Cubberley, Professor of Education, Stanford University.

Address, "Social Progression in Childhood," Mrs. Ella F. Young, University of Chicago.

Music—(a) Roundelay (Ledge), (b) Vocal solo, "Roses in June" (German), Miss Jennie Winston, Los Angeles.

Address, "The Coming Oxford-American," E. M. Hopkins, University of Kansas.

Election of officers for 1903.

Thursday, January 1, 1903.

Reception by the Los Angeles Teachers' Association, Cumnock School of Expression, 1500 South Figueroa street.

Holiday—Given up to sight-seeing and excursions to various points of interest in and around Los Angeles, arranged by a committee of Los Angeles teachers.

Friday, January 2, 1903.

Hazard's Pavilion.

Music—"On the Sea" (Dudley Buck), Euterpean Quartet, Los Angeles.

Class Exercise—A practical illustration of the German system of physical culture. Karl Ross, Director of Physical Culture, Turn Verein Germania, Los Angeles.

Address, "Education and National Character," Elmer E. Brown, Professor of Education, University of California.

Address—Booker T. Washington, President Tuskegee Normal and Industrial Institute, Alabama.

Immediately following this address the Los Angeles Chamber of Commerce tendered a reception to the teachers of California.

Friday, January 2, 1903, 7:30 P.M.

Hazard's Pavilion.

Music—"Habanera" (Bizet), Laurel Quintet.

Music—Vocal solo, "Lend Me Your Aid" (Queen of Sheba, Gounod), Chas. A. Bowes, Los Angeles.

Address, "The Solution of the Race Problem in the Black Belt of the South," Booker T. Washington.

Saturday, January 3, 1903, 9:00 A. M.

Simpson's Auditorium.

Music—(a) "Sigh No More, Ladies" (Schnecker), (b) "Song of Illyrian Peasants" (Stevens), Laurel Quintet.

Address, "Selection and Appointment of Teachers," Cecil W. Mark, San Francisco.

Address, "The Ideal Normal School," H. M. Bland, San Jose.

Music—"Polonaise," (Wieniawski), by Miss Holladay.

Address, "The Child Study Circles and Their Connection with the Public Schools," Mrs. W. W. Murphy, Los Angeles.

Reports of Council of Education and other committees.

Miscellaneous Business.

Reports of Officers.

Installation of Officers for 1903.

Adjournment.

Schedule of Department Sections

Monday.—Council of Education, Normal Auditorium, 9:30 to 12 and 1:30 to 3:45. Los Angeles County Institute, Blanchard's Hall. Los Angeles City Institute, High School Auditorium.

Tuesday.—Council of Education, Normal Auditorium, 9:30 to 12 and 1:30 to 3:45. Los Angeles County Institute, Blanchard's Hall. Los Angeles City Institute, High School Auditorium. Legislative Section, High School Building, room 14, 9:30 to 12.

Wednesday.—High School Association, High School Auditorium, 9 to 12. Grammar School Section, Normal Auditorium, 9 to 12. Primary Section, Blanchard's Hall, 9 to 12. Legislation Section, High School Building, Room 14, 9 to 12. Child Study Section, High School Building, Room 19, 9 to 12. Kindergarten Section, Commercial High School Building, Room 12, 9 to 12. Physical Culture Section, High School Building, Room 2, 9 to 12.

Friday. — High School Association, High School Auditorium, 9 to 12. Grammar School Section, Normal Auditorium, 9 to 12. Primary School Section, Blanchard's Hall, 9 to 12. Legislation Section, High School Building, Room 14, 9 to 12. Child Study Section, High School Building, Room 19, 9 to 12. Manual Training Section, High School Building, Room 3, 9 to 12. Music Section, Cumnock School of Expression, 9:30 to 12.

Sessions of Departments

Council of Education

Chairman, Frederic Burk; Secretary, J. W. McClymonds..

Normal School Building, Los Angeles.

First Day, Monday, December 29, 1902.

Morning sessions—9:30 a. m. to 12 m. Afternoon sessions—1:30 p. m. to 3:45 p. m.

1. Report of Committee upon the pro-

posed amendment to the constitution, relative to High Schools, since the amendment has been adopted, were made on the lines of needed legislation to make the adopted amendment most beneficial to the secondary schools of the State. O. W. Erlewine, Thomas J. Kirk, Robert Furlong, J. A. Barr, E. E. Brown.

2. Report of Committee on Compulsory Education. E. C. Moore, Thos. J. Kirk, R. H. Webster, A. L. Mann, J. W. McClymonds.

3. Report of Committee on Measures for the Betterment of State Text Books. J. W. Linscott, Jas. A. Foshay, R. D. Faulkner, A. L. Mann, O. W. Erlewine.

4. Report of Committee on Free Text Books, for use in the California schools. E. M. Cox, R. H. Webster, E. E. Brown, O. W. Erlewine, Thomas J. Kirk.

5. Report of Committee on Enforcement of Code of Professional Ethics. John Swett, Robert Furlong, E. P. Cubberley, E. E. Brown, C. C. Van Liew.

6. Report of Committee on Plan of Appointment of Teachers, which shall furnish the schools with the best available teachers, and prevent violation of the code of professional ethics. J. A. Foshay, A. L. Mann, J. A. Barr. R. L. Sandwick, C. E. Keyes, R. H. Webster, R. D. Faulkner, A. E. Shumate.

7. Report of Committee on Relation of Course of Study of Normal Schools to those of High Schools. C. C. Van Liew, M. E. Dailey, Robert Furlong, A. E. Shumate, S. T. Black.

8. Report of Committee upon the best preparation of teachers by State Normal Schools to fit them for practical work in public schools. M. E. Dailey, J. A. Foshay, J. W. Linscott, C. E. Keyes, C. C. Van Liew.

9. Report of Committee on the best preparation of teachers by universities to fit them for practical needs of the public High Schools. O. P. Jenkins, E. M. Cox, E. C. Moore, E. P. Cubberley, M. E. Dailey.

10. Report of Committee upon systems of promotion in use in cities of California, the value of these systems to the educational interests of the pupils, also the value of the systems for convenience in administration. J. W. McClymonds, J. A. Foshay, A. L. Mann, R. D. Faulkner, O. W. Erlewine.

11. Report of Committee on systems of promotion in use by the various County Boards of Education in the State, the value of these systems to the educational interests of the pupils as distinct from considerations of convenience of administration and ease of bookkeeping, and if deemed advisable, to recommend a substitute system, or modification for approval by the Council. Robert Furlong, S. T. Black, P. M. Fisher, E. M. Cox, O. P. Jenkins.

12. Report of Committee on the value to the educational interests of pupils, of the present system of supervision in rural schools by County Superintendents and Boards of Education, and to recommend, if deemed advisable, a substitute system and legislative action, for approval by the Council.

13. Report of Committee upon weaknesses of the present state series of Arithmetics, and to recommend specific omissions and supplementary devices. A. L. Mann, J. A. Barr, J. W. McClymonds, R. H. Webster.

14. Report of Committee upon the teaching of Geography in the Grammar grades and recommendations of methods and supplemental material of presentation, which shall avoid the word memorizing of the text now so currently common. J. A. Barr, R. D. Faulkner, C. C. Van Liew, O. W. Erlewine.

15. Report of Committee on relative number of boys and girls in California schools who withdrew from school during the last three years of the Grammar schools, and in grades of the High School, the report to determine roughly how far these withdrawals from school are due to external causes, and how far they are due to internal causes, such as failure in written examinations for promotion, lack of adaptibility of school work to the real needs of the pupils. R. D. Faulkner, J. W. Linscott, M. E. Dailey, J. W. McClymonds, J. A. Foshay.

16. Report of Committee upon the funds of common general information current among citizens of average intelli-

gence, which is necessarily omitted in the High School courses, and to recommend modifications in the courses to remedy this defect. R. L. Sandwick, E. M. Cox, Frederic Burk, C. C. Hill, E. P. Cubberley.

17. Report of Committee concerning effects upon High School education of the system of University requirements, which develop the line of special knowledge to the neglect of that general information commonly current among people of average intelligence and culture, and to recommend specific modifications of such courses. P. M. Fisher, E. C. Moore, E. M. Cox, C. C. Van Liew, O. P. Jenkins.

Second Day, Tuesday, December 30, 1903

Reports of Auxiliary Committees appointed by the Council of Education for the purposes set forth in the following:

1. To compile a report upon the system of union school districts and of transportation of pupils to school at public expense, and consider its adaptability to conditions in California. Miss E. M. Hilton, County Superintendent of San Mateo, Chairman; George Gordon, Superintendent of Amador county; Miss Kate Ames, Superintendent-elect of Napa county; H. M. Shafter, San Diego Normal School; Miss Lena Polhamus, President of San Diego County Board.

2. To compile a special report upon the specific weaknesses of the present State Series History, and to recommend special omissions and supplementary devices to serve while it shall continue in use. Miss Agnes Howe, San Jose Normal School, chairman; Superintendent J. D. Graham, Pasadena; E. J. Miller, Chico Normal School; Superintendent F. A. Wagner, Pomona; P. E. Davidson, San Francisco Normal School.

3. To compile a report upon the function of the present course of Algebra in accredited schools, aside from preparation to meet university courses in the mathematical department, and to determine its value relative to other material which must be omitted if this course is taken. Superintendent J. D. Graham, Pasadena, chairman; A. W. Stamper, Chico Normal School; F. F. Bunker, San Francisco Normal School.

4. To compile a report upon the present High School courses in Latin in accredited High Schools, aside from meeting the requirements to the Latin courses in the universities, and to determine its value relative to other material which must be omitted if this course is taken. E. Hohfeld, Principal Auburn High School, chairman; F. E. Thompson, San Francisco Normal School; Miss Lena Schopback, Pasadena High School; R. L. Sandwick, Pacific Grove; Dr. John Gamble, Haywards.

5. To compile a report upon the function of the present course in Literature in accredited High Schools, aside from meeting the requirements of the English courses in the universities; to determine the relative value to general culture of the present course of the prescribed material, to one of wide election or one permitting and requiring broad general reading. Principal G. W. Wright, Concord High School, chairman; Miss Margaret I. Poore, Superintendent of Schools, Shasta county; Dr. John Gamble, Haywards High School; Superintendent F. A. Wagner, Pomona; Leroy D. Eley, Pasadena High School; J. C. Templeton, Superintendent of Schools, Santa Ana.

6. To compile a report upon the function of the present courses in chemistry, botany, zoology and physics, in accredited High Schools, aside from preparation for corresponding university courses; and to determine the value of these courses relative to courses in these subjects which should offer a broader horizon in general information of their application. Charles D. Snyder, Lowell High School, San Francisco, chairman; Superintendent C. L. McLane, Fresno; L. B. Wilson, San Jose Normal School; Superintendent F. A. Wagner, Pomona; R. L. Sandwick, Pacific Grove; Ray Chase, Chico Normal School.

7. To compile a report upon the proper relation of county superintendents to the local affairs of school districts, and to recommend such plans as may be deemed for the best educational service. Miss Kate E. Ames, Napa, chairman; Superintend-

ent J. H. Strine, Los Angeles; Superintendent Gorge Gordon, Amador county; E. J. Miller, Chico Normal School.

8. To compile a report upon existing systems of using the district libraries in the State, the abuse of them, and to recommend a plan, requiring County Board regulations or legislative action, which shall make these libraries of the highest practical service to school work. E. I. Miller, Chico Normal School, chairman; L. B. Wilson, San Jose Normal School; Superintendent George Gordon, Amador county.

9. To compile a report upon existing systems for supervisions of rural schools by county superintendents, to estimate its value and to recommend such modifications as may be deemed for the best service to the educational interests of pupils. Superintendent J. A. Imrie, Napa county, chairman; Superintendent J. H. Stripe, Los Angeles; Kate E. Ames, Napa; E. J. Miller, Chico Normal School.

10. To compile a report upon the appointment of teachers in rural schools which shall offer a specific and practical means for furnishing the schools with the best available teachers and prevent violation of the code of professional ethics. Superintendent A. S. McPherron, San Bernardino county, chairman; A. W. Stamper, Chico Normal School; H. M. Shafer, San Diego Normal School; Superintendent J. H. Strine, Los Angeles.

11. To compile a report from views of experienced county superintendents and others upon the system of county institutes and to recommend modifications for approval by the Council. Superintendent J. H. Strine, Los Angeles county, chairman; Superintendent J. A. Imrie, Napa county; Miss Agnes Howe, San Jose Normal School; H. M. Shafer, San Diego Normal School; Miss Kate Ames, Napa.

12. To compile a report upon the function and scope of a business course in the High Schools and to determine the relation of such course to the rest of the High School curriculum. Superintendent C. L. McLane, Fresno, chairman; J. H. Francis, Los Angeles High School; D. A. Mobley, Stockton High School; P. M. Fisher, Central School, Oakland.

High School Association

Auditorium of High School Building

Chairman, Chas. L. Biedenbach, Berkeley; Secretary pro tem., J. C. Templeton, Santa Ana.

Wednesday, December 31, 1902, 9 A. M.

9:00. Opening, "The Cruiskeen Lawn" (Sir Stewart), Laurel Quintet.

9:10. Review of the Year's Work, C. L. Biedenbach.

9:30. General Report of Committee of Ten, D. S. Snedden. Reports of Sub-Committees.

9:50. "Function of the High School as Fitting for Life," G. A. Merrill.

10:20. "Why Pupils Leave the High School," A. C. Barker.

10:50. Intermission.

11:00. "The Transition from the Elementary to Secondary Schools," C. E. Keyes.

11:30. "Secondary School Work as Fitting for Normal Schools," C. C. Van Liew.

Friday Morning, January 2, 1903.

9:00. Music, Pasadena High School Glee Club.

"The Elective System," D. S. Snedden.

9:30. "Prescribed Admission Requirements," W. D. Housh.

9:50. "The Accrediting System," Edward Hohfeld.

10:20. "Evolution and Educational Method." Mrs. Ella F. Young, University of Chicago.

11:00. "Formal Discipline as Related to Secondary School Studies," E. C. Moore.

"Foreign Modern Languages," Valentine Buehner.

"Classical Languages," Frank Morton.

"English," Miss Gertrude Henderson.

"Mathematics," A. W. Scott.

"Sciences," S. E. Coleman.

Election of Officers.

Adjournment.

California Teachers' Association

Grammar School Section
Auditorium of State Normal School Bldg.

Chairman, Chas. C. Hughes, Alameda; Secretary, Miss Lois Peckham, San Francisco.

Wednesday, December 31, 1902, 9 A. M.

Music—Violin solo—"Madrigale" (Simonetti), Miss Holladay.

"The Training of the Grammar School Teacher," Henry Suzzallo, San Francisco Normal School.

"The Function of the Grammar School Principal," G. Dudley Kierulff, Principal Mastick Grammar School, Alameda.

"Is the Course of Study Overcrowded? Is There a Remedy?" Geo. S. Wells, Principal Lincoln Grammar School, San Jose.

"Teaching of Literature in the Grammar Grades," Miss M. R. Duraind, Hamilton Grammar School, San Francisco.

"American History in the Elementary Schools," Mrs. Ella F. Young, University of Chicago.

Discussion, "The Advisability of Forming a Permanent Elementary School Association."

Friday, January 2, 1903, 9 A.M.

Music—"The Bells of St. Michael's Tower" (Sir Stewart). Laurel Quintet.

"The Grammar School Course as a Preparation for Life," Supt. F. A. Wagner, Pomona.

"What the High School Expects of the Grammar School," Lewis B. Avery, Principal Union High School, Redlands.

"Historical Chart Teaching," Miss Christine Hart, Vice Principal Longfellow Grammar School, San Francisco.

"Domestic Science," Mrs. Jessica Hazzard, Director of Domestic Science, Los Angeles Normal School.

"The Grammar School and Secondary Subjects," C. E. Keyes, Principal Lafayette School, Oakland.

"Teaching of History in the Grammar Grades," Miss Julia C. Coffey, Spring Valley Grammar School, San Francisco.

Primary School Section
Blanchard's Hall.

Chairman, Miss Rebecca F. English, San Jose; Secretary, Mrs. Fannie Byram, Los Angeles.

Wednesday, December 31, 1902, 9 A.M.

9 to 9:15. Primary songs, Second Grade, Los Angeles schools.

Introductory remarks, Miss Rebecca F. English.

9:15 to 10. "Morals and Manners," Ellwood P. Cubberley, Stanford.

10 to 10:30. "Card-board Construction," C. A. Kunou, teacher of manual training, Los Angeles schools.

10:30 to 10:40. Violin solo, Miss Holladay.

10:40 to 11:15. "Ought the School to be Made More Like the Home?" Prof. Elmer E. Brown, University of California, Berkeley.

11:15 to 11:40. "The Ward System of Reading," M. L. Westover, Fresno, Cal.

11:40 to 12:00. "Reading in Lower Grades," Miss Julia Dwire, Ventura, Cal.

Wednesday, December 31, 1902, 9 A.M.

9 to 9:10. Violin solo, selected, Miss Holladay.

9:10 to 9:50. "Personal Initiative vs. Methods in Teaching," Prof. E. M. Hopkins, Kansas University.

9:50 to 9:10. "Correlation Between Kindergarten and Primary School," Mrs. Frances Holden, Santa Ana, Cal.

10:10 to 10:30. "Arithmetic Without a Pencil," Miss Edith M. Joy, Los Angeles Schools.

10:40 to 11:10. "The Teaching of Number in the Primary Grades," A. H. Suzzalo, State Normal School, San Francisco.

11:10 to 11:35. "Primary Grade Literature. The Possibilities of the Bible Story and Fairy Tale," Helen Ballard, San Diego.

11:35 to 12. Address, Dr. W. S. Small, Los Angeles.

Kindergarten School Section

Commercial High School, Room 12.

Chairman, Mrs. Frances B. Gould, Oakland; Secretary, Miss Mary F. Ledyard, Los Angeles.

Wednesday, December 31, 1902, 9:30 A.M.

"The Isolation of the Kindergarten," Dr. E. E. Brown, Professor of the Science and Art of Teaching in the University of California.

"How to Overcome the Isolation of the Kindergarten: The Training of Kindergarten Teachers," Dr. C. C. Van Liew, President State Normal School, Chico.

"How to Overcome the Isolation of the Kindergarten: The Primary Point of View," Miss Cora A. Reavis, Los Angeles School Department.

School Legislation Section

High School Building, Room 14.

Chairman, Hugh J. Baldwin; San Diego; Secretary, J. H. Strine, Los Angeles.

Tuesday, December 30, 1902, 9:30 A.M.

The Necessary Legislation to put into operation the Recent Constitutional Amendment relating to High Schools, W. H. Housh, Principal Los Angeles High School.

Discussion by P. M. Fisher, Principal Commercial High School, Oakland; Charles T. Meredith, San Diego Normal School; James A. Barr, City Superintendent of Schools, Stockton; F. P. Davidson, City Superintendent Schools, San Diego; William Carey Jones, University of California.

Some Needed Legislation in Reference to Teachers' Institutes, Harr Wagner, Editor Western Journal of Education.

Discussion by Pres. Benj. Ide Wheeler, University of California; Edward T. Pierce, President Los Angeles State Normal; Samuel T. Black, President San Diego Normal; C. C. Van Liew, President Chico State Normal; Frederic L. Burk, President San Francisco State Normal; Maurice E. Dailey, President San Jose State Normal.

Wednesday, 9:30 A.M.

Debate—Resolved, That the best interests of the California school system demand legislative enactments that will permit the combination of school districts and the transportation of school children, Elwood P. Cubberley, Leland Stanford Junior University. Discussion by Miss E. M. Tilton, Superintendent of Schools, San Mateo county; T. O. Crawford, Superintendent of Schools, Alameda county; W. C. Doub, Superintendent of Schools, Kern county; W. S. Edwards, Superintendent of Schools, Santa Barbara; A. S. McPherron, Superintendent of Schools, San Bernardino county; Geo. L. Sackett, Superintendent of Schools, Ventura county.

Judicial Consideration of Juvenile Offenders, Henry H. Klamroth, Pasadena. Discussion by Hon. J. H. Foley of Los Angeles Board of Education; J. W. McClymonds, City Superintendent Schools, Oakland; O. W. Erlewine, City Superintendent of Schools, Sacramento; R. H. Webster, City Superintendent of Schools, San Francisco; Sam. F. Smith, City Board of Education, San Diego.

Friday, January 2, 1902, 9 A.M.

Some Needed Legislation for the County Superintendent's Office, Edward Hyatt, Superintendent of Riverside county. Discussion by J. P. Greeley, Superintendent of Orange county; J. W. Linscott, Superintendent of Santa Cruz county; Minnie Coulter, Superintendent of Sonoma county; S. A. Crookshanks, Superintendent of Tulare county.

General School Legislation to Promote the Educational Interests of the State, James A. Foshay, City Superintendent of Los Angeles. Will speak on a compulsory educational law. Discussion by President George A. Gates, Pomona College; Albert Currlin, proprietor of Oakland Journal; W. J. Washburn, President Los Angeles City Board; George A. Merrill, Principal Lick Polytechnic, San Francisco; Mrs. J. E. Chope, Superintendent of Schools, Monterey.

The Advantages and Disadvantages of a Free Text-Book System, S. D. Waterman, City Superintendent of Schools, Berkeley. Discussion by W. W. Tritt, Assistant Superintendent of Schools, Los Angeles; N. B. Coy, Principal San Diego High School; E. C. Norton, Pomona College; F. B. Dresslar, University of California.

Manual Training Section

High School Building, Room 3.

Chairman, Walter A. Edwards, Pasadena; Secretary, Claude A. Faithfull, Los Angeles.

Friday, January 2, 1903, A.M.

"Manual Work for the First Grade," Mary F. Ledyard, Supervisor of Kindergarten Department, Los Angeles.

"Manual Training in Secondary Schools—A Cultural or a Vocational Subject?" E. E. Brown, University of California.

"The Future of Manual Training," T. H. Kirk, Superintendent of Schools, Santa Barbara.

"Experimentation by Pupils in Domestic Science," Mary L. Gower, Los Angeles.

The reading of each paper will be followed by a general discussion of the topic, in which any one may take part.

Physical Culture Section

High School Building, Room 2.

Chairman, H. J. Baldwin, San Diego; Secretary, Edward Hyatt, Riverside.

Wednesday, December 31, 1902, 9 A.M.

Address by Chairman, H. J. Baldwin.

"Physical Culture Viewed from a Medical Standpoint," Dr. Joseph Kurtz.

"Merits of the German System of Physical Culture," Fred Detmers.

An illustration of physical exercises by pupils of Turn Verein Germania, Karl F. Ross, Director.

General discussion.

Music Section

Cumnock Hall, 1500 Figueroa Street.

Chairman, Miss Kathryn Stone, Los Angeles; Secretary, Leon I. Stanton, Coronado.

Friday, January 2, 1903, 9 A.M.

"Meditation" (twenty violins), Bach. Solo by Mr. Edwin Clark.

Paper—"Voice Quality," Miss Estelle Carpenter, San Francisco.

Songs—Selected, Miss Beresford Joy, Los Angeles.

Paper—"Beginnings in Music," Miss Ida Fisher, Alameda.

Class songs, Fifth and Sixth Grades, Los Angeles.

Paper—"Rhythm," Mrs. L. V. Sweesy, Berkeley.

Violin solo—Ninth Concerto, De Beriot. Mrs. Hazel Dessery, Los Angeles.

Child Study Section

High School Building, Room 19.

Chairman, Edwin D. Starbuck, Stanford University; Secretary, H. M. Bland, San Jose.

Wednesday, December 31, 1902

9 to 10:10. The Child Study Circle. (b) How organized, Miss Mary F. Ledyard; (c) Relation to Citizenship, Miss Mary E. Foy; (d) Relation to Home, Mrs. Kate Tupper Galpin.

10:10 to 10:30. "Voluntary Association Among Children," D. S. Snedden.

10:30 to 10:50. "Some Phases of the Growth of Children's Minds," C. J. C. Bennett.

10:50 to 11:10. "Esthetic and Ethical Influence of the Kindergarten," Miss Leesie Byrd.

11:10 to 11:20. "Education Through Activity," Miss Harriet M. Scott.

11:20 to 11:40. Address, Mrs. Ella F. Young.

11:40 to 12. "Sex Differences," I. D. Perry.

Friday, January 2, 1903, 9:30 A.M.

9:15. "Value of Tests to Teachers," J. Fred Smith.

9:15 to 9:30. "The Possibility of Tests of School Children by Teachers," C. C. Van Liew.

9:30 to 9:45. "Description of a Few

"Simple Tests," Miss Frances C. Holden. 9:45 to 10. "An Outline for Tests and Observation," H. M. Bland.
10 to 10:15. "Correlation of School Tests," W. S. Small.
10:15 to 10:30. "A Report on the Literature of the Subject," F. E. Thompson.
10:30 to 10:45. "The Practical Question of Introducing a Child Study Specialist," Harry M. Shafer.
10:45 to 11. "What Is Being Done in Eastern Cities," W. F. Snow, M. D.
11 to 12. "The Next Step for the State of California," general discussion, led by Elmer E. Brown.

* * *

CONSTITUTION OF THE CALIFORNIA TEACHERS' ASSOCIATION

PREAMBLE.

For the purpose of furthering the educational interests of the State, of giving efficiency to our school system, of furnishing a practicable basis for united action among those devoted to the cause in which we are now engaged, and of securing and maintaining for the office of teaching its true rank among the professions, we, the members of this Association, do hereby adopt the following

CONSTITUTION.

NAME.

SECTION 1. This organization shall be known as the California Teachers' Association.

MEMBERSHIP.

SEC. 2. All persons who are now, or who may be hereafter officially connected with the public or private schools of the State, or interested in the cause of education, may become members of this Association by signing the Constitution, and paying the annual fee of one dollar; provided further, that no member shall have a vote in the management of the Association unless he has been for the preceding year a member of the Association, and has paid his dues for the current year. The Secretary of the Association shall annually publish in the November number of the "Educational Journal" of this State, without expense to the Association, a list of the members; provided, however, that before dropping any member for non-payment of dues, such member shall, one month before that publication, be notified that dues for the current year are now payable.

OFFICERS.

SEC. 3. The officers of the Association shall be a President, two Vice-Presidents, a Secretary, an Assistant Secretary, a Treasurer, and a Railroad Secretary, whose duty it shall be to make arrangements for the rate of transportation of members of this body; and these officers shall constitute an Executive Committee.

Term.—All officers shall serve for a term of one year.

Election.—The election of the foregoing officers shall be by ballot, and any member may place a name in nomination for any office; provided, however, that no nominating speeches shall be permitted, and that if no person shall receive a majority of the votes cast for any office upon the first four ballots, at each ballot thereafter the name upon the list receiving the lowest number of votes shall be dropped, and so on until the majority of the votes shall have been secured by one candidate; and this election shall take place at the opening of the afternoon session of the second day of the winter meeting.

DUTIES AND POWERS OF THE EXECUTIVE COMMITTEE.

SEC. 4. It shall be the duty of the Executive Committee to fix the time of holding general meetings of the Association, to prepare programs, to procure attendance of lecturers and other speakers, and to make all the necessary arrangements for the meetings.

Indebtedness.—They shall not incur any indebtedness in excess of the funds in the hands of the Treasurer.

Vacancies.—They shall have power, by majority vote, to fill all vacancies in office occurring between meetings of the Association.

Annual Report.—They shall make the Association, on the last day of its winter meeting, an annual report of its finances and membership, which report shall be submitted in writing.

Order of Business.—The Executive Committee shall have power to arrange the order of business at all the meetings, provided that reports of standing committees shall be heard on the afternoon of the second day of the winter meeting.

MEETINGS.

SEC. 5. There shall be a general meeting during such days as the Executive Committee shall determine, at a point to be determined by the vote of the Association, in the same manner as heretofore prescribed for the election of officers, so that the claims of each city to consideration may be presented by one speaker, who shall not occupy more than five minutes; and the Executive Committee may call a second meeting in June or July at such place as they may determine.

CLAIMS.

SEC. 6. All claims against the Association shall be paid by the Treasurer upon the order of the President, countersigned by the Secretary. Whenever the Treasurer shall doubt the validity of any claim, for which an order on the Treasurer may be presented, he may submit the same to the Executive Committee.

AMENDMENTS.

SEC. 7. The Constitution may be amended or altered, provided at least one day's notice, in writing, embodying the amendment or amendments to be made, be given in open session of the Association; and provided, further, the same shall be approved by a two-thirds vote of the members present, which vote shall be taken not later than the next to the last day of the general session.

COUNCIL OF EDUCATION.

SEC. 8. The Advisory Board of this Association shall be composed of fifteen members, who, together with the State Superintendent of Public Instruction, shall constitute the Council of Education. Its duty shall be to consider and report to the general body the desirability and means of securing reform in educational legislation practice.

The term of office for members of this Council shall be five years; provided, however, the first list of members shall be appointed by the President of the Association immediately upon the adoption of this section; three to serve for one year, three for two years, three for five years, three for four years, and three for five years; and annually thereafter three members shall be appointed by the Executive Committee of the General Association to serve the full term of five years. The Executive Committee shall also have power to fill all vacancies occurring in the Council between the meetings of the Association; the appointments so made to be subject to the confirmation of the General Association at its ensuing meeting.

And it is further provided that the President of the Association shall, in appointing the list of members, designate the State Superintendent as Temporary Chairman, and shall also designate a Temporary Vice-President and Secretary, and these three shall act as Temporary Executive Committee of the Council, prepare its first program, and serve until a permanent organization is perfected.

The first meeting of this body shall be held in the month of July, 1902, at a time and place to be designated by the Executive Committee of the Council herein provided for, and thereafter the Council shall meet semi-annually, alternating its sessions between the cities of Oakland and Los Angeles.

Amendment to Section 8 (December, 1901):

"The Executive Committee of this Association shall elect ten additional members of the Association, two of whom shall serve for five years, two for four years, two for three years, two for two years, and two for one year. The Executive Committee of this Association shall have power to fill all vacancies occurring in the Council.

"All members of the Council must be members of the Association, and should any member of the Council permit his membership in the Association to lapse, he shall be considered as having withdrawn from the Council, and the vacancy shall be filled by the Executive Committee of the Association.

"The Council shall have power to hold such meetings and elect such officers as it may determine. Eleven members shall constitute a quorum of the Council. All members shall be notified in writing of the time and the place of the meetings of the Council of Education. The Council shall have the power to make expenditures of money under such provisions and prohibitions as may be imposed by the Executive Committee. The Council shall have power to prescribe rules for its own government. Such rules may prescribe forfeiture of membership in the Council for lack of attendance on regular meetings of the Council."

THE COUNCIL OF EDUCATION
Frederic Burk, Chairman J. W. McClymonds, Secretary

Relation of Course of Study of Normal and High Schools

C. C. Van Liew

Normal schools, especially state normal schools, have been in existence in this country a good many years. The first normal school was established in 1838. Since then, and especially since the close of the Civil War, they have increased rapidly in number and efficiency. Every one of the younger states and territories has established one or more of these schools, and most of the older states have either fallen in line with the normal movement, raised the standard of efficiency in training teachers, or greatly increased the number of normal schools—sometimes all three. The growth has been very steady and very marked, and not lacking in the cultivation of a wholesome popular sentiment in favor of trained teachers, and of special schools designed, theoretically, to select naturally fit individuals for teachers and to give them readier efficiency in the use of natural powers.

Yet the status of the normal schools, at least in many sections of the country, is problematic. They seem to be firmly established; but their position with respect to other fields of the educational system, e. g., those of secondary and university education, is decidedly enigmatical. Here is the dilemma:

1. The normal schools have been claiming and aiming to achieve a rank equal to that of other training schools for the higher professions in both the dignity and quality of work. Yet among such professional schools many normal schools stand practically alone in still receiving students without some sort of secondary education. For such they provide three or four year courses devoted to both academic and professional training. As a result we have in this state, for example, the anomaly of normal schools which undertake to equip students in eight semesters or one hundred and sixty weeks with sufficient knowledge and spirit to teach most of their thirty to forty subjects, each one worthy of a specialist in the normal faculty itself. It is needless to argue that normal schools organized on that plan are not

going to achieve that high professional rank which is to be expected of them, and for three reasons: (1) True and thoro professional training must needs be sacrificed to a greater or less extent to academic training. (2) Even some academic branches, worthy of careful attention for their educative power in elementary education, must yield to the still more imperative demands of others. (3) No normal school in the state is equipped to give that relative mastery of subjects which will soon come to be recognized as a desideratum in the elementary school teacher, in more than a few lines. These are the matters which at present militate against the professional standing of normal schools, however much credit we undoubtedly should give them for past achievements.

2. In view of the preceding it is natural that the movement should have been set on foot to make graduation from first rank high schools the entrance requirement to normal schools. Done, in some instances; but, as this report proposes to show, with *increased* difficulties on the side of academic training.

3. The last suggestion has been that all teachers, elementary as well as secondary, should be trained at the universities. For is not the university vastly better equipped for special academic work? In point of fact the university is organized for purposes of high specialization, while our elementary schools, as they are organized today, require of their teachers a very great deal of general culture and only moderate specialization. One would not know where to turn to find a university doing work both academically and professionally suited to the preparation, e. g., of a primary teacher; and most universities give no attention whatever to three-fourths of what should make up the professional training of the elementary school teacher.

For these reasons, and for the additional one that normal school plants already exist, there is no immediate prospect of relief. Undoubtedly, however, the institute should give place to the university as post graduate work for the teacher in the elementary school.

Hence the normal school must still grapple with its dilemma, whose unusual peculiarity is that, instead of the traditional two, it has three horns: 1. There is a sacrifice of professional character and academic quality to academic quantity; 2. It has no immediate prospect of cultural relief on the academic side from the high school; 3. Its work is not such as to rank it, professionally, with the university, nor is it at present such as the university can either recognize as preparatory, or duplicate itself.

Undoubtedly the normal school has done a very great deal for the cultural and professional standing of the elementary school teacher; but at the cost of how much tension, pressure, stress, waste and clashing only he knows who is personally acquainted with the internal life of such institutions. Evidently these schools are here to stay, for their field is, professionally, a very special one—one which their faculties know much more about at present than do the faculties of any other institution. Yet it is but natural that they should seek relief, on the academic side, from secondary education. It is with this special problem of the relation between secondary schools and normal schools from the point of view of the latter, that this report has to do.

It is altogether probable that the further solution of the normal school's problem, assuming that it has yet a problem to be solved, will be along lines indicated by demands for greater maturity and culture of its trained teachers, and more careful and thoro tests of fitness to teach. The selection of those possessing native teaching ability, and the development of that ability into the most economic and efficient teaching practice, may be regarded as the prime grounds for the existence of normal schools. Normal schools in the future, then, will be called upon (1) to pass upon the native fitness of their candidates for the teacher's office, and rigidly to exclude the naturally unfit, recognizing that no amount of long endurance can make acceptable teachers out of radically poor material. No institution should be so well able to accomplish this vital work of selection, as those whose faculty have specialized in the field of elementary education. (2) The normal school of the future will be called upon professionally to train this selected material to its greatest efficiency. The status of the normal school, professionally, will depend upon the extent to which it realizes these two ideas fundamental to its unity. But they inevitably presuppose both maturity and liberal culture in the candidates. The moot question now is, whether the normal school must still continue to develop greater and more liberally trained maturity of manhood and womanhood at the same time that it is grappling with the work of professional selection and training. It seems to your committee that it should not be called upon to do so. A reference to the catalog of any normal school which attempts both academic and professional work for its candidates having no secondary training, invariably reveals both an indefensible attempt to deal with very many things in too short a time, and a resulting handicap to the strictly professional function for which such a school exists.

On the other hand, none of the training of those candidates who have had secondary education before entering the normal, has been able to devote itself exclusively to professional work and to dispense with academic. The two year courses for high school graduates are practically a confession that secondary education does not yet furnish the sort of candidates which normal schools are looking for. For purposes of elementary education they have to be hastily repaired in matters vital to the liberal culture of an elementary school teacher. There is a practical concensus of opinion on this subject. In evidence of this, your committee would submit the results of a "questionnaire" which it issued to all the leading normal schools of the country. It has received replies from most of the representative normal schools. The questionnaire read as follows:

In the present development of normal schools in this state (California) there is a strong tendency to prefer graduates of secondary or high schools as the material out of which to make teachers for elementary schools, and eventually to make graduation from a good high school, or equivalent preparation, the sole standard of admission to the normal schools, with a view to a teacher's course of about two years devoted to almost strictly professional culture and training:

1. In your normal school have you now such a course for students admitted upon such a standard?

2. Is it the only course?

3. If high school graduates are to be preferred for admission to normal schools, it is fair to assume that the knowledge and training imparted by good high schools will represent that *general* culture best for the elementary teacher prior to her two years' professional training. Do you find graduates of good secondary schools so prepared?

4. If not, in what lines of culture and training, in your experience, have

they been found most deficient when they came to take your professional course?

5. In what lines have they shown most power and efficiency?

6. What changes in high school courses would you suggest from the point of view of a general training prior to the later professional training of their graduates for elementary schools?

7. Is your normal course for high school graduates now shaped at all with a view to supplying deficiencies in their general culture or training?

8. If so, in what respects?

The consensus of experience which is given herewith is based upon reports from normal schools which, like those of Massachusetts, receive only graduates of high schools on the same basis that would admit them to a university, as well as upon reports from schools not yet maintaining so high a standard.

It appears from the reports that a normal school, by virtue of its professional aspect, is a good place in which to discover how much one knows and how effectively he knows it. Of course, your committee has to keep in mind that no school reaches its ideal and that any general culture school is at a disadvantage seen thru the processes of a professional school. In fact this is one thing which this report should bring out. But from the normal school point of view the reports unquestionably show that in the main, graduates of high schools do not possess that general culture most desirable in the elementary school teacher. To be more specific, they are deficient in most of those lines of general information (geography, social sciences, etc.) which are today the common stock in trade, in the power readily and effectively to use the English language and the principles of arithmetic, in scientific knowledge, in power of independent thought and interpretation.

They are stronger on the side of higher mathematics, the formal side of classical studies, and in the power to memorize and to get assigned lessons from textbooks. Some of the expressions contained in the reports are both typical and striking, e. g., "the comprehensive defect is absence of *culture*." Again, "they fail to appreciate and love good literature and they have little idea of the meaning of history." Again, "they cannot read," i. e., independently and understandingly. The reports also reveal that it is memorized knowledge which the average high school graduate possesses, rather than significant knowledge, or knowledge with points of view. He has come thru secondary education too exclusively under the influence of methods still prescribed by a pedagogy of memory and formal general mental discipline, and the world of human life with its significant sciences, history, arts, industries, has hardly been opened to him. Reality has too largely given place to the formal study of dead languages and high specialization in mathematics; and what time could be devoted to neo-humanistic culture has perforce been reduced to a minimum.

Your committee concludes, therefore, that as the high school is now generally constituted, graduates from secondary schools do not offer material for the teaching profession which the normal school can proceed to train solely in professional lines. Indeed, if we may judge from the reports in our hands, some of the eastern normal schools which have experimented extensively in this field, are beginning to suffer some decided lapse of enthusiasm.

We believe furthermore that the chief function of the high school is not preparation for entrance to a university (that is, its incidental function); but the many sided development of the adolescent in the direction of more effective and worthy manhood or womanhood along lines of general culture, with some specialization along the line of special bent; and that when the high schools are permitted to give greater prominence to real literary and English training, to the social and natural sciences, to arithmetic, music and art, and by methods that shall more generally provoke real thought as well as exercise memory, their graduates will be in much better condition to undertake normal school work proper. Normal schools must not be understood to be in the position of making any demands upon the constitution of the high schools; for the latter have already been too much hampered by such purely external considerations as that of preparation for universities. But the truth remains that when the high school graduates stand closer to the demands of present day citizenship, character and mental equipment, it will be possible for the normal school to undertake their professional training far more effectively. Most of the remaining defects in culture will be those arising from the new or more perfect viewpoint which a teacher must always bring to the subject matter, and from lack of skill in execution; and these defects can best be met in connection with, and under the stimulus of the teacher's professional problems. Moreover, wherever secondary training in such lines as social and natural science, English composition, literature and mathematics, has dealt with the function of thought as well as that of memory, the student's grasp of method should enable him readily to do what every teacher in practice should be able to do—to supply his own lack of information and to do so accurately.

Finally your committee believes that under present conditions, the two years' course at the normal school for high school graduates must continue to recognize the needs of such candidates for some purely general culture courses.

In conclusion, therefore, the mere restriction of the requirements for admission to normal schools, to high school graduation or its equivalent, does not definitely settle the normal school's chief problem—that of real, vital professional training. As a matter of fact, that problem involves a re-analysis and a reconstruction of secondary education, and of the influence which shape it. We suggest, furthermore, an active campaign of open forum and journalistic discussion in behalf of the liberalization of secondary education and of normal school professionalism.

* * *

The Present High School Course in Reference to Average Intelligence

R. L. Sandwick.

We are asked to compile a report "upon the funds of common general information current among citizens of average intelligence, which is necessarily omitted in the present high school course, and to recommend modification in the courses to remedy this defect."

In approaching this subject our attitude is rather that of a student than of an advocate. We have not started out to reform the high school course but to study it, for the purpose of seeing how far it may fit into the general scheme of education, the aim of which is preparation for life. There is no claim of originality for the ideas herein contained. Your committee has been at pains to consult some educators of national reputation and the principals and superintendents of some schools and cities. The report is therefore rather a compilation of current opinion than the views of any single individual or group of individuals.

While much credit is given the high schools for the great gain in efficiency they have already made, it is generally admitted that they have not yet reached a point in the evolution of a curriculum where they can afford to become fixed. High school education seems to leave the student suspended at a height from which he can step neither into a professional school nor into business life. He seems to be forced into the university for a career. Even there a difficulty awaits him; for the high school course has been so narrow that he is unable to elect a university course with sufficient intelligence. He has no knowledge whatever of the content of half the departments of university instruction. On the other hand he has no eagerness to enter commercial or industrial fields. Social organization and the everyday business world is a thing still more vague than university departments; and the unknown is never attractive.

The average student of secondary schools in California takes about these subjects: Four years English, five periods a week; four years Latin (or French and German,) five periods; three years mathematics (algebra and plane geometry,) five periods; three years history (U. S., med., mod., ancient,) five periods; one year science (usually physics,) five periods. Total points.

fifteen. This does not mean that only the subjects here listed are taught in the schools; but as a rule students take about these subjects. If they elect to take more science, as they often do, it is at the expense of history, or some other subject quite as important.

Let us consider what funds of general information this typical course omits. There is nothing in it of zoology, botany, chemistry, physiology, geology, astronomy, political economy; no business courses and no work that would promote industrial skill or acquaint the student with industrial life. The narrow scope of a typical course in California high schools is, however, no more remarkable than that found to obtain elsewhere; tho there are some exceptions. At the largest high school in Chicago, about two hundred graduates out of a probable two hundred and fifty, will hav taken the following course: Four years English, four periods a week; three years French or German, five periods; four years Latin, five periods, except first year when four periods; two years mathematics, four periods; two years science, one of which is physiography, four periods; two years history, ancient and United States, four periods.* Most of the students from this, the Hyde Park High School, are preparing for the university; so that this course with its maximum of science and history, is probably found most desirable to offer as university preparation.

It is questionable whether either of these typical schedules affords the best education a high school is capable of giving its students. This intensive study of but a few subjects, mostly language, leaves the student unacquainted with the world of nature and society, with no basis of interest that would urge him to

* Students take also physical culture, music and drawing.

learn more about it, and with little food for thought since there is no wide oasis of truth on which to generalize.

In spite of these defects high schools have been advancing; and whatever scheme is offered to remedy them, it must not sacrifice what has already been gained. High schools will not go back to the superficial methods in vogue a quarter of a century ago. We must hold fast to all that is good while working toward better results. Thoroness must not give way to superficiality. Cramming must not be substituted for learning. A multiplicity of undigested facts and details from whatever source gleaned will not make education. In fact the number of details crammed and the amount of thought engendered are usually in inverse ratio. Again the length of time required for graduation must not be prolonged unduly. There is a feeling that too many years of a man's life are spent in school as it is; and this feeling exists in the highest educational circles as well as in the business world. Many high school students do not finish before twenty; add to this four years in the university and four years in the professional school, and it will be seen that the period of tutelage and dependence on others for support has encroached too far upon manhood, especially considering how few the years remaining after twenty-eight in the average human life. Whatever scheme is introduced therefore to remedy defects in our present high school course, it must not be at the expense of thoroness, nor should it add to the twelve years already required before graduation.

Another consideration must be prominent in the minds of those who would revise the curriculum. The present elasticity of the high school course should be preserved and rather increased than diminished. Regard must be had for the varying individuality of the student. Neither high schools nor colleges will ever return to the former method of grinding all thru the same mill. Individuality is promoted by allowing a choice of subjects to which a student may devote himself. This is the justification of the elective system. But in order that it may be consistent, every interest should be represented in the curriculum; and there ought to be a distinction between those courses on the one hand where the student devotes four years to a single subject, and those courses on the other where he can devote but a limited time to the subject. To take a concrete instance for illustration. Few if any high schools in California offer a course in *general history*. To the student whose natural bent leads him to elect three or four years study in history, this is no loss. But certainly it is essential to the student who can devote but a single year to it that he should get a general view of the great names and great movements of history as a whole, rather than spend all the time at his disposal on the details of a narrow period. Especially is this apparent when we remember that the facts of history stand in the relation of cause and effect, and that the significance of no period can be adequately comprehended except in its relation to the whole. Another reason for choosing general history when only one year is devoted to that subject, is that thereby the desultory reading of after years and the numerous historical allusions of literature, may be related and find a place of association in the mind in that period of history where they belong.

What thus applies in history applies also in science. There should be a general course in science to fit the needs of those students who can spend but a year in that subject. Some science teachers have latterly adopted the old discipline theory which science itself compelled the classics to abandon: they talk much about the value of *scientific training* and say that in order to get this scientific training, a student must devote himself to the details of a single science.

Without stopping to discuss this assertion, it may be well to state our point of view as to the object and aim of high school education. Briefly it is the view of modern pedagogy, which considers the chief end of education to be not the discipline and training of the so-called faculties, but the acquisition of such a knowledge of the world as will enable a student to deal most intelligently with its problems. From this point of view useful information is more valuable than drill of any sort on empty forms; and the value of any particular subject is measured by its usefulness for the purposes of life.

This will appear to some like a very narrow interpretation of the function of education, i. e., the mere providing students with useful information. The word *information* is unfortunate in that it connotes the encyclopedia. So much has been written and said about character-building, training the will, developing the ethical and esthetic nature, teaching self control, etc., that these seem to outweigh completely the value of studies in and of themselves. But it is the opinion of your committee that all these higher qualities of character, so far as they may be determined by school-work, are best inculcated when the student comes to regard that he is, in high school, laying hold of the earnest realities of life, instead of blindly playing at gymnastics with stuff that is essentially no more than a bag of wind and useful only that by it he may some day be strong enough to handle the truth. It is well for the teacher to regard character as more precious than learning; but learning is precious too. Earnestness of effort, honesty, sincerity, reverence—these which alone make for character—are present only when the student sees the essential reality and the practical importance of all that he is learning and doing.

With this point of view, and with the limitations necessary to retain what advantages of thoroness, brevity and elasticity the present course possesses, we will consider four plans which have been submitted to remedy the existing defects by adding to the sum of general information which a high school student may acquire. They are (1) that a general information course of one year be given, devoting as many days or weeks to each subject as the students need to get an understanding of the broad facts of science, history and business; (2) that high schools offer a year course in general history, a year course in general science under the caption physiography, and a year course in business; (3) that the time spent on grammar school subjects be cut down, so that the high school course, covering more time, may be made to embrace more subjects for each student; and (4) that by a combination of the second and third plans, the general courses be introduced and time given to complete them by taking a year from the common school.

It seems necessary at this point to meet an objection that may be made at first sight to each and all of these proposals. It will be said that these general courses are superficial, and will result in giving a mere smattering. It must, however, be borne in mind that these plans involve the retention of all that is now learned thoroly and in detail. They insist on a union of general and special knowledge, not upon the former at the expense of the latter.

They would impart general information only where the present intensive course fails to give any knowledge whatever. It must also be borne in mind that *from the point of view of a specialist, all high school work is superficial.* It would take the entire time at his disposal to teach a high school student all there is to know, or even what a university specialist is expected to know, about physics, Latin, history or any single one of the studies pursued. Yet no one would insist that for the sake of thoroness a high school student should devote all his time to any one of these subjects. He ought rather to get a rudimentary knowledge of all of them. We see then that it is not a matter of relative value as between studies, so much as it is a matter of relative value between the broad facts on the one hand and the details on the other in the content of individual studies. It is not whether we should teach physics or botany to the student who can take but one year of science, but how much of both should we teach him.

This is an important point in the theory of high school education. Special knowledge is a thing that comes later, in the university or professional school; and it ought to be based on a wide general foundation. It has been questioned whether there can be any special knowledge, productive of results, that is not based on general. The best thinkers are agreed that science is a universal thing— a unit in itself, of which the so-called sciences are but parts. Hence no one science can be understood fully except from a knowledge of all the rest. When possessed of a truth discovered in one science men are enabled to discover analogous truth in other sciences: witness the universal application of the laws of evolution first discovered in biology; again it was a learned physician applying himself to economics after Harvey's discovery of the circulation of the blood, that first conceived of the circulation of money and acquired a conception of human society as an organism. There is then a need of general knowledge as well as specific. If so, probably all agree that it is the high school rather than the university that should supply this general knowledge.

Of the four plans submitted to give this general knowledge, the first provides a general information course of one year. The introduction of such a course would probably disturb existing conditions less than would any of the alternatives. But two considerations militate against it. In the first place, the field is so wide, and so much is likely to be attempted, that uncertainty and a hazy understanding on the part of the students would be likely to result. A still greater difficulty would arise from lack of teachers competent to handle such a course. We will therefore consider this plan impractical and give it no further attention.

The second plan offered is that of providing three general courses: one in science, another in history, and a third in business. The course entitled *business* needs explanation. In such a course your committee would include an introduction to bookkeeping and commercial forms, commercial arithmetic, commercial geography, and commercial law. This course would also give an elementary view of political economy, including such matters as the division of labor, public finance, the relations of labor and capital, and the corporations engaged in public service and requiring state control. These matters hold a large share of public attention, but because they are not in the schools, profound ignorance often exists as to the underlying facts and principles. In short, the course in business is designed to make the student a practical and efficient member of society.*

In order to introduce these general courses and render them effective, time will have to be found for them; and with students already crowded to the limit, this would seem a difficult matter. It is necessary to review the organization and methods employed in the high school to see whether there is any waste time that can be utilized. Your committee suggests that the usual method of conducting a recitation may involve waste, due to lack of pedagogic training among high school teachers. Too much time is ordinarily spent going over what the student already knows; too little time in developing and explaining new material. To take a concrete example. In algebra a common method is to assign a certain number of problems to be solved out of class, and the recitation period is spent going over the same problems and explaining such ones as any member of the class has had difficulty with. For those who understood the problems on coming to class, this time is largely wasted. The work might better be done in class under the supervision of the teacher who, passing from student to student, can help where help is really needed. It has been found that with sixty minutes of this work, a class can accomplish more than with an hour and forty-five minutes spent in the usual preparation and recitation.

There is often waste in conducting a recitation in English literature. Here it is sometimes forgotten that good literature can be relied upon to teach its own lesson. If the ethical and æsthetic qualities are not apparent on the student's reading, they are not likely to become more clear thru the teacher's explanation. Above all, literature should not be regarded as so many facts to be learned like history and recited. There should be some critical analysis, but enough of that is usually found in the rhetorics. Literature may be appreciated even tho the experience of years and the results of a wide culture cannot be read into it. It is not necessary that the student see at once all that the teacher sees. The aim of literature is to please; and it is questionable whether it becomes any more pleasing by making hard work of it. That English may not be known as a "snap" course, teachers have erred in striving to make it just as difficult as Latin or mathematics. We venture to suggest that if the four lessons a week usually devoted to English literature were cut down to one, and if the time thus saved were devoted to private reading, the students might not only gain a wider knowledge of literature than at present, but they might go much further toward acquiring a taste for future reading.

In the study of foreign languages, also, the recitation period may be so conducted as to involve waste. Here, too, the class often mark time when they might be advancing. Students are assigned a passage to translate at home, and the whole recitation period is often spent in translating it again, instead of only stopping to clear up the difficulties and then going on to the mastery of new material. The justification of this method of hearing individuals translate all of the lesson is that thus only can the teacher know whether the lesson has been prepared; but teachers should look to larger results than this, and by set papers, in which every student in the class is translating at once, seek to learn the progress of each. This does not mean that there should be no oral translation in class of work prepared beforehand, but it raises the question whether the constant practice of such translation does not involve waste, especially after some progress has been made in language.

---

* Special courses giving a detailed knowledge of business should exist side by side with this general course, and covering two or three instead of one years' time.

We have seen that unpedagogic methods of conducting recitations in mathematics, English and foreign languages may result in a loss of time. No doubt if the inquiry were pushed further into science and history, the same thing would be found to apply. The principal of a large high school in the East recently said in our hearing that that school had accomplished excellent results by lengthening the period of recitation and holding recitations on alternate days, in order to do away with the stereotyped method of conducting them.

No doubt some time can be saved by instituting right methods. If it is impossible to find enough time in this way to enable students to carry two or three additional courses, it may be advisable to take a year from the common school. In a recent discussion of "The High School of the Future" before a conference of schools and colleges affiliated with the University of Chicago, nearly all the speakers dwelt upon the need of a six-years' course in the high school following six years in the common school, thereby enabling two years of university work to be done in the high school. It is questionable whether such a scheme can be realized in full. However, already some cities have but seven years in the common school. In an interview with the principal of the Central High School of Kansas City, the chairman of the committee learned that such a reduction of the years below the secondary school in that city had lead to no apparent weakening of secondary work, while it had added greatly to the number of students pursuing high school courses. The same testimony comes from Decatur, where, owing to the fact that first-year primary children are in school but half a day at a time, less than seven years precede the high school. In the city of Chicago the principal of the Lewis Institute asserts that students admitted upon examination from the seventh grade of the city schools actually show a better standing than those who have been regularly admitted upon promotion from the eighth grade. These are isolated instances, it is true, but whatever may be inferred from them seems to bear out the statement of Superintendent S. Louis Soldan, of St. Louis, that "one year can profitably be taken from the common school without weakening its efficiency." He stops short of the position of Dean Russell of the New York Teachers' College and others when he grants seven years to the common school, for they recommend but six. However, the one year thus gained, if added to the high-school course, will be ample to widen and enrich its curriculum. The people recognize their own. Wherever high-school work has thus enlarged its scope, the school has enlarged its enrollment. The city of Galesburg, with a population of 19,000, has put industrial and commercial courses in her high school. As a result, the latter has had an average enrollment the past three years of 562 and a graduating class of 106 while Quincy, a neighboring city with twice the population, but with a traditional high-school course, has but 259 as an average enrollment, and 25 in the graduating class—less than half as many students, less than a fourth as many graduates. Of course, such figures as these are apt to be deceitful, other factors coming in for consideration; but we can take it for granted that high schools meet with popular support in proportion as they minister to all the needs of their respective communities in preparing the young people for life.

In conclusion, we would recommend that high schools seek to impart a wider fund of general useful information by adding to their curricula general courses in history, science and business, and that, where possible, one year be taken from the common school and added to the high school to make room for such courses.

Addenda.—The above is not regarded as a complete report. If upon discussion the Council of Education agrees that such general courses are needed in the high school, it then becomes necessaray to consider the courses in detail and determine just what should be the scope of each. Adequate general histories may perhaps be found. But text-books in physiography might have to be supplemented in order to make a full year's work, and they might profitably be made somewhat more experimental. The course in business matters, however, are details which may be deferred until there is agreement as to fundamentals.

I concur most heartily in the general conclusions of the chairman's report, but I would emphasize certain of his theses, expressed or implied, and would dissent in a few particulars as follows:

I. I would emphasize the importance of the theses that the goal of any course of study must always be specific, and not one of the vague products of the disrupted theory of general disciplinary value of studies, scientific training, observation, reasoning, etc. The facts studied must have worth in themselves, and the supporters of the disciplinary dogma must compromise to the extent of agreeing to obtain these general powers by dealing with problems or facts which yield material of intrinsic value.

II. I would emphasize the chairman's urgency for general information, which I would define to be that fund which the average person of general intelligence possess regarding any field of knowledge. The high school should aim for general intelligence, and, since its time is limited, it cannot profitably undertake any of those courses which give training or knowledge special to any class of society or occupation.

III. Therefore I would dissent from the chairman's plan of a business course, as I understand it, in so far as it undertakes to give training or knowledge special to any of the departments of business life. But I would commend such a course in so far as it provided that of commercial conceptions and abilities required of every intelligent citizen.

FREDERIC BURK.

The conclusions in the report by the chairman meet with my hearty concurrence. I wish to place emphasis on what he has said on the following points:

(a) The high schools are devoting too much time to language study.

(b) There should be no lengthening of the course of study. New subjects should be added only as they can crowd others out.

(c) The tendency toward elastic courses to suit individual needs should be encouraged.

(d) There is too much specialization in our high schools. Some general courses should be added, but they should avoid the superficiality that was so common in science, history, etc., not many years ago.

The text-books on commercial subjects are generally too superficial. They are too much inclined to offer quick trips to something that can only be obtained by hard, continued study. With satisfactory texts and teachers, business subjects, excepting those ultra technical, should have equal standing with others in our courses.

E. M. Cox,
Superintendent of Santa Rosa City Schools.

* * *

Promotion of Pupils in Rural Schools

Robert Furlong

Gentlemen: Your committee appointed "to compile a report upon the systems now in use by the boards of education of the various counties of the State for promotion of pupils in the rural schools, to consider the value of these systems to the educational interests of the pupils as distinct from considerations of convenience of administration and ease of bookkeeping, and, if deemed advisable, to recommend a substitute system, or modification, for approval by the Council," respectfully submits the following as its report:

The work outlined for committee in appointment notice sent to its members appeared to require data from every county in California. Much effort was made to obtain a full knowledge of all the various methods in use for the promotion of pupils in the different counties. It was the aim of the committee to make in this report a complete exhibit of all systems employed outside of the large cities of this State. Approximately only has this end been attained. In September last a letter of inquiry containing blank forms for answers to questions submitted was sent to every county superintendent in the State. Forty-eight of the fifty-seven counties, including in that number, perhaps, all counties of good standing educationally, have made returns. Data from these returns form the basis of this report.

The inquiries made of County Superintendents were as follows:

1. What are your standards or bases for promotion?
2. By whom are promotions made in the primary grades?
3. In the grammar grades?
4. What tests for fitness, if any, are employed?
5. If written examinations are given, who conducts them?
6. In what grades are they given?
7. By whom are the questions prepared?
8. If "Teacher's Estimate" plan obtains in your county, upon what do teachers base their judgment?
9. Do your teachers, or any of them, keep records of standing in recitation, or other form of book accounts with their pupils?
10. Have you any schools "accredited" by the County Board, from which pupils are graduated without examination?
11. Conditions for graduating pupils from schools not so "accredited" where the accrediting system prevails?
12. Is the system of promotion in your county satisfactory? If not, what would you suggest instead?
13. In your work of school visitation, do you find many pupils that have been "prematurely promoted"—that is, put into classes or grades beyond their developed powers?
14. Please give your views on promotion systems in general and their value in a scheme of education.

To the first question, "What are your standards or bases for promotion?" thirty-five counties answer in substance: "Ability to do the work of a higher grade, as determined either by class standing for term, or by monthly, quarterly, semi-annual or annual examinations in which a certain per cent must be obtained by the pupil. While no two of these accounts appeared to have precisely the same basis for promotion, each employed some modification of the general plan stated.

Eight counties simply answered a certain per cent, varying from 70 to 80 per cent, evidently for a final test.

Four counties appeared to have no standard, yet answers to other queries showed that something akin to an examination system obtained. One county reports its basis for promotion the completion of the course of study for each year.

To the second question, "By whom are promotions made in the primary grades?" forty-three counties answer, "By the teachers"; three counties, "By the teacher, supervised by the County Board"; two counties, "By the teacher, aided by tests sent out from County Superintendent's office."

Answers to query three show that in eight counties promotions in the grammar grade are made by the County Board of Education; in ten counties by teachers, and in thirty counties by teachers and board, either jointly or acting separately, for certain grades. "What tests for fitness, if any, are employed?" is answered by twenty-seven counties: "Oral and written examinations." "Written tests, combined with daily work," is the answer from seven counties; "Left with teachers," eight counties. Certain conditions, such as age of pupil, length of time in grade, marked ability, etc., are grounds for modifying rules to fit individual cases, reported from a few counties.

Questions prepared by the County Board appeared to be the test given for graduation in all counties where any test is given. Two counties appeared to have no test for graduation further than the completion of the course of study.

Where written examinations are given, teachers conduct them as a general rule. In eight counties, however, the County

Board conducts the examination for graduation, and in all cases the papers of graduating pupils are inspected by the Board.

6. In what grades are they given? Thirty-five counties report the examinations are given in the grammar grades only. "May be given in any grade" is the answer from three counties. "Left with the teacher, except in the ninth grade," one county. "By whom are the questions prepared?" is answered: "By the teachers," in seven counties; "By the County Board in grades above the fourth," in five counties; "Above the fifth" in eleven counties; "Above the sixth" in eight counties; "Above the seventh" in twelve counties; and for ninth grade in six counties.

Promotions are made chiefly on the teacher's estimate of the pupil's ability to do higher work in twenty-six counties, as reported. It would appear, however, from the record previously read that the teacher's judgment governed only in the primary and intermediate grades. In eight counties teacher's judgment is not a factor in the work of promotion. In two counties examination record counts one-half and class record one-half.

Forty-one counties report many teachers keeping records of standing of pupils in their daily work, also other forms of book accounts with their schools.

In four counties no such records are kept. Three failed to report in this particular.

"Have you any schools accredited by the County Board from which pupils are graduated without examination?" is answered "No" by thirty-two counties. Nine counties have accredited schools. In such counties schools not so accredited have to take the regular board examinations for graduation.

One county reports having tried the accrediting system, and, finding it unsatisfactory, discarded it. One county has a system of honorary promotion and graduation for particularly deserving pupils.

To the questions, "Is the system of promotion in your county satisfactory? If not, what would you suggest instead? one Superintendent says: "Unsatisfactory, but do not know of any plan better." Nineteen Superintendents say, "Partly satisfactory"; sixteen say "Satisfactory," and ten "Very satisfactory." In no instance is there a suggestion for a better plan given, or of any plan other than the one in use.

While Superintendents report the promotion systems of their respective counties satisfactory, or nearly so, yet in answer to question thirteen, twenty-two Superintendents have found in their work of school inspection many pupils in classes or grades beyond their developed powers. This condition is variously attributed to "Poor judgment of teacher," "Want of conscientiousness in teacher," "Want of courage on part of teacher," "Pressure from outside of school," etc. Nineteen Superintendents have seldom found pupils that had been prematurely promoted. One reports not any.

To the final request that Superintendents give their individual views on promotion systems in general and their value in a scheme of education, opinions were not as freely or fully given as the committee expected. The views of many Superintendents were implied in their answers to a former question, in which they indorsed the system of promotion in use in their county as being *"quite satisfactory."*

However, a number of the Superintendents expressed their opinions as requested. Some of these views, quite opposite in their conclusions, are here given to show what diverse ideas are held on the subject of promotions:

One Superintendent says: "The teacher who is untrammeled should be the one to promote through all grades, though examination for graduation may be conducted and determined by others."

Another says: "I think some system should prevail. Am not ready to discard examinations for promotion. If the teachers were all perfect in all ways, the teacher's estimate and the accrediting plans would no doubt be ideal."

Another: "Some promotion system, uniform in its operations, is necessary where a uniform course of study is prescribed for schools. The pupils' interests should be the first consideration. He (the pupil) should be protected from the common error of being 'prematurely promoted.' Premature promotions — the bane of all rural schools — will prevail where a strong central power does not control."

"Promotions should be made only on merit. The great desire teachers have to score what is called a success—which in some instances may mean to retain their places—make the present system very objectionable. I do not see a practicable remedy at hand."

"The final examination is not an ideal system, but it is the best that I know. It has done much to keep up the interest in our schools to the last of the term, keeping the big boy in school regularly and holding him until he graduates. I have watched both systems in their operations and am convinced that for the country school of one teacher the final examination by the County Board of Education is better than to leave the whole matter with the teachers."

"The Superintendent should be a more potent factor in the promotion and graduation of the children."

"In country school districts teachers' popularity and chances for re-election depend too much on promotion of pupils. I would like to see some system in use relieving the teacher of this responsibility."

"I believe the best method of promotion is a judicious use of the examination combined with the teacher's estimate. In primary grades, estimate of the teachers should be the principal basis."

"I am convinced that the efficient teacher knows better than any other person when the pupil is strong enough to go ahead. Because of outside pressure and danger to position, teachers sometimes promote against their own judgment. Our board tries to relieve the teacher's responsibility by giving the final examination and marking results."

"So far as possible, I think promotions should be based on the teacher's judgment, and children should be promoted whenever they can do the work of the next higher grade."

"Any plan for promotion that will give an incentive to study is beneficial, and I know that the plan we have adopted makes the schools more uniform in their work." (Board examinations in higher grades.)

"Under present conditions, I believe a system of promotion to be indispensable. It must be flexible, however, and the true teacher with the careful Superintendent must be the main factors."

"It is my opinion that promotions from grade to grade should be determined by the teacher of the school rather than by examination by the County Board of Education, excepting in subjects completed for entrance to high school."

"I think it is generally safe to trust the teacher's judgment and honesty, as she knows better than any one else the standing of her pupils."

"Pupils' fitness for promotion should be determined by the teacher, but the Superintendent should have a voice in selecting the teacher and power to uphold the teachers doing honest work."

"Basing my opinion upon observation and experience, I think there should be an incentive for proficiency in scholarship and deportment other than the standard suggested by the teacher."

"For rural schools some uniform system is certainly desirable. This system, whatever it might be, would be of broader usefulness if it could be made in all essentials uniform throughout the State. Undoubtedly the promotion system at present used in this county (County Board examination system) gives definite point to a teacher's efforts, stimulates pupils in a helpful way, gives the necessary uniformity when children move from place to place, and enables teacher, parent and the pupil himself to more accurately gauge the progress made. Not until the millenium dawns and children — all of them — study from love of intellectual progress, can examinations in some form be discarded."

"With our graded system of schools, we must have some system of promotion. All systems seem naturally to have objectional features. The value of any one system depends much upon conditions, as, for instance, the difference between a school of eight or ten pupils and one of eight or ten hundred. Assuming that the teacher is honest and possessed of good judgment, the 'accrediting system,' if under closer supervision than at present, might be made the best method of promoting pupils. But without this closer supervision I think the County Board should direct examinations which should count at least half in the standing for promotion."

"It all goes back to the stuff the teacher is made of. If she is right in training, breeding, health and moral fiber, all goes well. She won't promote improperly and won't receive improperly. If she isn't right, outside powers cannot do much to help her or to make her over."

"In this county we have found that examinations prepared and conducted by the Board of Education are the most satisfactory, relieving the teachers of responsibility and any charge of favoritism. By this system, also, we find the work thorough and uniform throughout the county."

"In primary grades promotions should be left with the teacher, but in grammar grades they should be directed by the County Board."

"I believe the promotion of pupils should be left very largely to the estimate of the teachers."

"Some system of promotion is indispensable. That system which best combines the daily work of the pupil with a final examination I believe to be the most nearly perfect. Punctuality and regular attendance should also be considered."

"A promotion system seems to be absolutely necessary as long as we plan mass instruction. To the system of written tests for promotion I attribute the lack of original thinking among public school children. A practical substitute seems hard to find, however."

The quotations here given, from the reports of some twenty-five Superintendents, appear to favor a promotion system in which the teacher is the *chief*, if not the *only*, factor. It must be remembered, however, that, as previously stated, nearly one-half of the Superintendents reporting did not write their views further than to commend as *good* the promotion system in use in their respective counties. In a large majority of such counties promotions are directed by the County Board, and on the examination plan.

Enough data has been given and enough opinions quoted to make an exhibit that is nearly complete for our State.

But the practices are so varied and the opinions so diverse that satisfactory conclusions can not well be drawn from this material. Perhaps in no other particular are the public school practices of our State so lacking in uniformity. Every county appears to have a system of promotion of its own, and every school district has probably a modification of its county system. At least this state of affairs is the outlook presented at first view. It is possible that a closer study of the promotion methods described in this report might lead to conclusions of value.

An analysis of the data will show that the various methods in use may be reduced to two distinct heads or systems, viz: Promotion by the teacher; promotion by some central authority, such as the Superintendent or County Board. It is the various and peculiar combinations of these two systems for the different grades that result in the complex practices described. Each of these two methods of promotion has earnest supporters; each has strong opponents. There is evidently an honest difference of opinion as to their relative merits. To some minds the difference is irreconcilable. Doubtless each of these methods of advancing pupils can be employed with advantage in the different grades. The relative values of the two systems will not be discussed in this report at this time. The main consideration is, How are the *pupil's interests* affected by these or any other methods of promotion? This is the vital question, for presumably all systems of promotion have been devised to aid pupils in their progress through the school course. This committee has no evidence that any scheme for promotion is or has been employed in the schools of this State for such unworthy considerations as "convenience of administration and ease of bookkeeping." On the contrary, a promotion system directed by a Superintendent or by the County Board greatly increases the work of such officials. The different School Boards of the State have doubtless exercised their best judgment in selecting systems of promotion that seemed to them best adapted to the conditions in their respective counties. And various as the methods of promotion are, they are perhaps not more varied than the school conditions existing in the different counties of California.

Here the question arises, Is uniformity desirable? Would a method of advancing pupils in the grades of the schools of Los Angeles county, and suited to the conditions here, be also adapted to the school conditions of Tehama and Humboldt? But in considering the pupil's interests, which alone should have weight in determining this problem, a deeper question arises, viz: Is *any* scheme of promotion necessary for a pupil's progress through a school course?

For a full consideration of this and other questions of perhaps equal significance pertinent to our subject, your committee must plead for further time.

ROBERT FURLONG,
E. M. COX,
Committee.

County Boards of Education

A. E. Shumate

As chairman of the special committee on County Boards of Education, appointed by President Frederic Burk, I beg to submit the following report:

The subject to be investigated by the committee was phrased as follows: "The value to the educational interests of pupils of the present system of supervision in rural schools by County Superintendents and Boards of Education and the average cost of maintaining the County Board in each county during the past ten years, and the proportionate cost per pupil for such supervision."

On July 28, 1902, the chairman of the committee mailed to all the County Superintendents of California a circular letter stating the subject to be investigated, in the words quoted above, and soliciting information in the following language:

"(1) What has been the average cost per year of your County Board of Education (including your salary as secretary) for the past ten years? (2) What has been the average number of pupils enrolled in your county, outside of cities having Boards of Education and City Superintendents for the past ten years? While it will take some little effort for you to get these statistics together, doubtless your time will be well spent. If you have given these matters any attention, or have any decided views upon them, we should very much like to hear from you.

Hoping to get a reply at your earliest convenience, etc."

Between the dates of July 28th and September 20th (the date of the preliminary meeting of the Council for the consideration of reports of special committees) replies were received from twenty out of the fifty-seven County Superintendents of the State.

These replies are as follows:

Alameda County.—"I must plead entire lack of time to look up the statistics you want. There is but one deputy for this entire county. If you care to send anyone here, the records are here to be examined, etc."

Amador.—"I estimate that the meetings have cost the county $380 per year for the ten years just past.—2,300 pupils (approx.).

"*George A. Gordon.*"

Colusa.—"Average enrollment for the past ten years, 1,561; average cost of the County Board, including my salary as secretary for the past ten years, $667.22.

"*Lillie L. Langenour.*"

El Dorado.—"(1) $450; (2) 1,734 pupils."

Glenn.—"(1) $616.06, $116.06 of this being for mileage; (2) 1,190.
"*F. S. Reager.*"

Humboldt.—"I realize that the time it will take to hunt up and segregate the financial statistics of this county for the past ten years in order to answer truthfully the two questions submitted is not at my disposal at present, nor will it be for months to come, if ever.
"*J. B. Brown.*"

Lake.—"(1) $630; (2) 1,452 pupils.
"It is my opinion that for counties such as Lake County all duties now falling on the Board of Education could and should be performed by the County Superintendent."

Marin.—"(1) $682; (2) 2,026 pupils.
"My dear Sir: With regard to the future usefulness of County Boards of Education in California's educational scheme, I am of the opinion that boards properly constituted can render valuable service to the work of education. In the past their work has been chiefly that of an examining board to qualify teachers by issuing them certificates. New duties contemplating work of far greater value have been assumed by some boards since the new certification law came into effect.

"Inefficient supervision, chiefly due to the multiplicity of duties imposed on the Superintendent, can to a great extent be made efficient through the work of Board members. Space will not permit me to give a detailed plan for such work. I believe that the Marin Board has been of more service to the schools during the past year than for any previous year. It is no longer a mere 'Board of Examiners.'

"By 'properly constituted Boards' I mean Boards not appointed for political reasons, Boards the members of which are earnest school men and women whose purpose is to aid the teachers in advancing the work of the schools. If Boards are to be dominated by politicians, the sooner they are eliminated from our system of education the better. Changes in the statutes contemplating some different system of selecting Board members, perhaps limiting the number to three, and assigning new duties for Boards could be worked out and made effective under the California system.

"I am only suggesting these things as practicable and having in them the possibility of much usefulness.
"Sincerely yours,
"*Robert Furlong.*"

Modoc.—"(1) $500; (2) 902 pupils.
"*Annie L. Williams.*"

Mariposa.—"(1) $500; (2) 1,000 pupils.
"*Julia Jones.*"

Monterey.—"(1) $1,100: (2) 2,191 pupils. Secretary of the Board receives no salary.
"*Mrs. J. E. Chope.*"

Nevada.—"(1) $600; (2) 3,100 pupils.
"*W. J. Rogers.*"

Orange.—"(1) $900; (2) 2,540 pupils. Secretary receives no salary.
"*J. P. Greely.*"

Riverside.—"(1) $400 to $500; (2) 3,000 pupils. Secretary of the Board receives compensation. The Board does good work.
"*Edward Hyatt.*"

San Benito.—"(1) $689; (2) 1,697 pupils. During the past four years the Secretary has received no salary as such.
"*John H. Garner.*"

Santa Cruz.—"(1) $765; (2) 3,800 pupils.
"*J. W. Linscott.*"

San Joaquin.—"(1) $900; (2) 3,300 pupils.
"*E. B. Wright.*"

Sierra.—"(1) $382 (approx.); (2) 756 pupils.
"*Josie Finane.*"

Stanislaus.—"(1) $635; (2) 1,630 pupils.
"*J. A. Wagener.*"

Tulare.—"(1) $900: (2) 4,840 pupils.
"*S. A. Crookshanks.*

Ventura.—"(1) $850; (2) 2,000 pupils.
"*George E. Sackett.*"

At the September meeting of the Council, held in Oakland, A. E. Shumate, Chairman of the Committee, because of stress of other duties, requested P. M. Fisher, second named on the Committee to relieve him and complete the report.

Additional letters were sent to the Superintendents, from whom no report had been received offering to send each upon his request a copy of the report when completed, and making the following and direct specific request: (3) "If prepared and willing to do so, will you please state your approval, or disapproval, of the work of the County Board in the supervision of the schools?"

To these inquiries replies were received as follows:

Alameda.—"(1) $1,400; (2) 7,124 pupils. Outside Oakland, Alameda and Berkeley. (3) See below."

Calaveras.—"(1) $700; (2) 2,191 pupils; (3) The work of the County Board of Education in the supervising of the schools of this county has met with my approval.
"*John Waters, per P. M. T.*"

Mendocino.—"(1) $1,250; (approx.); (2) 2,500 pupils; (3) While the work of the County Board is not ideal, at the same time I consider the County Board absolutely necessary.
"*J. F. Barbee.*"

Napa.—"(1) $750 salaries, $50.00 printing; (2) 2,940 pupils; (3) I believe in the County Board as a supervising body, but under the law at present not much can be done.
"*J. A. Imrie.*"

Sacramento.—"(1) $750; (2) 1,950 pupils; (3) I approve of the work of the County Board of Education in the supervision of the schools of its jurisdiction.
"*Benj. F. Howard.*"

Santa Clara.—"(1) $1,250; (2) 5,677 pupils; (3) No reply."

San Diego.—"(1) $3,000; (2) 3,200 pupils; (3) If the County Superintendent aided in the selection of the Board to free it from politics, I think the time of the Board would be better invested in that way.
"*Hugh J. Baldwin.*"

San Mateo.—"(1) $715.03; (2) 1,599 pupils; (3) In this county I feel that the work of the Board has been a success. I do not see how the schools could be touched otherwise and kept up to a standard, except through the efforts of the Board of Education in co-operation with the Superintendent of Schools.
"*Etta M. Tilton.*"

Solano.—"(1) $950; (2) 2,367 pupils; (3) I approve the work of the County Board in the supervision of schools.
"*D. H. White.*"

Trinity.—"(1) $250 (approx.) (2) 440 pupils; (3) With the co-operation of the County Board of Education, I think the rural schools of Trinity County have been raised to a standard of excellence; but if more progressive and effective means were suggested for the best interests of our schools, I would gladly indorse the movement.
"*Lizzie H. Fox.*"

San Bernardino.—"(1) I have not time to search the records; (2) 3,500 pupils (approx.); (3) The work of the County Board has been satisfactory to teachers and trustees in the main.
"*A. S. McPherson.*"

Alameda.—"(3) I find that the supervision of the County Board is salutary and helpful. It tones up the schools, putting teachers and pupils on their mettle. The teachers, pupils and the patrons have become accustomed to this supervision, and expect it as a matter of course. The personnel of the membership of the Board is high, and the Superintendent finds their co-operation of great service to him. The Board's duties in the promotion of pupils should be enlarged at the next session of the Legislature.
"*T. O. Crawford.*"

Placer.—"(1) $675; (2) 2,679 pupils; (3) I approve of the County Board's work of supervision of the schools. The secretary receives no compensation."

Santa Barbara.—"(1) $1,040; (2) 2,727 pupils; (3) Not what I should like to have it, but possibly this is for want of direction in the work. I am not in favor of dispensing with the work of the County Board.
"*W. S. Edwards.*"

Tuolumne.—"(1) $500; (2) 1,300 pupils; (3) The County Board in this county has not had any hand in supervision. Don't like it. 'Too many cooks spoil the broth.' Makes too much work for teachers in preparing for examination, etc., which time can be utilized for direct benefit of pupils.
"*G. P. Morgan.*"

Yuba.—"(1) $750; (2) 775 pupils; (3) It has been *very satisfactory—entirely satisfactory.*
"*James A. Scott.*"

Total for thirty-four counties: Expense, $26,576.31; number of pupils, 78,588; average per capita, 33.8 cents; average expense of maintaining County Boards per pupil, 33.8 cents. Being a clear majority of the counties of the State and representative of the various local conditions, this may be taken as a fair average for the counties.

The delay in receiving replies from the Superintendents of the State in a matter that would seem to be of such interest may be attributed fairly to several reasons, chief among them being that it was election year, and nearly all were before the people for re-election, and also that they doubtless were requested to furnish information for many other committees of the Council and they felt that there was a limit to their time for these things. A few may have taken no interest in what they may have deemed a useless investigation.

From the reports themselves and from personal acquaintance with the duties and work of County Boards, the Committee would respectfully summarize conclusions as follows:

Expense.—The question of the expense as it foots up, cuts no great figure in this case, distributed, as it is, over more than thirty counties, the compensation shared among more than one hundred and fifty persons, and the educational benefit, whatever that may be, conferred upon so many thousands of pupils. In the great majority of counties it will be observed that the total expense of maintaining the County Board is not equal to the salary of one competent deputy.

Powers and Duties.—The County Board was created by the Constitution of 1879 chiefly because of a protest against the scandals rising from the certification of teachers by the State Board of Education. Whatever may be thought now of this as a remedial measure, it was a change, and its local and democratic character commended it to a popular convention.

Since 1879 the Legislature has added to the Board's duties the adoption of courses of studies, text-books not issued by the State, library books and apparatus, and the supervision of promotions, the last named, except graduation from the grammar grades, having been omitted in the law as amended by the Legislature of 1901. During these years there has grown up through the agencies of Teachers' Institutes and Associations, biennial conventions, journals of education, and the natural influence of the universities and the Normal Schools a fair degree of uniformity and reciprocity in the work of County Boards, *without the aid of the law.* During the past five years an attempt to return to State control has been very apparent under various forms, with a consequent curtailing of the powers of County Boards by law. We need not look far for the cause of this movement. It is in the nature of men, whether acting alone or in a body, to exercise all the power they have and to gradually reach for more. Men magnify their offices. There has been a wonderful increase in growth in the High School during the past decade. The two great universities have made their influence felt in the remotest corners of California.

The entire system of public education in the State has been shaken and stirred by the spirit of investigation. The County Board of Education has not escaped challenge, and at the session of the last Legislature its power was shorn in the very direction and upon the very matter concerned in its creation. It was ascertained some years ago that there was a surplus of teachers in California. It was natural, therefore, when this was discovered that those concerned in professionally educating teachers would see to it that the teachers so educated should be preferred, and they set themselves about to accomplish it by limiting the powers of local Boards to grant certificates upon examination. Again it was argued that as high schools were to prepare students for the universities, they should be taught by thoroly prepared teachers. The only qualification named in the law for members of the County Board of Education was that at least a minority of them should hold grammar-grade certificates. It was contended, therefore, that Boards so constituted were not competent to pass upon high-school certificates. The power of the County Boards in this matter has, therefore, been confined to the clerical one of granting certificates only upon credentials issued by the State Board. It will be conceded by all that some measure of protection was needed for the high schools, and the movement took this form. The examination for the issuance of grammar-grade certificates has been made an annual one instead of semi-annual, and the primary certificate has been abolished. To these two changes there has been no objection made known anywhere. The Committee are of the opinion, however (an opinion shared by the Superintendents, who were asked the direct question, and whose replies are a part of this report), that the County Board has been, and may be, made even to a greater degree a most helpful agency in the educational system of the State.

The test of the value of every agency in the school system must be two-fold:

First—Does it tend to promote intelligent interest in and support of the schools by the public?

Second—What is the influence upon the pupils themselves?

Under the first, it will be remembered, that four of the members of the County Board are chosen from different sections of the county, with a responsibility to, not the appointing Supervisor alone, but the people who create Supervisors. Each member so appointed will take a lively interest in the schools of his section and do all in his power to advance them, so that they may compare well with those of other sections.

Each member will find it to his interest and will make it his pleasure to familiarize his immediate constituents with the work and aims of the schools. The County Superintendent meets the citizens only occasionally; the local representative on the County Board goes in and out before them daily, and thru him teachers and patrons have a bearing before the Board.

The people elect the local School Trustees; they can also secure appointment of proper persons upon the County Board. It is better that they should make mistakes sometimes than lose their voice in the matter. Local responsibility in school management is a means of educating the citizen himself. The school reflects the community; the improvement in local standards may well be permitted to come naturally, from contact and comparison with higher standards, and from the "University at large" in a country where the schools and the press are free.

In the second place, members of the Board may well be trusted to care for the humane and social side of the schools. Of this care, the emulation that grows up among schools and pupils, the recognition of good work done by individual teachers, the graduation exercises, in which members of the Board participate, the emulation among members of the Board themselves, are evidences.

That the work of the schools since the adoption of the Constitution of 1879 has been effective, witness the welcome given to the new University at Palo Alto, the generous support accorded the State University, the growth of high schools. Where have these high schools found their students? In the grammar schools and under courses of study prepared and enforced by the County Board.

All this may well be taken into consideration in judging of the value of the present system to the public and the pupils.

Recommendations

First—In view of the character of the work done by County Boards and its comparatively small cost, and in view of the additional burdens which the people of the State will in all probability be called upon to assume by the next Legislature, we would make no recommendation looking to an increase in the cost of county supervision of schools.

Second—We would respectfully recommend that the duties and powers of the County Board of Education should be more clearly defined by law and should be extended so as to include the supervision of schools jointly with the Superintendents, such supervision to cover the power of promotion in the grammar grades at least, in such manner as the Board may determine. That in all counties having high schools, at least one member of the Board shall be the holder of a regular high-school certificate.

Third—That the law relating to special certificates should even more specifically than it does now give County Boards discretion in certificating teachers to instruct in subjects not required in preparatory courses for the universities. The argument in favor of taking from County Boards the initiative in granting high-school certificates was that high schools prepared for the State University. This argument silenced opposition that would otherwise have been made to the change on the ground that it was a violation of the Constitution. Your Committee thinks it wise, therefore, and proper, and consistent, too, that no attempt should be made to abridge the powers of the local Board any further. There have been cases where hardships have been conferred and embarrassments met with in local administration because Boards have been obliged to wait for the action of a State Board, a body remote, and which meets infrequently, and such embarrassments have been without compensating features.

* * *

The Present High School Courses in Latin in Accredited High Schools

Edward Hohfeld

This report consists of two parts, which may be stated in the form of two questions:

First—Are the present high-school courses in Latin in accredited schools best adapted to the needs of the high school aside from meeting the requirements to the Latin courses in the universities?

Second—What is the value of Latin relative to other material which must be omitted if this course is taken?

It should be understood at the outset that the purpose of this paper is to consider the place of the Latin courses in the high schools, as indeed the high-school course as a whole, solely from the standpoint of its function in preparing for life irrespective of preparation for the universities. But as the true function of the university, also, is to prepare for life, in so far as the high-school course of study is adapted to prepare best for life, just that far will it best fit into the university course, if that, too, be adapted to prepare for life. There ought, thus, to be no conflict between the two.

In considering the first question, How far the present courses in Latin are best adapted to the needs of the high school, aside from meeting the requirements to the Latin courses in the universities, I should say that in so far as there is a Latin course at all in the high school, the division of work should be into the elementary course covering the first two years, both years of which must be pursued to obtain credit, and the advanced course, covering the last two years, the first half of which may be taken irrespective of the second half. Thus there should be offered a two-year, a three-year, and a four-year course.

The first year's work should consist of a drill in the forms of declension and conjugation, and abundant practice in reading the simplest possible Latin illustrative of the forms, and just so much syntax as is necessary to do the reading. There should be little or no translation from English into Latin during the first year, except so much as the teacher may give spontaneously from time to time to illustrate the use of forms or rules of syntax. I certainly think that a partial return to the old method of giving the declensions and conjugations as wholes and not split up into detached parts, as is the tendency in most of the beginners' books at present, would materially aid the beginner. This does not imply that the forms may not be presented inductively, if so desired, but only that the declension, conjugations, etc., be presented as wholes and not in detached parts. For a full discussion of this matter the reader is referred to Chapter II of Bennett and Bristol's "The Teaching of Latin and Greek in Secondary Schools."

The second year should be essentially a "Caesar" year, for simplicity and vigor of style his is unexcelled; his Gallic War treats of an important period in history, and is sufficiently varied to hold the interest of a class, especially if some work be done with the map in following his campaigns, and if, besides, some attention be given to the military methods of the Romans and Gauls. Caesar's vocabulary and style are also practically the same thruout, so that the student may rapidly gain in his ability to read "Caesar." This latter aspect is very important, too, in that he thus becomes a most excellent author to furnish sight reading in the second year, as will be explained later. For making the transition to "Caesar," some such book as Brittain's "Introduction to the Caesar" will be found an admirable help.

For much the same reasons which make "Caesar" an admirable author for the second year, "Cicero" seems to be at least as good an author as any other for the third year, and furnishes good material for sight reading in the fourth year.

For the fourth year Virgil's "Aeneid" is unquestionably the best work. Aside from its intrinsic worth, which is very great, the fact that this author and this work of his in particular, has influenced for so many centuries the literature of the world, makes it the classic of classics for high-school Latin. It is likely that a little easy reading from "Ovid" will be found helpful to serve as an introduction to the "Aeneid."

Thus the courses in Latin as now organized for the most part, as far as the authors and their works are concerned, seem to be about the best for high-school work in Latin. The amount of work to be required needs next to be considered. The amount of work for thoro preparation at present required of high-school students is too great. If students do excellent work, or even thoroughly satisfactory work, in their Latin, it requires too much home preparation; if they do not put on the necessary home study, their work immediately falls below standard, and interest decreases to a minimum. It is a familiar fact to all high-school teachers that most high-school students, in order to do even moderately well in their Latin, are obliged to put at least one and a half to two times as much home study on it as on any of their other studies. This causes them either to overwork or slight other studies, usually the latter.

It seems to me that the amount of Latin read is entirely subordinate to the quality of work done and to the amount of time devoted to it in the classroom. The home preparation in any study is entirely subordinate to the classroom work. If only half the amount of "Caesar" were prescribed for thoro preparation, only half the present time would be required for home study, only half the present time would be required for class recitation on that work, and the simplest Latin available, such, for instance, as is used at the end of the first year for home study—that found in the average gradatim. Thus, while only half as much "Caesar" would be read the second year, yet more Latin altogether would be read than at present, since it is possible to read at sight in the classroom more Latin than could be assigned for thoro preparation. Yet the knowledge of "Caesar" would be practically as great as far as vocabulary and syntax are concerned. The opportunity furnished for learning how to study and attack a Latin sentence, under the guidance of the teacher, would be invaluable, and would, in addition, require all students to depend on themselves for the work done in the classroom, and to exert themselves daily toward interpreting their Latin, a thing which far too many students of Latin are not obliged to do under the present system of only home study where various devices are employed to reduce their effort to a minimum.

In the same way, if but half the present amount of "Cicero" were required to be studied intensively in the third year, and the remaining half of the time in school were devoted to sight reading from "Caesar," far better work could be done in "Cicero," and a better knowledge and appreciation of "Caesar" be obtained. "Caesar" is most certainly an excellent author for sight reading in the third year.

In the fourth year, if about half the amount of "Vergil" were read for thoro preparation, far better work could be done in that which was read, and the remaining half of the time of classroom recitation could be devoted to sight reading from "Cicero."

Thus in the aggregate there would be fully as much Latin read, if not more, under the new system as the old. Only half the time would be required for home study, and thus much of the well-known "grind" would be done away with, and interest correspondingly stimulated. I doubt not in my own mind that the power of interpreting Latin would be greatly increased, and the knowledge of the vocabulary and syntax fully as great.

Latin prose composition will have its place in the second, third and fourth years of study. The composition work should be based on those parts of the author's work which have been critically studied beforehand, when the vocabulary, style and spirit of the passage has been grasped. The exercises should not, however, be haphazard and fragmentary, but should be adapted to develop the several points of syntax systematically; thus a systematic study of syntax should go on *pari passu* with the practice in reproducing the thought of the author in slightly different form. The distinction between the writing of detached sentences and connected passages is largely an artificial one; there is not a sharp line of demarcation between them. Rather is the progress from writing the most simple, straightforward sentences to writing those of greater length and more involved constructions. If the ability be developed to write good single sentences, that of writing those of connected discourse will follow as a matter of course. But for the purpose of style and illustrating the use of connectives, some attention should be devoted to the writing of connected discourse in the fourth year.

To sum up, I should say that in much the same way as in the high-school course in English, so in the Latin course, about half the amount of Latin should be studied intensively, and the remaining half should be read in the classroom under the personal supervision of the teacher, to be studied not so much for the sake of syntax as to cultivate the proper habits of study in the subject, to promote spontaneity and power of interpretation, and to foster individual effort. Latin prose composition should be begun in the second year and continue *pari passu* with the intensive study, and, besides re-enforcing the knowledge of the passages studied, it should develop systematically a knowledge of syntactical principles.

In order intelligently to consider our second question, viz: What is the value of Latin relative to other material which must be omitted if this course is taken? it becomes necessary to state, at least briefly, what are the subjects which may legitimately claim a place in a high-school course of study, and, this done, to examine the relative value of Latin with reference to these.

The different studies which may reasonably enter into high-school education may be divided broadly into three groups, viz: First, the Humanistic Group, that is, those studies dealing primarily with the history and life of man; second, the Naturalistic Group, that is, those studies dealing primarily with the history and life of nature; third, the Technical Group, that is, those studies dealing primarily with the learning of a trade. Of course, the lines of demarcation are not drawn absolutely between these groups, but I think we should all agree upon the broad distinctions made between these groups.

To the first, or humanistic group, belong the subjects of literature, including both the ancient and modern languages, art and history. To the second, or naturalistic group, belong the natural sciences and mathematics. To the third, or technical group, belong mathematics, the commercial branches, and the courses in manual training and mechanical arts.

The student's education must inevitably embrace, in the main, the subjects comprehended under one of these three groups. None of us can know equally well the record of both man and nature, and still less in addition, be proficient in the technical branches. It is indeed true that history does afford examples of a few such polymaths, such as Aristotle, Francis Bacon, Leibnitz, and Goethe, but these are exceptions to the rule. The great multitude of us must choose that line of study to which our bent inclines, and thenceforth depend for our acquaintance with the others, except for an elementary knowledge, upon the saving friction of our necessaray intercourse with the great thinking and writing world.

If the different studies naturally group themselves thus, all that need be done is to make such provisions as may be deemed necessary concerning choice and sequence of studies which would apply irrespective of which of the three main courses is studied, and then let the student decide absolutely for himself as to the balance of his course. Naturally, he will often be influenced in his choice by the advice of parents or teachers, but in the last resort he is to be left free to decide for himself.

It would seem that the following principles should be operative governing the course of study in the high school:

First—The minimum number of subjects should be prescribed and the maximum number elective.

Second—The courses should be so arranged that the student would not be obliged to decide finally on his group until after the second year, thus affording every student an opportunity to change his course at the end of his second year.

Third—Graduates from any of the three courses should be equipped to enter a corresponding course in the universities.

Fourth—The minimum of subjects or units which the high school finds best to prescribe for all courses, or for each course, should be the maximum number of subjects or units which should be required for entrance to the universities, the balance of units required for entrance being elective.

Fifth—A full high-school course should consist of sixteen units, a unit of work representing approximately the pursuit of a subject one year five times per week.

It is my belief that the following subjects should be prescribed for all, irrespective of which course is pursued:

	Units.
English literature and composition.	2
History	2
Science	2
Mathematics	2
Foreign language (ancient or modern)	2
Total	10

There would thus be left six units for elective work, two of which are to be determined by which of the three courses is chosen; if the technical course is chosen, these two units would consist of technical work; if the naturalistic course, two units more of science; if the humanistic course, two units more of foreign language, either ancient or modern. There would remain four units, or the equivalent of one year's work, to be chosen without any limitations whatever. Thus a student in the humanistic course could also take two extra units of science and two units of technical work, thus combining the distinctive features of all three courses in one; or he could concentrate on one particular line of work. There should exist no prestige of one course over another— all should be regarded as being of equal worth, considered absolutely; relatively, that course is best which is worth most to the individual student who has certain tastes, desires, aptitudes, and intended vocation in life.

The value of Latin relative to other courses which must be omitted if this course is taken, is to be determined by each individual according to his tastes and aptitudes. For those who have the time and taste for linguistic study, a knowledge of Latin such as would be acquired by at least a two-years' course, would be invaluable in any line of work; for others who have but a limited time, or perhaps have no taste or capacity for linguistic study, it would unquestionably be best not to take Latin at all. But for those whose tastes lead them to pursue the humanistic studies, at least a two-years' course in Latin is a *sine qua non,* and, apart from those studies prescribed for all, is worth more, by far, than any other subject in the whole high-school curriculum. In the humanistic course, therefore, four units of foreign language should be required, the first two units of which should be Latin, and so prescribed; the remaining two units may be Latin or Greek, or a modern language.

For hundreds of years Latin and Greek have held a leading place in the educational systems of the foremost countries in the world; they still hold it. Much has been said about the superior mental training furnished by their study, but I am not disposed to claim any pre-eminent disciplinary value for them that I should not claim for science, or history, or English when properly taught. Much has been said about the superior aesthetic training which these languages give but I am inclined to think that while for a certain few this may possibly be true, yet for the great majority this aesthetic training would come equally well, if not better, with the study of an equivalent amount of the best English or any other modern literature. While, in short, I might claim for the study of the classical languages a disciplinary value equal to that given by any of the other leading subjects taught in the high school, I should not claim that their study furnished any superior training when the other subjects are properly taught. If in the past greater disciplinary value has been associated with the study of the classics, this has been due to the fact that better trained teachers and better methods of instruction were found in these branches, but of late years, with the greatly improved methods of teaching science and history, and English, this superiority of teachers and methods has almost entirely disappeared.

To my mind it appears that unless we can defend the study of the classics in the high school by showing that even a moderate proficiency of the English language is impossible without at least some knowledge of them, we can not defend their study at all.

But we can thus defend the study of Latin, to confine our present discussion to it. It is not my intention to thrash over old straw in arguing the case for Latin, since the arguments pro and con have already been thrashed over ad nauseum. I shall simply cite a few facts which are outside the forum of debate, and though the soundness of the recommendations of the authorities quoted may be disputed, the burden of so proving rests with the opponents of Latin.

First—Two of the most renowned educational committees which ever met in this country, the Committee of Ten, and the Committee on College Entrance Requirements, have with a single voice insisted again and again on the indispensable need of at least some knowledge of Latin in order to gain even a fair appreciation of the English language.

Second — Hon. William T. Harris, United States Commissioner of Education, in his "Brief for Latin," published in the "Educational Review" some three years ago, stated that over 75 per cent of the words in our English lexicon are of classical origin. He insists that for this and many other reasons Latin should be retained as one of the staples in American education.

Third—The classics serve as a norm for our English; this is especially true of Latin. Being a dead language, it is unchangeable; successive generations being trained in it, drink ever anew at the fountain of perennial vigor, and nourish and foster the higher literary quality of the English language. Who knows but that, if the study of Latin were neglected altogether, the English language, instead of being practically uniform over the whole English-speaking world, maintaining everywhere its pristine strength and vigor, would begin to degenerate and split up into dialects. Indeed, with the standard of ages gone, and none other to take its place, would it not be the most natural thing to occur? At any rate, I think we should all admit that with a considerable proportion of the cultivated people of every generation trained in the Latin, and who would naturally be the ones to set the standards in literature, we have therein one of the surest, if not the only, safeguard, for the preservation of the unity and vigor of the English language. Perhaps some day we may spell our English words according to sound; perhaps some day we may prefer to use all words in no other than their most common every-day meanings, losing sight of the finer shades of meaning, and the mental pictures which the words contain. Surely, if that time ever does come, as it probably never will, then, with equal pace, will our literature degenerate into the commonplace and fast travel the downward path. If, however, that times does come, but not till then, will Latin cease to demand for itself a leading place in the education of those who want a literary training, and this includes all who have the time and capacity to give at least some attention to it.

The study of literature will enter into the course of all students in the high school; with some who have but a limited time to spend in high school, their study may perforce end with the study of their vernacular; with others, whose tastes and aptitudes are primarily scientific, their study may end with—say, a two years' course in a modern foreign language; but with those whose natural bent is literary or historical, those who wish to turn their attention to the history of man rather than to the history of nature, some acquaintance with Latin, at least, is necessary. For Latin lies at the foundation of all subsequent literature, and the nation that ignores it altogether does so at its peril. Literature is the living record of the life of humanity. Can any pains spent on the improvement and amplification of that record be adequate to such an object? If our life would gain depth and strength, it must rest on the memories of the past; humanity will not be willing to drop its connection with its own past, nor to renounce its powers of imagination and its love of beauty. It is for the production of these and such like qualities, after all, that civilization exists; the destruction of these qualities would result in the destruction of humanity itself.

If it be worth while to afford a training which develops those qualities which make our poets, writers of fiction, lawyers, statesmen, teachers, and the great mass of cultivated citizens found in all the ranks and walks of life, then will the education of such take its root firmly in the study of Latin. The same reason which makes a knowledge of mathematics necessary in Physics or Astronomy, makes Latin indispensable in the study of English. Without mathematics, to be sure, one may gaze at the stars, and sun and moon, and perhaps talk knowingly of what he has read or heard others say, but to make the science a living reality we must travel the same toilsome path which all others have traveled who have achieved anything in the science worthy of the name. So it is in the realm of literature and the humanities in general; if we desire to gain anything more than a superficial knowledge of literature, we must go back to the same source whence others have derived their standards.

It is true that some educators go so far as to maintain that Latin has absolutely no place or function in a high school curriculum. But I am inclined to believe that either they exaggerate their own views in order to bring forward the question of the function of Latin as strongly as possible into the forum of debate, or I fear they are afflicted with some sort of inanition, such as Darwin complained of in his autobiography when he said: "For many years I cannot endure to read a line of poetry. I have tried lately to read Shakespeare, and found it so intolerably dull that it nauseated me. I have also lost my taste for pictures or music. . . . My mind seems to have become a kind of machine for grinding general laws out of large collections of facts. . . . If I had to live my life again, I would have made a rule to read some poetry and listen to some music at least once every week; for perhaps the parts of my brain now atrophied would thus have been kept alive thru use. The loss of these tastes is a loss of happiness, and possibly may be injurious to the intellect, and more probably to the moral character, by enfeebling the emotional part of our nature."

A brief summary will conclude this paper:

1. The courses in Latin as at present organized in the secondary schools of California seem to be the best possible as far as the general arrangement of authors and their works are concerned.

2. The amount of work in Latin required for intensive study is too great at present. It should be reduced by a half, and the balance of the time now devoted to Latin should be given to reading in the class room under the supervision of the teacher. The present grind would thus be done away with, and interest and power increased.

3. The value of Latin relative to other courses in the curriculum of the high school which would have to be omitted if Latin is taken, depends on the tastes and aptitudes of the individual pupil, and the total amount of time he has to give to his education. For those who have the time and aptitude, at least a two years' course in Latin is most valuable, irrespective of what special line of work is afterwards followed. For those who intend to devote themselves to the humanistic studies, at least a two years' course in Latin is indispensable, and is worth more than any other subject, aside from those prescribed studies which ought to enter into the course of all students irrespective of their special line of work, and which should represent the round whole and be a complete circle of general subjects.

* * *

Commercial Course for High Schools

J. H. Francis

The committee appointed by your president "To compile a report upon the function and scope of a commercial course for the high schools, and to determine the relations of such a course to the rest of the high school curriculum," reports as follows:

This report will be somewhat brief, owing to the limited time given in which to secure data and compile the report. The following list of questions was prepared by your committee, and sent to twenty-three of the leading high schools in California, and to twelve other western high schools outside of California. Owing to the limited time, no data was secured from the Eastern schools:

1. Have you a Business Course in your high school?
2. How many years does it cover?
3. Are diplomas or other certificates of graduation given to those completing the course?
4. How long has your Business Course been established?
5. What is your high school enrollment?
6. How many pupils are taking work in the Business Course?
7. How does the proportion of boys and girls compare with that of other high school courses?
8. How many pupils have completed the Business Course?
9. Does the Business Course include-

any of the regular high school subjects, such as English, history, mathematics, etc.?

10. How many are taking subjects in the Business Course merely as "extras"?

11. What is the attitude of your superintendent and board toward a Business Course?

12. Should commercial subjects be accredited for college entrance?

13. Are Business Course subjects accepted toward graduation in regular high school courses?

14. Give, in brief, your opinion as to the scope and value of a commercial course in high schools.

Out of the thirty-five schools, to which the list of questions were sent, twenty-six answers were received, of which the following is a summary:

1. Twelve have regular commercial courses in the high-school curriculum, three have separate commercial high schools, five have commercial branches taught as electives, and six expect to introduce commercial work next year.

2. Out of the twelve schools having regular commercial courses seven have a two-years' course and five a four-years' course. Of the seven schools having a two-years' course, three hope to change to four years. Of the five schools having a four-years' course, none express a wish to change to two years. One school expects to establish a two-years' course next year.

3. All schools having four-year courses grant diplomas. Those having a two-years' course give some sort of certificate of attainment.

4. The greatest number of years which any school reporting has been conducting a commercial course is ten. The average for all is four and one-third years.

5 and 6. The highest percentage of commercial course students enrolled in any school reporting is twenty. The average is 13 per cent of the total enrollment.

7. Every school, except one, reports a higher percentage of boys in the business course than in the other high-school courses.

8. Out of a total enrollment of 6,365 in all schools reporting, outside the larger cities having commercial high schools, the total number of graduates from the business courses, from the time the courses were established to the present, is eighty-four.

9. All schools reporting, with one exception, include some of the regular high school subjects, such as English, mathematics, history and science, in the commercial course.

10. But eighty pupils taking regular work, in all schools reporting, are taking commercial subjects as "extras."

11. Sixteen schools report the Superintendent and Board as favoring commercial work in the high school, while three are reported as unfavorable.

12. Eight principals favor accrediting commercial work for college entrance. Four favor it conditionally, while nine are oposed to such accrediting.

13. Fifteen schools accept commercial work toward graduation in regular high-school courses, five give part credit, and three do not accept such work.

14. But two principals out of the entire number reporting are opposed to commercial courses in high schools. A few express themselves as favoring a straight four-years' commercial course, requiring from one-half to three-quarters of the work to be regular academic work, while a great majority seem to favor offering commercial work as electives.

It is only within recent years that the subject of commercial education has become a problem for the public schools to solve. It is not worth while to discuss the advisability of introducing commercial work in our high schools, that question having been settled already by 95 per cent of the leading schools, of this State at least. The question now is upon the scope and efficiency of this work.

It is hardly possible, with the limited time at our disposal, for your committee to prepare a complete discussion of the reports received from the various high schools. We, therefore, present to your honorable body the following points as setting forth our conclusions:

I.

The High School Should Offer Either a Commercial Course, or Commercial Subjects, Elective.

This proposition has already been settled by 95 per cent of the leading high schools, of the State. It is hardly within the scope of a report of this kind to enter into a discussion of the general educational value of commercial subjects. Suffice it to say, that this class of work is a demand of the times; that the subject matter taught is valuable for young people to know; that the discipline is good; that such courses bring many worthy young people within the general uplifting influence of the high school who might otherwise go no farther than the grammar school; special training is demanded for all other lines of activity; why not for business?

From the fact that only eighty-four pupils have been graduated from all of the twenty-six schools reporting to your committee, representing an annual enrollment of over 6,000, it is evident that pupils do not choose commercial work merely as an easy road to graduation.

II.

The Time Required to Complete the Commercial Course Should Not Be Shorter Than That of the Other High School Courses.

It should not be the purpose of the high schools to bid against the business college for patronage, in the way of *endeavoring* to prepare students for special positions, as stenographers or bookkeepers, "while the position waits." While it might not be best to prohibit pupils from taking special work in this department, it should certainly be discouraged by the school management; and pupils should be expected, under certain limitations, to follow the general order of the course, as outlined.

While many of the schools of the State are still working on the two-years' course, the tendency is entirely in the direction of the longer period. Several schools report change from two to four year courses, while not a single change is reported in the opposite direction.

III.

The Work Required in the Commercial Course Should Not Be Lighter Than That of Other Lines of Work in the High School.

The commercial course should be neither a short-cut nor a down-hill road to graduation from the high school. The course should not be crowded with pupils who have failed in other lines of work. It must be admitted, however, that many students who are not adapted to the study of Latin, or even higher mathematics and the sciences, are found to have their aptitudes and interests running along the line of more practical subjects. The selection of the pupil's course of study in the high school should hinge on the following points: What is he expecting to do after finishing his school course? What are his capabilities for general academic work? What is the direction of his interests and aptitudes?

IV.

In Elective High School Courses Commercial Subjects Should Have Equal Rank With Other Subjects.

The plan of offering one general elective course, with about half of the work prescribed, is becoming more and more popular among the high schools of the State. As a large percentage of those attending the high schools will never enter college, the plan of offering commercial subjects as free electives will not only increase the efficiency of our high schools, but will increase their popularity as well. This plan will attract many good boys and girls who might otherwise never attend the high school. It will bring them in contact with the inspiring influence of high-school teachers and students, and thus influence many to undertake higher educational work.

V.

The Following Subjects Should Be Required in Commercial Courses: Bookkeeping and Business Practice, two years; Commercial Law and International Law, one year; Commercial Arithmetic, one-half year; Commercial Geography, one-half year; Also, two years of English, two years of Mathematics, one year of Science, and one year of American History and Civics.

Besides these required subjects, the school should also offer economics, industrial history of the United States, penmanship, stenography and typewriting, as electives. Under this arrangement five-eighths of the work of the course is prescribed, leaving three-eighths to be chosen from the other commercial subjects offered, and from the regular academic subjects of the school.

VI.

The Educational Qualifications of Teachers for the Commercial Department Should Be Up to the Standard Required of Other High School Teachers, Not Only in General, but in the Particular Subjects to Be Taught.

The carrying out of this provision will do more toward placing commercial departments on an equal footing with other departments of the high school than anything else that can be done.

Respectfully submitted,

C. L. McLane (Chairman),
D. A. Mobley,
P. M. Fisher.
Committee.

I am in full accord with the general spirit of this report.

Conclusion No. 2 is desirable, but, as a matter of fact, the students who elect a commercial course do so, as a rule, because they feel they cannot take a full high-school course of four years.

Conclusion No. 6 is good as a general proposition, but should not be so stated in cold law. The present statute seems to me to fit the case quite well for commercial work.

Supplementary Report.

I wish to add the following suggestions to the foregoing report:

1. The data given does not include in every instance that collected from the commercial high schools of the State. Since the enrollment of these schools represents so large a percentage of commercial students, this fact should be remembered in drawing conclusions from this data. Not only do the commercial high schools represent a large percentage of enrollment, but they probably represent the highest degree of organization of commercial work, and possibly of efficiency in such work.

2. Commercial subjects should be given equal standing with other subjects toward graduation, and high-school graduates should be admitted to our State University because they are graduates. Unless commercial branches have equal worth with other high-school studies, they have no place in high-school work. If it requires their disciplinary value plus their practical value to balance the equation, our universities should be willing to give credit to the practical worth of any high-school subject.

I believe, however, that those having experience in commercial as well as academic work will agree that its disciplinary value is on a par with other high-school subjects.

3. Statistics showing the percentage of boys enrolled in the commercial courses, compared with the other courses, are significant, and, in view of the fact that high-school enrollments are showing a disparity of boys, these statistics are worthy of consideration.

4. The time required to complete the commercial should be equal to that required to complete any other high-school course, but the subjects should be arranged to place a large proportion of the distinctively commercial work in the first two years. Following are some reasons, briefly stated, for the last suggestion:

(a) It will increase high-school enrollments. To the question, "Would you have entered high school had there been no commercial studies offered?" 328 of our pupils gave definite answers, 132 replying in the negative and 196 in the affirmative. This gave a percentage above 40 who would not have attended high school except for commercial work. This percentage will be materially affected by the arrangement of subjects in the course.

(b) I believe the proposed arrangement is educationally correct. The manual work in bookkeeping, penmanship, stenography and typewriting relieves the strain of continuous and purely intellectual work. These studies at the same time compel habits of concentration, neatness, order, accuracy, and close application— qualities very essential to higher commercial work, and not usually highly developed in pupils entering high school.

(c) Distinctively commercial subjects appeal strongly to the interests of pupils entering high school. This interest is a great incentive to work. To the question, "Which study do you most enjoy?" 60 per cent of our entering class gave bookkeeping as their favorite study and 32 per cent gave stenography. This made a total of 92 per cent who enjoyed these studies most. At the end of one and one-half years' work the percentage had changed from 92 to 57, and pupils were enjoying more the subjects more nearly academic in character, such as economics, history, modern languages and mathematics.

(d) This arrangement would result in a larger number completing the course. It has been thought necessary by some to reserve the commercial work for the last year's work in order to hold pupils in school. This I believe to be a fallacy. Pupils who are liking their work and doing well in it will be inclined to remain in school. The large percentage leaving school before completing their work do so during the first two years. Those having remained two years see the necessity of a higher education, and, having successfully passed one-half of the work and having formed school ties arising from associations, desire to remain and finish with their class.

(e) The proposed arrangement offers to those who are compelled by force of circumstances to spend a limited time in school an opportunity to secure a working knowledge of commercial branches. This reason, next to the educational one, is to my mind the most worthy. This arrangement solves the question of length of courses.

5. In giving the points upon which the choosing a course by a pupil should rest "What are his capabilities for general academic work?" should be excluded or worded differently. The inference seems to be that if the pupil has capabilities for general academic work, he should take a course offering such work. This inference is probably correct, but it applies with equal force to pupils having capabilities for commercial or any other kind of work. If stated at all, the question should read, "How do his capabilities for general academic work compare with those for commercial work?"

6. In a course having a definite accomplishment in view, electives, if allowed at all, must be comparatively few. Commercial branches as electives in a general academic course will be valuable, but they will not accomplish the purpose for which commercial courses are instituted. In courses designated for general culture, much wider latitude could be allowed than in a commercial course.

7. Economics and penmanship should be required rather than elective subjects, and commercial arithmetic cannot be successfully done in one-half year unless the subject is moved farther up in the course than is practical.

8. If the sixth suggestion of the committee means that commercial teachers should have academic training equal to that required of other teachers, I am opposed to it at this time for the reason that such teachers who are at the same time qualified to handle some of the commercial branches are not available, and such recommendation would tend to cripple the work.

While it is true that the percentage of university men among the commercial teachers has probably not equaled that of other high-school courses, it is also true that commercial work has had teachers with more worldly experience and a wider business training than other courses. As between this and present academic training for commercial teachers there is probably not much choice.

The rating of commercial work below other work by high schools is not done to any material extent to the lack of scholarship of commercial teachers. It is due rather to the fact that the University does not recognize commercial work, and to the ignorance of high schools as to the educational and disciplinary value of commercial subjects.

J. H. FRANCIS.

* * *

Uniformity of the High School Course

S. D. Waterman

At the request of Dr. Burk, a short paper has been prepared upon the subject suggested in the headlines. It is not in the nature of a stated report but, largely, suggestive and intended to call out discussion and a full expression of opinion. All subjects relating to the high schools will, doubtless, be fully discussed in the high-school section.

The value of a uniform course of study in the secondary schools of the State, so far as they are strictly preparatory schools, must be apparent to all. There is every argument in favor of it, since, by vote of the people, an amendment to the organic law of the State has been ratified by which the State may become a direct supporter of these schools. In the older States, where the population is fixed, such uniformity is not so essential, but in California, where the population is constantly shifting, it seems to be necessary. If, then, there is value in a uniform course for the strictly preparatory work of the high schools, such uniformity is surely desirable, not only in the order of subjects, but also in the text-books. The studies and the texts for the elementary schools are provided by law, insuring uniformity in these schools. If the State, through a board established by statute, is to assume the management of the secondary school, and if the State aid is to be given to these schools, the State would doubtless have the same right to prescribe the courses of study and the text-books for these schools, as for the elementary.

We are aware that local feeling and the desire for non-interference with local school management is strong, and we would urge this uniformity only so far as the courses that are strictly preparatory to the universities are concerned. State aid to the high schools is sure to bring State supervision in some form.

In all of the larger schools, aside from the preparatory courses, which should be uniform both in subjects and texts, provision should be made for courses giving the widest possible range of electives, such as are best suited to the tastes and wishes of any who do not wish to avail themselves of university training. Special attention in these courses should be given to commercial, manual and industrial training, and the arranging of these courses should be left entirely to the local school authorities.

The solution of the problem, so far as the centers of population are concerned, is simple. The perplexing question arises with regard to the schools in the sparsely populated portions of the State. The question to be determined is to what extent these schools are to be treated as preparatory schools. Unfortunately, perhaps, the idea prevalent in many of these smaller communities, that a high school, to be worthy of the name, must at once be an accredited school, tends to cripple the efficiency of the school. In very many of these schools, having one or two teachers, the effort is made to give courses that will prepare for Palo Alto or Berkeley, whether any of the graduates of the school ever take university work or not. As a result, the energies of the teaching force, as well as of the taught, are exerted in trying to carry out a line of work which is not the best suited to the actual needs of the community, but only such work as will result in the accrediting of the school. The utilitarian side of the high-school course is left entirely out of the reckoning, and the school which the district supports fails to do for its patrons the work for which it was established. If these schools are to be preparatory schools, then uniformity is necessary; if not, the local authorities should be left perfectly free to arrange such a course as shall best suit the demands of the people.

In this connection I desire to quote from the report of Superintendent Fultz, of the Burlington, Ia., schools. This tends to show that the same questions as to the status of the high school in a system of education are to be found in other States as well as in California. He says: "We desire to correct the too-prevalent idea that a high-school education is only for those who expect to teach or go to college. The mission of the high school is to give the school training necessary to fit, as far as possible, for the appreciation of the best things in life, whether the person so trained shall afterwards remain in the home, enter business, run a farm or go to college. Our school has been examined and accredited, but while this is true, we do not wish it to be understood that we aim to be simply a preparatory school. The high school of the future has a wider mission. The colleges are also coming to recognize that whatever fits for life ought to be accepted for college entrance."

It must also be remembered that but a very small percentage of the high-school students ever go to the universities. From the report of Hon. Frank A. Hill, Secretary of the Massachusetts Board of Education, published in 1898, we quote the following: "In round numbers, 13 per cent of the students enrolled in the high schools are fitting for college, while 87 are taking courses that do not fit for college. The people have generously co-operated with the colleges for the sake of the 13 per cent, and even at the expense of the 87 per cent. If the colleges would co-operate more fully with the people for the sake of the 87 per cent, all of the high schools would receive an uplift, but none more than the smaller schools."

The same conditions prevail in California. In fact, the per cent of those fitting for college, except in a very few of the largest schools, will fall far below 13 per cent. However, the University of California has done much in fostering a sentiment in favor of secondary schools by the system of accrediting, which has been in use for the last fifteen years.

So far, then, as the secondary schools are to be preparatory schools, the contention is made that uniformity in courses of study and in text-books is valuable and desirable. In arranging courses not preparatory, there should be left to the local boards the fullest liberty to adopt any which will secure the best possible results for the community.

As to the practicability of any scheme to secure this desired uniformity, but little need be said. The way is open, and a little careful thought will be sure to bring about what little legislation is necessary.

There is no time for any further discussion in this paper, which is already too long. We must see to it, however, that, in some way, the needed legislation upon this and other matters pertaining to the welfare of public-school education in California be secured at the hands of the Legislature which is about to meet.

* * *

Algebra

J. D. Graham

As chairman of your committee selected to report on "The functions of the present course in algebra in accredited schools, aside from preparation to meet university courses in mathematics, and to determine its value relative to other material which must be omitted if this course is taken," I beg leave to submit the following:

It is assumed by your committee that

the course referred to is the course in elementary algebra, requiring one year's work.

The main question for consideration is, What should a year's study of algebra do for the pupil? How does it epuip him for success in the battle of life, and for enjoyment during the intervals of peace?

If this subject provides a means for learning one or more of the trades or professions, a knowledge of which is dependent on a previous knowledge of algebra, it will help him in his preparation for life's work. If during its study he is furnished with the opportunity for close logical thinking, it will give to the mind a training that will open up to the student wider fields whether for profit or enjoyment.

Algebra does both. As a whole, it consists of a series of demonstrations of methods for the solution of problems which do not yield to arithmetical treatment, together with a series of methods or operations for applying these propositions to the solution of problems. The study of the first division of the subject trains the mind to the logical habit and gives general culture, while the second provides the means of continuing in the higher fields of analysis, or of branching out into any of the subjects of applied mathematics.

Aside from the training given in logic and in mathematical processes, algebra has additional educative value. It is based on a series of definitions and on processes derived from them. These are stated in a technical language, each word of which has an exact meaning, the use of which must be mastered, thus training the pupil to be discriminating in the use of words.

In the solution of problems there are several helpful steps. The pupil must study the exact meaning of the sentence; he must determine the known conditions given; these must be translated into terms of algebra and put into the form of an equation, according to the terms of the question. He must also recall the possible processes available and determine how he can best combine these to secure the desired result. In this he exercises reading, memory, imagination and judgment.

The consideration of the question of what algebraic material shall be used in this course—whether the logic of the subject or application of its methods should be given prominence—must be dependent on those for whom the course is planned. Two considerations impel me to the conclusion that it is best to make it largely applied to algebra. First, these pupils have just completed a course in arithmetic, and, applied algebra being largely a continuation of that subject, it will be taken up more readily than will a purely logical discussion; secondly, the logical discussions of algebra are so much more difficult than those of geometry that any algebraic theory essential to its application should come in the last year of the course, after geometry has been studied. A third reason for taking the application of algebra before the theory is that the application is much simpler than the theory, and, therefore, should come first.

Among the topics that should receive careful attention, even when the shortest time is given, are:

First—The technical language of the subject, since in every science the best thought on the subject is incorporated in its special words. These words must be understood and used in order to become proficient in its application.

Second—Since algebra is so largely operated by means of the equation of condition, the difference between it and an identity should be made clear:

Third—The subject of quadratic equations should be taken up as early in the course as possible and taught so thoroly that the pupil will remember what it is and how to solve it. This being the most important subject in elementary algebra, should be frequently reviewed in order to fix it in the pupil's mind.

Where more than a year is available, a number of useful and interesting subjects may be introduced, such as:

Horner's Method of Division, with the Factor and the Remainder theorems.

The Elements of Graphics, with the Indeterminate Equation to Illustrate Simultaneous Equations.

The corollary to the law of signs, viz: "If an odd number of minus signs affect a term, the resulting sign is minus; if the number is even, the sign is plus, to be used in removing parentheses by one operation. The Arithmetical and Geometrical Progressions, Elementary Determinants for the Solution of Simultaneous Equations, and other topics that will doubtless be thought of by teachers of this interesting subject.

In conclusion, I beg leave to summarize my report as follows: It is the sense of your committee that the function of the course in algebra in secondary schools is:

First — To furnish means for solving problems that do not yield readily to arithmetical methods.

Second—To teach the technical language of the subject and to provide thoro instruction in the fundamental processes upon which are based all subsequent processes in pure and applied mathematics.

Third—To train the mind to logical methods, to clear, accurate expression and to furnish for general culture a means of comprehending a wider field of literature than would be possible without this training.

Fourth—As to the relative value of this course and of other subjects that must be omitted in order that this course may be taken; it is the opinion of your committee that the general scope of the subject is well covered, all essential features being presented, and none required that can properly be omitted. The course in itself is a minimum requirement, which, if taught without additional matter, will enable a student to pursue advanced courses in mathematics or science, while it is not so full that additional matter may not be introduced at the will of the teacher.

* * *

Algebra

A. W. Stamper

As a member of your committee selected to report on "The function of the present course in Algebra in accredited schools, aside from preparation to meet university courses in mathematics, and to determine its value relative to other material which must be omitted if this course is taken:"

I submit the following:

I agree with the chairman, Mr. Graham, that logical Algebra should be preceded by applied Algebra. But I do not agree that Algebraic reasoning should be left for the last year in the high school. The simple Algebraic processes should be introduced in the seventh and eighth grades, then in the one year devoted to Elementary Algebra the student can appreciate some Algebraic reasoning.

I agree that the student can reason better in Algebra after some work in Geometry. Hence teach Algebra and Geometry simultaneously the ninth and tenth years.

With reference to the function of the Elementary course in Algebra, the four points summarized by the chairman have essential value, and are agreed to, but I wish to emphasize that Algebra should be taught as it adds to the sum total of all truth, in particular to fundamental mathematical truth and, having such a function, it should supplement and aid Arithmetic and Geometry.

Performing such a function, the practical phase of the subject should be stressed—its aid and relation to the physical and applied sciences.

In the above whatever has been said of Algebra, applies to the Elementary Course.

The course as laid down by the university is meager enough to meet its demands. Its scope is not too broad nor technical for the student not going to the university. If one is to study Algebra at all, the course as laid down is no more than adequate. But it should not be taught merely as preparatory to advanced work; the work should be enriched as indicated.

One important addition should be included in the Elementary Course. The graph should be freely used in particular reference to simultaneous equations. It has important scientific value.

The State Arithmetic

A. L. Mann

The following are, in the judgment of your committee, the principal defects of the State Arithmetic:

1. Lack of working forms and directions, making the book almost useless for individual study, unaided by the teacher.

2. Many of its problems are unbusinesslike, some are too technical, others are too long, puzzling, and complicated.

3. Contractions in multiplication and division are confusing to young pupils and should be left for later study.

4. Denominators of fractions are frequently too large.

5. Stone and Brickwork, Carpeting, Plastering, Duties, Stocks, Exchange, Alligation, Average of Payments, Compound and Accurate Interest, and most of the work in Compound Numbers should be omitted.

The work for the average child's mind should be limited to the ground rules, common and decimal fractions, a few ordinary and simple applications of Percentage, Simple Interest, and Partial Payments on Promissory Notes by the Merchants' Rule.

All problems should be clearly expressed, generally contain but one operation and conform to a lucid method of solution, given in the book, at the head of the problems proposed under each topic.

All complex, difficult problems should be grouped under the head "Miscellaneous," at the end of the book and used as mathematical recreations for the quarter of the class standing highest in arithmetic, or such pupils as obtain more than ninety per cent in the examinations usually given to the whole class.

AIDS.—Good forms for working examples will be found in Robinson's and Wentworth's Arithmetics, and in Bailey's Comprehensive Arthmetic.

A variety of usely practical problems may be drawn from Walsh, Baird, and McLellan and Ames.

Other helpful authors are Milne, Hornbrook, and Cook and Cropsey.

* * *

Supervision of Rural Schools

Kate Ames

Your committee appointed to compile a report upon existing systems for supervision of rural schools by county superintendents, to estimate its value, and to recommend such modifications as may be for the best service to the educational interests of pupils, beg leave to report as follows:

1. The present system of supervision of rural schools by the county superintendent, altho working under many adverse conditions, is of great value to the schools of the state. It serves to enforce the course of study and to promote in a general way the educational interests of a county. The superintendent is a valuable advisor of teachers and trustees.

2. We believe that the best results are to be obtained when the superintendent is a vigorous, progressive, practical educator—one who can work in harmony with teachers and school boards. The spirit of co-operation is an essential element of efficient supervision.

3. The office of county superintendent should be removed from politics. The office should be an appointive one—the appointing power to be the State Board of Education or a non-partisan County Board appointed by the Superior Judge.

4. The superintendent should be furnished a deputy or deputies sufficient to do the clerical work of the office, over which the county superintendent should have general supervision.

5. We believe that the superintendent should have more power in the selection of the teaching force of his county. He should be an ex-officio member of every Board of Trustees in a county, and his

authority should be either to nominate for positions, or to confirm all appointments.

6. We believe that the consolidation of rural schools will greatly improve the conditions of supervision. A superintendent would then have fewer schools, and his visits could be more frequent and of longer duration, and greatly enhance the efficiency of the work of supervision.

7. The County Board of Education should have no part in the supervision of rural schools. Unless the county superintendent have a voice in their appointment they should in no case serve as deputy superintendents.

With the major report of your committee to report upon the existing systems of supervision of rural schools, I agree in the main, but can not add my signature to numbers *three* and *five* of the report.

3. There is no assurance, from experience, that the appointative power will not make as many mistakes as are at present made where the choice of superintendents is made by popular vote. This places the responsibility for the correction of mistakes where it should be—with the people, and is one of the chief means of raising the educational standard of the community, beyond which no superintendent can go, except that as a leader the ideals toward which he is striving and leading his community must be a little in advance of the community standard. Therefore, I believe that the choice of superintendent should rest with the people.

5. The superintendent's work is educative. His chief duty is to educate his community so that poor teaching will not be permitted. The superintendent should not be subjected to the criticism of favoritism and self-seeking to which an appointative power is usually subjected. He should never be looked upon as a person thru whom to secure positions, but his personality and training should be such that the trustees will have such confidence in his integrity and judgment that they will consult him when appointing or dismissing teachers. A superintendent who can not get the best teaching force in this way will not be able to do so with the law behind him, for the community, to obtain best results, must be in active sympathy with the educative efforts; therefore, I believe the superintendent should not have appointing power and there are many instances in which veto power would not be granted.

* * *

Teachers' Institute

J. H. Strine

Your committee appointed to compile a report from views of experienced county superintendents, and others, upon the system of county institutes, and to recommend modifications for approval by council, beg leave to report as follows:

Questions covering the value of our system of schools for the present annual institute; the question as to whether the amount of practical good derived from the present system of institutes compensates the state (thru increased efficiency in the schools) for the time and outlay as to whether the common plan of having nearly all subjects in the course of study discussed at each and every institute is a good one, or whether it would not be much more beneficial to take up instead but two or three subjects, have these presented by experts only (to be followed by general discussion of the teachers themselves), were sent out to the various county superintendents and normal schools of the state, as well as to a few individuals in other schools that have had institute experience.

A very large majority of replies concur in the facts:—

1. That our annual institutes are of great value to the schools.

2. That the state is indirectly, if not *directly* compensated for the time and money expended.

3. That the common plan of bringing up a whole course of study for discussion in any one institute is not a *good* one, and that vastly greater benefit would result if but two or three subjects were

presented for discussion, these led by specialists, and the insistance upon a general discussion by the body of teachers themselves.

Among the suggestions for improving the work of our present institutes given by our many correspondents, and worthy of note, are the following: The establishment of a higher and more thoroly enforced code of professional ethics; by taking pains to secure for each institute men or women of first-rate power in their departments of educational activity; if practicable, to have teachers witness actual teaching by one or two thoroly good instructors; by having less of the "pouring in" work and more of that kind which gives opportunity and *requires* teachers themselves to think and express themselves; and by arranging programs upon some principle of unity and coordination running thru the work of each institute.

**

NOTE—The report on "Compulsory Education" by Dr. E. C. Moore, and the report on "Free Text-Books," by Supt. E. M. Cox, were published in the February issue of the WESTERN JOURNAL OF EDUCATION. The report on "The Formation of Union School Districts" will be published in the June number of THE JOURNAL. Extra copies of these JOURNALS may be secured.

* * *

GENERAL SESSIONS

A. E. Shumate, Chairman   Mrs. M. M. FitzGerald, Secretary

Address of Welcome

Mayor M. P. Snyder

As the city's executive, it affords me much pleasure to extend to you a most hearty welcome to Los Angeles on the occasion of the 36th Annual Convention of the Teachers' Association of California. It is indeed a pleasure to welcome so distinguished, so intelligent, so representative a gathering.

Here are ladies and gentlemen, who by reason of their calling play a most important part in supplying the materials out of which is constructed the mighty rudder which steers our grand ship of state.

It is you ladies and gentlemen, who first teach the little ones how to creep in the world of letters, in the world of science, in every branch of useful knowledge.

The scene of your labor and devotion to a grand calling is laid in a land of wonderful possibilities. The little freckled-faced, red-haired youngster who exhausts your patience at times with his uncontrollable desire to engage in mischief, and who knows vastly more about marbles, tops and kites than about spelling and mathematical problems, may some day sway a great convention with his eloquence; he may some day be President of Harvard, Yale or Princeton; he may be a financial Napoleon; he may be President of the United States.

I believe that teachers oftentimes make a mistake in the way they deal with characters such as the one I have just mentioned. It takes a wonderful lot of patience, I presume, for one to daily try to hammer knowledge into the head of a youngster who seems utterly indifferent, and yet, as the history of all nations will serve to illustrate, these same freckly uninteresting youngsters have in many instances shined brightest in the world's history, while other boys whose prospects had been brilliant as the noonday sun never reached even the first round of the ladder of fame.

We need not turn to the dusty volumes of oldentime history; we need not go back to the Colonial period. Take, for instance, our illustrious U. S. Grant. It is said of him that his mother called him Useless Grant in his boyhood days. He considered it a prouder distinction to excel in equestrianism than in scholarship.

But that was when he was a mere boy. There came a time when his whole being changed; the little that the country school master had hammered into his head was there treasured as gold by the young man. An appetite for knowledge suddenly developed, and you know the rest.

The name of U. S. Grant will last as long as American history shall endure

There is no need of my speaking extensively on this subject, for you know that history is full of cases such as the one just mentioned.

So don't lose interest in the slow boys; pound knowledge into their heads whether they want it or not, and some day when one or two of them has made a good name for himself he will not forget you. Do not understand me, ladies and gentlemen, as taking sides with the slow, uninteresting boy as against the live, energetic boy. With me they both have the same weight in the scale of success.

All were created equal and all were put on earth for a purpose, and such being the case, you who have their futures in hand have a grave responsibility which each of you fully appreciates, and which you will not, I know, permit to pass from your hands, slighted.

And now as to your association, permit me to say that it is one of the grandest and best organizations in the State of California. It is engaged in a noble work. This gathering shows its strength. Here are the men and women in whose hands rests, to a large extent, the success or failure in life of the rising generation of the vast territory of California.

It is to our interest that the young should become noble men and noble women. We want them to fill our places with honor to themselves and with honor to the land of their birth.

We are wonderfully blest. Here under one sky live a contented people—a people the peer of any in the world in point of intelligence, refinement and citizenship. Our homes are fragrant with the perfumes of the rose and the violet; out on the grassy hillsides and upon the fertile mesa, the spring sunshine bathes vast fields of golden poppies fanned by the balmy breezes off the Grand Old Pacific. Here are permitted our young as well as old, to admire and gather what God in His infinite wisdom has so generously provided for them.

Brought into the world and reared in the atmosphere of such Paradisiacal conditions, the sons and daughters of California should some day become shining lights in the firmament of national greatness.

No round in the ladder of fame should be too high for them.

The members of this association are engaged in a noble work. All the conditions are favorable to them. I wish each of you unlimited success in your labors and bespeak for you the reward which comes to deserving ones.

Permit me in conclusion again to extend to you a most hearty welcome to our fair city.

May the convention prove a source of much benefit to yourselves and to California.

* * *

Address of Welcome

James A. Foshay

With the many busy cares that come to a superintendent of schools in a growing city, there is much pleasure, and among the pleasantest things that have come to help in a very busy life have been the warm friendships which are formed in such meetings as this. I believe that California is second to no other state in generous care and liberality towards her public schools, and I congratulate you, teachers and friends of education, that the people of this state, at the last general election, made it possible for California to take the child of four years, and carry him thru the kindergarten, the primary and grammar grades, and high school, and finally thru the university, thus perfecting the conditions as suggested by Professor Huxley, many years ago. He said: "I believe no educational system in this country (England) will be worthy of the name of national, or will fullfill the great object expected of it, unless it be one which establishes a great educational ladder, the bottom of which shall be the gutter, and the top of which shall be those universities of which we are justly proud."

A few years ago, in an address, I called attention to the fact that in 1895 Los Angeles city employed 290 teachers in her public schools. Today we have an able corps of 600 teachers, faithfully endeavoring to train more than 23,000 children for citizenship. Our city has recently voted $680,000 for additional school accommodations, and when this sum is converted into modern school buildings, we shall be a very happy people. But I would not have you think that growth and prosperity in a financial way is the aim of our people; we realize that our great work is to train our boys and girls so that they shall grow into true and honest men and faithful and conscientious women.

You are here as the advance guard of the large number of educational people which shall fill our hotels and homes on the last part of the old year and the first few days of the new year; and, like the advance guards, of course you are the choice of the army.

The teachers of northern California have the Northern California Teachers' Association; those of central California, the San Joaquin Valley Teachers' Association; those of southern California, the Southern California Teachers' Association; but, after all, northern California, southern California and central California are one. We do not seem so far apart when we realize that our work is along the same lines, and that we all come together at this time to join in harmonious tones the notes of universal advancement, and to unify all discordant elements, in one body known as the California Teachers' Association: and we are very glad to welcome this grand organization of the noble men and women of the Golden State to our city. I believe that the State Association and the several district associations, with the Teachers' Institute and other local associations, have done much to diffuse good, sound educational thinking, and to encourage good fellowship, and inculcate respect for others in our profession.

I see many faces before me that are very familiar, many whose hand grasps I take with a thrill of pleasure, but several are missing. I remember distinctly that in 1889, the president of this great association was none other than Ira Moore, President of the State Normal School located in this city. I remember his anxiety over the success of the meeting, that it should be a good one, and that among other features we should have good music. It was my pleasure to work on the music committee, and to lead in some of the songs on that occasion; and when I would say to him: "I fear that I cannot do this," he would say: "Talk with Fanny Quesnel about it. She will assist you." And I found his advice true. Several other faces we miss at this time, one of them known not only in Los Angeles city and county and in Southern California, but in the northern and central portions of California. I refer to our much loved and respected friend, Mr. Ennis who, but a short time before his death, conducted and presided over one of the most successful educational meetings ever held in our state. Another faithful worker, well known in this association, was Mrs. C. P. Bradfield who, for more than twenty years, had charge of the Drawing in this city.

The more we consider the business of teaching, the more important and exalted does the position of teacher become. The world is progressing very rapidly, changes are being made in all departments, and there perhaps was never a time when so many changes were taking place as at the present. In consequence of these, it is very essential that we meet together semi-occasionally, to consider those matters which pertain to our work. Twenty-three hundred years ago, the famous philosopher Plato gave his views on education as follows: "The office of the teacher is to educate and nurture the soul; gently to draw it out from the barbaric slough in which it has so long lain buried, and lead it to look upward; to turn it from the shadowy illusions of sense to the idea of Good, which is the dispenser of truth and reason, and to point out the best way of life."

No doubt many of us have thought that this sentiment is comparatively new, and are surprised to find that it was said by the Greek philosopher, so many centuries ago. Archimedes once said that if he had a place on which to stand, he, with a lever, could move the world. The teacher's strong lever is inspiration. Without this, the work in the schoolroom will be dull and of comparatively little value; for whatever subject is being considered, there must be inspiration on the part of the teacher.

The California Teachers' Association may well be the California teachers' legislature, where educational questions shall be considered and acted upon, and the final results reported to the State Legislature at Sacramento, that school laws may be enacted in accordance with the recommendations made at this session.

Los Angeles entertains august bodies, and is accustomed to distinguished gatherings, but I feel sure she entertains none for whom she has higher esteem than the teachers of our state and nation.

But we are here to welcome you; our honored Mayor has welcomed you on behalf of our city; and I am glad to state that on behalf of the Board of Education, the superintendents, and the six hundred teachers, we bid you welcome.

* * *

Response

Mrs. J. E. Chope

In behalf of the California State Teachers' Association, it is my privilege to respond to the very cordial welcome extended by Mayor Snyder and Superintendent Foshay.

A recent writer has said, "You'll find that education is about the only thing lying around loose in this world, and it's about the only thing a fellow can have as much of as he is willing to haul away. Everything else is screwed down tight and the screw driver lost."

Such a sentiment would be heresy in Los Angeles. Your Mayor and Superintendent have certainly given us permission to haul away more than educational ideas, and I don't believe anything is screwed down here!

Your welcome is a royal one. I presume that I but voice the unanimous sentiment of this Association when I say that any welcome less cordial would have been something of a disappointment in the light of the reputation Los Angeles has for its munificent hospitality, a reputation which is unrivaled, even in this state of glorious greetings.

A year ago I had the pleasure of welcoming the members of this Association to beautiful Pacific Grove, where the ocean rolls its ceaseless swell against the rocky shore, where the pines stand silent sentinels, and where the purple shadows rest upon the hills thru all the day; to old Monterey where early in the history of our state were initiated efforts to claim the natives from the wild freedom of the forest, to establish education and to sow in an unbroken wilderness the seeds of civilization and progress—where first was raised the symbol of the union, the stars and stripes, in token of American supremacy and American authority.

Tonight the scene is changed We are welcomed to the Minerva of California, sprung in the magnificence of her panoply, full grown from this southern Paradise; to the beauty and charm of a semi-tropic land, luxuriant in the wealth of sunshine and foliage denied to more rigorous climes.

Truly, inspiration is to be found amid scenes like these, groves with their golden fruit, wide spreading palms, tropical flowers—a very wilderness of color; scenes that transport us to the groves of ancient Greece where, in the centuries of long ago, arose that philosophy which has made an ineffaceable impress upon the world and which has been the fountain head of the great classics in the world of literature.

Upon the subject of education we are of one mind. Its universal importance is conceded; its pre-eminence as a factor in our commonwealth is admitted; it is the only certain foundation of a free state.

A subject of such importance, a subject fraught with such far-reaching consequences, a subject ultimately the concern of all, should be discussed under the most favorable circumstances.

With this beautiful environment as our inspiration, and with your cordial and gracious welcome as an additional incentive to work, surely we owe a great measure of gratitude to you and your fair city.

It is our hope and desire that the conclusion of this convention will be worthy of so auspicious an inauguration. And when we leave you, when our task is done, I assure you it will be with the kindliest recollections of Los Angeles and her lavish hospitality.

In behalf of the officers and members of our association, I earnestly and sincerely thank you, and trust that we may not prove unworthy of so spontaneous and genuine a welcome.

* * *

Habit

Ella F. Young

Your attention is invited not to the question, "How desirable, or undesirable, is a certain habit?" but to the questions "How is a habit formed?" "What is its origin?" "How is it perfected?" "How can it be changed?"

Had we hours at our disposal it would be interesting to attempt answering these questions along two lines of investigation: that of biology, the study of organic or physical life; and that of psychology, the study of psychic or mental life. In the part of an hour, which will be spent in discussing the questions of origin, perfection, and change of habit, the inquiry will be made along psychologic lines only.

Before beginning the search for the origin of a habit, let us come to some conclusion as to what Habit is. In so doing, I shall appeal to the experience of those among you who are singers, vocalists. When you were first conscious that you ought to sing well, was it after you had practiced long and faithfully upon the tones in the scale, the runs and the trills; after you had acquired power in pouring forth your self, your soul, in song and hymn? or was there before the acquisition of power, was there in the beginning a something of rhythm, of melody, that could be satisfied only by expression in song? Was there a something of music that made you feel, that to be yourself, you must sing? Was not the tendency to give yourself to your family and your friends thru song, there when you first sang, and then did not you repeat and repeat the score, not only for the purpose of getting control of your vocal chords, but also, for the very pleasure of making the beloved musical phrase perfect?

If memory would bring before each one of us the beginnings of that habit which most perfectly illustrates the individual disposition and aims, we should find them to be like the beginnings of the distinguishing, the characteristic habit of the talented and the gifted. Not in dull repetitions, made because we were told to repeat, but in impulses and tendencies which were afforded an opportunity for play, for action, for gratification, did our habits that indicate our real natures begin.

From this brief survey, habit may be defined as the expression of native impulses. This is only one element in the definition, however. Were we merely to give play to our impulses, we might never pass beyond the beginnings of habit; we might be mere creatures of impulse. But it is well to pause and emphasize the fact, that we recognize as ours, only that habit which began in a reaching forth on our part.

How, let me ask, did it ever come about that with all of our insight, we teachers begin training habit by setting up repetition as the basis, the beginning, instead of securing the training and the repetition, the final perfection thru the desire of the learner to gain control of the activity which originates in the native endowment?

Go into the school and see the child co-ordinating his sound image and his vocal apparatus in singing a new musical phrase.. Why does the teacher encourage the learner by praising the feeble attempt? Simply because in knowing humanity, she knows that to make that co-ordination a habit, the child must have not only the consciousness that his voice, his singing impulses, given play, have produced something that sounded like that which his ear had helped him to enjoy, but also that his emotion of pleasure over his success must be regarded, so that he will have heart, have courage to sing again and again until he has acquired thru *self directed* repetition the singing habit within that range.

In this development of the singing habit, there are the singing impulses, some of which must play freely; there is the recognition of the result of the co-ordination of the auditory image and the vocal apparatus, there is the pleasurable emotion, and all of these combine to make the little one repeat and repeat until he has ease in singing the phrase or song.

That ease, that facility, is Habit. But the impulse, the act, the image of the doing, the pleasurable emotion, are all finally lost to view; and we, noticing simply the repetitions—we, blind leaders of childhood—say we develop habits by having the children repeat.

- - -

Culture and Its Enemies

E. M. Hopkins

When Matthew Arnold formulated his definition, or rather his explanation, of the nature of an ideal culture, and when he proceeded to enumerate its opposing forces on both sides of the Atlantic he implied that the chief enemies of culture in America were commercialism and a sense of self-importance. It may be that we have still to reckon with these, but I believe that we have ceased to overestimate ourselves in the Arnoldian sense, and that the war we are waging against selfish materialism is not a losing battle, however much of it may remain to be fought. In any event, we are on our guard against this enemy; we are in no danger of surprise from that quarter.

Far more dangerous than the open enemy, though such may still exist, is the false friend, the traitor in the camp, ostensibly contributing to its maintenance and defense, in secret lending unsuspected aid and comfort to the enemy. Some of these false friends have been pointed out long ago. It has been a truism for years that scholarship, however great, is not necessarily culture; that the possession of talent, the acquisition of knowledge, the study of books, of nature, of men, time without end, may have in itself no culture significance. Perhaps we forget this sometimes. And I suspect, also, that when we strive to foster taste and sensibility to beauty of form and spirit we sometimes forget that even these do not lie at the summit of culture.

I have here suggested two points: First, that culture studies do not always make for culture, while other studies may, and, second, that culture which consists of a liking for the things that please the sense or the sensibility, tho it is a real appreciation of a real beauty, is not a complete culture. And on the other side, with the cultured teacher as the essential, and with a reasonable proportion of other conditions favorable, and natural science or mathematics even, or language may be made contributory to culture in the best sense, however little culture value they may have regarded apart from the teacher. To utilize such culture elements as are afforded by existing subjects and existing conditions in lower schools must ultimately be the solution of the problem, for as the lower schools move so will society move, nor have I said that I should elect mathematics first of all as a culture subject. But while I assert that we are not absolutely compelled to depend upon so-called culture studies for the development of culture, I have not said that they are not to be preferred for that purpose when in good hands, nor do I deny that even in ineffectual hands they may and often do exert the desired influence upon mind and character, if mind and character have not lost their responsiveness. Often, however, they fail; and because they fail the cause of culture suffers even in its chief stronghold, the college. The culture course, then, in art or literature, for instance, seems sometimes to be one of the traitors in the camp, and we may notice for a moment how this comes to pass.

The college culture course par excellence, the most popular course in every college, is the course in English literature. Sometimes a college course in literature, like the old-fashioned high-school course, is not a course in literature at all, but a course in somebody's text-book. Or the college course may be a lecture course of inferior type, in which the instructor substitutes himself for a text-book, and requires the members of his class to reproduce his own statements of fact and opinion from their note-books on examination day. Or the course may be a philosophical one, devoted to the study of the relation of one literary period to another, of the interrelations of various literatures, of all the causes that may be traced in the production of a work or a class of work, and of all the effects that followed from it. All these things are of importance toward the greater end in view, all of them are in some sense useful toward accomplishing that end; but a student may devote a considerable proportion of his time to them for four long years, and emerge at the end without a single spark of love for literature for its own sake, and without having had his own thought and motives, his own life, influenced thereby in the least degree.

Even under the happier condition that a lecturer is himself an artist, or that he is himself on fire with the love, the enthusiasm, the power that it is desirable to awaken in those whom he addresses, and even tho every student be positively required to spend a proportion of his time in reading, in actual mental contact with literature, spiritual contact may still be lacking, and the culture influence of the interpreter or of the thing interpreted may still be unfelt. There are fortunate exceptions, but for the many it is likely to be true that so much idle or worthless or vicious reading is forced upon them before they have an opportunity to form better associations, that better associations have no effect; between the chaff and husks of the newspaper and the highly spiced sweetmeats of the magazine, the taste for solid, nutritious food and the capacity for digesting it may have been almost or entirely lost. Proof of this may be found every day and any day in the freshman class of any college, nor in most colleges would one have far to seek for it in the senior class also.

For some persons, that is, for some students, it is doubtless true that to be in the presence of art, of painting, music, or poetry, or even to listen to a lecturer or to read a critic who is fired with appreciation of ideal beauty or significance in art, may enable them to feel the inspiration of the subject, even though they may not understand why it is inspiring, and, indeed, may not care to know. For a greater number this appreciation or inspiration, if it is felt at all, must be the result of conscious insight into the purpose or end of art product, literary or otherwise, and into the adaptation of means to end. In our work of to-day, accepting this as true, we are trying all sorts of plans to impart to students this technical knowledge of means, from which we hope will come in time an appreciation of the results obtained thru those means, when that appreciation is not a part of a student's original equipment. It is not unusual for an instructor to advocate and advertise some particular plan or method which, as it seems to him, is sufficient of itself to accomplish the thing desired, and to confine his own teaching to it as the one thing needful.

Of all these plans it may be said that there is perhaps not one that may not be in some degree helpful toward the ultimate end in view, and there is not one that may not defeat that end if followed too exclusively and too far. Whatever means we may use to rouse to activity a dormant part of an artistic consciousness, there comes a time to cease and to listen for the still small voice; and in point of fact, as the artistic consciousness is not usually entirely dormant in any pupil, it is a matter of duty to stop often to listen—that is, to stop often to direct the pupil's attention to the fact that all this analysis of means has no other or higher object than to reveal the nature of the art work that has been done, and to make clear its ultimate beauty and its ultimate significance (as expressing the ideal of both experience and imagination).

It is possible to direct a pupil's attention and to secure his attention to these things, but the appreciation of a work of art must spring from within. It cannot be compelled, but it is probable that in every personality the capacity for it is present in some degree; and the most generous and most worthy teaching is that which aims to develop that capacity as far as may be in every student, in preference to developing it greatly in a few, and neglecting all the rest. So far as methods are concerned, every method has its place and function; and it is as unjust to deride one kind of teaching as "chatter about Shelley," as it is to deride another kind of teaching as a mere raking over of bones and sawdust, provided each is rightly understood.

When, by whatever means, students have come to the appreciation of art product, we still have to ask whether culture is anything more than this. The answer is that one may possess all this and lack something of greater value; that one might possess all this and miss the essence of culture. The end of culture is not in the cultured self. If the result of training, of growth, of enlightenment, however much it may contribute to the individual's understanding and enjoyment of beautiful things, is not to make his living itself more beautiful, more interesting, more lovable in the eyes of other individuals, his culture is incomplete; and if his training results in intellectual or artistic Pharisaism, if it makes him draw himself apart from others, regarding himself as more wise, more refined, of deeper sensibility, as having entered into a higher sphere of existence, that result, because it is unbeautiful and unlovable, is not culture at all. Even at best there can be no complete attainment of culture, for in fact it is not something to be realized at a certain stage in a man's education or at a certain time in his life; it is an aspiration or struggle toward an ideal, and the aspiration is more significant than is the ideal. Culture is not being something, but becoming something. It is for this reason that culture is possible for every personality without limitation or exclusion; for however much ideals may vary with conditions in life, the controlling desire to rise toward them, the unending aspiration to make by any and every means the best of one's own daily life may be the same everywhere. Like happiness, culture cannot be sought for its own sake, not in any particular place, not by any predetermined method. It is no more surely to be found in a four-year college course than in a two-year course, or in a college than in a kindergarten, provided that time and opportunities are utilized. The college has certain culture advantages if it profit by them; but every school may foster culture, and the process is aided or hindered by every personality that comes in contact with that of the pupil at any stage of training or of life. Training at every stage may be so directed as to develop ideal elements in conduct and character thru the appreciation of those elements in conduct and character, as seen in life, or as reflected in literature or in any expression of life. Pupils may be surrounded from the beginning with culture influences and with the greatest of these influences, the cultured teacher—the aspiring, self-sacrificing, labor-loving teacher, always imagining and planning better things—other influences become relatively unimportant. But still they are not insignificant. Mark Hopkins at the end of a log is indeed a college, according to the dictum of President Garfield, but Mark Hopkins in a library is a better college. Whatever aid may be derived from time, subjects and environment must be sought for; and there is at least one subject taught in every school that may be made distinctively a culture subject, whether we call it reading or literature.

Finally, if we are acquainted with all these familiar enemies of culture, and are not able to cope with them, where is the trouble? Why does our work fall short of what we wish it to be? For one thing, we have not had time to accomplish great things since we began to set about them. We have been content to accept conditions and wait for somebody else to change them for the better; we have accepted others' definition of our duty and responsibility, even though that definition restricted growth and narrowed culture. There have been enemies in our own household, teachers whose example, or neglect of duty, or weakness, served to counteract the effort of others. A distinguished college president, of whom we have heard a great deal of, deeply laments that certain and numerous evils continue to exist in society, notwithstanding the influence of the schools; but the fact, though not less sad, is assuredly less strange when we find that against some of these evils the school has scarcely tried to exert any influence; that indeed some of them flourish within the schools themselves; that not only the students but the teachers are sometimes infected. Surely, if the schools are ultimately to clarify society and re-establish social relations upon a new, more wholesome, more altruistic basis—that is, if society is to become cultured throughout according to the broadest standard of culture, the teachers must move first into the light and move as a body. Yet never in the history of education and of educational results have we moved so directly and so rapidly toward the ideal of culture as during the last ten years; and I am inclined to believe that never in any single year have there been so many evidences of vitality and progress as in the present one. To be living today in touch with the world's thought and the world's action has in it more of interest, more of fascination, more of elevating excitement and of stimulus to high purpose and high endeavor, and is provocative of more intense curiosity as to what shall be the outcome than can be found in the pages of the most thrilling romance that ever was written. We may look forward all the more hopefully to the development of the plot, because we ourselves take a part in it as creators and actors, and because nobody else can have a more influential part than ours. If we rise to our responsibility, the ultimate result is certain, however long it may be delayed, but rising to our responsibility means coping quietly and individually with all sorts of petty difficulties, each of us in his own corner, and seeing what others are doing, largely with the eye of faith. In this way there may come some realization of the breadth and power of our ideal culture, such that every pupil in every school must to some degree be vitalized thereby, and perhaps develop motives that shall keep him advancing toward the light as long as he lives. If we have not the opportunity to make use of special art agencies in this development, we can always make use of such agencies as are at hand; if we cannot have the subjects which we should prefer, we can make others do; and there will always be beauty and inspiration in fresh air, pure water, in birds and trees and flowers, in men and women, and in little men and little women. Somehow, it ought always to be possible to teach everybody everywhere how much it means to like things that are likeable and to be liked for things that are likeable; and if we can influence our pupils to like those things and to be liked for those things, if we can win little victories over the common and commonplace enemies of culture as we go along, there will be no use to worry about the result of the campaign. As we begin a new century, perhaps the tide is turning toward the social uplift that must come before there shall be brightness, hope, upward development in every life, before the gain of the individual shall always be the blessing of society, and before what Arnold phrased as: "The end of culture shall be accomplished and the will of God shall prevail."

President's Address

A. E. Shumate

Officers and Members of the California Teachers' Association and Friends of Education: We have again assembled, in annual session, what is now the most important teachers' organization on the Pacific Slope—an organization in which we have ample cause to feel a pride.

In looking over the educational history of our State for the past eight or ten years I am sure it can be said with safety that we have kept fairly in touch with educational growth and well abreast of the times.

The fact that the permanent and prominent improvements in the organization of our schools during the period to which I refer have originated, in the main, with our association is sufficient occasion for congratulation.

The two years just passed have seen the consummation of a number of changes in our laws leading to the betterment of our school conditions.

The certification law, passed by our last Legislature has proved itself a step in the right direction.

The adoption of Constitutional Amendment No. 4 at the last election has made it possible for our high schools to receive State aid, so that in a short time we hope to point with pride to the fact that we have a complete system of schools; that any boy or girl in California may receive a free education in all grades from the kindergarten thru the university.

The gradual placing of the basis of entrance to our normal schools at the equivalent to a good high-school education is slowly but surely raising the standard of our great teaching body to that of the very best in the land.

The increased attention and care which county boards of education are giving to the grading and promotion of pupils is having a stimulating effect, and the lines of practical drift in courses of study for our elementary and grammar schools augur well for the educational future of our State.

Our two universities, now ranking with the best in the Union, are in a marked degree responsible for the educational Renaissance we are experiencing, and, with their magnificent endowments and increased facilities for investigation, they are bound to exercise an influence upon the civilization of the Coast which will increase as the years go by.

In my judgment, the crying need of the teachers of this State to-day, as well as of the nation, is unity of effort. We are in the midst of an age of organization. All crafts and kinds of business are receding from the sharp lines of competition that marked the life of the individual toiler or investor of a score of years ago, and are gradually working to each other's interests. I know of no class of wage-earners, other than school teachers, of whom this may not be said.

The least the teaching profession (if I may call it such) ought to do, in duty to itself, is to work unitedly for the uplifting of the standard of the calling and to form a solid front in securing legislation for the advancement of its condition and that of the schools.

To the end that the State Association's influence may be made more effective than it has been in the past, I suggest the following plan: Let a committee be appointed to correlate and concentrate the recommendations of the various sections and departments which will be presented at the close of this session, and to further consider the work of said departments and make recommendations, based upon it, for legislation at the coming session of our lawmakers.

I would suggest that this committee be composed of the chairman of the Legislation Section, the chairman of the High-School Section, the chairman of the Council of Education, and of such other members of the association as you may provide. Personally, I am of the opinion that we should instruct this committee to meet at an early date, and as often as may be found necessary, to eliminate all recommendations upon which they cannot agree, and to go before the Legislature as a unit and in the name of the association. * * *

Finally, I recommend to the serious consideration of the association the various movements that have been inaugurated in different parts of the State looking to the formation of a Teachers' Federation. It goes without saying that if the influence of the teachers upon the community is to count for all it may, there must be some stronger organization, one of more continuity, than we have now.

It is not my purpose to burden you with any extended address, since we have a full program for this afternoon. I wish, however, to thank you, as members of the association, for your disinterested zeal in helping to make this meeting a success, and to express our sincere gratitude to the teachers, citizens and officials of Los Angeles for the valuable assistance they have given us, and I hope that when we shall have concluded our work, each and every one of us may return to his labors with fresh ideas, renewed energies and a feeling that his money and his time were profitably spent.

* * *

Our Country School Problem

E. P. Cubberley

Forty years ago there was no particular country school problem. The country schools constituted the great bulk of all our schools. The cities were few and far between, and six out of seven of our population lived on the farm or in the small village. Many of our States had but two or three cities. But the past forty years have seen great changes. To-day cities are numerous, even in the West, and one-third of our population is congregated in cities of 8,000 or over. So great has been the rush to the cities that in many States the country districts have sustained an absolute as well as a relative loss in population. Forty years ago the country school and the city school were much alike. Each had small, cheap buildings, poor equipment and practically no teaching apparatus. Each drew its teachers from the same source and paid them about the same salaries. Higher education, trained teachers, skilled supervision, teaching equipment, kindergartens, manual training, special instruction—these and other things with which we are now so familiar were equally unknown in city and country.

But forty years have seen wonderful changes in American education, and in these changes the country school has been left behind. The equal taxation of every man's property for schools, regardless of whether or not he has children to educate, has been of great service to the cities. With the development of trade and commerce, the building of railroads and factories, and the consequent concentration of wealth, the cities have come to have a per capita wealth far in excess of that of the smaller towns and the country districts. Property values in the cities have increased enormously, while in many parts of the country the value of farm property has decreased. The cities, too, have offered and still continue to offer attractions which have drawn to them the best, the strongest, and the most capable, as well as the weak, the inefficient and the corrupt.

The concentration of wealth has made it possible and the concentration of population has made it necessary that the cities should develop a class of schools capable of meeting greater exegencies and more advanced needs than those of the country. It has accordingly happened that the cities have provided more liberally for their schools. They have built larger and better school buildings, paid salaries that would draw the best teachers from the surrounding districts, developed supervision and paid liberally for it; organized high schools, provided equipment for laboratory instruction; organized kindergartens, added manual training, cooking, drawing and nature study, provided for proper supervision of the instruction in these subjects, and done other things which have made city schools attractive to parents who are solicitous to the education of their children. Cities of 8,000 or 10,000 inhabitants have made similar progress, and even the small village has a graded school, and often a high school, good teachers, a system of supervision, teaching equipment, a course of study which includes some of the special branches, and a social spirit pervading the school which is of fine quality and of the first importance in the education of children.

The country school, on the contrary, is little ahead of where it was a generation ago. In many States it has been graded, to be sure, and uniform text-books and a uniform course of study introduced. With the better preparation of teachers in general, the quality of the country teacher has been improved. But, even in our own State, where we pay good salaries, comparatively speaking, and where we have, thanks to a wise law, probably the best rural schools in the United States — even here we must admit that, except in a few instances, the country school is poor compared with a good town school, due to its numerous classes, overburdened program, lack of equipment, and, above all, to its isolation and lack of that stimulus that comes from numbers. In most schools the average daily attendance is small, say fifteen to twenty. The children come from the same locality and have the same interests. A majority are from the same or related families. They bring no new interests to the school, there is little impulse to activity of any kind, and the school suffers from lack of new ideas and impulses to action. What the school is, it is because of the teacher and in spite of its limitations. In less favored States the country school, lacking financial support, is in a most pitiable condition. No wonder parents are willing to live by miscellaneous day labor in a town or city rather than on the farm in order that their children may have the advantages of a better education.

It will probably always be true that the city will attract the ablest men which a community produces. The prizes worth working for are larger there; are much more worthy the energy of a man who feels within himself the ability to master large things. The opportunities, too, are greater for the man of ability, though the struggle for existence is much more fierce. But while the city may be the best place for the man of brains and energy, it is not the best place to educate the great majority of the children of a future generation of our people, and the premium ought not to be on that side, as it is now. Whatever can be done legitimately should be done to encourage people to remain in the country.

The last decade has witnessed the introduction of many new things which have tended to make country life more attractive. Rural postal routes, daily rural paper routes, the general introduction of the bicycle, suburban trolley lines, lines traversing the country carrying cheap electric light and power, barbed-wire telephones, rural delivery routes of many kinds, bringing to the homes of the rural residents the products of hundreds of labor-saving machines. These and many other things have tended to make country life more desirable and to free the farmer from much of the drudgery of life. Even a few of these comforts and conveniences have made their way into communities somewhat sparsely settled and somewhat remote from centers of civilization.

But the little country school continues about as it used to be. An attempt has been made to enrich the course of study, but this has only increased the burdens of the teacher and decreased the time given to classes. The schools have been graded and the uniform examination introduced as a test of efficiency, but this has too often served as a temptation to the teacher to neglect the younger children for the sake of the older ones. Whenever the number of pupils has risen to a number sufficient to make possible the employment of two teachers, the desire to have "a school close at home" has led to the division of the district into two. The quality of the teacher has improved, but even the best of teachers can make little progress against such tremendous odds, and the good teachers leave at the first opportunity. Under present conditions the country school realizes but a small per cent of its possibilities.

In regions where it is possible to change this condition there is no longer any excuse for failure to do so. The remedy is to concentrate a number of these small, scattered, inefficient schools into one, three or four room union school, provide a good principal, good teachers, with two or, at most three, grades to a room, and transport the children from their homes to the school each morning and to their homes each night, paying the expense for transportation out of district funds. The remedy is neither new nor untried One-fourth of the States of the Union already have such a permissive law. In Massachusetts, Connecticut, Ohio, Indiana, Wisconsin and Iowa the plan has been tried, with great success, and at the coming session of our Legislature a law should be enacted for California which will permit the adoption of this plan where possible. The plan, in brief, is as follows: Three, or four, or five, or more existing school districts, acting on the advice of a county superintendent, teacher, or group of residents, vote to unite their schools into a union school. A three or four room schoolhouse, built on modern lines and well heated, lighted, and ventilated, is erected at a central location. The old schoolhouses and sites are disposed of. Arrangements are made for the transportation of all children living at a distance. One of the teachers is usually a person of some experience, often a man, and is designated as supervising principal. Often three or four of these union schools unite in employing a superintendent, who devotes such time to each school as may seem necessary, and is paid in proportion by each union. In a number of places where this plan has been tried the stimulus to better schools has been such that the same unions which have united to employ a superintendent have united to form a union high school, thus providing higher education for all the children of the region. The result has been the perfecting of a city school system in the country, consisting of a high school, graded elementary schools, superintendent, principals, teachers and janitors. Instead of a city on a small area, it is a city spread out—a city on a large scale. The graded schools of the small towns of Santa Clara or San Gabriel valleys, with their well-arranged, and often artistic, schoolhouses, supervising principal, graded school system and favorable school conditions, are types of the schools which might be formed here and there in each of the valleys of this State by the union of a number of adjoining rural schools; while the school system of that large area known as the city of Riverside, with its scattered elementary schools, its central high school, and its city superintendent, with an area to supervise almost as large as an Eastern county, is a type of what might be developed in twenty or thirty different rural districts in this State. Of course such unions cannot be formed everywhere. Schools in mountain districts, or where the roads are impasable, or where population is very sparse, cannot well be united. These will have to remain about as they are until conditions change. But in all the settled valleys there are certain natural concentrating centers, and what is wanted is a permissive law which will enable a few superintendents to form one or two unions and demonstrate their efficiency to the people of the county and the school men of this State. The future will then take care of itself.

Co-operation of communities for greater effectiveness is the central principle, and the advantages are those which come from organized co-operation. The new element which makes this co-operation possible is transportation—the carrying of the child to the school. This is only an old idea in a new form. For sixty years we have maintained that it was the duty of the State to provide each child with the opportunity to secure an education. In carrying out this principle we have carried the school to the child. This has led to the division of districts and the multiplication of small schools. These have been found to be expensive and inefficient. We now propose to reverse the principle and carry the child to the school—even more, to carry the child some distance to a still better school. While doing this we will save him the exhaustion of a long walk, protect his health, eliminate tardiness and increase his attendance at school.

Now what are some of the chief advantages of and objections to such a plan? The first and most important point in its favor is that such concentration means better schools. Fewer teachers will be needed, but better ones will be demanded and can be retained. The union school will be such as to offer inducements to good teachers. With two or three grades to a room, far better teaching can be done than with eight or nine. Primary children need not be neglected that older ones may be prepared for the annual examination. Due to the larger number of pupils in each grade, there will be present in the recitation work that stimulus which comes only from numbers. Due to the large number of pupils in the school as a whole and the new interests which this larger number will bring, there will be a social spirit present on the playground and in the school which will contribute greatly to the value of the education given. Due to the presence of a number of teachers in the school, there will be a professional enthusiasm which is almost unknown in the isolated country school to-day. Finally, due to the presence of a supervising principal, and eventually to a rural superintendent, there will be a supervision of the work which will be most valuable.

A second great advantage will be a partial equalization of opportunities and advantages as between the boy in the city and the boy in the country by bringing an approach to a well-organized city school within reach of the boy on the farm. The division of labor in such a school will make possible the introduction of lines of special work which will make the instruction more suited to the needs of the country child. This in connection with the other improvements in rural life which I have previously mentioned will do much toward making the country a more desirable place in which to live.

A third advantage is that such combination of schools for greater effectiveness is also cheaper, though this, of course, cannot be made a chief argument for union. The experience of every Eastern State has been that, in general, a better quality of education and a longer term of school, as well as transportation, can be provided at no greater expense than the aggregate cost of maintenance of a number of separate inefficient schools. In many unions a decided saving has been effected, even after providing a better school. But let me repeat that greater efficiency, not saving in money, is the real argument for union.

Another great advantage of the plan is the greatly increased interest taken in the school by the people of the union district. The larger and better school develops a broader and a better educational spirit. More interest is taken in the larger school, better men are selected as trustees, and the attitude of the community toward it is changed. The school becomes a matter of community pride, instead of community indifference. The testimony on this point is almost universal. The oft-repeated question of how to improve the school trustee may receive a partial answer here.

In districts where the plan has not been tried it is often bitterly opposed, while districts which have given the plan a fair trial are strong in its support. In Massachusetts, Connecticut, Ohio, Illinois, the most vigorous opponents of the plan at the time of its introduction, are now often among its strongest supporters. Let us consider a few of the objections usually advanced. It is argued that the plan is impracticable. The experience of a dozen States disproves this. Some parents dislike to send children "so far away from home," but what difference does it make whether the distance is one mile or five, if the children are well cared for. The ride is objected to by some, but is it not better to take the child from his door and deliver him at the schoolhouse in the morning and return him each night safe, protected from wind and rain, and with dry feet and clothes, than to have him walk a mile each way and miss school whenever the weather is bad? The argument that the exercise is good for him is no argument; we all know that the country child has more than enough exercise at home.

A common argument against the plan is that the removal of the little local schoolhouse causes a depreciation of farm property in the immediate neighborhood, with a corresponding increase in valuation of property about the concentrating center. This is a hard argument to answer, as it appeals to local jealousy and touches the pocket-book. Once get this idea started in a community and it takes hard work to eradicate it. Experience elsewhere, though, is all on the other side. A schoolhouse on the farm does not necessarily make land valuable. What is wanted is that the opportunity of attending a good school be within easy reach of the children, and the better the school which may be attended the more it adds to the value of the farm. A good school six miles away, with transportation, will add more to the value of a farm than a poor school brought to within a quarter of a mile. Such, at least, is the experience of every Eastern State.

The newness of the idea is to many an objection. Many communities move and think slowly. There are those who are content with things as they are, and are willing to live and die without an effort at improvement. With many there is a certain amount of sentiment connected with the little country schoolhouse, and they object to its removal. All such people need education, and no amount of argument is so effective as a successful union in an adjoining section. In northern Ohio the first centralized schools were hard to start, and the movement began slowly; now centralization is in process throughout the entire region.

The country school problem of to-day is how to materially increase the efficiency of the schools and develop a better school spirit in the community, without increasing the cost of the schools. Any increase in the efficiency of the rural schools means an increase in the desirability of country as opposed to town or city life. For sparsely settled or mountainous districts there is as yet no remedy, but for the valley regions of our State the remedy lies in centralization and transportation. The success of the plan elsewhere should secure to the schools of California a chance to try it.

* * *

Social Progression in Childhood

Ella F. Young

Not many years back there was a generally accepted theory which made morals and manners one and inseparable in every child during the period of his life spent in the elementary school. There was an equally well-defined idea that made, before the school age of six years was attained, obedience and manners one and inseparable in the little one. In going on to the high school we find that neither social nor educational terminology contains a term compounded of the two elements which stand one for the attitude of mind of the high-school boy or girl toward others, and one for the manners which express or objectify that attitude.

There is, nevertheless, a theory by which the manners are interpreted. It is that the manners of the lad or miss just in the dawn of manhood or womanhood depend upon the breeding of the young person. The manners are rough or gentle to or well-bred. But few persons, however, or well bred. But few persons, however, are content to pass the judgment ill-bred upon the rollicking, light-hearted high-school pupils that are over-boisterous in the noisy crowd. Most hearts go out in hope and faith toward those who are soon to enter into the labors and anxieties that ever press upon the mutitude in the great economic struggle. And so they temper their language and say: Breeding and manners are not all of it; we must know something of their honesty and kindliness; their earnestness and straightforwardness. In short, we cannot pass upon their conduct without some insight into the character that is back of the conduct. It is the degree of development of thoughtful or reflective sympathy that marks the social progression of the child. Through its activity the social world is not seen chaotic, tossing human beings mercilessly about.

It is seen as the great organization in which each individual must have recognition as a co-operative worker.

The school is successful in its field in just so far as it develops intelligent sympathy in its children as they work in the kindergarten, the elementary school, the high school and the college. It is impossible to comprehend the great questions of life without that insight into other minds which is born of sympathy. Sympathy is the quality that in its highest degree becomes charity—the greatest of the three. Sympathy imparts the buoyancy of hope to the heavy laden; it realizes the kinship of humanity.

* * *

Address by Booker T. Washington on the Tuskegee Institute

I never come before an audience of educators without recalling my own first contact with education. First, I had no name; I had all my life been called just "Booker"; I thought that was enough name for anybody, but I found other boys in the school having two or three names, and I thought it was partiality. I went to the teacher about it and asked her if we could not find another name. "What shall it be?" she asked. I studied over it a moment and then I said: "Call me Washington," and ever after that I was Washington.

Then I had no hat; other boys had hats— store hats— and they pointed their fingers at me. I told my mother and wanted her to buy me a hat. This is what she said:

"My boy, I sympathize with you, but there is one thing I'm not gwine to do— I am not gwine to get something for you that I can't pay for."

She took two pieces of cloth and sewed them together, and that was the first hat I ever owned. Since then I have had several hats, but I have never had anything to cover my head that I prized like that. I valued it because my mother was too honest to go into debt that I might have a better one, and again because it was made by my sainted mother.

When we went down to breakfast we were asked by the colored woman who waited on the table whether we would have long or short sweetening in our coffee. He nudged me and I nudged him, and finally my friend said he would take long. The woman dipped her finger into a jug of molasses and stirred it into his coffee. Without the least hesitation, I then said I would take it short. Then she took from a bowl a lump of something that looked like maple sugar. She bit it in two and put one portion in her own coffee and the other portion in mine.

I wish to assure you that both my long and short talks are very disagreeable.

As I came into this hall a gentleman asked me if I would not undertake to prove that the North and not the South was responsible for slavery. I'll illustrate that by telling you the story of Uncle Zeke and his pig:

Uncle Zeke sold the pig to a white man for $3, but before he got it home it broke away and returned to Uncle Zeke. About that time another white man came and wanted to buy the pig, and Uncle Zeke could not resist the temptation, so he sold it again for $3, and the new purchaser started off with the pig, only to meet the first purchaser coming back after it. They compared notes, and then went to Uncle Zeke with the question:

"What kind of way is this you have of treating us white folks?"

"Well, 'fore God; can't you white folks go off an' settle dat 'mong yourselves?"

I am not seeking to educate you educators; I was born a slave; I am pretty sure. I was born some time and some place. I was twelve years of age before I ever slept in a bed; my place was on the floor, wrapped in a bundle of rags.

One morning I remember going to the master's house with my mother, and hearing some papers read, and my mother leaned over to me and said: "Now, my son, we are free."

The speaker then recounted the story of his life, which took him to West Virginia, where he worked in a coal mine. While at work in this mine came the turn in the life of the obscure slave boy. He overheard two miners talking about Hampton Institute, and what they said about the possibilities open to any colored boy, through the good offices of the institution, made him at once determined to find his way there. He tells graphically of all the hardships encountered; how he begged rides between long walks, and finally arrived penniless at Richmond, Va., slept in a coal cellar, and worked at loading pig iron on a ship. Of his first night in Richmond he said:

"I found myself there with neither money nor friends, so I walked the street. You know when a fellow gets hungry he begins to walk. I don't know how it is with you, but I've been that way many a time."

A GOOD EXAMINATION.

After a while he reached Hampton with fifty cents in his pocket and applied for admission to the institution, but he said he was at once impressed with the fact that the teacher looked upon him as an unfit subject for examination, and in order to get rid of him as easily as possible she gave him a broom and told him to sweep one of the rooms.

"I swept that room three times,' said Washington, "and I dusted it four times. Just as I was through the teacher came in with her handkerchief in her hand. She was one of those New England Yankees who knew just where to find dirt every time. She took her handkerchief, but she couldn't find one iota of dust anywhere, and she said, "I guess you'll do."

"Now that, fellow-teachers, was my college examination, and I believe it was the best one I ever passed.

"It was while I was working my way through Hampton that I promised to give my life to the work of benefiting my race in the 'black belt.' In 1881, in a district where my race outnumbered yours as ten to one, I began my work.

"It was said that nobody but a black man and a mule could live there, and when you found one you found the other. I've felt rather lonesome since I came to this Coast."

He illustrated this phase of his subject with several laughable stories about the old darkies and the mules, and then turned to a more serious side.

" I speak to you not merely in the interest of Tuskegee, nor yet strictly in the interest of my own race. At first I confess I did this, but now, thank God, I have outgrown that idea, and my work is for the people of the entire South."

He said when he started he had a student stand in the old shed and held an umbrella over him to keep off the rain, as the roof let more in than it kept out. He enlarged his facilities by drawing on an abandoned henhouse, and when he asked an old darky to help him clean it out he responded:

"What you mean, boss? You done gwine to clean out dat henhouse in de daytime?"

HOW IT GREW.

"In 1881 Tuskegee Institute began with one instructor and thirty students. It now has a corps of 112 teachers and 1,400 students; with the families of the instructors, the total population is about 1,600. We have sixty-two buildings, all of which except four were built by the labor of the students, and the total value of the property, including 2,600 acres of land, is $450,000. The annual running expenses are $120,000.

"Very soon after starting the Tuskegee Normal and Industrial Institution in Alabama I made, as far as possible, a careful analysis of the conditions and needs of the people in that section of the South. In doing this I found that at least 80 per cent of our people depended for their daily living upon some form of agriculture. Since this was true, it seemed to me that the natural, logical and common-sense thing was to make a course of study which, as far as possible, should meet this condition and need; hence, from the first, at Tuskegee we have emphasized agricultural training, making that, in a very large measure, the basis for our industrial work.

"We began teaching agriculture very soon after the institution was started, in 1881, with one hoe and a blind mule. This feature of our work has grown until, at the present time, we cultivate by the labor of the students over 800 acres of land, and not only make the teaching of agriculture productive and valuable from an economic standpoint, but at the same time we make the farm in its stock raising, poultry raising, bee keeping, dairy and other features, an object lesson for our students and the people in that section, where 80 per cent of them depend upon agriculture for their living.

"Agriculture provides that which they shall eat, and you cannot put any nation upon its feet religiously, morally or physically until you have settled that greatest industrial problem.

"Counting those who have graduated from our full courses, together with those who have taken a partial course to the extent that they are able to do efficient work, we have sent out from the Tuskegee Institute over 2,000 men and women, who are engaged as teachers in the schoolroom, teachers of industries, or are themselves engaged in direct industrial effort. Our graduates are not only in demand among our own people in the South, but the demand for them to take charge of farms, dairies and other industrial enterprises for the Southern white people is greater than we can supply. I believe that our people will get upon their feet and solve what is known as the race problem in the South, just in proportion as they can become useful. Usefulness in the highest sense will constitute our most lasting and potent protection. Our people must be taught to do a common thing in an uncommon manner—to do a thing as well or better than someone else. Any race or individual that has learned to do some one thing better than anyone else has solved this problem.

CHRISTIANIZING LABOR.

"What our people need to know is that there is a moral, physical, Christianizing influence goes with labor of the hands. The greatest lesson for them to learn is the lesson to work—the difference is between working and being worked. They must learn to put brains, skill and dignity into the common services of life."

Mr. Washington used as an illustration the advanced farmer riding under a red umbrella on his patent corn planter, as compared with the barefooted black man and an old mule going a half-mile an hour, saying that the latter could not expect to compete with the former.

"You are going to buy your corn from the farmer who gives you the best corn and the cheapest, whether he be black, white, brown, yellow or ginger-cake color.

"I can recall the time when I hated the sight of a white man because of the oppression of my race, but now, thank God, that is all gone and I love all races. I teach our people that the way for them to do is to take their places, and if others are small, they must be great. The way to test a true gentleman is not when he is with his own, but when he is in contact with those beneath him.

"The way to belittle themselves is to learn to hate somebody; the way to lift themselves up is to learn to love somebody. That's what we're doing at Tuskegee."

* * *

The Race Problem

Extracts from an Address by Booker T. Washington

If we would discuss what is known as the race question with any degree of benefit, we must bring ourselves to the point where we can so far rid ourselves of sectional and racial prejudice to the extent that we can in a large degree place ourselves in the position of the Southern white man and at the same time put ourselves in the place of the negro. Nothing will be gained for either race or for any section of our country by bitter attacks and criticism. When we consider the past and the tremendous difficulties that have grown out of the presence of the negro in this country, I think that when we take a broad, generous view, all of us must agree that while there is much to be accomplished, we have some reason, North and South, to congratulate ourselves that the situation is as hopeful and satisfactory as it is.

I confess that when I first began the work of educating my race in the South I did so with a selfish ambition—that of seeking the interests of my race, but I have learned that a broader and more practical thing is to seek to do that which is going to serve the highest interests in the end of both races.

* * * *

Beginning in poverty, with not a dollar's worth of property, the Tuskegee Institute has now grown into a seat of learning where there are 1,200 students gathered from twenty-eight States, under the teaching and guidance of eighty-six instructors. In addition to training in religious and academic branches, we give constant instruction in twenty-eight industries, and all of them are industries at which our students can find immediate employment as soon as they leave the institution, and all of them are industries which are in great demand in the South.

The property of the institution consists of 2,300 acres of land, fifty-two buildings, large and small, and is valued at $370,000. The annual expense of carrying on the institution is over $100,000. We have an endowment fund of $271,000. The institution has $100,000. We have an endowment fund of $400,000. The institution has been built very largely by the students, so far as the buildings are concerned, but we are dependent largely upon gifts of friends for our current expenses. The State of Alabama assists in our expenses to the extent of its ability.

* * * *

In the present condition of my race, industrial education in connection with mental and moral training is of the highest value. The mere fact that through our twenty-eight industries we give our students the opportunity to help themselves is of great importance. The mere effort on the part of the student gives to him a certain amount of self-reliance and moral backbone that he would not get without such effort on his part. The salvation of my race will, in a large degree, be secured just in proportion as it learns to put brains, skill and dignity into the common occupations of life. In proportion as it learns to do a common thing in an uncommon manner, to lift the common occupations up out of drudgery into that atmosphere where labor will become in the eye of the individual beautiful and dignified. For 250 years the negro was worked. What he wants to learn now is to work. There is a vast difference between working and being worked. For one to learn that work is honorable and to be idle is dishonorable is at the foundation of civilization.

* * * *

Our effort, however, at Tuskegee would mean little except as we are able to impress upon each man and woman who is being trained there the idea that they are not to get education merely with a view of going out and leading a selfish life, but are going out and give themselves in an unselfish manner to the lifting up of their fellows. Counting those who have finished the regular course, together with those who have had a partial course, it is safe to say that we have over 2,000 men and women who have been trained at Tuskegee who are working in various parts of the country, materially, mentally or spiritually toward the welfare of the communities in which they live will be long left without encouragement. It is the quiet, earnest, persistent, unostentatious effort to do good that is going to tell. I repeat that nothing can be gained by stirring up strife between the races or between one section of country and the other. Race hatred when indulged in by a black man or a white man is degrading and hurtful. Broad, deep, generous interest in the elevation of all races is elevating and helpful. The time and place to test a true gentleman is to note his conduct not when he is in contact with those who are in his own station of wealth and culture, but to note his bearing when he touches those who are beneath him in these respects. The true gentleman is always considerate of the unfortunate race of the unfortunate individual.

* * * *

The demand for graduates from Tuskegee, not only from the members of my race, but from members of the white race in the South, is great. Our graduates are employed by white men to take charge of farms, dairies, blacksmith shops, wheelwright shops, etc., to a very large extent; indeed to such an extent that we cannot begin to supply the demand.

While we have difficulties in the South with which to contend, there is one advantage which is often overlooked at the North, and that is in the entire field of business and labor the negro has an opportunity that is perhaps not offered him in any other part of the country, or perhaps in the world. A negro can borrow money at the bank with equal security as quickly as a white man. If he has a business and conducts that business with skill, intelligence and progressiveness, I notice that he is patronized not only by the members of his own race, but by the white man.

While there is a tremendous work yet to be done, I see no ground for discouragement, but much reason for hope, and every reason why we should push forward with a stronger spirit and determination than ever before. It should always be borne in mind that the problems growing out of the presence and influence of my race in this country were not of the negro's seeking or making. The South is not alone responsible for what is known as the "Negro Problem." It is the Nation's problem, because the Nation as a whole was responsible for its creation, and the time has come when all of us, black and white, North and South, should in a broad, generous, unselfish manner do our part in making conditions more happy for all concerned.

* * *

Education and National Character

Ellmer E. Brown

It is the purpose of this paper to persuade teachers to become politicians. We have been informed that this undertaking is uncalled for. A writer in the Los Angeles *Herald* has declared that "all men in the profession are politicians." And a well-informed woman in the profession, a teacher in one of our great American cities — said to me many years ago: "There is not a political power in this city, from the highest to the lowest, which cannot be influenced by some member of our corps of teachers." Yet it may well be believed that there is still need of urging our teachers to become politicians. A politician I understand to be one who sets the public good above private advantage— one who serves the common weal. Our topic takes us into a consideration of education from the public point of view, or, to use large terms, from the national point of view.

"The laws of education," said Montesquieu, "will be different in each species of government; in monarchies they will have honor for their object; in republics, virtue; in despotic governments, fear.'

This is a different conception from that commonly put forth in our theories of education. We American teachers understand that we are directing our efforts to the perfecting of human character, and as such we would make this the ideal of education everywhere—in France, in China, and in the planet Mars. We should call it a perversion of the true spirit of education to turn it from the making of men to the making of subjects or the making of kings—to turn it from human ends to Abyssinian, German, or even partisan-American ends. But the subject will stand a closer examination.

For the sake of brevity, I will suggest some conclusions, without going much into the processes by which they have been reached. And first, and comprehensively, let us say that the more enlightened a people becomes, the more nearly will its national idea of education coincide with the universal, human ideal.

We must admit at the outset that the

two ideals do not, in experience, exactly coincide. Education is not, in practice, a free cultivation of the garden of childhood, but a bending of young twigs to predetermined forms. Our theory of education must not ignore this fact, and must not simply push it aside. We may go further and say that the political influences which play such havoc in our systems of schools, even the meaner political influences, the petty intrigues and brutal injustices which now and then appear, are not to be regarded as mere obstacles and hindrances. They are to be expected in the development of any truly public system of education. They are an evidence of the fact that education is interwoven with all of the other interests which enter into our social existence. They are an expression of minor phases of that national character with which education has to do.

Political science, as distinguished from political philosophy, inquires into the most ordinary, every-day workings of political bodies and seeks to understand their processes and their significance. Any scientific theory of education must in like manner take account of the actual processes of educational administration, and of all forms of educational procedure, whether regarded as good or bad, and seek to understand how they arise out of the relation of the schools to actual life.

Still we may repeat that in the more enlightened nations the making of good citizens is pretty much the same thing with the making of good men. Probably all rulers believe that the making of good subjects is the same as the making of good moral beings. And we think we have good reason for believing that the best possible American is the best possible man. We have a check on our own notions, however, in the comparison of our own education with that of other civilized peoples. Roughly speaking, with no attempt at strict exactness, we may say these things in education in which all cultured nations think and act alike are universal elements —human elements pure and simple; while those things in which nations differ are national elements, and indications of national character.

The principle which has already been set forth may, then, be restated as follows: As nations become more enlightened, they tend to drop off their educational differences and become more alike in their educational ideals.

This does not mean that what is distinctive in the education of a given people at a given period must after a time be discarded. It may be that some elements, now national, will so lead the thought of other nations that they will become universal, ecumenical. So the nationality of one people may serve the peoples of the world. And that will be a glorious achievement.

Now, what are some of the universal characteristics of modern education? There are three of these which we may stop to consider: The scientific spirit, the ethical spirit and the spirit of freedom.

The pure search for truth, the aspiration after liberal culture, which has appeared in various guise in the history of education, has taken on new strength and significance under the influence of our modern natural science. The scientific spirit, in its uncorrupted simplicity, is one of the cleanest and noblest things with which modern education has to do. It is a powerful force in all of the better educational systems of our day, and in the best of them it affects schools of every grade, for it is not allowed that the science of the lower schools may be a science contradicted by the more complete knowledge of the upper schools. To value scientific knowledge, to aim at scientific accuracy for oneself, and to appreciate and put confidence in the scientific competence of those who are really expert in other fields, are correlated aims in modern education. They know no national bounds, and they are of incalculable importance in every civilization.

If modern education, under the stress of religious differences, has come to lay less emphasis than was once laid upon formal instruction in the divergent doctrines of various religions, it prizes more highly than ever the aspirations after righteousness which lies at the center of all Western religions. The teachers of religion seem in our day to lay their first emphasis on this same ethical core of their several creeds. Not infrequently we hear apology offered for the non-religious character of our public education, as if it were an unfortunate result of untoward circumstances. If, however, it calls forth new attention to this vital thing in all religions, and does not in the meantime show any tendency to positive irreligion, it may contribute directly to the highest religious purposes, and certainly will contribute to the highest purposes of this life. Not all modern educational systems agree with those of the United States in their non-sectarian character; but all, I think, agree in this new stress upon the aspiration after righteousness. In this we find another element in modern education of incalculable worth which knows no national or ecclesiastical bounds.

The spirit of freedom is intimately bound up with the ethical and the scientific spirit, already referred to. Freedom of instruction, too, is bound up with freedom of the press and with all real freedom of every other kind. No education is modern education in which the spirit of freedom is wholly wanting, and it belongs in some degree to schools of every grade which strive after the ideals of truth and righteousness.

American education is full of imperfection. In many particulars it is inferior to that of other nations. It has very much to learn which they can teach. Yet after all is said and done, I believe it to be intrinsically the best education in the world, because I believe that it is most pervaded by that universal spirit of excellence which has been described, and because that which is distinctively national in it is most nearly in accord with universal modern tendencies.

What are our national characteristics which affect our education? There are doubtless many such characteristics, but the two that we will consider are these: The spirit of democracy and the missionary spirit.

The first of these will be recognized and acknowledged without question. The Declaration of Independence asserted the equality of all men as regards the most sacred of human rights. The only safe view of the equality of men is that which counts every man as of infinite worth. This is the view of our democracy. Every man is of infinite worth, for every man is different from every other man, every man is unique. Therefore every man should be judged by himself, according to what he is, and not according to anything of an extraneous nature. And every man should be given the best possible chance to give an account of himself. Such is the spirit of our democracy, and when we find it in its purity in American schools, we have found a thing of great price.

The prevalence of the missionary spirit in our American character may not be so generally recognized, but when we look into our case carefully we find evidence of its presence. The bell that rang out the first note of independence had been set in its place to "proclaim liberty throughout all the land unto all the inhabitants thereof." Our people have interpreted all the land to mean all the world, and for one-eighth of a millenium they have carried on a propaganda of liberty and democracy to the nations of the earth. When that little band of students made a Williamstown haystack the point of departure for the first American foreign mission of a religious character, they were so far in accord with what was already an American tradition. At their hands the message took the form: "Ye shall know the truth, and the truth shall make you free." In welcoming numberless immigrants, and offering them full citizenship on easy terms; and in spending a million lives to liberate the slaves; we have carried on this propaganda of freedom in its noblest political forms.

There is that in our political system which has greatly facilitated this program of democracy and liberty. The experiments in government which have gone on since the beginning of human society, seem to have culminated in the Federal system, as we understand the term. A strong government of the whole with self-government in each of its parts — this forms a mighty agency for the development and extension of those higher human qualities in which we are interested. With a democracy and a disposition to spread abroad the spirit of democracy and a governmental system lending itself powerfully to such purposes, all in the free field of a new confinement, it is perhaps small wonder that we have so greatly expanded in the short term of our existence, and that our influence among the nations has grown so great.

It is not to be supposed for a moment that we are wholly different from other peoples in these particulars. Yet in them we enjoy some sort of pre-eminence, and they are things deeply grounded in our American character. Democracy and federalism, too, are things which are likely in time to become a common possession of all highly civilized lands, and to mingle more and more with those universal forces of education which we have touched upon. Education will doubtless become more and more, in every land, a dealing with those universal elements which make for simple manhood. The number of those elements which are the common property of all well-developed civilizations will go on increasing. We in America will concern ourselves largely with those things which the thought of the world recognizes as proper to man irrespective of his nationality, and to those high and notable aspects of our national character which we expect to see accepted eventually by that world-thought. We shall not cease to teach democracy because Austria or Russia is not democratic, but shall rather hold it as a part of our mission to teach our own, and indirectly to teach the world, the meaning and majesty of democratic principles. But minor national characteristics will not receive so marked an emphasis. It is of no great importance that we insist on different spellings and pronunciations than those of other English-speaking lands. Most fortunately, too, we are not so circumstanced that nationalism requires us to teach hatred of any other nation.

The fact that our education has in it few provincial elements, and is mainly concerned with the strengthening of manhood for all the uses of manhood,, is due to that other fact that our Nation is frankly progressive. It is not so much concerned with being exactly what it has been as with being the best that it can be. So it expects from the schools highly trained, high-minded citizens, who may become intelligent critics of our national past and present, and free molders of a still better national future. Its spirit is not the spirit of those who forget nothing and who learn nothing. It remembers reverently the past, but will not let even the most glorious recollections tyrannize over the present. In the modern view, that nation is not best protected from revolution which steels itself against change, but rather that nation which forestalls revolution by continuous reform. To this end, the freest, the most scientific, the most moral education is greatly to be desired.

It is a sound procedure in education to begin with that which is near at hand; go on to that which is remote, and then return to a clearer understanding of the things at home. As regards the bearing of our education upon national interests, we may follow something of such a course. The beginning will then be with the things of the immediate neighborhood, which are under the local government. Later there will come a study of things national, and the final stage will be the attainment of more adequate insight into home affairs and better preparation for home employments. In a larger way, we may make an education which has much of nationalism in its elementary period, rise in its secondary period to the study of world-literature, world-history, world-civilization. But it is not complete till it comes back to the common things of daily occupation—to the ennobling of daily life. It is well that the education of our youth should have some period of dwelling among the stars; but not unless it shall come back from those high associations to lay upon itself "the lowliest duties" of our common life.

It all comes to this, that the Nation expects teachers to be politicians—statesmen, if you please—that they may bring up citizens prepared for the large demands of modern life. It does not wish to have its young citizens educated away from the ordinary business of life, nor educated away from the small political affairs of the home community. But it would have them educated up to the highest possible view of those commonplace affairs, and made ready to contribute their share to the betterment of society. It welcomes, not so much the occasional reformer as the continuing and co-operating reformer, who shall promote that everlasting readjustment which modern life demands.

In the economy of modern life, a new and larger part is assigned to education. It is a fair question whether our educational institutions can fulfill the expectations that are centered upon them. An old Roman symbol was brought to light some years ago which will illustrate our present case. It pictures a chariot drawn by a healthy dragon. The driver is a tiny butterfly, sitting on the chariot rail. It is supposed that this ancient cartoon represented Seneca, the teacher of Nero, in the attempt to guide his vigorous and refractory pupil. It represents equally well our modern education, charged with new responsibilities in its relation to modern life. This modern life is full of brutal energy. There is in it enough and to spare of commercialism, materialism and other isms that may make it terrible. But there is in it, too, unbounded promise of better things. Will the butterfly be able to fulfill its part? Yes, if the butterfly be indeed a soul. If education will hold steadily, in its several parts, and in all its parts unitedly—unitedly—to the highest spiritual ideals, to truth, and freedom, and self-sacrifice, it shall not utterly fail.

* * *

The Ideal Normal School

H. M. Bland

In the few minutes alloted to me I am to speak of an ideal normal school based on the relation of the child to society. I do not expect to dwell so much on the equipment of such a school as to attempt to point out the essential qualities of the mental and spiritual life of the school.

Every great educational movement has been an exponent of some feature of the intellectual life in the midst of which it has run its course. The schools in which Abelard played so important a part represented the spirit of reaction against the acceptance of assertions as truth merely on the authority of the teacher or textbook; or a reaction against the acceptance of teachings which cannot be rationally demonstrated. The schools of Froebel and Pestalozzi had for their dominating idea that wonderful world-sympathy so strongly characteristic of the latter part of the eighteenth century. The true university of to-day is born of the spirit which would advance to the outposts of a line of truth, and then push them a little further into the unknown. We have in California an extensive system of normal schools—a system of which the State is rightfully proud; yet is it not time to ask ourselves what our normal schools ought to stand for besides the perfunctory process of turning out of teachers certificated to carry the formal drill work of the schoolroom? What trends in our life does or can the normal school represent?

If we examine the average Californian at his vocation—that is, at the work at which he earns his living—we are easily forced to the conclusion that the capital worth most to him is a fund of experience, not drawn from books or the advice of friends, but the product of actual observation and experiment in doing school work. In other words, that which is most valuable to the average man is the power to acquire rapidly and unerringly the experience necessary to carry on his chosen work.

Since the normal school has to do indirectly with the education of the average man, it is easy to see that one contribution to our civilization ought to be the equipment of teachers, skilled in the giving of that kind of education which will enable the average man to acquire experience which he can use effectively in earning a living, which will enable him to get an insight into the mastery of the elemental forces of nature, or, in other words, which will give him power.

The question then is, What is that quality of normal school instruction which will educate so as to best correlate school life with real life?" To answer this question quickly and to the point, I should say that the work of the normal school should be that which as soon as possible, in every line taken up, puts the student upon the original solution of problems bearing upon life, that is to say, the teachers' preparatory training should be largely an exercise in research. The process of normal education should be a finding-out process, a searching for for fact, a delving for truth in libraries and laboratories, a practice in manual-training shops in constructing out of materials easily available such apparatus as is needed in the schoolroom, a gaining of an insight into nature by watching her in the fields, on the hills, along the creek-bottom, and by the sea-shore; a study not about children, but of children; a study of the child in that essential feature of the normal school, the child-study laboratory. In a word, the ideal normal school will lead its students to find truth through the medium of their own efforts. To put the proposition in another form, there will be in the training of the twentieth-century teacher less of the receptive and more of the encouragement of the power of initiative. There will be more of that teaching which leads the individual to discover and make use of nature's forces, and thus lead him toward the ultimate discovery of truth.

All these educational processes the normal student will carry over into the public school of which he is given charge, and thus they will aid in giving the public school its true function, which is to keep the lights of civilization burning.

This much with reference to the normal school's contribution to practical education, the giving of power to the child, which is, after all, but one phase of the complete education.

The ideal normal school will realize that there are certain social demands in the education of the child. The child must be taught not only how to live for himself, but how to live in helpful co-operation with others. This is part of what is meant by the Christian doctrine: "It is not all of life to live." A selfish man may live very successfully as a hermit or a Robinson Crusoe, but put him in a camping party and he soon puts the whole company out of tune. Jack London in his short story, "In a Far Country," gives a fair picture of the degree of "out-of-jointness" with his fellows that extreme selfishness will lead a man to, and of the terrific suffering to which selfishness ultimately leads. The hardship, the suffering, the disease, the insanity, the death of Carter Weatherbee and Percy Cuthfert were, in the case of both men, the direct result of an inability of the one to put himself in a relation of helpfulness to the other.

A man must not only be able to live; he must be able to live in harmony with others. He must not only be able to produce wealth; he must be able to increase his power of production by working conjointly with his fellows. Five men working together can do twenty-five times as much as one man working alone.

Society is placing greater and greater value on the man who makes a living in the actual process of wealth-production; on the man who toils and at the same time adjusts himself to the interests of others. On our public schools rests the tremendous responsibility of giving our boys and girls a rational attitude toward co-operative activity. Are we ready to meet the responsibility? The ideal normal school will teach the children to do, and at the same time be helpful in their doing, will drop the mediaeval idea that the school is for the mastery of erudition, and will substitute that it is a place for the mastery of the forces of life, and for the mastery of self in relation to others.

There is a third phase of life which the ideal normal school will emphasize. That phase is the esthetic. The immediate environment which will be used in California in dealing with it will be the wonderful natural beauty everywhere around us. Nature in California, if we would but let her, is exceeding kind to the child. Her infinite variety she is ever ready to flash before his eye. She stands ready to deluge his every sense with the host of her beauties and glories. Her orange groves and her vine-clad hills make him dream of treasures richer than the wealth of "Ormus or of Ind," and fairer than those that bewildered the brain of Caliban on Prospero's enchanted isle. The odors from the flowers, the fruits of her autumn, her balmy airs woo him. Her wild animals and her flashily dressed birds offer him wisdom and companionship. Her trout streams, her creeks and her rivers, her giant oaks and her ancient redwoods allure him to the sacred precincts of the forest, where she flashes on her inner eye "the light that never was on sea or land." The brilliance of her sunsets, the infinite stretch of her ocean, the eternal sweep of her snow-capped mountains, all lead him to glimpses of those ancient beatific visions which were at once the inspiration of the imaginative Athenian and the glory of the venerable Hebrew.

The ideal normal school will be keenly alive to the nurturing of this esthetic instinct which, in California, finds its best exercise in listening to winds which, in their sighing, tell of perpetual summer and in dreaming over landscapes richer and more varied in color than ever painted in fantastic Arabian story.

This esthetic phase of the life of the individual is the essential basis of his ethical development. It is only through the emotional attitude of the nature-lovers and the artist, an attitude that every man has in him to a certain degree, tho he may not know it, that one rises to the conception of the divine harmonies existing thruout the national world; and comes to regulate his own life more and more in accord with the divine harmony. Just as the serene, well-balanced beautiful life of her philosophers was the culminating point of the art of Greece, so the ethical life of the man is a growth of his earlier esthetic nature.

In fact the world's greatest religions and philosophies have been reached thru an esthetic attitude which, founded upon a love of nature, was developed into higher phases by a meditation upon or a contemplation of natural objects, gradually idealized, such as beautifully adorned altars, the Jewish Ark of the Covenant, the Athenian Parthenon, the Temple of Solomon; and then higher in the scale by a contemplation of the wonderful beauties of the New Jerusalem, the city or temple not made with hands, and finally by a meditation upon the harmonious beautiful life that must be led by those who would dwell in the New Jerusalem.

It was this relation between the esthetic and the philosophic that Milton thought of when he wrote:
How charming is divine philosophy!
Not harsh and crabbed, as dull fools suppose,
But musical as is Apollo's lute,
And a perpetual feast of nectared sweets,
Where no crude surfeit reigns.

The cultivation of this phase of our nature is what will rescue us from the baneful social influences of the time, which have a tendency to wither the individual and sacrifice him to the social whole. It is what rescues from the drugery of the man with the hoe and from the sensuality of Falstaffs and Swivillers, and finally crowns our lives with what for us is a glory and honor, bringing into our souls what the poet sighs for as the "music and the dream."

I have dwelt somewhat briefly upon the three fundamental phases of education which it seems to me it will be the function of the normal school of the twentieth century to lay the foundation for. I next wish to call your attention to a unifying principle, with which the teacher must be acquainted in order to carry out the ideals.

The new normal school will be fully awake to the bearing of psychology upon the destiny of the child. Hence the methods of the school will grow more and more scientific and rational. The school will not hamper its students with dogmatic plans of instruction. Nor will it soar away into an impractical idealism; but will pursue a steady conservative policy which will permit the constant modification of methods to meet the requirements of an increasing scientific knowledge of the child's mind. This psychology will lead to the establishment in the mind of the teacher and through him in the mind of the child a sound philosophy of life and will lead both ultimately toward a true conception of spirituality.

This philosophy will be the outgrowth of a knowledge of human nature. It will be based upon some form of the theory, which now seems to be fairly on the way to be established, that the world is, thru a process of differentiation or development, gradually approaching a state of perfection; and that it is the destiny of every one to contribute, through the medium of his conscious activity, to the final harmonious adjustment of human troubles. This philosophy will be optimistic. It will lead to the knowledge as well as the feeling that life is worth living, that the sum of its pleasures is greater than the sum of its pains.

The effect of this philosophy upon school work will be tremendous. It will go far in its effect to secure a healthy attitude both on the part of teacher and of pupil towards the school. It will bring about the unification of school work. It will enable teachers to measure children according to their true worth by enabling the teachers to see inherent defects, and to remedy the defects by developing compensating powers. It will create in the school a healthful moral tone, because by a reactionary process between pupil and teacher the pupil will take on the former's attitudes to life. It will prevent teachers who are over-zealous in their own particular line of work from emphasizing this line to the detriment of the child and perhaps to the arrest of the child's development. It will enable teachers to see clearly the relation between the phases or processes of the child-mind. It will, when well comprehended, enable the teacher to merge into one whole the conflicting social, economic and esthetic elements of his own nature, and lead him towards that region of mental calm which philosophers dream of.

In carrying these ideals of education into effect there are certain problems, now before us, which the normal school must boldly meet. The first of these is the unification of the normal course of study. Since all interest in the ideal normal school is in the child; and since the acquirement of academic knowledge is a matter of secondary importance; it is easy to be seen that the training school for teachers must come to be a laboratory for the purpose not only of getting as close as possible to the inherent nature of the child, but for the purpose of allowing observation on the part of student teachers of actual instruction of public school classes taught by skilled teachers. That is to say, the training school should be the center from which every interest of the whole normal school must radiate. The pursuance of this policy will bring it about that pupils of the training school will have the advantage of expert instruction, and that the student-teacher after long observation of expert work only will take charge of a class with which he has become thoroly acquainted in order to get his first experience. This plan eradicates the ten or twenty weeks of aimless experiment upon pupils which student teachers usually go thru, greatly to the detriment of the pupil, gives student-teachers a schoolroom standard toward which they can work, and enables them to get a rational hold upon scientific method.

An important aid in unifying the normal-school curriculum will be the child-study laboratory. This laboratory will be equipped for the study of the children of the training school, especially, from all points of view. It will not only be equipped with apparatus for applying ordinary pedagogical tests, but with aquaria, with aviaries, with cages for the keeping of animals, with work benches and tools, with simple gymnasium apparatus, with collections of natural objects and all sorts of curiosities, with sewing tables and kitchen equipment—in fact, with all those contrivances which will permit the student-teacher to get close to the spontaneous life of the child.

The child-study laboratory in our normal schools will have to grow from small beginnings, but it is bound to come, and will be an essential feature of the new normal school.

A second vital problem, which the State is looking to our professional schools to solve is that of keeping our boys in school until they have at least finished the grammar grades. At the ages of thirteen or fourteen the California boy, as well as other boys, develops ideals which find scant means of realization in the school, and our system, as at present organized, seems entirely inadequate to hold them. How vitally this matter is influencing our State is seen when we remember that statistics recently collected by the Superintendent of Public Instruction, and published in his biennial report, show that the number of boys in proportion to the number of girls completing the work of California public schools is decreasing at a rate that should alarm us. Without attempting to state the causes, except in a general way, responsible for the situation, I will say that it seems to me that the growing boy thirsts for that fibre of thought and life which comes from a contact with men. He grows interested at the vital ages I have mentioned, in trade, in adventure. He would rough it every Saturday and during vacations, over marshes. He would climb mountains, and chase over hills and thru forests after birds and wild animals. He would boat, he would ride horses. In other words, he would get right into the heart of life and nature by means of methods which only boys can sympathize with. There is a great deal in our boys which goes to make up the fibre of such men as Nansen, who would know the secret of the frozen North, or Stanley, who would know the heart of Africa, or our own ideal of all that is strong in life, Theodore Roosevelt. The problem before us is to give our boys more of an opportunity to feel the dash and hum of the strenuous life and so fit them to meet the vigorous demands of American civilization.

The ideas, let me say, finally, that I have presented in the foregoing, are professedly ideal. They will have served their purpose if they have in any way thrown light on what may be done to better our schools. It is always to be remembered that to reach any ideal we can only do with our might what our hands find to do, not attempting at all to reach the goal at a single bound. The problem in education, as it is in all life, is

"Not to fancy what were fair . . .
Provided it could be—but, finding first
What may be, then how to make it fair
Up to our means."

* * *

The Child-Study Circles

Mrs. W. W. Murphy

Extract

Was it only yesterday that women frantically followed a fad to go slumming? The awful woes of the distressed, degenerate and deformed children were dinned continually into our ears, until to a stranger it might have seemed that our world held no other kinds. The men, God bless them, every one, smiled on us and opened their hearts and pocket-books. Meanwhile the common, everyday boys and girls all about us were saved from a mad effort to emulate the abnormal and unfortunate classes, if only to secure a bit of sympathy, by the sudden awakening of the Mother's conscience. Too long, mothers have been lulled to security by the many eulogies about the sacredness of the mother's love; while she hugged the sweet sentiment to her soul, that in some magical way she would be constrained to do the very best for her child, through maternal instinct.

A thoughtful interest in childhood and its environments, has taught the lesson that knowledge and co-operation is more to be depended upon than intuition, and that the sacredness of parental love consists largely in the amount of reasoning and reasonable common sense used in fitting the children to meet the responsibilities of life. The world needs formation rather than reform. The children's birthright is justice rather than pity.

At meetings such as this, the duties of teachers to parents have been carefully taught. Now and then some bolder soul among you may have thought that parents owe duties to the teachers, but you hardly dared breathe it even to yourself, lest you be accused of disloyalty to your profession. You feel the need of help and council in your work, and organize State Associations. You come here to exchange ideas and to confer as to up-to-date methods. You evolve beautiful theories, each holding promise of success in child culture. Too often your plans have come to naught, because of lack of interest, understanding and co-operation in the home. By united effort the home may be made a powerful ally to the school. The way to a perfect understanding is plain and very simple. It is thru the Child Study Circles. There is no mystery about this, but there is a sort of free masonry among those who meet once a month for an hour, to talk about things of vital interest to the children.

To be able to piece out our own best efforts by calling to our aid the experience and co-operation of those who are, with us, alike interested in childhood, is a great gain in power. Conference brings a spirit of tolerance and thus we are raised above all pettiness and self-seeking. Many things in which we have always taken pride suddenly grow small and unworthy in our eyes, and the Circles are doing much in putting aside silly social formalities. There will always be persons with special gifts to look after the unusual child, with unusual environments. The work of the Circles is to gain knowledge concerning the everyday life and needs of the average boy and girl, and to apply that knowledge to the common good of all children. To do the best for our own, means bettered environments for all. The wisest mothers are those who seek to inform themselves most thoroughly regarding those things which their children are doing. Women were a long time realizing that the school needs them, and that they need the schools, but now, by this practical study of the child, they are beginning to know their own capabilities and limitations. Many mothers have expressed the feeling that thru a newly awakened interest, they have been making a post graduate course, and now know why certain things are included in the curriculum, and why others are prohibited. To visit the school her child attends, to make the acquaintance of the teacher, to know the mothers of his playmates, is to equip herself for co-operation in every good work. The very busy life of fathers in general prevents them from visiting the school and learning its needs. It is the mother's special privilege, and duty, to confer with the teacher and with other mothers, and then see that the fathers of the neighborhood are intelligently interested in the cause of education. One is never deeply interested in things he knows little about. The father loves his children not less than their mother does; his pride in them is often greater than hers, and once his attention is called to their needs, there will be no lack of school houses and appliances, for has he not the voting power, and are not his children's rights dearer to him than his own?

The object of the California Congress of Mothers and Child Study Circles is to raise the standard of home life; to promote conference among parents and teachers upon questions vital to the welfare of children, and to bring into closer relations the home and the school, that parents and teachers may co-operate intelligently in the education of the children in the impressionable years of their life, to co-operate with educators and legislators in securing the best mental, moral and physical training of children; to further develop the manifold interest of the home and the school; and to these ends to encourage the formation of the Child Study Circles in the school and elsewhere. * * *

A spirit of helpfulness pervades the Circles and parents and teachers turn confidently the one to the other, for knowledge and counsel and for sympathy and friendship. The Child Study Circle is not a fad, to be cherished today and flung aside tomorrow. Where introduced it is as much a part of the school curriculum as music, drawing or sloyd. Mothers have been caught in the tidal wave of enthusiasm, and, with quickened consciences, they have no longer the wish or the power to escape their responsibilities, and a new era is dawning for all children.

High School Association.

Chairman, CHAS. L. BIEDENBACH, Berkeley.
Secretary pro tem., J. C. TEMPLETON, Santa Ana.

Review of the Year's Work.

C. L. BIEDENBACH.

After a brief statement concerning the organization and purposes of the association, Mr. Biedenbach spoke of the work accomplished during the year, in part, as follows:

Much labor was spent in securing the passage of Constitutional Amendment No. 1, which provides for state aid for high schools. It is a significant fact that most votes were cast upon the amendment. Furthermore, it was carried by the largest majority. These facts show that the State was thoroughly aroused.

It is now important that this Association take a hand in seeing that proper legislation is passed to carry out the evident wishes of the people. I do not advocate the framing of a bill. There is no doubt that too many bills will be presented to the Legislature, as it is. But a watchful interest must be taken to prevent the passage of any bad measure. To this end it would seem best that a committee be appointed to act with the Committee on Legislation of the State Teachers' Association.

For many years the relations between the high schools and the State University have been—delicate. It is not right to say that they have been strained or even that there has been friction. Certain it is, however, that there has been much unfortunate misunderstanding. The two departments of education have never fully understood each other. There was no channel of intercourse between the two and nobody that could act for the high schools as a whole. This Association ought to supply that need and has already proven itself most effective. Through your executive committee, the views of the high school teachers connecting the entrance requirements proposed in December, 1901 were obtained in succinct form and presented to the University. Two conferences were held with a committee of the Faculty, the basis for discussion being the following requests:

1. That the requirement in Latin be reduced from three units to two.
2. That Latin, two units, be made optional with Greek or French or German.
3. That admission to the College of Natural Sciences be made possible without any requirements of Latin or Greek.

A joint committee consisting of three members of the Faculty of the University of California, Professor Stringham, Professor Lange and Profesror Lange, and three members of our Association, C. L. Biedenbach, F. H. Clark and A. W. Scott, were appointed to recommend satisfactory modifications of the published schedule of entrance requirements. As a result of the labors of that committee a revision of the entrance requirements was made that, so far as it has been possible to ascertain, has given satisfaction to all high schools. Needless to say, no one feels that the matter is now settled for all time. As conditions change and as further study throws new light, so will further change follow. But I regard it as the most significant fact of the year's work that a matter so vital to the best interests of high schools and University was settled by amicable conference. *That* principle has been established for all time—that matter pertaining to the best interests of the two departments of state education are proper subjects for discussion by the two bodies jointly. Definite action should be taken only when the wishes of both have been fully and fairly presented and are clearly understood.

. . . .

As an evidence of the University's attitude in this matter, I take great pleasure in reading a letter that reached me just before leaving Berkeley.

BERKELEY, December 22, 1902.

Dear Mr. Biedenbach: The conference between the representatives of your association and representatives of the University on the subject of the entrance requirements demonstrated so clearly the advantages of such co-operation between the schools and the University, that I have thought it would be wise and proper to suggest that now, in view of the somewhat radical change we are proposing in our system of examinations for the next academic year, a committee of conference should be appointed by the High School Teachers' Association to join with a University committee, which I will designate, for conference upon the whole subject, and particularly upon the practical execution of the plan of examination. I appreciate very much the spirit in which the teachers met my suggestion for the last conference, and I hope I may count upon their willingness to co-operate in this case. From such co-operation and the mutual understanding arising therefrom, I believe great good will come to the school system of this State.

Very faithfully yours,
BENJ. IDE WHEELER.

Principal C. L. Biedenbach, President California High School Teachers' Associalion, Berkeley, California.

Recent changes in the University curriculum practically place prescription upon a six years' basis. All preparatory work must be done before entering the Junior year — the University proper. This will bring about a closer articulation and will cause a better choosing of free election in the high schools. Those preparing for the University will naturally choose such as will help in higher work there. At the same time, the requirements will be so arranged that no student will be prevented from entering who may have chosen with a view to discontinuing his work at the end of his high school course. Students who have taken extra work, as post graduation, for instance, will receive full credit for all work done in excess of requirements for matriculation.

It may be interesting to mention here that the required studies in the University Colleges of Natural Sciences and of Social Sciences have been made identical. And the only difference between them and the College of Letters is six hours of Greek. It follows that a matrioulant can already go into either the College of Natural or of Social Sciences in the University, no matter which he prepared for in the high school. In other words there is now no distinction between the two.

In the matter of accrediting schools, the university policy is to throw responsibility more and more upon the principals of the high schools. A new man is to be put into the field during the first term of the next Academic year who will give his whole time during that term to visiting high schools. The second te:m he will be engaged at work at the University, while the regular university examiners are in the field. Such an inspection would be a standing link between this Association and the University.

We cannot help but feel that the outlook for good work along all lines of enquiry concerned with secondary education are most encouraging. Beside the problems we are already at work on, there are some, more particularly concerned with the internal affairs of the high schools, which will be attacked during the coming year. Even though no immediate conclusion can be reached, I feel strongly that the question of athletics, fraternities and other societies should be earnestly studied by competent committees with a view toward determining their effect upon the moral and intellectual tone of the schools. Salaries and commercial courses are also proper subjects for investigation and report.

On Formal Discipline.

DR. E. C. MOORE.

"Wrestlers," said Socrates, "have heavy shoulders and thin legs, runners thick legs and narrow shoulders, but dancers are strong in every muscle, for dancing unlike other physical exercises calls into play not a part of them but the muscles of the entire body. Dancing is the best of all bodily exercises for it makes the entire body strong.

Two kinds of exercises are here indicated — exercises which fit or train for a particular work as wrestling, running, jumping, etc., and exercises which employ every muscle and make the whole body stronger.

And with regard to mental training the same division has long obtained. Studies are divided into two classes, those which prepare for special occupations or train a special function of mind, and those which train the mind as a whole and the pursuit of which renders the intellect capable in any sphere whatever.

It has long been believed that the study of medicine prepared men for the practice of medicine; the study of law prepared men for the practice of law; the study of architecture prepared for the practical work of an architect; that of mechanical engineering prepared for mechanical engineering; in short, that certain forms of study developed certain forms of skill, while at the same time it was urged that the study of Latin, Greek and mathematics did not merely make Latin and Greek scholars and mathematicians, but trained the mind as a whole, making it capable in every muscle or strengthening all its powers. Of late vigorous efforts have been made to gain for the study of science the same sort of recognition to claim for it also a wholesale disciplinary value.

Our question then is, are there some studies whose pursuit trains the mind as a whole, making it stronger in every function, and by what marks are they to be distinguished from other studies which cannot do more than exercise it in special directions.

This division of studies into qualitatively different kinds, has led to great confusion in educational practice and to even greater confusion in pedagogical discussions. The enemies of formal discipline have often gone so far as to say that learning to do a thing simply fits one to do that special thing, forgetting that as men never think the same thought over again so they never perform the same act over again, and the essential difference between living and non-living things, lies in the fact that living things are constantly changing, and not merely changing under the influence of external surroundings "but that any change which takes place in them is not lost but retained and, as it were, built into the organization to serve as the foundation for future actions."

The radical enemies of formal discipline make the mistake of supposing that the acts of mind are limited to simple imitation — that it repeats or can repeat without variation an action once performed, whereas the characteristic behavior of man is through persistent imitation in which the first reaction is never repeated, but always revised through fusion with a new experience and reapplied. To the question "how learn to do anything?" they are apt to answer "by practicing it and it alone." This was the Spartan theory of education, but Aristotle was able to point out that this method succeeded only while the condition which confronted Sparta were crudely simple and utterly failed to fit the Spartans with skill to war with the armies of developing peoples. And Aristotle's criticism of the Spartan system of making soldiers, applies equally well to every department of human activity today. One cannot learn to do a thing by practicing it and it alone. That is narrow specialization, too narrow for human use, which must always be condemned—for to know a thing as the wants of society demand that it shall be known, involves knowing it in its ramifications and relations; knowing it together with its background : knowing it as an articulating member in the organism to which it belongs. This means that education to be special must be general. Take an instance of the need for general education, and what, if nothing but it, can do for a people.

The president of the British Association for the Advancement of Science in his address before the Belfast meeting of that body, drew an interesting contrast between the state of applied chemistry in Great Britain and Germany, a form of industry which has expanded marvelously during the last thirty years, and which Germany has all but monopolized. The actual money value of these industries in Germany, is estimated at not less than fifty millions sterling, per annum, and an army of workers is employed in them. How must we account for German superiority in this regard; "I give it in a word," says President Dewar—"want of education. We had the material in abundance when other nations had comparatively little. We had the capital and we had the brains, for we originated the whole thing, but we did not possess the diffused education without which the ideas of men of genius cannot fructify beyond the limited scope of an individual. The root of the mischief is in the want of education among our so called educated classes, and secondarily among the workers on whom we depend. It is the abundance of men of ordinary plodding ability, thoroughly trained and methodically directed, that Germany at present has so commanding an advantage. It is the failure of our schools to turn out, and of our manufacturers to demand men of this kind, which explains our loss of some valuable industries and our precarious hold upon others. Let no one imagine for a moment that this deficiency can be remedied by any amount of that technical training which is now the fashionable nostrum. It is an excellent thing no doubt, but it must rest upon a foundation of general training. Mental habits are formed for good or evil long before men go to the technical schools. We have to begin at the beginning, we have to train the population from the first to think correctly and logically, to deal at first hand with facts, and to evolve, each for himself, the solution of a problem put before him, instead of learning by rote the solution given by somebody else. There are plenty of chemists chock full of formulæ; they can recite theories and they know text books by heart; but put them to solve a new problem freshly arisen in the laboratory, and you will find that their learning is all dead. It has not become a vital part of their mental equipment and they are floored by the first emergence of the unexpected. The men who escape this mental barrenness are men who were somehow or other taught to think, long before they went to the university. To my mind the really appalling thing is not that the Germans have seized this or even that they may have seized upon a dozen industries. It is that the German population has reached a point of general training and specialized equipment which it will take us two generations of hard and intelligently directed educational work to attain. It is that Germany possesses a national weapon of precision which must give her an enormous initial advantage in any and every contest depending upon disciplined and methodized intellect."

It is this very demand for general training which has ennobled the so-called disciplinary studies to impose upon us. The champions of these studies, like the Sophists of old, go about everywhere crying, only study with us and every day you will go away a better man. And there have been all too few men like Socrates going about asking, "In what way a better man?" Does learning to do one thing well, cause us to do all things well? The Sophists claimed for the study of rhetoric that it was the very best preparation for any calling in life — a much better preparation for any calling, indeed, than the study of its own subject matter.

Socrates, indeed, knew better and condemned them as well as the artisans of Athens for professing to know all about the building of states because they knew how to build a sentence or a house.

How far does the training of one function train all?

Habituating a given area of the skin to the impressions of two compass points not only increases the sensitiveness of neighboring areas but also that of the corresponding part of the body on the opposite side. Training of the touch of one finger will affect the sensitiveness of the others, even on the other hand. It is believed that learning to write with one hand aids learning to write with the other; and experiments indicate that this transference of ability from one hand to the other applies to other manual acts as well. In short, it is an established principle that the training of a specific function trains in a measure its homologous bilateral function, and in a lesser degree, structurally, all others identical with it in the nervous system. The unity of organs in the brain or identical centers governing different peripheral areas seems fully to account for these cases of seeming vicarious education, but by no means to warrant the conclusion that acts of will, memory, imagination or thinking affect each other in the same fashion.

While the strain of consciousness presents itself under the three different aspects of feeling, thinking and willing, and these three aspects of its being can never be separated, yet the energy of attention is a somewhat constant quantity; so that if it be used in thinking, "the native hue of resolution becomes all sicklied o'er with the pale cast of thought, and feeling, too, subsides."

While the limitation of the man of thought is that he does not act, the limitation of the man of action is that he does not think, and the sentimentalist or the mystic of whatever sort who revels in an orgy of feeling is subject to the same limitation. It can hardly be claimed for any one of these forms of mental activity that it develops the whole mind.

Our greatest objection to the upholders of formal discipline is that they perpetuate the false theories of the old faculty psychology in the realm of education long after they have been abandoned by psychologists.

Teachers are told that they must train the faculty of observation, attention, imagination, memory, reasoning, etc., in their pupils, and that certain studies have been provided, providentially as it were, to enable them to train these faculties.

Train the senses or the faculty of observation is a command that is everywhere given to teachers, and they are told that this is to be accomplished by the aid of those deformities of science called Nature Study. Suppose they do drill their pupils in examining bugs and worms, caterpillars and grass, do these exercises train them to observe all sorts of phenomena or merely bugs and worms? It is a well known fact that the natural scientist is lame, halt and blind, and, what is much worse, bound to be dogmatic when called upon to investigate the phenomena of social life, and that though he has been trained to observe, he almost never does so outside his own immediate sphere of interest unless prompted by necessities other than those of his training. The veriest gamin of the city streets can give him any number of points and still score against him in researches into moral delinquency and human depravity. The social scientist is hardly more successful in dealing with the facts of animal life. The wild Indian of the woods and the polished gentleman of the drawing room, each of them specialists in the lore of his own life, are the veriest babes at sea when transplanted each into the others environment. The phrenologist has been trained to observe heads; the physiognomist, faces; the palmist, palms; the oculist, eyes; the aurist, ears; the pugilist, biceps; the runner, legs; and they continue to be interested and collect data on their specialties. The geologist observes rocks; the philologist, speech; the socialist, wrongs; the capitalist, wealth; the revivalist, sins; and so thoroughgoing is the one-sidedness of trained observation that the very classes of our society are based upon it, and human birds of a feather flock together simply because they have no eyes or ears for the notes of other birds. No single form of exercises can be prescribed which will cultivate an all-round observation. It cannot be taught as an art, for there is no faculty of observation which can be trained, since we have not one observation but many, each aroused, guided and directed by the mental interests we keep.

It is less fashionable among pedagogues at the present time to talk of training the memory, for it is commonly recognized that the memory is not a fixed thing — a faculty, but rather a function of the content remembered, depending upon our interest in and thoroughness of comprehension of it. In other words, that we have a different memory for each particular thing.

The same is true of imagination, though less commonly recognized. The form of image that we employ depends upon nature and early training, but the thoroughness with which we shall image any mental happening varies directly with our experience of it.

Attention, like observation, is a mental trait which schoolmasters have been most unwilling to submit to the psychologist. They still believe it to be a faculty, or power which can be trained as a whole; and while they scout memory drills, many still cling fondly to exercises and studies which train the observation, the imagination or the attention.

But this fetish also must be given up. Attention, like the others, is no fixed power or faculty, but varies with each experience, being as surely as memory, a function of content, not an organ of mind.

Reasoning is the detecting of identities. It also depends upon our interest in and knowledge of the particular subject matter involved. Familiarity with the things involved and our mental attitude toward them are the chief determinants of our ability to reason concerning them. It is evident, therefore, that power to reason cannot be engendered in toto;

and verification of this position is to be found everywhere about us. Scientists make ridiculous philosophers; philosophers and theologians, ridiculous scientists. And with regard to no mental operation is the ancient warning, "Shoemaker, stick to your last," more binding than with regard to the special forms of reasoning.

Psychologists, with one accord, deny the existence of any sort of power, force or faculty which can be trained or exercised as a whole. Individual acts, thoughts and feelings are absolutely all that the teacher can consider in his work. Since there is no study which disciplines the mind as a whole or trains any faculty of it, we must inquire what are the objects of instruction. In a phrase, it is enlightened action. It is one and inseparable, but for purposes of investigation may be divided into three parts or phases. Instruction must have for its object the imparting of facts needful to be known; 2nd, of methods of reacting to such facts; 3rd, methods of learning facts and the necessary methods of reacting to them, or methods of study and investigation. Instruction exists to impart facts. It is evident that each fact must be learned by itself, and that there can be no training of any sort which will stand proxy for this process or learning them one by one. It is true that the parts of an organized or interrelated whole of knowledge are learned with different degrees of ease. The first elements are difficult to acquire, the last come almost of themselves; but this facility in learning a subject after a beginning has been made is due to the representative and apperceptive character of the facts first learned, to what things one knows, not to any mysterious mental powers that may have been developed within him.

When we consider methods of reacting to facts or of dealing with them, we must note a great difference.

Mr. Baldwin finds an element of imitation in all human action. Every act is different from every other, but every act in some form or other reproduces past acts. "Every new thing is an adaptation, and every adaptation arises right out of the bosom of old processes and is filled with old matter." The motor attitudes are fewer than the sensory. The nervous organization may be compared to a funnel, of which the sensory part is the wide mouth, the motor the small neck. What does this mean but that experiences are not gotten one by one? The very conception of a living being is one which is constantly assimilating new experiences through old, constantly adapting old methods of reacting to fit new needs, constantly readjusting or accommodating its methods of reacting to meet the ever new situations which confront it. Indeed, this constant process of readjustment or accommodation is the most familiar thing in the history of living beings. To facilitate it every precept is immediately generalized as a concept. Experiences of all sorts are treated as typical of future experiences and consciously or unconsciously classified and formulated as rules of action. New contents are searched for familiar elements or overlaping characters in order that known methods may be applied to them.

Any general power, ability, or faculty can only mean a familiar method of reaction which has a wide applicability and may be generally used. There are no wholesale exercises which can be employed in instruction, and with good reason, for complete disorganization would be their effect. There are no general disciplines, but there are disciplines which have a general usefulness, whose methods have a wide range of applicability. The difference between these two conceptions is the difference between a "general act" and an act which is generally or commonly performed. There are mental processes which are commonly used, which form as it were, basic habits which can readily be accommodated to fit many varying human needs. Plato in speaking of mathematics calls it "that general thing which all arts and dianoetic powers and sciences employ and which every one ought, in the first place necessarily to learn; for is it not that every art and every science must of necessity participate in these." [R. viii-522] Every one knows that the person who uses a typewriter need not practice so religiously upon the piano and will continue to play as well. Methods of observation, methods of attention, of imagination, of remembering and of thinking, which will be generally useful may be acquired. Processes or ways of doing things generally applicable, may be learned, but not powers or faculties trained. Not *the* attention or *the* senses or the *the* memory, but ways and habits of attending, observing, remembering, etc., constitute the objective of all teaching. To learn typical things, to form habits which have a general applicability then, is the chief task of education. It cannot be doubted that every thought is a new thought; that every act is a new act, and it is just as true that each is generalized and shaped into an instrument with which to manipulate its successor.

What are the limits of this process? The limits of class recognition itself. Whatever new experiences can be brought under a familiar class will be reacted to in ways already in part at least, familiar.

The study of mathematics, it is said, begets habits of carefulness and thoroughness. Habits of carefulness and thoroughness in all things, or only in mathematics? And one does not have to pause long to recall mathematicians who seemed to be careful in nothing but mathematics, whose personal appearance, treatment of creditors, and conduct in general was anything but careful. The same thing is true concerning the characteristic virtue of almost all the special industries. A Pythogorean or any Greek who came under that beneficent influence was able to apply mathematical methods and precepts far beyond the range of a modern mathematician, simply because he had learned to regard the field of mathematics as practically coterminous with life itself. It taught him justice in his dealings with his fellows, simply because ethical situations were conceived as falling within its sphere and aroused its reactions. How absurd it is to expect the man who has never consciously made this connection between sensory element and motor reaction to exhibit the motor reaction in the presence of the sensory element habitually. Your scientific man is careful in his work and nowhere else. Does this prove that scientific training may not impart general carefulness? I hardly think so. His training has enabled him to be consciously careful, and perhaps to be habitually careful, in reacting to certain situations. If it had been more thorough and lasting, and had been consciously generalized to a wider range of activities, it would most certainly have rendered him careful in many things. It equipped him with the method of scientific carefulness, ready to be applied whenever he choose to do so.

A series of experiments conducted by Professor Thorndyke, of Columbia University, in an effort to determine the influence of the improvement of one mental function upon another, has revealed some very interesting results.

Four subjects were requested to estimate the areas of a series of papers of various shapes and sizes. In front of them was a card on which three squares 1, 25, and 100 sq. cm. in area, respectively, were drawn to guide the eye in estimating the areas of the papers given. After being thus tested, the subjects were given a series of paper rectangles from 10 to 100 sq. cm. in area; and after they had been trained to guess the areas of these, by ascertaining the real area after each judgment until the average error was 2.3 per cent, they were required to estimate the areas of the figures already estimated before training, with the following result:

On Formal Discipline

The percentage of error, in estimating figures from 20 to 100 sq. cm. of the same shape as the training series, fell from 15.4 to 6—or 9.4.

In figures of 140 to 200 sq. cm., from 34.5 to 20.5—or 14; 200 to 300 sq. cm., from 30.8, rose to 31.3.

In figures of different shapes, 10 to 60 sq. cm., from 10 fell to 6.3—or 3.7; 100 to 140 sq. cm., from 28.2 fell to 13.9—or 14.3; 140 to 100 sq. cm., from 41.5 fell to 32.4 — or 9.1; 200 to 240 sq. cm., from 50.5 fell to 43.4— or 7.1; 240 and over sq. cm. from 75.6 fell to 58.1 — or 17.5

The improvement in the estimation of rectangles from 10–100 is not equaled in all the other functions, but marked improvement followed the training in every case but one. Change of size decreased the amount of improvement, but change in shape and size decreased it only in about the same degree.

While these experiments indicate that training of one function does not improve others closely allied to it, in the same degree, they do show that other allied functions are greatly improved by such training, and it is not claimed by those who conducted them that they were exact or thorough-going enough to decide the question involved. They do not bear at all on that phase of the matter most interesting to teachers—on the effect of training on the ability to improve, for say those who conducted them: "The experiments were all on the influence of the training in efficiency, on ability as measured by a single test, not on ability to improve. It might be that improvement in one function might fail to give an another improved ability, but succeed in giving ability to improve faster than would have occurred had the training been lacking." Indeed, the tabulated reports of the tests seem to indicate not only great improvement but also, therefore, ability to improve, which any theory of mental development would require.

The question of the influence of improvement in one mental function upon the efficiency of another cannot yet, perhaps never can be, answered in detail. Fortunately, we do not need to wait for such a detailed answer. That experience is cumulative, that accommoda is a function of habit, that there is a stant reapplication and revision of knowledge to meet new needs, do wait to be proven. Our question is so much in what degree this is true under what conditions can it take pl Ideas and acts, contents and meth are not separated in the brain. They one there. Under what conditions new experiences be brought under methods? Only when the old cont middle terms, common elements to readily found in the new; only when old contains somewhat of the new. other words, training for life must through familiarity with the thing life. One cannot learn methods of servation, thought or anything else will fit him for life without using t upon the very problems which he n handle in life. If the skill in estima square figures of a given size is los large part when one attempts to estin square figures but a little larger, is it reasonable to conclude that the skil thought engendered by translating L sentences or reiterating Euclid's pr or Darwin's theories is almost of effect when in after years one come the forum or the farm? It is not s cient that the appropriate method reaction should be established in yo The very ideas which call them f must be in large part the same as tl which shall call them forth in after The ideas which are associated them in the school must represent situations which shall call them fortl the world. The typical method and ideational approaches must be ricl social ramifications to the eager min the child who is acquiring it, else he seldom be able to apply it in after Education prepares for life only by b life while it is education; and ther more than a half truth in the statem of many men that as it is now pract it unfits for life in a great many case

Enriching the meaning of the cesses acquired in the school is perl the chief work of the teacher.

Music, said the Greeks, gets into soul and harmonizes it with the harm which it brings, and that it did so among them is not a theory but a fact. And did it do so because it was a superior discipline indifferently taught or well taught for a brief period? By no means. Every Athenian citizen taught it to every other. One simply could not escape learning its lessons in connection with every lesson that he learned. Its application to every act of life was everywhere pointed out. No one could fail to learn the lesson of its directive reference to all things, for its meaning was so thoroughly socialized. Socrates might have said to the carpenters of Athens, most likely did say to them, you are good carpenters, you saw your boards straight and make their joints fit, but you do not recognize the same need of sawing your conduct and making it fit into the structure of State. The method could not be carried over into a realm so remote, but the homely lessons of the Great Teacher generalized the method and taught the lesson by illuminating homely experiences in such a way that they became guides to the kingdom of heaven.

And that such a revitalizing of much of our teaching is needed today I am assured by my friend, a Professor of English literature, who tells me that he greatly prefers students of biology to students of Latin as candidates for his instruction, for the former have learned to imagine things clearly, while the latter have become so familiar with words that they convey but little meaning to them. Anyone who has attempted to teach ancient history to students who have for years been in the habit of regarding the characters involved as but names, knows how well nigh impossible it is to make the past live again for them. Studies must be embedded in a broad and deep matrix before they can even be used, let alone used profitably, in life.

Turn to the socalled disciplinary studies. What warrant have they for claiming to discipline the whole mind or whole departments of it — none whatever. If by any chance they did posses this mysterious prerogative, all other studies might claim it with as good a right.

They are of value, then, in the degree in which they impart ideas and methods of action which do not prepare for life, but pertain to life, or are life. The so-called disciplinary studies are inherently less teachable than the information bringing studies. They self-confessedly offer fewer opportunities to the apperceptive interests. They do not readily articulate with human life, or serve its social wants. The attention of pupils is apt to be divided in following them. Their lessons are not readily learned nor easily remembered, because native desires, interests, impulses, do not move in their direction. They do not by arousing thought, lead to organization and reorganization of the lessons of every day experience. They are not a criticism of life, but mere addenda to it, leading indeed, to disorganization and lack of unity. In so far as disciplinary studies or any other studies offer a subject matter not readily fusible with ordinary experience, they are positively harmful.

It is sometimes said that these studies are superior because they are perfected disciplines offering a graduated series of progressively difficult tasks. But perfected and over logical disciplines are apt to be schoolmaster's machines wholly unlike the problems and situations of the world; work, exercise, labor which is merely work, even though it be a system of graduated tasks is of no avaail whatever. Mere work is a curse, because it kills the soul and robs the body, and more work in school which is known by the name of *exercise*, is a curse also. Let me illustrate: I do not write well now; I shall write a great deal this year, and until the end of life, but I shall not learn to write any better for the exercise of all the years to come. Exercise alone is not good but harmful. "Only continued effort and not effortless exercise" improves. Compelled and formal disciplines do not develop a progressive series of interests, and cannot therefore, provoke continued effort. The work which children do in school must grow out of the needs which children feel. It must not be let down upon them from the heaven of the past, through tradition or scholastic stubbornness.

A subject to be worth teaching, must involve a mastery of methods such as are actually fundamental in the affairs of life, and these methods, no matter how useful, must not be presented in connection with a dead or abstract system of grammatical, mathematical or scientific problems. . If the methods which are learned in the class room are to be applied elsewhere than in the class room, they must there be woven about the body of the very things to which they are expected to have reference. If you are to learn contingent reasoning in the study of the ancient languages, you must in the study of the languages be constantly applying your methods of contingent reasoning to the very matters to which you expect to apply it in after life. Like the Talmud, all things are in these studies. "The mind" indeed "takes fiber, facility, strength, adaptability, certainty of touch from handling them when the teacher knows his art and their power." But this goodly result comes not from treating them as parsing blocks or philological opportunities. Declaming, conjugating, expounding, scanning, phrasing, and that infinity of schoolmasters' devices for concealing the essence of the language studied, might be better left alone.

Our interminable writing and grammar lessons prevent our entering into the rich heritage of the past—actually keep us from reading the wisdom literature of the ancients. We need to adopt the program of the German schoolmasters promulgated in the year 1892. The study of humanism has for its object the "historical comprehension of antiquity." The study of mathematics, too, to be disciplinary must be a study of its applications; practical or applied mathematics a study of means in connection with ends; a series of graduated commercial and engineering exercises which train in computation, because they involve computation, and not a series of barren exercises framed to expose seemingly self-existent principles.

The instrumental character of science is so important that it is less likely to be overlooked. Its main object is the imparting of methods of discovery. It is not so much knowledge bearing as knowledge finding, and the teacher who makes the most of the subject will constantly call the attention of his students not to their results but to how they got them.

Our interpretation of the principle of formal discipline leads us then to the conclusion that the chief object of studies is the imparting of social methods, which can only be done successfully where these methods are well interwoven with the material upon which it is desired to operate by their use. Our chief objection to the so-called disciplinary studies is that their methods are taught in a vacuum and not in reference to the living world. History is full of the most convincing evidence to prove that beyond a question these studies are of the greatest benefit when taught as guides to life.

I believe that no statement will summarize this whole matter better than a passage from Bishop Potter's recent work, "The Citizen in His Relation to the Industrial Situation." Speaking of the conditions of labor before the coming of the factory system, he says: "It mattered little, comparatively, to a workman where he was, *e. g.*, a mechanic making a whole thing, whether he found employment in the manufacture of that particular thing or something else; for the knowledge and aptitude which he had acquired in mastering his peculiar craft or art, even though directed ordinarily toward the making of a single thing, had given him deftness and facility sufficient to enable him to turn his industrial activity to half a dozen things."

In other words, an art thoroughly learned involved a knowledge of many things and processes by which to handle them; and a subject thoroughly mastered with a keen perception of its kinship with all things human is not merely one subject learned but indeed goes a long way toward fitting for life.

* * *

Disciplinary Value of English.

GERTRUDE HENDERSON.

What is the disciplinary value of English? I should like to begin my answer to the question with this: while I think English has great disciplinary value, and that in various ways, yet I think *the* value of it is something else, so that if it were of no value at all as discipline, still I should think it of the highest importance that it should be taught. The great and characteristic usefulness of it, not disciplinary, is that it opens to people resources of joy that are very little dependent upon their circumstances or the other people among whom it is their lot to live. A person who knows to read books has the entrance into much and permanent pleasure. And the second strong claim it has, not disciplinary, is that an acquaintance with literature does add to people's agreeableness as companions to their fellow men, both directly, and also, through enriching their souls any brightening their minds as it does, indirectly. There are many children who would get these two desirable things, the reading habit and acquaintance with literature, from living with their families, without aid of schools; but there is also a very large multitude whose only chance of getting either is in the English classes. So, quite aside from mental discipline, English seems to me to have a high claim upon the High School time.

I suppose disciplinary value in any subject of study means the power in it to give the mind some training that helps to fit it for extremely practical living — for earning one's living or running one's household, or helping to run one's town, or in any other way holding one's own and making one's self felt.

There is a mechanical part of the task of English classes, and the practical value of that lies on the surface and is perfectly obvious to any one. To be able to write grammatical English and punctuate it intelligibly, and spell it right, every one needs; and although in the nature of things it is impossible for one department to train people to those habits without the active help of all the rest, yet the burden of the training falls chiefly and always upon the English department. And that, too, seems to be in the nature of things.

The second sort of training I wish to speak of is beyond mere mechanical accuracy. It is a training of the habits of thought, and the ways of collecting the materials out of which thought is made. The trained and the untrained mind read differently. The trained mind reads with such attention as to get the author's thought; the untrained reader is very apt to get, not the author's thought, but his own hasty misconstruction of it, generally incomplete, often curiously mistaken, sometimes directly contradictory of the thing he thinks he has read. People read books with this slovenly misunderstanding, read newspapers so, read public affairs and their own so, and from misread data think unsound thoughts, and from mistaken thinking misdirect their actions. The habit of reading what's *there* is an extremely valuable habit. It is the continual, plodding care of the teachers of English that their pupils shall read what's *there*, without vagueness, without misconception, without the fragmentary realization and frequent skipping that seems the native tendency of the indolent human mind. By requiring that the daily English lessons shall be so read, and seeing that they are so read, and talking much about the exact and whole meaning of the text, it is the daily labor of the English teachers to get their pupils settled in the habit of reading right; which means reading accurately, sincerely, comprehendingly and completely; that is, reading in the ouly way by which reading can be made to furnish one materials for reasonable thinking. And as most people get much of the material of their thought out of newspapers, magazines and books, it is important to do what can be done to give them the habit of reading in the way that gives their snbsequent thinking the chance of being reasonable.

Every day's lesson is a drill toward this habit of reading understandingly; and every day's lesson is a drill to the pupil, too, in the ability to speak his own thoughts clearly and without encumbering verbiage — not to vapor, but to say the *thing*, and then not to say it over, but to stop.

The opportunity for this drill English affords, in common with most other High School studies. The last sort of training I shall speak of, however, is peculiar to English, except in so far as the study of history contributes towards it. It is the training in the comprehension of people, below their surface manners. The great novels and the great dramas have usefulness beyond the mere giving amusement. Through the power of the mind that has that genius for seeing into *people* that makes the great novelist or dramatist, one can make keen one's own understanding of living people; through the wisdom of the printed story one's eyes get opened to the possibilities, good and bad, of one's own human nature, and the inexorable law of effect that follows cause, action that follows action, moral rectitude or crookedness tomorrow, that inevitably follows one's moral rectitude or swerving today. It is very easy, convenient and general to read even great novels and dramas without getting any other ideas out of them than just that the story is more or less entertaining. It is in the power of the English course to give people the habit of reading them differently, so that they are training in understanding, which alone makes possible handling one's fellow men and one's self. It is never for any one novel alone that an English course includes that novel, nor for any one play or play writer alone that it includes that play, but, through reading these right, to get people into the habit of reading all sorts of things right, afterwards. And the great thing about reading this sort of literature right is reading it in such a way that you see the better for it what living people and their live stories mean, without seeing which clearly you are bound to be an inadequate person always, no matter how big or how little a position you are trying to fill.

The Educational Value of Mathematics.

DR. A. W. SCOTT.

Previous to ten, or fifteen years ago, when election in secondary schools was confined to a choice between fixed traditional courses of study, it would have seemed a waste of time and energy to apologize for, or demonstrate the educational value of, any of the time-honored subjects constituting the backbone of the curricula of those schools.

But the reports of the Committee of Ten and of the Committee of Fifteen; the influence of such men as President Elliot, Dr. Harris, President Butler, Dr. Hanus and Professor Hinsdale; the efforts of Mr. Search and others to cause us to concern ourselves more with the intellectual condition and needs of the individual pupil; the resulting plea for election in subjects, as well as in courses, in order to allow for those different conditions and needs; the rapid development of industrial activity, necessitating our taking into consideration the demands of the business world for commercial and constructive subjects of rather immediate utility; — all of these elements have caused a condition of ferment in secondary educational thought, in which all kinds of educational theories have been advocated concerning the function of the high school, and the educational value of the many subjects knocking at its door and demanding recognition. We have run the gamut from the dictum of the strict humanist, who ignores his concrete surroundings, to that of the narrow man of science, who is so intent on getting recognition for his subject that he can see nothing but waste of time and energy in the study of a dead language. We have had the doctrine of the five coordinate groups of Dr. Harris and its polar, that of the educational equivalence of subjects.

The outcome of all this agitation has been that we have placed all the subjects demanding consideration on trial and are now requiring them to justify their place in the curriculum of the modern high school.

In determining the educational worth of these subjects, we are ultimately compelled to take a utilitarian view of them and to ask ourselves what we expect them to accomplish in attaining the end or aim of education; and we are also compelled to be utilitarian in requiring that the final results obtained from them be more or less appreciable and measurable at some time or other. These two requirements must be kept in mind in discussing the disciplinary and content value of mathematics.

At the outset, we must recognize what Mr. Froude in his "Short Studies on Great Subjects" insists upon, that education has two aspects; that on the one side it is the cultivation of man's reason, the development of his spiritual nature, from which we derive our inspiration, our social and ethical ideals; on the other side, it is the necessary equipping a man with the means to earn his own living. Each of these aspects is a noble and necessary one — in fact they are complementary to each other. General culture and immediate utility must both be recognized in the school curriculum. But in doing so we must not be misled by the low standard set by those who look on the school almost wholly from the vocational standpoint. It is not the business of the school to teach a trade or to fit for any particular vocation; it is rather to develop in the boy the ability to adapt himself to his future environment by training him in the ability to think clearly, broadly and deeply, to know and appreciate the motives that have impelled man to arrive at his present social, political and industrial condition.

The general culture subjects, under the guidance of teachers who have correlated themselves with their environment and epoch, will prove to have a not very remote utility value. The value of any particular subject in the curriculum will depend largely on the degree and manner in which it satisfies the requirements that the demands of social and industrial life make upon man. The demands that the various activities of life, with which every man may expect to be thrown in contact, make upon him, such as, first, those that conduce to his happiness at home and in society — the social and ethical activities, and second, those that conduce to his proper conception of the phenomena of life, organic and inorganic, as he daily comes in contact with them, must appeal alike to all; while the demands made in particular professions, trades or callings, will appeal only to those following them.

Now, in as far as the intelligent study of mathematics produces results that satisfy and harmonize with the social and ethical activities of life, and enables man to live in intelligent sympathy with the activity of man and of nature, in so far, other things being equal, should it form part of the curriculum of all students. Again. in as far as it is a prerequisite to the study of science, as physics, astronomy, etc., or a profession, as engineering, it appeals only to the specialist.

The value of mathematics on its content side is, of course, unquestioned. We all recognize the necessity of training the mathematical sense of all pupils, of storing the mind with a stock of necessary mathematical facts, concepts and methods. We cannot avoid this, considering that we live in a material world, come in contact with tangible objects, involving the concepts of number, form, size, distance, etc. The placing, then, of arithmetic and objective geometry in the elementary school needs no apology. They are the means by which all the commonplace phenomena of Nature, animate and inanimate, are measured and interpreted. The only topics justifiable here are the fundamental operations on integers and fractions, the translation of fractions into percentage and its application in simple interest, and perhaps proportion. The study of objective geometry should be purely informal, involving the formation of judgments, the acquisition of facts concerning the geometric magnitudes and their relations, the development and constructive faculties and the use of drawing instruments. This geometric work will naturally be intimately correlated with nature study work, and will be largely inductive in its character. Because of the facts and operations learned, it will be almost entirely utilitarian; and, because observation provokes thought, and thought begets further observation, comparison and judgment, leading under skillful direction to a conception of the unity of nature, the work will possess a culture value. For these reasons the mathematics of the elementary school should not be elective; it appeals to and comes within the experience of all.

In the secondary school the world of knowledge begins to be regarded as a multiple unit consisting of intimately related and correlatable yet recognizable single units. Knowledge begins to be classified, and the analytical as well as the synthetical point of view begins to be assumed. It is a period of anticipation and bewilderment, and therefore a critical time in the student's life, intellectual, moral and physical. His tastes, either permanent or evanescent, are just beginning to be evolved. It is here, during the first year of his high school course, that the principal who directs his work finds his most important and most difficult task, that of so directing and encouraging him that his needs and tastes may be discovered and interest aroused where apparently lacking. In choosing the different lines of work to present to him as he enters the high school, the end to be attained becomes paramount.

Man differs from all other animals in that he reasons. Every social or industrial act that he performs throughout his life, either individually or collectively, is the result of a process of reasoning. Only children, unlettered adults and leaderless mobs act reflectively, i. e., impulsively. Man, in order to be an active member of society, is constantly called upon to form judgments, i. e., to gather facts, arrange, compare and classify them and draw conclusions. In other words, he is constantly called upon to reason. Now reasoning is an orderly and an abstract process. In its rudimentary form it begins with the concrete and gradually passes over into the abstract. Mathematics, more than any other high school subject, is the best vehicle for traveling in the realms of the abstract. It affords development in orderly consecutive thinking, inductively in algebra, and deductively in geometry. Each of these methods of reasoning is conditioned on, and developed by, habits of close observation, acute discrimination, the elimination of unnecessary details, insistence on sound premises, and absolute accuracy of language in the expression of ideas. The conclusions of mathematical reasoning, even the inductive, are absolutely exact; and the mind, especially the flexible, impressionable mind of the secondary student, receiving that feeling of satisfaction and power induced by the definite results obtained by his own unaided efforts.

If the object of education be to develop power, — power to arrange the facts and ideas at one's command, and to draw therefrom valuable results, power to seize the salient point in any issue, power to influence one's fellow man along desirable lines, power to think out and solve the different problems that arise, to do the things awaiting doing, then the dynamic culture value of mathematics in subserving these ends is unquestionable. And this value is largely and almost wholly due to the habit of *orderliness* that all mathematical study is conditioned on and develops. On this one essential feature I would base the chief claim of mathematics to a recognized place in every secondary school curriculum.

The different isolated steps in an algebraic investigation are, as a rule, easy of comprehension. The difficulty that confronts the average student is to know in what direction to reason, and his success in arriving at his result is largely dependent on his removing the difficulties that lie in his way, gradually, one by one, getting each time a simpler and simpler expression, until he finally gets one that he can interpret. The same holds true in the solution of a geometric problem. In both lines of work he finds that the key to success is orderliness. And this orderly habit of mind that mathematical work develops, influences and controls in other related and unrelated subjects.

There are, as we all know, students who seem to be lacking in the mathematical sense, and yet who are capable of development in imagination, sympathy and the social and ethical instincts. Such students must and can be provided for in a flexible course of study. I would not, however, accept the self-diagnosis of the student as to his lack of ability for mathematical work, and I would compel him to demonstrate to me by at least one term's work under intelligent supervision that he was deficient in the mathematical sense, and then I would excuse him from further mathematical work, either permanently or until he should become more mature. While providing for such one-sided pupils, and recognizing the fact that they may prove to be strong in literature and linguistics, I would venture to affirm that it is the experience of many high school principals that the pupil who is lacking in the mathematical sense, as a rule, shows his weakness in other lines of work or less well-defined carelessness, disorderliness and inexactness. A few words will suffice concerning arranging and handling of the work. As the subject-matter in the better text books on the reorganized algebra, such as Stringham's, Smith, Hall & Knight, etc., is difficult and intense, I would prefer beginning it in the second year of the high school when the pupils have presumably developed the ability to work. I would prefer this to beginning the work in the first year with a simpler book, because, otherwise, many of the definitions would have to be modified to suit the new conditions, and a waste of time would result from repetition of subject matter. Where the conditions are favorable, the simultaneous handling of geometry and algebra is desirable, as it enables the teacher to correlate the two intimately, and to express and illustrate the same principle in both languages. The statement of the conditions of a problem or the facts of an equation or formula should be taught as the translation of a statement from one language into another. The standard formulæ of algebra should be discovered heuristically, and illustrated by all possible means, in order to avoid that extreme carelessness and inaccuracy in their handling which is so common. The pupil should be taught that the possession of the final formula is not the only end in view, but that the processes used in arriving at it, and the proper interpretation of it — the ability to generalize — give him the logical training for the securing of which he studies algebra. The end of the course, rather than the beginning, will be the time for stating formal and general definitions. Of course this will not conform to deductive sequence, but the main idea in algebra teaching is to discover and formulate principles. After the course has been evolved inductively, then a retrospective survey can be made and the work arranged synthetically into its proper sequence.

In the teaching of geometry, the teacher should by all means at his command prevent the pupil from comitting demonstrations to memory. The subject had better not be taught at all, if the ability to discover and invent is not definitely developed. No particular attempt should be made to follow the order of theorems in the particular text used. The logical order of theorems can well be reserved for the end of the year. In unfolding the subject, take the basic geometric principles, such as the congruence of triangles, and use them to illustrate the different methods of attack, such as the genetic and analytic. This latter method and the subject of loci should be central subjects in a course of geometry.

In conclusion, I have attempted to show that the study of mathematics satisfies the demands of the social and ethical activities of life, and therefore subserves the purpose of formal discipline by developing the habits of order, integrity of thought, accuracy and intellectual sequence, and that this orderliness of thinking necessarily reacts on thinking in other fields of knowledge. And these results, in my judgment, can be appreciated and almost measured, not only after the student has gone out into life, but even while he is under instruction.

The Educational Value of Modern Languages

Valentin Buehner

In his lecture on the study of modern languages before the Modern Language Association in 1889, James Russell Lowell says that before 1808. there was at Harvard University no regularly appointed tutor in French, but a stray Frenchman was caught now and then, and kept as long as he could endure the baiting of his pupils. If he failed as a teacher, he commonly turned dancing-master. By hook or by crook, some enthusiasts managed to learn German, but there was no official teacher of German until about 1825, when Dr. Follen was appointed. Another old Harvard student relates that it was with so little difficulty that a volunteer class of eight was formed. They were looked upon with very much the amazement with which now a class in some obscure dialect of the remotest Orient would be regarded.

But today, all this has changed. There are now at Harvard University more professors and assistants employed in teaching modern languages than there were students of them when these men attended college.

Many causes have worked together to bring about this change. Modern inventions, such as the railroads, steamships, and the telegraph, have annihilated distances. The immense progress in the manufacturing industries has made it desirable to enter the markets of the world. The unusual activity in all departments of science and learning has made it necessary to know the chief European languages, so as to be in closer touch with the new discoveries and theories that are continually advanced by the scholars of the various nations. Not the least cause, however, of the greater esteem in which the modern languages are held, has been their being themselves raised to a higher level through the investigations and achievements of modern philology. While before the great labors of Grimm and others, only the classical languages were considered worthy of the attention of scholars, it has since then been found that in the modern languages, philology first gathers its real blossoms and fruits. The growth of the languages can only then be traced to its ultimate conclusions, when the modern languages are made the starting point as well as the culminating point of philological investigation.

The question immediately before us today is, What claim have the modern languages to be an integral part of the secondary school course? Our commercial age clamors for a practical education, an education that will assist the student to enter the race in the struggle for existence with a chance to compete successfully with his fellow-competitors. It is my opinion that the schools should not too readily yield to this clamor, but should rather assume a conservative attitude; for it is they that link the present to the *past* as well as to the *future*. They should, therefore, look farther than the immediate demands of the time. They cannot make it their object primarily to turn out artisans, or artists, scholars, or professional men, but they must direct their efforts towards producing all-round human beings, educated up to the culture of the present day. The education for special callings must follow the general training.

It is remarkable, however, how few of the patrons of our schools look at education in this way. With them, the "bread and butter" question is the most important and it demands recognition. The interest which the common man takes in education, especially in this country with its democratic institutions, has gradually caused the schools to come in closer contact with actual life. It is, therefore, desirable that the subjects taught at school should have a practical as well as an educational value.

The modern languages answer these requirements in an eminent degree. They give the student a valuable linguistic discipline by making him compare the idioms and constructions of his own language with those of the foreign tongue. They open up to him a beautiful literature and the thoughts and sentiments of another race, and thus enrich his own soul and intellect. They make him more broad-minded by teaching him that there are other races who have fought the battle of existence and of civilization outside of his own, and that there are other nations beyond the confines of his own that have written pages of history.

Of the practical side we need say little here. The commercial spirit which has entered the lists of the world, in the conquest of new markets, takes care of that. We will only say that the professors in our universities find it necessary to direct their students to study the modern languages if they would do the best work in their various departments.

With the growing importance of the modern languages there has also taken place a corresponding development in the methods of teaching them. At first, they were taught either without any system whatever, merely with the object of learning to speak them, or in the same manner as the dead languages. Then there were the adherents of the "natural method," who promised to make the learning of the language as pleasant and as facile as the child learns its mother tongue. They produced, however, only superficial results. In Europe the advocates of the *phonetic* method found many followers within the last few decades.

But of late there has been a revulsion from all of these special methods. It is now recognized by the most advanced educators that the study of a foreign language must at the same time furnish linguistic discipline, i. e., it must give the student a better command of his mother tongue. The severe drill of the ancient languages must be combined with the advantages which the modern languages offer as such. To this end, the grammatical laws of the language are made the basis of instruction; with this is combined drill in the spoken language; the student is introduced into the foreign literature as early as possible, and his literary taste is appealed to and developed; he is made acquainted with the manners and customs of the people whose language he studies by being brought in direct contact with their modes of feeling and thinking; all kinds of helps, such as maps, illustrations, etc., are used to enliven the instruction; in short, "Let there be Life!" is made the watchword, in order that the student's interest may be aroused to the highest pitch, for it is recognized that interest is the soul of instruction. But not the least important of all, his conception of the human race is broadened by making use of the achievements of modern philology: the history of words, and their changes in form and meaning, are occasionally brought to his attention; the close relationship existing between English and other European tongues is made clear, and he learns the important lesson that language is not something dead and petrified, but that it is a living and ever growing organism.

It is apparent that such teaching and such learning possess a high educational and disciplinary value. But to teach the languages with such results, *we need competent teachers*. It is only too true that in the past the modern languages have too often occupied the position of a stepchild in the school course. Any one that could speak a few words in the foreign tongue, or had acquired it by some lightning process—perhaps in a six weeks' course, or had taken it a year or two at the university—was considered good enough to teach the class. On the other hand, no other teacher is so readily criticized as the teacher of modern languages. Anybody that has a smattering of the language or knows some dialect of it, considers himself called upon to find fault with the teacher's accent, and everybody claims to know much better than the teacher, by what method he should teach. What we need, then, is teachers who are masters of their subject, who have a thorough knowledge not only of the grammar of the language, and who can speak it, but who also have a good literary and philological training, as well as a liberal education in other branches. Such teachers will not be easily swayed by criticism, for they know what they want, and they are confident that the results of their teaching will be generally satisfactory in the end.

Some of the arguments in favor of the study of foreign languages apply as well to the study of the ancient languages. But we think that the modern languages have a few advantages over the ancient ones, from an educational as well as from a practical point of view. They come nearer home; we find in them modern life and modern ideas, brought down to the present day, and not removed from us by thousands of years; they are more or less similar in construction with English; for that reason, the student makes better progress in them and sooner obtains actual results. The argument that Latin makes the acquisition of modern languages easier, is unpedagogical, for such study makes the pupil proceed from the more complex to the simpler. It often happens that, owing to the wide gap existing between English and Latin, the student is discouraged and abandons all language study forever. A modern language is a much better introduction to Latin than *vice versa*. This is recognized in European secondary schools, where the tendency is to begin with a modern language, and it has been found that, under those circumstances, as much is accomplished in Latin in *six* years as formerly in *eight*.

It is to be regretted that the study of the modern languages is not more encouraged by our State University, but, on the contrary, is discouraged by discriminating in favor of the ancient languages. The present entrance requirements compel smaller high schools who can afford to teach but one foreign language to decide upon Latin in order that their students may be enabled to enter the chief departments of the University, when a modern language would often be of greater benefit to the majority of the students and more acceptable to the community. Some of the Eastern universities have recognized this and have removed Latin from the list of subjects *required* for admission, but it seems those liberal views have not yet reached our university. We representatives of modern culture ask nothing unreasonable. All we ask is that the modern languages be given a fair chance, and that they be placed on an equal footing with the ancient languages, and we are confident that the relation between them will in time adjust itself.

In conclusion, I wish to refer to a conference of principals and teachers of secondary schools which was recently held in Cleveland, and which has made the following recommendations: The triennium should be made the basis of the school system; the primary and grammar schools should consist of three years each; then there should be a lower and an upper high school, each of three years; the college course giving the degree of A. B. should be three years; special studies and post-graduate work should then be pursued for three years more, leading up to the degree of Ph.D. (The secondary schools of France have recently been reorganized on the same basis.) The conference further recommends that a modern language should be begun in the first year of the lower high school, and Latin in the third. Greek should be taught at college. These suggestions seem to be admirable, and it seems desirable that we here in California should work toward the end of obtaining such a well organized educational system.

I close with the plea that the modern languages be given a proper place in the school course, and that they be put in the hands of teachers who are well prepared, and we are confident that they will win for themselves the position which they by rights ought to occupy.

* * *

Latin as a Formal Discipline

Frank Morton

The subject has been so long and thoroughly discussed that one cannot hope either to shed new light upon it or even to say old things in a new way. But the "new education" is putting the old to the test, especially by urging a new viewpoint, education for action by action, and the old must show its efficacy to give the desired product or fall. Oddly enough, while the "new" is gaining many a convert, the old, so far as the subject of Latin is concerned, has gained tremendously in students, 174 per cent in ten years ending with 1898, in which year, out of 554,814 secondary-school students in the United States, 274,293 were studying Latin. This proportion was exceeded only by the students of that other formal study, algebra, whose per cent of increase for the ten years, however, was less than that of Latin—141 per cent. The claim that the adherents of the study of Latin are driven to the last ditch is rather amusing in face of these facts, just as if a general, with an army in point of position, numbers, and *discipline,* far superior to that of his enemy, should be put in desperate straits because, forsooth, cut off from his base of supplies. On the other hand, the "content" studies have made much less gain, with the exception of history, for which Dr. Hall has given a lame excuse, and a lamer explanation for the increase in Latin students.

Is there such a thing as formal discipline of mind, has it value, and does the study of Latin give it?

We have heard much in these latter years of the "dogma of formal discipline," an expression used as a term of reproach for such studies as Latin. In common understanding, we mean by formal discipline of mind the training and development of the various powers or qualities of mind, "powers" being here understood to mean, not as in the old-fashioned psychology, but the various functions of the mind or the modes in which its acts. Thus, the mind acts now as memory, now as discrimination, now as judgment, always as attention. By discipline or training we develop an ability to remember, to discriminate, to judge, to attend. The mind, oft exercised in these various fashions, acquires a habit of remembering, of discriminating, of reasoning, of attending. We may go a little farther and higher. The mind as form and subject works on the material as object, recalling, discriminating, analyzing, synthesyzing, relating; in other words, organizing the unrelated matter into a thoroughly related whole.

This development and training is just as real and useful as is the training of the hand in skill and delicacy of touch, and in habits of work—also a formal discipline. And as this skill and delicacy, these habits, trained by one sort of material have an acquired power good for use in other sorts, so, in greater degree, good memory, discrimination, attention developed by one study, have value for other fields, although, in both instances, new material presents new qualities for exercise.

In fine, aside from those studies which provide the common mental tools to enable us to exist, what would all the material presented to the mind by education count for, except as furnishing the means for acquiring power and momentum? At best, we store up but a modicum of useful facts for common life, and retain these only by frequent repetition in experience. In the specialized field of our life-work we gather and retain a body of facts whose magnitude is in direct proportion to narrowness of life.

There is, then, such a thing as formal mental discipline, and it has value.

Does the study of Latin give it?

The study of Latin, in the first place, trains the memory, not by repetition of mere meaningless words and sounds, but as images or ideas in relation to other images or ideas. It develops an ability to remember, not alone Latin vocabulary and forms, but also anything worth remembering in any sense. (In all this argument I, of course, assume a proper method of teaching Latin.)

The study of Latin increases the power to discriminate. This power is constantly exercised, as in discriminating the different form endings and the different meanings of words. Following close upon this is the power of analysis, by which the pupils take apart the words of a sentence, investigate their relations to one another as shown by their form and position, and relate them into a connected whole. Through this necessary constant analysis and relating there is also acquired a habit of concentration, a power to focus and hold attention upon the matter in hand.

Finally, the study of Latin gives an

ability to put forth effort. Latin is a strenuous subject. Consciously the pupil meets and overcomes difficulties. He gains courage, nay, desire to meet and overcome others. Here we come upon the ground of the "new school" that wishes everything translated into terms of action; but we cannot allow action to be restricted to physical, muscular action, as one might easily infer is meant by the great apostle of this school, Professor John Dewey, in his "School and Society," although Professor Dewey certainly does not intend so to restrict it. Mental effort, even of the purely intellectual sort, is the best form of action, and the study of Latin provokes it.

It may be asked if Latin is of superior or even equal value as a formal discipline to algebra or science or manual training. To this question reply is made that it is of superior value in the writer's judgment to any of these subjects in the training of the memory—its value in this respect would be considerably greater if the study were begun two years earlier than is the present general custom in our high school—and at least their equal in the training of discrimination and ability to make effort, this latter being perhaps of the purely mental sort.

But, it is argued, you have no proof of these claims you make for the study of Latin. The only absolute proof, by the nature of the case, lies in the argument, and if the writer or any one else cannot make it logical and conclusive it is insufficient and the thesis is not proven. Outside of the argument, the proof is the same that the natural scientist has for all his conclusions, namely: I have found my hypothesis true in all the cases examined; hence I infer it to be generally true. Of course, this is not absolute proof, but it finds general acceptance. Unfortunately, we cannot get at the mind with the scalpel, or even with the microscope, hence cannot demonstrate probabilities by the senses and cannot satisfy those whose convictions come to them only through the senses. After allowing 50 per cent of a person's mental make-up to inheritance from parents, 25 per cent to inheritance from grandparents, five per cent to acquired qualities from a vigorous stepmother, if he is so fortunate as to have had one, and ten or fifteen per cent to the various influences outside the school, Latin has little left on which to leave a mark. Besides, we could come closer to a satisfactory judgment in the matter if we could take a student, put him through a course of Latin with other studies, evaluate the product; and then, dispossessing him of everything that came to him after he began the Latin, put him through exactly the same experiences, but putting in place of Latin whatever study we wished to make comparison with, and again evaluate. Again unfortunately, we must compare one mind with another, neither of whom has had anything like the same experiences and heritage as the other.

In the school in which the writer has been employed for a number of years we have had curricula containing strong Latin courses, curricula containing strong modern language courses instead of Latin, curricula containing no foreign language courses, their place being supplied by an equivalent amount of work in English, science and mathematics. We have also had a sprinkling of students coming from good manual-training schools. Of all our students, those having Latin courses were —on the average—the strongest, especially in alertness of mind, in discrimination, in memory, in power to think and get at thought. This has been true with students of equal equipment in other respects, so far as we could determine, and this is a formal discipline. How much of the advantage came from the study of Latin, who can say?

In my experience with teachers, those are the best in ability to instruct, in method and clearness of presentation, who have studied Latin; and this is true of science teachers, as well as of history and English, and this is formal discipline. How much of this superior ability is due to Latin, who can say?

GRAMMAR SCHOOL SECTION

Charles C. Hughes, Chairman   Miss Lois Peckham, Secretary

Minutes

The Grammar Grade Section of the State Teachers' Association of California was called to order in the auditorium of the Los Angeles State Normal School building, at 9 o'clock, A. M., December 31, 1902, by Charles C. Hughes of Alameda, chairman.

The following program was carried out:

Music — Violin solo, "Madrigale" (Simonetti), Miss Holladay.

"The Function of the Grammar School Principal," G. Dudley Kierulff, principal Mastick Grammar School, Alameda.

Is the Course of Study Overcrowded? Is There a Remedy?" George S. Wells, principal Lincoln Grammar School, San José.

"Teaching of Literature in the Grammar Grades." Miss M. R. Duraind, Hamilton Grammar School, San Francisco.

"The training of the Grammar School Teacher," Henry Suzzallo, San Francisco Normal School.

Mrs. Ella F. Young, who was to have given a paper on "American History in the Elementary Schools," failed to appear, claiming that the time allotted her was too short for the lengthy paper that she had prepared.

Moved by Mr. Henry Suzzallo, seconded by several, that we organize a permanent Elementary School Association, and that a committee of three be appointed by the chair to draft a constitution and to also act as a nominating committee to make a report on Friday morning, January 2, 1903. Carried.

The chair appointed R. D. Faulkner, Miss M. R. Duraind, and George D. Kierulff.

The Section then adjourned to meet Friday, January 3, 1903.

January 2, 1903.

The Grammar Grade Section was called to order at 9 A. M. by Charles C. Hughes of Alameda, chairman.

The following program was carried out:

Music—"The Bells of St. Michael's Tower," (Sir Stewart), Laurel Quintet.

"The Grammar School Course as a Preparation for Life," Supt. F. A. Wagner, Pomona.

"What the High School Expects of the Grammar School," Lewis B. Avery, principal Union High School, Redlands.

"The Grammar School and Secondary Subjects," C. E. Keyes, principal Lafayette School, Oakland.

"Teaching History in the Grammar Grades," Miss Julia C. Coffey, Spring Valley Grammar School, San Francisco.

"Historical Chart Teaching," Mrs. M. M. FitzGerald, for Miss Christine Hart, vice-principal Longfellow Grammar School, San Francisco, who was unable to be present.

The report on "Formation of Permanent Elementary School Organization and Nomination of Officers," was then presented by the chairman of said committee, R. D. Faulkner.

It was moved and seconded that the first two recommendations of the report be adopted.

1. That a permanent association of those interested in elementary education be formed, the same to be known as

the "California Elementary School Association.
2. That the general constitution drafted and submitted by your committee be adopted as that of the association.
Carried.
R. D. Faulkner then takes the chair and a motion is made, seconded and carried, that the third recommendation as given by the committee be adopted, viz:
3. That the following nominations for the offices to be filled for the ensuing year be adopted: Mr. C. C. Hughes, president; Miss R. F. English, vice-president; Mrs. Fannie Byram, secretary and treasurer.

The Section now adjourns to the Domestic Science Department of the Los Angeles Normal School and a paper on "Domestic Science" is given by Mrs. Jessica Hazzard, Director of Domestic Science, Los Angeles Normal School.
Adjournment.

LOIS PECKHAM, Secretary.

* * *

Organization of Elementary School Association

Your committee reports the following three recommendations:

1. That a permanent association of those interested in elementary education be formed, the same to be known as the "California Elementary School Association."
2. That the following general constitution drafted and submitted by your committee, be adopted as that of the Association.
3. That the following nominations for the offices to be filled for the ensuing year be adopted: Mr. C. C. Hughes, president; Miss R. F. English, vice-president; Mrs. Fannie Byram, secretary-treasurer.

Constitution of the California Elementary School Association.

ARTICLE I.

This association shall be known as "The California Elementary School Association."

ARTICLE II.

Its objects shall be to advance the interests of elementary education thru unity of effort in the study of educational problems and in the recommendation of needed legislation.

ARTICLE III.

Its regular time and place of meeting shall be the same as that of the California Teachers' Association. Other meetings may be held at such time and place as the association may designate.

ARTICLE IV.

All persons interested in elementary education are eligible to membership.

ARTICLE V.

SECTION 1. The officers shall be a President, a Vice President and a Secretary-Treasurer to be elected at the annual meeting.

SEC. 2. There shall be an executive committee consisting of the officers and four other members to be appointed by the President.

SEC. 3. The duties of the officers and executive committee shall be such as usually devolve upon such officers and committee. In addition, it shall be the particular business of the executive committee to act with the President in arranging and providing a suitable program for the annual session of the association, and in appointing such committees for the investigation of elementary school problems, and the recommendation of needed legislation.

SEC. 4. The Executive Committee shall meet at the call of the President. Four members shall constitute a quorum.

Literature in the Grammar Grades
Miss M. R. Durain

The importance of the study of literature in our elementary schools is universally conceded. For the past ten years the attention of the educational world has been focused upon this branch with the result that, all over the length and breadth of the land, it occupies a more or less prominent place on every school program. Teachers' institutes, educational conventions, and school reviews have discussed the subject from almost every point of view until it seems that nothing more remains to be said. Under these circumstances, it is exceedingly difficult to find anything new to place before you for your consideration this morning, and I claim your kindly indulgence if what I have to say sounds trite. At the outset, I must frankly disclaim all pretensions to originality, for I am sensible of the fact that "abler minds have said with masterly good sense precisely what I have thought and felt all the time."

No one can overestimate the importance of literature in the life of a people. The sociologist is just beginning to perceive that literature in some form is at the basis of almost every social movement. It is literature that creates the thoughts and sentiments of a people and molds their entire course of action. Literature is the handmaid of religion. It affects legislation. It changes habits and customs. It preserves and perpetuates the highest ethical and intellectual traditions of a country. It is the only living voice that goes echoing down the ages. In it the very soul and spirit of a race are preserved for the benefit of civilization. It inspires the national conscience with the highest ethical ideas, spreads among the masses the love of the beautiful, sounds the warning note of revolt against the tyranny of oppression and injustice, enlarges human sympathies, inculcates hope and courage, and calls forth the latent energy and creative power of man

What does America stand for? Pre-eminently for political liberty and self-government. In a recent address, Professor Eliot, of Harvard University, enumerates among America's contributions to civilization, the principles of arbitration, of religious toleration, of manhood suffrage, of political equality and freedom for all races, and of the diffusion of material well-being among the population. We Americans are an intensely practical people. We have entered upon an era of great prosperity and are making rapid strides towards the commercial and industrial supremacy of the world. Our energies must not be expended wholly in the amassing of material wealth, but the acquirement of mental and spiritual riches must receive increased attention. We must teach our children higher aims and train them to nobler purposes. To quote the language of Morley: "The great need in modern culture, which is scientific in method, rationalistic in spirit and utilitarian in purpose, is to find some effective agency for cherishing within us the ideal. That is the business or function of literature."

Realizing that our chief aim in the study of literature must be the cultivation of the ideal, what are the books and what the methods best adapted to further this end? Clearly we need here what De Quincy calls the "literature of power," the masterpieces of the world, that represent the life and character of a people in "thoughts that breathe and words that burn." History is the record of the heroic deeds of brave men and fair women, but literature breathes the breath of life into the "cold, inanimate clay," and lo! the dead "live and move and have their being," clothed in the picturesque garb of a by-gone age, instinct with a sturdy faith, a simple piety, and a brotherly love that have their lesson for this selfish, sordid, money-getting age; displaying even in their little foibles, harmless vanities, and childish superstitions, that provoke our smiles, yet somehow bring them nearer to us, that "touch of nature which makes the whole world akin."

Because it enlarges and informs the spirit as to the deeper meaning and mysteries of life, the appreciative reading of a good book is the greatest of all educators. To read intelligently, children must have clear ideas of the meaning and value of words; not isolated words, but words "in their social order," linked together in the phrase that illuminates the mind. This knowledge can come only from study, not of the dry bones of philology, but of the literature illustrative of high thought and tinged with strong emotion. Reading simply to pass away the time counts for nothing. It is only when we raise ourselves to the spiritual level of an author and enter into his creative thought, making his experience wholly ours, that we can be said to understand him. We want then, to teach children how to read so as to get at the heart of books. The effort to concentrate the attention at that formative age when the brain is "wax to receive and marble to retain," will bring a rich reward in the future by filling the mind with ideas, stimulating thought and exciting interest and ambition.

The one thing necessary is that the pupils rightly *understand* and *feel* what they read. All explanation, comment and collateral reading should be subordinate to this vital purpose, else the pupils' minds will be lost in a maze of petty detail and fail to grasp the principle of unity, which is the first and fundamental law of every true classic. Full comprehension of meaning on the part of the child is not necessary. As Colonel Parker says, "A taste of a great thought is far better than the full comprehension of a small one." Hence do not labor over the grammatical construction of sentences. Reserve the analytical processes of thought for a later period. Read to the children, read with them, help them to get the thought, help them to see the picture; let them drink in the beauty of the language, the music of the verse, the melody and rhythm of sound. It is better that the children should love poetry and be stirred by its beauty and intensity of feeling than that they should be able to define every obscure phrase and dissect every figure of speech. "Gee! that goes right thru you," said a homely little urchin in the sixth grade, on hearing his teacher read "The Midnight Ride of Paul Revere." That is the effect we want to produce; to make the children *feel* the poem, to stir their emotional nature and so reach into that finer world of spirit where grammar and analysis can never enter.

Every true poem possesses an indefinite spiritual element which makes an appeal to our own spiritual nature, and according to the degree of response which we make to this appeal may we be said to know the poem. The point that I wish to make very clear is this: the primary object of all our teaching must be to get this spiritual response. For there is something of infinitely more importance than the acquirement of knowledge or the training of the intellect, namely, the development of the soul, the basis of individual character building.

Probably no more forcible illustration of the value of literature for ideal and ethical training could be given than the following brief passage from Darwin's autobiography: "Up to the age of thirty or beyond it, poetry of many kinds gave me great pleasure, and even as a schoolboy I took intense delight in Shakespeare, especially in the historical plays. I have also said that pictures formerly gave me considerable, and music very great delight. But now for many years I cannot endure to read a line of poetry. I have tried lately to read Shakespeare, and found it so intolerably dull that it nauseated me. I have also almost lost my taste for pictures or music. * * * My mind seems to have become a kind of machine for grinding general laws out of large collections of facts, but why this should have caused the atrophy of that part of the brain alone, on which the higher tastes depend, I cannot conceive. * * * If I had to live my life again I would have made a rule to read some poetry and listen to some music at least once every week, for perhaps the parts of my brain now atrophied would thus have been kept alive through use. The loss of these tastes is a loss of happiness, and may possibly be injurious to the intellect, and more probably to the moral character, by enfeebling the emotional part of our nature." Could the most ardent enthusiast of poetry as a means of training the super-intellectual faculties present a stronger argument in its favor than this pathetic admission from the great scientist who discovered the laws of evolution?

After this momentary glimpse into the deficiencies of a life wholly absorbed in scientific pursuits, we can well understand what Robert Chalmers meant when he said that he raised statues in his heart to the great masters of fiction who first taught him to see beyond the narrow circle of his natal village. In fact, as the lives of many of our greatest writers attest, before the scientific or reasoning powers of the mind are developed, very young children can appreciate through the emotions the concrete forms of human experience as expressed in literature.

Therefore, as soon as children have mastered the externals of reading, let us put in their hands the best and noblest books suited to their age and capacity; and each succeeding year open up new realms of thought and imagination, creating in them that thirst for good literature which is the best and only means of counteracting the flood of cheap juvenile books and pestilential fiction that inundates our land, sapping the brains and undermining the virtue of our growing boys and girls.

But this result never can be accomplished so long as we make examinations the test of proficiency and apply to the literature lesson the same methods pursued in other studies.

For "it is only what people take pleasure in that shapes and determines their characters," and if we wish to cultivate a love for good reading we must make the literature lesson the happiest and most enjoyable period of the day. All must look forward to it with feelings of pleasant expectation and eager longing. The selections must be read again and again until their beauty and charm penetrate into the growing mind and heart. There should not be too much explanation or questioning. Let the text do the work of teaching and conveying the author's message to the hearts of the children.

In my own experience, I have often found that descriptive poetry does not appeal to children, because they have not been taught to observe the changing phenomena of sky and sea, of field and forest. They are much more easily interested in narrative selections. The story charms and interests them from the beginning, the gradual development of the characters heightens their interest, and the final culmination of the plot brings into play their keen sense of justice.

Hence the fairy tales and myths of the primary school should be followed by ballads, lyrics, nature poems and other works of the creative imagination, so as to people the child's thought world with grand and noble forms cast in an heroic mold and animated by singleness of purpose. Not only is it necessary to place the best books in the hands of the children, but the work should be so correlated and bound together as to present a gradual unfolding or development of the world's progress in literature.

In the first two grammar grades short poems, such as Bryant's "White-Footed Deer," Whittier's "Gift of Tritemius," Browning's "Pied Piper of Hamlin," and Arnold's "Forsaken Merman," should be chosen for special study.

After the children have grasped the idea of unity and learned to trace the logical sequence of thought, the study of longer poems, such as Longfellow's "Building of the Ship" and "Evangeline," Lowell's "Vision of Sir Launfal," and Scott's "Lady of the Lake," may be taken up in the last two grammar grades.

Hand-books of methods and devices are so numerous and accessible that it seems superfluous to outline any particular plan of study.

However, if definite topics and special questions be assigned for preparation, better results will be gained than by leaving pupils to their own unaided resources, though sometimes very great interest is excited by making the children ask instead of answer the questions. They will read the selection with eager and absorbing interest to find material for thought questions. Before studying the poem much preliminary work is necessary to bring out the proper geographical and historical setting. Yet it must never be forgotten that "great literature is universal in its appeal, because its essential interest is in the realm of the mind and feelings and not primarily in the realm of historical or geographical fact."

Try to interest the pupils in the personality of the various authors by characteristic anecdotes and interesting details of their early life. Children are always intensely interested in what other children do. Occasionally have ten or twelve pupils read a poem of their own choice, aiming to give full expression to the thought. It is not necessary to make a special study of all the poems read in the class, but aim always to have the pupils grasp the central thought and see the poem as a whole. Be not in too great haste for results. Mere word knowledge comes rapidly, but growth in ideas is a "slow, silent and mysterious process," as are all the great natural processes of life. Be content to sow the good seed, and, in the fullness of time, the plant will blossom and bear abundant fruit. What though other hands than yours gather the harvest?

"To strike or bear, to conquer or to yield,
   Teach thou, a topmost crown of duty, teach.
Though calm and garlandless, thou may'st appear,
   The world shall know thee for its crowned peer."

* * *

Historical Chart Teaching

Miss Christine Hart

In teaching United States history, our aim should be not only to give the pupils a clear idea of the founding and development of their own country, to bring out prominently the striking points connected therewith, and to present those points as simply as possible, but also to develop an interest in the study of history which shall inculcate a desire for historical reading.

This will lead to a recognition of the dignity of character and of the significance and value that it bears in the molding of the world's events.

A knowledge of these things will tend inevitably to develop in the student a sense of love for, and pride in, his own country.

Every teacher has her own method of irradiating with a warm human ray the dry and dusty details which might tend to chill the enthusiasm of the student.

But there is one practical aid upon which every teacher should to some extent rely.

She should be ready with wall maps and blackboard maps, as no history lesson can be properly presented without them.

But the pupil, also, should make charts for himself, filling in the places and events of which he is studying. These are of value not only for giving a clear understanding of questions involved, but are a great saving of time.

Some of our best authors of school histories object to the stories which are so often used to interlard the main facts that the students are called upon to remember. But why?

All children like stories. So do the majority of grown people for that matter. There can be no feasible objection to the pupils reading the romantic and interesting tales of Spanish exploration while at the same time they are learning of Spain's failure to plant successful colonies north of Mexico.

Their hearts cannot fail to be stirred and their imaginations kindled when they read of the struggle of the brave pioneers who settled the Atlantic coast. The stories of the French missionaries and fur-traders of the new world and their contests and compacts with the Indians are full of interest for the children. All of this makes good supplemental reading for the lower grades. But a short time is given in these grades to the actual study of history. Still they should have acquired from their reading a lasting impression which should fix in their minds the historical facts connected with the permanent settlements made by the English, the French and the Spanish. They are then prepared to take up, when they enter the grammar grades, the struggle for supremacy on the North American continent.

We all remember a name or a date when presented to the eye much more readily than when simply heard.

So, when we *tell* children that the English occupied a strip along the Atlantic coast, although claiming the land from ocean to ocean, that the French claimed the whole of the Mississippi Valley, and that Spain claimed all land west of the French possessions, they will certainly remember these facts better if we also *show* them a picture in colors of each nation's claims.

I have here a device, embodied in a series of maps, which will serve to illustrate the point I wish to make.

Let us then place before the pupils a map which illustrates in color the territorial apportionment just mentioned. Let them see for themselves the extent and boundary of the English, the French and the Spanish territory. Let them make similar maps for themselves. A free hand map of the continent of North America, filled in with colored crayons or water colors, can be quickly done in their "busy work time," and they will more surely remember the relative position and territory occupied by each nation after they have drawn and colored them for themselves.

The only one of the inter-colonial wars which should be actually studied is the French and Indian war, which was closed by the treaty of 1763. This was the real struggle for supremacy.

Again, we turn to a colored map to bring clearly before them the terms of the great treaty.

This is a notable landmark. The war for supremacy was ended. On the first map the children see the enormous territory claimed by France represented in the blue. On the second map the blue is no longer to be seen on the continent. France has withdrawn. They will see also that Florida has changed its color from Spanish yellow to English red. They will *see* how these powers of the old world disposed of millions of square miles of territory, and how these vast areas, through the medium of battle and barter, passed from one owner to another.

Then comes the study of the Revolutionary War, with its story of the struggles of eight long years and the birth of the little nation which has since grown to such enormous dimensions.

In studying any war, pupils should of course learn the causes, the decisive battles, and the results.

But what purpose is served by burdening their minds with the dates of every engagement that took place! As one of the best historians says: "A few significant battles are far better than many minor engagements and military details to enable pupils to understand the character of the fighting."

After they have studied the Revolutionary War, let them discover by referring to the changes of color what changes of territory take place. Let them place beside the map that they have drawn and colored a third map showing the territory claimed by England, Spain and the United States after the treaty of 1783.

We have now a new color—green—to represent the new nation, our own United States.

We have the thirteen original states, and the land in dispute between the United States and the different States.

Florida has again changed its color, and wears the Spanish yellow once more, but for a time only.

Oregon is claimed by both Spain and England, as the two colors show, but they will learn later how the growing nation of the United States got a foot-hold there through the cruise of the venturesome American explorer, Captain Gray, who pierced the estuary of the great Columbia and thus led the way for the settlement of the fertile valleys and once trackless forests where rolls the Oregon.

Next year the children all over our land will hear of the celebration in St. Louis over the purchase of Louisiana. They have learned that, by the terms of the treaty which closed the French and Indian War, France withdrew from the continent, giving up all of her American possessions except two small islands in the Gulf of St. Lawrence. How then could the United States purchase from France the enormous territory of Louisiana, comprising over a million square miles, an area greater than the United States of that day?

Again, they turn to the map which shows that in 1800 the enormous valley of the Mississippi has once more taken on blue, the color of France.

True, they have read and repeated that during the Napolionic wars, Spain has ceded the territory back to France, but how much more lasting the impression if they see the *blue* restored to the map, and draw it in miniature with their own hands.

They are now prepared for the fact that this enormous territory takes the United States color green after its purchase in 1803 for $15,000,000. By the gradual introduction of each map, they perceive that the area of the United States is steadily expanding and can realize what tremendous weight this accession of territory must have on the question of free and slave territory which agitated the people later.

We now use a new color—violet—to show how the slavery controversy was settled in 1820, by the Missouri compromise.

Pupils will readily commit to memory the conditions of that compromise, and they will often as readily forget them.

Let them *see* how Missouri, although north of the dividing line, is a slave state, as shown by its violet color, while the remainder of the new territory preserves the green color, which we have selected to represent the United States.

Let the pupils now make a map of the United States territory at the close of the Revolutionary War in 1783, and then add with its date, in a lighter shade of the same color, the different acquisitions. The Louisiana purchase of 1803; Florida, whose purchase was completed in 1821; Texas, annexed in 1845; the Mexican concession of 1848; the Oregon country, which has been claimed by Spain, England and the United States, but which finally became ours in 1846 and the Gadsden purchase of 1853.

Yellow, red and blue have each in turn disappeared, and only green is left to represent a nation which, freed of all conflicting claims, would seem to be embarked upon its triumphant way toward a glorious future of peace and prosperity.

But now comes the re-opening of a vexed question.

In studying the Mexican war, the children will learn how the difficult slavery question was opened afresh by the Mexican cession.

The Omnibus bill of 1850 was not enough to settle this perplexing problem. In 1854 we have the Kansas-Nebraska Act, repealing the Missouri compromise.

Place map No. 8 beside map No. 6, which shows the division of free and slave territory. The pupils see on map No. 6 that no new territory north of 36 degrees 30 minutes, *except Missouri*, is colored violet. Through map No. 8 they learn that by the new law an enormous territory was opened to slavery. Their text books will tell them of the tremendous uproar the Kansas-Nebraska Act occasioned in Congress.

They are now prepared to take up the study of the great Civil War, which for a time tore the country in two, but freed it from the burden of slavery.

Let them make an outline map of the United States, giving the States which remained loyal, green, the color which they have kept throughout, for the United States, the Gulf or Cotton States, which seceded first, black, and those which seceded after the bombardment of Fort Sumpter, pink.

They learn that one of the objects of the Federal government was to gain control of the Mississippi river. The children see from this map whether the battles were fought in Union or Confederate States. They can perceive how the Confederacy was cut in two when the Union forces got control of the Mississippi River, and the "Father of Waters," as Lincoln declared, "once more rolled unvexed to the sea."

Last, let the pupils take an outline map of the world showing the United States with all of its possessions. No nation is represented by a color except the United States.

We have the original territory as they drew it in an earlier map. We have Alaska, purchased in 1867. We have Porto Rico and the Philippines, which they learn that Spain ceded at the close of the Spanish-American War, and the Hawaiian Islands, which were annexed during that same war.

When children study geography, they have their text-books, maps of the divisions, counties, etc., etc.

But the teacher has besides, some larger maps to place before the class, where they can see at a glance such important points as she wishes to call attention to.

The text-books of history have also a few small maps, but it is quite as important that the teacher of history should have larger maps to place before the children to impress upon their memories the changes that take place in the territory of the nations that they are learning about.

Every teacher will, of course, draw blackboard maps to illustrate different points that come up, but the value of the colored map is obvious.

An appeal to the Visual Memory is made and psychologists tell us that the more avenues through which we appeal to the pupils receptivity, the more firmly we implant any idea in the mind. These maps are then strictly psychological in concept, and as they hang around the room as a sequential illustration of the country's development, they form a sort of continued story, whose chapters are distinctly separate, and yet closely linked in a complete whole.

The maps alone will not teach History. They are simply helps.

As I said earlier in my paper, every experienced teacher has her own methods, but a suggestion from a fellow-worker will often bring a ray of light to a perplexed and harassed teacher, who feels as if she had exhausted her resources.

* * *

What the High School Demands of the Grammar School

Lewis B. Avery

There was a time when the high school found it a matter of no small difficulty to make clear to the community its reason for being. That time has passed, and the high school is an accepted part of the school system in many States, and its popularity has been shown by its unprecedented growth and expansion. It has now, for the first time, been admitted to equal rights with its sister institutions above and below it in the matter of depredations upon the California State treasury. For a child of its age, it has shown remarkable vigor and maturity, as its sister institutions can testify. It has not yet succeeded in getting the University well halter broken, but is making steady advancement, and in the midst of this struggle for supremacy it is encouraging to thus receive the capitulation of the grammar school, for to an optimistic mind the request to state our demands can be translated only as unconditional surrender, it yet remaining to decide whether we shall allow you to retain your side arms, State series of text-books and other heirlooms.

When our conquest shall be complete we shall be able to glory in a unified school system—that is, if we can get rid of the small boy, who constitutes an uncertain factor, and will, unfortunately, be very apt to get mixed up in the gearing of any delicately adjusted educational mechanism.

Now, for fear that I may not be able to formulate *all* that the high school demands, it might be well for you to consult all the high-school people of the country, when you will doubtless get a view, as pleasing in its variety as in its expansiveness, of the rich field of labor laid out for you by your dictator and late sister institution, the high school. But should you be unable to follow all the advice thus contributed, just consign it to the crematory—with the exception of my suggestions—and follow your own good sense—enlightened by what I am about to say.

An architect builds his castle in the air. He outlines his plans and specifications. The builder calls his workmen together. The merchant and the manufacturer minister to the material part of the plan. Soon the picture that the architect saw stands for the world to see.

It may be beautiful, but it is dead.

In no such way may the gardener presume to dictate to the growing plant. He may induce the apple tree to bear a larger and more luscious load, but he can never make it bear oranges. It is the tree that decides the fruit. He may picture happy combinations as much as he pleases and undertake to recommend them to nature. He may obtain all the aid that wealth can give, but he cannot get a plant to violate the hidden laws of its own being.

Though one be master of many secrets and learned in all the arts, to accomplish the simplest transformation in the realms of life he must come to the throne of Nature, not as a dictator, but as a suppliant. In dead nature man may dictate. In living nature, the humblest plant may dictate to the king, and the gardener will be its interpreter.

Now when the University dictates to the high school and the high school to the grammar school, we are treating the education of the child as though it were the building of dead material instead of the growth of human life.

It is the need of the child that should dictate, and the teacher and the parent should be the interpreters.

Therefore, I must say that we cannot dictate forms or ideals to you of the grammar school. We can, however, demand that you shall be good gardeners, that you discover the real nature of the plants under your care, and that you so nurture them that you you may turn them over to us vigorous growers. We do not always find them so.

A higher school may not, in my opinion, define the course of study for a lower school except as a temporary expedient, where the lower school has not reached any agreement as to its faith and practice—has not acquired a sufficiently consistent body of belief to be self-directive—has not attained its educational majority.

Prescription by absent treatment is a necessary but unfortunate part of this direction of lower schools by higher. In order that justice may be rendered, all must be served alike, and it is calomel for whatever is the matter as it was with the good old doctors. But this is a necessary evil when the prescribing power knows the individual pupil and the individual community for which the school really exists, only as an average of statistics or as a composite picture. It rests, then, with the teacher to protect the child —to translate the needs of the child and see that they are supplied. If the teacher cannot do this, one who can should be substituted. I would rather trust the present family physician than the absent expert, and not infrequently the good old grandmother can give them both pointers.

I prefer the advice of the teacher who is personally interested in my child to that of the psychologist who knows children only. I do not, in this, reflect upon the value of the expert or of the psychologist. Final responsibility rests on the one who has the individual in charge. It is the present teacher who must break the bread of life to the child. No course of study can relieve her of this responsibility or deprive her of this privilege.

The first thing I would ask, then, is greater opportunity in the grammar-school system for the personality of the individual teacher.

I will send you to the books to find recipes for realizing this happy condition, but I will take time to point to one change that will accompany this accession of a larger freedom for the teacher.

The teacher will be allowed greater liberties with the prescribed work for each grade. The extent cannot well be lessened, for the realm of knowledge is daily becoming more complex. But the teacher will do much more than is now common to create a true perspective founded on the relative importance of the parts. I do not think I misstate when I say that the average teacher is insisting on the nine-tenths that is comparatively unimportant, so far as retention in the mind is concerned, just as strenuously as on the one-tenth that is the key to the subject. Superintendents have been known to fall into the same error. As for County Boards of Education, that is just another case of absent treatment. They do the best they can without seeing the patient, and have to prescribe for Tommy on the supposition that the same thing ails him that killed his brother Johnny.

But if you ask me if there are not some things that the grammar school may do that will directly aid in making the high school more effective, I can say "Yes" with decision.

The high school will be glad of even a small body of knowledge on the part of the entering pupil on which it could depend. At present it has none. The pupils have a large fund of information, more or less accurate, but it is in assorted lots, and it is hard to find a majority of an incoming class that are sure of the same thing. The result is an enormous waste of time on the part of high-school teachers, who have to go over all the ground of preparation for a part of the class. I think I speak of an experience that is not uncommon even where grammar schools are the best.

The field of the grammar school course cannot be decreased. It will rather increase. What, then, is to be done? The same solution that I mentioned as bringing relief to the teacher will equally aid the school in getting a more consistent body of knowledge. In each subject the teacher must give the pupil a few points of view—must separate the material into important and unimportant so far as retention is concerned. To insist on all alike is to get nothing. The bane of the grammar school is attempted thoroughness in non-essentials, which means real thoroughness in nothing. This difficulty will increase with the increase of general knowledge. To insist on everything is to get nothing.

Listen to a reader who emphasizes every word, including his a's, and's and the's, and you are soon wearied. An easy speaker or reader makes so clear the inter-relation of the facts of the sentence that the auditor's effort is not wasted on the machinery of thought.

So the teacher should economize the effort of the pupil. Failing to do so not only kills the subject in hand, but stifles interest.

Let there be a few absolutely certain points in each subject and the rest of the subject will arrange itself.

If we could name to you a thousand words on which we should like absolute accuracy of spelling and you could guarantee them to us, the rest of the words we could care for.

If we could be certain of absolute certainty and speed in a few fundamental processes in arithmetic, the remainder of the book might do for an exercise ground, and I may add that there are yet better exercise grounds than the book.

If we could be assured of the easy use of correct grammatical forms most common in speech and an accurate understanding of the more elementary interdependencies of the parts of the sentence, we would gladly make allowances for the rest.

A body of knowledge cannot be assured without drill, and some seem to think that drill is not in harmony with the doctrines of interest, inductive learning and the like. The understanding of these doctrines has rendered incalculable service to the education of today. Interest is the door to apperception and apperception is the entrance to understanding and all that education means. But teaching so frequently stops short of getting anywhere! Interest is the road, but the road is not a good stopping place—except for tramps. We are apt to make our children educational tramps—always moving, but with no place to lay their heads. Why let them dig out nuggets of gold and leave them ungathered? Why pick up pearls to throw them away? Moreover, the essential things in the field of knowledge are the more essential because they are the keys to future doors.

Inductive learning is the best learning, but when a principle is comprehended, if it is worth formulation, why not impress that formula past effacement if you can? When a classic is appreciated, let it become a part of the soul's furniture for life.

Cut down the essentials as much as you please, but see them everlastingly fixed, and send us pupils with at least a small list of accomplishments on which we can depend. We leave you to prescribe them.

Beyond this small but definite list let the horizon of the pupil sent from the grammar school extend as broadly as it may, to include all the individual can grasp of nature, man and God. Let him revel in biography, literature, travel and science, which he can comprehend and enjoy and come away with what may stick to him.

I have named the more definite part of what we would require if we could. Let me now tell you of an indefinite part that is of much greater importance than anything I have yet given.

We want pupils whose characteristics in certain lines have been largely and definitely developed. With all that is said about the character side of teaching, I am doubtful if much is definitely done in the matter of cultivating those most important characteristics that we of the high school so frequently find wanting. We realize that the task is not an easy one. All we ask is that careful and systematic attention be given to it—not incidental and desultory.

We want girls and boys with ambition to be and to do. Such ambition will necessitate high ideals, responsiveness, persistence and courage.

I believe high ideals are generally instilled in the grammar schools, but the responsiveness, persistence and courage necessary to their accomplishment are too frequently systematically stifled by the predominance of system over teacher. While a teacher is struggling to keep her own head above water she cannot do much to inspire her pupils. She therefore follows the program. The result is the assignment of tasks that are frequently impossible for the pupil or test his willingness past the breaking point, which amounts to the same thing. A horse set to pull against a post is almost sure to become balky, and the higher the spirit the greater the danger, and one already having a balky tendency must be hitched to a load—not that he ought to be able to pull, but that he will pull, and it should be seen that he pulls it.

The difficulty of selecting sufficiently simple work in sufficient variety and amount is increased by poor classification, large classes, and especially by such poorly graded books as California furnishes her children—at the highest market price.

I am presuming that the teacher is endeavoring to keep the work well within the grasp of her pupil. This is sometimes not the case. I know of those who contend that the brain fibers should be stretched a little beyond their capacity every day. The idea used to prevail that heavy clubs and dumbbells were necessary to produce strength, but it soon became evident that it is movement, not resistance, that gives strength. Light weights that can be moved many times to each movement of the large ones will produce not only more and better muscle, but more volition—more willingness to move, and that is half the battle.

Large amount of simple work is what our grades want. That will develop the characteristics I have enumerated.

Responsiveness comes naturally, because it is a pleasure to do what you feel sure you can accomplish. There are no lions in the way.

Activity becomes the normal condition. There is always something doing. They are not satisfied to be educational tramps moving at a jog-trot pace. That is the pace that kills, by the way. They die of *ennui*. Why, it is a common experience, I think, that pupils that are held back till the eighth year before entering school get thru the grades as early, in spite of the hurdles in their path, and I have several instances in mind where they have shown much more life and energy in the high school, and I have thought it was because they never had a chance to become satisfied with the jog-trot gait of repeated failure and conventional dullness.

Courage and persistence are the natural result of simple and abundant requirements. Pupils that do not know what it is to give up will not balk. It is the work that the pupil cannot, or thinks he cannot, do that makes friction in the school and between the home and school, and its certain product is discouragement and indifference. With these qualities in the ascendent, hope gives place to fear as a motive power and real teaching is at an end.

Bring us pupils who have become accustomed to success and do not know failure and we shall have a spontaneous, responsive and courageous army that we can lead to battle with certainty of victory.

One thing more: Send them to us with certain formal habits well established—good use of speech in common conversation. Let them be good readers and writers if you know how to make them—not writers in copy-books, but those who will put up a page with readiness and with care as to form and neatness. Finally, let them be habituated to study effectively.

To accomplish these things, the teacher will have to give up hearing so many lessons and do more teaching. Teaching consists mainly in directing study, not in hearing recitations. I fear it is too largely left to chance as things are now. If the parents are to have any part in the school work, let them hear the lessons and you see them taught. Reversing this process with young children is not only a dismal failure in immediate results. It is productive of evil. It is an educational mistake.

President Eliot says "American teaching has been chiefly driving and judging; it ought to be leading and inspiring."

While the course of study must remain, it is time that teachers took their proper place with regard to it and used it rationally for the attainment of the purpose for which it was planned. They must be freed from the minutiae of the Pharisaic code and advance to the gospel of a genuine—not an assumed—interest in and love for the children under their care.

In summing up, I have asked for more drill on fundamentals and less dull and more inspiration on the remaining nineteen-twentieths of the work; for a simplification of the work with elimination of the difficult material and an increase in variety and amount thus rendered possible; that the teacher shall create perspective in every subject, and in every lesson, that time and effort may not be wasted on the unimportant; that certain characteristics may thus be established, which I have summed up under the general head of "ambition to be and to do"; that some three formal habits be established by deliberate supervision of study; this requires that the teacher teach to study and to do rather than hear recitations to the extent now in vogue. It also requires that the teacher be freed from the burden of minutiae of a fixed course of study.

This deficiency in tools, characteristics and habits seems to me worthy of your attention, teachers of the grades. The suggestions I have made may not be in the line of the correct solution of the problem, although I think they are. They are my personal suggestions from personal observations, and I cannot claim for them that they represent any concensus of opinion or experience.

In conclusion, let me say that we demand of you only what you may equally demand of us, and what every parent of right demands of all teachers of his children—that we shall not be so engaged in running the machine as to overlook individual character as the chief aim of education—that with all our interest in theories we shall share in some degree the parents' anxiety about results—not on the average, but in the individual case.

Less of judging; more of leading.

The Course of Study in the Grammar Schools--Its Limitations

George S. Wells

It is my purpose in this paper to discuss the value of a fixed curriculum and the inadequacy of the present one and to suggest in a general way a possible remedy.

First, let us address ourselves to the proper evaluation of a course of study— Its function. Is it a help or a limitation?

In the olden days of the log schoolhouse, with its puncheon benches, of which we so often hear, there were but two factors of importance in the make-up of the schools —the pupil and the teacher. The course of study was a compromise between the whim of the teacher and the wish of the pupil. The equipment was meager. The house and furniture, as already mentioned, of books and supplies the measure was small. The teachers varied more in the quality than in the quantity of their learning. Few of them had received much school training. Some, however, possessed the true instincts of the scholar and a genius for teaching. Fortunate was the lad who early found companionship with such a teacher. Dr. Dewey says that "The real course of study is the personal face-to-face contact of teacher and pupil." In those olden days this close relation was not limited, except by the capability of teacher and pupil.

Going back to a still older civilization, one loves to think of the Greek philosopher and his group of boys working out those glorious results for the few.

The older schools regarded the individual pupil as the unit, and tho they were greatly handicapped by poor equipment and lack of trained teachers, they were sufficient for the bright pupil. The term's work and subject taught were not primary things. The training of the pupil was viewed as a whole; it was the personal growth and development of the individual that was of primary consideration.

We live, however, in the days of machine-made products. We pass up to the high school and out to the world a large supply, all shaped after one model—that is, our over-systematized schools attempt to give the same training to all, and vainly hope for an equality of development, but, fortunately, the varying quality of the raw material resists our effort and partly defeats us.

I would not be understood as longing for a return to those "golden days." Such methods would be entirely inadequate to meet the complex conditions of the present. The modern graded school is a vast advance, if we consider the total of the results. What I would do is to ask, Is our system the best possible working machine that our intelligence can devise?

It seems to me that our schools have two glaring weaknesses: Lack of flexibility—trying to fit all pupils to the same pattern —over-supervision—trying to fit all teachers to the same pattern. The old schools had too little supervision and system; ours have too much. I do not cry out against a wise and judicious supervision, a supervision that instructs and assists a teacher in personal growth along individual lines, but against a meddling, nagging supervision that hedges in and dwarfs.

The President of one of our universities has said that a good university might consist of an earnest student on one end of a log with an instructor who gets his knowledge at first hand on the other end. That is in valuing the elements that make for the training of youth, the attitude of the student and the ability of the instructor are of the first importance — equipment and organization auxiliary.

We find many of our universities stamping the same approval upon all their graduates, coming from whatever department they may. They may not hold that all learning is of equal worth, yet they rate all training of equal value, and allow a very wide liberty to each department.

Those who are doing supervision work know that a good teacher rises superior to the weaknesses and deficiencies of a course of study, and exercises much freedom in spite of the completeness of the machine organization. She does not teach subjects, but children. She sees education as a realization of the individual through the mastery of subjects. We know also that most of us who teach partake but smally of greatness, and we needs must have our guiding lines; we cannot escape entirely from a schedule of requirements—a course of study.

Yet I fear the expression "course of study" calls up to many teachers visions of uniform examinations, a low class average and all such nightmares, all of which has a tendency to drive a teacher into cramming and grinding, vainly hoping to smooth out the inequalities, and to bring the class to a right dress with toes on the line. Alas for the sparks of genius that may have burned in the souls of some of them when they left their homes at six years of age! Indeed, I know of nothing that tends more to bring our children to the dead level of machine work than the fear of final examinations. Since our schools must be taught by teachers of average ability, geniuses being few, we must be tied by a specific curriculum. Without it I fear the ship would be sailed into unknown seas, among rocks and shoals, and would fail to reach any port at all.

Let us now examine our grammar-school course of study, or rather the results obtained by following it. I suppose I will not be far wrong if I take the course of study of any city or county of California as typical. I will not offer closet opinions, but will present quantitative results, obtained from the careful study of the schools of two cities.

The following questions were asked as to the various classes in these two cities, which I shall designate as City 1 and City 2: "How many pupils have done the school work up to the last promotion in less than the prescribed time?" "How many have done the work in the prescribed time?" "How many have been held over once?" "How many have held over twice?" "How many have been held over more than twice?" "What per cent were held over at last promotion?"

These questions were carefully answered as to 2,353 pupils in City 1, including the whole eight grades in the primary and grammar schools. In City 2 I obtained answers as to 1,822 pupils; here the first grades were omitted on account of known inaccuracies in the statistics; all the other grades were included. In both cities invalids and pupils of less than normal intelligence were omitted.

I find that in City 1, 45 per cent of the pupils in the school at the time of writing this paper (December, 1902) have been held over at least once; 23 per cent have been held over twice; 9 per cent more than twice; about one-third have been held over more than once. I would report, also, that in City 1, 57 1-2 per cent of all pupils that have reached the eighth grade have failed of promotion at least once, and 20 per cent more than twice. At the last promotion in the same city 20 per cent of eighth-grade pupils failed. Now if the same average should hold at the next promotion, we must add about 9 per cent in the failures, making 66 per cent of all those promoted to the high school who will have spent more than eight years in the primary and grammar schools.

In City 2, 50 per cent of the pupils now in school have failed of promotion at least once, 31 per cent have failed twice, and 13 per cent have failed more than twice. In this same city 47 per cent of the pupils now in the eighth grades have failed of promotion at least once. Estimating the per cent of probable failures at next promotion by the per cent of failures at last, we must add to this 4 per cent, which will give us 51 per cent of all pupils promoted to the high school as having made at least one failure.

In each of the two cities the number of failures from the first to fourth grades are much smaller than the number from the fourth to the eighth. Throwing the data of the two cities together, we find that about 9 per cent of the pupils now in school have been able to skip grades; by the same reckoning we find that 42 per cent have been able to keep with their grades and do the work in just the prescribed time.

We shall now attempt to draw some conclusions from this data: What does it signify? What changes should be made?

It is evident that the attempt to fit these 4,000 pupils to the same bed, or to fashion them after the same model has failed. Our figures show conclusively that the attempt in these two cities to have all the pupils do the same work in the same time has failed as to the 58 per cent of the pupils now enrolled, and for 62 per cent of those now in the eighth grade. This, however, only partly shows the inequality of results. Every teacher well knows that the pupils passed at any promotion vary widely in their attainments and abilities. We not only fail to get the same work done in the same time, but fail to get the same done at all.

Our figures do not show, indeed they could not, the number of pupils who have kept along with their classes so easily that they have never been called upon to do their best work. At least the upper one-third of the class waits for the teacher to push or drag the lower third along. When one sees the impatient expression on the face of a bright pupil in a recitation-room he thinks of the impatient youngster on the Fourth of July waiting for the procession to move. These figures show that about one out of every ten have been allowed to push on and do the work in less than the schedule time.

Whether or not eight years hath a magic significance and is the only proper time in which to do the elementary school work, I shall not discuss here. Suffice it to say that it has been substantially agreed on as the proper time, and that the age of six is the proper time to begin the work.

Without discussing the questions fully, basing my opinion upon my experience, I will hold that pupils are not able to do seventh and eighth work before the ages of thirteen and fourteen; that boys and girls do not acquire a maturity and judgment before the ages of fifteen that will enable them to do high-school work in a manner most profitable to themselves. If I am right in this, it would not be desirable to arrange the elementary course of study so as to hurry bright pupils over it in a shorter period than it now requires. Not only would we push our children into work that is beyond their grasp, but we would fail to give sufficient time for the work to sink in and find its proper setting and arrangement in the mental storeroom. The boy cannot learn to swim in one day, nor can he master his fractions in one day or one month. We must give time for the nerve centers to make the adjustments.

There is undoubtedly much waste of time by our bright pupils—an enforced waste of time. Some one may say, no matter, they reach the high school and university young enough. Quite true, and they are well enough qualified educationally to do the work when they get there. A more vital question, however, confronts us. What is their attitude when they get there? Have they lost that thirst for knowledge and desire to do things that they had when they first came to conscious existence? Where is that zeal they had when they were first committed to the teacher's care? Have they lost it? It is the world's right to demand of us an accounting. I would not discount the value of superior mental endowment, yet I believe that the thing to be most highly desired is ability and inclination to work up to one's fullest capacity. Our attention is often called to the success of the plodder. The person long thought mediocre suddenly does something that stamps him as great. In the battle of life nothing but success counts, and success depends not alone upon the strength of the forces, but upon the skill in marshaling them. The boy or girl who passes the first eight years in school with credit so far as per cent is concerned, but who gives not a full measure of effort, has partly failed. That pupil who leaves the grammar school with the ability and inclination to do his uttermost in each undertaking has possessed himself of forces that will carry him to sure victory. The ability to spend the whole self with judgment, when occasion demands, is greatness. Where is the valedictorian? At the front or rear according as he has learned to use all or a part of his resources. "Not failue, but low aim, is crime." A cynic once said in speaking of a boy's chance in the race of life: "If he escape the elementary school teacher his chances are good." I would say if the teacher can escape machine requirements and grow as God started her, the pupil need not escape her.

I would not argue that any course of study could cure all the ills and make us to avoid all the errors of our profession, but that a course of study might be so arranged as to help in developing a pupil along the lines of his individual powers and bent. In a course of study a machine teacher finds her refuge, an original teacher her limitation, but, at the same time, her escape from chaos.

That more than 50 per cent of our pupils who are enrolled in our grammar schools have already failed one or more times to do a term's work in a term's study, and that 63 per cent of those who finish the work of these schools fail of promotion one or more times demand an investigation. Not only the loss of the time of the pupil, but the loss of zeal and the discouragement on the part of the pupil claim our attention. O that he might remain "open-doored to God and opportunity!"

We cannot lay all this at the door of poor instruction unless we rate all our teachers as poor. The work must be done by the teachers that we have, and let us not scold, but make all we can of the situation, hoping that a higher culture will be demanded of the new enlistments into our ranks; but let us remember that these additions are made slowly, and we must always look to the forces in hand for our results.

Any supervisor who will begin at the highest grade and pass down through the classes, noting the attitude and bearing of the pupils, must be struck with the increase of freshness and originality as he approaches the first grade, and when he reaches the receiving class, what a restful and hopeful feeling possesses him! Here he finds the joy of work, that springtime of endeavor that holds the minds of the great in the world. I know it is not possible to retain all of this condition of mind and heart, as the child passes on through the years; that were, indeed, attributing greatness to all, but I do think it possible to save much more of it than we do. A bright pupil will lose much of it if we do not call for his best and whole self; a dull pupil may lose it by being called for accomplishments which lie beyond his resources. One is in danger of perishing of *ennui*, the other from bewilderment.

If you find in the face of a pupil an expression of worry which is likely to pass to indifference, you may safely attribute it to one of two causes: it is a physical disinclination or the effect of poor teaching; the laziness we are responsible for to the extent that we have fostered it by poor teaching; poor teaching may consist in the matter taught or in the manner of teaching.

The manner of teaching is not primarily under discussion here, but the matter that is to be taught, and I will now call your attention to that phase of the question. Notwithstanding the cry against machine uniformity, we are still striving for uniform results—still trying to have the pupils learn the same amount of the same things in the same time. This has a partial justification. It is necessary that everybody should learn to read. How well? As well as his powers will admit of. The only equality of results we are here justified in expecting is the full measure of each individual's capacity. Each pupil should learn to write. How well? Well enough to make the art of the greatest possible use to himself. In fact all the various elements of learning and accomplishment that come near to the every-day life of the individual is his just inheritance, and we are the administrators; they are entitled share and share alike.

The plan of individual instruction does not commend itself as workable unless we go back to the simplicity of the Greeks and let each teacher have a few self-selected pupils. This is not to be thought of where the many are to be educated. Yet it seems possible that we may replace some of the worst features of our system by what would be an approach to the individual system.

Let us have a course of study that prescribes a minimum amount of work for the eight years; one that demands an acquirement of knowledge that is within the possibilities of any child that possesses enough capacity to class him above feeble-mindedness. This should be fundamental, and should answer as nearly as possible to the demands of every-day life. This minimum course should be limited by the capacity of the lower fraction of the class—say one-third. To the next third give the same fundamentals, but enriched by that which will give a wider development and greater growth. To the higher third give all this with still greater enrichment. I would not, however, give opportunity for a shortening of the time for the brighter pupils, but give greater chance for individualizing. At the end of a period I would promote to the next grade to a like classified grouping. It should always be possible at any time for a pupil to be passed from a lower to a higher or from a higher to a lower grouping, as effort and capacity justified, but to not advance in grades ahead of time, thus always keping the pupil upon work suitable for his years. The number of groups to the class that I have suggested is only tentative. That is a matter to be worked out by trial. It is the grouping plan that I offer, though not claiming originality for it. At least I am not the first to present it.

I do not say that this would entirely redeem us from the "lockstep," nor do I think we should be wholly redeemed. When we consider the multitudes of men and women that constitute the moving world, we are struck with the multiplicity of individuality, and, at the same time, with the wonderful sameness of pattern.

To be wholly individual is to be a freak. The world, moves in a large measure in "lockstep." Your knowledge and mine, your wants and mine, your experiences and mine have many points in common. In this somewhat indifferently suggested plan we have still our groups of pupils from whom we demand an average of results, but the groups are much smaller than the present ones. The possibility of a pupil placing himself in the proposed groups where his effort and ability justify would put a premium upon individuality. This plan would also unfetter the original teacher and give her a chance to work out her individuality; she could be judged by the ability she showed in making these optional increments to the minimum course. The genius of the teacher, if she possessed any, would have opportunity of development in the guiding and encouraging of personal effort and originality in bright pupils, for the possible increments to the course of study should not be rigidly prescribed, but suggested only. Best of all, this would be the dull pupil's opportunity. He would not be swamped and disheartened in vain endeavor to do things which do not appeal to him, nor cannot connect themselves with his life as he is enabled to see it. By working upon things that come within his comprehension and touch his life, his originality would be called out, for he has it as well as the bright pupils. Indeed, it would seem to offer a chance for the self-realization of both teacher and pupil, whatever the natural resources of either might be.

In this paper I have tried to show the necessity of a course of study and the unworkableness of the whole individual plan, things assumed by most teachers, yet cried against by our critics. I have offered evidence tending to show that the present course is not adapted to the capabilities and possibilities of all pupils; that it offers too little for some and too much for others and meets the needs of but few. I have somewhat vaguely suggested a plan upon which a course might be constructed that would meet the needs of the pupils better and come nearer to them, and make it possible to save a larger measure of that mental freshness that is a part of God's endowment to us all.

The Scope and Duties of the Principal in Relation to the School

George Dudley Kierulff

The scope and duties of the principal in relation to the school fall under three general heads:

I. In relation to teachers as supervisor of:
1. Professional training.
2. Discipline.
3. Class.

II. In relation to pupils as supervisor of:
1. Manners and morals.
2. Studies and methods.

III. In relation to parents as supervisor of:
1. School interests.
2. Pupils and teachers.

He stands as the pivot betewen the central power and the school; between the pupil and the teacher; between the parent and the teacher. He stands for the combination of unified control with diffused responsibility. He must be an educational officer of zeal and intelligence if he would secure the betterment of school conditions; progressive, and knows how to inspire his teachers and pupils with high ideals.

The world turns aside to let a man pass, if he knows whither he is going.

The principal of a modern school cannot be dogmatic, yet his ideas, his principles, must contain the element of conciseness, for without a syllabus of methods analyses and classifications and provisionally formulated laws, he has no basis for organization and supervision. The question of environment, of conditions, also, must be considered. He must possess a summary of opinions slowly evolved through daily experience.

The principal has a three-fold function:

1. He examines in order that he may test the possession of knowledge on the part of teachers or pupils.

2. He inspects in order that he may determine the quality of work and so control or organize the management.

3. He supervises in order that, as an adviser and friend, he may point out errors and suggest remedies, encourage honest efforts and welcome signs of improvement in methods of instruction or discipline.

He must be more than a teacher. It is only by regarding each of these functions that the principal may bring his work into accord with that of the teacher and that of the pupil, and thus unite for a common purpose all the interests of the school.

I. In relation to teachers:
1. Professional training.

The principal must be looked to, to encourage and promote the professional training of his assistants. He should be the mediator between the teacher and archives of learning. He cannot shift the burden of subject matter to the text-book. His own personality interjected into the subject will be the residuum which his teachers will carry away. He should cause teachers day by day to see, and to understand as a whole, the structures they are molding and developing. His attitude must be such as to inculcate methods of observation and interpretation. If he cannot give direct information, he should be able to sugest a way of finding out.

The exercise of personality, directive influence, gives a teacher encouragement and self-confidence. Teachers young in experience crave a little sympathetic guidance. It enables them to overcome difficulties, to gain interest. Frequent conferences, then, should be held by the principal with his teachers, at which questions of doubt should be thoroughly discussed and settled; the course of study considered; new books criticised; new work outlined. These conferences may be (1) with all the teachers, or (2) with groups, or (3) with individuals; but conferences there should be. The principal can lose power or gain by these meetings. His influence, his personality, should be adaptive and creative. No teacher can be dull or spiritless under a principal of enthusiastic research and productive energy.

2. Discipline.

Give teachers to understand, in the first instance, that indiscreet acts of discipline will be disavowed. It does not lower a teacher's dignity to acknowledge an error to pupils. Drill your teachers in the ethics of the profession and insist upon their observance. Discountenance gossip for the mere sake of gossip. It belittles the opinion of those that listen and discredits the one that tells it.

Teachers have a right to demand that a principal know children's ways. No teacher will respect her principal if he do not know. There must be no debatable ground over which teachers can wrangle.

He must allow his teachers to exercise as much personality and individuality as possible. He should stand ready to shield them from criticism for general management, from politics; to counsel them from probable difficulties. Those who know how to control themselves will control others; that have learned to obey, will be obeyed.

He should demand from them as little clerical work as possible, yet sufficient to give all necessary information. Blanks properly ruled and worded will be of great assistance to them and will insure him uniformity and conciseness of records.

He must be guarded that his supervision and organization do not trend too much toward officialism and formalism. They become a burden to teachers in their classroom when they do not work for true pedagogical ends. This kind of discipline, too, reacts on pupils and distracts their attention from study for its own sake. It lowers the *esprit de corps* of the teachers, the tone of social solidarity of the school. The principal whose teachers do not break down from fatigue is always on the lookout for excess of energy. He aims to make his teachers quiet, positive, strict, forward, for these secure best results with the least expenditure of energy. The teacher should be energetic, but the energy should count. She should be direct, clear, plain.

A principal never should criticise a teacher unless his criticism is based upon a full technical knowledge, expressed from an empirical standpoint—not by way of attack or defense or ridicule, but just a fair, truthful statement. He must be enough suggestive and informing to carry teachers over difficult places.

A careful study of his teachers and a conscientious report of them to his superiors will seldom fail to bring about better results in the personnel of his corps. Work for cheerful and pleasant surroundings for them in the building.

3. The class.

The methods of instruction which make for individual initiative, independence and freedom of action should obtain amongst his teachers. The principal must strive to place before his corps and his pupils American ideals in the social, industrial and political life, thus fitting for citizenship and for life.

It is the business of the principal to see that his teachers come down to the pupils and meet them on their own plane; not on all planes of their being, but on their highest. He must have the discernment to see this higher plane if his teachers cannot.

He must work uphill, uphill till he get to the point of uphill maximum. See that his assistant makes the subject yield up what it has to give and then quit it. Care must be exercised that just enough work be given in a given time, and that it be done. Proportion is one of the chief things the supervisor must work for. We can be too thoro. Children must be led many times thru a subject. Be watchful of the teacher that insists on constant thoroness.

A wise principal will work for and secure co-operation among his assistants. There must be this co-operation to make a unification of the studies and to make organization. He will foster and promote a close sympathy of the teacher with the pupil. The vital point is personal contact of pupils with teachers of fine principles, fine personal qualities, cultivation, ideas and sentiments.

Success will come to the principal who has the ability to arouse, to set on fire, to animate his assistants. He needs constantly to advise and direct here, stimulate and inspire there. Under such a man the highest type of school spirit will prevail among both teachers and pupils.

II. In relation to pupils:

1. Manners and morals.

Comprehensive and patient inquiries, observations and experiments, form the basis in dealing with the moral and intellectual delinquent pupils. Theoretical categories must be filled in with concrete material. Such pupils cannot be created except individually.

I believe that idealism in discipline will not prevail.

The principal who has in view to make his pupils good citizens, to prepare men and women to live well and helpfully with other men and women will train them to three duties: (1) obedience; (2) reverence; (3) order.

1. Obedience: To do what they are told. Obedience is a habit, and that is what we want children to get—the habit of minding. They must take orders; they must fall into line. Society demands respect for authority.

2. They must be taught reverence.

(a) Reverence for authority, for things that are great.

(b) Reverence for life's beauties.

(c) Reverence for life's nobilities—the church, society, the home.

They shall have faith; you must have religion if you want reverence, if you would build up the ideals and the enthusiasm.

3. They must be taught order; a sense of duty, conscience, a sense of responsibility.

The school is here to prevent anarchism. The school is here to rebuke anarchism. The school is here to root out anarchism.

Almost all discipline in school could be obtained by "customary courtesy," the cultivation of amicable relations. It gives the school the tone and feeling of social solidarity. Children get the basis of acting and doing from individuals about them. We cannot bring children to distinguish between right and wrong life, doing, by merely giving it to them in literature. They must see it enacted. They must be able to see the bottom of the dark pit. Knowing and doing come from imitation. Their character, conduct, truth side, intellectual side, come from seeing these sides in others around. They must be able to discriminate.

If he would be successful with his pupils in his discipline, let the principal seek to know their native interests and natural tendencies. He cannot leave this to his assistants alone. He will maintain the position of constant preparedness. He will carefully grade motives and make the punishment fit the crime.

Let his rules be so cast as not to call to mind the thing to be avoided, but rules for governance there must be and there *must* be obedience.

Oftentimes the troublesome pupils are such because they need some new work; they have reached the plane where a change takes place, and the new wants must be met. They should be dealt with as individuals, not with the mass. The undisciplined boy often is of the purest gold within, but he needs a careful, analytical, refining process to bring out the good character traits. If this method fail, it is high time his presence should cease to be a menace and a contamination. Remember, we are preparing for citizenship, and that the lives of a body politic *must* be lived *within the circle of the law.* In the matter of infractions of rules, the intent and consciousness of the offender always must be considered. I said above that motives should be graded.

The greatest need in the matter of discipline, however, is to reach the parent. The principal will meet with greater success if he communicates with the parent or can meet the parent personally at the school. Such a policy seldom fails to bring immediate and satisfactory co-operation, and, at any rate, it throws the responsibility for future misconduct on the parent. In my own experience in a school of nearly 800 pupils I never have failed to find this method the most expedient.

Again, I believe in the axiom that certainty is better than severity—in proportion to the offense.

Be constant and uniform in your dealings with your pupils and teachers. No one is keener to note negligence or omission, and preference shown, or to feel it, than the pupil. We have incipient anarchism engendered when one pupil is refused a condition that another has granted to him through influence. The first child believes that government is unfair, while the second believes that influence will secure anything.

2. Studies and methods.

Do not work on the basis that the presence of young people in school is explained by the fact that they want an education, but rather that they need it. Create the want and supply the need.

A response to the emotional methods of a teacher by the pupil is good, but, better still, is the calling out the individuality of each. The springs of action, the motives to learn, to keep at a thing, to understand it—these are the things to get at. Most of our endeavor is vague to the child. We must understand the emotions the children get from us, and we can do this only by association, observation, experiment and verification.

Study motives, tendencies, trends, attitudes of types, by induction and deduction; observe children's development, their animal instincts and habits; social phenomena as phases of individual life and individuals as they are affected by known social conditions. Watch effects on character, of changes introduced into school life.

Character is at the bottom of everything, and we should attempt to understand it before we can hope to teach it for the best. Personal contact is worth everything. Education must be warm with life, warm with the teacher's interest and sympathy. Study method, the curriculum, discipline, the standard set and attained, from the standpoint of what they are *to do* for the children. Look at everything from the standpoint of character. No one can correlate character by merely correlating courses of study.

Give children big, generic habits—psychical, sympathetic and self-assertive, and make them relational—rather than specific. Finer specific habits will be formed from these.

If it be borne in mind that gregariousness, play and acquisitiveness are character traits of children, a basis for methods of control and character training is given the principal to work upon. Habits of work, of attention, of bringing out subjects of experience, however obscure, and connecting them with real and concrete facts, instincts and motives — these are plans for training, for proper supervision.

The first thing to do with children is to give their self-assertion an awakening; to rouse them, to make them respond; but the self-assertive should not cut out the psychical. The mind must start to work at the same time to secure a balance.

There is great scope for the capacity of the principal in dealing with children through their plays and games. A greater hold on children can be gained through their spontaneousness, for this is the true element showing individuality and character. Work and play where character is developed form the basis of life. *Adaptive* work and play very often become *expressive*. The first goes along the industrial line and makes for peace, order; the second goes along the aesthetical line and shows itself in art. The necessity, then, for organization and supervision of children's play, as well as of their work, is manifest. It is an aphorism among schoolmasters that the greatest amount of control and order over children can be obtained when we know the play side of their lives, and lead up through the weak to the strong.

All animals go through methods of play which tend to fit them for life. This is our basis for kindergarten work—to humanize the animal element of children. Play is teachableness—a diligence to receive, an anxiety to acquire. This view of play includes the ability to receive most and to give up most, and also includes spontaneous work. I cannot lay too much stress upon the necessity of a principal being a factor in children's plays and games. He must be cautious, however, not to affect their true spontaniety.

For success in supervising and in teaching, both for knowledge and discipline, there should be all possible play, for the intensity of activity in any exercise and the beneficence of its results increase with the pleasure involved. To acquire alert minds, children must be alert, and alertness comes only when play instincts are aroused.

The principal must exercise constant

supervision over classrooms. Too often there is work by the teacher without proper response, the lack of registration of a sensation and its passing over into impulse. The child must be given habit rationally and judiciously. When he responds to the "have to," when he can force himself, then can the supervisor feel that his work has been rewarded properly. Habituation is the prime thing, but we want rational habit, not the irrational we so commonly find in the schoolroom. Here is where the judicious work of the principal manifests itself. We want an organic habit, an internal habit, that will assert itself without pressure from without.

A judicious mixture of the Herbartian method and the "go and find it out yourself" method oftentimes makes men and women of children. A principal needs to note closely, therefore, that the pupils and not the teacher do most of the work in a classroom. It is what children do that educates them. I believe children do not work enough in school. They should be taught to use the school hours with the spirit that they must study. Work should not be sent home; it should be done in the time allotted in school.

The directive influence of a principal is felt strongly at promotion time. His judicious guidance should be felt during the term in having the class up to the standard. He is well qualified to do this, for he has had the great advantage of comparative study of the classes above and below any particular one.

The course of study should be considered ever as temporary, lasting only till experiment verify its strength or weakness. No one is better qualified than a principal to note the value of given work at a given time in a given class. His judgment is from a practical standpoint. In a course of study the lines of work should have proportional and fitting space, each adjusted to fit the others, and all giving unity.

The principal should be slow to criticise or to offer objection to a policy, or program, or course of study from a theoretical standpoint. Theory may be taken in conjunction with directive experiment or practical demonstration, and then his objections can be made specific and can be backed up by positive proofs. Criticising can best be given, with probably safer and surer results, in the form of suggestions for change or experiment backed by reasons.

With close supervision he best should be capable of classifying pupils, of grading their intellectual powers. Close contact with teachers and classes tells him that too much nervous strain is put on this class; the teacher hurries that class too much. A nice discrimination, a tactful method, will correct conditions.

No principal can supervise till he knows things. It is he who looks out for details that makes the successful supervisor and administrator. He guards the classes against poor ventilation, enforced stillness, prolonged efforts of attention, improperly adjusted seats, defective light, pernicious system of rewards, valueless devices, unskilled and tactless punishments, and a thousand other things which, corrected, make the work of the teacher far more a success and her pupils worthy products of the time and energy spent upon them. These seem trivial, but by prevention and formation, secured through broad and intelligent prevision and supervision, both the mind and the body of the child may be symmetrically, if not perfectly, developed, and a healthy growth given to both. The principal must have within his grasp the directive control and guidance of every thread of detail. His prevision and supervision must be not only extensive, but intensive.

III. In relation to parents:

1. School interests.

It rests with the principal to make his school a pride to the city, a source of authority in methods and system for all teachers. He is the responsible head to the community. The people go to him for explanation of the policy of the school, so that they may understand the outline of work and the objects to be attained. He must be able to meet the criticism of the public in the right sort of spirit, as well as his superintendent. It often rests with him to show the parent how little that parent knows of school. It is not necessary, however, to defend everything in regard to the school. A certain amount of dignity, of respect, is due to his profession and his position.

His relation to the community can be shown further by his influence in regard to the libraries, lectures for school purposes, school entertainments, school exhibits, etc. He should be able to awaken public concern and strengthen the entire tone and trend of thought as it is directed toward the promotion of educational interests.

2. Pupils and teachers.

Be judicious in dealing with complaining parents and patrons. A tactful and conciliatory attitude, where he has nothing to lose, means much to the principal. He should endeavor to deal, in the first instance, with parents, and, assured of the justness and righteousness of his attitude, he should be firm in maintaining it. No good will accrue to a weak, vacillating man who says one thing today and another tomorrow. Professional knowledge and the ability to control himself will not permit the whims of parents to militate against him. Parents will appreciate the fact if presented to them in the right way, that "success at school demands that attention to school duties shall be made paramount to almost every other duty, and above every consideration of convenience or pleasure to parent or pupil; that punctuality adds greatly to the efficiency of school as regards progress of pupils in their studies and the formation of correct habits of thought and action in the performance of duty."

He should profit by mistakes—his own and his teachers'.

He should work with his superiors always. He must work in harmony, though he may not agree; he may know even that a mistake is being made, but there must be harmony. Opportunities will come for suggestion, and no principal should feel constrained in presenting his idea or objection in conference.

If he has a policy marked out which he desires to pursue, he should work with several of his assistants as a sort of committee before he brings it before the corps. He can work it out with a strong hand by sympathetic action on the part of his teachers. He should undertake what his best self is in sympathy with. There must be no personal selfish motive; we fail when we use our public position to bring about personal ends and aims. Do whatever is of merit.

Bear in mind always that the community believes teachers to be only an incident, and when you advocate anything for them you run the risk of failing. Whatever is good for the pupils, however, is good for the teacher. Work for betterment. Keep self subordinate to the good of the children. Be prepared to take advantage of circumstances for betterment. Do not attempt to secure legislation or change when there is any fact that will call out opposition.

The principal should endeavor, always, to create a teaching profession; should dignify it and make the teacher's position worthy of the man.

From a generic point of view, California demands the school principal shall be a man of noble character, high ideals, generous impulses, broad and accurate scholarship and technical skill, and, above all, a gentleman, a patriot and an educator.

* * *

Teaching of History in the Grammar Grades

Julia C. Coffey

To the teachers of America is given the noble task of transmitting the history of our country to the present generation. We are asked to lead every child into those rich and verdant fields of inspiration and thought, and thus broaden and deepen that mental scope which is within him, making him feel that there is a grand and glorious future opening up before him, full of great results, for which he must strive with all the energies of his soul. At best, we know we can only begin the work of training the coming citizen, trusting that the home circle, the world of books and the world of labor will add a goodly portion.

The feeble child of the schoolroom must become the strong, earnest man of the world of action, and those who have the sacred trust of his mental, moral and physical development in their charge are molding, or fashioning, as it were, the destinies of this great republic. As we have accepted our share of the duty, we should devote our best energies to sound, uplifting work at every step of the way. In our efforts we should keep in mind a high aim. We are fitting the child to take an honorable place in the actual, practical world. The rising generation must be sent forth in the struggle for existence armed with the proper qualities of manhood. American youth must have a deep appreciation of the value of the institutions of freedom, a willing obedience to law, a kindly feeling toward all American citizens, an intelligent respect for all parts of the country and a sincere love for the Union.

We wish to point with pride to the American gentlemen, those gentle enough to soothe the troubles of the smallest child and men enough to fight single-handed a legion of temptations. The past of our Nation was wrought out of just such spiritual material. Our forefathers knew only one word where self came first, and that word was self-command. In my imagination I have pictured them placing that as the keystone of the Union. No man is a worthy citizen of this republic who does not hold that word as his highest mark, and we shall feel that our country is safe when every citizen knows truly how to rule himself. We must so imbue our students with this spirit of American history that they will accomplish every noble undertaking, right every wrong that's done, and stand unflinchingly by the banner of truth and justice.

Every child must be so trained that he gets a sensible grasp of the complex world in which he must move. Our present society and government have grown from very simple elements and conditions, and the child must recognize these, step by step, building his knowledge on solid foundations, just as his forefathers built the Nation. With such a training he will know how to direct his efforts amid the multitude. His spirit will be aroused so that he will desire to be an honest worker in the field of achievement. He will learn to give much to those about him, and also to claim something from them.

We as teachers, then, must recognize that history holds a high place among studies, not only in school days, but all through life, as it is a most direct guide in the conduct of affairs. We must respect the subject, seek to understand its merits, and labor to find the best means of imparting the knowledge contained. All of the work must be done according to the high standard which I have set, but the material must be studied in different lights, according to the age of the pupil.

The ideal graded system is one in which every teacher knows her relation to every other one. She must build for those above her and fully appreciate what has been done before her. Although each teacher has only a little share in the work, she must ever feel that her portion fits into the noble plan. I shall endeavor to show more particularly, yet very briefly, how the teaching of history in the grammar grades must hold to this high aim, strengthen the previous training of the child and send him out with definite ideas that will serve him well, whether he goes on to another school of books or stands out in the field of labor. My view point is that of a grammar-grade teacher in the San Francisco schools and the field from which I select my material is the course of study outlined for the eight years of elementary instruction.

The child reaches the sixth grade with a knowledge of historical personages. He has cultivated a number of social ideas, his imagination is alive, and he is able to picture. He has gone from the stories of imaginary heroes and child life of the past on through pioneer stories of real heroes. He has heard of Columbus, Washington, Lincoln and other great men, and has developed some appreciation of these characters as they appeared in the stirring scenes of their times.

In the sixth year he is asked to secure a text-book of United States history, and you know that every child will begin to turn its pages with eager curiosity. The book is his, and the wise teacher will find in that very fact the keynote of grammar-grade work. She will need all her tact and skill to establish the right relation between the pupil and the text. Her time is to be devoted to encouraging self-activity on the part of the child.

History must be no longer a simple story of adventure, but must be a well-directed study, teaching him about the discovery, exploration, settlement and government of his country, combined at every step of the way with a record of the deeds of the people. The child's interest must be aroused until he is convinced that the book contains something he wishes to know. How he shall get at that knowledge rests with the teacher.

She must approach these first simple lessons with a clear mind, a noble heart and a devoted spirit. Like a skilled general, she surveys the whole field, but at every attack she has a distinct, objective point. As she leads the child outward in his search of knowledge, she does so with a consciousness of her power and mastery of the task. No matter how humble the lesson, she must approach it in the spirit of the student and keep constantly in mind its bearing upon the desired end.

The outcome of the history work must not be merely a mass of facts. We must have these, of course, but the child must be trained to think correctly, to be accurate and painstaking, to cultivate an interest in books, and to use every resource within himself. All work should tend toward a definite, sound personality.

The teacher, then, must carefully plan the work by topics and unfold the plan to the pupils as the study proceeds, so that they become sharers in outlining their progress. As she opens up the new work to them, she must keep well in mind their previous efforts. The children know that Columbus discovered America, and they know many other points in history, gathered in story form, so the ground must not be gone over again in the same way. They must be led to a discovery of relations. They must see at the start that our history does not stand isolated from the world's story, but that it had its beginnings in Europe, and that most of its great events stand linked to the history of other nations as well as to one another.

The eyes of the pupils will brighten eagerly when the teacher asks them if they would like to know how the discovery of this great land came about; if they would like to know what people were doing at that time, or if they would like to study as Columbus did to reach his conclusions. They will thus be carried forward from their previous work to the opening topic of their new work, "The Commerce of Western Europe with the Far East in the fifteenth century."

Under this main topic will fall many sub-topics, such as:

(a) A knowledge of geography possessed by the people of Europe at that time.

(b) Beliefs in the shape of the earth.

(c) Size of the known world.

(d) Routes of commerce.

(e) Description of India.

(f) Value of Oriental trade.

(g) The two great religions of Europe at that time, and their relation to commerce.

(h) The fall of Constantinople.

These sub-topics are suggested merely to bring out certain essential points which should characterize the whole training of our pupils.

When a subject is presented, the chief requirement of the student is to seek out the important points which will make the matter live before him. The sub-topics mentioned above fall naturally into their places, as they tend to give the pupils a clear idea of commercial relations at the given time. The teacher having planned the work and aroused the interest of the pupils, sends them to earnest study. They are shown the exact place to get the material and must return full of it to the recitation. They are not told to learn so many pages to recite under the spur of gentle help, but they must respond with all the essential points in relation to the topic or sub-topic assigned for the lesson.

Beginners in United States history should not be sent to wander in a library, but should do some reading outside of the text-books. The teacher, after assigning a topic and hearing the recitation, should read from some good history, and thus show the pupils how the work is done. Gradually the list of references must be enlarged and the pupils be expected to bring forth their results of study from them.

The recitation must be full of spirit. No teacher can afford to accept a faulty piece of work. The boy who has been told exactly where to get a piece of information and returns without it must be sent promptly back again to find it. His teacher has had the good judgment to give him something she knows he should be able to do, but she has to convince the boy that he is able to do it. That one piece of clear-cut work may be the making of him, and every future recitation must be held to the same standard. A training in this definite response, carried through the grammar grades, will send out pupils trained in the habits of obedience, respect for a command and decision of action.

In assigning sub-topics, the parts must be closely related when presented to the pupils. The teacher may point out these relations and discuss them in class, but the work will not go far before the pupils will begin to make these relations themselves. She will then be able to let them suggest topics in proper order. Their work may be crude and not acceptable at times, but it will tend to train them in connecting their present work with past efforts, and making it build for future study.

Thus when they study the fall of Constantinople they view it as the outcome of what went before, and from it they look out on a field of new thought. They learn its relation to the problem of the sea-road to India and its relation to the discovery of America. The work will unfold with increasing interest, and the teacher must act as a guide to keep some from wandering too far afield, and to encourage others to seek to the full extent of assigned study.

The pupil will draw help from as many directions as possible, and will soon master the period of discovery and exploration. Every recitation in history will have a definite background in geography, and, to summarize various parts of the work, the pupils will do some simple map drawing. This is extremely interesting to children, and is less confusing than the ordinary school map, as only the salient features suited to the historical matter are portrayed. The pupils take pride in watching the product grow under their efforts. When the first part of the sixth-grade work is completed they will have a good idea of the historical geography of North America at that time. Their map work will illustrate the parts held by the various European powers, will arouse questions as to the future territorial conflicts and progress of these people, and will be a fitting preparation for a study of the period of settlement.

In studying the colonies, the pupils will derive great profit by entering into the spirit of colonizing, discussing the purposes of the various colonists, their efforts in establishing homes, their occupations, religions, education, government and other vital interests of all communities. When a few colonies have been studied separately, they may be grouped and reviewed according to points of similarity or contrast. This latter work will be done entirely by the pupil if the teacher has insisted on clear knowledge in regard to the essential points of the separate colonies. This constant drill of comparison and contrast, carried through the term, will maintain interest and form the most valuable kind of test work. The study of relations with the mother country and of the geographical features of the region must be well understood, as they are a necessary preparation for the new work.

In the seventh grade the pupils begin to answer some of the questions which arose in the previous year in regard to the claims of England and France. The geography of the country showed them that there were natural openings between the parts held by these people, and that there was bound to be a meeting, as each sought for territorial expansion. This conflict will be watched with eagerness by the pupils, as it has a many-sided interest. At its close they will summarize its geographical result in a new map, making a little more definite the claims of Spain, France and England.

The preparatory work in grasping the relations between the colonies and England is now brought forward and applied to discovering the causes of ill-feeling which led up to the Declaration. The pupils should so realize the existing conditions that they will appreciate the meaning and force of the Declaration of Independence. It must awaken the deepest feelings of their nature and carry them on in their study with zeal for the interests at stake. The children must move in spirit with their forefathers through the gloomy periods of the war, the distress of finances, the deceit of traitors, the kindness of friends, the worries of Government and the victories of heroes.

The great struggle over, they will begin to see the need of a strong government for the new republic. The teacher who has awakened their sincere patriotism will now find them willing workers in mastering the meaning of the Constitution. No partisan spirit pervaded it, no selfish interests clouded its bright lines, no weakness clung to its well-wrought sentences. Its founders were guided by the words of Washington: "Let us raise a standard to which the wise and honest can repair; the event is in the hands of God."

The new republic stands before the world proud in its strength, but not secure. The unsettled conditions at home soon adjust themselves, but the vital work of commerce on the sea must be set right. The struggle for commercial independence must be closely followed by our earnest little students, and its great results, reaching down to the present day, must be appreciated.

The pupils enter the eighth year and pause for a survey of the road over which they have traveled. They are assigned some valuable work to summarize the line of study. Like wise citizens, they are asked to view the work of political parties and discover what our legislators did to establish a firm government. They are led to realize that "A man is great as he contends best with the circumstances of his time." This topic is a study of duty well performed and worthy of the highest praise. Passing on, they summarize the territorial development of the Nation, and look out on a country ready for the arts of peace.

Industrial history now stands in first place, and its many interests hold the attention. A break is made in the progress of the Nation, and the slavery question calls for settlement. A careful study of this great event brings out lessons of permanent value, and stamps upon the minds of the pupils a deeper respect for the Union. The students continue with a survey of State and local government, the rights and duties of citizenship and prominent events of recent occurrence, until they stand face to face with the problems of today.

Their study throughout has been marked by truth, right and duty; they have learned to love their country and their fellow men, so they will be in sympathy with the world movements about them. Problems as great as any in the past are calling out to the thinkers of the day, and our earnest men are studying them in the light of previous experience. We know that such men have grasped the meaning of history, and we can only hope that the pupils whom we have aroused to a persistent exertion of their powers may attack the problems of the morrow with the same ready will. All that a teacher may ask from the man of the future is the message: "You awakened me to myself, and for that I thank you." Let us strive that this message may be oft repeated.

Our educational system is very complex, and teachers must work closely together to develop the best interests of their pupils. As we expect them to be definite in presenting their work, we must be definite in directing it. If earnest thinkers devote themselves to perfecting methods in all the great industrial fields dealing with material stores, how much more should we put forth our efforts to discover the best means to further our work with the living, creative material put into our hands; yea, intrusted to us, for we know, despite the petty attacks we sometimes hear, that the people have faith in us, the parents look to us as skilled workers in guiding the human soul.

Let us prove always worthy of the trust. Let us plan together, work together, counsel together, so that we may go higher and higher in perfecting the details of our profession—the one profession that must labor with the strictest practical material, and yet can never, like other fields, turn out a finished product. For truly do we educate, do we train man, the agent of all other fields. Our greatest glory is that every stroke we make gives a practical fact and also furnishes power.

No examination can test our whole work, no supervision measure it. All tests may help us, all criticism enlighten us, but the real result of our labor must be the story of every pupil who passes thru the public school.

* * *

The Elementary Course of Study

C. E. Keyes

[Extract]

During the last seven or eight years there has been a remarkable increase in the number of articles and books written on educational subjects. The whole educational field has been plowed, subsoiled, harrowed and plowed again. Seed has been sown, some good, and some otherwise. Crops have grown in abundance, albeit some are of hothouse growth, while elsewhere the seed has fallen into rocky ground, or else the weeds have grown up and choked it.

This great educational activity is worldwide, and is a part of the wonderful awakening of mankind in religious and sociological matters. As incidents in this great activity came the reports of the Committee of Ten and the Committee of Fifteen. These reports are of themselves epoch-making.

You are all familiar with the questions submitted by the Committee of Fifteen, the answers to which formed the basis of that report. Two or three only of these I shall quote, for this paper is an echo of some of the discussions concerning those questions.

1. Should the elementary course be eight years and the secondary course four years, as at present?

Or, should the elementary course be six years and the secondary course six years?

2. Has each of the grammar-school studies—language, mathematics, geography, history, natural science, penmanship, drawing, etc.—a distinct pedagogical value? If so, what is it?

3. Should other subjects than those enumerated in the second question, such as manual training, physical culture, physics, music, physiology, Latin, or a modern language, be taught in the elementary school course? If so, why.

In this paper I shall discuss three points concerning the course.

First, shall the course be shortened? Second, can the gap between the elementary and secondary courses be removed? Third, shall the course be enriched?

It is agreed on all hands that there are serious defects in our educational system. Best results are not obtained. Time is wasted. Children leave school earlier than they would if conditions were better. In this matter statistics show that the situation is appalling. Of one hundred children only twenty-five reach the sixth grade, twelve the high school, and two finish the high-school course; the greatest decrease being between the fourth and sixth grades.

In answer to the questions about the

length of the elementary and secondary courses, a variety of opinions have been given. On the part of a large number the opinion prevails that the time of the elementary course should be shortened and the secondary course remain as it is.

From early times there has been the three-fold or tripartite division of educational courses: The elementary school, the high school and the college. Usually eight years has been given to elementary work, four years to the high school and four years to the college. In addition to this three or four years are given to graduate or professional studies, so that the professional man does not get well started before he is twenty-eight or thirty years of age. It is very desirable that the time of preparation for the life work be shortened. In the case of those who cannot attend the university, but must drop out at the end of the secondary school or earlier, it is even more important that the elementary course be as short and as rich as possible.

Many of our best schools have enriched their programs by introducing nearly all that is called for by the "new" education. The "three R's" have been supplemented by drawing, music, natural science and manual training, and reading itself has made incursions into literature, and geography and history to a degree unthought of in our own school days. At first thought it seems ridiculous with all this added material to think of shortening the time of the elementary course. Teachers of the elementary schools feel that the work is already too heavy.

But the burden rests upon us to send our young people into active life well prepared for that life at as early an age as possible. Experiences in actual life furnish means of growth which the school cannot give. There is a certain dependence on others in school life, which, if continued too long, does not give that strength which leads to highest endeavor. Longfellow graduated at eighteen, and was a professor of modern languages at twenty-two; Webster graduated at nineteen, Emerson at eighteen, and Bancroft at seventeen.

A recent Controller of the Currency graduated from the college at eighteen and from the law school at twenty. Not able to practice law on account of his age, he spent the year in important engineering work on a railroad. He was made Controller of the Currency at the age of thirty-one. At thirty-six he is thought to have executive ability to take the presidency of a bank with $10,000,000 capital. Cases like these are exceptional and belong to men of exceptional ability, you say. This is doubtless true; nevertheless, it is probably true that a measure of their success is due to the fact that they were early thrown on their own resources.

Many reasons suggest themselves to everyone of the desirability of early entrance into one's life work. But is it feasible to shorten the time of preparation? If so, shall the so-called new studies of the curriculum be dropped, or shall there be a condensation of some sort in the work? Is it possible to crowd the work now done more closely together in point of time? Or would it be better to shorten the time by some method of selection and omission? Much of that which is best in our school work is the so-called "new." Professor Dewey speaks of the conflict between the old and the new, and asks "Why it is that the newer studies and the older ones practically conflict instead of re-enforcing one another?" In the same connection he speaks of the transition period we are now in.

We have not yet been able, as a body of teachers, to adjust the new and the old. This is not to be wondered at. It is always true of advancement in any direction. The traditions in teaching, as elsewhere, are tenacious in their hold upon us. The new studies are valuable. Of their value I shall speak later.

Superintendent Soldan of St. Louis says: "If there is any change in the duration of the course of study to be made, it cannot be made by condensation exclusively, but must be largely brought about by selection and omission." Dr. Butler says: "I believe there is waste in our educational system. It seems to me patent that this waste occurs chiefly at two points in the educational work. I am distinctly of the opinion that the four lower elementary grades, the primary grades as they are called, and the four years of secondary work in the United States are, on the whole, thoroly well and economically occupied. I am convinced that the waste is serious in the four upper elementary, or the so-called grammar grades, and in the college, and I believe, and firmly believe, that we must shorten the time given to upper elementary grades, and shorten the time given to the college, because we are now taking longer than we need to do the modicum of work allotted by common consent to the students in these two stages of their education."

Dr. Butler gives it as his opinion that this waste is due to two causes. First, lack of sufficient scholarship on the part of the teacher, and, second, the growing tendency to exaggerate the importance of method in teaching.

To me it seems possible to do all the work now done in less time if conditions are favorable; and there is no doubt, I think, that omissions may be made which will materially shorten the time. This is especially true in geography and arithmetic.

Finally, I wish to speak of nature study. We do not realize the value of nature study to the child.

G. Stanley Hall says: "Science, art, literature, religion, human history and society are the five great objects, not only of education, but of human interest. These all root in the love and study of nature."

Titles of books like "Through Nature to God" indicate the feeling of great men that Nature is truly great. Someone has said that instead of saying nature study we should say nature sympathy.

I have wondered how anyone can condemn nature study in the schools. How much we should lose if the love of Nature had been wanting in many of our great writers. How we should miss Lowell's "Good Word for Winter," and his equally good word for summer in "Sir Launfal," and elsewhere; Whittier's "Snowbound," Burns' "To a Daisy," Bryant's "To a Waterfowl," Tennyson's

"Flower in the crannied wall,
I pluck you out of the crannies;
Hold you here, root and all, in my hand,
Little flower—but if I could understand
What you are, root and all, and all in all,
I should know what God and man is."

There are a thousand other matchless writings no one of which would have been possible without the author's sympathetic knowledge of nature.

The problem of the course of study is still with us unsolved. The course of study now in use is better than that of a century or even a decade ago. The earnest students who are endeavoring to bring better conditions have increased a hundred fold. Something better is before us.

What we have now is good, however, only when it reaches the pupil through the wise and true teacher. When the better course of study shall come it will fail of good results if mechanical instruction takes the place of vital instruction and routine work the place of the individual teacher.

* * *

The Grammar School Course as a Preparation for Life

F. A. Wagner

[Extract]

Constantly preparing, but never prepared, for life that is not, but is to be. An explosion in Havana harbor quickens the heart-beat of nations and announces the death of a degenerate civilization. A boxer uprising turns our faces toward the Orient, there to behold a people aroused from the stupor of twenty centuries. As a result, we enter upon a new era of commercial, industrial and political life. We realize anew our obligations to other nations and are confronted with more complex and intricate international problems.

In the industrial world steam and electricity have unharnessed the horse and have lifted the load from the shoulders of men. Type-setting and type-casting machines have forced their thousands into other channels of labor. Edison and Bell have completely transformed the business and social world. Great corporations, with giant intellects to grasp the details of their business, to plan and to carry out large enterprises involving three or more continents, foreshadow a world's trust to cheapen necessities and provide luxuries to the humblest toiler of our land. National councils and civic federations for the adjustment of the vital relation between labor and capital, and international councils to arbitrate differences between nations, may suddenly change the civilization of today from one of peace and quiet to one of war and desolation. The Emancipation Proclamation revolutionized the social and industrial conditions in the South. Who can foretell the changes that will follow the emancipation of the slaves to the modern competitive system — the dwellers in tenement-houses, sweat-shops and slums?

Yet, if we may use the searchlight of experience to sweep the skies prophetic of the future, certain elements of the life into which our pupils go may easily be discerned.

The coming years will be years of intense mental and physical activity. There will be need of greater powers of endurance. Competition will compel the youth to fight successfully the battles of a strenuous life, or be trampled under the foot and become as the worm that crawls in the dust. Our grammar schools are laying the necessary foundations by giving special attention to the physical development of the child. Systematic physical culture, more or less of manual training, sanitary school buildings, well-lighted and well-ventilated school furniture that makes possible symmetrical growth, instruction in hygiene, and in the proper preparation of foods and clothing, expert medical supervision, correct habits of sitting, standing and walking becoming a part of each child's nature (warning against the danger of alcoholics, narcotics and other drugs, against the destructive power of vice of all kinds)—these are some of the many aids which the modern school brings to nature in developing the sturdiest possible physique. But the competitive system enters our doors and drives the pupil to excessive study, to the point of fatigue and worry, exhaustive waste of nerve force. It has entered the home and society and has added to a day's work in school, another day's work at the accomplishments, music and painting, and, in the upper grades, a half night's work in social amusements carried to the point of dissipation of energy. Our constructive efforts for stronger and more vigorous children have been undone at the command of that reckless dictator, competition.

Civilization will demand not only toughened muscle and iron nerve, but muscle and nerve that is trained to the most delicate impressions and to accuracy and precision in execution. "The complexity of modern industrial life, the minute division of labor, and the specialization of function in almost every trade, craft, and profession "compel everywhere a higher technical skill, a more complete mastery of the principles involved in one's own narrow line." Greater power needed to help multiply inventions and commodities, greater intelligence to manage and direct the machinery, greater intelligence to understand instructions given. The delicacy and costliness of machinery compels a higher standard of morality. Capitalists and corporations can not afford to employ dissipated men who wreck their trains and ruin their business. Smokers are now barred from the United States signal service. Railway companies will not knowingly continue in their service men who use alcoholics while on duty. Exact and painstaking effort, the ability to do some one thing, however small, surpassingly well will continue to be at a premium. The existence of technical schools, agricultural schools and universities compel more general information among the masses. What use is the agricultural experiment station if the farmer and orchardist cannot understand and apply the results of the investigations? Technical schools will develop architects, machinists, pattern-makers, but the rank and file must be able to read the designs and give the designer's thought expression in the materials used. 'A carpenter, no matter how skillful in the handling of tools, must be able to read the architect's drawing or else he can not construct the dwelling. A paper-hanger without an eye for beauty and harmony will utterly destroy the design of the artist. Clothed in silks of discordant color and out of proportion with her size and form, a woman is not well dressed, and deservedly receives the censure of her more cultured sisters. The civilization of tomorrow will have more of art and stately architecture —our own universities leading the way. Men and women will have the taste and leisure to admire and the wealth to construct buildings of incomparable grandeur and stateliness — a style of architecture that shall develop from our own civilization.

* * * *

The elementary school must continue to strengthen, in the course of study, those elements which "show the origin and value of our institutions," "the rights and duties of citizens," "political questions having an economic basis," and social ethics should have a larger place in the curriculum. It is of more value to know that speculation was the cause of the panics of 1837, 1873 and 1893 than to know the detailed movements in every battle during the Rebellion. Infinitely more important to catch the spirit of "Paul Revere's Ride" than to parse every word in the poem. The conditions that made one panic may again become operative. If, in teaching history, you illuminate the past with the conditions that now confront the student, the past will be freighted with a new significance. The spirit of Paul Revere still lives. Let the pupil drink in the coolheaded patriotism of our time, let him feel his heart leap and his blood boil at the thought of treason when he finds soulless corporations withholding $2,226,000 worth of taxes from the city treasury of Chicago, thereby robbing the teachers of that city of their just dues. Thanks to that noble, patriotic woman who had the courage to bring these thieves to justice— thieves who would as surely wreck our Government as any band of anarchists. While your pupils are on fire with this thought, putting down foes more dangerous than redcoats, let them read the poems that tell of Paul Revere and Gettysburg. What the elementary course needs is more vital teaching—teaching that shall make the past in art, literature, history and song to live anew in and through present thought and activity. All teaching that helps the pupils to mold from the past an expression of his present social and natural environment becomes interesting and immeasurably effective. The teacher must therefore be in touch with our bounding industrial, commercial, political and literary life—she herself must "be filled with the thought of our time" if she would inspire her pupils with the highest ideals and noblest aspirations possible to human race. As more and more of our teachers realize the need of larger views of our present civilization and fit themselves for more complete living, we shall hear less and less of courses of study and their fitness to prepare for life. A course of study is dead without a wideawake, up-to-date, life-inspiring teacher.

PRIMARY SCHOOL SECTION

Miss Rebecca F. English, Chairman   Mrs. Fannie Byram, Secretary

Introductory Remarks

Rebecca F. English

Fellow Teachers and Friends: The time has come for the opening of our meeting. Looking around upon this vast assemblage, I am convinced that the importance of the primary section is esteemed by you as second to none on the program of the State Teachers' Association. If further proof of this fact were necessary it would be found in the prompt and favorable responses of those who were requested to talk to you and the hearty good wishes expressed by them for the success of our deliberations.

In the name of the primary teachers of the State of California, I cordially thank these educators for their cheering words of encouragement and for their helpful contributions to the work of our section.

It has been our purpose to bring before you leading educators from all parts of the State, and we have even been so fortunate as to secure the services of a well-known speaker from our sister state of Kansas. These gentlemen have in turn brought ideas, gained by recent sojourn and study in the East and Europe. They will discuss not so much the methods as the relation of the teacher to her pupils and her work, such relation as is being emphasized in the best of educational thought and practice of the world today. For example: Dr. Brown of Berkeley will bring out the relation of the school and the home; Professor Cubberley of Stanford will talk of morals and manners as related to school life; Professor Hopkins of Kansas University will discuss "Personal Initiative versus Methods" in teaching; Professor Suzzallo of the San Francisco State Normal School will present some views of that much-abused subject, arithmetic in the primary grades; and Dr. Small of the Los Angeles Normal School has selected as his topic of discussion, "Teaching and Health."

A no less practical feature of our program will consist of talks by successful primary teachers, showing the correlation of kindergarten and primary school work, and giving practical experiences in the teaching of reading, literature and number; also manual training, constructive work in the lower grades.

We sincerely regret that time is too limited to consider more of the branches in the primary school curriculum, or even to give to each speaker an opportunity for a full presentation of his subject. In order to carry out the program as arranged, it will be necessary to begin promptly, listen attentively, and to hold each speaker as nearly as possible to his allotted time.

Limited as the time must be, however, much good will undoubtedly be gained by the coming together of this great number of earnest, conscientious, sympathetic teachers—one in interest, one in purpose and one in aspiration—from the leaders of our highest state educational institutions to the teachers of our smallest district schools away off in the mountains.

Indeed, a movement is already hinted at for the purpose of more closely unifying the grammar and primary sections. It has been suggested by interested members of these two sections that an association be formed similar in character and purpose to the High School Association. This matter will probably be considered before the adjournment of the present State Association.

And now may the lessons brought to us by our leaders—the acquaintances formed with other teachers and their ways and means, but, most of all, the clasp of hands that are working in God's noblest field of creation, the heart of a little child—go with us to inspire, comfort and brighten the work of the new year. May our daily supplication be for "Light to see, a heart to close with and power to do" the great work that lies before us.

Morals and Manners

Ellwood P. Cubberley

[Professor Cubberley had no manuscript, but talked from pages 236 to 241 of the San Francisco Course of Study, of which the following is a part.]

This subject does not need a set time in any grade. Better results can be gotten by bringing in the topics at what seem to be appropriate times rather than by giving set talks at a stated time. Such work, to be valuable, must not be given in the form of preaching. Children resent moral lectures, but accept easily that which comes as a natural emanation from the life of the school and the spirit of the teacher. The important thing in moral teaching is that the teacher should be, first of all, an example of what he wishes to teach; that she be fully conscious of the transcendent importance of the subject; that she use the many opportunities of the school life and the school studies to enforce the principles she is trying to teach; and that she keep the ideas she wishes to teach before her own mind constantly. Keeping these moral principles constantly in mind does not mean constantly hammering on them. Great tact must be used by teachers that the approach to the subjects be such as will make a lasting impression. Opportune moments must be used, and, so far as possible, pupils be led to formulate moral truths for themselves. There certainly are times, particularly in the primary years, when a moral talk is valuable, but it should be at a time when the school or the lesson has presented an opportunity that will make a talk of a moral nature of lasting value. To illustrate: Suppose the class is studying "The Building of the Ship," and the lines

"For his heart was in his work, and the heart
Giveth grace unto every Art."

And the teaching will aim to lead the pupil to feel the dignity of skilled manual labor, and the especial importance of a knowledge of domestic science to rich and poor alike.

The course will also give a knowledge of the preparation and the relative values of raw materials, and some ideas as to the nutritive values of different kinds of food and how to live economically and at the same time have a good, wholesome diet.

The Rational Method of Reading

Mrs. M. L. Westover

[Extract]

A noted educator in an article to "The Forum" says: "Methods for learning to read come and go across the educational arena like the march of supernumeraries upon the stage. Each is heralded as the final solution of the problem of learning to read, but each in turn gives way to some later discovery."

This paper has to deal with the claims of the latest discovery, namely, Ward's method of learning to read.

Professor Ward's dissatisfaction with the three methods known to every teacher, that is, the a, b, c method, the purely phonetic method, and the word method, led him to devise a better one, which he styles The Rational Method.

It is an outgrowth of the author's study and experiments in the schools of Brooklyn, N. Y., of which he is superintendent.

In describing his system he says: "The rational method is a peculiar combination of the sentence and phonetic methods. It utilizes each for that part of the work to which it is particularly adapted.

"The sentence method is used first as

principal, because of its value in developing a habit of reading thoughtfully, and afterwards as auxiliary, to remedy the shortcomings of the phonetic method and increase the stock of word phonograms.

"The phonetic method, which is introduced by easy stages during the ascendency of the sentence method, finally becomes itself the principal means of growth and progress. Its proper use develops great power, while it supplies the key which the word method is inadequate to give."

Mr. Ward claims for his method, when intelligently followed, that it makes the child a thoughtful reader.

That it not only makes him independent in his reading, but it also assists greatly in making him generally self-reliant.

That it enables him to read a vastly greater amount than heretofore in a given time, and thus to acquire both a fuller vocabulary and greater maturity of mind.

That it puts him into possession, during the first year and a half of school life, of a complete key to the language, so that no matter how soon thereafter his schooling may cease, his ability to read is assured.

Also, that in the schools where the method has been mastered the time formerly devoted to the acquirement of a vocabulary of 200 words now gives the children one of more than a thousand, while their enunciation is clearer and their reading is more spirited and in every respect better than formerly. * * * *

* * *

Primary Reading

Miss Julia Dwire

In writing a paper of this kind, many details and many devices must be omitted. Much depends upon the class you are teaching. However, I have a plan which I hope may be suggestive.

On the first day of school I should work to get the children to talk in sentences by showing objects and talking about them. Take some object that is interesting to the children—for example, a kitty. Get them to talk about their kitty; let them play that they are kitties. Write one of their sentences, as "I see a kitty," on the blackboard. Tell them that the chalk has made a picture of that story. Then let the children find a word that says kitty, see and I. Write these words in many places on the board and have the children find the words. Call attention to peculiarities in words, as the child's power to recognize and name different words depends upon his power to see resemblances and differences between forms. He must learn to observe forms attentively. You can help the child make the new words his own by letting him use them in various ways. He may write the words, use them in oral statements, illustrate them, find them among others. After a number of words have been taught in this way, closely related sentences, which to the child is an interesting story, may be written upon the blackboard. Supply your lack of words by using pictures. As the child's vocabulary grows, the use of pictures may be dropped. These blackboard stories should compose the reading lessons for at least seven or eight weeks. Never let a child read a sentence until he is ready to do so without a break. Have the class read each line silently, then call upon some one to read it aloud. After going through the lesson in this way, let them read the story as a whole. If the children read without expression, draw it from them by questions or remarks upon the subject. Failing in this, read the sentence for them exaggerating the expression. A helpful exercise is to question the class upon the sentences before they read them aloud.

While the first words may be taught by the word method, the children may begin the study of phonetics at once. The first lessons should be to help the children distinguish sounds. In this work, as well as in all other, the child should live his lessons and "to live it means to play it." For example, I say today we will play that we are going on a picnic and I will tell you in a new way what we are to have to eat. See if you can tell me what I say. Then spell by sound as c-a-k-e—b-r-e-a-d, etc. Be particular to see that each pupil gives the sound correctly. Do not give the letter names, give only the sound. Teaching as ing, ight as ight, at as at, all as all, etc. Put the sounds on the board as they are learned and review them every day. When you teach a new sound to the class give many words containing the sound, as need, see, feed, tree. Avoid diacritical markings. There are no markings in the book and there are many devices to help the child to determine what the sounds are as final e makes the vowel long.

I select the word from the book which I expect to give the children to read first; about two weeks before you wish to give the book to the children place upon the blackboard the words in both script and print. Let them find the script word first, then show them the printed form, calling their attention to the likenesses and differences in the two forms. After considerable practice in this way give them their books. Tell them to find certain words. If any of them fail to find a word, write it upon the blackboard for them. A little practice will enable them to recognize readily the printed forms in their books. They are now ready to read the lesson in the book. I proceed as we did the blackboard lessons, having the class read each sentence silently, then have each child read the lesson as a whole. When the children have read about thirty pages in the state reader, I give the Wheeler's Graded Primer, which is a very interesting little book. It furnishes much new reading matter, with but few new words to be learned. The two books are read together. An average class should read at least six books during the school year.

* * *

Correlation

Frances Cook Holden

[Extract]

A large number of cities and towns of California have made the kindergarten a part of the public-school system, and year by year the number of public kindergartens increase. But while the kindergarten has been legally adopted, in spirit and practice it too often remains an alien. The child may begin his school life in either the kindergarten or the receiving class.

If he enters the kindergarten he is promoted not because of his fitness or ability, but because, in the course of time, he reaches the age of six! The first grade does not take into account the training which the child receives in the kindergarten and make it the foundation of his work in the grade. Thus the kindergarten is compelled to be its own excuse for being, its activities commencing and terminating within itself. It is evident that such a condition cannot long continue. Six-year-old Johnnie in the receiving class is not very different from five-year-old Johnnie in the kindergarten. He is a little larger, a little stronger, somewhat more active, but his interests are in large part the same, and they find their natural expression aproximately through the same channels. Therefore an organic union of the kindergarten and primary school must seek its true basis, not in the attempt to make either conform to the other, as they now exist, but rather look for such a union in the child's growth stage, in his nature and needs, as they are manifest during this period in his development.

* * *

We see that the child in the kindergarten and primary school is in the same stage of development, and any real correlation between the two must be based on his nature and needs. The exercises of both should spring from the sensory and motor activities, especially in case of the formal studies of the primary grade. Play is the child's normal means of expression and of acquisition and should be utilized to further his development. He should be allowed all the freedom consistent with the good of the whole. He should be brought face to face with situations which contain incentives for exercising his own initiative. His sense of his own worth should be given wholesome expression, as well as his appreciation of the worth of others. Through suggested ideals, imitation and obedience and little acts of helpfulness and good will the child becomes established in moral and social habits of action.

From the teacher's standpoint the correlation is effected by transferring the center of interest from the means to the end —from the product or curriculum to the child; by getting a basis of understanding and interpretation of both departments through conferences, visits and exchange of work.

* * *

Arithmetic Without a Pencil

Edith M. Joy

[Extract]

Once upon a day a mother brought her boy to me to enter him in school, and she said: "I want my son to get an education, for I want him not to have to work when he becomes a man." Was the mother's wrong conception of life responsible for the boy's wrong view? He manifested from the first a disposition to acquire and a contempt for all legitimate effort.

This opinion that education is to be desired because it will bring immunity from manual labor is held by many persons who ought to know a better reason for educating children. Those to whom has been assigned the duty of teaching the little ones must not expect to be excused for failing to rightly understnd what education is and what is its purpose.

Truth is within ourselves; it takes no rise
From outward things, whate'er you may
   believe.
There is an inmost center in us all,
Where truth abides in fullness; and
   around,
Wall upon wall, the gross flesh hems it in,
This perfect, clear perception—
   * * *   And to know
Rather consists in opening out a way
Whence the imprisoned splendor may
   escape
Than in effecting entry for a light
Supposed to be without."

To what an extent has the erroneous opinion prevailed that education adds something to the individual? It does not, nor is it education if it unfold not the good that is within. I wish we could lead our children to see that learning is but growing; that we could help them to a belief in themselves—not a belief that savors of self-conceit or one that rests in self-confidence, but a belief that is self-reliance. The self-reliant man, I think, is the one whom Dr. Jordan means when he speaks of the man who knows whither he is going and says the world stands aside to let him pass.

No other study that we teach holds the possibility of developing self-reliance through a recognition of the power that comes through knowing and doing things in accordance with law as does arithmetic. What is the first lesson numbers should teach a child? Belief in unchanging, unerring law, as exemplified in his experiments. Hand in hand with the growth of belief, develop exactness and accuracy. After he has learned to be exact and accurate in the demonstration of a few facts, his belief becomes faith as regards other facts, and faith is ever opposed to fear—to fear, that great dissipation of energy. The mind, unhampered by fear, is easily directed in the line of logical thinking, and our own opportunity to train in habits of logical thinking, as well as in exactness and accuracy, is found in the arithmetic lesson. * * * *

Time is lost in many ways. Perhaps it would not be amiss to briefly consider some of the causes of this. Interruptions for discipline kill an arithmetic lesson, for they disturb or destroy concentration, without which connected reasoning is impossible. If you lose a pupil during the recitation, better let him go, unless you can quietly and unnoticed, get him back. No words that would not show manifest connection with the development of the lesson, were all taken down and reduced to print, should be spoken during the lesson.

Time is lost by teaching any portion of arithmetic apart from the need for it. The most glaring illustration of this is the popular method of teaching g. e. f. and l. c. m. before beginning fractions. The only use a pupil will have for g. c. f. is in reducing fractions to lowest terms, and for l. c. m. in changing fractions to least common denominator. Why not teach them at a time when even a child can see a purpose in the work? Teaching fractions in accordance with the pages devoted to them in our state arithmetic is rich in illustrations similar to the above, illustrations of work without system or purpose.

Now fractions are easy, if intelligently treated, and I say it deliberately, that they come pretty near being the arithmetic. However good the teaching has been in third and fourth grades; however strong it may be in sixth and seventh grades, the school that lacks strong teaching in fractions will graduate pupils insufficient in arithmetic. We must make our work strong right here, for weak teaching in fractions is very grave, since it causes pupils to become hopelessly muddled.

KINDERGARTEN SECTION

Mrs. Frances B. Gould, Chairman   Miss Mary F. Ledyard, Secretary

How to Overcome the Isolation of the Kindergarten

Cora A. Reavis

How shall we overcome the isolation of the kindergarten, or, in other words, how may we carry at least a part of its good work into the first grade? This burning question of the last decade is slowly being answered, and the breach between the two is gradually being narrowed and becoming easier, for the little people who are vitally concerned, to cross.

That the kindergarten be not isolated, there must be sympathy between it and the grades above, the deep sympathy that will certainly follow mutual understanding and knowledge. Though their application differs in the different grades, the laws governing education are the same for all.

In time past the first grade teacher has labored under numerous difficulties. With fifty active children to be given the first care-demanding lessons in new subjects, with no material at hand with which to continue work already familiar to them, coming from a room with at least a teacher to every twenty pupils, she has a problem which only those who have tried to fill her position can realize. But she is one of the bravest of the brave, and she begins her work each morning with a firm resolve that, in spite of many hindrances and seeming impossibilities, whatever is good shall be made to serve its purpose in her work.

Believing that individual effort on the part of the person to be educated is essential to full development, and that the child is in the largest sense drawn out by what he does for himself both with mind and hand, we may wisely follow the kindergarten by giving opportunity for free efforts at self-expression in speech, in drawing, in color work, and in constructing, paper folding and cutting, forming a foundation for the creative imagination, and training in deftness and accuracy. All instruction and all training must appeal to the interest of the children. How to find time to satisfy varied interests among so many is one great problem. For young children do not look below the surface of things, and change their interests in quick succession from one thing to another. Therefore, they may with much benefit consider in the same day a larger number of subjects than older students. They demand variety in their work, lest they tire. Short periods of work, with games often interspersed, such as may be conveniently played in a first grade room, marching, and like forms of exercise, form a wise continuation of kindergarten practice. For this reason I advocate a first grade room furnished with movable tables and chairs, as an improvement over stationary desks and seats, thereby furnishing conditions for more naturalness and freedom.

The "morning talk" and the "story hour," with free use of the blackboard as the story progresses, have become as essential to the first grade as to the kindergarten. Another subject started in the kindergarten profitably to the child is the study of nature. We should consider that we had lost a valuable opportunity if we did not continue to make our collections and our observations. When the little child comes to us he has not forgotten the little basket of seed babies that he himself collected, nor the fallen leaves and their study, nor has he forgotten about the beautiful butterfly that came from the carefully watched chrysallis and the game that followed. We first grade teachers can not but appreciate the love for school and the freedom which the kindergarten has developed in the little one, and we feel it our duty to do all in our power to continue the good work.

We would not burden the kindergarten child, still, we believe that stress should be laid upon the acquiring of good habits, especially as to the careful use of material,

neatness of work, perseverance and independence, and consideration for others. After his entrance to first grade, owing to the large number under one teacher, he must from necessity often be left alone to accomplish some assigned task. During the last part of the kindergarten year, in order to prepare for this necessity, a wise practice would be that of assigning work with proper directions, and leaving the class alone to follow the directions given. At the close of the given period, examine each child's work, and hold him responsible for all work not accomplished.

Just here will come in the necessity for consideration for others. The child must be made to feel that it is his duty to aid his companions by giving them the proper conditions for work, quiet and freedom from all hindrances by their neighbors. I believe that one of the greatest problems of a first grade teacher, working with a class fresh from kindergarten, is the tendency to interfere with each other's work when left alone. This difficulty arises, of course, from the fact that they have not become accustomed to working alone, but have always been under the immediate direction of a teacher. They only need a little more training along the lines of independent work and self-control. However, the suggestion as to a remedy may be neither practicable nor advisable. This the kindergarten can decide most wisely.

The happiness of the child should be one of the chief ends in view during the first regular school year. The child's school days are not merely days for the preparation for mature living; they are a part of his life. If we withhold happiness, we withhold one of the essentials to proper child living, as well as to proper growth. As far as it is possible to have it in a first grade room, I would encourage the joyous freedom of the kindergarten. How full of love it fills the heart of a teacher when a dear little tot, entertaining herself by reading hardly aloud from her reader, unconscious of those about her, laughs her low, baby laugh over some story she feels she has mastered!

In our own city, the wisdom of a plan

that has greatly benefited us in our work is evident. The "Kindergarten Director" has been made "Supervisor of Manual Work" in our first grades. Besides giving us valuable instruction to be applied, she visits our rooms at short intervals. The children know and love her; and welcome with true enjoyment either a story or some lesson in manual work. In my estimation, a deeper bond of sympathy and mutual knowledge of methods has been in this way brought about than could have been in any other.

This leads us to the thought that "manual work" has been one of the links which have drawn us nearer together. I am glad to say that we can no longer make the plea that we have no materials furnished; but by wisely ordering and using we can easily have sufficient material for the work.

That there are obstacles in the work no one will question. But a love for children—not for the dainty little tots only, but a love that sees the lovable in every child, come from whatever quarter he may—this love, coupled with a common-sense view of conditions, and a faith that though results are not always what we desire, yet time will develop the seed sown; these will help to surmount all the difficulties—difficulties that stand in the way of overcoming the isolation of the kindergarten as well as all others.

* * *

SCHOOL LEGISLATION SECTION

Hugh J. Baldwin, Chairman　　　　　　J. H. Strine, Secretary

General School Legislation

James A. Foshay

The Legislature of California meets biennially, but does not act, as a rule, in accordance with the wishes of the school people of the state. Many bills are introduced, both in the Senate and Assembly at each Legislature, many of which are very desirable, and have received much careful consideration from the school people, but these bills do not finally become laws.

It is one thing for us as superintendents and teachers to say what we need and quite another to have it reduced to the proper form, and then receive the necessary consideration at the hands of those who compose the Legislature. Your committee believes that the school people should meet and inaugurate a movement which shall receive the co-operation of the school people in all parts of the State.

We believe there should be established what might be called a Committee on Publication, whose duty it shall be to publish and disseminate literature on the educational needs of the state, and to especially call the attention of the members of the Legislature to those needs. To do this there must be money, and we as teachers and friends of education must take the initiative, and either furnish the money ourselves or enlist others in such a way as to have them furnish it. And if we are to succeed in this we must have that very efficient aid, the press.

The laws which we seek to have enacted must be carefully and thoroughly considered and formulated by persons able to draw legal documents and make them in accordance with our Constitution and other laws. These should receive the attention of our most mature school people and those competent to carefully consider such matters.

. Then, too, we should perfect our state organization for personal work with the Assemblymen and Senators from each part of the state. In our opinion there should be a central committee composed of different members selected from the several sections of the State, and each member responsible for his section. There may be sub-committees appointed of faithful, diligent men and women, who have tact and common sense, to present properly the different issues to the members of the Legislature for their several sections. Our trouble has been that we have not been able to forcibly present the matters from the different sections of the state to those who represent those sections in the Legislature.

We should not be discouraged, for we go on the assumption that we have the sympathetic attitude of the Legislature and the Governor, and will continue to hold this idea until we are otherwise convinced.

There were about twenty-five Assembly bills and Senate bills introduced in 1901 session of the Legislature concerning education. Some of these bills were carefully drawn and should have become laws, but the great amount of work to be done in sixty days caused those matters which did not have personal attention from their friends to be laid aside, and others, very frequently of less importance, to receive attention instead.

We believe that one of the greatest needs in the educational department of California is to have enlarged facilities placed in the State Superintendent's office. President Merrill E. Gates, in speaking of the State Superintendent, says:

"To stand between the people and the schools, to help shape public opinion with reference to schools and educational work, while at the same time he shapes the work of the schools; to be in close relations with political boards and politics and committees, yet to keep the school system out of politics, and politics out of the school system—these are not slight demands. And I have not alluded to the Superintendent's relations to his teaching force of men and women, in itself a complicated problem, requiring for its successful solution intelligence, inspiring power, keen perceptions of justice, wise, courteous, thoughtfulness, much knowledge of men and affairs."

All examinations for certificates should be uniform, and the State Superintendent in charge. This would eliminate from the teaching profession a large majority of the school-keepers and place in their stead a class of earnest, conscientious and qualified teachers who would be an honor to the profession and to the state.

With closer supervision from the State Office, there would come a unifying of the interests of the different sections of our state.

Your committee believes that the organization of an educational commission, similar to the one recently organized, would be of great value to the school interests of this State in establishing unity of purpose in all parts of the state. We also believe that the teachers' institutes do not give a value received for the amount expended. The sessions are too short, and more normal work should be done. Let specialists in the several branches be employed by and sent out under the direction of the state office and reports made to the State Superintendent, and thus give to the State Superintendent a knowledge of the conditions and needs of the several portions of the state which would enable him to plan the work more efficiently and acceptably and employ the conductors more advantageously than can be done with so many heads. Of course co-operation is highly essential with local school authorities, and the institutes should be planned for their convenience.

Your committee would emphasize the needs of a compulsory education law to enforce the educational rights of the children of the state, and provide penalties in order for the enforcement of the law.

There should be truant schools established in cities and supported by the common school funds of those cities. In addition to the truant school in cities, a state school for truants, similar to the one we have for incorrigibles at the present time, where there can be an extensive farm cultivation and training in farm work, should be established. If we can have such a school, and knowledge on the part of the public that truant children will be systematically picked up and placed in these schools, the number of actual truants would be very much diminished. A report from the Brooklyn Truant School shows that of the 146 boys sent there in one year only three were returned the next year. It is the fact that truants will be picked up which causes them to attend school.

No pupil should be admitted to this school who has been arrested for any cause other than truancy. Such a school should be thoroly organized and equipped on the most humane plan possible, with high-minded teachers, who are in thoro sympathy with the children and their work.

The state should care especially for her unfortunate children. In cities there should be in addition to the ungraded room, which solves the problem in part, one or more rooms for defective or feeble-minded children. Such children should have much individual attention, more than can be given in the regular school or the ungraded room.

It is a surprise to know of the large number of children of school age who are either congenitally deaf or hard of hearing. We believe the state should make special provision for these children. The education of the deaf children in the public schools has progressed to such an extent that it is no longer an experiment; hence those of California thus afflicted should receive the education which is guaranteed to all our children.

In cities, the government of the school department should be vested in a Board of Education to consist in numbers as shown in their respective charters. The members should be elected for a term of four years. At the organization of the Boards first chosen after the bill shall have become a law, the members shall by lot designate the number, which shall be one less than half of the number elected, or half the number elected, if an even number be elected, who shall go out of office at the end of two years: Thereafter, all members shall be chosen for the full term of four years.

Some Needed Legislation

Edward Hyatt

Friends, I am not among those who would constantly be altering the school laws, radically *changing* them, *experimenting* with them all the time.

I would rather have them a conservative body of laws, slow to change and hard to reach. We are apt to get a notion in our heads that a certain change is absolutely necessary; to think that the world will go round in a very wabbly way without it; but in most cases it *isn't so*.

You all remember that before the last legislature there was a period of eight long years or more, with no change whatever in the laws; no thanks to us, for we demanded many changes every year, changes that we couldn't possibly get along without—yet the world wagged on, and the best school system in the American Union went serenely on its way. And since change *has* come; there are those who *are* sure we went out of the frying pan into the fire—in the matter of high school certification, for instance.

It has been my experience that we have as much to hope for and work for along the line of learning how best to use the laws we already have—as in adding new ones or making over old ones. A part of the energy we spend in bucking the center of the legislature for new enactments might well be used in unifying and improving our manner of *using* the laws as they *stand*.

For, no two counties use the same law in exactly the same way. No one who has not looked into the matter has the faintest idea of the different constructions that are put upon the same section by different minds.

Take the matter of drawing requisitions upon the county auditor. That is the most laborious and important of the county superintendent's duties; and it is the one that your chairman has particularly requested me to touch upon.

The law tells, apparently as plainly as words *can* tell, exactly how this duty shall be performed. The law has stood as it is for a score of years. The state furnishes the blanks to show how the work shall be done. Yet, I venture the assertion, and challenge anyone to prove the contrary, that there are no two counties in all this great state that do this work in the same way. And some are as different as day is from night.

Some superintendents are putting *twice* as much time and eyesight and labor upon it as others; some auditors do four times as much labor on it as others; some treasurers put ten times as much labor on it as others. Yet all are working honestly upon *their* understanding of an apparently plain and obvious law. Fifty superintendents, guided by fifty district attorneys and influenced by fifty sets of precedents, will naturally differentiate and adapt themselves to their conditions. Here and there will naturally work out short-cuts, and original methods and labor-saving devices. Naturally, there is a field for each to use his thought, his brains and his experience in most skilfully adapting his work to his conditions—in using the law to the best effect. To illustrate: (Here the speaker showed on the blackboard how a little forethought can save a deal of labor in the drawing of requisitions.)

In some counties *this* is the procedure; for the superintendent, the auditor and the treasurer to keep an exactly parallel set of books, both journal and ledger, with an account for each fund of each school district in the county, and to carry thru all these books every one of the eight or ten thousand transactions that take place. This requires an enormous outlay of clerkly industry; it chains the superintendent to his desk and transforms him from an active, wholesome school man to an austere, constipated bookkeeper. It is unproductive labor, it is vain repetition, it cannot be defended on any ground. For the trustees to laboriously draw up a paper showing the date, the name, the fund, the price, the items, the purpose of an expenditure is all right—it must be on record. But when the superintendent must write out, with anxious care, another paper showing the *same* date and name, and fund and price, and items and purpose—that's a little too much of a good thing. And then when the auditor must draw up still another paper, showing for a third time the same date and name, and fund and price, and items and purpose—that's a good thing gone to seed! And when all these particulars must be set down in four great ledgers, to be added and subtracted and juggled with for a year—why, then it becomes a weariness to the flesh! There's no *need* of it. Every repetition is a chance for an error. When it is *once recorded* and the original paper is put on file, open to inspection, that's enough, in all conscience! A regiment of bookkeepers could do no more.

Most counties, however, find a legal way to avoid more or less of this burden. Sometimes the superintendent or the auditor or the treasurer does not keep any accounts with the separate districts—perhaps only one of them does so—sometimes they do not separate the funds, and so save a thousand troubles; sometimes the auditor puts his rubber stamp on the superintendent's requisition, passing it on to the treasurer as a warrant, and sometimes the superintendent does the same with the original order that comes from the trustees. Sometimes, instead of keeping a register and a journal and a ledger in the three great books, they are combined into one small one. If a man will use his head to think with, he will find a hundred ways to simplify and improve his work. If we can get him to *do so*, we have done a better job than when we try to do it for him with a law, from outside. We cannot formulate a precise plan that will fit the counties all the way from Siskiyou to San Diego; it is better to leave a good deal of freedom for us each to work out his own salvation, under all the exhortations and encouragements we can give each other.

In this matter of requisitions I see no reason why the original paper, as it comes from the trustees, should not be stamped with the superintendent's approval and the auditor's, and then passed on to be paid by the treasurer. Permissive legislation would be better than mandatory; and it would be well to add or subtract a phrase from the present law, perhaps, so that superintendents might do this when they chose. It would certainly greatly reduce their office work and give them more time among their schools. A superintendent, however, must continue to keep an account with each of his districts and should be the custodian of the original orders after payment. If he loses touch with the purse strings of the separate schools, his power goes. He must not do anything to become unfamiliar with the financial condition of each district if he would have any real influence in the school system.

My modest dictum, then, of this one little phase of the legislative problem would be this: change the present law but little, and that little in the direction of greater freedom; and then find means for us to get our heads together on our different methods of carrying it out. The superintendents' biennial convention affords a good chance for this, as Superintendent Kirk discovered at our last meeting. I believe that an *exhibit*, showing how the books are kept and how the blanks are prepared and the funds handled in the various counties of the state, would have more actual *effect* than any change in the law that could be framed. By spending time in seeing and discussing such an exhibit, the superintendents of the state would get something *real* and *present*, something they would take home and go to work on at once, more tangible than haggling over imaginary amendments for the sweet by and by. Mr. Kirk's step in this direction deserves our approval; while it isn't exactly *legislation*, it is along the same line; and we will do well to encourage him to "push the good work along."

The Advantages and Disadvantages of a Free Text-Book System

S. D. Waterman

In general, the less tinkering with existing laws and the fewer changes the better; but there are some things in connection with the schools that will demand the attention of our law makers at the coming session of the Legislature.

First in importance, is the demand for some legislation which will give us better text-books for the elementary schools. Undoubtedly, the very best thing to be done would be to repeal every section of the law which provides for the publishing of the text-books by the state, or by constitutional amendment, however necessary, and to enact a law authorizing the State Board of Education to select such books in every branch as seem to be to them the very best, and to contract with the different publishing houses for the furnishing of these books for a specified time and at a specified rate. If this cannot be done, it is to be hoped that, at least, some such provision as was passed at the last session of the Legislature, but which was declared inoperative, may be enacted by which the copyright for certain books may be purchased for a specified number of years, these books to be printed at the state printing office. It would, however, be vastly better if the printing of text-books by the state were entirely abolished. The whole plan has been a costly experiment and has proved to be an ignominious failure in every respect. It is the height of folly for any state to go into the publishing business. A higher order of text-books can be obtained and at a lower rate under free competition.

A most important enactment, and one carrying with it more benefits to the elementary schools than any other except the one already mentioned, is a law providing for "free text-books" for the use of every pupil in the primary and grammar schools of the state. This law should not be merely permissive, nor should it partake of the nature of a "local option," but to insure the best results it should be of general application for every county and school district.

The system is in effect in some shape in the following states:

Obligatory—In Delaware, Idaho, Maryland, Maine, Massachusetts, New Hampshire, New Jersey, Pennsylvania, Rhode Island.

Permissive or Local Option—In Colorado, New York, Connecticut, Iowa, Kansas, Michigan, Wisconsin, Minnesota, North Carolina, South Dakota, North Dakota and Vermont.

In the following states, boards must furnish indigent pupils with text-books: California, Indiana, Kentucky, Montana, Nevada, Virginia, Washington. From these statistics it seems that the system, in some form, is in general use in at least twenty-seven states.

I am presuming that there is no difference of opinion as to the necessity of state uniformity, especially in California. In many of the older states in which the population is permanent, it may be so essential; in fact, in many localities, adoption and purchase by local authorities seems to be quite the thing.

State Superintendent Ranger, of Vermont, writes: "In Vermont, municipalities are required to furnish free text-books, and local school directors have the power to select and purchase books and supplies according to their judgment. The law works finely, and is eminently satisfactory. Our people would no more leave such things to a state commission than they would suffer local officers to be appointed by the Governor. This is the extreme state in democracy and local control."

Frank J. Dimond, superintendent of schools, Tonawanda, N. Y., writes: "In our state each community decides whether books shall be free or not. The cost is thus a local charge. The system has been in use here for ten years. We buy of all publishers and it is our own fault if we do not get the best. The expense after the first year has not exceeded fifty cents per pupil, each year. We are satisfied that there is great economy and great added efficiency under the 'free text-book' plan. There is everything to commend it."

"The system of 'free text-books' prevails in Greater New York. No one would think of returning to the old system under which the pupils bought their own books."—Superintendent W. H. Maxwell.

"The system of 'free text-books' has been in use in Philadelphia for eighty-four years. The board of education adopts a series of books on different subjects, the principals select their books from the list. The system works well in our city; in fact, without such a system a large number of the children would be without books, as their parents are not able to furnish them."—Edward Brooks, Superintendent.

"I am pleased to say, after years of experience under both systems, that I am uncompromisingly in favor of free text-books. The other side has no argument. After the first investment, the annual expense is not 20 per cent of what it is by the old plan."—Superintendent Boynton, Ithaca, N. Y.

"The free text-book system has been in operation in the city of Duluth for the last fifteen years. It would be utterly impossible to go back to the old plan of having the children purchase their own books. The present system is perfectly satisfactory. The books owned by the Board of Education are better cared for, and, therefore, last longer, and in this way the cost is very materially reduced. I believe that it is the only way in which children can be economically supplied with books. Trouble as to contagion is no greater than when the pupils purchase their own books."—Supt. R. E. Denfield.

A circular issued by Hon. L. D. Harvey, State Superintendent of Wisconsin, contains the following:

"There are now about 1,700 districts in this state, outside of the cities, that furnish free text-books to pupils. Seventeen cities also furnish text-books free of charge. Experience has shown that this system is cheaper and more satisfactory than any other that has been devised. There is no loss of time at the beginning of the term for lack of books, there is constant and absolute uniformity in the various classes, there is the best classification with the smallest number of classes possible, and the teacher can give the largest amount of time to class work and individual help. The convenience of making transfers from one grade to another, and the educating influence of the requirement to take care of books are also valuable factors incident to the plan. Experience has shown that books are serviceable for not less than six years, and after the first introduction, only those worn out need to be supplied. The cost of the books to the district is reduced at least two-thirds."

Michigan has a free text-book law which is giving universal satisfaction. The state superintendent. estimates that there is a saving of at least 50 per cent to the taxpayers.

State Superintendent Baxter of New Jersey says: "We have had a free text-book law since 1894. It has proved such a benefit to our schools that our people are practically unanimous in its support. We find that the system is more economical than the old, and that the loss of time at the beginning of the term is reduced to a minimum."

Quotations almost without number might be given, but enough have already been written to indicate the success of the system wherever it has been tried, even in those states where local adoption is the law. How much more easily and successfully the plan can be put into effect in a state like California, where there is a state adoption of books.

In order to bring the subject fully before you, I quote from the school law of a few of the states:

Massachusetts—"The School Committee of each district shall, at the expense of the town, purchase text-books and other supplies used in the public schools and, subject to such regulations as to their care and custody as it may prescribe, loan them to the pupils of such school free of charge," etc.

New Hampshire—"They (the school boards) shall purchase at the expense of the city or town in which the district is situated, text-books and other supplies required for use in the public schools; and shall loan the same to the pupils of the school free of charge, subject to such regulations for their care and custody as the school board may prescribe. They shall make provision for the sale of such books at cost to pupils of the school wishing to purchase them for their own use."

Maine—"Towns shall provide school books, apparatus and appliances for the use of the pupils in the public school, etc., provided, however, that any parent or guardian of any pupil in the public schools may at his own expense, procure for the separate and exclusive use of such pupils the text-books required to be used in such schools."

Nebraska—"District school boards and the boards of trustees in high school districts and boards of education in cities of the first and second class are hereby authorized and it is made their duty to purchase all text-books necessary for all of the pupils of the district; and they are empowered to contract for a uniform price for a term not less than three years," etc. The contractors must contract to furnish the books at as low a rate as they are furnished in any part of the United States.

From the report of Hon. F. A. Hill, secretary of the Massachusetts state board of education, we find that the expense of text-books per pupil for the last year, in Massachusetts, was $0.59. The average for the past ten years, $1.62.

Secretary Hill names the following as among the most common of the adverse comments that are made:

1. The books may become carriers of disease.

2. They may be kept in use too long.

3. It does not favor the gathering of educational books at home.

4. Their proper care diverts the teacher unduly from his main work.

The first objection would be justly made with regard to the ordinary circulating library; yet we never hear this objection made.

The second really has no force, as the

renewal of the supply rests entirely with the board.

In answer to the third it may be said that a lot of old text-books do not form the most valuable educational library for the home.

Arrangements could easily be made as to the care and the issuing of these books which would relieve the teacher and at the same time be of positive educational value to the school.

A few of the advantages are given as follows:

1. The removal from parents of a serious burden of expense.

2. The ending of the friction that so often arises when parents are asked to buy new books.

3. The banishing of the obnoxious distinction between those who are able to buy and those who are not.

4. A more varied and generous supply of text-books at school with absolute uniformity, whenever desired.

5. Greater ease in keeping the supply fresh and modern.

6. Increased respect for books as shown in the care of them.

7. Great saving in time and energy at the beginning of each term, because of having books on hand in ample supply.

8. A larger and more permanent attendance.

9. A closer approach to an ideal public school system.

On any subject that we have not actually tried, our opinion must be largely formed from the testimony of those who have had experience. The opinion of those who have tried the free text-book system is practically unanimous in its favor. A bill to put into operation the free text-book system in California should be the second bill referred to the Educational Committees of the Legislature, the first being a bill to repeal the present fraud which authorizes the books to be printed by the state.

Hon. E. B. Andrews, of the University of Nebraska, has written a very clear and comprehensive review of the whole subject. The article referred to appeared in the *Cosmopolitan* for January, 1902. It is well worth careful perusal. A few quotations are given:

"It is significant that those states and cities in the Union commonly considered the most advanced educationally have adopted free books as indispensable to the proper working of a free school system, and that wherever this has occurred, the number of pupils in attendance has increased, the average duration of pupils' attendance has lengthened, a greater number and proportion of pupils continuing their studies up to the highest grades, and the whole efficiency of the schooling has been improved. I have before me a great mass of favorable testimony from able and discriminating superintendents who have had experience with the free system. All arguments against it are theoretical. Wherever free text-books have been tried, support of them is, I believe, practically unanimous. Only by resort to the gratuity system can classes be promptly organized at the beginning of sessions. Do our best, the opening of a session sees more or less delay in waiting for pupils who could not take up the work with the class at the proper time. If school books are not free this difficulty becomes appalling. It is not at all uncommon for a pupil to be kept from school for weeks for this reason. Again, without free text-books, classification cannot be just or complete. Promotions and reductions are certain not to occur as deserved. If a pupil has begun a session in a given grade and purchased the proper books, no principal would wish, and few would dare, to "demote" him to the next lower grade, even if the pupil's interest and the interest of the grade demanded this ever so imperatively. The same difficulty renders due promotions. Ascending a grade, the pupils must, of course, have new books. Even well-to-do and sympathetic parents complain at such demand."

More might be written, but enough testimony has already been given to convince any one that there is great good to be accomplished for the schools by the adoption of the free text-book plan.

A third subject which demands attention is the passage of a law making operative the amendment recently adopted by the people by which the state may levy a tax for aid of the high schools. This question, however, will be discussed fully at another time and place.

If the three enactments referred to in this paper can be secured, great good for our school system will be accomplished.

* * *

MANUAL TRAINING SECTION

Walter A. Edwards, Chairman   **Claude A. Faithfull, Secretary**

Manual Training in Scondary Schools

Elmer E. Brown

With reference to the abstruse question whether in the secondary school the work in manual training is work generally cultural or vocational, I would say yes, and no, and both; and it is neither. The history of the subject has been of much interest to me.

A kind of manual wave has swept over this country. Away back in the twenties and thirties of the nineteenth century, partly under the influence of the denominational schools and partly as a spontaneous development of our own country, there grew up a great demand for manual labor schools. They were different from the manual training school but something of the same sort. Manual labor schools became very popular in connection with theological seminaries; they nearly all had them as attaches. The idea was double: they were dealing with theory which took them away from the ground and these schools were added to put them back into the ground; and another reason was, the students could work their way through the school. In a way it was a liberal culture movement, but it is hard to define just what it was. The main thing about it was that the boys could make their way and get an educational result which was the inculcation of the spirit of industry.

These schools were in a large measure farm schools in which the pupils were getting regular instruction in school half a day and during the other half of the day worked on the farm. But part was also shop work of various sorts. I have not very definite information as to just what that shop work was but it was some ordinary carpenter work as near as I can find out. These attached schools were distinctly, though not primarily, cultural schools. That movement has not entirely died out; there exist at present two or three schools that are known as manual labor schools.

After the Civil War there came a new interest in manual training and that was more of the sort that we are dealing with. It was an interest that had arisen in Russia, Germany and Sweden before it touched this country to a very great extent. There had been some interest in it here before the Philadelphia Exposition in 1876, but the exhibits there from Russia especially gave a new impetus to it, and the great time of expansion was in the early part of the 80's, when there was an enormous interest in manual training, and that interest has never died out. We think of it as being a movement of the last two or three years, but there is no break between this movement and that of the early eighties. That of the eighties was distinguished from the earlier manual labor schools in that the schools of the 80's had more of the shop work and less of the farm work; it was different from it as being distinctly, and vitally, a cultural movement. The leaders emphasized the fact that they were not engaged in teaching trades, but were interested in it for the sake of making a manhood. Great claims were made for it. It was supposed to have tremendous educational value. There is a tendency in these days to moderate the more extravagant claims made then as to their cultural value. Emphasis was laid by some of the more enthusiastic leaders upon the moral value of this training, especially in the planing of boards or the drawing of a chalk line, because there was something between them and the rule of conduct that brings the mind to a moral line. This is a question that has come to a new discussion; it is not definitely settled, and so it is coming up again. This question goes by the name of "Formal Culture." This arose not in connection with manual training, but arose in Germany in the early part of the nineteenth century in reference to the educational value of the classes of mathematics, that in the educational process there is a certain virtue which relates not to the particular subject upon which the process is applied or to schools of that subject, but which gives results of a universal character, which produces a certain kind of power in the person instructed, which he can carry with him, from, say the field of Latin, to the field of geology or engineering, or to any other field. That is, that education, in any one of its special fields gives some sort of educational result which is in the nature of current coin that can be employed in any of the vocations of life. Now, is there any result of education that can be passed on from one field to another, and if so, is there any difference in studies?

It was maintained in the earlier part of the nineteenth century by the advocates of the classics and mathematics in the German gymnasium that the subjects referred to were peculiar subjects which gave large results of this sort; subjects, the mastery of which meant not simply the mastery of those subjects, but in addition, a certain power that could be used in all the employments of life, so that the person who had mastered a subject of that kind had a residuum of power which increased him as a man, pure and simple, without reference to what he was engaged in. This same doctrine was applied to manual training and it was held that in learning to saw a board a boy did not only gain some ability to do that one thing with that one sort of material, but it made him more of a man. As regards intellectual results he gained power of close discrimination, and as a moral result it was supposed he gained a certain power of self-mastery and a certain ideal of rightness that was very closely connected with righteousness. If that sort of claim were fully justified, and if the additional claim that manual training occasioned a particularly large result, were also justified, it would seem that manual training as a cultural subject would have an assured place and one of very great importance.

Now this doctrine of "Formal Culture" was settled. It was found out that there was nothing in it; that there is no general result of education, and that the only result of education in a certain subject is ability to handle that subject; that there is nothing universal.

The results of past investigation along this line have not been entirely satisfactory, and certainly we have reason still, without violating the laws of common decency, to think that there may be something in manual training other than a mastery to do these special things. I will suggest one which is coming out pretty clearly, namely, that whether much or little of "Formal Culture" is possible as a school result, formal culture varies greatly with the individual; that is, there are men who from sawing a board will get lessons which they will carry into the fields of morals. I presume there are boys who from the making of a basket will get something that will go with them into the field of morality. There are certain endowments of mind that enable some people to utilize these lessons in their fields of action, while in others it never could be.

We have got to the place where we think we ought to apologize for any possible trade tendency in our education. I hope we are coming to the point where we realize that vocational training is just as dignified, worthy and significant as any other kind of training. We are getting to the point, I think, where it is possible. I think we are to hold two ideas in our heads at the same time; it is possible for us to be loyal to two ideals. when we see they are not inconsistent one with another, and the idea of liberal culture, I believe, is consistent with the idea of technical competence with a man's business in life. We are coming to the belief that it is important in a correlative way that a man should both be liberally educated and should be educated to do something honest for a living. I think we are tending toward that view of education which is represented by a happy remark of President Butler when he says: "The world does not need narrow men, but it does need broad men, sharpened to a point," and that is exactly what we are tending toward in our view of public education—we are tending toward men made broad by liberal culture sharpened to a point by vocational training; men, accordingly, who can make an honest livelihood and still be men of liberal culture. I think there is something mightily fine in that sort of idea.

I do not think that according to our advancing views of educational theory manual training is ruled out as a cultural subject. I think we are prepared to recognize cultural elements and cultural value in manual training. Secondly, I think we are coming to the point where we will demand that manual training shall come in in some sort of school somewhere, for many of our boys to definitely, sharply mark vocational training. I think it is desirable that we should have general cultural schools and probably with manual training in them. We should have a broad, concrete, common system of liberal training that we Americans lay so much stress upon, for I might say that we have a tendency toward a consecutive, well-articulated system of general culture. As we go back over the history of our American education we see there a deep-seated movement of the American people toward the maintenance of great consecutive systems that should give liberal culture and without any bars, without any leadings off, lead up to the highest attainments. Probably, there is no more marked characteristic in our American educational training than the fact that we can congratulate our American future that the highest political office that goes the way to the Presidency is open to every child, and the way to the highest possible culture in preparing for public service should be open to every child. But at the same time that this is true there is going to be a distinct demand that there shall be a school, definite and distinct from the school of general culture which has for its purpose the preparing of men and women to become honest, skilled, bread-winners, so that at the completion of the course at such a school they shall be fully prepared to go out and quit themselves honorably in some definite occupation in life, and I think we should be able to emphasize both of these sides and not feel that either is subordinate to the other.

* * *

Manual Work for the First Grade

Mary F. Ledyard

[Extract]

For the benefit of those who never believe what they hear and only half of what they see, I have caused to be exhibited here today a little raphia work, collected very hurriedly from some of our first-grade classes just a few days before Christmas.

Of course the product is crude in many ways, but this fact is true of it—the work is the work of the child, and in many cases represents the almost unaided effort of the child, for our method of using the medium raphia has been to introduce it as busy work as soon as the child has a small working knowledge of it or power over it, and he is expected to go on independently while the teacher is employed with the other children of her class. Of course our use of raphia is so far only tentative, but of this little exhibit I will have more to say later on.

Since first becoming actively interested in the work of manual training as an outgrowth of the principles laid down by Froebel, using it as a means of bridging the gulf between kindergarten and first grade and on thru the grammar and high school as a golden line holding and binding all together, I have sought more earnestly than ever before for the key—the deep, underlying principle which fixes and holds with a magic charm this innate tendency to create—to make something at once beautiful and useful, to overcome crude and elemental materials and transform them into an image conceived in the brain and worked out thru the finger tips.

Many students of economics claim that the great problems that rend our land concerning the relation of labor and capital "will never be solved until there is greater respect for manual labor; until there is more joy to the worker in his labor, which should be the expression thru his hand of the thought of his head and the feeling of his heart. We absorb only so much as we can interpret in terms of our own active experience." I claim, on the other hand, that there is very real and inborn "joy of the worker in his labor"; that this joy is God-given and almost universal when called out; that there is no age limit, and that we have all history to bear us out in this position. From the ancient Egyptian and the cliff-dweller, deftly modeling his beautiful potteries from the clay at his hand, unaided by tutor or tool, to the child of today fashioning a crude little basket from some simple nature material, the impulse, the motive is the same; the educative result is the same; the yearning to create, to bring into being something that never before existed and to stamp upon it something of personality, making it a means of inarticulate expression, is the same. * * * * * * * *

Living in a land so rich in natural material, it is sad indeed that the above should be in any measure true. So far, we have made use of some of these,
that is, palm, tule, yucca, reed and raphia; the latter, as you all know, we import from Madagascar, one of the East African archipelago. It comes to us with but little preparation, and we use it with no change except to moisten it for some purposes. * * * * *

Raphia grows as a covering on the under side of the leaf spur of the raphia palm. It is simply stripped off with a knife, and this is done by women, dried in the sun and, knotted or twisted, the material is ready for use. The natives use raphia for fish nets, rice winnowers and fine mats, and use it in many ways, both useful and beautiful. The fascination which this form of manual work possesses seems to be very persistent and as pronounced in the case of grown people as in children, as exemplified by the great wave of interest in basketry which has swept over the whole country since the work has been seriously introduced into the school. Of course this has largely taken shape as a fad, but as a means of education and aid to manual training work I think it has come to stay, whatever may be said of it as a godsend to the vast army of unemployed rich and idle people. If Neal Burgess is right, however, its chances are good in this field, for he says:

"One by one we outlive the joys of youth, the zest of travel, the beatitudes of emotion; the familiar games lose their savor; the dance gives way to the drama; we tire of seeing and begin to read, but the joy of creation does not fade, for in it lies our divinity, our claim to eternity. Each new product arouses the same thrill, the same spiritual excitement, the same pride of victory. It is not the completion of an object, but the construction which holds us enthralled; not the last stroke, but every stroke brings victory. It is like the climbing of a mountain. Do we endure the toil merely for the sake of the view from the summit? No, but for the primitive passion of conflict, the inch-by-inch fight against odds—the joy of overcoming."

Experimentation by the Pupil in Domestic Science

Mary L. Gower

Under this heading I wish to group, for consideration and discussion, the following problems:

1. How shall domestic science aid in developing the child intellectually?
2. In what way can the work in the cooking-room be made to help the other school work, as well as obtain the most help from it?
3. How much experimenting can be successfully done?
4. Will there be gain or loss in substituting experiment for lecture, or dictation (oral or written)?
5. What advantage has individual experiment over demonstration by the teacher?

In a talk delivered before a parents' association on the University Elementary School of Chicago, Mr. John Dewey says: "We started with four problems: 1. What can be done, and how can it be done, to bring the school into closer relation with the home and neighborhood life. * * * ?

This does not mean * * * that the child should simply take up in the school things already experienced at home, and study them, but that, so far as possible, the child shall have the same attitude and point of view in the school as in the home; that he shall find the same interest in going to school, and in there doing the things worth doing for their own sake, that he finds in the plays and occupations which busy him in his home and neighborhood life. It means, again, that the motives which keep the child at work and growing at home shall be used in the school, so that he shall not have to acquire another set of principles of actions belonging to the school—separate from those of the home. It is a question of the unity of the child's experience, of its actuating motives and aims.* * * * "

By substitutions we may make this problem ours. In substance it would question how to connect more closely the cooking and other school work, so that pupils may look upon both as interdependent, and, while thoroly enjoying the activity of the cooking-room, appreciate the theory which raises the preparation of a meal above a purely mechanical plane.

Children are naturally impatient of what does not give visible or tangible results, and only too well satisfied to follow a given recipe as the shortest road to reach a desired end. In "cooking school" they expect to *cook* and either *eat* the finished article at once or bear it home in triumph as a specimen of their handiwork.

Next to this they appreciate cleansing processes as having a practical value. For theory as such they have scarcely tolerance, being willing to take at second hand what receipts they can find; and thinking every lesson on theory so much time lost.

One little girl in a most earnest tone asked: "Why do they waste a whole lesson that way?"

Of course a ready and truthful answer is that the time allowed each lesson is not sufficient to combine the necessary lessons on materials and all the subjects they should understand, with cooking; hence the lessons must be separate. * * *

In this connection the desire for action may be utilized in actual discovery, following certain suggestions at first, noting results; then suggesting other points and the method of experimenting.

Mr. Dewey, in another lecture, speaks of this phase of the work—the desire of the child to "mess around," imitating "the activities of older people."

He says: "Here, too, if the impulse be exercised, utilized, it runs up against the actual world of hard conditions, to which it must accommodate itself; and there, again, come in the factors of discipline and knowledge." * * *

In order that the work should be truly educative, note-books and pencils should be used freely to record the results and state deductions.

The experiments should be performed

by individuals, under sufficient guidance to prevent aimless work, following a definite outline. Results should be discussed and verified that the student may be certain of correctness of work. Conclusions should be reached as to the application, and the theory stated by the class. Following this, application may be made of the theory in some dish, or in cleansing, etc.

We should not lose sight of the right of the child to know if her results are correct. In thus stimulating her to exercise thought and judgment, and to express results, we cause an increase of intellectual power.

The work in other lines is thus helped, and work in domestic science is helped by the use of the methods employed in general subjects.

There will be no loss, but rather gain, in substituting experiment for lecture and dictation.

The advantage in having each student perform the experiment is seen in the close attention to each point that is needed to gain correct results, or exact knowledge.

* * *

PHYSICAL CULTURE SECTION

H. J. Baldwin, Chairman Edward Hyatt, Secretary

In Relation to Physical Culture

Louis Fritz

Health and strength of body and mind should be the first requisite of every good educational system. Intellectual attainments are of secondary importance. This proposition may appear strange to some, particularly to that class who can see in education nothing but the training of the mind. But if one is attained to the detriment of the other, which of the two could we best afford to dispense with? Surely, if we have any regard for the preservation of our race, in a healthy and vigorous state, we must admit that the former is the most essential, as without it we would be like a top-heavy vessel on the mighty waves of the ocean, lacking the necessary ballast to guide us safely thru tempests and storms that may chance to overcome us on our travels thru life.

The dual principle of education of the body and mind co-ordinately was strictly adhered to by the Hellenic people of old; and well did they succeed in not only planting the banner of their mighty physical power on the highest pinnacles, but that remarkable period was also fruitful of that grand wisdom and profound knowledge which every investigator of basic learning of our time must study in order to lay for himself a proper foundation on which to build his future intellectual researches. Not only this, but we go back to that period for our ennobling inspiration, in beauty of form, sculpture and architecture, by admiring and copying those beautiful designs and types and consider them today models of perfection. As the photographic lens gives us an exact reproduction of things, so can we take it for granted that the great masters of art of that age have given us representations of beauty, graceful form and awe-inspiring grandeur, as seen with their eyes. Art today without those classical designs to gaze upon, to admire and to emulate, would be like a barren wilderness lacking the beautiful and inspiring touch of the master in nature's garden. We should strive with all the power that we are possessed of to rekindle that noble spirit which will lead us on to open up all the avenues of physical development for our children and children's children. There is no reason why every man, woman and child of the future should not be a model of beauty, strength and vigor, worthy of the master's art, if we make our educational system as perfect as the advanced spirit of the time demands. Give to every child the opportunity and a practical physical training and in due course of time during the period of its growth the sharp curves and ungainly angles will have a tendency to disappear, and a well-rounded and symmetrical form will be the final reward. Let us not forget that the time at which to begin physical development is during the earliest stages of school life, because whatever part is neglected then cannot by any means be regained, no matter how perfect they may otherwise be. We should therefore consider it a great obligation we owe to ourselves and to posterity to give to child life that attention that its physical well-being is above all other things entitled to. Competent authority on the subject has said that from three to five hours a week should be devoted to the physical body and its systematic training. It would seem that this time allowance is but a reasonable demand when we consider the benefits to be derived. Every child in normal physical condition has a natural desire for recreative plays and exercises which should be controlled by rational methods under competent supervision, but if these plays and exercises are unnaturally restricted, by adding too much mental exertion, the muscular forces will become relaxed, so that the child in such instances will seek a state of rest rather than of activity, and consequently the initiatory way has been opened for the undermining of that child's bodily powers. Does it not seem clear, then, that our first efforts should be directed to maintain that which is dearest to all—health of body and mind—where it can be secured at such trifling cost, even if we have to cut short some studies, to which many do not naturally incline, and which can safely be left to the private and home departments. We may feel kindly toward any character of study that will contribute to the attainment of the highest type of education, but we should not favor the teaching of things at the expense or to the detriment of the child's physical well-being, particularly if such studies are not susceptible of a general application. When the state takes a child under its guardianship, at the kindergarten or primary stage, it certainly also assumes the responsibility of preserving that child's physical welfare, at least to that extent, as not to contribute anything to its injury. But, is it not conceded generally that too much mental work is imposed on the children of today, both in the schools and at home, crowding out the time and the opportunity for beneficial exercises and healthful recreation? The burden of the responsibility rests upon the state to apply all the precautionary measures in order to safeguard the health and strength of these tender lives while it has charge of them, and also to assist in developing and improving the physical condition of our race.

To leave the carrying out of this important feature of education to the whims and wills of county and district boards of education, as the matter now stands, is to go begging for something that ought to be as secure to us as the sunlight that we enjoy. School boards usually have neither time nor the inclination to take hold of the subject in the proper spirit, knowing that whatever action they might take may be overturned by the next incoming board. The subject being purely of an educational character, the State Board of Education should control it, protected by the proper enactment of law, defining the principle and the manner in which physical culture should be applied throughout the state.

Section 1668 of the present school laws, termed: "Hygienic Directions," is the only law we have in this state on the subject under consideration, and, as it now reads, is evidently not sufficiently explicit, in that it does not distinguish as between physical training and hygienic requirements, which is also plainly shown by Rule 18 of the State Board of Education, limiting the requirement to its hygienic aspect, that is, breathing exercises within the schoolroom not to exceed five minutes. This is merely a measure to give the teacher a needed opportunity to open the windows of the schoolroom for ventilation and the entering of fresh air. Physical training, in the proper acceptation of the term, should be practiced independently from hygienic regulations, and in this state should be preferably carried on outside of schoolrooms, either on the school or adjoining grounds or in public parks, suitably arranged and adapted for this purpose, under the supervision of learned and competent teachers for this work. If our aims and conclusions as here stated are correctly taken, one of the first-needed steps is to ask the Legislature of this state to enact an additional section to the school laws plainly defining physical training, making the same mandatory, and placing the power of the State Board of Education for its execution.

Another important phase of the benefits of physical training is found in the duty the state owes to our common country towards safeguarding of our institutions against any foe within or without. There is nothing that will contribute more to our everlasting peace and happiness than the consciousness of our ability to make our position impregnable, in case of danger or necessity, as a means of national defense. It will probably be strange to some in what manner the public schools can have any connection with a purely military question, but when we consider the results to be achieved by a thoro physical training, then we can more readily see the close relation the two bear to each other. Among the aims of physical culture may be briefly stated: Health, strength of body and limb, uniform and symmetrical build, erectness of body and ease of movement, agility, quickness and speed of action, exactness and precision, power of endurance, graceful and easy carriage.

The ethical aims closely related to the above are: Discipline, will power, manliness, self-reliance, respect for self and others, presence of mind, sense of beauty in form and action, quickness of though and perception, and last, but not least love of country.

Now, it does not need any stretch o our imagination to be able to discern tha a good defender of his country should b possessed with all of the above-mentione requirements. In order that the averag citizen may attain these, the groundwor must necessarily be laid at the base of eac rising generation, or, in other words, i must be made an essential part of our edu cational system. California should tak particular pride in this matter as a com monwealth to raise her sons, yes and he daughters, so that they may be capable de fenders of our country's institutions wher ever occasion should require it. I do no mean by this that we should instill in th youths of our state any desire or taste fo the arts of warfare; on the contrary, suc an outgrowth should be summarily sup pressed whenever or wherever it shoul appear, but by a comprehensive and wel governed system of physical trainin brought home to the individual units tha will make up our great aggregation o future citizens we shall have created barrier which, on the shortest notice; ca be molded into a massive, movable huma avalanche, irresistible in aggression an unconquerable in defense. Large standin armies would thus become useless appen dages in our country, where the popula will alone should control its destinie when the blessings of a permanent peac would be more secure.

Having arrived at that cherished stag of American civilization and advance ment, of commanding superior physica and intellectual qualities, we could the look down from our exalted position an proclaim to the world that fond desire To be in peace and unity with all mar kind.

The German System of Physical Culture
Fred Detmers

Although physical training as a part of the public school course is supposed to be of very recent date and often referred to as an addition to the modern curriculum, yet forty-one years ago, in the school report of Providence for the year 1861, there is found mention that "a decided step forward in our school economy was made during the past year in provision for physical exercises in the high school. A building was erected upon its premises and appropriate gymnastic exercises freely indulged in by the pupils, fostered by teachers and the committee." This movement is parallel with the gymnastic revival of 1860 throughout America, dating from the meeting of the American Institute of Instruction at Boston in that year, at which meeting Dr. Dio Lewis made his famous plea for "calisthenics and gymnastics a part of school teaching." This report of progress in 1861 in the Providence schools concluded with these words: "More attention than usual has been paid in all our schools to this indispensable branch of culture, and we augur favorably for the increased mental development of the pupils from this bodily training." In the school statement of 1865 a special report was made upon the same subject, and the prophecy made "that the mind of the child might become emasculated by too much teaching, while his energies may not be properly developed in consequence of over-much study and confinement during school hours."

Since that time the agitation for the introduction of physical training in the regular school course has never stopped; it sometimes lagged, but in recent years, again, has been taken up with much earnestness and zeal by leading educators all over the country. It has become self-evident to teachers and parents alike that the ordinary course of study alone taxes the mental faculties of the children to their utmost capacity, and if some means are not found to counteract this strain a collapse seems inevitable. The most sensible, the most rational of all means employed to support the mental activities under all circumstances is a graded and well-balanced course in physical culture. It is hardly necessary to dwell at any length upon the urgent need of such exercises; they are the need of the hour, and no one who sincerely and thoroly studies our present school conditions will deny it. But the question arises, Who shall instruct the children in this branch, and what system shall we employ, what rules shall we follow to obtain the best results? To suppose that the regular teacher, already burdened to the limit with the educational tasks, should accept this responsibility and assume the role of physical instructor seems little less than unreasonable. We must have special teachers who will take up the study of physical training as their life's work; teachers who have been properly fitted and prepared for this arduous task, and who are willing and capable to devote all their energies to the upbuilding of the physical faculties of their pupils.

To decide which system shall we teach there is really but one before the American public today, and that is the German system. Its aim is the harmonious development of all the different parts of the body, resulting in health, strength and agility, ease and grace in the carriage of the body, as well as in the movement of its different parts. A hundred years or more ago Johann F. Gutsmuths, the first writer on German gymnastics, defines it as "Work in the garb of youthful pleasure and merriment." It distinguishes between educational, medical, military and society gymnastics. The educational branch is divided into six large classes or groups of exercises, namely:

1. Tactics, or order movements, embracing marching in all its forms.

2. Calisthenics, consisting of free exercises and such with hand appliances, as

short and long wands, dumbbells, rings and Indian clubs.

3. Fancy steps, mainly for girls and ladies.

4. Apparatus work on the horizontal bar, parallel bar, long and side horse, buck, rings, ladders, poles, ropes, round swing, balance board, see-saw, swinging board and vaulting table.

5. Popular exercises, as high, far and deep jump, hop, step and jump, running, hopping, putting the shot, throwing the javelin and discus, lifting and putting up iron weights, pole vaulting, swimming, skating, fencing, boxing, wrestling and shooting.

6. Innumerable games and plays, the first publication of which was made in 1793 by Gutsmuths, and to which a large number of pedagogues have added constantly ever since.

The enormous abundance of physical movements is due to the chief characteristic feature of the German system as a progressive and all-embracing system. Since the time of its origin hundreds of able and experienced educators have been busy arranging this vast wealth of exercises into a logical system, and at present it may be said that there is no other system in existence that has so carefully prepared and graded its material, so as to be properly adapted to every age, to every institution of education, and to both sexes. Music is considered a great aid in the practice of the exercises in this system, and is largely employed in it. The exercises may be executed by words of command as well as in rhythmical time. While dealing with the instruction of large masses simultaneously it never loses sight of the special needs of the individual.

These, in the main, are the features of the German system of physical training. It stands today unapproached by any other, contains all the necessary requisites for the needs of our educational institutions, and is in perfect conformity with the wants of our country and the character of our people.

Surprising as it may seem, it is a fact, nevertheless, that very much ignorance still prevails at present as to the merits of physical training, especially among members of school boards, who really ought to know better. In a great many cities in the United States physical culture is looked upon as a branch, which, in the opinion of an exalted school board, may be introduced or abolished at will, or maintained as a sort of compensation for political pressure or influence. It should be our aim to remove this question entirely from the sphere of politics and to establish physical training firmly and permanently in all of our public schools. For this purpose the hearty co-operation of you, the teachers, is absolutely essential. Let us, then, one and all, resolve to put our best efforts forward to attain this end. Let us not relax our vigilance until every schoolhouse in this great and glorious land is equipped with a gymnasium, in charge of a qualified instructor; until all the children, from the kindergarten to the high school, enjoy the benefits of a rational physical education, and then from millions of youths will you receive hearty blessings for having given them a brighter, better and healthier condition of both body and mind.

MUSIC SECTION

Miss Kathryn Stone, Chairman
Leon I. Stanton, Secretary

Minutes

Friday, January 2, 1903, 9:30 A. M.

Cumnock Hall, a most appropriate place for the meeting of musically inclined teachers of the state, had its capacity fully tested upon the date and hour above mentioned. To fully describe the sight presented by so many intelligent faces, surrounded by such environs as the building of this school of expression presents, would take more space than might be allotted to the subject. Enough to say that those taking active part in the program will ever have the picture before them, so harmonious was the thought.

The program, having been arranged by the chairman of the music section, Miss Katherine Stone of Los Angeles, assisted by Mrs. Mary E. Dunster and Miss Jennie Hogan, was well worthy the attention it received, the opening number being an air of Gounod's, arranged by Bach as a "Meditation," for twenty violins, a solo being played by Mr. Edwin Clark.

Miss Estelle Carpenter of San Francisco was then introduced and read a thoughtfully prepared paper upon "Voice Quality," interspersing it with a number of unique examples, which were appreciated by the listeners.

Miss Beresford Joy of Los Angeles gave pleasure in the rendering of vocal selections entitled "The Shephard," by Somerville; "Little One a-Crying," by Oley Speaks; "The Gingerbread Man;" also, "The Slumber Boat," by Gaynor, Miss Showater accompanying.

Miss Ida Fisher of Alameda read a paper which she had prepared upon "Beginnings in Music," amplifying the same with numerous examples of an instructive character.

Following the singing of class songs, "Santa Lucia" and "The Violet," also very good examples of sight singing by children of the fifth and sixth grades of Los Angeles schools, being a representation of the effective work done by Miss Katherine Stone, Miss Hogan of the Normal School asked for the privilege of stating that, "after all," thought papers are a great benefit, such work as an example of what can be done with the children in preparation for the Normal was to her mind the most effective.

Mrs. L. V. Sweesy of Berkeley talked upon "Rhythm" and received a very pretty compliment (by the singing of a class "yell" from a chorus of Pasadena high-school girls), which she had composed during her regime in the music section at that institution. Unfortunately, the notes taken during the presentation of the subject were lost, and, as it was not in the form of a paper, as mentioned in the program, I am unable to give to you the details of the same. Suffice to say, it was interesting and instructive.

The final number, a violin solo, "Ninth Concerto," by De Beriot, effectively played by Mrs. Hazel Dessery of Los Angeles, closed, perhaps, the best program ever presented to the California Teachers' Association.

An invitation was extended to the Musical Supervisors present, by Miss Katherine Stone, to attend a round table at her home the same evening, at which several matters of importance were discussed. Among those present were Mesdames Mary E. Gorden Dunster, L. V. Sweesy, Misses Estelle Carpenter, Ida Fisher, Katherine Stone, Messrs. A. D. Hunter, Allan B. Martin and Leon I. Stanton. Miss Stone, being hostess, served the most dainty and appropriate refreshments. Just before adjourning it was decided by vote of those present to recommend the adoption of the "movable do" system as against the "fixed do," now being taught in some districts of our state.

Your secretary received a communication from Mrs. Jennie L. Thorp, together with copies of a very pretty song for school work, entitled "California, Queen of Old Columbia," also a "Rote Song Book," being first steps in music, and a "New Natural Music Primer," edited by Frederick H. Ripley and Thomas Tapper, published by the American Book Company, and he would personally recommend them to the use of teachers of the first grades as containing a great fund of helpful information and music. Papers upon the subjects of "Voice Quality" and "Beginnings in Music" are to be found in detail below.

LEON I. STANTON,
Secretary of Music Section.

* * *

Beginnings in Music

Miss Ida Fisher

The child's progress in music depends much upon the way the subject is presented to him. It is important to begin so that the best possible benefits may be derived through its study. "Build the oak with the proper essence in the acorn."

Upon entrance into school, only about one-third of the children can sing. Shall we first give the scale or even difficult songs, when more than half the class sing along on one low tone or up and down regardless of the melody? It would be as reasonable to attempt to teach reading to children before they have learned to talk. Vocal freedom must be brought about for these little so-called "monotones," and it must be done in such a way that those who can sing will not become discouraged.

Watch the child on the playground and see how quickly he learns the games. He forgets himself completely and becomes a part of the game. The boy and the game come together with unity. Every attribute appeals to his whole nature. Many things come to the little child very easily in play, when all his senses are alert and active. Then he often does unconsciously that which would seem impossible otherwise, and what is learned in this way is not easily forgotten. I have seen children perfectly delighted when playing "Poll parrot," and have been surprised to note such gratifying results gotten so quickly. Have the class imitate polly by calling such phrases as "Polly, pretty bird," "Polly wants a cracker," etc. In this way the child can be taught to sound a high tone, then hold it, and last change the pitch of his voice. To begin by giving chants is another interesting way. Chant first with one tone, then gradually introduce new tones in the scale succession. Start, if possible, with G, second line, and add the tones upward. Many beautiful songs that appeal to the child may be learned, and he loves to sing them, for it is not always the most difficult songs that give him the greatest pleasure. It is more often the rhythm, sentiment or action that takes.

It is natural for a child to learn more easily that in which he is interested. By singing he will learn to sing. We must take him as he is; give songs that appeal to him and that he can understand. Many of us, in our ambition to make of the pupils good readers of music, are apt to begin the formal side of music prematurely, forgetting for the time that, while this should not be neglected, for to make real the study of music in the schools, the science should be taught, it is out of place before the pupil is prepared for it. Of what use are sharps, flats and the value of notes to him if, through all his school work, his soul lies dormant, never touched by a tender strain? There are many who at the end of their school work are able to answer any question put to them, but who have never once received the real joy and pleasure that would have been theirs had music been rightly presented.

Every person represents a dual nature, animal and spiritual; the one made up of material elements, fed three times a day, the other as a living soul received direct from God. Impressions made upon the senses stimulate action on the soul. Song should express both the animal and spiritual natures. In the body, at first, there is but little heart and little mind. The body, mind and heart should harmonize in song. If there be too much will, it becomes cunning; if excess of body, brutal; the heart predominating, the song becomes sentimental.

We must first get the spirit of music. The breath is the spirit. It is important to have good use of the breath. Little children should be led to take the breath correctly, more by example than by explanations. Take a deep breath as if smelling a flower, let it out and give all plus your own nature. There is great power in the breath. Grasping the hand, take a long breath, looking into the eyes of a near friend in trouble, expresses more sympathy than words.

One who can talk with a fervent voice learns easiest to sing expressively. It was the fervor in Patti's voice that brought the tears to the eyes of the audience when she sang "Home, Sweet Home." We must take away the prosaics from the voice and talk and sing with different moods. Some people sing like the fashionable handshake, touching but the tips of the fingers. One should take hold of music with a firm grasp. It is not so much the tone you sing as what you sing through it. Too much of the school singing is like the outer ring of the bell, the proclamation. Let us have the inner tones, the over tones, that go to the heart.

Along with the development of the voice the ear should be trained. Have children listen to the music in the air. It can be heard in the sighing of the breeze, the moaning of the sea, the hum of the insect, the laugh and the groan. Let them listen to the songs already learned and tell what has been sung. It is peculiar that often the worst monotone never makes a mistake. This shows a good ear for music, but inability to make the tones.

Music is a gift from God, generously given, for more than ninety-five per cent of the people can learn to sing, but song must usually be developed. This is our mission. But for our work in the schools many children would never attempt to sing, and numerous beautiful voices discovered there would never be heard.

Deep in the center of the boy is music. Get right at him and touch the bubble and the song will spring forth. It may at first be rough, but when once rightly brought out, will reflect most beautiful colors. What sound is more delightful to the ear than the child's sweet voice expressing the emotions of his soul?

When once the interest has been awakened and a love for music created, the way is well paved for thoughtful work. The child is willing and anxious to learn that which has become necessary to him. He now sees the use of scale, clef, sharps and flats. As soon as the majority of the class can sing several songs with expression and good voice, and that need not take long, then, and not until then, are we ready for formal work in music. This should begin with the major scale, which is the foundation of tune, through which all the tones can be taught.

Begin to teach the scale descending, as a little song with such sentences as:

"The little lambs are in the field,
I hear them say 'ba-ba-ba-ba.'"
"The little birds are in the trees,
I hear them say 'coo-coo-coo-coo.'"
"Down the hill we're sliding, sliding."

Then give it with different rhythms. It is safest to carry the head register down rather than the chest tones up. Guard against using the chest register at first. Keep the voice as much as possible on high pitch, with light power, and see how the tones improve.

Many people possess the mistaken idea that for a song to suit a child's voice, especially a boy's, it should be written low. They have only to listen to the child at play to hear the natural high pitch of his voice.

By taking the child where he is, giving him songs that interest him, without catering to all his whims and fancies, and leading him onward unconsciously to himself to a liking for better music, we soon find that he enjoys only the good, the true in song. The pupil who can appreciate good music is more apt to select the best in life and reject that which is unwholesome.

We, who are given the supervision of this great culture study, should aim to make California second to no state, musically, for it is only through the education of the masses that this can be accomplished. Let us make its study a real thing by beginning it with a high ideal in mind, working ever to reach it, not simply aiming to attract the attention of the public. We must make the results show that our work is fit.

* * *

Voice Quality

Estelle Carpenter

[Extract]

It is a well-known fact that where the air is soft and mild, where the climate is semi-tropical in character, that the quality of the speaking and singing voice is much richer, purer and sweeter than the voice found in northern climes.

In different countries we find different peculiarities in the languages. The voices of each country are influenced by the language. If there is a tendency toward the nasal, gutteral or musical sounds in the language of any land, there will also be that tendency in the singing voices of that country.

The languages of the Latin lands are particularly flowing. The majority of the Italian, Spanish and French voices are round, full, smooth in sound, and they indicate the happy and easy-going temperament.

The languages of the Anglo-Saxon and Teutonic peoples are not very musical. There are many consonants used. The voices in these countries are ringing, clear and brilliant, and indicate the sturdy, stern and energetic character of the people.

The Americans are a strange mixture of the different nationalities, and, consequently, there is to be found a great variety in the quality of their voices. But nowhere in the United States is there such a cosmopolitan population as right here in California. Therefore, there are many kinds of voices here in our own land. And with few exceptions there is no better environment for the perfect voice than in our Golden State.

Here there is a cosmopolitan population, favorable climatic conditions and much good training for the adult voice. But can there not be more done for the child-voice?

The voice is like a most delicate flower, which must be handled lovingly, wisely and well, or else the treasure will be lost or so irretrievably injured that it can never attain its highest use. And it is when this flower is young and frail and tender that it should be watched carefully and guarded from harm. When it is unfolding and developing; when it is small and starting, then it is time, fellow-workers, to watch this soul-stirring plant and start it aright.

Just through the years that the teacher is helping to form the character of the child, then guard and assist the golden bud of its voice, and one day of its own accord it will blossom into a flower of dear delight, a very treasure indeed to comfort and uplift all who may hear it. * * *

The wise teacher will watch for the change of voice and be governed by the individual case, and parents and teachers should caution their boys that during this time they must be careful not to shout; that it is dangerous. I think if the boys were told that carelessness at this time might injure the fullness and roundness of their speaking voices that they would strive to spare their throats. In singing in class, the boys should be put on the part that comes in the range of their softest tones. On no condition should the heavy voice be used during this time. The altos must use the head voice. There are a number of exercises I would wish to give you. First in breathing:

Breathing two positions, on back and standing straight with thumbs on the small of back.

1. Inhale quickly—and exhale quickly.
2. Inhale quickly—and hold.
3. Inhale slowly—and hold.
4. Inhale quickly—slow exhalation.
5. Inhale slowly—then hold.

Vocal exercises.

Begin on high tones and softly say "ha ho, he," then "no na num." Then hum down, using sustained tones, and little exercises of all descriptions on vowels.

For enunciation a good rule to follow is to give different parts of organs proper exercise—tip tongue "la ta na edda." Lips "oo o a a," and then practice vowels separately, and then always hold the vowels for tone, easily but softly touching the consonants. These exercises must especially be given playfully, even to the older children. It is wise to practice words of a sentence alone for enunciation.

The jaw should receive proper attention as well as the middle tongue—yaw— and sticking tongue out. Watch for the stiff-jawed singer in the room. Practice whole songs on vowels alone. Be sure each child breathes at will. This gives a wonderful continuous tone.

There is so much to say on my subject. There is so much to do in this line. I can but hope that you may have gained some points and that you will be interested enough to read and study up on this subject. The folowing books are most helpful and are authorities on the subject:

"The Art of Singing," by Bach.
"Philosophy of Singing," by Rogers.
"Child Voice in Singing," by Howard.
"Mechanism of Voice," by Emil Bahake.
"Practical Hints on Boy Choir Training," by Edward Stubbs.
"Voice, Song and Speech," by Behuka and Brown.
"The Child Voice," by Behuke.
"The Boy's Voice," by Curwen.

But to simplify everything, have children breathe easily often; be interested, have free use of lips and tongue, and use entirely the head voice. And may you learn in your teaching, for experience is the best teacher.

If we cannot get the correct tone in our children's voices, who knows what may come to California? We may be known for our wonderful voices, and called the "Italy of America."

Written and read by Miss Estelle Carpenter.

. . .

CHILD STUDY SECTION

Edwin D. Starbuck, Chairman   H. M. Bland, Secretary

The Passing of Child Study

Edwin D. Starbuck

There was a day when the child-study section of teachers' associations was the best-attended and most enthusiastic of all the sections. Fortunately, at the present time, it has ceased to be the rallying point of the people who are hunting a sensation. It must be confessed that little of permanent value came out of those early enthusiasms. What has remained is the continued work and activity of the few persons who were the nucleus of the "movement" and who were actually doing something. What has passed by is the nervous fever of those who catch the contagion whenever something new is going the round. Happily, now, most of those are immune to any farther attack of the same fever. The chief thing those people have bequeathed child study is something of an ill-repute among serious, thoughtful people. So we have witnessed not only the period of enthusiasm, but also a period of languishing. That period is largely the natural cooling after the fever, the depression following the boom, the "backsliding" that normally succeeds extreme religious zeal.

There are unmistakable evidences, I believe, of a steady development of child study, even during its years of diversity, and also of an increased interest—an intelligent interest—in it at the present time. It has gradually found its way into the courses of study of a good proportion of the leading colleges, universities and normal schools. It is no longer limited to the few psychologists, who have at the same time to be students and advocates. Psychologists of recognized standing are more and more giving it their attention and making contributions to it. Without trying to give more than a suggestive list, one might mention the work of Scripture and Gilbert at Yale, Hall and Sanford at Clark, Thorndyke and Cattrell at Columbia, Kirkpatrick at the Fitchburg Normal, Bryan and Lindley at Indiana University, Dexter at the University of Illinois, Smedley and Kranskopf at Chicago, Kirkpatrick, Seashore and Bolton at the University of Iowa, O'Shea and Jastrow at the University of Wisconsin, Allin, Lancaster and Phillips of Colorado, Wolfe and Luckey at the University of Nebraska, and Yoder at the University of Washington. It is a sign full of significance that the school authorities of the City of Chicago have not only adopted the method now becoming common of systematically taking note of the physical condition of children throughout their school life, but are supporting as an organic part of the school system psychological experts who make observations of the mental life of the children for both practical and scientific purposes. It takes no prophet to know that something of that kind will finally be a fixed part of the educational regime of the country—not soon, but gradually, as the experts are trained, as our wisdom increases in respect to methods and problems, as it proves itself useful, and as funds are available. It is a significant thing, too, that one of the ends in view in this session of our Child Study Association is to determine what can be done this year and the succeeding years in bringing to bear upon the practical school work of the state the facts that are already well established in regard to the mental and physical life of children. The growth in this direction ought to be a slow one. Whatever is done should be safe and sure. In my opinion, the time is ripe for a beginning.

The first and great essential in the teacher is right personal relationship. The teacher is in the truest sense an artist. Her highest training is in her equipment by Nature with a native mother instinct. Such a procedure, if done in the right proportion and in the right way, can but increase the rapport of teacher and pupil and work toward making of the teaching profession a progressively more refined art.

* * *

Sex Differences

I. D. Perry

[Extract]

Upon entering the field of sex-psychology one finds himself on much disputed territory. And in selecting that little portion which may be called logical sex differences he finds himself on the most hotly contested ground of all the field. In this subject he has approached the most complex part of a very complex subject. This is against the canon of the German laboratory psychologists, who would confine research to the simplest mental operations until our knowledge of them becomes more perfect. He must proceed by methods which cannot be reduced to the exactitude of laboratory conditions. The possible sources of error will inevitably be numerous.

Then he must go against a sentiment which is well voiced by Professor J. R. Angell in a recent number of the *Popular Science Monthly*. Professor Angell says: "When one comes to speak of the influence of native abilities, native tastes, and intellectual interests in the election of courses, the available data are altogether less tangible. The prevalent doctrine concerning the mental differences of men and women are matters of dogma, readily susceptible of neither proof nor disproof. In polite letters, as in society, woman has long figured as the adorable parent of men, not of ideas; as the repository of delicate sentiment rather than of accurate knowledge, and in general as the residuary legatee of all those interests which men do not care to cultivate. The evidence adduced in the support of the correctness of this view is often proclaimed as conclusive, and ranged behind it is the authority of sundry psychologists, physiologists, sociologists and men of fashion. The contrary view in accordance with which women are allowed to possess ideas, some of them even original, is supported by evidence almost as intelligible, and by partisans quite as eminent and quite as confident. The fact seems to be that it is extremely difficult to demonstrate how much of a woman's bent is due to the sexual bias of her mind, and how much to the influences which surround her from the cradle to the grave."

The purpose of this study is to determine, if possible, something of the characteristic ways by which the sexes come at knowledge, ideas, ways of reaching conclusions, to inquire, in short, whether there be a sex-psychosis, and if there be, wherein the two sexes differ in their mental life; and secondly, to seek to know whether it is the result of native nervous organization, or, to use the words of Professor Angell, quoted above, "influences which surround them from the cradle to the grave."

We may pertinently use, in justification of this study the argument employed by William Binet and Henri for individual psychology. The higher and more complex a process is the more it varies in individuals; sensations vary from one individual to another, but less so than memory; memory of sensations varies less than the memory of ideas, etc. The result is that if one wishes to study the differences existing between two individuals it is necessary to begin with the most intellectual and complex processes, and it is only secondarily necessary to consider the simple and elementary processes.

Concerning the question of the variation of mental processes in the sexes we have the widest range of opinions. There are writers, such as Colin Scott, who see in all art only an irradiation of sex, as Clifford Howard, who makes sex-worship the basis of all religion, and Krafft Ebing, who makes all intellectual life only an irradiation of sex. On the other side of the question we have considerable writing from a philosophical standpoint, but very little that is analytical. There is certainly in Havelock Ellis's statement: "Sex lies at the root of life and we can never learn to reverence life until we know how to understand sex," a strong challenge to our attention.

Miller's tabulation of the major subjects of the graduates of Stanford University is interesting in this connection. In this institution the elective system has been in vogue since the opening, in 1891. But the tabulation includes only those graduating with the class of '94 and since, as before that time many of the graduates had taken work in colleges not elective in their courses. He says: "The women form from 69.45 per cent to 90.91 per cent of the graduates in all language studies save Greek and classical philology. Whether taken by separate years, by four-year periods, or for the whole time, the women tend to elect the language studies (save Greek and classical philology), education, drawing, painting and botany. Men tend to elect mathematics, Greek, classical philology, philosophy, history, economics, physical and biological sciences (except botany).

This study seems to indicate that under existing conditions of society men and women have different intellectual preferences if they are allowed freedom of choice."

Investigators in all lines of work that have to do with life have learned to look at their problems from the genetic standpoint. While knowing the origin of a thing does not explain it, much light comes to us from its process of becoming. We also wish to know the bodily accompaniments of mental states, if perchance we may find the relation between them. So the psychologist seeks the aid of the biologist and the psychologist.

If there be any fundamental differences between the sexes we should expect, a priori, to find it in the beginnings of life. The earliest differentiation of sex-cells ought to show characteristic features. And empirical study confirms this, both in the phylogenic and the ortogenic series.

The studies of Geddes and Thompson have made us familiar with a theory of sex, which makes the biological difference, when reduced to its lowest terms consist in a difference in nutrition. The female cell is characteristically well nourished, anabolic. The male cell, on the other hand, is ill nourished, restless, active, kotabolic. Dr. Schenck of Vienna thought that the determination of sex depends upon nutrition and organic exchange, which is in line with the thought of Geddes and Thompson. What is more natural than that this fundamental difference should persist up thru the highest reaches of life, that is, up into the intellectual?

Continuing from the biological standpoint, we may quote Dr. Jordan, who says in his footnotes to evolution: "The egg-bearing sex becomes, in comparison with the other, sessile, expectant, conservative. The feeding of the young and its protection from external enemies falls to the lot of the female. The male becomes, in varying degrees, the food winner, the fighter, the one who struggles against outside foes. Greater physical strength is co-ordinated with the need for greater activity. Increased force demands increase of size of body. Increased muscular development necessitates increase in the size of the sensorium, or brain, which controls it."

"Because of the needs of life, man has been differentiated in motor directions, woman in directions of feeling and response. Man has been compelled to face external nature. Woman must face humanity. Thus the initiative in action is thrown more and more on the male; the response of feeling on the female. In the division of labor mental and physical characters are correlated. Women excel in delicacy, in devotion, in sympathy. They are not noted as explorers in new fields. As investigators, judges or warriors their efforts are on the whole ineffective. Such activities are not in the line of duty assigned them in the division of labor. As defenders of the young the female puts the male to shame. No creature is so dangerous as the female beast at bay. The defender of the young or the weak must be a partisan, not a judge."

Thus we find a biological and evolutionary reason for expecting to find logical differences. Let us now turn to the physiologist to see if our expectation will be verified in his case.

* * * * *

In Munsterberg's "Action Theory" we find a psycho-physical reason for expecting to find logical differences. Briefly stated, it is this: The kind of mental process is determined by the external part of the body stimulated, the strength of the mental process upon the force of the stimulation, the value of the mental process upon the course that the nervous discharge takes and the vividness upon the quantity of the discharge, that is, the energy thrown into the innervation of the motor system."

The "Action Theory" is not peculiar to Munsterberg, though he has given it concise shape. Preyer, in saying the only way the will can express itself is thru the voluntary muscles, puts forth the same idea. James, in saying that all consciousness is motor in its tendency, gives us the same thought. Baldwin's circular reaction is the same thought elaborated in another way. In short, it is the commonplace of psychology that vividness of mental life depends upon the force of the motor response. Following this idea, we should expect from two beings of equal sensoria the intenser forces of mental life from the one having the more vigorous motor reaction. But from the greater m[...] development of the male, correlated with the larger sensorium, this would be the more emphatically true. * * *

Child Study from the Teacher's Point of View

J. Fred Smith

[Extract]

The most wonderful thing in all the world is a little child. The most responsible position in all the world is that which imposes the care of a child. The mother comes to her responsibility thru the course of nature and accepts it with its flood of love and joy as one of the choicest gifts bestowed upon woman. The teacher seeks the place, on the other hand, with complex motives; love for children, desire for a livelihood, quest of a pleasant, honorable vocation being among the most prominent.

The average teacher enters upon the work with a conscious mastery of the subjects to be taught and of the approved methods of instruction.

The state looks carefully after our professional training and proper certifications. We have been instructed in all the best devices for securing moral as well as mental development, and know the various symptoms, stages, remedies, of all possible forms of disorder; the solutions of the problems before us lie clear and distinct in our minds. Given a definite group of children of definite preparation and grade; also, a definite amount of time and material. Required, a definite degree of advancement, a definite conformity to an accepted standard of law and order. Boards of Education often take particular pains to emphasize this view of the great problem of education; and the teacher is compelled to acknowledge the fact that a vigorous system is necessary from an economic standpoint, and that things as they are are the outgrowth of the world's experience in trying to deal with the children of the masses. That grades and tests, examinations and promotions are among the great realities in education at the present time. Fortunately, a large number of our teachers have a saving instinct that guides them thru and above the set bounds of regulations of their work and leads them to teach school rather than to keep it. Sympathy with children has been the strongest factor in inspiring child study and in the development of some of the world's greatest teachers. The names Rousseau, Froebel, Pestalozzi, Arnold, suggest a galaxy. Kindergartens and play schools have been some of the legitimate results. While modifications of school courses and the introduction of new work of great interest and profit to the child have been probably by far the most valuable fruits of this awakening, no child study can be more helpful than a retrospection of one's own youth. How vividly I recall sitting in a dull class myself, listless and inattentive, saying in turn, four plus eight are twelve, five plus eight are thirteen, etc. Then listening with every nerve in tension, while the upper class in Colburn's struggled over concrete problems. How shy I felt as I approached the teacher one day and asked if I might try the work of the upper class. The wise teacher kindly assented. The uplift of soul that came to me with my victories then abides with me still. A little later in the high school I had another experience that stamped itself upon my whole after life. It was in algebra. It was in the days of Legendre and Greenleaf. The laws of the signs in operations and the meaning of signs prefixed to quantities were in a helpless chaos in the minds of the pupils. The teacher told us to accept them all as facts and to let the whys and wherefores go. He might as well have told some of us not to breathe. Sleepless I lay upon my bed that night, while the typical combinations came and went at my bidding. A little after midnight the solution came, positive and negative were *kinds* of quantities; a negative operation was simply the opposite of the ordinary positive operation. With a light step and glad heart I walked my three miles of New England hills to school next day. When the algebra class was called I stood with face aglow. I feel those proud blushes yet, and said: "I have found out the reasons for those laws of the signs." The class was held in the main study-room. Instantly every sound was hushed; very eye was centered upon me; the teacher looked in surprise around the expectant room and remarked: "Remember, the next class will be expected to recite in fifteen minutes!" Then turning to me, he said: "Well, what is your solution?" "It is perfectly clear, sir, but I prefer to explain it to you at some other time." There the matter dropped, but oh, how I felt. It seemed as if I could never go to that school another day. That man became a fine physician, but he never was a teacher.

I call that a wasted hour in which the master does not bring a glow upon some face in the class before him; does not make some eyes kindle with the consciousness of overcoming some obstacle in the path of knowledge; with the consciousness of the acquisition of the power of a new thought. True teaching makes a tremendous drain upon the nervous energy of the teacher, but the reaction keeps the true teacher ever young. The life chords must beat in unison or in discord. One is success, the other failure. It is our duty to get all the knowledge possible concerning the child in general and the individual children under our care. I believe in child study most thoroly. There are probably some lines of investigation that will lead to small results, but in the main it must be helpful. I have charge of a high school and supervision of the grades tributary to it. I plan to have a record of each child in the whole system thru as many of the twelve grades as possible. These records are to show the development of each child, so far as simple modern tests can reveal it. They certainly should materialy aid a set of earnest, intelligent teachers in bringing to each child his rightful heritage, a true education, and in bringing to the community its just recompense, a body of well-trained, well-balanced, forceful citizens.

* * *

Education Through Activity

Ella M. Scott

[Extract]

We have arrived at a new day in education. The activity and the spontaniety which manifest themselves in commercial life, in the multiplication of inventions, in social organizations, and which are recognized as characteristic of Americans, must make themselves more evident thru the schools. There may have been times when the ideals of the schoolroom became the standard for the outer world, but at present the stirrings of the outer world are pressing hard upon the schools. The influences are both bad and good. However that may be, the age of mere negative, passive absorption has passed; it cannot meet the needs of the present day. To merely absorb from the printed page, to memorize the text, to study and recite, to express the thoughts of others chiefly by word of mouth or assigned writings, may have satisfied one age, but the world-spirit decrees other things for the age that is dawning.

* * * * *

It is in the grades, however, that I wish to appeal particularly for a recognition of the meaning and value of activity in education. Let me illustrate correctly what I mean: In the first grade one of the characteristics of the development of the children is the growth of the limbs. In the natural state the evidence of this is the child's incessant activity. The child runs, jumps,, balances, digs, pulls, constantly exercising his limbs, and thereby acquiring control, precision, alertness and grace. It would seem evident that lack of exercise, repression, would interfere with growth, but in school the hands must be kept in position and the feet must be kept still. I do not recommend turning the children loose to lawless freedom, but to turn to account for educational ends this wonderful activity. Let the limbs be developed to their highest power, and by means of their activity let the child acquire experiences possible thru this activity. Thru the exercise of the sense organs, also developing at this time, and thru imitation, the child should register a rich store of impressions from nature and human life, instead of having to get his mental images *mainly* from the printed page and lists of combinations and separations and to express these interesting impressions thru written symbols, which have not the life and reality dear to this age, to say nothing of the dangers of such work which others have pointed out.

* * *

The Influence of the Kindergarten

Miss Leesie Byrd

The investigation from which the facts were taken in order to reach the following conclusions was begun in September, 1900, and the work carried on at various times up to the present. As far as possible school official records were used as the basis for the material. The facts concerning esthetic and ethical attitudes were obtained from the joint observations of the experienced teachers of the city schools of San Jose and the San Jose Normal Training School. There was no particular aim in view with the observers while the facts were being collected. The process was simply a matter of gathering statistics and not at all of interpretation.

In all there were four hundred papers—two hundred reports on children who had attended the kindergarten and two hundred on those who had not attended the kindergarten.

For the sake of convenience in this report, we have referred to these as kindergarten children and non-kindergarten children.

The points which have been placed in your hands were observed and comparisons made between the two groups.

It was soon seen that there were marked differences between the records of the boys and the records of the girls, so comparisons were made between kindergarten girls and non-kindergarten girls, and kindergarten boys and non-kindergarten boys.

In the seventh grade the average age of the non-kindergarten girls was 13 2-5 years, of the kindergarten 14 years.

In the sixth grade the average age of the non-kindergarten girls was twelve and one-half years and of the kindergarten thirteen and one-half years.

The number of times tardy was: Non-kindergarten, 17; kindergarten, 51.

Number of times absent, non-kindergarten, 269; kindergarten, 221. In justice to the non-kindergarten girls we state that there were two extreme cases of absence, one girl having been absent 33 times and another 25 times.

Number of times corporal punishment was received, one by a non-kindergarten girl.

Seventy-five per cent of the non-kindergarten girls were neat in their work and **62 per cent of the kindergarten.**

Imagination—Non-kindergarten, 48 per cent; kindergarten, 41 per cent.

Sixty-eight per cent of the girls who had attended kindergarten were prompt in responding to school tactics, and of those who had not there were 59 per cent.

An equal number were found to be stubborn, or 23 per cent in both cases.

The number that kept step well in line were: Non-kindergarten, 76 per cent; kindergarten, 81 per cent.

Looked up to by other children,: Non-kindergarten, 64 per cent; kindergarten, 53 per cent.

Well kept at home: Non-kindergarten, 93 per cent; kindergarten, 92 per cent.

Neat in personal appearance: Non-kindergarten, 93 per cent; kindergarten, 90 per cent.

Likes to sing: Non-kindergarten, 87 per cent; kindergarten, 92 per cent.

Likes to draw: Non-kindergarten, 85 per cent; kindergarten, 81 per cent.

Likes to speak pieces: Non-kindergarten, 69 per cent; kindergarten, 68 per cent.

Appreciates music: Non-kindergarten, 91 per cent; kindergarten, 93 per cent.

The number that appreciated pictures were equal to 95 per cent.

Generally amenable to school rules: Non-kindergarten, 93 per cent; kindergarten, 95 per cent.

Quarrelsome: Non-kindergarten, 27 per cent; kindergarten, 20 per cent.

Variable in conduct: Non-kindergarten, 22 per cent; kindergarten, 25 per cent.

We find that the girls who attended kindergarten were at a disadvantage in thirteen out of twenty-one points, and at no advantage in two points.

Of the seven points in which the kindergarten girls were at an advantage three are ethical attitudes and three are esthetic. The seventh does not classify with these.

Esthetic—Likes to sing, 1; appreciates music, 1; keep step in line, 1.

Ethical—Amenable to school rules, 1; quarrelsome, 1; corporal punishment, 1.

Now we will compare the kindergarten boys with the non-kindergarten boys.

The average age in the seventh grade was: Kindergarten, 13 1-2 years; non-kindergarten, 14 1-2 years.

In the sixth grade the average of the kindergarten boys was 12 4-7 years, and non-kindergarten 13 2-7 years.

Number of times tardy; Kindergarten, 70; non-kindergarten, 69.

Number of times absent: Kindergarten, 153; non-kindergarten, 380.

Number of times truant: Twice by non-kindergarten boy.

Number of times corporal punishment was received: Kindergarten, 6; non-kindergarten, 4. Causes: Kindergarten, disobedience, 2; disorder, 3; impudence, 1. Non-kindergarten: changing note, 1; truancy, 2; noisy in hall, 1.

Appearance of paper on board work: Kindergarten, 42 per cent were neat; non-kindergarten, 30 per cent.

Imaginative: Kindergarten, 36 per cent; non-kindergarten, 29 per cent.

Prompt in responding to school tactics: Kindergarten, 57 per cent; non-kindergarten, 45 per cent.

Stubborn: Kindergarten, 30 per cent; non-kindergarten, 28 per cent.

Kept step well in line: Kindergarten, 71 per cent; non-kindergarten, 66 per cent.

The numbers looked up to by other children were the same in both, or 49 per cent.

Well kept at home: Kindergarten, 90 per cent; non-kindergarten, 86 per cent.

Neat in personal appearance: Kindergarten, 85 per cent; non-kindergarten, 81 per cent.

Likes to sing: Kindergarten, 67 per cent; non-kindergarten, 63 per cent.

Likes to draw: Kindergarten, 82 per cent; non-kindergarten, 73 per cent.

Likes to speak pieces: Kindergarten, 50 per cent; non-kindergarten, 40 per cent.

Appreciates music: Kindergarten, 84 per cent; non-kindergarten, 77 per cent.

Appreciates pictures: Kindergarten, 84 per cent; non-kindergarten, 82 per cent.

Generally amenable to school rules: Kindergarten, 83 per cent; non-kindergarten, 80 per cent.

Quarrelsome: Kindergarten, 29 per cent; non-kindergarten, 27 per cent.

We find that in 17 out of 22 points the boys who had attended the kindergarten were at an advantage.

In one point they had no advantage, and the four in which they were at a disadvantage are ethical attitudes.

Tardiness, corporal punishment, stubbornness and quarrelsomeness. We learn these facts with you as indicating on their face the influence of the kindergarten on the ethical and esthetic nature of the child.

* * *

Some Results of Kindergarten Training

H. M. Bland

The results of child study may be grouped under two general headings: First, Results from the observation of the spontaneous activities of individual children as represented by Preyer and others; second, results from tests along definite lines to determine the growth and abilities of children. The results of the second group seem infinitely more valuable to the teacher for the following reasons, viz: Deductions from the observations of the spontaneous activities of children do not lead to any definite end by which school conditions can be improved. But it is said, and rightly so, that by teachers observing the activities of children they are brought into closer sympathy with the child. It is just this unconscious and natural interest and love for children which have led men and women to observe them more closely.

In some cases this has resulted in the popular phases of child-study which have come into disrepute; but in a few cases a deeper interest has been awakened, due to observations of wide individual differences in children. Some of the differences are due to defects of sight, hearing and bodily symmetry. As a consequence of these individual characteristics there has been a definite study of children in order that the individualities may be taken into account in our teaching. Consequently the one, two, or three specific observations have resulted in the physical and mental examination of children in order to determine as far as possible (1) the laws of child growth, (2) results of particular training, and (3) the existing relation between physical conditions and intellectual activity. And all this effort has had the sole purpose of evolving the most efficient educational system.

A discussion of the results of the work done by such men as Bodwitch, Byran, Porter, Peckham, Gilbert, Roberts and others who are familiar to us all, is unnecessary, since these articles are well summarized and accessible to all. I shall confine myself to the second statement—that is, some results of particular training. And this will be confined to only one phase of the problem studied. The subject of this paper will be: "Is the two years' training in the kindergarten an advantage to the child afterwards?" But before answering this question it will be well to state the theory of the kindergarten and some criticisms made against it.

The heart of the kindergarten idea is the application of the principle of self-activity, love, fellowship, sympathy, together with the doctrine of organic development. The kindergartner says the "special senses receive careful systematic training; give skillful use of the hands, and arouses and exercises powers of comparison, of judgment and of foresight which will be the child's possession for life." Within recent years the system of gifts formulated by Froebel has been criticised by some educational men, such as G. Stanley Hall. Certain neurological facts have been theorized upon educationally and applied against the methods of the kindergarten as to whether the training received by children in the kindergarten is detrimental or beneficial.

SECRETARY'S MINUTES

The program as published was carried out in detail.

President Shumate announced that Mr. Philip Prior's name was inadvertently omitted from the Committee on Resolutions.

A motion was carried that the president appoint a committee of eleven, of which he shall be chairman, to consider the suggestions made in his annual address.

President Shumate declined to serve as chairman, naming R. D. Faulkner in his stead, and announced the following Legislative Committee of Eleven: R. D. Faulkner, Thomas J. Kirk, James A. Barr, C. L. Biedenbach, Hugh J. Baldwin, Frederic Burk, George L. Sackett, D. S. Snedden, P. M. Fisher, A. E. Shumate.

At the business meeting of the Association San Francisco was chosen the meeting place for 1903, and the following officers were elected: President, O. W. Erlewine, Sacramento; Vice-President, Mrs. J. E. Chope, King City; Vice-President, Edward Hyatt, Riverside; Secretary, Mrs. M. M. Fitz Gerald, 1627 Folsom street, San Francisco; Assistant Secretary, Charles C. Hughes, Alameda; Railroad Secretary, Job Wood, Sacramento; Treasurer, Philip Prior, San Francisco.

The Secretary reported the following action of the Executive Committee as to vacancies on the Council of Education:

Dr. Elmer E. Brown, Robert Furlong, R. H. Webster, E. C. Moore and S. T. Black, whose terms expired in 1902, were reappointed for the full term of five years.

Mr. R. L. Sandwick was dropped for non-residence and Mr. H. M. Bland appointed to fill the unexpired term of two years.

Mr. Carl H. Nielsen was dropped for non-payment of dues, and Mr. W. D. Kingsbury named to fill the unexpired term of one year.

Mr. George S. Wells, chairman of the Committee on Organization of an Elementary School Association, made the following report, which had been approved by the members of the Grammar and the Primary School Departments of the California Teachers' Association:

Your committee reports the following three recommendations:

That a permanent association of those interested in elementary education be formed, the same to be known as the "California Elementary School Association."

That the general constitution drafted and submitted by your committee be adopted as that of the association.

That the following nominations for the offices to be filled for the ensuing year be adopted: Mr. Charles C. Hughes, Alameda, President; Miss R. F. English, Vice-President; Mrs. Fannie Byram, Secretary-Treasurer.

GEORGE S. WELLS,
Chairman of Committee.

* * *

CONSTITUTION CALIFORNIA ELEMENTARY SCHOOL ASSOCIATION.

Article I.

This association shall be known as "The California Elementary School Association."

Article II.

Its objects shall be to advance the interests of elementary education through unity of effort in the study of educational problems and in the recommendation of needed legislation.

Article III.

Its regular time and place of meeting shall be the same as that of the California Teachers' Association. Other meetings may be held at such time and place as the association may designate.

Article IV.

All persons interested in elementary education are eligible to membership.

Article V.

Section 1. The officers shall be a President, a Vice-President and a Secretary-Treasurer, to be elected at the annual meeting.

Sec. 2. There shall be an Executive Committee, consisting of the officers and four other members, appointed by the President.

Sec. 3. The duties of the officers and Executive Committee shall be such as usually devolve upon such officers and committee. In addition, it shall be the particular business of the Executive Committee to act with the President in arranging and providing a suitable program for the annual session of the Association, in appointing committees for the investigation of elementary school problems, and the recommendation of legislation.

Sec. 4. The Executive Committee shall meet at the call of the President. Four members shall constitute a quorum.

Mr. Erlewine reported that the High School Committee of the Council of Education had discussed ways and means of distributing money for state high school support, the following Committee of Five having been appointed to consider the matter, namely: State

Superintendent of Schools; President of California Teachers' Association; Chairman of Council of Education, C. T. A.; Chairman of High School Section, C. T. A.; Chairman of Southern High School Section.

Mr. Housh presented resolutions agreed upon by joint committee of High School Section and Council of Education and thought they should be referred without reading to the Legislative Committee of Eleven appointed by President Shumate.

Upon motion and second, it was so ordered. They read as follows:

REPORT OF COUNCIL COMMITTEE ON THE CONSTITUTIONAL AMENDMENT PROVIDING FOR STATE AID FOR HIGH SCHOOLS.

The committee respectfully submits the following sugestions with reference to the proposed legislation providing for state aid to high schools.

General Principles.

Any legislation for the distribution of state aid to high schools in California should guard well the following points:

1. It should preserve the local initiative and local control provided under our present laws.

2. It should aim to pay only a portion of the cost of maintaining high schools from the treasury of the state, leaving the greater portion to be provided by local taxation.

3. It should give the opportunity which the present laws provide of offering special courses of secondary instruction adapted to local needs.

4. It should preserve the high standard guaranteed under our present laws, and should give no encouragement to schools other than genuine high schools.

5. It should encourage existing schools to become better schools, and should promote the establishment of new schools in portions of the state which are not well provided with such schools, but it should not encourage the multiplication of such schools in regions where they already abound.

6. It should look to the provisions in the near future of free high school instruction for all qualified pupils in the state.

Revenue.

That the funds for this purpose be raised by a general tax of two cents on every one hundred dollars of taxable property in the state.

Distribution.

That the State Superintendent of Public Instruction apportion to every district, county, city, union or joint union high school the sum of four hundred dollars annually, and that the remainder of the annual appropriation be apportioned among such high schools upon the basis of the average daily attendance as shown by the official reports for the last preceding school year, or that one-third of the annual appropriation be apportioned equally to the high schools and the remaining two-thirds be apportioned on tne basis of the daily average attendance; provided, that such high schools have been organized under the laws of the state, or have maintained the grade of instruction required by law of the high schools; and provided that no school shall be eligible to a share of the state aid that does not employ at least two teachers for a term of at least nine months with an average daily attendance of not less than twenty pupils, except it be for the first year that such school is organized, when the minimum number of pupils in average daily attendance shall be twelve; and provided further, that the law shall not operate to disqualify any existing school from receiving state aid for a period of one year.

That the State Superintendent of Public Instruction draw his order on the State Controller in favor of the county in which there is a high school entitled to aid in accordance with the above provisions for the amount apportioned to the high schools of the county, the same to be paid out in support of the high schools of the county in the manner provided. In the case of joint union high schools, the order shall be drawn in favor of the treasurer of the county in which the high school building is located.

SCHOOL STANDARDS.

The Elementary School.

The standard California elementary school course should be eight-year grades in length, but where the school year is less than nine months in length the work may fairly be distributed over nine grades. In schools having exceptionally short school terms it is desirable that the County Superintendent should arrange for definite periods, longer than one school year, in which the work of a given grade should be covered. In arranging for the general recognition of the eight-grade course as the standard for the state sufficient time should be allowed for the making of readjustments in cities now organized on the nine-year basis with a school year of nine or ten months.

The Secondary School.

The standard high-school course should be four years in length, beginning where the elementary school leaves off.

Instruction in the high school should be given only by persons holding the teacher's certificate of high-school grade.

The high school should provide one course of study such as will prepare for admission to one of the colleges of the University of California, as under the present law, but should be allowed to offer other courses without reference to college-admission requirements.

Before receiving state aid each school should furnish satisfactory evidence of the possession of a reasonably good equipment of building, laboratory and library, and of having maintained the preceding year proper high-school instruction for a term of at least nine months.

No school should be recognized as a complete high school which does not employ at least two teachers and a sufficient number of teachers to give adequate instruction to the whole number of pupils in attendance and in the full number of courses undertaken.

At a meeting of the Committee of the High School Teachers' Association, held this day, it was unanimously voted to indorse the report of the Committee of the Council on High School Legislation, with the following exceptions, viz:

It is our opinion that the provision limiting state aid to high schools of two or more teachers should be stricken out.

It is also our opinion that a clause should be inserted providing for an appropriation of $200 to a high school having but one teacher.

The Secretary was instructed to report the action of this committee to the chairman of the Legislation Committee of the State Association.

Executive Committee: C. L. Biedenbach, L. B. Avery, A. E. Shumate, E. M. Cox, F. E. Clark, A. W. Scott, W. H. Housh, J. D. Graham, W. A. Sheldon, Edward Hohfeld, G. W. Wright.

Upon being questioned as to the status of the high school and the elementary school associations, the Secretary answered that in the past similar associations had been accorded the privilege of presenting to the California Teachers' Association at its annual session a program of their own preparation, all expenses of each subordinate association being borne by itself.

Messrs. Templeton and Faulkner suggested that the Executive Committee for 1903 bring forward amendments to the constitution to cover the conditions arising from the formation of such associations.

The following resolutions were adopted:

I—Text-Books.

Resolved, That the Committee of Eleven be and is hereby instructed to memorialize the Legislature to the end that better text-books may be provided for use in the schools of the state at the earliest possible date; that the committee shall point out specifically the unfitness of certain text-books now in use; and, further, that they shall recommend the passage of appropriate legislation that will permit the purchase or leasing of plates, maps and engravings "of the first order of excellence," such texts to be printed, published, distributed and sold as directed by the Constitution of the state.

II—Physical Culture.

The Department for Physical Culture of the State Teachers' Convention, after a thoro investigation of the subject of physical training in the public schols of the State of California, recommends the practicability of making physical exercises a permanent feature of education in this state, and respectfully suggests the following substitute for Section 1668.

Physical Training.

Physical exercises must be regularly practiced in the public schools according to an approved and rational system, and under competent and qualified teachers. The State Board of Education shall adopt the necessary regulations to make this section effective.

II—Juvenile Court.

Be it resolved, That the California Teachers' Association hereby heartily indorses the bill proposed by the civic department of the California Club for the establishment of the Juvenile Court in our state.

IV—Consolidation of School Districts.

Resolved, That we indorse the movement for legislative enactments that will permit the consolidation of school districts and the transportation of school children of said consolidated districts.

V—Secretary's Salary.

Resolved, That the sum of $150 be paid to Mrs. M. M. FitzGerald, the Secretary of the association, for her services during the past year.

VI—California Roadmakers.

Believing in good highways for the industrial and economic development of our state, we indorse the movement for the improvement of roads and apply for membership in the California Roadmakers.

VII—California Historic Landmarks League.

Resolved, That the California Teachers' Association most heartily indorses the work of the California Historic Landmarks League in collecting material for future historical use and in the preservation of those remnants of the early occupation of this state by Spanish, Russian and American pioneers.

VIII—The Press.

Resolved, That the press be tendered the thanks of the association for the good work done in reporting the proceedings of this convention.

X—Local Committees.

Resolved, That the thanks of this association be extended to the local committees for the excellent entertainment and other attentions extended to us during our stay in this city, and to those who assisted in carrying out the program of this association.

* * *

Treasurer's Report

March 1, 1902, to May 1, 1903.

RECEIPTS

Cash balance, March 1, 1902	$229 18
Membership fees	2165 00
Ticket sales	949 50
J. H. Strine, Supt. Los Angeles Co.	120 00—$3463 68

DISBURSEMENTS

Miscellaneous printing,	$107 50
Advance bulletins	57 50
Programs	93 75
Proceedings	485 00
Postage	100 00
Advertising	13 50
Telegrams, telephones, expressage, etc.	32 05
Badges	148 55
Incidentals	252 66
Halls	261 00
Services	1079 10—$2630 61

Total receipts............$3463 68
Total disbursements...... 2630 61

Cash balance, May 1, 1903.....$833 07

Respectfully submitted,
PHILIP PRIOR,
Treasurer California Teachers' Association.

*

Minutes of the Proceedings of the Council of Education of the California Teachers' Association.

The Council of Education met in the Normal School building at Los Angeles on Monday, December 29, and Tuesday, December 30, 1902, daily, from 9:30 A. M. to 12 M., and from 1:30 to 3:45 P. M.

Present—Frederic Burk, State Superintendent of Schools Thomas J. Kirk, Robert Furlong, E. E. Brown, E. C. Moore, S. T. Black, E. M. Cox, M. E. Dailey, John Swett, E. P. Cubberley, C. C. Van Liew, James A. Barr, A. L. Mann, C. E. Keyes, O. W. Erlewine, A. E Shumate, R. D. Faulkner and J. W. McClymonds.

Absent—R. H. Webster, G. H. Howison, C. H. Nielson, P. M. Fisher, J. W. Linscott, R. L. Sandwick, O. P. Jenkins.

The minutes of the adjourned meeting held in Oakland September 20, 1902, were read and approved as recorded.

On motion, it was decided that the Executive Committee of the Association be asked to include in the report of the proceedings of the Association the reports of the Council of Education. A committee consisting of Mr. E. M. Cox, Mr. M. E. Dailey and Mr. J. W. McClymonds was appointed to draft a resolution making this request of the Association, and also to request the appropriation of money for the publication of reprints of certain of these reports for more general distribution than can be had through the publication of the general report.

The following reports were read and referred to the Executive Committee of the general body for publication:

E. C. Moore, on compulsory education, submitted an extended report on the history of compulsory education in the various states, and submitted figures showing the absolute necessity of a compulsory education law in California.

E. M. Cox submitted an exhaustive report on free text-books for use in the California schools, favoring some legislation to bring about the desired result.

O. W. Erlewine and State Superintendent Thomas J. Kirk each submitted a minority report agreeing in general with the main committee, but disagreeing with some of the findings.

From C. C. Van Liew, of the Committee on Relation of Course of Study of Normal Schools to those of High Schools.

From Robert Furlong, an exhaustive report on systems of promotion in use by the various County Boards of Education in the state.

From A. L. Mann, of the Committee on Weaknesses of the Present State Series of Arithmetics.

From R. L. Sandwick, report on common general information current among citizens of average intelligence, which is necessarily omitted in the high-school courses. This report was read by Professor D. S. Snedden.

From James A. Barr, report upon the teaching of geography in the grammar grades.

From E. Hohfeld, principal of Auburn High School, report upon the present high-school courses in Latin in accredited high schools.

From Principal G. W. Wright of Concord

High School, report upon the course in literature in accredited high schools.

From S. D. Waterman, Superintendent of Schools of Berkeley, report upon the value, desirability and practicability of uniformity in high-school courses throughout the state.

From James D. Graham, of the Committee to Compile a Report Upon the Functions of the Present Course in Algebra of Accredited Schools.

From J. A. Imrie, report upon existing systems for supervision of rural schools by County Superintendents.

From J. H. Strine of the Committee Upon System of County Institutes.

From C. L: McLane of the Committee to compile a report upon the function and scope of a business course in the high schools, accompanied by a supplemental report by J. H. Francis of the Los Angeles High School.

The following submitted partial reports and asked for further time, which was granted by unanimous vote of the Council:

James A. Foshay of the Committee on Plan of Appointment of Teachers.

M. E. Dailey of the Committee on the Best Preparation of Teachers by Normal Schools.

J. W. McClymonds of the Committee on System of Promotions in Use in Cities of California.

R. D. Faulkner of the Committee on relative number of boys and girls in California schools who withdraw from school during the last three years of the grammar schools and in grades of the high school.

Mr. O. W. Erlewine of the Committee on needed legislation to make the adopted amendment most beneficial to the secondary schools of the state reported recommending that a tax levy of 2 cents be raised by the state, to be distributed to the high schools already organized in the state, partly to the schools and partly on average daily attendance. State Superintendent Kirk and others spoke in favor of the report. J. W. McClymonds opposed the report on the ground that he thought the money ought to be apportioned to the counties, and not to the school. Further consideration of the report went over until Tuesday, the second day's meeting of the Council.

John Swett of the Committee on Enforcement of the Code of Professional Ethics, tendered his resignation from the committee, and Professor E. P. Cuberley was appointed in his stead.

Dr. Frederic Burk was elected President of the Council and J. W. McClymonds Secretary of the Council for the ensuing year.

On motion, it was decided that the Council meet several times during the year for the purposes of discussions and hearing reports of committees.

J. W. McClymonds, Secretary.

* * *

COUNCIL OF EDUCATION.

Ex-Officio — Hon. Thomas J. Kirk, Sacramento, State Superintendent of Public Instruction.

Term expires 1903—G. H. Howison, Berkeley; W. D. Kingsbury, San Francisco; P. M. Fisher, Oakland; E. M. Cox, Santa Rosa; M. E. Dailey, San Jose.

Term expires 1904—J. W. Linscott, Santa Cruz; E. P. Cubberley, Palo Alto; John Swett, Martinez; H. M. Bland, San Jose; C. C. Van Liew, Chico.

Term expires 1905—J. W. McClymonds, Oakland; James A. Barr, Stockton; Frederic Burk, San Francisco; A. L. Mann, San Francisco; C. E. Keyes, Oakland.

Term expires 1906—James A. Foshay, Los Angeles; O. P. Jenkins, Palo Alto; A. E. Shumate, San Jose; O. W. Erlewine, Sacramento; R. D. Faulkner, San Francisco.

Term expires in 1907—Elmer E. Brown, Berkeley; Robert Furlong, San Rafael; R. H. Webster, San Francisco; E. C. Moore, Berkeley; S. T. Black, San Diego.

Respectfully submitted,

M. M. FITZ GERALD,
Secretary California Teachers' Association.

* * *

List of Members California Teachers' Association

A

Abbott, A. M., Florence; Abbott, Clara L., Los Angeles; Abbott, Emilita, Los Nietos; Abbott, Mae H., Los Angeles; Abbott, Mary, Los Angeles; Abel, G., Milpitas; Abel, M. A., Milpitas; Adams, Ella A., Los Angeles; Adams, Laura, Downey; Adams, Madge, Downey; Adams, Mary B., Petaluma; Adams, Mary, Long Beach; Agnew, Frank J., Oakland; Agnew, Mrs. F. J., Oakland; Aitken, Mrs. Helen, Los Angeles; Allen, Blanche, San Diego; Allen, E. C. San Bernardino; Alexander, Evalyn, Los Angeles; Allen, Grace, Los Angeles; Allen, Lyman, Berkeley; Allen, Mrs. Mary, Los Angeles; Alexander, O. A., San Jose; Allender, Mrs. Nellie M., Los Angeles; Allison, Camille, San Jose; Ames, Mary, Rutherford; Amos, Caroline B., Los Angeles; Anderson, Augusta T., San Jose; Anderson, Elizabeth V., San Jose; Anderson, Fidelia A., Los Angeles; Anderson, Grace, Los Angeles; Anderson, Ida F., Redlands; Anderson, J. T., Covina; Anderson, Mrs. J. T., Covina; Anderson, Mary F., Riverside;

Andrews, Fern, Los Angeles; Angell, Amelia M., Los Angeles; Anthony, John H., Napa; Arbuthnot, Elnora, Pomona; Archambeault, Bell, San Jose; Ardito, Isabel F., Los Angeles; Armer, Evelyn D., San Francisco; Arnick, Myrtle, Los Angeles; Arnold, Bessie, Long Beach; Arnold, Martha W., Los Angeles; Ashby, Jennie, Claremont; Ashby, Sara C., Redlands; Ashley, R. L., Pasadena; Atherton, Ruth B., Los Angeles; Atwood, Stella M., Riverside; Averill, N. S., Los Angeles; Avery, Lewis B., Redlands; Ayer, Lillian E., Los Angeles; Aylward, Grace, Livermore; Ayers, Sophie, Long Beach.

B

Babcock, Martha M., Pomona; Babcock, Mary D., Los Angeles; Backus, Viola, Los Angeles; Bacon, C. E., San Francisco; Bacon, E. E., Berkeley; Bacon, Laura, Los Angeles; Bahr, Lulu C., San Bernardino; Bailey, Arline L., Los Angeles; Bailey, Bessie, Santa Cruz; Bailey, Florence R., Los Angeles; Bailey, Harriet B., Santa Cruz; Bailey, Kate, Long Beach; Baker, Arthur, Berkeley; Baker, A. E., Los Angeles; Baker, Mrs. Estelle, Redlands; Baker, M. L., Fernando; Baker, M. S., San Francisco; Baker, Nettie L., Pasadena; Balcomb, E. E., Palo Alto; Baldwin, Abby G., San Diego; Baldwin, Grace M., Santa Cruz; Baldwin, Hugh J., San Diego; Baldwin, Ruth A., San Diego; Balis, Lola, East San Jose; Banks, Belle, Los Angeles; Ball, Hannah M., Los Angeles; Ballard, Ben F., Santa Rosa; Banning, Mrs. F. A., San Francisco; Bannon; Mrs. Fannie S., San Diego; Barber, Leeta, Azusa; Barkelew, Amber, Riverside; Barker, Katharine, Los Angeles; Barmby, Martha, San Jose; Barmby, Mary, San Jose; Barnard, Grace E., Oakland; Barnes, Adda, Los Angeles; Barnes, Earle, Ventura; Barnes, E. A., Chicago, Ill.; Barnes, Laura C., Monrovia; Barnes, Laura M., Redlands; Barnes, Mabel, Los Angeles; Barnes, Nellie, Los Angeles; Barnhart, W. C., East Highlands; Barnwell, Sue, Glendale; Barr, James A., Stockton; Barron, Flora M., Los Angeles; Barron, Emma, Covina; Barron, Ida E., Compton; Barron, Pearl, Compton; Barry, Emma, San Jose; Barry, Lottie, Ventura; Barry, Marcella J., San Jose; Bartell, Nora, Shasta county; Bartell, Alice, Shasta county; Barthel, F. K., San Jose; Barton, G. C., Palo Alto; Batchelder, Lizzie E., Pasadena; Bates, Alice L., Los Angeles; Bates, Edith, Berkeley; Bates, Elizabeth, Los Angeles; Batty, Kate S., Los Angeles; Baxter, Minnie S., Los Angeles; Beale, F. E., San Jose; Beatty, Anna, Ocean Park; Beamer, M. A., Stanford University; Bear, Mary E., Los Angeles; Beebe, Mrs. Eva, Corona; Beem, Eloise, Nordhoff; Beers, C. W., Nordhoff; Beers, Mrs. Zelia W., Nordhoff; Belfrage, William F., San Francisco; Bell, Edith, Punta Gorda; Bell, Lillie V., Monterey; Bemis, Grace L., Los Angeles; Benedict, Mae, Pasadena; Bennett, Florence E., Los Angeles; Bennett, Mary E., Los Angeles; Benson, Christine M., Los Angeles; Benson, Saidie, Los Angeles; Berry, Vida H., Long Beach; Bertola, Dominica C., San Francisco; Best, Gertrude, Riverside; Best, Lucy, Riverside; Beswick, B. F., Santa Ana; Bettinger, M. C., Los Angeles; Betts, Mrs. E. J., Los Angeles; Biddison, Mrs. N. S., Palmdale; Biedenbach, Charles L., Berkeley; Biffer, Mary, Los Angeles; Bigley, Alpha N., Redlands; Billingall, J., San Jose; Billings, Anna H., Long Beach; Bisbee,, Henrietta, Los Angeles; Bisby, Mrs. M. K., Los Angeles; Bixby, Mae, Los Angeles; Black, E. C., Pasadena; Black, Lester, Murrietta; Black, S. T., San Diego; Blanchard, Ada T., Los Angeles; Blanchard, Milton E., San Francisco; Blanchard, J. Maud, Los Angeles; Blanford, Carrie M., Los Angeles; Bland, Henry M., San Jose; Bland, Maud, Norwalk; Bledsoe, N. C., Los Angeles; Bletso, Leah, Los Angeles; Blend, L. E., Los Angeles; Blockman, Mrs. Ida M., Santa Maria; Blumb, Mrs. Joseph L., Sespe; Blythe, M. R., Oakland; Bodham, Byron J., Los Angeles; Boehncke, Frieda C., Prospect Park; Boehncke, George, Prospect Park; Boggs, G. J., San Bernardino; Bohan, Martha, Los Angeles; Boke, H. J., Perris; Bont, Josephine; Los Angeles; Boor, Edith, Santa Paula; Booth, Menetta M., Florence; Boring, Ora, Riverside; Bossuet, Philana, Los Angeles; Boswell, Jennie L., Los Angeles; Bostwick, Isabella C., Pasadena; Bouelle, Frank A., Los Angeles; Bonne, Jennie, Los Angeles; Bovard, F. G., Colton; Bovard, Helen, Compton; Bowman, Jennie, Los Angeles; Boyd, J. C., Glendora; Boyden, M. G., San Francisco; Boyle, Maude, Los Angeles; Boynton, E. C., Los Angeles; Boynton, J., Stanford; Boynton, W. P., Oakland; Boynton, Mrs. W. P., Oakland; Brackett, S. H., Redlands; Bradford, Mrs. L. P., Los Angeles; Bradshaw, D., Stanford; Brainard, Frances V., Berkeley; Brainard, Maud, Riverside; Breen, Nellie, Los Angeles; Brenclamond, Frank, Colorado; Bremzier, Pearl, Long Beach; Brewer, Annie W., Oakland; Brewer, John M., San Francisco; Bremzer, Nettie, Long Beach; Briggs, H. E., Berkeley; Briggs, Mary, Santa Paula; Brink, Mrs. E. A., Pomona; Bristor, Frances, Los Angeles; Brodbeck, Mrs. Kate, Los Angeles; Brodbeck, Mrs. H. W., Los Angeles; Bronson, Mrs. Fannie P., San Francisco; Brooks, Ada, Pasadena; Brooks, Elisha, San Francisco; Brooks, Ethel D., Los Angeles; Brooks, Imelda, Pasadena; Brookman, Thirmuthia A., Redlands; Brown, Addie R., Alhambra; Brown, Agnes, Los Angeles; Brown, Alice, Petaluma; Brown, Arthur C., Los Angeles; Brown, A. P., Merced; Brown, Mrs. C. F., Merced; Brown, Corris M., Whittier; Brown, Elmer E., Berkeley; Brown, Ethel, San Jose; Brown, Frances, Los Angeles; Brown, Isabella R., San Francisco; Brown, J. H., Goleta; Brown, Kaloola, Pasadena; Brown, Maude, Los Angeles; Brown, S. W., San Jose; Brown, Thomas P., Santa Monica; Brownell, E. E.,

San Jose; Browning, Leona, Monrovia; Brubaker, N. J., Temecula; Bruch, Louis, San Jose; Bruere, Clara, Los Angeles; Bruere, Cornelia, Santa Paula; Bruere, Julia, Los Angeles; Brunson, Jessie, Alhambra; Brunson, May, Downey; Bryan, Mrs. J. S., Lemoore; Buck, Nellie, Bardsdale; Buckman, Mary H., Walters; Buehner,Val., San Jose; Buell, Margaret, San Jacinto; Bullock, M. L., Alameda; Bulson, Mrs. Bertha, Riverside; Purdy, Mrs. Ida M., Riverside; Burgess, C. M., Colton; Burgess, Elizabeth, Long Beach; Burgess, Louise, El Rio; Burgess, M. L., Colton; Burt, Francis S., Pasadena; Burk, Frederic, San Francisco; Burke, Agnes, Rivera; Burke, Mary, San Quentin; Burke, Sara, Los Angeles; Burnett, Jessie E., Oxnard; Burnett, May, Los Angeles; Burton, Eva, Redlands; Burton, M., Pasadena; Button, Allie, Sierra Madre; Butler, Isolda, Los Angeles; Butler, Jessie, San Dimas; Butler, Julia R., Downey; Butler, J. B., Fullerton; Byram, Fannie H., Los Angeles; Byrd, Lessie, San Jose.

C

Cady, C. B., Los Angeles; Cahalin, Lillian, San Jose; Cain, Grace S., Los Angeles; Cain, Mary M., Los Angeles; Caldwell, H. N., Lompoc; Caldwell, Mattie B., Los Angeles; Caleff, Emma V., Los Angeles; Campbell, Amy T., San Francisco; Campbell, Nannie B., San Francisco; Campbell, Blanche, Fresno; Campbell, Cora, Redlands; Campbell, Frank C., Whittier; Campbell, Laura J., Los Angeles; Candee, Katherine, Riverside; Cannon, H. D., Oxnard; Carew, Mrs. L. M., Gilroy; Carhart, Augusta, Los Angeles; Carmichael, C., San Jose; Carmichael, Emeline, San Jose; Carpenter, Estelle, San Francisco; Carpenter, M. Grace, Pomona; Carpenter, W. C., Fullerton; Carr, Katherine, Los Angeles; Carr, Lincoln, Hollister; Carick, Ida O., Los Angeles; Carroll, Agnes, San Jose; Carroll, Anna M., Los Angeles; Cassassa, Rose, San Francisco; Case, Jean, Los Angeles; Case, M. Ellen, Los Angeles; Casey, F. Lorena, Pomona; Cassidy, Mrs. K. R., San Francisco; Catey, Minnie, Compton; Cathedral School, Los Angeles; Chaffee, Kate, Pasadena; Chaffey, Mrs. Susie, Los Angeles; Chamberlain, Grace A., Redlands; Chamberlain, J. F., Los Angeles; Champlin, Anna, Los Angeles; Chandler, H. P., Pasadena; Chandler, Jessie, Long Beach; Chandler, M. W., Rivera; Chandler, W. R., Tropico; Chappelow, Amy, Prospect Park; Charlton, Mrs. O. A., Chatsworth Park; Chase, Joneta, Los Angeles; Chase, Lydia M., Pasadena; Chewning, Mrs. M. L., San Diego; Chilcate, G. H., San Francisco; Childers, W. E., San Jose; Childers, Mrs. W. E., San Jose; Chipman, L. J., San Jose; Chope, Mrs. J. E., King City; Christian, Lena, Norwalk; Christie, Mrs. Kate E., Pasadena; Christensen, Clara M., Garden Grove; Christensen, Serena, Garden Grove; Churchill, Grace, Santa Paula; Claney, Agnes E., Santa Rosa; Clark, A. M.,
San Rafael; Clark Effie, De Luz; Clark, Emily, Ontario; Clarke, E. Louise, Los Angeles; Clarke, Grace E., Highland; Clarke, H. A., Palmedale; Clark, Helena, San Jacinto; Clark, Katharine, Los Angeles; Clark, Lelia, San Jose; Clarke. Mary J., Los Angeles; Clarke, Mattie, Los Angeles; Clark, Walter, Petaluma; Clay, Ida Bell, Pomona; Clayton, Elizabeth, Downey; Clayton, W. M., Santa Ana; Claypool, Alice, Los Angeles; Claypool, Mary F., Los Angeles; Claypool, Mildred, Santa Rosa; Cleveland, A. C., Pasadena; Climie, Jessie, Pasadena; Coates, W. W., Pomona; Cobb, Benjamin, Ventura; Coblentz, Ethel, Pasadena; Cocke, Amy F., Los Angeles; Cocke, Mabel, Downey; Codington, Lida, Berkeley; Coffey, Julia, San Francisco; Cole, Mrs. Mary Stone, San Francisco; Cole, N. P., San Francisco; Coles, Ida E., San Francisco; Colegrove, Jennie, Chatsworth; Colehower, Josie, Watsonville; Coleman, S. E., Oakland; Collings, Mrs. D. R., Orange; Collins, A. H., Redlands; Collins, A. Kate, Monrovia; Collins, Blanche, Santa Ana; Collins, Laura, Los Angeles; Compton, Mrs. M. R., Los Angeles; Connelly, Mamie, Ventura; Conkling, Harriet, Pasadena; Conklin, Kate, San Francisco; Conover, Flora, Pacific Grove; Conrad, F. W., San Bernardina; Conrad, W. E., Gilroy; Cook, Annice, Los Angeles; Cook, Frances G., San Francisco; Cook, Jessie, Ventura; Cook, Lita C., Ethanae; Cook, W. H., Santa Ana; Coon, Charles D., Lamanda Park; Cooney, Ella L., Los Angeles; Cooney, Katharine M., Los Angeles; Cooper, Alice C., Los Angeles; Cooper, Francis S., Hayward; Cooper, Rebecque, Los Angeles; Cooper, Ruth M., Pasadena; Copeland, Lewis, Beaumont; Copp, Marion, San Diego; Corey, Althea S., Riverside; Cornell, L. C., Watsonville; Corson, Anna, Pasadena; Couch, George, Los Angeles; Couchman, H. H., Norwalk; Coulter, Minnie, Santa Rosa; Cowan, Estelle A., Los Angeles; Cowan, J. W., Stanford; Cowan, Rose E., Los Angeles; Coward, Beulah, Norwalk; Cox, Bessie M., Los Angeles; Cox, E. M., Santa Rosa; Coy, Nathan B., San Diego; Coyne, Isabelle, College Park; Coyne, R. J., College Park; Crandall, Jessie M., Los Angeles; Crandall, Jessie M., Pasadena; Crawford, Lida, Downey; Crawford, T. O., Oakland; Cree, Mrs. Bettie, San Jacinto; Cree, Ray, San Jacinto; Crew, Ethel, Los Angeles; Crittenden, J. L., San Francisco; Crolic, Leah, Los Angeles; Cronkite, Minnie, Los Angeles; Crowell, Alice G., Los Angeles; Crowell, Mrs. Ida S., El Modena; Crowley, Elizabeth, San Francisco; Crowley, Kate, San Francisco; Crum, Mabel, Ocean Park; Crumpton, Clara, Sausalito; Cubberley, E. P., Palo Alto; Cubbison, Sedalia, Santa Ana; Culbertson, May, Claremont; Culver, Carolyn, Corona; Culver, H. E., Los Angeles; Culver, Susie B., Oakland; Curley, Kate, San Jose; Curley, L., San Jose; Curlett, William, San Francisco; Curran, Pauline G., Los Angeles; Curry, Eltha, Norwalk; Curtis,

Mrs. Emma G., Viru City; Curtis, H. M., San Bernardino; Curtis, Laura A., San Bernardino; Curtis, Louise, Los Angeles; Curtis, Mrs. Mary W., Los Angeles; Curtis, Nellie, Placer county; Curtis, Sara M., Iowa; Cushing, Alice J., Los Angeles.

D

Dailey, M. E., San Jose; Daley, Ysibel, San Jose; Daman, A. O., Chatsworth; Daniels, Agnes E., Los Angeles; Daniels, Aimee, Pasadena; Dannals, Marion E., Whittier; Davies, Grace, Newbury Park; Davis, Mrs. Angie, Daggett; Davis, Blanche, Hollister; Davis, Bernice G., Pomona; Davis, B. M., Los Angeles; Davis, Corinne, Los Angeles; Davis, E. M., Fresno; Davis, Helen, Los Angeles; Davidson, F. P., San Diego; Davidson, James B., Sausalito; Davidson, J. P., Stanford; Davis, L., Stanford; Davisson, Mabel, Los Angeles; Davis, Mary A., Los Angeles; Davis, M. B., Los Angeles; Davis, Meredith, Redlands; Davis, Nellie, Los Angeles; Davis, Rose A., Los Angeles; Davis, Rosa, LakeView; Dawson, Mrs. Ella C., Santa Monica; Day, Mrs. F. B., Palo Alto; Deacon, Mary, Long Beach; De Berri, A. I., East Highlands; De Berri, Josephine, East Highlands; De Cou, J. Allen, Berkeley; De Fremery, Grace, Perris; De Luna, Edith Ocean Park; De Pencier, Mabel, Sierra Madre; DeVose, Mary, Redlands; Demmon, Adelaide, Pomona; Denman, James, San Francisco; Denton, Franc V., Los Angeles; Denton, Joey, San Jose; Denton, Lyman W., Los Angeles; Denton, V. L., Rivera; Desmond, Kate, Los Angeles; DeVin, Minnie, Los Angeles; Devine, May E., San Francisco; Dexter, Yetta F., MonroVia; Dick, Nettie M., Los Angeles; Dick, Ona V., Los Angeles; Dickerson, Roy, Ontario; Dickey, Ethel, Pasadena; Dickison, Mae, Los Angeles; Dickson, Etta M., San Gabriel; Dickson, Lucile, Los Angeles; Dietrich, Florence, Pasadena; Diffenbacher, Lulu, Los Angeles; Dill, Minnie, Los Angeles; Dilworth, Anna, Ventura; Doyle, M. J., Berkeley; Dayle, M. P., Berkeley; Dimmick, Carrie, Los Angeles; Dixon, Clara, Los Angeles; Dixon, Ella M., Los Angeles; Dobbs. Ella V., Pasadena; Dobsynsky, Sarah, San Francisco; Dolland, Edward, Los Angeles; Dole, M. M., Auburn; Dole, Sara L., Long Beach; Donnell, B. H., Los Angeles; Donahue, Jennie, Los Angeles; Donohue, Rebecca, Berkeley; Donovan, Laura, Dimond; Dooner, Mabel, Los Angeles; Doran, A. E., Los Angeles; Dorn, Clara H., Los Angeles; Dorn, Olga H., Los Angeles; Dornberger, A. L., Mayfield; Dorsey, S. M., Los Angeles; Doty, Jessie P., Hueneme; Downes, C. S., San Francisco; Downey, Helen, Los Angeles; Downing, Margaret, Los Angeles; Dozier, Melville, Los Angeles; Drapér, Alice G., Pasadena; Drewey, Ida, Arlington Station; Du Bois, Mrs. C. G., Los Angeles; Dunbar, Sue H., Oakland; Duncan, Mattie, Redding; Duncan, Luella A., Los Angeles; Dunham, Florence A., Los Angeles; Dunlap, Knight, Berkeley; Dunn, Emma M., Los Angeles; Dunn, Francis, Berkeley; Dunn, H. E., Los Angeles; Dunn, W. A., Hollywood; Dunster, Mrs. Mary G., Los Angeles; Duraind, May R., San Francisco; Duren, A. M., Oakland; Durfee, L. A., Hollywood; Durham, A. B., Aguanga; Durkee, Ellen I., Pomona; Durrell, C. E., San Mateo; Durward, Arthur, Pomona; Dwire, Carrie, Ventura; Dwire, Julia, Ventura.

E

Easton, Edith, Riverside; Eckert, D. A., Santa Monica; Eckford, Annie, Los Angeles; Edgerton, C. L., Montalvo; Edwards, Elizabeth, Petaluma; Edwards, Eva D., Pomona; Edwards, Mrs. E. W., Los Angeles; Edwards, Hazel, Stanford; Edwards, Mary G., Glendale; Edwards, Mary M., Los Angeles; Edwards, W. A., Pasadena; Edwards, W. H., San Francisco; Edwards, W. S., Santa Barbara; Eells, Georgiana, Los Angeles; Egan, May, Los Angeles; Eisenberg, Winifred, Los Angeles; Elder, Ada A., Tustin; Elliott, Agnes, Los Angeles; Ellithorpe, Ada, Aguanza; Ellis, F. E., Stockton; Ellis, Fred, San Jose; Ellis, W. A., Los Angeles; Ellsworth, Mrs. De Grace, Santa Ana; Ellsworth, Anna M., Los Angeles; Ely, Roy D., Pasadena; Emery, Lottie, Los Angeles; Emery, R. B., Los Angeles; Endicott, Stella, Los Angeles; English, Mrs. M. A., Los Angeles; English, Rebecca F., San Jose; Ensign, Olive L., Los Angeles; Erickson, Mrs. J. A., Los Angeles; Erlewine, O. W., Sacramento; Eshbach, Mrs. E., San Jose; Espy, Edna, Pasadena; Estabrook, Lois, Pacific Grove; Evans, Ann, Nordhoff; Evans, B. L., Colton; Evans, I. L., Long Beach; Evans, Maria, San Bernardino; Evans, M. O., Berkeley; Evans, P. L., Redlands; Everett, A. W., Perris.

F

Fackler, Mary, Pasadena; Faithfull, Claude, Los Angeles; Fall, H. C., Pasadena; Fanning, Mamie, Los Angeles; Farley, C. M., San Jose; Farnsworth, Grace, Los Angeles; Farrier, Mrs. E. J., Lakeport; Farrington, E. A., Downey; Faulkner, R. D., San Francisco; Fay, J. A., Stanford; Feddersohn, Mrs. P., Los Angeles; Fenton, E. S., San Francisco; Ferguson, Hattie I., Los Angeles; Ferguson, Rose, Alameda; Field, Elizabeth, Los Angeles; Finch, Eunice M., Los Angeles; Finch, Mrs. E., Los Angeles; Fine, Anna, San Bernardino; Finley, Emma, Lordsburg; Finley, Lulu B., Santa Ana; Finley, Sallie H., Needles; Finney, Venna O., Los Angeles; Fishburn, Rosetta, South Pasadena; Fish, Chestina, Bardsdale; Fisher, Ida M., Alameda; Fisher, Philip M., Oakland; Fisch, Ida, Los Angeles; Fitting, R. U., Stanford; Fitz Gerald, Mrs. M. M., San Francisco; Fitzmier, Bertha, Los ..geles; Fleishman, Helena, Los Angeles; Fleishman, Mrs. J. B., El Monte; Flentjen, Anna, Los Angeles; Flentjen, Augusta, Los Angeles; Flint, Ora, Los Angeles; Flood, Florence, Pomona; Floyd, Annie, Hollister; Flynn, Louise C., Los Angeles; Foley, Mary, Alhambra; Ford, Anna S., Los Angeles; Ford, Gertrude, San Jose; Ford, Hannah B., Los Angeles; Ford, James —, Los Angeles; Forst, Antoinette, El Monte; Forst, Cathrine, El Monte; Forsyth, Lillian, San Francisco; Forsythe, Lucy, Dimond; Foshay, James A., Los Angeles; Foster, Mrs. A. M., Los Angeles; Foster, B. B., Fairmount; Foster, May, Downey; Fox, Charles J., Los Angeles; Fox, C. J., Los Angeles; Fox, Daisy E., San Jose; Fox, Lizzie H., Weaverville; Fox, L. O., Saticoy; Fox, Nettie I., Pomona; Frackleton, Lena, Garvanza; Frackleton, William B., San Pedro; Francis, J. H., Los Angeles; Frank, E., Oakland; Frank, Eva M., Los Angeles; Frasier, Alice M., San Pedro; Fraser, Anna G., Santa Monica; Fraser, Maude, Petaluma; Fraser, Jessie, Santa Paula; Fraser, Mrs. J. D., Ventura; Frazer, J. D., Ventura; Frazee, Isabelle, Pasadena; Frazier, Aranetta, Long Beach; Freeman, Mrs. Cora B., Los Angeles; Freeman, Ethel, Los Angeles; Freeman, Jacob H., South Pasadena; Freeman, Mrs. G. N., Fowler; Freeman, G. N., Fowler; French, Charles E., San Francisco; French, Helen G., Monrovia; French, Mary L., Los Angeles; French, W. B., Pasadena; Frew, Will L., Compton; Frink, Clara B., Los Angeles; Fruhling, Millie, Agenda; Frye, Joseph C., Garlock; Fryer, Roy, Santa Rosa; Fuller, Grace, Azusa; Fuller, Mabel B., Pomona; Furlong, Judith M., Los Angeles; Furlong, Robert, San Rafael; Fussel, Mrs. S. E., Pasadena.

G

Gage, Harriet, Los Angeles; Gaines, Mrs. Nettie, Clipper Gap; Gallup, Anna F., Pomona; Gallup, Luke C., Compton; Ganahl, Antoinette, Los Angeles; Gardner, Arthur B., Santa Ana; Garey, Julia, Los Angeles; Garlick, E. F., Oakland; Garlick, J. B., Oakland; Garner, J. H., Hollister; Garner, Mrs. J. H., Hollister; Garst, Mrs. Dollie, Riverside; Garwood, B. V., Fullerton; Gastrich, J. W., Berkeley; Gaud, Margaret, Pasadena; Gearhart, Edna, Azusa; Gearhart, Frances H., Merced; Gearhart, May, Berkeley; Geddes, Ethel, Rochester; George, Mrs. M. W., San Jose; Geotz., J. J., Anaheim; Germain, Jennie Los Angeles; Getchell, Nettie, Los Angeles; Getz, K. C., Los Angeles; Gibbs, Mrs. Ellen, Berkeley; Gibson, Annette, Los Angeles; Gibson, Elizabeth, Los Angeles; Gibson, Elizabeth J., Los Angeles; Gibson, Marguerite L., Los Angeles; Gifford, Wilhelmine, Los Angeles; Gildsey, M., San Jose; Gillespie, Augusta M., Los Angeles; Gillespie, Cora, San Jose; Gillespie, Effie, Los Angeles; Gillespie, Harriet, Los Angeles; Gilman, Myrtle, Whittier; Gilott, Iva, San Jose; Glasscock, Ida, Ventura; Glass, Jeannette, Los Angeles; Gleason, Charles B., San Jose; Gleason, E. M, Pasadena; Gleason, Laura, Pasadena; Glenn, Elston, Pasadena; Glenn, Maud, Pasadena; Glick, Margaret, Los Angeles; Glover, Estelle, Redlands; Glover, Mrs. J. M., Evergreen; Glover, J. M., Evergreen; Goldberg, David, Los Angeles; Goldsmith, Lulu, Los Angeles; Good, S. V., Ventura; Goodenow, F. G., Los Angeles; Goodin, Anne, Los Angeles; Goodhart, Katherine, Riverside; Goodhue, Elsie, Los Angeles; Goodrich, Alice, Orange; Gooch, Rivera; Gooch, Emma, Covina; Gordon, A. W., Stanford University; Gordon, Bertha E., Los Angeles; Gordon, Mrs. E. A., San Jose; Gordon, George A., Jackson; Gould, Mrs. Frances B., Oakland; Gould, Jennie C., Los Angeles; Gourley, Jessie, Calaveras county; Gower, Hattie F., Los Angeles; Gower, Mary L., Los Angeles; Gracier, Addie J., San Francisco; Gray, Laura, Redondo; Graf, Louise, Banning; Graehe, Mattie, Los Angeles; Graham, Pearl, Los Angeles; Gray, Alice C., Los Angeles; Gray, Catharine, Somis; Gray, Mabel T., Los Angeles; Graff, Mrs. G. L., San Jose; Graff, George L., San Jose; Graham, Daisy B., Los Angeles; Graham, Elizabeth A., San Francisco; Graham, Frances, Los Angeles; Graham, James D., Pasadena; Gray, Mabel, Los Angeles; Graves, Ethel W., Pasadena; Gregg, E., San Diego; Gregory, Mrs. Anna C., Los Angeles; Gregory, Elizabeth A., Los Angeles; Gregory, Lyman, Los Angeles; Gregory, Mabel, C., Los Angeles; Greeley, J. G., Santa Ana; Green, Bonnie, Los Angeles; Green, Frances M., Los Angeles; Green, Grace A., Whittier; Green, G. M., Colton; Green, G. W., Riverside; Green, Hephzibah E., Benicia; Green, Jennie, Piru; Green, Louise, Winchester; Green, S. Maud, Sacramento; Green, H. Viola, Redlands; Green, Marian, Los Angeles; Greene, Rebecca, Salinas; Greenwood, Barbara, Pomona; Grey, Grace J., Los Angeles; Griffith, Anna L., Monrovia; Griffith, B. W., Los Angeles; Griffith, Mabel, Long Beach; Griffith, Julia W., Pasadena; Grinnell, Mrs. E. E., Banning; Grinnell, E. E., Banning; Grinnell, Joseph, Palo Alto; Griswold, Anna S., Los Angeles; Griswold, Mabel, Pomona; Grovenendyke, Elizabeth, Los Angeles; Gross, Bertha, Riverside; Grow, Jessie C., Los Angeles; Gude, Alberta, Los Angeles; Guillon, A., Hueneme; Guirvits, Nettie M., Los Angeles; Gulick, C. T., Fruitvale; Gundrum, F. F., Stanford; Gunn, A. F., San Francisco; Gunn, Mrs. A. F., San Francisco; Gunn, F., Los Angeles; Gunning, Alma E., Ocean Park; Gunning, Mabel R., Ocean Park; Guthrie, F. W., Azusa City.

H

Haas, Charles E., Irvington; Haas, Clara J., Los Angeles; Hackenson, H. A., San Pedro; Hadley, G. E., Santa Ana; Hadley, Myra L., Iowa; Hafford, F. S., Hemet; Hahn, Jean M., Santa Ana; Halberstadt, Leonore, Los Angeles; Hale, Marguerite, San Jose; Haley, Anna T., San Francisco; Hall, Alice, Los Angeles;

Hall, Bertha, Los Angeles; Hall, Ida L., Los Angeles; Hall, W. S., The Palms; Haller, Dora A., Los Angeles; Halvorsen, C. Marie, Los Angeles; Hamilton, A. L., Pasadena; Hamilton, J. E., Santa Marie; Hamilton, Kate, Pasadena; Hamilton, Myrtle L., Pasadena; Hamlin, Elizabeth, Ocean Park; Hamlin, Lillie J., Berkeley; Hammack, Eleanor L., Los Angeles; Hammond, Florence, San Jose; Hammond, P. H., Claremont; Hancock, Inez E., Riverside; Hancock, J. E., San Jose; Hanna, E. G., Stanford; Hanna, Ross, Los Angeles; Hanlon, Annie, Los Angeles; Hanlon, Harriet, Los Angeles; Harcus, Mrs. H. E., Los Angeles; Harden, Isabel, Los Angeles; Hardenberg, Rose, Los Angeles; Hards, M. G., Los Angeles; Harnden, Mrs. F. W., San Francisco; Harnden, F. W., San Francisco; Harnett, Jane E., Long Beach; Harrington, Kate, Stanford; Harrington, Helen, Los Angeles; Harris, Caroline E., Los Angeles; Harris, Edna A., Redlands; Harris, Flora, El Monte; Harris, Gertrude, Santa Rosa; Harris, Mabel A., Pasadena; Harron, Frances V., Los Angeles; Hart, Elizabeth, Los Angeles; Hart, Pauline, San Francisco; Harwood, Helen L., Los Angeles; Huskey, F. G., San Francisco; Haskins, Edith L., Tustin; Haskins, Myrtle, Ventura; Haskins, Rose, Petaluma; Hastings, Ida, Los Angeles; Hastings, Mary A., Los Angeles; Hathaway, Chat., Santa Rosa; Hathaway, E. M., Sebastopol; Hauselt, E. E., San Francisco; Haveman, Mrs. William, Los Angeles; Havemam, J. Jeannette, Los Angeles; Haver, S. C., Stanford University; Hawkins, Effie I., Palo Alto; Hawkins, Jessie, Artesia; Hawley, Agnes G., Berkeley; Hawley, Mary, South Pasadena; Hawley, Sadie, South Pasadena; Hayden. James A., Sutter Creek; Haydock, R. B., Oxnard; Hayes A., Stanford; Haynes, D. M., Stanford; Hays, Fannie, Los Angeles; Hazard, F. A., Whittier; Hazard, Mabel, Los Angeles; Hazen, Lillian D., Los Angeles; Hazzard, Jessica C., Whittier; Heald, Clara E., Los Angeles; Healy, Clara, Ontario; Heap, Jennie L., Los Angeles; Heaton, Thomas L., Berkeley; Hecht, Grace A., Los Angeles; Heineman, Ada J., Los Angeles; Hendershot, Frances, Glendale; Henderson, Anna W., Santa Paula; Henderson, Gertrude, Los Angeles; Henderson, Janet M., Los Angeles; Henderson, Mary A., Los Angeles; Henning, M., Ventura; Henry, J. N., Los Angeles; Henry, Mrs. M. J., Los Angeles; Hendrie, Anna, Redlands; Herrick, Zoe C., Redlands; Hibbard, Gertrude E., Pomona; Hibbard, Elizabeth, Pasadena; Hickcox. Gail, Eliwanda; Hickman, Sue, San Jose; Higgins, Eliza, San Jose; Higley, Alice D., Pasadena; Higley, Rosa, Palo Alto; Hiett, M., Santa Paula; Hill, Charles C., Salinas; Hill, Edith, Stanford University; Hill, Edith L., Alhambra; Hill, Ethel L., San Francisco; Hill, Jessie L., Pomona; Hilliard, Justine, Long Beach; Hill, Lillian R., Pomona; Hill, Merton, Compton; Hill, S. E., Berkeley; Hilliard, M. A., Glendora; Hilliard, Olive M., Redlands; Hillis, M. E., Los Angeles; Hite, Mary F., Puente; Hoagland, Clara, Redlands; Hobe, Sophie A., San Francisco; Hodge, M. C., Rialto; Hodgson, S. J., Oakland; Hodgkins, S. J., Oakland; Hodgkins, Edith M., Los Angeles; Holdel, Robert, Berkeley; Hoffman, Hattie, San Jose; Hogan, Helena M., San Francisco; Hohfeld, Edward, Auburn; Hohfeld, Lily, San Francisco; Holcomb, Mamie, San Bernardino; Holden, Mrs. Frances C., Santa Ana; Holland, Mrs. W. H., Los Angeles; Holland, W. H., San Gabriel; Holleran, Nora, San Pedro; Holling, Louise, Berkeley; Hollingsworth, Mrs. Hattie, Los Angeles; Holmes, Julia K., Los Angeles; Holway, R. S., Palo Alto; Hollywell, Florence, Los Angeles; Hook, Julia, Montalvo; Hoose, J. H., Los Angeles county; Hopkins, Edwin, Kansas; Hopper, Florence, Los Angeles; Hopkins, Leoline, Pomona; Horgan, Gertrude, Los Angeles; Hostetter, Grace M., Oakland; Houghton, Clara H., Hynes; Houghton, Laura L., Los Angeles; Houser, Lila E., Los Angeles; Houseworth, Mrs. F. A., San Francisco; Houseworth, F. A., San Francisco; Housh, Frances M., Pasadena; Housh, W. H., Los Angeles; House, Mabel, Ocean Park; Houston, H. A., Berkeley; Hovey, Grace V., Los Angeles; Howe, Agnes E., San Jose; Howell, Minnie, W., Stockton; Howard, B. F., Sacramento; Howard, Florence G., Fernando; Howard, Maude, Montalvo; Howard, W. B., San Francisco; Hubbard, Mrs. G. W., Tustin; Hubbard, H. C., Stanford; Huber, Louise, Los Angeles; Huber, Mrs. O. H., Azusa; Hudspeth, B. F., Colfax; Huffaker, Ernest L., San Francisco; Huff, William F., Anaheim; Hughes, Mrs. C. C., Alameda; Hughes, Charles C., Alameda; Hughes, Minnie E., Downey; Hughes, M., San Francisco; Hugunin, May E., San Pedro; Hull, Lulu, Santa Paula; Humphrey, Alice L., San Jose; Hunt, Barta, Santa Ana; Hunt, Bertha R., Santa Monica; Hunt, Caroline L., San Francisco; Hunt, Helen E., Los Angeles; Hunt, R. D., San Jose; Hunter, Mrs. A. D., Pomona; Hunter, A. D., Pomona; Huntley, Wenona, Los Angeles; Huntoon, Carolyn L., Pomona; Huston, Margaret, Los Angeles; Hurley, Anna M., Pasadena; Hurry, Kate, San Jose; Hurtt, Bertha, Cucomonga; Hursey, G. W., Upland; Hutchinson, M. I., Los Angeles; Hutchinson, M. Louise, Los Angeles; Hutchinson, Ollie, Downey; Hutton. Charles E., Los Angeles; Hyatt, Edward, Riverside; Hyde, Kate, Elsinore; Hyde, Olive, Los Angeles; Hynding, Cecelia, Redwood City.

I

Imrie. John A., Napa; Ingham, Mrs. E. C., Fernando; Ingham, E. T., Fernando; Ingraham, L. L., Riverside; Ingram, Stella B., Los Angeles; Inskeep, L. D., Oakland; Inskeep, I. N., Los Angeles; Ismert, Rose I., Ventura; Izumi, A., Stanford.

J

Jack, H. M., Stanford; Jackson, Bessie E., Pasadena; Jackson, Emma L., Redlands; Jackson, Mollie A., Los Angeles; Jacobs, L. Foster, Los Angeles; James, L. G., San Jose; James, Margaret, Abbotsford Inn; James, Mary K., Los Angeles; James, M., Pomona; Jamison, Rachel, Los Angeles; Jarmick, J., Stanford; Jeffers, F. F., Stanford; Jeffreys, Catherine, Corona; Jenkins, O. P., Stanford University; Jensen, P. J., Stanford University; Jenson, Mrs. P. J., Stanford; Jessup, Ruth, Bancroft Jensen, P. J., Stanford University; Jensen, Alice E., Los Angeles; Jodon, Beatrice, Pasadena; Johnson, Annette, Los Angeles; Johnson, Clara O., Riverside; Johnson, Emily F., Los Angeles; Johnson, Edna L., Los Angeles; Johnston, Eva E., Berkeley; Johnson, Fred P., San Luis Obispo; Johnson, Gretchen, Los Angeles; Johnson, Ida J., Ontario; Johnson, Julia E., Ontario; Johnson, Jean, San Francisco; Johnson, Mabel, Whitter; Johnson, Margaret C., San Lucas; Johnson, Mattie, Los Angeles; Johnston, S. Grace, Pomona; Johnston, A. E., Anaheim; Jones, Adelaide, Los Angeles; Jones, D. R., Berkeley; Jones, Jennie L., Los Angeles; Jones, Jessie H., Alameda; Jones, Julia, San Jose; Jones, Melvania, Los Angeles; Jones, Mary I., Laguna; Jones, Mrs. C. B., Sierra Madra; Jones, Zella, Riverside; Jordan, L. A., San Francisco; Joy, Edith M., Los Angeles; Junkin, A. M., Los Angeles; Junkin, Mary, Los Angeles.

K

Kallenbach, Lizzie, Los Angeles; Kane, Mrs. T. L., Ventura; Kauffman, P. W., Ventura; Keach, Ninta, Los Angeles; Keaton, Ellen M., San Jose; Keefer, Alice F., Berkeley; Keiller, Anna B., San Diego; Keeler, C. D., San Bernardino; Kellogg, A. E., San Francisco; Kellogg, L. F., El Mone; Kellogg, Minnie, San Pedro; Kelly, Alice E., Pacheco; Kelly, Helena, Aromas; Kelly A., Laura, Gonzales; Kemp, W. W., Menlo Park; Kenny, Maud L., San Diego; Keppel, Mark, Los Angeles; Keppel, Mrs. Mark, Los Angeles; Kerlin, Ada M., Los Angeles; Kerlin, C. W., Monterey; Kerns, Alma, Los Angeles; Kerns, Fannie, Los Angeles; Kerns, Page, Los Angeles; Kerr, Henry, Monrovia; Kesling, M. C., San Jose; Kevane, Kate, Long Beach; Keyes, C. E., Oakland; Keys, Stella, Orange; Kidder, Louise, Berkeley; Kidwell, N. C., National City; Kierneff, G. Dudley, Alameda; Killifer, Mary, Los Angeles; Kimmell, Marian, Hemet; King, Anna A., Loomis; King, Anna V., Los Gatos; King, Edith, San Jose; Kingery, Frances, Los Angeles; King, Mary F., Los Angeles; Kingsbury, Rae W., Los Angeles; Kingsbury, W. de L., San Francisco; Kinney, Burt, Los Angeles; Kinney, L. C., Berkeley; Kirk, Alice, Los Angeles; Kirk, T. H., Santa Barbara; Kirk, Thomas J., Sacramento; Kirkpatrick, Eunice, Los Angeles; Knepper, E., Los Angeles; Knight, Agnes, Los Angeles; Knight, Della, Los Angeles; Knight, Franc R., Pasadena; Knoch, C. A., Pasadena; Knox, Bena I., Elsenore; Knox, Bertha, Oakland; Knox, M. E., Los Angeles; Kuma, T., Stanford University; Kunou, C. A., Los Angeles; Kurtz, Edith, Petaluma; Kyle, A. D., Santa Paula.

L

Lacey, Benjamin O., San Diego; Laird, Anna M., Los Angeles; Lamb, Cora E., Los Angeles; Lambert, Mabel J., El Monte; Lambie, Grace V., Los Angeles; Lane, Robert H., Los Angeles; Lang, Carrie J., Pasadena; Lane, Edith L., Los Angeles; Lang, Ellen, Los Angeles; Lang, Mary G., Los Angeles; Langheim, Lillian E., Los Angeles; Langdon, W. H., San Francisco; Langman, Nellie, El Rio; Langenour, Lillie, Colusa; Larkey, George E., Los Angeles; La Sage, Estella, Los Angeles; Latham, C. E., Los Angeles; Lattig, Mrs. F. J., San Francisco; Latty, F. J., San Francisco; Laughlin, Grace A., Los Angeles; Layne, Mary, Los Angeles; Lawley, Grace E., Middletown; Lawson, Gertrude, Los Angeles; Lawton, Frances, Los Angeles; Lavallie, E. I., Hayward; Leach, Pauline, Santa Monica; Leathers, Martha, San Bernardino; Ledford, Mrs. Carrie F., Los Angeles; Ledyard, Mary F., Los Angeles; Leffen, Isabella, San Bernardino; Lee, Robert A., San Jose; Leet, Cynthia P., Oakland; Leland, Anna, Los Angeles; Lemon, Addie, Salinas; Lemon, Anna E., Pasadena; Lennon, Lida, Chico; Lenton, Levinia E., Fullerton; Leslie, George, Los Angeles; Le Van, Mary E., Los Angeles; Leviele, Blanche, Los Angeles; Lewers, C. R., Stanford; Lewis, Jesse, Ventura; Lewis, Josephine, Los Angeles; Lewis, Sada L., Pomona; Libby, Anna L., Redlands; Libby, Lucy A., Fredalba; Lietzan, Cora, Los Angeles; Lietzan, Emily, Los Angeles; Lillibridge, Clara, Los Angeles; Lillie, Emma E., Los Angeles; Lindsay, E. M., Ross; Lindsay, Ruby V., Los Angeles; Linn, Mary, Los Angeles; Linscott, H. A., San Leandro; Linscott, J. W., Santa Cruz; Linscott, Louise, Berkeley; Linscott, Stella, Berkeley; Lipe, Clara, Los Angeles; Lipe, Mary, Azusa; Lipley, W. J., Alhambra; List, B. F., Los Angeles; Little, F. E., Los Angeles; Littler, T. M., San Jose; Livesey, J. J., Berkeley; Livingood, Anna, Los Angeles; Livngstone, May, Los Angeles; Lobbett, F. J., San Francisco; Loeke, Charles E., Los Angeles; Lockwood, Elizabeth, Los Angeles; Lockwood, Kate, Los Angeles; Lodge, E., Stanford; Lodge, Leta, Los Angeles; Longenecker, H. E., Berkeley; Longley, Florence, Los Angeles; Loomis, Jean, Pasadena; Lorbeer, M. W., Glendale; Loree, W., El Monte; Loring, Grace M., Los Angeles; Lotshar, Sarah R., Lemon; Lotspeich, Jessie A., Los Angeles; Loucks, Annie, Pacheco; Lovejoy, Lena G., Santa Monica; Loveland, N. B., San Jacinto; Lovell, Olivia, Anaheim; Loon, Annie C., Los Angeles; Lowe, J. M., Agunnga; Lucy, Estelle, Oakland; Lunt, H. L., Los Angeles; Lyon, Sarah, Los Angeles; Lyons, Mrs. Edith H., San Francisco.

M

Maag, C., San Jose; Machado, Ylara, Ocean Park; Machold, E. M., San Pedro; Mackenzie, Anna, Los Angeles; Mackenzie, Helen C., Los Angeles; Mac Kenzie, Mary W., Los Angeles; Mackey, Mrs. Frances, Los Angeles; Madden, Delia, Redwood City; Madden, Emma L., San Francisco; Madden, Jennie, San Jose; Madden, Mrs. K. L., Los Angeles; Madden, Sara A., San Francisco; Madsen, Marion, Oakland; Magaw, W. J., Redlands; Mahoney, Elizabeth, Los Angeles; Main, Mrs. Lulu, Corona; Mainland, Sara, Riverside; Maitland, Mary F., Los Angeles; Malcolm, William, Tropico; Manley, Edna T. H., Los Angeles; Mann, Azro L., San Francisco; Mann, Laura, San Jose; Manning, Catherine V., Lang; Manning, Lura, Azusa City; Mantz, Anna M., Berkeley; Manzer, John, San Jose; Marbut, E. H., San Juan; Marbut, J. W., Goleta; March, Mrs. B. M., Los Angeles; Mark, Cecil W., San Francisco; Marks, H. F., Stanford; Maris, Leora, Los Angeles; Marsh, Alice L., Los Angeles; Marsh, Bessie L., Los Angeles; Martin, A. R., San Jose; Martin, F. N., Visalia; Martin, J. D., Oakland; Martin, Kittie O., Colton; Martin, Lillie, Riverside; Martin, Mabel T., Los Angeles; Martin, May, Pomona; Martin, Mimi, Pasadena; Martin, Nina, Covina; Mason, Mrs. L. I., Riverside; Matlock, Clara, Los Angeles; Matthews, B., Stanford; Matthews, Mrs. C. B., Oakland; Matthews, Ellen, Los Angeles; Matthewson, Helen E., Los Angeles; Maxwell, Jennie, Los Angeles; Maxwell, Josephine, Los Angeles; Maybach, S. P., Watsonville; Mayhorn, Mrs. M. J., San Francisco; Maynard, Los Angeles; Mayo, R. S., Santa Rosa; McCallum, Helen G., Los Angeles; McCarthy, Elizabeth C., Garvanza; McCarthy, Emma, Oxnard; McCarthy, Kate, Los Angeles; McCasky, H. L., Pasadena; McCharles, Mrs. Florence E., Tustin; McChesney, Alice, Los Angeles; McClelland, D. T., Los Angeles; McClenathan, Dell, San Jose; McClure, Mrs. Martha, Los Angeles; McClymonds, J. W., Oakland; McCollum, Alice, Los Angeles; McCormack, Ida M., Los Angeles; McCormack, Julia, Auburn; McCracken, C. A., Oakland; McCullock, A. L., Buena Park; McCulloch, Maria, Corona; McCutchan, H. H., Long Beach; McDaniel, Bertha, Los Angeles; McDaniel, Jean, Los Angeles; McDonald, L. J., Los Angeles; McDonald, Mary, San Jose; McDougall, Tena, Ontario; McEachin, Mamie, Los Angeles; McElroy, Louise, San Francisco; McFadden, Effie B., San Francisco; McFadden, E., Santa Ana; McFadden, Isabel, Los Angeles; McFeely, Agnes, Oakland; McGuffin, James A., Sacramento; McGovern, H. S., Sacramento; McGovern, Ina E., Sacramento; McGowan, Lucy G., Pasadena; McIlmoil, W. H., Lordsburg; McIntyre, Mrs. J. F., Ventura; McIsaac, Flora R., San Rafael; McKeehan, Annie M., Eureka; McKellar, M. Jose, Downey; McKendrick, Mary C., Pomona; McKenzie, Belle, Los Angeles; McKenzie, Lzzie, Los Angeles; McKenzie, L. M., San Jose; McKibben, Mary, Azusa City; McKinney, Mrs. Ida, Gilroy; McLane, C. L., Fresno; McLain, Leonora, Los Angeles; McMahon, A. M., Pasadena; McMillen, Clara, Los Angeles; McMullin, Rose I., Los Angeles; McNair, M. J., Pasadena; McNamara, Kate, Redwood City; McNaughton, Anna, Pasadena; McNeil, Grace, Pasadena; McPhail, Kathleen, Los Angeles; McPherron, A. S., San Bernardino; McPherron, Grace A., Los Angeles; McPherron, J. M., Los Angeles; McQuade, Mrs. C. M., Chico; McQuarrie, Mary, Los Angeles; McSweeney, Nellie, San Francisco; Meacham, Kate, Los Angeles; Meader, Margaret, Los Angeles; Meeker, C. H., Pacific Grove; Melton, Julia E., Downey; Melton, W. I., Downey; Merrick, Mrs. Rosetta, Corona; Merrill, George A., San Francisco; Merrill, Mrs. Minnie, Los Angeles; Metcalf, Beeda A., Los Angeles; Metcalf, Mrs. Nettie, Los Angeles; Metcalf, Ruby E., Los Angeles; Metkiff, Guenevere, Santa Monica; Meyer, Mrs. E., San Francisco; Meyer, Catherine, Sebastopol; Michaels, Abbie M., Pasadena; Miles, T. W., Bakersfield; Miles, Mrs. T. W., Bakersfield; Mignon, Helen, San Jose; Millard, Mrs. J. B., Los Angeles; Millard, J. B., Los Angeles; Miller, Ada J., Los Angeles; Miller, Mrs. C. A., Covina; Millar, Jess, Los Angeles; Miller, Charles M., Los Angeles; Miller, Elizabeth, Berkeley; Miller, E. I., Chico; Miller, Florence, Pomona; Miller, G. A., Stanford; Miller, Mrs. J. L., Los Angeles; Miller, Mrs. Louise J., Los Angeles; Miller, Mrs. L. M., Highbrove; Miller, Maude, San Jose; Miller, Narcissa, Los Angeles; Miller, Nellie, Perris; Miller, Therese, Hollywood; Milliken, Calla, Colton; Milliken, Luella, Colton; Millirou, Thyra L., Los Angeles; Mills, Catherine, Whittier; Mills, Mary, Los Angeles; Millspaugh, Nora H., Los Angeles; Milton, Marietta, Oakland; Minier, D. W., Berkeley; Minium, Willis, Petaluma; Mitchel, E. L., Fernando; Mitchell, Fanny, Los Angeles; Mitchell, Flora E., Oakland; Mitchell, Georgia, Pasadena; Mitchell, Jessie R., Pasadena; Mitchell, Mary B., Pasadena; Mishler, Grace, Pomona; Mock, Nannie E., Pomona; Moffitt, J. K., San Francisco; Mohan; Rose E., Los Angeles; Mohr, Paul, Oakland; Mohr, Thekla T., Los Angeles; Moisson, L. C., San Jose; Monk, Grade E., Los Angeles; Monks, Sarah P., Los Angeles; Monlux, J. B., Los Angeles; Monroe, Emily, Los Angeles; Monroe, George, Whittier; Moody, Mabel M., Los Angeles; Moore, Emma A., Los Angeles; Moore, E. C., San Francisco; Moore, Maud, Los Angeles; Moore, Stella M., Los Angeles; Moore, W. S., Antioch; Moores,

Edna, Downey; Morey, Bernice, Watsonvlle; Morey, Fannie, Watsonville; Morgan, Jessie J., Lon Beach; Morgan, Mabel, Los Angeles; Morgan, Mabel B., Los Angeles; Morgan, Mira, Santa Barbara; Morgan, Sylvia, Berkeley; Morrill, Mrs. George E., Santa Monica; Morrill, George E., Santa Monica; Morris, Ella, Los Angeles; Morrison, Ida E., Los Angeles; Morrissey, Katherine, Los Angeles; Morrison, Lizzie, Pasadena; Morton, Ella J., San Francisco; Morton, Frank, San Francisco; Mosgrove, Ella, Los Angeles; Mosher, Ella D., Pomona; Mosher, Katherine, Long Beach; Mosher, Libbie, Los Angeles; Mosher, Mary, Los Angeles; Motsinger, Kate, N. Cucomonga; Mourrts, L. F., Roseville; Mower, F. O., Napa; Moyse, G. W., Glendale; Mudge, Carrie, Redlands; Muller, Irene, Berkeley; Mulligan, T. A., Morgan Hill; Murdoch, Mrs. E. S., Los Angeles; Murdoch, Grace R., Los Angeles; Murdoch, Maria E., Los Angeles; Murdoch, Mrs. M. M., Los Angeles; Murphy, Alice G., Los Angeles; Murphy, Mary S., Los Angeles; Murphy, W. R., Chino; Murphy, Mrs. W. W., Los Angeles; Murray, Elizabeth, Redondo; Murray, Mary B., Los Angeles; Myers, Katherine, Los Angeles; Myrick, Eliza P., Los Angeles.

N

Nasserth, Winnie, Los Angeles; Neel, Melvin, Los Alamitos; Neely, Mrs. Arthur, Duarte; Nellis, Frances, Los Angeles; Nelson, Marie, Santa Paula; Netz, Joseph, La Habra; Nevell, Ella M., Los Angeles; Nevins, Katherine, Los Angeles; Newham, Frances, Oceanside; Newkirk, Lizzie G., Los Angeles; Newby, Mamie, Whittier; Newberry, Maude, Petaluma; Newton, Esther M., Redlands; Neylan, Nellie H., Oakland; Nicholson, Annie, San Jose; Nicholson, Genevieve, San Jose; Niles, Beth E., Los Angeles; Nisbet, Mrs. Henrietta, Los Angeles; Noble, Annie R., Los Angeles; Noble, Emma, San Jose; Noble, Amy, Ontario; Noble, Mary, Ontario; Noonan, Lizzie, Riverside; Noonan, Mary, Los Angeles; Norris, Mary M., Tropico; Norton, Cecelia, Los Angeles; Norton, Mina, Los Angeles; North, Helen, Stanford University; North, W., Stanford University; Norver, A. L., Stanford University; Nourse, J. P., Palo Alto.

O

O'Brien, Nelle, San Jose; O'Connor, Joseph, San Francisco; O'Hara, Maud F., Sespe; O'Neal, Mrs. M. L., San Francisco; O'Neil, Florence, Los Angeles; Oden, Helen R., Hueneme; Oman, Mrs. M. E., Los Angeles; Oliver, Andrew, San Francisco; Oliver, Bertha, Los Angeles; Oliver, Elizabeth B., Los Angeles; Oliver, Louise, Rialto; Oliver, Nellie G., Los Angeles; Oliver, Mrs. Sara T., Pasadena; Olmstead, V. A., Los Angeles; Orcutt, Mary, Santa Paula; Orr, Marie P., Berkeley; Ortley, Harriet R., Alviso; Ortley, O. I., Alviso; Orving, Mrs. Maud, Los Angeles; Osborn, G. V., Elk Grove; Osgood, Kate F., Los Angeles; Owen, Edna, Los Angeles; Owen, J. C., Santa Paula; Owen, Mae, Los Angeles; Overholzer, John, Lakeport.

P

Packard, Henry, Santa Barbara; Page, Alec, San Rafael; Page, Mary, Berkeley; Paine, Mae, Los Angeles; Palen, H. O., San Francisco; Palmer, Mrs. C. F., Stanford University; Palmer, Elizabeth, Los Angeles; Palmer, Mrs. Ellen H., Azusa; Palmer, Harriet R., Pomona; Palmer, Luella, Redlands; Palmer, Mabel E., Berkeley; Parcell, Zulema, Los Angeles; Parker, J. R., Goleta; Parker, Lulu V., Pomona; Parker, Maud C., Covina; Parkhurst, E. S., Willows; Parkman, Jessie A., San Jose; Parolini, Mrs. M. J., San Francisco; Parsons, A. M., San Pedro; Parsons, E. N., Los Angeles; Partridge, Annie M., Pasadena; Partridge, Mrs. Clara M., Berkeley; Paterson, Mary, Hollister; Patton, Herbert, Claremont; Patterson, Mahel, Arlington Staton; Payne, Ella, Los Angeles; Pease, Virgnia, Pasadena; Pechin, Mrs. C. R., San Francisco; Peck, Bessie, Ventura; Peckham, Mrs. Alice M., Bakersfield; Peckham, Edith C., Redlands; Peckham, Le Roy B., Bakersfield; Peckham, Lois A., San Francisco; Peckham, S. F., Los Angeles; Peet, Carrie, Pomona; Pendergrast, C. C., San Rafael; Pendleton, M. R., Downey; Pepper, Elizabeth N., Los Angeles; Perl, Ida M., San Francisco; Perrin, Mrs. A., Berkeley; Perry, Amy L., Los Angeles; Perry, Gertrude J., Sausalito; Perry, I. D., Palo Alto; Peter, Mary, Pasadena; Peters, E. A., Newhall; Peters, Louise, Ventura; Peterson, Louisa; Salinas; Petray, H. C., Haywards; Petray, Nellie M., Los Angeles; Petterson, H., Berkeley; Pfaffenberger, Selma, Los Angeles; Pfeninger, Leila I., Los Angeles; Phalin, A. M., Martinez; Phelps, Mary A. J., Los Angeles; Phelps, Mary M., Los Angeles; Philips, Maud, Los Angeles; Philipson, Margaret, Los Angeles; Phillips, Alice, Los Angeles; Phillips, Edith J., Los Angeles; Phillips, Fannie M., Los Angeles; Phillips, Sudie E., Los Angeles; Phillips, T. J., Los Angeles; Pico Heights Convent, Los Angeles; Pierce, E. T., Los Angeles; Pierce, Isabel W., Los Angeles; Pierpont, M. Olive, Santa Barbara; Pierson, Mrs. L. M., Goleta; Pierson, Mabel B., Los Angeles; Pillot, Mrs. Mary, San Jose; Pinney, Ellen B., Long Beach; Pittman, C. B., San Diego; Plummer, A. W., Los Angeles; Pobes, Fannie, Pasadena; Pollock, Mrs. Minne R., Ontario; Pond, Mrs. N. F. W., Los Angeles; Porter, Annette, Norwalk; Porter, Burney, Los Angeles; Porter, Roy, Norwalk; Post, Mary H., Santa Clara; Potter, E. F., Oxnard; Potter, Mrs. Nellie I., Los Angeles; Power, Alice Rose, San Francisco; Powers, E.

A., San Francisco; Powell, Bessie, Los Angeles; Powell, Katharine, Los Angeles; Powers, Mrs. Sylvia L., Pomona; Pratt, Abbie L., Los Angeles; Prentiss, Bertha C., Los Angeles; Preston, Charlotte M., Los Angeles; Preston, Clara M., Los Angeles; Prentiss, Luella, Los Angeles; Prentiss, S. L., Ontario; Prince, Geo., H., Los Angeles; Prior, Philip, San Francisco.

Q

Quayle, Mary E., Los Angeles; Quinn, Eliza, Los Angeles; Quick, M. Eva, Los Angeles; Quinn, Annie, San Francisco; Quinn, May, Sn Francisco.

R

Radcliffe, Emily, Los Angeles; Rainy, M., San Francisco; Ramboz, Ina W., Los Angeles; Ramsaur, B. W., Berkeley; Ramsdell, Mary A., Los Angeles; Randall, Nellie, Los Angeles; Raney, O. N., Los Angeles; Rapier, Rowen, Salinas; Rattan, Volney, San Jose; Rea, Kate, Anaheim; Read, Mud E., Amador City; Reager, Frank S., Willows; Reardon, C. E., Reedly; Reardon, Emma E., Selma; Reardon, Nellie F., King Cty; Reaves, Bessie F., Los Angeles; Reavis, Cora A., Los Angeles; Reavis, Ellen N., Los Angeles; Reavis, Mrs. T. C., Salinas; Reddy, Katharine, San Pedro; Redlin, Marie, Redlands; Redmond, Ella M., Puente; Redmond, Mamie, San Pedro; Reed, B. W., Los Angeles; Reed, D. C., Redlands; Reed, Mrs. Edith, San Bernardino; Reed, D. A., San Bernardino; Reed, Ida D., Los Angeles; Reed, Minnie, Santa Ana; Rees, Minnie E., Los Angeles; Reese, Mary W., Santa Barbara; Reeves, Alice, Los Angeles; Reeves, Mrs. E. A., Los Angeles; Reeves, Carrie, Los Angeles; Reese, Sara C., Los Angeles; Reeves, Sara W., Los Angeles; Reeves, Susan A., Los Angeles; Regan, Agnes G., San Francisco; Rehwold, Edith, Riverside; Reid, Laura, Palm Springs; Remmel, Alva, Alameda; Rengstorff, Mrs. Nellie, Mountain View; Reynolds, Ada M., Los Angeles; Reynolds, Annie, Los Angeles; Reynolds, Howard, Los Angeles; Reynolds, I. M., Sacramento; Reynolds, James B., Ventura; Rhodes, Alice M., Los Angeles; Rice, D. A., Stanford University; Rice, Hattie, Pasadena; Rice, J. A., Corona; Rice, Mary E., Monrovia; Rice, Mary E., Santa Ana; Rice, Nettie B., Los Angeles; Rich, Ednah A., Santa Barbara; Richards, Lucy R., Los Angeles; Richardson, Grace B., San Francisco; Richmond, Adah; Los Angeles; Richmond, Clara, Murietta; Richmond, Maud, San Jacinto; Rider, E. B., Stockton; Rider, William L., Stanford University; Riechers, J. H., San Jose; Ringo, M. Emma, San Jose; Ritchie, Florence A., Los Angeles; Ritter, C. M., Stockton; Robe, Frances C., Los Angeles; Roberts, Alma L., Los Angeles; Roberts, Mrs. Anna W., Los Angeles; Roberts, Carrie E., Anaheim; Roberts, W. C., Santa Rosa; Robinette, Mary, Los Angeles; Robinson, Ethel, Los Angeles; Robinson, Inez; Berkeley; Robinson, I. R., Pasadena; Robinson, Lucy A., Los Angeles; Robinson, Minnie L., Riverside; Rogers, Eleanor, Los Angeles; Rohrback, Minnie, San Jose; Rolfe, B. L., Long Beach; Ronick, Minnie, Pomona; Ronan, Julia C., Los Angeles; Rooksby, Clara A., Whittier; Root, R. C., Berkeley; Rosa, Lena A., Los Angeles; Ross, F. J., Stanford; Ross, Mrs. H. N., Etiwanda; Ross, Katharine B., Los Angeles; Ross, Maude E., Los Angeles; Ross, Mary, Berkeley; Rouse, Elizabeth, Redlands; Rowland, Emily, Oakland; Rowell, E. P., Los Angeles; Rubottom, Jessie, Los Angeles; Rucker, Ethel L., Santa Clara; Russell, Alice, Bakersfield; Russell, B. G., Bakersfield; Russell, Mrs. B. G., Bakersfield; Russell, Eleanor M., Whittier; Russell, John T., Redondo; Ruth, Anna F., Pomona; Ryan, Mrs. M. O., Burbank.

S

Sabine, Agnes G., Los Angeles; Sackett, Geo. L., Ventura; Sackett, Mrs. George L., Ventura; Samuels, Addie J., Los Angeles; Samuels, Minnie A., Los Angeles; Sanborn, Bertha, Los Angeles; Sanborn, Flora A., Pomona; Sandeman, Ethel F., Pasadena; Sanders, M. Frances, Los Angeles; Sandwick, R. L., Illinois; Satterlee, Louise J., Los Angeles; Saunders, L. Jessie, Santa Monica; Savage, Ada, Los Angeles; Saxton, Ella, Corona; Sayre, Ludema, Los Angeles; Schallenberger, Frances, San Jose; Schanck, Imogene, San Jacinto; Schimmel, H. L., San Jose; Schlegel, John, Inglewood; Schlicher, Mrs. Eda H., Santa Ana; Schmieding, Pauline, Los Angeles; Schofield, Blanche, Elsinore; Schopbach, Mabel, Pasadena; Schroder, L., San Diego; Schultz, C. Helene, San Jose; Schultzberg, George, Tehachapi; Schulz, R. E., San Mateo; Scott, A., Stanford University; Scott, A. W., Alameda; Scott, Bertha, Los Angeles; Scollard, Dora E., Los Angeles; Scott, Lillian B., Pomona; Seaver, H. W., Los Angeles; Seaman, J. E., Los Angeles; Seaman, W. W., San Francisco; Seegmiller, E. M., Imperial; Segerstrom, Christine; Los Angeles; Seidel, Mrs. Emma E., Berkeley; Senter, Katharine, Los Angeles; Serfling, G. A., San Jose; Sessions, Bessie M., Berkeley; Settle, Laura, Lawanda Park; Sexton, Mrs. Ella M., San Francisco; Sexton, Mamie G., Los Angeles; Seymour, Anna, Monrovia; Shaffer, Jennie L., Los Angeles; Shane, C. N., Auburn; Sharpe, C. O., Sausalito; Shattuck, Mrs. Charles, Alameda; Shaw, B. M. Hemet; Shaw, Ella B., Santa Paula; Shaw, Mrs. L. A., San Francisco; Shanklin, Martha B., Los Angeles; Shaw, Sophie, Long Beach; Sheldon, George M., Anaheim; Sheldon, Harriet, Ventura; Sheldon, W. A., Azusa; Shepherd, Emma, Sedgwick; Shephardson, Everett, Los Angeles; Shepherd, A.

E., Oceanside; Sherwood, Julia A., Lower Lake; Shields, Mrs. Alice, Los Angeles; Shields, Matilda, Los Angeles; Shine, Nellie, Los Angeles; Shoemaker, Fred W., Los Angeles; Short, Edith M., Los Angeles; Shumate, A. E., San Jose; Shrimplin, Rose A., Los Angeles; Shyrock, Mrs. Anna, Simi; Silvaria, Elsie, Redlands; Simons, Mrs. J. H., San Francisco; Simpkins, Florence, Los Angeles; Singer, Martin, Petaluma; Singletary, Clara, Murrietta,; Skofstad, Ada E., Los Angeles; Slate, Frederick, Berkeley; Slaughter, May, Los Angeles; Slaven, James, Paicines; Small, Myrtie, Orange; Small, W. S., Los Angeles; Smead, Elizabeth, Los Angeles; Smith, Albertina, Los Angeles; Smith, Bessie, Sebastopol; Smith, Bettie, Long Beach; Smith, Clara, Azusa; Smith, Clara, Santa Ana; Smith, Estelle B., Los Angeles; Smith, Franc W., Los Angeles; Smith, Gertrude A., Pasadena; Smith, J. Fred, Campbell; Smith, J. M. Redondo; Smith, Josephine, Eureka; Smith, Kate E., Los Angeles; Smith, L. A., Penryn; Smith, Mrs. Louise H., San Francisco; Smith, Maude, Los Angeles; Smith, Mary M., Los Angeles; Smith, Nathan F., Monrovia; Smith, Mrs. Reba B., Whittier; Smith, Rose F., Los Angeles; Smith, S. C., San Francisco; Smith, Mrs. S. C., San Francisco; Smith, Susan, Redlands; Smith, P. W. Auburn; Smith, W. Clifford, Berkeley; Smythe, Charlotte S., Pomona; Smythe, E. Louise, San Rafael; Snedden, Anna, Los Angeles; Snedden, D. S., Palo Alto; Snell, Francis E., Los Angeles; Snoddy, J. S., Stanford University; Snow, A. Emigh, San Jose; Snow, F. B., San Jose; Snow, D. A., San Jose; Snow, Ernest D., San Jose; Snyder, C. D., San Francisco; Snyder, Carrie, Lamanda; Snyder, Florence, Ventura; Soldner, Jonas, Turlock; Solomon, Alfred, Los Angeles; Spellmeyer, Loretta, Los Angeles; Spencer, Gay, San Francisco; Spencer, Mrs. H. A., Anaheim; Spalding, Jane, Stanford University; Spencer, Julia H., Sant Paula; Spreckels, Agnes, Alameda; Spreckels, Anna, Alameda; Spurlock, Sue, Los Angeles; Stacy, I. M., Los Angeles; Stafford, Helen M., Los Angeles; Stafford, W. A., Santa Barbara; Stahmer, Ella, Los Angeles; Stamper, Josie, San Francisco; Standley, Mollie, Waukena; Stanley, Mrs. E. A., Los Angeles; Stansbury, May, Los Angeles; Stanton, Carrie B., Los Angeles; Stanton, Leon I., San Diego; Stanley, Stella, Orange; Stanton, T. E., Berkeley; Starbird, Mary B., Wilmington; Starbuck, Edwin .., Palo Alto; Stark, Harriet, Los Angeles; Stearns, Alice, Pasadena; Stearns, H. M., Oakland; Stedman, Lulu M., Los Angeles; Steele, Mattie L., El Monte; Stewart, Effie, Long Beach; Stephens, Annie, Los Angeles; Stetson, Emily M., Covina; Steward, Alma R., Santa Ana; Stetson, M., Hollywood; Stewart, Anna, Los Angeles; Stewart, Mrs. F. E., Berkeley; Stewart, F. E., Berkeley; Stewart, Jessie A., Penrose; Stewart, J. N.,

Santa Barbara; Stewart, Lena M., Pasadena; Stewart, Mrs. M., Chino; Stewart, Rosia Lee, Whittier; Stevens, Otta. J., Gardena; Stevens, Roxana, La Crescenta; Stevens, Florence, Los Angeles; Stincen, Emma E., San Francisco; Stirling, Duncan, Salinas City; Stockdale, Mrs. H. M,. Los Angeles; Stoemer, Rosella, San Gabriel; Stokes, G. H., San Francisco; Stoltenberg, C. S., Stanford University; Stollenberg, Ella, Los Angeles; Stone, Florence, Banning; Stone, Kathryn, Los Angeles; Stone, Louis S., San Francisco; Stone, Mabel, Santa Monica; Stone, W. W., San Francisco; Storment, J. C., Pomona; Stradley, Mrs. Ella M., Viru; Strang, F. M., Redlands; Strauss, Esther F., Los Angeles; Strine, J. H., Monrovia; Strominger, G. W., Clearwater; Stuart, Grace, Los Angeles; Stubblefield, John S., Springville; Stubblefield, Mrs. John S., Springville; Stuhlman, Carrie, Los Angeles; Sturges, Selden, San Francisco; Sturtevant, Merta M., Covina; Suber, Georgia, Los Angeles; Sullivan, Anna, Prospect Park; Sullivan, D. J., San Francisco; Sullivan, Helen, Los Angeles; Sullivan, Kate E., Colton; Sullivan, Katharine, Santa Cruz; Sullivan, Mary E., San Jose; Sumner, D., East Oakland; Sutton, Mrs. E. G., Los Angeles; Sutton, Emilie V., Los Angeles; Sutton, John R., Berkeley; Sutton, Mrs. Sylvia D., Auld; Suzzalo, A. H., San Francisco; Svenson, Lillie, Pomona; Swasey, A. J., Oakland; Sweeney, J. D., Red Bluff; Sweesey, Mrs. L. V., Berkeley; Swett, John, Martinez; Sweezey, Irene, Los Angeles; Swerdfeger, Daisy, Santa Ana; Swerdfeger, Grace, Los Alamitos; Swerdfeger, Isabel, Azusa City; Swerdfeger, M. E., Azusa City; Swift, Mrs. M. H., Los Angeles; Sylvia, Isabel C., Wilmington.

T.

Tade, Fronie, Sacramento; Taft, Mamie, Clements; Tait, Elizabeth M., Pomona; Talbot, Mrs. J. C., Sawtelle; Talbot, Maude, Chualar; Tanner, W. G., Los Angeles; Taylor, Charles E., Anaheim; Taylor, C. S. Jr., Santa Monica; Taylor, Fannie R., Berryessa; Taylor, J. V., Berryessa; Taylor, Irene, Los Angeles; Taylor, Jefferson, Ontario; Teahan, Katharine, Los Angeles; Teale, Charlotte, Los Angeles; Tedford, Mattie S., Los Angeles; Teggart, Helen, San Diego; Templeton, J. C., Santa Ana; Theall, Mrs. K. J., San Jose; Thees, Emma T., Los Angeles; Thomas, Hannah, Ft. Bragg; Thomas, Helen, San Jose; Thomas, J. E., Escondido; Thomas, Katharine, Los Angeles; Thomas, Mary L., Hemet; Thomas, Maude A., Los Angeles; Thomas, Mrs. Mildred A., Los Angeles; Thomas, O., Santa Rosa; Thomas, Mrs. S. L., Gilroy; Thomson, J. G., Stanford University; Thompson; Annie H., San Jose; Thompson, Clar, Moreno; Thompson, Ellen F., Pasadena; Thompson, Frank E., Palo Alto; Thompson, F. L., Ventura; Thompson, G. S., Los Angeles; Thompson, Jessie, Redondo;

Thompson, Jessie, Simi; Thompson, Mrs. Laura I., Los Angeles; Thompson, Mary E., Pasadena; Thompson, Mrs. M. C., Los Angeles; Thompson, Susa, San Bernardino; Thompson, W. V. E., Santa Barbara; Thornton, Carlotta E., Los Angeles; Thornton, Emma T., Los Angeles; Thorpe, Charles, San Francisco;; Thorpe, Helena, Los Angeles; Thorp, Lula, Lodi; Thrall, Mrs. J. B., Cucamonga; Throop, Jennie L., Los Angeles; Thurston, I. P., Los Angeles; Tillman, H. C., San Jose; Tilton, Etta M., Redwood City; Timmons, Clara L., Los Angeles; Toland, Maie, Los Angeles; Tormey, Mary J., San Jose; Tower, Emily, Norwalk; Townsend, Mrs. Belle, S. Pasadena; Townsend, C. M., Pasadena; Townsend, Ella, Rivera; Trahm, C. G., Salinas; Tripp, R. H., Long Beach; Tritt, J. A., Los Angeles; Tritt, W. W., Los Angeles; Trobridge, Laura, Santa Paula; Trobridge, Verona, Santa Paula; Troconiz, Carmelita, Los Angeles; Trowbridge, G. S., Santa Paula; Tubbs, W. D., North Ontario; Tubbs, Mrs. D. D., Uplands; Tuber, A., Los Angeles; Tucker, Adelaide, Santa Ana; Tucker, Adella, Santa Ana; Tucker, Jenny E., Pomona; Turner, Bessie, Los Angeles; Turner, C. L., San Francisco; Turner, Grace M., Johannesburg; Tuttle, Joy, Prunedale; Tuttle Maude, Prunedale; Tuttle, Mrs. M. E., Perris; Tuomey, Honoria, Los Angeles; Twining, H. La V., Los Angeles; Twitchell, May, Santa Maria; Twogood, Blanche, Hemet; Tyrrell, M. W., Oakland;

U.

Uewby, Nellie J., Ventura; Uncapher, Mary, Agenda; Underwood, Annette, Pasadena.

V.

Van Cleve, Rae G., Los Angeles; Van Dompselaar, Theresa, Newbury Park; Van de Goorberg, W., Perris; Van Dementer, Rose, Redlands; Van Dusen, Marian, Redlands; Van Duyne, Mrs. E. M., Oakland; Van Gordon, A. I., San Mateo; Van Liew, Charles C., Chico; Van Nostrand, Lester, San Francisco; Van Winkle, Mae, San Fernando; Vaughan, Libbie A., Redlands; Vassault, Theodora E., Berkeley; Vassult, Virginia N., Berkeley; Vickers, Nan, Stanford University; Vischer, H., Pasadena; Vose, Adelaide, Los Angeles.

W.

Wade, Janet, San Francisco; Wagner, Fred A., Pomona; Wagner, Harr, San Francisco; Wagner, Minnie L., Los Angeles; Wagner, Mrs. Winona, Chino; Wagner, W. H., Los Angeles; Waite, Alfreda, Ocean Park; Waite, Margaret, Long Beach; Walker, S. J., Elsinore; Walker, A. L., Stockton; Walker, C. J., Visalia; Walker, Florence L., Santa Barbara; Walker, M. Edna, Monrovia; Wallace, Agnes, Los Angeles; Wallace, Belle, Los Angeles; Wallace, Cora B., Riverside; Walsh, A., San Jose; Walters, Lydia E.,

Los Angeles; Walsh, M., San Jose; Ward, Agnes G., Los Angeles; Ward, E. Grace, Redlands; Ward, Gertrude, San Jose; Ward, Lattie A., Riverside; Ward, Jennie, Alameda; Ward, Mrs. W. B., San Jose; Warner, Ruby, Riverside; Warnick, J. W., Berkeley; Warren, Lillie, Los Angeles; Warren, Lottie, Colton; Washburn, Marion, Los Angeles; Waterman, Mrs. S. D., Berkeley; Waterman, S. D., Berkeley; Waters, Lucy, Livermore; Waters, Sylvia, Los Angeles; Watson, Helen, Compton; Way, A. B., Redwood City; Weatherholt, Idell, Los Angeles; Weaver, G. B., Stanford University; Webb, Holton, Riverside; Webb, Margaret, Berkeley; Webber, Emily C., El Monte; Webster, Mary H., Pasadena; Webster, M. Lillian, San Bernardino; Webster, R. H., San Francisco; Weed, Benjamin, Oakland; Weeks, Hattie E., La Habra; Weh, Edna G., Los Angeles; Weil, Adele, Los Angeles; Welch, Maude L., San Jose; Wells, George S., San Jose; West, Nellie A., Los Angeles; Westerman, Mrs. Ellen, Pomona; Westfall, Augusta, Los Angeles; Westland, Nellie M., Redlands; Westphal, Clare, Fresno; Wetmore, Maybelle, Ventura; Weymouth, Ella, Berkeley; Wheat, A. C., Alhambra; Wheeler, Benjamin Ide, Berkeley; Wheeler, Eva M., Los Angeles; Wheeler, R., Salinas; Wheelock, A. N., Riverside; Whelan, Mary E., Santa Monica; Whelan, Mary, San Jacinto; Whims, M. V., Los Angeles; Whitcomb, Elizabeth, Los Angeles; White, Emily F., Los Angeles; White Carrie, Los Angeles; White, Florence A., Burbank; White, Gertrude, Los Angeles; White, Marie, Los Angeles; White, Mrs. M. A., Los Angeles; White, Nellie M., Los Angeles; White W. E., Norwalk; Whitlock, Bessie, Ethanae; Whitlock, Frances J., Los Angeles; Whitmire, Ethel, San Jose; Whiting, Mrs. Lillian M., Los Angeles; Widney, Emma, Monrovia; Wieneke, Ida, Colton; Wiggin, Chas. M., San Francisco; Wilher, Marie E., La Canada; Wilbur, C., Stanford University; Wiley, Cath., Los Angeles; Wiley, Elizabeth, Bakersfield; Willets, Mrs. S. J., El Monte; Willett, Mrs. Martha, Whittier; Williams, Mrs. A. T., San Miguel;. Willams, Carrie San Jose; Williams, Hallie San Diego; Williams, Helen W., Redlands; Williams, M. Ida, Pasadena; Williams, Louise A., Los Angeles; Williams, L. P., San Francisco; Williams, Marietta, Los Angeles; Williams, Wirt C., Duarte; Williamson, Anna, Los Angeles; Williamson, Edward T., Chico; Williamson, Jessie, San Jose; Williams, Lillian, Los Angeles; Williamson, Marinda, Los Angeles; Willis, Bessie, Los Angeles; Willis, O., Redlands; Wisler, Mrs. Emma C., Los Angeles; Wittich, M. K., Compton, Witman, Anna, Los Angeles; Witman, Elizabeth, Los Angeles; Witmer, Marie A., Redlands; Wolcott, Mrs. L. M., Compton; Wolfe, Berenice, Oxnard; Wolff, Fred, San Jose; Wonner, Lucy C., Pasadena; Wood, Job Jr., Sacramento; Wood, Mrs. Job. Jr., Sacramento; Wood, Maud, Los Angeles; Wood, M. C., Pasadena; Woodford, Mary, Alhambra; Woodin, Grace, Norwalk; Woodsum, Edith, Redlands; Woodward, Mary, Alhambra; Woodworth, Mary A., Ventura; Woolsey, Mrs. Jeanne, Palmdale; Woolsey, P. E. M., Hollywood; Willis, Mrs. M. T., Los Angeles; Willson, Mrs. E. E., Gilroy; Wilman, Beatrice, Riverside; Wilson, Emma H., Hesperia; Wilson, George W., South Pasadena; Wilson, Jessica A., Santa Monica; Wilson, Mrs. L., San Francisco; Wilson, Louise S., San Bernardino; Wilson, Mrs. Lucy S., Los Angeles; Wilson, Mabel, South Pasadena; Wilson, Mrs. Mary T., Berkeley; Wiltshire, Grace, Long Beach; Winslow, M. M., Pasadena; Winston, Mrs. E. M., Los Angeles; Winter, W. S., Newhall; Wirt, Mrs. M., Santa Rosa; Wise, H. S., San Francisco; Wooster, C. E., San Jose; Workman, Mary J., Los Angeles; Wright, Carry T., Redlands; Wright, Clara, Los Angeles; Wright, Ella M., Los Angeles; Wright, G. W., Concord; Wright, John E., Whittier; Wright, Martha, Florence; Wright, May E., Los Angeles; Wright, Minnie M., Whittier; Wurtz, Lucy S., Los Angeles; Wylie, Jennie B., Los Angeles; Wylie, Jennie, South Pasadena.

Y.

Yates, Mabel, Elsinore; Yeazell, H. A., Berkeley; Yoch, B., Stanford University; Yoch, Elizabeth, Stanford University; Yoch, Josephine, Los Angeles; Yoder, J. P., Los Angeles; Young, E. R., Los Angeles; Young, Lottie, Los Angeles; Young, Roy J., Berkeley; Young, Stella, Los Angeles; Younglove, Emma, Ventura.

Z.

Zahn, Edwin L., Santa Paula; Zilian, J. J., Tustin; Zumbra, C. A., Riverside; Zumbra, E. A., Riverside.

* * *

Official Department

State Board of Education

GEORGE C. PARDEE, *President of the Board* .... Governor, Sacramento
MORRIS ELMER DAILEY .... President State Normal School, San Jose
E. T. PIERCE .... President State Normal School, Los Angeles
C. C. VAN LIEW .... President State Normal School, Chico
BENJAMIN IDE WHEELER .... President University of California, Berkeley
ELMER E. BROWN .... Prof. of Theory and Practice of Education, University of Cal., Berkeley
SAMUEL T. BLACK .... President State Normal School, San Diego
FREDERIC BURK .... President State Normal School, San Francisco
THOMAS J. KIRK, *Secretary of the Board* ...... Superintendent Public Instruction, Sacramento

The State Board of Education is called to meet at the office of the Superintendent of Public Instruction, in the Capitol, Sacramento, on Saturday, June 6, 1903, at 10 o'clock, a. m.

* * *

County Boards Cannot Examine Pupils for Promotion

To School Superintendents, County, City and County, and City Boards of Education of California: The Attorney-General, in an opinion given on the 23d inst., reciting the statutes and sundry court decisions bearing upon the subject, decides that county or local boards of education have no authority to examine pupils for promotion from grade to grade in the public schools.

But the opinion does not, as some have supposed it does, question the right of such boards to provide for a final examination, and for the conferring of diplomas of graduation upon pupils that satisfactorily complete the course of study prescribed for the grammar and primary grades.

The opinion will be published in full in the May number of the official journal, *The Western Journal of Education.*

Sacramento, April 30, 1903.

Examination for Promotion by County Boards of Education

State of California, office of Attorney-General, etc.

SAN FRANCISCO (Cal.), April 23, 1903.

Hon. S. T. Black, Member State Board of Education, San Diego, Cal.

Dear Sir: Your favor of March 30, 1903, received. You state:

"At a meeting of the State Board of Education, held at Sacramento March 28th, by request, I made a motion that the opinion of the Attorney-General be asked upon the question concerning the powers of county boards of education in the matter of holding examinations for promotion in the elementary schools of the state. Section 1663, prior to the amendment of 1901, directed that county boards of education should require that promotions upon writen examinations, or otherwise, 'shall take place at stated periods, at least once in each school year.' It also provided for the conferring of diplomas at the end of the course of study in the grammar schools. The section as amended in 1901 continues in force the provision for a final examination and the conferring of diplomas of graduation, but is silent on the matter of examinations for promotion from grade to grade."

In addition to the above section allow me to direct your attention to Section 1771, Political Code, which, in part, provides:

"County Boards of Education have power:

1. To adopt rules and regulations, not inconsistent with the laws of this state, for their own government. * * *

5. To adopt a list of books and apparatus for district school libraries, and, except in cities having a city board of education, to prescribe and enforce in the public schools a course of study and the use of a uniform series of text-books."

Section 1521 Political Code provides:

"The powers and duties of a state board of education are as follows:

1. To adopt rules and regulations not inconsistent with thé laws of this state for its own government, and for the government of the public schools and district school libraries."

Article IX, Section 7 of the Constitution, relating to the powers of county boards of education, is as follows:

"The Legislature shall provide for a board of education in each county in the state. The county superintendent and the county boards of education shall have control of the examination of teachers and the granting of teachers' certificates within their respective jurisdictions."

It would be well, also, to refer to certain of the provisions in regard to district boards. Section 1617 Political Code provides:

"The powers and duties of trustees of school districts, and of boards of education in cities, are as follows:

First—To prescribe and enforce rules, not inconsistent with law or those prescribed by the state board of education, for their own government and government of schools, and to transact their business at regular or special meetings called for such purpose, notice of which shall be given each member.

Tenth—To enforce in schools the course of study and the use of text-books prescribed and adopted by the proper authority."

It is from these provisions that we must discover whether it is still within the province of the county boards to require that promotions upon written examinations shall take place at stated intervals.

By a comparison of Section 1521, supra, and Section 1771, supra, it will appear at once that the rules and regulations of a general nature, which the county board may adopt, are restricted to its own body and have nothing to do with the schools.

By a comparison of Section 1617, supra, with the two sections first referred to, we find that the city boards may enact rules for the government of the school system in the cities if the state board has not enacted rules relative to the same matters.

Further, a reading of the first subdivision of Section 1617, supra, would direct us to the conclusion that the only sources for rules governing schools, are the State Board of Education and the law of the state, comprising statute law and case law.

It must be remembered that the school system in the state today is a state system, not a local system. The control of the system is in the state and not in the counties. This was determined by Section 7 of Article IX, quoted above, which is a new section ratified by the people in 1884.

Mitchell vs. Winnek, 117 Cal., 526

The power of the Board of Education to "require that promotions upon written examinations, or otherwise, in each of said courses shall take place at stated periods, at least once in each school year," was not an additional power of said board, but was, prior to 1901, derived from subdivision 2 of Section 1663 Political Code, to which you refer.

In Section 1663, as amended in 1901, this provision is not preserved, and if the right of the board in this particular still exists, it must so exist by virtue of the language found in the section, prior to the amendment of 1901. The amendment of 1901, however, appears to be a complete revision of said Section 1663, and the new section stands in lieu of or as a substitute for the section as it previously read, and the old section by virtue of such revision, is repealed.

"A subsequent statute revising the whole subject matter of a former one, and evidently intended as a substitute for it, although it contains no express words to that effect, must on principles of law, as well as in reason and common sense, operate to repeal the former."

Section 154 Sutherland on Statutory Construction.

I am, therefore, of the opinion that the county boards of education have not now the authority to hold examinations for promotion.

Very truly yours,
(Signed) U. S. WEBB,
Attorney-General.

* * *

Hon. Thomas J. Kirk, Superintendent of Public Instruction, Sacramento.

Dear Sir: Your favor of March 3, 1903, received. You say:

"I respectfully request, at your earliest convenience, your opinion whether or not the reading or use of the Bible as a text-book in the public schools of this State is in violation of the provisions of Section 1672 of the Political Code."

At the outset I am constrained to take cognizance of the fact that there are a great many versions of the Bible in use in the world. Honest differences prevail as to what books should be included within the meaning of the words "Holy Bible." Witness the Jew, who regards the Old Testament as alone inspired; the Catholic, who adds the Apocrypha; and the Protestant, who repudiates the Apocrypha. There is the King James version of the Bible, which the Protestants accept; the Donay version, which the Catholics accept as, alone, correct and complete; besides the sacred books of other religions, which may be called "Bibles," as "bible," in its literal sense, simply means "the book."

It is impossible to find any version of the Bible which does not represent and promulgate the teachings of some religious sect or society, or the opinions of some founder of a religion.

There is no such book in existence as a Universal Bible, which would appeal to all people, in all climes, at all times.

You will, therefore, understand that with the truth or efficacy of any of these versions of the Bible, this opinion does not deal. In endeavoring to determine the law on the subject, I have no concern with the truth or error of the doctrines of any sect. I am to be guided solely by the Constitution and laws of this State now in force. I am not called upon to decide what religious doctrines, if any, ought to be taught, or where, by whom, or to whom it would be best they should be taught. These are questions which belong to the people and to other departments of the government.

I have no doubt that the Bible to which you refer in your request for an opinion is the King James version, which is in very common use in this country. My opinion will be confined to a discussion of the question as to whether the reading or the use of this version of the Bible in the public schools as a text-book would contravene the Constitution and Political Code of the state.

Article I, Section 4, of the Constitution of 1879, provides as follows:

"The free exercise and enjoyment of religious profession and worship, without discrimination or preference, shall be forever guaranteed in this State; * * *"

Article IX, Section 8, provides as follows:

"No public money shall ever be appropriated for the support of any sectarian or denominational school, or any school not under the exclusive control of the officers of the public schools; nor shall any sectarian or denominational doctrine be taught, or instruction thereon be permitted, directly or indirectly, in any of the common schools of this State."

Section 1672, Political Code, was passed to effectuate the above provision of the Constitution, and reads as follows:

"No publication of a sectarian, partisan, or denominational character must be used or distributed in any school, or be made a part of any school library; nor must any sectarian or denominational doctrine be taught therein. Any school district, town or city, the officers of which knowingly allow any schools to be taught in violation of these provisions, forfeits all right to any state or county apportionment of school moneys; and upon satisfactory evidence of such violation, the Superintendent of Public Instruction and school superintendent must withhold both state and county apportionments."

It is well settled that neither Christianity nor any other system of religion is part of the laws of this state or of the United States.

Cooley says in his Constitutional Limitations, Chapter XIII, 472:

"Christianity is not a part of the law of the land in any sense which entitles the courts to take notice of and base their judgments upon it, except so far as they can find that its precepts and principles have been incorporated in and made a component part of the positive law of the State."

Also, at page 469, he says:

"Those things which are not lawful under any of the American constitutions may be stated thus:

"1. Any law respecting an establishment of religion. The legislatures have not been left at liberty to effect a union of church and state, or to establish preferences by law in favor of any one religious persuasion or mode of worship. There is not complete religious liberty where any one sect is favored by the state and given an advantage by law over other sects. Whatever establishes a distinction against one class or sect is to the extent to which the distinction operates unfavorably, a persecution, and if based on religious grounds, a religious persecution. It is not mere toleration which is established in our system, but religious equality.

"2. Compulsory support, by taxation or otherwise, of religious instruction. Not only is no one denomination to be favored at the expense of the rest, but all support of religious instruction must be entirely voluntary. It is not within the sphere of government to coerce it."

Andrews vs. Bible Society, 4 Sandf. 156, 182;

Bloom vs. Richards, 2 Ohio St. 387.

Our constitutional theory regards all religions, as such, as equally entitled to protection and equally unentitled to preference. Where there is no ground or necessity upon which a principle can rest but a religious one, then the Constitution steps in and says that it shall not be enforced by authority of law.

Ex parte Newman, 9 Cal. 513;

Ex parte Andrews, 18 Cal. 684;

State ex rel. Nevada Orphan Asylum vs. Hallock,, 16 Nev. 373.

Ex parte Newman was overruled by later decisions, but not in the fundamental principles laid down as regards religious doctrines.

We may also refer to Article II of the

Treaty with Tripoli, concluded November 4, 1796 (8 U. S. Stats. at Large, 155): "As the government of the United States is not in any sense founded on the Christian religion," etc.

It is, therefore, clear that the Christian religion, as such, has no preference under the law of the state over any other religion, though its precepts may have largely molded the common law upon which our laws are based. The doctrines of many ancient religions entered into the formation of the laws under which we live, and the Christian religion contains what is best and truest of them all. I quote from the Supreme Court of Ohio in the case of Board of Education of Cincinnati vs. Minor, 23 Ohio St. 247:

"The only foundation—ratner, the only excuse—for the proposition, that Christianity is part of the law of this country, is the fact that it is a Christian country, and that its constitutions and laws are made by a Christian people. And is not the very fact that those laws do not attempt to enforce Christianity, or to place it upon exceptional or vantage ground, itself a strong evidence that they are the laws of a Christian people, and that their religion is the best and purest of religions? It is strong evidence that their religion is indeed a religion 'without partiality,' and therefore a religion 'without hypocrisy.' True Christianity asks no aid from the sword of civil authority."

This leaves us free to take up the question as to whether the use of King James's version of the Bible as a text-book in the public schools would be sectarian instruction within the meaning of the above provision of the Constitution and Codes.

We may approach this question in two ways: First, if this version of the Bible represents and is the organ of any religious sect or society, then its teachings may be called sectarian; second, if it contains within its pages the doctrines of a number of sects, then its teachings may be called sectarian.

In the first place, the Christian religion is divided into two great branches, the Protestant and the Catholic. The members of either body consider themselves entitled to be called Christians, but they each present the claims of a different version of the Bible which they believe to be inspired. The King James version, with the Apocrypha excluded, is the Bible of the Protestant religion. In contradistinction to the Catholic version, which includes the Apocrypha, the King James version would necessarily be sectarian in its doctrines.

A number of courts have defined the meaning of the word "sect." The Supreme Court of Nevada has held that the Catholics were a "sect," as distinguished from Protestants. The fact that they controlled St. Mary's School, which is a part or branch of the Nevada Orphan Asylum, and introduced their religious exercises there, made the Nevada Orphan Asylum a sectarian institution. I quote from the opinion of the Court in the case, State of Nevada vs. Hallock, supra:

"From all the preceding facts, it seems to us that but one conclusion can be arrived at, which is, that the Nevada Orphan Asylum is a sectarian institution. Webster defines 'sectarian,' as follows: 'Pertaining to a sect or sects; peculiar to a sect; bigotedly attached to the tenets and interests of a denomination.' He also defines the word as 'one of a party in religion which has separated itself from the established cnurch, or which holds tenets different from those of the prevailing denomination in a kingdom or state,' and it was argued by petitioner's counsel that the word was used in this sense in the Constitution. We do not think so. It was used in the popular sense. A religious sect is a body or number of persons united in tenets, but constituting a distinct organization or party, by holding sentiments or doctrines different from those of other sects or people. In the sense intended in the Constitution, every sect of that character is sectarian, and all members thereof are sectarians. The framers of the Constitution undoubtedly considered the Roman Catholic a sectarian church. (Const. Debates, 568 et seq.) The people understood it in the same sense when they ratified it."

The case of State vs. District Board of School District No. 8, 76 Wis. 177, was a case decided under a provision of the Constitution relating to "sectarian instruction" similar to ours. In that case certain taxpayers prayed for a writ of mandate from the circuit court, compelling the school board to cause the teachers to discontinue the practice of reading daily to the pupils during school hours certain portions of King James's version of the Bible, selected by the teachers. The Supreme Court ordered the writ to issue. Their opinion, in part, is as follows:

"This opinion will be confined quite closely to a discussion of the question whether the adoption of the Protestant, or King James, version of the Bible, or any version thereof, in the public schools in the city of Edgerton, as a text-book and the reading of selections therefrom in those schools at the times and in the manner stated in the answer, is sectarian instruction, within the meaning of that term as used in Section 3, Article X, of the Constitution, which ordains that no sectarian instruction shall be allowed in the district schools of this State. * * *

"It should be here said that the term 'religious sect' is understood as applying to people believing in the same religious doctrines, who are more or less closely associated or organized to advance such doctrines and increase the number of believers therein. The doctrines of one of these sects which are not common to all the others are sectarian; and the term 'sectarian' is, we think, used in that sense in the Constitution. * * *

"That the reading from the Bible, in the schools, 'although unaccompanied by any comment on the part of the teacher, is instruction,' seems to us too clear for argument. Some of the most valuable instruction a person can receive may be derived from reading, alone, without any extrinsic aid by way of comment or exposition. The question, therefore, seems to narrow down to this: Is the reading of the Bible in the schools—not merely selected passages therefrom, but the whole of it—sectarian instruction of the pupils? In view of the fact already mentioned, that the Bible contains numerous doctrinal passages, upon some of which the peculiar creed of almost every religious sect is based, and that such passages may reasonably be understood to inculcate the doctrines predicated upon them, an affirmative answer to the question seems unavoidable. Any pupil of ordinary intelligence who listens to the reading of the doctrinal portions of the Bible will be more or less instructed thereby in the doctrines of the divinity of Jesus Christ, the eternal punishment of the wicked, the authority of the priesthood, the binding force and efficacy of the sacraments, and many other conflicting sectarian doctrines."

In the case of Board of Education of the City of Cincinnati vs. John D. Minor, supra, certain taxpayers sought to prevent the school board from carrying out the resolution abolishing the opening exercises of the public schools, which included reading the Bible. The Court discussed the question at great length, and held that the Christian religion was not the only religion under a clause of the Constitution requiring religious instruction in the schools; that to permit the Christian Bible to be used was to prefer the Christians to any other sect. The Court then proceeds:

"Counsel say that to withdraw all religious instruction from the schools would be to put them under the control of 'infidel sects.' This is by no means so. To teach the doctrines of infidelity, and thereby teach that Christianity is false, is one thing; and to give no instructions on the subject is quite another thing. The only fair and impartial method, where serious objection is made, is to let each sect give its own instructions, elsewhere than in the state schools, where of necessity all are to meet; and to put disputed doctrines of religion among other subjects of instruction, for there are many others which can more conveniently, satisfactorily, and safely be taught elsewhere. Our charitable, punitive, and disciplinary institutions stand on an entirely different footing. There the state takes the place of the parent, and may well act the part of a parent or guardian in directing what religious instructions shall be given."

These are the leading cases on the subject, and the consensus of opinion seems to be that Protestantism, as distinguished from other branches of Christianity, is a sect, and that Christianity, as distinguished from other religions, is a sect. It surely began as a sect, for the followers of Christ were dissenters from the principles of Judaism and were known as a sect all to themselves.

In the light of the above decisions, King James's version of the Bible is sectarian in its tendency. In fact, each version of the Bible extant is sectarian in its tendency. But, assuming that King James's version is the version of no particular sect, it contains within its pages the doctrine of any number of sects or denominations.

Upon this phase of the question, the Court says in the case of State vs. District Board, supra:

"3. The courts will take judicial notice of the contents of the Bible, that the religious world is divided into numerous sects, and of the general doctrines maintained by each sect; for these things pertain to general history, and may fairly be presumed to be subjects of common knowledge. (1 Greenl. Ev., secs. 5, 6, and notes.) Thus they will take cognizance, without averment, of the facts that there are numerous religious sects called Christians, respectively maintaining different and conflicting doctrines; that some of these believe the doctrine of predestination, while others do not; some the doctrine of eternal punishment of the wicked, while others repudiate it; some the doctrines of the apostolic succession and the authority of the priesthood, while others reject both; some that the Holy Scriptures are the only sufficient rule of faith and practice, while others believe that the only safe guide to human thought, opinion and action is the illuminating power of the divine spirit upon the humble and devout heart; some in the necessity and efficacy of the sacraments of the church, while others reject them entirely; and some in the literal truth of the Scriptures, while others believe them to be allegorical, teaching spiritual truths, alone, or chiefly. The courts will also take cognizance of numerous other conflicts of doctrine between the sects; also that there are religious sects which reject the doctrine of the divinity of Christ, among which is the Hebrew or Jewish sect, which denies the inspiration and authority of the New Testament."

These denominations of the Christian church carry on a continual controversy among themselves which often reaches to violent lengths. They divide, and are founded, often on the simple meaning of words and expressions in the Bible. It appears to me impossible that the Bible should be used as a text-book in literature, and its language, meaning, and literary value discussed without precipitating a theological dispute and calling forth the prejudices of teachers and pupils.

It has been held, as appears above, that the mere reading of the Bible as a morning exercise is sectarian instruction within the meaning of the state constitutions. For a state officer or school board to take action establishing King James's version of the Bible as a text-book in the public schools approaches very near to a discrimination in favor of the Protestant religion.

Suppose any school board should be authorized to cause the reading of the Bible as a morning exercise in the schools, Protestant taxpayers could mandamus the board to compel the reading of the version of King James, Catholic taxpayers could mandamus the board to compel the reading of the Donay version, German Lutherans could mandamus the board to compel the reading of the Lutheran version; the public schools would be turned into religious institutes. Otherwise, the school board, when brought to the alternative, would have to discriminate in favor of one or the other of these sects and thereby violate Section 4 of Article I of the Constitution.

Wise and good men have struggled and agonized through centuries to find a correct interpretation of the Scriptures, and the version which they finally accepted, their children read and study today and believe the only infallible guide to right conduct. When we force our citizens to pay for and send their children to public schools where the Bible of another faith is read to them, I believe we come dangerously near intruding upon freedom of conscience.

There are a number of cases in different states, bearing upon the main question, which would seem opposed to the views here set forth, but none of the states in which those doctrines were made have in their constitutions a direct prohibition of sectarian instruction in the public schools.

The Constitution and laws of this state appear to have in view the maintenance of exact equality of all sects, creeds, or religions; that all shall have equal rights, equal opportunities, and be subject to equal restraints. And this accords well with that rule of human conduct, which is of higher wisdom and wider application than human laws; commending itself to the administration of the law and to every field of human action, and which is found with almost verbal identity in the sacred books of all religions:

"All things whatsoever ye would that men should do to you, do you even so to them, for this is the law and the prophets."

I am, therefore, of the opinion that the reading of King James's version of the Bible, as a religious exercise, or its use as a text-book in the public schools, is prohibited by the Constitution and the laws of this state.

Very respectfully,
U. S. WEBB, Attorney-General.

* * *

CIRCULAR No. 8.

To County and City and County Boards of Education of California: In view of the fact that the State Department of Education has taken every means possible to supply the school authorities of the state with all the laws relating to education and the public schools that were enacted at the last session of the Legislature, by publishing the same in the official journal and by sending out copies of the different measures so long as copies of the bills could be obtained, it is strange that in several counties there seems to be a disposition to disregard the law in some matters. This is particularly noticeable in advertisements for consideration and adoption of school text-books. The passage and approval of the so-called state text-book measure entirely changes the law that was formerly found in Section 1874 of the Political Code. There is now no provision for advertisement and adoption of text-books by County, City, or City and County Boards of Education.

My advice is that until this new law has been set in operation the school text-books last heretofore in use in the different counties, cities, and cities and counties of the state be continued in use until by proper authority it may be determined what and how changes may lawfully be made. The State Text-Book Committee is moving in the matter delegated to it as rapidly as circumstances and the light before it will permit. Surely no great injury can come to the schools by failure for a time to adopt new books. Certainly there is at present no law authorizing county boards, as heretofore, to enter into contracts for text-books, and persistence in attempting to do so may be of serious consequence.

* * *

CIRCULAR No. 9.

Information in Reference to the Special High School Credential

The law authorizing the State Board of Education to grant the document known as the "Special High School Credential" is found in (2) (b) Section 1521 of the Political Code, which reads as follows:

The said board shall also consider the cases of individual applicants who have taught successfully for a period of not less than twenty school months, and who are not possessed of the credentials prescribed by the board under the provisions of this section. The said board, in its discretion, may issue to such applicants special credentials upon which they may be granted certificates to teach in the high schools of the state. In such special cases, the board may take cognizance of any adequate evidence of preparation which the applicants may present. The standard of qualification in such special cases shall not be lower than that represented by the other credentials named by the board under the provisions of this section.

In pursuance of the above provision of law, the State Board of Education has adopted the following rules for its guidance in the granting of said document:

1. Under the provisions of Section 1521 (2) (b), and Section 1775 (1) (a) of the Political Code of the State of California, the State Board of Education may issue special credentials for high school certificates to those who have taught with decided success at least twenty-seven months as regular teachers in schools of the academic grade and character of California high schools. The success of such teachers will be determined by confidential letters and such other reliable information as the board may be able to obtain.

2. A graduate of a college of recognized high academic standing, who has had pedagogical training equivalent to that prescribed by this board for graduates of the University of California, and who has taught two years (twenty months) subsequent to graduation, may be granted the Special High School Credential, upon which a county or city and county board may grant a high school certificate. The success in teaching of those making application for credentials under this provision will be determined by confidential letters or by any other reliable information which the board may be able to obtain.

It will be the policy of this board to demand high scholarship and marked skill in teaching of all successful applicants for special credentials, whether they be college graduates or not. In order that the Board may be able to satisfy itself thoroughly concerning the fitness of an applicant, ample time will be required for the necessary investigation before final action is taken. No one will be granted the special credential who is diseased or lacking in normal bodily vigor.

3. In accord with an opinion rendered by the Attorney-General, the State Board of Education will not grant a credential for a teacher's certificate to an applicant who is not a resident of the State of California.

4. Every application for a teacher's credential under the foregoing rules must be accompanied by a reputable physician's certificate, to the effect that the applicant is in sound bodily health.

METHOD OF APPLICATION

This Department does not furnish any blank upon which to make application for the Special High School Credential, nor is there any special form of application required. The applicant should write a letter to the State Board of Education or to the State Superintendent of Public Instruction, its Secretary, giving in full his academic training and professional experience, with names of places and dates where and when he has taught. This statement should be sworn to. The applicant should also give names of those to whom the State Board may refer for information respecting his character and qualifications as a teacher. With letter of application must be sent *diplomas of graduation, courses of study pursued and of the schools in which the applicant has taught,* together with *letters of recommendation* and *physician's certificate of health.*

In order that action may be expedited as much as possible, applications are referred to the Committee of the State Board of Education on High School Credentials as soon as they are received at this office, and such committee is generally able to report on an application at the first meeting of the State Board after it has been received. No application, however, will be considered at any meeting that has not been filed at least fifteen days prior to the date fixed for the next ensuing meeting of the Board.

* * *

Proceedings of Joint Board of State Normal School Trustees

The Joint Board of State Normal School Trustees met at San Diego, April 10, 1903. The following persons were present:

Governor George C. Pardee, ex-officio Chairman.

Superintendent Public Instruction, Thomas J. Kirk, ex-officio Secretary.

San Jose Normal School—President, Morris E. Daily, Frank H. Short, Dr. P. K. Dow. Los Angeles Normal School—Chairman, John Wasson, President, Edward T. Pierce, E. J. Louis, J. P. Greeley. Chico Normal School—President, C. C. Van Liew, Senator Clifford Coggins, T. H. Barnard. San Diego Normal School—Chairman, Dr. R. M. Powers, President, Samuel T. Black, C. C. Chapman, Senator M. L. Ward. San Francisco Normal School—Chairman, S. C. Denson, President, Frederic Burk, H. G. Dinkelspiel, Frank Marston. Absent—Thomas Adison, Chairman San Jose Normal, and F. C. Lusk, Chairman Chico Normal.

The following subjects were discussed:

(a) Reading and consideration of the law, Section 1492 of the Political Code, as amended by the Legislature of 1903, under which the Joint Board of Normal School Trustees is created and by which its duties are prescribed.

(b) Consideration of text-books to be prescribed and made uniform as required by law.

(c) Consideration of Course of Study and time and standard for graduation, as required to be prescribed and made uniform in all the Normal Schools.

(d) Consideration of standard of admission of students to the Normal Schools and for transfer from one school to another.

(e) Matters of arbitration concerning management neding adjustment.

(f) If, as claimed, there is great need of more men teachers in the public schools, what may the Normal Schools do to encourage more young men to attend Normal Schools and prepare for teaching?

(g) Continuous sessions of one or more of the Normal Schools.

(h) What arrangements desirable and practicable to be made with the city boards of education in the cities where the Normal Schools are located in regard to maintenance of the training schools?

(i) Value and importance of Kindergarten departments in the Normal Schools.

(j) Gymnasiums or facilities for systematic physical training in the Normal Schools. To what extent uniform in the different schools?

(k) Why not Latin as a part of the curriculum in the Normal Schools?

(l) The policy which the different Normal boards may legally establish and wisely pursue with reference to vacations to be granted Norman instructors after a lengthy period of teaching service.

(m) Academic studies in the Normal Schools. Why should not the course of instruction be purely professional?

Respectfully,

THOMAS J. KIRK,
Superintendent of Public Instruction.

PUBLISHERS' NOTICE.

THE WESTERN JOURNAL OF EDUCATION succeeds to the subscription lists, advertising patronage, and good will of the Golden Era, established in San Francisco in 1852.

Subscription, $1 50 a year. Single copies. 15 cents. Remit by check, Postoffice order, Wells, Fargo & Co., or by stamps.

ADVERTISEMENTS—Advertisements of an unobjectionable nature will be inserted at the rate of $3.00 a month per inch.

MSS.—Articles on methods, trials of new theories, actual experiences, and school news, reports of teachers' meetings, etc., urgently solicited.

Address all communications to THE WESTERN JOURNAL OF EDUCATION, 723 Market Street, San Francisco.

HARR WAGNER, Editor.
THE WHITAKER & RAY COMPANY PUBLISHERS.
Entered at the San Francisco Post-office as second-class matter.

The Official Organ of the Department of Public Instruction of the State of California.

PRESIDENT ROOSEVELT will address the students of the University of California on May 14th.

* * *

THE JUNE number will contain sixty-four pages of matter relating to the union of elementary school districts. This material has been specially prepared for the JOURNAL by Prof. Ellwood Cubberley of Stanford University.

* * *

THIS issue is heavy with the educational material presented at the meeting of the State Teachers' Association at Los Angeles. The citizens of the state will find in this number discussions of practically every current educational problem. The papers of the Educational Council, the General Sessions, the High School, the Grammar School, the Primary School, the Kindergarten, Manual Training, Music, Administration, Child Study and Physical Culture, are all represented by well prepared addresses. By arrangements with the Executive Committee three thousand two hundred and seventy copies of the proceedings are distributed to the trustees and the district school libraries, one thousand copies to city and county superintendents, to pedagogical libraries and individual subsribers, and over two thousand copies to members of the C. T. A.

THE meeting of the Educational Council in the State Normal School building, April 25th arose to the distinguishment of an affair. There was a notable absence of afternoon tea style of presenting ideas. The arguments were strenuous. President Burk presided and introduced Gov. Pardee, who spoke of the need of the schoolmaster in politics, and the masculinization of the elementary schools. The free text book problem was discussed by Supt. Cox, A. L. Mann, and others. The Council passed a resolution requesting the State Text Book Committee to secure new geographies first, arithmetics second. It was not, however, until President Burk called upon Philip M. Fisher to discuss *Tenure of Office* that the amplitude of incisive argument was noticeable. Mr. Fisher in a few terse sentence that fell with a grating sound like the pulling of one sand board over another aroused a debate that might be called chilling or warm according to the mental attitude of the listener. Prof. Cubberley, Dr. E. C. Moore, L. A. Jordan, Supt. Coulter. A. L. Mann, R. D. Faulkner and J. W. McClymonds took part in the discussion. It would be unfair to state that certain speakers were against and others were for tenure of position. Leslie A. Jordan

Editorial

replied hotly to what he considered reflections on tenure of position in San Francisco, and the general tendency to refer to San Francisco teaching force as incompetent. It was the first time that the "tenure of position" has ever been discussed with fearlessness. There is no reason why it should not be. No legislative enactment will effect the teachers who have tenure of position under the present law. Then again practically the unanimous sentiment of the people is in favor of the teacher holding his or her position doing good service, and if any law is enacted it will be to strengthen this sentiment so that teachers in the public schools should not be disturbed by political whims, personal bias or sectarian influences.

* * *

Summer Session of the San Jose State Normal School.

[The following editorials on the "Summer Session at the San Jose State Normal School," and "More Men in the Elementary Schools" were written for THE JOURNAL by W. C Doub, ex-superintendent of schools of Kern County.]

The educational interests of the State are to be congratulated on the new policy of the State Normal School at San Jose. This new policy is the establishment of a summer normal session at that institution, and is the direct result of the recommendation of its president, Morris E. Dailey. It has become the settled policy of the larger universities to require their professors to accept a "year's leave of absence" at intervals of from four to six years, and devote the time to travel, to study and to advance research in other institutions. This is done in order that a professor may keep "abreast of the times", and will not become influenced too much by the environment of the institution in which he is teaching. If an occasional change of intellectual environment, and some time devoted to study and advance research, is found to be necessary for a teacher in a university, it is just as true of the teach the secondary schools and in the ele tary schools. The university te increases his efficiency as a teache travel and advance research; in fornia the secondary school teacher so by attending the summer sessi the State University; and one of main objects for establishing the sui session at the San Jose Normal is to vide similar opportunity for the ele tary school teacher. There are a five thousand men and women tea in the elementary schools of Calif who have never attended a normal s or a university, and whose prepar for their work has been restricted t grammar school and to the high sc The summer session at the San Normal will give those teachers a ch to do some advance work, to com contact with the most advanced meth and to learn more of the techniqu their profession. For the work do the summer session regular credit ing toward graduation will be g This, of itself, is a valuable consi tion, for the tendency of school off to place a premium on special traini growing constantly.

It is hoped that the teachers wil courage the authorities of the San Normal School by attending the sui session in large numbers. If the mand for this summer work become enough, it will no doubt be taken t some of the other state normal sch If teachers generally would attend a school during the summer vacation efficiency of the teaching force of State would be increased materially. all lines of work the successful mer women are those who are always loc for new methods—new tools—and m of self improvement. Increased effic on the part of teachers will lead to t salaries, and better salaries must

The Western Journal of Education.

he permanent efficiency of the public ool system is to become higher and ter. Good work demands good pay; r work demand and should receive ll compensation.

rom an educational standpoint and m a monetary standpoint, also, the ing summer session of the State rmal School at San Jose should be gely attended by the teachers of the te. From an educational standpoint, ause better preparation means better rk; from a monetary standpoint, be- se better preparation means a better ary.

re Men in the Elementary Schools.

According to the press reports Governor George C. Pardee and State perintendent T. J. Kirk are very xious that more men should enter the te normal schools. It is the opinion these gentlemen that it would be tter if more men were teaching in the mentary schools. Those who have ade a close study of and are familiar th school work are also emphatically the opinion that the public school stem would be much more effective in veloping strong citizenship if there re more men teaching in the elementary hools. The man as a teacher is just much superior to the woman in the gher grammar grades as the woman is the man in the lower primary grades. efore he graduates from the grammar hool every pupil should have as a acher for at least one year, a man of rong individuality. The physical and tellectual changes which take place in e pupil during the last years in the rammar school demand this influence. o deprive the pupil of it is usually an reparable injury.

Governor Pardee and Superintendent irk state that some means must be found to induce more men to enter the profession of teaching, and especially grammar school work. There is one thing that must be done in order to ac- complish this, and it is absolutely neces- sary, and it will accomplish it, and this thing that must be done is to pay better salaries. It is unbusinesslike from the standpoint of government, and it is an outrage as well, for the state to ask men to work for it for a salary on which they cannot hope to raise and to support a family. Is it reasonable to suppose that many men of common sense and ability will deliberately choose teaching as a life profession when it means throwing away the prospects of marriage and the enjoy- ment of home life? Is it right for the State to ask a man to do this? More than ninety per cent of the teachers in the elementary schools of this state re- ceive a salary which amounts to less than $600 per annum, which is only $50 for each month in the year. It is usually impossible for them to secure other work during the summer vacation, and they should use this time for rest and better preparation. This inadequate compen- sation is the reason more men do not choose teaching for their life work. Nearly all of those who do enter it do so as a temporary expedient. This is also true of the women. Most of the girls who prepare themselves for teachers do not intend to remain in the work for any great length of time. Like the men, they consider it a temporary expedient only.

It is worth while to compare the sal- aries which the state pays teachers and other school officials with the salaries which it pays its other employees. Al- most without exception the county super- intendents in this state receive a smaller compensation than any other county official who is supposed to devote all of his time to his official duties. The dep uties in the county offices, the constables, and other petty county and district officials receive annual salaries which will average at least fifty per cent more than those paid to the teachers of the county. Most of these county and district officials are engaged in suppressing crime or the violation of law of one sort or another. They are dealing with an element that it would be well for society to be rid of. The teacher on the other hand is engaged in developing a citizenship that will be clean and strong, both morally and intellectually. It would seem but the exercise of common sense and business judgment for the state, if it discriminate at all in the matter of salary, to discriminate in favor of the teacher, who is doing the constructive work, and not in favor of those whose duties are merely clerical or the suppression of an element that is injurious to society.

The major part of the blame for this condition of affairs rests justly on the parent. While to him the education of his children is more important than anything else, he usually frowns upon the proposition of increasing the salaries of teachers, altho he finds but little fault with paying much higher salaries to officials whose duties are much less valuable to himself and to society as a whole. In palliation of this the statement is often made that the teachers' hours are short. Now, anyone who understands school work at all, knows very well that altho the number of hours actually devoted to teaching in the schoolroom is extremely hard work, it does not represent more than half of the work which any good teacher does. The examination of much of the work which her pupils have done thru the day and the planning and preparation of the work for the next day require time and close application. It would be well to have the officials named who devote as much actual time to work as the teacher does to actual teaching in the schoolroom, to say nothing about her school work outside of the schoolroom.

Constant reference is also made to the fact that teachers receive much better salaries now than they did twenty-five years ago. Will those who harp upon this statement please consider the salaries paid now and paid then in other lines of work. Skilled labor in nearly all lines of work receives a much better salary than teachers receive, and certainly the teacher's work is just as valuable to society. It is also very important to note the preparation required of a teacher today and that required twenty-five years ago. California today requires from four to six years' preparation beyond the grammar school, of all those who wish to teach in the elementary schools. In other words, this state requires expert knowledge and thoro preparation, on the part of her future teachers. A grammar school education was ample preparation twenty-five years ago.

To conclude. The elementary schools are badly in need of more men teachers— are badly in need of a larger number of able teachers who select the work for their life work. As is true in all other lines of work, men and women will not enter the profession of teaching for their health or for the sake of philanthropy. If the State wishes the service of strong, able and well prepared teachers, the compensation must be adequate. No teacher in the elementary schools should receive less than seventy-five dollars per month for each calendar month in the year, and in large cities where living expenses are high, the minimum should be larger than this. The salaries of principals and superintendents should be increased accordingly. Better salaries than these are now being paid by the state to officers whose duties are far less valuable to society.

WESTERN SCHOOL NEWS

MEETINGS

National Educational Association, President, Charles W. Eliot, Boston, July 6-10, 1903.

California Teachers' Association, O. W. Erlewine, president; Mrs. M. M. Fitz Gerald, secretary, 1627 Folsom Street, San Francisco; December 28 to 31, 1903.

Summer Normal School, State Normal School, San Jose; Morris E. Dailey, President. June 29, 12 weeks.

Summer Session, University of California, June 25 to August 5, Berkeley, Cal. Application should be sent to the Recorder of the Faculties, on or before June 15.

National Summer School of Music, 2014 Van Ness Ave. July 6 to July 18; Selden C. Smith, 325 Sansome st., S F

Augsburg's Summer School of Drawing, Oakland, Cal. Beginning July 20. Address, F. J. Lobbett, 809 Market street, San Francisco.

NOTES

There is a movement on foot to establish a high school in Modoc county.

E. E. Balcomb of Stanford University has been appointed the representative for California of Henry Holt & Co.

D. R. Augsburg of Oakland has been invited to deliver a series of addresses before the State Teachers' Association of Minnesota.

Supt. Tillie Namoni Kruger and Miss Rose McIntosh of Plumas county spent several weeks visiting schools in and about San Francisco recently.

J. W. Graham, ex-superintendent of Kings County, has returned from Texas where he is interested in large land deals, and is now in San Francisco.

Mrs. Rose V. Winterburn, the well known teacher of history who has been spending several years abroad, has just published a book on the early history of California.

Robert French, formerly of the Monmouth State Normal School has been elected president of the State Normal School at Weston, Oregon. He was also elected president of Inland Empire Teachers' Association.

J. C. Shipley, a pioneer school teacher of Tulare county, met with an accidental death on Saturday evening, May 2d, in San Francisco. It is presumed he fell from an electric car and had his head crushed.

Dr. Elmer E. Brown has been offered the Department of Education in the University of the City of New York at a much larger salary than he is receiving at Berkeley. It is not probable, however, that he will leave the University of California.

The article on page 388, "Some Results of Kindergarten Training," is an extract from a paper by N. H. Bullock and not by H. M. Bland. Mr. Bland's paper on "An Outline for Tests and Observations," will appear in the July number.

The preliminary program of the N. E. A. has on it a number of noted names. Edward Everett Hale will pronounce the blessing. President Eliot's address, "The New Definition of the Cultivated Man" will be followed by E Benjamin Andrews, chancellor of the University of Nebraska, Lincoln, Nebraska, on "The Jeopardy of the Culture Element in Education." Benjamin Ide Wheeler, Elmer E. Brown, James A. Foshay, A. H. Chamberlain, J. H. Francis are Californian names on the program.

The drawing and manual training teachers of Northern California met in annual convention Saturday, April 25th, in the Normal School. The sessions were well attended and full of interest. The following teachers were present: Miss Gearhart, Berkeley; Mr. Doyle, San Francisco; C. H. Meeker, Pacific Grove; Olcott Haskell, San Rafael; Mrs. Goodell, Alameda; Mr. Felton, San Francisco; Mrs. Jones, Alameda; Mrs. Coldwell, Alameda; Miss Reibsam, San Jose Normal; Miss Brown, San Jose Normal; Miss Amy Campbell, San Francisco; Miss Bradbury, San Francisco; Miss Kate Whitaker, San Francisco; Miss Rebecca English, San Jose Normal; H. C. Bagot, Miss Nina Davenport, Miss Enid Kinney, San Jose Normal; Miss Cora Boone, San Francisco; A. B. Clark, Stanford; Miss Calthea Vivian, San Jose Normal; D. R. Augsburg, supervisor of drawing, Oakland; E. R. Snyder, manual training, San Jose Normal; Mr. Thorpe, manual training, San Francisco; Walter Tenney, manual training, Oakland; E. E. Goodell, supervisor of manual training, Alameda; Miss Cowden, San Jose; Bertha Warren, Santa Clara.

County Institutes

Supt. W. H. Langdon held the institute of the City and County of San Francisco in the Mission High School April 7, 8, 9. The principal speakers were Ellwood P. Cubberley, Henry Suzzalo, President Benjamin Ide Wheeler, T. L. Heaton, Supt. Langdon and Director Woodward. The musical features of the program were most excellent. The teachers were particularly responsive to the practical work of Prof. T. L. Heaton and the talks on Primary Arithmetic by Henry Suzzalo.

Supt. J. G. O'Neil of Nevada county held his institute in Nevada City, April 13, 14, 15. The instructors were President Morris E. Dailey of San Jose, Agnes Howe of San Jose and D. R. Augsburg of Oakland, Cal. The meeting was very successful and Supt. O'Neil is to be congratulated on the excellent manner in which he conducted the first institute of his administration. Supt. O'Neil supplied the teachers with a very neatly illustrated program.

Supt. T. O. Crawford of Alameda held his institute March 30-31 and Apr. 1—one day in Oakland, one day in Berkeley and one day in Alameda. The instructors were Dr. Brown, Dr. Busk, P. M. Fisher, A. W. Scott, Morris Elmer Dailey, Prof. W. H. Dudley, W. P. Montague, Supt. McClymonds, Supt. Waterman, Supt. Hughes, Prof. H. Morse Stephens.

Sonoma County Institute

The Teachers' Institute of Sonoma County was held at Santa Rosa. The officers were ex-officio Pres. Minnie Coulter, Vice Presidents H. R. Bull, Walter Clark, Mrs. M. B. Williams. The instructors were F. L. Burk, Effie B. McFadden, F. F. Bunker of San Francisco Normal School, Ellwood Cubberley, Stanford University, E. C. Moore, University of California, Thomas J. Kirk, Supt. of Public Instruction. The principal topics discussed were: F. F. Bunker—1, "Methods of Teaching Division"; 2, "Relation Between Formal and Abstract Number"; 3, "The Essentials of Geography and Method of Presentation." Effie B. McFadden—1, "Some Easy Experiments in Physical Geography"; 2, What to do Now in Nature Study"; 3, What Use can be Made of Nature Study in Language and Composition". F. L. Burk—1, The Confusion of Tongues in Method"; 2, What the School can Do for Citizenship"; 3, "What are the Educational Problems in California Today"? Ellwood Cubberley—1, "Reading and Literature in the Grades"; 2. "Concentration of Schools, Transportation and Supervision"; 3, "Education in England". E. C. Moore—1, "The Old Education and the New"; 2, "The Next Step in Education;" 3, "My Definition of a Teacher". Thomas J. Kirk—1, Some Changes in the School Law."

The special features of the Institute were as follows: Discussion of Dewey's "School and Society" by the teachers and a discussion of the various subjects taught in the High School when considered as a direct preparation for life. These topics were discussed by members of the Sonoma County High School Teachers' Association.

San Mateo County Institute

The Teachers' Institute of San Mateo County was held April 28, 29, 30 at Redwood City. The officers were Pres. E. M. Tilton, Vice Presidents Mr. Gilcrest, Mr. Hall, Mrs. Hartley, Miss McLellan. The instructors were Prof. Cubberley, Prof. Starbuck, Prof. Alden, Prof. Wilson, Mr. Suzzalo. "Popular Errors in Geography, Reading and Literature". "The New Course of Study", "Teaching of Numbers and Language in Elementary Schools" and "Union of Schools" were the principal topics discussed. The evening entertainment was as follows: First evening—Reunion of the teachers; second evening—Illustrated lecture, Fog Phenomena—Prof. Alex McAdie.

The special features of the Institute were: The Revision of the Course of Study; Criticism of the old course by the teachers and suggestions for improvement. Discussions led by Prof. Cubberley.

Santa Clara County Institute

The Teachers' Institute of Santa Clara County was held on April 27, 28, 29 at San Jose High School Building. The officers were D. T. Bateman, Pres. ex officio and Supt. of Schools; A. E Shumate, R. D. Hunt, Vice Presidents; Secretary-in-Chief, Mr. Hobart Hesken of Almaden; Assistant Secretaries, Miss Sullivan of San Jose, Miss McIntyre of Guadalupe, Miss Rose Daly of Gilroy. The instructors were Prof. David S. Snedden, Stanford; Prof. T. L. Heaton, Berkeley; Prof. Edward Hyatt, Riverside Co. Supt. of Riverside; Mrs. George, San Jose State Normal; Prof. Wm. Baker, San Jose State Normal; Prof. L. B. Wilson, San Jose State Normal; H. M. Bland, San Jose State Normal; Miss Belle Mackenzie, Principal of Kindergarten, San Jose. The principal topics discussed were: "Training to Study", "Literature Reading"—T. L. Heaton; "Geography of Desert", "Letters to Teachers"—Edward Hyatt, (Riverside Co.); Geography—Mrs. Mary George; Arithmetic—Prof. Wm. Baker; Geography—L. B. Wilson; "Literature Reading", Illustrated—H. M. Bland; "The Function of the Story"—Miss B. Mackenzie; "Rocks of California"—Ed. Hyatt; "Reading Circles"—David S. Snedden of Stanford.

The special features of the Institute were as follows: The Institute was divided off into Primary, Grammar and High School sections. High School section, E. E. Brownell, Chairman, H. S. Dutton, Secretary; Grammar section, F. K. Barthel, Chairman, R. A. Lee, Secretary; Primary section, Alice Jones. Chairman, Genie Gairand, Secretary. Edward Hyatt conducted a section for three days on "Rocks of California". These sections met every morning at 9:30 to 12. Afternoons were devoted to lectures from Professors Heaton, Snedden and Hyatt.

The teachers of this county divided themselves off into Geographical subdivisions, for the purpose of professional reading during the next year. Eleven centers were selected, with a leader for each—each leader being a member of a central committee, which will meet at intervals yet to be named, at various times during the following year.

The books selected by this committee are "James' Talks to Teachers", "Chubb's Teaching of English." These books are to be read by the teachers and discussed in the various sub-circles with a view of making this study a basis for discussion at the next institute. From time to time during the year speakers of more or less prominence who are capable of handling the subjects, will be sent out to address these several sub-sections. Also certain meetings of the General Committee will be held, at which time speakers will be present who will be able to discuss these subjects and to give us encouragement and assistance along the special line of our reading.

San Luis Obispo County Instiute

The Teachers Institute of San Luis Obispo County was held April 22, 24 at San Luis Obispo. The officers were: President, Frederic P. Johnson, Co. Supt.; Vice Presidents, F. E Darke, S. S. O.; A. G. Balaam, Arroyo Grande; D. H. Foree, Cayucos; Irvin Passmore, Paso Robles. The Instructors were Dr. Frederic Burk, Job Wood, Herbert Bashford, A. J. Walker. Dr. Leroy Anderson spoke on "The Aim of the California Polytechnic School", Mr. Henderson of the International Correspondence School on "Spanish Lessons by Phonograph". The principal topics discussed were: By Job Wood—"Practical School Problems", "Discipline", "Management", "Arithmetic", "Reading". By Dr. Burk—"California's Educational Problems,," "Professional Training of Teachers". By H. Bashford—"Literature of the West", "Interpretation of Poetry". By A. J. Walker—"The Philippines and Education". The evening entertainments were as follows: April 22—H. Bashford gave readings, and local talent furnished good music, vocal and instrumental. April 23—A. J. Walker spoke on "From San Francisco to Manila" and on "Experiences and Observations in the Philippines", with a musical program of six numbers.

The special features of the Institute were as follows: The teachers expressed their enjoyment of Mr. Bashford's day lectures; were interested in Mr. Walker's vivid description of the Philippines, and made good use of the question box. The musical program was very satisfactory.

The *Daily Breeze* spoke in particularly complimentary terms of the institute work of Job Wood, Jr. Supt. Johnson is to be congratulated on the success of the first institute of his administration.

* * *

Perham Nahl received the prize for the best poster at the recent carnival. The Polytechnic High School, the Stockton High School. Sutro School and Douglas School received prizes. Adolph Beck of the Clement Grammar School received the prize for the best individual poster. Florence Locke of the Edison School, fourth grade. Alice R. Power teacher, received the $25 cash prize for the best individual poster from primary schools.

The California School Masters' Club gave a banquet at the California Hotel Saturday evening, April 25th. Dr. C. C. Van Liew of Chico presided. Gov. George C. Pardee, Hon. James Phelan, John McNaught of the *Call* and Abraham Reuf discussed the question of whether or not young men should participate in politics.

Manual Training Supplies

Basketry Materials

BOOKS ON BASKETRY   We carry a large stock of **RAFFIA**

REEDS (plain and colored), etc., and can fill orders promptly.

☞ Price Lists of materials and books, *free*

MILTON BRADLEY COMPANY

H. O. PALEN,
Manager

122 McAllister Street
San Francisco, Cal.

NOTES

Ex-Superintendent Robert H. Furlong was presented with an elegant secretary's desk and chair by the teachers of Marin county during the recent institute.

The National Summer School of Music will open July 6th. The instructors are E. E. Chapman, Miss A. M. Fleming, Mrs. L. V. Sweesy, Miss K. E. Stone, Mr. P. A. R. Dow, Miss M. H. Mills. Teachers desiring the Course of Study should address Selden C. Smith, care Ginn & Co., 325 Sansome St., San Francisco, Cal.

D. C. Heath, of D. C. Heath & Co., Boston, has been spending several months on this coast, and in Honolulu. He has confirmed the appointment of G. H. Chilcote as local representative of the house. Mr. Chilcote is an experienced teacher, a graduate of the University of California '03, and is a man of virile enterprise and ability.

The Summer Session of the University of California will open June 25th and continue to August 15th. Scholars from the chief American universities will be present to instruct the attendants. There will be a number of those engaged in school administration in California to lecture on problems connected with administration work in elementary schools. The session promises to be of unusual interest.

The trustees of the State Normal School at San Jose have arranged for a continuous session. This is one of the most important innovations yet made at the San Jose Normal. It will give the teachers in service an opportunity to prepare for better work. It was recommended by the faculty that the school year be divided into four quarters of twelve weeks each, the work of each quarter constituting a full unit on which credit be given whenever the work was completed. The school will open on June 29th and continue until September 18th. The work will be exactly the same in character method, credit values as the other terms of the year. The school will not conflict with the Summer Session of the university, for the reason that the course of study will not be on the lines of advanced study, but more particularly on the training of the teachers for the elementary schools. A lecture course will also be maintained.

An election was held May 2d to consolidate the school districts of Merle, Hope and Encinitas. Supt. Hugh J. Baldwin has received several other petitions and is taking an active interest in carrying out the provisions of the new law for the Union of School Districts.

When the vacation season begins the Californian Northwestern Railway Company will be ready to make thousands happy. Its lines run thru one of the most picturesque regions of the state, and every :e and there are ideal places for rest and reation. Lakes and mountain streams, cosy corners in beautiful valleys, comfortable farm houses, mineral springs, natural springs, camps in the wildwood, all these are offered, and each has the advantage of being only a short distance from the city. Only a small expenditure is needed for railway fares, and in each instance the other charges are very reasonable.

The Perry Pictures
ONE CENT EACH
for 25 or more on paper 5½ by 8. Postpaid. Assorted as desired.
120 for $1.00
Send three two-cent stamps for catalog containing 1,000 miniature illustrations and two sample pictures.

The one-cent pictures are 20 to 30 times the size of this picture.

The Perry Pictures, Extra Size
On paper 10 by 12 and larger. 5 for 25 cts; 11 for 50 cts; 23 for $1.00.

New York Edition of the Perry Pictures
On paper 7 by 9. 10 for 25 cts; 50 or more, 2 cts. each

Pictures in Colors
Birds, Animals, Minerals, Fruits, etc.
Two Cents each
No orders for Pictures in Colors for less than 25 cents.

The Perry Pictures, Small Size
On paper about 3 by 3½. One-half cent each for 50 or more.

Large Pictures for Schoolroom Decoration
On paper 22 by 28. 75 cents each.

The Perry Magazine
Monthly except July and August. $1.00 per year.

The Perry Pictures Company
Tremont Temple, Boston   Box 4, Malden,
146 Fifth Avenue, New York   Mass.
Send all mail orders to Malden, Mass.

DIPLOMAS

We carry a fine line of

Grammar chool {Diplomas} High School
Promotion Certificates   Reward Cards
Report Cards, etc.

Write for prices
The Whitaker & Ray Company
723 Market Street, San Francisco

NOTES

"The First Year of Latin," based on Caesar's War with Helvetii, by Walter B. Gunnison, Ph.D., Principal of Erasmus Hall High School, Brooklyn, N. Y., and Walter S. Harley, A.M., instructor in Latin, Erasmus Hall high School. Pages IX, 319. Cloth. Illustrated. Introductory price, $1. Silver, Burdett & Co. A thorough knowledge of the essential part of Latin grammar and a definite preparation for the reading of Caesar are the two things which "The First Year of Latin" should accomplish. The book has materialized from many years of classroom experience, from a careful study of the difficulties that confront the beginner in Latin and the most effective methods of presenting the subject to him. The student—his needs, his interests, and his comprehension—has been kept in mind constantly in the making of the book.

Don't You Find Trouble

in keeping your pupils interested in

BOOKKEEPING?

If you will use the ELLIS SYSTEM you will have no further trouble. It was prepared by men who have had years of experience not only in the schoolroom but in the business world. This system teaches the kind of business and bookkeeping that business men want.

The Gregg System of Shorthand is particularly adapted to High School work on account of its simplicity, rapidity, and legibility.

We have made arrangements with the leading business college in San Francisco to give a special course in these subjects to teachers. Write us for full information.

ELLIS PUBLISHING COMPANY 1236 Market Street, San Francisco

YOU

will make no **MISTAKE** if you order your

LIBRARY BOOKS, FURNITURE

and SUPPLIES

from *C. C. Adams,*

131 Bridge Street, Stockton, Cal.

Busier Than Ever

The Royal Cloak and Suit Co.

Makers of popular priced Ladies' Suits, Jackets, Capes and Skirts.

Have been rushed with orders ever since they have thrown open their factory to the general public.

WHY
ARE WE BUSY?

Correct Styles   Small Expenses
Perfect Fit   Small Profits
Artistic Tailoring   Large volume of business

VALUE VERIFIED TO THE LAST STITCH

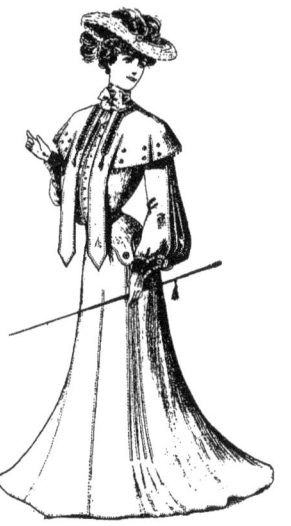

Suits made to order from $15.00 up

From the hands of the skillful designer through all its stages of completion, the utmost care is exercised in our production. We make every garment to order to your own individual measurement, and being first hand, we save you the middleman's profit. If you are in the city call at our factory; if not, we would be pleased to send you samples of cloths.

ROYAL CLOAK & SUIT COMPANY

Factory and Salesroom, 523 Market Street,   San Francisco, Cal.
Our Fall Catalog will be out August 1st. **Write for it.**

Book Reviews

Macmillan Company have issued a new edition, revised and enlarged, of the "Elements of General Method," based on the principles of Herbert. Price, 90 cents.

D. Appleton & Co. have issued the revision of Cassell's Standard French Dictionary. Professor Boielli has done the work of revision. This will undoubtedly become the standard French dictionary for popular use. Price, $1.50.

"Galdos. Marianela," edited by Edward Gray, A.B. Cloth, 12mo, 264 pages. Price, 90 cents. American Book Company. This touching and pathetic story of the popular modern Spanish author is here presented with the necessary assistance for reading in elementary classes.

"Merrill's Studies in Zoology, by James Merrill. Cloth, 12mo, 232 pages. Price, 75 cents. American Book Company. The directions in this laboratory guide are simple and suggestive as well as comprehensive. The plan of the work was tested, before publication, with pupils of all grades in the high school.

"Andrew's Botany all the Year Round," by E. F. Andrews, High School, Washington, Ga. Cloth, 8vo., 302 pages. Price, $1. American Book Company. This book is admirably adapted for botanical work in the average high school, and requires no expensive equipment. It is based on observation, and in this respect meets the popular demand.

"Galdos. Electra," edited by Otis G. Bunnell, M.S. Cloth, 12mo, 185 pages. Price, 70 cents. This drama, which was first presented at Madrid on January 30, 1901, made a deep impression on the Spanish people. It was written to give expression to the author's ambition for his country and his countrymen, and to urge them to social and political renovation.

GILLOTT'S PENS.

Grand Prize, Paris Exposition, 1900.

This is the highest award ever made, and no other pen-maker has it.

For Slant Writing: 404, 303, 604 E. F., 603 E. F., 601 E. F., 351, and 1047 (Multiscript).
For Vertical Writing: 1045 (Verticular), 1046 (Vertigraph), 1065, 1066, 1067.
For Semi-slant: 1089, the Semyslant Pen.

From the beginning of the Steel Pen industry Gillott's Pens have been the recognized standard.

Joseph Gillott & Sons, 91 John St., New York.

Notes

A meeting of the California Council of Education was held on Saturday, April 15th, in the San Francisco State Normal School Building. Powell street, near Clay, at 2 P. M. Topics for discussions were: 1—Free Text Books; 2—Compulsory Education; 3—What State Texts Book need Revision? 4—Life Tenure of Teachers. The discussion was informal with a view of getting these subjects pegged out for later committee work looking to future legislation. The attendance was good and the discussions lively. Frederic Burk presided and J. W. McClymonds acted as secretary.

SUMMER SCHOOL
Throop Polytechnic Institute

PASADENA, CALIFORNIA

July 6——August 1

Elementary and advanced courses for Teachers and others in Wood-Working, Cardboard Construction, Free Hand Drawing, Clay Modeling, Pottery, Wood Carving, Basketry, Cooking, Sewing, Pyrography, Elocution.

For circular and further information address

HARRY D. GAYLORD, Secretary,
Throop Institute,
Pasadena, California.

WANTED—AGENTS AND SALESMEN
FOR SCHOOL FURNITURE AND SUPPLIES

C. F. WEBER & CO.

☞Give references

526 Market Street, San Francisco, Cal.

210-212 N. Main Street, Los Angeles, Cal.

ts per copy $1.50 per year

June, 1903

SPECIAL NUMBER ON

Consolidation of School Districts and the Transportation of Pupils

CONTENTS

		PAGE
I.	Introductory Statement........ELLWOOD P. CUBBERLEY	421
II.	Report of the Auxiliary Committee of the Council of Education..MISS E. M. TILTON	422
III.	Report of a Visit to the Centralized Schools of Northern Ohio....SUPT. O. J. KERN	437
IV.	The Schools of Gustavus Township..........TRUSTEE C. G. WILLIAMS	452
V.	What Massachusetts is Doing in the Matter of Consolidation and Transportation........STATE AGENT G. T. FLETCHER	454
VI.	Consolidation and Transportation in Connecticut.....SEC. CHARLES D. HINE	463
VII.	Consolidation of Rural Schools in Indiana......SUPT. FRANK L. JONES	467
VIII.	Consolidation and Transportation in Wisconsin......SUPT. L. D. HARVEY	477
IX.	Consolidation and Transportation in Iowa......SUPT. R. C. BARRETT	483
X.	Consolidation and Transportation in Kansas........	485
XI.	Contracts for the Transportation of Pupils........	490
	(a) Notice to Bidders........	491
	(b) Contract forms for Drivers........	491
XII.	The Plan in California........	493
	(a) The Purpose of the New Law......MARSHALL BLACK	493
	(b) The Possibilities of the New Law......SUPT. THOMAS J. KIRK	493
	(c) Putting the Law Into Operation......ELMER E. BROWN; EDWARD HYATT	495
	(d) The First Union Formed Under the New Law, SUPT. HUGH J. BALDWIN	496
	(e) Lessons to be Drawn from the Attempt to Form a Union at Fowler, Fresno Co.	499
	(f) A Possible Union in Riverside County....ELLWOOD P. CUBBERLEY	500

Official Department............THOMAS J. KIRK, Superintendent of Public Instruction. 501

Editorial.   Western Schools News.   Teachers' Institutes.   Book Reviews.

THE WESTERN JOURNAL OF EDUCATION.
723 Market St.
San Francisco

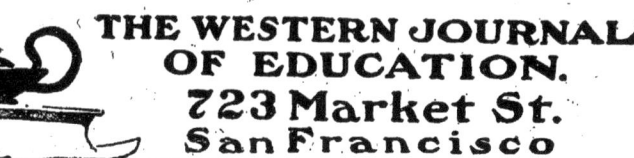

Winterburn's The Spanish in the Southwest . . . 55 cents
By ROSA V. WINTERBURN

THE discovery and early history of California are in this book vividly and attractively presented for young readers. Commencing with the life of the Indians, it takes up next the coming of the Spaniards, then their explorations in search of gold, the founding of the missions, and the life on the pueblos and the ranches. The book brings the history down to the end of the Mexican rule in 1848.

The narrative element and the purely historical are so skillfully combined as to make this book a story of history, a collection of stories so selected and arranged as to present historical characteristics and tendencies of periods. The style is adapted both to the subject-matter and to the age of the pupils for whom the book is intended. The illustrations are numerous and artistic, and maps show the places mentioned. At the end of each chapter are suggestive questions which serve as a helpful review drill. A list of the principal books consulted in the preparation of this work is also included.

The contents and scope of the work may be gathered from the titles of its chapters given below. It is equally suited for the school and the home, and the children of the Pacific slope who read and enjoy it will find in and between its lines an uprising of love and respect for their native state.

The Spanish in the Southwest

Part I. Before the Coming of the Spanish
- Chapter I. Indian Life in California
- Chapter II. Indian Legends

Part II. Discoverers and Explorers
- Chapter III. Cortes
- Chapter IV. Reports of the Seven Cities
- Chapter V. Fray Marcos de Niza
- Chapter VI. Coronado and Alarcon
- Chapter VII. The Spanish Claim to the Pacific Ocean
- Chapter VIII. Cabrillo and Viscaino
- Chapter IX. The English in the North Pacific

Part III. The Missions of Alta California
- Chapter X. The Desire of a Youth—Father Serra
- Chapter XI. Expeditions into Alta California
- Chapter XII. Founding of San Diego Mission
- Chapter XIV. The Last Days of Father Serra
- Chapter XV. Life at the Missions
- Chapter XVI. The Slavery of the Missions
- Chapter XVII. Secularization

Part IV. Spanish California
- Chapter XVIII. Life in the Pueblos and on the Ranches
- Chapter XIX. Foreigners on the Pacific Coast
- Chapter XX. Spanish Governors of California

Popular Text-Books

Baldwin's School Readers
Eight-Book or Five Book Series
New Education Readers
Books I and II, each $0.35
Book III, $0.40; Book IV .45
Patterson's American Word Book .25
Rice's Rational Spelling Book
Part I, $0.17; Part II .22
Barnes's Natural Slant Penmanship
Eight Books per doz. .75
Four Charts per set 1.50
Baird's Graded Work in Arithmetic
Eight Books for Eight Years
Maxwell's First Book in English .40
Introductory Lessons in English Grammar .40
Advanced Lessons in English Grammar .60
Webster's School Dictionaries—Revised
Natural Elementary Geography .60
Advanced Geography 1.25
McMaster's Primary History of the United States .60
School History of the United States 1.00
Overton's Applied Physiology
Primary, $0.30; Intermediate .50
Advanced .80

Newest Supplementary Reading

Abbott's A Boy on a Farm $0.45
Bakewell's True Fairy Stories .35
Horne & Scobey's Stories of Great Artists .40
Krout's Two Girls in China .45
Monteith's Some Useful Animals .50
Pitman's Stories of Old France .60
Pyle's Stories of Humble Friends .50
Simms's Child Literature .30
Wood's The Children's First Story Book .25

Send for descriptive circulars

AMERICAN BOOK COMPANY PUBLISHERS
NEW YORK   CINCINNATI   CHICAGO   BOSTON   ATLANTA   DALLAS
204 PINE ST., SAN FRANCISCO

THE WESTERN JOURNAL OF EDUCATION

Established 1852.

Consolidation of School Districts and Transportation of Pupils

I.—INTRODUCTORY STATEMENT

The matter of framing a bill to permit the consolidation of scattered rural schools was first discussed in the meetings of the sub-committee on Legislation of the Educational Commission, now almost three years ago. After careful consideration of the matter a bill was drawn, approved by the Educational Commission when it met, revised by the lawyer employed by the commission, and introduced in the legislature of two years ago. The bill passed first reading, but died on the files.

At the Los Angeles meeting of the California Teachers' Association, held last December, Miss E. M. Tilton presented a report on the subject to the Council of Education, and the plan was discussed by those present. Miss Tilton's report is printed in full in this issue. It is a good statement of the reasons for and the advantages of the plan. I also read a paper before a general session of the association on "Our Country School Problem," in which I sketched the many changes which have taken place in American life and education within the past thirty years, and pointed out the need of such a permissive law as we now have. This address was printed in the May number of THE JOURNAL (pp. 278-282).

The bill of two years ago was introduced again in the last legislature by Assemblyman Marshall Black of Palo Alto, who deeply interested himself in its passage, and to whose efforts, both in the assembly and before the senate, the enactment of the bill into a law is largely due. The new law, known as Section 1674 of the Political Code, was printed in full in the April number of THE JOURNAL (pp. 180-186). In a general way it follows the lines of the high school law. It was made purposely hard to start a union, so that when one was formed it would be only after careful discussion and thoro understanding of the plan. In many communities the population is so sparse, the distances so great, or the country so rugged that consolidation is not possible, but in places where consolidation is possible the new law will permit of the introduction of economies in administration and an effectiveness in teaching and supervision which have not been possible in our rural schools in the past.

In preparing this issue of THE JOURNAL it has seemed to me that what is wanted now is not a theoretical consideration of the question, but the presentation of a large amount of the experience of other people in other places, and that this should be presented in as concrete a manner as possible. Accordingly, with the exception of the council report by Miss Tilton, which is a statement of experience as well as an argument for the plan, I have presented only a series of statements as to methods and results in other places, and a few letters and statements as to the introduction of the plan in California. In making the selections from the great mass of literature on the subject I have tried to select that which would be most instructive to those who have to deal with California conditions. I have tried to get together such statements and illustrations of methods as I should like to have at hand if I were a county superintendent, or a village principal or a district trustee, and wanted to inform myself on the subject with a view to meeting objections and forming a union in my territory. The statement by Superintendent Baldwin, who has formed the first union district in this state, and the statement of lessons to be learned from the failure at Fowler, will be suggestive to California workers. The possible union in Riverside county, which is illustrated and calculated out, shows how to calculate the financial possibilities of a union.

The plan is a new one in this state, and needs careful discussion. It ought not to be taken up too hastily. It seems to me that it would be well if some time were taken in the institutes of our valley counties next year for a careful discussion of the subject, so that teachers, as well as trustees and parents, may become familiar with the possibilities and limitations of the plan. Using this number of THE JOURNAL as a basis, county superintendents could conduct a very effective discussion. Of other easily accessible literature on the subject, the article in the December, 1902, number of the *Review of Reviews*, and the article in *The Outlook* for December 27, 1902, will be found very useful.

ELLWOOD. P. CUBBERLEY.

* * *

II.—REPORT OF THE AUXILIARY COMMITTEE OF THE COUNCIL OF EDUCATION

Miss E. M. Tilton.

Under the laws of California a new school district may be formed, upon complying with the procedure pointed out by the statute, upon the petition of the parents or guardians of at least fifteen census children, residents of such proposed new district, and residing at a greater distance than two miles by a traveled road from the public schoolhouse in the district in which said parents or guardians reside.

This provision of the law has been very generally resorted to, and the result is that, in this state, there are a large number of districts, with but small attendance, formed on the outskirts of cities, villages, and well-populated school districts; and again, in sparsely populated territory, there are a number of contiguous small districts.

The primary object of the school system is to give the particular pupil the best education possible for him, which result, however, must be accomplished at lying schools, and were transporting, at public expense, nearly 2,000 pupils to adjacent or village schools.

Ohio, Indiana, New York, Maine, New Hampshire, Vermont, Connecticut, New Jersey, Nebraska, Pennsylvania, West Virginia, Kentucky, and other states of the west have followed the lead of Massachusetts, and this principle of consolidation is now in operation in most of the states east of the Mississippi River. It has also been adopted in Victoria, in Australia, whose minister of public instruction reports that 241 schools have been closed, at an annual saving of over $70,000.

California, however, has not at the present time (December, 1902,) any statute upon its books permitting trustees to contract with another district for the education of its pupils, or to expend the public moneys for the transportation of pupils to and from school, and this report is compiled for the purpose of calling the attention of educators, and also of the state legislature to this system of education, and this want of legislation to put it into effect, so that this plan may be adopted in this state wherever practicable.

So large is the area of California, and so comparatively sparsely settled is it in many of its counties that no arbitrary, or uniform plan of consolidation would be beneficial; of necessity, many school districts, with small attendance, must exist apart, in mountainous territory. But wherever schools are more favorably situated these small schools may be united with a larger central district, or several small districts consolidated, to the advantage of all. In every county there are many school districts which might thus unite for their mutual benefit; on the other hand, there are many other districts where it would be both impracticable and impossible to unite them. The general topography of the country, and the distance to be traveled in transporting the pupil to and from school, would determine the practicability of a union of districts.

The law of the State of New York on the transporation of pupils is as follows:

"Whenever any district shall have contracted with the school authorities of any city, or village, or other school district for the education therein of the pupils residing in such common school district, the inhabitants thereof entitled to vote are authorized to provide, by tax, or otherwise, for the conveyance of the pupils residing therein to the schools of such city, village, or district with which such contract shall have been made, and the trustees thereof may contract for such conveyance when so authorized, in accordance with such rules and regulations as they may establish."

An additional law is neecessary in California, *i. e.*, to permit a district, in its discretion, to discontinue its school, and to transport its pupils to the union schools, at public expense. Inasmuch as such a plan cannot be made generally operative or compulsory, efforts must be made by the school authorities of the several counties to induce the progressive trustees of one or more of these small districts in each county to try the experiment of transportation, and their example will be more effective than any other force to make such consolidation general as practicable.

KINGSVILLE, OHIO.

Kingsville township, Ashtabula county, Ohio, first in the west, adopted this plan of consolidation, and Edward Erf, of Ashtabula, Ohio, writing of the "Kingsville plan" of education, says:

"Those who have any acquaintance with district schools know that their advantages are meager, as compared with those of the town or city school. There are thousands of these rural schools which furnish their pupils scant preparation for the duties of life. As a rule they are not graded; the studies taught are the most elementary; the classes are small, and the attendance is irregular. Many districts are so sparsely settled that it is impossible to raise by taxation sufficient funds to build good schoolhouses, or hire a sufficient number of teachers. And, even if this be possible, the attendance is such as to make the per capita cost of maintenance unduly large, so that even a common school education becomes very costly.

"To overcome the many disadvantages of the subdistrict system, and for the purpose of offering an advanced graded-school education to every boy and girl of the proper school age, in Kingsville township, Ashtabula county, Ohio, its citizens have adopted a plan of consolidation, or centralization, of the subdistrict schools of the township into a common central school, conveying the pupils from every part of the township to and from school by means of coaches.

"The plan was not original with the citizens of Kingsville, Ohio; it was adopted by the citizens of Quincy, Mass., in 1874, and reported as successful. In Concord, Mass., it has been in operation since 1878. Up to the time the "Kingsville plan" went into effect, a large proportion of Massachusetts towns had consolidated their schools. No similar plan, however, had been tried in the state of Ohio, or in any states of the west. Generally speaking, the people were ignorant of this advance in the methods of common school management. The plan was favored by many educators, but up to the year 1892 no practical step had been taken to introduce a system of consolidation.

"While the township is the unit of

school organization in Ohio, and is the school district proper, it is divided into subdistricts for the regulation of school attendance, and to serve as a unit of representation in the township board. Previous to 1892, a board of directors, consisting of three men elected by the voters of the school district, employed the teachers and carried on the schools. In the year 1892 all the old powers of the directors were transferred to the township board, which was now represented by one director from each subdistrict. It was this year that the question of building a new schoolhouse in district No. 4, in Kingsville township, came up for discussion before the school board of the township. The schoolhouse was a necessity, but the school attendance was small. The board hesitated about expending the money for a new building. In was at this juncture that Prof. F. E. Morrison, then the principal of the village high school, urged upon the school board the adoption of the plan suggested the year before, that the few scholars of district No. 4 be brought to the village high school at the expense of the taxpayers of the township. As the expense of conveying the children of that district to the high school was far less than the cost of hiring a teacher, to say nothing of erecting a new building, the board of education favored the idea. Upon investigation it was found, however, that there was no law on the statute books of the state, which authorized the expenditure of money out of the public fund to pay for conveying children to and from a centrally located school.

"While discussing the question of conveyance, the idea of school consolidation took deeper root. A bill was passed in the Ohio state legislature, which enacted that any board of education in any township which by the census of 1890 had a population of not less than 1710 nor more than 1715 may, at their discretion, appropriate funds derived from the school tax, for the conveyance of pupils in subdistricts, from their homes to the central school of said township, provided such appropriation for any subdistrict shall not exceed the amount necessary, in the judgment of the board of directors, for the maintenance of a teacher in such subdistrict for the same period of time. The law was based specifically upon the rate of population for Kingsville township, and was passed for the benefit of that township only, so as to gain the support of legislators from other sections of the state who were attached to the old plan, but who did not object to a trial of the plan, which they regarded as chimerical.

"The system was put in operation in Kingsville township with but little opposition, which came wholly from the teachers and their friends, who saw that by the consolidation of the schools the number of positions open to them was lessened. Each subdistrict was admitted upon a written petition signed by the taxpayers of the school district. At first only three subdistricts availed themselves of the privilege. A fourth followed later. At present there are only two subdistricts which still maintain separate schools; but these, it is confidently expected, will follow within a year.

"When the taxpayers of the subdistrict have by petition signified their willingness to abandon the school of the subdistrict, and send their children to the central school, the board of education employs a teamster to convey the pupils of the subdistrict thither—one teamster employed for each subdistrict. These teamsters work under a special contract, and agree to construct covered wagons, approved by the board of education, to be used in the conveyance of the pupils. These wagons are provided with side and end curtains, which may be raised or removed on warm days, and tightly closed in cold or stormy weather. They have steps in the rear by means of which the pupils enter or leave the coach. The seats are arranged lengthwise, and are provided with cushions, and suitable blankets for the covering and comfort of the pupils. Each coach carries from eighteen to twenty-four persons.

"The contracts for conveying the pupils from each subdistrict are let out to the lowest responsible bidder; the board, however, reserves the right to give the contracts to those whom they deem fit to be entrusted with the care of the pupils. The moral character of the bidder, as well as the lowness of the bid, is considered. The teamster enters into a written agreement that he will get the pupils at their homes, convey them to the central school, at a time set forth in the contract, and be ready to return them within a specified time after the school is out. He also agrees that no profane, immoral or indecent language shall be used by himself or others, during the transportation of the pupils to and from the school building. He further agrees that he will allow no tobacco or spirituous liquors to be used by any person in the conveyance. Every morning during the school year the teamster drives to the homes of the pupils on his route, makes his presence known by ringing a bell, or blowing a horn, to which the pupil responds by promptly entering the wagon. If he does not appear within a few minutes, the wagon drives on, and the pupil is marked tardy. Thus far, there have been very few cases of tardiness. The price per day, for each wagon, varies in the different districts. During the present school year, the price per wagon for conveying the pupils from the four outlying subdistricts is one dollar and fifteen cents a day. Up to the present time, there have been more bidders than contracts to award. While the price is low, it offers fair and sure compensation to those who accept the contracts.

"The experiment was watched with much interest by educators, and those interested in education, thruout Ohio. Some thought the plan impracticable, others championed it with ardor. The latter looked upon it as the most practicable and economical solution of the vexed country-school problem. This was specially true among educators of neighboring townships and counties. They saw realized in this plan their hope of giving to the country pupil all the advantages of education which the city boy or girl enjoys. And they urged the, adoption of the plan in the localities in which they taught school. Accordingly, two years later, a more general law was passed, which provided for the extension of the Kingsville plan to other townships. It has also been adopted in townships in New York, Pennsylvania, West Virginia, Kentucky, and other states of the west since its trial in Kingsville, Ohio.

"The residents of the subdistricts of Kingsville township which have adopted this plan, would deem it retrogression to go back to the old subdistrict plan. It has given the school system of Kingsville an individuality which makes it unique and progressive. Pupils from every part of the township enjoy a graded school education, whether they live in the most remote corner of the township, or at the very doors of the central school. The line between the country-bred and village-bred youth is blotted out. They study the same books, are competitors for the same honors, and engage in the same sports and pastimes. This mingling of the pupils from the subdistricts and the village has had a deepening and broadening influence upon the former, without any disadvantage to the latter. With the grading of the school and the larger number of pupils, have come teachers of a more highly educated class. Higher branches of study are taught, the teachers are more conversant with the needs of their profession. The salaries are larger; the health of the pupils is preserved, because they are not compelled to walk to school in slush, snow and rain, to sit with damp, and perhaps wet feet, in ill-ventilated buildings. Nor is there any lounging by the wayside. As the use of indecent and obscene language is prohibited in the wagons, all opportunities for quarreling, or for improper conduct, on the way to and from school, are removed. The attendance is larger, and in the subdistricts which have taken advantage of the plan it has increased from fifty to one hundred and fifty per cent in some cases; truancy is unknown. It has lengthened the school year for a number of the subdistricts; it has increased the demands for farms in those subdistricts which have adopted the plan, and real estate therein is reported more salable. The drivers act as daily mail-carriers.* All parts of the township have been brought into closer touch and sympathy.

"The cost of maintenance is less than that of the schools under the subdistrict plan; the township has had no schoolhouses to build; it has paid less for repairs and fuel. Since the schools were consolidated, the incidental expenses have decreased from eight hundred to eleven hundred dollars per year, to from four hundred to six hundred dollars per year. In the first three years following its adoption, Kingsville township has actually saved one thousand dollars."

State Commissioner of Common Schools O. T. Corson, in his forty-third [1896] annual report to the Governor of Ohio, referring to the Kingsville experiment, states that "the expense of schooling the children has been reduced nearly one-half, the daily attendance has been very largely increased, and the quality of the work done has been greatly improved."

Prof. J. R. Adams, superintendent of schools of Madison township, Lake county, Ohio, says that "under the new plan the cost of tuition per pupil, on the basis of total enrollment, has been reduced from sixteen dollars to ten dollars and forty-eight cents; on the basis of average daily attendance, from twenty-six dollars and sixty-six cents to sixteen dollars and seven cents. The total expense will be about the same in this district as under the old plan, but the cost per pupil will be much less." This is because the school attendance has increased in Madison township from two hundred and seventeen to three hundred pupils, since the plan went into operation.

In the townships where the Kingsville plan has been adopted it has met with general favor, and has received the warmest support of educators, who regard it as a long step forward toward placing the country schools upon a higher plane of efficiency. Superintendent Adams, referred to above, writes: "A trial of this plan of consolidating our schools has satisfied me that it is a step in the direction toward whatever advantages a well-graded and well-classified school of three or four teachers has over a school of one teacher with five or eight grades. I am more thoroly convinced than ever that centralization is the true solution of the country-school problem."

Prof. F. E. Morrison, to whom its

---

*In some districts they also act as truant officers for the district.

adoption by the board of education in Kingsville township was in a great measure due, speaks of it as "a system of education superior to any in the State of Ohio, and one which is to be the system of the future."

Again, in the forty-fifth [1898] report to the Governor of Ohio, State Commissioner O. T. Corson, referring to the "Kingsville plan" says: "I anticipate none the less an increasing tendency in all parts of the state, year by year, to make the law serviceable in reducing school expenses, and in extending the benign influence of well-graded instruction. Incidental to the operation of this law, township high schools will be established, township libraries will be built up, and possibly it is no idle hope that the same wagons that carry the children to and from school may also carry, under government contract, the mails, and distribute them free to our farming communities."

Prof. L. E. York, superintendent of Kingsville school, in writing concerning the system, says: "The best physical laboratory in America is the well-regulated American farm. Here the boys and girls study nature first-handed. Here they observe the growth and life of plants and animals. Here they breathe pure air, become familiar with the beauties and wonders of the natural world. Here they make character. To have added to all these opportunities the advantages of a high school education, without any of the disadvantages that attend the spending of evenings, without chores or home duties, in the town, is an educational condition that is almost ideal.

"The pupils like the system, as do the teachers employed. It has gained the favor of parents, and in general is regarded by those who have studied it and understand its workings as a most practical advance in methods of rural education."

Extracts from Reports

The experiment in consolidation now in progress in northeastern Ohio is of such interest and promise as to warrant extracts from the annual reports for 1895-6 of the two superintendents who have been most prominent in the work. This recent movement may have an interest for some minds that earlier movements would not possess.

KINGSVILLE, OHIO.

Extract from the report of Mr. F. E. Morrison, superintendent of the Kingsville, Ashtabula county schools.

"The new school system, which is known as the Kingsville system of education, has been formulated and introduced with marked success.

"By this system the pupils of the subdistricts are given the same advantages for obtaining an education as the village pupils, and this result has been obtained without working any disadvantage to the village pupils, for we have been enabled to open a new room and supply another teacher in the village schools, thus reducing the number of grades in each room and giving all the pupils better school advantages. We have sufficient room yet for several more pupils without crowding the rooms.

"The pupils of the subdistricts have not only been given the advantage of more extended associations and larger classes with which to recite, but they have also the advantages of a school where the teacher has fewer recitations and can give more time and attention to each recitation; thus the pupil's progress is much more rapid than is possible in a school where there are three times as many classes and one-sixth the number of pupils. It is a fact that the work of the teacher depends more upon the number of classes to recite than the number of pupils in attendance. It is a pleasure indeed to note that the attendance in the subdistricts that have availed themselves of the new system has increased from 50 to 150 per cent. in some cases, and a larger increase in all cases; the daily attendance in the same subdistricts has increased from 50 or 60 per cent. to 90 or 95 per cent., thus increasing greatly the returns from the school fund. This has been accomplished at a saving of more than one thousand dollars to the taxpayers in the three years.

"The Board of Education and citizens of Kingsville are to be congratulated for their progressive and energetic spirit in being pioneers in formulating and placing in operation a system of education superior to any in the state of Ohio, and which is to be the system of the future. The Board of Education has been enabled under the new school law, to conduct its financial matters by better business methods, buying its supplies in larger quantities, and letting its contracts on competitive bids, and by centralizing the schools, thus saving many needless expenses."

MADISON TOWNSHIP, LAKE CO., OHIO.

Extract from the report of Mr. J. R. Adams, superintendent of Madison township, Lake county, Ohio.

"In my report to the board one year ago I called attention to the very low average attendance in some of our schools, the great expense per capita of educating the pupils in those small schools, and to the fact that, on account of the lack of interest and enthusiasm therein, good results could not be obtained, and suggested the plan of consolidation as the proper solution to the difficulties.

"Acting upon my suggestion the board, having in view only the best interest of the children for whom our school exists, voted to consolidate three subdistricts at North Madison, No. 16 and No. 3 with No. 12, and also three at Unionville, No. 10 and No. 11 with No. 4, arrangements being made with the school board of Harpersfield township whereby the pupils of subdistrict No. 1 of said township, might attend the school at Unionville upon payment by the board of education of Harpersfield to the board of education of Madison township of the sum of $140 tuition.

"Our school opened with two teachers and with an attendance of ninety-three pupils. This was certainly more than the number for which we had planned, and was a great surprise to me, for from No. 10, in which subdistrict there had been the previous year an attendance of only ten pupils, there came eighteen; from No. 11, in which there had been an attendance of only eight pupils, there came eighteen, and from the Harpersfield district, in which there had been an attendance of fourteen pupils, there came twenty-three. The number of pupils enrolled in this school was 107, with an average attendance of seventy-three.

"Having tried the new plan for a year, it is no longer an experiment, but an experience with us; therefore, let us now candidly look at the results. First, I wish you to know what the patrons of the consolidated school think of the plan, and then to give you, as briefly as I can, some of my own observations. All the patrons in the school of subdistrict No. 10 of Madison, and in subdistrict No. 1 of Harpersfield, have signed a paper stating that they are well pleased with the plan and its results, and asking their respective boards to continue the plan another year. While there has been no canvass at Unionville, subdistrict No. 4 to ascertain what the people there think of the plan yet, from what I have heard, I am confident that they are unanimous in its support. The foregoing represents the opinion of patrons who send 89 of the 107 pupils to this school. A large majority of the patrons in subdistrict No. 11, who send 18 of the 107 pupils to the school in question, have publicly expressed themselves as being dissatisfied with the plan, and that under it their children have not received the educational advantages which they ought to have received. Further comment is unnecessary.

"The following are some of the good results which have come under my personal observation:

1. A much larger per cent. of enumerated pupils enrolled.
2. No tardiness among the transported pupils.
3. Irregular attendance reduced, the per cent. of attendance of transported pupils from two subdistricts being each 94 per cent., the highest in the township.
4. Pupils can be better classified and graded.
5. No wet feet or clothing, nor colds resulting therefrom.
6. No quarreling, improper language, or improper conduct on the way to and from school.
7. Pupils under the care of responsible persons from the time they leave home in the morning until they return at night.
8. Pupils can have the advantage of better schoolrooms, better heated, better ventilated, and better supplied with apparatus, etc.
9. Pupils have the advantage of that interest, enthusiasm, and confidence which large classes always bring.
10. Better teachers can be employed, hence better schools.
11. The plan insures more thoro and complete supervision.
12. It is more economical. Under the new plan the cost of tuition per pupil on the basis of total enrollment has been reduced from $16.00 to $10.48; on the basis of average daily attendance, from $26 66 to $16 07. This statement is for the pupils in said subdistricts Nos. 10 and 11.
13. A trial of this plan of consolidating our schools has satisfied me that it is a step in the direction toward whatever advantages a well-graded and well-classified school of three or four teachers has over a school of one teacher with five to eight grades, and with about as much time for each recitation as is needed to properly assign the next lesson.

"I am now more thoroly convinced than ever before that consolidation, or centralization, as it is sometimes called, is the true solution to the country school problem."

IN NEW YORK STATE.

Hon. C. R. Skinner, State Superintendent of Public Instruction of the State of New York, thus forcibly urges the need of consolidation in the schools of that state:

"In 1860 the school population of the state outside of its cities was 894,432. At the close of the school year of 1895 the school population of the state outside of its cities and villages, containing upwards of 10,000 people, was 609,146, a decrease of 285,286, or upwards of 31 per cent. While the number of school children has decreased during that time nearly one-third, there has been substantially no decrease in the number of rural school districts. It needs no argument to show that the antiquated school district system, which served the people so well in 1860, has outgrown its usefulness, and that, if the State of New York desires to keep pace with adjoining states in the advancement of her educational interests, some new system must be devised.

"The township system, or some unit larger than the present system, in my judgment, is the only solution of the difficulty, and until the state shall have adopted that system its rural schools will continue to decline in efficiency. There is, in my opinion, no better school in America than the union free school and village school of our state, but the results there obtained cannot possibly be achieved in the weak rural districts, where the average attendance is less than twenty pupils, and, as shown above, in nearly 3,000 districts less than ten. The ambitions and rivalries of the students—incentives to greater exertion on the part of the pupils—which prevailed thirty-five years ago in these country districts no longer exist. The school is lifeless, cannot be graded, there is little enthusiasm among the students, and that activity and earnestness which come from numbers are entirely lacking."

IN MASSACHUSETTS.

The arguments for the reform have been luminously stated by Mr. A. W. Edson,* one of the agents of the Massachusetts State Board of Education, as follows:

"There is a decided tendency on the part of intelligent and progressive communities to close the small schools in remote districts and to transport the children to the graded schools of the villages, where better classification, better grading, and better teaching are the rule. This is done not so much from an economic standpoint as because of the firm conviction that the children receive greater educational advantages than in the small, ungraded schools.

"The number of children in the back districts is small, and growing less every year. With few children and small classes there can be but little enthusiasm and progress.

ARGUMENTS FOR THE PLAN.

"The leading arguments in favor of the movement are:

1. It permits a better grading of the schools and classification of pupils. Consolidation allows pupils to be placed where they can work to the best advantage; the various subjects of study to be wisely selected and correlated, and more time to be given to recitation.

2. It affords an opportunity for thoro work in special branches, such as drawing, music and nature study. It also allows an enrichment in other lines.

3. It opens the doors to more weeks of schooling and to schools of a higher grade. The people in villages almost invariably lengthen the school year and support a high school for advanced pupils.

4. It insures the employment and retention of better teachers. Teachers in small, ungraded schools are usually of limited education, training or experience, or are past the age of competition The salaries paid in cities and villages allow a wide range in the selection of teachers.

5. It makes the work of the specialist and supervisor far more effective. Their plans and efforts can all be concentrated into something tangible.

6. It adds the stimulating influence of large classes, with the resulting enthusiasm and generous rivalry. The discipline and training obtained are invaluable.

7. It affords the broader companionship and culture that comes from association

8. It results in a better attendance of pupils, as proved by experience in towns where the plan has been thoroly tried.

9. It leads to better school buildings, better equipment, a larger supply of books, charts, maps, and apparatus. All these naturally follow a concentration of people, wealth, and effort, and aid in making good schools. The large expenditure implied in these better appointments is wise economy, for the cost per pupil is really much less than the cost in small and widely separated schools.

10. And, again, it quickens public interest in the schools. Pride in the quality of the work done secures a greater sympathy and better fellowship thruout the town."

---
*Fifty-eighth Annual Report of the Massachusetts Board of Education, 1893-4, pp. 215-17.

OBJECTIONS URGED.

Mr. Edson reports that the following objections have been made in Massachusetts:

1. Depreciation of property; decreased valuation of farms, in districts where schools are closed.
2. Dislike to sending young children to school far from home, away from the oversight of parents; and to provide a cold lunch for them rather than a warm dinner.
3. Danger to health and morals; children obliged to travel too far in cold and stormy weather; obliged to walk a portion of the way to meet the team, and then to ride in damp clothing and with wet feet; unsuitable conveyance and uncertain driver; association with so many children of all classes and conditions; lack of proper oversight during the noon hour.
4. Insufficient and unsuitable clothing; expense to parents of properly clothing their children.
5. Difficulty of securing a proper conveyance on reasonable terms or, if the parent is allowed compensation, of agreeing upon terms satisfactory to both parties, parents and town officials.
6. Local jealousy; an acknowledgment that some other section of the town has greater advantages and is outstripping any other locality.
7. Natural proneness of some people to object to the removal of any ancient landmark or to any innovation, however worthy the measure, or however well received elsewhere.

OBJECTIONS ANSWERED.

To these objections Mr. Edson, who is one of the most competent of authorities, replies:

"The first one is more imaginary than real, for any level-headed man with children to be educated will place a higher value on the quality of the schools and the school spirit in the community than upon the number and accessibility of the schools. Experience has demonstrated the fact that property in towns committed to this plan has appreciated rather depreciated in value.

"The second and third objections are the most serious. It behooves school authorities to see that the danger is reduced to a minimum. Suitable conveyances, covered, should be provided, and competent, careful drivers selected. No risks should be taken. During the noon hour some teacher should remain with the children who carry luncheon.

"The fourth, fifth and sixth objections have no great weight. The last one has great influence with those people who choose to live, move and die as did their ancestors, on the theory that this is the last generation, and that any special efforts at improvement are just so much more than is wise or necessary."

CONVEYANCE OF CHILDREN TO SCHOOL.

The Secretary of the Massachusetts State Board of Education, in his report to the board for 1894–95, says:

"The question of the consolidation of rural schools continues to receive the thoughtful attention of educators. It has been frequently demonstrated, and is generally conceded that it would be better, both on economical and on pedagogical grounds, to unite the many small and weak schools of a township, dispersed over a large extent of territory, into a few strong, well-equipped and well-conducted graded schools, located at convenient points.

"The adoption of the town system in the management of school affairs in several states has rendered this procedure more feasible, by placing the control of all the schools under one central authority, with power to locate and discontinue schools wherever needed in its discretion, and which is competent to reduce the disjecta membra of a school system to healthy and well-rounded educational organisms. The chief hindrance to consolidation now to be considered lies in the distance some of the pupils would have to travel from their homes to reach the nearest union or graded school, in thinly populated sections.

"The expedient has been tried on a considerable scale in Massachusetts, and is being favorably considered elsewhere, of transporting the more distant pupils to school at the public expense. The importance of this experiment and the influence it may exert in determining the future character of rural and village schools, would seem to render it advisable to recapitulate what has been undertaken and accomplished in this direction.

"A law of Massachusetts, approved April 1, 1869, reads as follows:

Any town in this Commonwealth may raise by taxation or otherwise, and appropriate money to be expended by the School Committee in their discretion, in providing for the conveyance of pupils to and from the public schools.

"The then Secretary of the State Board, Mr. White, refers to this act as 'introduced into the Legislature thru the efforts of a practical man from one of our rural towns of large territory and sparse population, where the constant problem is, how to bring equal school privileges to all without imposing undue taxation.

"'In too many cases the town seems to have forgotten that the most important element in the solution of the problem has been the character of the school, and have bent their efforts to making them accessible to all. This has led to such an unwise multiplication of them as not only to shorten the time of their continuance, but greatly to diminish their efficiency, while at the same time the expense of maintaining them has been largely enhanced.

"'The act recognizes the fact that it is a far better policy for the town to spend a few dollars in conveying, in severe and stormy weather, and thru drifts of snow, children who have no means of conveyance, to a well-appointed and good school, rather than to waste hundreds in planting small and feeble schools at their doors.

"'I have little doubt that the future history of not a few of them will amply justify the wisdom of the grant.

"'It is to be remembered that the law is not compulsory. It simply gives the power to the towns, whose citizens are amply qualified to judge as to the propriety of exercising it. Certainly there is little danger of its abuse.'"

MR. EATON'S REPORT.

The first general statement of the results in Massachusetts of the law authorizing the public conveyance of pupils to school was made by Supt. W. L. Eaton, of Concord, in 1893, in a pamphlet prepared for the Massachusetts public school exhibit at the World's Columbian Exposition. In it he said:

"Since the year 1869 the cities and towns of Massachusetts have been authorized by law to appropriate and expend money for the conveyance of pupils to and from the public schools. At first this authority was used, in accordance with its apparent purpose, mainly to convey pupils to the high school, as generally there was but one such school in a town. Within a few years, however, many communities have used this authority to increase the educational advantages of the children—constantly decreasing in numbers—who live in the districts at a distance from the centers of population. This has been accomplished by closing many district schools and transporting, at public expense, their pupils to the neighboring school or to the village.

"In order to secure full information regarding this important movement, a circular letter of inquiry was sent to 165 cities and towns. Replies have been received from 135, and the answers tabulated. The following summaries are of interest:

1. The cities and towns that reported an expenditure for 1891-2 of $33,500, will expend for the current year $48,300.

2. Fifteen towns and cities report conveyance to high school only at a cost of $8,650 20 for 462 pupils.

3. It appears that in the remaining 120 towns and cities there were, prior to the beginning of this movement to consolidate, 632 outlying schools. Of this number 250 have been closed within the past 12 years, and to-day nearly 2000 pupils are being conveyed to adjacent district schools, or to the village schools

4. To the question, Is it the policy of your town ultimately to close all the schools outside the centers of population, twenty five answer yes, without qualification; forty answer no, and nearly all the others reply that their towns are working for that end, or are considering the question, or hope to accomplish such a result.

5. To the request of a brief statement of the reasons that determined the towns to close district schools and transport the pupils to other schools, the replies indicate two distinct purposes—one financial and the other educational. In many of the towns of the state the depopulation of the districts outside the villages has made it cheaper to transport to other schools the few pupils living in the districts than to teach them in situ. In other towns the desire to make strong central schools, and the purpose to give all the children of the town the benefit of better teachers, better appliances, and better supervision, have been the dormant motives to determine consolidation.

6. To the question whether the results have been satisfactory, there is a substantial agreement in the affirmative. The most emphatic expressions of satisfaction come from those towns in which the educational motives have been the dominant ones. Repeatedly comes the assertion from this latter class of towns that the parents would not return to the old system of isolated schools if it were possible.

BRISTOL AND NORFOLK COUNTIES, MASS

State Agent John T. Prince, in 1894, on the school of Bristol and Norfolk counties as follows:

"Increased attention has been given in recent years to the consolidation of schools, either for the purpose of better grading, for bringing together small schools, or for uniting small outlying schools with a central school. In either case it becomes necessary frequently to convey children from one neighborhood to another or from an outlying district to the village center. Three different plans of conveyance are followed:

1. Conveyance by carriage from some central point, as, for example, the abandoned schoolhouse, to the school or schools which the children attend.

2. Conveyance by carriage which passes thru the principal thoroughfare of the neighborhood from the most distant point, the children being obliged to walk to the carriages from homes which are situated on the side roads.

3. Conveyance by carriage from the homes of all the school children of the neighborhood.

"It is evident that the latter plan, altho more expensive than either of the other plans, is the one most convenient for the pupils, and it has been found by experience to be the one which gives the greatest measure of success.

"The amount paid for conveyance and the basis of payment vary greatly according to circumstances. Some towns pay so much a week or mile for each pupil carried, and some so much by the season for carriage and driver. Experience has demonstrated the importance of making a careful selection of a driver who can take proper care of the children and keep them in control."

WESTERN MASSACHUSETTS.

In the Massachusetts school report of 1894-5 are given the results of an inquiry regarding the rural schools of three counties in the western section of the state, conducted by State Agent G. T. Fletcher. The questions touching consolidation and conveyance submitted to the school committees and the gist of the answers thereto, as given by Mr. Fletcher, are as follows:

"Do you favor the consolidation of small schools, and the conveyance of pupils when necessary? Give reasons for your opinion."

Nearly all the replies are in the affirmative, so far as the theory is concerned, while many committees find difficulties and sometimes impossibilities in the way of application.

The reasons for consolidation of schools by conveyance of pupils are as follows: Increase in the size of the schools, rendering it possible to have better classification; better attendance, because the school is more interesting and profitable, and the pupils can ride in comfort and safety when weather conditions would be unfavorable for walking; and the saving of money by closing small schools, making it possible to employ better teachers.

Some maintain that the contact with a larger number of pupils excites a healthy emulation, and that the small district school does not bring the pupils into touch with the conditions of life which they must meet later.

"To what extent has the plan of uniting schools been tried in your town, and with what results?"

"80 towns report of a trial of the plan. 50 of them state that results are favorable. 6 report some favorable results but much opposition from parents. 4 towns of the 80 do not favor the plan."

QUINCY, MASS.

Quincy, Mass., was probably the first town in America to try the experiment of concentrating schools and transporting pupils. The following extract from the School Report of Quincy, Mass., for the year 1874-5 will prove of interest:

"A reference to the former reports of the School Committee of the town will show that for many years the condition of the little school at Germantown has been steadily unsatisfactory. Isolated and small, classification was impossible, emulation unfelt, and enthusiasm absent. Ten pupils ranged from the primer to the proper studies of a high school. The most conscientious teacher soon lost hope and energy in such surroundings. For years committee after committee has striven in vain to afford a remedy. During the past summer, the teacher, who has been laboring there for a considerable period declared her intention of resigning in despair. The committee, profoundly dissatisfied with the backwardness and lethargy of the school, was unable to assign the fault either to the teacher or to the pupils. At the same time, it became evident that the school building was unfit for occupation during another winter without extensive repairs. It was indeed shamefully dilapidated, decayed, and dirty. Competent mechanics, after careful survey, estimated the expense of necessary repairs to be at least $500. Besides this extraordinary outlay, the regular expense in salary, care of house and fuel, incurred to maintain this school of ten scholars, was $560 a year. And yet this large expense availed those ten scholars but little or nothing. The committee, therefore, determined to try by experiment whether or not at one and the same time in this department the outlay might be reduced and the returns increased. It ascertained that it could contract for the transportation of all the school children in that school district to the Coddington school for about $420 yearly, and it thought it probable that when there they would be aroused and stimulated by the transfer to a large and graded school. The result has fully justified its anticipations. The whole number upon the register of the old Crane school was 12, and of these the average number of attendance was never more than 10. Now 17 are daily transported to the Coddington school from the same territory; and so great has been their interest that the attendance among them has been almost absolutely perfect. Meanwhile, both from the reports of teachers and from personal observation, the committee is thoroly satisfied that they are making a progress in their studies which they never had approached at Germantown For these reasons the committee thinks it decidedly for the interest of the town, and clearly beneficial for the pupils concerned, that the present experiment should be prolonged for at least a year more. It is persuaded that this policy will approve its wisdom to those who are now most doubtful if it can be fairly tried. The day of small, ungraded, remote and isolated schools in a town like Quincy has passed away. Only absolute necessity can now justify it. Even if the plan we recommend was as much more costly as it is really less costly than the old one, we should not hesitate to urge its acceptance as decidedly the cheaper and better.

CONSOLIDATION OF SCHOOLS IN OTHER STATES.

A Maine law of 1897, says: "The superintendent of schools in each town shall procure the conveyance of all public school pupils residing in his town to and from the nearest suitable school, for the number of weeks for which schools are maintained in each year, when such pupils reside at such a distance from the said school as to render such consolidation necessary."

A law of New Hampshire provides that town school boards may use a portion of the school money, not exceeding twenty-five per cent., for the purpose of conveying children to and from schcols.

A similar law existed in Vermont in 1894. A new law goes into effect in February of this year, whereby, "upon application of ten taxpayers in any town, the school directors shall furnish transportation to any and all children residing one and a half miles or more from any school; but the aggregate cost of such conveyance shall not exceed twenty-five per cent. of all the school moneys." Vermont is now expenping twice as much for transportation as ten years ago.

A provision of the school law of Connecticut authorizes town school boards to unite schools "when in their judgment, the number of pupils is so small that the maintenance of a separate school is inexpedient," and provide transportation for the pupils.

In Rhode Island the state pays a bounty of $200, in addition to all other funds, to each union school.

The New York law of 1896 provides for a tax for conveyance of pupils by vote of the inhabitants.

A law of 1894 in New Jersey and one of 1897 in Nebraska provides for transportation of pupils.

From the report of the Minister of Public Instruction for Victoria, in Australia, the following extract is taken: "Under the system of conveyance 241 schools have been closed. The saving in closed schools amounts to about $71,000 per annum. The attendance is so regular and the system so popular that applications are constantly made for its extension."

III.—REPORT OF A VISIT TO THE CONSOLIDATED SCHOOLS OF NORTHERN OHIO

O. J. Kern.

County Superintendent of Schools, Rockford, Winnebago County, Illinois.

[A report to the school officers and patrons of the schools of Winnebago County, and reproduced here by the kind permission of Superintendent Kern.]

In company with State Superintendent Bayliss and Supervisor Black Owen, Chairman of the Committee on Education of the Winnebago County Board, I had the great pleasure of visiting the Centralized Schools of Northeastern Ohio in October last. It was an extremely interesting and profitable trip. So numerous have been the inquiries for information concerning the improved system for district schools in Ohio that, as a result, this report is given in the hopes that what is herein described of our visit to Ohio may lead to better things for Illinois. We left Chicago on the morning of October 8th and our first stop was at Painesville, 29 miles east of Cleveland. Our tour of inspection was through Lake, Ashtabula, Trumbull, and Geauga counties, some of the finest portion of the Western Reserve. This country was originally settled by people from the New England states. We were received with utmost kindness wherever we went, and no pains were spared to make our visit pleasant and profitable. Last, but not least, the weather was all that could be desired, and our drives over a beautiful country with every evidence of prosperity, were thoroughly enjoyable. Enough frost had touched the maples to make the leaves scarlet and golden, and with the glimpses of the blue waters of Lake Erie, made a scene never to be forgotten.

The first place we visited was Perry, Lake county, where there is a township high school. The principal, Professor Morrison, is a pioneer in the matter of centralization. He assured us that the experiment was no longer an experiment, that the new movement was the logical solution of the country school problem, and that centralization of districts with transportation of pupils had come to stay.

It gave much better schools with but a slight, if any, increase in the cost of the township. The opposition to the plan has long since died out. This has been the testimony at every place visited thus far. At this particular place, however, there was only one wagon drawing children. So we drove on to North Madison, in Madison township, where three wagons are used. On our way there we saw the first wagon. We stopped at the farm house and talked with the driver. He carried all the children from one district, about twenty in number. His route was five miles long. That is to say, starting at the first home to pick up a child until he arrived at the central school was five miles. Then he drove back home after delivering the children, thus covering ten miles in the morning. Of course he traveled the same ground after school, thus making twenty miles in all. He got $1.20 a day for his work. We asked him if he made any money at it. He said he did as he was working a small farm that did not require all the time and labor of himself and team. We asked him if he had any trouble with the children and he replied none. He said he was employed by the Township Board of Education who put him under bond to be careful with the children; to have a safe team; to provide a suitable wagon. covered and provided with curtains, and containing soapstones and laprobes for the severest weather. We asked him what objections the parents along the route had to the new plan. His reply was that the only objection was on the part of two or three at the beginning of the route, as they had to get their children ready somewhat earlier than they used to when they went to the district school. Of course the children must be ready when the wagon came. He aimed to start at 7:30 and arrive at the building not later than 8:45. Thus there were no children tardy; none came with wet feet or clothing; the attendance was greatly increased and much more regular. The driver believed the movement had come to stay; that the people would not consent to go back to the old way. A short distance on towards the centralized school we had a very interesting conversation with Mr. Fuller, a member of the Township Board of Education. Mr. Fuller is a public spirited, prosperous farmer, and believed in giving the county children the best educational advantages possible. And while the new plan did not materially increase the cost, yet the amount of taxes was not the first consideration. He had four boys. One was at home on the farm; another was in Delaware University; a third was in school in Cleveland, while the fourth was in business in Cleveland. His girls were in the centralized school. He knew the value of the plan and was sure the people would not go back to the old method. The opposition had long since died out, and the bitterest opponents three or four years ago are now the most enthusiastic supporters. They had seen the value of a well graded school, with good teachers, over an ungraded one, with oftimes indifferent teachers. We visited the school house during the noon hour and did not have time to see the school in operation. We next drove to Unionville, and had a pleasant visit at a two-room school. The children were fine specimens of the American public school. The principal, Mr. Adams, was township superintendent for Madison township, and has had considerable experience with centralized schools. His testimony as to the value of the movement was stronger, if anything, than that which we had heard at Perry and North Madison. The cost had not been increased.

MADISON TOWNSHIP.

Madison township, Lake county, presents an excellent illustration of what may be called partial centralization, that is, a grouping of two, three or four schools into one without attempting to bring all the schools to the geographical center of the township. The latter method would not be practical because of the shape of Madison township. It is one of the townships along the shore of Lake Erie and is nine miles long by five miles wide. Most of the townships of the Western Reserve are five miles square, while in other portions of the state, where centralization is successful, the townships are even larger than six miles square.

Centralization in Madison township has been in successful operation since 1896. We visited the schools at Unionville and North Madison. Supt. J. R. Adams, principal of the Unionville school and superintendent of Madison township, during the months of December, 1901, and January, 1902, sent me the following facts and illustrations:

1—They have now only three one-teacher schools in the township.

2—Since centralizing the per cent of the enrollment of children on the enumeration (census returns) of school age, between 6 and 21, has increased from 60 per cent in 1894 to 86 per cent in 1901.

3—For year ending June, 1901, 20 pupils were taking high school studies. (This is more than can be said of some Illinois townships.)

4—The total cost for the township for educational expenses in 1896 was $7,555; for 1901, $7,243.

5—Cost of transportation in 1896 was $332; for 1901, $1,618.

6—Incidental expenses for the township in 1896 were $2,509; for 1901, $902.

7—Total enrollment in 1896 for township was 390; for 1901, 414.

8—Per capita cost for education for the township based on total enrollment for the year was $19.36 for 1896, and $17.50 for 1901.

THE KINGSVILLE SCHOOL.

We next visited Kingsville in Ashtabula county, 401 miles east of Chicago. This was our farthest point east. Kingsville is a small village with a township high school. To the school are brought all the children of the township, with the exception of two districts. Four wagons are used at a cost of $20, $25, $24 and $28 per month, respectively, for a month of twenty days. The school year is nine months. Five teachers are employed in the building. The testimony of the principal of the school, the town clerk, and Mr. Kinnear of the Board of Education, was that there was an actual saving in the total cost to the township under the new plan; and while money was expended for transportation of pupils, it was more than saved in the fewer schools operated. And as to the increased efficiency of the new centralized school over the scattered schools, that was beyond a question of doubt.

It was here that the Ohio plan of centralization had its origin in 1892. The erection of a new building in one of the districts of Kingsville township brought up the question whether or not it would be better to abandon the school in that district and take the children to the village school at the general expense. In this first case of consolidation in Ohio the schools were centralized at the village school, a village situated about a mile and a half from the railroad. The results, educationally, in the small districts, were far from satisfactory. In order to con solidate and transport children at public expense, special legislation was necessary. So the Ohio legislature passed the following bill, April 17, 1894:

"SECTION 1. *Be it enacted by the General Assembly of Ohio,* That any Board of Education in any township, which by the census of 1890 had a population of not less than 1,710 nor more than 1,715; of any county, which by the same census had not less than 43,650, nor more than 43,660 inhabitants, may, at their discretion, appropriate funds derived from the school tax levy of said township for the conveyance of pupils in sub-districts from their homes to the high school building of such township; provided, such appropriation for any sub-district shall not exceed the amount necessary, in the judgment of the board, for the maintenance of a teacher in such sub-district for the same period of time."

The Kingsville plan proved such a success that on April 27, 1896, the Ohio legislature passed a bill for the relief of the counties of Stark, Ashtabula and Portage, which provided that the Board of Education of any township of those counties may, "when in its opinion it will be for the best interest of the pupils in any sub-district, suspend the school in such sub-district and provide for the conveyance of said pupils to such other district or districts as may be convenient for them; the cost of such conveyance to be paid out of the contingent fund of said district; provided, the board of any special school district in any county mentioned above, may provide for the conveyance of pupils out of the contingent funds, the same as townships aforesaid."

Since then a general law has been enacted, permitting the people of any township at the annual town election to vote "yes" or "no" on the proposition to centralize the schools of that township: i. e., to abandon the small districts and transport the children at public expense to the central school. Such, in brief, is the history of the legislation. And as to the result of the Kingsville experiment, I can do no better than to quote from the *Arena* for July, 1899. It was a beautiful day in October, 1900, that we visited Kingsville, and our inspection of the school, our conversation with the teachers and school officers, our seeing the children loaded into wagons and driven to their homes, made a deep impression on me, at least. But the quotation:

"The residents of the sub-districts of Kingsville township which have adopted this plan, would deem it a retrogression to go back to the old sub-district plan. It has given the school system of Kingsville an individuality which makes it unique and progressive. Pupils from every part of the township enjoy a graded school education, whether they live in the most remote corner of the township or at the very doors of the central school. The line between the country bred and the village bred youth is blotted out. They study the same books, are competitors for the same honors and engage in the same sports and pastimes. This mingling of the pupils from the sub-districts and the village has had a deepening and broadening influence on the former without any disadvantage to the latter. With the grading of the school and the larger number of pupils have come teachers of a more highly educated class. Higher branches of study are taught, the teachers are more conversant with the needs of their profession. The salaries are higher; the health of the pupil is preserved, because they are not compelled to walk to school in slush, snow and rain, to sit with damp and perhaps wet feet, in ill-ventilated buildings. Nor is there any lounging by the wayside. As the use of indecent and obscene language is prohibited in the wagons all opportunities for quarreling or improper conduct on the way to and from school are removed. The attendance is larger, and in the sub-districts which have taken advantage of the plan it has increased from 50 to 150 per cent., in some cases; truancy is unknown. It has lengthened the school years for some of the sub-districts; it has increased the demands for farms in those sub-districts which have adopted the plan, and real estate therein is reported more saleable. The drivers act as daily mail carriers. All parts of the township have been brought into closer touch and sympathy. The cost of maintenance is less than that of the schools under the sub-district plan; the township has had no school houses to build; it has paid less for repair and fuel. Since the schools were consolidated the incidental expenses have decreased from $800 to $1,100 per year to from $400 to $600 per year. In the first three years following its adoption Kingsville township actually saved $1,000."

We left Kingsville feeling that we had

Kingsville Centralized School, Kingsville, Ashtabula county, Ohio.
Centralization of schools in Ohio began here in 1892. The picture shows the children ready to start home from school.

traveled nearly 500 miles to a good purpose. Before leaving we had an amateur photographer take snap shots of the wagons, children, school building and ourselves.

GUSTAVUS TOWNSHIP, TRUMBULL COUNTY

But we wished to find centralized schools in a purely country township, where there was no village or village school, a place where country life was being preserved. We went thirty-five miles south of Ashtabula and visited Gustavus and Green townships in Trumbull county. The first place visited was Gustavus. This

The Consolidation of School Districts

township is exactly five miles square, as are all the townships of the Western Reserve with the exception of those along the shore of Lake Erie. In Gustavus township the town hall is situated exactly in the center of the township, as is the case in Green township. Here was a church, the post office, a country store and a few houses.

I had a picture of the centralized school of Gustavus township and was anxious to see the real thing. We saw it and all was as represented. The school building is located in the center of the township. The school has been in operation two years.

grounds at 8:45 a. m., which does away with tardiness, and to leave for home at 3:45 p. m. The wagons call at every farmhouse where there are school children, the children thus stepping into the wagons at the roadside and are set down upon the school grounds. There is no tramping through the snow and mud and the attendance is much increased and far more regular. With the children under the control of responsible drivers there is no opportunity for vicious conversation or the terrorizing of the little ones by some bully as they trudge homeward through the snow and mud from the district school.

Going Home from School, Gustavus Township, Trumbull County, Ohio.
These wagons are fitted with curtains, laprobes, and if necessary, with oil stoves for severe weather. Longest route, 4¼ miles. Average price per wagon per day, $1.25.

It is a four-room school, having a principal and three assistants. All the children of the township are brought to this central school and nine wagons are employed in the transportation.

The wagons are provided with curtains, lap-robes, soap-stones, etc., for severe weather. The Board of Education exercises as much care in the selection of drivers as they do in teachers. The contract for each route is let out to the lowest responsible bidder who is under bond to fulfill his obligations. The drivers are required to have the children on the school

During the school year 1898-99 there were enrolled in the grades below the high school eighty-two boys and fifty-two girls; in the high school room seventeen boys and thirty-five girls; making a total in the building of 186 pupils. The average monthly enrollment for the entire school the past year was 163, while the average daily attendance was 77.4 per cent of the total enrollment. This is a fact of great significance. The children are regular and are getting the benefit of such a course.

Keep in mind that this school is not

in a village and the children are scattered over twenty-five square miles of territory. The children are not tardy. How do they do it? you ask. Well, they do it and that is enough for me. Any one who stands in that building, looks at those children and wagons, must be convinced that here is

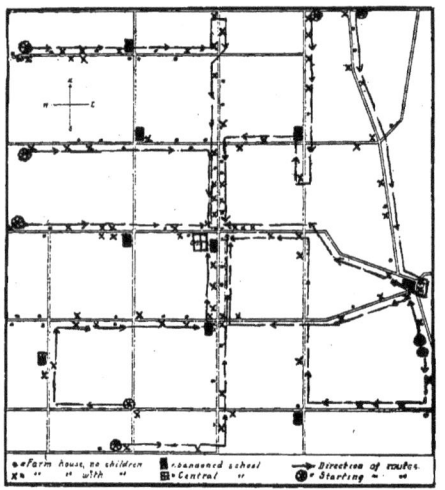

Diagram of Gustavus Township, Trumbull County, Ohio. Showing transportation routes, farm houses, and schoolhouses.

The average price per day per wagon is $1.25 and the length of the longest route is five miles.

THE ROUTES PAY AS FOLLOWS.

ROUTE	AMOUNT	MILES TRAVELED
No. 1	$1.55 per day	5
" 2	.98 "	3¼
" 3	.69 "	2¼
" 4	1.50 "	5
" 5	1.25	3¾
" 6	1.45	4½
" 7	1.40	4½
" 8	1.48	5
" 9	.95	3½

the solution of the country school problem. Because this problem is being solved in the country over six miles from the nearest railroad. There is an organ in every room and the walls are being decorated with pictures. They have started a library. In the high school room were fifty-two enrolled, with fifty present. Here was an opportunity for the big boys on every farm to get higher education and still be at home evenings, secure from the temptations and dissipations of city life. They rode home in the wagons with the children of the lower rooms and thus were able to be of service on the farm.

The building is a frame structure erected at a cost of $3,000. It is heated by steam. The principal gets $80 per month, while his assistants each received $27.50. The wages of the assistants should be larger. The drivers receive respectively $22, $30, $18, $25, $30, $32, $16, $30, and $17 per month, making an average of $1.25 per day. Before t' e adoption of the centralization the average daily attendance was 125 pupils. It has increased to 144 at the end of the second year and the principal told us the attendance is increasing all the time. Before the schools were centralized the cost for the entire township was $2,900. Now it is $3,156, being an increase of only $256 annually. And as to the character of the school, who will claim that the nine scattered schools were doing the work of a well-graded four-room school? There is absolutely no comparison. In order to keep up the school and pay off the school bonds, the Township Board of Education made a levy of nine mills on a valuation of $373,000. There was opposition to the plan at first.

The people who were opposed simply took the ground that the thing had not been done and therefore could not be done. Just as there are always people opposed to any progress. When I was a boy sensible people said a man was a fool to think about binding grain by machinery. They were not ignorant; they were simply mistaken. So those who were opposed to centralization of schools frankly acknowledge their mistake and are found among the staunchest supporters. We have found this true every place we have visited.

A special committee was sent from an adjoining county to investigate the Gustavus school. The committee was composed of one person opposed to the system and one in favor. They traveled over the township and talked with the people as we did. In their report, out of fifty-four families interviewed only one person with children was opposed; seven of those in favor were formerly strongly opposed, while none that were first in favor of the system are now opposed. The same committee adds: "although the system costs a little more (the belief is that it is cheaper after building is paid for) yet the people as a whole are highly pleased and are very enthusiastic and proud of their schools. Several of the neighboring townships, after carefully watching the system, have decided to centralize, and the growing opinion is that centralization is in harmony with educational progress.

The committee's report is certainly correct. Bear in mind, the roads in this township are but a trifle, if any, better than the average of Winnebago county. In fact, two or three townships of our county have as a whole, better roads. The people are simply determined to have better schools and will not allow obstacles to remain in the way of their children's fullest and freest development, even if it does cost a few hundred dollars more per year for the entire township. What would $1,000 more per year on the $373,000 valuation of Gustavus township amount to? The average tax-payer would not know it. The testimony has been that after the new school building has been paid for that there is an actual saving per capita of children of school age in the township. Then think of the superior value of the new school over the old. It cannot be a question of a few hundred dollars.

While we were at the Gustavus school the principal advised us to drive five miles to the west into Green township, where the people had centralized and put up a fine new brick building at a cost of over $6,000. The people of Green township had watched the school in Gustavus township for two years and believed so thoroughly in the new plan that at the last

The typical rural schoolhouse.
One of "those miserable box-car, one-room structures."

April election they voted to centralize and bond the township for a long term to erect a new building. The vote was overwhelmingly in favor of the new school. We drove west to the center of Green township, which is five miles square. This township is eleven miles from one railroad and six miles from another. So it is distinctly rural. To be sure, there is the town hall, a post office, a church or two, a country store and a few dwellings. That is New England brought to the Western Reserve. We all were enthusiastic over this building for country children. We never saw the like before in the country

Centralized Country School Building, Green Township, Trumbull County, Ohio. Erected in 1900.
To this school are brought all the children of the township, and nine wagons are employed in the transportation.

to take the place of miserable box-car, one-room structures. And the possibilities of such a school, who can measure it?

This building stands in the center of the township in a community distinctly country. There is no village beyond a store and post office, a town hall, a church or two, and a few dwellings. It is eleven miles from one railroad and six miles from another. It was built in 1900, at a cost of $6,000. There are six school rooms with two additional, one of which may serve as a library and the other as an office and reception room. There is a basement under the entire building, part of which may be utilized for laboratory and gymnasium. The building is heated by steam.

To this building are brought all the children of the entire township. The educational influence of a building over that of eight or nine widely scattered, neglected district buildings, is beyond controversy, to say nothing in the way of sanitary improvement in the way of seating, lighting, heating and ventilation. Such a building may be had in hundreds of townships of Illinois. It would not be a burden to any of the tax-payers of any township of Winnebago county. Bonds could be issued for thirty years' time, money could be borrowed at 4 per cent. The annual interest on $6,000 at 4 per cent would be $240, an amount no larger than the repairs on seven or eight district school houses from year to year if kept up as they should be. One-thirtieth of the principal or $200, plus the annual interest, $240, would make a total cost of $440 for building purposes for the first year, decreasing every year afterwards as bonds were paid off. The total valuation of Owen township, according to the Winnebago county Board of Review, for 1900 is: real estate, $253,622, and personal, $310,038, making a total valuation of **$563,660.** An annual tax of $440 for such a central building here shown, on a valuation such as the township of Owen has, is cheaper in the long run than under the present plan.

They began this school in September last. The enrollment is 180 over 150 of last year in the scattered schools. Four teachers are employed. All the children of the township are brought to the school and eight wagons are employed in the transportation. The campus has about three acres. Shade trees, school decoration, library, etc., will come. How that school can be made the social, literary and musical center of the entire township! What an inspiration it must be to a corps of teachers to work in such a community as that!

In the primary room were all the little ones of the entire township in a beautiful room, while in the high school room were many large farmer boys getting an education they could not otherwise gain. On the playground all the boys of a township play baseball. Think what it is to get all the boys of a township, country boys, I mean, on one playground. There will grow up a unity. Each boy, having studied and played with the other boys of the entire township, will be stronger for it. When the football team or baseball team or literary contests of Green township compete with Gustavus township, on athletic ground or in town hall, each team will have the backing of an enthusiastic township. In a great many districts there are hardly enough boys to play "two-cornered cat." Can you wonder that the children get tired of district school after a certain age? I am not sure that I have yet grasped the full significance of what we saw here. If that is good for Ohio boys, why not the same for Illinois?

The day spent at Gustavus and Green township schools was by far the best one in the Western Reserve. As far as educational matters are concerned, it was ahead of anything I had ever seen.

We returned to Ashtabula, fully realizing that it was a good day, well worth our coming nearly 500 miles. Superintendent Bayliss and Mr. Black returned home from here. I paid a visit to Thompson Center, Geauga county. They did not have centralization, but the special district plan, a modification. It is not so good as centralization, but much better than the old way. They wish now they had complete centralization as in other townships. But the special district plan was the best they could do then. Certain sections of the township were jealous of the other, and after the most determined opposition, those in favor of better schools at last, by a decree of the probate court, succeeded in getting two districts consolidated. A new school house was built; a graded school was organized with three teachers; and the children transported themselves. Now, instead of nine small schools, there are five on the special district plan. They expect to reduce the number.

On my way from Thompson Center I stopped at a district school house where the school had not yet been centralized. It was a small building, with no shade trees in the yard. On entering the house I found a teacher and four pupils. There were no more in the district. I asked the teacher why this school was not centralized. She replied that it would be next year. The teacher was getting $30 a month to teach four pupils. She said that for the same money she would rather teach a room of thirty pupils in a graded school than to teach the four she had. Besides the possibility in the way of enrichment of country life which the centralized school promises, it also will bring better roads.

At the Green township central school, where the new $6,000 brick building has been erected, I asked a high school class how the roads were when they were bad. A young lady said they were real bad, while a young man said they sometimes found it necessary to put four horses to the wagon. The principal said the people were preparing to improve the principal roads over which the wagons ran. Thus better schools bring better roads. But more about the centralized schools later. The grounds are beautiful. The Garfield memorial monument in Lake View cemetery, Cleveland, is well worth a visit, as is also the monument in honor of soldiers and sailors, in the public square. Here I saw the trophy of the Spanish-American war, a cannon from Viscaya, Santiago, July 3, 1898.

My first day's visit in the Cleveland city schools was full of interest to me.

At the city normal school I had the pleasure of meeting again Prof. J. E. McGilvery, whom the Winnebago county teachers will recall because of his work with them at the last two annual institutes. The city of Cleveland supports a normal school, with a corps of instructors numbering fourteen, to train prospective teachers after they have graduated from the city high schools. That is how they believe in professional training for teachers in Cleveland. I was especially interested in the city cooking schools and visited one most of the day. But space here will not permit of further mention of the most excellent work witnessed in the Cleveland city schools.

On my return from Ohio I visited the Indianapolis schools, to learn about the new buildings and school room decoration as described in "School Sanitation and Decoration," a new book being studied by Winnebago county teachers. While there I spent half an hour with State Superintendent Jones, who informed me that centralization of district schools is going on in some parts of Indiana and proving satisfactory in the main. Superintendent Jones was busy digesting reports from all his county superintendents, with reference to the subject of centralization of county schools, thus getting matter together for his biennial report to the governor.

THE SYSTEM APPLIED TO WINNEBAGO COUNTY.

But let us discuss the practicability of this system in Winnebago county. There are 118 school districts in the county outside of Rockford. If we deduct from this number the six village and two suburban districts of the county there will remain 110 one-room country schools. Out of these 110 districts, from reports of teachers on file in my office for the school year of 1899-1900, there are five districts that had an enrollment of exactly ten pupils for the entire year; thirteen districts had an enrollment of fewer than ten (three of the thirteen having fewer than five pupils), while one school has been closed, there being only one pupil in the district. The cost per capita is very high in such cases, to say nothing of the character of the school. From the reports of township treasurers to me on Sept. 15, 1900, I give the following from one of the representative townships of the county, in which there is no village:

	Expenditures for year ending April 1, 1900.	Number in District 6 to 21, June 30, 1900.	No. Enrolled in School for year	No. Months School.	Salary of Teacher per Month.
District 1	$378 53	34	25	8	$35
District 2	293 40	26	21	8	30
District 3	314 75	33	17	9	30
District 4	436 29	42	28	9	35
District 8	321 15	47	32	9	30
District 9	243 65	22	12	7	30
District 10	194 80	51	28	6½	25
Total	$2182 57	255	163	av8	av30

Several other townships have reports of the same general character. From the above table it will be seen that it costs $2,182.57 to educate 163 children (for none of this expenditure is for building purposes), a per capita of $13.39. Of the 255 persons of school age only 163 are in the district schools. A few may go to the Rockford high school or business college. It is not true that the most capable boys and girls are the children of parents of the most means, while the poor children can never hope for school education any better than the common country school affords.

To quote from an article by "Taxpayer," in an Ohio paper of December 26, 1899: "We believe that in this age of steam and electricity, in which human ingenuity and human endurance are taxed to the utmost and in which the educational qualifications were never more imperatively demanded, that our boys and girls of the country districts should have educational advantages as nearly equal with those of the boys and girls of the city or special district schools as possible. We do not believe that the centralized system is a great panacea that will cure all the ills with which our educational system is afflicted, but we do believe it is an improvement over the old methods; that it has advantages that will more than repay the expense and inconvenience incident to reorganization. If centralization is a good thing, we want it; if it is not, we want to know why it is not. Because some one we know is in favor of it, or opposed to it, is not sufficient ground upon which either to approve or condemn it. Let us investigate it thoroly, study over it carefully and form conclusions slowly; also, in forming our conclusions, let us be careful that we consider the merits and faults of the system of centralization, and that we do not approve or condemn it on account of merits and defects that do not arise out of centralization itself, but exist in the school system as a whole, or arise from its sources."

In such a spirit as the above we should discuss centralization in relation to the schools of Winnebag county. Naturally one of the first considerations will be the condition of the roads for the transportation of pupils to the central schools. Two or three townships in Winnebago county have as good if not better roads than those of Gustavus and Green townships, Ohio, where the experiment is a success. Centralization of schools and free delivery of mail are bringing better roads which are needed by the farmer for many things Under present conditions our farmers manage to get a load of milk to the factory over the worst of roads. The other day I saw a load of milk drawn by three horses, while over the same road a little child was trudging thru the cold and mud to the little old school house. The creamery was fitted up with improved machinery, while the schoolroom was lacking in nearly everything that goes to make a school. Perhaps there is money in getting a load of milk to a central depot, while there is no money in getting a load of children to a central school. This is where we are mistaken. Good roads and a central graded school will do more to keep our boys on the farm than any other agency. To quote from a circular received today, with reference to better roads: "Under the inspiration of the flag we love, and the matchless system of free popular education, the youth of the land have awakened to the possibilities that lie within them; they are restless and pulsating with energy; they

The Ordinary Road to Learning.

realize that this is an age of mighty possibilities, hence their intense desire to keep in touch with the outside and everchanging world. The youth of the farm dreams and longs for the intenser life of the city. He feels an almost irresistible desire to get closer to the nerve center. He is not content to be shut in mud-bound for weeks and months at a time. The great outside world is calling him, and his nature answers the call. Country life demands and must speedily have free rural mail delivery and the daily papers delivered on the date of publication; it demands the telephone; it demands above everything else a complete system of good, hard, every-day-in-the-year roads. They make country life better worth living, they broaden, educate and uplift this most important branch of the commonwealth."

With the free transportation of children our youth can be educated at home; be at home evenings and not on the streets of a distant city. What I have written above will not appeal to all. There are objectors and always will be. Progress is rarely along the path of the least resistance. The opponents of the movement in Ohio were very determined. But the successful operation of the system has won their approval. It is possible, I suppose, to travel over Illinois and find people who

Wagon used in Springfield Township, Clark County, Ohio, for Transporting Children to School. Good Weather Dress.

Route of this wagon, 6 miles; time, 1 hour 10 minutes; capacity, 28; transports, 18. The township owns the wagon, which was built for the township by the National Wagon Works, Chillicothe, Ohio. Cost for transportation, $1.66⅔ per day.

The Same Wagon in Stormy Weather.

are opposed to better schools, especially if it should cost a few cents more on the hundred dollars. It is possible to find people in Illinois who believe in low wages for the teachers, short school terms, with no library books or apparatus in the schoolroom in order to keep down taxes. It is possible to find people in Illinois who don't care for the school because their children are gone. But to the man, rich or poor, who has a family of growing children, living in a country district, far from a city, any reasonable proposition to better the educational facilities for his children ought to receive from him a candid consideration.

ADVANTAGES OF THE PLAN.

Such common sense reasons as the following must appeal to the great majority of the district school patrons of Winnebago county and win their support to the centralization of the schools, the logical step to improve country school facilities:

1. By centralization all the children of a township can be brought together in one building, and thus will result the inspiration that always comes from numbers. A school of seven or eight pupils is not calculated to stimulate a boy or girl to do the best work possible. With only one in a class there is no competition, that rivalry which calls forth all the powers of the child. By centralization strong classes can be formed and thoroughly graded as advancement is made. Such classes call forth the best efforts of the members. Such classification and gradation furnish longer recitation periods, thus giving the teacher more time for instruction. There will be uniformity of text-books, thus securing unity of study.

2. By centralization there will be fewer but better teachers in our schools. It will be a case of survival of the fittest. Better salaries will be paid those who do teach, thus enabling a person to make it possible to acquire a high school and normal training before attempting to teach. There is no inducement for a person to spend time and money in training when the only prospect ahead is a small school at a salary of $20 or $25 a month, for six or seven months of the year. Many directors want to hire a cheap teacher, as the school has only a few scholars and it costs too much to teach those few. When a person teaches for $25 per month, does his own janitor work, pays $10 or $12 per month for board, the sum left at the end of each month is not such as would induce a normal graduate to take up such a school. Of course a small school is expensive. Thus in one district in Harlem township the total expenditures for the year ending April 1st, 1900, was $233.60. They had school seven months of the year and a total enrollment of four. Thus the per capita cost for education on the enrollment was $58.40. A school in Burritt township for the same period had a total expenditure of $217.99 for a seven months' school with an enrollment of eight. The per capita in this instance is $27.25. A school in Pecatonica township had a total expenditure of $158.03 for seven months' school, with an enrollment of six. The per capita is $26.34. A school in New Milford township had a total expenditure of $269.65 for eight months' school, with an enrollment of ten. The per capita, $26.96. And so on for the small schools of the county. Thus a premium is put on poorly prepared teachers who are willing to teach for $20 per month or less. *Centralization will decrease the cost per capita for education, give longer school years, and furnish a more efficient force at better salaries.* There are facts that cannot be disputed. One more phrase of the financial question. The following figures show the inequalities of taxation. One district levied $176 on a valuation of $38,835; another, $200 on a valuation of $31,422; a third, $230 on a valuation of $23,826; a fourth, $200 on a valuation of $64,250; a fifth, $250 on a valuation of $12,696; a sixth, $300 on a valuation of $27,944; a seventh, $150 on a valuation of $11,052; an eighth, $100 on a valuation of $32,154; and so on over the county. Centralization of schools will equalize the cost of education.

3. By centralization all the children of the township have the same chance for higher educational advantages, which un-

der the present plan only five or ten percent are able to get by leaving home and going to the city. With a central graded school and a high school course the children can be at home evenings under the care of their parents. The people of the country districts are entitled to receive the fullest benefits for money expended. Better means of education, better training, stronger characters; the possibility of all these must appeal to every parent and to every public spirited citizen of any community. The course of study may be so enriched that all the farmer boys may be taught some of the fundamental principles of agriculture, horticulture, etc., without sending them away to a university to learn what may be learned at home. Such a township high school, with good teachers, ought to be able to teach the boys and girls something about formation, composition and care of the soil; feeding standards and selection of animals for the dairy; rotation of crops; constituents of plants, and fruit growing. The State Farmers' Institute of Illinois has asked that the country school do something along this line. In obedience to their request, an elementary course in agriculture has been added to the state course of study for the common schools of Illinois. The farmers of Illinois are doing well in having a college of agriculture built up in connection with our State University at Champaign. But don't stop there. Let the influence of that work extend to every township in the way of an enriched course of study in the township union graded school and one result will be that more boys and girls will go to the university. The poor man who has been able to send his children only to ungraded district schools, will have the pleasure of seeing his children given the best education the township can afford, and that at a *less per capita cost* to his rich neighbor than heretofore.

4. By centralization the health of the children is guarded. With transportation to a central school there are no wet feet and clothing and consequent sickness and impaired constitutions. Regularity and promptness of attendance are secured.

These things do affect the character of children. The average daily attendance is so increased that as a result from 25 to 35 per cent more schooling is secured in a township at a *decrease in the cost per capita.*

5. By centralization we go a long ways toward the solution of the problem, "How to Keep the Boys on the Farm." We bring to the farm that which he goes to the city and town to secure. Such a school may become the social and intellectual center of the community life. With a library room, music, debating club, etc., our boys and girls will hesitate to leave home and such a school for the uncertainties of city life.

And the centralization of country schools has a most vital relation to the cities. It is just as important that there be good schools surrounding Rockford (or any other city) as it is that there be good crops or good roads. I can do no better than quote an excellent editorial from the Rockford *Register-Gazette* of December 1, 1900, entitled "A New Day for Rural Schools":

"The city as well as the country is interested in the new question of the consolidation of the country schools and the promotion of their efficiency as brought about by that policy. The changes brought about by the rural free delivery and the rural electric lines are radical, but they are not so important as this advance in the character of the schooling offered to a larger part of the rural children.

"The interests of the larger centers in this small revolution is self-evident. The city draws about half of its best men from the country and is dependent on the country for their healthful constitution, their character and a good start, including schooling. How many a young man has felt the handicap of having his boyhood fortunes cast where a small school, an unfit or indifferent teacher and the lack of rivalry or emulation failed to arouse his interest and threw away his one opportunity. The merging of half a dozen or more inefficient country schools in one good one, with large attendance, inviting school-house and well systematized and graded work, is a complete remedy for this drawback, in so far as good schooling can remedy it, and both city and country will profit by the results.

"The photographs obtained by Superintendent Kern of the school accommodations under the new order of things in Ohio, and of the vans which convey the children to and from their homes, are a demonstration to the eye which scarcely needs further argument. The system has made such progress in Massachusetts that it is now taken for granted. Illinois cannot afford to be behind in such a procession or to let time and opportunity run to waste. Let the young people and the children take it up, as well as the older members of the community, and hurry the matter forward. The legislature has something to do in the premises. It were well if no time were permitted to lapse in that duty, too."

Now if Ohio, Indiana, Iowa, Kansas, Massachusetts and New Jersey can centralize and transport pupils, why not Illinois? If it be important that the country boys and girls of those states be given the benefit of higher educational facilities, why not the youth of this state have the same opportunities? Justly have we prided ourselves in the past on the district school. Changing conditions of life, the demands of a higher civilization demand the evolution of the district school, the people's college to the township graded school, the people's university. Such an evolution must come. The spirit of the twentieth century, the inspiration of grander, nobler things in national thought and character, urge us to make the most of our opportunities. There is not the faintest desire on my part to force this system upon the people. I have not the power and would not exercise it if I had. There must be further legislation on the subject in the state before any township can centralize, providing the people are a

Stables connected with the central high school in Bethel Township, Miami County, Ohio.

The township furnishes the stable and the children transport themselves. This is possible where horses are plentiful and not in constant use.

unit in favor of the change. My duty is to find better methods, to inform you of them, yours to adopt or reject. I hope to confer with you in your school-houses about this subject during the coming months. The twentieth century problem in education is the evolution of the country schools (with all the possibilities in the way of the enrichment of country life), the better training of country youth, the hope, the salvation of American democracy.

Rockford, Illinois, December, 1900.

IV.—THE SCHOOLS OF GUSTAVUS TOWNSHIP

C. G. Williams

Member of the Board of Trustees of the Consolidated School, in "The Ohio Teacher" for September, 1902.

Gustavus is a typically rural township of the Western Reserve, covering twenty-five square miles, with a little hamlet composed of eighteen dwelling-houses, two churches, town hall, school building, one store, and finally a blacksmith shop at the center, and some eight hundred population scattered promiscuously over the township, with a school enumeration of about two hundred and forty.

DECREASE IN POPULATION.

In common with many rural communities, there has been a falling off in population in recent years. In fact there are fewer people living in our township to-day than there were sixty years ago. No manufacturing, and nothing save agricultural and live stock interests. Less population and fewer children in our schools. The time came when it seemed impolitic to maintain our usual number of sub-district schools. Up to August, 1898, we had maintained nine sub-district schools as conveniently located as possible, with a free high school at the center of the township, which any pupil was at liberty to attend when he could pass the required examination. Some few of these sub-district schools were attended by twenty to twenty-five pupils; others had an attendance of five to ten, and one school was kept up for several months for only two pupils. Since the above date we have been accommodating our school population in a five-room building located near the center of our township, to and from which every pupil living more than one-half mile from the center is conveyed at public expense.

NINE COVERED WAGONS,

Built expressly for this purpose with a view to comfort and health of occupants and owned by the route contractors, call at the home of every pupil in the morning, and return every pupil to his home after school. Our routes vary in length from two and one-half to five miles, and cost us from 68 cents to $1.55 per day. These routes are let to the lowest responsible and satisfactory bidder. In the letting of routes the moral character of contractor is taken into consideration, and he is put under strict bond, not only to do the work, but is held responsible under the Superintendent of Schools for both the comfort and the moral condition and order in his wagon in transit.

CHEAP TRANSPORTATION.

To many people the price at which we are able to let our routes is a matter of surprise. It should be remembered that during the greater part of the year both trips can be made in four hours or less, and that during the balance of the year when more time is required, our contractors (usually farmers with few acres who have to keep a team of horses anyhow) are not very busy upon their farms. We have never yet had any trouble in letting our routes, and of late we have not had enough routes to supply all who would like them.

PROVIDING FOR EMERGENCIES.

Before this system was put into operation some prospective patrons worried a little as to what might happen should a child be taken ill at school, in some instances a long way from home. Our Board of Education has thought best to provide against that trouble by contracting with a man to take any pupil immediately to his home that the Superintendent thinks should for any reason go home. We have not as yet had to expend over $3 any year for this purpose. It surely is a comfort to a parent to know his child will be brought home if occasion demands it.

Speaking of opposition, it should be recorded that when the proposition came before our voters for indorsement four years ago at our annual spring election, it was defeated upon a tie vote. Three

The Consolidation of School Districts

weeks thereafter the same, or a very similar proposition, was submitted to our voters, and, with practically every vote in our township cast, centralization carried by a majority of only seventeen votes. It will be seen that public sentiment was pretty evenly divided and that the new system and the new school would have very many critics.

THE REAL TEST.

It is a fair question to ask, how have these opponents been pleased? Perhaps as good evidence as I can bring to the readers of *The Ohio Teacher,* is the result of an investigation and canvass of our township made by a visiting committee from another county of the State in their efforts to determine how the new system was working. This visiting committee was composed of two members, one of whom was sent here as an opponent, the other as a friend of centralization. Their canvass was made after our school had been in operation two years. This committee spent several days in our community visiting not only the school but many of the parents of the pupils at their homes, and particularly those people who resided farthest from the school. Their report to their own Board of Education (afterward published) shows seven out of fifty-four people interviewed to be yet opposed to centralization. But of the seven opposed to the system *six* were without children in attendance upon school. This was two years ago. I think public sentiment is even more in favor of the "new way" now than then.

CENTRALIZATION IS HERE TO STAY.

As further evidence that centralization is here to stay attention should be called to the fact that while Gustavus was the first township in this county to adopt this system, since we have adopted it every township adjoining us have adopted it, and at the present time has in operation similar schools. Those who are nearest us seem to be most favorably impressed with its benefits.

As to the comparative expense of our public schools conducted in the old and new way: The last year in which worked under the old system our exper were as follows: Teachers, $2,400; ot expenses, $555; total, $2,955.

Under the new system, for the y ending August, 1901: Teachers, $1,3 hauling pupils, $1,755; other expen $200; total, $3,275.

Deduct from this $75 received f foreign tuition (not received un old system) and we have an e expense of $245 for the well supervi and graded central school as compa with the "hit-or-miss" sub-district v For the year ending August, 1902, we ployed an extra teacher at an expense $240 more. With a larger daily atte ance under centralization the per ca expense is about the same. Our tax property is in the neighborhood of $3 000, and our tax rate for school purpo 9 or 10 mills on the dollar.

ADVANTAGES OF GRADED SCHOOLS

I need hardly take any of your spac considering the advantages of a g graded school as compared with the a age sub-district school. Under a com tent superintendent, with large num and consequently greater interest and thusiasm, with better teachers, more isfactory apparatus, more regular atte ance, and absolutely no tardiness, it without saying that we have a school yond all comparison with our former district school. It costs a little m money in our case, but we are get more than value received for it, and w this is true the tax payer who has the terest of the public at heart is satisfied

OUR COURSE OF STUDY

Is likely very similar to the ordinary lage special district school, with the sible exception that we have more w along the line of nature study than is ally given. This is true of all grades

Among the advantages not alre mentioned I should not fail to include fact that we are able to keep the o boys in school longer. Under the old tem most of them dropped out be reaching the high school. There is no now to bridge over—no changing from an isolated sub-district school to a high school elsewhere.

A PRACTICAL SOLUTION.

The following editorial appeared in the following number of the same journal:

It must not be forgotten that centralization of small rural schools is a *practical* solution of the problem. Small schools cannot have the vitalizing force that comes from larger numbers. The environment and associations necessary to the most desirable results cannot come from a small school, especially if this small school is taught by an inexperienced, poorly trained and poorly paid teacher, as is likely to be the case. It must not be forgotten that children who are transported in comfortable covered wagons are not exposed to the inclemency of the weather. Their clothing will be better cared for, and their general health will be improved. Tardiness and absence would be almost unknown. Parents would become more deeply interested in their schools. Pupils would take a deeper interest in their work, because of the added rivalry. Better school buildings, better sanitary conditions, better equipment, and better teachers would be a few of the inevitable results. It must not be forgotten, also, that wherever there was decided opposition to the plan at the start, the successful operation of the system almost always wins unanimous approval. The plan was first tried in Ohio, but it is now spreading into several other states. The Michigan State Grange recently sent Hon. A. E. Palmer into Ohio to investigate the claims of centralization. He came as an opponent of the idea, but returned as a convert and advocate.

* * *

V.—WHAT MASSACHUSETTS IS DOING IN THE MATTER OF CONSOLIDATION AND TRANSPORTATION

G. T. Fletcher.

The following is taken from a report by Mr. G. T. Fletcher, Agent of the Massachusetts Board of Education, and gives in detail the status of the work in that state:

DISTRICT SCHOOLS FIFTY YEARS AGO.

The question of the consolidation of schools has for many years received the attention of educators. Conditions pertaining to changes in the population and the wealth of communities as well as the increasing educational demands of the times have rendered necessary a certain centralization of forces for economy and efficiency in school work. Fifty years ago a large percentage of the people of Massachusetts belonged to the "original stock," and lived in country towns. District schools were numerous and large. Seldom did a school register less than twenty-five pupils; not infrequently seventy-five were enrolled during the winter term, ranging in age from four years to twenty-one. An attendance of forty or fifty pupils was a common occurrence. Many of the schools were taught in winter by college students—often the brightest young men from the rural communities, whose example was a stimulus to the boys of the district to get an education. In the summer the teacher was often a young woman from the country, whose scholarship and character were an inspiration to the children. The district school was a center of interest and influence in the rural community. The range of studies was narrow, but the few branches then taught are regarded to-day as fundamental in a broader system of education. The independent thinking and the individual doing of pupils, whose age gave maturity to mind, were educating. The school was a "consolidation" of numbers and ability sufficient for the educational needs of the times. Similar conditions exist in a few country towns now, and such schools may well be nurtured by town and state in the place of their native growth. A home life of frugality, simplicity and industry is a potent factor in the upbuilding of body and mind. But there were many poor schools then, as there are now.

CHANGES THAT HAVE COME TO THE DISTRICT SCHOOLS.

Within the last fifty years great changes have been wrought in social life and conditions. The increase of population and wealth in centers of commerce and manufacturing is both a cause and a result of an exodus of the farming population to the cities and large towns.

In many rural communities farms were abandoned, or only the "old folks" left at home, to pass there the remnant of their days, while the farm constantly depreciated in value. The young, vigorous element of the population left home to work in store or factory. Families remaining in the "hill towns," or coming to them, had few children; and, as a result, the schools became small, the local interest in them often decreasing in the same ratio. These changes came in different degrees of severity to different towns. Those most favorably situated for farming purposes "held their own," to quite an extent, in adult population and wealth, but the number of children constantly lessened, and the schools, though not generally reduced in number, were reduced greatly in attendance. Occasionally schools were united, to increase the number of pupils, or a winter term was held at the center of the town for the older pupils of all the districts. Just when and where consolidation on a small scale began we can not tell. The cause and the fact of a beginning are both evident. There came to the people, slowly at first, a realization that the interest, economy and efficiency that had in many cases characterized the large schools of former days were wanting. The struggle to retain the same number of schools as when the adult population was greater, the property valuation was twice as large and the town had three times as many children of school age, was as painfully evident then as it is now. The school had been the common center of interest, and the thought of its closing was a shock to the people. No wonder a deep-seated feeling existed, and still continues, that home interest and property valuation would suffer from the discontinuance of the local schcools.

People are now coming to see that educational advantages are not represented by the number of near-by schoolhouses. From one of the annual reports of Dr. Harris, U. S. Commissioner of Education, we quote as follows:

"It has been frequently demonstrated and is generally conceded that it would be better both on economical and on pedagogical grounds to unite the many small and weak schools of a township, dispersed over a large extent of territory, into a few strong, well-equipped and well-conducted graded schools, located at convenient points."

MR. EATONS' STATEMENT.

The first general statement in print of the results of the law of 1869 was probably the pamphlet prepared by Superintendent of Schools W. L. Eaton, of Concord, in 1893, for the Massachusetts public school exhibit at the World's Columbian Exposition. As the combination of schools in Concord was probably more complete than in any other town in the state, the selection of Superintendent Eaton to prepare the pamphlet was highly appropriate. Mr. Eaton says, in part:

"At first the authority was used mainly to convey pupils to the high school. Within a few years, however, many communities have used this authority to increase the educational advantages of the children, constantly decreasing in numbers, who live in districts at a distance from the center of population. This has been accomplished by closing many district schools and transporting, at public expense, their pupils to the neighboring district schools or to the village."

Superintendent Eaton sent circulars of inquiry to 165 towns and cities, and received replies from 135. These replies indicated a gradually increasing number of schools as closed yearly. The reasons for closing say:

"In many of the towns of the state depopulation of the districts outside of the villages has made it cheaper to transport to other schools than to teach them in situ. * * * In other towns the desire to make strong central schools, and the purpose to give all of the children of the town the benefit of better appliances, better teachers and better supervision have been the dominant motives to determine consolidation. * * * There is a substantial agreement in the affirmative that results have been satisfactory."

CONSOLIDATION AS SEEN BY THE STATE BOARD OF EDUCATION.

In the report of Agent G. A. Walton to the State Board of Education, in 1889, consolidation of schools is recommended. In more recent reports of the board many facts and opinions, based upon observation and upon information received by the secretary and agents, may be found. Some of the reasons advanced by them for the consolidation of schools and the conveyance of children may be briefly stated in abridged form, as follows:

Diminished school population, rendering the schools small and expensive, making it difficult to secure competent teachers for the wages that can be paid.

The cost in some small schools of five pupils was $50 per pupil, while in schools of twenty-five pupils the cost was only $10 per capita.

Two essential things must be kept in view—efficiency and economy. To secure these, there must be comfortable, convenient schoolhouses, necessary appliances, intelligent teaching, skilled supervision, and no more schools than are needed for the number of pupils.

In some towns two or more schools may be united, according to convenience of location. In others, most of the outlying schools can be accommodated at the center by transportation of pupils.

In a few towns of large area, bad roads and scattered population, little or no combination can be effected. In such cases the schools, small or large, must have such attention by the town, and, if necessary, such aid by state, as will make them as good as possible.

One of the results that follow from consolidation is a better grading, a better classification of pupils, by placing them where they can work to the best advantage. Consolidation gives a better opportunity for special instruction in music, drawing and nature study, and brings all the schools under closer oversight by the superintendent.

It insures better school buildings, appliances and teaching force.

The money saved in a small town by reducing the number of teachers is often large enough to furnish better school accommodations to the children, better wages to better teachers, such transportation as consolidation requires, and longer schooling.

OBJECTIONS TO CONSOLIDATION.

It must not be supposed that policies of consolidation are adopted without earnest discussion. In some cases the opposition has been so strong as to stave off favorable action for years. Among the reasons urged against consolidation the following may be cited:

Injury to the district, by removal of the school.

Risk to the health of children, because of long rides in cold and in stormy weather.

Association in carriages and during the long noon intermission at the schoolhouse.

Injury to health by cold dinners hastily eaten.

Long absence of young children from home.

It may be questioned whether the objection regarding injury to the property valuation of the district is a serious one. People having children to educate are not slow to see that educational advantages are not represented in their fulness and completeness by near schoolhouses. This property objection is well met in the replies to questions submitted to the towns, to which later reference will be made.

The objections to the risks of conveyance and of the noon intermission are of serious import, and can be met only by making transportation safe to health, manners and morals, as well as comfortable, and by requiring the presence of a teacher at the noon intermission.

PROGRESS OF CONSOLIDATION.

The progress of consolidation in Massachusetts through transportation is indicated by the tabulation of expenses, beginning with the first year in which such expenses were reported:

AGGREGATE COST OF CONVEYANCE FOR THE STATE.

Year.	Amount Expended	Year.	Amount Expended
1888-89..	$22,118 38	1895-96..	$91,136 11
1889-90..	24,145 12	1896-97..	105,317 13
1890-91..	30,648 68	1897-98..	123,032 41
1891-92..	38,726 07	1898-99..	127,402 22
1892-93..	50,590 41	1899-00..	141,753 84
1893-94..	63,617 68	1900-01.	151,773 47
1894-95..	76,608 29		

The expenditure in 1900-01 ranged from $6.25 in the town of Hatfield to $2,640.75 in the town of Lexington. The Massachusetts Legislature has never made any requirement about the limit of distance beyond which children should be conveyed to school at public expense except in a single instance. Chapter 541, Acts of 1898, provides that the town of Boxford may use the Barker Free School as a high school upon complying with certain conditions, one of which is that the town shall furnish free transportation to the school for pupils who live more than two miles away from it.

CURCULARS OF INQUIRY.

To secure as complete information as possible regarding the history, progress, means and results of consolidation of schools and conveyance of children in Massachusetts, circulars containing inquiries regarding the different phases of the plan were sent to the school officials of all the cities and towns of the state. Nearly 200 replies have been received, representing conditions and practices in all sections of the commonwealth, from the largest cities to the smallest towns.

When their gist is contained in a few similar words or sentences, these replies are given only in percentages, or in a general way. Special facts, opinions and suggestions are quoted as fully as space will allow. As the circular calls for information upon more than twenty different phases of the subject, it is not possible, in the space allowed in this report, to name the towns responding. The returned circulars are on file at the office of the secretary of the State Board of Education in Boston.

The circular of inquiry began with the following letter:

Northampton (Mass.), Dec. —, 1898.

To the Chairman of the School Committee or the Superintendent of Schools of ———:

Many inquiries come to the State Board of Education, not only from our own towns and cities but from those of other states, regarding the need, operation and results of plans for the consolidation of schools and the conveyance of children that naturally accompanies such plans. That such inquiries may be answered fully and intelligently, your co-operation is earnestly desired. Will you favor me, therefore, with such information about your own town's (city's) experience with consolidation and conveyance as is called for under the heads herewith given? Please forward your reply as soon as possible to

G. T. FLETCHER,
Agent of the State Board of Education.

The inquiries are given in full, as follows, the answers to each inquiry being given in immediate connection with it, and with various degrees of abridgment:

I. GENERAL CONDITIONS FAVORING OR REQUIRING CONSOLIDATION.

Changes in population, property valuation, etc., that have impaired the efficiency of your schools by reducing their size, increasing their cost, making it harder to get good teachers, etc.—

More than 50 per cent of the towns report changes in population and property valuation in the towns as a whole, or in sections of them, that have affected the school conditions.

The following statements are samples of those coming from a large number of rural towns:

Attendance of pupils reduced; cost in a small school per pupil for a year, $46.82; in the central building, $16.30.

Difficult to retain good teachers.

Population diminished more than a half and property valuation more than a third since 1875.

Loss in population and property valuation makes it hard for us to meet increasing educational demands.

Good teachers command better wages than we can pay.

In one district that formerly had 60 to 80 pupils there are now 13. The farming population has disappeared.

Farming population once over 1,100; now only 605. Valuation reduced from $375,000 to $309,000.

Population reduced from 2,300 to 1,400 in thirty years; loss of $70,000 in valuation in five years.

Farms abandoned; not enough children in any district to keep a school.

In many towns the loss in population and wealth is only in sections, usually in outlying districts, and so affects certain schools only. Many towns have gained in the villages as much as they have lost in the rural sections. Some towns and all of the cities have gained in population and wealth; yet most of them in some quarters have had to deal with diminishing schools.

II. WHAT THE TOWN HAS DONE TOWARDS CONSOLIDATING ITS SCHOOLS.

The number of schools that have been closed, whether the consolidation is partial or universal, whether it has gone on gradually or was brought about at one stroke, whether any children are sent to schools in adjoining towns or not, whether higher grades are taken to the high school building or not, etc.—

More than 65 per cent of the towns and cities reporting have found it necessary or advantageous to close and consolidate some schools. Movements of population within town or city limits as well as the exodus of people from many towns have led to the closing of schools, but have not always involved the transportation of pupils.

Probably Quincy was the first town to act under the law of 1869, having closed two schools in 1874 and transported the children to other schools.

In the year 1893 Seymour Rockwell, the veteran school committeeman of Montague, said:

"For eighteen years we have had the best attendance from the transported children; no more sickness among them, and no accidents. The children like the plan exceedingly. We have saved the town at least $600 a year. All these children now attend a well-equipped schoolhouse at the center. The schools are graded; everybody is converted to the plan. We encountered all the opposition found anywhere, but we asserted our sensible and legal rights, and accomplished the work. I see no way of bringing the country schools up but to consolidate them, making them worth seeing; then the people will be more likely to do their duty by visiting them."

This statement indicates that consolidation of schools was heroically completed in Montague in 1875.

Prior to that time and for many years afterward there was a rapid diminution of school population in the outlying districts. Of late the school population of these districts has increased. We attribute this to the willingness of young married people to settle on these farms, since transportation secures to their children educational opportunities as good as the town provides. Consolidation begun as an experiment, was carried to completion, at the desire of the population affected.

From another town came this suggestive statement:

Once when a man wished to sell his farm he advertised, "A school near." Now he advertises, "Children conveyed to good schools." Farms sell more readily now.

Other towns report as follows:

We have closed only one school, and that for two terms during the year, as the lot will revert to the former donor unless a school is kept in the building.

The scattered population renders consolidation undesirable in our town.

Planned at one time to close a school, owing to smallness of numbers, and convey the pupils to the next village. After consideration, decided that only an unwise parsimony on the part of the town could favor the project, and it was abandoned forever.

A few years ago the town tried to "double up" the schools, and convey the pupils, but the people would not listen to the suggestion, mainly through ignorance.

Attempted to build a new schoolhouse and grade the schools, but bitter opposition upon the part of the older people defeated the plan.

We believe in closing the schools when it can be done.

Our rule is to keep a school as long as there are ten pupils in it.

From one to ten schools have been closed in different towns. Consolidation is generally partial; in a few towns, complete. Most frequently it has been accomplished gradually; in some instances, at "one stroke." In twenty-five instances pupils belonging to higher grades are taken to the high school building.

III. Appropriations for Conveyance

Whether the town raises money for the purpose by a specific appropriation separate from the regular school appropriation or by making the regular school appropriation include transportation—

About 60 per cent of the towns reply, "By a specific appropriation, separate from the regular school appropriation." It seems evident that the law requiring towns to raise money for school purposes should include in the amount so raised whatever sum may be needed for transportation.

IV. Distances.

(1) The conveyance of children—whether they are conveyed all the way to school or only a part of it, whether the carriage goes to the house in every case, or some pupils have to meet it at designated points, etc.—

More than 50 per cent of the towns report that they "convey all the way from the home to the school." Other towns say that, unless the conveyance, carriage or car passes their homes, the children walk to the main street, or to designated points, or to the closed schoolhouse, or to the streets through which the electric cars run, etc. In a few towns the carriage goes to every home in stormy weather, to take and leave the children. In some towns conveyance is furnished only in winter or in stormy weather. In some cases children are conveyed to school, but not from it unless the weather is stormy or the traveling bad.

(2) The distances children are conveyed —whether any are fixed absolutely or approximately, what they are and what conditions determine them, etc.—

Those who interpret this question to mean the distance within which children will not be transported to school at public expense make the distance from one mile to two miles. In one town small children will in some cases be conveyed to school if the distance from home is less than a mile. There seems to be no consensus of opinion regarding what is a "reasonable walking distance." Age, sex and strength of pupils, nature of the road, the amount of money appropriated and the disposition of the committee seem to be determining factors. It is the one difficult question which committees must settle for themselves, making such judicious provisions as will insure school attendance for all without undue hardship to any.

The majority of committees and superintendents understand the question to refer to the maximum distance of conveyance, and reply that they convey pupils "all the way from home to school," or "from the closed schoolhouse to the new one," or two, four, six or eight miles, as the case may be.

(3) Questions of conveyance and distances — whether in deciding them young children are considered more than older ones, girls more than boys, the lower school more than the high school, wooded, lonely or difficult routes more than open, easy and populous ones, etc.—

Approximately, 45 per cent of the towns report that they give equal consideration to young children of both sexes.

Ten per cent report that they give a preference to girls in their plans.

In 12 per cent of the responses the character of the routes was mentioned as an important factor in determining plans.

Thirty-two per cent make no discrimination as to children, schools or routes.

V. PAYMENTS FOR CONVEYANCE.

Whether payments for conveyance service are made to the parents of the pupils or to persons hired for the purpose, whether they are made by the trip, the week, the term or the year, with or without reference to the precise number carried, or in accordance with a fixed charge per pupil or a fixed rate per mile or some other system, with one or two illustrations of the amounts paid or rates fixed for definite services—

Payments are sometimes made to parents for the actual attendance of their children—so much per day a child, the teacher keeping a record. It is noticed in such cases that the attendance is very regular, and that the children are able to walk most of the time. Payments are most frequently made to persons hired for the purpose, or in some towns and cities to steam and electric railroad companies. Illustrations:

One parent was paid 50 cents a trip for conveying his children three miles.

A parent carries his children for $10 a term.

A parent transports his children two miles for $15 a year.

The foregoing may be cases in each of which the father takes his children to school as he goes to his work.

Some parents carry the children of several neighbors with their own for a moderate sum.

Five cents a day for each pupil attending school.

Many pupils ride on electric cars at half fare, tickets being furnished by the school committee to be distributed by the teachers.

Carriages hired by the week: $9 for transporting twelve children two miles; $4 for transporting four children one and three-fourths miles.

Some make yearly payments as follows to persons hired for the purpose:

Seven pupils, three miles, for $75; twenty-nine pupils, one and one-half miles, for $80; eleven pupils, two and one-half miles, for $85; seven pupils, two miles, for $70.

Six hundred dollars a year, without regard to the number of pupils.

One school, one year, $175; another school, one year, $195.

Two hundred dollars and $300 a year, without regard to number.

By the week for a certain number of pupils, one route, $2.10; another and shorter route, $1.30.

One route, $5 a week; on a bad road, two children, $6.25 a week.

VI. DETAILS OF TRANSPORTATION.

Persons who are charged with the duty of bargaining for and settling the details of transportation; the vehicles selected whether covered or otherwise made comfortable; the drivers—whether selected with reference to their trustworthiness and fitness to care for children, etc.—

In 43 per cent of the towns the school committee makes bargains and settles details; in 10 per cent a sub-committee of the school committee; in 5 per cent, chairman of school committee; in 12 per cent, the superintendent of schools; in 4 per cent of the towns arrangements are made by the committee and the superintendent. In about half of the towns vehicles are covered and comfortable; in the others, not covered excepting in bad weather.

Nearly all of the drivers are reported to be "trustworthy." Some are said to be "as good as we can get." Some are of "doubtful qualifications." All committees and superintendents regard trustworthiness and fitness in the driver of the highest importance. One committee says:

"Only such persons should be employed as we would trust with the care of our own children."

A few committees say that they have to watch drivers of conveyances, and hold them to strict account. Some complain that children are not under proper control in the carriages; but, upon the whole, there seems to be a good degree of satisfaction with such vehicles and drivers as have been employed.

VII. ADVANTAGES OR DISADVANTAGES OF CONVEYING CHILDREN.

(1) Effect, if any, on promoting attendance—

The testimony upon this point is nearly unanimous that attendance is improved by conveyance of pupils. Some speak of the increase as very decided; a few say, "No effect."

(2) Effect, if any, on health of children conveyed—

A majority see "no effect upon health." A large number say, "Effect good," and add that there is less exposure to rain, snow, cold weather, sloppy or muddy traveling; consequently, fewer colds. A few speak of the unfavorable effect of cold dinners, hastily eaten. A few others say, "Not healthy." Much depends upon the vehicle and the driver.

(3) Any trend toward needlessly short distances for conveyance or toward reduced self-reliance and sturdiness on the part of the children conveyed?—

The larger number of replies are to the effect that no such trend is noticeable, but about three-fourths as many replies are to the contrary effect. Comments:

Depends upon the firmness of the school committee.

We have a rule, and when parents and children know what it is, nothing more is said.

We meet all reasonable demands, then stand firm.

Pupils have so much done for them that they are not willing to do anything for themselves.

(4) Effects as regards (a) the character of the school buildings and equipment, (b) the classification or grading of pupils, (c) the quality of the teachers and their work, (d) the efficiency of the pupils, and (e) the general spirit of the school—

The larger number of towns report under (a) an improvement in the character of the school buildings and equipment resulting from consolidation. Some say, "No effect yet." Under the remaining subdivisions of (4) there is a very marked accord that in all respects improvement is very evident.

A few comments:

Better ventilated rooms; hence more healthful.

Costs less for repairs; better janitor service.

Houses closed were in poor repair; good teachers would not remain in them.

Pupils better classified; three teachers do the work of five in ungraded school.

Too strict grading not beneficial.

Petty local jealousies lost in the larger school.

I question if the too-closely graded school of 50 pupils reciting in one division is not inferior, from the pupils' standpoint, to the ungraded school of 20 pupils. Advantages of the ungraded school lies in the greater freedom of the individual pupil to advance at a rate best suited to him.

Pupils are more studious in the graded schools with only their classmates with whom they must compete.

Greater incentive and enthusiasm.

In the graded schools pupils lose the

personal oversight of the teacher which in small schools is of so great advantage.

(5) Any further results, good or bad, to be expected from the extension of the consolidation policy?—

None but good.

Pupils become better acquainted with people; hence less bashful and awkward.

The time lost by the superintendent on the road is saved by consolidation of schools.

It becomes possible to give all the pupils of the town the advantages of special teachers in drawing, music, etc.

Real estate men think it will reduce the value of their property in the rural districts.

Objection to having small children so long from home.

Our people would as soon think of havin district churches as district schools.

Association with others whose lives are less restricted than their own is a gain in social graces.

Much is to be expected in moral influences, as conditions are better in the graded than in the ungraded schools. This is especially true as regards outbuildings or basements in their sanitary arrangements, and the oversight had in and about them.

Economy and efficiency.

I do not favor too great efforts to consolidate. Drivers are not and can not be expected to be men who control children and hold their respect.

A compact neighborhood with a good school should be let alone.

(6) The cost of the schools after consolidation — whether less or greater than before or the same, and whether with poorer, equal or better results—

Sixty per cent of the towns report the cost as less, but the results as better; 15 per cent, cost the same, but results better; 8 per cent, cost more, but results better; 8 per cent, cost more, but results not stated; 8 per cent, cost less, but results not stated.

Duval County, Florida, in transporting 176 pupils at $303 per month, having closed fourteen schools. They began with two schools two years ago, and the plan has been very popular. Extra teachers hired cost $145, making a total cost of $448, for what had before cost $490 per month, thus saving $42 per month. Schools of three teachers and eight-year grades were formed. They are planning now to reduce forty-five schools to fifteen. The superintendent says: "We furnish wagonettes carrying 8, 12 and 16 passengers, so there is no difficulty in getting farmers to furnish teams and harness; this is an improvement over other ways."

(7) The public attitude toward the policy —whether one of approval or not—

Reports of approval, in some cases of modified approval, are related to cases of strong opposition about as 70 per cent to 30 per cent. Comments:

At first opposed; later approved.

Those favored by the plan approve it; those not, oppose it.

Sanctioned when committee advocated it.

Opposed to extension of policy.

No "public attitude" here.

The policy is never questioned.

Opposed.

Toleration.

VIII. CONSOLIDATION NOT DESIRABLE OR FEASIBLE.

(1) Any large rural schools—schools of twenty-five to forty pupils—that probably would not be helped by processes of consolidation?—

More than half the replies indicate that there are rural schools that would not be helped by consolidation. Several towns report having one or more rural schools with an attendance of 20 to 40 pupils. Some special replies:

Distance and size render transportation difficult and expensive.

Retain such schools if good teachers can be secured.

Would not consolidate a school of over 20 pupils.

One school six miles from the center.

We have a large rural school of 50 pupils with two teachers.

I would prefer that a child of mine should be educated, up to the high-school grade, in a school of 30 pupils under a superior teacher rather than in the ordinary graded school with the average classroom instruction. I think there is a tendency to grade too much. In a well-organized and conducted ungraded school there is an unconscious review all the time and an anticipation of what is to come. The whole is there and the part in relation to the whole.

A good district school, with 25 pupils and an efficient teacher, can be made equal to any closely graded school, and better than most of them.

Consolidation has disadvantages as well as advantages.

Thirty towns report that consolidation would help all of their ungraded schools; it would provide better houses, appliances, teachers and superintendence at equal or less expense.

(2) Conditions that largely or wholly forbid consolidation—

About fifty towns mention objections of various degrees of seriousness that have been urged against consolidation:

Too long distances; bad roads, blocked in winter for weeks.

Pupils too young to ride long distances.

Lack of money to pay the expense of suitable transportation.

Strong opposition of the people to the machine-like system of conveyance of pupils.

Saloon at the center; can not have a schoolhouse near.

Invasion of individual rights.

Belief of farmers that closing rural schools reduces the value of their property.

IX. IN OTHER STATES.

From the reports received by Prof. N. A. Upham and published in a bulletin by State Superintendent L. D. Harvey, of Wisconsin, it appears that eighteen states have a law allowing the transportation of pupils at public expense, and thirteen are availing themselves of the privilege. The following is the list:

Connecticut,	Wisconsin.
Florida,	Vermont,
Indiana,	South Dakota,
Iowa,	Rhode Island,
Kansas,	Pennsylvania,
Maine,	Ohio,
Massachusetts,	North Dakota,
Nebraska,	New York,
New Hampshire,	New Jersey,

These states have nearly half the population of the United States.

* * *

VI.—CONSOLIDATION AND TRANSPORTATION IN CONNECTICUT

C. D. Hine.

From the Report of C. D. Hine, Secretary of the State Board of Education of Connecticut, for 1900.

In the year 1893 the following act was passed:

"Whenever any school shall be discontinued . . . the school visitors may provide transportation for children to and from school.

"The expenses of transportation, when approved by the board of visitors, shall be paid by the town treasurer, upon the order of the selectmen."

This act authorizes school visitors and town school committees to expend money for the conveyance of children to and from the public schools.

Within the seven years since the passage of the act about sixty towns have used the authority conferred by the act to increase the educational advantages of their children. This has been accomplished by uniting schools and transporting the children to the nearest schoolhouses.

The following summaries are of interest:

1. The number of schools closed was 85.

2. The number of scholars conveyed was 773.

3. The expense was $10,752.38.

In reply to the question whether the plan was satisfactory to parents the table shows:

Not replying directly, 13.
Satisfactory, 21.
Satisfactory "to most" or "generally," 12.
Not satisfactory, 3.

In reply to inquiry whether beneficial to schools the table shows:

Not replying directly, 15.
Beneficial, 33.
Not beneficial, 1.

The financial arrangements include:
Payments to parents by town dependent upon distance or attendance.
Payment of carfare by town.
Town hires horse and carriage by day.
Town owns vehicle and hires driver.
Town contracts with individuals by day or year.

The following table exhibits comparatively the facts of the two years reported:

TABLE LXXX.

Year	Number Towns	Number Schools Closed	Number Children Carried	Expense
1897-8	44	84	849	$11,416.25
1898-9	49	85	773	10,752.38

There are two distinct purposes in closing schools and transporting children—the financial and the educational.

1. It is cheaper to transport children than to maintain very small schools.
2. The desire to make strong schools with better teachers, more apparatus and good libraries, and some supervision has been added to the economical view.

There is substantial agreement that the result, financially and educationally, has been satisfactory. The most emphatic expressions of approval come from those who were influenced mainly by the educational motive.

An experiment was tried, in a small way, during the winter, in the transportation of children to and from school. A special car made a morning and afternoon trip to convey pupils living at Shippan and attending at William Street school. In my judgment the experiment was successful. I believe, as I said in a former report, that it would be to the advantage of the town, pecuniarily, and very greatly to the advantage of the children affected, could several of our ungraded schools be consolidated and the pupils (residing in districts where school is discontinued) conveyed to a centrally located school which, under conditions that would then prevail, should be developed as a graded or semi-graded school. I would recommend that a special committee be appointed to make a study of this plan as worked out in Massachusetts.—Stamford, E. C. Willard, Supt.

A feature which added to the size and interest of several schools was the transportation of children to them from the sparingly-populated sections, which, although quite unpopular at first, became more agreeable and grew in favor as the necessity for such action and the benefits accruing therefrom were apparent.

People who reside in the outlying districts, where children are not as numerous as in the years gone by, should bear in mind that it is hardly fair to expect the town to support a school for four or five scholars. The majority cannot be expected to submit to the minority, when it becomes largely a financial matter.—Griswold, John Potter, Acting Visitor.

Some of the advantages are:

1. Children are less exposed to storms and bad weather and are healthier
2. Attendance is increased ten to twenty per cent.
3. The advantage of graded or larger schools is secured.
4. The cost is reduced because
   (a) fewer teachers,
   (b) less fuel and incidentals.

Inquiries are frequently made as to the duty of the town officers if schools are closed.

1. It is the duty of towns to "maintain" schools and the district or the town must provide schoolrooms.

2. School visitors or town school committees may close a small school and unite the closed school with that of an adjoining district.

3. In case a school is closed the school visitors or town school committee may provide transportation, but are not under legal obligation to do so.

4. Clearly the town furnishes schooling if the school house is within reasonable walking distance or conveyance is furnished to those not within reasonable walking distance.

5. The law does not determine what reasonable distance is—that may be settled by the school visitors.

6. It is the legal duty of a parent or guardian to send his child to school even if the distance be great.

7. The law does not give the state board of education any authority to open a school closed by the local officers or to decide what a reasonable distance is. The matter is wholly in the hands of the local school officers.

Young children with their delicate frames should not be required to walk a long distance. Older children may easily walk a mile and a half or even more, but these limits may be modified. If the roads be muddy, storm-swept, unfrequented, or near dangerous places, a mile and a half may be too long or too dangerous. If the road be well kept and there are houses at short intervals, there is no hardship in a walk of a mile and a half or more for a sturdy child in ordinary weather. There are many who have walked greater distances for years without danger and with self-reliance and pleasure. If ever there is doubt, the convenience of the child should determine the case.

The following table is compiled from returns of town school officers:

TABLE—CONVEYANCE OF CHILDREN IN CONNECTICUT.

Town	Number Schools Closed	Number Children Carried	Cost for Year 1898-9	REMARKS
Ashford	4	12	$85 75	Caused better attendance. Satisfactory to parents. Expense should be paid to parent for actual attendance.
Bozrah	1	3	27 00	
Bristol	1	35	343 00	Children carried from all outside districts to high school. No criticism.
Brooklyn	1	3	10 00	10 cents per day per pupil. Beneficial to school. Satisfactory to parents.
Columbia	1	6	46 50	Conveyance began Jan. 12, 1899. Common wagon to and from school. Scholars meet at point near schoolhouse in district.
East Haddam	1	1	15 00	Sum paid to parent. Beneficial to school.
East Haven	1	1	15 00	Sum paid for car fare.
East Lyme	1	8	222 55	Exceedingly beneficial to the school. Children taken from and to their own doors.
East Windsor	3	15	400 00	Beneficial to the schools.
Easton	2	10	120 00	Decidedly beneficial to the schools. In most cases satisfactory to parents.
Ellington	2	15	292 00	Children taken at district schoolhouses and left there at night. Satisfactory to most parents. Better schools.

CONVEYANCE OF CHILDREN IN CONNECTICUT—(*Continued*).

Town	Number Schools Closed	Number Children Carried	Cost for Year 1898-9	REMARKS
Enfield	5	48	741 00	Thirty children by electric cars at expense of 2½ cents each way. Contracts made in each case. Satisfactory to parents. Beneficial to schools. High school scholars all carried to ThompsonVille.
Fairfield	2	40	340 00	Beneficial to the schools. Responsible driver. Supervision over pupils to and from school. Covered conveyance in stormy weather. Robes and blankets for cold weather. In most cases satisfactory to parents. "There are always grumblers, always have been, and always will be."
Farmington	3	14	350 00	Team was hired at an expense of less than $200, when it formerly cost $1,400. If schools be small, no doubt children are greatly benefited if brought to a common center, and expenses greatly reduced. Plan satisfactory to parents. Very beneficial to schools. Five children carried by trolley at $1.00 a week.
Franklin	1	3	90 00	
Griswold	4	14	229 00	Definite sum paid per day according to distance and number transported. Satisfactory to parents, beneficial to schools.
Hampton	1	6	84 00	Children carried from schoolhouse for 50 cents per day. Satisfactory to most parents.
Harwinton	1	6	135 00	Distance about 1½ miles. Conveyance met children at corners nearest residence at definite times in morning and left them at night. Generally satisfactory to parents. Beneficial to schools. Sensible people see the advantage. Nearly all think a school of 12 better than one school of 6 each.
Hebron	1	3	31 50	Definite sum paid per day to parent. Saved maintaining separate school for few children. Persons who conveyed children paid from 75 cents to $1 per day. Satisfactory to parents, beneficial to schools.
Killingly	4	43	570 40	
Lebanon	2	12	126 00	Private arrangements for conveyance in each case. Generally satisfactory to parents. Beneficial to schools.
Lisbon	1	1	26 00	Parents paid $1.00 per week. Not satisfactory to parents because pay too small.
Madison	1	5	135 00	Cost 75 cents per day. Beneficial to schools. More might be done at saving of hundreds of dollars and with a great improvement to schools, but parents are not willing to have schools closed.
Mansfield	1	1	18 00	Voted to pay 10 cents per day for each day's attendance.
New Britain	1	20	398 05	$9.95 per week. Covered carriage to school in the morning and returned at night. Generally satisfactory to parents. Decidedly beneficial to schools. Objection is raised that closing may effect real estate unfavorably. Objection confined to two or three, and not well taken.
New Hartford	1	20	230 00	$1.25 per day. Generally satisfactory to parents. Beneficial to school. Transportation done in a very satisfactory manner in every particular.
Newington	1	14	275 20	Cost $50.00 less than pay of teacher. Very beneficial to school; attendance more regular; no tardiness, and children had graded school.
North Branford	1	4	119 00	Children gather in the morning at some central place and are carried to school and brought back daily. Satisfactory to parents. Beneficial to schools.
No. Stonington	1	5	90 00	Satisfactory to parents. Beneficial to schools. Two or more schools might be combined with advantage and economy. The difficulty is to make people see the matter in that light.
Old Saybrook	3	80	260 04	
Plainfield	2	8	115 40	Satisfactory to parents. Beneficial to schools. Allow each family 20 cents a day for each day their children are in school, whether carried or whether they go on foot, and this for all who live 1½ miles or more from school. Mr. ———, living 2½ miles to 3 miles, allowed 40 cents, and he furnishes two boys a horse to drive.
Plainville	1	30	264 00	Covered vehicle at $24 a month for 7 months, and $32 a month for 3 months. Entirely satisfactory to parents; decidedly beneficial to schools. Punctual attendance secured. Plan adopted twenty years ago.
Plymouth	1	8	60 00	Three months during winter and spring. Satisfactory to parents; beneficial to schools.
Redding	1	2	10 00	Money paid to parents. Schools could be much improved by closing several and transporting children.

Town	Number Schools Closed	Number Children Carried	Cost for Year 1898-9	REMARK
Scotland	4	60	$536 04	Agreements made to transport children for year from each section of town at certain price per day. Several teams driven by school children. Satisfactory to parents generally. Beneficial to schools. Attendance improved. Able to secure better teachers at same expense.
Simsbury	1	5	180 00	Contract satisfactory to parents. Distance 1¼ miles.
Somers	1	8	234 00	Satisfactory to parents.
Southington	1		198 00	Person who conveyed children provided wagon and horse. On the whole satisfactory to parents. Beneficial to schools. Some objected, saying it was detrimental to value of property, tho children were benefited.
South Windsor	1	6	150 00	Not satisfactory to parents. Have not heard of benefits to schools.
Stafford	1	2	135 00	Children carried in season to be present at opening of school. Satisfactory to parents; beneficial to scholars.
Stamford	1	20		Street car one cent per trip. Satisfactory to parents and beneficial to schools
Sterling	2	14	315 00	Covered carriage at school at 8:45 a. m., and returned to homes at night. Satisfactory to parents; beneficial to schools. Schools to which children conveyed improved by extra scholars. Children more interested and better taught.
Stonington	2	7	152 50	Definite sum for each day children were carried. Plan satisfactory to parents. A little dissatisfaction in one case.
Union	1	7	47 00	Fall and summer terms Verbal contract to carry children from house to school and return. Satisfactory to parents; beneficial to schools.
Waterford	1	7	215 15	Persons hired to carry all children at so much per day. Satisfactory to parents. Made attendance of school stand first in the town.
West Hartford	3	58	850 00	Town furnished omnibuses and paid drivers for horses and service a stipulated daily price Satisfactory to parents; beneficial to schools. Enabled us to grade our schools more thoroly.
Windham	6	67	1370 30	Contracts awarded to lowest bidders. In most cases satisfactory to parents. Decidedly beneficial to schools. Our policy is to transport pupils from all small districts to graded schools.
Wolcott	1	6	35 00	Spring term. Not very satisfactory to either party.
Woodstock	1	10	50 00	Satisfactory to parents in most cases, but not all. Beneficial to schools.
Total, 49 towns	85	773	$10752 38	

VII.—Consolidation of Rural Schools in Indiana

Frank L. Jones

State Superintendent of Public Instruction in Indiana

[Extracts from the Biennial Report for 1902]

The rural schools have been the subject of so many excellent magazine articles and special reports during the last four years that it seems unnecessary in this report to discuss at length their conditions and needs. It is intended, only, that this section of the Biennial Report present in a brief form some of the agencies now at work to do away with the small, expensive school, and to improve the social and educational conditions among the people of rural communities.

THE SMALL SCHOOL.

Attention is called to the report of this department for the year 1900, in which statistics were given to show that more than one-half of Indiana's rural schools are too small to be maintained with profit. Indiana is not unique in this respect. The reports from all of the States in the central and western portions of the United States show the prevalence of schools enrolling from one to fifteen pupils each—all of which are too small. The large per capita cost, lack of social spirit, absence of educational enthusiasm, and almost total absence of vigorous exercise and play in these small schools have been emphasized in all of the state, county and township meetings, so that we have come to an almost unanimous view, namely, that the small school must be abandoned. The only proper question now is one of means.

RE-ORGANIZING AGENCIES.

Both the sentiment of the public and the laws of the State are helping local school officers in the matter of the consolidation of schools, and it seems to be progressing as rapidly as any new movement should. A gradual adjustment will be looked upon with favor by the patrons, the majority of whom should at all times be in accord with it. At the present time one or more groups of schools have been consolidated in 51 counties, 181 wagons are used in transporting children to school, and 2,599 children were carried last year.

THE CONSOLIDATED SCHOOL

HAMILTON TOWNSHIP, DELAWARE CO., INDIANA.

If any one has doubt of the wisdom of the consolidation of schools he should visit this school located just outside the small village of Royerton, under the supervision

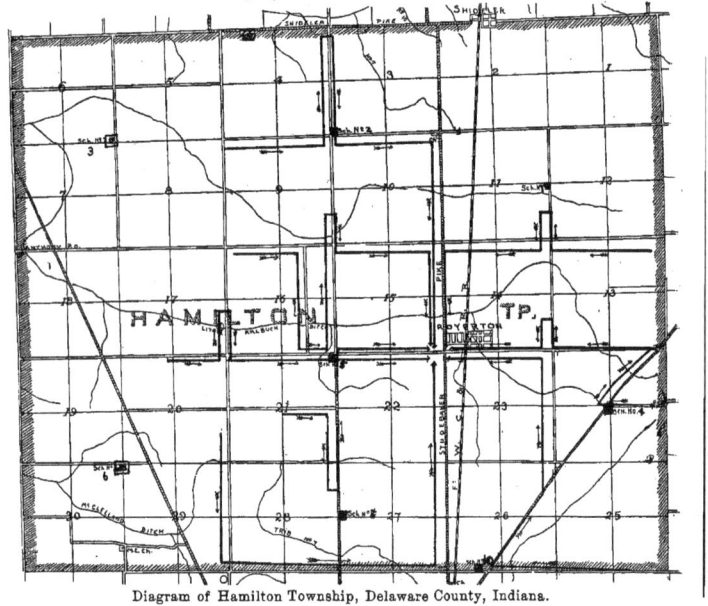

Diagram of Hamilton Township, Delaware County, Indiana.
Showing transportation routes, position of abandoned schools, and schools still in use.

Township Trustee John M. Bloss and County Superintendent Chas. A. VanMare. Here are gathered each day 192 pupils, 118 of whom are conveyed at public expense in wagons owned by the township. Seventy-four pupils belong to the original Royerton District and, of course, continue to walk to school. The distances the children who ride are as follows:

Route No. 1—
  2 children ride 3 1-2 miles.
  1 child rides three miles.
  2 children ride 2 1-2 miles.
  3 children ride 1 3-4 miles.
  1 child rides 1 1-2 miles.
  3 children ride 1 1-4 miles.

Route No. 2—
  2 children ride 3, 1-2 miles.
  3 children ride 3 1-4 miles.
  2 children ride 2 1-2 miles.
  1 child rides 1 1-6 miles.

Route No. 3—
  4 children ride 4 1-2 miles.
  3 children ride 5 1-2 miles.
  3 children ride 3 miles.
  2 children ride 2 1-2 miles.
  4 children ride 2 miles.
  2 children 2 1-2 miles.

Route No. 4—
  6 children ride 5 3-4 miles.
  3 childre nride 5 1-2 miles.
  1 child rides 4 miles.
  5 children ride 3 1-2 miles.
  1 child rides 3 1-4 miles.
  3 children ride 2 1-2 miles.

Route No. 5—
  8 children ride 5 1-2 miles.
  3 children ride 5 miles.
  2 children ride 4 miles.
  3 children ride 3 1-2 miles.
  4 children ride 3 miles.
  1 child rides 2 1-2 miles.
  1 child rides 2 miles.
  2 children ride 1 1-2 miles.
  1 child rides 1 1-4 miles.

Route No. 6—
  4 children ride 3 1-2 miles.
  6 children ride 2 1-4 miles.
  3 children ride 2 miles.
  2 children ride 1 3-4 miles.
  1 child rides 1 1-2 miles.
  1 child rides 1 1-4 miles.

Route No. 7—
  6 children ride 3 1-2 miles.
  3 children ride 2 5-8 miles.
  1 child rides 2 miles.
  1 child rides 1 3-4 miles.
  1 child rides 1 1-2 miles.

Route No. 8—
  1 child rides 5 1-2 miles.
  3 children ride 4 3-4 miles.
  2 children ride 4 1-4 miles.
  2 children ride 2 1-2 miles.
  1 child rides 1 3-4 miles.

The first distance shown in each case is the extreme length of the route. This is the distance of the child from the school. In determining the length of a route no consideration is taken of the residence of the driver. He may live at either end of the route or anywhere along the route. The prices paid for driving are as follows:

Route No. 1, W. Holliday, 3 1-2 miles, $1.00 per day, 12 children.

Route No. 2, S. S. Alexander, 3 1-2 miles, $1.00 per day, 8 children.

Route No. 3, Otto Sharp, 4 1-2 miles, $1.25 per day, 16 children.

Route No. 4, H. Gumpp, 5 3-4 miles, $1.60 per day, 19 children.

Route No. 5, J. M. Snyder, 5 1-2 miles, $1.60 per day, 25 children.

Route No. 6, Geo. Sheets, 3 1-4 miles, $1.25 per day, 17 children.

Route No. 7, Fred. Besser, 3 3-4 miles, $1.25 per day, 12 children.

Route No. 8, H. J. McClellan, 5 1-4 miles, $1.50 per day, 9 children.

I made personal inspection of this school on October 6, 1902. I asked the pupils to tell me what they thought of the plan and lacked one vote of having it unanimously in favor of transportation. The one pupil who did not like it said that he could state no objections. The enthusiasm, happiness, industry, and good health of the pupils was more marked than in any other rural school that I have visited. Here are gathered enough pupils to have in one class an active competition and genuine class enthusiasm. The "hum-drum" of a one-pupil class is not seen here. The collection of enough country pupils with good habits, good health and industry, with all the graded school advantages, makes here a school even better than the best city graded schools. All of the teachers are qualified, well-trained and experienced. A music supervisor visits them each week, and the consolidation enables the county superintendent to supervise when necessary. In addition to the grammar schools there is an excellent high school department under the direction of two qualified teachers. There are 27 pupils doing high school work, four of them young men who act as drivers for the wagons and are thus kept in school. There is almost entire absence of contagion in this township, and during the last school year the school continued without interruption, though the schools in adjoining townships were closed by health boards. The attendance is always good and punctuality is nearly perfect, tardiness being almost unknown. The wagons are owned by the township and cost from $80 to $125 each.

The teachers of grades, one to four inclusive, give the following figures in attendance:
Per cent. of attendance in Grades 1 and 2 of those who walk, 93.4.
Per cent. of attendance in Grades 1 and 2 of those who ride, 93.7.
Per cent. of attendance in Grades 3 and 4 of those who walk, 96.8.
Per cent. of attendance in Grades 3 and 4 of those who ride, 96.8.

One of the Delaware county papers published the following article a few weeks ago. It is in a nutshell a good view of the experiment:

"Thus, in the Royertin school there are 192 pupils and instruction is given by five teachers.

"In the primary grades, where the pupils need the most help and direction of the teacher, the recitations are about twenty-five to thirty minutes and the same subjects in different forms are pursued during the day.

"In the intermediate grades there are but three classes of pupils and the recitations can reach about twenty minutes.

Type of Transportation Wagon in Use in Indiana.

The teachers who have charge of the eighth year and the high school practically have charge of two grades, and here the recitations can be made longer. In fact, this school has about the same advantages as the city school, and with boys and girls coming to it from the home upon the farm, as a majority do, full of energy, with abundant time for sleep and willingness to work, it is not surprising that they can do in seven months what it takes the city pupil nine months to accomplish.

"The trustee of Hamilton township has been particularly fortunate in the selection of teachers for this school—all the teachers have had experience; all have had more than ordinary school advantages; four of them have had normal instruction and three of them are graduates of normal schools.

"If the pupils constituting this school were returned to the several districts from which they have come the following traditions would obtain:

"First. Loss of teachers specially fitted for the work of the several grades. This loss can not be made up by a 'good all-around' teacher.

"Second. The high school could not be maintained. Two of the graduates of this high school last year are now doing the fourth year work in the Muncie high school, and according to the reports of their teachers are maintaining their rank well in their classes.

"Third. The school spirit, which can only come from numbers doing the same work in the class, would be wholly lost. If there are only two in a class, or many times only one, the zeal for work on the part of the pupil and teacher is largely lost. The pupil does not know whether he is doing well or not; he has no one with whom to compare himself.

"Fourth. The attendance is better than it would be if the pupils attended the several separate schools. The attendance of those who are transported to school is from 5 to 10 per cent. better than those who walk from the home district, and no one is ever tardy.

"Fifth. A larger number attend the school in the sixth, seventh and eighth year grades who would not attend at all in the separate schools. This was found to be true when the wagons were put on. Pupils reported to have quit school for one or more years discovered that their education was deficient and determined to begin anew. These pupils will be a positive gain to good citizenship—and some of them will find their way into the college and university. This of itself will be worth all that it costs many times over.

"Sixth. Parents who are observant say that the cost of shoes worn out in walking to the separate schools and the cost of medicine and doctor bills more than pay for the transportation.

"Seventh. Transportation makes it easier to maintain a quarantine in case of disease and prevent the spread of contagion."

Three Wagons used in the Transportation of Children in Perry Township, Delaware County, Indiana.

Consolidation in this township is quite as satisfactory, though not on as large a scale, as in Hamilton township.

LETTERS FROM PATRONS OF THE CONSOLIDATED SCHOOLS

THE FINANCIAL PHASE OF THE CONSOLIDATION OF RURAL SCHOOLS.

I mailed uniform letters to the patrons of the consolidated schools asking them to write me full and frank expressions of their opinions in relation to the success of the plan. The following are all of the replies received up to date:

"October 21, 1902.

"Mr. Jones:

"Dear Sir—I received your letter, wanting my opinion on the consolidation of schools. I think it is far better than the district school system. I think we need a larger building, large enough for all of the grades to be in one building, or better rooms for the first, second and third grades. Our children did very well last winter and so far this winter.

"HENRY GRUMPP."

"Shideler, Ind., October 21, 1902.

"Mr. F. L. Jones, Indianapolis, Ind.:

"Kind Sir—Your request at hand and contents noted. As a patron of the consolidated schools, I wish to say that I have reasons to favor and reasons to oppose the consolidation of our schools.

"Yes, I think the consolidation of our schools give our children better advantages than do the district schools, for the reason, first, we are able to get better qualified instructors, because we do not have to hire so many. And then a well-qualified man will not go into a small district school. So, you see, it is a long step toward enabling us to perfect the profession of school teaching. Next, it throws a larger number of children of the same grade together, enabling them to exchange ideas. Next, it enables us to get more and better apparatus, for one school is easier supplied than eight or ten. Next, a saving in fuel. Next, and of much importance, our children step out of the homes into a nice, dry (and warm, if need be) of age, to send to school. She is now taking the first year of high school work. Under the present system I will be able to give her a full high school course and yet have her under my care and protection. I find that the school spirit is increased by having the larger number of pupils assembled together as compared to that of the small district school.

"I find that the health of the children is much better. There is no exposure to storms in bad weather. The wagons protect them from the wind and rain, consequently there is little trouble from coughs and colds. There is some saving in the wear and tear of clothing, particularly shoes. I am not inconvenienced from my work to see that my child is placed in school or returned during stormy days. The wagon is in charge of a competent driver, who takes my child from my door in the morning and returns her there again at night. This is a great relief to me.

"There is some talk of combining the entire township into one school. I am heartily in favor of so doing. A commissioned high school could then be established, with all the advantages of gradation in the lower grades. In conclusion I will say that I approve of the system.

"Very truly,
"J. C. KAUFFMAN."

"Muncie, Ind., October 24, 1902.
"Superintendent F. L. Jones, Indianapolis, Ind.:

"My Dear Sir—Your letter of inquiry concerning the consolidation of schools in my township—Hamilton township, Delaware county, Indiana—is at hand. In reply will say that I am very much satisfied with the movement. I am sending

A Small Consolidated School, Bloomfield Township, Lagrange County, Indiana.

one child to the school. Under the present plan I am relieved of all concern about the child's getting to and from the school during bad weather. The wagon passes my door each morning and evening. I find that the health of my child is better. There is not so much trouble with coughs and colds which may result from wet feet. The wagons are warm and dry and there is no necessity for the child being exposed. There is some economy in the cost of clothing.

"The gradation of the school is much better. The school spirit is high and the children take a deeper interest in the work. It is much easier to keep the larger children in the school than when sending to the small district school. I will now have a high school at hand, and can feel that my child will be under home protection until she is old enough to care for herself.

"I am in favor of the entire township being united into one school. I think it is possible to do this. I am a member of the Township Advisory Board, and am ready to give anything that will advance the interests of my township my most earnest support. I think that the consolidation of schools is a movement in the right line. Very truly,
"JOSEPH SHEETS."

"Muncie, Ind., October 19, 1902.
"Mr. F. L. Jones, Inidanapolis, Ind.:

"Dear Sir—In reply to consolidation of schools I will say that I think it is a greater benefit to children than public schools for this one reason, that the teacher can more plainly explain the matter to the children and make them understand much better by teaching one or two grades than teaching seven or eight. I am well pleased with consolidation of schools.
"Yours truly,
"GEO. F. WISSEL."

"Royerton, Ind., October 20, 1902.
"Mr. F. L. Jones, Superintendent, Indianapolis, Ind.:

"Dear Sir—Your letter or request is at hand asking my opinion about consolidation of schools. While I have not fully considered the subject, and at the same time the consolidation of schools being almost in infancy, it is yet too soon to determine what is best. But will reply. In the beginning I was not in favor of consolidation of schools. Can not say that I am yet. While the children may learn some faster, having the advantages of being in larger classes and have most likely better teachers and other surroundings, yet there are some objections of vital importance. While we all love to have our children educated, we must not force them too fast. At the same time we must learn to look after their health, whether it is best to crowd so many in one room or house them like sheep in a fold. One great objection of consolidated schools over the district schools is this, if fatal diseases are carried or start in these schools, then most all of the children of the township are exposed to it. Then under the ruling of the Board of Health of our county the school must close from thirty to forty days, while in district schools, if one is exposed, the other schools not exposed can go on. Still more, I am not certain the hauling of the children is best for them at all times. True, there are days in stormy weather of rain and sleet, the hauling of them is nice, but in general is it not better for them to walk to school for health, by having exercise, than to leave a warm room, jump into a cold wagon and ride from one to three miles? There are thoughts that must come into the mind of every parent if the hauling system is to go on. I would have the township trustee to be very careful in hiring the teams, to get good, gentle teams and careful drivers.

"Now to the point: I have been in Hamilton township, this county, over forty-seven years; have paid my taxes to help build all the schoolhouses in the township, and we had good schools; the people were satisfied. Now, under the consolidation, the schoolhouses are going down, school lots not cared for, windows being broken; good many of the people are feeling sore as to the property loss of thousands of dollars; and now, if the consolidation of schools is to hold good, there must be greater temples built. More rooms to accommodate the children—more taxes. The American people are progressive, but they are going at a rapid rate. I am not an old fogy on the subject at all. You wanted my views. I do not think it will be long till the schools will fall back to the district schools. Many of the profound scholars of the day never saw a consolidated school or were hauled to school in a wagon. While this system may prove better than many believe, yet it is to be thoroughly tested before final decision. Not condemning the school so far as it has been going on and hope it may prove bet-

ter for all than many of us think, yet with what advantage children have over the district schools will hardly warrant a success. Yours truly,
"T. F. Kirby."

"Royerton, Ind., October 14, 1902.
"Mr. Frank L. Jones, Indianapolis, Ind.:

"Dear Sir—The per cent. of attendance in grades one and two, and grades three and four, are as follows: Those who ride, 93.7—96.8; those who walk, 93.4—96.5. Yours very truly,
"Mabel E. Blazier.
"Bessie Stretcher."

. . "Muncie, Ind., October 26, 1902...
"Mr. F. L. Jones, Indianapolis, Ind.:

"Dear Sir—Your letter dated October 16th at hand requesting a statement from me on the advantages of consolidation of schools, or rather, what advantage it is to us in our township.

"There are several different ways in which we find it an advantage. In the first place, as in our case, where we have children ready for the high school work, they have an opportunity for that work without the extra expense and trouble of sending them to the city. Then again, the convenience of having a wagon for transportation to and from the school while the distance is much greater, the time taken up in going and coming is very little more than if they were walking the one and one-fourth miles to the district school.

"Again, with six years' personal experience in teaching and a part of that time in a graded school, I know of the advantage in having large classes, namely, where they are not too large there is more enthusiasm, more interest taken in the recitations.

"As to the primary work in the consolidated school, one advantage is in getting the little fellows to school dry and warm. However, I am afraid that our wagon is hardly warm enough for very cold weather. . .

."Another advantage in the primary work is that each teacher has fewer grades and is enabled to give more attention to each separate grade.

"The disadvantages that seemed to appear at the beginning are now in the background and are disappearing as the plan becomes older and more in use. One of the most prominent disadvantages talked of was the effect of contagious diseases getting into the school infecting so many more at once than in each separate district, but the danger of spreading such disease is prevented by the co-operation of the trustee and the drivers of the different wagons.

"There are many other advantages that might be enumerated here, but these few thoughts will show you that I am decidedly in favor of consolidation as conducted in Hamilton township, Delaware county.

"Yours very respectfully,
"O. M. Sharp."

The Financial Phase of the Consolidation of Rural Schools.

As a solution to the rural school problem, the school at Royerton, Ind., is a fruitful field for study. Six districts, comprising an area of about eighteen square miles, have been combined into one. The union school is located at Royerton. Under the separate-district plan seven teachers were employed—two at Royerton and one in each of the other districts. Now five are employed in the union school, a difference of two teachers resulting from the change. Three teachers are doing grade work, one does high school work, and one divides his time between grade and high school work. Some little high school work was given when there were but two teachers in the Royerton school, but no high school work was given in the district schools outside of the Royerton school. Under the separate-district plan seven rooms were maintained. Now there are but four, and a small room used for recitations, which adds no expense. No additional buildings were needed at Royerton, due to the fact that there was an old building which had not been used for several years. Thus there has been a saving in tuition by reducing the number of teachers. Not considering the high school, four teachers do the work formerly done by seven teachers—a difference of three. The cost of fuel, supplies, and repairs for seven rooms has been reduced to the cost of four. There are 190 pupils enrolled in the school, 129 of whom are conveyed from the abandoned schools—about two-thirds of the number enrolled in the union school. The daily expense for transportation is $8.75. The following will show the comparative cost of the two plans:

DISTRICT PLAN.

Salaries for seven teachers for seven months	$2,492 00
Institute fee for seven institutes	124 60
Fuel for seven rooms at $30 per room	210 00
Supplies for seven rooms at $10 per room	70 00
Repairs at $20 per room	140 00
Total	$3,036 60

CONSOLIDATION PLAN.

Salaries for four teachers for seven months	$1,442 00
Institute fee for seven institutes	72 10
Fuel for four rooms at $30 per room	120 00
Supplies for four rooms at $10 per room	40 00
Repairs at $20 per room	80 00
Total	$1,754 10
Transportation, at $8.87 per day	1,225 00
Total	$2,979 10
Difference in favor of consolidation	57 50
	$3,036 60

The salaries shown in the above estimate are the actual salaries paid the teachers. The cost of the fuel has been estimated upon a coal or wood basis. The supplies include maps, globes, charts, desks, books of reference, etc. The repairs include fencing, wells, pumps, floors, windows, papering, janitor work, etc. These are only estimates. If there is any error, it has been in making them too low. However, this would only make the saving greater, and does not interfere with the argument. Buildings are not included. There was no additional expense for buildings.

PER CAPITA COST.

	Consolidated Plan	District Plan
Tuition per day	$0.060	$0.100
Transportation per day	0.067	....
Other items	0.012	0.041
	$0.139	$0.141

The pupils of the original Royerton school are not transported, which makes a reduction from 14.1 to 7.2 cents per capita. There are about sixty pupils in this district.

In the township in which Royerton is situated there are other schools not centralized at Royerton. Each of them enrolls more than thirty pupils. The cost of tuition cannot be greater than 8 cents per capita, using as a basis the same rate as used in the other estimates—$2.50 per day. The cost of transportation can not be much less than six cents per day per capita, considering that the average cost of driver, wagon and team is $1.25, and that a wagon may convey from twenty to twenty-five pupils. If there be thirty pupils two wagons may be needed, which would increase the per capita cost. To consolidate such schools would be more expensive than to maintain separate schools.

MONTGOMERY COUNTY, IND.

(a) CONSOLIDATED SCHOOL, UNION TOWNSHIP, MONTGOMERY COUNTY, INDIANA.

This schoolhouse, which is very similar in outward appearance to the schoolhouse built in Sugar Creek township and shown below, was erected in the summer of 1901. The cost of the house, two acres of ground and furniture, was about $12,000. The children from four former school districts are accommodated in this building. There are four rooms, two large halls and basement, and the building is heated by two furnaces, using coal. There are two large wagons to haul the children, and the cost of the two drivers is about $3 per school day. There are also many children who come in private conveyances, and their horses are housed during the school hours in sheds built by the township, upon the back of the lot. The territory from which the children come is about three miles square, the longest drive being about five miles.

The New Consolidated School Building of Sugar Creek Township, Montgomery County, Indiana.

(b) CONSOLIDATED SCHOOL, SUGAR CREEK TOWNSHIP, MONTGOMERY COUNTY, IND.

This school building, shown in the picture above, is a modern four-room structure located on two acres of ground in every way suited to the needs of the schools. The cost of building, grounds and stables was $10,500. Four new wagons, with a capacity of twenty-five pupils each, are required to haul the pupils. Each wagon is finely upholstered and well heated, so that the pupils are always comfortable. The cost of each wagon was $150. The routes covered by the wagons embrace twenty-three square miles, and are six to seven miles in length. The average time required for making the trips is one hour and twenty minutes. Six schools are centralized here; 135 pupils enrolled. The school is modern in every respect.

* * *

VIII.—Consolidation and Transportation in Wisconsin.

[From a Bulletin issued by the State Superintendent of Public Schools]

This age is rightly termed the age of progress. We see evidence of it on every side. In rural communities the crude log houses have given way to comfortable and commodious dwellings. The ramshackle buildings in cities have been replaced by stately stone mansions and towering edifices filled with offices and stores. The self-binder and header have taken the place of the sickle and scythe. Machinery is supplanting labor in every phase of industrial life. Steam and electricity are annihilating distances and are bringing to our doors the favorite products of other countries and climes.

In education, also, the last few decades

have witnessed great progress. Twenty years ago waves of anti-high school sentiment swept this continent from the Atlantic to the Pacific; now, the high school, the people's college, is firmly entrenched in the hearts of the American people. In 1875, the first free high schools were established in Wisconsin; today we have 222 free high schools, and about thirteen other high schools of equivalent rank.

RURAL SCHOOLS HAVE NOT KEPT PACE WITH PROGRESS.

In one phase of education alone has progress not kept pace with the improvements in other directions. I refer to the district school. While improved conditions exist as to text books, apparatus, and to some extent, in the school buildings, yet on the whole, the rural school ranks very much lower, in comparison with other educational institutions, than it did thirty years ago.

large. Boys and girls of maturity and ability attended the sessions every winter. Even twenty years ago it was no uncommon sight to find a class of twenty mature students, ranging in age from sixteen to twenty-one, in the district school. Today, when the child in the rural school has reached the age of thirteen, he feels that he has outgrown it. Then the school was taught in winter by the brightest young men in the community. Frequently college students were employed, whose example furnished a stimulus to the pupils to procure an education. The school was a center of influence and interest. Spelling matches, debates and discussions made the school the center during long winter evenings. It is different today. Now, these schools to a large extent are taught by young, inexperienced girls. The salary that these districts can afford to offer is too low to command the services of strong teachers. Yet even at the low sal-

A Typical One-Teacher Rural School.
Such a school suffers from isolation, lack of numbers, lack of enthusiasm, and lack of impulses to action.

ATTENDANCE IS NOW SMALL AND PUPILS ARE YOUNG.

Thirty years ago in most localities, especially in the older parts of the country, the rural school was far different from what it is today. The attendance was

ary of $20 or $25 a month the cost of maintaining schools in small districts proves a heavy burden upon the taxpayers. The decline of the rural school, or if you choose to say, its failure to progress, is due to many factors. Division of labor has opened many new fields for the young men and women, causing them to flock in large numbers from the country to the city. The excitement of city life induces others to change their abode. Furthermore, the great advantages incident to a well-graded high school in cities and villages cause many families to leave the homestead and remove to those places for the purpose of giving their children an opportunity of securing an education that will enable them to compete with others in the battle of life.

$1,588,715.41 WASTED IN RURAL SCHOOL EDUCATION IN WISCONSIN IN 1901.

Our state in 1901 had a school population of 731,063 persons, of which number 316,833 were enrolled in the rural, village and small city schools having no city supervision. The average daily attendance was 179,913, making the per cent of attendance 56.7 per cent. This per cent of attendance is very low indeed. For the rural schools of the state the percentage is materially lower, since, in the estimate here given, are included the enrollment and attendance of graded schools in villages and cities where the regularity of attendance is relatively high. For the maintenance of these schools during the year 1901, $3,669,088.77 were expended. The teaching force, equipment, apparatus, and school buildings were ample to accord school facilities to the entire enrollment of 316,853 pupils every day of the school year. However, the average attendance was only 179,913. The capital invested was, therefore, not utilized to its full extent. In fact, only 56.7 per cent of the capital was thus fully utilized, because of the lack of regularity in attendance. This makes a loss of $1,588,715.41, or 43.3 per cent of the capital invested. This large amount was lost to the cause of education in one year through irregularity in attendance.

THIS AMOUNT WOULD HAVE PAID FOR THE TRANSPORTATION OF PUPILS TO CENTRAL SCHOOLS.

This means that the state paid out for teachers' wages, fuel, and supplies more than one-half million dollars to provide school facilities for pupils not in school. The loss is sustained mostly by rural communities because the irregularity of attendance is greater than in villages and cities. This amount is four times as much as would be required to furnish all pupils in the public schools with free textbooks and free supplies, and it is far more than is needed for providing for the free transportation of the children of the rural schools to central graded schools.

ADVANTAGES OF CONSOLIDATION OF DISTRICTS AND TRANSPORTATION OF PUPILS.

COSTS LESS FOR BUILDINGS AND REPAIRS.

Consolidation of districts results in the concentration of money and effort upon one or a few serviceable buildings, doing away with ill-ventilated, badly lighted and poorly equipped schoolhouses. It is far cheaper to heat a few well-constructed schoolhouses and keep them in repair than to heat a large number of scattered schoolhouses, as a rule poorly constructed, and keep them in good condition.

COSTS LESS FOR TEACHERS.

In nearly a thousand schools in the state in 1901, the average attendance was less than ten. Even with the low-priced teacher usually found in these schools, the per capita cost of maintenance is very high. In a well-graded school a teacher can easily take care of thirty-five pupils, and do justice to the class and individual. In this way, by engaging fewer teachers, even at higher salaries, it enables the taxpayer to lessen the expense and yet enhance the efficiency of the educational work done.

WILL INCREASE VALUE OF LAND.

Many families yearly move into cities to educate their children. They would remain upon the farm if they could have within easy reach of their homes a graded school, offering to the children educational advantages equal to the town school. The large influx into cities has greatly enhanced the value of real estate in those places, while the increase in value of farm lands has not been nearly so great.

In many places where consolidation of school districts has been effected and a strong central school established, the value of the land has increased very materially, since many parents are desirous of having their children enjoy a good school education without being compelled to give up the farm associations and consequent moving into cities. Good schools always enhance the value of land in their vicinity.

THERE IS LESS SICKNESS OF CHILDREN.

This plan is more conducive to the preservation of children's health. The central buildings are far better adapted for school purposes than the small district schoolhouses. They are properly lighted and provided with modern heating and ventilating apparatus, and with proper seating facilities. Therefore, there will be no wet feet and clothing, and consequent colds with their attendant ills are largely avoided.

PUPILS WILL ADVANCE MORE RAPIDLY.

While the cities have been perfecting the organization of their graded school system, the rural schools have been unable to make advancement in this direction. One teacher cannot very well carry on the work of an entire school and do justice to the individual pupils, or even classes, on account of the large number of recitations which thorough gradation makes necessary. It is a physical impossibility for one teacher to divide a school into separate grades and then give each class the amount of time needed for securing the best results. Consolidation of districts gives the country communities the many advantages of graded and high schools now enjoyed in cities, without any of the disadvantages. The pupils will be in well-graded schools, under close, systematic supervision of principals and county superintendents. They are taken out of the isolation of the district school and brought in touch with other children, and by this association with their fellows they are broadened and developed. The spirit of emulation in the larger school is greater than in the smaller one, as the pupils have an opportunity to measure themselves with others of their own age.

SPECIAL AND ADVANCED SUBJECTS MAY BE TAUGHT.

It enables the school authorities to make arrangements for instruction in special subjects, as music, drawing, agriculture, domestic economy, etc. Instruction in advanced subjects may also be offered. This plan often results in the organization of a free high school, thus bringing excellent facilities within the reach of rural communities.

LENGTHENS THE SCHOOL YEAR AND INCREASES REGULARITY AND PUNCTUALITY IN ATTENDANCE.

Longer and more regular terms of school will be possible as the result of uniting the several small districts into one strong central school. The children will be more regular and punctual in attendance, since the larger and better school arouses greater interest. In places where transportation of pupils has been tried, the attendance has been increased from fifty to one hundred and fifty per cent. Tardiness is practically unknown, since the vehicles arrive at school before the time set for the beginning of the session.

CHILDREN MAY REMAIN AT HOME WHILE SECURING AN EDUCATION.

This plan enables the children to secure a good education and yet remain at home under the influence of father and mother, at the time when they are most susceptible to bad influences incident to city life. It will tend to keep the boys and girls on the farm, instead of encouraging them to leave it and go to the towns.

WILL MAKE FARM LIFE MORE ATTRACTIVE.

This plan will improve the farm surroundings and add attractions to country life, by leading to an appreciation of Nature and a desire to know more about her work. Lectures and public gatherings, debating societies, etc., made possible by this plan, will also greatly add to the enjoyment and attractiveness of farm life.

EXTRACTS FROM LETTERS OF COUNTY SUPERINTENDENTS

RECEIVED MAY 12-14, 1902.

"The present status of affairs in this respect will be greatly improved by the opening of the next school year. We are having this year the transportation at public expense into the village of Cartwright. Two teams are employed. At least one other school three miles from Cartwright will close next year and transport the children; possibly *two will close.* A good many children from country schools have been attending the village school at Bloomer, also at Boyd. But their own people have furnished the teams. *Two,* and possibly *three,* schools will close near Bloomer next year and the children will be transported. I cannot tell just yet how many teams will be required for this. The determined effort made this spring to bring about *country* consolidation in the town of Eagle Point, and the *large vote* in favor of it at spring election shows that people are in earnest about the matter. There is little doubt but that another year will find a large central school ($3,000 building) in the town of Eagle Point, to accommodate the four schools in that end of town.

While we have only just *begun* the good work of consolidation, yet the sentiment in its favor is growing rapidly. The air is full of it, and it will come before long, *with a rush.*

Supt. ANNIE E. SCHAFFER,
Chippewa County.

[From the Superintendent of Dunn County.]

"In reply to your favor of the 9th inst. will say that transportation of pupils is in operation in Jt. District No. 2, towns of Red Cedar and Tainter, in this county. The driver contracted to make two trips daily over a route of about eight miles,

A Carryall used for transportation of children in the Cedar Falls district, Dunn County, Wisconsin.
This shows a cheap, home-made transportation wagon.

carrying at most eighteen pupils, if there are that many desiring to ride, for the sum of two hundred dollars for nine months. I know of no criticism on the plan at present.

"To bring this about a small mixed school in one part of the district was closed and the pupils are taken to the graded school at Cedar Falls, in the same district.

"We have one case where two small districts were united a year ago and now support a strong mixed school.

"I believe that by proper agitation of the question Jt. District No. 1, towns of Eau Galle. Dunn and Waubeck might be consolidated with District No. 1 of the town of Eau Galle and a three-department school maintained where there is a two-department school now in the village of Eau Galle."

Supt. N. O. VARNUM,
Dunn County.

[From the Superintendent of Gates County.]

"There are two towns in Gates county where children are transported to school at public expense. The school officers believe this is cheaper than to maintain small schools. In the town of True, four carriages are used to bring children to the graded school at Glen Flora at an expense of $25 a month for each team. Twenty-five children are transported. More children can be carried at a much less expense when roads are built connecting the main roads. There is one team hauling children to the school at Ingram.

"There is a strong sentiment in favor of building a central school at Bruce and transporting children from Atlanta and Beldenville, each about two miles from Bruce. This would make a school of about three hundred pupils. The plan could be carried out with success.

"There are five schoolhouses within three miles of Island Lake. The attendance in the five schools is about 60. The leading people there are talking of selling the small schoolhouses, building a large one, and transporting the children to the central school. The people here would like pictures of barges and an estimate of the cost and the carrying capacity of a suitable barge.

"There is still objection to consolidation in some districts. At the town meetings this spring, three districts voted to build schoolhouses, none of which will be more than three miles from good graded schools. The average attendance in each of these will be between five and fifteen. The opinion was that many settlers are not yet able to clothe their children well enough to go to village schools. It would seem that this is a wrong impression, as children ought to be dressed plainly in going to any school."

Supt. W. N. MACKIN,
Gates County.

[From the Superintendent of Wood County.]

"There are going to be some changes in the schools (for the better) this summer. I think there will be one or two more graded schools established. This will mean a change in some districts, though it is not fully decided yet just what they will be.

"No 4 Remington has had transportation for some time."

Supt. O. J. LEU, Wood County.

[From the Superintendent of Eau Claire County.]

"Considerable attention has been devoted to the subject of the consolidation and transportation of children. The following are the figures for one township (six miles square) in this county. There are 243 children between the ages of 4 and 20 years. The average daily attendance last year was 76. The total number enrolled was 163. It certainly appears evident that a township central plan would be the cheapest in a town of this stamp and would result in better work. Two schools have been closed and joined with neighboring districts."

Supt. E. A. CLEASBY,
Eau Claire County.

" FORWARD ! "

Consolidation of school districts and transportation of pupils is one of the most important movements in recent years for bettering the school facilities of rural communities. It is in line with the progress that is being made in industrial fields. This is the era of concentration. The foregoing discussions indicate sufficiently that the small country school, with the frequent accompaniment of poorly prepared teachers, does not give the children the preparation that is now needed for success in life. It also shows that it is expensive when the number of persons in attendance is taken into consideration. Consolidation of districts always results in better organization of schools, in stronger teaching force, and in taking pupils out of the isolation found in many small schools. One of the most important things in the education of the child that he shall come into contact with a [go]odly number of children of his own [ag]e; without this contact he is missing [on]e of the most important elements in ed[uca]tion.

Experience in more than twenty states, [Wi]sconsin included, has shown that con[sol]idation may be effected and pupils [tra]nsported without a material increase in [th]e expenses for school purposes in the [ter]ritory covered. This experience is [str]ongly in favor of consolidation. Had it not been a success we should have heard unfavorable reports from localities where this plan has been tried. So far it has been found eminently satisfactory.

This is a very important question and should receive the serious consideration of all communities favorably situated for consolidation of schools.

"Forward" is the inspiring motto of our state; let us be true to it.

L. D. HARVEY, State Supt.

Madison, Wis., 1902.

* * *

IX.—Consolidation and Transportation in Iowa

[From the report of State Superintendent R. C. Barrett for 1901.]

Consolidation has been tried in twenty-[eig]ht counties, transportation in thirty-[fiv]e, and both in nineteen. Consolidation [ha]s been adopted by sixty-three districts, [an]d eighty districts have transported pu-[pi]ls at the expense of the district. In nine [co]unties districts have been consolidated [w]ithout providing transportation at the [ex]pense of the districts. In sixteen coun[ti]es pupils have been transported where [th]ere was no consolidation.

The most notable illustration of this [pl]an is found in Buffalo Center. Buffalo [C]enter township, Winnebago county, in [18]95, formed an independent district, em[br]acing the entire civil township, six [m]iles square, and voted bonds running for [a] period of ten years for the purpose of [er]ecting an eight-room building.

BUFFALO CENTER SCHOOL PLAN.

The board, which consists of five mem[be]rs, is chosen on the second Monday in [M]arch by the qualified electors, and is [go]verned by the same provisions of law [wh]ich apply to independent districts.

At the time the township became inde[pe]ndent it was not proposed to close the [ru]ral schools and transport the children. [T]his was an after consideration, and arose [fr]om the demand upon the part of the [pe]ople of the rural districts for better [sc]hool facilities.

On August 23, 1897, the residents of what was formerly known as sub-district No. 3 requested the board to furnish transportation for their children to a central school. The request was granted, and the outlying school closed. On August 30th of the same year the board arranged for the transportation of children in districts No. 2 and No. 4. On August 17, 1898, the board, upon petition, arranged for the transportation of children from another ward. In April, 1899, the board, having noted the success with which their efforts had been attended, ordered all of the rural schools in the district closed except those in the extreme northeastern and southeastern parts of the township.

By refeerence to the accompanying map it will be observed that the central school is located only one mile from the western boundary line of the district, thus making it extremely difficult on account of the distance to transport the children from these two remote portions of the township. The two rural schools maintained by the board are considered superior in many ways to the ordinary school, since they are under the supervision of the principal of the central school, and are maintained for the same length of time each year as the central school.

Contracts for the year 1900-01 provide for the transportation of ninety-eight children. Six routes are laid out, and one team is provided for each. For convenience the routes are numbered 1, 2, 3, 4, 5 and 6, beginning with the one running north from the central school. (See plat.)

The greatest distance the children most remote from the central school on the different routes are conveyed is as follows: Route 1, three and one-fourth miles; route 2, four and one-half miles; route 3, five and one-half miles; route 4, five and three-fourths miles; route 5, five and one-half miles; route 6, six and one-fourth miles. The average distance the children are conveyed on the longest route is about four miles.

What can be said of the roads? Comparatively speaking, Winnebago is one of the newer counties, and roads have not been so thoroughly graded and drained as in old-settled sections, consequently the roads are not so good as in many parts of the state.

What length of time is required to convey children to and from the central school? The time required depends upon the condition of the roads. When very muddy, as was the case when the writer visited the district in 1900, the drivers began collecting the children from 7:15 A. M. to 8:15 A. M., according to the length of the route, and returned them to their homes from 4:45 P. M. to 5:45 P. M.

The compensation paid drivers is $30 per month, except on route 1, where only $25 are paid. For this amount they are required to furnish their own properly covered, strong, safe, suitable vehicles, subject to the approval of the board, with comfortable seats, and a safe, strong, quiet team, with proper harness, with which to convey and collect safely and comfortably all of the pupils of school age on the route, and to furnish warm, comfortable blankets or robes sufficient for the best protection and comfort for each and all of the pupils to and from the public school building and their respective homes. They agree to collect all of the pupils on the route by driving to each and all of the homes where pupils reside each morning that school is in session in time to convey the pupils to school, so as to arrive at the school building not earlier than 8:40 a. m. nor later than 8:45 a. m., and return the pupils to their homes, leaving the building at 4 p. m., or later, as the board may determine.

They are required to personally drive and manage the teams, and to refrain from the use of any profane or vulgar language within the hearing or presence of the pupils; nor may they use tobacco in any form during the time they are convey-

By "starting of routes" is meant where teams start. The most remote children are as a rule gathered first.)

Diagram Showing the Consolidated Schools of Buffalo Center Township, Winnebago County, Iowa.

The figures by the x indicate the number of children at each farm-house.

ing children to and from school. They are not permitted to drive faster than a trot nor race with any team, and are required to keep order and report improper conduct on the part of pupils to the principal or president of the board.

It is further provided between the driver and the board that one-half of the previous month's wages shall be retained to insure the faithful performance of the contract.

In 1894 the district township was composed of six sub-districts, and required six buildings, six teachers, six sets of apparatus—in fact all of the equipment necessary for one district was required by each of the others.

* * *

X.—Consolidation and Transportation in Kansas

The movement began in Kansas in 1898, and a general permissive law was passed by the Legislature in 1900. The best way to show with what favor the plan is received in Kansas will be to reproduce a number of letters from County Superintendents which were published in the last (1902) Report of the State Superintendent of Public Instruction of Kansas:

DICKINSON COUNTY.

"The consolidated school district which was organized in this county last April has about completed its new stone structure. When completed the building will comprise a basement, two schoolrooms on the first floor and a large hallroom on the second. The upper room is so arranged that it may be used for classrooms at any time it may be required. The basement will contain living-rooms for the janitor, or principal, as the case may be. The building is thoroughly modern in appearance, and will be heated by furnace throughout.

"This year the school will have an enrollment of about sixty, in eight grades, under two first-grade teachers, receiving $55 and $45 respectively. At the present time there are no pupils for the ninth grade, but it is believed, however, that as pupils advance an additional grade can be maintained with the present force of teachers. If this proves true, more thorough work will be done in the seventh and eighth grades than under the old system, and an extra year's work will be brought within the reach of these pupils. But this is not all. The lower grades will receive better instruction than under the old plan, because the primary teacher will have about thirty pupils in four grades, whereas before they had thirty in eight grades. When the successful working of this plan has been fully demonstrated by practical results, and the surrounding towns are organized on the same plan, enough territory can be added to this district to make it necessary to employ three teachers.

"This movement is being watched with great interest by school patrons all over this county. At Moonlight there is situated a creamery and country store, so located that the tributary territory includes the greater part of five school districts. These pupils could be placed under three teachers in a consolidated school, receive a more thorough training, and under more favorable conditions, in pleasant schoolrooms, presided over by teachers especially adapted for the work of their respective grades, at a cost of about the same to the parent. Pupils can drive five miles in a modern rig with less exposure than they can walk one and one-half miles. At Acme the conditions are about the same as at Moonlight. Talmage, Carlton, Elmo, Detroit and Woodbine are each so situated that, by the addition of adjacent territory, enough pupils might be added to make it profitable to employ three teachers instead of two. This would result in better work in each grade, and an additional grade to each school.

"I believe that this plan will help the county high school in this, that it will secure older and better-trained pupils at admission. Personally, I do not think it a good plan to send children only twelve or thirteen years of age away from home. Consolidated schools will make it possible for them to remain under the home influence at least one or two years more.

"To summarize: To the pupils consolidated schools mean pleasant schoolrooms, uniform heat, large classes of the same grades and teachers thoroughly trained to teach those grades; to the parent they mean the advantages of a city school in the country, with the vices of the city removed—it will mean obedient, healthful, moral, educated children at home at about the same price they are now paying; to the teacher they mean longer terms, better wages, and the most favorable conditions for successful teaching; to the superintendent they mean larger enrollments, in fewer school buildings, a better class of teachers, by reason of the fact that the higher wages will retain the best, fewer cases of discipline, because the changed conditions will result in better-trained boys and girls; to the future they mean a more thoroughly educated class of young men and women among the masses of our people.

"The old fords and wooden bridges every eight or ten miles of the early '70's were useful, but have given way to beautiful structures of iron on every section line. The stone churn and the busy housewife working butter by hand are no more. The creamery and skimming station have proven better economy. The farmer who spent at least one day of each week to go to town for the mail now has it brought daily to his door. The log schoolhouse of our childhood days has passed. The neat one-room school of the present has fitted many a young man and woman for successful citizenship; but the consolidated union graded school in the country is a blessing that the future holds in store"—R. V. Dyer, County Superintendent.

CLOUD COUNTY.

"'In union there is strength.' To get best results, efforts and interests must be centralized. Each of our district schools represents fragments of disjointed efforts, each working out its own salvation without definite plan or system. As a result, our boys and girls are found drifting with the current of indifference, and have no definite object in view of completing the work that should be done. Is it any wonder that fifteen-year-old Fred says that he does not care to go to school any longer? He feels there is nothing there worth his while, and this is probably correct.

"A young teacher goes to an isolated school with few pupils in attendance. She does not have much enthusiasm, and the district has less, as they are all intensely occupied with their their home affairs. In a few weeks the teacher loses what interest she has, and so school is too often 'kept' until the close of the term. The present system presents too great an opportunity to neglect the work. There is every chance of poor teaching for those who wish to take advantage. The present system encourages unqualified people to begin the work, and well qualified to either not begin or quit; as a result we have 33 1-3 per cent new and untried teachers, about 50 per cent who stay with the work three or four years, 10 per cent give their entire time and attention, and the remainder farm and teach, but mostly farm. No teacher can be much interested in the work under three or four years' service; hence we must do something to keep our best teachers in the service and get others to enroll who are well qualified.

"Cloud County has as fine schools as can be had under our present system, but we must change our system to keep abreast with the times. The schools are not keeping pace with commercial interests. They are yet in the last century, and we must unite to bring them up to the present. Centralization is the only thing that can do it. We are spending much force, with meager results. I have in mind seven districts in which all pupils are within six miles of the center. Average length of term is seven months; average wages for the year is $238; number of pupils for each teacher is nineteen. Now, where is there a preacher or an editor who can live on $238 a year? Four teachers could do this work and each receive $416 a year. A teacher who is not worth $400 a year is not ready to be a teacher; yet we cannot pay this amount under our present system. Many people will not enter the work who should, because there is no just compensation. We cannot have better schools until we get better teachers; we cannot have better teachers until we have better pay; and we cannot have better pay until we have better teachers, etc.

"Under consolidation the county superintendent would have supervision, as he should spend an hour in each school at least once a month. As it is, he cannot make but two visits in a year. The county superintendent must waste too much precious time in traveling. Last year I traveled 3,000 miles. Allowing one hour's time for each six miles traveled, we have 50 hours wasted, and no one is benefited. A superintendent will make some necessary objections or plans to each school, but he cannot see that they are executed; hence his supervision cannot have much weight. Under consolidation he would be able to execute his plans. I have spoken to many with whom I have come in contact the last two years in regard to consolidation, and find that all but two or three are enthusiastic over it.

"*Conditions of Schools under Present System*: Too many poorly qualified teachers. Great opportunity for neglect in isolated schools. No permanency. A constant change of teachers. Not sufficient interest. Irregular attendance. Petty troubles of community. No place for a teacher to board (in many districts). School board not thoroughly organized. Carelessness on the part of board in transacting business of the schools. Poorly equipped and poorly kept schoolhouses. Must wait till the wheat is gathered to get the necessary supplies. John Smith has the privilege of attending but six months each year, and has an inexperienced teacher each year; his cousin, James Brown, who lives in a wealthier district, may go eight months, and always have an experienced teacher.

"*Schools Under a System of Consolidation*: Closer supervision. Better teachers. More thoroughly organized. A graded school and country home, which is the best combination. Longer term of school. Boys and girls will not quit school at fifteen. Could have a music supervisor. Could have lectures. Country people would have what they move to town to get. Closer interest in community. All children would have equal school privileges.

"We claim justice to all, special privileges to none. This is an 'iridescent dream' in the schools, since they are scattered. Consolidation of schools will bring about the greatest reformation Kansas has ever had. This is one of the most important questions of the day for Kansas to solve. All honor is due to our present state superintendent, Hon. Frank Nelson, who has worked early and late to bring it about. This is a great monument he has erected to his memory, and every child and every parent directly interested in our schools owe him a lasting debt of gratitude. Cloud county will be in the foremost ranks when this great wave comes."
—Bertha Marlatt, County Superintendent.

ANDERSON COUNTY.

"The consolidation of rural and village schools is receiving a great deal of consideration in this county, especially among the districts in which the valuation is low. We have held one election for the purpose of consolidation, and it resulted almost unanimously in favor of the union district. There is a general tendency on the part of pupils and patrons to patronize the village schools in order to get the benefits of a high-school course, if located within a reasonable distance. One village with a four-room school, carrying a two-years high-school course, has twenty-five tuition pupils from four adjoining districts, whose aggregate attendance is forty-eight pupils. One more additional room in this village school would accommodate all pupils of the adjoining districts and would enhance the valuation of the union district $150,000, thus giving all pupils of these four districts the advantage of a high-school training instead of only a few fortunate ones whose individual circumstances enable them to take advantage of their location."—J. B. Cox, County Superintendent.

HARPER COUNTY.

"The subject of school consolidation has received a good deal of attention in this county, but as yet no schools have been consolidated. A vote was taken in two districts a few weeks ago, with the result that one district favored consolidation by a large majority, while in the other there was a light vote and a majority of one against consolidation. The question is being discussed in a number of districts at the present time, and it seems probable that a number of these schools will consolidate in the near future. We have in this county a number of large tracts of grazing land, where residence houses are far apart and only a few families reside in each district. In many cases the taxpayers in such districts oppose long terms of school and high salaries of teachers. It is difficult to make some of them understand that the children in those sparsely settled regions need as many months' school in the year as do those who live elsewhere. Many of the parents are now beginning to think that the remedy for this condition is in school consolidation, whereby better schools may be maintained with little or no increase of expense. School consolidation is often favored by our best teachers, for while the number of teachers would be reduced, those who remained in the profession would have better positions and receive better wages. The demand for better schools is increasing rapidly."—Lee B. Wilson, County Superintendent.

REPUBLIC COUNTY.

"In Republic County no rural schools have yet been consolidated, although the question has been agitated in at least three portions of the county. The question has been discussed in our county associations for the past year or so, and it has a prominent place on the program for the meetings this year. Persons other than teachers, interested in the movement are asked to discuss the question.

"The first attempt made looking toward consolidation was in the town of Courtland and the four surrounding districts. Courtland maintains a school of two rooms and a number of the pupils are from the country. It was thought that if the four districts whose territory is contiguous to the Courtland district could be induced to unite, an excellent high school might be maintained. The proposition met with considerable favor in at least three of these neighboring districts at first, but the matter was never brought to a vote. Later, White Rock township north of Courtland, began to discuss the question. Five different districts were interested, and several public meetings were held to forward the movement. Considerable sentiment in favor of the consolidation of the five districts was created, but in this case, as well as in Courtland, the stumbling-block proved to be the matter of the transportation of pupils. The friends of consolidation, finding that they would be outnumbered if the matter were brought to a vote, did not ask for this privilege.

"At the time of the teachers' institute, the school boards and others of the county were asked to meet and hear something of consolidation. Owing to the very busy season at that time, only a limited number could attend.

"At present the matter is being agitated in a quiet way in Albion township. There are six school districts in the township, and the town of Narka is located in the center of the township. The condition of roads is superb, and the other conditions necessary for consolidation are almost ideal. It is not probable that the question will be brought to a vote at this time, but if the necessary sentiment can be awakened it is possible that a consolidated district consisting of an entire township may be effected.

"Other localities in Republic County favor the plan of consolidation if it can be shown that the total expense of school is not greatly increased. The one thing

that seems to most persons the least feasible is the transportation of pupils. Could this objection be met by practical experience with similar conditions, Republic County would have, within a year, a number of these strong centralized districts."
—E. E. Baird, County Superintendent.

ELLSWORTH COUNTY.

"It may appear strange to many that the sentiment in favor of consolidation of schools has not 'taken' this entire county, ual districts are willing to do this, nothing definite can be done.

"If pushed by the county superintendent or other outside parties, no matter how disinterested they may be, the people are inclined to look upon it as a scheme. Two years ago we had a county-high-school proposition. Well, that proposition is *just five times dead,* which explains some of the danger of outside influence being brought into any school proposition.

"As for the Lorraine school, it is prov-

The Consolidated School at Lorraine, Ellsworth County, Kansas. One of the first of the Kansas Consolidated Schools.

since our single consolidation district was organized in the spring of 1898. But other districts in the county waited for this school to prove the success that was claimed for it. It has done so; but it still requires time for new ideas to take root and grow. I believe there is a widespread sentiment in this county in favor of consolidation; in fact, I know there is. But in each district there are some parties who are opposed, and those who look with favor on the plan are not willing to take hold of such a movement and push it to a successful conclusion or to defeat; and until influential taxpayers in the individ- ing very succeessful. I think it would be impossible to find more than one man in the district who would be willing to go back to the old district plan. I am sure you could not find a boy or a girl in the school who would not object. The attendance last year was eighty-five per cent of the enrollment; this was ten per cent higher than the average for the entire county, and fifteen per cent higher than the average attendance for the country schools. Of the total number of county graduates forty per cent was from the Lorraine school. A two-years high-school course has been adopted. Last year there were two graduates from this course. This year's class in the high-school work numbers eight. The school year was longer and the teachers' salaries higher than the average for the county. The tax levy of 13 mills is but 1.2 mills higher than the average levy for the county.

"Ellsworth County schools (village and city included) cost $20.16 per capita on the average daily attendance. The Lorraine school on the same basis costs $22.44 per capita. This includes all expenditures. The school is a success in every respect. The slightly increased cost of maintenance is so small as to be unworthy of consideration. The taxpayers are unanimous in their approval of the plan. Of three adjacent districts, one has not maintained school for three years; the others have been sending the older pupils to Lorraine, and now talk of uniting with Lorraine. I assure you that a consolidation so far adopted in this county is an unqualified success."—W. W. Maze, County Superintendent.

RUSSELL COUNTY.

"We have no union graded schools in Russell County at present, but I see no reason why we should not soon have two or three. Many of us are in favor of the plan, and we have several places where it would work admirably. I favor the consolidation plan, because it would be the means of putting better teachers in charge of our schools, and those teachers would be much better paid for their services than they are at the present time. Fighting and the use of vulgar and profane language by pupils on the way to and from school would no longer be the cause of so much trouble. Tardiness would be practically wiped out and attendance greatly stimulated. No longer would half-frozen children be seen crouching and shivering around the stove each morning, and no wading to school through slush and mud and sitting all day with wet, cold feet. Schoolrooms would be larger, better furnished, better ventilated and kept cleaner than under the present system. Literary and debating societies, so much needed by our boys and girls, could be organized to better advantage on account of larger numbers taking part in the work, and, being under the direct supervision of the teacher, the low order of exercises so common in the old-fashioned evening lyceum would no longer exist. A taste for the good in literature would take its place.

"At present many of our schools, especially in the western part of the state, have an enrollment of but three or four pupils. Supposing two of those are small, the others can't even get up a game of 'two old cat,' to say nothing of baseball, basket-ball and football, which our boys and girls like so well and should have an opportunity to enjoy. Neither can there be any great amount of enthusiasm in the preparation or reciting of lessons where one pupil is in a class by himself or with a single classmate. The little ones would have a better opportunity to sing, and in every way our country boys and girls would have the same advantages, and on account of their quiet surroundings would do perhaps better work than those who live in the city and attend the city schools. And, if rightly managed, the cost of maintenance need not exceed what it is at tthe present time."—P. C. Smith, County Superintendent.

* * *

XI.—Contracts for Transportation of Pupils

Many different arrangements as to transportation exist. In some places a definite allowance is made to the head of the family and he transports the children, being held to account for their attendance; in other places contracts are made with suburban electric car lines to furnish transportation; in one place in Connecticut an allowance of $20.00 for the year was made to one boy who lived mosewhat off the regular routes, and with this sum he purchased a bicycle and transported himself; in a few other places where horses are plentiful the school has furnished a good stable and the pupils ride their own horses to school; but by far the most common and most desirable form of transportation is that by wagon, a contract being made with some reliable person to transport the pupils to and from school each day.

In making such contracts a common mistake is to agree to award the contract to the lowest bidder. This is bad. The trustees should always reserve to themselves the right to reject any bid and award the contract to the person who, in their judgment, will look after the interests of the children best. The awarding of these contracts is not a matter which can be lumped off to the lowest bidder. It should be entirely proper for the trustees to fix the amount that will be paid and then select the best man obtainable for the work at that price.

To give an idea as to the method of letting contracts two forms, one a notice to bidders and the other a form of contract used, are reproduced:

(a) NOTICE TO BIDDERS.

(This form of advertisement was used in Madison Township, Lake County, Ohio).

Bids for the transportation of pupils of the Madison township schools over the following routes will be received at the office of the Township Clerk until Friday, July 24 at 12 M.: —

Route A. Beginning at County Line on the North Ridge road and running west on said road to schoolhouse in Dist. No. 12.

Route B. Beginning at Perry Line on the North Ridge road and running east to schoolhouse in Dist. No. 12.

Route C. Beginning on Middle Ridge road at residence of N. Badger, running thence west on said road to the residence of Rev. J. Sandford, thence north to schoolhouse in Dist. No. 12.

Route D. Beginning at Perry Line on River road, and running thence east on said road to schoolhouse in Dist. No. 6.

Route E. Beginning at the Hartman farm, thence by Bennett road to Chapel road, thence east to A. R. Monroe's, thence west on Chapel road to schoolhouse in Dist. No. 13.

Route F. Beginning at residence of J. H. Clark and running east on Chapel road to schoolhouse in Dist. No. 13.

All whose bids are acceptable will be required to sign a contract by which they agree:

1. To furnish a suitable vehicle with sufficient seating capacity to convey all the pupils properly belonging to their route, and acceptable to the Committee on Transportation.

2. To furnish all necessary robes, blankets, etc., to keep the children comfortable; and in severe weather the conveyance must be properly heated by oil stoves or soap stones.

3. To provide a good and reliable team of horses, and a driver who is trustworthy, and who shall have control of all the pupils while under his charge, and shall be responsible for their conduct. Said driver and team to be acceptable to the Committee on Transportation.

4. To deliver the pupils at their respective schools not earlier than 8:30 A. M., nor later than 8:50 A. M., and to leave at 4:05 P. M. (sun time).

Each contractor shall give bond for the faithful discharge of his contract in the sum of $100 with sureties approved by the president and clerk of the board.

The committee reserves the right to reject any and all bids.

By order of the committee,
C. G. ENSIGN, Clerk.

(b) CONTRACT FORMS FOR DRIVERS.

At a recent meeting of the County Board of Education of Lagrange County, Indiana, it was decided to have a uniform contract for transporting pupils. It was felt that such a method would assist in a clear understanding of all concerned and encourage co-operation in this work. Blank lines are introduced in several places for such "additional considerations" as the contractor and the township may desire to agree upon.

The following is the form adopted:

School Conveyance Contract.

....Township, Lagrange County, Indiana.

This article of agreement made and entered into this .... day of........ 190..., by and between . ... , of Lagrange County, in the State of Indiana, and........................School Township, in the said County and State.

Witnesseth, That the said........... ......party of the first part, doth hereby agree to and with the said............. School Township, party of the second part, as follows, to wit:

That the said..............will convey by spring hack all children herein stated:

....
....

and such other children of school age whose parents may later reside on the route or in the district.

The transportation route shall be as follows:

....
....

The said party of the first part further agrees to arrive at............between ..A. M. and ...A. M., standard (sun) time and to leave said schoolhouse promptly at the close of each day's session and convey the foregoing pupils to their respective homes as expeditiously as possible in the same general manner as in the morning. He shall strictly prohibit profane or obscene language and boisterous conduct in or about the back. The said party of the first part further agrees not to use tobacco while in charge of the children, neither will he permit its use by any pupils while in his custody. The pupils shall be conveyed with due regard for their comfort and the team shall not only be safe but reasonably speedy.

(Additional considerations.) ....
....
....

The services of the said party of the first part shall commence on the....day of......... ..... 190..., and continue thruout the school year for such days as the school shall be in session.

The said party of the first (or second) part shall provide a comfortable and safe conveyance, and said vehicle shall be so constructed that it can be entirely closed during inclement weather.

(Additional considerations.) ....
....
....

The said party of the second part in consideration of the prompt fulfillment on the part of the party of the first part contracts and agrees to pay..:......... dollars per day for services rendered as above stated.

In case party of the first part fails, neglects or refuses to faithfully do and perform each and every one of the covenants and agreements herein specified on his part to be performed, then this contract shall be void at the option of the party of the second part, and the party of the second part may immediately bring suit on the bond annexed hereto for any damages sustained to the party of the second part by reason of the failure of the party of the first part to perform his covenants and agreements herein contained.

In Witness Whereof, the above named parties have signed the above contract this....day of . ....., 190...

Party of First Part............
Party of Second Part.... .....
By............Trustee

Know All Men by These Presents, That we............and.............. are held and bound unto the State of Indiana in the sum of.... .. dollars, fo - the payment of which we do bind our- selves jointly and severally. The condition of this obligation is such that we do hereby guarantee the full performance of all conditions specified in said contract on the part of said............to be kept.

Now if the said.................shall faithfully fulfil all the requirements mentioned, then this obligation to be void, otherwise to be and remain in full force.

Witness our hands and seals this.... day of.................190..
....[SEAL]
.... [SEAL]

XII.—The Plan in California

(a) THE PURPOSE OF THE NEW LAW.

A Statement by Mr. Black.

(Mr. Black, who makes this statement, was a member of the Assembly in the last Legislature, and introduced the consolidation bill in the Assembly. He also looked after the bill in the Senate, and was largely instrumental in securing its adoption as a law.)

PALO ALTO, CAL., May 20, 1903.

Assembly Bill No. 532 passed both houses of the Legislature with but little opposition and became a law by receiving Governor Pardee's signature March 21, 1903. This bill in its provisions closely follows the Union School Laws in successful operation in many eastern states, notably Ohio, Indiana, Iowa, Minnesota, Nebraska and Kansas. Its purpose is to effect the consolidation of the small and weak districts of our rural communities and provide for the transportation of pupils to and from the union school by means of wagons, and to pave the way for more perfect supervision of rural schools.

That the country schools of California need to be improved, goes without saying. They have not kept pace with the progress made by the city school systems. The only practical way to bring the benefits of a graded school system to our rural communities appears to be thru the adoption of the Union School plan. This plan of school organization contemplates the disorganization of small districts and uniting them into one strong, well-graded school. Consolidation can, in some cases, be made with adjoining rural schools, and in others, with the schools of a village, where oftentimes the nucleus of a graded school already exists.

The novel part of the new plan is the transporting of the pupils, the carrying of the children to the school, instead of carrying the school to the children, as has been our policy in the past. This is merely applying the lesson taught by the remarkable success of the Rural Mail Delivery system. The wagons go over a specified route, collecting all the children living on that route and conveying them to school with a promptness which could not be secured under the old way. The school board lets the contract for each route, and bonds should be required, to insure responsible drivers.

By this plan of consolidation and transportation, the Union School Law proposes to strengthen the country schools of our State. It will make possible the employment of better teachers. It will secure more thoro superintendence, and it will undoubtedly stimulate school attendance. Another great advantage will be the richer social life it will develop in our rural communities. It will do away with the feeling of isolation that often exists, and by stimulating lecture courses and literary entertainments, will prove of educational value to all the people of the district. All this can be accomplished, I believe, at a less cost to the rural tax payer than is possible under present wasteful conditions. I am hopeful of splendid results from the adoption of this plan in the more thickly settled portions of our State.   MARSHALL BLACK.

* * *

(b) THE POSSIBILITIES OF THE NEW LAW.

A Statement by State Superintendent Thomas J. Kirk.

State of California,
Department of Education.

SACRAMENTO, CAL., May 19, 1903.

The scheme of consolidation of school districts and transportation of pupils to a centrally located schoolhouse is one that has come along with rural mail delivery, country telephone lines and other improvements for life in the country. Every one knows how great has been the increase of population in cities during the past three decades and how it has correspondingly dwindled in the country.

Among the many attractions of the city are the superior school facilities, such as large, well-equipped, sanitarily constructed school buildings, with laboratories, larger libraries, picture galleries and rooms and classes sufficient for a teacher for every grade. These are among the causes that have led parents to give up the farm and move to town for the better education of their children. The result is a congested condition of population in the cities and a dearth of people and home life in the country. President Jordan uttered a patent truth not long ago when he stated that about 25 per cent of the people now living in cities have no business to be there; that they would be far better off if they would return to the country.

The atmosphere and surroundings of life in the country, where there is freedom from the noise and bustle of the street, where the individual is away from the influences that counteract good precepts and right training, have ever been recognized as ideal conditions for the growth and development of youth. Hence the thought and attention given by thoughtful parents to ways and means for the improvement of country schools and the efforts to secure in some measure to the rural communities what has hitherto been enjoyed only by the cities and towns. The thought has been to preserve all the good features of the country school and to supplement them as far as possible with the advantages of the city school. Among the things admittedly necessary to a good school are the aggregation of a reasonably large number of pupils, graded and classified to best possible advantage, and an up-to-date, commodious, comfortable, well-furnished, well-equipped school building. Sewage and general sanitation, heating and ventilating, matters which have been well-nigh impossible in the case of the isolated country school, are also problems which, it is believed, may be satisfactorily and successfully solved by this new scheme.

The Legislature of California, at its session which closed March 14th last, adopted a measure which its advocates believe permits and provides for the carrying out of some of the foregoing ends. It is purely permissive in its operation. There is nothing compulsory about it. It enables two or more contiguous school districts to go into partnership in order to secure better school facilities. The initiatory steps to be taken and the method of organization and of management have been adopted from the law relating to the establishment and government of union high schools. The scheme is practicable and to be recommended only for reasonably well populated communities and in sections where there are fairly good roads. In my judgment it would not be reasonable to expect the plan to succeed for an area greater than 100 to 125 square miles —that is, for a territory of from ten to twelve miles square.

Before voting upon the question of a union school district, the trustees of the different local districts should carefully consider the matter, and should call meetings of the people of their districts to discuss and weigh the advantages and disadvantages likely to accrue from the proposed change.

The different districts that may combine to form a union district retain their identity for the purpose of census enumeration and for the apportionment of school moneys, except that one census marshal will take the census of all the districts in the union, and the money that would be received by the respective districts is apportioned and credited to the union district.

For purposes of taxation, bonding and other matters of revenue, and for admission into and withdrawal from a union district, the same general provisions apply as now apply in the case of union high-school districts. Provision is also made for dissolution of the union in the event that after three years conditions and results have not been found satisfactory. But so far as unseen and untried plans can be prejudged the scheme is most promising. It may be added, however, that it is not entirely an untried experiment. Several States, notably Ohio, have adopted and are carrying out a similar plan in many communities with highly gratifying results. No legislative school measure enacted in recent years promises more at the present time. If undertaken and carried out in the proper spirit, it is believed that some of the highest ideals in education and in public-school work are soon to be realized.

THOMAS J. KIRK,
Superintendent of Public Instruction.

* * *

(c) PUTTING THE LAW INTO OPERATION

Letters by Dr. Brown and Superintendent Hyatt.

University of California, Department of Education.

Berkeley, Cal., April 30, 1903.

My Dear Mr. Cubberley: It seems to me that the bill relating to the consolidation of school districts, which you prepared with so much care and the Legislature has passed in substantially its original form, is a measure of very great significance for the development of sound education in the rural portions of our state. As the bill stands, it seems to preserve all that is good in our rather remarkable California provision for district schools, and at the same time to make it possible for the more enterprising portions of the state to forge ahead along the lines which have proved so successful in the East and Middle West.

The carrying out of this scheme will depend in the first instance upon a few friends of education in communities that are favorably situated as regards the conditions of consolidation. I think county superintendents would do well to look over their several counties and select the groups of districts which they regard as most likely to carry the consolidation into effect, readily and advantageously. By a little judicious prompting, the school trustees and other public-spirited citizens of those districts can be led to take the preliminary steps — to talk the matter over with their neighbors, study the provisions of the law, and work up a local sentiment in favor of the change. As soon as the plan has been got well under way in two or three counties, it would be desirable to have full accounts of the movement and how it was brought about published in the newspapers and in the official journal, so that other portions of the state may be able to profit by the experience of the pioneers.

The plan is well worth any effort it may cost to put it into operation. It will give our pupils in the country districts some of the advantages now possessed by those living in towns that are provided with good graded schools; it will pave the way for the establishment of small high schools in counties which are not yet adequately provided with such schools; and by calling attention in a new way to the educational interests of the community will, I believe, cause a new wave of educational activity and enthusiasm to move over the counties in which the new plan is tried.

Hoping most earnestly that this movement will fulfil all these expectations and more, I am, very truly yours,

ELMER E. BROWN.

* * *

Office of the County Superintendent of Schools.

Riverside, Cal., May 9, 1903.

Dear Sir: In relation to the permissive law concerning consolidation of districts, I feel moved to say that I think it will be a fine thing for certain places in this state, where the conditions are favorable — places that have been subdivided into the many weak districts, districts so weak that they can barely eke out an existence. This law offers a chance for a new birth, under richer, better conditions. I shall take much interest in watching the experiment tried in a few places favorable to its success.

I would not *urge* it, however, indiscriminately upon the schools of a county or state, or recommend it as a cure-all for the ills of the body politic. There will be many ready to rush into this new thing without understanding it, without knowing whether the chances for its success are favorable. In most cases it will be well, I think, to watch the experiment for a year or two somewhere else before trying it yourself. If discordant elements are bound together, if people go into it not understanding what they must give up, then trouble comes—and with trouble in the family, with divorce in the air, success is not probable—is hardly possible.

Very truly yours,
EDWARD HYATT.

* *

(d) THE FIRST UNION FORMED UNDER THE NEW LAW—SAN DIEGO COUNTY

On May 2d an election was held in San Diego county to vote on the proposition to unite the districts of Merle, Hope and Encinitas into a union school district. The election was carried, and this becomes the first union under the new law. The future of this union will be watched with interest. The following letter from Mr. Baldwin, County Superintendent of Schools of San Diego County, gives a good idea as to his views on the matter and his missionary work in the county.

Office of the County Superintendent of Schools, San Diego County.

San Diego, Cal., May 20, 1903.

"Rah! rah! Stanford! Rah! rah! Berkeley! Rah! rah!—High School!" are bursts of enthusiasm that still linger and charm my ear from jubilant and happy students singing praises to their Alma Mater. Similar loyal expressions may be heard from any of the grammar schools of our cities; but never do you hear this organized "Rah! rah!" of enthusiasm from the rural schools of the state.

Through an act of the recent State Legislature, which endows the country youth with educational possibilities far beyond the present regime, a morning of a brighter day is dawning upon them, for there may be established in many of their localities opportunities to possess that class spirit of the strong institute and rend the air with their school shouts of jolly hurrahs.

Adjacent communities are now permitted to consolidate their schools and transport the children from the old districts to a central school where numbers and educational facilities will generate that true inspiring atmosphere that stimulate the student to his highest personal effort.

Ever since the state took upon itself the education of the youth, the city authorities have constantly been appealing to the Legislature and securing from it higher power and greater facilities, through which they have expanded and developed the city system until to-day every municipality points with pride to the evolution of its school system. This action has inaugurated in each state two distinctly marked educational systems, the one for the city boy, the other for the country boy. The question now arises which boy has the advantage?

It is not necessary to go very deeply into this discussion, a few will suffice.

Nothing is so dear to a parent's heart as the welfare of his family. He will sacrifice his money, his residence and his business all for his child; hence the best school is none too good for him, and the State thinks the same. The abandoned farms are eloquent reminders of this love, and the moving of parents into cities to educate their children demonstrates that the city school system is worthy of this sacrifice. In their judgment the city schools are superior to those of the country.

They say the country school system has fossilized; that the country schools are still the nurseries and experiment stations for the cities. They develop the teachers and are soon deprived of the best, for the cities pay the higher salaries and command their services. The tenure of office in the city is more satisfactory, and is a strong attraction. The excellent buildings, with modern equipment in apparatus and the opportunity of doing special work in harmony with one's training, are further inducements that tend to take from the country boy the strong teachers of the state. The five-minute recitations, extending from the lisping child learning the elements of the language to the advanced pupil plowing his way to graduate from a school of eight or nine grades, where "hearing lessons" constitute the employment, and where true teaching is almost an impossibility, are further weaknesses in comparison with the graded school of the day.

It is poor political economy to develop the educational facilities of our cities and retain the rural schools of our grandfather's days. If our cities have the better system, then it is the duty of our educators and statesmen to establish in the rural communities wherever possible a school system up to date and equal to the best the cities afford.

At the Biennial Convention of Superintendents held in Fresno May, 1902, by request of State Superintendent Kirk, I spoke on the "Necessity of laws that would permit the consolidation of school districts and the transportation of school children." The debate showed that several of the superintendents were strongly opposed to the innovation. On investigation it was discovered that misinterpretation of the desired law was the source of the confusion. After considerable discussion a resolution was unanimously adopted by the convention recommending the above measure, and a committee of three was appointed, consisting of Ellwood P. Cubberley of Stanford University; Miss Minnie Coulter, Superintendent of Schools of Sonoma County, and Hugh J. Baldwin, Superintendent of Schools of San Diego County, to induce the State Legislature to furnish measures permitting freedom to school districts along this line.

The Legislature granted the request of the convention, and the law is now in force. All school trustees that desire to avail themselves of the benefits of this act during the next fiscal year must see that the petition to the County Superintendent and election are attended to immediately, as all the requirements of the law must be performed before the first day of July of each year.

Too much credit cannot be given to, nor can too much honor be conferred upon Professor Ellwood P. Cubberley of Stanford University; President Frederic Burk, State Normal School, San Francisco; and State Superintendent Kirk for the great missionary work these eminent educators have done to secure the passage of this law and for their constant efforts to renovate and invigorate the rural schools of the state.

We cannot ask the people for more money to aid the country schools, for, so far as apportionments of school funds go, the rural school has a decided advantage. The cost per capita on average daily attendance is far greater in the country schools than in the city. The expenditure of the school department of San Francisco per capita on average daily attendance, high school and all, is close to $35, with salaries averaging $97; while Alpine County's expense on same basis is almost $40, and teacher's salaries averaging only $61.65.

The consolidation of naturally united districts, throwing their school funds together for united action, is the only solution to enrich the rural schools.

What should be done to inaugurate this measure? What difficulties will probably be met and how shall they be overcome?

The County Superintendent should arrange a series of local institutes in the districts that by nature can be combined and transportation of children practicable. He has then an opportunity to do the necessary missionary work and explain the great virtue of the innovation. The welfare of the child must be his platform, for opposition may come from local pride to retain the school; from false impression as to reduction in value of real estate if school be suspended; from those receiving perquisites — janitor's work, hauling water and wood and making repairs, and from boarding teacher.

These must be overcome by the attack that the school funds are exclusively for the child, and he is entitled to the highest possible returns for the expenditure of this sacred fund.

The strongest argument that I have heard in opposition to the plan was that it savored too much of paternalism, but I readily overcome this by proving that whatever paternity existed in the support of the public school system of the State of California, the adoption of this measure neither increased nor diminished it; it simply permits the disbursement of the people's money more intelligently and systematically, giving to the children of the country communities equal possibilities with the city children, far beyond the present possibilities of the rural schools.

I advocate the preservation of the local schoolhouse in the discussion for Sunday school and community interests, and many of the large taxpayers of the district consequently removed their objections and now support the measure. The proper missionary work will meet with success.

I had no serious trouble in securing a consolidation of the district of Encinitas, Merle and Hope after the people understood the operation of the law.

At a recent local institute held in Oceanside, the evening session was devoted to the discussion of the application of the law. I outlined what could be done there. At the conclusion of my address a resolution was passed by the citizens of Oceanside that a committee of seven, including the County Superintendent, be appointed by the Chair to represent the six surrounding districts for the purpose of ascertaining the feasibility of the measure for that locality. This committee will be called together by the 30th of May for report. We must remember that all of our districts cannot avail themselves of the benefit of this act. We must encourage the plan where success is evident.

After the organization, it is absolutely necessary to secure teachers in sympathy with the enterprise. The heart and hand must go together to secure the desired results, for in the pioneering many problems will arise that must be met with a determination to solve successfully. It may be difficult to secure suitable persons to drive the teams for the amount that may be spared for that purpose, and under such conditions I recommend that the teachers reside in the localities most favorable to meet this condition and gather the children along the line. In fact, I have had already several excellent teachers speak to me as very willing to take charge of the conveyance. This plan is decidedly more advantageous to the child. The parents, who have given much thought to the transportation, are more and more entranced with the arrangement.

In conclusion, I state that the successful application of this law is now in the hands of the County Superintendents in particular, and the county boards of education and school trustees in general. With these bodies working in harmony, we may look forward within the next decade to a transformation of the present rural school system to a well-organized and supervised ideal plan.

Being relieved of the unfavorable surroundings that so frequently meet one's eyes in city communities, it will be so educationally marked thru the great possible evolution that the suburban consolidated system provides, nourished by the high, noble and pure elements of the interior that these schools will be the most popular resorts for the education of the child.

. HUGH J. BALDWIN,
County Superintendent Schools.

(c) The Proposed Union at Fowler, Fresno County

Lessons to be Drawn from the Attempt.

The town of Fowler is well situated to serve as a natural concentrating center for at least three surrounding districts. The school at Fowler has an enrollment of about two hundred pupils, and employs four teachers. It was proposed to form a union district by uniting two or three surrounding districts with the town school, transport the pupils, and develop a good strong union school, thus providing a good city education to the children of the surrounding country. A meeting of the trustees of the town district and of three adjoining districts was held at Fowler on Saturday, April 4th. The meeting was called by the trustees of one of the adjoining districts, and not by the trustees of the town school. This was certainly very tactful. All of the districts were represented by all the trustees, and the law was explained and the advantages of consolidation pointed out. As there was some opposition in one of the districts, it was thought best to leave that district out for the present, and admit it to the union later on, if it so desired.

The next step in the procedure was to obtain the signature of a majority of the heads of families to a petition asking the County Superintendent to call an election to allow the voters to determine the question. Persons who understood the purpose of the law and the arguments for consolidation accompanied the trustees who circulated the petition, and carefully met all arguments against the plan. In this way the signature of every head of a family in each of the three districts who had children of school age was secured. So far good, but right here the mistake was made. In each district there were one or more *voters* who were not *heads of families*, and these were not seen, as they should have been.

The petition was sent to the County Superintendent, and, in accordance with the law, an election to determine the question was called for Saturday, May 16th. After the election had been called opposition developed in one of the districts, chiefly from men who had not been interviewed when the petition was being circulated, and who, consequently, did not thoroly understand the purpose of the plan, and when the votes were counted it was found that the union had been defeated in two districts, tho the total vote cast was in favor of the plan. The law requires that there shall be a majority in each and every district. In the district where the opposition was strongest, out of 28 votes on the register, 24 voted, the result being 16 against to 8 for the union. In the town district, where there are several hundred voters, only 26 votes were cast, 23 for and 3 against. In the Third district, where no opposition was expected, a very light vote was cast, and the plan was defeated by a small majority, those who were in favor of the plan not voting because they thought there would be no need of their votes. Had there been any opposition in the town of Fowler it might have been defeated in the same way there.

To sum up the whole matter, consolidation was defeated chiefly by those who would not be affected by it one way or the other, because they had no children of school age, and by those who favored the plan and did not think it necessary to go to the polls and vote. The lesson is plain: To consolidate, *see every voter* when circulating the petition regardless of whether he has children of school age or not, and then make an effort to get every man who is in favor of the plan to go to the polls and vote when the election takes place.

ELLWOOD P. CUBBERLEY.

(f) Type of a Possible Union in Riverside County

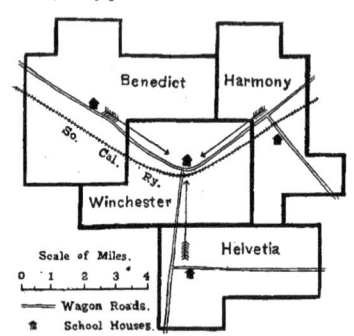

Map of the districts, showing boundaries, wagon roads, school houses, and distances.

The adjoining illustration shows a group of four districts suitably situated for consolidation. The region is comparatively flat and level, and the schools are only about three miles apart. Winchester is a natural concentrating center. The following table shows the financial status of the schools as they now are:

If these four schools were to unite to form a union a great economy could be effected, as well as a great increase in the efficiency of the school secured. The school could be managed with two teachers if confined to the primary and grammar grades only, but as there is no financial reason why this need be done, it would be best to put in as a third teacher a strong man who could act as principal of the school and teach some ninth and tenth grade work to those boys and girls who want to go farther than the grammar grades. Such a school ought to do the first year of high-school work well, sending the pupils on to the larger central high schools for further work. With three teachers, one teacher would teach the first, second and third grades; another would teach the fourth, fifth and sixth grades; and the principal would teach all grades from the seventh up. This would permit a degree of specialization in the work which would be of great benefit to all the children of the school. Instead of schools from seven to eighteen pupils, there would be a school of about seventy, with from twenty to thirty in each room; and instead of classes of one or two there would be classes of from six to ten. The recitation periods could be made three times as long as at present, and the increased interest in school and the stimulus to action which would come from the increased numbers in the school and in each class would be an educational factor of great importance.

The better school would keep pupils in

ITEMS.	Benedict	Winchester	Harmony	Helvetia	TOTALS.
School Census	13	21	19	24	77
Total Enrolment	11	19	23	24	77
Average Daily Attendance	7.5	18	14.5	16	56
Length of Term	8 mos.	8 mos.	8 mos.	8 mos.	
Apportionment on Census	$400 00	$500 00	$400 00	$500 00	$1800 00
" on Average Daily Attendance	75 00	180 00	145 00	160 00	560 00
Total Apportionment	$475 00	$680 00	$545 00	$660 00	$2360 00
Teachers Salaries per Month	$50 00	$55 00	$55 00	$50 00	
Teachers Salaries per Year	$400 00	$440 00	$440 00	$400 00	$1680 00
Library Fund	10 00	15 00	10 00	15 00	50 00
Repairs, Census, Fuel, etc.	65 00	50 00	95 00	161 00	371 00
Total Expense for Year	$475 00	$505 00	$545 00	$576 00	$2101 00

it longer than at present. At present only about two-thirds of the enrollment is in average daily attendance. With a strong union school and transportation of pupils the average daily attendance ought to be increased from 56 to at least 70. This increase of fourteen in the average daily attendance would mean an increase of $140 in income for the union school.

Let us now see what would be the financial aspect of such a union:

INCOME.	
Total apportionment at present	$2360 00
Increase for 14 in average daily attendance	140 00
Total income after consolidation	$2500 00
EXPENSE.	
1 Principal at $70.00 for 8 months	$560 00
2 Teachers at $55.00 for 8 months	880 00
Library Fund, as at present	50 00
Repairs, Census Fuel, Etc.	210 00
Total expense for maintenance	$1700 00
Left for transportation of pupils	$800 00

After maintaining a far better school, with better-paid teachers, better teaching, better supervision, with the first year of high-school instruction provided for free, there still remains $800 to provide for the transportation of the children. Three different routes would be required. Judging by prices paid elsewhere, this ought to be sufficient, tho transportation is likely to cost more the first year than ever afterward. The distances are short, and the maximum number to be transported would be 11, 23 and 24—a total of 58 if all enrolled attended. Considering the short distance, the good roads and the dry climate, it ought to be possible to get each route contracted for at a rate of $30 a month; this would be a total of $720 for the year for the three routes. This would leave a net surplus of $80 for other purposes.

These four districts are types of many other possible unions which might be formed in this state, with great gain in the quality and quantity of the education provided for the children of these favorably situated districts, and with no additional expense to the taxpayers of the

ELLWOOD P. CUBBERLEY.

* * *

Official Department
State Board of Education

GEORGE C. PARDEE, *President of the Board* .... Governor, Sacramento
MORRIS ELMER DAILEY .... President State Normal School, San Jose
E. T. PIERCE .... President State Normal School, Los Angeles
C. C. VAN LIEW .... President State Normal School, Chico
BENJAMIN IDE WHEELER .... President University of California, Berkeley
ELMER E. BROWN .... Prof of Theory and Practice of Education University of Cal., Berkeley
SAMUEL T. BLACK .... President State Normal School, San Diego
FREDERIC BURK .... President State Normal School, San Francisco
THOMAS J. KIRK *Secretary of the Board* .... Superintendent Public Instruction, Sacramento

The Meeting of the State Board of Education, June 6, 1903.

The State Board of Education met at Sacramento June 6, 1903. The following were present: Benjamin I. Wheeler, Frederic Burk, Morris E. Dailey, Samuel T. Black, C. C. Van Liew, E. T. Pierce, Thomas J. Kirk. President Wheeler acted as chairman of the meeting.

The request for the reconsideration of the B. F. Wulff case was denied. The revocation of life diploma of Thomas C. Welch was revoked upon the charges of unfitness preferred against him by the County Board of Education of Riverside County.

The Committee on the OFFICIAL JOURNAL OF EDUCATION reported in favor of Harr Wagner's suggestion of appointing an advisory board of editors. The report was adopted. The following were selected by ballot: President C. C. Van Liew of Chico; President Morris E. Dailey, San Jose; Hon. John Swett, Martinez; Supt. C. C. Hughes, Alameda; Dr. E. C. Moore, of the University of California.

The Committee on High School Text Books reported formally on adding an additional number of books to the list. Bulletin giving the list in full will be issued at an early date by State Supt. Kirk.

The Western Journal of Education.

Action on code of professional ethics was postponed until the next meeting.

The Normal Schools of Willimantic and New Briton, Conn., and of Cape Girardy, Mo., were placed on the accredited list. The applications for accrediting of the Michigan State Life Certificate was denied.

The Chicago Kindergarten College and Golden Gate Kindergarten Association of San Francisco were placed on the accredited list for the granting of kindergarten primary certificates.

* * *

The following Diplomas were granted:

University Documents.

Ella Castelhun, San Francisco; Frances Hammel Gearhart, Merced; Kate Herrick, Sacramento; Maud B. Jones, Sacramento; Edith Rosine Kurtz, Sonoma; Margarethe H. E. Meyer, Sacramento; Louise S. Wilson, San Francisco.

Normal Documents.

Annie Louise Adams, San Jose; Florence Anderson, Chico; Clara F. Boardman, San Jose; Annie J. Brook, San Jose; Evie Kate Burt, Chico; Rebecque M. J. Cooper, Los Angeles; Viola Crum, Chico; Ysibel Irene Daly, San Jose; Edith V. Duncan, San Jose; El Vira V. Johnson, San Jose; Ada W. Karr, San Jose; Harriett W. Phelps, San Jose; Minnie E. Rees, San Jose; Margaret Cecilia SaVage, Los Angeles; Mary Barbara Starbuck, Chico; Mrs. OliVe Thornburg, San Jose; Jessie A. Tritt, Los Angeles; L. Grace Turner, Chico; W. E. Ulrici, San Jose; May Wilson, San Jose.

Special Life Diplomas.

John K. Daniels, Bookkeeping, San Francisco; Louise E. Freese, Penmanship, San Francisco; Dora Kozminsky, Stenography, San Francisco; Dora Warshauer, Typewriting, San Francisco.

High School Diplomas.

Evelyn D Armer, San Francisco; Helen Eliot, Butte; Margarethe H. E. Meyer Sacramento; Elmer I. Miller, Butte; Viva B. McArthur, San Francisco; Mary E. G. Morton, Sacramento; IrVing E. Outcalt, Merced; Emily P. Rhine, San Francisco; Robert Cromwell Root, Alameda; Adella Tucker, Orange.

Grammar School Diplomas.

Elizabeth O. Agnew, Alameda; Besse Baker, Placer; Wm. H. Banks, Yolo; Carleton T. Bartlett, Amador; Marcella Barry, Santa Clara; E la Louise Bennett, Kern; Chas. F. Black-tock. Ventura; Joseph Blumb, Ventura; Jennie L. Boswell, Los Angeles; Margaret Bradley, Alameda; Lola Bray, Yolo; Annie E. Britton, Santa Clara; R. Gertrude Brokaw Yolo; Margaret Clare Burke. Sonoma; Grace Bickford Chadwick, Glenn; Martha S. Case, Los Angeles; Margaret G. Cashin, San Francisco; Rose G. Daly, Santa Clara; Anna L. Dodge, Kings; Virginia V. Dollarhide, Napa; Mildred I. Farrell, Sonoma; Clara L. Finnegan, San Francisco; Kate J. Foley, San Luis Obispo; Calla Frazier, Kern; Louise E. Freese. San Francisco; Birdeen M. Freeman, Alameda; Edith M. Frost, Sonoma; Matie I. Gardner, Santa Clara; Mira J. Glidden. Fresno; E. May Grant, Santa Cruz; W. H. Greenhalgh. Amador; Mrs. Abby M. Griffith, Glenn; Della Pearl Hague. Fresno; Adele Harrington, Tehama; Salena Heckle, Tehama; Daisy G. Hewitt, Contra Costa; Ida I. Hill, Tuolumne; Mary Lane Hines, Fresno; Iosie H. Inglis, San Joaquin; Lena M. Jones, Marin; Eva Jones, San Joaquin; Ada W. Karr, Sonoma; Beulah Kozminsky, San Francisco; Bessie Lonsdale Leavitt, Fresno; Alice Lewis, Marin; Rose F. Lewis. San Francisco; Edna Locke, Sonoma; Katie E. Lynch, Butte; Amy Marcus, Tuolumne; Mary A. McKay, Sonoma; Mary R. McCall. Napa; Alice Catherine McCarty, Orange; Lucile McCargar, Santa Barbara; James A. McGuffin, Sacramento; Mrs. J. R. Murdo, Tuo umne; Mathilde Meysan, Inyo; Clara Belle Miller. Tehama; Evalena Van Winkle Miles, Sonoma; Emeline R. Miller, Santa Clara; Winifred E. Moon, Sutter; Mabel Lucy Morrell, Contra Costa; Alice Mulcahy, NeVada; June G. Painter. Alameda; Pearl L. Phelps, Tehama; Henrietta Post, Amador; Elizabeth D Potter, Butte; Jesse F. Prestwood, Sonoma; Luella R. Prentiss. Los Angeles; Stella Reynolds, San Joaquin; Amanda Rickey. Sacramento; Eliza Ann Rixou, San Francisco; Edna Mae Robinson, Sonoma; Zilda M. Rogers, Sonoma; Anna M. Schulz, Placer; Callie G. Shartzer, Santa Clara; Frankie Shomate, Kern; Esther Smith. San Joaquin; Minnie SteVens, Kings; Mrs. M. E. T. Stevens, Inyo; Mary Storer, Fresno; Myrta M. SturteVant. Los Angeles; Esther Rose Sullivan, Sutter; Helen M. SulliVan, Alameda; Lizzie Stewart, Contra Costa; Elizabeth M. Tait, Los Angeles; Mrs. Emma T. Thees, Los Angeles; Carlotta E. Thornton, Los Angeles; Hattie May Tilson, Monterey; R. Izer Turner, Orange; Mrs. H. A. Van Housen. Sacramento; Herbert Walker, San Joaquin; Mrs. Katie High West, Glenn; Mrs. Minnie Weems, Kings; Eliz beth Estella Webster. Los Angeles; E. Mabel Wheeler, Amador; Mamie D. Wheeler, Amador; John H. W llms, Stanislaus; Wm. S. Williams, Amador; Odile G. Woody, Kern.

High School Credentials.

Clara P. Ames; Frank J. Browne; A Percy Brown; Geo. A. Connolly; C. M. Carpenter; Jennie M. Deyo; E. G. Donaldson; F. L. Fenton; John L. Mulrein; A. Oliver; Mary E. Rice; Margaret S. Robbins; Walter R. Rutherford; W. E. Schlieman; Geo. A. Sorrick; M. Pauline Scott.

* * *

Resolutions Adopted by the State Text-Book Committee.

1. It is the purpose of the State Text-Book Committee to secure the consideration, compilation or reVision of texts, for use in the schools of California, on the basis, first of merit, and secondly, of economy; and without reference to any other considerations whatsoeVer. All persons who may in any way haVe to do with the presentation, examination, and choice of texts are requested to co-operate with the committee with a view to the full realization of this purpose.

2. EVery publishing house desiring to submit texts for adoption and use by this committee is requested to furnish the committee with the names of all agents who are authorized to represent such publishing house in its relations with the committee. All such representatiVes will be notified of the intention of the committee to compile or reVise text-books in any giVen subject, in time to present proposals for the use of copyright matter in such compilation or reVision.

3. All representatives of publishing houses or those having text matter to offer are requested to address their communications relating to text-books or text-matter, in writing, to the committee at Sacramento and to have no separate communications with reference to such matter, either directly or indirectly, with any individual member of the committee or with its secretary. But the several members of the committee would be pleased to be furnished with identical copies of any important communications addressed to the committee as a whole and to receive copies of texts offered for adoption. All communications received by the committee will be kept on file, under charge of the secretary and open to the inspection of all members of the State Board of Education.

4. Full publicity will be giVen to all acts of the committee The committee holds that, under the statute which created it, the approval of the State Board of Education is necessary to the Validity of all of its acts, with the exception of those relating to the employment of a secretary.

THOMAS J. KIRK, Supt.

PUBLISHERS' NOTICE.

THE WESTERN JOURNAL OF EDUCATION succeeds to the subscription lists, advertising patronage, and good will of the Golden Era, established in San Francisco in 1852.

Subscription, $1 50 a year. Single copies. 15 cents.

Remit by check, Postoffice order, Wells, Fargo & Co., or by stamps.

ADVERTISEMENTS—Advertisements of an unobjectionable nature will be inserted at the rate of $3.00 a month per inch.

MSS.—Articles on methods, trials of new theories, actual experiences, and school news, reports of teachers' meetings, etc., urgently solicited.

Address all communications to THE WESTERN JOURNAL OF EDUCATION, 723 Market Street. San Francisco.

HARR WAGNER, Editor.
THE WHITAKER & RAY COMPANY PUBLISHERS.

Entered at the San Francisco Post-office as second-class matter.

The Official Organ of the Department of Public Instruction of the State of California.

The material for this issue was furnished by Prof. Ellwood P. Cubberley of Stanford University.

* * *

In the report on the "Supervision of Rural Schools" in the May number, the chairmanship of the committee is credited to Supt. Kate Ames. It should have been credited to ex-Supt. John A. Imrie.

* * *

The commencement exercises at the University of California was made particularly notable by the address to the graduates by President Roosevelt. The address should be read in every public school. The following is an extract:

President Wheeler, Fellow Members of the University:

Last night, in speaking to one of my new friends in California, he told me that he thought enough had been said to me about the fruits and flowers, that enough had been said to me about California's being an Eden, that he wished I would pay some attention to Adam as well as Eden; and much though I have been interested in the wonderful physical beauty of this wonderful State, I have been infinitely more interested in its citizenship, and perhaps most in its citizenship in the making.

This same friend last night suggested a thought to me that I intend to try to work out in speaking to you today. We were talking over the University of California, and from that went on to speak of the general educational system of our country. Facts tend to become commonplace and we tend to lose sight of their importance when once they become ingrained as part of the life of the nation. Although we had a good talk about what the widespread education in this country means, I question if any of us deeply consider its meaning. From the lowest grade of the public school to the highest form of university training, education in this country is at the disposal of every man, every woman who chooses to work for and obtain it. The State has done much, very much. Witness the university. Private benefaction has done much, very much. Witness also this university.

Each one of us who has obtained an education has obtained something for which he or she has not personally paid. No matter what the school, what the university, every American who has a school training, a college training, a university training, has obtained something given to him outright by the State or given to him by those, dead or alive, who were able to make provision for that training because of the protection of the State, because of existence within its borders. Each one of us then who has an education, school or college, has obtained something from the community at large for which he or she has not paid; and no self-respecting man or woman is content to rest permanently under such an obligation.

Where the state has bestowed such an education the man who accepts it must be content to accept it merely as a charity unless he returns it to the state in full in the shape of good citizenship.

I don't ask of you men and women here today good citizenship as a favor to the state. I demand it of you as a right, and hold you recreant to your duty if you fail to give it. Here you are in this university, in this state, with its wonderful climate, which is going to permit the people of a northern stock for the first time in the history of that northern stock to gain education under physical circumstances, in physical surroundings, somewhat akin to those which surrounded the Greeks. Here you have all those advantages, and you are not to be excused if you do not show in tangible fashion your appreciation of them and your power to give practical effect to that appreciation. From all our citizens we have the right to expect good citizenship, but most of all from those who have had the training of body, of mind, of soul, which comes from association in and with a great university.

Of those to whom much has been given we have Biblical authority to expect and demand much in return, and the most that can be given to any man is education. I expect and demand in the name of the nation much more from you who have had training of the mind than from those of mere wealth. Now, to the man of means much has been given, too, and much will be expected from him, and ought to be, but not as much as from you; because your possession is more valuable than his and if you envy him I think poorly of you. Envy is merely the meanest form of admiration, and the man who envies another admits thereby his own inferiority. And we have the right to expect from the college-bred man, the college-bred woman, a proper sense of proportion, a proper sense of perspective, which will enable him or her to see things in their right relation, one to the other, and when thus seen, while wealth will have a proper place, a just place, as an instrument for achieving happiness and power, it will not stand as high as much else in our national life.

Now, I ask you to take that, not as a conventional statement from the university platform, but to test it by thinking of the men whom you admire in our past history and seeing what are the qualities which have made you admire them—what are the services they have rendered. For, as President Wheeler said today, it is true now, as it ever has been true, that the greatest good fortune, the greatest honor, that can befall any man is that he shall serve, that he shall serve the nation, serve his people, serve mankind; and, looking back in history to the names that come up before us, the names to which we turn, the names of the men of our own people which stand as shining in our annals, the names of those men typify the qualities which rightly we should hold in the highest reverence; those names are the names of the statesmen, the soldiers, the scholars, the poets; the architects of our material prosperity also, but only also.

Don't misunderstand me. The average man, the average woman, must earn his or her living in one way or another, and I most emphatically do not advise any one to decline to do the humdrum, every-day duties because there may come a chance for the display of heroism. Let me just tell you one anecdote, and I shall be through. When I raised my regiment prior to going to Cuba, we had of course every variety of person come into it, and some of them without a very clear idea of what was ahead of them, and I had one youthful enthusiast who got down there having portrayed to himself a cavalry regiment and its career as depicted in the story books, and the reality struck him as different. And about the third day he came to me and said: "Colonel, I came down here to fight for my country, and I am treated like a serf; they have put me to burying a dead horse." And at that moment his captain, who was a large man from New Mexico, and not wholly sympathetic with him, came up and explained to him that he would go right on burying that dead horse, and that the next task ahead of him was digging kitchen sinks, and that if he did all that well we would attend to the hero business later.

I ask of you the straightforward, earnest performance of duty in all little things that come up day by day in business, in domestic life, in every way, and then, when the opportunity comes, if you have thus done your duty in the lesser things, I know you will rise level to the heroic needs. Good-by.

⁂ WESTERN SCHOOL NEWS ⁂

MEETINGS

National Educational Association, President, Charles W. Eliot, Boston, July 6-10, 1903.

California Teachers' Association, O. W. Erlewine, president; Mrs. M. M. Fitz Gerald, secretary, 1627 Folsom treet, San Francisco; December 28 to 31, 1903.

Summer Normal School, State Normal School, San Jose; Morris E. Dailey, President. June 29, 12 weeks.

Summer Session, University of California, June 25 to August 5, Berkeley, Cal. Application should be sent to the Recorder of the Faculties, on or before June 15.

National Summer School of Music, 2014 Van Ness Ave. July 6 to July 18; Selden C. Smith, 325 Sansome St., S F

Augsburg's Summer School of Drawing, Oakland, Cal. Beginning July 20 Address, F. J. Lobbett, 809 Market street, San Francisco.

NOTES

The Text-Book Commission of Montana will adopt books June 15th.

The Text-Book Commission of Texas will adopt a uniform system of books for Texas July 3.

The State Printer will have the New McMaster's History ready for the opening of schools.

J. W. Kemp, formerly of Hoitt School for Boys at Menlo Park, has been elected principal of one of the schools of Alameda.

Mr. Codrad has been elected city superintendent of San Bernardino, and W. S. Brown has been elected principal of the high school.

The San Francisco Board of Education will hold a competitive examination for teachers June 15th. About thirty new teachers will be elected.

Frank J. Browne, author of Browne's Series of Arithmetics, has been re-elected headmaster of Hoitt's School for Boys at a largely increased salary.

Supt. Hugh J. Baldwin of San Diego spent his vacation in visiting the Lick Mechanical School, grammar schools of San Francisco, the University of California, and other points of inspiration.

Guy H. Stokes, formerly teacher of Latin in the San Francisco High School, and former principal of the Marysville High School, is manager and editor of the "Orchard and Farm," Los Angeles, Cal.

J. H. Strine of Los Angeles county has been appointed secretary to the Text-Book Commission of the State Board of Education. Mr. Strine was born in Pennsylvania, educated at University of Missouri, and has taught in the primary, grammar, and high schools. He served Los Angeles county as superintendent from 1899 to 1903.

The board of trustees of the San Francisco State Normal School re-elected Frederic Burk as president for a four year term, and upon recommendation of the president elected to positions F. A. Wagner, superintendent of the schools of Pomona, and David Rhys Jones, reader in education, University of California, formerly principal of the Escondido schools. Mr. Thompson and Mr. Davidson resigned.

Supt. W. H. Langdon has appointed Henry Suzzalo and T. L. Heaton as deputy superintendents. Mr. Suzzalo is a graduate of the San Jose Normal, Stanford University, and spent a year in the Teachers' College, Columbia University, New York. He taught a rural school for one term in Santa Clara county, served as principal one year in Alameda, and, for a short time served as an instructor in Stanford University and at the San Francisco Normal School. Prof. T. L. Heaton has had a wide experience with public school teachers and as a public school teacher. His principal work in this state has been as city superintendent of Fresno, city superintendent of Eureka, and as instructor in education in the University of California.

Professor Elmer E. Brown, head of the department of education, will represent the University in various educational matters in the East this summer. He will be a delegate to the golden jubilee in commemoration of the union of Franklin and Marshall colleges at Lancaster, Pa.; attend a meeting in New York of a committee of the National Municipal League; participate in the meeting of the Council of

Education in Boston; take part in the program of the department of higher education, over which President Wheeler will preside; address the Eastern Manual Training Association, and attend the meeting of the committee of eleven on contemporary educational doctrine.

Throop Polytechnic Institute, Pasadena, California, announces the return of Professor Chamberlain as follows: The president and trustees take great pleasure in announcing that Professor Arthur Henry Chamberlain, who is devoting the current year to professional study and research at Teachers College, Columbia University, will return to the Institute and next September resume his duties as Professor of Education and Instructor in Sloyd. Students in the Normal School of Throop Institute and all teachers who are planning to spend a year or two at Throop studying one or another form of manual training, are to be congratulated upon the special interest and value which Professor Chamberlain's advantages at Teachers College will add to the work of the Institute.

* * *

Boston Meeting National Educational Association 1903

The next annual meeting of the National Educational Association will be held at Boston, Mass., July 6th to 10th, 1903. The Executive Committee has announced that the rate of one fare for the round trip, plus the usual $2 membership fee, has been secured for the Convention, excepting that the special rate from the Pacific Coast will be $91.50 or $94.50, for the round trip.

Tickets to Boston and return, from either Los Angeles or San Francisco, will be $72.50, to Chicago. To this will be added $2 membership fee, and either $19.00 or $22.00, according to the route taken from Chicago to Boston, proportionate rates via other points than Chicago.

The dates of sale will be four, viz., June 24, 25, 26, 27.

Ticket extension is to September 1st.

An excellent program is being prepared by President Eliot, and the local entertainment committee is making elaborate arrangements for excursions to many points of general interest. Harvard College will keep open house.

California Headquarters will be at the Nottingham Hotel, which is centrally located. This hotel will give preference to applications from California.

Teachers and friends of education who contemplate a trip east this summer should take advantage of this opportunity to receive the low rates by becoming members of the Association.

There are certain advantages which active memberships furnish, and it is desirable that such memberships should be increased in our State. I would therefore call the attention of teachers and others interested in education, who are not already enrolled as active members, to this opportunity to thus permanently indentify themselves with the interests of the Association.

JAMES A. FOSHAY,
State Director N. E. A., Los Angeles, Cal.

* * *

Chas F. Blackstock, principal of the Hueneme School, last month passed the examination before the Superior Court, and was admitted to the Bar.

On Saturday, May 23, 1903, the corner stone of the $18,000 New High School Building at Oxnard, Cal. was laid. Pres. Edwards of Throop Polytechnic School of Pasadena, delivered the address.

President Benjamin Ide Wheeler of the University of California delivered the address at the dedicatory exercises of the new High School building, Saturday afternoon, May 23d. The structure is completed and the Board of Education has recommended its acceptance by the City Trustees.

Supt. of Public Instruction Thomas J. Kirk, has written the following in reference to Mrs. Jennie L. Thorp's song, "California": The song, both for words and music, should find large and ready sale to the public schools of the State, and I wish you all possible success as the author.

Beginning June 29, 1903, the State Normal School at San Jose, California, will be open for four terms of twelve weeks each during the calendar year. The work for the summer term is arranged with special reference to the needs of teachers who desire to take a course during their vacation with a view to ultimately securing a diploma, and also to meet the wants of graduates who desire to take advanced work. The summer term is exactly the same in character, method and credit value as each of the other terms, except that the Training School will not be in session. Three terms constitute a year's work for students, and no students, except by special permission from the faculty, will be allowed to attend more than three terms during one year.

* * *

For Sale.—A scholarship in leading business college, price $100; will sell for $50. Address "Business," care JOURNAL, 723 Market street, San Francisco, Cal.

TEACHERS' INSTITUTES

Santa Clara County

The teachers thought it was a good institute—and surely the teachers of Santa Clara county ought to know, for they have peculiar opportunities for cultured judgment. The city of San Jose the oldest of the state normal schools and the famous university, are all within the county's boundary.

The Institute was called for April 27, 28 and 29, and was managed by Supt. D. T. Bateman. It was one of the largest institutes of the state, with over three hundred teachers in attendance, yet in the halls and classrooms of the San Jose High School there was plenty of room for every purpose.

Superintendent Bateman summoned three outside helpers to the institute; one from the State University, one from Stanford and one from the common schools of the state, viz., Prof. T. L. Heaton of the pedagogical department of Berkeley, Prof. David Snedden of the educational department at Stanford and Edward Hyatt of Riverside county.

Prof. Heaton gave a most valuable lecture on practical education, followed by a talk on "Art." Prof. Snedden talked on "Teachers' Reading Circles" in a most forcible and sensible way, and arranged for the organization of circles for the county. Mr. Hyatt conducted section work in nature study for the three days of the institute and gave besides some general talks on the way to use school libraries and upon geographical topics.

One feature that seemed to please the teachers was the absence of roll call, a tedious formality. The attendance was quietly looked after by several secretaries. Another good thing was the fact that not more than one or two formal lectures were given in any one day—the rest of the time being occupied by section work and general exercises of a varied nature.

The institute closed harmoniously on Wednesday evening, and the teachers scattered to the four winds, pleased and refreshed with their week's work.

Marin County

The teachers' institute of Marin county was held April 13-16, at San Rafael. The officers were C. O. Sharpe, R. H. Van Horn, J. F. Seaman, vice-presidents; Miss M. Boyd, Secretary; Miss Maggie Keating, assistant secretary, and James B. Davidson, president. The instructors were F. F. Bunker, Dr. Elmer E. Brown, Frederic Burk, E. P. Cubberley, Miss Estelle Carpenter, Robert Furlong. The topics discussed were "Essentials of Geography," by F. F. Bunker; "The New in Education or Some Notes on Eastern Schools," Elmer E. Brown, "Changes in the School Law," Robert Furlong; "American Citizenship," Frederic Burk; "Phonics," E. C. Cubberley; "Reading and English Literature," E. P. Cubberley; "Music," Miss Estelle Carpenter: "Professional Ethics," Robert Furlong.

The special features of the institute were as follows: Short sessions—two lectures a day. An aim to interest the teachers in the institutes so that promptness and regular attendance would arise from professional spirit rather than the law's injunction. An attempt to carry the spirit of professional work and study thruout the year rather than to confuse it to institute week. To do this clubs or reading circles were formed thruout the county and a certain time for work recommended. An aim to build up a profession, to arouse and foster a professional spirit.

***

D. C. Heath & Co. have issued a new series of Arithmetics. The type page is very attractive and the cover is especially beautiful for those who like the combination of flaring red and modest white. The features which will attract the attention of teachers are as follows:

In this Arithmetic, while the Spiral Plan is followed thruout, exercises and problems have been so arranged as to afford at once the thoro and practical drill of the Topical Method and the alertness, skill in analysis, and thoro review that are secured only thru the use of the Spiral Plan. Many new exercises, problems and definitions, explanation of processes and numerous directions and aids to the teacher have been added. We believe that this Arithmetic, which offers a combination of the Topical and Spiral Methods and which is richer in problems than any other arithmetic published and which is pedagogically correct in every detail, will prove better balanced, more helpful to the student and more readily teachable than any other text in this subject available for American schools. The prices are: Primary, 30 cents; Grammar School Part I, 40 cents; Grammar School Part II, 45 cents.

* * *

Frank J. Browne has completed his series of Arithmetics. The primary and advance books will be issued this month by the Whitaker & Ray Co.

Teachers ⚜ Vacation

To the East
The Yellowstone
Boston

NORTHERN PACIFIC — YELLOWSTONE PARK LINE

and the
National
Educational
Association

TEACHERS deserve a holiday. Above all they need a change. The Northern Pacific Railway traverses a cool latitude, and the most interesting regions of America. About half way across the continent is the Yellowstone National Park, which affords a delightful rest on an overland trip. Then again a trip by the Northern Pacific is just the "Correct Thing," for their train service is unsurpassed. The Pullman Tourist Sleepers are as clean and comfortable as Pullman Palace Cars. Our "North Coast Limited" is the finest train in America; the observation car

Liberty Cap in Yellowstone Park.

attached is a bower of beauty, and a joy to the traveler. Special rates have been secured for teachers and others that wish to take advantage of the opportunity to visit Boston during the N. E. A. Convention to be held July 6th to 10th. Tickets will be on sale in California June 23d and 24th. Good 90 days, allowing stop-over going and coming. Send six cents in stamps for "WONDERLAND 1903". Address, T. K. Stateler, General Agent, 647 Market Street, San Francisco, Cal.

cents per copy $1.50 per year

July, 1903

CONTENTS

		PAGE
A Study of the Health of University Girls..........Dr. Mary E. B. Ritter		509
Queer, Is'nt It?..........D. R. Augsburg		516
An Honest Critic..........Alice M. Mitchell		517
The Teacher and the City..........Charles F. Thwing, LL.D.		518
Things to Remember..........		519
A Social Clearing House..........Josiah Strong, D.D.		520
Current Educational Thought..........		523

The Individual and the Nation, Senator Hoar; College and Commercial Spirit, President Jones; Why Technical Training is Desired, President Birge; College Man's Duty to Society, Rev. Dr. William E. Barton; The Education of the Filipinos, Ossian H. Lang; The Society of Educational Research, Dr. J. M. Rice.

The Essentials of Geography..........F. F. Bunker and Effie B. McFadden		526
The Rational Method for the Study of Children..........Henry Meade Bland		530
Homemade Busy Work..........Mabel Kimball		532
The Ideal Rural School..........Charles S. Ball		534
Earl Barnes on Truth Versus Lies..........		536
Extent and Causes of Pupils Dropping out of the High School......A. C. Barker		538
Official Deparment......Thomas J. Kirk, Superintendent of Public Instruction		543
Editorial..........		544
Western School News..........		546
Book Reviews..........		550
Miscellaneous..........		551

THE WESTERN JOURNAL OF EDUCATION.
723 Market St.
San Francisco

Winterburn's The Spanish in the Southwest . . . . 55 cents
By ROSA V. WINTERBURN

THE discovery and early history of California are in this book vividly and attractively presented for young readers. Commencing with the life of the Indians, it takes up next the coming of the Spaniards, then their explorations in search of gold, the founding of the missions, and the life on the pueblos and the ranches. The book brings the history down to the end of the Mexican rule in 1848.

The narrative element and the purely historical are so skillfully combined as to make this book a story of history, a collection of stories so selected and arranged as to present historical characteristics and tendencies of periods. The style is adapted both to the subject-matter and to the age of the pupils for whom the book is intended. The illustrations are numerous and artistic, and maps show the places mentioned. At the end of each chapter are suggestive questions which serve as a helpful review drill. A list of the principal books consulted in the preparation of this work is also included.

The contents and scope of the work may be gathered from the titles of its chapters given below. It is equally suited for the school and the home, and the children of the Pacific slope who read and enjoy it will find in and between its lines an uprising of love and respect for their native state.

The Spanish in the Southwest

Part I. Before the Coming of the Spanish

Chapter I. Indian Life in California
Chapter II. Indian Legends

Part II. Discoverers and Explorers

Chapter III. Cortes
Chapter IV.   Reports of the Seven Cities
Chapter V.   Fray Marcos de Niza
Chapter VI.   Coronado and Alarcon
Chapter VII. The Spanish Claim to the Pacific Ocean
Chapter VIII. Cabrillo and Viscaino
Chapter IX.   The English in the North Pacific

Part III. The Missions of Alta California

Chapter X.   The Desire of a Youth—Father Serra
Chapter XI.   Expeditions into Alta California
Chapter XII. Founding of San Diego Mission
Chapter XIV. The Last Days of Father Serra
Chapter XV.   Life at the Missions
Chapter XVI. The Slavery of the Missions
Chapter XVII. Secularization

Part IV. Spanish California

Chapter XVIII. Life in the Pueblos and on the Ranches
Chapter XIX.   Foreigners on the Pacific Coast
Chapter XX.   Spanish Governors of California

Popular Text-Books

Baldwin's School Readers
  Eight Book or Five Book Series
New Education Readers
  Books I and II, each $0.35
  Book III, $0.40; Book IV .45
Patterson's American Word Book .25
Rice's Rational Spelling Book
  Part I, $0.17; Part II .22
Barnes's Natural Slant Penmanship
  Eight Books per doz. .75
  Four Charts per set 1.50
Baird's Graded Work in Arithmetic
  Eight Books for Eight Years
Maxwell's-First Book in English .40
  Introductory Lessons in English Grammar .40
  Advanced Lessons in English Grammar .60
Webster's School Dictionaries—Revised
Natural Elementary Geography .60
  Advanced Geography 1.25
McMaster's Primary History of the United States .60
  School History of the United States 1.00
Overton's Applied Physiology
  Primary, $0.30; Intermediate .50
  Advanced .80

Newest Supplementary Reading

Abbott's A Boy on a Farm $0.45
Bakewell's True Fairy Stories .35
Horne & Scobey's Stories of Great Artists .40
Krout's Two Girls in China .45
Monteith's Some Useful Animals .50
Pitman's Stories of Old France .60
Pyle's Stories of Humble Friends .50
Simms's Child Literature .30
Wood's The Children's First Story Book .25

Send for descriptive circulars

THE WESTERN
JOURNAL OF EDUCATION

ESTABLISHED 1852.

A Study of the Health of University Girls

Mary E. B. Ritter, Berkeley, Cal.

[Read before the Medical Society of the State of California at their Annual Convention in Santa Barbara.]

We are hearing constantly of the ill effects of higher education upon the health of women.

My personal observations in the University of California for the past thirteen years have led me to believe that the majority of college girls and boys *improve in health* during the four years of their college life—at least those students who take their work seriously and rationally. There are, of course, the social butterfly who tries to dance all night and study all day, and the "dig" who burns the midnight oil too assiduously in a close stuffy room; and these unwise young people of both sexes do not as a rule make a success of either education or health. But certainly such failures can not be charged against the necessary regime of college life, but rather to lack of common sense. On the other hand it is not uncommon for a thin anæmic girl to gain 12, 15, 20, or 25 pounds during the first year in college. However, "there is no smoke without some flame." and there is so much smoke here, so much agitation over this question of the relation of education of women to health, that the reasons for this should be carefully investigated.

My work as Medical Examiner has led me to study the condition of health of these young women before they undertake the taxing years of their university work, to determine, if possible, whether the causes of the later breakdown are present *before* this time, or whether they develop during the college course and in consequence thereof. Not only do I find as a rule the causes of later collapse present when they enter college, but I also find that the impaired health can often be traced back to some illness incident to childhood, to improper food for the growing child and other unhygienic conditions. And following back from branch to stem, from stem to root, in striving to answer the various "whys" in these cases, I have come to feel that the relation of the physician to the families of his patrons is largely responsible for the present sad condition of health of our primary, grammar and high school children, for it is at these ages that the damage is done.

As it is now, and has been in the past, the medical profession alone has been generally trained in the branches of Hygiene and Sanitation, and upon them the community at large have depended for direction. Has the medical profession fulfilled its duty in this respect? Has the individual physician noted and corrected the unhygienic conditions in the homes of his patients as minutely as he should for their best weal? Has the family doctor, when attending the contagious diseases of childhood, carefully instructed the mother about the various sequelae which might bring lifelong injury in their train; has he noted the faulty postures of the growing child, the pallor of oncoming anaemia in the girl approaching puberty, and warned the mother of its dangers—directing proper food, outdoor life, a rest from the nervous strain of school works, and all the other essentials to sensible and hygienic living at this important period? I wish to enter a plea for more careful observation of the home and the growing children by physicians, and particularly for more minute instructions to mothers about the care of their children whether sick or well—not to be content with prescribing only for the prominent symptoms which necessitates the professional call. Especially I make a plea for more careful instruction about those diseases so frequently neglected because such common incidents of childhood as to be considered almost natural—such diseases as whooping cough, rheumatism in its lightest forms, so light and so common as to be dubbed "growing pains" (as if it were painful to grow), yet so *very* relentless in their effects, so frequently accompanied by a slight endocarditis and resulting in a lifelong injury to the cardiac valves.

It is doubtless fair to presume that the girls who enter the University of California are an average lot, neither stronger nor weaker physically than their sisters who attend other institutions of equal rank in their own State or in Eastern States. Fully two-thirds of the women in California who aspire to college life enter the University of California. Gymnasium work is required of all students during the first collegiate year, and before being admitted to this work a physical examination must be submitted to (1) of an examination of heart and lungs, (2) history of bodily functions and of previous health, (3) family history as regards constitutional tendencies or the so-called hereditary dyscrasia, and (4) measurements to determine the symmetry and posture of body. With the young women particular attention is paid to the history of the menstrual epoch.

During the past two college years I have examined 660 freshmen girls, and upon these I base my remarks, as there is but little variation in percentage from year to year, hence larger numbers are not necessary to establish their approximate correctness. Of this number 176, or 26 2-3 per cent are subject to headaches; 193, or 29. 1-4 per cent, are habitually constipated; 86, or 13 per cent, are subject to indigestion; 3, or 1-2 per cent, had defined tuberculosis; 7, or 9-10 per cent, had goitre; 57, or 9 per cent, were markedly anaemic; 105, or 16 per cent, had abnormal heart sounds; 62, or 9 1-3 per cent, had rapid or irregular pulse; 193, or 29 1-4 per cent, were subject to backaches; 443, or 67 per cent, were subject to menstrual disorders; 10, or 1 1-2 per cent, gave histories of having broken down in grammar or high school, two from "nervous prostration"; 149, or 22 6-10 per cent, reported themselves as free from all aches or pains or functional disturbances.

I cite this disheartening list to emphasize my point that most of the ills are sown in early girlhood, from which the harvest of semi-invalidism is reaped in mature womanhood. I also wish to emphasize the fact that the majority of these ills are preventable; that more wisdom on the part of the mothers could avoid these deplorable conditions. My personal experience with mothers leads me to consider the majority of them as unwise as their daughters regarding hygienic laws. In the future, when more and more educated women have become mothers, and when it has become a part of every college curriculum to require of all students instruction in Hygiene and Sanitary Science, I feel sure these high percentages of "unhealth," as Huxley terms it, will be notably lessened.

That this prediction is founded on fact seems indicated by quite extensive data collected by the American Association of Collegiate Alumnæ, in which they show that the ratio of infant mortality is decidedly lessened among the children of college women. Surely we should expect that the mental discipline they have received in college would fit them better to fulfill any vocation in life, especially the responsible vocation of motherhood.

I shall not take your time to discuss the minor ills of the above list. In the 105 cases of abnormal heart sounds 22 have left college and been lost sight of. One gave a history of having been a "blue baby," but is apparently a healthy girl now, but is easily fatigued. Another had been treated for a year for acute cardiac dilatation resulting from too vigorous mountain climbing when very anaemic. Fifty-five histories pointed to a rheumatic diatheses, with combinations of the following diseases:

Acute articular rheumatism..........12
Rheumatism followed by endocarditis.. 4
Rheumatism and pertussis............ 8
Severe growing pains...............18
Growing pains and tonsilitis (repeatedly) 10
Growing pains and tonsilitis and chorea 1
Growing pains and scarlatina........... 3
Growing pains and typhoid.......... 1

Combinations of diphtheria, scarlatina, spinal meningitis, pneumonia and severe pertussis occurred in 19 cases more. Endocarditis had been recognized as a complication of one case of each of the following: Typhoid-pneumonia, malaria and purpura. Malaria for years was the history of three coming from districts noted for the *anopheles maculipennis*. One interesting case of exophthalmic goitre had been sent from Colorado to see what change in climate and altitude would do for her. She improved somewhat. In fifty-nine cases out of the 105 compensation was good, and the girls were unaware of any disturbance. With the others the record shows a report of palpitation and of getting out of breath easily. Forty-six were markedly anaemic. Evidently many of the murmurs were haemic, for with improved health 20 per cent have nearly or quite disappeared.

It has been especially amazing to note the improvement in many of these anaemic cases. Girls whom I advised to go home—to take at least a year's leave of absence in which to regain their health before beginning their college course— have many times persisted in remaining in college and have gained 10, 20 and 25 pounds, and in one case forty pounds. This remarkable gain I ascribe to several factors: (1) change of climate, for fewer of the resident girls have made such phenomenal increase in weight, (2) to the regular but gentle and selected exercise required four times a week in the gymnasium, followed by a tepid spray bath and a brisk rub, (3) the required gymnasium work brings the girls under constant supervision, and they have been urged to take plenty of sleep, outdoor air, etc., and have been required to report frequently upon these matters. The fact remains, nevertheless, that the gain has been made during and in spite of the nervous strain of college life.

To sum up, all of these abnormal hearts seem attributable to one of two causes— either sequelæ of infectious diseases or the result of anaemia. Both causes are largely preventable. We all know that sufficient care for a sufficient length of time will at least mitigate the effects of the endocarditis, which so frequently complicate certain infectious diseases of childhood. We all know that hygienic living—the right kind of food, plenty of air, exercise and sleep—will prevent anaemia in the adolescent girl.

Dr. C. B. Brown, in a statistical report before the Medical Society of the State of California in 1896, demonstrated that among 1,000 San Francisco and 287 Oakland schoolgirls insufficient breakfasts, cold lunches, lack of outdoor exercise and inadequate sleep were prevalent factors in those years when girls are apt to show the first signs of failing health, *i. e.*, in the ninth grade of the grammar school and first two years of the high school, the ages being from 14 to 16 years. At this time the social life of girls begins, and also more arduous study, so that among these 1,300 girls scarcely any went to bed before 10 o'clock habitually, and frequently much later. Late nights, lack of sleep, is the *bete noir* of the student's life. I repeat, with plenty of sleep, proper food and exercise there is very little danger of mental application injuring the health of any one.

In studying the menstrual history of these 660 girls I find the California girl matures at 13.5 years and that the period averages 4.6 days. This average, while exact for the majority, is made up of wide extremes, the epoch beginning from the 10th to the 18th years, and lasting from 1 to 21 days. With regard to the 443 reporting menstrual disorders, 51.6 per cent suffer from dysmenorrhœa, varying from slight cramps for a few hours to being confined in bed for two or three days— 117 reporting severe, 109 moderate and 113 slight pain. 26.3 per cent reported irregularity, 18.3 per cent too late, 8 per cent too frequent. Of courses many of these cases overlap, *i. e.*, pain and irregularity being most commonly coincident.

Thirty-three gave a history of some form of uterine or ovarian disease, for which they had previously had local medical treatment or operative procedures; in eleven cases displacements, in two metritis, one stricture of os uteri, twelve menorrhagia, and five ovarian inflammation.

These figures seem appalling, and I hesitated to report them, yet we all know that within the limits of our personal observation the majority of women are more or less inconvenienced by the menstrual period—a normal function, or one that should be normal, and it behooves us to look to the causes when we find this condition so prevalent among young girls.

Allowing for the natural monthly rhythmic ebb and flow of the feminine system and the fact that all the vital activities seem to be highest a few days before the menstrual epoch and lowest at its close, there is here an added range that is abnormal. Allowing for the evil effects of the all-too-prevalent constipation, for the chilling due to wet feet in the rainy season, often producing endometritis, there is still too high a percentage of suffering.

Judging from the fact that eleven of the thirty-three cases which had had pelvic examinations are known to be due to displacement of the uteris, and to the large number of such cases diagnosed by the gynecologist and the general practitioner in later years, it is fair to presume that a much larger percentage of displacements of the pelvic organs is present at the onset of the menstrual function, and is accountable for a considerable degree of the suffering experienced by young girls. In one of the largest gynecological clinics in Berlin the head surgeon assured me that the majority of such cases in women who had not borne children were congenital. This is a hard position to either prove or refute, but until we have removed all probable causes *during growth* it seems unfair to fall back upon the untenable and undemonstrable "prenatal" conclusion.

In watching school children and University students it has been impressed upon me that the almost universal faulty posture in which the body is held is largely responsible for this particular abnormality. When the body is held erect the pelvis is tipped at such an angle that the symphysis pubis forms the lowest bony point of the trunk, and is a support for the pelvic and abdominal organs. The inner surface of the sacrum forms almost a right angle with the perpendicular plane of the body, and a plumb line dropped from the anterior surface of the third or fourth lumbar vertebræ passes *in front of the symphysis pubis*, and one from the middle of the sternum two and one-half to four inches in front. Thus the weight of the abdominal viscera should not fall *upon* the uterus and ovaries, but in front of them. The upper edge of the symphysis pubis and the abdominal muscles attached to it and to the wings of the false pelvis should support the abdominal organs. But what do we find?

Taking school children of all ages, as they are examined by the directors of physical culture, we find the bodily posture is almost universally incorrect. The first thing noted by the eye, perhaps, is the asymmetry due to standing on one foot. This almost universal fault lowers the shoulder and makes the hip more prominent on the side used habitually, while the spine curves slightly to the other side. This deformity is not, as a rule, sufficient to cause any discomfort, but it does not add to the beauty of the form divine, and the beauty of form is certainly a desideratum in life. A well-poised body, a stately carriage, is always attractive, while a misshapen body with a slovenly posture and gait detracts in a like degree.

But *the* reprehensible posture, and the one most universal, is a faulty poise of the body antero-posteriorly. So common is this that if a student enters the examination room with head erect, chest elevated, the various curves of the spine in normal position, with the pelvis at an angle of 30 to the perpendicular and with knees firm, the reply to the question, "You have had gymnasium work before?" is usually answered in the affirmative. The ordinary posture is relaxed knees, pelvis tipped upward, shortening the distance between symphysis and sternum protruding the abdomen, the lumbar curve lessened, the dorsal exaggerated, the shoulders drooping forward, chest flat and chin projecting. The plumb line from the sternum then falls *behind* the symphasis, and that from the lumbar vertebræ thru the middle of the pelvis. That this position robs the pelvic and abdominal organs of their natural support of the symphisis pubis is evident. That it must result in displacement of the pelvic organs seems, also, evident. And this, it appears to me, must be *one* prolific cause of the very large percentage of menstrual disorders, to say nothing of the injury to the general health by lessened room for lung expansion and for stomach, liver and intestines to perform their functions. And when to the weight of the abdominal viscera is added that of heavy skirts and the pressure of tight corsets the above abdominal conditions are increased in large measure. With the body erect and the pelvis at its normal angle, the center of gravity of these heavy organs and the line of direction of their weight falls in front of the uterus, or, at least, only impinges upon the superior and posterior surface, but the moment the pelvis is rotated forward the lumbar curve is lessened, allowing the abdominal viscera to move relatively backward, while the pelvic organs move forward, hence the weight of the superimposed organs bears directly upon the fundus of the loosely swung uterus and ovaries, causing downward pressure, and as this pressure is downward and backward, tends to produce prolapsus, retroversion, and perhaps retroflexion. Dr. E. M. Mosher of Brooklyn, ex-dean of women and Professor of Hygiene in the University of Michigan, has studied this subject carefully and made digital examination of the pelvic organs in a large number of cases, with the patient standing in her habitual posture. She discovered "exaggerated intra-pelvic pressure in all cases when the pelvic inclination was more than 57 degrees, and the pressure increased as the angle increased. If one of these patients was placed for a few moments in the *modified* knee chest position (with abdomen well supported) to drag the intestinal loops out of the pelvic cavity, and re-examined with the pelvis in normal position (at an angle of 45 degrees or less) the intra-pelvic pressure was not observed. It returned slowly, however, when the habitual posture was again resumed."

This posture of the body is *so* common among both men and women, and assumed so generally by children, that there must be some deep underlying cause, some instinctive tendency that produces it. Doubtless most of us can remember being chided in childhood for not standing erect. This is one of the constant battles mothers try to wage with their growing children, altho frequently they lessen the efficacy of their corrections by a bad example. Telling a child to throw back its shoulders is trying to relieve the effect without removing the cause, and the physician who orders shoulder braces for the ordinary round shoulders is decidedly putting the cart before the horse, or would be like strapping the top of the leaning tower of Pisa to the adjacent cathedral to try to draw up the sunken foundation. In our human frame, as in an architectural structure, when the mass is out of plumb, the difficulty lies in the foundation, and, in the instance of our bodies, in relaxed knees. This seems an easier posture, and doubtless does require less exertion of leg and back muscles—at least until those muscles are developed by practice. The military position, with "knees locked," requires the use of all the leg, thigh and back muscles, especially of the posterior femoral and tibio-fibular regions. To hold them thus for any length of time is fatiguing, especially to the rapidly growing child, and it is only long muscular training that makes the posture habitual. A public speaker who stands unusually erect recently told me that whenever he arose to make an address and felt his knees firmly locked, his inner consciousness reverted to the military discipline of his college days.

It is impossible to assume the correct posture without straight, firm knees, and, again, if knees are "locked" and pelvis held in place, it is impossible to let the shoulders droop forward. One must then hold the shoulders back, the head erect and elevate the chest in order to keep the body in equilibrium.

My own theory of this almost universal propensity, to stand with knees relaxed, is that it is a cause of inherited tendency to certain muscular co-ordination, i. e., a phylogenetic tendency. The mammalian body was originally constructed to go on four limbs, and the change to the erect posture has been acquired with great difficulty. In all quadrupeds the knee joint of the hind leg is bent forward at a decided angle. This angular limb has thru evolution become the straight leg of man, but even in our nearest anthropoidal ancestors who *can assume* the erect position the knees are still bent at a wide angle, and whenever a chimpanzee or orang wants to stand his straightest he clasps his hands behind his head to balance himself. Ordinarily these manlike apes stand so stooped that it is necessary for them to rest their hands upon something for support. As their arms reach almost to the ground, this is very easy.

In developing from the quadruped to the biped, the relative position of the pelvis has not been much changed, i. e., it points backward almost as in the quadruped. In assuming the erect posture, the spine has bent upward almost at a right angle at the juncture of sacrum and lumbar vertebræ.

Looking at the human body from an architectural standpoint, we find the feet, or pedestals supporting two immovable columns, spanned by an irregular arch, the pelvis, which is itself oblique and fitted by loose ball and socket joints to the oblique heads of the femurs. This unstable keystone supports a heavy movable and curved column, the spine, to one side of which is attached the weight of the trunk organs, and from the superior corners of which hang two heavy movable columns, the arms, and on the summit is a movable ball, the head. All these weights, all these mobile supports, must be held in place by the constant play of muscles, contracting and relaxing with every movement of the body.

From a phylogenetic standpoint the posterior muscles of the legs are comparatively undeveloped, at least for their present task, for it is only in man that these limbs even approximate the perpendicular. Hence the erect posture is a matter of education of the muscles in mankind, and it seems to be the natural tendency to revert to ancestral type and stand with knees slightly relaxed.

The young child from the time he learns to walk until five or six holds himself more erect than his ten or twelve year old brother who is going to school. Two reasons may be assigned for this: The body of the small child is more compact, not only being much lighter in weight, but the legs are both actually and relatively shorter, and the shorter, proportionately, a muscle is the more easily it can perform its work. In the second place, the young child has no duties imposed upon him, never has to hold his body in wearisome positions for any length of time; during his waking hours he is constantly on the move, contracting and relaxing different sets of muscles, so that none become overstrained. But there comes a time when the chubby child begins to stretch out rapidly into the lean boy or girl—the skeleton and its muscles grow often with marvelous rapidity, and with each added inch of bone the muscles have a more arduous task to keep the loose-jointed architectural pile in plumb, and just at this age commence the long hours of confinement in school, and the ill-fitting seats. The restless child that heretofore has been only a free young animal twists and turns in his seat until he finds the position requiring least muscular exertion, which is to deposit the upper portion of his weight on the desk in front, resting his elbows or forearms, thus losing the normal spinal curves. Standing in class is a most unrighteous interference with his natural freedom, and a very few moments serve to fatigue him, and he shifts from one foot to the other and back again until he finds the posture of least resistance, which is either the one-sided posture first noted, or the second posture, with knees relaxed, and generally is a combination of the two. That these postures throw the body out of plumb any one can demonstrate upon the nude body of a child —or, better still, comparing the body of a child who holds himself erect with one who has assumed these improper attitudes.

The evolution of the practice of medicine from the old-time family doctor, who was physician, surgeon, obstetrician, and everything needed in one, has been in two directions, which are more or less antagonistic—the one being specialization, the other preventive medicine. No one will deny for a moment the advantages of specialization. The fields of medicine and surgery have become too broad for any one man to cover, and the man who devotes himself to one branch can undoubtedly do better work than the medical man who is Jack of all branches and master of none.

On the other hand, those great provinces of research which have yielded such rich returns concerning the causes of disease— all that has been learned concerning fermentation, bacteriology, immunity and asepsis, tend to develop the profession along the line of "prevention of disease." It is better to keep the human body healthy and in full possession of its powers than to resurrect a maimed body from the operating table or a weakened system from the ravages of the tubercular parasite, so the rule of the physician who bends all his energies to preventing illness of any kind is no less noble, even if less spectacular, than that of the great healer, be his results obtained by scalpel or medicine chest.

There is no time to develop this thought. I can only refer to an address on the "Practice of Medicine in the Twentieth Century," in which the development of this tendency was predicted. The writer pointed out the great need of more attention to preventive medicine and how it could be fulfilled, and he prophesied that before the end of the century specialists on this line would be more numerous than in any other; that before the year 2000 a young couple, upon starting a home, would select their physician, whose office it should be to keep them and their children in health. To him should be given all the information possible about their own physical beings, and, as the children came along, he should watch over them and guard them—not only from disease, but also from those insidious unhygienic conditions which undermine the health of our young people of to-day.

This seems Utopian, and would of course necessitate a change from the present fee system—so much per visit or per consultation. But changes are the wellspring of progress, and more than one conscientious physician realizes that the existing relation between patient and practitioner is not ideal.

But this is in the future. What can be done now? No physician hesitates to spend his time over the microscope, the test tube of the chemical or bacteriological laboratory, to determine for his patient the cause of the attacking malady. If he would only spend as much time in instructing the parents how to make their homes truly hygienic, what kind of food to give their children; the *urgent* necessity of plenty of sleep, of regularity in the bodily excretions, the ill effects of incorrect postures *and how to correct them,* the care necessary during and subsequent to the lightest forms of infectious diseases, the conditions so prevalent among our young people, and which pave the way for our invalids, would be largely obviated.

Summary:

I have not expected to establish the positive proof of facts by the figures here presented. The personal equation of the individual questioned enters too largely into such statistics to make them entirely reliable, but they may be safely taken as indices pointing toward the main conclusions, and these I would sum up as being:

1. College education does not necessarily injure the health of women.
2. The seeds of subsequent ill health are sown at an earlier age, and do not develop in consequence of the college curriculum.
3. The causes of ill health are mainly avoidable and due to unhygienic living or the sequelæ of infectious diseases.
4. That in a large proportion of women students the regular routine of college life, with the mental stimulus of a purpose, improves their health and fits them to become better disciplined and more intelligent mothers.
5. That more careful observation on the part of physicians with instructions to mothers would in large measure obviate the present unsatisfactory conditions.

* * *

Queer, Is'nt It?

D. R. Augsburg.

Is drawing an important study? Yes. it is one of the four fundamental means of acquiring and expressing thought. (Language, number and music being the other three.) Drawing is the language of form, the medium thru which form is expressed on paper before it assumes its permanent position. It is the universal medium of making, and tells the appearance of form, the facts of form and the decoration of form. The queer part is this:

While drawing is placed by many prominent educators the equal of number in value, both educationally and commercially, yet *number is given the honors in the school curriculum to less than one given to drawing.*

Superintendents and learned professors will meet in solemn conclave and talk about the weakness in the language, number, geography and grammar without the least suspicion that perhaps there may be some of the elements lacking. *Perhaps a weakness in form may have something to do with it.* Again, these same parties will wax eloquent over some poor little branch, like writing or spelling, but when the subject of drawing is approached it is almost humorous to see the shrug of the shoulders or the patronizing condescension with which it is met. Has not any one the courage to grapple with the subject of drawing? Yes, there is one. He will stand up and tell all about it: what it is, and how it should be taught, and the next moment say he *can't draw even a straight line or a cat that one can tell from a rooster.* Yes, educators generally will speak of the great value of drawing, will admit that it is fundamental in character and a great aid in teaching, in learning and grasping the form elements of other studies, in laying the foundation of technical education, and valuable in all work in which the hand and mind work together; that it is really the only study we have in our common schools in which skill of hand is systematically taught, and then these same teachers will put these ideas in force by *letting their pupils copy a little or draw on the blackboard some Friday afternoon.*

Yes, it's queer, but if a drawing teacher speaks of it, "Oh, he's an enthusiast—a crank on the subject; he's tooting his own horn," etc., and forthwith he is put out of the synagogue. Put out, did I say? Of a truth, he has never been let in. He is there in person, he can come to the meetings, but as for being one of us—no, no. *Brethren, this ought not to be.*

An Honest Critic

Alice M. Mitchell.

The eighth grade in the Copa de Oro School were wrestling with problems in surface and areas and solid contents. The leader of the class was a bright boy who took such enthusiastic interest in his work that he was a continual incentive to teacher and to the lagging members of the class. When he was a fourth-grade boy, from which time teacher dated her acquaintance with him, he was just the same. A, B and C, those mythical characters who figure in so many transactions, were flesh and blood to him, and his explanations of their remarkable pedestrian feats were so vivid that teacher felt quite guilty in not encouraging him to take off his jacket, gird up his little knickerbockers and give a realistic illustration of the race on the spot.

Later on he was equally alive. He would plaster and paper a room to the last square inch with skill and dispatch, and then carpet the same accurately, making due allowance for matching the breadths; even going so far as to design a large figured carpet which would necessitate waste.

It was about this time that he began to be critical, and to wonder why the ceilings of the rooms on which he figured were not papered as well as the walls. He thought this must be an oversight on the part of the compilers of the State Series Text-Book, and asked teacher if he might not count up the cost, and add it to the given result. "It wouldn't look right," he objected, "to have a papered wall and a bare ceiling, and see, the cost isn't very much more."

He was also quite sure that there was a serious error in compelling a man to pay for double work and material in the angles of a stone wall, and was not satisfied until teacher allowed him to deduct the two feet of thickness from the corners. "They didn't think about that, did they?" he said sweetly, but pityingly.

"Oh, yes," said teacher, "it's the rule to measure a wall on the outside. Don't you think its nice for the man who builds the wall?"

"It wouldn't be right," he insisted stoutly. "He'd be cheating, counting his work twice."

And so he had gone on, till now he was absorbed in finding out the number of square feet necessary to make a piece of stovepipe two and one-half feet long and five inches in diameter, and directly there was vexation of spirit.

"They haven't allowed any lapping," he announced, "and there must be a seam in it. The answer isn't right. It would take more iron to make it." And the same grave omission occurred in the next example, where the amount of material needed to make a tin pail is required.

He found consolation for his wounded feelings in measuring the rusty school stovepipe, and allowing a generous inch in width for the join, and he figured out the contents of his own little dinner pail labeled "Cottolene," to his entire satisfaction, and fired the rest of the class with a similar ambition; so that one morning the desks were adorned with pails of various sizes—the former contents of which were plainly proclaimed, "Dixie Queens" and "Cottolenes" predominating, while busy fingers measured depths and diameters, and busy brains calculated results.

In due course of time the boy arrived at the conical pile of oats two feet high and twelve feet around it at the base, and the number of bushels it contained was correctly obtained. Then came the next problem: "Anticipating rain, the above pile is covered with tent cloth — how many square yards?" The boy was soon in visible distress.

"What's the trouble?" teacher inquired. "You must find the slant height; remember your rules."

"But the answer isn't right. It would take more canvas, and you'd have to make it loose to fit over that pile. Besides, they wouldn't do it that way at all. If it was going to rain, they'd just hurry up and throw a square piece over the pile and fasten down the corners."

"But you musn't be so particular," said teacher. "They just want you to find the surface area."

"Why don't they say so, then?" answered the boy. "It isn't a sensible question."

When the committee meet to revise the school text-books, teacher recommends that this honest little critic be given a hearing.

* * *

The Teacher and the City

Charles F. Thwing, LL.D.

President of Western Reserve University and Adelbert College.

The teacher of the American public school is the most important force for the improvement of society. He represents the chief power recognized and constituted by the law for the enrichment and preservation of the state. The state determines the character of the men, who shall practice law before its courts. The state also determines the character of the men who, as physicians and dentists, shall practice their healing arts among the people. The state turns over to the Church the determination of the character of the men, who shall be its priests and ministers. But in the case of the teacher, the state determines not only who may and who shall not teach in its public schools, but also the state pays out of its own treasury for the teaching thus rendered. The state, furthermore, determines that boys and girls, up to a certain age, shall submit themselves to this teaching for a certain number of weeks of each year. It seems, therefore, that the state commits to the teacher in a way of special significance and responsibilities most serious, and peculiar duties for its own preservation and enlargement.

What is thus said in reference to the function of the state in general applies with special significance to the city. For the forces of the commonwealth are centralized in the city. The powers of the city for righteousness are the most potent. Its tendencies toward wickedness are the most evident. The forces of the whole state of every sort are here found raised to their *tenth* power. The best and the worst, the richest heritage and the most promising assurance for the future, the finest personalities and the most degraded characters, the noblest generosities and the most miserable meannesses, are here found in evidence. Therefore, the city represents the supreme opportunity and the most useful tool for the teacher of the American public school.

There are several forces which help to constitute civilization. Among them are the family, the church, the government, literature, commerce and personality. The family represents love; the church represents religion; the government represents authority; business represents force; literature represents truth; and personality represents inspiration. Love, religion, authority, truth, force, inspiration are the mightiest forces constituting civilization and promoting its progress.

But these powers are the powers which the teacher uses. The teacher represents the love of the family. If a teacher fail to love his students, he is not worthy of being a teacher. If he be unable to see the soul of character in the midst of these little bits of humanity, he has no right to stand in the schoolroom. He must love. Be it said, too, that the teacher *is* a lover. He puts his own heart into the lives of these children.

The teacher also uses religion. I do not

mean that the teacher should use the Protestant faith or the Roman Catholic faith, or any other faith. I recognize the obligation of the statute, but I do mean that religion represents the relation of man to ultimate reality. Concerning the notion of that ultimate reality people differ. One man says it is a person; another man says it is an impersonal power; but whatever it be, the teacher has a right to use a broad interpretation of that ultimate reality for the formation of character. Respect and obedience to that reality, he has a right to teach. Without such teaching, instruction lacks the highest relationship; with it, instruction takes upon itself a sky and a firmament.

The teacher also uses the essence of governmental authority. He represents the government; he is constituted by the government; to the government he owes allegiance. This officer of the law himself should so impress upon students the duty of respect for authority, that each shall become a better citizen, as well as a better man or woman.

In the administration, too, of the school the teacher represents the essence of commerce, force. He uses executive skill. He is to be active and strong in doing. The man of human force entering into the administration of the public school system is akin to the man of human force that enters into great commercial undertakings.

It is also to be said that the teacher represents the power which constitutes or helps to constitute literature, truth. Truth is the chief element of his work; truth is the atmosphere of his life; truth is the instrument of his service. The book as embodying truth is both his companion and his servant. The shield of the oldest college in America consists in part of an open book, across which is written the word *Veritas*. Such a shield would be a proper symbol for every public school.

The teacher also represents personality. As a personality he embodies that supreme quality of life known as inspiration. This is life itself. The most valuable force in every schoolroom is not the room, is not the tools, but is, or ought to be, the teacher himself. He should be a great "human" to quicken, to arouse, to enlarge, to uplift his students.

Therefore, in the use of these forces, love standing for the family, religion standing for the church, government standing for authority, commerce standing for force, literature standing for truth and personality standing for inspiration, the teacher is the mightiest power for the enlargement and the enrichment of the American city.

* * *

Things to Remember

"Fellow citizens, let us remember the oneness of our American derivation and destiny. Let us be thankful that in the baptism of blood all serious causes of division and reproach were purified away. Let us be grateful for the years of peace thru progress and of progress thru peace. Let us hail them as but the prelude of still better days to come. From this table land of time, looking backward on the past, and forward on the future, let us strike hands for the betterment of politics; for the cleansing of rule; for the moral trusteeship of private wealth and of public office; for the lifting of poverty, thru self help, into comfort; for the considerate leadership of ignorance into knowledge; for the transmutation of provincialism into patriotism and of patriotism into philanthropy. In this work, while our country is our solicitude, let our field be the world. While our countrymen are our preference, let humanity be our client. By recasting ourselves on the lines of God's laws in our hearts, our State shall prosper, our cities shall come to honor, our communities shall conquer the pinnacles of material and of moral achievement and our Nation shall attain to the benign purposes of deity in its discovery and in its development. And from the vantage ground of this republic will sweep streams of blessings to all the race of man. If to this we here dedicate and here consecrate ourselves, the North of our homes and the South of your hearts, the North and the South of our country will eventually be constrained to admit that we sought well and thought well and wrought well for their behoof and for our own."—St. Clair McKelway.

* * *

A Social Clearing House

Josiah Strong, D.D.
President American League for Social Service, New York.

Civilization at the beginning of the twentieth century is something radically different from civilization at the beginning of the nineteenth. We might almost say of our country as a Japanese said of his, "Nothing remains the same except the natural scenery." Material civilization has changed more during the past 100 years than during all the past preceding history of the race.

The fundamental cause of this change was very simple, but its results are far-reaching beyond calculation. It was the substitution of mechanical for muscular power. Glance briefly at some of the results. One set of muscles could do little more than provide for the necessities of their owner and of those dependent on him. Such food or fuel meant so much sweat. In order to double the output it was necessary to double the number of muscles, which meant doubling the number of mouths, and that meant doubling the demand on the increased product, so that there could be little accumulation. In 1820 the entire property of the American people amounted only to about $200 per capita. Under such conditions the wealth of a few implied the poverty of the many.

When, however, men substituted mechanical power for vital energy this limitation was removed. It was possible to double the number of steam engines and then double them again without increasing the number of mouths by one. Hence the possibility of boundless wealth and of abundance for all.

With the increase of wealth there has been an increase of intelligence and culture, and consequently a marked rise in the standard of living. But while knowledge has been multiplied and popularized, wealth has been multiplied and centralized; hence popular discontent.

True, the workingman today has, say, three times as much as his grandfather had, but he knows six times as much, and, therefore, wants six times as much. The workman with the aid of machinery and organization produces, on the average, about fifty times as much as the workman of one hundred years ago, and believes that he does not receive his due share of the increase. The problem of production has been solved, but not the correlative problem of distribution. Hence the question is being asked, What more is due to the workman than his wages?

Capital and labor are both being massed, and are entering into new relations with each other. What are their mutual obligations has not yet been made clear: at least men are not agreed as to those obligations.

In other words, society is not yet readjusted to the new conditions created by the sudden increase of wealth. Spain was demoralized by the torrent of gold and silver which was poured into her lap from the New World. But a hundred Lands of the Incas could not furnish the wealth now being created by manufacturers. The forces of nature, brought under control, are gold mines which can never be exhausted. It is estimated that the wealth created in the United States from 1890 to 1900 was equal to the assets of the entire world in 1776. This is a more sudden increase of riches than that which overwhelmed Spain. This enormous wealth may be made an unspeakable curse or an inestimable blessing, and which it becomes will depend on the success of the process of readjustment.

When man's working power was in his muscles or in those of his horse and oxen, he could go apart by himself and do his work alone. But when the stationary steam engine became the source of power, men had to gather around it; hence the factory, and hence the redistribution of population and its concentration in centers of industry. This process was emphasized by the application of machinery to agriculture as well as to manufactures, for it drove away many from the farm to the city. At the beginning of the nineteenth century less than one-thirtieth of our population was urban; at its end about one-third.

So rapid has been the growth of the city that we have not yet learned how to live in it. As a rule, the more dence the population, the higher is the death rate, of which there is no need. It can be shown that between city and country in the United States there are every year more than 150,000 unnecessary deaths in our cities. Here is a great problem of readjustment.

Again, so rapid has been the growth of the city that we have not yet learned how to govern it. The fathers worked out for us the principles of state and national government, because at that time the city practically did not exist; it had not become a problem. We accordingly have today no generally accepted problems of municipal government. Ofter cities in the same state have radically different charters. We are told that no two cities in Ohio have the same. Here we see the confusion which attends the process of readjustment. The process is being attended also by maladministration and by gross corruption. And generally speaking, the larger our cities the greater is the mismanagement and the grosser is the corruption of their government, so that our great cities are usually under the control of those elements of society which are least capable of self-government, and themselves most need to be controlled.

The natural results of such conditions have as yet appeared only in part, because state legislatures have taken from the cities some of the powers of self-government. But because the tendency of population toward the city is permanent, the city will in a few years be able to outvote the country. It will then control not only its own affairs, but also those of the state and of the nation. What if the city is then incapable of self-government? Here is another great problem of readjustment; and we have only about one generation of time in which to solve it.

Mr. James Bryce, who has made a more exhaustive study of our institutions than any other foreigner, recently said to a company of Americans about to sail for the United States: "Go back to the splendid world across the sea; but don't you make a failure of it. You cannot go on twenty-five years more in your great cities as you have been doing.

Don't you do it. If you do, you will set us liberals back in Europe five hundred years."

When power was furnished by muscles it was individualistic; industry was, therefore, individualistic, and so was society. The steam engine deindividualized industry and organized it; and this industrial revolution has created social revolution with the result that civilization, which one hundred years ago was individualistic, is now collective.

In the age of homespun, the farmer and his wife together knew ten or a dozen trades. In the age of the factory, each trade is represented by dozens of machines, and each machine has its operative, and each operative is dependent on dozens of others for the finished product. Thus in the old civilization, industrially speaking, the family was a little world; in the new, the world is rapidly becoming one great family. In the old, men were independent; in the new, they are interdependent. In the old, relations were few and simple; in the new, they are many and complex. In the old, the great problems with those of the individual; in the new, they are those of society.

Conditions are new and strange, and this is a period of transition and of social readjustment. Geologists tell us that at certain periods in the history of the earth some forms of animal and vegetable life, which had been common, suddenly became rare or extinct, while other fauna and flora, formerly rare, suddenly multiplied. The explanation is that an important change took place in the climate or in the food supply; and those forms of life which could not adapt themselves to the new environment perished or became rare, while whose forms better adapted or more adaptable, covered the earth and filled the sea. This illustrates the vital law that there must always be a certain correspondence between all life and its environment; and if there is a radical change in the latter, there must be a corresponding change and readjustment in the former, or it must perish.

For lack of readaptation to the changed conditions of the new civilization numberless business men have failed, thousands of churches have died, and, as we have seen, many thousands of lives are yearly sacrificed in our cities. For lack of such readaptation we have bitter strife between capital and labor, strikes and lock-outs, discontent and riot, anarchy, murder and suicide.

When the process of readjustment is blind and unintelligent, it is terribly costly in time, in money, in suffering and life. The process of readjustment to new conditions, so far as it is conscious, is one of experiment. Thousands of experiments are now being made in legislation, in government, in sanitation, in philanthropy, in charity, in religion, in reform, in the reconciliation of capital and labor; in every department of human life and activity. Many of these experiments fail; some of them succeed. All these results, whether positive or negative, cast some light on the great problem of readjustment.

The American Institute for Social Service serves as a lens to gather up these scattered rays, focus them, and then reflect them to all who are willing to profit by other people's experience.

In other words, the League gathers from all civilized countries facts of every kind which bear on this great problem of readjustment, interprets them, and then in many ways disseminates them so as to educate public opinion. Thus the Institute has become a great reservoir of experience, a much-needed Social Clearing House.

Current Educational Thought

Vigorous Thoughts from Addresses to Graduates

THE INDIVIDUAL AND THE NATION.

The fate of the Nation depends, in the last resort, on individual character. Everything in human government, like everything in individual conduct, depends, in the end, upon the sense of duty. Whatever safeguards may be established, however complicated or well adjusted the mechanism, you come to a place somewhere where safety depends upon somebody having the will to do right when it is in his power and may seem to his interest to do wrong. When the people were considering the adoption of the Constitution of the United States, one of our wisest statesmen said that the real and only security for a republic is when the rulers have the same interest as the people. If they have not, constitutional restraints will break down somewhere, except for the sense of duty of the rulers.

All elections depend upon this principle. You may multiply election officers and returning boards, you may provide for an appeal to courts of first resort or last resort, but in the end you must somewhere come to a point where the sense of public duty is stronger than party spirit, or your election is but a sort of fighting, or if not that, a sort of cheating. The same thing is true of the individual voter, or of the legislator who is to elect a Senator, or the Governor who is to appoint the Judge, or the executive officer or the Judge who is to interpret the Constitution or the statute and decide the cause, or the juror who is to find the fact. On these men depend the safety and the permanence of the republic. Each has to decide whether he will be influenced by ambition or by party spirit or the desire for popular favor or the fear of popular disfavor; by the love of money on the one side, or by the sense of duty on the other.—From Senator Hoar's address to the Graduates of the University of Iowa.

COLLEGE AND COMMERCIAL SPIRIT.

College men of the present day have been accused of not having the lofty aims of the college men of twenty-five years ago. It is often said that they now view everything from a money-standpoint. I wish to take exception to this. We have to acknowledge that colleges in this country do not stand apart from the rest of American life. The spirit of America is commercialism, and the college shares in the spirit, but I believe we are gradually slipping away from the commercial ideal.

It is also true that many a college man is unwilling to meet the test of a business career. Hence many a college graduate has been lost to the business world simply because he would not prepare for the test. I think, however, that I need not exhort you to work. Average Americans work enough, in fact they work too much. The strenuous life need not be recommended to the average American. Therefore I would advise you to find some object for your work. If you cannot do this enlist yourself under the banner of some acknowledged leader. For if you cannot lead the next best thing is to follow the banner of some great leader.—From President James' Address to the Graduating Class at Northwestern University.

WHY TECHNICAL TRAINING IS DESIRED.

Technical training has become a motto in a day, a motto which the universities must recognize. Those who would push aside this movement with a sneer as "bread and butter" studies wholly fail to understand the significance of the movement or to read aright the signs of the times. The demand means no less than an educational revolution. The community is coming to feel its dependence upon the training which the university can give, not merely for culture but for the needs of life. This relation necessarily means the connection of the university course with affairs—a relation of studies to life, and not merely or mainly to a livelihood.

Those who see in this demand for increased technical studies a mere wish for increased future earning power are quite out of touch with the students, as they quite fail to comprehend the spirit of the age. It is not with a bread and butter spirit that the students of to-day ask for courses which shall prepare them for the study of law or of medicine.

The student is not looking for larger earnings by their aid. He asks them because he sees the greatest chance of the field of knowledge which he must explore if he is to gain that intellectual view of his profession which is the foundation of true happiness to his exercise. He sees that the three or four years of the professional school are quite too short for the purposes. He therefore asks a broad foundation of specific scientific knowledge on which to build his later professional studies. His demand is in its way exactly parallel to that for social studies at the university by him who is to be an active member of society. It is for success, for happiness in the practice of his profession that he is looking, not for the wealth that may or may not come to him as the result of his success.—From the Baccalaureate Address of President Birge, University of Wisconsin.

COLLEGE MAN'S DUTY TO SOCIETY.

The college man represents a considerable cash investment. Joseph Cook estimated that his father had spent $16,000 on his education, and that was a small part of the real cost. The educated man has been spared four or five years from the ranks of the producers at a time when his friends and companions are doing something for society. He has been made the beneficiary of large endowments, and for his sake a body of picked men has been set apart to teach him a great many arts and sciences. He is a man for whom more is done than for any other man in modern life, and society has in store for him a judgment day if he does not render account for what he has received.

I can bear with the student charitably if he counts the classics of little importance compared with the ability to make a home run on the diamond, or kick a goal on the gridiron. But if mere muscle were the end of education, the hay field is a cheaper and more effective way of producing it than the college.

I bring no railing accusation against the college man for battling out his course with soft electives, and doing a minimum amount of work to secure his diploma, while he devotes the heavy end of his work to club life and the cultivation of good fellowship, though I maintain that we can find men who are willing to live in this way without the necessity of hiring teachers and accumulating endowments to enable them to do it.

It is said that one-third of the graduates of European universities die prematurely of bad habits or overwork. Another is conspicuously useless, and the remaining third rules Europe. I do not doubt that education pays by reason of the good society gets out of the one-third which actually does the work, but it is the business of modern economics to utilize the waste, and society will some day demand the reason for any waste among men for whom the world has done so much.—From the Baccalaureate Address of Rev. Dr. William E. Barton of Oak Park (Chicago) to Yankton College Graduating Class.

ideas of our present common-school system. The Italians, Russian Jews, Chinese and representatives of other nations and races who like to gather by themselves in city quarters would have to be left to develop by cultivation of their own peculiarities as best they may. Turks, Bulgarians and Albanians may do as they please. Disharmony lends weirdness to the Eurasian concert. At any rate, it is pleasing to Dr. Chamberlain and his sympathizers. Theories and facts are often out of tune in education. We others who prefer to be persuaded by actual results rather than professional anxieties will meanwhile take courage in the progress made in Philippine education along the lines of American civilization.—By Ossian H. Lang in the July-September "Forum."

The Society of the Educational Research

Primarily, the association has been organized for the purpose of maintaining a Bureau of Research intended to act as a center of information for those who are desirous of knowing with what degree of success the various educational methods and processes in use in our country have been rewarded. To illustrate: Every conscientious school superintendent is anxious to base his work upon a sound and rational course of study. But what may be said to constitute such a course? Broadly speaking, our educators would answer the question in two different ways. On the one hand, there are those who believe that the value of a system must be judged by its disciplinary power, that is, by its power to develop the faculties, not by results subject to measurement on a scale of percentages. On the other hand, we find those who believe that the value of an educational process must be judged by the tangible results which follow its use. In accordance with these views, the former school of educators, in constructing a course of study, seek guidance in *a priori* reasoning, while the latter prefer to be guided by experience.

The Society, of course, will base its conclusions upon tangible results. However, in doing so, it will not by any means make light of the views of those who believe that the end and aim of education is the development of moral and educational strength, views with which it is absolutely in accord. It simply takes the stand that intellectual power is subject to demonstration; that the arithmetical faculty has been more highly developed among children, who find no trouble in solving difficult problems than it is among those who show but little comprehension of very much easier problems; that the language faculty has been more highly developed among those who are able to interpret intelligently the thoughts expressed by others, and to express their own thoughts in elegant and forcible English, than among those who show but little comprehension of what they read, and whose own written expressions are crude and faulty, etc. And as to the ethical traits, which, naturally are not subject to measurement, the Society takes the stand that the English schools that train the children to do well what they are taught to do, and to be neat and accurate in their work, are doing more toward the development of the intangible elements than the schools where the children show but little knowledge of what they have been taught, and are untidy and inaccurate in their work.

For those who believe in looking to experience for guidance, the Bureau will serve a unique purpose in endeavoring to render it possible for them to become acquainted with the experiences of the educational body as a whole.—By Dr. J. M. Rice in the July-September "Forum."

* * *

THE ESSENTIALS OF GEOGRAPHY

There is a very general movement among educational leaders and thoughtful teachers looking toward the evaluation of the studies usually included in our curricula. We are beginning to realize that under the impulse given teaching by the so-called New Education the course of study is overcrowded. We are dissipating our energies and the energies of our children by virtue of too many subjects. The consequence is that some of those studies, which time and experience have shown to be fundamental and necessary in the training of children, have been neglected to a considerable degree. The inevitable reaction has set in, and, as a result, teachers and supervisors are carefully examining the claims of these several studies with a view to an intelligent and conservative pruning of the course.

This tendency toward the elimination of those studies which are not *most* essential for the sake of more efficient work in the teaching of those which *are*, has not stopped with the mere consideration of the relative value of the several studies as *wholes;* but this critical examination has extended to the details usually comprehended in the text-books of those subjects considered most essential. Thus, for example, it is universally agreed that arithmetic deserves a place in the curriculum. But the notion is also becoming quite general that the teaching of exchange, of stocks, of alligation, of cube root, does not belong in the arithmetic of the grammar grades. Further than this, it is pretty generally agreed that the subject of fractions should be taught to children. But it is also becoming a prevalent notion that it is a waste of valuable time to have children change mixed numbers of large dimensions to improper fractions. So this process of evaluation has not stopped with the subjects of the school curriculum as wholes, but rightly extends to the most minute details of these subjects.

Geography is coming to be recognized as the study of Man, his home, and his activities; and as such it deserves a much larger place in our school work than it has ever been accorded. Along with this change in our estimate of the value of Geography, there has come an epoch-making shift in the matter of the details which should be presented and in the method of their presentation. Instead of blindly following the older texts, instead of sitting back in our chairs as teachers and idly running our fingers down the dry and sterile wastes of map questions, as we solemnly propound them to our children, we miles north of the Niger River, near the Sahara Desert?

Geography treats of the elements of many of the sciences. It draws its data from astronomy, from anthropology, from ethnology, from ornithology, from meteorology, and from geology, not to mention others. Among the million and one interesting details which might be taken from these sciences and legitimately included under the term Geography, it is not to be wondered at that many non-essentials have crept into our school treatment of this most important subject. I presume it is in just this matter of the separation of the essential from the non-essential that teachers feel least confidence in themselves; and being hazy, confused, and uncertain in their own minds, the natural tendency is to fall back upon the traditional and authoritative treatment to be found in the several text-books of Geography.

It will help us in looking at this question of "What is essential in Geography?" to consider Geography in its two-fold aspect: (1) its formal elements; (2) its content or cultural elements.

In the advanced text of the California State Series Geography, there are about two thousand geographical names; and included in the maps there are approximately seven thousand more. Of this number the ordinarily well-informed man could probably step to a series of outline maps and accurately locate no more than four or five hundred. As a child in school his list was very much larger, but upon leaving he straightway forgot the most of it. As Mr. Redway says: "The average pupil on leaving the grammar school undoubtedly possesses a much larger stock than this—and promptly proceeds to forget all but about one hundred, or, possibly, half as many more. He then adds to his stock the names that may be called the 'unexpected,' that is, the names that come into use through discovery, political change, industrial movement, or change of environment." It would seem to be a waste of time to require our children for the sake of the "unexpected" to spend their time in the indiscriminate mastery of these nine thousand names.

Of this body of geographical map facts, from the standpoint of general, usable knowledge, the adult needs to know the location and situation of London, but he has little use for Timbuctoo. He needs to know New York, Chicago, St. Louis, San Francisco, but has little need for Milpitas or Deadwood City. He needs the Mississippi River, the Ohio, and in his own State, the Sacramento and the San Joaquin, rather than the Red River of the North or the Santa Marguerita of San Diego County. He needs these facts because that body of information which passes current and which affects the world and its people in a large and vital way has to do with New York and London, with the Mississippi and the St. Lawrence, with the Amazon and the Nile. So from the standpoint of those map facts which are common to people of general intelligence we could easily make a minimum list with respect to each continent which children should know and know perfectly.

With this idea of the essential formal elements in mind let us turn to South America. I presume that however much we disagree on minor points, there will be no disagreement with the conclusion that the child should have the power of calling up before his mind's eye the picture of the contour of South America enlivened with the following details: The principal water partings, the Andes Mountains, the Brazilian Highlands, and the Guiana Highlands, together with their corresponding drainage basins; the specific names and location of the Amazon, the Orinoco, and the La Plata rivers; the location of Para, Rio Janeiro, Buenos Ayres, Santiago, and Lima. He should be able to point out and name at sight the several political subdivisions. Besides these formal facts to be gotten from the study of the map, he should be able to see South America in relation to the other continents of the world, to the chief water masses, and to the several zones of light. Whatever map information there is over and above this, and there is much besides which is required by your text, to my mind is *special* information, the learning of which, if it ever becomes necessary, should be entrusted to the initiative of the child, which initiative will be operative if the teacher has been careful to instill in him the necessity for constant reference to an atlas when he is reading.

This is the minimum list of geographical map facts which I have already suggested one needs of South America in order that he may be in touch with that body of knowledge of South America which today passes current. Not only for this reason are these facts needed, but for the further and important purpose of affording a foundation for work on what may be called the content side of geography teaching and study.

At this point, for the sake of clearness I wish to summarize in a sentence or so what I have presented.

Our school curricula has become overcrowded, and in consequence the work of some subjects which all recognize as having proven their right to retention has suffered. This among other factors has set students to re-evaluating studies. This process of evaluation with a view to separating the essential from the non-essential is rightly being applied not only to studies as wholes, but to the details as well. Geography, because it includes the elements of many sciences, is peculiarly likely to contain much which is of less than the greatest value. In this consideration of what is essential, it is helpful to consider first, its formal elements, by which I mean map facts mainly; and second, its content or cultured elements, by which I mean the associations one builds in and around the map facts. In connection with the formal elements, I pointed out that the basis of selection was to be found by putting and intelligently answering the following question: "What map facts does one need to know in order that he may be in touch with that body of current information which affects the world and its people in a significant way?" I answered this question in regard to South America.

I wish now to consider the more difficult, though no more important part this question of essentials, that pertaining to the content or cultural elements.

To our minds our own State of California naturally breaks itself up into certain geographical areas, the characteristics of which differ. It has, speaking roughly, its valley region characterized by grain and fruit raising, and its mountain region characterized by lumbering and mining. So with South America, with Africa, or, for that matter, with any of the other continents; each is naturally broken into certain characteristic areas. For our purpose, I presume those of South America may be said to be: the Amazon region; the Orinoco region; the La Plata region; the Andes region; and the Patagonian region. With each of these areas the popular mind has associated certain facts and certain feelings.

To illustrate this point, take the Amazon region. If I were to ask what the Amazon region means to you, I presume among other things you would tell me that to you it is a region of dense, tropical, luxuriant vegetation; that it has a hot, humid climate; that its chief product is rubber; that its forests are the homes of myriads of insects, of brilliant-plumaged birds, and of tree-climbing animals; and that it is a region sparsely populated by semi-civilized Indians and negroes.

That the Amazon region has 50,000 miles of navigable waters draining 2,000,000 miles of area, and that the river itself inundates a region 1,000 miles long and 200 miles wide, are bits of special information readily accessible in any good encyclopedia, and therefore should not be required by the teacher.

By contrast let us turn to the Andes region. Again I ask, "What does the popular mind associate with the Andes region?" To most of us without special information this is a region of great altitudes and of precipitous slopes; a region whose climate ranges from the equatorial heat of the foothills to the arctic cold of its mountain peaks; and a region characterized by its silver mines worked by natives who employ crude and wasteful methods.

That Chimborazo is 20,478 feet high or that Quito is exactly on the parallel of latitude which we call the equator are, again, bits of special information which can be found in any reference book on the region, and being special in their nature and application would better be eliminated from classroom work.

In like manner we might take the Sahara region, the Nile region, Japan, China, India, or the several characteristic areas of our own country. In the case of each it is possible to write down specifically some half dozen or more facts or feelings which fall outside the field of special knowledge and which in themselves constitute the measure, which I am seeking, by which to estimate the worth of the details of the recitation.

Then, since the facts and feelings which the popular mind has associated with their respective geographical areas constitute the essentials of given regions, and since a child, when he completes his school course, should have at least these definitely associated with their proper area, then it follows that we can judge each of the lesser details of the recitation in the light of its efficacy in establishing in the child's mind some one or more of these essential associations. Whether a teacher should spend time in having children tell the time-worn, but, I fear untrue, story of the monkeys in the forests climbing cocoanut trees and throwing the ripe fruit at the heads of passing travelers depends on whether this story will give them the basis for drawing some one or more of these characteristics as inferences. Whether the teacher should spend time in giving one lesson or a series of lessons on the boaconstrictor, on the blowgun of the natives, on the cow-tree of the forest, or on the process of gathering rubber depends, not upon the amount of interest which these details will command (they are all interesting if the teacher is interesting), but upon the grasp, either direct or by inference, they give the child on some one or more of the aforesaid essentials. If a given lesson or a specific detail of that lesson affords the basis for an inference on the part of the child in terms of one of these essentials, then that lesson or that detail should take its proper and worthy place in that teacher's scheme of lessons.

To summarize: From the standpoint of intelligently entering into that part of current information which is of significance there are a minimum number of formal map facts which children should know and know well. On the content side general intelligence recognizes that each natural geographical area has certain characteristics which differentiate it from every other area. This minimum list of map facts on the formal side, and these characteristics on the content side, constitute, to my mind, the essentials of the geography of the grammar grades, and being the essentials afford the teacher that basis for the selection of the details of her recitation which we have been seeking.—From Bulletin No. 2, San Francisco State Normal Schools, on "The Essentials of Geography in the Primary and Grammar Grades," by F. F. Bunker and Effie B. McFadden.

* * *

A Rational Method for the Study of Children

Henry Meade Bland, State Normal School, San Jose.

The proper beginning of any science is with the facts of the science. These facts or systems of concrete knowledge must be sought out through the processes of observation and experimentation. The ultimate aim in the science is to deal with facts collected so as to permit truth to evolve or generate from them. There is to be no forcing of conclusions, no inferences not warranted by the data, no hasty generalizations.

If the study of children is to become a science, it must yield to the processes of science. What the study now needs most of all is a body of fact carefully collected by laboratory method from which to get our insight into the child's nature and development.

The facts of our science must be collected with no narrow point of view in mind. We must consider all sides and conditions of the child which we study. We must study him in all environments: in the nursery, in the later home life, in the school, at play. We must know the fundamental points of his nervous development, even from the earliest stages of the embryo upward. We must consider him psychologically and sociologically. We must know his interests. In fact nothing will lead to the truth but a possession of all the facts bearing upon the object of our study.

It may be easily seen that we must get our facts by the study of the individual and not by the collection of material from classes in school. The mere fact that a certain conclusion with reference, say, to fatigue, is reached concerning a certain class in school, studied as a whole, tells but little of the facts or conditions leading to the fatigue of an individual. The investigation should be of the individual, and the facts thus found used in arriving at results.

While it follows, as a matter of course, that the more skilled the experimenter the more accurate the results, yet it does not necessarily follow that studies by the rank and file of teachers is valueless. While the public school teacher may not be able to broadly generalize, yet a concrete knowledge of the child on the teachers' part is greatly to be desired, as it enables the teacher to see the child in a clearer perspective.

Through this concrete knowledge of the child health conditions and their bearing on the child's studies are more clearly understood. Phases of arrested development in individual cases come clearly to light, and the teacher can better deal with them. The teacher gets at the natural instincts and tendencies of the child, and so is able to do the most for him.

My function of this program is to present an outline of points for observation. The outline in your hand is tentative. Its very fulness is indicative of the broad point of view from which we must look at the child. There are a great many questions and considerations which naturally arise as to the value of the various points outlined. Suffice it to say that the ultimate value of the facts cannot now be seen. Let us be satisfied to collect phenomena, and when we have gotten together a mass of material, without any preconceived opinions to bias us, let us proceed to scientifically draw our conclusions.

OUTLINE FOR THE STUDY OF CHILDREN.

1. Date of record.
2. Sex.
3. Age, years, months, days.
4. Height.
5. Height, sitting.
6. Weight.
7. Length of arm-span.
8. Circle of arms at biceps.
9. Circle of forearm.
10. Circle of leg at thigh (boys).
11. Circle of leg at calf.
12. Girth measure.
13. Chest measure.
14. Inion to ophryon.
15. Lambda to ophryon.
16. Pre-auricular pt. to pre-au.
17. Pre-au to bregma.
18. Pre-au to chin-point.
19. Eyesight (a) color-blind—Yes. No. (b) sight. Normal. Defective. (c) astigmatism. Present. Absent.
20. Hears watch tick with right ear. With left ear.
21. Touch. On finger tip. On back of hand.
22. Taste. Threshhold.
23. Flesh. Hard and firm. Medium. Soft and flabby.
24. Appearance of skin. Ruddy. Medium. Pale.
25. Color of eyes. Brown. Blue. Gray. Hazel.
26. Gait. Steady and firm. Medium. Awkward and loose-jointed.
27. Shoulders. Right higher. Left higher.
28. Head. Symmetrical. Asymmetrical.
29. Right-handed. Ambidextrous. Left-handed.
30. Grasping power.
31. Lung power.
32. Respiration.
33. Temperature.
34. Pulse.
35. Condition of the teeth (a) milk. Good. Medium. Poor. (b) second. Good. Medium. Poor.
36. Endurance.
37. Heredity—(a) Country or State born in. (b) Nationality of father, age of father. (c) Nationality of mother, age of mother. (d) Nationality of paternal grandfather. (e) Nationality of paternal grandmother. (f) Nationality of maternal grandmother. (g) Nationality of maternal grandfather. (h) Number of children in family. (i) Relative age. (j) Remarks on distinct traits or physical features inherited. (k) Occupation of father. (l) Of paternal grandfather. (m) Of maternal grandfather.
38. Apparent condition of ill health.
39. Evidences of general nervousness.
40. Attitude. Erect. Medium. Approaching that of embryo.
41. Love of pets. Extreme. Medium. Absent.
42. Love of flowers. Extreme. Medium. Absent.
43. Love of nature. Extreme. Medium. Absent.
44. Specific instances of moral conversion.
45. Likes poetry. (a) For its rhythm. (b) For the story. (c) For the reflective. (d) Name favorite short poem.
46. Likes pictures. (a) For the color. (b) For the dramatic. (c) For the experience suggested.
47. Likes music. (a) For the rhythm. (b) For the melody. (c) For the harmony.
48. Likes to sing. Yes. No.
49. Likes to speak pieces or recite poetry. Yes. No.
50. Likes to play what game best.
51. Likes to imitate what adult activity best.

52. Spends leisure time in doing what.
53. Is successful in organizing and commanding what game or games among his fellows.
54. Is he or she looked up to as an ideal by other children? Yes. To a medium degree. No.
55. Game played well on the school ground.
56. Likes to make collections. Yes. No. (a) Collects systematically. Yes. No. (b) Collection carefully kept. Yes. No. (c) Collections all of one kind. Yes. No. (d) If of several kinds. What? (e) Attempts to classify. Yes. No.
57. Most permanent interest observed.
58. Five books liked best (prose).
59. Likes to do things requiring physical activity. Yes. No.
60. Likes purely mental activity. Yes. No.
61. Grade in school.
62. Scholarship. (1) Excellent. (b) Good. (c) Average. (d) Below average. (e) Poor. (2) Likes best. Mathematics. English studies. Art (including drawing, music.) Poetry. History. Science. (3) Character of work. Neat. Medium. Careless. (4) Regularity of attendance. Good. Medium. Poor. (5) Punctuality. Good. Medium. Poor. (6) Obedience. (7) Industry. Good. Medium. Poor. (8) Attention. (9) Reasons. (a) Accurately. (b) Inaccurately.
63. Entered school at what age.
64. Number of months' attendance at kindergarten, if any.
65. Attended one or two roomed country schools. Months.
66. Record in department last month. Good. Medium. Poor.
67. Remarks.

* * *

Homemade Busy Work

Mabel Kimball, Yuba City, Cal.

When we come from our normal schools, where the deep, wide pocket of the State is open for all needs, to our own schoolrooms, the securing of busy work material becomes a problem.

Yet here are fifty restless little hands, and as many mischievous little brains, incapable as yet of continuous mental application, they must have something to do.

The district can give us but little more than the usual supplies, and, as we cannot have what we wish, we must put our ingenuity and invention to work and make things.

I have found that a few tubes of bright colors in oil paints, a fine brush and some sheets of cardboard can be great helpers.

With them I make alphabets in large, small and writing letters, and each child can have his own box and make the words of his lesson upon his desk. A great number of words can be painted upon larger cards to use for sight reading, and imitation dominoes can thus be developed for number work.

In teaching the primary colors, I painted the rainbow on a large sheet of stiff, white board to hang up like a chart, then each child had an envelope given to him with the seven colors or slips of cardboard.

What a child really sees he knows, and the rainbow has been a source of delight to my class.

After they know it with the colors and chart, we used the prism, and for days in little pockets could be found a bit of glass from mamma's lamp or the stopper to a perfume bottle to make that wonderful thing to childish eyes, the beautiful, elusive rainbow.

For the youngest readers small charts of two or three sentences can be painted in great variety. A bright picture may be cut to finish the sentence.

"Do you see the girl?" has greater fixative power in the child's mind, if the laughing face of another child smiles down upon him, than the same words written coldly in chalk on the board.

One little boy said to me when we came to the sentence, "She is a pretty girl": "I don't like to read that because I don't think she is pretty."

Then I saw that my artistic productions must consult the child's taste that his veracity be not troubled.

Home-made stencils are a great source of pleasure to my children, and I think by their use drawing is made easier. I select a number of outline designs, such as a cup and saucer, a lamp, a cat, mouse, bird, elephant or bear, then I cut a number of pieces of printer's paper the right size and place under them a thickly folded cloth. Laying the design upon these, I follow the outline with a tracing wheel, and my stencils are ready. The children use them by passing an eraser over the stencil, thus making the outline on the blackboard, and develop it with chalk, occasionally with colored, but that is a luxury.

My little folks are very fond of stenciling, and on holidays and birthdays we have many gay borders and pictures.

Among my busy-work material I have large numbers of small pictures pasted on stiff cardboard. These are passed around, and the children look at and arrange them, and select one to tell a story about. We have a few minutes, and each child comes up to the platform and, holding up his picture before the school, tells a little story about it, and some of them are very good, too.

I have a picture wire stretched above the blackboards all around the room, and on this I hang pictures mounted on dark, heavy board, fastening them by hooks over the wire with a clasp attached to hold the picture. These pictures I frequently change, that the children may have new ones to look at.

Flags of different nations painted on cambric, and grouped around our own Stars and Stripes, make a pretty wall decoration.

* * *

COLLEGE MEN ARE ALWAYS ON THE CONTRARY SIDE.

I heard a man say the other day that the University men were not on his side of a certain question. In fact, he said, the college men are always on the contrary side on every question. This is probably true in the sense he meant, for it is the province of college men to judge intentions and pretenses by ultimate results. When the final end, according to the experience of human wisdom, is sure to be bad, wise men must oppose the beginning. The universities have many times stood in opposition to the popular feeling of the time, but they have never found their condemnation in the final verdict of history. Only he who has studied the affairs of men critically, impartially, coldly, can discover the real trend of forces in the movements of to-day. This the university has means to do. It does not carry elections; in fact, it has seldom tried to do so; for the results of an election play a very small part in the evolution of democracy; not to carry elections, but rather to carry wisdom to the people; that is something worth doing. The words of experience which are wasted in the noise of the hustings become potent as the tumult passes by.—President David Starr Jordan in the July "Atlantic."

AN INTELLIGENT HORSE.

Will Wadsworth owns a horse that his children drive to school mornings, and upon arriving at the schoolhouse they all go in, leaving the horse to go home alone, which he does without accident or loss of time. At night Mr. Wadsworth harnesses him to the wagon and the intelligent animal goes after the children. If he arrives before school is closed, he waits patiently at the door until it is out and his charges are all aboard and then conveys them home. The distance that the sagacious brute thus travels alone is more than a mile. Such an instance of intelligence and sagacity in an animal is rare, and can hardly be accounted for on the theory of instinct alone.—*Gilbertsville Journal.*

The Ideal Rural School

Charles S. Ball, Springfield, Ohio.

Some one has said that every great principle has first been worked out among the people, and then taken up and adopted by the universities and those in high places. The hard-headed conservatism of the people, the grip with which they hold on to the old and existing customs and institutions, and their tardiness in accepting any new thing, has sometimes checked and sometimes aided the progress of civilization, yet the truth holds good that the leaven of progress must work from the top downward.

In any new country, as in America, the first thought has never been the highest development of each individual, but the training of leaders, statesmen, preachers, jurists, physicians, teachers for the masses. To that end here in America our fathers established colleges and universities before free schools for all the people were thought of, or even the secondary school system. Later the secondary school system came in—the academies and high schools. These were few in number at first, and even till within the last few years they have not been numerous. During the last ten or twelve years these schools have multiplied rapidly, and their rapid increase is one of the most hopeful signs of the times, as it is the most effective step yet taken to bring the higher and better education to the common people. The rapid increase of secondary schools is, of course, due to the fact that each year more and more graduates are sent out from the colleges and universities to live among the people and establish these schools. Now, our educational system is incomplete and far short of accomplishing its whole work till it has been so perfected that it can reach and seek out each individual and give him the training for life's work best suited to his native powers, with a careful eye always to what that individual expects to do and where he expects to live.

Education may be worth something—may *happen* to be useful when given by instructors who have taken no account whatever of what the student is best fitted for, the tendencies of his life, and the kind of people among whom he will probably live and labor. But who will deny that it may be, and, indeed, is in most cases, worth tenfold more when these things are taken into account? We have had enough waste in educational work. At this period of our effort we need to become utilitarians. What sadder spectacle than to see a man educated out of his sphere and work, a loafer with a well-trained mind, yet having no special fitness for any work.

The college cannot reach the people directly. It reaches them very effectively indirectly through its students who go back to the people. The purpose of this paper is to show that the academy, or high school, as it is commonly known, put into the place of the present inefficient public school system, will be the most effective and satisfactory means of reaching the people of the rural districts. The city graded school is handling the problem of giving the best training to the masses with much success, the great drawback being that too few as yet finish the course or go through a sufficient number of grades. If the rural public school in its present condition is inadequate, and it is admitted that the secondary school, that is, the academy or high school, is the nearest approach to the right kind of country school, would it not be well to examine the work these schools are doing, and see if they may not be made the means of perfecting our educational system among the very people intended to be reached by the rural public schools? These schools do not thrive nowadays in the towns and cities. The graded school has supplanted them. They thrive well and seem well adapted to rural life and conditions.

Speaking briefly, the course of study in the secondary school of the country is as follows: There is a primary department doing the same work intended to be done by the rural public school, but doing it much more efficiently. It also has higher courses of study, which, in many branches, go beyond the highest grade in the city schools. Many of these schools have a good business course, and in almost any of them thorough preparation for college may be had. The course of study in these schools is often broader than in the city graded schools, and may be varied to meet the special requirements of almost any student.

But some may desire to ask if the city graded school is a good thing, why not put one in each country district? There are several reasons for not doing so, chief among them being the following: (1) The people are too poor. (2) Rural districts are thinly settled. (3) To unite sufficient territory, wealth and children to get the buildings and teachers necessary for the eight grades would throw many of the children too far away from school, even if they should be transported at public expense. At any rate the efficient country school cannot be conducted as is the city graded school. In the rural school three or four teachers must do the work, and in some cases only two will be needed. These must have broad and thorough preparation, as they must be prepared to teach more subjects than is required to be taught by the average city school teacher, there being fewer teachers.

Having studied the problem, I am free to say that uniting small rural schools everywhere in the South, or, what would be more effective, redistricting the country and forming larger and better schools, will not operate against any child, as is often argued, but will be a decided advantage to all, even if it does remove the school farther from some children. Being thrown a little farther from school is not half so great a disadvantage as attending school in the little one-room school building, poorly furnished, where pupils of all ages and ranging in advancement from the first to the seventh and eighth grades are taught by one teacher.

This school will be made possible by redistricting or uniting small schools, voting a local tax, securing aid from friends of education and by private subscriptions in the community of the school. The most difficult aid to secure at present is the local tax. The towns and the cities of the South have gone forward nobly in the matter of local taxation, laying aside prejudices, overcoming poverty. I believe the rural districts of the South only need to be more deeply aroused on the subject of education for all the people, in order to secure local taxation for the schools.

The question of what should be taught in the ideal rural schools is one of great importance. The word "education" has changed its meaning in the last few years. Children *must* be taught to read and write. Other kinds of training are impossible without these acquirements. But it is now recognized to be an important educational truth that industrial and manual training should be a part of the course of study in the rural public school. Elementary science, nature study, agriculture, drawing, woodwork and domestic science should be added to the course of study in the country school as soon as possible. The course of study must be broad enough and thorough enough to be a finishing course for at least nine-tenths of the people, as at least that number will never attend a higher school.

One or two such schools as I have outlined above in each township, taking the place of the present rural public school, would bring good high school advantages to all the people—a thing much to be desired. It would furnish the opportunity of bringing out the best there is in each child in a school of high grade, under well-trained instructors; for the poorly prepared teacher would find no place in this grade of schools.—*Atlantic Educational Journal.*

Earl Barnes on Truth Versus Lies

The theory that controls this course of lectures is this: We are all born with certain fundamental appetites; for example, the appetite for food, the appetite for admiration that creates the arts, the appetite for the right which impels men toward doing the best they know. The earlier conception of this appetite for the right, this conscience, said that it knows the right. I should maintain instead that all these fundamental appetites of the soul are blind, that the appetite of hunger will lead the individual to eat mushrooms and live, or to eat toadstools and die. What guides these fundamental appetites is the judgment of each individual. . . . We are placed in the world with this obligation on us of finding the truth, of perfecting judgment, and all the time this great desire of all humanity for the right pushes us on. This appetite for the right may be neglected, and so many dwindle away; it may be overstimulated and become sentimental; it may be perverted, and led in the wrong direction. We must keep it in a condition that is real, sane minded. With a steadily growing appetite for the right, steadied by judgment, the human being is working toward the higher development.

Truth may be understood in two ways: (1) the absolute truth of a fact, or (2) the attitude for truth. I say you are a true man when you tell me two and two are four. Or I say you are *not* true when, ignorantly, you say that two and two are five. In today's study I shall not try to distinguish these things. I find the truth of them as one common truth.

Whenever you go back to the earlier forms of life you find truth strangely lacking. The cunningest fox, the craftiest coon, is the one that receives the highest reward, that survives in the struggle for existence. At most you find the animal telling the truth to its mate and its young. The charm of Uncle Remus' stories is due to the fact that the rabbit, the least crafty of animals, is put in a position where he can outwit Bre'r B'ar and Bre'r Fox. The stories of Ernest Seton Thompson take us into a world where deceit is the highest form of virtue. . . .

Do children lie? Yes; constantly, persistently, and universally. A child does not tell the truth because he cannot. He does not know the truth, and his approximation to the truth is very much vaguer than ours. And there are certain qualities of his mind which make it inevitable that he should pervert the truth. In the first place, truth is synonymous with knowledge. He does not know what truth is. He has not yet come to a plane where he can think truly, not even to our plane. His movement of thought is fragmentary; he deals with little bits. A child was told the story of "Peter, the Goose." The story runs that a little girl named Alice had a tame goose. Her mother told her that when she went out of the yard to roll her hoop she should close the gate. But Alice forgot to do this and the goose wandered out. Tom came along with his dog, which chased the goose and caught it. But Alice got the goose away from the dog and carried it home. This child, in illustrating the story, drew a picture of Alice and of Tom, two pictures of the hoop, and two of the dog, but none of the goose, although the story was of "Peter, the Goose." This shows the fragmentary nature of the child's knowledge. The pictures drawn were absurdly untrue to life.

In the second place (and it is the same with us), we gradually approximate the truth. Children have their ideas of truth. We speak the truth to our friends and the false to our enemies. When I was a boy, if I said, "Hope to die if I don't tell the truth," or something of that sort, I felt more sure of getting a better article than if I didn't take such a precaution. It is something mediæval and primitive. The child has a feeling that it is worse to lie to his mother than to a stranger. It is the same thing which makes difficulty in the police courts, where the authorities have to watch the ignorant witness to prevent him from kissing his thumb instead of kissing the book with the idea of escaping the penalties that would follow if he kissed the Bible.

In the third place, the child's imagination drives him often to tell what is not true. Joan of Arc and other child prophets are illustrations. This imagination drives them to every form of perversion of the truth. The child has an imaginary companion. She knocks on the bars of the gate and leads the imaginary companion into the house. They have a party. When the cake comes around the child takes a cake through the little girl. The child, of course, must do everything for the little girl, and so she eats her cake for her. The next morning her mother finds her toothbrush out in the garden. When the child is questioned about it she says the little girl took it there to brush her doll's curls. If you want to read a story on this point, read "Sentimental Tommy," by Barrie. In the second volume you come to the almost inevitable conclusion. Was Sentimental Tommy a liar? In the same way that all children are. As a boy, his vivid imagination came into play.

The first difficulty—that which comes through lack of knowledge—must be met by education. Nothing else will help us out. The child must be brought constantly in contact with palpable truth and made to feel its existence! This other disorder must be met by the most subtle education. Stamp out the imagination and you have a being unfit for the relations of social life. Somewhere in the process there should be the child's imaginative vision.

In the fourth place, you have egotism as a source of untruthfulness. One lies because he wants to show off, or because he wants to get into the background. In the one case he lies because he is a bravo; in the other case, because he is a coward. A boy in school was made to stand on the floor because he had written a love letter to one of the little girls. He got some paris green, carried it to school, and took it there. Doubtless every one of us with any imagination has lingered over the thought of some dramatic ending of our life which would bring us for once conspicuously before the community.

Contagion is the fifth cause. In the sixteenth century one hundred thousand people were put to death for witchcraft. I have looked over with some care the records in regard to witchcraft, both in Germany and in America. The singular thing is that a great mass of these people were children, and nearly all the witnesses were children, generally girls from twelve to fourteen years old. The children's crusades are another illustration of the same thing.

Children lie over and over again under the contagion of ideas. All the community is talking about witches and what they have done. Some one perhaps hints that a certain old one is a little peculiar. The rumor grows by continued repetition and the added imagination until it grows in definiteness and becomes a conviction. That is the way with a lot of the church quarrels and squabbles.

The sixth cause of children's lies is selfishness—they want something.

If I am right in my treatment of lies, if it is true that we are growing up from deceit to a franker transparency, then we must expect to find people all along the line. If a child misrepresents the truth it is a secondary symptom; it is because he is timid or afraid, perhaps; you whip him, and he is more timid than before. It is because he is a bravo and wants to show off; you stand him on the floor; he has exactly what he wants. He misrepresents the facts of life; you punish him and thereby introduce more difficulty into the understanding of facts of life than before. In every case of lying you have an indirect symptom, and what you want is to get back to the right thing. . . .

If the child lies because it is selfish, then it is a simple problem; in any other cases you must treat the child indirectly. We have some subjects who never will tell the truth if they can avoid it. They are on that plane of development. The difference between your telling a lie and the child's telling a lie is the difference between a million and two.

—*Atlantic Educational Journal.*

Extent and Causes of Pupils Dropping Out of the High School.

A. C. BARKER.

At the request of the executive committee of this Association, I undertook last spring to gather statistics to show the extent and causes of pupils dropping out of the high school. Inquires were sent to all the public high schools in the State asking how many of the pupils enrolled in the entering class of 1898-1899 have since left school, when, and for what reasons. The replies received from twenty-five principals indicate that approximately thirty per cent have since then reached the senior year. For the rural schools the percentage is higher and for the city schools considerably lower, reaching in several cases a total of twenty per cent. About forty per cent of these pupils left during the first year, thirty per cent the second, and ten per cent the third. In regard to the time and reasons for leaving, the replies were in many cases, owing to the lack of systematic records, unsatisfactory. In some instances all records had disappeared with the change of principal. The Association, by adopting and recommending a record card for uniform use, would render a substantial service to the high schools of the State.

These replies show that ten per cent left on account of ill health. Nearly all of the cases reported were girls. In one large school twenty per cent dropped out because of illness. The percentage of illness is certainly large enough to raise the question, "Are not the requirements for graduation too high?" One school reports seventeen recitations per week as the regular requirement; seventeen report twenty; two, twenty-one; and two, twenty-five. These requirements are in excess of those of Phillips, Exeter, and Andover, which rank among the best preparatory schools for boys in this country. The public high school of today, however, is not a boys' school; for it contains a much larger percentage of girls than boys. The fact that girls can not carry as many hours as boys without undue danger to their health is too well established to need discussion. The girls to be sure will do the required work, yet many will break down under the strain. I have personally known of several exceptionally bright girls who entered the high school in robust health and left little better than physical wrecks. Twenty hours (which seems to be the average requirement) would not be excessive if a larger proportion of the time were given to teaching or to actual instruction in the class room, rather than to the hearing of recitations. In my opinion the high school should not require more than fifteen prepared recitations per week.

The reports again indicate that twenty-nine per cent left school on account of failure in studies. In two schools, each with an enrollment of over two hundred, the failures exceed one half the whole number of pupils. Fifty-two per cent of these occurred in the first year. Undoubtedly many failures were due to want of ability; for the incompetent and unfortunate will always be with us. But the fact that such a very large number occur during the first year can be explained only by the lack of articulation between elementary and high schools.

This gap between the lower grades and the high school seems every year to be widening, owing to the fact that the former has not kept pace in improvement with the latter. The work of the last two years of the elementary school has too frequently been a dead mechanical routine, possessing little interest and requiring little or no mental effort except the exercise of the memory. Professor Hanus declared that "the total permanent result of the first eight years of the pupil's school life is the ability to read, but not the reading habit; the ability to spell and write words, but no power of expression with the pen; a varying ability to add, subtract, multiply, and divide simple numbers, integral and fractional, but much uncertainty in other operations; some fragmentary book knowledge of names and places, and some scrappy information relating to the History of the United States," most of which information is found to be useless and is soon forgotten. The Seventh and Eighth Years' curriculum is mainly a review of the Sixth Year, and it does not require serious application. During these years pupils are likely to acquire indolent habits, which in the first year of the high school render failure almost certain. The introduction in the Ninth Year to four new and formal subjects will severely tax even the most diligent and ambitious student. When he passes from the elementary to the high school he finds an even greater change in teaching methods than in subject matter. For example, the instruction in English has so changed that it is to all purposes a new subject. Formal and mechanical reading has given way to a study of literature, and the pupil in consequence for the first few months flounders wretchedly. Of course it sometimes happens that high school teachers expect too much of beginners, and many consequently fail or become discouraged and leave school. This is partly due to the fact that the teachers are frequently not conversant with the work of the grades and do not realize the difficulties with which beginners in the high school have to contend; partly to the change from the one teacher to the departmental system. There is undoubtedly too much explanation in the lower grades, the work is made too easy, and the habit of dependence is formed. Inexperienced high school teachers frequently assume that the pupils have acquired independent habits of study, and therefore often adopt methods better fitted for seniors than beginners. Each teacher is a specialist, a fact which naturally begets the idea that his subject is all important. Too often he does not know what is required of his pupils in other subjects. His own work must be done or the pupil is mercilessly dropped. It is the old story of each one for himself and the devil take the last one.

We now come to the question, How shall this gap between the elementary and the high school be bridged? In my opinion it can be brought about only by a revision and an enrichment of the elementary school curriculum; the employment of better teachers, and the adoption in at least the last two years of the course of the departmental system of teaching. I suppose that most educators would agree that the greatest loss of our educational system occurs in the Seventh and Eighth grades, and that all the essentials of the elementary school could, without overstraining, be learned in six years. A few years ago one of the most progressive educational cities in the State required a ten years' elementary course. The same work is now better accomplished in eight years. Another generation will see the same results satisfactorily secured in six or seven years. An examination of the pupils of any good grammar school will show that the acquirements of Eighth Year pupils are but slightly in advance of those of the Sixth Year. The Seventh and Eighth Years' program should undoubtedly be greatly modified; the lumber should be discarded; the present course should be sufficiently cut down to admit of new subjects. There should be more rational instruction in reading and composition; commercial arithmetic should be greatly abridged, and the time given to geography should be reduced by one half. The elements of algebra, geometry, physical and biological sciences, should be added to the course; a foreign language should also be provided for those who desire it. These changes can be brought about in two ways, either by the employment of thoroughly trained teachers in the grammar school with qualifications equal to high school teachers, or in communities maintaining a high school by incorporating the Seventh and Eighth Years with the high school and extending the course of the latter from four fo six years. Personally I am of the opinion that the latter method would be better for districts supporting a high school, although of course either method would necessitate an increased expenditure. The best private schools now provide a curriculum such as I have outlined. President Eliot in an address to the Rhode Island teachers recently declared that unless there is an "enrichment of programs for the years between nine and fourteen the public schools will cease to be resorted to by the childéen of well-to-do Americans. The private and endowed schools offer a choice of foreign languages; for instance, as early as ten years of age or even earlier; and everybody knows that this is the age at which to begin the study of foreign languages, whether ancient or modern. In large cities it seems to be already settled that the private and endowed schools get the children of all parents who can afford to pay their charges." Of course such changes as I have advocated would necessitate the adoption of the departmental system of teaching; but given trained teachers, there seems to be no reason why it should not be as successful in the grammar as in the high school. I have no sympathy with attempts to enrich the course by adding elective subjects to be taught by special teachers. Such experiments have generally produced congested courses resulting inevitably in failure. Most attempts to improve the present curriculum have failed for want of thoroughly trained teachers. The Normal schools have emphasized the study of psychology, pedagogy, methods and fads to the neglect of academic training; and in consequence many Normal graduates are deficient in scholarship. It is useless to hope that attempts to "enrich" the course of study will prove very successful until the standard for the certification of teachers is raised, and until more adequate provision is made for supervision.

The replies also show that fourteen per cent leave owing to lack of interest on the part of either of the parent or the pupil. It is well nigh impossible to determine all the causes for this lack of interest, yet it is clear enough that the main ones are the absence in the curriculum of sufficient scope and flexibility. Until recently the high school program consisted of a single course in which college preparatory and classical interests largely predominated. A few schools of this type still exist. The inadequacy of the course to meet the demands of a large body of students has resulted in the establishment of several group or parallel courses. Three objections to the group system may be noted: some courses are inferior to others, it compels pupils to make a choice too early in the course, and it results in undesirable and unnecessary segregation of pupils. In a few schools the parallel courses have been abolished and a single flexible course substituted therefor, in which certain subjects are required of all pupils, and other subjects are freely elective. In practice the single elastic course has proved very satisfactory, and it will undoubtedly soon supersede the group system. It is certainly a distinct advantage for all pupils whether preparing for business or college to be brought into closer contact than is possible with the parallel courses.

There is a wide dissatisfaction because the high school does not offer instruction of a more practical character. The lack of manual training and commercial subjects perhaps tends more than any other cause to reduce the attendance. Not only do large numbers leave because they are unable to pursue such subjects as they desire, but a much larger number for the same reason never enter the high school. The demand for vocational training is shown by the increased attendance at high schools offering commercial and manual training and the large attendance in private commercial schools. There is no good reason why commercial subjects cannot be better taught in the high school than in the business college. The traditional business course should of course find no place in the high school. Dr. E. J. James has shown clearly enough what sort of commercial education the high school should undertake. Students electing commercial subjects should be required to take the identical prescribed courses in English, Mathematics, History, and Science with those preparing for college. The accrediting system has undoubtedly resulted in making the high school mainly preparatory, for both teachers and principals are frequently unwilling to admit subjects that do not have a credit value for admission to the University. The high schools at present are too largely concerned with academic interests. Too often college entrance requirements rather than the needs and interests of the pupils have been the determining factor in secondary education. Dr. G. Stanley Hall has recently stated that the "present almost feudal dominance of colleges over high schools is without precedent in other countries or the history of education." The high school ought to be broad enough to serve the interests both for pupils preparing for college and life. According to the "Committee of Ten" the best preparation for college is also the best for life; but as Professor John Dewey states, this does not "determine whether the preparation for college or life should furnish the criterion." "The callings that are represented by manual training and commercial studies," he continues, "are absolutely indispensable to life, and to indict a whole nation were a grateful task compared with labeling such occupations as low and narrow—lacking in all that makes for training and culture. With the rounding out of the high school to meet all needs of life, the standard changes. We are no longer concerned with abstract appraisal of studies by the measuring rod of culture and discipline. The problem is rather to study the typical necessities of social life and the actual nature of the individual in his specific needs and capacities."

In conclusion, the results of this investigation have shown that over fifty per cent of the students who entered twenty-five California high schools in the year 1898-1899 dropped out of school for the following reasons—illness, failure in studies, and lack of interest. No attempt has been made to determine the external causes, but only those for which the schools may justly be held responsible. The high school of the future should more adequately meet the needs of its constituency. This can be brought about by a modification or rather an extention of the curriculum in the interest of the large class of pupils who have no intention of entering college. It is to be hoped that these changes will arrest the threatened effeminization of the high school.

* * *

England is the Land of the Free

It is a fair question nowadays if England be not after all the true land of liberty. I believe it is the present fashion in America to admit it. Some estimate in terms of the domestic problem, though England has one too. But our household mechanism is more complicated and more brittle than the English, and the American housewife is bowing into slavery beneath the cooks and butlers, and city families are fast becoming driven into hotels and boarding-houses. Others estimate in terms of other slaveries. One is the slavery to publicity. England has spared more refuges for privacy. The garden wall more frequently rebuffs the street, and the homes that count even the telephone a noxious intrusion of the outer world are more the rule than the exception. Again, there is the slavery to a something we call public opinion, but which is not really the opinion of the great public, so much as a congeries of various sets of opinions publicly set forth, each under the guarantee of some organization or institution. Public opinion has indeed of late years yielded so largely to the organizational form that it becomes difficult to discover what public opinion really is. Every proposal for reform or for standing pat, every phase of view or plan of procedure, must have its organization with pages of officers and honorary councilors. One by one the subjects concerning which a public man may with immunity from organizational attack freely express himself are withdrawn from the open field and lodged behind entrenchments. The result is, naturally, that for the tactful statesman—and tact has of late years been forced high above par—a chief stock in trade has become the cautious list of taboos. I pray you, my promising young man, embroil not thyself in the days of thy youth with those various combinations of initial letters which are nowadays the powers that be; so speaks the voice of carnal Wisdom. This is undoubtedly a land of freedom and free speech, but freedom of speech means that one is at perfect liberty to express such of his convictions as he dares to.—President Benjamin Ide Wheeler in the July "Atlantic."

The Richest of Western Material

The West is rich in literary material. There are mountain ranges comparatively unexplored, which aboriginal tradition veils in haunting mystery. The struggles, trials and heroism of the early pioneers have scarcely been touched upon, and what dramatic strength and picturesqueness is contained in this old-time life of the border! And there exists to-day throughout the length and breadth of the Pacific Coast a peculiarly fascinating freedom not easily comprehended by those who have known nothing but the restraints of an older and more conventional civilization. This, as I have attempted to show, will leave its impress upon the future literary production of the region. As the lands of the olive and the vine have ever figured prominently in the history of Old World letters, it is not unreasonable to expect that California, with its tropical sun and gorgeous coloring, will add luster to the literature of America. Perhaps I have dwelt too strongly upon scenic grandeur as a factor of literary growth, but vast forests, icy summits, somber canyons, and beetling cliffs must stimulate the imaginative powers and lead to creative effort. What has been accomplished thus far by the writers mentioned at least offers glorious promise of future achievement — of work, if I may be so bold as to prophesy, that shall draw its freshness and color from California's sun-clad hills, and its strength and beauty from the white radiance of her eternal peaks. — Herbert Bashford in the July "Atlantic."

Official Department

State Board of Education

GEORGE C. PARDEE, *President of the Board* .... Governor, Sacramento
MORRIS ELMER DAILEY .... President State Normal School, San Jose
E. T. PIERCE .... President State Normal School, Los Angeles
C. C. VAN LIEW .... President State Normal School, Chico
BENJAMIN IDE WHEELER .... President University of California, Berkeley
ELMER E. BROWN .... Prof. of Theory and Practice of Education, University of Cal., Berkeley
SAMUEL T. BLACK .... President State Normal School, San Diego
FREDERIC BURK .... President State Normal School, San Francisco
THOMAS J. KIRK, *Secretary of the Board* ...... Superintendent Public Instruction, Sacramento

State Text-Books

To County, City and County, and City Boards of Education of California:

In answer to a number of questions concerning the completion of the new Grammar School History of the United States, will say that the committee confidently expects it to be printed, seasoned, and ready for distribution by September 1st, next. The price cannot be determined by the State Board of Education until after the State Printer shall have filed an itemized statement covering cost of material, labor, etc., but will probably not *exceed* one dollar per copy.

Boards of Education may, then, safely incorporate the new History in making their courses of study for next school year. McMaster's School History of the United States is the basis of the new book, and will serve as a guide in the division of work by years—allowing for an added chapter, 25 pages, on California.

Under the present law, no county, city, or county and city is *compelled* to use a new book until one year after its completion, and until after the Superintendent of Public Instruction has given his official order for its use, "but nothing in this Act [the law above referred to] shall be construed to prevent any county, city, or city and county from adopting any one or more of the State series of school text-books whenever said book or books shall have been published and is ready for distribution."

The matter of *supplementary* work should remain the same as for the year just closing (see Superintendent Kirk's "Circular No. 8," dated May 1, 1903), as it is not expected that the Committee will be in a position to consider this matter in time to affect the coming year's work.

To County, City and County, and City Superintendents of California:

In proceeding with the revision of the State text-books—provided for in Section 1874 of the Political Code, as amended March 18, 1903—the Committee, in order to determine the order of such revision, is desirous of learning from those actually engaged in teaching the present series what books, in their opinion, are most in *need* of revision.

Will you, therefore, kindly consult as many of your teachers as possible within the next three weeks, and send to the Committee tabulated answers to the question, "In what order should the State text-books be taken up for revision?"

Please have each consider the subject of Primary History, the *Grammar* School History being now in press.

These answers will, of course, be in no way *binding* upon the Committee, but will serve a good purpose when the matter comes up for consideration, as it probably will at the next meeting.

Respectfully,
J. H. STRINE,
Secretary State Text-Book Committee.

PUBLISHERS' NOTICE.

THE WESTERN JOURNAL OF EDUCATION succeeds to the subscription lists, advertising patronage, and good will of the Golden Era, established in San Francisco in 1852.

Subscription, $1.50 a year. Single copies, 15 cents.

Remit by check, Postoffice order, Wells, Fargo & Co., or by stamps.

ADVERTISEMENTS—Advertisements of an unobjectionable nature will be inserted at the rate of $3.00 a month per inch.

MSS.—Articles on methods, trials of new theories, actual experiences, and school news, reports of teachers' meetings, etc., urgently solicited.

Address all communications to THE WESTERN JOURNAL OF EDUCATION, 723 Market Street, San Francisco.

HARR WAGNER, Editor.

THE WHITAKER & RAY COMPANY PUBLISHERS.

Entered at the San Francisco Post-office as second-class matter.

The Official Organ of the Department of Public Instruction of the State of California.

The Selection of Teachers. The building of schoolhouses, the providing of school gardens, the furnishing of school supplies, are important duties of school trustees. The most important duty, however, is the selection of teachers. It is a Duty. The best system of schools in the country may be afflicted and inflicted with acute indigestion by poorly prepared and badly equipped school teachers, whether the preparation and equipment be a part of nature or a part of a pedagogical school. The teacher is the most important element in the success of any school. The trustees in every district should be most careful in the selection of the teacher. The record of a teacher should be investigated, not by an examination of the letters she may have, but by direct consultation or communication with the county superintendent and with the trustees of the school where she has taught.

Ready made, general testimonials, "To Whom it May Concern," are of very little value. An occasional general testimonial may give some important data, but as a rule it requires no trick of the mind to interpret the letter of recommendation, phrase by phrase, before it is opened.

The general testimonial, however, is not as bad as the detective-like, secret communication. There are some natures so small, so mean, so unchristian, that if given the opportunity to write a secret communication to a teachers' agency or a board of school trustees, cannot resist the impelling force of their minute souls to create an incapacity on a teacher, and then exaggerate the incapacity. The promise that the communication shall be confidential has given many a mean, cowardly spirited man the opportunity to use his latent abilities.

The confidential report has been miserably abused. Trustees should not give it too much weight.

Professors in our normal schools and universities, superintendents, and trustees should be strong enough, brave enough, honest enough, to criticise the weaknesses of a teacher in an open communication. It may not be the most agreeable thing to tell a teacher "she loses control and respect of her pupils because she talks too much"; or, "She failed in our school because she lacked the ability to organize her work in a systematic manner." Yet, frank, straightforward criticism, if given in the spirit of helpfulness, freedom from prejudice or ill-will, is sure to be corrective. Trustees should therefore demand from superintendents and others an open opinion, an expert opinion, as to the abilities of a teacher.

The selection of teachers should be made on merit, and merit alone.

The merit should be based on:
1. The natural aptitude of the applicant for the work.
2. Experience.
3. The preparation for teaching.
4. The special consideration of the qualities of the applicant for the particular place in view.

Trustees should know that a teacher who has succeeded admirably in a graded school with forty pupils may fail in an ungraded school of only thirty pupils. There are many things to take into consideration. The trustees are not likely to make any serious errors, if they consider: first, the needs of the children; second, the teacher in relation to the children.

* * *

The Certification of Teachers. There are not sufficient teachers on the Pacific coast to supply the demand! The five normal schools of California, the two universities, the two normal schools of Arizona, the four of Oregon, three of Washington, one of Montana, and one of Idaho, are not graduating sufficient number of teachers to meet the demand. This is due largely to the fact that trustees desire teachers who have received professional training. It is also due to the fact that it requires greater preparation under the present laws in Washington and California to get certificates than formerly. Again, our California certification law is not favorable to holders of certificates of other states.

Before August 1st practically every teacher in California with a good record will have secured a school. And Oregon and Washington will have to advertise for teachers. It is to be hoped that this situation of affairs will lead our strong young men and women to enter the normal schools and prepare for the work of teachers. There is an absolute demand for young men. There is no immediate danger of a surplus of teachers. This state will always stand for a certification law that will require both strong academic and professional training. A certificate, therefore, in California, will mean something. To graduate from our normal schools means a position at a good salary.

It is important, therefore, that our young men and women take advantage of the facilities offered them for professional training.

* * *

Prof. Payne was in the habit of saying: "Whatever is altogether new in education is not true and what is entirely true is not altogether new." Swinburne has emphasized this in a poetic way when he says:

"Change never lays its hand on truth."

* * *

M. Fitzpatrick, formerly superintendent of Omaha schools, but now manager of the American Book Company for the New England States, is authority for the following: "There is a growing tendency today to give applause, not to what is said, but to the man who is saying it."

The present department of education in Harvard university is to be enlarged into a school of education with an endowment fund of $2,000,000 and an additional $500,000 for an administration building. College men who wish to adopt teaching as a profession will be given a theoretical and practical training in education.

WESTERN SCHOOL NEWS

MEETINGS

National Educational Association, President, Charles W. Eliot, Boston, July 6-10, 1903.

California Teachers' Association, O. W. Erlewine, president; Mrs. M. M. Fitz Gerald, secretary, 1627 Folsom Street, San Francisco; December 28 to 31, 1903.

Summer Normal School, State Normal School, San Jose; Morris E. Dailey, President. June 29, 12 weeks.

Summer Session, University of California, June 25 to August 5, Berkeley, Cal. Application should be sent to the Recorder of the Faculties, on or before June 15.

National Summer School of Music, 2014 Van Ness Ave. July 6 to July 18; Selden C. Smith, 325 Sansome St., S. F

Augsburg's Summer School of Drawing, Oakland, Cal. Beginning July 20 Address, F; J. Lobbett, 809 Market street, San Francisco.

NOTES

Prof. Alexander B. Coffey has been called to Washington for some special institute work.

Miss Margaret I. Poore, ex-superintendent of Shasta County, is now teaching.

The National Summer School of Music, under the direction of Selden C. Smith, is very successful.

S. A. Crookshanks, ex-superintendent of Tulare county, is attending the summer school at Berkeley.

Thomas J. Kirk, Superintendent of Public Instruction, wife and daughter, are in attendance at the N. E. A., Boston

W. W. Welch, superintendent of public instruction of Montana, has been given the degree of L.L.D. by Nashville College.

Miss Kinney, Miss Vivian, Mary W. George, and J. E. Addicott of the State Normal School of San Jose, were all given leave of absence for one year.

Prof. F. C. Thompson, formerly of the State Normal School of San Francisco, has been elected to a position in the State Normal School at San Diego.

J. A. Wagener, ex-Superintendent of Schools of Stanislaus county, has been engaged by the trustees of Newman school district as principal of the Newman schools.

Supt. James A. Foshay of Los Angeles has been re-elected for a four year term with a raise of salary. He will receive $3600 per year. The salaries of the high school principal and teachers were also raised

J. W. Graham, ex-superintendent of Kings county, has been appointed the western representative of the Playa Plantation Company, with rubber lands in Vera Cruz Mexico. The rubber tree is the greatest natural producer of wealth known to mankind. It is reported that Mr. Graham will not only make himself, but all his friends, rich. His address is 723 Market street, San Francisco, Cal.

Dr. Eli F. Brown, formerly superintendent of city schools at Riverside, Cal., and well known as an institute instructor on the Pacific coast, has been selected to lecture on Psychology and Child Study in the State School of Methods at Dover, Delaware, during June and July, and as institute instructor in Ohio during August. For many months he has been employed in writing and editing the instruction sheets of the National Correspondence Schools at Indianapolis.

Prof. Van der Naillen of the Van der Naillen School and a well-known writer, has recently been created Chevalier d l'Ordre de Leopold by the King of Belgian, by royal decree, June 6, 1903. This honor has been granted Prof. Van der Naillen on account of his honorable career as civil engineer and founder of the Van der Naillen School of Engineering, and of his relations to the Belgian government and his kindness to a fellow countryman. The jeweled insignia of the "Order of Leopold" is suspended on a scarlet ribbon, presented by the King to the members of his order. The insignias are worn on important occasions only; in everyday life a scarlet ribbon alone is worn in the button hole. The motto is " L' Union fait la Force.".

Tehama County

The schools are all closed and teachers have largely been selected for the coming term. The Red Bluff Union High School closed a very successful term under Principal J. A. DeCou. A class of five graduated and most of them will enter the universities Principal DeCou, Glenn Allen, and Miss Elizabeth Herman have been re-elected. Miss Ruth Atterbury, who has endeared herself to all, will engage in the school of matrimony. Miss Delia Fish takes her place. Miss Fish is a Red Bluff girl, a graduate of the Chico Normal and of the State University. She formerly taught in the Red Bluff Grammar School, but recently has taught in the Chico Normal.

J. D. Sweeney has been re-elected principal of the Red Bluff city schools. J. M. Osborn will be vice-principal. Mr. Osborn has been principal at Corning during the past year. The attendance in the Red Bluff schools was about one hundred more than last year. Mr. Sweeney has been honored by being elected a commissioner to the Presbyterian General Assembly at Los Angeles; also by election to membership in the California Schoolmasters' Club. Miss Clara Miller and Dora Lages have been added to the teaching force of Red Bluff. The other teachers were re-elected. During the term Vice-Principal E. B. Warmoth resigned to become deputy sheriff, and R. L. Douglas, formerly vice-principal, completed the year. Miss Estella Matlock also resigned and Miss Asenath Grier took her place.

The Corning people voted by a large majority to have a union high school. It is too early to give corps of teachers. A. W. Glover was elected principal of the Corning Grammar School. Mr. G. was formerly principal.

During the school year death called two of our teachers, Miss Jessie Nickle and Miss Bessie Hartle. Miss Nickle was one of our best known and most efficient teachers. Miss Hartle had charge of her first school.

The county board of education examined the eighth grade in all topics completed therein in order to lessen the amount of work in the ninth grade. A large class graduated from the latter grade, many of whom will enter high schools. The board also turned out about a dozen new teachers at the May examination. The supervisors appointed Miss Clara Miller, vice E. B. Warmoth, resigned; Miss Jemima Lang, vice Clara Miller, term expired; and Paul Henderson, vice A. W. Glover, term expired.

None have high school certificates as required by law.

Miss Grace Williams was married upon the close of her school term to Frank Ward of Red Bluff.

Miss Ellen A. Lynch, in her few months of office, has made many friends by her apparent desire to act for the welfare of the county schools. She has been honored recently by being elected a Grand Trustee of the N. D. G. W.

Miss Naomi Baker, one of Red Bluff's primary teachers, was made State Superintendent of Junior Christian Endeavors by the San Diego convention.

THE UNION OF DISTRICT SCHOOLS IN SAN DIEGO COUNTY.

From a business standpoint I see nothing in the way of bringing the children of Earle, Montecito and Santa Maria districts to Ramona as a common center. It is now costing from fifty to sixty dollars a month to give each of these districts an eight months' school per year. Taking the cost of delivering the U. S. mail as a basis, it would not cost more than about half that sum to bring the children to the central school during the school months. Not all the balance of the money from each district would be needed to carry on the graded school, the result being an actual saving to the taxpayer and a much superior school available for every child in the territory embraced in the four districts.

Much might be said in regard to the building up of Ramona as an educational as well as a business center, but as that is a matter only indirectly affecting other than the business people of the town, I will leave that for others to discuss, but the better education of ones nearest our hearts today, and who are soon to take our places, is our particular care. I am sure if our people think over this matter, acquaint themselves with its merits and purposes, as well as the practical business side of the question, there will be a general desire to make the change.

O. E. M. HOWARD, Trustee.

* * *

The summer school of the University of California will reach an enrollment of nearly one thousand attendants. Montana, Utah, Oregon, Washington, California, and Arizona are represented.

Text-Books in Montana

The Text-Book Commission of Montana, consisting of W. W. Welch of Helena, J. M. Lewis, Helena; J. P. Monroe, Dillon; J. M. Hamilton, Missoula; J. N. Lenning, White Sulphur Springs; W. E. Harmon, Bozeman, and O. S. Harvey of Billings, met at Helena, June 15th, and adopted common school text-books. The members of the commission were representative teachers.

The commission devoted six days to the consideration of the books presented, and were generous in granting personal interviews night, noon and morning. There were twenty-seven bids. The following books were adopted:

Spellers—American Book Company.
Readers—Ginn & Co.
Copy Books—B. H. Sanborn & Co.
Arithmetics—D. C. Heath & Co.
Browne's Mental Arithmetic—State Publishing Company.
Geographies—Ginn & Co.
Grammars—Maynard, Merrill & Co., and Rand. McNally & Co.
Harr Wagner's Pacific History Stories, Montana edition—The Whitaker & Ray Co.
Physiologies—American Book Company.
Histories—Scribner & Co.
Music—Silver, Burdett & Co.
Drawing—Webb, Ware & Zaner.
Civics—F. C. Kress.
Supplemental Reading—Silver, Burdett & Co.
Supplemental Drawing—Prang Educational Company.
Supplemental Civics—American Book Company.

Among bookmen present were the following: American Book Company, F. A. Fitzpatrick and Mr. Todd; Ginn & Co., O. P. Barnes and Mr. Gilsen; Silver, Burdett & Co., Farr and Maddock; D. C. Heath & Co., Ed. Smith; Crane & Co., Hoehenshell; Educational Publishing Company, W. G. Smith; Rand, McNally & Co., A. W. Schroyer; Ainsworth & Co., W. I. Fraser; Maynard, Merrill & Co., J. D. Williams; Globe Company and Newson & Co., Captain R. L. Edwards; Scribner & Co., Mr. Cheney.

The Commission thanked the bookmen for the many courtesies extended and for the honorable methods pursued in presenting the merits of the various books. In turn the bookmen expressed their appreciation of the Commission.

The Text-Book Commission of Montana deserves to be placed on record for courtesy and fair and honorable treatment of the bookmen, and for careful consideration of the needs of the schools of the state in reference to text-books.

Superintendent Welch requested that he be permitted to present the one thousand and more sample books submitted to the district libraries, which were in need of books.

The bookmen expressed themselves as pleased to have the samples disposed of in the manner proposed.

* * *

A Teacher's Letter.

MENDENHALL SPRINGS, June 8, 1893.

My Dear Estelle: Eureka! I have found the very place for a tired teacher (and we are all tired) to spend her vacation. The very place for us, Estelle. Climate, altitude, mountain scenery, buckeyes in blossom, shady retreats and hammocks, and the cosiest little cottages, big cottages, all sorts of cottages. We can have a bachelor girls' hall, or live in lonesome grandeur apart. The springs will cure us of all our ills, either real or imaginary; and last, but not least, the finest meals and the best and cleanest cooking, and the loveliest landlady, you could find anywhere. Sweet milk without any water in it, delicious rich cream, ice cream, and — oh, well, no use wasting time telling about the good things. Pack up your old clothes —thin ones, mind you—and come at once, before the cottages are all taken, and the jolly time we'll have will be something to tell about. All for $8 per week.   Yours as ever,
CASSIE.

P. S.—Take Southern Pacific to Livermore, and the carriage from the springs will be in waiting.

Write to J. B. Short, Mendenhall Springs, Livermore, Cal."

* * *

Augsburg's Summer School of Drawing has enrolled students from the principal counties in the state.

The continuous session at the State Normal School at San Jose has awakened considerable interest. The teachers in attendance were highly appreciative of the excellent courses offered.

Mrs. Jane L. Stanford has been elected president of the board of trustees of Stanford University. Under the new regime in the administration of Stanford University affairs the board of trustees will have a voice in the selection of the faculy.

Statistics of Examination

M. O. HOLT.

The following statistics were compiled from the reports of the examinations of pupils and from the classification of pupils from the fifth to the ninth grades inclusive, in the public schools of Placer county:

In schools in which the teacher had one, two, or three grades, the average per cent of the pupils was 78; in schools in which the teacher had four, five, or six grades, 77; and in schools in which the teacher had seven, eight or nine grades, 76 per cent. That is, the fewer the grades under the charge of the teacher, the higher the percentages of the pupils, illustrating that with fewer grades the teacher can do much more effective work.

The ninth grade pupils received in the examination an average of 83 per cent, the eighth grade 80, the seventh 77, the sixth 76, and the fifth 73 per cent. Since an average of 75 per cent was required for promotion, the fifth grade failed to obtain the required standing. According to the foregoing statistics, the lower the grade the lower the percentage. Why? A number of reasons might be given. The lower grades contain the largest proportion of dull pupils, who drop out of school before reaching the higher grades. Then the pupils of the lower grades cannot always write answers to the questions they know. Their stock of knowledge is not assimilated. They have it in a disorganized condition but are unable to use it when it is wanted. All teachers, in correcting examination papers, find that pupils in the lower grades cannot always write answers to written questions which, if put orally, they could readily answer.

Taking the five grades from which these statistics were compiled, the average standing was 78 per cent nearly.

The standings in the different studies were as follows—100 credits being the standard:

*Morals and manners 92, composition 90, penmanship 84, physiology 80, music 80, reading 78, bookkeeping 78, civil government 78, geography 77, history 76, word analysis 76, drawing 76, arithmetic 73, grammar 73, spelling 72, mental arithmetic 66. Morals and manners head the list with a good showing for the conduct of the pupils. These statistics show that

*The teacher marks the standings in morals and manners in accordance with the general deportment of the pupils during the term.

since the standings in mental arithmetic, written arithmetic, and grammar are low, more attention should be given these subjects.

Ninety-three per cent of the ninth grade pupils obtained a sufficient standing for graduation—a good record; 85 per cent of the eighth grade, 75 per cent of the seventh, 63 per cent of the sixth, and 69 per cent of the fifth grade obtained a sufficient standing for promotion.

This makes 77 per cent of all pupils who were examined successful, the smallest proportion of promotions being in the sixth grade, and not in the fifth, as one would suppose. Why? Would the average age of the pupils of the grades help to answer the question?

The average age of the pupils in the fifth grade was 12 years, in the sixth grade 13.1, in the seventh grade 14.6, in the eighth grade 15.2, and in the ninth grade 16.4 years, making the average age of the pupils from the fifth to the ninth grade inclusive, 14.3 years.

Summing up, then, the higher grades obtained proportionately higher standings, the probable reasons being given elsewhere in this paper. Greater thoroness should be observed in teaching mental arithmetic, written arithmetic, and grammar. The teachers having the fewest grades, securing the highest standings, the result is a plea for more teachers in the schoolroom.

The July number of "The Atlantic Monthly" is a California number. The leading article, on "The Literary Development of the Pacific Coast," has been written by Herbert Bashford, Editor of *The Literary West*. John Muir contributes a fascinating paper apropos of the appearance of the final volume of Professor Sargent's monumental work on American Silva. President Jordan furnishes an essay on "The Voice of the Scholar," President Wheeler one on "A National Type of Culture," and Professor Gayley an important paper entitled "What is Comparative Literature?" Jack London has a characteristic sketch, "The Gold-Hunters of the North," and Ethel J. Hussey writes of "Lift at a Mountain Observatory." Among the stories dealing with California subjects are "The Last Antelope," by Mary Austin, and "A Lochinvar of the East," by Mabel Clare Craft. There are poems by Charles Keeler, Clarence Urmy, Rebecca Foote, and other verse writers, and contributions by California writers of distinction

Book Reviews

There has just been issued by the San Francisco State Normal School, Bulletin No. 2, The Essentials of Geography in the Primary and Grammar Grades, by Frank F. Bunker and Effie B. McFadden, Supervisors of Geography. This Bulletin is worth $1.00, but will be sent to any teacher for the price of the postage, six cents. Address F. F. Bunker, State Normal School, San Francisco, Cal.

Teachers and Superintendents who have heard Herbert Bashford, the editor of the *Literary West* in his original readings and talks on Western literature, will be interested in the leading article in the July *Atlantic* by Mr. Bashford, entitled "The Literary Development of the Pacific Coast."

Joaquin Miller has published an unique book. It is called the Stork Book, or "As It Was in the Beginning." It is a great poem of 3,000 lines in length with the color of the Yukon, Hawaii and Japan. It is questionable whether on account of its strenuous treatment of President Roosevelt's ideas against "Race Suicide" whether it will not be tabooed the same as was Walt Whitman's "Leaves of Grass." The price of the book is $1.00. A. W. Robertson, publisher, San Francisco, Cal.

Browne's Series of Arithmetics for Primary and Grammar Grades by Frank J. Browne, formerly Superintendent of Public Instruction, State of Washington; Head Master of Hoitt's School, Menlo Park, California. Graded Mental Arithmetic adopted Stockton, Cal., State of Montana, Utah and various counties in California, Washington and elsewhere. Graded School Arithmetic, Book One.

This book is for use in the primary grades, and prepares for Book Two, which should be introduced in the last half of the fifth year. It follows the inductive method, leading up to principles by practical operations with objects and quantities. Graded School Arithmetic, Book Two. This book is designed to follow Book One, and to complete the work required for the grammar grades. The first 60 pages are for a general review of the subject after completing Book One. This review may well be done in the last half of the fifth year. The publishers believe these books to be superior in style, and up-to-date both in subject matter and methods of presentation. Teachers or school officers looking for the latest and best books are invited to correspond with the publishers. The Whitaker & Ray Company, 723 Market street, San Francisco, Cal.

The Glory of California Scenery

As long as there remains the love of beauty in the human soul, so long will the glory of California scenery, and that of the whole Pacific Coast, prove a source of inspiration to the poetic mind. Descriptive verse has been from the beginning a marked feature of the literature of this region. In fact, the term "landscape poets" may be properly applied to this bevy of song birds which seemed to the late Maurice Thompson to have taken "complete possession of the entire Western seaboard." Suffice to say, that if a volume of verse were written by a Californian which reflected nothing of the State's scenic beauty or its warmth of color, it would not only come as a surprise to most reviewers, but the loyalty of the poet might be seriously questioned .... While all this display of local color may seem too apparent an effort on the part of Californians to place upon their work the stamp of a definite locality, and may be considered by some a cheap form of art, it is this very sensitiveness to the beauty and grandeur with which nature has clothed the West that offers the most promise of its rapid literary advancement—a sensitiveness, moreover, that will become more and more acute with the civilization of the higher faculties through increasing educational growth. — Herbert Bashford in July "Atlantic."

* * *

Some Important Changes in Positions

P. W. Kauffman of Ventura has been elected superintendent of Pomona, salary, $2100; E. E. Muller has been elected principal of Point Richmond schools, salary $1000; J. B. Hughes has been elected principal of the Merced High School; Edith Jordan, daughter of President Jordan, has been elected as a teacher in the Merced High School; Mr Davidson, formerly of the San Francisco Normal, has been elected principal of one of the San Diego grammar schools; H. C. Hall, formerly of Menlo Park, has secured a position in the San Francisco School Department; Irving Outcault, formerly of Merced, has been elected to a position in the San Rosa High School; A. D. Tenny, formerly of Humboldt county, has been elected to the principalship of the Ventura High School.

The Western Journal of Education

cents per copy $1.50 per year

August, 1903

CONTENTS

		PAGE
A New Definition of the Cultivated Man	PRESIDENT CHARLES W. ELIOT	552
The Length of the Baccalaureate Course	PRESIDENT BUTLER	555
The Educational Progress of the Year 1902-3	WILLIAM DeWITT HYDE	558
Saving Time in Elementary and Secondary Education	ELLA F. YOUNG	560
Surroundings of Rural Schools	CHARLES R. SKINNER	560
A Friend of Children	THOMAS PEARCE BAILEY, JR.	562
The Progress of Arbitration	MAJOR-GENERAL O. O. HOWARD	564
Organized Industry and Peace	JOSIAH STRONG	566
Teaching as a Fine Art	PROF. GEO. HERBERT	558
Arithmetic	W. H. BAKER	559
Official Deparment	THOMAS J. KIRK, Superintendent of Public Instruction	561
Editorial		565
Western School News		569
Book Reviews		570
Miscellaneous		583
A Struggle for Success—The Building of a Business College	R. L. DURHAM	584

THE WESTERN JOURNAL
OF EDUCATION,
723 Market St.
San Francisco

Winterburn's The Spanish in the Southwest . . . 55 cents
By ROSA V. WINTERBURN

THE discovery and early history of California are in this book vividly and attractively presented for young readers. Commencing with the life of the Indians, it takes up next the coming of the Spaniards, then their explorations in search of gold, the founding of the missions, and the life on the pueblos and the ranches. The book brings the history down to the end of the Mexican rule in 1848.

The narrative element and the purely historical are so skillfully combined as to make this book a story of history, a collection of stories so selected and arranged as to present historical characteristics and tendencies of periods. The style is adapted both to the subject-matter and to the age of the pupils for whom the book is intended. The illustrations are numerous and artistic, and maps show the places mentioned. At the end of each chapter are suggestive questions which serve as a helpful review drill. A list of the principal books consulted in the preparation of this work is also included.

The contents and scope of the work may be gathered from the titles of its chapters given below. It is equally suited for the school and the home, and the children of the Pacific slope who read and enjoy it will find in and between its lines an uprising of love and respect for their native state.

The Spanish in the Southwest

Part I. Before the Coming of the Spanish
- Chapter I. Indian Life in California
- Chapter II. Indian Legends

Part II. Discoverers and Explorers
- Chapter III. Córtes
- Chapter IV. Reports of the Seven Cities
- Chapter V. Fray Marcos de Niza
- Chapter VI. Coronado and Alarcon
- Chapter VII. The Spanish Claim to the Pacific Ocean
- Chapter VIII. Cabrillo and Viscaino
- Chapter IX. The English in the North Pacific

Part III. The Missions of Alta California
- Chapter X. The Desire of a Youth — Father Serra
- Chapter XI. Expeditions into Alta California
- Chapter XII. Founding of San Diego Mission
- Chapter XIV. The Last Days of Father Serra
- Chapter XV. Life at the Missions
- Chapter XVI. The Slavery of the Missions
- Chapter XVII. Secularization

Part IV. Spanish California
- Chapter XVIII. Life in the Pueblos and on the Ranches
- Chapter XIX. Foreigners on the Pacific Coast
- Chapter XX. Spanish Governors of California

Popular Text-Books

Baldwin's School Readers
  Eight Book or Five Book Series
New Education Readers
  Books I and II, each . . . $0.35
  Book III, $0.40; Book IV 45
Patterson's American Word Book 25
Rice's Rational Spelling Book
  Part I, $0.17; Part II 22
Barnes's Natural Slant Penmanship
  Eight Books per doz. 75
  Four Charts per set . . . 1.50
Baird's Graded Work in Arithmetic
  Eight Books for Eight Years
Maxwell's First Book in English 40
  Introductory Lessons in English Grammar 40
  Advanced Lessons in English Grammar 60
Webster's School Dictionaries—Revised
Natural Elementary Geography 60
  Advanced Geography . . . 1.25
McMaster's Primary History of the United States 60
  School History of the United States . . . 1.00
Overton's Applied Physiology
  Primary, $0.30; Intermediate 50
  Advanced 80

Newest Supplementary Reading

Abbott's A Boy on a Farm . . . $0.45
Bakewell's True Fairy Stories 35
Horne & Scobey's Stories of Great Artists 40
Krout's Two Girls in China 45
Monteith's Some Useful Animals 50
Pitman's Stories of Old France 60
Pyle's Stories of Humble Friends 50
Simms's Child Literature 30
Wood's The Children's First Story Book 25

Send for descriptive circulars

AMERICAN BOOK COMPANY   PUBLISHERS
NEW YORK   CINCINNATI   CHICAGO   BOSTON   ATLANTA   DALLAS
204 PINE ST., SAN FRANCISCO

THE WESTERN JOURNAL OF EDUCATION

Established 1852.

Old Series: Golden Era, Vol. XLVI.   San Francisco, August, 1903.   New Series: Vol. VIII. Number 8.

The New Definition of the Cultivated Man*

President Charles W. Eliot of Harvard University.

The ideal of general cultivation has been one of the standards in education. It is the object of this paper to show that the idea of cultivation in the highly trained human being has undergone substantial changes during the nineteenth century.

I propose to use the term, cultivated man in only its good sense—in Emerson's sense. In this paper he is not to be a weak, critical, fastidious creature, vain of a little exclusive information or of an uncommon knack in Latin verse or mathematical logic; he is to be a man of quick perceptions, broad sympathies and wide affinities, responsive but independent, self-reliant but deferential, loving truth and candor, but also moderation and proportion, courageous but gentle, not finished but perfecting.

There are two principal differences between the present ideal and that which prevailed at the beginning of the nineteenth century. The horizon of the human intellect has widened wonderfully during the past one hundred years, and the scientific method of inquiry has been the means of that widening. The most convinced exponents and advocates of humanism now recognize that science is the "paramount force of the modern as distinguished from the antique and the mediæval spirit" (John Addington Symonds—Culture), and that "an interpretation of humanism with science and of science with humanism is the condition of the highest culture."

Emerson taught that the acquisition of some form of manual skill and the practice of some form of manual labor were essential elements of culture, and this idea has more and more become accepted in the systematic education of youth.

The idea of some sort of bodily excellence was, to be sure, not absent in the old conception of the cultivated man. The gentleman could ride well, dance gracefully, and fence with skill, but the modern conception of bodily skill as an element in cultivation is more comprehensive, and includes that habitual contact with the external world which Emerson deemed essential to real culture.

We have become convinced that some intimate, sympathetic acquaintance with the natural objects of the earth and sky adds greatly to the happiness of life, and that this acquaintance should be begun in childhood and be developed all thru ado-

*Extract of address delivered before the N. E. A., Boston.

lescence and maturity. A brook, a hedgerow, or a garden is an inexhaustible teacher of wonder, reverence and love.

The scientists insist today on nature study for children, but we teachers ought long ago to have learnt from the poets the value of this element in education. The idea of culture has always included a quick and wide sympathy with men; it should hereafter include sympathy with nature, and particularly with its living forms, a sympathy based on some accurate observation of nature.

We proceed to examine four elements of culture:—

Character.—The moral sense of the modern world makes character a more important element than it used to be in the ideal of a cultivated man. Now, character is formed, as Goethe said, in the "stream of the world," not in stillness, or isolation, but in the quick moving tides of the busy world, the world of nature and the world of mankind. To the old idea of culture some knowledge of history was indispensable.

Now, history is a representation of the stream of the world, or of some little portion of that stream, 100, 500, 2,000 years ago. Acquaintance with some part of the present stream ought to be more formative of character and more instructive as regards external nature and the nature of man, than any partial survey of the stream that was flowing centuries ago.

The rising generation should think hard, and feel keenly, just where the men and women who constitute the actual human world are thinking and feeling most today. The panorama of today's events is an invaluable and a new means of developing good judgment, good feeling, and the passion for social service, or, in other words, of securin[g] cultivation.

But some one will say the stream [of] the world is foul. True in part. Th[e] stream is what it has been, a mixture [of] foulness and purity, of meanness a[nd] majesty; but it has nourished individu[al] virtue and race civilization. Literatu[re] and history are a similar mixture, an[d] yet are the traditional means of cultur[e]. Are not the Greek tragedies means [of] culture? Yet they are full of inces[t,] murder and human sacrifices to lustf[ul] and revengeful gods.

Language.—A cultivated man shoul[d] express himself by tongue or pen wit[h] some accuracy and elegance; therefo[re] linguistic training has had great im[-] portance in the idea of cultivation. Th[e] conditions of the educated world hav[e,] however, changed so profoundly sinc[e] the revival of learning in Italy that o[ur] inherited ideas concerning training i[n] language and literature have require[d] large modifications.

In the year 1400 it might have bee[n] said with truth that there was but on[e] language of the scholars, the Latin, an[d] but two great literatures, the Hebre[w] and the Greek. Since that time, however, other great literatures have arisen[,] the Italian, Spanish, French, German[,] and above all, the English, which ha[s] become incomparably the most extensiv[e] and various and the noblest of litera[-] tures.

Under these circumstances it is im[-] possible to maintain that a knowledge [of] any particular literature is indispensab[le] to culture. When we ask ourselves wh[y] a knowledge of literature seems indis[-] pensable to the ordinary idea of cultiva[-] tion, we find no answer except this—[-] that in literature are portrayed all huma[n] passions, desires and aspirations, an[d] that acquaintance with these huma[n] those which enable him, with his individual personal qualities, to deal best and sympathize best with nature and with other human beings.

It is here that the passion for service must fuse with the passion for knowledge. We have learned from the nineteenth century experience that there is no field of real knowledge which may not suddenly prove contributory in a high degree to human happiness and the progress of civilization, and therefore acceptable as a worthy element in the truest culture.

Imagination.—The only other element in cultivation which time will permit me to treat is the training of the constructive imagination. The imagination is the greatest of human powers, no matter in what field it works—in art or literature, in mechanical invention, in science, government, commerce or religion, and the training of the imagination is, therefore, far the most important part of education.

I use the term constructive imagination, because that implies the creation or building of a new thing. The sculptor, for example, imagines or conceives the perfect form of a child ten years of age; he has never seen such a thing, for a child perfect in form is never produced; he has seen in different children the elements of perfection, here one and there another. In his imagination he combines these elements of the perfect form, which he has only seen separated, and from this picture in his mind he carves the stone, and in the execution invariably loses his ideal—that is, falls short of it and fails to express it.

Constructive imagination is the great power of the poet, as well as the artist, and the nineteenth century has convinced us that it is also the great power of the man of science, the investigator and the natural philosopher. The educated world s to recognize the new varieties of tructive imagination.

)lo, in "La Bete Humaine," con-:s that ten persons, all connected . the railroad from Paris to Havre, l be either murderers or murdered, oth, within eighteen months; and he ; two railroad slaughters criminally ured. The conditions of time and e are ingeniously imagined, and no il is omitted which can heighten the :t of this homicidal fiction.

ontrast this kind of constructive im-1ation with the kind which conceived great wells sunk in the solid rock be-Niagara that contain the turbines ; drive the dynamos, that generate electric force that turns thousands of els and lights, thousands of lamps · hundreds of square miles of adjoin-territory; or with the kind which con-es the sending of human thoughts)ss 3,000 miles of stormy sea instan-:ously on nothing more substantial 1 ethereal waves. There is going to ·oom in the hearts of twentieth cen-/ men for a high admiration of these ls of imagination, as well as for that :he poet, artist or dramatist.

; is one lesson of the nineteenth cen-/, then, that in every field of human wledge the constructive imagination .s play—in literature, in history, in)logy, in anthropology, and in the)le field of physical and biological re-:ch.

'he great century has taught us that, the whole, the scientific imagination uite productive for human service as literary or poetic imagination. The gination of Darwin or Pasteur, for mple, is as high and productive a form imagination as that of Dante, or :the, or even Shakespere, if we re-d the human uses which result from the exercise of imaginative powers, and mean by human uses not meat and drink, clothes and shelter, but the satisfaction of mental and spiritual needs.

It results from this brief survey that the elements and means of cultivation are much more numerous than they used to be; so that it is not wise to say of any one acquisition or faculty—with it culti-vation becomes possible, without it im-possible.

The one acquisition may be immense, and yet cultivation may not have been attained. We have met artists who were rude and uncouth, yet possessed a high degree of technical skill and strong powers of imagination. We have seen philanthropists and statesmen whose minds have played on great causes and great affairs, and yet who lacked an ac-curate use of their mother tongue, and had no historical perspective or back-ground of historical knowledge. We must not expect systematic education to produce multitudes of highly cultivated and symmetrically developed persons; the multitudinous product will always be imperfect, just as there are no perfect trees, animals, flowers or crystals.

Let us as teachers accept no single element or variety of culture as the one essential; let us remember that the best fruits of real culture are an open mind, broad sympathies and respect for all the diverse achievements of the human in-tellect at whatever state of development they may be today—the stage of fresh discovery, or bold exploration, or com-plete conquest. The moral elements of the new education are so strong that the new forms of culture are likely to prove themselves quite as productive of mor-ality, high-mindedness and idealism as the old.

The Length of the Baccalaureate Course*

In my judgment most participants in the discussion now going on thruout the land as to the length of the baccalaureate course and the preparation for the professional schools, err in supposing that the two questions are necessarily reducible to one and also in taking hold of that one by the wrong end. The nature, content and proper length of the baccalaureate course are matters quite independent of the proper standards of professional education and are entitled to consideration on their own merits.

The one question to which the two are usually reduced is taken hold by the wrong end when it is said that the baccalaureate course should be of a stated length, say four years or three years, and that everything else in education and in life must adapt itself accordingly. Those who take this stand give us no clear notion of (1) where the baccalaureate course begins, (2) what it consists of, or (3) what it exists for. They assume that all of these points are clearly understood and generally agreed upon. Nothing could be farther from the truth. Not even the so-called reputable colleges are in anything approaching agreement as to the standard to be enforced for admission to the baccalaureate course; and while there is an external pretence of unanimity as to what the baccalaureate course exists for, that course is, nevertheless, in two many instances, fearfully and wonderfully made. Dr. Wayland said over sixty years ago that "there is nothing magical or imperative in the term of four years, nor has it any natural relation to a course of study. It was adopted as a matter of accident, and can have, by itself, no important bearing on the subject in hand." To suppose that a four years' baccalaureate course is necessary *semper ubique, ab omnibus*, is to elevate an accident to the plane of a principal.

Others take hold of the question by the middle. They fix an arbitrary age at which professionally trained men should be ready for active work in life, and after subtracting the sum of the years that they propose to allot to the elementary school, the secondary school and the professional school, the remaining years, three, or perhaps two, are held to be sufficient for the college.

Both of these methods appear to me to be arbitrary and unscientific, altho the former is the usual academic mode of settling the question and has behind it the support of uncritical public opinion.

One of the worst of all educational evils is that of quantitative standards, and it persists surprisingly in the discussion of college and university problems. Every higher course of study that I know of, except only that of graduate work leading to the degree of doctor of philosophy at the best universities, is primarily quantitative. These courses are all based on time spent, not upon performance. The adjustment of the period of work to the capacity of individual students, now so common in elementary schools and not unusual in secondary schools, is almost wholly absent from the colleges. The "lock-step" is seen there to perfection, and class after class of one hundred or even two hundred members moves forward (with the exception of a few delinquents) as if all its members were cast in a common mold. The place of the baccalaureate course and its standards will never be established on sound principles until the question of its length is made subordinate to

---
*Abstract of a paper by President Butler of Columbia University, read before the department of Higher Education of the National Educational Association, at Boston, Mass., on Tuesday, July 7, 1902.

those relating to its content and its purpose. Moreover, it is quite unreasonable to assume that the baccalaureate course should be of one and the same length for everybody. By the term "baccalaureate course" I mean those liberal studies in the arts and sciences that follow the secondary school period.

My own views on the question at issue are, briefly, these:

1. The baccalaureate or college course of study of the liberal arts and sciences should be preserved at all hazards as an essential part of our educational organization. It is distinctively American and a very powerful factor in the upbuilding of the nation's culture and idealism. It should be treated as a thing of value in and for itself, and not merely as an incident to graduate study or to professional schools.

2. The college course is in serious danger by reason of the fact that the secondary school is reaching up into its domain on the one hand and the professional school is reaching down into it on the other. Purely professional subjects in law, medicine, engineering and architecture are widely accepted as part of the baccalaureate or college course by university colleges, and now independent colleges in different parts of the country are trying various devices with a view to doing the same thing. If this tendency continues unchecked, at many institutions there will soon be little left of the old baccalaureate course but the name.

3. To preserve the college is (a) to fix and enforce a standard of admission which can be met normally by a combined elementary and secondary school course of not more than ten years well-spent, and (b) to keep out of the baccalaureate course purely professional subjects pursued for professional ends by professional methods. The college course, in other words, should be constructed for itself alone and for the intellectual, moral and spiritual needs of the youth of our time, without reference or regard to specific careers. This course must be widely elective, and so offer material to enrich and develop minds of every type. This course is the best preparation for the professional study of law, medicine, divinity, engineering, architecture and teaching, simply because it does what it does for the human mind and the human character, and not because it is so hammered and beaten as to serve as a conduit to a particular career or careers.

4. This course should be entered upon at seventeen, or in some cases at sixteen. Eighteen is too late for the normal boy; the boy who has had every educational advantage and is not ready to meet any existing college entrance test at eighteen has been dawdling and weakening his mental powers by keeping them too long in contact with merely elementary studies.

5. For the boy who enters college at seventeen and who looks forward to a career as scholar, as teacher, or as a man of affairs, four years is, ordinarily, not too long a time to spend in liberal studies. On the other hand, a boy who, entering college at seventeen, proposes to take up later the study of a profession in a university, ought not to be compelled to spend four years upon liberal studies just at that time in his life. To compel him to do so is to advance the standard of professional education arbitrarily without in any way raising it. It is a fallacy to suppose that the more time a boy spends in study the more he knows and the more he grows. Whether he grows by study depends entirely upon whether he is studying subjects adapted to his needs, his interests and his powers. Pedagogs suppose that the more time a boy spends in school and college, the better; educators know the contrary.

There is a time to leave off as well as a time to begin. A boy *can* develop intellectual apathy in college as well as knowledge, weakness of will as well as strength of character.

6. The earlier parts of professional courses in law, medicine, engineering and the like are most excellent material for the boy of nineteen or twenty. He should begin them at that time and complete his four years of professional study by twenty-three or twenty-four. To postpone his professional course later than this is not only to waste his time, but to waste his mind, which is far worse.

7. There should be a college course two years in length, carefully constructed as a thing by itself and not merely the first part of a three years' or a four years' course, which will enable intending professional students to spend this time as advantageously as possible in purely liberal studies. The university colleges can establish such a course readily enough; the independent colleges will have to establish such a course or see their influence and prestige steadily decline. To try to meet the new situation by simply reproducing all present conditions on a three-year scale instead of on a four-year scale, is a case of *solvitur ambulando*. The shortening of the college to three years for all students involves an unnecessary sacrifice. As usually defended this policy involves no educational principle, but merely concedes a year of liberal study to the modern demand for haste and hurry.

8. Whether the completion of such a two-year course should be crowned with a degree, is to me a matter of indifference. Degrees are the tinsel of higher education and not its reality. Such a two-year course as I have in mind would imply a standard of attainment at least as high as that required for the degree of A.B. in 1860, which had many characteristics that we of today persistently undervalue. If this discussion could be diverted from degrees to real educational standards, it would be a great gain. The compromise plan as to degrees, now becoming so popular, whereby the baccalaureate degree is given either for two years of college study and two years of work in a professional school or for three years of college study and one year of work in a professional school, is disastrous to the integrity of the college course. It deliberately shortens the college course by one year or two while proclaiming a four-year college course. It is a policy that only university colleges can adopt; independent colleges must suffer if it becomes a fixed and permanent policy.

9. The most difficult point to establish, apparently, is that at which the baccalaureate course should begin. Colleges with courses nominally four years in length are admitting students with from one to two years' less preparation than is demanded by other colleges with four-year courses. The lax enforcement of published requirements for admission, together with the very general acceptance of certificates from uninspected and unvisited schools, has demoralized college standards very generally. It does not make much difference how long the baccalaureate course is if it does not begin anywhere.

10. A university ought not to admit to its professional schools students who have not had a college course of liberal study, or its equivalent. A minimum course of two years of study should be insisted upon. A four-years' course should not be required for the two reasons (1) that it delays too long entrance upon active life-work and (2) that

it does not use the time and effort of the intending professional student to the best advantage.

11. For a university to admit professional students direct from the secondary schools is to throw the weight of its influence against the spirit and ideals of college training, and to prepare for the so-called learned professions a large body of very imperfectly educated men. To say that any other procedure is undemocratic is not only a grave misuse of words, but is to imply that the universities should not struggle to give this democracy what it most needs, namely, well-educated and highly trained professional service.

* * *

The Educational Progress of the Year 1902-3

President William DeWitt Hyde, Bowdoin College.

The death of Mrs. Alice Freeman Palmer has left us the ideal of the educated woman; scholarship without a particle of pedantry; optimism with no blinking of unpleasant facts; efficiency unsevered from winsomeness. By a splendid educational campaign leading to increased state appropriations and local taxation, better schoolhouses, free summer schools for teachers, consolidated schools, improved courses of study, the South has made the greatest progress within the year.

The kindergarten idea is improving teaching in all the primary grades; the two-session kindergarten, where the same teacher meets the same pupils twice, involves excessive strain for both and is being abandoned. The wiser kindergartners are learning that the spirit of Froebel enables them to dispense with a good deal of the letter of the law and to make their teaching a helpful preparation for the primary work. The reflex influence of Hampton and Tuskegee and the industrial development of the country have led to a great extension of the manual training. School buildings, school grounds, and, especially, school gardens, are receiving more of the attention they deserve.

Vacation schools, summer playgrounds, free evening lectures and evening classes and clubs are utilizing the school plants in our cities for social as well as intellectual purposes at times when they have hitherto been idle, and widening our idea of public education to include the elevation of the entire community. An expenditure of $130,000 last year for this school extension in New York City made available for 400 hours $35,000,000 of municipal property which otherwise would have been unused.

By introducing the school physician, by asking parents to report health and home habits of children, we are treating home and school as parts of a single; healthy, happy, useful life, and seeing that the avoidable breakdown of a child's health is murder in the first degree for which parents and school officers are jointly responsible.

The tendency is toward small school boards, nominated and elected on the general ticket or appointed by the mayor, confined to legislative work alone, and employing experts for all executive work. Such boards are introducing the merit system of appointment of teachers, uninfluenced by considerations of politics, religion or residence; increased salaries to teachers of proved ability and tenure of office after adequate probation. There is a wholesome reaction from the refinements of pedantic methodology in vogue a dozen years ago and an insistence upon thoro and advanced knowledge of the subject taught as the prime qualification of the teacher.

The consolidation of rural schools, authorized in twenty states, is giving better buildings and better teaching, better supervision, larger attendance at less expense; and, by affording a centre for the intellectual and social life of widened neighborhoods, is enriching rural life and keeping the prosperous farmer on the farm.

The certificate system of admission to college is spreading, and the colleges of New England and of the North Central Association and the University of California are taking steps to tighten it at points where it has come too loose. The college or university which entices students to leave the secondary school before they have thoroly completed a preparatory course, is understood to be guilty of the folly of killing the goose that lays the golden egg; the crime of taking its students' money under false pretences; the parasitic vice of sucking lifeblood out of an educational system of which it professes to be the crowning ornament. Yale and Dartmouth have added their weight to the degree of A.B. without Greek. Yale and Williams have extended the elective system.

Williams and Dartmouth have adopted the group system of electives, with the requirement of a major study in one group which gives coherence and continuity to the individual's choices. The proposition to cut the college course in two and throw the better half away by granting the degree of A.B. at the end of two years has met emphatic and universal condemnation.

By reducing the number of grades; by offering high school studies in the upper grammar grades; by counting secondary work and requirements for admission to college by points or credits; by stating the requirements for college degrees in units of work rather than in lapses of time; in some cases by counting the same work for the last year in college and the first year in the professional school—we are reducing the time required to prepare for a profession, and at the same time making graduation from either grammar school, high school, college or professional school mean as much as it ever did.

Chicago University, in defiance of the educational tradition of the West, has partially segregated the women students during the first two years. This is a brave declaration that co-education is no mere question of administrative detail, but is a profound sociological and social problem: that it cannot permanently be solved in one way in the East and in another in the West; that there will always be those who from circumstances or conviction, will prefer co-education; and others who, for social or pedagogical reasons, will prefer more or less separation; and that henceforth each institution must determine its policy, not by doctrinaire devotion to abstract theory, but by inductive study of its specific circumstances and resources and the preference of its special constituency.

Professional schools are being divided into two groups, according as they do, or do not, require the college degree, or its equivalent, for admission. The larger institutions are establishing professorships wholly or mainly devoted to research. The wise administration of the Carnegie Institute has sidetracked the sentimental agitation for a Washington Memorial University; has made what might have been a rival a stimulus and ally to all our universities, and is proving itself the worthy crown and consummation of our national educational system.

Saving Time in Elementary and Secondary Education

Ella F. Young, University of Chicago.

Turning to the elementary and secondary schools, we find a situation analogous to that which obtained formerly in the college and the professional school. With the development of the high school, the differentiation between it and the grammar school has been made sharper and sharper, until the time spent upon covering the work offered by the two combined has become excessive. The treatment of subjects in the elementary school seems to fit the pupils in very slight degree for the work planned in the secondary school.

In many cities the separation between the two schools has come to be felt so keenly, that within the last few years conferences have been held, in which the high school teachers have told the eighth grade teachers wherein their work was poor, and the eighth grade teachers have reciprocated the courtesy by telling the high school teachers wherein they have failed. Some high school principals have expressed a willingness to take the seventh and eighth grades under their care, and some elementary school principals have expressed an equal willingness to keep their pupils a year or two longer and instruct them in the ninth and tenth grades. These straws indicate the general trend of thought

By a system of grouping the required preparatory subjects the colleges have opened the way for group electives in the secondary schools These college preparatory courses, together with manual training, school economics, nature study, the school arts, offer abundant material for continuous lines of work in the elementary and secondary schools, if systematized.

The time has come when the aims of elementary and secondary education must be unified. The courses of study must be reduced to reasonable proportions, and then intelligently apportioned between the grammar and the high school with a clear understanding of the relations and responsibilities involved.

The National Council could undertake nothing greater than the solution of this problem.

* * *

Surroundings of Rural Schools

Charles R. Skinner, LL.D.

State Superintendent of Public Instruction of New York State.

Millions of school children thruout this country are seeking education under most wretched conditions; in miserable buildings, poorly equipped, with no playgrounds but the fenceless yard, the highway or the hillside, where the thrifty farmer's cattle wander at will. If we expect our children to live the beautiful and love the beautiful, we must surround them with beautiful influences in home and school. A child is educated by every influence with which he comes in contact, is being changed for better or for worse every moment of his life. I pity the man who has no pleasant recollections of his school days, but how can he have such happy memories if his school life is associated in his mind with a tumbledown building, a barren schoolroom, and constant contention to preserve the school playgrounds from the encroachment of animals and tramps.

It is in the power of teachers and friends of education to change these conditions—will they do it? A movement is already well under way, and this association of educators should encourage and co-operate in this reform. Parents and patrons should be stimulated to properly fence and improve the school grounds, and the children should be encouraged to feel that the school grounds belong to them, that they have an opportunity to make them what they should be.

If this is done, we shall find we have taken an important step toward giving the principles taught inside the schoolhouse an opportunity for expression in the life of the child. When we talk of enriching courses of study, let us not forget how much of life's course of study is furnished by environment, and that its enrichment makes possible nobler tastes and more refined ideals. Ruskin has said: "What we like determines what we are, and is a sign of what we are; and to teach taste is inevitably to form character."

School grounds may be made beautiful without restricting free play, and the work may be so done as to bring rich returns to hand, head and heart. School authorities, farmers, fathers, and particularly the mothers, should be interested in this cause. The school grounds should be properly fenced and suitably graded. In the decoration there should be a definite and well-considered plan. "School ground committees" of boys and girls should be selected to care for the yards during the hot, dry vacation months, in order that the work of the springtime and early summer may not be wasted.

The public school aims at a development of all the faculties, with the ultimate purpose of leading to better citizenship and nobler character. It must not, therefore, neglect any opportunity for broadening the experience upon which to build the essentials for a complete life. It is in helping Nature that the child feels the influence which makes for his greatest good. If we can educate a child to love a flower or care for a tree, we have helped to lay the foundation of character.

An outline was given of the extensive work in the matter of decoration of school grounds done in the state of New York, under the direction of the state department of public instruction, and the speaker also referred to the excellent service rendered by the Perry Mason Company, publishers of "The Youth's Companion," Boston, which is helping on the good cause in all sections of our country by offering prizes for improvement in such schools.

* * *

I, Louis Agassiz, Teacher

I do not know in recent times a more stirring answer than that of Lacordaire, the famous Dominican, to the court of peers in France, who asked him what his profession was, when he replied simply, "A schoolmaster," unless it be the answer of his friend, the Compte de Montalembert, the noblest specimen, I sometimes think, of the modern French laity, to the same question: "A Schoolmaster and a peer of France." Nay, it was but the other day that a learned and humble man of science, who will live in history as having declared that he had "no time to make money," began his will with the modest words, so great in their modesty, "I, Louis Agassiz, teacher."—Contemporary Review.

A Friend of Children

Thomas Pearce Bailey, Jr., University of Mississippi.

Few Californians realize fully that in Charles T. Wilkinson the state lost one of the noblest, most successful and most original teachers ever vouchsafed to a commonwealth. He made the blind children of the institution to see with their minds and hearts; he helped them to find the self-respect and joy that come with skilful hands and with minds that work. He found the blind children doing odds and ends of futile handwork; before he died he saw some of them holding honorable positions in business life and the professions. But altho one might well point with admiration to the results wrought by this man in the higher education of certain talented pupils, it is the work this apostle of light did for the development of character that we need to ponder most deeply.

He embodied a trinity of pedagogical virtues—interest, sympathy and tact. First, he was profoundly interested in each blind child and in all of them as a class and as a school. He constantly spoke of what "we" are trying to do. Thus, while his sympathy was true and abiding, it was based on interest. Not his the sympathy of condescension, but rather that of comprehension. For nothing pertaining to the blind or to children in general lacked stimulating interest to him. Each child was God's child, one of Christ's little brothers or sisters, and therefore *his* little brother or sister. Yes, he saw the normal and the perfect in spite of the closing of the greatest window of the soul. So deep was this teacher's vital interest in his blind friends that in working for them and for their advancement in college and in life, he often lost sight of his own affairs, and sometimes, I fear, forgot to care for his health. His devoted wife had often to remind him that he must preserve his health for the work's sake.

Most of us teachers grow weary of our profession at times. We are glad to banish "shop"; indeed, we often feel like apologizing for naming our calling a profession. But this teacher was always enthusiastic, always planning improvements, always gaining deeper insights into the peculiarities of the blind and into the character of individuals. He used to say, "What do you make of this case, I have been studying it for six months, and I can't get it off my mind." Indeed, his interest in his work extended to every detail of the paraphernalia of teaching. He made raised maps, repaired typewriters, manufactured apparatus for teaching physics, attended to the minutest details of the printing for and by the blind, and yet found time to read books like Lloyd Morgan's Psychology for Teachers and the last edition of Dr. LeConte's work on "Sight," to attend meetings of literary clubs, of the Philosophical Union, to charm many dear friends by his genial conversation and to take an active interest in affairs of state and church. But in all of these activities, his one consuming interest was to understand and help the blind children. His call from God to his vocation unified and vitalized all his other interests. When enjoying his delightful hospitality on his ranch at El Verano, in the lovely Sonoma Valley, I have seen a faraway look in his eyes show whether his thoughts were tending, and I knew that he would soon say something about his beloved blind. When Charles Wilkinson and Joseph LeConte talked together, as they often did under Mr. Wilkinson's friendly roof-tree in Sonoma Valley, one could but feel that like "communism of saints" and the "blessed company of all faithful people" are phrases of wider and deeper import than we realize.

Mr. Wilkinson's sympathy was instructive and habitual, an aroma from the flower-cup of love. He did not obtrude it on the blind children, those sensitive plants. But they sensed its soothing presence, and their hearts responded thereto. They learned to know that he would help them to aid themselves, instead of giving the easy help that enervates the spirit, and his sympathy was active as well as sensitive. Let any one look down on the blind as a class or fail to give a fair chance to a blind boy or girl, then Mr. Wilkinson would rise in his righteous wrath and would fight for the rights of the blind far more strenuously than he would contend for his own rights. In fact, the rights of the blind became his by virtue of heart sympathy. From his interest in the children and his sympathy for them, flowed his abounding tact. How he soothed and guided and comforted and cheered! I have watched him sometimes with a sense of shame for myself and my fellow-teachers, because there is so little living interest and sympathy in our tact. Instead of making the blind feel their deficiences, he acted as if he were simply the oldest and most experienced in the group about him, and his irrepressible cheerfulness toned them up, even as it often toned him down, for the man was always giving himself for others. Verily, he followed the Master-teacher's example.

A few words about his practical methods: Fully realizing how much of nature and society is denied the blind, he strove to enlarge their "many-sided interest." The blind cannot see the stars, but a little astronomy helped them to feel the immensity and the fullness of space. The physics of everyday life and common-sense made their world more intereresting and significant. History and literature were the vehicles for teaching practical ethics. But he did not neglect the formal side of training. I have before me a number of letters from his pupils—warm, loving, appreciative letters. They all show correct spelling and sentence-structure. For our teacher was himself interested in the ever-varied rhythm and movement of drill-work. Isn't that in large measure the secret of success in the formal drill of mathemathics, language and manual training? Mr. Wilkinson would not tolerate slovenliness, but did all in his power to form the work habit and the love of work in his pupils.

One of his experiments deserves more particular notice. He tried to find out whether the pupils naturally tended to study general outlines by free particulars or vice versa. Watching them at work with raised maps he found that they first strove to gain the general outlines, then to place particular localities, and he instinctively at first and afterwards consciously, laid much stress on having the pupils gain a conspectus on general systematic outline in all their studies. Thus there was a beginning, a middle and an end in Mr. Wilkinson's teaching. Thoroness, mastery, significance, clearness, system—these were some of the traits he aimed at securing and secured.

Perhaps the best summing-up of his work as a teacher is this: He adopted course of study, methods, principles of discipline to the nature of childhood in general and to the character and aptitudes of each individual in particular.

I like to believe that in the Heavenly city of the hereafter he will be known as the Friend of Children and the Brother of the Blind.

The Progress of Arbitration

Major-General O. O. Howard.

Webster's definition of arbitration is: "The hearing and determination of a cause between parties in controversy, by a person or persons chosen by the parties." Once I had a very terrible experience by submitting a cause to arbitration. My adversary chose an arbiter and I chose one. My friend decided that I ought to pay nothing whatever for a sand pit whose lease clouded the title of the large estate upon which it existed. The friend of my adversary brought in his judgment that I should pay $20,000; the two chose a third man and the amount settled upon in compromise was $10,000, my own friend, however, declaring that the final decision of the two against him and me was a fraud and showed previous collusion. They might possibly have been a small loss to the lessee due to the action of the lessor, but it was not plain to me why I, the purchaser, should pay the lessee $10,000. I was merely anxious to have a clear title from the original owner or lessor of the property. This simple case indicates the danger that may be found in arbitration.

We have had a long experience with our northern boundary, reaching back to many years before I was born. Again and again since its beginning at the Atlantic Ocean and its arrangement portion by portion along the entire northern boundary to the Pacific Ocean, lines more or less extended have been settled upon by arbitration. It has cost both countries several million of dollars to carry thru the courts of arbitration the questions that have been at issue, and as a rule the United States has had to give way and give up territory that was plainly intended to belong to our nation in the original treaty or treaties. These difficulties have arisen mainly from the reputed boundary up to which our settlers, being citizens of the United States, have pushed their positions. The boundary being disputed by great Britain or our citizens has caused often great excitement, even leading to the drafting of men and marshalling of troops on both sides, as at the northern boundary of Maine and the later bitter conflict at San Juan Island, north of Puget Sound, on the Pacific.

I was but eight years old when the Maine controversy arose, and remember distinctly the terror of war inspired thruout my native county and the principal towns in the vicinity. My own father was drafted and furnished a substitute. There were military gatherings and intense excitement everywhere and a steady marching, amid the tears of women and children, toward the frontier. I remember the fear of the situation was relieved at once when our government and Great Britain determined to settle the question of disputed boundary by arbitration. General Winfield Scott was our representative and succeeded in bringing about a compromise which effected a later settlement.

The case of *forty-four forty* along the northwestern boundary, to which our claim ran, caused a national commotion and troops were encamped on both sides within sight of each other, and at one time war seemed inevitable, but at last the apparent difficulties were overcome after much time had been given to the matter by surveys, by treaties, and by arbitration proceedings.

All of the expense, terror and loss to us could have been avoided by a little more careful settlement of the lines in the outset. The two governments were indeed careless and derelict in the beginning. It would have been easy enough to fix the lines of demarkation from ocean to ocean, but the careful reading of history will show that there was need of a proper feeling, such as exists today between the two governments, that of the United States and of Great Britain. I do hope that while this feeling exists all such matters relating to the remaining portion of our boundaries, as that between Alaska and British Columbia, may be carefully, definitely and unmistakably established. It can best be done now by arbitration, for there would be no disposition to overreach on the part of the one or the other of any commissioners appointed at the present day.

The habit of referring questions like those arising in Venezuela to an impartial court is gaining upon the nations of the world. It seems hard for a government like Germany, for example, to submit to such a reference and to do it when she is very able in her army and her navy to enforce her demands. It is fortunate for Venezuela that the United States has lately demonstrated her magnificent naval power. This admitted power behind the Monroe doctrine fearlessly demands that European nations shall not seize and hold American territory, and strongly holds in check every nation which seeks reprisals from Venezuela. Poor, weak, foolish and constantly revolutionary, this South American nation is like every other poor debtor; but by the help of friends she is safe guarded in her material interests, and the great court of arbitration at the Hague will settle all the difficulties in the case and give to each creditor nation a fair proportion of all that can be paid by Venezuela.

If the people of that country could understand the situation and breast it with courage and patriotism, little by little the debts would be paid off and the nation might regain an actual independence, and so secure the future weal of the people within her borders. The very presentation of the case makes us cry out from the bottom of our hearts, "How much better is peaceful settlement by arbitration, the arbitration of a great and impartial tribunal, than the arbitrament of war!" The hostile nations could have shaken the little one in pieces and torn out its vitals, as once I saw a tiger seize and destroy a spaniel, but the woe of it would have forever gone against any such tiger nations.

But while there are cases which we cannot submit to arbitration, cases which involve the safety and the life of the nation itself, still the time may come, and I hope will speedily come, when by mutual agreement one nation will not encroach upon the interests of another, and if by accident there is such encroachment there will be a willingness to submit questions which arise to the arbitration of a faithful and impartial body like that which has been organized at the Hague.

General Sheridan said that the improvement in modern arms, which made the destruction of human life so enormous that a thousand men may keep ten thousand at bay, will hasten the day of arbitration. These improvements have not yet caused wars to cease, as we know by painful experience. The invention of smokeless powder has increased the peril of life and its destruction, but where nations are in any way nearly equal in strength, these improvements are as much an aid to one as to another, and however far cannon may reach and rifles carry, the hills, the mountains, and the kopjes remain as natural protections, and fortifications can be held and barricades constructed of sufficient strength to guard a defensive force.

However, the improvements make wars brief compared with those under the old regimes, and the great peril to human life sets statesmen and rulers and enlightened people generally to thinking and planning for better ways of settling controversies than by warlike methods.

I remember in 1861 how we were associated at West Point, officers and cadets; and when the first rumors of war came I wrote to my friends, "Is it possible that we must shed each others' blood?" and we went out, officers who had been companions and friends, many who had been intimate associates, and cadets who had been for years as intimate and friendly as young men could be—we went out to lead regiments and brigades and divisions and corps and armies against each other. It was an unnatural war, a dreadful conflict. How I longed for some preliminary settlement, but then there seemed no other way to defend the unity of the nation but war.

I am glad, indeed, that we have fallen now upon better days and that the prospect is so grand that it makes our hearts rejoice that the twentieth century has advanced many steps in securing the settlement of controversies without the shedding of human blood.

Perhaps the reaction in Venezuela will show that nation and the other small republics of South America, and indeed all the Latin republics of North America, the utter folly of changing their administrations by revolution rather than by the quiet and peaceful method of the ballot box. Of course it requires intelligence and education of the common people of every name, race and color within a given state to bring this about, but the quick transmission of information and the force of good example will soon go far, as it has already done in Mexico, little by little to bring about this desired method of changing and of continuing a veritable government of the people, by the people and for the people. And may our Heavenly father bless the efforts of his servants in the distribution of right principles of government and right precepts for individual action till peace on earth and good will to men shall be the accepted song in the skies of every land.

* * *

Organized Industry and Peace

Josiah Strong, D.D.
President American Institute of Social Service.

At the beginning of the twentieth century, after the advent of the Prince of Peace, the nations are beating their ploughshares into swords and their pruning-hooks into spears. Never before in history have the armaments of the nations been so great or so costly. In view of this fact, it would seem as if the progress of the world had not been toward that time when the "nation shall no longer lift up sword against nation."

But if we should draw this inference we should be as mistaken as possible, for there are today causes at work in the world which are destined to wage successful warfare against war and ultimately to destroy its destruction. Foremost among these causes is modern or organized industry.

Philosophers of history are very apt to ascribe the progress of civilization chiefly or wholly to some one cause, as, for instance, religion, or climatic or physical conditions, or the evolution of thought, or the action and reaction of institutions upon each other, or the embodiment of great ideas in great men. All of these causes have been profoundly operative. Some have been more effective in some ages and among some peoples than others; some are more influential at certain stages of civilization than other stages. But there is one cause which has had a scant attention at the hands of the philosopher, which is profoundly effective among all peoples, at every stage of civilization, and in every age, and every day of every year of every age, and that is the necessity of something to eat.

Tell me one thing about a people— namely, what is the form of their industry, how they get their living—and I will tell you a hundred things about that people. Do they get their living by the chase? Then they are savages. Do they get their living directly from domesticated animals? Then their government, their social institutions, their usages, their customs of life, their domicile are all such as characterize a nomadic life. Do they get their living directly from the soil? Then the tent becomes the house; government, laws, social institutions, customs, all these are profoundly and radically changed, and they have all the characterics which belong to an agricultural civilization. Do they get their living by traffic? Then their merchants and sailors returning from afar bring back new and stimulating ideas, and these people develop an art, a literature, laws, customs, a government, virtues and vices as different from those of the ploughman and the herdsmen as their occupations are different. We must not be then surprised that the industrial revolution of the past century has produced and is producing a new civilization, profoundly different from the other civilizations already named.

The new civilization, introduced by the industrial revolution, has been reproduced primarily by the steam engine, or to speak a little more broadly, by man's gaining forces which were not muscular, by tapping the great reservoir of force which has always surrounded him, but which he had never known how to use until a few generations ago. The steam engine deindividualized and centralized power, and that is the fundamental cause for the transition from the individualistic to a collective type of civilization. This produced the factory, the organization of industry, the division of labor, the redistribution of population; in short, the social or collective civilization.

As industry becomes more and more organized and labor becomes more and more specialized, we find a growing interdependence. And as a facility of intercommunication increases, the area of competition enlarges; the successful manufacturer drives his inferior competitor into some other business or absorbs him. Thus, as industry is progressively organized, we find that interdependence becomes wider and more complete. For instance, New England does not now attempt to produce her own grain. It is not agriculturally impossible for her to do so, but it is commercially impossible. It is much cheaper for her to buy her grain from the Dakotas, and to pay for it with manufactured products. She brings her sub-tropical fruits from Florida and southern California; her meats from the West, her cotton from the South; her iron from Pennsylvania; her precious metals from the Rocky Mountains, and she pays for all these with her manufactured products. And in so doing she receives better service, her workmen get better wages and larger returns for their work.

Thus we have developed thru this organized industry of the nation an intimate and interdependent national life, so that the interests of one section have become the interests of all sections. Suppose a frost kills a cotton crop, or drought greatly injures corn or wheat, every industry shares the loss. All the great industries have become allied one with the other; they have common interests.

Now, what has taken place in the United States and in Great Britain and is taking place in all other nations as the industrial revolution makes its way around the world, is destined to take place in a still larger sense in the organization of a world industry. Indeed, we have already entered upon this final stage; the world industry life. The nations are just now entering into severe international competition with one another; and no nation is so well fitted for that competition than the United States.

The great conditions of successful competition in this day of organized industry are five—cheap coal, cheap iron (for coal is king and iron is his sceptre), low labor cost—I do not say low wages, but low labor cost, which is a very different thing—cheap raw materials and ready access to markets. Now all five of these conditions belong to us supremely here in the United States. And these five advantages are like the five fingers of a mighty hand stretched out to grasp the industrial supremacy of the world's future. Many of you will say that the low wages of European nations give them an advantage, but investigation shows that while wages are higher here, our labor cost is low, for the reason that we are making more use of machinery, and of better machinery than any other nation.

And we have still another advantage in this industrial competition, for the European manufacturing nations are handicapped with great standing armies. The manufacturing people who are our rivals in Europe are England, Germany, France and Belgium. We will confine our attention for a few minutes to them. The standing army of France on a peace footing is 579,000 men; of Germany, 691,000 men; of Belgium, 57,000 men; of Great Britain, 254,000 men; while our standing army is, at the highest, only 100,000 men.

Without stopping to tell you precisely how many men must co-operate to support a soldier in each of these countries, let me say that the four European nations to which I have referred are from seven to fifteen times as much handicapped by a standing army as are the people of the United States. Now this is a tremendous disadvantage where competition is sharp, as it is sharp today and growing sharper between four European powers and the United States.

Gladstone prophesied some thirty years ago in words like these: "The day will come when America will be what England is now—the greatest servant in the world's great household." Even in 1880 that prophecy began to see its fulfillment, for the manufacturers of the United States that year exceeded those of great Britain by upwards of six hundred million dollars, but the world took no note of the fact because the products were consumed here at home. The year 1898 was a notable one in the world's commercial history, because then for the first time our manufactured exports exceeded our manufactured imports. European manufacturers have already become alarmed, so that officials of state are beginning to discuss the question of an industrial combination against the United States.

What does this signify? When a manufacturer is very much undersold he must do one of two things; he must either cheapen his production or go out of business. The European nation cannot go out of business; they must have something to eat. Not one of the four manufacturing nations referred to can produce its own food supply. Food must be imported, and they must exchange their manufactured products for that food. They must resort to every possible means to cheapen the cost of production, and that means ultimately the destruction of the standing army. I cannot stop to develop that point, however.

The natural result of the international competition upon which we are now entering will be to drive capital out of the unprofitable industries and compel it to seek some more profitable field of investment. Thus the production of certain articles of commerce will become commercially impossible in western countries, precisely as it has become commercially impossible to raise wheat in New England. England and Germany, for instance, will discover in time that they cannot compete with the United States in producing iron and steel. When the world's industries are fully organized we shall make most of the steel and iron for the world.

Thus, by reason of natural resources, or of climate, or of some peculiar skill on the part of the people, the great industries will be localized and divided among the various nations, just as our national productions, for similar reasons, are divided between the various states. And as we have developed a national life in which the various states are dependent on each other, there will in time be developed a world life in which the various nations will be dependent on each other. When that time comes, a nation will no more think of making war upon another nation upon which it is dependent for the necessities of life than would Massachusetts think of making war on the source of her wheat or her cotton supply. All this means that the progressive organization of industry is developing a world-wide brotherhood. It means that notwithstanding racial antipathies, and notwithstanding the prejudices of religion, notwithstanding international jealousies, notwithstanding the selfishness of human nature—

> For 'a that, and a' that;
> It's coming yet for a' that;
> That man to man the wolrd o'er
> Shall brithers be for 'a that.

It was one of the sayings of Mathew Arnold that "force and right rule the world—force until right is ready." It seems to me that, religious considerations aside, it does not require the eye of the prophet, but only the eye of reason, to see Right putting on her royal robes and making ready to ascend her throne, where will be committed to her the sceptre of peace with which forever she shall rule and bless the world.

* * *

Arithmetic

[Extract from Bulletin No. 1, State Normal School, San Jose, by W. H. Baker.]

If properly taught, arithmetic, besides fitting the boy or girl for performing the necessary calculations in the ordinary business relations, will also perform an important educational office. *Besides the acquisition of knowledge, education should give three things: Mental attitude, mental strength, and good mental habits.* To each of these arithmetic contributes no small share. It tends to give stability and balance, and a feeling of certainty; it trains in thinking and in the concentration of thought; and it aids in the formation of habits of neatness, conciseness, system, and investigation.

It should rest on a basis of intelligence, and, as far as possible, should appeal to the understanding. This is possible to a much greater extent than is generally supposed.

In arranging the course given below, the following points have been kept in mind:

1. THE HOW AND THE WHAT.

It is one thing to be able to perform a given operation; it is quite another to determine in a given instance what operation should be performed. A pupil may be able to perform all the arithmetical operations, yet be helpless in an attempt to deal with a given problem. The *how* deals with the mechanics of number and may be mastered by rule. The *what* has to do with mind and can be mastered only as the mind grows. Any rule for this work would defeat the purpose of arithmetical study. Arithmetic does not need to wait on this growth. By well arranged exercises and proper methods it may and should minister to it.

2. LEARNING AND FIXING FACTS.

It is an easy matter to learn that 6 times 7 gives 42. This may be done with or without the aid of objects. To fix this fact in the mind so that 6 times 7, the 42 will immediately present itself, requires skillful teaching, and more or less frequent repetition. In order to be effective, this repetition should be methodical and should require the present active mind. It should require the use of the eye, the ear, and the vocal organs, and thus reach the mind through various avenues. It may be greatly aided by the proper use of rhythm. It should be accompanied by exercises requiring the immediate use of the knowledge obtained.

3. ACCURACY, SKILL, SPEED, INDEPENDENCE.

No effort should be spared that the pupil shall get right results at first, for first impressions are apt to be deep, and if wrong, they are hard to overcome. Skill comes through practice in the use of good methods. The pupil is trained from the beginning in the best methods. Interested mental activity can be maintained without tiring, where dead repetition would result in fatigue. Where wise and economic methods are used, practice will produce speed.

The wise teacher seeks to "liberate" her pupils—to make them self-reliant, and to lead them to a point where they can proceed without further assistance. When a pupil has grasped the law on which a process depends, he is ready to become his own master as far as that process is concerned. It is the teacher's duty to lead the child to discover the law, and to fix that law by appropriate exercises.

4. AVOIDING BAD HABITS.

Most bad habits in the handling of numbers are formed in early years, and defy the efforts of later years to overcome them. The counting habit is formed because pupils are put to using the combinations in addition and subtraction before these combinations have been fixed.

Children do mere rote work because they are put to work which they do not comprehend, and with them it must be rote work or nothing.

The Hindu notation furnishes an easy method for handling large numbers mechanically; hence the tendency of authors and teachers to push the children in the lower grades into the handling of numbers entirely beyond their comprehension, with consequent surrender of the understanding. "Carrying" is easily taught with splints or other devices, but these can not increase the number grasp. There is no necessity for such costly haste. The burden of the work is in the learning of the combinations, not in the handling of large numbers. Abundance of work with small numbers may be found for exercising the child's number faculty in the early school years. Many of the bad habits which cling so tenaciously in later years may be traced to this forcing of the processes with large numbers.

5. INSPECTION.

So common has the handling of large numbers become that the child feels that he must literally cipher out his results. The power of inspection receives little or no encouragement, so lies dormant until stimulated in later years by the exigencies of business or the necessities of a professional life. In this course inspection receives encouragement and exercise from the first, and when later in the course mechanical methods are of necessity introduced, still the form is such as stimulates the fullest use of inspection. Processes and methods in common use by business and professional men are at the proper time taught to the pupil. It is believed that in this way a keener interest can be awakened, and that the pupil, conscious of increasing power, will pursue his work with greater pleasure.

6. DISCOVERY, EXPLANATION, TELLING.

The discovery of a law or principle gives great pleasure. We waste valuable time and frequently do serious injury to pupils when we tell them what they can find out for themselves. Most of our mechanical processes for handling large numbers are abbreviations of fuller work. If the full work is given first and the child is left to himself, he discovers and appreciates the reason for the present practice. Thus the inversion of the divisor in division of fractions can not be explained abstractly so that the child can grasp and appreciate the explanation, but after solving problems for a while by the full process, the pupil is prepared to understand and appreciate the shorter way.

It sometimes happens that a teacher wishes to use a principle which the child is not prepared to understand. In such a case it is best to give the principle and defer the explanation. For instance, a child may need to find the circumference and area of a circle. But he can not understand the process by which these rules are obtained until he has studied geometry. Any attempt to deduce the rule by making a rectangle out of reversed sectors will only cause him to question the accuracy of results obtained by methods so obviously incorrect.

7. VISUALIZING.

Children habitually make use of mental pictures. If objects have been seen, their mental pictures correspond very closely to their earliest experience with such objects. If the pupil has only read or heard about an object, his mental picture represents the notion formed at the time of the hearing or reading. The word *alphabet* suggests to different persons different pictures, dependent on the arrangement of the letters when first learned. Most children see numbers arranged in some definite manner, and make use of this arrangement in getting the combinations. Consequently in this course, when the child is taught to represent numbers with figures, they are presented to him in a tabular form, which is most convenient for reference and future use. This number table should be made in large figures and hung in a conspicuous place in the schoolroom.

In the solution of concrete problems, the pupil relies largely on mental pictures. If the problems are about things foreign to the child's experience, he falters or fails, because he is unable to visualize the given relations. Problems involving the metric weights and measures always confuse a child who has not had direct experience with metric units. Problems relating to geometric figures never fail to interest the pupil who has been made familiar with such figures. The geometric explanations of square root and cube root, when properly given, make a more lasting impression than the algebraic explanations.

Because of its great value, visualization is made use of in this course of tables for teaching the combinations, in concise forms for various operations with whole numbers and fractions, and in illustrative diagrams to aid in the solution of concrete problems.

* * *

Teaching as a Fine Art

Prof. Geo. Herbert Palmer of Harvard University gave an address on July 22nd to the students of the summer session of the University of California, of which the following is an extract:

"A characteristic of the art product is that it can never be quite complete. The essential artistic traits in a teacher's work are four—aptitude for vicariousness, an already accumulated wealth of knowledge, power of ennobling through life, readiness to be forgotten.

"Vicariousness must be wrought in the teacher's moral fibre. He must not enter teaching because he loves books, for a teacher's work is not in obtaining knowledge but imparting it. 'Thought transference' is what I mean—getting hold of others' minds. It is a double-ended process. You must discover where the truth rises—scrutinize its genesis—and also where it falls. Find the line of least resistance where knowledge may enter. The teacher must have an imagination and must be busied with it all the time. He must get rid of his condition so he may enter into that of his pupil's. He must be an altruist—to be able to bear the burdens of his weakest pupil. His imagination should be artistically trained, for this is his great business. It is to be able to appreciate other minds than our own. It is to reach the child's innocent point of view.

The teacher should have an already accumulated wealth of knowledge, constantly accumulating. He ought to be master of his subject. I have to work hardest on the things I don't say. I never teach up to the edge of my subject for fear of falling off. The confidence of the teacher creates the impression of largeness in the subject and he must work with a big background. I was not convinced that there should be a graduate school at Harvard until President Eliot said that 'the teaching here will never be satisfactory until the students are convinced that there is no limit to the teaching.' The graduate school has been the most ennobling factor that has ever come to Harvard.

"The power of ennobling through life is essential. Knowledge buffets. Every fragment of knowledge is repulsive, yet this fragmentary condition is inevitable. A child cannot understand this and his confidence in knowledge must be restored by the teacher.

"The teacher must train himself to forget himself. The desire for praise is common but it certainly can have no place in the makeup of the teacher. The teacher is a colorless medium through which the child is brought to look on truth. It is the teacher's greatest compliment to be passed by. It is futile for attempt to trace results. The teacher casts his bread upon the waters—it may return."

Official Department
State Board of Education

GEORGE C. PARDEE, *President of the Board* .... Governor, Sacramento
MORRIS ELMER DAILEY .... President State Normal School, San Jose
E. T. PIERCE .... President State Normal School, Los Angeles
C. C. VAN LIEW .... President State Normal School, Chico
BENJAMIN IDE WHEELER .... President University of California, Berkeley
ELMER E. BROWN .... Prof. of Theory and Practice of Education, University of Cal., Berkeley
SAMUEL T. BLACK .... President State Normal School, San Diego
FREDERIC BURK .... President State Normal School, San Francisco
THOMAS J. KIRK, *Secretary of the Board* ...... Superintendent Public Instruction, Sacramento

To County, and City and County Boards of Education of the State of California;

Please take notice that a meeting of the State Board of Education has been called for Saturday, the 29th day of August, 1903, at 10 o'clock, a. m., at the office of the Superintendent of Public Instruction, in the Capitol, Sacramento, Cal.

You will please note that under the rule adopted at the meeting of the State Board on July 2, 1902, all applications for diplomas, credentials, or other teacher's document, must be filed in this office at least fifteen days prior to the date fixed for the meeting of said Board.

* * *

To the National Educational Association

[State Superintendent of Public Instruction Thomas J. Kirk writes the following comments on his trip to Boston.]

Educators in Boston.

"The meeting of the National Educational Association in Boston was the most largely attended in the history of the association. Boston people proved themselves the most royal and whole-souled of entertainers. President Eliot of Harvard University is very popular with the people of Boston, and his being President of the association this year explains in large part how everything that could be done was done for the visiting educators. Then, too, Boston and vicinity is full of historic interest and attracted the educational forces from every section of the country. To see and have explained the many old landmarks, guides were provided for every group of twenty or more teachers. The houses in which once dwelt Emerson, Longfellow, Lowell, Holmes, Hawthorne, Louisa Alcott, Thoreau and others of fame were thrown open and were thronged with visitors. For six days, from morning until night, a long line of pilgrims was constantly seen wending its way to the graves of those mentioned, and to those of Agassiz, John Hancock, James Otis, Samuel Adams, Paul Revere and to Bunker Hill Monument, Fanueil Hall, Old North Church, Old South Church, King's Chapel, to Lexington and Concord, to Salem and Plymouth.

PROSPERITY EVERYWHERE.

"On every hand, from the Pacific to the Atlantic, are manifestations of material prosperity. In the grain-growing States of Kansas, Missouri, Illinois, Indiana, Ohio, New York and in Canada the crop prospects could hardly be better. Here and there too much rain, but all in all a propitious season. The factories and mills in the New England States are running to full capacity, and it is not infrequent that manufacturers are obliged to call in their traveling salesmen, being already unable to fill their orders.

IRON AND COAL REGIONS.

"In the great iron and coal regions of Pennsylvania every furnace and oven is aflame. I was informed," says Superintendent Kirk, "that in Pittsburg, notwithstanding the great and constant output of steel rails from the Pennsylvania steel and iron mills, they were more than a year behind orders, and that many American customers on this account are forced to buy some things in foreign markets.

CALIFORNIA FRUIT SOLD EVERYWHERE.

"In every city and town from Reno to Boston California fruit is offered for sale. The names of well known California fruit growers and shippers are seen on every hand. There is a prominent corner building.in the trade center of Boston designated 'Los Angeles,' and in it all products of Southern California are displayed. Some products, perhaps, that came from north of Tehachapi, but credited to Southern California, are on exhibition. Southern California energy and enterprise have been heard and felt in the East. Lick Observatory, even, is supposed by most Bostonians to be located in Los Angeles. The guides to 'Seeing Boston' so announce as they pass, and compare the observatory building in Cambridge with the great institution on Mount Hamilton.

OGDEN EXHIBIT NEEDS RENEWING.

"The Sacramento exhibit at Ogden needs renewal or revision; samples of fruit in many of the jars are rapidly decaying. The exhibit is attractive, being in a most favorable location to catch the eye of the overland passenger, but it should be kept up to date.

STATE AID FOR EDUCATION.

"There were some strong papers read and many valuable discussions had on educational topics in the various departments of the N. E. A. Among the resolutions adopted at the close of the general sessions was one expressing the belief that general or State aid for public education should be only supplementary, and that local aid should be depended on for the main support. This, in my opinion," says Superintendent Kirk, "should be taken in a restrictive sense, because the principle of public education at State expense has long been fundamental, and one of the great educational measures for which Horace Mann so faithfully and successfully labored. The theory that prevailed in his day was that those who had children to educate should bear the burden of the expense, and this he counteracted with all his great ability. He believed that the welfare of the entire people depended upon liberal education of the masses and sought to uproot the idea of district or local taxation and planned in its stead a strong system of State and general taxation. This theory has always prevailed in California, and her public school system is far in advance of that of most of the States for this very reason. Under our State system a public school must be maintained at least six months in every school district every year.

CALIFORNIA'S SCHOOL PLAN.

"A law has long been upon the statute books of California that requires a general State levy every year sufficient to provide not less than $7 per census child, and in every county the mimimum represented by county tax for school purposes must not be less than is sufficient to raise $6 per census child in addition to the State school fund. The theory in California is that by local pride school buildings and their equipment shall be supplied by local tax, and that the State and the county will mainly bear the burden of the other expenses, such as teachers' salaries and running expenses. Our public schools, particularly the primary and grammar schools, have been brought to their high degree of excellence by being sustained on this well established State plan. High schools which differ from the lower schools only in degree having been declared a necessity by the people and having been incorporated into the State system may rightly demand liberal support from the same general public."

Official Department 575

SCHOOL CENSUS OF CALIFORNIA

A Comparison of the School Census of the State for 1902 With that of 1903, by Counties

Counties.	Census of 1902	Census of 1903	Increase	Decrease	Counties.	Census of 1902	Census of 1903	Increase	Decrease
Alameda	34,415	35,063	648	......	Plumas	964	984	20	......
Alpine	81	77	......	4	Riverside	5,280	5,430	150	......
Amador	2,718	2,550	......	168	Sacramento	9,711	9,504	......	207
Butte	4,407	4,406	......	1	San Benito	1,753	1,718	......	35
Calaveras	2,927	2,789	......	138	San Bern'dino	8,128	8,318	190	......
Colusa	1,950	1,873	......	77	San Diego	7,937	8,035	98	......
Contra Costa	4,565	4,746	181	......	San Francisco	82,391	91,386	8,995	......
Del Norte	644	678	34	......	San Joaquin	7,500	7,516	16	......
El Dorado	1,935	1,921	......	14	San L's Obispo	5,474	5,074	......	400
Fresno	10,157	11,119	962	......	San Mateo	3,454	3,344	......	110
Glenn	1,258	1,241	......	17	Santa Barbara	4,799	4,741	......	58
Humboldt	7,328	7,541	213	......	Santa Clara	15,550	15,697	147	......
Inyo	945	907	......	38	Santa Cruz	5,626	5,615	......	11
Kern	3,922	4,047	125	......	Shasta	4,486	4,190	......	296
Kings	2,697	2,667	......	30	Sierra	761	818	57	......
Lake	1,556	1,517	......	39	Siskiyou	3,782	3,774	......	8
Lassen	1,064	1,098	29	......	Solano	5,232	5,059	......	173
Los Angeles	45,167	51,898	6,731	......	Sonoma	10,188	10,155	......	33
Madera	1,487	1,559	72	......	Stanislaus	2,344	2,533	189	......
Marin	3,557	3,494	......	63	Sutter	1,294	1,279	......	15
Mariposa	1,136	1,038	......	98	Tehama	2,803	2,865	62	......
Mendocino	5,248	5,206	......	37	Trinity	756	759	3	......
Merced	2,401	2,491	90	......	Tulare	5,749	5,722	......	27
Modoc	1,505	1,434	......	71	Tuolumne	2,530	2,379	......	151
Mono	421	413	......	8	Ventura	4,345	4,017	......	328
Monterey	5,367	5,419	52	......	Yolo	3,119	3,183	64	......
Napa	3,584	3,564	......	20	Yuba	2,098	2,040	......	58
Nevada	3,871	3,640	......	231					
Orange	6,251	6,353	102	......	Totals	373,999	390,141	19,230	3,088
Placer	3,391	3,267	......	124	Total gain				16,142

Review of School Census for Year Closing June 30, 1903, and Comparison with the Census for the Year Closing June 30, 1902.

Number of children between five and seventeen years of age.

White—	1902.	1903.	Gain.	Loss.
Boys	184,679	192,990	8,311	....
Girls	180,299	187,685	7,386	....
Total	364,978	685,380	15,697	....

Negro—				
Boys	1,221	1,311	90	....
Girls	1,143	1,279	136	....
Total	2,364	2,590	226	....

Indians—				
Boys	1,817	1,785	....	32
Girls	1,621	1,666	45	....
Total	3,438	3,451	13	....

Mongolian—				
Boys	1,868	2,154	286	....
Girls	1,351	1,271	....	80
Total	3,217	3,425	206	....

Total census Children	373,999	390,141	19,230	3,088
Total Gain for Year			16,142	

Number of children between five and seventeen years of age who have

	1902.	1903.	Gain.	Loss.
Attended Public School	289,993	289,751	....	242
Attended Private School	24,350	29,300	5,850	....
Attended No School	59,656	71,190	11,534	....

Number of children under five years of age.

	1902.	1903.	Gain.	Loss.
White	115,934	115,227	....	707
Negro	647	636	....	11
Indian	1,173	1,125	....	48
Mongolian	941	904	....	37
Total	118,695	117,892	....	803

Nativity of Children	1902.	1903.	Gain.	Loss.
Native Born	484,867	498,849	13,982	....
Foreign Born	7,827	9,184	1,357	....
Total	492,694	508,033	15,339	....

Number of deaf children in state between five and seventeen years of age, 294. Number of children between five and seventeen years of age not Vaccinated, 126,112. The last-named items were not reported previously to the present census.

There is a gain of 16,142 in the number of children between five and seventeen years of age, the principal gain being in Alameda, Fresno, Los Angeles, and San Francisco counties. There is a loss of 803 in the number of children under five years of age.

The striking feature of the comparison is the loss of 242 children in the enrollment in the public schools, a gain of 5,850 in the private schools and a gain of 11,534 in the number of children who do not attend school. JOB WOOD JR.

TO SCHOOL BOOK PUBLISHERS

The State Text-Book Committee of California hereby invites publishers of primary histories of the United States to send sealed proposals for the sale or rental of the plates of such books, subject to the following conditions:

"* * * Whenever any plates, maps, or engravings of any publisher or author are adopted for use as hereinbefore provided, the State Text-Book Committee shall enter into a contract for not less than four nor more than eight years for the use of the same, and shall require a good sufficient bond of such plates, maps, or engravings, guaranteeing that the same shall be kept revised and up to date, as may be required by the State Board of Education."

The proposal to lease such plates, maps, or engravings should be a royalty proposition; that is, a fixed amount upon each volume printed and sold by the State of California.

The committee expects these plates to be placed in the hands of the State Printer at Sacramento, California, at the cost and risk of the owner, and desires that all representations concerning the character and the merits of the book or books in question be made in written or printed form.

All proposals should be the hands of the committee by August 15, 1903.

Respectfully,
J. H. STRINE,
Secretary.

PUBLISHERS' NOTICE.

THE WESTERN JOURNAL OF EDUCATION succeeds to the subscription lists, adVertising patronage, and good will of the Golden Era, established in San Francisco in 1852.

Subscription, $1.50 a year. Single copies, 15 cents.

Remit by check, Postoffice order, Wells, Fargo & Co., or by stamps.

ADVERTISEMENTS—AdVertisements of an unobjectionable nature will be inserted at the rate of $3.00 a month per inch.

MSS.—Articles on methods, trials of new theories, actual experiences, and school news, reports of teachers' meetings, etc., urgently solicited.

Address all communications to THE WESTERN JOURNAL OF EDUCATION, 723 Market Street, San Francisco.

HARR WAGNER, Editor.
THE WHITAKER & RAY COMPANY PUBLISHERS.

Entered at the San Francisco Post-office as second-class matter.

The Official Organ of the Department of Public Instruction of the State of California.

The State Normal School at Los Angeles

The publication in leading newspapers of a resolution assuming to represent the Alumni of the Los Angeles State Normal School, stating that it was not up to standard under the administration of President Pierce, and that he should be removed for incompetency, cast an unjust shadow on every diploma from that institution issued during the past ten years. It is necessary that a plain statement of the facts be made.

First, the charges against President Pierce were not based on any fundamental principle of administration, but on mere details of management.

Second, the Alumni meeting was not attended by five per cent of the graduates.

Third, although President Pierce was re-elected for four years, he placed his resignation in the hands of the Board of Trustees and requested an investigation. The trustees, at the close of the investigation, reinstated him for the coming year.

Without entering into the details of the

case at all, it is due to the graduates, the students, and to the people to know that under President Pierce's administration, laboratories, Manual Training, Domestic Science, Art and Library work, have been established. Strong correlation between the training and academic departments has been secured, and the highest of professional work has been inaugurated, bringing such educational leaders as Dr. F. B. Dresslar and President C. C. Van Liew to the State.

The growth of such a school as that of the Los Angeles State Normal is not spontaneous. President Pierce has had his part as the Executive in the building up of an efficient State Normal School.

* * *

The Declaration of Principles. The resolutions of the National Education Association adopted at the Boston meeting, embody to a large extent the educational thought of the nation. The "Principles" consist of the following demands:

"The Bureau of Education at Washington should be made an independent administrative department, such as were the departments of Agriculture and Labor before their elevation to Cabinet rank. Sufficient appropriation should be made by the Congress to enable the Commissioner of Education to extend the scope and add to the usefulness of his work." Provision should be made by Congress "by which the people of Indian Territory will have power to establish and carry on a system of public schools so that all classes of citizens in the Territory may have ample educational advantages." "Teaching in public schools will not be a suitably attractive and permanent career, nor will it command as much of the ability of the country as it should, until teachers are properly compensated and are assured of an undisturbed tenure during efficiency and good behavior." "State aid is to be regarded as supplementary to and not as a substitute for local taxation for school purposes. In many parts of the United States a large increase in the amount of the local tax now voted for school purposes is a pressing need if there are to be better schools and better teachers." "The highest ethical standards of conduct and of speech should be insisted upon among teachers. It is not becoming that commercialism or self-seeking should shape their actions or that intemperance should mark their utterances." "School buildings and school grounds should be planned and decorated so as to serve as effective agencies for educating not only children but the people as a whole in matters of taste." "It is the duty of the schools so to lay the foundations of character in the young that they will grow up with reverence for the majesty of law. Any system of school discipline which disregards this obligation is harmful to the child and dangerous to the State."

* * *

THE superintendents will soon have to decide on the program for the Annual Institute. Under the present law much of the success of the Institute depends upon the selection of lecturers and instructors. After a careful study of the institute problem we believe that the best results can be obtained by securing specialists along certain lines of educational work for day and for evening sessions popular lectures and entertainments. We give the names and addresses and line of work of some of those who are available this season:

Dr. E. C. Moore, University of California, Berkeley— Professional topics. Has two popular lectures.

Dr. Elmer Ellsworth Brown, University of California—May possibly accept some invitations.

Prof. Ellwood P. Cubberley, Department of Education, Stanford—Professional topics and administration problems.

Alex. B. Coffey, Palo Alto, Cal.—Professional topics and psychology applied to common school work. Three popular lectures.

Prof. David S. Snedden, Stanford University—Professional topics.

T. H. Kirk, Santa Barbarr, Cal.—Professional topics, methods, common branches.

D. R. Augsburg, Oakland, Cal.—Drawing; popular evening lectures.

Herbert Bashford, 723 Market street, San Francisco, Cal.—Specialist in literature, reading, etc. Evening entertainment, original readings.

Frederic Burk, State Normal School, San Francisco, Cal.— May accept a few invitations. Professional topics.

Frank Bunker, State Normal School.—Specialist in methods in arithmetic, geography, etc.

Jenne Morrow Long, 2152 Sutter street, San Francisco, Cal.—Specialist in reading. Has several evening entertainments.

Edward Hyatt, superintendent of Riverside county, Riverside, Cal.—Specialist in common school branches and school problems.

J. W. Linscott, superintendent Santa Cruz county, Santa Cruz—Professional topics and common branches.

Henry Meade Blande, State Normal School, San Jose, Cal.—Professional topics and methods in common school branches.

President David Starr Jordan, Leland Stanford University—May accept some invitations.

Joaquin Miller, the Poet of the Sierra, will give an evening lecture on "Lessons Not Found in Books," with a prelude on "The Orient."

State Superintendent Thomas J. Kirk and Deputy Superintendent Job Wood Jr., will follow the usual custom, and one or the other will be at the various institutes.

* * *

THE next issue of THE JOURNAL will be edited with the assistance of the advisory board, consisting of Dr. E. C. Moore of the University of California, Hon. John Swett, Supt. C. C. Hughes, C. C. Van Liew, president Chico State Normal, and Morris E. Dailey, president of the San Jose State Normal.

* *

LITERARY NOTES

Rural School Agriculture, Bulletin No. 1, University of Minnesota, St. Anthony Park, Minnesota. Price 60 cents, or in lots of five or more, 50 cents; carriage prepaid.

This bulletin is a unique attempt to place in the hands of the rural school teacher detailed plans for leading the country pupils to study the things of the farm and the farm home. It was edited by Messrs. Hays, Robertson and Wojta, but was in part written by other members of the faculty of the Minnesota Agricultural College.

It contains 237 exercises to be carried out by the pupils. Each exercise is complete in itself. It gives the object to be sought, the materials to be used, and the plan in detail which the teacher is to have the pupil carry out in doing the work of each experiment. The materials required are such as may be available at the school, or in the farm home.

WESTERN SCHOOL NEWS

MEETINGS

California Teachers' Association, O. W. Erlewine, president; Mrs. M. M. Fitz Gerald, secretary, 1627 Folsom Street, San Francisco; December 28 to 31, 1903.

Humboldt County Teachers' Institute, Sept 14-18. Supt. Geo. S. Underwood.

Summer Normal School, State Normal School, San Jose; Morris E. Dailey, President. June 29, 12 weeks.

NOTES

G. W. Beattie has been appointed principal of the Normal School at Manila.

Supt. T. O. Crawford of Alameda county is in the east on his wedding trip.

L. H. Grimm of Arcata has been elected principal of the Mayfield School.

E. E. Balcomb of Stanford has been elected to a position in the Fresno High Schools.

An election was held at Ione, Amador county, recently, and a union high school formed.

H. F. Sheldon of Fresno has been elected principal of the San Luis Obispo High School.

Prof. W. W. Fogg of Crescent City has been elected principal of the Oroville Union High School.

C. T. Meredith, formerly of the San Diego Normal School, has been elected principal of the Fallbrook High School.

Dr. Edwin Starbuck is absent from Stanford on a years's leave of absence. He will deliver a course of lectures in Edinburgh.

W. B. Creager, formerly city superintendent of Phoenix, has been elected principal of the Twelfth-street School, Los Angeles.

Kendric C. Babcock of the University of California has been elected president of the University of Arizona, located at Tucson.

T. H. McCarthy has been elected to succeed T. B. White as principal of the Washington Grammar School, San Francisco.

David Starr Jordan has returned from his trip in northern waters, where he made a special study of fishes for the United States Government.

Mr. L. Kilkenny has been elected principal of the Salinas High School to succeed C. C. Hill, who has been elected principal of the Palo Alto High School.

W. J. Meredith, professor of English literature in the University of Washington and formerly a member of the State Board of Education, has accepted a position in Hoitt's School for Boys, Menlo Park.

Prof. Thomas Pierce Bailey Jr. has been appointed professor of psychology in the University of Mississippi. The department of character-study and culture history was created especially for Professor Bailey in the University.

R. H. Webster, ex-superintendent of schools of San Francisco, has opened the Metropolitan College at 403 Van Ness Ave., San Francisco. Mr. Webster's splendid ability as a teacher and executive will make the new enterprise a success. Superintendent Webster will establish an ideal commercial school. He has secured able assistants. The formal opening of the school will take place August 17th.

D. R. Augsburg, author of Augsburg's Drawing Books, and special teacher of drawing in the Oakland schools, conducted two summer drawing schools, one in Chicago and one in Oakland. Both schools had a large attendance, and the teachers were more than pleased with the instruction.

Superintendent of Public Instruction Thomas J. Kirk has written the following in reference to Mrs. Jennie L. Thorp's song, "California": "The song, both for words and music, should find large and ready sale to the public schools of the state, and I wish you all possible success as the author." This song was rendered at the National Summer School, San Francisco, and was highly complimented by the special teachers of music.

The Four Great Languages

D. R. AUGSBURG.

The four great languages thru which we formally acquire and express thought are:
The language of Communication—Talking.
The language of quantity—Number.
The language of form and color—Drawing.
The language of harmony—Music.

These are the four great lines of work that run thru our entire educational system. These are the foundation of which all other studies are the superstructure. These are the fundamentals which, if acquired thoroly, make such studies as geography, history, physiology, and the sciences—studies in which the language, number and form elements are united, comparatively easy.

These four great languages merge into each other at almost every point, more especially in the advanced steps. For example:
The music of language is *poetry*.
The music of number is *rhythm*.
The music of drawing is *the artistic*.

Poetry, rhythm, the artistic, are but another name for music. Take from a building its music and it offends the mind and is only fit for shelter. As music permeates thru these sister languages in like manner they permeate one another. It's useless to try to leave one out, or to get all thru the study of one. We have tried it and failed. Why continue to fail?

Language and number are on a good basis. Why not stop beating the bush and place drawing on a good basis. It can't be done by copying a little once in a while, by making it the tail for language or number or using it as busy work or to patch out the week as a Friday afternoon exercise. The way to get drawing is to *go for it*. To take up the elements the same as we do in number and *conquer them*. The elements of drawing are only four, but like the simple elements in number, are far-reaching. Let's take hold of the question. Let's do it for the sake of the children. You lose many children—perhaps more than half. With drawing we will gain and hold many more, for let me look you square in the eye and with all the earnestness I can command, say: The doing-with-the-hand part of our education is weak, and drawing is the only study we have in our common schools in which the element of doing with the hands enters systematically into education—the only study in which skill of mind is carried into skill of hand.

Oakland, Cal.

The Consolidation of Rural Schools

Department of the Interior,
Bureau of Education,
Washington, D.C., June 23, 1903.

My Dear Professor Cubberley: Your June number of THE WESTERN JOURNAL OF EDUCATION has come and I have to congratulate you on the production of a very great document. We have sent (thru our agent here) for one hundred and twenty copies of it. I hope you have kept it in type long enough to reprint it in case your supply should run out, because it ought to be purchased all over the country as the fullest statement thus far of the consolidation and transportation system. It is a great movement that will in time spread all over the United States and do more than anything else to give the rural parts of the country as good schools as can be had in the cities.

The State Superintendent of Nebraska, William K. Fowler, needs a copy of this number at once, and I have written him to order one, but perhaps you will send him one in advance, taking it out of my one hundred and twenty copies.

Yours very truly,
W. T. HARRIS,
Commissioner.

* * *

A Popular State Song

California, Queen of Old Columbia.

Words and Music by Jennie L. Thorp.
Has been indorsed by leading Musical and Literary Critics; is highly commended by our State Superintendent of Public Instruction, Hon. Thomas J. Kirk, and by County and City Superintendents generally. **Price 10c. per copy; special price in quantities.**

It is also approved by *teachers* as far as it has become familiar to them, and both *County* and *City Boards of Education* are rapidly adopting it for use in their schools.

It will be noticed that "California, Queen of Old Columbia," is valuable as an incentive to the study of Geography and History. Thus the first and second stanzas are descriptive, referring to the natural resources of the State, the places of interest, etc., Yosemite and the Sequoia Gigantea receiving special recognition, as also does Southern California, the "land of genial balm," with its orange blossoms, etc., and where the "desert blossoms as the rose."

The third stanza refers to the history of the Golden State and mentions the days of '49.

The whole, as an ovation to California, our own beloved queen, as she poses in her majesty beside the sea, stimulates a sense of love and patriotism, which becomes intensified in the last stanza and chorus.

Order from Jennie L. Thorp, Healdsburg, or The Whitaker & Ray Co., San Francisco.

Manual Training

ZAMBOANGA, Mindanao, P. I.
June 5, 1903.

Harr Wagner, Editor Western Journal of Education, San Francisco—

DEAR SIR: In your April number you express such sound opinions on the value of "manual training" in the Philippine schools that it is cause for sincere regret that you seem to have fallen into some errors as to the local situation. In saying, "The Commission and Superintendent had no prejudices except their own to overcome," you seem to be doing these gentlemen an injustice.

The Filipino was, and to a great extent is, suspicious of us. When we undertake something out of the way of his experience and observation, he looks for a hidden motive. The teaching of reading, writing and arithmetic he understood from past experience and was not afraid that this proceeding boded him ill; but "manual training" was a different proposition. His idea was, and to a great extent is, that an education is intended to relieve its possessor of the necessity of working with his hands; and just so far as it secured this immunity from toil, it was successful. Here seemed a scheme for binding the educated Filipino to labor, and it was to be watched from a distance. I think it will be the testimony of all in a position to speak from first-hand knowledge that the Filipino prejudice against work and all training for work, especially that proposed in schools, was so very prevalent as to be almost universal. It is true that some of the more intelligent Filipinos have advocated this class of education strongly and intelligently, and there have been found communities where the response to offers of "manual training" or "industrial education" has been hearty and gratifying. Yet the Manila Trade School, organized and equipped for work equal to that done in the better class of such schools in America, had to depend for some months almost exclusively on the American colony for pupils. Gradually, however, it has been gaining in favor, and it is hoped that it will soon be one of the most prosperous institutions in the Islands. Its success will depend upon its ability to overcome prejudice other than that of the men who organized it and equipped it so liberally.

The introduction of "manual training" features in the primary schools has received serious consideration and considerable effort. This effort has been rewarded to some extent, and it is hoped that further progress in this line can be made gradually; but it is my opinion, based upon observation and experience, that nothing revolutionary in this line can be accomplished at present. Parents look upon all that is new in this line with singular suspicion. They fear that we are trying to educate their children in such a way as to make working persons of them, and this they could not think of tolerating. Even the little children seem to take abnormally little pleasure in making things—probably on account of the spirit of the home. It is proverbially hard for an Occidental to understand an Oriental; but we say less about the fact that it is equally difficult for an Oriental to understand an Occidental. As mutual understanding is reached I have no doubt that industrial education will make such progress out here that we shall be in a position to give points in California.

Now a word as to the attitude of the Commission and the Superintendent toward "manual training." I have been a persistent advocate of what I prefer to call industrial education, and I have never yet proposed a plan for work in this line which was not heartily approved by the Superintendent. While some of my plans have seemed to the commission, or rather to a Commissioner, to be impracticable, I have never yet heard a word of disapproval of the end sought in any of these plans from any member of the Commission.

Now, Mr. Editor, go ahead with your advocacy of industrial education for us; tell your numerous and important constituency among our teachers that we ought to make our work every day and in every grade tell directly upon the home life of our pupils; tell them that we should keep constantly in view the home conditions of the pupils and should try and fit them for good service in the midst of these conditions. But do not judge that we shall not still have suspicions and prejudices to encounter, and do not judge us harshly if we do not accomplish great things in short time.

Yours very truly,
HENRY S. TOWNSEND,
Division Superintendent of Schools.

Literary Note

The "Atlantic Monthly" for August contains "Daphner," a complete novel by Margaret Sherwood. "The Widder," a story by Alexander Black, and a full table of contents, including a pecially interesting Contributors' Club.

SAN FRANCISCO STATE NORMAL SCHOOL BULLETINS ON METHODS

The San Francisco State Normal School has taken a new and important step in sending out, free of charge, to all teachers or school departments in the State of California, bulletins of methods of teachers the various subjects of the elementary course of study. The Board of Trustees and faculty of this normal school have taken a right view of the largeness of their duty to the state and very properly recognize that it includes aid and assistance to teachers already teaching as well as the preparation of teachers. Bulletin No. 2, which has just been issued, has been prepared by Mr. Frank F. Bunker, Miss Effie B. McFadden and Walter J. Kenyon, supervisors of geography, who personally direct and supervise the work of the student teacher in the training school and the bulletin is therefore practical, since it represents methods in actual operation. Its central purpose is to offer an escape from the prevalent bad habits of text-memorizing. The first few chapters deal with the purpose and aim of geography teaching, seeking to point out what is essential. Here follows a course of study for map knowledge and methods of instruction by means of map drawing, filling in outlines and other means of building in the child's mind a visual image of the maps. A chapter follows giving detailed directions by which teachers may learn to draw maps as pictured relief. Then comes the work in descriptive geography, and the authors give about fifty pages of references to library and supplementary books of travel, geography, etc., characterizing each reference briefly and stating the grade in which it may be used. The final chapter is by Miss McFadden upon Physical Geography, presented by inexpensive experiments. This chapter is made up of reports by student teachers giving pen pictures of just how their recitations were conducted.

Oakland, Los Angeles, Pasadena, Berkeley, San Jose, and some eight counties have already availed themselves of the opportunities and have secured enough copies for every teacher in their department. Their courses of study will be adjusted to the use of the Bulletin.

Bulletin No. 1 on the teaching of Primary Arithmetic, by Frank F. Bunker, was issued last year. Bulletin No. 3, by Miss Alma Patterson, upon Methods of Primary Language Teaching, will be issued in a month. Superintendent McClymonds of Oakland has printed Bulletin No. 3 in his new course of study, but separate copies will be ready for distribution by the Normal School by September 1st. Any of the Bulletins may be obtained by sending the cost of postage to the State Normal School at San Francisco, Powell near Clay. The postage upon Bulletin No. 1 is two cents, on Bulletin No. 2 six cents, on Bulletin No. 3 four cents.

* * *

University of California Graduates

The University of California reports that graduates have been placed in the following positions:

High School, Literary— Elizabeth J. Adams, Fresno; Annie A. Allen, Winters; A. S. Anderson, Colusa; Clara Bailey, Santa Ana; Lucile Bailey, National City; Violet E. B. Baugh, Easton; Bertha Bradley, Berkeley; Antoinette Chevret, Eureka; Helen Clapp, San Pedro; Cecelia Cronise, Berkeley; Mrs. Abbie Curran,Grass Valley; Harriet Curtis, San Bernardino; Oma DaVies, Santa Ynez; Monroe E. Deutsch, Eureka; Grace Dibble, San Jose; Grace Belle Edson, Lompoc; John M. Eshleman, Merced; Maude M. Fraser, Sonoma; EVie M. Gilbert, Gilroy; Marcella Glazier, Sonoma; Blanche Graham, Arcata; Bertha Green, Monrovia; Edna Grinnell, Vacaville; Rose Hohfeld, Alameda; Bertha Hutton, Santa Monica; Almira J. Kelshaw, Paso Robles; L. E. Kilkenney, Salinas; J. M. Koford, Auburn; Herbert Lee, San Jose; Maria de L. Lopez, Los Angeles; Arleigh Lemberges, Los Banos; Sarah Luuny, Concord; Earl Mc-Colliser, Livermore; George C. Mansfield, Ventura; M. Nina Marin, San Pedro; Hannah Oehlman, Fullerton; Florence Preble, Bishop, Inyo county; R. C. Root, Berkeley; Florence Sollman, Lompoc; Grace R. Southwick, Santa Barbara; Mary Stewart, Suisun; Grace Swain. Grass Valley; Ruth Swett, Martinez; Seth Van Patten, Escondido; Allison Ware, Lemoore; Elise Wartenweiler, Auburn; S. Bruce Wright, Alameda; Florence H. Young.

High School, Scientific—R. C. Balaam,Arroyo Grande, M. Bannon, Auburn; Grace Burnott, Hollister; Fred Durst Jr., Esparte; W. F. Fogg, Oroville; Roy Fryer, Sacramento; Edith Hadley, Escondido; May Haworth, Alameda; Lucile Hewitt, Marysville; Loye Miller, Centerville; W. F. Minium, Alameda; Grace Moody, Long

Beach; Ella J. O'Connell, Gilroy; Mabel E. Sharp, Selma; G. M. Sheldon, Banning; H. F. Sheldon, San Luis Obispo; Roge Sprague, Lompoc; Ella J. Sullivan; Santa Ynez; A. D. Tenny, Ventura; Gertrude Ticknor, San Pedro.

Grammar School—Ethel Bartlett, Oakland; Lillian G. Chace, Berkeley; Harley P. Chandler, San Diego; Blanche DuBois, Fresno; Amy E. Cox, Hanford; Elsie Gunn, Oakland; Alice C. Johnson, Rio Dell; Ethel Jones, Loomis; Maude Lanktree, Tacoma; Alice M. Lewis, Bodega; Clinton Miller, Alameda; Edna Monroe, Monrovia; Grace Parish, Santa Barbara; Clarence Peck, Fresno; Edna Patwin, Mount Hamilton; O. H. Roesner, Fowler; Daisy M. Steele, San Pedro; Elsie Sullivan, DaVisville; R. Webster, Fresno.

Private Schools—Viola Brainerd, Miss Head's Berkeley; Josephine Colby, Miss Head's, Berkeley; Albert G. Colton, Anderson Academy, Irvington; Lucile Graves, Paul's School, Walla Walla, Wash.; Allen P. Matthew, St. Matthew's, San Mateo; Roger S. Phelps, St. Matthews; Evelyn Ratcliffe, Miss Head's, Berkeley; Marian Whipple, California School of Mechanical Arts, San Francisco

* * *

Classification of School Children

Superintendent Langdon has sent the following important communication to the San Francisco Board of Education:

The problem of the classification of school children has become one of the most important school problems in the city of San Francisco, as in all the other large and growing cities of the United States. It is a difficulty that requires particularly urgent action in this city for three reasons: (1) The number of children assigned to a class has always been too large in the city of San Francisco. (2) the impending enforcement of the compulsory education statute will bring into the schools thousands of children for whom no provision has been made in space equipment, (3) the present rapid growth of the city is giving an increased school population that will soon levy additional burdens on the school department.

Something must be done immediately for the relief of the pressure of crowded classes before the additional pressure of an increasing population becomes too excessive. Nothing less than the full quota of schools asked for by your Board of Education in the projected issuance of bonds will meet the necessities of the coming few years. In the meanwhile we must lay down an ultimate working standard for the size of classes to which we must bring our classification.

* * *

The National Summer Music School

The National Summer Music School, the first school in America established to promote the cause of music in the public schools, has been a strong organization in Chicago for seventeen years. It has offered a practical training to teachers and supervisors, and numbers among its sixteen hundred graduates many leaders in the profession.

Two years ago, in response to a call from the Pacific coast, a western session was organized in San Francisco, which immediately preceded the eastern session. The enthusiasm and interest shown by the large attendance of teachers and supervisors proved, at an early date, that the California Session need no longer be considered an experiment.

The school is largely made up of supervisors of music who wish to discuss the latest method of presenting their delightful subject, and of grade teachers who wish to teach music better as a part of their regular work. Supervisors and teachers from ten states were in attendance.

The session was held this year the same as last in San Francisco, at Miss West's School for Girls, 2014 Van Ness Avenue. It opened July 6th, ending July 18th. The following six of the forty-five students in attendance were graduated, having passed successfully the required examinations: Miss Margaret Bradley, Merced; Miss Alice Freeman, Oakland; Mr. E. T. Nesbit, Fresno; Miss Hattie T. Rice, Pasadena; Mrs. Jennie L. Thorp, Healdsburg; Mrs. May T. Wilson, Berkeley.

The Faculty consisted of Mr. Frederick E. Chapman of Cambridge, Mass., Miss Ada M. Fleming of Chicago, Mrs. L. V. Sweesy of Berkeley, Cal., Miss Kathryn E. Stone of Los Angeles, Cal., Mr. Percy A. Dow of San Francisco, and Miss Mary H. Mills of Berkeley. These instructors brought years of experience to the National School, and gave practical demonstrations of actual schoolroom methods. The aim of each member of the Faculty seemed to be, to give to each student just the help needed in a definite, practical way. The school has for its motto the following lines from the pen of Richard Burton:

" The hours are yours 'twixt dawn and night,
And since that youth's sure aftermath
Is memory—use the day aright."

I am sure that music thruout the state cannot fail to have a fresh impetus from the work accomplished in this school.

The social side, during the two weeks, was not forgotten. Two evening recitals were given to the students and their friends, and while the hours from 8:30 to 4:15 daily were full to overflowing with earnest work, the evenings were left free to social pleasures.

In conclusion let me not forget the name of Mr. Selden C. Smith, business manager, who was ever ready to look after the missing trunks, find boarding places, cash checks, etc., and whose geniality and good humor were much appreciated.

A STUDENT.

A Struggle for Success
THE BUILDING OF A BUSINESS COLLEGE
By R. L. Durham
President of California Business College

One day two men were standing together watching the almost endless stream of employes pouring out, at quitting time, of one of our great manufacturing concerns. One turned to the other, the man who had built up the great business from a most humble beginning, and asked, "John, how did you do it?" The man addressed, a quiet, keen, determined man, replied, "Dave, it just grew." "True," said his friend, "but you brought together the elements of growth." "The opportunity and the elements of growth were already here. I have simply tried to mix them in the proper proportions," said the other, quietly.

And in those words, he expressed the real secret of the growth and development of every great business of the present time.

So, when the editor of THE JOURNAL, being somewhat familiar with the brief history of California Business College, stood with me observing the hundreds of students emerging from our college doors, turned to me and asked me "How did you do it?" I replied in the language above quoted, "It just grew." He then asked me to write out for the readers of this magazine the story of how I "mixed the elements in the proper proportions," and without wishing to make this article in any sense one of self-praise, I shall tell as simply and directly as I can how I built California Business College from an enrollment of one student to an enrollment of over four hundred students in four and one-half years.

The Beginning of the Struggle

In the fall of 1898, after a number of years' experience in teaching in business college work, and believing that the time was ripe for me to make the beginning, of a business college in which I could have free scope to carry out some of my long cherished ideals of practical education, I began preparations for opening a small night school of shorthand. With the kind assistance of a friend, I managed to get together about one hundred and fifty dollars, with which to launch the future college. After a great deal of interviewing of agents of buildings, I finally found a suitable room in the old Mercantile Library building on Van Ness avenue and Golden Gate. This building was selected for three reasons: First, reasonable rent; second, desirable location in the residence portion of the city where students could reach the college without paying car fare; third, the arrangement of the floor space offered ample accommodations for future growth. Somehow, I seemed to have an intuition that more room would be needed.

The first investment in school furniture consisted of one dozen good oak chairs, and some lumber, with which to make a long table for typewriters. I did the carpenter work and the painting myself. For tables, I secured some old and time-scarred chess tables, which were formerly used by the chess club of the library, the janitor rather reluctantly stipulating that I should have the use of them "for a while." One of the tables did honorable service as "roll top office desk" for some time to come. I then rented a few typewriters, and sent out invitations for an "opening night."

On October the 17th, about thirty of my friends and former students gathered to "see the new school start off." On the next night, two of them returned for "complimentary" dictation in shorthand. On the night following, a third was secured, who paid me one dollar for one week's dictation, the first pay student of the future school, and one of blessed memory when my mind turns back to those days of struggle and disappointment.

but I would not admit defeat, though often after a day of hard and apparently fruitless work, I went to bed late, tired and discouraged.

The end of the first month was coming, and with it rent day. My little capital, which I was most carefully guarding, was

R. L. DURHAM
President and General Superintendent

The next week brought a few more stenographer friends, who had, after earnest persuasion on my part, joined the class for "complimentary" dictation. But there were few pay students.

Early and late, until time for evening school, I was out among my friends, looking up new students. Disappointment after disappointment came on every hand,

fast dwindling away, and no money was coming in. Then, fortunately, and at a most opportune time, a student entered and paid for her course in advance, one hundred dollars. While this was a godsend at the time, in providing for most urgent necessities, and in giving me encouragement at a time when I most sadly needed it, it was not altogether a blessing, as it led me to "figure on futures," so to speak, the rock on which many a promising business college has met its fate.

Opening of a Day School

I paid the rent, gathered myself together and completed arrangements for opening a day school. A friend of mine in the printing business offered me sixty days' time on forty thousand circulars and one thousand copies of a booklet. I put out the booklets, audaciously outlining a curriculum and a policy of a full-fledged business college, and quoting the prices of tuition prevailing in the oldest and largest business colleges in the West. This fixing of prices turned out to be about the wisest thing I did during these days, as it gave me a good rate from the students I did secure, and relieved me from the embarrassment attending the raise in price on an established rate, later on.

The day school consisted of some two or three former students of mine, temporarily out of employment, who kindly consented to write circular letters to prospective students for me, in order "to keep in practice."

The First Dash for Business

Taking advantage of the offer of my printer friend, I put out the forty thousand circulars, announcing that for the next eight weeks, I would give away a six months scholarship in shorthand on each Monday morning, on a lot drawing basis. Applicants were to write a letter beforehand, and then appear in person at the drawing.

This first dash for business brought a good many replies, gave me each week a new student, and in addition the names of quite a number of young people interested in taking up shorthand, and, best of all, afforded me an opportunity to meet them face to face and talk business to them. By the time the eight weeks were over, I had some fifteen day students, one-half of whom were paying me regular rates of tuition.

In the meantime, the night school was growing, so that within three months after starting, I had a fairly good nucleus of both a night school and day school. The teaching day and night, the handling of the business end of the undertaking, together with my personal solicitation outside of teaching hours, and even the janitor work, kept me very busy, and I often went to bed too tired to sleep. It was during those long hours of nervous fatigue that many plans for the extension of my business and the perfection of the educational system of the school were evolved and either elaborated or discarded.

Business Expansion and Educational Development

It was in these early days that I began to give most careful consideration to the development of my little school along two lines that have ever since been followed and that have resulted in whatever degree of success California Business College now enjoys,—the extension of the business as a business and the perfection of the school as a school. It was difficult for me then, and is still difficult, to tell which of the two is of the greatest importance. Undoubtedly the temptation is, as borne out by the experience of innumerable schools that have long since been entered in the great book of failures, to get business first, last and all the time, and let the school take care of itself. But subsequent events have proven the correctness of my theory that, no matter how advanced and progressive were the methods employed to secure new business, an educational proposition, such as a business college, could not endure unless thorough, progressive, earnest methods of instruction prevailed in the school room.

The First Enlargement of Quarters

The little room soon became too small to accommodate the increasing attendance, and a very bold stroke was decided upon, namely, to double the floor space, and consequently, the rent, and to invest in one

Cashier's Office

Reception Room

Private Office of President

hundred dollars' worth of furniture suited to school purpose. But in those days, in the exuberance of faith and inexperience, to feel an inspiration tugging away at the heart strings, was to act. The students were all enthusiastic over the proposition, and when we were fairly settled down in our new quarters, our present location, at 305 Larkin street, in the Supreme Court building, they went to work most willingly and loyally to build up the school. The net result of our first months' combined work was sixteen new students.

From this on, the success of the enterprise was assured. Our own enthusiasm, backed by the visible evidence of a few good oak tables and the presence of about thirty students began to create confidence in others as to our stability; and though the school did not have a rating in Bradstreet's or Dun's, and though many of our callers did look a little suspiciously at a man who tried to do business in an office that could boast of nothing in the way of furniture except a roll top desk, a revolving chair and a wall telephone, with neither carpet, rug, nor picture to relieve the bareness, still we kept getting an occasional student.

Additional Departments

The demand was now being made for other studies besides shorthand and typewriting, and the necessity was upon me to open up some of the departments I had advertised. This meant additional teachers, and additional teachers meant additional expenses. Where the money was to come from to pay teachers, and how teachers could be secured without visible means to pay them, were problems that only my unlimited faith in the business could solve. As for myself, I had no complaint if my salary at the end of the week was represented by just what I had eaten at the restaurants during the preceding days, but who else would work for me on such a basis? Here was where my real and most embarrassing difficulties began. Even now I do not know how I ever steered my little craft through the rocks and reefs of the next six months, but somehow we got through, my one teacher stood by me, and we were compelled to put on an assistant.

We had now a department of shorthand, one of typewriting, one of bookkeeping and one of penmanship. Crude as were these departments in their beginnings, I tried to put into them and into the teachers the spirit of thoroughness in everything that was done. Therein, and therein only, is there a resemblance between the elaborately equipped and scientifically arranged departments of the California Business College of today and their humble prototypes of those earlier days.

From this point, the college seemed to "just grow," as it is doing today. The forces were at work, and growth followed naturally until we have

California Business College at Present,

with its one little original room expanded into a whole floor in one of our large office buildings; with its original single student multiplied over four hundred times; with its one crude department enlarged into a great number of perfectly equipped and organized departments covering all the phases of business education; with its time-scarred little chess table for office desk replaced with a large suite of offices fitted up with modern furniture; and with its original faculty composed of one, grown into a faculty and working force of twenty-one earnest men and women, striving by conscientious and enthusiastic service to make California Business College the one school of the West.

What some of the forces are that have been at work in the building of the school may be appropriately outlined as follows:

The Spirit of Thoroughness

Running through the warp and woof of the whole fabric of this college, is now, and has been from the beginning, a spirit of thoroughness in all things. One illustration will show how thoroughly our teachers became imbued with this spirit of thoroughness. The next day after a full meeting of the faculty, during which an interesting discussion was had on the old old question "of how to teach the careless boy to become thorough," I was showing some visitors through one of the departments just at a time when the teacher in charge had the most notoriously lazy and careless boy in the whole school before his desk for a lecture on his bad habits. At length becoming exasperated at the boy's indifference, the teacher exclaimed in none too pleasant tones, "Young man, your first duty in life should be to do something, or die, and if you don't do it right, die anyhow."

The spirit of thoroughness has been a silent, positive force, carrying conviction to student and parents, friends and business man, that nothing but absolutely good work was done here.

Social Life and College Spirit

Another of the contributing causes to the rapid growth of California Business College has been the recognition of the social side of our students' lives. The social instincts are strong within us all and no scheme of education is complete that overlooks them. A large hall on the same floor on which the college is located made it possible to gather the students daily in a general assembly during the day time, and for lectures and socials in the evenings, to which they had the privilege of inviting their parents and their friends. The general assembly during the day gave a unity to the school that could not have been secured in any other way, as well as affording a most excellent occasion for giving students talks on the affairs of the day, the principles of character building, success, and all kindred topics. The assembly is today one of the strongest and most interesting features of the whole work of California Business College, and one in which our students take great personal pride, and it has done more to develop that loyal and aggressive college spirit so characteristic of students of California Business College, than any or all other things put together.

Securing Positions for College Graduates

In those early days, California Business College was sadly deficient in that department which is of most vital concern to every one taking up a business course, namely, the position department. Few business men knew of such a school, much less of the character of work done by its students. But soon our students began to demonstrate what they could do, and we began to get an occasional call for our graduates. Here again a fixed policy early prevailed, never to recommend a student unless he was fully competent to do the work. The policy has resulted in two things: First, better and more thorough work by each student; second, a flood of applications from business houses for our graduates. So great was this unsolicited demand in 1902 that over two hundred applications for graduates were filed away marked, "No recommendation for the reason that we had no competent person to recommend."

No Man Builds Alone

California Business College stands today, not the result of one man's work, but of the work of many. One plan, one inspiration, may pervade it, but other hands and other hearts have had to do with its building, and I wish here to express my appreciation of the constructive work of those who have labored with me, and particularly to those who passed through the days of trial. Of our large faculty now, only one of the old guard remains, but without the aid of those who are no longer with us, the college could never have become a great school.

For the benefit of those who do not understand the work of a business college, or the difficulties in this line of work, it is well to make here a statement of the

Educational Problem of a Business College

In no line of educational work is the problem so complex as in the business college work.

First, because a business college is a

SEMI-ANNUAL GRADUATING CLASS, JULY 18, 1892.

Reading from left to right, the third figure in the second row from the top is Hon. W. H. Langdon, Superintendent of San Francisco Public Schools.

business venture; students must be secured in the first place, and kept satisfied in the second place, or the college must close its doors.

Second, the varying age of the students, running from fourteen to sixty, and the varying educational qualifications, ranging from the eighth grade graduates of our public schools and mature men and women of limited or no education to graduates of colleges and universities, make it exceedingly difficult to devise a curriculum to fit the needs of each individual.

Third, the method of instruction must be individual in order to perfectly meet the needs of each student.

Fourth, to properly discipline such a heterogeneous mass of students without having too much control for the mature students and too little control for the immature ones, requires consummate skill.

Fifth, the customary time limit for covering such a course, still further complicates the problem. Each student enters the college with a definite notion as to how long it will take him to complete such a course, regardless of his lack of preparation or his adaptability to such lines of work.

These are a few of the problems confronting us that are not, to any appreciable extent, met with in any other line of education that has assumed anything like the proportions of business education in this country, and to conduct a large business school on lines broad enough to meet all these conditions fairly and fully gives the business college manager a larger task than he is ordinarily supposed to be able to carry, but the splendid business schools throughout our land bear ample testimony that we have plenty of men in the work, fully equal to the emergencies.

A Personal Word on Success

I have often been asked for my opinion on success. It can be expressed in three words: Preparation, grit, work, and the greatest of these is work. Sprinkle this liberally with salt of confidence and throw in a dash of the pepper of audacity and go out and make your opportunity. Don't lose your grip on life sitting around waiting for an opportunity to come. Life is too short.

Opposition from Established Schools

Such were some of my early struggles. Just a few are given here in bold outlines to show a sample of the difficulties before a young man with no capital, who attempts to build a college in a large city in the face of sharp competition from established schools. Opposition was to be expected of course, but my faith in the innate justice of the average man was rudely shocked, when I found that my character was assailed, my reputation made malodorous, my business methods classed with those of the impostor, and even the affairs of my private life so twisted and distorted, that I myself did not recognize them, all to the end that a little insignificant school might be kept from securing an occasional student. But these malicious flings so straightaway became a boomerang and returned with such disastrous effects to those who had thrown them, that I learned once for all the valuable lesson that, in business, it does not pay to run down your competitors.

Looking to the Future

So stands California Business College, in its vigor and strength of youth. What of the future? According to the law of cause and effect, since the same forces that have been at work in the up-building so far are still at work, there should be similar growth in the future, and perhaps better, because these forces can now work under better conditions.

I am, and have been convinced, that the Pacific Slope could maintain a university of practical education of at least one thousand students, comfortably housed in its own building and backed by the unanimous good will of California's intelligent citizens. Whether or not California Business College ever attains to that high sphere of usefulness, some school will reach it, and I cannot resist saying here that California Business College is a competitor for that place.

Book Reviews

The Origin of American State Universities, by Elmer Ellsworth Brown, has just been issued by the University Press. Price, 50 cents.

* *

"The Delineator" for August is an excellent midsummer number. It presents a charming array of Fashions, as well as numerous other features of deep interest to women, and stories and articles of a high literary standard. In fiction there are four storiettes that will furnish good reading for lazy summer afternoons, also the fourth installment of Mrs. Catherwood's story, "The Bois Brûlés," in which the action becomes very thrilling. Lillie Hamilton French writes entertainingly about some of her city neighbors, including the very poor and the very rich. "Our Summer in a Barn," by Frederick J. Burnett, is the narrative of a novel manner of spending the warm season in the country. For the children there are the engaging pastimes, the Firelight story and other features. The various departments are up to the usual standard.

SCHOOL FURNITURE

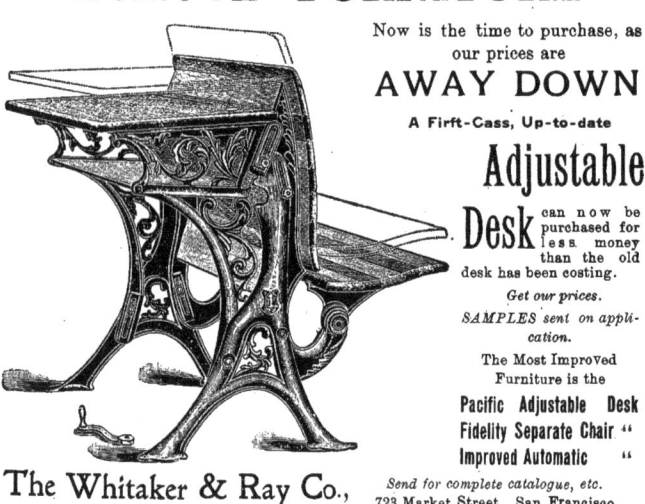

Now is the time to purchase, as our prices are

AWAY DOWN

A Firft-Cass, Up-to-date

Adjustable Desk

can now be purchased for less money than the old desk has been costing.

Get our prices.

SAMPLES sent on application.

The Most Improved Furniture is the

Pacific Adjustable Desk
Fidelity Separate Chair "
Improved Automatic "

The Whitaker & Ray Co.,   *Send for complete catalogue, etc.*
723 Market Street, San Francisco

THE WESTERN JOURNAL OF EDUCATION

September, 1903

	PAGE
PHYSIOLOGICAL PROBLEMS, *Jacques Loeb*	593
THE ALCHEMY HIDDEN IN BIOLOGY, *Wilhelm Ostwald*	597
DISCIPLINARY VALUE OF ARITHMETIC, *Frank F. Bunker*	613
THE INSTITUTE, *Charles C. Van Liew*	630
SUMMER SCHOOL AT SAN JOSE, *Marguerite Winceslow*	634
DEPARTMENT OF METHODOLOGY	636
The Teaching of Reading—The Teaching of English—Long Division—Method of Teaching the Sentence	
OFFICIAL DEPARTMENT, *Thomas J. Kirk*	639
Normal Schools Accredited—Kindergarten Training Schools—High School Text-Books—New Books—Bulletin No. 21, Relating to the use of Text-Books—Bulletin No. 20, Relating to New History—Notes of State Text Book Committee—Credentials Granted	
EDITORIAL	647
The Western Journal and Advisory Board of Editors—Tribute to Martin Kellogg	
BOOKS AND MAGAZINES	651
WESTERN SCHOOL NEWS	658
ADVERTISING DEPARTMENT	661

THE WESTERN JOURNAL OF EDUCATION
723 MARKET ST., SAN FRANCISCO

Volume VIII
No. 9

$1.50 Per Year
Single Copy 15c

NOTEWORTHY NEW BOOKS

Just Published

The Baldwin Speller

By S. R. Shear, Superintendent of Schools, Kingston, N. Y. Assisted by Margaret T. Lynch, Principal of Public School No. 2, White Plains, N. Y.

Cloth, 12mo, 128 pages. Price, 20 cents.

The words in this speller were selected by classroom teachers after observing the class vocabulary for a year. They include, therefore, those words which require special attention, and which will be of most immediate practical use to the child. They are arranged according to difficulty. The words for each year's work are divided into groups of four lessons, each group forming a week's work, the fifth lesson of each week being an oral review. In the earlier review lessons the accentuation and pronunciation of the words are marked. Illustrative sentences show the uses and meanings of words with the same sound. Among the selections for study are such favorites as Whittier's "Barefoot Boy" and Longfellow's "Children's Hour." The book is based upon actual conditions in the school, and not upon mere theories.

A Practical Book

Milne's Primary Arithmetic

By Wm. J. Milne, Ph.D., LL.D., President of the New York State Normal College.

Cloth, 12mo, 160 pages. Price, 25 cents.

In this book each number from 1 to 100 is developed by the spiral system through all the fundamental operations. The work in connection with each number is elaborated and carefully developed. Among the special features of the book are—

1. The illustrations are particularly well chosen and admirably adapted for their purpose.
2. There are many devices to arouse the interest of the child.
3. There is active work to sustain the interest of the child.
4. The problems are practical and deal with matters in connection with the child's experience.
5. Reviews are frequent and well planned.
6. Inductive work leads the child to discover facts for himself.
7. Fractions are developed in connection with integers.

Other Recent Text-Books

Abbott's A Boy on a Farm	$0.45
Baird's Graded Work in Arithmetic Eight Books for Eight Years	
Barnes's Natural Slant Penmanship	
Eight Books, per doz.	.75
Four Charts, per set	1.50
Barnes's Elementary History of the United States	.60
School History of the United States	1.00
Baskervill-Sewell English Course	
Language Lessons	.35
School Grammar	.50
Horne and Scobey's Stories of Great Artists	$0.40
Krout's Two Girls in China	.45
Monteith's Some Useful Animals	.50
New Education Readers	
Books I and II, each	.35
Book III, $0.40; Book IV	.45
Roddy's Elementary Geography	.50
Complete Geography	1.00
Simms's Child Literature	.30
Smythe's Reynard the Fox	.30
Winterburn's The Spanish in the Southwest	.55

AMERICAN BOOK COMPANY Publishers

204 Pine Street, San Francisco, Cal.

New York   Cincinnati   Chicago   Boston   Atlanta   Dallas

The Western Journal of Education

SEPTEMBER, 1903

I

PHYSIOLOGICAL PROBLEMS*

American universities are just taking their first steps toward giving research that place which it has occupied for several generations in European and especially German universities. If one of the recognized leaders of scientific thought and research in the Old World is willing to interrupt his work and participate in the inauguration of a laboratory on the Pacific Coast we may be sure that the new departure of American universities has won for this country the sympathy of the best and therefore real representatives of the European nations.

It is customary to indicate on an occasion like this the general direction and tendencies of the work which will be carried on. I need not dwell upon the importance of physical chemistry for physiological problems, as I have often discussed this before. It is realized by all biologists that the source of energy in life phenomena is chemical, while many of the manifestations of life are physical in character. From this alone it is evident that physical chemistry must form the foundation of biology.

It is clear that the more fundamental the problems are which a laboratory undertakes, the more it may hope to accomplish, but it is also true that at each period the number of tasks which might be undertaken successfully is limited. What we call the explanation of a phenomenon is, according to Mach, the possibility of presenting it as an unequivocal function of those variables upon which it depends. Each generation can hope to successfully solve only those scientific problems whose variables it adequately knows and controls. One of the fundamental problems of biology is to find a definite answer to the question whether or not it is possible to make living matter out of dead matter. No one has thus far succeeded in transforming dead matter into living matter, and

---

*Prof. Loeb gave the above interesting address at the dedication of the new physiological laboratory of the University of California. The address is taken from a newspaper reprint.

no one has thus far observed the spontaneous generation of an organism in nature. In consequence of this fact Arrhenius assumes that living matter has eternally existed and has been carried through the universe from star to star in the shape of extremely minute particles, such as spores at or below the limit of microscopic visibility. He has calculated that electrical charges of those particles and radiation pressure suffice to bring about a transmission of living particles from one star to another in a comparatively short time. On the other hand, however, we are warned by a number of reasons not to be too hasty in assuming the impossibility of abiogenesis. As far as we know the substances found in living organisms are chemically well characterized and can be obtained outside of living organisms. Moreover, the growth of an animal or plant from a microscopic germ to its adult state depends upon a constant transformation of dead matter into living matter. Did this transformation not occur constantly in all living beings no living organism would be left today. As far as the dynamics of this transformation of dead matter into living matter inside of an organism is concerned, we know that no other specific agencies are involved than enzymes. The action of enzymes, however, does not seem to differ in any way from the action of inorganic catlytic agencies. I do not think it too bold to prophesy that the general physiochemical character of these enzymes will sooner or later be cleared up. As regards the oxidizing enzymes the goal seems to be already in sight.

DEAD MATTER INTO LIVING.

In going over in detail all the features of life phenomena we find that many of them can either be imitated in inorganic nature in all their details, or can be controlled unequivocally by physical or chemical means. In fact this is the case to so great an extent that it almost causes surprise that the experimental transformation of dead matter into living has not yet been accomplished. But we must consider the fact that the peculiar complex of physical conditions which we call the structure of living organisms is absolutely essential for life phenomena. If an organ, a brain for example, be ground to pulp its function ceases. When the kidney is ground to pulp it loses the power of transforming benzoic acid and glyccoll into hippuric acid, provided all the cells are destroyed. From this the conclusion was drawn that possibly all the synthetical processes of an organism depend upon the normal structure of the tissues. This certainly goes too far for we now know that soluble enzymes which can be extracted from the tissues, for example lipase, not only accelerate hydrolitic but also synthetic processes. But it can certainly not be denied that the physiochemical peculiarities which we call the structure of the living tissue form an essential part in the complex conditions which determine life phenomena. In regard to the question of abiogenesis the biologist is therefore placed before two possibilities. Biologists will either succeed through a series of discoveries in transforming dead matter into living matter, or they will finally discover that there is as definite a discontinuity between dead matter and living matter as there is between two chemical elements.

ONE SPECIES TO ANOTHER.

Another problem of transformation faces the modern biologist, namely, that of transforming one species into another. If living organisms have arisen from dead matter the first forms of living matter must have been simple in structure, and perhaps not more complicated than spores. If, on the other hand, living germs are as old as cosmic matter the transportation of germs from star to star is only imaginable if the germs were extremely small and consequently simple in structure. In either case it is necessary to assume that the present fauna and flora of the earth must have developed from structures of no higher degree of differentiation than, for example, spores. If an investigator were asked today which he considered more difficult, to make a highly organized plant or animal from the spores of a fungus, or to make a spore from dead matter, I am afraid he would hesitate to decide.

Yet the majority of investigators have been convinced since the days of Lamarck and Darwin that such an evolution must have occurred. We are better off in regard to our observations concerning evolution than in the question of abiogenesis, for there can be no doubt that hereditary transformations within narrow limits at least have occurred. I need only mention the positive observations of DeVries. But all the variations which have thus far actually been observed are extremely slight, so that it is still difficult to grasp an evolution from cosmic spores or protoplasmic material of the simplest structure, into such highly developed machines as human beings. As far as I am aware no one has yet found a method of bringing about a rapid variation in animals or plants. I am inclined to believe that this failure is at least partly due to the existence of mechanisms of regulation. We know that our bodies possess automatic regulators to keep our temperature constant, etc. Any too sudden and extensive change in an organism probably interferes with these automatic mechanisms, and therefore leads to the destruction of the organism. We again meet with two possibilities; we shall succeed by a series of continued slight changes in one and the same form in bringing about a large transformation from the original form, or we shall obtain the result that in each form the possibility of evolution is limited and that, at a certain point, the constancy of a species is reached. Either result if guaranteed by adequate observations will be a welcome discovery.

UNBIASED TREATMENT.

Before closing allow me to make one additional remark. It is quite common to find that even scientists are inclined to assume that the restrictions or limitations to research in biology are greater than, or of a different order from those in the field of physics or chemistry. This is not true as long as we treat biological problems in the same unbiased and unprejudiced way in which we deal with the problems of physics and chemistry. The alchemists tried to solve the problem of perpetual motion and of making gold. No one, however, would say that the phycist or chemist is limited in his search for truth because perpetual motion is impossible and the chemical elements are constant. On the contrary, it is fully recognized that the discovery of such constants as the quantity of energy of a system or the chemical elements were the most fertile discoveries ever made, and, in fact, are among the pillars on which not only modern physics, chemistry and biology, but indirectly our whole modern civilization rests. Why should we change our attitude when we leave the field of biology, and why should we consider it a restriction or limitation of knowledge if it should turn out—which is far from certain, however—that it is no more possible to transform dead matter into living than to transform copper into gold?

JACQUES LOEB

University of California.

II

THE ALCHEMY HIDDEN IN BIOLOGY*

The event which we celebrate today is like the launching of a beautiful ship. The keel has been laid with great care, slender and powerful the hull is made, and the engine and propeller are of the newest and best construction. Above all, we know that the captain is a man who understands how surely and fearlessly to steer the ship over the high seas of science.

If it were only a matter of discovering new lands our ship might sail one course as well as another; it would only be a matter of time when the new land would be sighted. Only one thing is certain, and that is that we do not know the land, and therefore have no right to predict anything about it.

The answer to this is that it is by no means so impossible to look into the future as we ordinarily think. Nowhere is the struggle toward fundamental explanation so great as in biology.

WHAT WILL HAPPEN?

On the other hand, a very gifted broker might predict the condition of stocks a week from now, but not further, while the great majority of men would not be able to make any prediction at all. Thus our notions of the future are made up of a wonderfully complicated and tangled tissue, varying in its nature from the greatest certainty to the most doubtful possibility. And in every one of these most diverse cases it is necessary to distinguish between the contents and the degree of probability. We recognize immediately that in the struggle for existence he will be the most skilled who in any field can answer the questions, "What will happen?" and "What is the probability that will happen?" more accurately than his fellow men. This is the cause of the high honor and slavish fear in which peoples of low development hold their prophets and medicine men. If the Roman Republic wished to declare a war, it first questioned the oracle as to what would be the outcome of the war, and when, in 1870, Mismarck saw that the clash between Germany

---

*The dedication of the Laboratory of Physiology of the University of California August 19, 1903, was a great event. Prof. Wilhelm Ostwald came all the way from Germany to deliver the address at the dedication. It is printed, in part, in this issue of THE JOURNAL. This will give the trustees and teachers of the state an opportunity to read and have on file this masterly exposition of modern investigation in the realm of physilogical sciences. The laboratory was donated to the state by Rudolph Spreckels.

and France was unavoidable, he asked Von Moltke the self-same question. The augurs prophesied with the aid of the internal organs of a sacrificed animal, while Moltke predicted upon the basis of a scientific investigation into the military conditions of both countries. Here we have the difference between the old and the new civilization clearly in view, and the word which expresses this difference is "Science."

This is what science, as a matter of fact, really means. Its aim is to make a glimpse into the future possible, and science is so much the more perfect the broader and more certain this view is. Probably each of us has at some time dwelt upon the question of what may be the essential thing in science. The answers to this question are very different from the other. Corresponding to different conditions of my own mind, I have answered the question to my self very differently at different times. However, since I have possessed the definition which I have given you above (and which I find already given in Locke) I find myself in a position to solve many problems more readily and with more certainty than was possible to me up to that time.

SCIENCE MUST FIND IT.

And now, ladies and gentlemen, when we had strayed apparently very far away from the subject of our discourse, we find ourselves again in the very midst of it. Science must find us the means to choose the course which our ship must sail in order that she shall, with the greatest possible probability, be able to reach those unknown fields upon which we place the greatest value, and she must also show us how, when we have reached the desired shore, we can best cast anchor, and how we may best make a landing.

Here we have to do with a science of sciences. Special questions of mathematics and chemistry have no place here. Rather shall we have to do with the questions as to how each individual science develops, irrespective of its contents. Such a science as this scarcely exists at the present time. There have, it is true, appeared several valuable preparatory studies along this line. On the other hand, the special histories of the various individual sciences have been very thoroughly and comprehensively investigated, and the definition of concepts in the philosophy of today comes very near to his problem. Still one misses the discussion of the historical development for the most part in this part of philosophy, as well as of the common factors in the individual sciences. But, from both sides one can see the undoubted tendency toward the development of just this field of knowledge, and we may expect to see in the near future the development of a "biology of sciences."

In reality we have here to do with a true biological problem. A rock or a comet has no need of science, because, in so war as we are capable of judging, their existence has no meaning to them. But we, who not only wish to maintain our position, but also to better it, need science in order to do this, for in order to attain to anything we must know our conditions of existence, and in order to improve anything we must know the possibilities of influencing these conditions. The broadest and surest road we have of these things is that which we call science.

TO FORESEE IS STRENGTH.

When we picture to ourselves the most primitive conditions in the development of mankind, we see that without doubt that individual and that people that best foresaw the conditions of the future in the end has always been victorious in the struggle for existence, for it knew best how to influence conditions. There are indeed conditions in which the fist-fight, i. e., physical strength, seems to decide the point. But even here we see skill, that is, the intellectual or scientific factor, counterbalance a very considerable portion of mere brute strength, and this portion increases as development progresses. The greatest leaders of humankind have always been those who more clearly foresaw the future.

Possibly the objection will be made here that we are accustomed to look upon the lawmakers and political organizers, and not upon discoverers and inventors, as the leaders of mankind, and it will be well to bring this apparent contradiction into order at this point. We indicate both the regularities of natural processes and arbitrarily influenced action of mankind with one and the same word, namely, "law." The truly great thing which the moral and political lawmakers have done lies in the fact that they have brought certain fields of human action to the possibility of prediction. Since they did not know the internal causes of these actions, it was necessary to give the external rules, or laws in the jurist sense. These may agree more or less with the psychological and biological laws which are applicable to the phenomena in question. The closer this agreement, the more permanent have been these laws, and the greater and more influential have these lawmakers been. Thus every political and moral organization is subject to biological conditions, and at the same time these fields are shown to be such as are destined to fall under the irresistible conquest of science.

INFLUENCE ON ART.

Many of my friends, and particularly those whom I especially esteem, have made a most strenuous objection to this point of view, when we have discussed these matters, from which I hold that it is probable that this objection has occurred to you. We are accustomed to connect sensations with those things which we have discussed, to which we ascribe a great value and which we permit to exert a great influence upon us. We look at the moral and political laws with a different feeling from that with which we look at the law of physics or chemistry, with a feeling which we call reverence. And then there is another great field that seems to be entirely withdrawn from the influence of science and which, nevertheless, exerts a great and valuable influence on our lives—namely, the field of art. Here, also, there are more or less stirring sensations which move us and lead us to believe that art is something which carries us beyond our common nature and ordinary condition. This sensation of the beautiful, the great, the strong, the eternal, we do not wish to destroy or to diminish, and, therefore, those who see the value and charm of life in these things protest violently against their absorption by science, ascribing to science sobriety and coldness, the exact opposites of those sensations.

TRUTH EVER PRESENT.

Now, in such an audience as this, where each of us in some way or other has dedicated the better part of his life to science, I do not need to speak of so elementary a thing as the fact that science certainly demands soberness and coldness from its children, in so far as matters of criticism are concerned—i. e., in so far as the proving of their work is concerned, to determine whether it is sound and trustworthy or not. But none the less science demands of us reverence; reverence before that which is the most enduring thing that we know; reverence before truth; we all know that it will nevertheless be discovered and driven forth; that the inner life of science knows how to put to rout all such foreign enemies with irresistible power. And indeed, this process takes place the more rapidly and energetically the more free the communication between the true and the false members of the organism, because in this way the unbearable character of the false is sooner realized. Only such errors can maintain themselves in the scientific organism for considerable periods as exist in isolated portions of the organism, like an inclosed foreign body, and have only a mechincal relationship to the other portions of science. . Therefore, there is no better way to test the truth of a scientific concept than to bring it into connection with as many parts of science as possible. We all shall have occasion to discuss this matter more thoroughly later.

WORTHY OF REVERENCE.

The fact that we do not as yet recognize this irresistible power of science as a subject of daily thought and experience is the reason why the feeling of reverence does not arise in us with such strength when we think of science as it does when we think of those things whose greatness and strength we have been accustomed to honor from our youth up. But when we have once learned to look upon science as that which controls our whole life, then we know of nothing more powerful nor more worthy of reverence.

And now what is the position of the beautiful, of art? In the first place, it is beyond all doubt that the development of art is dependent upon the development of science. When one recalls the history of any one of the completed periods of art—for example, that of Greek sculpture—one sees how, step by step, the development of this art has been dependent upon increasing knowledge; knowledge of the anatomy of the subject, the human body, and its expression by movements, as well as knowedge of the sculptor's materials, marble and the metals. One also sees how, in such cases, the degree of artistic development always corresponds to the degree of technical and scientific development. Just as science always needs more and more exact knowledge of its materials, so it is with art. And just as a great scientific genius can produce most extraordinary results with very limited materials, as was the case with Newton's law of gravitation and Mayer's law of energy, so a great artistic genius, with the limited materials of his time, may produce works that will live for hundreds and even for thousands of years, as for example the dramas of Aeschuylus and the ninth symphony of Beethoven.

Here, also, we are, to a certain extent, impressed with the superiority of science, for, while we do not doubt that such scientific results as were cited above will last so long as culture itself lasts, we hesitate to utter the same judgment upon the artistic productions. We cannot deny that there are traces of age in Aeschylus—i. e., passages which most certainly do not produce the same effect upon us as they most certainly did upon the people of Aeschylus's own times. And it is likewise possible to think of times when the ninth symphony will no longer be able to produce any greater effect than is now produced by a symphony of Haydn's.

ELEVATING INFLUENCES.

This points to the possibility that art itself is destined to become gradually absorbed by science. I am willing to believe that this point of view will find very active and even angry denial. I wish to say, therefore, that personally I have to thank art for many elevated and beautiful hours; poetry, music and painting have refreshed me and given me courage when, exhausted by scientific work, I have been forced to lay my tools aside. But I cannot but feel that this is a sign of imperfection, and not so much of the imperfection of science as of my own self. For science, in the sense in which I speak of it today, exists only in its beginnings, and the human organism has not progressed far in its adaptation to it. Thus all of us suffer more or less from atavistic tendencies, which find their clearest expression in our perpetual complaining about the uninterrupted growth of science in scope and complexity. Thus we, and likewise our children and grandchildren, will still enjoy many beautiful and grand hours under the influence of art, for there will always be fields of human experience into which science has not yet penetrated, and in which art will rule without any limitations. But it is likely that to a future race, which has gained control of the science of psychology, many a treasured psychological drama of the day will appear as naive and insufficient as the first attempts of a four-year-old child at picture making.

But we will not dwell longer upon these questions, because there are more fundamental matters to be discussed. We have entered into these considerations only in order to apply them to the case which we have under consideration—that is, to gain as clear an idea as possible, by the methods of prediction, of the direction in which the special science of biology may find its best development. In order to gain the right to say anything whatever upon this point, it was necessary to convince ourselves that such a prediction might be in any case possible, and now one other little preparatory matter must be settled, and that will bring us directly to the problem itself.

FIRST LAW OF NATURE.

Science is an organism that steadily struggles for self-preservation and development. Therefore it is provided with organs for self-regulation, by means of which the useful is furthered and the harmful suppressed. Now, such organs can only come into action after these processes which are to be regulated are themselves in action. Thus each regulator cannot, under any condition, act without a certain lag. From this it follows that science, like any other self-regulating apparatus, must oscillate about an average condition. The average condition is not necessarily unchangeable with the time; on the other hand, it is, in our case, in a state of uninterrupted progress, because science may only increase, it can never diminish. Further, we have several sources of energy, each with its own regulating apparatus; therefore we have to do with a number of superimposed periods, which will give us a rather complex picture, and occasionally, for example, by the addition of several maxima or minima, which are in themselves small, a very large elevation or depression may be produced. We will try to determine in what condition of elevation or depression science in general and biology in particular exists at the present time.

One of the most influential components of these movements is at the present time especially easy of recognition. We have just passed through a period of specialization, in which all science has been most strictly divided into its separate fields, and are now entering an epoch where the synthetic factors are acquiring a greater and greater significance. Consider for a moment, ladies and gentlemen, what you see today! In the lecture room of a biological institute there speaks to you on this important occasion a man who is not only no biologist, but who, on the other hand, was expressly invited because he is known as the representative of a sister science. And this man is, again, the product of the synthesis of two other regulated sciences, physics and chemistry. And, furthermore, when this man seeks to gather for you the best that his garden offers, he brings you no word of physics nor of chemistry, but, rather, thoughts whose subject is the triad, physics, chemistry and biology, and whose object is a group of problems which include these and many other sciences. This is no accidental matter, but the genuine expression of the struggle of which these days are full.

TRY TO GIVE LIGHT.

Everywhere the individual sciences are seeking to find their points of contact with one another; everywhere the investigator examines his own special results, to see what bearing they may have on the most general questions; in short, all sciences are beginning to philosophize. Nowhere is the struggle toward fundamental explanation so great as in biology. A glance into biological literature shows us at once with what a vast deal of earnestness and energy the biologists are struggling to throw light upon the fundamental principles of their science.

The chief interest of the biologists here, is naturally to determine their relationships to the neighboring sciences, particularly to the inorganic sciences of physics and chemistry, and the conflict of opinions upon this point has given rise to the two battle-cries, "Vitalism" and "Mechanics." In all such cases there arises one great danger, namely, that one names a manifold complex for a single one of the many properties by means of which it is determined. Thus we see a well-known investigator call himself a mechanist, while the mechanists themselves reckon him a vitalist. In trying to treat these questions here from my own point of view, I prefer to take sides with neither of these parties; I wish to attempt to determine, upon the basis of the most elementary principles possible, the relationships that exist between the sciences in question.

When one attempts a general classification of the sciences, one coomes soon to the result that they do not exist along side of one another, but rather that they include one another, and in a remarkably reciprocal manner, which allows of a somewhat imperfect geometrical representation. Human experience is the direct object of all sciences. Every experience is composed of an unlimited number of components; of these components, only a few are taken into consideration, according to the specific purpose; all others are left out of consideration. Thus a given science includes the more experiences, the smaller the number of components considered; and it includes conversely, the more components, the narrower the choice of experiences. Thus, that science which, from the one point of view is the broadest, is from the other point of view the narrowest, and conversely. In order to give you at least an opproximate conception of these relations, I wish to call your attention to this sketch, in which the number of experiences is represented horizontally, and the number of components vertically. Thus you can see that the theory of manifolds is the most inclusive and narrowest of sciences because it includes all experiences, but considers these experiences from only one side, namely, that each is a distinguishable object; on the other hand, psychology is the narrowest and most inclusive science, because it deals only with phenomena which had to do with the human brain (or, if one prefers, the human soul), but takes into consideration all possible components. Thus, if we start with the theory of manifolds, arranging the sciences in a regular series, we see that each science in the series involves the preceding, but reaches beyond this, in that it deals with new components with which the preceding science had nothing to do. Its scope is thereby made narrower, as it has to do only with experiences which possess the new components. Thus mathematics has to do with the theory of manifolds, but only with such as possess the properties of space. Physics treats of spacial objects, but only in so far as the different forms of energy are active upon them, while chemistry has to do with physical objects which are distinguished from one another by qualitative differences, apart from those due to the presence of any other forms of energy. In this system, biology is that science which has to do with such chemical objects as show a stationary condition of energy; that is, such as show the phenomena of nourishment and of propagation. Psychology, finally, has to do with life processes only in so far as they exhibit spiritual functions, from which it is easy to see that the intellectual processes of mankind are almost the only things concerning which we possess moderately certain knowledge.

BIOLOGY INVOLVES ALL.

It is very essential for our problem, however, that we clearly understand that biology involves all of the preceding sciences, from the theory of manifolds to chemistry; that is, all biological phenomena are subject to the laws of these sciences. In exactly the same way all chemical phenomena are subject to the laws of mathematics and of physics, and indeed in such a way that no chemical law will, if it is correct, contradict any law of physics, or of mathematics. But the laws of mathematics and of physics do not by any means exhaust all that can be said about chemical phenomena, and the qualitative differences of substances, which form the subject matter of chemistry, cannot be sufficiently nor completely worked out by the implements of those sciences. The cause lies in the fact that in chemistry we have to do with a richer manifoldness than in the preceding sciences. Whether we charge a sphere of gold or an equally large sphere of carbon to one hundred volts makes no difference, so long as we are considering only the physical, i. e.: here, the electrical phenomenon. But whether we burn a sphere of sulphur or an equally large sphere of carbon makes, chemically considered, an irreconcilable difference. Thus, also, the chemical composition of a living man is not different from that of a dead one, while, biologically considered, the difference is a great one, since the first one can nourish itself and propagate its kind, while the second cannot. Here you may perhaps find some objections, but I scarcely believe that you will be able to change matters much. At the most, it might be necessary to our definition of life to be somewhat more exact.

From what has been said, there follows the answer to the much discussed question as to whether the laws of chemistry and physics are sufficient to explain all biological phenomena. In one sense the answer must be yes, in another sense no. Yes, in so far as all biological phenomena lie within the realm of possibilities given by those sciences. No, in so far as within this realm undoubtedly a greater manifoldness will be given than can be completely represented by physics and chemistry.

CONCEPT OF QUANTITY.

Perhaps it will make matters clearer if we look into the analogous relationship that exists between mathematics and physics. Most certainly all physical phenomena are to be classified under the concept of quantity, and to this extent physics may be considered as a part of mathematics. But just as certainly is it impossible to completely represent a physical phenomenon with the aid of mathematics alone. We can, for example, mathematically represent the phenomena that are connected with the conduction of an electric current, with that degree of accuracy which is attainable by the present methods of analysis. But we cannot mathematically represent the difference between this process and the conduction of heat through the same body, for here there are found new sorts of manifoldness which are not treated in mathematics, but first receive attention in physics.

Since now the mechanists and the vitalists look at the matter from opposite sides, we have the remarkable phenomenon that in both camps prominent and thoughtful investigators maintain apparently contradictory points of view, while it is impossible that there be more than one truth. And we know the members of both camps to be earnest and upright seekers after truth.

Truly these general considerations only become valuable for the problem which we are treating, when we investigate more thoroughly the new components of biological objects, which distinguish them from other chemical objects. We are accustomed to summate these differences in the word "life." If we inquire as to the recognizable and measurable properties of this concept, we find the following: Living beings are not stable, but rather stationary systems; rapid changes occur in them in such a way that gain and loss approximately counterbalance one another, so that the whole system experiences only very slow changes. Furthermore, these slow physical changes may be looked upon as displacements of energy in space and time, so it is also characteristic of living organisms that they hold their energy content approximately constant, both as to form and quantity, while a constant current of the various forms of energy passes through their bodies. In accord with the general principles of energetics, this can only occur in such a way that the living organisms take up energy at higher potential, and give it off at a lower. In the meantime the energy has been utilized for those transformations which constitute the activities of life, namely, motion, production of heat, reproduction, etc., etc.

"THE FLAME OF LIFE."

These characteristics apply not only to a living organism, but also to many inorganic systems. A burning candle whose wick is supplied with melted fat at the same rate at which the fat burns; or a gasoline motor, which regulates its own gasoline supply by means of a ball-governor in such a way that its velocity remains constant; both of these have exactly the same properties as the living organism. This has given rise to the expression, "the flame of life," and "the machine of the body." But we do not reckon these things among living organisms, because their existence is not selfmaintaining. When the fat is used up, or the gasoline gone, the flame goes out, and the motor stops, for the candle cannot produce new fat, nor can the motor obtain new gasoline.

But another regulator is imaginable, which could pump gasoline from a larger tank into the tank of the motor when the supply in the smaller tank became exhausted. But finally this will also become exhausted, or perhaps some part of the machine is broken, so that in the end the machine must stop. Thus the machine in or to maintain itself or its life, on the one hand, must be able to voluntarily replace the broken part, or else voluntarily create a new machine. If such a machine were in existence, we should be forced to call it a living organism.

Such a conclusion may seem to you, ladies and gentlemen, to be perhaps arbitrary; furthermore, among others, a very able investigator has given utterance to the opinion that even if it were possible to produce a system which possessed all of the properties of a living organism, still it would be no genuine living organism. To this one has only to interpose the question, assuming that by some means or other such a thing actually should occur, How is the genuine organism to be distinguished from the artificial? Since both are by assumption identical in all properties, at least in all recognized ones, it is impossible to distinguish between them. And according to fundamental laws, things that cannot be distinguished from one another are identical.

CHEMICAL SUBSTANCES.

Now, as to the arbitrariness of the conclusion, it is really less than one would think. How do our concepts arise? In this way: We collect that which is common to many phenomena and neglect that which is not common. In the case of the stable chemical systems, the concept of a chemical substance is that concept under which we collect those objects which possess identical specific properties, and we are able to build this concept because the individual substances, as for example, sulphur, when they are found or produced under the most different conditions always show the same specific properties. It is a much more different matter to form concepts in the case of those systems in which chemical changes are occurring. In order that under any conditions these systems may serve as the subject matter for the formation of a concept they must be at least externally stable, since otherwise we should have absolutely no means of identification. In other words, since they are by definition not stable they must at least be stationary. But even stationary systems will not lead us to the formation of a concept unless they are always to be found again in like form. Examples of such physical stationary systems are rivers, clouds and waves. They are characterized by esentially definite spacial form and the conditions for the reproduction of these forms occur easily and frequently. Chemical stationary systems occur more rarely on account of the greater difficulty of bringing about the necessary conditions. The only case which occurs to me is that of the flame. The conditions for the formation of such a system are the everywhere present oxygen, the readily found plant residues and, finally, a temperature of from four to five hundred degrees. And yet this constellation of conditions occurs voluntarily—i. e., without the intervention of mankind—only extremely rarely.

SOURCES OF ENERGY.

It is evident that the voluntary formation of such systems as possess, along with their stationary nature, also the power of self-maintenance—i. e., the power of seeking out the sources of energy necessary to self-maintenance—must be looked upon as an extremely rare phenomenon. And only when such a system, in addition to all this, also possesses the power to reproduce its kind, would one be willing to admit that it would submit itself to our observation so frequently as to lead to the formation of a corresponding concept. Looked at from this point of view, the condition of affairs seems to be the following: These considerations teach us nothing whatever as to how the organism may have been formed; but they do show us, on the other hand, that we should never have attained to the concept of a living organism as a stationary chemical system, if such living systems had not in addition possessed the powers of assimilation and reproduction. These, then, are the properties which are always found in those stationary chemical systems that we call living organisms, which constitute the new and the specific of biology in distinction to chemistry. Upon this point, then, the vitalists are wholly in the right.

But when, in connection with this view, it is also maintained that "consequently" life can never be explained, it is manifestly a confusion of scientific systematics with experimental investigation. Explanation in this case, as in any other, means simply the recognition of actual relationships between different series of phenomena. One chemical explanation of life we have already. No one of us has the shadow of a doubt but that life is unthinkable without chemical processes in which free energy is available. That which is lacking is a complete analysis of each of these chemical processes which occur in the living organism. In a general way we know many of these processes, as those of oxidation in the tissues and many of the processes of digestion in the intestines, etc. Most of them are, however, wholly unknown to us. We are therefore not in a position to decide as to whether or not it might be possible, in case all of these processes were understood, to create a living organism. We have conceived and explained many things without being able to create them, and whether organisms belong to this class, or to that other class of things which we can create, can only be determined in a future epoch.

ELECTRICITY PRESENT.

In order to make my meaning a little clearer, I will give an illustration. In a space where there is no electricity, we can at any time produce some; in other words, we can transform other forms of energy and obtain electricity with its two factors, quantity and potential. On the other hand, we cannot, in the same sense, produce gravitation energy, but only make it greater or less by bringing heavy bodies closer together, or farther apart. The cause of this is easy to see. Quantities of electricity are always produced in equal parts of the positive and negative kinds, so that their algebraic sum is always equal to zero. As a result of this, one can create any desired quantity of electricity without in any way running contrary to the law of the conservation of capacity, since the total value of this factor remains always zero. The corresponding factor of gravitation energy is proportional to the mass, and therefore has of necessity a positive value, which live mass itself can be neither created nor varied. At the present time it is most certain that we cannot foresee whether or not the complete analysis of life will show the presence of such non-creatable factors. However, from the fact that life may be arbitrarily destroyed, it seems to me somewhat probable that its arbitrary production is at present impossible on account of technical, and not of fundamental difficulties.

What then are these difficulties? The answer has already been often given. They lie in the fact that every organism, even the most simple, is a very complex apparatus, in which numerous different reactions along with one another in such a way that they mutually support one another in operating for the vital purpose of self-maintenance. For this purpose many different things are necessary, and above all it is essential that all reactions shall so occur that their velocities are so regulated that they all act together in unison for the purpose in question. A machine would dash itself to pieces if the movements of all its parts did not occur in the proper phase. In this case the problem is solved in such a way that the different parts work in compulsory unison, so that no motions except those that are suited to the purpose can occur. Such compulsory unison is very likely to exist in the case of the chemical processes of the living organism; they occur, for example, in the digestive apparatus, where the substances necessary for the reactions are specially separated in different parts of the intestine, and are then mixed with the previously prepared chyle by means of a motion in one direction. But in the case of interiors of a single cell, such a mechanical explanation is not very probable. Furthermore, the problem is solved by the organisms in very different ways according to the conditions.

ENZYMES OF ORGANISM.

A further means of accomplishing this purpose is found in the regulation of the various reaction velocities by means of catalysors or enzymes. The occurrence of such substances in the different parts of the organism was already known to Berzelius. He, and later, Ludwig, have expressed themselves as convinced that the enzymes play a very general and important role in the organism. Later investigations have confirmed and deepened this view. There seem truly to be very few tissues in which enzymes are not present, and in most cases large numbers of them occur together. But, while the older investigators on account of the condition of science in those times, ascribed to catalysors the power of actually producing reactions, thus of producing substances, we are now in a position to widen and deepen this conception, in that we know that the enzymes also regulate the velocity of the reactions. That this may produce a sort of compulsory unison is seen, for example, from the results of some of the later investigations upon the germination of seeds. During this phenomenon there appear in succession the starch-dissolving, the oxidizing, the assimilating, etc., enzymes, and in such order, such quantity, and such kind that the extremely complicated process of development of the young plant takes place regularly and economically.

Here there arises a question of fundamental importance, and one that to the present time has scarcely suggested itself to biology, because the general knowledge necessary to build upon has only been acquired in recent times; and the question as to the time-sequence of the processes in the living organism. Biology's scope has shown us the special sequence and, ladies and gentlemen, I need all of that little help which this instrument has given us.. Biology has busied itself for many years with certain questions of time relationships, especially such as are concerned with evolution, but time-microscopy, if I may use the word, has given us the most of that which takes place in each instant of life, in particular the time-microscopy of the chemical processes of life; this is a problem toward whose solution much already has been done, but which must be solved if we wish to go earnestly into the questions of those deeper problems which life offers to us.

PROBLEM OF CO-ORDINATION.

Where and how we are to attack these problems you will undoubtedly realize better than I; probably the best way would be to start from as many different points as possible at the same time, for the problem is of inconceivable complexity. As I have never busied myself with the problems of biology, I naturally cannot wish to offer suggestions to those who have. The one thing, however, which I can do is to indicate general points of view which come from a consideration of the facts of science. The problem of the co-ordination of a great number of different amounts of data to a united system scarcely occurred in the development of all the sciences previous to chemistry, and when it did occur it was usually settled by means of the principles of addition or of superposition. That is, the whole phenomenon concerning a given thing was considered as the sum of all the single phenomena which made up the total, and each individual phenomenon played its own part just as if the others were not there. The sound waves cross one another in the greatest variety of ways, without disturbing one another, and in the same way two, three or even more rows of waves cross in different directions and each retains its order and character. But here one sees already the limits of the application of this principle. When the big wave breaks, the little ones disappear in the breakers, never to be seen again. This comes from the fact that the waves are stable only to a certain limit. If this limit is overstepped, the forms of energy which are present become converted into others, as when treated by the principle of superposition, offers no longer a definite solution.

This last sort of reaction is universal with organism. A small change in one factor of a given condition will, in the first place, bring about proportionately small changes in the other factors, but only in the rarest cases will a case of superposition be recognizable. When one allows a string to vibrate, the change in temperature will produce a change in pitch, but this is simply due to a change in the elasticity of the string, and with the determination of this factor the problem is solved. If one raises the temperature of an organism, there results not only the corresponding change in the physical properties of the tissues, but at the same time the reaction velocities of all chemical reactions which occur in the organism are changed, and, indeed, each reaction is influenced in a different way. As a result, the proportionality between these reactions is disturbed, and it can happen that through small influences of this sort the limit within which the organism remains a stationary system will at some point be transgressed; then death occurs. It appears to me certain that, as I suggested some years ago, the remarkably careful and fine self-regulation of the higher mammals, whereby they have become thermostats of extraordinary constancy, has its origin in the necessity of holding the proportionality between the various chemical reactions constant in order that the life processes shall run normally.

MOST IMPORTANT SIDE.

Here, in the problem of co-ordination, it seems to me, lies the most important side of the problems of biology which have to do with time. In this field, at the same time, lie those phenomena for whose intellectual conquest new concepts are necessary, and which in the more general sciences, up to chemistry, are not needed.

In these fields biology will rule as an autonomous science, although not independent of physics and chemistry, but within the limits of the empirically possible as given by those sciences. These limits and conditions the biologist must know and respect, if he wishes to solve his problems; he must know the methods and ways of general chemistry and of physics if he wishes to understand the methods and ways of the organism. And this leads us back to the chief question, on account of which we have undertaken these considerations, namely the question: How blows now the wind upon the sea of science? The answer is, toward synthesis. The most beautiful and the richest results are to be expected there, where the different sciences reach out to one another for mutual support. And therefore you can see why we have been able to predict for our ship a most happy journey. The direction, which was found by means of observations from the highest standpoint to which I could attain, is the same which the steersman of the ship has already followed for many years. He needs only to steer the accustomed course in order to reach the best for which one may hope, and it only remains for us to wish him and his crew a "happy journey."

PROF. WILHELM OSTWALD.
University of Leipzig.

THE DISCIPLINARY VALUE OF ARITHMETIC.*

I have observed in our discussions of this question of formal discipline that we have opinions. Mr. McClymonds says that he does not believe in formal discipline, but admits that he does not know why. Dr. Burk says there is nothing in it, but while he will not admit it, it is probable that he does not know why either. We approach this question as we do questions of theology and politics —with prejudices. In consequence, so far as I can see, we stand just where we did at the beginning of our discussions. Those who believed in formal discipline believe in it more firmly than they ever did; those fought it first still fight it all the harder. And the good-natured part of it all is, not one of us really knows why.

Yet tremendous consequences, educationally, are involved. For upon the basis of our opinions and prejudices on this question courses of study are planned and the work of our schools shaped. We ought, therefore, to persevere in our attempt to get beyond mere opinion and endeavor to find by an unbiased survey of the evidence submitted, what the truth is concerning this problem, the solution of which is fraught with such far-reaching consequences.

It seemed to me well, then, to consider as impartially as I can the nature, bearing, and value of the evidence which has been submitted on this question. My hope is that thereby we may see more clearly the nature of the issue and the point we have reached in its consideration.

For my purposes, at least, the evidence which has been submitted as having a bearing on this question may be said to be:

1. The testimony of tradition, which means in the main the testimony of philosophers and psychologists of the old school.
2. The testimony of the newer school of psychologists.
3. The testimony of reflection based on introspection and observation, which, to distinguish it from the other categories, we shall call the testimony of "common sense."

To consider first, then, the traditional notion: I remember very well my first experience as a boy with arithmetic. My teacher put before me a text-book with the request that I learn certain definitions, pointing to a page in the book as he made the request. One of those definitions, for some reason, stuck to me to this day, and that is, that "arithmetic is the science of numbers and the art of computations." Singularly enough, yet I presume naturally enough too, in this definition we have suggested that two-fold aspect of

---
*Read before the Scholia Club of California.

arithmetic which was recognized by the earliest civilizations. Notions of arithmetic came into existence among the ancient peoples, on the one hand, because of the demands of practical life, and on the other hand because of the scientific spirit of individuals who held that arithmetic should be studied for a higher reason than for its utility. The Greeks, for instance, differentiated the science into arithmetic and logistic, the former having to do with the theory of numbers and the latter having to do with the art of calculating. In consequence, when these two branches were united in our modern treatment of arithmetic, the subject naturally came to be defined, as I remarked a moment before, as the "science of numbers and the art of computation."

But in the time of the Greeks, while the philosophers recognized this distinction, that part of arithmetic which was taught to the Greek youths was the part which had to do with the utilities. So with the Egyptians and, I may add, the other countries of the far East, arithmetic was given a place in the curricula solely that the boy might gain sufficient knowledge of the fundamental processes for the common vocations of life.

Among the Romans, also, the development of arithmetic took a purely practical turn. Rome's commercial interests extended to the limits of the known world. Under the pressure of her spirit of commercialism a business education, of which arithmetic was an important element, became obligatory for a large class of her citizens. The arithmetic of the time went no farther than dealing with simple operations and with problems which grew out of controversies regarding questions of inheritance, of private property, and of reimbursement of interest.

For exactly the same reason, though independent in its operation, the Semitic peoples laid much emphasis on the study of arithmetic. They were a people with strong trading instincts. Very early they recognized the utility of arithmetic, and in consequence they made its study, together with writing and the study of the Pentateuch, the sole work of the child from the sixth to the tenth year of his school life.

Occasionally, however, even in these ancient times, there appears a suggestion of another and a higher reason for the study of arithmetic.

Pythagoras, who was the first great mathematician, and who lived six centuries before Christ, saw in arithmetic something more than its utilitarian value. Gymnastics, music, and mathematics were the three grades of his curriculum. "By the first," he says, "the pupil is strengthened; by the second purified; and by the third perfected and made ready for the Gods."

Plato, a century later, says of arithmetic: "No single instrument of youthful education has such mighty power, both as regards domestic economy and politics, and in the arts, as the study of arithmetic. Above all, arithmetic stirs up him who is by nature sleepy and dull, and makes him quick to learn, retentive, shrewd, and, aided by art divine, he makes progress quite beyond his natural powers." He does not go so far in his notion of the transference of power, however, as to say that arithmetic will develop morality, for he continues: "This (the study of arithmetic) will be an excellent and suitable instrument of education if the legislator by laws and institutions can banish meanness and covetousness from the souls of disciples. But if he cannot do this, he will unintentionally create in them instead of wisdom the habit of craft, which evil tendency may be observed in the Egyptians and Phœnicians."

In another one of his dialogues Socrates says to Glaucon: "And have you further observed that those who have a natural talent for calculation are generally quick at every other kind of knowledge; and even the dull, if they had an arithmetical training, gain in quickness, if not in another way?"

The followers of Plato, among the philosophers so far as can be inferred from obscure references, held essentially the same views in regard to the value of mathematics in general, and arithmetic in particular. So in characterizing this ancient period we may say that down to the period of the Middle Ages arithmetic was taught to children solely because of its utility. That arithmetic had a value for general mental training was a view advanced by but a few philosophers, Plato and Aristotle being the chief exponents.

The striking thing of the Middle Ages was the attempt to reconcile theology and the rapidly awakening human reason. This struggle culminated in that outburst of philosophical activity which we call Scholastic. The Church had rendered certain decisions which were regarded as infallible and irrevocable. Her philosophy was a static one while the awakening Western mind displayed a tendency to advance. The schoolmen did not question the truth or soundness of the theology of the Church; they accepted all the writings of the Fathers, the canons and decrees of the Popes and Councils as true. They argued that there must be a reason for these decrees and God has given us our reasoning faculty that we might search out final causes. So with nothing else to work with but Aristotle's logic, which had come to them through the Saracens, they fell upon the piles of dogma and legends of the Church with the purpose of reducing all to order, harmony, and system. Under the pressure of rivalry between individuals and between schools these schoolmen looked about for a means of training themselves for their disputations. At this time arithmetic was taught in their cloisters and ecclesiastical schools mainly for the purpose of computing the date of Easter, which to them was a very important matter. Whether or not they got their hint from Aristotle or got it independent of the Greek philosophers I haven't the data to determine, but at any rate they saw in arithmetic, aside from its utility in making computations, a means for sharpening their wits. It thus became the business of teachers to "discipline" the minds of their pupils, and the most suitable means for this purpose was thought to be the study of mathematics. With this idea in view, they sought to make arithmetic as obscure and as difficult as possible, thinking that much mental stumbling about would give greater exercise, and hence be more productive of power. In consequence of this notion there arose a mass of catch problems—problems which contained some ambiguity of language, and which would therefore provoke discussion.

Alcuin, the famous teacher of Charlemagne's palace school, wrote an arithmetic entitled: "The Propositions of Alcuin, the teacher of Emperor Charles the Great, for Whetting the Wit of Youth." One of his problems was this:

"After an ox has plowed all day, how many steps does he take in the last furrow?" The answer is, "none, because the last furrow covers his tracks." Again:

"When a farmer goes plowing, and has turned thrice at each end of his field, how many furrows has he drawn?" Alcuin said six, but Venerable Bede stoutly maintained seven.

In another proposition Alcuin requests that 300 pigs be killed in three batches on successive days, an odd number to be killed on each day. After allowing the boys to puzzle their heads a while on this problem, which is impossible of solution, he cries in great glee, "Here's a go. There is no solution. This fable is only to provoke the boys."

In the thirteenth century Lord Bacon expresses the current view of his time when he says:

"In the mathematics I can report no deficience, except it be that men do not sufficiently understand the excellent use of pure mathematics, in that they do remedy and cure many defects in the wit and faculties intellectual. For if the wit be too dull, they sharpen it; if too wandering they fix it; if too inherent in sense they abstract it."

Essentially the same view was held in the seventeenth century. Dr. Barrows, a famous English mathematician of this (seventeenth) century says:

"Mathematics serve to inure and corroborate the mind to a constant diligence in study; to undergo the trouble of attentive meditation, and cheerfully contend with such difficulties as lie in the way. They wholly deliver us from credulous simplicity, most strongly fortify us against the vanity of skepticism, effectually restrain us from rash presumption, most easily incline us to due assent, perfectly subjugate us to the government and weight of reason, and inspire us with resolution to wrestle against the injurious tyranny of false prejudice." He continues:

"If the fancy be unstable and fluctuating, it is, as it were, poised by this ballast, and steadied by this anchor; if the wit be blunt, it is sharpened by this whetstone; if it be luxuriant, it is pruned by this knife; if it be headstrong, it is restrained by this bridle; and if it be dull, it is roused by this spur."

In the eighteenth century a number of the leaders of educational thought both in England and on the continent, still under the influence of the schoolmen and the philosophers, perpetuated the views already held. Thus Hubsch, about the middle of the century, remarks in the same strain that "Arithmetic is like a whetstone, and by it one learns to think distinctively, consecutively and carefully."

Pestalozzi, at the beginning of the nineteenth century, while radically opposing much of the educational theory then extant, was in hearty accord with existing views regarding the purpose of arithmetic, as he maintained that its aim was to develop and strengthen the mental powers in general.

It is very easy, then, to see how this notion of the disciplinary value of mathematics came to dominate educational theory in our own country when we remember how our colonial forefathers in rearing their children followed with remarkable fidelity the philosophy as laid down in the writings of John Locke; and when we remember also the influence which Pestalozzi and his school have exercised in moulding our educational theories and practice.

This disciplinary view is the legitimate corollary of the faculty psychology which originated with the Greek philosophers, and which dominated the philosophical world until it received its death blow at the hands of Herbart about a century ago. And not until this time, so far as I can see, was there ever a question raised as to whether power developed in one field could be applied in another. Authority had said dogmatically that it was so, and so it was to each successive generation. Ziller, an enthusiastic follower of Herbart, about fifty years ago, was the first to attack this traditional notion in a forceful way. He maintained at much length:[*]

"That a good memory for places does not necessarily bring with it a good memory for names or for numbers."

"That active imagination and sound understanding in one sphere is consistent with positive dullness in another."

"That formal culture, the benefit of which extends from one

---

[*]Prof. E. E. Brown; "How is Formal Culture Possible?"—Public School Journal, December, 1893.

thought circle to another, is not possible so long as these thought circles are not brought into close connection with each other."

"That it cannot be said that the study of languages, or of a particular language, or the study of mathematics, will train the power of thought in general."

This attack on the traditional notion by Ziller, followed a few years ago by Hinsdale's well-known article on the dogma of formal discipline, marks the extent of the contributions to the opposition by speculative psychology.

For the sake of clearness permit me at this point to summarize the evidence submitted by tradition.

From the most remote times arithmetic has been valued for its utilities and for its power in mental training. The rank and file of business men, men in close touch with practical daily affairs, little giving to theorizing, but wanting tangible results from their schools, have held to the former view. The other, the disciplinary view, seems to have originated with the Greek philosophers 2,500 years ago, to have passed from them to the scholastics in the Middle Ages, and to have been handed down to us in the nineteenth century by a few philosophers who, while breaking away from the ideals of the scholastics in many ways, yet perpetrated this notion, that certain studies have peculiar power in general mental training. This notion was the legitimate outcome, as we saw, of the conception that back of the several states or moods of the mind there were certain positive agencies or units interacting with each other, called faculties. Not until the fallacy of faculty psychology was pointed out, at the beginning of the nineteenth century, were the extravagant claims of the formal disciplinists questioned. Opposition to this dogma, first raised by Herbart, and followed later by Ziller and Hinsdale, seems to be gradually gaining ground, but as yet it has effected our educational practice but little.

A word regarding the value of this evidence. Personally I want to say that I have no sympathy whatever with that idea one hears forcibly expressed at times, that a thing is to be damned because it is traditional; again, I have less patience with those people who, in listening to the voices of the past, do not hear those sweeter and more alluring ones of the future. The true spirit of the earnest seeker after truth demands that he respects the words of the world's great reformers and thinkers, else he drifts about at the mercy of every idle breath of opinion. It does not demand, however, that these notions be accepted implicitly: if this were done there could be no progress. It merely asks that what is best in the past be held, and thrown aside only when its error is shown by other and conclusive evidence.

Looking at this evidence as impartially as I can, however, I am forced to conclude that as mere evidence it is weak. When we consult Davies, who in 1850 wrote a work on the "Logic and Utility of Mathematics," we find that he dogmatically asserts the disciplinary value of arithmetics, backing up his assertions only by referring to Locke and Barrows, who lived in the seventeenth century. We consult these writers, who again back up dogmatic assertions by referring to Lord Bacon, who wrote in the thirteenth century. I have gone through Bacon carefully, but can't find the data or the line of reasoning by which he arrived at his very positive conclusions. I am forced to conclude that he merely gave expression to the popular notion which the Scholastics of his time held, and which they in turn seem to have gotten from Plato and Aristotle. I have gone through the dialogues of Plato to find why he held that arithmetic excelled all other studies in its power of training the mind. But here, again, I am stopped with mere assertion. I have wandered down the whole line of tradition from Pythagoras to Com. W. T. Harris searching for a man who backed up his assertions in this connection with some data other than authority. Com. Harris is the only one who makes the attempt, so far as I can see.

We are forced to conclude, therefore, that the traditional notion of the disciplinary value of arithmetic rests in its last analysis upon either personal opinion or opinion based upon nothing more substantial than the unsupported authority of the great philosophers of the past, whose conclusions are rendered less worthy of credence by reason of the fact that they were based on a psychology which is now generally held to be false.

I wish now to consider the evidence submitted on this question by the so-called "New Psychology." For my purpose the new psychology breaks itself up naturally into two classes of investigations.

(1) The investigations in the field of psychological psychology.
(2) The investigations in the field of child study.

The physiological psychologists have worked very patiently with their dissecting needles and their microscopes in the attempt to apply rigorously the methods of science to physical and psychical phenomena. Up to a certain point they have done their work well, but at a certain point they have reached the limitations of their method, and at this point they drop their knives and chemicals and go to speculating, at which game they prove as resourceful as did the philosophers of the old school. In our consideration of their contribution to this question of discipline we must carefully distinguish between fact and fancy; between what they have demonstrated and the hypotheses which they hope to prove.

They have shown that physically the brain is a mass of nerve cells and fibers.

That it is connected with the sense organs on the one hand by sensory nerves and on the other hand with the muscles by motor nerves.

And that exercise modifies the brain structures by developing latent cells.

At this point in their examination of physical and psychical phenomena the rigorous scientific method breaks down and they fall back upon introspection and speculation.

The very premise upon which their interpretations turn, that every excitation of brain area is attended by a concomitant psychical process which ceases when the excitation ceases, is undemonstrable by the methods of science alone.

The theory of levels, suggested by Dr. Hulings Jackson and elaborated and applied educationally more recently by certain students of Clark University, has no basis in anatomical fact. It is but an ingenious hypothesis to explain what introspection and experience has shown to be true.

In fact, even the notion that the nerve cells of the brain are joined by nerve fibers, along which stimuli pass, can not be determined by the most powerful microscope yet invented. Such phraseology as "cell discharges," "association paths," "neural processes," "plasticity of cells," "stored nerve force," have no justification so far as the most rigid examination of brain anatomy has shown. A century later these terms may be as nearly obsolete as are now such phrenological phraseology as "amativeness," "combativeness," "secretiveness," and "philoprogenitiveness." In this field, then, it is apparent that there is little evidence, scientifically demonstrated, which bears directly on our problem of mental discipline.

It has been shown, however, that the excitation of a brain area which accompanies any psychical process draws a larger supply of blood to itself than when the mind is doing no conscious thinking. The blood brings with it food and nourishment and takes away with it waste materials. It is reasonable to suppose, therefore, that the exercise of a portion of the brain, and the increased flow of blood which it causes, will aid in the development of other nerve cells just as physical exercises not only energize the particular muscles involved, but by stimulating the circulation exercise a beneficial effect on other parts of the body as well. In consequence of such exercise one has a better nourished brain and nervous system and fatter nerve cells with which to work. A game of chess or a game of poker, from this point of view, will give as much general brain power as a lesson in arithmetic or one in grammar. And whatever gives better brain stuff will presumably give greater power on the thought side.

But given a good, well-fed nervous system, the greatest development of nerve cells comes from successive "nervous excitations and discharges." Laura Bridgman at three years of age was stricken with scarlet fever and left entirely deaf; and blind in her left eye. Five years later she became blind in her right eye as well.

Presumably her brain was well nourished in a physical sense, but upon examination after her death, at the age of sixty, the cortex of her brain was seen to be thinner and less developed than that of the average person who retains the use of his sense organs. The cortical center of her right eye, the eye of which she had the use for eight years, was much thicker than that of her left. It is a reasonable inference that the cortical center of the right eye was more highly developed than the other, because sensory stimuli from the eye poured into it five years longer. This illustrates my point, that the ebb and flow of the blood alone is not sufficient to secure adequate nerve development—there must be the incoming stimuli from the sense organs energizing and discharging the stored-up energy of the cell. The general power of which I spoke a moment before will not accomplish this. An excitation of the visual centers will not necessarily excite or discharge the cells of the auditory centers, or vice versa. We may handle, touch and feel boards and rocks and tables all the days of our lives and never develop our centers of smell. Our centers of smell may be so delicately attuned as enable us to detect all the odors in Christendom, yet to save our lives, if blindfolded, we couldn't distinguish between white wine and red.

A few months ago I was out rabbit-shooting with a friend of mine who has a keen eye for a drawing, whether it be a map or a landscape. So keen is his eyesight that he can see a blot on a drawing across the room. On our trip rabbits jumped out from the bushes under his very nose, but he couldn't see them. The difference between us was that as a boy I tramped the hills with a shotgun and learned the habits, the homes, the appearance of game, and consequently knew where to look and what to look for, while he had spent his time working with drawings. In consequence, I can scarcely distinguish one line from another in a drawing and he can't see the rabbits.

So it seems safe to conclude that from the standpoint of physiological psychology, mental exercises as mental exercises assist in a very general way in the development of brain power, but that the finer adjustments, the closer co-ordinations between centers, the great sensitiveness of the nerve cells to external stimuli, in fact all that really goes to make what we mean when we speak of a finely organized brain cannot be the result of any circumscribed series of exercises.

I turn now to the evidence which has been gathered by that method of securing data in the field of child study called the method of the questionnaire.

In this connection there are some interesting studies being carried on at the University of Columbia under the direction of Professor Thorndyke.*

Those engaged in the work state the question in this way: It is commonly supposed that ability—and by ability they mean speed, accuracy and whatever else helps to make goodness in anything—ability with one kind of data or in one subject is commonly supposed to mean ability also in some other subject, or with other data. They ask, "Is this true?" They ask, what is the degree of probability that ability in science carries with it ability in mathematics? Even in different branches of the same general subject, as algebra or geometry, what is the degree of certainty that ability in one implies ability in the other? Does improvement in one imply improvement in the other? And can the extent to which the training of one's ability "spreads" to other abilities be measured? Is there an overflow from the exercise of ability in Latin to ability in English, as is often contended? This is the problem they are seeking to solve. Their method of procedure is as follows:

They obtained the rating, that is, the grading in terms of E. G., F. P., or as given in per cents, extending over a period of about three years, of 1,500 children. These were carefully examined with this theory in mind: that if ability in arithmetic gives ability in English, then those pupils who are graded excellent in arithmetic would be graded excellent in English. In other words, the specific purpose of the examination of the gradings was to determine the amount of correlation between abilities involved in the study of grammar-school subjects. By certain methods used in tabulating statistics this degree of correlation between pairs of mental abilities as shown in the ratings could be determined.

In one of the studies, that carried on by Mr. Smith, six questions were asked:

1. How far does ability in English imply ability in geography?
2. How far does ability in English imply ability in mathematics?
3. How far does ability in English imply ability in drawing?
4. How far does ability in mathematics imply ability in geography?
5. How far does ability in mathematics imply ability in drawing?
6. How far does ability in geography imply ability in drawing?

An examination of the results show the absence of any close relationship between the pairs of abilities just mentioned.

Another study carried on by Mr. Fox, in which the same method was used had for its specific purpose the determination of the relationship involved in the study of the several phases of arithmetic.

*Columbia University. "Contributions to Psychology."—Vol. XI, No. 2.

An examination was given to a number of pupils involving exercises in
1. Column addition,
2. Multiplication,
3. Easy fractions,
4. Rational computation,
5. Problems.

As a result of the study it is pointed out:

That our common notions concerning reasoning in arithmetic are purely speculative.

That the vast majority of pupils do no reasoning whatever in arithmetic.

That the real abilities in arithmetic are many and are largely independent of one another.

That the relationships among the several phases of arithmetic are no larger than between high school subjects, that is, there is no closer correlation between ability in adding figures and working out a problem in fractions than between arithmetic and Greek.

In other words, the conclusion seems to be that the thing which we call arithmetic ability is a composite made up of a number of separate abilities.

These conclusions in the main are borne out by my observation of practice work with children. I have long observed that a child in school may be able to handle perfectly a problem of a given type, but will flounder most woefully when given one which is slightly different either in principle or in language form from those he has had. Though, as I say, my conclusions, based on observation, are in entire accord with those reached by the above method, yet I am frank to say that I do not believe the method is a reliable one. The value of the conclusions, as those conducting the experiments admit, rests entirely upon the reliability of the data with which the method deals. And it must occur to all that there are many reasons for questioning the data which is obtained in the manner I have indicated.

In itself, then, this method of the questionnaire proves nothing. It is suggestive, it points out a tendency, when repeated a great many times, and when its conclusions are supported by evidence drawn from other sources and other fields and gotten by other methods, it should and will have weight.

If you remember, the third and last class of material which I wish to consider is that gotten through reflection based on introspection and observation; that body of testimony which, for the want of a better name, I called "common sense."

The other day I was on a car on one of the down-town streets. I glanced up to a sign which read, "Importing Tea House." I jumped off the car and entered the office. The first man to whom I spoke happened to be a professional tea-taster. He told me that the stock examination given by the firm to a young man learning the business was to lay before him forty samples of one general kind of tea—as for example the black tea of the market. To my eye these samples were all alike. He was expected by tasting the tea made from the samples to classify them properly and state their value at market prices. It takes ten years of hard daily practice for a young man to become efficient in this work. I asked him if an expert tea-taster made a good coffee-taster. He replied, "One never is both; it takes too long to learn." He said, however, that an expert tea-taster could learn tasting coffee in less time, he thought, than one who had no training in either.

At the Union Iron Works there is an immense steam hammer, I do not know how much it weighs, but there are some in the Eastern shops which have hammers weighing eighty tons, and which strike a blow equal in force to a weight of 800 tons dropping fifteen feet. To show how easily these hammers are manipulated, and what skill the operator develops in their use, it is said that frequently a watch is laid on the anvil, face up. On it is placed a moistened wafer. This ponderous weight drops with its full force, strikes the wafer, but is stopped by the operator before it touches the watch. On raising the hammer, the wafer is found adhering to its surface. Again, a wine glass is placed on the anvil, and in it an egg which projects above the rim of the glass. The egg is chipped open by a successive series of blows of the immense hammer, but the glass remains unbroken.

It is said of Mr. Theodore Thomas, leader of the famous orchestra of ninety-two pieces, that his auditory centers are so highly developed that when his men are all playing he can instantly detect the instrument that strikes a wrong note, and can usually designate the player.

I might cite many more concrete instances of the high degree to which our sense organs and centers can be developed through exercise, but it isn't necessary.

My point is just this: that the hard-headed, matter-of-fact business world, the world which hasn't much use for theory, but which holds in high esteem the man who *does* things, whether he be a bootblack or a preacher— I say this old practical world, while recognizing that there may be some basis for formal discipline, doesn't for a moment build up its system of education and training for the handicrafts or industries upon any such basis. When she has need for an expert tea-taster, she goes and gets a man who has been testing tea for ten years, and, by the way, she pays him for his been tasting tea for ten years, and, by the way, she pays him for his goes and gets a man who has been bred and nurtured in an atmosphere of music and art. When she wants a man steady of hand and clear of eye to drive her steam hammers, she doesn't go to a jewelry shop, nor to the coffee house, nor to the teaching profession on the strength of the formal discipline there may be in these trades and professions, but she takes the man who, as a boy, has played about the machine shops, who has watched the steam hammer at work, and who knows her as he knows his best-beloved brother.

My illustrations so far have had to do with the training of the physical senses. Let me take up briefly the mental process which we call memory and see what the world of experience says of it.

I was talking with a young lady recently who has remarkable aptitude for remembering poetry. She says it is just as easy to remember prose as poetry, but she has no knack for remembering the names of people whom she meets.

A friend of Mr. Teggart, the Librarian of the Mechanics' Library, says he has a remarkable memory for the names of books, and that he can tell whether a given book is on the shelves. But this friend also reports that he can't remember to mail his wife's letters any better than the rest of us.

The cashier of my bank has wonderful success in remembering faces and signatures, but deplores his lack of memory in general reading.

Last week I saw several policemen standing on a street corner. I asked them if they had any good stories of men in their department who had developed particular skill in doing things. They began to tell me some wonderful stories of the feats of memory of one they called Bainbridge. These stories sounded so incredible that I decided to go to headquarters and get some which were true. At the office of the Chief of Police I found them very ready to relate stories of this man's remarkable ability, and for which they vouched. One of these stories was to this effect:

A man who called himself James Howard was arrested the other day for attempting to blow open a safe down town. When brought before Bainbridge, Bainbridge ejaculated at once: "Hello, Fernando, back again, are you?" The prisoner disclaimed ever having seen him. Bainbridge then remarked: "Did you ever know a man by the name of Peterson?" The prisoner glared a moment and replied: "Well, Bainbridge, you've gotten me at last." The gentleman who gave this information said that the prisoner had been arrested eighteen years ago; that at the time he had been brought before Bainbridge for inspection, just as hundreds have since; that his real name was Fernando, though he at that time went under the name of Peterson; that he had not been in the city since until his arrest a few days ago; and that in consequence Bainbridge could not have seen the man but the one time in eighteen years.

They told me, upon inquiry, that he has no particular power in remembering data in any other field than the one in which he is now working.

There seems to be as many memories as there are categories of knowledge.

What has been said of memory applies equally well to imagination, which, though differing from memory, is yet separated from it by no sharp line of demarcation. The imagination of the business man is not identical with the imagination of the artist; neither is the imagination of the architect of the same quality as that of the novelist. This can easily be shown by reference to concrete instances which any one of you could furnish in abundance.

Though there seems to be no such thing as building up a general memory or a general imagination by circumscribed studies, yet when we come to consider the method by which we develop the power of mental concentration or voluntary attention as it is called, we are forced to acknowledge that the formal disciplinists have the best of argument. A baby has no power of voluntary attention. Neither has an ignorant, uneducated adult. They are the creatures of the moment, wholly dependent upon immediate interests. They find it impossible to hold the thought down to the less interesting, but frequently the more important, object. For them it is impossible to turn away from those things which are of immediate interest to the things which the judgment affirms to be of greater and more lasting worth. This power of taking your mind by the nap of the neck, as I heard President Wheeler once remark, and forcing it to attend to that which is temporarily distasteful is an attribute of the well-trained mind only. Now, is the power of voluntary mental concentration a general power which can be applied to other fields than those in which it was developed? I say most emphatically "Yes." I have never studied Hebrew, I have no interest in the language whatever, but I do not think any one of you will say that I could not sit down at my desk with a Hebrew grammar, or, for that matter, in a crowded street car, and not become oblivious to the sights and the sounds about me. How have I gotten this power of mental concentration, this control over my voluntary attention, if not through long-continued study, frequently along lines which temporarily were highly distasteful to me? I dare say in this my experience is in entire accord with your own. This increased power of voluntary attention is one result, then, which comes from thorough instruction in arithmetic, or, for that matter, in any subject, and which may be carried over and effectively applied in any other field of knowledge however remote.

There are certain emotional qualities, also, which admit of the same transference. We have all experienced the bracing-up effect which came through the successful accomplishing of some undertaking which we approached with fear. We have all seen the timid, reticent, self-conscious child transformed by the realization of the fact that he excels in some thing. There is much truth in the old saw, that nothing succeeds like success. But it succeeds not so much because success inspires others with confidence in us, but because it inspires *us* with confidence in *ourselves*.

Just so with that quality which we call reliability. There are a few people of whom we say, "They always keep their engagement." If they are ten minutes late at an appointment, we say that something serious has happened. There are others who are careless and negligent in these and larger matters. We say one is reliable and the other unreliable. The one we entrust with our most important and serious work; the other never understands why he is given no responsibility nor why confidence is never reposed in him. I believe that much of the reliability which Mr. McClymonds has shown in his school work was gotten on the farm and in the field. If Mr. McClymonds were suddenly transported to New York and given the presidency of the great steel trust, which carries with it a salary of $1,000,000, I believe he would prove the same careful, painstaking, reliable man that we find him in his present profession. In other words, he has formed the *habit* of reliability, the operation of which is independent of specific trades or professions.

Besides these emotional qualities which I have mentioned, there are also qualities which might be termed moral. I refer to what Professor E. E. Brown means when he speaks of "that ardent love of truth and that fine feeling of intellectual responsibility" which some scholars and students possess, and which others do not. These, like the qualities already mentioned, are the product of thorough and proper instruction in the studies of our curriculum. And they are the qualities which our observation and experience show us can be applied in fields of thought widely remote from those in which they were gained. If these, and these only, are the general qualities or powers which specific studies develop in any considerable degree, then it is pertinent to ask, Are these powers, emotional, or intellectual, or moral, the product of arithmetic more than of history; of grammar more than of nature study? In other words, is arithmetic the *open sesame* that unlocks the hidden mysteries, or is it grammar, or is it history? Is it the so-called group of formal studies, or will these qualities and general powers come from cultural studies as well? Will arithmetic give you any greater control over voluntary attention than the study of English? Can you develop that love for truth, in whatever guise it is to be found, any better through the study of arithmetic than through the study of history? Does it offer any greater opportunities for the development of what we have termed self-confidence and reliability than any of the other of the subjects usually comprehended in our courses of study? I think "common sense" will reply, "No; these qualities refuse to be circumscribed by the narrow limitations of any one subject." If this be true, that these qualities or powers are the product rather of the *manner* of our study than of the *subject-matter*, it seems to me that mathematics must justify the large place which it occupies in our courses of study on other grounds than on its efficacy in mental discipline. The only other legitimate plea it can make is its utility, and on this ground arithmetic would be much reduced in scope and the time given to its study lessened. There is still much of the mediæval notion clinging to teachers, that it is well that the child should be worried and perplexed in education, and that out of this agitation of nerves and strain upon the mental powers proceed health and vigor. An examination of the problems given to-day in most text-books will show that a great many of them are merely logical puzzles without any connection or relation with the present-day methods of arithmetical application. At one time, in past ages perhaps, most of the arithmetic was of use, but times have changed, business men have found better ways of doing things, but the school teacher and the text-book writer have not discovered the change, so they go on treating the several phases of arithmetic essentially in the way they were treated decades ago. If one chances to point this out and ventures to ask why the teacher treats it so, the reply is, "Oh, it trains the mind to think." And so this traditional notion of the disciplinary value of arithmetic is made to cover a multitude of sins in the present-day method of teaching the subject. Lest I be charged with drawing on my imagination, at this point let me cite some specific instances to show that many of the notions we are now teaching are either obsolete or else are not used by practical men.

In the usual text-book treatment of percentage there are five cases or general classes of problems. In business only two are ever used. These two are:

1. Eight per cent of $650 is how much?
2. If 106 per cent of x equals $4.24, what does x equal?

In the text-book treatment of discount we find considerable attention to that aspect called "true" discount, by which is meant the difference between the present worth of an amount and the amount itself. This is not used in business.

Take the text book treatment of interest. A business man never has any occasion to find the time, when the principal, rate, and interest are given. The child has also little use for compound interest and for partial payments.

Equation of payments was once of practical value, but improved methods of banking have rendered it obsolete. The same can also be said of partnership.

Since the adoption of standard time in the greater part of the civilized world, the subject of "longitude and time" has ceased to have much importance in a practical way.

So I might pass in review each of the phases of arithmetic and point out many aspects which have long outlived their usefulness, but retained because of the notion of their disciplinary power.

The arithmetic of the future, when that part which is now retained only for its so-called disciplinary value is sloughed off, will, to my mind, lay greater emphasis on two things: (1) on accuracy and rapidity in the simple fundamental operations with figures, and (2) on the application of these processes to the everyday activities going on about us, instead of seeking to apply these operations to problems of an antiquated type. Instead of forcing children to puzzle over the "A, B, C," problems, or over those which have to do with hounds chasing hares, or again over those in which pipes fill cisterns in certain times we shall have our children estimating the cost of producing an acre of wheat in the Sacramento Valley, or running the municipal government of their own town or village. This is by no means a new idea in arithmetic. It is being worked out, and worked out successfully in some quarters.*

The testimony of "common sense" then on this question seems to show that there is good and sufficient reason for concluding that the qualities of mental concentration, of intellectual reliability, of self-confidence, and of love of truth, are all general powers capable of application in widely varying fields. It also shows that no one subject of study is any better adapted to producing these results than any other and consequently arithmetic should not be retained on the ground of its supposed efficacy in producing these results.

If these conclusions are well founded then it seems to me that the truth of the whole matter is this: that in our school training, as in the training for industrial pursuits by the world outside the schoolroom, while we recognize that there is a basis in fact for the doctrine of formal discipline, yet we should construct our courses of study as if there were no such basis. Since formal discipline, limited as it seems to be to a few emotional reactions, is the product of no one study or group of allied studies it can and should be allowed to take care of itself, and the time thus gained devoted to developing an all-round, versatile product through actual experience with the essential parts of a great many subjects.

*Teachers College-Record, Columbia University, Vol. IV, No. 2.

FRANK F. BUNKER.

THE INSTITUTE.

The days in which teachers in general are becoming more intelligent and in which the professionally selected and trained teacher is rapidly receiving a more liberal recognition, are the days in which the old time institute becomes more and more a problem to the superintendent who has it to plan and to execute.

Just here it might be well to emphasize that what an institute is, is largely due to the personality, ideals and energy of the superintendent who undertakes it. Occasionally an institute worker brings up in a gathering whose atmosphere betrays but too plainly that the institute is being held merely because the law requires it, not because any real personal energy, spirit or thought have been put into it by the superintendent, nor yet because the assembled body of teachers feels a call for it. It is dead and nothing the lecturer can do can bring it to life. Only a spirit of vigorous, enthusiastic leadership on the part of the local authority, the superintendent, felt for months by the teaching body, can bring them together with life and *esprit di corps* in an institute.

To the thoughtful superintendent, however, the problems which the institute must solve are by no means few or simple. It may well be asked whether, after all, the County Institutes, an outgrowth of older conditions, most of which no longer exist for many counties, is not fundamentally weak. Except for the fact that they are all teachers, there is almost no interest in common which offers a basis for work in common. The average institute has already come to represent more or less professional differentiation among its attendants, and that fact complicates the problem of rendering it effective. Commonly, kindergartens, primary, grammar and high school teachers, often also special teachers, principals and supervisors are brought together in one body. There are neither sufficient numbers nor funds to warrant any division of work, even in part. The only lecturer who can approximate the common interests of this audience educationally is necessarily the one who talks in most glittering generalities. The problem is still further complicated by the varying experience, and time in service of the teachers. Side by side are the experienced, the trained and untrained. Whatever of subject matter and methods is adapted to the needs of these classes is bound to be either trite to one class or beyond the other, *i. e.*, if real substance is presented. It is just this total situation which very often makes the average institute an exceedingly hard place in which to work with satisfactory effectiveness.

Finally, the time ordinarily devoted to an institute, one week, seems very short and inadequate to the instructor who really desires to leave some lasting and serviceable impression, rather than merely to talk, draw his pay, and get away.

The writer has worked in many institutes in a number of states and has found the conditions practically the same everywhere. Everywhere there is evidence that the conditions which originally created the annual week's institute are passing away; and that it is becoming increasingly difficult to make it meet modern conditions with their enlarged and complexer demands. It is, perhaps, not too early now to predict that these needs will be met in the future by something like the university and normal summer schools, which shall offer courses postgraduate to the ordinary training and experience of the teacher.

But the requirements of the law in the matter of institutes still stands; the practical issue before the institute conductors, superintendents and instructors is, what shall be done with it?

In general the institute may serve about four useful functions. First, then is the social function, certainly not invaluable among the ends which may be met at any gathering of teachers. It is commonly remarked at great conventions that the opportunity to meet many, and to compare experiences and ideas with a choice few, is not the least of these advantages. The same holds good to a very appreciable extent, of the county institute. And the time spent and pains taken in behalf of such social functions as will give opportunity for acquaintance, conversation and exchange of experience are not necessarily less unwarrantable than the time and pains spent upon lectures.

In the second place the institute may stand for general educational inspiration and the renewal of professional spirit. The collective effect of a teaching body makes for this, in part; in part, lectures of general educational significance. But the thing which needs most to be said, perhaps, is that there is a very definite limit within which an institute may indulge in the general educational lecture which is given for the sake of inspiration and stimulus. Such lectures, which deal with the common stock in trade of the teacher, and aim to recall the ideal aspects and ends of the profession, cannot, in the nature of things, contain much that is new; they are chiefly an appeal to the teacher's emotional stock in trade, to her professional pride, enthusiasm, and ambition. They are intended to leave her with a fresh fund of motor power to charge the storage batteries. In so far they are very good. But the moment an institute becomes committed to that sort of instruction and nothing else, that moment it runs the danger of becoming either nerve-wearying because of emotional intemperance, or humorously trite. For this reason I believe that an institute should indulge in only a very limited number of lectures on the general, directly educational themes. Let the emphasis be thrown on something at once more concrete and practical.

Third, the field of method in the special subjects offers one of the best opportunities for live, effective institute work. Every teacher that has seen service still has problems touching practical teaching on which she would like further light and suggestion. When it is possible in such work the teachers institute should be segregated on the basis of experience, or of special lines of work. In order that the instructor may bring his work as close to the individual teacher as possible, he should use the seminar, rather than the lecture method. The exclusive use of the lecture method always results in a needless repetition of what is perfectly familiar to the experienced teacher. During the lecture, furthermore, she will undoubtedly preserve her inalienable right to be skeptical or critical of a good deal the lecturer is saying. At the same time it is the experienced teacher who is probably the instructor's most attentive and devoted auditor. It is all this which renders her a most valuable presence at an institute, provided she can be called out. There is no exercise, of a pedagogical nature, more practically productive than the seminar which calls out the exchange of experience and the general discussion of problems that have arisen among the individual teachers present. It is, indeed, under the conditions of the carefully conducted seminar alone that methods and logical instruction can be made effective. This is true, in part, because the seminar limits the amount of ground that can be covered. It is not the quantity of material which should constitute the instructor's aim, but its quality. Has it taken hold of the teacher thoroughly enough to be remembered, to react in her practice? The seminar method is effective, again, because it is about the only method that permits of any individual adaptation at once to the experienced and the inexperienced teachers.

Fourth, Probably the prime need of the experienced and inexperienced teachers alike is the constant renewal and enrichment of their culture. For this reason the cultural aim of the institute stands second to none. But it should not be assumed that the institute itself can be a direct source of culture in any adequate sense. Five days devoted to lectures up on literary, historical, or scientific themes, holding the teachers to their chairs six hours by day time and two by night in the steady effort to be attentive and to absorb, become simply a protracted period of one sort of intemperance. Just here it may be well to say that one of the common errors of institutes is the overcrowded program, and that the unreflective eagerness and enthusiasm of the teachers themselves is very commonly the cause of it. If the institute is to do anything, it must be largely by suggesting lines and pointing out the way. The writer sees no good reason why one or two good university instructors, selected to meet the needs or wishes of a majority of the teachers, should not be able to initiate work which would last most of the teachers a year—at least most of those with any professional pride or ambition. There are counties in this state which have carried through good courses of reading for most of their teachers, and have made some connection between these courses and their institutes. There are counties which have, in various ways, even by travel, done a great deal for the cultural enrichment of their teachers. Let us suppose that a university teacher in literature and one in history are employed, and that each is given an hour in the forenoon and one in the afternoon—in all four hours a day. Each selects some part of his field fitted to his audience and devotes his brief time to a discussion of its purpose, a general survey of the ground to be covered, perhaps from sylabus, to a discussion of the best methods and the requirements of studying it, and to the best and most available sources, adapting his suggestions always to the possibilities of the teacher's independent study. Ten hours spent upon this sort of work would open to ambitious teachers something of interest for a year. It would not be university work; but it would be worth while. It would probably result also in more teachers availing themselves of what, after all, is to become the ultimate substitute for the week's institute—the university summer school. Two such lines of work alone would be enough for a week's institute work, with the possible exception of the evening lecture. But it is to be remembered that their subject matter should be of the order of general culture, rather than of the hackneyed professional order. As we grow in experience, as teachers, our pedagogical technique rightly tends to pass over into the unconsciousness of habit. What the institute needs is a broader, more vital cultural outlook, and less pedagogy.

CHARLES C. VAN LIEW.

President State Normal, Chico, Cal.

SUMMER SCHOOL AT SAN JOSE.

M. E. Dailey, President of the San Jose Normal School, is initiating a new departure in normal school work in this State by establishing a summer school for teachers and conducting his school with a session continuous throughout the year.

This is a school of teachers, not pupils training for teachers, but teachers who are utilizing part of their vacation for self-improvement. In a few weeks they will disperse and become the teachers of this and other states, whereas they are now acting in the capacity of pupils.

This is the first regular school held in the summer in the State. Berkeley has held a summer school of university work, but this is the first normal work done in the State toward which the pupils may work to obtain a normal diploma. The regular normal pupils are not allowed to attend this summer school except in special cases and by special permission of the faculty. Thus the attention of the faculty can be centered on the needs and directed along the lines of interest to teachers already in the schools. It is intended as a school for teachers and of teachers, helping those who have not had normal training to obtain it during vacation; and to enable those who have had normal training to come in contact with the latest methods and ideas, and to freshen those subjects which may need it. The work done is the regular normal work, and by attending its sessions any teacher not a normal graduate may become such. This is filling a long-felt want among teachers, for they realize that the time is not far distant when none but normal trained teachers will be accepted.

Realizing their need of a normal training, the city of Phoenix, Arizona, sent its fourteen teachers to the San Jose Summer School and paid all their expenses. They are a bright lot of attractive, progressive ladies and made quite an impression among their fellow students. They are alert and eager to grasp all that is newest and best. This certainly was a compliment to the educational advancement of California to have a body of teachers sent with their expenses paid to our first normal summer school. Miss Hicks, teacher of the Sacaton Indian School, had her expenses allowed while she attended. Thus the government is complimenting the State also.

In an interview Mr. Dailey said: "The summer school idea, as an idea, is growing all over the East and is bound to succeed. Every teacher who comes in contact with the best methods, if only for a few weeks, is bound to carry away some inspiration, which will result in better work for the coming year. Normal school training is being demanded more than ever before. It will not be many years before it will be nearly impossible for any but normal graduates to find positions in the grades."

As proof of this he cited the large class which graduated the 19th of last June. Of the 117 students graduated, 86 have been elected to positions and not less than 20 others have been recommended to positions and are certain of them. Practically nine-tenths of the class have already obtained positions. Yet some are continually advising promising young people not to train as teachers, saying the profession is over-crowded.

In Illinois the first normal summer school had only a very few pupils. This was three years ago. This summer Prof. Cubberly of Stanford reports that this school had more pupils than it could accommodate. If this be true in Illinois, with its disagreeable climate, what may we not expect from San Jose, with its superior coast climate?

The enrollment at San Jose is far greater than was expected, as the circulars announcing this session were not sent out until nearly the first of May. By this time many teachers had made their plans for the summer. The present session has enrolled 170 pupils. Of these, 118 are not normal graduates. One-half the counties of the State are represented by these pupils. With an enrollment of 170, it is conclusively proven that there is a demand and a place for the summer school, and fully 250 or 300 pupils may be expected next year. The San Jose Normal now has a continuous session of twelve months. Under this plan the instructors teach three terms out of the four, but not four successive terms. This gives the instructors a chance to take vacations in different parts of the year. The faculty of the summer school this year is composed of the following instructors: M. E. Dailey, School Law and Management; L. B. Wilson, Physics and Physical Geography; Calthea C. Vivian, Drawing; Rebecka F. English, Primary Methods; N. H. Bullock, Nature Study and Physiology; W. N. Baker, Arithmetic, Algebra, Geometry and Trigonometry; Anna M. Nicholson, Literature, Grammar and Literature Methods; Agnes E. Howe, History Methods; C. J. C. Bennett, Psychology, Pedagogy and History of Education; H. L. Schemmel, Music; Ruth Royce, Librarian.

MARGUERITE WINCESLOW.

Department of Methodology

THE TEACHER OF READING.

To teach reading successfully in any grade, one must first have the courage to interpret the selection according to his own best understanding. Elocutionary skill is not necessary, but the teacher must be able to speak distinctly, enunciate clearly, pronounce correctly and use the voice with a natural conversational inflection. If added to these qualities are enthusiasm and energy born of real interest, the teacher may be said to have entered on the highway to success.

It now remains for her to acquire ability to detect errors of speech immediately, refer them to their cause, and apply the proper remedy; to formulate drill exercises for the formation of good habits, and to create conditions for bringing the class in close touch with the subject matter.

Teach the children that drill exercises are necessary for the formation and fixing of good vocal habits, and the correctness of bad ones, and have a place for active, wide awake practice with these objects in view. Then when it is time to read, *read,* do nothing but read, keeping up the enthusiasm of the class through genuine interest in the subject matter, and recognition of power to understand, interpret, and give back the thought of the selection.

THE TEACHING OF ENGLISH.

Forty-seven out of sixty applicants for admission to Stanford failed in the English test. It ought to be interesting to learn what the trouble is. This problem assumes greater proportions every year. Something is wrong in our accepted theories of teaching English. Every language teacher, from the primary to the high school, inclusive, is fully aware of the two ends—formal correctness and free expression. The problem is, how to secure both. Formal correctness, according to a prevailing current belief, is wholly subservient, and worthy only of incidental treatment.

The solution of the problem points to an isolation of aim during each recitation. The language period can be so adjusted that there is an opportunity to emphasize and not confuse these almost conflicting ends. Formal correctness should have its place. This need not be by a time-consuming, lifeless exercise.

The teacher, by jotting down to the account of each individual his glaring characteristic mistakes in oral and written expression, can in individual consultation directly aid him to recognize and thereby correct these mistakes. Errors, more or less common to a class, can be made the subject of class discussion, followed by drill in the correct forms. Tune the ear to correct sounds, train the eye to correct forms. This can be done only by patient, tactful repetition, sometimes called old-fashioned. How many a moment of mortification, how much of the embarassing consciousness of incorrect usage, some of the "grown-ups" might have been saved!

LONG DIVISION.

To the beginner, long division presents two difficulties; he must become familiar with the form, and he must acquire skill in approximating and testing his results. These difficulties should be overcome singly. Teach the form by first using divisors, not exceeding 12. Write the quotient over the dividend, placing each quotient figure directly above the right-hand figure of the dividend used in obtaining it. There can then be no doubt as to which figure should be next brought down.

In approximating our results, we never use more than the two figures on the left of the divisor. Train the pupil to approximate his results by giving him much practice, using such divisors as 21, 31, 41, 211, 312, 417, etc., in which the left-hand figure may be used as a trial divisor. Have the estimated results tested. Then use such divisors as 49, 59, 69, 795, 892, etc., in which the number next larger than the left-hand digit may be used as a trial divisor. Be satisfied with slow progress. The child must grow. Give him time and helpful experience.

METHOD OF TEACHING THE SENTENCE.

The habit of using sentences in composition cannot be taught by means of defining a sentence to be "a group of words which make complete sense." The correct use of the sentence is an acquired habit. The following series of exercises are designed for primary grades, to give this systematic drill:

Purpose.—To connect, with the notion of "sentence" in the child's mind, the mental picture of a period at the end and a capital letter at the beginning.

Exercise 1. Select from the pupils' readers, or write upon the board, some paragraphs made up, so far as possible at first, of simple declarative sentences. Read these to pupils and have pupils read them, calling their attention to the capital and period. The following selections, from Miss Smith's "Four True Stories," will serve as good illustrations:

"Columbus went to the new land twice after this. The last time he was put in chains again. Then these cruel men sent him home in chains. This last time he had no friends to help him. The good queen was dead. Columbus was now too old to work. Soon he grew very poor. Day by day he grew worse. In a little while the kind old man was dead."

Exercise 2. Read to pupils a selection, containing simple declarative sentences, so far as possible without phrases, and accentuate the falling of the voice at the period. Have pupils count the number of sentences, determining these by the falling of the voice.

Exercise 3. Dictate the same sentences, of a connected narrative, keeping the pupils' attention alive to capitalizing the beginning word and inserting the period at the end.

Exercise . Write upon the board parts of a sentence, as:— "Columbus went to ——." Drill pupils in recognizing this as only a part, both by the absence of a period and by ear. Continue this exercise for several lessons, gradually using more complex forms such as phrases, dependent clauses (commencing with when, where, unless, if, etc.), until pupils recognize a phrase or clause as incomplete.

Exercise 5. Write upon the board (or hectograph upon separate slips of paper so that each pupil may have one), complete sentences and also incomplete parts, arranged indiscriminately, and drill pupils to select the complete sentences and discard the parts.

Exercise 7. (a) Write upon the board compound sentences connected by a comma and "and." Point out that when the comma and "and" are used the sentence does not end until the period is reached. (b) Write clauses of compound sentences upon the board and drill pupils in discriminating the two. (c) After the connective "and" is thus recognized, introduce "or," "nor" and "but," drilling in the same day.

Exercise 8. After the sentences ending in a period are easily recognized and errors in the use of sentences of this type practically disappear in the original compositions, begin a similar drill upon sentences ending with an interrogation mark. Do not bother with exclamatory sentences in the primary grades, as this is a matter which will adjust itself in the upper grades without special drill.

Official Department

STATE BOARD OF EDUCATION

GEORGE C. PARDEE, *President of the Board*..............Governor, Sacramento
MORRIS ELMER DAILEY............... President State Normal School, San Jose
E. T. PIERCE........................ President State Normal School, Los Angeles
C. C. VAN LIEW .... President State Normal School, Chico
BENJAMIN IDE WHEELER............President University of California, Berkeley
ELMER E. BROWN ..Prof. of Theory and Practice of Education, University of Cal.
SAMUEL T. BLACK ....President State Normal School, San Diego
FREDERIC BURK...... ....President State Normal School, San Francisco
THOMAS J. KIRK, *Sec. of Board*.. Superintendent Public Instruction, Sacramento

Report of the Proceedings of the Meeting of the State Board of Education held August 29, 1903

NORMAL SCHOOLS ACCREDITED.

Pursuant to the provisions of Sub. 1 (b), Section 1775 of the Political Code, the following Normal Schools were placed on the accredited list:

New York City Normal College, New York;
Northern Arizona Normal School at Flagstaff, Arizona;
Washington State Normal School at Whatcom, Washington, *advanced course only*.

KINDERGARTEN TRAINING SCHOOLS.

The following were added to the list of accredited Kindergarten Training Schools, under the provisions of Sub. 1 (c), Section 1775 of the Political Code:

Kindergarten Training Department of the Nebraska State Normal School at Peru, Nebraska;
Oakland Kindergarten Training School, Oakland, California.

HIGH SCHOOL TEXT-BOOKS.

The following corrections were made in the list of recommended High School texts issued June 9, 1903:

From Milton to Tennyson and *Four English Poems*, by L. DuPont Syle, are published by Allyn & Bacon, the announcement of their publication in the circular being incorrect.

NEW BOOKS.

Under the heading "History," two titles were added, the same having been omitted from the published list by mistake:

Ancient History—West—Allyn & Bacon;
Essentials of Ancient History—Wolfson—American Book Company.

The State Board refused to make any changes or additions to the list of high school texts at this time, except in correction of error; and the Secretary of the Board was directed to call the attention of school officers and publishers to the rule of the Board under which changes in the list of recommended texts may be made *only* at the last meeting of the Board or before the close of any school year. All books which are to be considered for addition to this list should be submitted to the State Board of Education as early as possible in the school year, in order that they may be properly examined and reported on by readers designated by the Board.

* * *

BULLETIN NO. 21.

To the County, City, and City and County Boards of Education of the State of California:

Some complaints have recently been made to me that the State law relating to school text-books is being disregarded by sundry school boards, and that I am derelict in the discharge of my official duty in not pointing out the penalty and inflicting it, as provided for such violation of law.

I am fully cognizant of the widespread desire for better school text-books, and I am pleased to inform you that hopes long deferred in this direction promise very soon to be realized. A new U. S. History of the State series, suitable for the advanced grammar grades, composed in the main of text matter that is well known and recognized by all educators as of the highest order of excellence, has just been published under the general direction and approval of the State Board of Education and is now going out for use in the schools. A tabulated statement of the opinions and criticisms of the State Text-Book Secretary and a number of expert history teachers on subject-matter for a primary U. S. History is now before the Committee, and a selection of such matter will be made within a few days, and publication of the book will be pushed to completion at the earliest possible date. It has been decided by the Committee that in addition to the two books on U. S. History, new text-books on both Geography and Arithmetic shall be completed and ready for use in the schools by July 1, 1904.

The entire list of subjects to be taught in the primary and grammar schools, and for which text-books may properly be required, will be prepared and published just as speedily as the Text-Book Committee can do the work, and do it as in its judgment it should be done.

The Committee will, in accord with its interpretation of the law, designate texts for supplementary use just as soon as the State series principal text in a given subject has been prepared and published. Text-books for supplementary use in the subject of advanced United States history will probably be announced in a few days.

Members of school boards, superintendents and teachers, those school officials who have taken an oath of office, particularly those who are drawing public school money, should feel under both a legal and a moral obligation not only to abide by the laws of the State, but to assist in carrying them out. It ill becomes such persons to ignore or evade the laws. State publication of school text-books is a constitutional requirement, and in pursuance of this fundamental law, the Legislature passed an Act, approved March 18, 1903, creating a State Text-Book Committee, and said Committee is directed to compile, or cause to be compiled, and to manufacture such books, subject to the approval of the State Board of Education, as it may deem proper for use in the primary and grammar schools of the State. It is to prescribe and enforce the use of a uniform series of text-books, and to adopt a list of books for supplementary use in primary and grammar schools.

The law relating to this matter in one instance reads as follows:

"Any county, city and county, city, or school district that refuses or neglects to use the State series of school text-books in the grades and in the subjects * * * and at the time as required * * * must have the State money to which it is otherwise entitled withheld from it by the Superintendent of Public Instruction."

I have regard for my oath of office, and in the event of its being conclusively shown to me that the authorities of any county, city and county, city, or school district have violated the provisions of the law above quoted, I shall surely not shrink from the discharge of the duties imposed upon me as Superintendent of Public Instruction. I have specific directions from the Attorney-General as to how to proceed in the event of its being necessary to withhold State funds from a single district.

* * *

BULLETIN NO. 20.

To County, City and County, and City Boards of Education of the State of California:

Pursuant to the provisions of law, I, Thomas J. Kirk, Superintendent of Public Instruction of the State of California, do hereby notify you that a new State Series United States History for use in the advanced grades of the public schools of the State has been compiled, published, and adopted, and that the same will be ready for distribution on or about the 10th of September, 1903. The uniform use of said book in all the upper grammar grades of the public schools under your jurisdiction will be required after one year from April 24, 1903, the date contract was made for the use of the plates of said book; but nothing is to prevent any county, city and county, or city board of education from adopting and requiring the immediate use of said book in the upper grammar grades of the public schools under their charge.

The State Board of Education at its meeting today has, pursuant to law, fixed the price of said book as follows:

    Cost price at Sacramento...............81 cents.
    By mail ....95 cents.
    Price to pupils from retail dealers........95 cents.

The attention of County, and City and County Superintendents is called to Subdivision 1 of Section 1874 of the Political Code, as amended at the last session of the Legislature, which provides that they shall order a sufficient number of each new text-book to give at least one copy to every public school library within their jurisdiction.

NEW STATE SERIES GRAMMAR SCHOOL UNITED STATES HISTORY.

The State Text-Book Committee submitted the itemized statement of the Superintendent of State Printing, showing cost per copy of 51 cents to manufacture, in an edition of 8,000, the new State Series Gramar School History of the United States, whereupon the State Board of Education passed a resolution adopting it in accordance with law and fixed the price of said book as follows (F. O. B. railroad or express):

    Offices in Sacramento ....81 cents.
    By mail, postage prepaid...............95 cents.
    Price to pupils from book-dealers.........95 cents.

                           THOMAS J. KIRK,
              Superintendent of Public Instruction.

* * *

NOTES ON MINUTES OF MEETINGS OF AUGUST 24th AND SEPTEMBER 3d.

August 24.—Adopted order of revision and compilation, between now and July 1, 1904, as follows:

1. A primary U. S. History. 2. A series of geographies. 3. A series of arithmetics.

September 3.—Met for purpose of considering subject matter for a text in primary history. Copyright and rental of plates of the following offered:

Barnes's Elementary U. S. History. Am. Bk. Co.

Blaisdell's Story of American History. G nn & Co.
Burton's New Era History of the United States. Eaton & Co.
Channing's First Lessons in U. S. History. The Macmillan Co.
Eggleston's First Book in American History. Am. Bk. Co.
McMaster's Primary History of the United States. Am. Bk. Co.
Montgomery's Beginner's American History. Ginn & Co.
Mowry's First Steps in the History of Our Country. Silver, Burdette & Co.
Tappan's Our Country's Story, Houghton, Mifflin & Co.
Thomas's Elementary History of the United States. D. C. Heath & Co.

Royalties asked ran from 8 cents to 18 cents for each copy printed and sold by the State. All bids rejected, mainly because majority were too high.

The following were adopted, subject to approval of the State Board of Education, as supplementary to the new Grammar School History of the United States:

Fiske's History of the United States. Houghton, Mifflin & Co.
Eggleston's History of the United States and Its People. Am. Bk. Co.
Montgomery's Leading Facts in American History. Ginn & Co.
Mowry's History of the United States. Silver, Burdette & Co.
Thomas's History of the United States. D. C. Heath & Co.

To Supt. J. W. Linscott, Supt. Edward Hyatt, Ex-Supt. Robert Furlong, Ex-Supt.P. W. Smith, Miss Anna C. Weeks of Sacramento and Miss M. Josie McKellar of Downey, members of the recent expert committee on subject matter for a text on primary history, and to Miss Agnes E. Howe and W. F. Bliss, the members of the committee of 1901 that responded to the recent request, the following vote of thanks was ordered sent:

"The State Text-Book Committee hereby expresses its appreciation of, and thanks for the services you have rendered the State by examining and reporting upon the several books submitted as history texts for use in the lower grades of our common schools."

Sincerely,

GEO. C. PARDEE,
THOMAS J. KIRK,
ELMER E. BROWN,
State Text-Book Committee.

♦ ♦ ♦ ♦

DIPLOMAS GRANTED

The following Teachers' Credentials were granted:

UNIVERSITY DOCUMENTS.

Harriet M. Curtis, San Bernardino; Agnes Frisus, Alameda; Maud L. Grover, Contra Costa; Edward Hohfeld, Placer; Jessie Ryan Hollenbeak,

San Joaquin; Agnes R. Jewett, Sonoma; Texaina Tyler Kurtz, Alameda; Teresa Hess, Colusa.

NORMAL DOCUMENTS.

Della Adulman, San Jose; Mono Aulman, San Jose; Ida E. Barron, Los Angeles; Pearl L. Barron, Los Angeles; Louis Drury, San Jose; Lois M. Estabrook, San Jose; Grace Helene Farnsworth, Los Angeles; Lizzie Farrell, San Jose; Viola D. Fisher, San Jose; Thana Hamilton, San Jose; Julia K. Holmes, Los Angeles; Emelie R. Houghton, Los Angeles; M. Louis Johnston, Los Angeles; Eva Viola Joseph, San Jose; Ida M. Keilbar, San Jose; Frances Kingery, Los Angeles; Jane Lawrence, San Jose; Maria de Guadalupe E. Lopez, Los Angeles; Grace Olivia Lovell, Los Angeles; Elizabeth M. Cudden, San Jose; Grace E. Monk, Los Angeles; Harriet R. Ortley, San Jose; Anna Snedden, Los Angeles; Josephine M. Stancer, Los Angeles; Mary E. Uncapher, San Jose; Lydia E. Walters, Los Angeles; Lillie Warren, Los Angeles; Marietta Williams, Los Angeles.

HIGH SCHOOL DIPLOMAS.

Will Lear Brown, San Bernardino; Elmer E. Brownell, Santa Clara; Valentine Buehner, Santa Clara; Katharine C. Carr, Los Angeles; Samuel A. Crookshanks, Tulare; Ulysses Grant Durfee, Shasta; William Willis Fogg, Del Norte; Grace Cecelia Morgan, Los Angeles; Jesse J. Morgan, Los Angeles; George Ulysses Moyse, Los Angeles; Irvin Passmore, San Luis Obispo; Carl A. Richmond, San Bernardino; Fred Grant Sanderson, Lake; Stella Young, Los Angeles.

GRAMMAR SCHOOL DIPLOMAS.

Ella A. Adams, Los Angeles; Daisy E. Allen, Humboldt; Isabella Ashfield, Shasta; Adalyn O. Bangham, Lassen; Lester Black, Riverside; Josephine A. Bont, Los Angeles; Lillian M. Bowland, Orange; Chas. S. Breaty, Sonoma; Mary F. Breaty, Sonoma; Mary Agnes Brennan, San Joaquin; Nora E. Brouse, San Bernardino; Mrs. Adelia Gray Brown, Placer; Enoch J. Buckman, Tulare; Algernon Butler, Colusa; Grace S. Cain, Los Angeles; Pearl D. Caldwell, Tulare; Ida M. Cambridge, Modoc; Nellie R. Cameron, San Bernardino; Margaret A. Campbell, San Mateo; Jennie D. Cavanah, Santa Barbara; Florence A. Cilker, Santa Clara; Florence Clark, Placer; Amey C. Cooper, Santa Cruz; Raymond Cree, Riverside; Agnes E. Crimin, Solano; Isabelle H. Critcher, Santa Cruz; Mrs. Jennie C. Conneghan, Yuba; Carolyn Culver, Riverside; John J. Dailey, Shasta; Lea Darrah, Inyo; Mary E. Davis, Los Angeles; Anna M. Dennis, Los Angeles; Miss Willie Downing, Santa Barbara; Caroline W. Eickhoff, Madera; Henry B. Everett, Sutter; Mary E. Ferguson, Sacramento; Kate C. Fox, Santa Barbara; Martha E. France, Alameda; Eugenie G. Gairaud, Santa Clara; Catherine E. Gloster, Modoc; Lulu Belle Goldsmith, Los Angeles;

Official Department

Lucy I. Gordon, Siskiyou; Ida Grafe, Solano; Rachael E. Green, Modoc; Frances Mabel Green, Los Angeles; Bessie L. Grenfell, Madera; Lucy Griffitts, Lake; John Hancock, Calaveras; Irene Hankenson, Santa Clara; Lycy R. Harper, Inyo; Iola M. Harris, Santa Clara; Mabel A. Harris, Los Angeles; Mary A. Harvey, San Francisco; Tillie W. Hassheider, Orange; Frances J. Heil, Orange; Dorathea H. E. Helms, Alameda; Alice A. Hight, Santa Cruz; Hattie E. Hinkson, Amador; Clara Hogan, San Joaquin; E. Blanche Holly, Solano; Avis Hopkins, Yuba; Fannie Hopping, Placer; Susie Hudson, Santa Barbara; Charles Eugene Irons, Siskiyou; Loretta B. Kaler, Calaveras; Josephine G. Kelly, Alameda; Della Kelso, Tulare; Estelle Farmer Laramore, Tuolumne; May Evans Larkin, Butte; Eva C. Larrison, El Dorado; Wm. Lemon, Modoc; Irma R. Levy, Sacramento; Belle Levington, San Francisco; Frances M. Leutzinger, El Dorado; Harriet B. Lewis, Placer; Margaret G. Liner, San Francisco; Albert G. Loomis, Lassen; Annie C. Love, Los Angeles; Mrs. Alpha A. Lyman, San Bernardino; Marion Madsen, Alameda; Edgar H. Marbut, San Benito; Gertrude McAdam, Humboldt; Mrs. Alice McCarty, Shasta; A. L. McCulloch, Orange; Eva Laura McPhail, Santa Barbara; Ella M. Miller, Santa Barbara; R. Garner Mitchel, Humboldt; Rose E. Mohan, Los Angeles; William J. Moore, El Dorado; Julia Mulcahy, Nevada; Lizzie Nixon, Calaveras; Mary R. Parks, San Francisco; Harry Renowden Painton, San Mateo; Carrie Peet, San Bernardino; Harriet W. Phelps, Santa Clara; Abbie L. Pratt, Los Angeles; Kate C. Orr, San Bernardino; Gertrude Owen, Santa Barbara; Mrs. Helen Ford Quilty, Santa Clara; Frances Quinlan, San Francisco; William Leonard Redding, Calaveras; Mrs. Minerva L. Reed, Calaveras; Susan H. Reeves, Los Angeles; Mary E. Riebsam, El Dorado; M. Lena Rice, Humboldt; Alice E. Rowland, San Francisco; Mamie Russell, Santa Clara; Lorinda M. Sauber, Lassen; Minnie M. Schulze, Sacramento; Mamie G. Sexton, Los Angeles; Jennie L. Shaffer, Los Angeles; Marion Olivia Shannon, Tulare; Mary B. Shell, Tuolumne; Della Smith, Modoc; Helen I. Smith, Placer; Ella Stahmer, Los Angeles; Grace J. C. Stewart, San Joaquin; Nettie Louise Stover, Plumas; Frank T. Sweeney, Solano; Clara E. Thompson, Riverside; J. E. Thurmond, Santa Barbara; Margaret Tungate, San Luis Obispo; Lillie E. Vilas, Shasta; Walter Burns Violette, Humboldt; Mrs. M. Winona Wagner, San Bernardino; Mary Adell Ward, Los Angeles; Marie Weiss, San Joaquin; Augusta M. Westfall, Los Angeles; Mary C. Wilcox, Santa Clara; Carrie E. Wilkinson, Santa Cruz; Mina Wolfe, San Joaquin; Geo. F. Willis, Inyo; F. L. Wright, Sonoma.

SPECIAL LIFE DIPLOMAS.

Katherine T. Black, San Francisco; Music.

SPECIAL HIGH SCHOOL CREDENTIAL.

Miss Helen Beardsley, Berkeley; Mr. Charles E. Cox, San Jose; Mr. John S. Donagho, Palo Alto; Mr. Edmund E. Knepper, San Rafael; Miss

Marie Jacobi, Stanford University; Miss Marion Alice Kendall, Palo Alto; Miss Jean Loomis, Pasadena; Miss Louisa McDermott, Berkeley; Miss Euphrasie Molle, Berkeley; Mrs. Mary A. Pillott, San Jose; Mr. George R. Ray, Oakland; Mr. Lewis A. Robinson, Berkeley; Mr. John A. Sands, Oakland; Miss Elizabeth Sellards, Ione; Mr. Alvah B. Way, Redwood City; Mr. Frances H. White, Redlands; Mr. Herbert O. Williams, Pomona.

The following were granted said credentials, but the same to be withheld by the Secretary of the Board until the applicants become residents of the State of California:

Mrs. Lana M. C. Conger, Minneapolis, Minn.; Miss Lillie Elda Moessner, Madison, Wis.; Miss Mary O. Pollard, Sherburn, Minn.

THOMAS J. KIRK, *Ex Officio Secretary*.

Editorial

At the request of the editor of THE WESTERN JOURNAL the State Board of Education at its meeting on June 6th appointed an advisory board of editors, whose names will be found elsewhere in this issue. This step was taken in the hope that THE JOURNAL might if possible become more closely connected with and more truly representative of the educational interests of California and the states of the Pacific slope. The sphere of public education has increased so mightily in recent years its interests have become so diverse and its workers so specialized that a journal which endeavors to reflect their efforts must be the work not of a single man but of many. And if possible the men who shape its educational policy should be in a measure identified with the actual work of the schools.

Such were the considerations which led to the call for assistance. While the advisory board is in the strictest sense a working body and corporately responsible for the utterances of THE JOURNAL, the initial responsibility as heretofore belongs to the managing editor. The general plan of THE JOURNAL will not be changed. It will be conducted as in the past in a spirit of conservative radicalism. The fixities and the fads of education will both be unsparingly dealt with. More attention and a larger space will be devoted to editorial comment which will, it is hoped, reflect the mature and careful judgment of the whole body of Western educators, and in the preparation of which the services of the leading educators of the land will be enlisted. Leading articles upon a variety of subjects will be prepared for each number by writers who have made a special study of the themes which they treat.

A department of methods will offer month by month a selection of the best schoolroom methods and devices taken both from the literature devoted to those subjects and from available current practice.

The department of school news will undertake to imform the readers of THE JOURNAL concerning educational events of general as well as of local interest.

The department of reviews is designed to serve as a sort of clearing house of current educational thought thruout the world.

Important discussions of educational matters which appear from time to time in the general as well as in the professional and technical magazines will be briefly summarized. The leading articles of German, French, English and American educational journals will be noticed. A list of the best books of an educational character will appear from month to month, together with a statement of the uses which they are designed to serve, will be found here.

It is believed that there is need at the present time for a magazine which shall do for education what is so ably done by a score of reviews and digests for the general news of the day. To meet this demand which, because of our geographical position is more keenly felt in the west than in the east, a sort of educational review of reviews has been planned whose editorial comments, contributed articles, section of methods and department of reviews will in a measure select the noteworthy from the common in the general field of education, and at small cost and little outlay of time enable the teacher in the most remote rural school district to keep in close touch with the educational progress of the world.

It is believed that the cause of education is one and indivisible; that a journal of education which shall best serve it must treat it as a whole; that the problems of the rural schools must be made known to the workers in city schools, and high schools and colleges as well; that the problems of the city schools, the high schools and the colleges belong to the entire educational profession and cannot be wisely discussed unless they are treated as parts of the whole nor solved by other than the united consciousness of the state. In an age of organization and coöperation the educational forces must be organized and coöperate in sentiment, in purpose, and in effort.

THE JOURNAL will stand for this unification. The whole field of public education, from the Kindergarten to the University, will be treated. Its pages will offer contributions from workers in each of these departments. It is hoped that they will become indispensable to workers in each of the subdivisions of the field. But while the general plan is to cover the whole field the perspective of importance will not be overlooked. The rural schools and the city schools of lower grades because they reach most will, as heretofore, be given most attention, but the schools of higher grade will not be slighted.

Such is the program of THE JOURNAL—time, patience, hard work, and the hearty support of the friends of education are needed to carry it out. The work is worth doing and therefore must be done. "The nation which has the best schools," said the distinguished French thinker, Jules Simon, "is the first nation in the world. If it is not so today, it will be tomorrow."

THE JOURNAL invites the cöoperation of all who believe in the future of the West. Its editors can do no more than avow the faith that "the art of giving shape to human powers and adopting them to social service is the supreme art; one calling into its service the best of artists; that no insight, sympathy, tact, executive power is too great for such service. That the teacher is a social servant set apart for the maintenance of proper social order, the prophet of the true God and the usherer in of the true kingdom of God."

Dr. Martin Kellogg, ex- President of the University of California and the oldest member of its faculty of instruction, died on August 26th, after a brief illness. Prof. Kellogg served the university from its inception, forty-three years ago, as a little college in Oakland. First he was appointed professor of mathematics, in 1860. Eight years after he was made professor of ancient languages. When the work was reorganized in 1874 he became head of the Latin department, a post which he continued to fill for nineteen years, then becoming President of the University. From the burdens of this position he resigned in 1898 and was made Emeritus Professor of Latin in grateful recognition of his long and valuable services as a teacher of that subject. The duties of that position he continued to perform until stricken but a few days ago. He died literally in the harness. Perhaps no man in California has served the cause of education so faithfully. In his classes the teachers in most of our high schools were shaped, and under his leadership the State Univsrtity grew into a great city of instruction. President Kellogg was an unostentatious man, of quiet bearing and reserve which forbade him to vaunt himself in the slightest degree before his fellows. No one who did not come into close touch with his work knew, or could know, how wisely, bravely and untiringly industrious he was in planning and working for the best good of the State. Too great credit simply cannot be given him for the material upbuilding of the university.

He was a humanist of that rare and kindly sort which has

learned to separate the pure gold from the dross of human nature by listening to the spirit voices echoed from an age long gone. Hundreds of men and women will recall his unfailing, cheerful salutation and personal inquiry which always came from the heart and went to the heart. He belonged to the generation of pioneers of the commonwealth. One by one they go into the quiet land, but their works live after them.

* * *

Advance orders for over ten thousand copies of McMaster's History, state series, have been received. The history is duplicate in text and illustration of the American Book Company's edition, with the addition of a chapter on the history of California. The book is well printed and bound. The Albion paper used is most excellent for text-book purposes.

* * *

The following names should be added to the list of instructors available for institute work: Prof. T. L. Heaton, deputy superintendent of schools, San Francisco; Kate Ames, superintendent of schools, Napa county; Mrs. L. V. Sweezy, Berkeley, music.

BOOKS AND MAGAZINES

Preliminary
New books in English appear at the rate of over thirty a day, and magazines are inaccessibly plentiful. He who reads them will be kept busy. A reader with less time may profitably employ the services of a directory. That is what this department aims to become—a monthly directory of educational literature. From month to month it will publish a list of the best books upon educational subjects which have appeared. Comment upon them will be confined almost entirely to a statement of their purpose. Praising and blaming is not essential to this plan and will, it is hoped, be indulged in but infrequently. It is true, in education as in other departments of work, that the fugitive literature of the subject to be found in pamphlets, reports and magazine articles, is on the whole of greater value to the working teacher than the more modest and conservative utterances which find their way into books. Causes are not usually fought out in books. If one would catch truth in the making he must find it in the stages preceding formulation. For this reason much attention will be given to the preliminary and polemical literature of education.

* * *

English
Few teachers of English can be so confident of their unaided ability as to disregard any real help in the teaching of what is commonly regarded as the most difficult subject which falls to the lot of the schoolmaster. The help which this book offers is real and considerable. Indeed it is a sort of encyclopedia of the subject. It is the composite work of three distinguished specialists. It treats primary, secondary and college English with equal emphasis, and its bibliographies are practically exhaustive. The first division of the work is devoted to "History and Method." Its first chapter, written by Prof. Carpenter, discusses the Study of the Mother Tongue, pointing out the superior claims of the study of English to those of Latin and defining in a forceful and just manner the ends and purposes which should be sought and attained in it. Eighty-five pages of the book are assigned to the chapter on English in Elementary Ed-

(1) The Teaching of English, by C. R. Carpenter, F. F. Baker, and Fred. N. Scott. [The American Teachers' Series] Longmans, Green & Co.

ucation by Professor Baker. The various methods of teaching reading, spelling, grammar, are evaluated, and the place, kind and method of literature teaching in elementary education is ably set forth. Language is the first subject discussed in the section which treats of secondary education, language including grammar, rhetoric and composition, etc. Literature in the secondary schools is then treated and college entrance requirements in English, and the course of study next follow.

The second division of the work is on the Teacher and His Training, contributed by Prof. Scott. General and special qualifications for the work, the philosophy of the assignment and essay-correcting are the subjects discussed here.

* * *

One expects of a text-book on Literature that it will be accurate, exhaustive, instructive—even interesting. Professor Trent's book has all these qualities and more, for it has also distinct charm. For out of the mass of very necessary facts important for the student of American Literature, he has chosen with humorous good sense to place a good deal of emphasis upon what might almost be called the lighter side of life. The result quite justifies the practice, giving to the whole a particularly human and vital aspect and showing no lack on the side of knowledge because dealing with fresher views of old subjects. The chapters regarding the earlier writers from 1607 to the times of Dwight and Edwards, have a quality of their own decidedly rare. The book is by no means a chronicling of events in proper order, with equally correct quotations placed at set intervals. It has the spice of individual criticism and evidences a balance of judgment unafraid of what has been said before or may be said hereafter.

Teachers—or lay readers—who turn over, perforce, many a text book which is that simply and no more, will take a fresh breath of courage here and feel a real delight and joy in the use of so cheerful and wise and pleasant a work concerning the long unfolding of our literary growth, today so robust and vigorous a plant.

* * *

Agriculture   In April, 1901, a law was passed by the State Legislature of Minnesota requiring the introduction of the teaching of agriculture and household economics into the rural schools of the state. A liberal appropriation was made and an official text-book—the volume now in hand —prepared for the purpose. It is a series of 237 exercises of observation and experiment fully explained and easily conducted.

(1) American Literature, by William P. Trent. D. Appleton & Co.

(2) Rural School Agriculture, Willet M. Hays. (Bulletin No. 1) Dept. of Agriculture, University of Minnesota.

The purpose of these experiments is to lead rural school pupils to a deeper and more systematic knowledge of the more or less familiar facts of farm life. The work is not offered as a final or sufficient basis for the study of agriculture, which should as in Canada be conducted on a miniature farm. The experiments collected here have been selected with the greatest care and seem to be admirably adapted to the purpose of the book. As an addition to the literature of practical nature study it should have a wide circulation.

* * *

Tools

The value of this book will depend entirely upon the way in which it is used. If a teacher is satisfied to place it, instead of the tools, which it so admirably describes, in the hands of his pupils, he will have done them but an ill service. If on the other hand it be used as supplementary reading for classes that have much practice in shop work, it will be found of real service, for it describes the more common tools, tells something of their history and explains their use and care. But no teacher should use it without a prayer, "Lord, deliver my students from books that keep them away from things."

* * *

Ethics

This book professes to be an account of the virtues and their reasons, designed especially for high schools, academies and seminaries. While it has several commendable features, it is pervaded throughout by a spirit of philistinism which will be sure to antagonize the class of students for whom it has been prepared. The author writes down to his reader—an unpardonable fault in the teaching of any subject, most of all in ethics. One may indeed question whether the introduction of any text book on ethics to students of the class for which this is designed, is desirable. For ethical action is only the right doing of the ordinary acts of life, and not a superadded subject matter. All teachers must study the subject carefully and teach it in all they teach, but they ca nderive little benefit from a book defective both in form and in matter.

* * *

Pedagogy

This work is a worthy attempt to discuss and systematize current educational doctrine with a view to contributing to a broader and richer elementary education. It opens with a good discussion of the conflicting automatic and free-will theories of mind. The fundamental error, however, into which the author falls at once, is that this distinction has anything to do with the remainder of his book, or with shaping

(1) Tools and Machines, by Charles Barnard. Silver, Burdett & Co.
(2) Ethics for Schools, by Austin Bierbower. Hinds & Noble.
(3) A Broader Elementary Education, by J. P. Gordy, Ph.D., L.L.D. New York: Hinds & Noble, 1903.

educational practice. As a matter of fact, adherents to each view engage in much the same sort of practice, side by side, and produce like results, dominated largely by the ends and the spirit of their civilization. So, too, our author, after disposing of the errors of automatism, devotes himself assiduously to the *mechanics* of instruction and education.

In discussing the aim of education Mr. Gordy's efforts are directed, first, to pointing out that all educational systems inevitably reflect the purposes of the civilization in which they operate, that the democratic ideal develops the only logically consistent political form upon which a philosophy of education can be based, and that a true philosophy of education must reckon with the inalienable right of every individual to his best possible self-development. His final cast of the educational aim ("to promote the intellectual and esthetic culture, enlarge the sympathies, strengthen and purify the friendships and domestic affections, and make devotion to duty the governing principle") draws somewhat nearer to the concrete, in the discussions, than many of his predecessors. Formally modified, again, it becomes a demand for knowledge, discipline, a true estimate of the value of things, an effective will. It is to be realized in the effort to combine right and high values of living with the needs of the bread-winner and citizen. Then follows a clear and temperate discussion of the "child's capital," or the instinctive basis of education, in which he recognizes the innate as a legitimate foundation for the selective and directive functions of the teacher. Especially good is the treatment of imitation, which he seeks to rescue from the dominant position it has assumed in the minds of some and to give it one (1) of ready adaptation to environment, especially the social, (2) as a source of experience, (3) as a basis of reflective activity. Equally sound is his refusal to attribute paramount character-building powers to subject matter and formal instruction. It is personality which makes most for character. He has given a good critical treatment of what he calls the Herbartian General Method, by which he means the Formal Steps of Instruction, though his criticism is based upon the narrow interpretation of those steps. He makes a strong plea for adaptation of school work and gradation to individual needs, and for the specialization of teaching in the grammar grade for the sake of vitality and soundness of subject-matter. His discussion of the educational value of school branches is mild, but compares favorably with current discussions of this sort. The final chapter of "The Small High School" is worthy of a second reading for its aggressive stand, and because it is the only chapter in the book that does deal radically with a vital and moot issue. The author would have the small high school relieved of the dominance of tradition and adapted to practical life and citizenship and local needs.

On the whole the work is neither new, positive nor agressive, and consequently not very stimulating. It is temperate, fairly well compiled, a good work in which to make a first acquaintance with current educational thought without suffering noticeable bias. Occasionally it is troubled with logical distinctions (vide, lower immediacy, mediacy and higher immediacy, conceptions which the author goes out of his way to analyze and rename without making anw appreciable use of his terms thereafter) and it contains an expose of about all the educational blunders committed by great thinkers from Plato to Dr. Eliot and Dewey. His defense of Dr. Harris' view of reading as mental training superior to objective study is weak, (1) because, with Dr. Harris, he overlooks the fact that the double mental gymnastics disappear as soon as the recognition of symbols has become a mental process, (2) because he forgets that all image building that is connected with reading is conditioned strictly by previous observation and discrimination in the objective world. Finally the book, like most modern works of its kind, is dominated from start to finish by the dogma of general formal mental discipline.

* * *

Psychology The writer has sometimes been asked to suggest a work on psychology suitable for the lay reader. The request is usually preferred by teachers and it is exceedingly difficult to answer. The work with a good style is apt to be lacking in substance, while the books which contain the substance of psychological doctrine are almost certain to be couched in a style too profoundly soporific to be thought of for the purpose.

The editor of the Teachers' Professional Library has offered substantial help in this difficulty. Prof. Royce's "Outlines of Psychology" is intended particularly to meet the needs of studious teachers. Its style is readable, its content substantial, and its price is acceptably small.

The work is as its name indicates, a statement of principles rather than details. "I presuppose a serious reader," says the author, "but not one trained either in experimental methods, or in philosophical inquiries. I try to tell him a few things that seem to me important, regarding the most fundamental and general processes, laws, and conditions of mental life." The phenomena of mind are treated under three general heads, Sensitiveness, Docility and Initiative. The chapters on Sensitiveness deal with the elements of all experience. The chapters on Docility discuss the questions, How we acquire knowledge, and How our habits of action become moulded by our environment. The section on Initiative contains a discussion of the bases of the intellectual life. The practical charac-

Outlines of Psychology, by Josiah Royce, Ph.D., L.L.D. (Teachers' Professional Library). The Macmillan Co.

ter of the work will be apparent from this outline; besides it is full of practical applications. It is not a "pedagogical psychology" but a scientific psychology, written in such a way as to make readily accessible to teachers a deep and true knowledge of the nature which they seek to influence.

* * *

Readers who are already acquainted with the field of general psychology and are interested to become somewhat familiar with the experimental side of that science will find Professor Stratton's volume a pleasurable as well as a profitable discussion of the objects, methods and results of laboratory work. The chapters on Memory and the Influence of Time, and Imitation and Suggestion, have a very direct bearing upon mental growth.

* * *

The Elementary School Teacher

The June number of the "Elementary School Teacher" is devoted to the Laboratory School. As this school has been conducted as a pedagogical experiment station, in connection with the University of Chicago, for the last eight years, a report of results should be of general value. The first article on the Teaching of Science calls attention to the well known fact that nature study in the schools has led neither to a knowledge of facts nor of scientific method. The methods of teaching are responsible for this deplorable condition. In general they are of four sorts: First, the knot-hole method; second, the method which organizes the world of forces which play about the child on the theory that because these natural forces play about him he must be interested in and profit by learning of them; third, the Agassiz School proceeds by abstraction and formulation to underlying laws in a purely objective way. The fourth method is "evolutionary." It seeks to arouse and encourage the animistic love of nature in the hope that it will mature in a scientific interest. A more satisfactory method of science-teaching is promised in the next number.

The article which follows outlines the results of a systematic attempt to apply Froebel's ideas of the use of occupations and plays in the teaching of children more than six years old.

The next article attributes the artistic poverty of modern life to the unsatisfactory teaching of art in the schools. Art must be taught as expression and not confined to copying. A detailed discussion of the art impulse in children follows.

The teaching of music, history, cooking, textile work and literature are described each in a special article prepared by the teacher in charge. This one and the next number in which these articles are completed will be a great assistance to any working teacher who is thinking about her work.

(1) Experimental Psychology and Culture, by G. M. Stratton, Ph.D. The Macmillan Co.

The World's Work The August issue of the *World's Work* is an educational number. Beside pertinent editorials upon several educational matters, Mr. Booker T. Washington, in a well illustrated article, tells the story of "The Successful Training of the Negro." President Taylor of Vassar writes on "The Education of Women." Prof. Frederick J. Turner contributes "The Democratic Education of the Middle West," locating the distinguishing feature of the higher education of that region in the state university, which is doing more than any other institution to elevate the whole body of the people to a higher intellectual life. The keynote of the present educational situation is struck in the statement that the state university of a democracy could be carried to as high a point of efficiency as the state university of a monarchy.

The thesis, "Farmer Children Need Farmer Studies," is advocated by Mr. C. H. Poe. At present the entire course of study leads away from the farm. School arithmetic, geography, penmanship, bookkeeping and reading are all dominated by the clerk and trading point of view. The teaching might even seem to be undertaken to create discontent with country life. Arithmetic need not expound the problems of banking to the exclusion of those of agriculture. A right point of view might be developed in all the studies, but agricultural studies are so cryingly important that they must be taught in the public schools also. President Hyde's address before the N. E. A. on "The Year's Educational Progress" is reproduced and President Eliot's "New Definition of the Cultivated Man" follows. Prof. M. V. O'Shea discusses "The Right Physical Start in Education." Careful investigations have shown that at least twenty per cent. of school children have some defect which handicaps them in their work. Thirty to fifty per cent. of the pupils may be expected to exhibit visual defects; eighteen to thirty per cent auditory defects. Eighteen per cent. of the school children of Madison, Wis., were found to be "mouth breathers," owing to the baneful presence of adenoid tissue. Perhaps more than 80 per cent. suffer from bad teeth. Mental work cannot be carried on under these conditions. Medical inspection is absolutely necessary. Organizations of citizens must help teachers to accomplish the needed reform.

# WESTERN SCHOOL NEWS

MEETINGS

California Teachers' Association, O. W. Erlewine, president; Mrs. M. M. FitzGerald, secretary, 1627 Folsom street, San Francisco; December 28 to 31, 1903.

TEACHERS' INSTITUTES

Humboldt County Teachers' Institute, September 14-18. Supt. Geo. S. Underwood.
Contra Costa county, A. A. Bailey, supt. Martinez, Sept. 8, 10, 11.
Del Norte, Mrs. A. M. Leishman, supt. Crescent city, Sept. 28, 29, 30.
Kings county, Mr. N. E. DaVidson, supt. Hanford, Dec. 21, 22, 23.
Mendocino, J. F. Barbee, supt. Ukiah, Oct. 27, 28, 29.
Modoc, Nellie Forest, supt. Alturas, Sept. 30, Oct. 1, 2, 3.
Plumas, Tillie Naomi Kruger, supt. Quincy, Oct. 7, 8, 9.
Sacramento, B. F. Howard, Supt. Nov. 23, 24, 25.
San Joaquin, E. B. Wright, supt. Stockton, Nov. 23, 24, 25.
Santa Barbara, Supt. W. S. Edwards. Santa Barbara, Oct. 5, 6, 7, 8.
Siskiyou, Grace Addis Johnson, supt. Shasta Retreat, Sept. 26, 28, 29, 30.

NOTES

Edgar T. Boughn, formerly of Riverside county, has been elected principal of the schools of Martinez.

The San Francisco Teachers' Club organized for 1903 and 1904, August 11th, with A. L. Mann as president.

Several of Dr. Frederic Burk's papers on pedagogy have been translated in Czech for the use of Bohemian teachers.

H. N. Caldwell, formerly of the Lompoc High School, has been elected principal of the Oakdale Union High School.

The city board of Los Angeles is making a special effort to carry out the provisions of the compulsory education law.

Ex-Superintendent J. A. Imrie of Napa county has been elected to a position in the San Francisco School Department.

The board of education of San Francisco has adopted a resolution requiring children to have their eyes and ears tested.

Ex-Superintendent Graves of Tehama county has been elected principal of the Corning school at a salary of $150 per month.

Five of the male graduates Class of 1903 of the State Normal School of Los Angeles have been elected to good principalships.

The board of education of Fresno has made a general raise in the salary of the teachers from Superintendent McLane to grade teachers.

The text-book board of Arizona adopted the Progressive Course in Reading. The Sprague Readers were adopted as supplementary.

Superintendent W. H. Langdon has inaugurated special teachers' meetings in the San Francisco School Department, with T. L. Heaton and A. H. Suzzalo as leaders in charge.

Prof. W. S. Holway, formerly of the State Normal School of San Jose, is now instructor in the department of theory and practice of education, University of California.

Prof. Bernard Moses, on his return from the Phillipines, delivered at the University of California an address on the educational work the United States is doing in the Islands.

The Board of Education of Los Angeles County has adopted a new course of study. The most noticeable change is the return from the vertical to the slant system of writing.

H. E. Miller, the man who attained considerable newspaper publicity in securing his diploma for the State Normal School at San Jose, has been elected principal of the Yuma schools.

The Sonoma County Board of Education has adopted rules establishing a standard of professional ethics. The Board has already tried a delinquent teacher under its rules and with good effect.

Charles C. Hughes, city superintendent of Alameda schools, has resigned to accept the management of the Pacific Coast Agency of Silver, Burdett & Co. Fred. T. Moore has been elected to succeed him at Alameda.

Miss Mae Streeter, deputy superintendent of Fresno county, has resigned, and Mrs. G. M. Freeman has been appointed in her place. The county board of education presented Miss Streeter with an elegant cut glass service.

Prof. Schafer of State Normal School, San Diego, has been elected president of the State Normal School, Cheney, Washington. Frank H. Thompson, formerly of San Francisco State Normal School, will succeed him at San Diego.

The district attorney of Tehama county has ruled that the county board of education of Tehama county is not a legal body, because the law requires at least one member hold a high school certificate. All the members hold grammar grade certificates.

Would'nt you like to go to the great Exposition at St. Louis next year? An absolutely free trip is offered ten teachers in each county of California. A postal will bring full information. Address, J. W. Graham, Associate Western Manager The Playa Viciente Plantation Company, 723 Market street, San Francisco, Cal.

County School Superintendent Mark Keppel has announced the appointment of Prof: M. A. Tucker as principal of the Wilmington Union High School and Prof. J. T. Anderson principal of the Norwalk Excelsior Union High School. These are the high schools that was organized not long ago. They will open Sept. 14 for fall term.—Los Angeles Times.

We, the students of the Augsburg Summer School of Drawing of 1903, desire hereby to express our appreciation of our beloved and efficient teacher. We have enjoyed every day of the session and every branch of the work, and we are of one sentiment in declaring that never has the subject of Drawing been presented to us in so interesting and clear a manner.

We shall take with us not only enthusiasm and inspiration, but the memory of a most beautiful example in gentleness, unselfishness and simplicity.

Lura Manning, Azu*; Mary E. Curtis, Visalia; Louise Foundeen, Proberta; Jeanette Scott, Selma; Ellen A. Cockefair, Dekoto; Anna L. Wells, San Jose; Frances S. Cooper, Haywards; Frances S. Woolsey, Fulton; Blanche McNeal, Winters; Florence C. Webber, Walla Walla, Wash.; Mary A. Huggins, Berkeley; Emma Turner, Howe; Maggie Hennessy, Stockton; Maude M. Green, Yuba; Lena M. Harry, New Almaden; E. Montgomery, Dinuba; Lillian Gibson, Haywards; Nellie E. Walubence, Bolinas; Elsie Sinclair, Oakland; Mary Kallenberger, N. Bloomfield; Anna B. Nelson, Visalia; Lida C. Clark, San Jose; Eliza Howell, Visalia; May Barnes, Orosi; Ella Monroe, San Francisco; Jeannette S. Bryan, Lemoore; Estelle Baker, Redlands; Georgina Cooper, Nevada City; Ella H. Palmer, Azusa.

* * *

SCHOOL BOARD TYRANNY

Professor Keppel, superintendent of the county schools of Los Angeles, strikes at a species of depotism that is growing up in the public schools, in this paragraph of his annual report:

"There is a general and growing tendency to diminish the freedom of the teacher. Trustees impose conditions, as for example, remaining unmarried, living in the district, boarding with a trustee, summary dismissal, etc.—conditions that seem good to the trustee, but which are irksome and harmful to teachers. Teachers should be required to live honorable lives and to do good teaching; and beyond those requirements they should be free."

It is good to see an experienced male teacher protesting against a system of social tyranny of which women are the chief victims. School boards all over the State have put wifehood and motherhood under ban by making marriage a capital offense calling for discharge. No one has the right to forbid marriage to another. The prohibition promulgated by school boards invades the most sacred of human rights. It is unknown to the law and unsanctioned by public policy. It is based upon the exercise of arbitrary power, which the law never intended to confer.

School boards have no more right to dictate where a teacher shall eat and sleep than they have to dictate where he shall get shaved or his clothes washed, or what church he shall worship in. Requiring the teacher to board with one of the trustees is a sort of petty "grafting." It is a selection under compulsion, is not contemplated by law, and is opposed to public policy. It is repugnant to every sentiment of fair play, and opposed to the free exercise of the most fundamental rights.—*Oakland Tribune*.

The State Text-Book Committee adopted at a recent meeting Thomas' Elementary History, published by D. C. Heath & Co., at a royalty of 15 cents per copy.

THE
WESTERN JOURNAL
OF EDUCATION

October, 1903

	PAG
EDITORIAL	66
Text-Books—Professional Ethics—University Graduates in Ungraded Schools—Compulsory Attendance—The Batavia System.	
CALIFORNIA EDUCATIONAL EXHIBIT AT LOUISIANA PURCHASE EXPOSITION	66
THE APPRECIATION AND INTERPRETATION OF POETRY IN THE PUBLIC SCHOOLS, *Herbert Bashford* . .	67
CARE AND TRAINING OF CHILDREN, *James A. Foshay* .	68
EDUCATION OF PEOPLE IN PEACE, *Warner Van Orden* . .	68
THE CALIFORNIA SCHOLIA CLUB	68
DEPARTMENT OF METHODOLOGY - - - -	68
A New Method in Long Division—Products of California—Topics in Geography for Special Study—Geography.	
BOOKS AND MAGAZINES	69
WESTERN SCHOOL NEWS	70
ADVERTISING DEPARTMENT	71

THE WESTERN JOURNAL OF EDUCATION
723 MARKET ST., SAN FRANCISCO

Volume VIII
No. 10

$1.50 Per Year
Single Copy 15c

Four New Books by California Authors

SIMMS'S CHILD LITERATURE — — — 30 cents
By Mae Henion Simms

This is the latest addition to the well-known and popular series of Eclectic School Readings, and is intended for First Reader grades. Its distinctive feature consists in its method of presenting attractive nursery rhymes and stories, popular poems, and Bible stories, simplified and told in short, easy words. The rhymes are afterward repeated in their original form. New words are naturally and gradually introduced, and the gradation of the matter is easy and well-maintained throughout. Written by a teacher in the Stockton, Cal., schools, it is the outcome of work done there and was thoroughly tested in the classroom before publication. The book is profusely illustrated, and will be welcomed by the many California teachers who feel the need of fresh and interesting reading matter for younger pupils.

"*I heartily approve of Mrs. Simms's new book, Child Literature. My faith will be shown by a liberal use of the book.*"
JAMES A. BARR,
Superintendent of Schools, Stockton, Cal.

WINTERBURN'S THE SPANISH IN THE
SOUTHWEST   55 cents
By Rosa V. Winterburn

The discovery and early history of California are in this book vividly and attractively presented for young readers. Commencing with the life of the Indians, it takes up next the coming of the Spaniards, then their explorations in search of gold, the founding of the missions, and the life on the pueblos and the ranches. The book brings the history down to the end of the Mexican rule in 1848. The narrative element and the purely historical are so skillfully combined as to make this book a story of history, a collection of stories so selected and arranged as to present historical characteristics and tendencies of periods. The style is adapted both to the subject-matter and to the age of the pupils for whom the book is intended. The illustrations are numerous and artistic and maps show the places mentioned.

CHAMBERLAIN'S FIELD AND LABORATORY EXERCISES
IN PHYSICAL GEOGRAPHY   50 cents
By James F. Chamberlain, Department of Geography, State Normal School, Los Angeles, Cal., Associate Editor of "The Journal of Geography."

This is a series of laboratory and field exercises designed to lead the pupil to interpret the geographical forms and processes about him, and to give him a practical knowledge of their principles. Each exercise is preceded by a list of necessary materials, which are easily obtainable. After each exercise ample space is left for the pupil to write a complete record of the work done. An important feature of the book is the plan for studying the geographical distribution of various phenomena, and plotting the data on outline maps of the United States and of the world, which are inserted. The manual is adapted for use with any text-book on Physical Geography, and will form a valuable adjunct for practical work.

COLEMAN'S PHYSICAL LABORATORY MANUAL   60 cents
By S. E. Coleman, Head of the Science Department, Oakland, Cal., High School.

In this manual the laboratory work is co-ordinated with the classroom study, and comprises 81 exercises, so arranged that the book can be used either with simple apparatus, or with a more fully equipped laboratory. The matter in connection with each experiment consists of (1) A definite statement of what the experiment is for; (2) References to leading text-books in physics, indicating what reading may profitably precede and accompany the laboratory work; (3) A list of the apparatus required; (4) Directions, suggestions, form of record, and discussion of the experiment. The book is the outgrowth of practical work, and shows throughout that it was prepared by a skillful teacher.

AMERICAN BOOK COMPANY Publishers
204 Pine Street, San Francisco.

New York   Cincinnati   Chicago   Boston   Atlanta   Dallas

The Western Journal of Education

OCTOBER, 1903

EDITORIAL

Text-Books
It is an important part that the text-book plays in our actual systems of education. Yet our pedagogical literature is strangely deficient in any adequate discussion of the make-up of such texts. What in general are the essentials of a good text-book? is a question worth asking and worth answering. And it may well be followed with more specific inquiries: What constitutes a good text-book in the history of the United States for the upper grammar grades? What is needed in a series of school geographies? And so on through the list.

Such questions as these cannot now be called "academic" in California, for the State is making a new and vigorous effort to get a good series of texts for use in the common schools. It seems likely, too, that we can get what we want if we know what we want. It is easy to say that we want the best, but how is the State Text-Book Committee or any one else to know what is the best? Any one who has any real light to throw upon this subject should lend his little lamp to the State Text-Book Committee. They are ready to welcome suggestions from any who know whereof they speak, and particularly from such as are actually teaching in the grades and in the country schools.

To know what we want in text-books we must know what we want in education. This is obvious. It may not be so obvious, but is equally true that to know what we want in text-books we must know what the actual text-books now available have to offer. It is only by a comparison of the best books now in use that one can appreciate fully the conflict of educational ideals which is going on in the domain of the several subjects taught in our schools. To read the claims put forth by the publishers of different books and compare these claims with the results of schoolroom experience is one way of defining a standard of excellence in the texts of any subject. Some help may be got from the book reviews of the better educational periodicals; but these reviews generally show the lack, already referred to, of any well-thought-out conception of what a good book should contain.

Two admirable studies in text-books have been published, which will serve to illustrate what we need in this pedagogical field. Dr.

Rudolph R. Reeder's monograph on *The Historical Development of School Readers and of Method in Teaching Reading* (Columbia University Contributions to Philosophy, Psycholgy and Education, vol. 8, no. 2, May, 1900, pp. 92) does not undertake any general survey of the series of school readers now in use. But it offers an indispensable introduction to the subject for any one who would make such a survey. The report on *Text-books in American History* prepared by the standing committee on text-books of the New England History Teachers' Association (*Educational Review*, vol. 16, pp. 480-502, December, 1898) compares some of the best available texts with reference to fairly definite but by no means rigid standards of excellence. This report was consulted with profit by some of those who had to do with the selection of a new history text for the grammar schools of California.

The California State Text-Book Committee is now proceeding in a systematic way to discover what we want in text-books in geography and arithmetic, and then if possible to get it. It is a difficult task to select and compile the text material which shall be used in many widely different schools, scattered over a great State, and taught by teachers of very different tastes and talents. In this undertaking the Committee should have, as it seems to have had thus far, the cordial co-operation of the teaching force of the State.

Professional Ethics

From time to time teachers' institutes have discussed the subject of professional or, rather, unprofessional, conduct. There seems always to be teachers ready to speak vigorously and feelingly on the subject, and at times resolutions are passed condemning certain indefinitely described practices which are supposedly characteristic of many teachers. It is usually argued that the professional courtesy commonly observed among lawyers and physicians should be equally the practice among teachers.

Why does not the action of teachers in this matter reach farther than institute talk and resolutions? If teachers are really in favor of more professional courtesy and believe in the punishment of unprofessional conduct, it is in their power to bring it about. County boards are controlled by teachers and these boards are of tremendous power through their control of certification.

The uncertainty of position and the low annual salaries of teachers make it necessary for their future welfare that there be a revival of professional spirit which will demand the enactment of regulations controlling the actions of thoughtless or unprincipled teachers and determining their punishment for violation of these regulations.

The California Teachers' Association and the Council of Education, at their meeting in 1901, adopted two resolutions which might well be made the beginning of a code of professional ethics for the teachers of California. These resolutions have not received the attention they deserve, and, so far as we know, they have had little effect upon the administrative powers.

The Sonoma County Board of Education last June took decided action in favor of professional spirit. This action followed the adoption of the resolutions by the county institute, which had been affirmed by the State Teachers' Association. The Sonoma County Board's resolution covered more ground, however. Their resolutions were as follows:

First—"It shall constitute *unprofessional conduct* for any one holding a teachers' certificate to submit any argument or plea in obtaining or retaining a position, other than those constituting evidences of professional competency; or knowingly to permit any other person in behalf of the applicant to do that which is defined above as unprofessional conduct on the part of the applicant."

Second—"It shall constitute unprofessional conduct for any one holding a teacher's certificate to seek a position which is not legally vacant or definitely known to become vacant at a specified time."

Third—"It shall constitute unprofessional conduct for any one holding a teacher's certificate to leave a position without the consent of the Board of Trustees concerned, until sufficient notice has been given; and if the teacher holds under a contract, either written or implied, the consent of the trustees must be secured."

These resolutions seem to have met hearty approval from the teachers and trustees. This board has given evidence that they are not intending to allow the resolutions to be considered idle words. Only a few days after their adoption a teacher was summoned before them and reprimanded for attempting to secure a position already promised to the incumbent.

The schools of our State need a greater permanency in teachers' appointments. The frequent changes are quite as much due to the teachers as to the trustees. The checking of the efforts of teachers to secure the positions of others and the enforcement of agreements and contracts will do much toward securing the continuance of good teachers in the positions they occupy.

University Graduates in Ungraded Schools

How many University graduates have taken ungraded country schools this year? "Few or none," is what most of the superintendents report. And pity 'tis tis true; pity for the young teachers and pity for the state. The young graduate needs the experience of life that the little rural school gives—the contact with children of all ages, the teaching of different branches, the mingling with all the people in their homes. And the people of the state need to come into close contact with the enlarged outlook and higher culture that the universities should give. Neither of these ends is served when the brilliant, specialized student passes direct from his university in the teaching of his one specialty to a special group of students in a big high school. He knows his own piece of music; but he doesn't know the great human harp upon which he must play it. There are so many, many things never dreamed of in his philosophy. He is so apt to become narrow and hidebound. He needs a dip in the broad sea of humanity, outside the limits of his one little pool.

The universities themselves recognize this and urge their graduate teachers to take a turn at the country schools; but when high school places are plentiful, with higher salaries than the rural schools can offer, such advice is apt to fall on deaf ears. How would it be to give the graduates of accredited universities grammar school certificates only, until they have had one or two years' experience?

* * *

Probably the very best teachers in our country today are college-trained men and women who have had an all round experience after leaving college. One who is preparing seriously for high success in the profession of teaching ought to consider a few years in the common schools as a part of his education, a "P. G. Course," as it were; and he ought not to be withheld by a few dollars difference in salary or by the greater ease of swimming with the current in his own special hobby.

* * *

It is a fine piece of experience, to tackle a difficult rural school. We have in mind a university girl whose school we chanced to visit last year. It was a hard, sodden, tough school, too, one that had been the despair of more than one pedagog.

But she was equal to the situation. She was so dainty and

fresh in her blue dress and white apron, so sprightly and spirited in manner, eye and gesture, so alert and quick in getting around —that it was a treat to watch her. She had resources, intensity, dynamic force, that were too much for those youngsters to stand up against. Everything went smoothly on. One big boy gave signals for marching; another opened the windows; a girl played the organ—somehow, the responsibility had been placed on them so that they liked to do it—the teacher apparently paid no attention, but all went on orderly and well. The point is this: this young graduate was having a pretty good time. She was doing the state good by brightening that rural community. She was preparing herself for greater usefulness as the highest type of the educated, cultivated teacher. She was doing better in everyway than to have gone direct to the teaching of third year Latin in the high school.

* * *

Compulsory Attendance

The last legislature passed a bill intended to guarantee to each child of California his right to the elements of an English education. The governor signed the bill making it a law. As yet almost nothing has been done anywhere in the state to put it into effect. Oakland and Los Angeles have appointed attendance officers, but their conduct was rather good before the law was passed. The worst sinner in the state, the community of San Francisco, has done nothing as yet to comply with the suggestions of this law, tho near 10,000 children of school age are not attending school there.

In the first place every child in the state has a right to attend school—a right which he will one day be keenly conscious of. In the second place no parent in the community has a right to deprive his child of this inalienable privilege, for the pupils belong to the state rather than to their parents. The legislature has attempted to throw a safeguard about the child. It is the duty of school boards thruout the state to assist in this matter. It is poor economy not to have all the children in school. The tax is distributed to them, the buildings are built for them, the teachers are hired for them. The state cannot afford to have them absent. Cannot afford it, not merely because the plant is thereby prevented from doing the work it was built for, but much more, because of the expensive lessons which they are learning in absentia. No family in this commonwealth is so poor as to require the children to support their parents. The state has said, and every state in the Union has said, that no matter how poor they may be they shall at least have this advantage.

It is time for carelessness to end, time for the debasing of the young to end, time for the stream of youths to stop flowing to Whittier and Ione, time for the work which was begun to proceed.

* * *

The Batavia System

For several years a system of instruction has been in operation in the public schools of the town of Batavia, in central New York, which offers a solution for one of the most serious problems that the rapid growth of our public school system has produced. In the necessarily large classes of graded schools the task of getting the whole class over a specified amount of ground in each subject without having many of the pupils fall far behind is often an impossible one for the teacher. The remedy proposed and carried into effect by Superintendent John Kennedy, of the Batavia public schools, is simply to put an extra teacher into a crowded room, "not to hear classes, but to give personal, individual instruction to the pupils who are falling behind." The experiment met with startling and instantaneous success in the one room in which it was at first tried. The teacher found that within a very short time the weak spots in her class were becoming the strong spots. The more backward children began to improve in scholarship with wonderful rapidity, and before very long to catch up with the brighter ones. In many cases they were even surpassing them, so that the leaders of the class found it all that they could do to keep up with the "dull" scholars. There are now seven individual instructors employed in the Batavia schools, one teacher in many cases going from room to room. In some cases, where the rooms are not overcrowded, one teacher acts both as class instructor and as individual instructor. The "individual" teachers are not regarded as assistant or under teachers in any sense, and they receive the same salaries as the class teachers of the same grade. The testimony of teachers, parents, and scholars is unanimous that the "Batavia system" is a success. Many authorities on educational subjects who have investigated the Batavia schools testify that a revolution has been accomplished. One says, "There cannot be found in America a healthier, happier, busier lot of pupils than are today in the public schools of Batavia. Teachers are equally well and happy. The scheme of individual instruction is so simple and practicable that it could easily be followed in every city in the country." A prominent English educator says, "These methods will revolutionize the schools of England."—*The Outlook*

CALIFORNIA EDUCATIONAL EXHIBIT AT LOUISIANA PURCHASE EXPOSITION

Robert Furlong, Chief, Department of Education.
Advisory Board—Thomas J. Kirk, Superintendent of Public Instruction; Dr. Elmer E. Brown, University of California; James A. Barr, City Superintendent Schools, Stockton; James A. Foshay, City Superintendent Schools, Los Angeles; Sam'l T. Black, President State Normal, San Diego.

To Public and Private Schools in California: As has been announced, California will have an educational exhibit next year at the Louisiana Purchase Exposition. Side by side with similar exhibits from other states and from foreign countries, California will display such material as may best illustrate the different phases of educational effort in her schools.

The material must come chiefly from the schools themselves. Historical monographs and official records will show the development of school systems and of institutions, but it is believed that the work of pupils will best represent education as it is in our state today.

The schools of California, public and private, are invited to have a part in the making of this proposed exhibit. This circular, addressed to all schools and institutions of learning in the state, is for the purpose of suggesting some material suitable for an exhibit, also the plan and the regulations that have been adopted.

MATERIAL.

All work from schools, whether of pupils in elementary classes, or of students in higher grades or institutions, should be a faithful representation of the curriculum.

It should comprise a series of lessons extending, if possible, thru a month, a term, or a year, in any study pursued, and should show (1) purpose, (2) method, and (3) results.

Such work of pupils may be literary, scientific, mechanical and artistic. When honestly prepared and intelligently labeled, it may be made to represent the work of a school with considerable clearness and fidelity.

Bound volumes of work arranged by years or grades, and illustrating fully the curriculum, are the solid, scientific and indispensable portions of an exhibit.

Graphic charts, maps of school grounds, models of school buildings in paper, cardboard, papier mache or other material, photographs of interiors and of exteriors of schoolhouses, of classes at work, freehand drawing, color work, map drawing, mechanical drawing, illustrations, nature study outlines, distribution charts, etc., are all suitable material for an educational exhibit.

Specimens of students' work in physics, chemistry, biology and the higher mathematics, of laboratory experiments, of art work, etc., are valuable as material from secondary schools and academies.

The results of manual training are appropriate in an exhibit of pupils' work.

Other material will suggest itself to schools. It is not here intended to restrict originally in exhibitors as to material. Those things that are distinctive of education in California should be emphasized. With all material mere quantity should be subordinated to variety and excellence of work.

PLAN.

Two forms of exhibit are included in the plan adopted.

CLASS A.

A general exhibit of (1) the state public schools at large; (2) the State Public School System.

CLASS B.

Distinctive or individual exhibits, as of (1) a city; (2) a county; (3) a private school system; (4) a single educational institution; (5) miscellaneous.

Exhibit material for Class A, carefully arranged, is to be submitted to this department unbound and unmounted. When approved by this Department it will be bound and mounted at the expense of the Commission.

Exhibitors of material in Class B must, at their own expense, prepare their exhibits ready to be installed—that is to say, material submitted must be bound uniformly as in books or albums, mounted on cardboards of standard size, in frames or in swing-leaf cabinets, and otherwise prepared in accordance with the uniform regulations hereafter stated.

REGULATIONS.

In preparing material a few specific directions must be

strictly followed. These are necessary for uniformity in the exhibit.

Flat exhibits (charts, drawings, photographs, botanical specimens, kindergarten work, etc.) will be shown in wall frames, wall cabinets, on mats or on cardboard. The standard dimensions of cards will be 22x28 inches, *the latter dimensions being vertical.* It is recommended that all cardboard used for this purpose be of a court gray color. Photographs for albums or for wall cabinets should be either 8x10 inches or 11x14 inches, and should be mounted directly on the full-sized cardboard.

WRITTEN WORK.

(1) Pupils' work should be written on paper 8x10 inches in size, except in the subjects of drawing and botany.

(2) The paper should be of a good grade, and at the left of each sheet a margin of 1¼ inches should be left for binding. Three-fourths inch margin is recommended on the other side. Pupils may write on one or both sides of the sheet, at the option of the teacher, care being taken to preserve the binding margin. Only the best ink should be used in preparing written work.

(3) In drawing, and in mounting botanical specimens, the standard sizes of paper may be used (22x28) and the same margin should be left as noted above.

(4) At the top of the first sheet of each pupil's work should be written the name, age and grade of the pupil, also of school, whether rural, village or city, public, private or denominational.

(5) Only regular class work is desired. As a suggestion, it is recommended that the first draft of the work by the pupil, with the teacher's corrections in different colored ink or pencil, be followed by an "improved" draft embodying the corrections. Volumes of selected work in any subject may be shown, provided its nature is fully set forth.

(6) Wherever the subject demands it, a single set of questions, neatly written or printed, should precede the answer papers in each subject. The answers should be numbered to correspond, but the questions are not to be copied on their answer papers.

(7) The written work in each subject should be preceded by a "Teacher's Statement" blank carefully filled out. Sample blanks will be furnished by this Department upon application from city or county superintendents.

(8) The work of one grade in one subject should be arranged for binding by itself.

(9) A photograph of the class as a frontispiece to each volume would add greatly to its interest.

DIRECTIONS AND SUGGESTIONS.

Superintendents are requested to direct the preparation and selection of exhibit material in their respective counties and cities. In this work they should have the assistance of boards of education, or of committees of teachers.

A copy of the course of study should accompany each separate exhibit, as of city or county.

So far as possible every phase of education suggested in the course of study should be represented.

It should be borne in mind that the material is more to illustrate the lines of work followed in the schools than to show excellence of pupils. This suggests that a bulky exhibit is not necessary; nor is it desirable, since space is limited.

SPACE.

The amount of space that will be assigned to any one exhibit, as of an institution or of a city, cannot be determined until all intended exhibitors have applied. Applications for space made after October 10th cannot be considered.

RURAL SCHOOLS.

It is desirable that the rural schools as well as town and village schools be well represented in the general exhibit. It is suggested as one attraction of a separate county exhibit that the work of a single typical rural school of one teacher, having all the elementary grades, be kept intact as a special feature.

County superintendents are urged to have the schools under their supervision select suitable material in conformity with the course of study. Especially is it requested that rural schools prepare such descriptive matter in writing, drawing, or object form as will best tell of their locality, its physical features, soil, climate, products, and the occupations of its people.

A large mass of material from the schools of a county is not desired. Select material from typical schools is what is wanted. It should pass the inspection of the superintendent and his associates before shipment to this department. One or two sets of papers from each grade in each study pursued, thru a series of lessons or a term, will suffice both to illustrate the course and show quality of work in a school.

So far as practicable the material from a county will be kept intact in Class A. A separate county exhibit can be made under the provisions of Class B. Public school exhibitors in Class B are requested also to contribute material to the general exhibit of Class A.

KINDERGARTEN.

An exhibit from this class of schools, such as would show scientific educational foundations and also give a detailed statement of the gifts, games, songs, etc., used in the course, will be encouraged. An illustration of this earliest phase of school effort in our state system will beautify and otherwise add to the general display, which, without it, will be incomplete.

Technical Schools, Manual Training Schools and other institutions of learning-having industrial training as the *distinctive feature* of their courses, are invited to have a representation in the exhibit. Material from such schools form an attractive feature in a display. Quantity of material must be limited, however, because of space limitations. Finished products of the handiwork of students will not so well illustrate the work as will material showing a series of progressive lessons by which skill has been developed.

Commercial or Business Schools are requested to make a display of material that will show the educational lines followed in their courses.

Private schools, academies, parochial schools, convents, and other denominational schools are all invited to participate in the exhibit, under the conditions previously stated.

BINDING.

The less expensive forms of binding, such as cloth, leatherette, boards, buckram, etc., will be approved. Fancy bindings, such as Russia leather, morocco, embossed-gilt, etc., will not be accepted. "Jewels appear brightest in plain settings." Uniformity is desirable in this matter.

CABINETS.

The swing-leaf cabinet appears to be a convenient device for presenting much material in a compact form, where it may be readily seen.

All special devices, including cabinets used for exhibiting material, will be subject to the approval of this department, as will also single exhibits as a whole, under Class B.

PACKING.

Material for the exhibit should not be rolled or folded, but should be carefully packed flat in the boxes or packages in which it is to be shipped.

FREIGHT.

All freight charges by rail or steamer will be paid by the Commission. All material used in the exhibit will be returned without cost to the owner, after the close of the Exposition.

Material may be shipped at any time during November, and not later than December 20th.

Address boxes to Department of Education, Louisiana Purchase Exposition, San Francisco, Cal.

EXPENSE.

There is practically no expense to exhibitors in Class A except for the simple item of school stationery. Exhibitors in Class B, having the privilege of a separate and distinct display of their own, must fit their material ready for installation, as has been explained. This expense will be moderate. The installing and caring for material at St. Louis will be done at the expense of the Commission.

It is believed that communities and institutions of learning will have sufficient pride, and boards of education sufficient interest, in having their respective schools participate in this great international display, that they will cheerfully bear the expense incident thereto.

Intended exhibitors should inform this Department at an early date of the nature and extent of their exhibit and approximately of the amount of the space needed.

In conclusion it may be said that, so far as an exhibit of the kind herein outlined reflects education in a state, the schools of California will next year be placed in comparison with the schools of the world. Every person connected with the work of education in this state should feel the responsibility. We must not, thru indifference, suffer in the comparison. Let us, thru honest effort, at least, sustain the high reputation that our schools now enjoy.

ROBT. FURLONG,
Chief Department of Education for California.

Approved:
Educational Advisory Board.
Approved:
California Louisiana Purchase Exposition Commission.
E. B. WILLIS, Secretary.

THE APPRECIATION AND INTERPRETATION OF POETRY IN THE PUBLIC SCHOOLS

It has been said by an eminent critic that the appreciation of poetry is entirely a matter of temperament; that it appeals to those people who possess a peculiar sensitive and emotional organism.

Certain it is that the man or woman who fails to see any beauty in the common things of field and sky cannot appreciate poetry in its highest form. I do not mean that to become a lover of verse one should make a scientific study of God's handiwork. Heaven forbid! If anything could possibly tear to fragments the airy creations of the poet it would be the study of science. In this connection you may recall Edgar Allen Poe's oft-quoted lines which make my ideas clearer in this regard than I myself could possibly express them:

"Science."

Science! True daughter of old time thou are!
Who alterest all things with thy peering eyes!
Why prayest thou then upon the poet's heart.
Vulture, whose wings are dull realities!
How should we love thee or deem thee wise
Who would'st not leave him in his wanderings
To seek for treasure in the jeweled skies
Albeit he soared with an undaunted wing?
Hast thou not dragged Diana from her car
And driven the Homadryad from the wood
To seek a shelter in some happier star
Hast thou not torn the Niad from her flood,
The elfin from the green grass and from me.
The summer dream beneath the tamarind tree?

Science, "whose wings are dull realities," never soars into the etherial realm of the imagination nor gives to "airy nothing a local habitation and a name." It keeps as close to facts as did Dr. Squeers. It analyzes and dissects after the manner of the novel of realism. It plants its feet firmly upon the earth and guesses at nothing. It deals with the real. It adheres strictly to mathematical calculation. The scientist says "two and two make four;" that a lily is "an endogenous bulbous plant having six stamens and a superior three celled ovary." The poet observes the lily and says "what thoughts the lily speaks in white." The poet sees deeper than the scientist. He sees the spiritual unity which underlies all and which manifests itself in nature—the loftiest function that nature, as related to man can have—the aesthetic and moral function.

The scientist may have a correct and rational comprehension of the parts that air and vapor, sky and earth, rock and trees, river and plants play as components of natural landscape; but after all, landscape must appeal for the truest and most elevating function— that of beauty— to other faculties than the understanding. Wordsworth's lines—

> "A primrose by a river's brim
> A yellow primrose was to him,
> And it was nothing more,"

illustrates this failure of one to discern the spiritual essence of things without which an appreciation of nature, as interpreted by the poet, is impossible. To appreciate poetry and to interpret its meaning it is essential that the pupil should be taught to observe the wonders of earth and sky, and while few may find, as did Wordsworth, who possessed the poet's mind, that the meanest "flower that blows can often give thoughts that lie too deep for tears," they will thru observation gain a deeper insight into the underlying soul of things. We may look on the plain material side of the great out-of-doors and a pine tree will ever remain a pine tree until an interpreter tells us that its "poet heart knows naught but melody," and having listened to its wild, sweet songs we see that the tree now possesses a rarer attribute, a greater worth and an added beauty. Of course, science steps in and says, "Impossible." A pine tree is inanimate. It knows nothing of melody. What you hear is simply the sound of the wind through its branches."

Nevertheless, the pine tree is somehow nearer and dearer to us since Taylor has said it is a "voice for every sky" and has been clothed in a personality by the poet. To make this study of nature effective teachers themselves must not only be keen observers of landscape, but they must read the best interpretations of nature, that they may be able to point out to their pupils the poetic beauty, the deep spiritual significance of the sunrise and sunset, of night and noon, of sea and sky and all the innumerable ways by which the Creator reveals himself to mankind. "Through nature up to nature's God is the only way by which we are able to ascend the holy heights.

Carlyle wrote: "There is a majesty and mystery in Nature, take her as you will. The essence of poetry comes breathing to a mind that feels from every province of her Empire," and a great German poet has said that if we have "no love for nature the earth will present a pitiful appearance, and in that case the sun is merely so many miles in diameter, the trees are good for fuel, flowers are classified by stamens and water is simply wet." "What are these maples and beeches and birches but odes and idyls and madrigals?" said Oliver Wendell Homes.

> "The earth is crammed with Heaven
> And every common bush afire with God."

It is to find "books in running brooks, sermons in stones, and good in everything" that an appreciation of poetry through nature-study should be cultivated in youth as in the molding of character it leads to purity and gentleness.

Now, what is poetry? Steadman, our greatest living authority, defines it in these words: "Poetry is poetry because it differs from prose; it is artificial, and gives us pleasure because we know it to be so; it is beautiful though expressed in rhythmical form, not half expressed or uttered in the form of prose; it is a metaphorical structure, a spirit not disembodied, but in the flesh, so as to affect the senses of living men." William Cullen Bryant said: "Poetry is that art which selects and arranges the symbols of thought in such a manner as to excite it the most powerfully and delightfully." There have been many other definitions given, but to my mind Poe, in his essay, "The Poetic Principle," comes the nearest to defining it. He says: "I would define the poetry of words as the nearest rhythmical creation of beauty. That pleasure which is at once the most pure, the most elevating and the most intense, is derived, I maintain, from the contemplation of the beautiful. In the contemplation of beauty we alone find it possible to attain that pleasureable elevation or excitement of the soul which we recognize as the poetic sentiment, and which is so easily distinguished from truth, which is the satisfaction of reason, or from passion, which is the excitement of the heart. I make beauty, therefore—using the word as inclusive of the sublime—I make beauty the province of the poem simply because it is an obvious rule of art that effects should be made to spring as directly as possible from their causes—no one as yet having been weak enough to deny that the peculiar elevation in question is at least most readily attainable in the poem. It by no means follows, however, that the excitement of passion or the precepts of duty or even the lessons of truth may not be introduced into a poem, and with advantage, for they may subserve, incidentally, in many ways the general purposes of the work, but the true artist will always contrive to tone them down in proper subjection to that beauty which is the atmosphere and the real essence of a poem."

A rhythmical creation that produces an elevating excitement of the soul is Poe's definition of poetry. We all know that everything that is written in rhyme does not produce this effect, and, though not stopping to analyze our feelings, we at once declare such a composition doggerel, the reason being that it has not thrilled our innermost being—has not appealed to the soul.

It is well to impress upon the minds of the pupils in advanced grades at least, as I know a girl of fourteen who can select the noteworthy lines in any poem she reads, the best definitions of poetry that they may not, as is frequently the case, confound the false with the genuine. In no better way can the appreciation of poetry be cultivated than by teaching the pupils to observe the world in which they live. How often do we hear the expression "I don't read poetry; it's too deep for me." Such persons have never noted the wonderful beauty of the dawn or listened to the grand oration of the sea. Their eyes are fixed on the ground, and to their ears the voice of the bird brings no message of happiness. When the student becomes imbued with the thought that nothing is commonplace, however common it may be, that he may find beauty in everything, then shall poetry become to him a pleasurable and elevating excitement of the soul.

"Wherever snow falls," says Emerson, "or water flows, or birds fly, wherever day and night meet in twilight, wherever the blue heaven is hung with clouds or sown with stars, wherever are forms with transparent boundaries, wherever are outlets into boundless space, wherever is danger, awe and love, there is beauty, plenteous as rain shed for thee."

Poetry cannot be correctly interpreted by the pupils unless they really appreciate it, and to gain this appreciation their attention should be called to the beauties of the landscape, of mountains, hill and dale. In a walk through the autumn woods, where they have watched the dead leaves whirled about by the sudden gusts, how much clearer to them is the line from Rosetti:

"The ground-whirl of the perished leaves of hope," or the quatrain from Aldrich:

"October turned my maple leaves to gold
  The most are gone now; here and there one lingers.
Soon these will slip from out the twig's weak hold
  Like coins between the dying miser's fingers."

The similarity of leaves to gold coins that are dropping from a dead man's fingers will arouse at once the imagination by the picture the poet creates, and the meaning is made clear. The pupil feels the effect of autumn in a way he never felt it before. And in that, too, he is adding to his store of knowledge.

"They knew not how he learned at all
  For idly hour by hour
He sat and watched the dead leaves fall
  Or mused upon a common flower."

An outing in the woods of autumn may fix upon the pupil's mind the beauty of Bryan't line in his "Death of the Flowers," used in the States Fourth Reader:
"The South Wind searches for the flowers whose fragrance late he bore
And sighs to find them in the wood and by the stream no more."

And when attention is called to the madrone and its picturesque appearance, the pupil notes how true in its description is the poem he has had for his day's lesson in reading, and how, as his imagination is stirred, the tree does possess a "scarlet hose" and is a very "captain of the western wood."

True, the ethical value of the poem should be the first consideration. In Joaquin Miller's "Columbus" we have a fine example of true poetry. The teacher will observe that the poet does not dwell upon the discovery of a large portion of the earth's surface. It is the fearless soul of Columbus that receives the tribute. While no word is spoken of his courage, the soul of the Admiral looms large against the pitiful weakness displayed by the mate and the crew:

"Behind him lay the gray Azores,
  Behind the gates of Hercules;
Before him not the ghost of shores,
  Before him only shoreless seas.
The good mate said, "Now must we pray
  For lo! the very stars are gone
Brave Adm'r'l speak; what shall I say?"
  Why say, "Sail on! sail on! and on!"

There is a mountain of meaning in those words, "Sail on!"

They not alone bore Columbus over unknown waters to an unknown port for which he had set his heart, but they speak for humanity as well. "Sail on" is the spirit in man which has conquered worlds.

"For lo! the very stars are gone."

Hope faded with the stars, and the weak mate is typical of life's temptations. "Shoreless seas" impress us with the feeling of the frightened crew.

> "They sailed and sailed as winds might blow
> Until at last the blanched mate said
> "Why, now not even God would know
> Should I and all my men fall dead.
> These very winds forget their way,
> For God from these dread seas is gone.
> Now speak, brave Adm'r'l; speak and say—
> He said: "Sail on! sail on! and on!"
> "These very winds forget their way,
> For God from these dread seas is gone."

are the powerful lines of this stanza. The pupil's attention should be called to the imaginative power herein displayed. The poet shows us that it is God who leads the winds and the intense feeling of the blanched mate is portrayed with wonderful effect when he says to Columbus that the "very winds forget their way." How far and in what a weird waste of waters did these men think themselves!

> "Then, pale and worn, he kept his deck,
> And peered through darkness. Ah, that night
> Of all dark nights. And then a speck—
> A light! A light! A light! A light!
> It grew, a starlit flag unfurled!
> It grew to be Time's burst of dawn.
> He gained a world; he gave that world
> Its grandest lesson: 'On, sail on!'"

Here the darkness of the night is put into sharp contrast with the light. No matter how dark may seem the way, the morn surely welcomes us—"Time's burst of dawn"—the light of liberty in America compared to the dark ages preceding the reformation. "The spiritual power of the poem Columbus," says a well-known writer, ' is all the greater because it celebrates in the language of Truth the most momentous event in the history of the world. One may read it with no thought of its spiritual quality and be impressed with the marvelous gift of the poet." The imagery, the startling sweep of the poet's mind, surely brings to every reader that *elevating excitement of the soul.* It is to be regretted that the poem in its entirety is not given in the fourth reader.

Now in the "Vision of Sir Launfal," beginning with "And what is so rare as a day in June," we have a fine example of the poetry of nature, which will be more and more appreciated by the pupils as they are taught to observe nature during the queen month:

> And what is so rare as a day in June?
> Then, if ever, come perfect days
> Then Heaven tries the ear if it be in tune
> And over it softly her warm ear lays.

There is beautiful imagery expressed in those lines. The hollow of the sky—the ear of Heaven—held close to the earth and listening if it be in tune.

> Every clod feels a stir of might
> An instinct within it that reaches and towers
> And groping blindly above it for light
> Climbs to a soul in grass and flowers.

Here we have that "subtle music strangely sweet." No one could explain from a purely scientific standpoint how it is possible for a clod to climb to a soul in grass and flowers, and yet while we cannot explain such a process of nature, there is something within us that thrills at the thought the poet has given us.

And in watching the brooklet in the rocky glen, how oft has the poet described it in these lines: "In its slender necklace of grass."

> "The little spring laughed and leapt in the shade
> And with its own self like an infant played."

For the pupil to fully comprehend the beauty of these verses, we see how very essential it is that he should be taught to observe the waters of the brook. Not until he has noted how it seems to laugh as it leaps can he rightly interpret the meaning of the poet.

It was from observing the smithy at his task that Longfellow conceived the thought:

> Thus, at the flaming forge of life
> Our fortunes must be wrought.
> Thus on the sounding anvil shaped
> Each burning deed and thought.

And it is quite as necessary that the reader, to fully grasp the meaning conveyed, should also have seen the sparks fly from the anvil as the iron is beaten into the form desired.

The beauty that unfolds itself from day to day has a sympathetic interpreter in every great poet, and the poet may have sympathetic interpreters of his work if his readers themselves observe the doings of nature. Poetry will ever remain an unsolved riddle to him who lacks in appreciation of the universe—of the wonderful beauty with which the Creator has surrounded him. To cultivate this appreciation of nature in the youth of our land rests with the teacher in the public schools. When we correlate nature-study and literature we give to each a manifold interest, as the greatest of American and English writers have been the most observant of nature's handiwork. Bryant, in watching the flight of the waterfowl, felt that a great lesson had been taught him.

> He who from zone to zone
> Guides through the boundless sky thy certain flight
> In the long way that I must tread alone
> Will lead my steps aright.

Emerson it was who said: "The wood is wiser far than thou," and from his study window looked out at the falling snow and felt himself "enclosed

> In the tumultuous privacy of storm."

The spirit of Longfellow drank the cool "cisterns of the midnight air," and Lowell saw the blue bird "shifting his light load of song

> From post to post along the cheerless fence."

We find that the study of nature and that of poetry are closely allied. Teach the pupil to observe closely; bid him note the effect of light and shade; the blue haze of the distance; the sunshine of the tawny hills; the streamlet singing down the glade; the delicate fringe of the pine grove; the breakers thundering in "with mouths afoam"; the old miracle of sunrise and sunset—bid him mark the marvelous beauty that is to be seen everywhere, and he will appreciate more and more the poetry of the best poets whose names will suggest themselves to him in that delightful way so beautifully expressed by Mr. Bailey Millard in his poem, "Voices that Abide," which permit me to quote in conclusion:

> "The sovereign will not cease to sing
> While notes arise from any living thing
> Of which he sang. Earth still will gladly hail
> The voice of Keats in its last nightingale.
> What soars above us softly? Hark, friend, hark!
> Blythe Shelley's song swells forth from that blythe lark;

And see where wings his soul! Yes, 'tis the same
With many more the clear fire of whose fame
Is fanned by sight of objects animate
Or void of life when they are seen with eyes
That look with fondness on the poet's state,
And are most blest when soft before them rise
His strains celestial. Doth not Wordsworth's voice
Speak from the modest primrose? I rejoice
When darkly flits a waterfowl alone
Through evening skies, for these I see mine own
Good Bryant soar; and if a broad sea marsh
Spreads green or gray before me I can hear
The voice of that sad Southron, never harsh,
But always sweet—the liquid-toned Lanier.
And where a rugged island greets mine eye
I hail the homely Stevenson and Skye.
The busy, singing brook I gaze upon
Gives glimpses glad of sweet-voiced Tennyson;
And when a bell booms sadly forth in low
Dirge tones it peals for me the name of Poe.
The stately arches of cathedrals old
Say "Emerson." When to mine ear I hold,
On any shore, beside which waves and foams,
A chambered shell, it whispers to me, "Holmes!"

HERBERT BASHFORD.

San Francisco, Cal.

* * *

CARE AND TRAINING OF CHILDREN.*

I would like to outline a plan of work for the year, but I can only touch on some of the vital points. As the teacher, so the school. Our system depends almost wholly on the individual teachers. In the first place there must be loyalty; not necessarily personal loyalty, but loyalty to the educational policy established by the Board of Education. We are all parts of one great system, which controls and shapes, in large degree, the education of the people. There must be no half-hearted interest. It is our purpose to ask for results, rather than to dictate as to how these results shall be accomplished. Every school teacher should be original and think for herself."

The superintendent followed with many hints for the teachers as to methods of controlling the school and gaining the best results. He urged promptness, kindliness and a firm rule. He decried the

*Extract of address delivered to teachers on the opening of the schools of Los Angeles by Superintendent Foshay.

use of certain methods of control that have become common, but which tend to decrease individual responsibility in the child.

EFFICIENT SCHOOL SYSTEM.

An efficient school system, he continued, is one in which superintendents, principals, teachers, pupils and parents work together with confidence and mutual helpfulness, but perhaps the greatest help to the attainment of respect and reverence for law and authority in the schoolroom is the teacher himself. His school will be, to a large degree, what he or she is. If the pupils find the teacher has little regard for the execution of some law or rule of conduct which has been made for the school, their respect for him is lost. The teacher who is conscientiously honest in all his work may well correct and reprove dishonest acts on the part of the pupils. Very few rules should ever be made for the schoolroom, but these should be rigidly enforced.

It is encouraging to note that there is a growing favorable sentiment on the part of the people toward the schools, and that the newspapers, monthlies and periodicals are giving more and more space to them each year. In all professions there is an advance in requirements. Teachers note the high standards of qualification set by Boards of Education and of examining boards in granting certificates. After all requirements have been met, and the work begun, the teacher finds a strenuous life is before him. The people who have the idea that the teacher works only from 9 until 2 or 3, or from 9 until 12, are beginning to realize that they make a serious mistake, for the teacher who succeeds is the one who throws his whole life into the work and makes it his chief concern.

CAUSE FOR TEACHER'S PRIDE.

The pride of every teacher should be, not that he has taught so much language, science or mathematics, but, that he has inculcated such habits of work and study as shall influence the character. The inspiration of the child receives from intimate association with efficient teachers, compensates for whatever loss there may be in the work for the time being.

Seek to have the pupils in harmony with you. We are all here working for a common end. Absolute harmony can never be established, and perhaps is not desirable, but I feel there should be more of it than is manifested at present. Let us continue to study the children and not hold too much to the theory of what they ought to be, but endeavor to know what they are. Look into the mental characteristics of each child. The physical characteristics, too, should receive more attention than has heretofore been given them. While it is true that much good has been accomplished by examining as to sight and hearing, we must go much further along this line. I believe we have made a mistake in supposing that our calisthenics would give relief to the brain. For when the child is required to be on the alert lest he make some mistake, his mind is on a tension quite as great as when he is preparing his lessons. There should be spontaneous freedom and play on the school grounds, and much should be made of the open air. There is no doubt that pupils will accomplish more in their studies if permitted occasional recesses in which to have their games and plays under the direction of teachers who are in sympathy with them. A fresh, wide-awake class, upon entering the schoolroom, after vigorous, healthful play, will learn more during the first hour than they would in a period twice as long if they began the work in a room poorly ventilated, and with their brains tired and overworked.

CHEERFULNESS IN SCHOOL.

I have noted, on occasions, that when there was a general feeling of restlessness among the pupils, it was a good idea to have them engage in a bright, cheerful song. If it be inconvenient to have the children sing, to my mind it is perfectly proper for them to have something to laugh at, instead of attempting to repress trouble by scolding. A restless feeling in the schoolroom is irritating to both teacher and pupils. The children need something to cause them to forget themselves, and are ready to be amused. Laughing is better for the health than scolding, and the teacher who occasionally smiles may be saved the appellation of "cranky."

Let us have the thorough training of the essential branches. Teach the boys and girls to read, to spell, to think, and train them in the power to do. Guard against waste, not only of school property, but of time and effort.

The subject of truancy will be emphasized this year as never before. At the last session of the Legislature a compulsory-education law was passed which, if enforced, will compel children from 8 to 14 years of age to attend school. Boys should not be allowed to roam the streets and alleys during school hours.

Some of the salaries have been increased for the coming year, and it is a matter of regret that all were not so treated. We sincerely hope that the day is not distant when we shall be able to retain our best teachers, not only because they are happy and contented in their work, but because their salaries are as good as those in the surrounding cities.

Teaching in the public schools will not be a suitably attractive and permanent career, nor will it command as much of the ability of the country as it should until the teachers are properly compensated and are assured of an undisturbed tenure during efficiency and good behavior.

STRENGTH OF THE SYSTEM.

The true source of the strength of any system of public education lies in the regard of the people whom it immediately serves, and in their willingness to make sacrifices for it. For this reason a large share of the cost of maintaining public schools should be borne by a local tax levied by the county or by the town in which the schools are. State aid is to be regarded as supplementary to, and not a substitute for, local taxation for school purposes. The highest ethical standards of conduct and of speech should be insisted upon among the teachers. The school is becoming more and more a community center, and its larger opportunities impose new obligations. Disregard for law and for its established modes of procedure is as serious a danger as can menace a democracy. It is the duty of the school so to lay the foundations of character in the young that they will grow up with reverence for the majesty of the law. Any system of school discipline which disregards this obligation is harmful to the child and dangerous to the State. A democracy which would endure must be as law-abiding as it is liberty loving.

I sincerely hope that the year will be pleasant, and in every sense of the word successful, and that as other years may follow you may always entertain pleasant recollections of the school year 1903-04."

JAMES A. FOSHAY.

EDUCATION OF PEOPLE IN PEACE.

There can be no question as to the unwisdom of war from a commercial standpoint; in whatever way we regard it, war is a great disaster to business men, to everybody except the few who make money out of it — the rest suffer in purse and credit, and in every possible way. A few contractors may get their living by it on the principle that "the rain falls upon the just and the unjust fellows, but more upon the just, because the unjust have the others' umbrellas."

We must assume an aggressive position; it is not sufficient to sit still and let the forces of civilization work out for themselves. Hence it is our duty to teach the people that war is a great horror and that peace is a great blessing. That may be, perhaps, called a commercial method, but we are living in a commercial age, and we are a commercial people. A man sets up a department store, does he sit still and wait for customers to come? No; he advertises it from morning to night; he exhausts all his ingenuity in informing the people what he has for sale, in making them believe in his policy and by and by success crowns his enterprise.

It must be confessed that the men who are successful are the far-seeing men, the men who look forward to the future. The man who is far-sighted is the one who makes the millions. We hear a great deal in the present time about anarchism and about social disturbances and the labor problem, and Macauley said of us that some day we would have men who had no breakfast and did not know where they would get their dinner, and unless some Napoleon arose our cities would be sacked as was Rome in the fifth century.

There is a great army marching towards us, now we can hear the tramp, tramp. They are coming to overrun our land, they will take possession of our farms, they will seize upon our workshops, they will go to Washington and sit in the seats of the Senators, one of them will come and sit in Mr. Roosevelt's chair, they will occupy our pulpits, they will even invade our homes. I allude to the great army of children that are coming on to fill the places of every one of us. They are the ones to wield the future power, and they are the ones that you and I ought to be educating today to be peacemakers for the future world and not war-makers.

We have often heard about the difficulty of changing human nature, but it is not impossible to make men see things in a new light. When Paul lay that night at Troas listening to the roll of the Mediterranean, when the voice beckoned him to Macedonia, there was not a single Christian in all Europe, and yet within three centuries that the new religion had blazoned the cross on the standards of the empire. If that could be done, certainly we can make progress with people today.

History since the advent of Christ is a sort of secondary Scripture, great in extent, covering all the continents, its initial stamped sometimes in blood and sometimes in gold, but the whole vast tangled and confused text holding in it still the song of the angels, "Peace on earth, good will to men," the Beatitudes on the Mount, the story of Bethlehem and of Calvary, the triumph of the Ascension and the Apocalypse.

Some of us can remember when the anti-slavery movement had no more momentum than the peace movement now has. This work is regenerating the race, and is hastening the time when the swords shall be beat into plowshares and the spears into pruning hooks. Sometimes you go into an artist's studio and you see there the marble form of a female face, of what we callled a veiled lady, every characteristic form and feature seen through what seems to be lacework, but which is itself worked out in marble. So the earth on which we stand is coming to show the face of the Christ wrought into it from above, and revealed through all the reticulated hardness of its slow-yielding civilization.

MR. WARNER VAN ORDEN,
President National Bank of North America.

* * *

THE CALIFORNIA SCHOLIA CLUB.

About a year and a half ago four men interested in education met in a San Francisco restaurant to discuss the feasibility of forming a small club which should be devoted to the co-operative study of educational problems in a scientific spirit. The outcome of this preliminary meeting was the formation of the California Scholia Club, whose membership is composed of representatives of the two universities, of the State Normal schools of Northern California, and of educators in the public schools around San Francisco Bay. The number of members was limited—in order that informal discussion around a table might be practicable. In electing members especial attention has been paid to their interest in and fitness for the study of fundamental educational questions.

The working organization of the club is very simple. A president (called "The Factotum") is elected annually and becomes entirely responsible for the program and other details of the meetings of the club, on Saturday evenings. Monthly meetings are held during the school year, after which the more serious work of the club is carried on.

At each meeting some member presents a paper in which a vital educational question is carefully discussed. The reading of this paper is followed by full and frank discussion on the part of all members, the sole object being the emphasis of strong points, the exposure of weak ones, and the contribution of additional suggestions. It can be easily understood that in preparing a study for such an audience the writer will be especially careful to present only well-digested conclusions. Inasmuch as the subject has been announced two months beforehand, it is also true that the members come well prepared to take an active part in the discussion.

With the exception of three or four papers bearing on special topics, the work of the club during the year and a half of its existence has centered around the general topic of "Formal Discipline in Education." This vital question has been approached from its philosophic, and from its psychological sides; and the study has been given greater concreteness owing to the fact that several papers have been devoted to the study of the disciplinary values of the individual subjects. Men who have given especial attention to such formal subjects as Latin, algebra, arithmetic, English, and manual training, have endeavored to indicate in some detail the training values of these subjects. While definite conclusions have been reached in few cases, the work of the club on this topic has nevertheless developed the fact that we stand in need of clearer light as to why such prominent places are given in elementary, and especially in secondary, curricula, to subjects which are chiefly defended on the grounds of their value as mental disciplines. It has been found that the respect with which these subjects has been regarded is largely due to the force of tradition, and that it is now necessary that educators have a careful stock-taking of educational values in the light of such knowledge of psychology and child development as we now possess.

As before stated, the members of the club have not been in agreement as to conclusions reached in discussion; but this was neither expected nor desired, especially in view of the fact that insufficient data exist for solution of the more pressing of educational problems. The club has fully attained its object in the fact that a number of thoughtful men, actively engaged in educational work, have co-operatively threshed over these problems, and have discovered their character, extent and importance. For the individual members the best results of the meetings are found in the clearer conceptions attained and in a more sympathetic appreciation of "the other fellow's point of view."

Several papers which have first seen the light in the club's meetings have already been published, and still others are yet to be published. For the coming year it is announced by the "Factotum" that special studies will be made of the subjects of the elementary curriculum with a view to determine their real educational value in other respects besides disciplinary.

It is believed that the work of the club has been very successful educationally and socially. This brief account has been prepared for the WESTERN JOURNAL OF EDUCATION in the belief that other organizations of educators should be formed in California along somewhat similar lines for the prosecution of careful studies in live educational questions.

Department of Methodology

A NEW METHOD IN LONG DIVISION

In the JOURNAL for September, Department of Methodology, is the statement that, to the beginner, long division presents two difficulties. I believe this can easily be reduced to one if the subject is taught correctly.

In this line let me offer two suggestions, either one of which will relieve the pupil of the necessity of using "skill in approximating" which, as yet, he has not:

First—Instead of writing the quotient over the dividend, place it at the right of a vertical line, as in the accompanying illustration. Proceed as in the usual way, but do not *require* the pupil to place (for example) 9 in the quotient when the divisor will be contained nine times.

Allow him to use a 7 if he select it. Then, when the remainder is found to be larger than the divisor, teach him to make the correction without erasing the 7, the remainder, or the product of the divisor by the 7, by placing a 2 under the 7, bringing down no figure, and proceeding from that point in the usual way. The work should then appear as in the accompanying illustration, the quotient being the sum of 470 and 28

```
745 ) 371629  | 47
      2980    | 28
      ----
      7362    | 498
      5215
      ----
      2147
      1490
      ----
      6579
      5960
      ----
       619
```

The pupil should be urged at all times to avoid the necessity of making corrections, and possibly, after some experience, a slight premium should be placed on the exactness of the first effort.

I believe that, throughout the school course, a student should never be allowed to erase a step in division unless he has used too large a figure in the quotient. This method is simpler and quicker than erasure, and obviously neater when pen or pencil is used on paper—simpler and quicker because, after multiplying by 7, it is much easier to multiply by 2 than to erase and multiply by 9.

Second—Carrying this idea to its limit, perhaps, we have the following form, which reduces to a minimum the necessity of approximating; and, whatever objectionable features there are about it, it has the redeeming features of making long division a very simple process and putting it in such shape that it becomes a comprehensible exercise instead of a mere mechanical process.

Let us assume that the pupil has been taught short division, also to divide by any one of the digits, followed by from one to three noughts, so that he has some ability in comparing the values of the dividend and divisor. He may, if he errs greatly in his comparison, decide to try the divisor in the dividend 40 times. He places the 40 in the quotient, multiplies, subtracts and finds that it is contained some hundred times. He may note the relative values of 29 and 37 and decide next time to try 400. He multiplies, subtracts and will probably next try 50, then perhaps 7 and then 1. The quotient is the sum of 40, 400, 50, 7 and 1, or 498 with a remainder, as before, of 619. The work then appears as in the illustration.

```
745 ) 371629  | 40
      29800   | 400
      ------  | 50
      341829  | 7
      298000  | 1
      ------  | ---
       43829  | 498
       37250
       -----
        6579
        5215
        ----
        1364
         745
        ----
         619
```

It makes no difference whatever, as far as corrections are concerned, what number goes in as part of the quotient so long as it is not too large.

J. M. HORTON,
Arcata.   Principal A. U. H. S.

PRODUCTS OF CALIFORNIA.

The following represents a method of escaping the word-memorizing system so frequent with exclusive use of texts. The references are given for teachers' reading. After she has prepared herself with the necessary information in concrete form, she gives this material to her pupils in the form of "chalk lessons." It is well to make these lessons as conversational as possible, the teacher drawing at the blackboard as she talks. It is also essential that after the concrete material is given to insist upon memory of the essential facts and conclusions. Then, and not until then, make use of the text. Of course, this study of products presupposes thorough knowledge of the map.

The Product Map.

California has four great characteristic products, which it seems well to teach in a group. These are gold, lumber, fruits and grain. It may be well at a later time, perhaps in another grade, to teach the products of secondary significance, such as petroleum, coal, wool, etc.

The accompanying product map, together with the reading later cited, concern only the big four first mentioned.*

Gold is mined throughout the length of the Sierra and in the northern and southern parts of the coastal region.

The lumber regions are so nearly identical with those of gold that, for simplicity's sake, one shade has been used to represent them both. Of course this coloration is correct only in a large way. But a scheme of more minute detail would hopelessly confuse the pupils.

So, also, while fruit is raised in nearly all portions of the State, the *characteristic* fruit areas are the southern counties, the Sierra foothills and some of the Coast Range valleys, notably the Santa Clara and Russian River.

Grain, principally wheat, is raised in several sections of the State. But the great grain area is the upper two-thirds of the central valley.

Following this scheme, the four principal produce areas are shown in the map by the use of the three shades of ink, these shades

---

* For those who purpose teaching other products there is a helpful mineral map (petroleum, salt, borax, coal and gold) on page 41 of the Tarr and McMurry California Supplement. And in "How We Are Fed" are to be found readings on "Beet Sugar" and "Where Salt Comes From." Both of these are California topics.

being explained in the legend on the map. This map could be enlarged for teaching purposes, and the areas tinted with crayon or water color.

Adams Commercial Geography, page 131, tells of California's rank as a gold producer. Accounts of the discovery of gold in California are given in Children's Stories of American Progress, 293-8; Golden Drys of '49, page 182-7; Side Lights on American History, page 248-51; Stories of American Life, page 71-7.

Gold mining in California is described in Great American Industries: Minerals, page 168-87; Side Lights on American History, page 251-7; King's Geographical Reader, V., 44-51; Stories of Industry, Vol. I, page 37-44; Primer of Political Economy, page 15-21; Information Reader, III, 207-26; Around the World, III, 133-9.

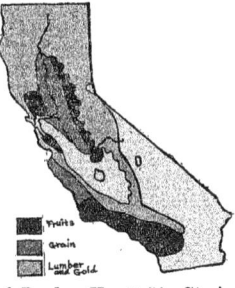

There are many lumber regions in the world, but California is the only producer of the variety called redwood. We use virtually all of it all at home. All California, so far as dwelling-houses are concerned, is built of redwood.

Reading on California's big trees is to be found in Carpenter's Geographical Reader, page 271-3; Our Country West, page 131-3; Johonnot's Geographical Reader, page 165-8; King's Geographical Reader, Book V, 123-8 and 165-71.

In addition to this immense supply of redwood, the Sierra counties yield great quantities of pine and spruce. Some of this is used in our own State and is railroaded west, down across the central valley to San Francisco and other centers of distribution. But a considerable part of the Sierra lumber is sent directly east over the mountains. Tuolumne is one of the great shipping points for this lumber.

Reading on California lumbering is to be had in Stories of California, page 111-20; Our Country West, page 135-7; Mountains of California, 139-225; Tarr and McMurray's California Supplement, page 43-5 and 69-70.

There are useful descriptions of lumbering, applicable in a general way to California, in Products of the Soil, page 12-36 and 46-

50; Information Reader, III, 195-206 and 241-52; Stories of Industry, Vol. I, 121-5; Stories of Country Life, 39-43 and 48-9.

California sends countless loads of its fruits to the Eastern States, and even further, to Canada, Europe and Australia. Some of these fruits, the oranges, for instance, are sent just as they come from the tree. But the great bulk of fruits for shipping are dried, or 'cured.'' For example, the prune, as it grows on the tree, is a small, sweetish plum. But before it is sent to market it is dried and afterward "dipped," to give it a gloss. This makes it the prune we buy at the grocery. Similarly raisins, before they are dried, are a kind of grape. Our peaches and apricots are cut into halves, dried and then bleached in sulphur fumes before they leave the ranch. In this dried form California fruits find their way all over the world, and particularly into the Eastern States of our own country. The money received for them comes back to California and enables the people here to buy other things, such as machinery, jewelry and clothing, from the East.

Grapes and raisins are told about in Information Reader No. 1, page 189-93, and How We Are Fed, page 174-83. Peaches, Information Reader I, 188-9. Pears, same, 181-5. Oranges, Tarr and McMurry, Cal. Supplement, page 107; 79; 61; Tarr and McMurry Geog., Second Book, page 300; King's Geog. Reader No. IV, page 9-10; Carpenter's North America, page 130-34; How We Are Fed, page 165-73.

Fruits in general, Information Reader No. I, 169-81; Tarr and McMurry, Book II, 299-301; California Supplement, page 37; 61; 107-8; How We Are Fed, 187-91 (walnuts) and 201-2 (almonds).

The central valley raises countless thousands of bushels of wheat. We use all we need of this wheat and send the rest to China. Most of it is ground into flour before it goes. Immense flour mills are busy in Stockton and other places constantly grinding this flour, including what we eat ourselves and what we send to China.

In How We Are Fed, the "Story of a Loaf of Bread" (page 7-17) is a useful study, applicable, in the main, to California wheat nd flour. Our Fatherland, page 103-4, deals with cereals in general.

We do not send our wheat and flour east because the great wheat areas there produce more than is needed. While we are producing these great staples to send away there are others which we have to buy. California is not producing any iron. The Union Iron Works and others have to send over the mountains for all the iron and steel they use. We have to buy in the East, also, nearly all kinds of manufactured goods, such as tools, furniture, cloth and medicines. We buy these things with the money we get for our fruits and our gold, lumber and wheat. Thus, as we sat at breakfast this morning, we used a spoon that was probably made in Connecticut, and the people of Connecticut are eating for lunch to-day some stewed peaches that once were grown and dried on a California ranch.

Books. Cited.

How we are fed. Chamberlain.—Macmillan.
Tarr and McMurry Geog. II.—Macmillan.
Tarr and McMurry Geog. California Supplement.—Macmillan.
Adams Commercial Geography.—Appleton's.
Children's Stories American Progress. Wright.—Scribner.
—Golden Days of '49. Munroe, Dodd, Mead.—Scribner.
Side Lights on American History. Elson.—Macmillan.
Stories of American Life. Eggleston.—Am. Book Co.
Great American Industries: Minerals. Rocheleau.—Flanagan.
King's Geog. Reader, Book V.—Lee & Shepard.
Stories of Industry, Vol. I, Chase & Clow.—Ed. Pub. Co.
Primer Political Economy. Wood.—Macmillan.
Information Reader III. Parker.—Boston School Supply Co.
Around the World III. Carroll.—Morse Co.
Carpenter's Geog. Reader. North American.—Am. Book Co.
Companion Series:
Our Country West.—Perry, Mason & Co.
Johonnot's Geog. Reader.—Am. Book Co.
Stories of California. Sexton.—Macmillan.
Mountains of California. Muir.—Century Co.
Products of the Soil. Rocheleau.—Flanagan.
Stories of Country Life. Bradish.—Am. Book Co.
Information Reader No. I. Beal.—Boston School Supply Co.
King's Geog. Reader No. 4.—Lee & Shepard.
Our Fatherland. Carver & Pratt.—Educational Publishing Co.

WALTER J. KENYON.

State Normal School, San Francisco.

* * *

TOPICS IN GEOGRAPHY FOR SPECIAL STUDY.

1. The geography of the tea-table: the manufacture, sources and transportation of foods, dishes, etc.
2. The geography of the wardrobe: the manufacture, transportation and raw material of the ordinary articles of dress.
3. History below the high school, and the relation it holds to geography.
4. Science below the high school, and the relation it holds to geography.

5. The text-book in geography, good and bad features, supplementary material and methods for using it at the least expense.

6. The daily paper in the school, its good and its evil.

7. Geography and travel: "A trip around the world; what I saw and whom I met"—an imaginary journey.

8. Geography and current civilization: closer trade relations, irrigation schemes, manufacturing trusts, grain famines, Nicaragua canal, strikes, etc. etc.

FRANK J. BROWNE.

Hoitt's School, Menlo Park.

* * *

GEOGRAPHY.

Some questions on local geography used with good results in Franklin Grammar School, R. D. Faulkner, principal:

1. How many counties in California?
2. Which is the largest?
3. Which is the smallest?
4. San Bernardino County contains 20,055 square miles. The City and County of San Francisco 42 square miles. The area of San Bernardino County is how many times greater than the area of the City and County of San Francisco?
5. In 1890 the City and County of San Francisco contained 298,997 inhabitants. The same year San Bernardino County contained 17,352. How many times greater is the population of the former than the latter?
6. How many people live on a square mile in San Bernardino County? (b) How many on a square mile in the City and County of San Francisco?
7. The total area of the State is 158,360 square miles. The population in 1890 was 1,208,130. How many people to a square mile?
8. How is the number of inhabitants of a city, city and county, state, or the United States found?
9. At $1.25 per acre what would be the value of all the land in California?
10. What is meant by density of population?

BOOKS AND MAGAZINES

This work is a human document of rare interest. For in a very peculiar sense Dr. Bushnell was one of the spiritual fathers that begat us. His life was typical of the cultured and humanized Puritanism of later New England which spread its beneficent influence over our whole land and set the standards for our American civilization. He lived the strenuous life of a leader of men in a great age.

This is no place to speak of the vigor and sanity of his intellect, of the piquancy of his wit, of the majesty of his character, or the spiritual power of his ministry. No one can read of these things and remain unmoved.

It is as the first President of the College of California that Horace Bushnell commands our attention. He came here in 1856, having about an even chance with death. He spent the first part of his stay in riding, tramping, fishing, climbing mountains, preaching a little, and glorying in the richly varied landscape. In July, 1856, he was offered the presidency of the little college which as yet existed only in the minds of a few sturdy friends of education, whose enthusiasm was not shaken even by the terrors of the Vigilante period. With the statement, "I am a Christian pastor, holding a very peculiar relation to my flock"—in Hartford—Dr. Bushnell neither declined nor accepted the office, but at once threw his energy into the work of finding a suitable location for the college, organizing its constituency and raising funds for its maintenance. The letters which tell of his search for water and an available location are of the rarest interest. Martinez, the Petaluma valley, the Sonoma valley, the ranch of Senor Sunole, the Mission San Jose, San Pablo, Napa, and Clinton or Brooklyn, were each reported as in a measure satisfactory. Of this pioneering in the cause of education Dr. Bushnell wrote: "If I can get a university on its feet, or only the nest-egg laid, before I return, I shall not have come to this new world in vain." The college was established and Dr. Bushnell returned home. But in 1860 the trustees moved it to the site at Clinton or Brooklyn, which had been most preferred by him. There, in 1860, a formal meeting was held and the name of the place changed to Berkeley.

* * *

"The beginning is the main thing, especially in dealing with a young and tender nature. For at that time it is most plastic, and the stamp sinks in deepest which it is desired to impress upon any one."

(1) The Life and Letters of Horace Bushnell, published by Charles Scribners Sons.

(2) The Jones First Reader, The Jones Second Reader, The Jones Third Reader, by L. H. Jones. Ginn & Co.

For this reason the Torah was the early reading book of the Jews, "The Iliad" of the Greeks, Virgil's "Aeneid" of the Romans, and the Gospels of the early Christians. The primer represents the witless and unnecessary degradations of modern education. Witless, because needless, for at no other period of a long life is the learner so full of questions as at the primer stage. He hungers for the substance of knowledge, and it is a well-known fact that he amasses more of it before he reaches the school age than in the subsequent years of his existence. Is it not, then, folly to put him to reiterating statements already repellantly familiar, in the hope that thus he will learn to read? From the standpoint of his interest, as well as from that of his future character, *what* he reads and re-reads, so often that he will never forget it is long as he lives, should be worth while. He asks for bread and is given a reading book. He is a learner literally running over with curiosity, and we put him to reading a reader. Some concessions of form should indeed be made, but when this process had once been started, substance fled away. Taken all in all, the writing of books for children has been a curse. What are called readers are generally not fit to read, and what are called children's books would usually be discarded by children if their elders had half the clarity of vision that they have, but cannot make effective.

I am loath to include these readers under this condemnation. Their print is so good, their illustrations so satisfactory, their author so reputed, their construction so careful, that at first look one is tempted to praise them. Upon examination, however, it will be found that they go the way of their kind. Their improvements are mechanical improvements. The substance of knowledge which active young minds hunger for, and should be provided with, is not in them. Facts of nature and human conduct which they impart are of too primary a character. Normal children are already familiar with them, and need more nourishing mental food. Practice has proven time and again that they can take it. The fact that supplementary reading books are not of so diluted a character is proof positive that readers need not be.

* * *

It would be difficult to improve upon this book as a text in civics. Its chief purpose is preparation for citizenship. To accomplish this the author believes that three things are necessary: First, an adequate knowledge of the structure and functions of our system of government. Second, some familiarity with present-day political affairs. Third, a training in seeing both sides of public questions, and in weighing arguments and reaching one's own conclusions cocerning them.

American Government; A Text-Book for American Schools. By Roscoe Lewis Ashley. The Macmillan Company.

The book is devoted primarily to meeting the first requisite, but the other two are nowhere overlooked. Each chapter closes with general references to other works which treat the same subject, and a series of questions for investigation by the pupil, together with a list of magazine articles which bear upon the themes proposed. In accordance with sound pedagogy, local government is treated first, state government next, and the functions of the national government last. These discussions are clever but thorough. Where the genesis of institutions would help to understand them, it is added. The illustrations are good and often quite suggestive. The study of this book should make the student pretty thoroughly acquainted with the institutions of our political life. It should also make him acquainted with current political discussions. And more important than either of these, if he follows the work outlined here he will have learned the method of investigating such problems and gotten into the habit of reading the literature pertaining to them.

* * *

This volume undertakes to cover a large field. It is written in vigorous and trenchant English. It is interesting, but it is hardly profitable, for it is rather too brief and too technical to serve as an introduction, and not exhaustive or technical enough for a basis of advanced study. As a fillip to the imagination of one already familiar with the subjects of which it treats it may be of service.

* * *

These two books belong to the same language series. While they have many commendable features, they are all offset by one most serious fault—their lessons are practically confined to literature. Consequently, they are thoroughly unpsychological, and will certainly be harmful. Language is expression—of one's own thoughts, not another's, though he be an archangel. It must be taught as it is. Aside from this, one may question the propriety of mutilating the passages quoted, and the purpose of the repeated memorizings prescribed.

* * *

The art of preparing text books in sciences has advanced more rapidly in recent years than that of making texts in other subjects. This volume is a good example of such progress. Its material is well selected, well arranged, and vital. Structural and systematic zoology is subordinated to comparative zoology. It is life, rather

(1) Swain School Lectures, by Andrew Ingraham. The Open Court Publishing Company.

(2) Language Lessons from Literature, by Alice W. Cooley. Houghton, Mifflin & Co. Elementary Composition, by W. F. Webster. Houghton, Mifflin & Co.

(3) General Zoology; A revision and rearrangement of Orton's Comparative Zoology by Charles W. Dodge. American Book Company.

than this or that kind of life, which is studied. It seems admirably fitted to meet the growing demand for general science—science as information, rather than classification or tabulation. Its style is excellent; its illustrations clear and intelligible.

* * *

Pennsylvania School Journal The September number reports the proceedings of the various departments of the State Educational Association. The Conference on Compulsory Education is particularly satisfactory. The tendency in all lands is toward compulsory laws. Most of the states of Europe have them. Ontario and Mexico, and seven of the countries of South America, have them. The immigrants of Australia carried with them this seemingly essential principle of modern civilization, and now it dominates the school systems of New South Wales, New Zealand, Queensland, South Australia, Victoria and Tasmania.

The bogy in the shape of threatened visits from the attendance officer and fines which do not materialize, must be abolished, and, in their stead, a wise, judicious policy be inaugurated which, while considerate and kind, shall be what the law anticipates—compulsory. The laws must be executed vigorously. When unnatural parents forget or ignore their duties to children, the state does not perform one of the functions for which it was established, if it does not compel the parent and secure the rights of the neglected children. It is recommended, that a department of registration be created, and empowered to keep a record of births, new arrivals, changes of residence, etc.; that no child be hired without a certificate of school attendance; that the establishment of truant schools be not left optional with school districts, but established by the state; that truant officers be not answerable to school boards, but to this department of registration.

The conferences on Secondary Education, Nature Study, Manual Training, the Kindergarten, County Supervision, Child Study, are all quite fully reported.

* * *

Education The leading article in the September number, by H. A. Peterson, of St. Louis, discusses in an able manner the subject of Classification in the Elementary School Curriculum. The purpose of classification is to sum up experience and make it readily accessible. Classifications have a use in suggesting short cuts in the experience of others. The abandonment of reading as a separate study, and with it the present composite readers, is practicable. The teaching of writing, spelling and elementary grammar through composition and occasional dictation, is the most natural way to give these studies a connected and interesting content, and to motivate their study. No difficulties of application will be experienced then. A quite successful solution of over-classification and isolation in arithmetic has been worked out in the same way. The educational kingdom of heaven is near at hand when superintendents begin to write in this fashion. The second article is a valuable statistical study of evening high schools in the cities of the United States.

― * * *

The Paidologist The July number of the organ of the British Child-Study Association contains the able address of the president of the Association, on "Child Study," and articles on "Preparation for Child Study," "The Mentally Defective Child," "Appreciation of Number," "Real Education," and "Adolescence."

* *

School and Home Education The place of honor is accorded an article by Supt. T. M. Balliet, on "The Saving of Time in Elementary and Secondary Education." "I believe that the most satisfactory solution will be found, in the end, in the establishment of special grammar schools, in which pupils who are to fit for college and higher technical schools may be given an abridged grammar school course of four years, instead of five or six, and be allowed to begin a modern language and the elements of Algebra. Such pupils could enter the high school at the age of twelve, or at most thirteen, better prepared to do the work of the high school than the average grammar school pupil is at fourteen or fifteen."

* * *

The Educational Review The September number contains five papers read before the Department of Higher Education of the N. E. A., on the general subject, "The Length of the College Course," Mr. Whitelaw Reid's Phi Beta Kappa address at Vassar, entitled "The Thing to Do," "The American College Course," by Grant Showerman, "Visual Inaccuracies in School Children," by Alida S. Williams.

A contributor arraigns the public schools as inadequate for the development of originality—over-worshipful of artificers of words —imbuing children with the idea that work is ignoble; giving undue prominence to language, and so filling "the learned professions" and emptying the productive ones; putting both sexes through the same mill; giving an exaggerated idea of the value of books; lacking totally a system of ethical instruction; developing the memory at the expense of the powers of initiative. He concludes: "Under the present system of public instruction a boy must steal something, or commit some other infraction of the law, in order to be sent to an institution where he may receive a training that bears some relation to the work of life."

* *

Science

The issue of August 21st contains a timely article by Prof. C. M. Woodward, on "The New Opportunity for Secondary Schools." There is an increasing tendency to extend the period of socially required attendance at school to include the high school. Throughout the land high school attendance has been growing rapidly. In Kansas City it increased one hundred per cent while the population increased but fifty per cent. What is being done to provide for the wants of this multitude of learners? If we agree with President Wilson that the college is for the minority, inasmuch as the average secondary school prepares for the college, we must agree that it also is not for the majority. We must not approve of educational features simply because they are fashionable. Let those who ask for them have the classics. An opportunity, however, is presented high schools of offering another sort of training—of giving a secondary education looking toward industrial occupations and technical professions, equal, at least, to those offered to students looking forward to clerical or mercantile occupations and the traditional professions.

The issue of Sept. 11th contains a very suggestive article by Prof. Rufus P. Williams, on "High School Chemistry in Its Relation to the Work of a College Course."

The subject is discussed under two questions: 1st. Who ought to decide what is the most suitable course for high schools, and how shall such decision be arrived at? The answer which is suggested is, that colleges can not shape their courses arbitrarily, stating that just so much ground must be gone over by just such a method, neither can the high school unadvisedly lay out its course. The course must be the result of co-operation, and must be worked out by frequent conferences of the teachers involved.

Second, What is the most notable defect in the present arrangement, and what is the remedy? The first part of this question, "In what part of the work do you find those offering chemistry most deficient?" was put to 23 colleges, and answered as follows:

1. Elementary general principles.

2. A comprehension of underlying principles. Pupils acquire facts but do not understand their relation to general principles.

3. Want of application.

4. Work is not thorough; mostly taught from books. Ground covered too great for time devoted to it.

5. Elementary logic. Students coming to college are very deficient in reasoning.

6. Equation and laboratory work.

7. Making, putting up, and using apparatus; a thorough knowledge of the non-metals; quantitative experiments.

8. Their failings will vary with the instruction they have received.

9. In general.

10. Perhaps theoretical, more than descriptive.

11. Have generally "done" a large number of experiments, but are sadly deficient in chemical laws.

12. In theory and in knowledge of metals.

13. Equations and familiarity with fundamental principles. Three-fourths of the time at high schools is wasted in trying to cover too much ground.

14. They fail because they will not study, and I think in many cases they were never taught how to study.

15. The preparatory schools are not in a position to give students anything like comprehensive instruction in elementary chemistry. An answer which the writer of the paper regards as both untrue and unkind.

The latter part of the question is answered by the suggestion that the colleges shall treat elementary chemistry as they do elementary English or mathematics, i. e., assign to high schools a definite work and begin their teaching of the subject at the point where the high schools leave it, and not at the beginning, as now is customary.

* * *

Harpers
There are two articles in the September number of *Harper's Magazine* of peculiar interest to educators. The first, by Stoddard Dewey, describes a Paris School Colony—an organized effort, supported by the municipality, to give 1,000 or more children from the poorer sections of Paris the benefit of three weeks of life amid almost ideal surroundings

in the country. The candidates are selected on the basis of need. Class records and conduct are not consulted. Only children who show signs of suffering and for whom the doctors in charge prescribe country air, whose parents are unable to provide this necessity, are taken. To them the city offers "assistance," not "charity," for the word is tabooed in republican Paris. At the colony they play, and tramp, and eat as much as they can. Lessons are forgotten, the one object of the undertaking being to send them back as much heavier and stronger than they came, as possible. Surely, this is a form of vacation school which might be developed to advantage in our country.

The second article of special interest is by Professor T. R. Lounsbury, on "The Standard of Promotion in English." It should be read by every teacher of English, as well as by every student in his classes.

* * *

Review of Catholic Pedagogy

It is a pleasure to welcome the newest comer in the ranks of educational journalism, the *Review of Catholic Pedagogy*. Its editor, Rev. Thomas E. Judge, has studied in the secular universities of our country as well as in the schools of the church, and beside has proven himself one of the ablest of her teachers. Principal Arnold Tompkins writes of the first number of the *Review*: "I have never seen a stronger pedagogical journal," and the second number is like unto the first. The first article, upon the "Necessity of Training Teachers of Religion" is contributed by Rev. P. C. Yorke of the Board of Regents of the University of California. An article by the editor entitled "The Alphabet of the History of Philosophy" almost attains the proverbial clearness hinted in the title. "The Attitude of the Early Church toward Pagan Culture," a subject of the utmost importance in the history of civilization, is ably treated by Prof. Turner of St. Paul's Seminary. "Art in the Elementary Schools," "Musical Pedagogy," "The Need of Technical Education," "The Teaching of Grammar" and a half-dozen other articles on kindred subjects, will indicate the solidity of its table of contents and the high standard which its editor has set for himself. The philosophic side of education, rather than its empirical phases, is here represented. The *Review* bids fair to distance its complacent and more commonplace secular rivals. Catholic teachers will of course read it but students of whatever faith will find it well-nigh indispensable. An undue fear of the centralization of responsibility and the prevailing drift of things toward "Socialism" may readily be forgiven a journal so thoroughly devoted to the cause of pedagogical scholarship.

The Review of Catholic Pedagogy. Chicago, Ill.

The Forum

The last number of the *Forum* contributes three articles on education. The first, on "The Educational Outlook," by Ossian Lang, outlines the plan recently adopted in Connecticut for the supervision of rural schools, and calls attention to the fact that the most satisfactory work on this continent for the improvement of the efficiency of rural schools has been undertaken, not in the United States, but in Canada. Not only are country schools consolidated and children transported there, but practical courses in agriculture are given wherever conditions warrant. The second article is an explanation of the purposes of the Society of Educational Research, which was organized last February to undertake an extensive study of the methods of teaching employed and the results attained by school work in various sections of our country. Education is still in the empirical stage. It cannot advance save by experimentation followed by careful induction. Varying daily school practice affords a wealth of experimentation which only needs to be interpreted to make it of the greatest value. It is to collect and study this mass of facts that the society was organized. If its work is conducted with a due regard for the limitations of the statistical method it cannot fail to be of the greatest value. The third article is contributed by Professor Ladd, on the oppressively present problem of the college course. He points out that the remedies proposed—the long, unorganized course, the too short course and the long mediæval course—each fails to meet the situation. "The American college curriculum of today offers the only deliberately planned and respectable environment which habitually tempts the man who does not wish to do honest and thorough work, and which actually cultivates his facility in escaping from such work. It affords largely, in fact, a training-school of shamming and shirking." The plan proposed offers a three years' course; modern, disciplinary, comprehensive, having continuity and a fair amount of symmetry. The fitting schools are to be freed from the intolerable burden of so many subjects. One of the two classical languages and one of the two modern languages well learned would be of far more value than two not learned at all. Some history, some English books and a part of the required mathematics could well be dropped also. Preparatory school teachers are frequently on the whole superior to college instructors. There is room for improvement here. The college course to be disciplinary and progressive throughout, must be mainly required and only subordinately elective. The required work must fall under three groups: (1) Language as the key to the interpretation of human thought and feeling; (2) so much of mathematics as is necessary to comprehend the simpler methods and principles of the exact sciences, and some knowledge of the methods and discoveries of some one of those sciences; (3) the scientific knowledge of man's own mental and moral activities, their problems and the answers given by human reason to them. Knowledge, factual and methodological, is the object of this course.

Such radicalism is refreshing. The plow is in new ground.

* * *

Notes

"The Sunset" for October is a particularly attractive number. The most notable articles are by Joaquin Miller, George Wharton James, E. O. McCormick, Victor Henderson. The circulation of "The Sunset" has reached over 25,000.

"Hello Bill"; "Toasts," is the title of a unique book of toasts suitable for banquets and social occasions. The toasts are gathered from many sources by Victor W. Williams. Published by the Whitaker & Ray Co., 723 Market street. Price, $1.25.

Mae Henion Simms, the well-known primary teacher of the Stockton schools, has written a most excellent book for first and second grades. It is published by the American Book Company. The subject is "Child Literature." Price, 30 cents. Among the well-known stories told are "Jack and Gill," "Twinkle Little Star," "Mother Hubbard," "Joseph," "Tom Thumb," etc,

D. Appleton & Co. have published "Lessons in Hygiene," by W. O. Krohn, Ph.D. (Yale). This text has been adopted as the state book in Washington, Utah, and other states, and in many of the large cities of the country. Bailey Millard, the review editor of the *Examiner*, devoted a page to the merits of the book recently. It is recognized as a valuable text-book. D. Appleton & Co., 809 Market street, San Francisco.

George Wharton James, explorer, ethnologist, author and lecturer, who has devoted the greater portion of his life to geological, geographical, ethnological and archælogical researches in the great Southwest. especially in the Grand Canyon region and among the various tribes of Indians, is the author of "The Indians of the Painted Desert Region," which will be published by Little, Brown & Co. of Boston. This book, like its author's valuable work on the Grand Canyon, is the result of experience, of personal adventures and hardships in a journey over the Western desert, fraught with many dangers on account of sudden storms and absence of shelter, besides scarcity of water. Mr. James visited various Indian tribes, discovering some very curious facts. Among the Hopie tribe, for example. men weave the women's clothing and knit their own stockings, and the women build their own homes and invite their husbands to marry them. When Mr. James first visited the Navahoes, the chief ordered his daughter to "shampoo" the stranger's head. This is considered a great luxury, one Indian divorcing his wife because she declined to shampoo his head.

WESTERN SCHOOL NEWS

MEETINGS

California Teachers' Association. O. W. Erlewine, president; Mrs. M. M. FitzGerald, secretary, 1627 Folsom street, San Francisco; December 28 to 31, 1903.

Northern California Teachers' Association, Willows, Nov. 12, 13, 14.

Southern California Teachers' Association, Los Angeles, Cal., Dec. 22, 23, 24.

TEACHERS' INSTITUTES

Mendocino, J. F. Barbee, Supt. Ukiah, Oct. 27, 28, 29.

Modoc, Nellie Forest, Supt. Alturas, Sept. 30, Oct. 1, 2, 3.

Plumas, Tillie Naomi Kruger, Supt. Quincy, Oct. 7, 8, 9.

Sacramento, B. F. Howard, Supt. Nov. 23, 24, 25.

San Joaquin, E. B. Wright, Supt. Stockton, Nov. 23, 24, 25.

Santa Barbara, Supt. W. S. Edwards. Santa Barbara, Oct. 5, 6, 7, 8.

Siskiyou, Grace Addis Johnson, supt. Shasta Retreat, Sept. 26, 28, 29, 30.

Kings county, Mr. N. E. DaVidson, supt. Hanford, Dec. 21, 22, 23.

Colusa County; Supt. Laugenour, Nov. 9, 10, 11.

Butte County, Supt. R. H. Dunn, Nov. 9, 10, 11.

Tehama county, Supt. Lynch, Nov. 9, 10, 11.

Shasta County, Supt. Mrs. Brieard, Nov. 9, 10, 11.

Yolo county, Supt. Mrs. DeVilbiss, Nov. 9, 10, 11.

CalaVeras county, Supt. Waters, Nov. 2, 3, 4, 5.

Los Angeles, Supt. Mark Keppel, Dec. 21, 22, 23, 24.

Merced, Supt. Anna Silman, Oct. 26, 27, 28.

Orange county, Supt. Nichols, Oct. 19-24.

Stanislaus county, Supt. Florence Boggs, Oct. 26, 27, 28.

Madera county, Supt. Estelle Bagnelle, Dec. 15, 16, 17.

Napa county, Supt. Kate Ames, Oct. 19-21.

Mariposa county, Supt. Julia Jones, Nov. 16, 17, 18.

Placer county, Supt. C. N. Shane, Oct. 12-15.

Eldorado county, Supt. S. B. Wilson, Oct. 26-28.

San Benito county, Supt. J. H. Garner, October 26, 27, 28.

NOTES

Mr. J. E. Hayman of Colusa has resigned his position and has located in Napa, Cal.

The board of education of San Diego has introduced physical culture into the schools.

The Northern California Teachers' Association will meet November 12, 13, 14 at Willows, Cal.

The California Schoolmasters will give a banquet Saturday, October 10. Prof. C. A. Dunniway will preside.

Superintendent E. B. Wright of San Joaquin county has inaugurated a series of Saturday afternoon teachers' meetings.

President Benjamin Ide Wheeler delivered the dedication address at the new high school in Colusa, September 14, 1903.

California had a membership of one hundred and fifty-five at the forty-second convention of the N. E. A., held in Boston, July 6-10.

J. O. Osborne of Fresno city has been elected principal of Mastick school. This is the third principal Alameda has elected from Fresno.

Judge Rhodes of Santa Clara County, has decided that the dismissal without cause of fourteen teachers of the San Jose School Department was illegal.

Superintendent W. H. Langdon delivered an address on the "Improvement of the Schools of San Francisco," before the Local Council of Women, September 5, 1903.

Ex-Superintendent R. H. Webster's new Metropolitan Business College, 403 Van Ness Avenue, is in a flourishing condition. He has enrolled upwards of fifty pupils.

The Supreme Court has ruled in the case of Webster vs. San Francisco Board of Education that the superintendent of schools has not the authority to designate his power to a deputy.

The government has advertised for 150 male teachers to take positions in the Philippines under civil service rules. Salaries range from $900 to $1000.

W. H. De L. Kingsbury, formerly deputy superintendent of San Francisco schools, has been appointed by the Methodist Conference to preach at San Mateo and South San Francisco.

A. Megahan has been granted a leave of absence by the city board of education of Oakland, and has gone east in connection with a large syndicate, of which he is western manager.

The Greek theatre that William R. Hearst presented to the University of California was dedicated Thursday, September 24. Aristophanes' comedy, "The Birds," in the original Greek, was produced.

H. A. Suzzalo, deputy superintendent of schools of San Francisco, has been given a scholarship in the Teachers' College, Columbia University, N. Y., and has resigned. A. A. Macurda has been appointed by Superintendent Langdon in his place.

The staff of teachers of the College City High School, Colusa, is as follows: Ira Abraham, principal; assistants—Miss Louise Johnson and Miss Ruth Henry, both graduates of the University of California.

The City of San Francisco voted three million dollars for new schoolhouses. There were less than 4000 votes cast against the school bonds. Bonds were also voted for children's playgrounds, parks, etc.

A. B. Anderson of the University of California is principal of Colusa High School this year. School opened in the fine new building September 14. Ethel Farnham of the University of California and Miss Bessie Strange of Stanford are the assistant teachers.

The California School of Mechanical Arts, founded by James Lick, observed Founders' Day at the school on Monday, September 21. The students and officers of the school participated in the morning exercises. From 1 to 4:30 p. m. the school was open to the general public.

The Drawing Teachers' Association held a meeting at Polytechnic High School Saturday, September 6. Miss K. Ball spoke on Japan. C. W. Mark,

Mrs. E. M. North, and E. E. Goodell spoke on Manual Training. The next meeting will be held in Alameda Saturday, November 28, 1903.

The executive committee of the California Teachers' Association met in Superintendent Langdon's office Saturday, September 12, to engage special speakers for the meeting in December in San Francisco. The committee has secured Arnold J. Tompkins, president of the Cook County Normal School, and author of Philosophy of Teaching and School Management; also, Prof. S. H. Clark of the University of Chicago. The following is a partial list of departments arranged for the December meeting: County Boards of Education—chairman, P. M. Fisher, Oakland; Physical Culture and Hygiene—chairman, Walter Magee, University California; Music—chairman, Estelle Carpenter, San Francisco; Industrial Arts—chairman, A. B. Clark, Stanford University; High School Department—chairman, C. L. Biedenbach, Berkeley; Elementary School Department—chairman, C. C. Hughes, Alameda.

* * *

San Francisco Normal School Bulletins

The editions of the first three Bulletins of Method, compiled by the San Francisco State Normal School, have been exhausted, and requests for over 1000 copies of Bulletin No. 2 are now received which cannot be filled. The editions of each were 2000, making 6000 copies in all, which have been distributed free upon application from teachers thruout the state. A circular has just been issued from the school stating that while there are no funds for the republication of a second edition now available, the school will republish any of the exhausted editions, provided those desiring them will pay the cost of printing. This cost, estimated upon editions of 2000, will be 15 cents for Bulletin No. 2 on geography, and 10 cents for Bulletins Nos. 1 and 3. Orders for these back numbers will be received, and when enough are filed to justify republication, they will be reissued; it is not necessary to send stamps until notification that the bulletin is ready for distribution, but orders should be filed promptly so that they may be issued as soon as possible.

Three new bulletins will be issued in the course of the next four or five weeks and will be distributed free of charge upon receipt of the postage. The graduate association of the school has undertaken to assume the expense of this free publication and have assessed themselves most liberally, in order to be of service to their fellow-teachers and the educational progress of the state. Bulletin No. 4 will be a course of study leading to an honorary diploma the school proposes to confer for marked efficiency of teaching, combined with certain professional study, but of a kind which directly helps in daily teaching. This course for the present will be open only to graduates of the school, but as soon as these are organized it is the intention to throw its privileges open to any efficient and earnest teachers who can comply with the requirements. Bulletin No. 5 will be a concrete illustration of teaching geography, using Scandinavia as the topic; it is prepared by Mr. Walter J. Kenyon. Bulletin No. 6 will be similar to No. 4, using China as the illustration; it is prepared by Mr. Frank F. Bunker and is a supplement to

Bulletin No. 2, in which he details just the method of using reading references, how to organize the essential things to be taught, and what points should receive emphasis. The postage upon Bulletins 4 and 5 will be two cents and on Bulletin 6 will probably be four cents.

* * *

Consolidation of School Districts

Many superintendents or trustees may want extra copies of the JOURNAL of last June containing the description and methods of the system of consolidating school districts as provided by the last legislature. The council of education, thru a committee appointed last Spring, ordered 1000 extra copies printed to be distributed at cost price of ten cents each when ordered in quantities. Such orders may be sent to Superintendent Minnie Coulter at Santa Rosa, or they will be filled by writing to the JOURNAL.

When it is desired to educate a community upon the plan, a number of the special issue will be found of service in leading to a true comprehension of the system. Some superintendents have suggested that a set of these JOURNALS could be legitimately made a part of the teachers' library, to be issued and circulated when occasion occurs and later returned.

* * *

Permanent Headquarters in San Francisco for Teachers of the State

For a long time the advantages that might come to the teachers of the state individually and collectively, by the opening and maintaining of suitable club rooms in San Francisco, have been apparent to all of us who have given the subject any thought. A detailed statement of the many advantages would require too much time and space. In order to assist in bringing this subject definitely before our teachers, a letter, of which the following is a copy, has been sent to the city and county superintendents, members of the State Board of Education, and also to many of the representative teachers in different parts of the state:

BERKELEY, Cal., September 24, 1903.

I am trying to perfect a plan by which the teachers of the state or the Association itself may be enabled to establish and maintain permanent "headquarters in San Francisco. I am sure that it will be of great adVantage for our teachers, and especially for visiting teachers and the cause of education generally, if suitable rooms can be secured and fitted up for this purpose. Teachers and others interested in educational matters will then have a common place of resort at all times during the year. The best educational journals should be kept on file and a competent person should be in charge all of the time. There might also be a "bureau of information" in connection with it. If one half of the teachers of the state will join the Association each year, the plan is feasible, as there will be enough money for this purpose, with a sufficient balance to pay the expenses of the Association. What do you think of the scheme? If you faVor it, will you assist? Very truly yours,

The teachers in the different cities and counties can readily be reached thru their superintendents. Aside from the personal advantages to be gained, there should be, it seems, a willingness and desire on the part of every teacher ("professional pride" it is usually called) to become a member of the association. Membership is worth to every teacher who joins, many times the cost, from the standpoint of personal advantage alone. When, in addition to this personal factor, it is remembered that membership in the association helps to unify and strengthen educational work thruout the state, that it makes it possible for us to come into direct touch with the leaders of educational thought in America thru the annual meetings; and, in addition to this, that it may result in the establishing of a permanent "home," we may say for all, there seems to be no good reason why any teacher should refuse to become a member.

If these rooms are established, every teacher in the state, as well as every visitor from any other state, will be made to feel that there is a community of interest that can come so fully in no other way. Co-operation of superintendents and teachers is all that is needed to put this plan into immediate effect.

The establishing of "headquarters" in San Francisco does not imply that the meetings of the association are to be held permanently in that city. For many reasons this is not desirable, not would it be practicable. The meeting of the association carries with it much of good to any community. Its influence should be as widespread as possible; hence, a change in the place of meeting from year to year is desirable. But the place of holding the annual meeting has nothing to do with the establishing of the club rooms referred to above.

This matter is commended to the immediate and careful consideration of every teacher in the state, whether engaged NOW in the schoolroom, or not. Can there not be secured such a hearty response as shall result in the successful carrying-out of the plan at the coming meeting of the association?

S. D. WATERMAN,
City Superintendent of Schools, Berkeley.

* * *

INSTITUTES

The institute season is upon us and no doubt many superintendents are earnestly considering ways and means of making their institutes interesting and profitable; and well may they, for institutes cost this state in direct expenses and teachers' time, one hundred thirty-five thousand dollars a year. When the expense is taken into consideration it is not surprising that now and then a taxpayer demands that institutes be abolished, and that there are not wanting among educators those who feel that the institute has outlived its usefulness. All this may be edifying, but it does not help the county superintendent who is required by law to hold an institute each year.

With all their faults, institutes have some redeeming features. The school ma'am has a chance to shake out the wrinkles of her last year's gown, and to come to town to buy a new hat. She has an opportunity to meet acquaintances and form new ones. She can listen to educators who are wrestling with current educational problems, and who may have pet theories to expound or fads to display. She may learn that the world is moving and that she must bestir herself if she would not be left behind. She may be made to feel her own insignificance, her ignorance, and alas, too often, her helplessness. She may get inspiration and help, and determine to investigate the problems for herself and master then. Blessed is her school if she has not determined to try in it some fad which has been presented in glowing colors; the good features of which she has not learned how to use, or the bad to avoid.

The institute is not a place for spouters to show the emptiness of their minds, or for pretty misses to read flowery essays on the beauties of nature; nor is it a place for tedious lectures on psychology or pedagogy, nor for the presentation of untried theories.

It ought to be a place where that which is practical and valuable is presented; where teachers are filled with a desire to know and a determination to find out; where much information on a few topics is given, and the means and methods of getting more clearly set forth.

To be specific, 1. Choose two or three related subjects for the week's work. It is not enough to rake away the ashes, stir the coals, and fan the embers; new fuel must be added, and the key to the coal-bin should be hung in a conspicuous place.

2. Take up other subjects at the succeeding institute so that all the subjects of the entire course of study shall be successively considered.

3. Engage two, or at most three, practical, experienced instructors, except where the number of teachers is very large, and have them devote the entire week to instruction. They should furnish beforehand such outlines of their work as will enable the teachers to prepare to receive the most good out of the instruction.

4. Divide the institute into two or three sections, graded where admissible. In populous counties more sections will be desirable and High School teachers should form a separate section.

5. Arrange for two, or at most three daily recitation periods, so that each instructor may, if possible, teach each section.

Suggested Program.—Monday morning, meet, organize, announce committees, make your speech, get acquainted. Monday afternoon, instructors meet sections, make general announcements, map out work and lay foundations. Monday evening, social function. Tuesday, Wednesday, Thursday and Friday mornings, 9:30-12 m, instruction in sections. Tuesday, Wednesday and Thursday afternoons, 2-3:30 P. M. sharp, entertainment in the form of lectures, essays, readings, music. Tuesday, Wednesday, Thursday evenings, Study, Relaxation, rest. Friday afternoon, closing up work.
WILLIAM HOWARD BAKER,
Teacher of Mathematics State Normal School, San Jose.

* * *

A MILLION A MONTH

By manufacturing and selling a million records every month the Columbia Phonograph Co. has achieved the end for which it has long been striving —the reduction in the price of its High Speed Moulded Cylindrical Wax records from fifty cents, each, Simultaneously with this reduction in price a new record, greatly superior to any that has ever been offered for sale is being furnished—a black, superhardened record, both durable and brilliant and combining sweetness and smoothness with remarkable volume. These records will fit all talking machines using cylindrical records and the facilities for manufacturing them have been increased to an extent that will enable the Columbia Phonograph Co. to produce a practically limitless supply.

While improved processes of manufacture and the simplifying of talking machine construction have resulted in the price of Graphophones being reduced, from time to time, until they are now sold at figures that bring them within the reach of all, the price of cylinder records has, in the meantime, remained at fifty cents each. For many insuperable reasons it has never been possible until now to sell records at the popular price that has finally been fixed for them. But continued and unceasing improvement in Columbia facilities has, at last, brought the output to a point where it is possible to cut the price in half while, instead of impairing the quality of the product to secure this end, a better article is to be furnished than ever before. This could only be done by increasing the sales to the enormous figures they have now reached and which are certain to assume bewildering proportions, with the reduction in the price.

The Columbia Phonograph Co., the pioneer and leader in the talking machine art, was the first to furnish a really meritorious record for fifty cents and while its records are far superior to those of previous years, the fact is admitted, on all sides, that Columbia records, in all stages of their development, have always been the best that were made. And this is truer now than ever before. While the superiority of Columbia records would justify their sale at a higher price than that of any competing record, their reduced price means that the purchaser is to have the very best records ever manufactured and to have two of them at the price he formerly paid for one.

Preparations have been made with the utmost thoroughness to meet the emergency which a reduction in the price of cylindrical records to twenty-five cents, each, was certain to precipitate. In anticipation of an unprecedented demand for the new and vastly improved records, the factory of the Columbia Phonograph Co. is running day and night and every possible arrangement has been made to fill all orders with reasonable promptness, however heavy those orders may become.

To make better goods than its competitors and sell them at popular prices has always been the aim of the Columbia Phonograph Co. Desirous that the public should test its claims as to the superior quality of this new product it offers, for a limited period, to give a record, free, to any user of a talking machine who will call at any of its stores and mention the type of the machine he is using. If not convenient to call, a record will be mailed on receipt of ten cents, to cover postage, and the information as to the type of the machine in use.

AN EXCELLENT COMPOSITION.

Mrs. Jennie L. Thorp,

Dear Madam: I am in receipt of several copies of "California, Queen of Old Columbia." Permit me to state to you that your very excellent composition was sung by a double quartet at our recent 9th of September celebration in St. Helena. It was splendidly sung, and received many very complimentary responses from those who had the pleasure of hearing it.

Thanking you for affording us an opportunity of becoming acquainted with the song and for the pleasure of hearing it well sung, I remain,

Yours very truly, E. L. CAVE.

* * *

Mr. Frank H. Ball, formerly of Throop Institute and last year connected with the Department of Manual Training of San Francisco, has recently been made Superintendent of Manual Training for the Island of Porto Rico.

* * *

SUGGESTION TO SCHOOL TRUSTEES.

To Trustees: Permit me to express to you my appreciation of the interest you have taken in the welfare of our schools.

You are called upon many times to sacrifice personal interests in the performance of your duties as trustees.

This you have done cheerfully, without compensation for time and labor lost, but your reward is the satisfaction of knowing that such duties, so well performed, are reflected in the efficiency of the schools of the county.

Without this co-operation of trustees our schools never could have attained their present high standard of excellence.

We must not weary in well doing, and must be on the alert to advance the cause of education whenever opportunity affords.

The efficiency of our teachers may be advanced by giving them an opportunity to visit other schools of the county.

I am very desirous of introducing into the schools of the county a "Visiting Day" for teachers, viz.: one day in the year to be allowed each teacher, without loss of pay, in which to visit some other school in the county doing similar work.

Thus the teacher has an opportunity of comparing her work with that of a fellow teacher doing similar work, and of making notes of such points as she deems helpful to her in her own work.

By this means each teacher will be strengthened and encouraged, and your school will be the gainer in this work.

I am confident of the good results to be thus attained.

The teacher will be expected to put in the full number of hours in her visitation as she puts in each day in her own school room, and will be required to report to this office, as well as to the Clerk of their respective Districts, the school visited, date of visit, etc.

This can only be accomplished by the co-operation of trustees with this office. Are you willing to grant this assistance to your teacher, and thus strengthen the work of your school?

If so, please sign the inclosed card and mail it to this office.

Yours in the interest of education,

    Geo. L. Sackett, School Superintendent.

* * *

NORMAL SCHOOL ATTENDANCE.

The gratifying start that the Normal School has had this term leads to the conclusion that it is on a good, firm footing, and has the confidence of the people.

The adoption of the "high school basis" has of course prevented so large an attendance during the past two or three years. That was expected. And it is not to be regretted. Whenever a standard of enrollment is raised the enrollment decreases. But what is the result, if not the turning out of better graduates?

Under he old basis of grammar school graduation, the school was filled with young students of an average of 16 years of age. The enrollment went as high as 766. They were a host of boys and mostly girls, who needed the same kind of discipline as in the grammar schools, would scarcely go into the library unless fairly driven, and didn't know how to make proper use of their opportunities. One girl, when asked by one of the staff what was the reason she had been so long in the school, replied: "It took me a year or two to find out what I am here for."

On the high school basis a student entering must be a high school graduate, and puts in two years at the Normal as against four years required under the former conditions. The consequence is that now the girls average 20 years of age. They are in fact young women, well developed mentally, and also physically fit to prosecute the severer studies required of them. Such young women—and the lonesome few young men who are brave enough to enter the noble profession where they, too, are needed—are better able to do the professional work requisite in their training for teaching than were the students who entered on the grammar school basis.

It is not enrollment alone that is needed. What the State demands is that the best quality of teachers shall be turned out. The Normal Schools are maintained, not for the purpose of accommodating boys and girls of the grammar grades who desire to become teachers, but for the purpose of fitting those for the profession who are ready to take up the professional studies demanded as qualifications for teachers.

There has been some talk heard here of a dissatisfaction of some people on account of the San Jose State Normal putting up the bars so high as to exclude many of those who wish to go into teaching, because they must wait to go through the high school. It must be remembered, however, that the Normal School located in San Jose is not a city but a State institution. What is best for the teaching profession in the State must be considered, not what is convenient for some San Jose girls and boys. San Jose is benefited and honored in having such an institution in her midst. She has also a first-class high school, in which to prepare her aspiring young men and women for the Normal course, so there is no special cause for complaint.

The fact that the State now imposes a tax for the support of high schools makes it all the more necessary that the Normal Schools should have a high standard for admission. Even in sparsely settled parts, for example, in Inyo county, high schools are springing up, and the more advanced education there obtainable is now within more or less easy reach of every home.—*Editorial in San Jose Mercury.*

* * *

Boynton & Esterly, Managers of the Fiske Teachers' Agencies, report a scarcity of teachers, and they will consider it a favor to have information of available teachers who will accept positions in district schools immediately. Address 518 Parrott Building, San Francisco, Cal.

* * *

The California Polytechnic School, located at San Luis Obispo, opened with about twenty students on October 1st. This school is well equipped and offers instruction in practical arts. There should be a large attendance from all parts of the State. Young men and women who desire to be the leaders of the greatest of all industries, agriculture, and kindred branches, should attend this school. Write to President Leroy Anderson for catalog. Tuition is free.

* * *

Wouldn't you like to go to the great Exposition at St. Louis next year? An absolutely free trip is offered ten teachers in each county of California. A postal will bring full information. Address, J. W. Graham, Associate Manager The Playa Viciente Plantation Company, 723 Market street, San Francisco, Cal.

STATE NORMAL SCHOOL.

President Pierce, of the State Normal School of Los Angeles, reports an unusual enrollment of new students for the fall term. Practically all who will come in this fall are now registered. The number of new students is 166, of which fifty-eight are from the ninth grade and the balance from high schools and academies. It is said that there are forty schools of every sort and in every part of the country represented in the enrollment. In the training school department there have been added accommodations for 400 extra children, and this will not only go a long way toward helping the city school department, but will provide additional material for the members of the normal school classes to teach.

* * *

TEACHERS WANTED FOR THE PHILIPPINES.

The United States Civil Service Commission announces that an examination for the position of teacher (male only) in the Philippine service will be held October 19, 20, 1903. This examination will be held to supply 150 teachers, with salaries as follows: Twenty-five at $1200, 70 at $1000, and 55 at $900 per annum. Appointments will be made at the salaries mentioned, based upon the experience and the relative standing in the examination. Those appointed will be eligible for promotion to the higher grades in the service, ranging from $900 to $2000 for teachers and $1500 to $2500 for division superintendents. The examination will consist of ten obligatory subjects and twenty optional subjects. One or more optional subjects may be taken if desired, but it will not be necessary for applicants to take any of the optional subjects. Applicants must indicate in application form 2, in answer to question 1, the optional subject which they desire. This examination will take place at San Francisco on the date mentioned. Age limit, 20 to 40 years. Persons who desire to compete should at once apply either to the Secretary of the Consolidated Board of Examiners, 301 Jackson street, San Francisco, Cal., or to the Civil Service Commission, Washington, D. C., for application forms 2 and 375, which should be properly executed and filed with the Commission at Washington. Persons who are unable to file their formal applications and who notify the Commission of this fact, either by letter or telegram, with the request that they be permitted to take the examinaion, naming the optionals, if any, will be examined, provided their requests are received at the Commission in sufficient time to ship examination papers.

▲ BLACKBOARD ▲

The Very Best is

Furnished in continuous lengths up to 12 feet. Furnished in widths of 3, 3½ and 4 feet.

Black or Green as Desired

Write for Samples and Prices. Try our

NEARSLATE DUSTLESS CRAYON

The Whitaker & Ray Company   San Francisco

FOR SALE—One hundred dollar scholarship in business college. Address, Editor "Western Journal of Education," 723 Market street.

Good Writing

IN 100 HOURS
Under Guarantee

Bixler's Physical Training in Penmanship has been before the public for 20 years, and it is the only system that can guarantee a good hand writing, a thorough mastery of the pen, in 100 hours practice. It is the best and only book recognized as a complete self-instructor. It employs only positive means, in every stroke of the pen, and the results must be satisfactory. You train the writing muscles by correct practice. "It is all in the practice," some say, but there are some 1,000 different ways of practicing NEGATIVELY, imparting NEGATIVE results. We give you the right way, and guarantee success, or will

Give 15 Cents an Hour for Your Time During the 100 Hours.

We do this because some folks lack the confidence and nerve to go ahead. Undertake the task at our responsibility and get your 15c. an hour if you fail. It is no big risk on our part, for we have 20 years to draw conclusions from. The book was a great event in the penmanship field 20 years ago; it is a bigger one today. It is necessary for learners of shorthand; making the course shorter by 50 per cent. as characters will roll from your pen rapidly and easily. Mr. Bixler is president and proprietor of Bixler's Business College, cor. Madison and Ogden, Chicago, founded in 1886, and in constant session ever since. 10,000 sq. ft. floorage, and the most practical school in the country. Price of book is $1, including time book, contract, and full directions. 100 lessons by mail in addition to book. Positions secured when competent. PRIZES, Pianos, Watches, Books, etc., to those making best improvements. Prof. G. BIXLER, Cor. Madison Street and Ogden Avenue, Chicago.

School Souvenirs

We print the best for the money. As teachers we know what you want. Beautiful designs, low prices, prompt work. Nothing is more pertinent to the occasion than these souvenirs for scholars on last day, holiday or any important period in school life. Send for free Samples and circulars, or better yet, send us your order with 3 cents, 4c or 5c for each souvenir, according to style. Only one style to each order. Photo Souvenirs, Booklet Souvenirs, Round Corner Souvenirs.

Prof. G. Bixler, cor. Madison St., and Ogden Avenue, Chicago.

THE
WESTERN JOURNAL
OF EDUCATION

November, 1903

	PAGE
EDITORIAL	719
The Future of the Teachers' Institutes—Freedom vs. Slavishness in School Work—Teachers Who Loaf—Compulsory Education and the Country Schools—The Adoption of a Series of Text-Books—Teachers' Meetings—To the Clerk of the School Board, etc.	
THE INFLUENCE OF BRAIN-POWER ON HISTORY	
Sir Norman Lockyer	727
A QUESTION OF ETHICS, *M. P. Donnelly*	740
READING AND LITERATURE, *W. W. Stetson*	742
EMERSON'S INFLUENCE IN EDUCATION, *Michael E. Sadler*	746
DEPARTMENT OF METHODOLOGY	749
Physiology-Digestion—Thanksgiving Day Program—History of Thanksgiving.	
BOOKS AND MAGAZINES	752
WESTERN SCHOOL NEWS	763
INSTITUTES	765

THE WESTERN JOURNAL OF EDUCATION
723 MARKET ST., SAN FRANCISCO

Volume VIII
No. 11

$1.50 Per Year
Single Copy 15c

Four New Books by California Authors

SIMMS'S CHILD LITERATURE — 30 cents
By Mae Henion Simms

This is the latest addition to the well-known and popular series of Eclectic School Readings, and is intended for First Reader grades. Its distinctive feature consists in its method of presenting attractive nursery rhymes and stories, popular poems, and Bible stories, simplified and told in short, easy words. The rhymes are afterward repeated in their original form. New words are naturally and gradually introduced, and the gradation of the matter is easy and well-maintained throughout. Written by a teacher in the Stockton, Cal., schools, it is the outcome of work done there and was thoroughly tested in the classroom before publication. The book is profusely illustrated, and will be welcomed by the many California teachers who feel the need of fresh and interesting reading matter for younger pupils.

"I heartily approve of Mrs. Simms's new book, Child Literature. My faith will be shown by a liberal use of the book."
JAMES A. BARR,
Superintendent of Schools, Stockton, Cal.

WINTERBURN'S THE SPANISH IN THE SOUTHWEST — 55 cents
By Rosa V. Winterburn

The discovery and early history of California are in this book vividly and attractively presented for young readers. Commencing with the life of the Indians, it takes up next the coming of the Spaniards, then their explorations in search of gold, the founding of the missions, and the life on the pueblos and the ranches. The book brings the history down to the end of the Mexican rule in 1848. The narrative element and the purely historical are so skilfully combined as to make this book a story of history, a collection of stories so selected and arranged as to present historical characteristics and tendencies of periods. The style is adapted both to the subject-matter and to the age of the pupils for whom the book is intended. The illustrations are numerous and artistic, and maps show the places mentioned.

CHAMBERLAIN'S FIELD AND LABORATORY EXERCISES IN PHYSICAL GEOGRAPHY — 50 cents
By James F. Chamberlain, Department of Geography, State Normal School, Los Angeles, Cal., Associate Editor of "The Journal of Geography."

This is a series of laboratory and field exercises designed to lead the pupil to interpret the geographical forms and processes about him, and to give him a practical knowledge of their principles. Each exercise is preceded by a list of necessary materials, which are easily obtainable. After each exercise ample space is left for the pupil to write a complete record of the work done. An important feature of the book is the plan for studying the geographical distribution of various phenomena, and plotting the data on outline maps of the United States and of the world which are inserted. The manual is adapted for use with any text-book on Physical Geography, and will form a valuable adjunct for practical work.

COLEMAN'S PHYSICAL LABORATORY MANUAL — 60 cents
By S. E. Coleman, Head of the Science Department, Oakland, Cal., High School.

In this manual the laboratory work is co-ordinated with the classroom study, and comprises 81 exercises, so arranged that the book can be used either with simple apparatus, or with a more fully equipped laboratory. The matter in connection with each experiment consists of (1) A definite statement of what the experiment is for; (2) References to leading text-books in physics, indicating what reading may profitably precede and accompany the laboratory work; (3) A list of the apparatus required; (4) Directions, suggestions, form of record, and discussion of the experiment. The book is the outgrowth of practical work, and shows throughout that it was prepared by a skilful teacher.

AMERICAN BOOK COMPANY Publishers
204 Pine Street, San Francisco.
New York Cincinnati Chicago Boston Atlanta Dallas

The Western Journal of Education

NOVEMBER, 1903

EDITORIAL

The Future of the Teachers' Institutes

In several sections of California a disposition has in recent years manifested itself to question the value of the Teachers' Institute as at present conducted. The Institute, it is claimed, served a very useful purpose in the early stages of education in California when there was no professional training of teachers, when an educational propaganda was periodically desirable both for teachers and communities, and when both the subject matter and the methods of education were relatively so unorganized that the work of a skilled Institute instructor, even for a day or two, might produce results that were immediate and effective. In those days, it is pointed out, teachers were largely independent of uniform courses of study and uniform systems of textbooks; consequently each was at liberty to put into practice the best that he could gather at teacher's meetings.

But conditions have changed, so it is asserted. Professionally trained teachers are found in every community, sometimes, indeed are in the large majority, to whom the average Institute conductor brings little that is worth while, since he must usually address himself to the untrained portion of the body of teachers. Teachers and communities have now well developed educational ideals, so that propagandist movements are no longer necessary. Knowledge of subject matter of education no longer troubles the average teacher, as is evidenced by the fact that Institutes no longer give subject matter, as such, any consideration. Detailed and special methods also are now seldom discussed at Institutes, owing partly to the fact that the professionally trained contingent already possesses these, and partly to the fact that these are available in equally good shape in books and journals. The Institute lecturer, therefore, is obliged to occupy himself with the more general aspects of education—ideals, aims, educational values, general principle of method, new theories, historical studies in education, and the like. But these, it is claimed, are not profitable subjects for the ordinary teacher for several reasons. The average teacher has neither time or power to pass from educational theory over into practice. She cannot profit by an understanding of educational aims and values because she has no control over the machinery of administration— the adopting of text-books, courses of study, examinations, etc. Finally, while it is possible to present in a few lectures an outline of some general principles of method, or a new field of subject matter, as manual training or nature study, it is by no means possible, even in several weeks, to give the teacher any command of the application of either the principles or the subject matter; that can come only after long and patient effort in learning under skilled direction. The net result of much of the presentation of educational theory is that the experienced teacher turns an indifferent ear while the younger and more inexperienced, if she be in earnest, acquires an uneasy conscience with reference to her already moderately good work.

On the other hand, it is claimed by those who are opposed to the present Institute, that these annual meetings cost the state something over $150,000 annually, if everything is taken into consideration. This money could be more profitably spent. It would be possible to endow teachers' reading circles; or to maintain University extension courses; or to support, in five or six centers of the state, short summer schools under skilled direction, where the best of new educational work could not only be studied, but where it could be illustrated objectively in actual class room practice and otherwise.

It is believed that the above is a fair presentation of the claims of those who would see the present Institute modified. It is probably not claimed by any serious educator that this form of professional training for active teachers should be entirely eliminated. Apart from the ministry, education offers the first example of a trade or profession whose members have been trained at public expense. This has been due to the social recognition of the importance of the teaching profession and the desirability of special inducement for professional training. But education progresses, and in these later years progresses rapidly. Public support, from a social standpoint, is still highly desirable to enable the teacher whose compensation is by no means in proportion to the importance of the service she renders, to continue her professional advancement. The question is, then, not one of the abolition of this particular form of professional encouragement and training, but rather has reference to the form it shall take.

Any serious discussion of the usefulness of the Teachers Institute at the present time should take into account two or three facts. In the first place, the teaching force in California is very heterogeneous. There are counties where the large majority of the teachers are professionally trained which have very low standards of educational attainment. There are many places where the old fashioned Institute serves a very useful purpose, both in giving the teachers new mastery of the art of teaching, and in arousing public sentiment in favor of more and better education. Again, while we can in no way measure the effect upon the work of the teacher of broad views, high ideals, and enthusiasm, it is very evident to the experienced educator that these count for much. Teaching fails of its end when it degenerates into mechanical routine, and a perpetual access of energy and interest is essential to prevent this degeneration. Not what the working teacher obtains in the way of definite ideas and methods is always the most importance; more valuable may be the spiritual uplift which comes from contact with the enthusiastic co-workers of her profession. Moreover, it is not true that teachers have little influence in administration. In the democracy of education new ideas and standards percolate thru the teaching force and gradually but surely work themselves into courses, text-books, and the other machinery of education. Finally, in elevating professional spirit and in expanding the social horizon of teachers, the present Institute which assembles for a week all the teachers in a county is of postive value.

The Teachers Institute has not lost its educational value when all sections of the state are taken into consideration. In many places it could doubtless be profitably replaced by some other form of professional training which might not be more expensive. At present the statutes allow no flexibility in this matter. The time has probably arrived when laws should be passed which would permit and encourage the development of new types of professional training for active teachers; but we are not ready for sweeping legislation to either destroy or greatly modify the present Institute.

722   *The Western Journal of Education*

Freedom vs. Slavishness in School Work

There is a thought in Booker Washington's interpretation of the negro problem that should be generalized. After the war, he says, "it was not unnatural that a large element of the colored people at first interpreted freedom to mean freedom from work with the hands. They naturally had not learned to appreciate the fact that they had been *worked*, and that one of the great lessons for freemen to learn is to *work*. They had not learned the vast difference between *working* and *being worked*." Their difficulty was not peculiar to their color. The great cause, in fact almost the only cause of dry rot in the schools, is that teachers have not learned the difference between working and being worked. The school law, the course of study, the rules of the Board of Education and the directions of the Superintendent all seem to them to be efforts to work them rather than suggestions to them in their work. The law, all law is a schoolmaster to bring one to the spirit of work, i. e., to provoke one to find its reasons, to think out its meaning and so make it an expression of his own wish and desire. If this cannot be done the law is insufficient and must be changed, but before it can be changed it must be "fulfiled." Mere outward compliance is never sufficient. Plato defined the slave for all time as one who in his acts does not express his own ideas. Measured by this standard it is to be feared that the work of our schools is slavish rather than free. We need an educational evangelization which should make us aware of the dignity of the calling whereunto we are called and of the ends and methods of our occupation. Ours is the supreme art; but an artist is one who has thought upon his business, lives with it by day, and dreams of it at night, and in his work expresses the ideas which he has made his own. Slavishness is the very opposite of this and slavishness should have no place in a free school.

* * *

Teachers Who Loaf

A text for a one-minute editorial sermon is furnished by an item which has recently been extensively copied in the daily press. It is entitled "Trained Nurses Who Loaf." It reads as follows:

"When a doctor finds a nurse reading a book about her profession, and not a novel, while she watches at the bedside of a patient," said an uptown physician, "that is the nurse he likes to hire and to help. If the case turns out well, the doctor sometimes makes her a present of a book with up-to-date ideas on her profession, which she might not be able to buy. One-half of the trained nurses of the city are dependent upon the recommendations of physicians, and half the success of a physician depends on a good nurse. Therefore, a doctor likes a nurse who reads about her business, attends lectures and keeps up with the times.

"You would be astonished to know how many lectures are given by physicians in New York every month that are open to trained nurses, but which few of them attend. There are a good many loafers among the trained nurses. They seem to think their study ended when they got their diplomas."—*New York Press.*

Change nurses to teachers and the application is plain. Their business requires more training, for it is altogether more difficult to keep a person well who is already well than it is to make a sick man well. Their work is professional whenever they approach it in the professional attitude. There was a time in the history of education when it was better to read novels than most of the books which were published about the profession, but praised be Allah, that time is passed. Not a single month passes which does not witness the appearance of several serious scholarly and helpful works of a professional sort. Are they being read? A superintendent said a little time ago, "I can't get my teachers to read, that is my great affliction. They won't take hold. The schools get no better. The teachers get worse as the days go by." It is safe to say that that superintendent will promote teachers upon the basis of their professional interest and growth. Civil service requirements are coming more and more to dictate the terms of pedagogical advancement. Pulls are ceasing to avail much and the teacher who cannot obtain and keep the esteem of his professional fellows will soon find himself high and dry without a position. On the other hand, a teacher who reads about his business, attends lectures, teachers' meetings and conferences, and takes part in them, not grudgingly, but with the enthusiasm that every worker should show for the work he has chosen, not only does his work better but is better protected in his calling than he could be by pages of tenure of office laws and old age pension provisions.

Compulsory Education and the Country Schools

There was a time when it was thought that virtue was synonymous with country life. Time has gone by. Now it is well known that carelessness, ignorance and indolence are more likely to exist in the country than in the city. The city child is surrounded with more of the instruments of law, with more of the spirit of lawlessness, with more incentives to work and more and plainer examples of the results of failure than to the country child. The small country town represents neither the organization of a city nor the equally vigorous and educative influence of farm life. Socially it is neither fish, flesh nor fowl, and because of its disorganization and looseness of ideals and purposes it is apt to supply more than its proportionate share of vagabons, idlers and criminals. The village is the pitfall of the country child. The loafers at the street corners, the idlers about the hotel, the indolent village wits are too apt to represent an ideal of freedom from toil which appeals to his youthful mind. For these reasons the compulsory education law should be vigorously enforced by village and rural school boards. Country children as well as city children have a right to an elementary education. The law was made for the whole state and should be diligently enforced in each school district.

* * *

The Adoption of a Series of Text-Books

The State Text-Book Committee, consisting of Gov. Geo. C. Pardee, Thomas J. Kirk, Superintendent of Public Instruction, and Dr. Elmer E. Brown, of the Department of Education of the University of California, created by the legislature of 1903, has arranged for a grammar gradeand a primary history, and have now under consideration a series of geographies and arithmetics. The committee is proceeding with due precaution. It is fortunate for the state that the selection of matter for a state series of books is left largely to men of wide experience in public schools. Superintendent Kirk has been connected with the primary and grammar schools for over twenty years. Dr. Brown has had practical experience as a teacher in the public schools, and has always been an earnest student of education in all of its phases. The committee selects as readers a number of men and women who are actually engaged in the use of text-books in the schools of California. It has been asked, "Why are not the teachers of California consulted?" The fact is that ninety-five per cent of those who have anything to do with the selection of matter for the state series of books are either practical public school teachers or have been. The text-book committee selected as secretary, J. H. Strine, a teacher. If the state fails to get the best books in the country it will not be due to the fact that public school men have not been given a voice in the matter. The committee under the law has no restrictions as to price or merit. The confidence of the people is with the State Text-Book Committee.

* * *

Teachers' Meetings

The stimulating influence of teachers' meetings gave Indianapolis a live corps of teachers. The local institute of Pennsylvania has made the great body of teachers in the common schools of that state most thoroly wide-awake on educational topics. The teachers' meetings when properly conducted are for good. Superintendent Langdon is to be congratulated on the inauguration of a series of meetings for the teachers of the San Francisco School Department. It is a question, however, whether it is practical to hold meetings immediately after five hours of hard teaching for the purpose of instruction in methods. The teacher who uses up all her vitality on fifty to sixty pupils does not have a great mental aptitude for professional work. Teachers' meetings should be in the morning, when there is an absence of mental and physical fatigue. Saturday morning will not do for the reason that the mental attitude of the teacher would not be right, and you cannot force nor inspire favorable attention. There would be no loss to the department nor to the pupils if an occasional hour was taken out of the morning's teaching and devoted to "plan" work. It might be difficult to educate the public to appreciate the use of school hours for teachers' meetings. It would pay.

* * *

To the Clerk of the School Board

The law in reference to the OFFICIAL JOURNAL is printed on the first page of this issue. The clerk of the board is requested to hand THE JOURNAL over to the teacher by the end of each month. There are important articles in each issue. The departments of "Methods," "Books and Magazines," "School News," etc., are of more than ordinary interest. Complaint has been made on the part of a number of teachers that THE JOURNAL is not filed with the teacher in accordance with law.

* * *

It is not the man who can do one *stupendous* problem, and then collapse, that the world wants, but rather the one who can do innumerable smaller problems—and continue doing them. To do this requires continued drill in one particular direction, as nearly in line with the work to be done as possible. For instance: Pugulist Jeffries has by careful training developed steel-like muscles which are well-nigh perfect, and yet the writer knows a small man who weighs not over 130 pounds, and who never took one hour's training for muscle building in his life, but who can go into the hay-field with Mr. Jeffries and in the parlance of hay-field workers, "run him to the shade" in one hot afternoon.

We are all familiar with the ponderous brain which has been developed to gigantic proportions by years of struggle with mighty (and useless) problems in arithmetic. We also daily see this "giant intellect" out-pointed by the practical little brain which can solve a dozen live problems with its "jaw" before the stuffed giant can get the machinery of his ponderous mind into working order. Modern education seems to be based largely upon the idea that we can learn to lift great weights of iron by constantly tugging at heavy loads of lead. This is a fatal error in principle, and dangerous because it is difficult to see. Senator Sanford gave California horses a world-wide reputation by abolishing the "jogging system." He began by putting the colts to doing precisely what he desired them to excel in on the track in after years. We may well learn a lesson educationally from the success of his experiments. Let us abolish the "jogging system" in education and put the children to doing that which we expect them to follow in after life just as soon as possible.

* * *

The improvement of rural school grounds is of the greatest importance. A model schoolhouse and model school yard will oftentimes influence the entire neighborhood for the betterment of homes. Trustees who fail in their duty in beautifying should be removed for negligence. The purchase of school supplies may seem important, but it is of far greater importance to plant a tree. The outhouses should be kept in the best sanitary condition. The ventilation of the schools should be perfect. The beauty of the walls of the schoolhouse and the school grounds should be an example to all. Now it the time of the year to start in to improve the school property. It is not in building expensive schoolhouses that proves the worth of a board of school trustees, but it is in the making the best out of the conditions that exist.

* * *

From an educational view point California has a publicity in the East that has a distinct material value. The "Literary Digest" of October 10th contains an article on "The Literary Development of the Pacific Coast," written by Herbert Bashford for the "Atlantic Monthly"; also a page on the Greek amphitheatre at the University of California. The article on the literature of the West and the dedication of the Greek amphitheatre are but incidents of publicity. California has a large way of doing things. Our state makes good. When California exhibits its wines, fruits and grains, its ores, big trees, and commercial supremacy there will also be recognition of the large way in which our educational institutions find expression in the development of the state. And the state in its appreciation of education, music, and literature has extreme felicity in the expression of its sane love of intellectual resources.

THE INFLUENCE OF BRAIN-POWER ON HISTORY.*

On this we may congratulate ourselves all the more because, I think, although it is not generally recognized, that the century into which we have now well entered may be more momentous than any which has preceded it, and that the present history of the world is being largely moulded by the influence of brain-power, which in these modern days has to do with natural as well as human forces and laws, that statesmen and politicians will have in the future to pay more regard to education and science, as empire-builders and empire-guarders, than they have paid in the past.

The most fundamental change wrought by the early applications of science was in relation to producing and carrying power. With the winning of mineral wealth and the production of machinery in other countries, and cheap and rapid transit between nations, our superiority as depending upon our first use of vast material resources was reduced. Science, which is above all things cosmopolitan—planetary, not national—internationalizes such resources at once. In every market of the world

> "things of beauty, things of use,
> Which one fair planet can produce,
> Brought from under every star,"

were soon to be found.

Hence the first great effect of the general progress of science was relatively to diminish the initial supremacy of Britain, due to the first use of *material* resources, which indeed was the real source of our national wealth and place among nations.

The unfortunate thing was that, while the foundations of our superiority, depending upon our *material resources,* were being thus sapped by a cause *which was beyond our control,* our statesmen and our universities were blind leaders of the blind, and our other asset, our mental resources, which was within our control, was culpably neglected.

So little did the bulk of our statesmen know of the part science was playing in the modern world and of the real basis of the nation's activities, that they imagined political and fiscal problems to be the only matters of importance. Nor, indeed, are we very much better off today. In the important discussions recently raised by Mr. Chamberlain, next to nothing has been said of the effect of the progress of science on prices. The whole course of the modern

---

*The address of the President of the British Association for the Advancement of Science, which perhaps has provoked more discussion and obtained a wider reading than any statement of the claims of education published in recent years. We believe that it is should be read by every teacher in California and therefore present this epitome of the address.

world is attributed to the presence or absence of taxes on certain commodities in certain cóuntries. The fact that the great fall in the price of food-stuffs in England did not come till some thirty or forty years after the removal of the corn duty between 1847 and 1849 gives them no pause; for them new inventions, railways and steamships are negligible quantities; the vast increase in the world's wealth in free trade and protected countries alike comes merely according to them in response to some *political* shibboleth.

We now know, from what has occurred in other States, that if our Ministers had been more wise and our universities more numerous and efficient,. our *mental resources* would have been developed by improvements in educational method, by the introduction of science into schools, and, more important than all the rest, by the teaching of science by experiment, observation and research, and not from books. It is because this was not done that we have fallen behind other nations in properly applying science to industry, so that our applications of science to industry are relatively less important than they were. But this is by no means all; we have lacked the strengthening of the national life produced by fostering the scientific spirit among all classes; and along all lines of the nation's activity; many of the responsible authorities know little and care less about science; we have not learned that it is the duty of a State to organize its forces as carefully for peace as for war; that universities and other teaching centers are as important as battleships or big battalions; are, in fact, essential parts of a modern State's machinery, and as such to be equally aided and as efficiently organized to secure its future well being.

Some years ago, in discussing the relations of scientific instruction to our industries, Huxley pointed out that we were in presence of a new "struggle for existence," a struggle which, once commenced, must go on until only the fittest survives.

It is a struggle between organized species—nations—not between individuals or any class of individuals. It is, moreover, a struggle in which science and brains take the place of swords and sinews, on which depended the result of those conflicts which, up to the present, have determined the history and fate of nations. The school, the university, the laboratory and the workshop are the battlefields of this new warfare.

But it is evident that if this, or anything like it, be true, our industries cannot be involved alone; the scientific spirit, brain-power, must not be limited to the workshop if other nations utilize it in all branches of their administration and executive.

It is obvious that the power of a nation for war, in men and arms and ships, is one thing; its power in the peace struggles to which I have referred is another; in the latter, the source and standard of national efficiency are entirely changed. To meet war conditions, there must be equality or superiority in battleships and army corps. To meet the new peace conditions, there must be equality or superiority in universities, scientific organization and everything which conduces to greater brain power.

All this refers to our industries. We are suffering because trade no longer follows the flag as in the old days, but because trade follows the brains, and our manufacturers are too apt to be careless in securing them. In one chemical establishment in Germany, 400 doctors of science, the best the universities there can turn out, have been employed at different times in late years. In the United States the most successful students in the higher teaching centres are snapped up the moment they have finished their course of training, and put into charge of large concerns, so that the idea has got abroad that youth is the password of success in American industry. It has been forgotten that the latest product of the highest scientific education must necessarily be young, and that it is the training and not the age which determines his employment. In Britain, on the other hand, apprentices who can pay high premiums are too often preferred to those who are well educated, and the old rule-of-thumb processes are preferred to new developments—a conservativism too often depending upon the master's own want of knowledge.

I should not be doing my duty if I did not point out that the defeat of our industries, one after another, concerning which both Lord Rosebery and Mr. Chamberlain express their anxiety, is by no means the only thing we have to consider. The matter is not one which concerns our industrial classes only, for knowledge must be pursued for its own sake, and since the full life of a nation with a constantly increasing complexity, not only of industrial, but of high national aims, depends upon the universal presence of the scientific spirit—in other words, brain-power—our whole national life is involved.

It is sufficient for me to quote Mr. Chamberlain:

"It is not every one who can, by any possibility, go forward into the higher spheres of education; but it is from those who do that we have to look for the men who, in the future, will carry high the flag of this country in commercial, scientific and economic competition with other nations. At the present moment, I believe there is nothing more important than to supply the deficiencies which separate us from those with whom we are in the closest competition. In Germany, in America, in our own colony of Canada and in Australia, the higher education of the people has more support from the Government, is carried further, than it is here in the old country; and the result is that in every profession, in every industry, you find the places taken by men and by women who have had a university education. And I would like to see the time in this country when no man should have a chance for any occupation of the better kind, either in our factories, our workshops or our counting-houses, who could not show proof that, in the course of his university career, he had deserved the position that was offered to him. What is it that makes a country? Of course you may say, and you would be quite right, 'The general qualities of the people, their resolution, their intelligence, their pertinacity, and many other good qualities.' Yes; but that is not all, and it is not the main creative feature of a great nation. The greatness of a nation is made by its greatest men. It is those we want to educate. It is to those who are able to go, it may be, from the very lowest steps in the ladder, to men who are able to devote their time to higher education, that we have to look to continue the position we now occupy as, at all events, one of the greatest nations on the face of the earth. And, feeling as I do on these subjects, you will not be surprised if I say I think the time is coming when Governments will give more attention to this matter, and perhaps find a little more money to forward its interests." (*Times,* November 6, 1902.)

Our conception of a university has changed. University education is no longer regarded as the luxury of the rich which concerns only those who can afford to pay heavily for it. The Prime Minister in a recent speech, while properly pointing out that the collective effect of our public and secondary schools upon British character cannot be over-rated, frankly acknowledged that the boys of seventeen or eighteen who have to be educated in them "do not care a farthing about the world they live in except in so far as it concerns the cricket-field or the foot-ball field or the river." On this ground they are not to be taught science, and hence, when they proceed to the university, their curriculum is limited to subjects which were better taught before the modern world existed, or even Galileo was born. But the science which these young gentlemen neglect, with the full approval of their teachers, on their way through the school and the university to politics, the Civil Service, or the management of commercial concerns, is now one of the great necessities of a nation, and our universities must become as much the insurers of the future progress as battleships are the insurers of the present power of States. In other words, university competition between States is now as potent as competition in building battleships, and it is on this ground that our university conditions become of the highest national concern and therefore have to be referred to here, and all the more because our industries are not alone in question.

Chief among the causes which have brought us to the terrible condition of inferiority as compared with other nations in which we find ourselves, are our own carelessness in the matter of education, and our false notions of the limitations of State functions in relation to the conditions of modern civilization.

Time was when the Navy was largely a matter of private and local effort. William the Conqueror gave privileges to the Clinque Ports on the condition that they furnish fifty-two ships when wanted. In the time of Edward III., of 720 sail engaged in the siege of Calais, 705 were "people's ships." All this has passed away; for our first line of defence we no longer depend on private and local effort.

Time was when not a penny was spent by the State on elementary education. Again, we no longer depend upon private and local effort. The Navy and primary education are now recognized as properly calling upon the public for the necessary financial support. But when we pass from primary to university education, instead of State endowment we find State neglect; we are in a region where it is nobody's business to see that anything is done.

We in Great Britain have thirteen universities competing with 134 State and privately endowed in the United States and twenty-two State endowed in Germany. I leave other countries out of consideration for lack of time, and I omit all reference to higher institutions for technical training, of which Germany alone possesses nine of university rank, because they are less important; they instruct rather than educate, and our want is education. The German State gives to one university more than the British Government allows to all the universities and university colleges in England, Ireland, Scotland, and Wales put together. These are the conditions which regulate the production of brain-power in the United States, Germany, and Britain, respectively, and the excuse of the Government is that this is a matter for private effort. Do not our Ministers of State know that other civilized countries grant efficient State aid, and further, that private effort has provided in Great Britain less than ten per cent. of the sum thus furnished in the United States in addition to State aid? Are they content that we should go under in the great struggle of the modern world because the Ministries of other States are wiser, and because the individual citizens of another country are more generous, than our own?

If we grant that there was some excuse for the State's neglect so long as the higher teaching dealt only with words, and books alone had to be provided (for the streets of London and Paris have been used as class rooms at a pinch), it must not be forgotten that during the last hundred years not only has knowledge been enormously increased, but things have replaced words, and fully equipped laboratories must take the place of books and class rooms if university training worthy of the name is to be provided. There is much more difference in size and kind between an old and new university than there is between the old caravel and a modern battleship, and the endowments must follow suit.

What are the facts relative to private endowment in this country? In spite of the munificence displayed by a small number of individuals in some localities, the truth must be spoken. In depending in our country upon this form of endowment, we are trusting to a broken reed. If we take the twelve English university colleges, the forerunners of universities unless we are to perish from lack of knowledge, we find that private effort during sixty years has found less than 4,000,000 pounds, that is, 2,000,000 pounds for buildings and 40,000 pounds a year income. This gives us an average of 166,000 pounds for buildings and 3,300 pounds for yearly income.

What is the scale of private effort we have to compete with in regard to the American universities?

In the United States, during the last few years, universities and colleges have received more than 40,000,000 pounds from this source alone; private effort supplied nearly 7,000,000 pounds in the years 1890--1900.

Next consider the amount of State aid to universities afforded in Germany. The buildings of the new University of Strassburg have already cost nearly a million; that is, about as much as has yet been found by private effort for buildings in Manchester, Liverpool, Birmingham, Bristol, Newcastle and Sheffield. The Government annual endowment of the same German university is more than 49,000 pounds.

This is what private endowment does for us in England, against State endowment in Germany.

But the State does really concede the principle; its present contribution to our Universities and colleges amounts to 155,600 pounds a year; no capital sum, however, is taken for buildings. The State endowment of the University of Berlin in 1891-2 amounted to 168,777 pounds.

When, then, we consider the large endowments of university education both in the United States and Germany, it is obvious that State aid only can make any valid competition possible with either. The more we study the facts, the more statistics are gone into, the more do we find that we, to a large extent, lack both of the sources of endowment upon one or other or both of which other nations depend. We are between two stools, and the prospect is hopeless without some drastic changes. And first among these, if we intend to get out of the present slough of despond, must be the giving up of the idea of relying upon private effort.

To compete on equal grounds with other nations we must have more universities. But this is not all—we want a far better endowment of all the existing ones, not forgetting better opportunities for research on the part of both professors and students. Another crying need is that of more professors and better pay. Another is the reduction of fees; they should be reduced to the level in those countries which are competing with us, to, say, one-fifth of their present rates, so as to enable more students in the secondary and technical schools to complete their education.

In all these ways, facilities would be afforded for providing the highest instruction to a much greater number of students. At present there are almost as many *professors and instructors* in the universities and colleges of the United States as there are *day students* in the universities and colleges of the United Kingdom.

What, then, is to be done? Fortunately, we have a precedent admirably in point, the consideration of which may help us to answer this question.

I have pointed out that in old days our Navy was chiefly provided by local and private effort. Fortunately for us, those days have passed away; but some twenty years ago, in spite of a large expenditure, it began to be felt by those who knew, that in consequence of the increase of foreign navies, our sea-power was threatened, as now, in consequence of the increase of foreign universities, our brain-power is threatened.

The nation slowly woke up to find that its enormous commerce was no longer insured at sea, that in relation to foreign navies our own had been suffered to dwindle to such an extent that it was no longer capable of doing the duty which the nation expected of it even in times of peace. At first, this revelation was received with a shrug of incredulity, and the peace-at-any-price party denied that anything was needed; but a great teacher arose (Capt. Mahan, of the U. S. Navy, whose book, "On the Influence of Sea-Power on History," has suggested the title to my address); as the facts were inquired into the suspicion changed into an alarm; men of all parties saw that something must be done. Later, the nation was thoroughly aroused, and with an universal agreement the principle was laid down that, cost what it might to enforce our sea-power, our Navy must be made and maintained of a strength greater than those of any two possibly contending Powers. After establishing this principle, the next thing to do was to give effect to it. What did the nation do after full discussion and enquiry? A Bill was brought in in 1888, and a sum of 21,500,000 pounds was voted in order, during the next five years, to inaugurate a large ship-building program, so that Britain and Britain's commerce might be guarded on the high seas in any event.

Since then we have spent 120,000,000 pounds on new ships, and this year we spend still more millions on still more new ships. If these prove insufficient to safe-guard our sea-power, there is no doubt that the nation will increase them, and I have not heard that anybody has suggested an appeal to private effort.

How, then, do we stand with regard to universities, recognizing them as the chief producers of brain-power and therefore the equivalents of battleships in relation to sea-power? Do their numbers come up to the standard established by the Admiralty principle to which I have referred? Let us attempt to get a rough-and-ready estimate of our educational position by counting universities as the Admiralty counts battleships. I say rough and ready because we have other helps to greater brain-power to consider besides universities, as the Admiralty has other ships to consider besides ironclads.

In the first place, let us inquire if they are equal in number to those of any two nations commercially competing with us.

In the United Kingdom, we had until quite recently thirteen. Of these, one is only three years old as a teaching university and another is still merely an examining board.

In Germany there are twenty-two universities; in France, under recent legislation, fifteen; in Italy, twenty-one. It is difficult to give the number in the United States, because it is clear, from the tables given in the Report of the Commissioner of Education, that some colleges are more important than some universities, and both give the degree of Ph.D. But of universities in title we have 134. Among these, there are forty-six with more than fifty professors and instructors, and thirteen with more than 150. I will take that figure.

Suppose we consider the United States and Germany, our chief commercial competitors, and apply the Admiralty principle. We should require, allowing for population, eight additional universities at the very lowest estimate.

We see, then, that instead of having universities equalling in number those of two of our chief competitors together, they are by no means equal to those of either of them singly.

After this statement of the facts, any one who has belief in the importance of higher education will have no difficulty in understanding the origin of the present condition of British industry and its constant decline, first in one direction and then in another, since the tremendous efforts made in the United States and Germay began to take effect.

If, indeed, there be anything wrong about the comparison, the error can only arise from one of two sources; either the Admiralty is thoughtlessly and wastefully spending money, or there is no connection whatever between the higher intelligence and the prosperity of a nation. I have already referred to the views of Mr. Chamberlain and Lord Rosebery on this point; we know what Mr. Chamberlain has done at Birmingham; we know the strenuous efforts made by the commercial leaders of Manchester and Liverpool; we know, also, the opinion of men of science.

If while we spend so freely to maintain our sea-power our export of manufactured articles is relatively reduced because our competitors beat us in the markets of the world, what is the end of the vista thus opened up to us? A navy growing stronger every year and requiring larger votes to guard our commerce and communications, and a vanishing quantity of commerce to guard—a reduced national income to meet an increasing taxation!

The pity is that our Government has considered sea-power alone; that while so completely guarding our commerce, it has given no thought to one of the main conditions on which its production and increase depend: a glance could have shown that other countries were building universities even faster than they were building battleships; were, in fact, considering brain-power first and sea-power afterwards.

Surely it is my duty as your president to point out the danger ahead if such ignoring of the true situation should be allowed to continue. May I express a hope that at last, in Mr. Chamberlain's words, "the time is coming when Governments will give attention to this matter"?

The comparison shows that we want eight new universities, some of which, of course, will be colleges promoted to university rank and fitted to carry on university work. Three of them are already named: Manchester, Liverpool, Leeds.

Let us take this number and deal with it on the battleship condition, although a modern university on American or German models will cost more than to build a battleship.

If our present university shortage be dealt with on battleship conditions, to correct it we should expend *at least* 8,000,000 pounds for new construction, and for the pay-sheet we should have to provide (8 x 50,000 pounds) 400,000 pounds yearly for personnel and upkeep, for it is of no use to build either ships or universities without manning them. Let us say, roughly, capitalizing the yearly payment at 2 1-2 per cent, 24,000,000 pounds.

At this stage, it is important to inquire whether this sum, arrived at by analogy merely, has any relation to our real university needs.

I have spent a year in making inquiries, as full as I could make them, of friends conversant with the real present needs of each of the universities old and new; I have obtained statistics which would fill a volume, and personally I believe that this sum at least is required to bring our university system up to anything like the level which is insisted upon both in the United States and in Germany. Even Oxford, our oldest university, will still continue to be a mere bundle of colleges, unless three millions are provided to enable the university properly so-called to take her place among the sisters of the modern world; and Sir Oliver Lodge, the principal of our very youngest university, Birmingham, has shown in detail how five millions can be usefully and properly applied in that one locality, to utilize for the good of the nation the enthusiasm and scientific capacity which are only waiting for adequate opportunity of development.

How is this money to be raised? I reply without hesitation, *duplicate the Navy Bill of* 1888-9; do at once for brain-power what we so successfully did then for sea-power.

Let 24,000,000 pounds be set apart from one asset, our national wealth, to increase the other, brain-power. Let it be assigned and borrowed as it is wanted; there will be a capital sum for new buildings to be erected in the next five or ten years, the interest of the remainder to go towards increased annual endowments.

There need be no difficulty about allocating the money to the various institutions. Let each university make up its mind as to which rank of the German universities it wishes to emulate. When this claim has been agreed to, the sums necessary to provide the buildings and teaching staff of that class of university should be granted without demur.

It is the case of battleships over again, and money need not be spent more freely in one case than in the other.

Let me say at once that this sum is not to be regarded as practically gone when spent, as in the case of a short-lived ironclad. *It is a loan* which will bear a high rate of interest. This is not my opinion merely; it is the opinion of those concerned in great industrial enterprises and fully alive to the origin and effects of the present condition of things.

If it be held that this, or anything like it, is too great a price to pay for correcting past carelessness or stupidity, the reply is that the 120,000,000 pounds spent recently on our navy, a sum five times greater, has been spent to correct a sleepy blunder, not one whit more inimical to the future welfare of our country than that which has brought about our present educational position. We had not sufficiently recognized what other nations had done in the way of ship building, just as until now we have not recognized what they have been doing in university building.

Further, I am told that the sum of 24,000,000 pounds is less than half the amount by which Germany is yearly enriched by having improved upon our chemical industries, owing to our lack of scientific training. Many other industries have been attacked in the same way since, but taking this one instance alone, if we had spent this money fifty years ago, when the Prince Consort first called attention to our backwardness, the nation would now be much richer than it is, and would have much less to fear from competition.

Suppose we were to set about putting our educational house in order, so as to secure a higher quality and greater quantity of brain-power, it would not the be the first time in history that this has been done. Both Prussia after Jena and France after Sedan acted on the view:—

"When land is gone and money spent,
Then learning is most excellent."

After Jena, which left Prussia a "bleeding and lacerated mass," the King and his wise counsellors, among them Kant, determined, as they put it, "to supply the loss of territory by intellectual effort."

What did they do? In spite of universal poverty, three universities, to say nothing of observatories and other institutions, were at once founded, secondary education was developed, and in a few years the mental resources were so well looked after that Lord Palmerston defined the kingdom in question as "a country of damned professors."

After Sedan, a battle, as Moltke told us, "won by the schoolmaster," France made even more strenuous efforts. The old university of France, with its "academies" in various places, was replaced by fifteen independent universities, in all of which are faculties of letters, sciences, law and medicine.

The development of the University of Paris has been truly marvelous. In 1897-8 there were 12,000 students, and the cost was 200,000 pounds a year.

But even more wonderful than these examples is the "intellectual effort" made by Japan, not after a war, but to prepare for one.

The question is, shall we wait for a disaster and then imitate Prussia and France? or shall we follow Japan, and thoroughly prepare by "intellectual effort" for the industrial struggle which lies before us? Such an effort seems to me to be the first thing any national or imperial scientific organization should endeavor to bring about.

SIR NORMAN LOCKYER.

* * *

The logical quality is above all to be cultivated by teachers. . . . To lead requires the sense of direction and of the fitness of things. It requires the ability to remain undistracted by the clamor of the hour, and to see things clearly, free from prejudice, or the approval of misguided majorities.—*Joseph Jastrow, Wisconsin State University.*

A QUESTION OF ETHICS

Ethics as defined by Webster is the science of human duty; the body of rules of duty drawn from this science; a particular system of principles and rules concerning duty; whether true or false; rules of practice in respect to a single class of human actions; as, political or social ethics.

In stating the meaning or particular meaning taken by me in discussing this subject, we will look first at the duty a teacher owes to himself.

It is the province of every teacher, and it may also be added of every person engaged in any calling, to make a thoro study of his limitations.

No teacher can succeed in his chosen work unless he find by a close analysis of his mental trend wherein lies his greatest strength as well as his peculiar weaknesses. Many are specially gifted in some particular line and yet fail to make the most of the endowment thru a sort of bashfullness or timidity. A shrinking backward, which dries up the fountain of inspiration and leaves only a mental desert of what might have been by proper stimulation and cultivation a mind refulgent with ideas which would prompt to actions that would brighten and enrich the lives of all it touched.

Again the more sensitively attuned natures of many shrink from a harsh criticism made either in a spirit of thoughtlessness or it may be of wantonness, down to the dead level of a mediocrity that is far worse than inferiority.

The thoughtless criticism wounds vastly more than the wanton one. For when made, strikes the energy expended in preparation and must perforce weaken the efficacy of the blow.

Scott realized this fully when he says: "Full many a shaft at random sent finds mark the archer little sent."

There are those also who from inattention or carelessness do not improve their opportunities and pass their shortcomings without ever reflecting that every omission of duty leaves them weaker than before, and soon they have only husks instead of luscious fruit to bestow upon those entrusted to them for materials to make a healthful mental growth.

To the teacher, then, I would say, study yourself even more carefully than you study your subject. This will lead up to a process of mental growth that will make a study of one's pupils a pleasure. A complete knowledge of self presupposes a complete mastery of self, and he who has mastered self has practically mastered all. For it is the petty things of life that wound and annoy, and a thru self-mastery renders the mental epidermis, if I may use the expression, impervious to the darts of pettiness.

For all the expenditure of time, energy and money made by the teacher in acquiring and developing the power to teach, it is a duty incumbent upon him to see that a proper reimbursement is made by the state he serves, or rather by the state's agents. The trustees and the teacher who fails in this respect works an injustice not only to himself but also to the whole teaching force of his vicinity. For the Good Book states that the laborer is worthy of his hire. So the cheap teacher is a millstone around the necks of his associates.

It is the duty of the teacher, therefore, not only to prepare himself to teach, but also to demand the highest possible salary for the services rendered. If the ability of the teacher be an established fact the price will be added thereto. It is not a question of supply and demand, but rather one of quality and amount.

George Eliot says, "The reward of one duty is the power to fulfill another."

Hence, having fulfilled his duty to himself, it is easy now to render his parent his due, and here also lies the duty to the pupil. The horticulturist look always to the quality and condition of the parent tree before choosing the scion or judging its merits. So a knowledge of human nature must be acquired by the teacher before he can successfully guide the children coming to him from homes of so many and such widely divergent character into proper channels of thinking and living. Right thinking is right living, and a proper study of the heredity temperament, environment, and mental status of the child enables the teacher to skilfully guide the mind of the pupil into proper channels, and the proper living will follow unconsciously.

As like begets like it is imperative that we study the child thru the parent rather than the parent thru the child. Such study, however, should never border upon familiarity. If it do so the result will be disastrous to the teacher. The duty of the teacher to the state is clearly set forth in Section 1702 of the California School Law, which says:

"It shall be the duty of all teachers to impress upon the minds of the pupils the principles of morality, truth, justice, and patriotism; to teach them to avoid idleness, profanity, and falsehood, and to instruct them in the principles of a free government and to train them up to a true comprehension of the rights and duties of American citizenship."

These things should not be taught incidentally, but specifically. I will hear remark that it took two jury trials to convince a few of my patrons that I did only my duty in teaching those things not only specifically but strenuously. I based my line of defense on this section of the school law and owe my acquittal to the intelligence of twelve of my peers, fair-minded and honest, who had been trained in accordance with this section of law, and who stand for the principle that the upholding of the law of our land must never be subservient to prejudice.

Fellow-teachers, read this section of the school law over carefully. More—re-read it; commit it to memory, and then reflect upon its vast possibilities when you have instructed your pupils thoroly in the rights, duties and dignities of a true American citizenship, you will have equipped them for life and diverted from the jails, almshouses and gutters of the future years the great tide of humanity, weak, frail, and untaught, that yearly fills them to repletion. Fellow-teachers, I doff my hat to the man that wrote Section 1702 of the school law.

A knowledge of professional ethics is to be obtained only as other knowledge—by study, thought, observation, and more than all, by experience.

There is no royal road, and all the theory you can ever read will not take the place of actual experience. The five state normal schools supported by our state and the pedagogical departments of our two universities are of unquestioned excellence, but are beyond the reach of many of great merit who must defer an attendance at such institutions for a financial reason.

There are many graduates of such institutions who, for all their training, are among our rankest failures. The untrained country boy or girl who, as a result of effort and energy, has attained even a partial sccoess, should reflect upon the larger field of opportunity that would open to them as a result of professional training. It is not well for talent to rest content with mediocrity.

The application of professional ethics depends upon the innate executive ability of the teacher and the extent to which he has been impressed by his training, reading or observation of the methods of others. I can say that I have never yet entered and visited a school without gaining some suggestions for the improvement of my own work. I have not always been favorably impressed by the ability or methods of the teacher, but a negative impression often produces a positive result.

The value to a teacher of an understanding of professional ethics is that it broadens his mind and quickens his perceptions to such an extent that he ceases to marvel that one small head can contain all he knows. Whatever tends to broaden the intellect of the teacher tends also to increase the regard in which he is held by his community. I have observed that the broad-minded and intelligent teacher is sought for by the community, and his standing and usefulness as a citizen is in proportion to his ability to perform the duties incumbent upon his station in life.

In conclusion I will say that professional ethics as applied to teaching is a system of rules of duty drawn from this science or the system of principles and rules to be applied to a successful instruction of the pupils of our schools.

And an understanding of professional ethics teaches us the duty we owe to ourselves, our patrons, and our state.

Such an understanding is attained by study observation and actual experience, but when once obtained broadens the teacher's field of usefulness immeasurably and increases his worth as a citizen.

It merges into that broad-minded charity that teaches us not to be too exacting of our fellows and that perfection is not of this earth. That when the angel of divinity has set the seal of peace upon the troubled brow of each child of man, then, and not until then, can we expect perfection.

M. P. DONNELLY.

"If the school has failed to kill the love of learning in its pupil, that is good; if it has failed to make him intellectually conceited, that is better; if it has kindled a divine interest in his soul, that is best."

READING AND LITERATURE.

THE STUDY OF WORDS.

Many students have vocabularies so limited they cannot understand or appreciate the subject matter studied. This deficiency is due to the fact that so little time is devoted to the study of words. Some teachers fail to do the work expected of them because their general and technical vocabularies are so meager they cannot comprehend what they read, or the force of what they say.

This knowledge can only be acquired by an intelligent and persistent study of words as individual items, and this work must be continued until the student has a knowledge of the sources from which the words came, an understanding of their original significance, the changes they have undergone and their present meanings. In addition to this he must know the part of each word which forms the root, which parts are the prefix and suffix and the extent to which each extends or limits the root-word.

The teacher must also study classical English until she has a knowledge of the finer shadings given to words by those who use them as means to embody beauty, express thought, stimulate emotion, defend opinions, re-inforce convictions and bless life. This reading will enable her to discern those delicate distinctions which give to words in certain relations their peculiar fitness and force. She will see that "They are apples of gold in pictures of silver."

While she must know the analyses and definitions of the words composing her vocabulary, yet she needs more than all this can give her. She needs such a comprehension of thought as a unit as will permit her to receive its message. This knowledge will make it possible for her to say with dignity and propriety what she knows, thinks, feels, believes, hopes, strives for. The subtle meanings of words, their skillful arrangement, the attractions of diction, the graces of style and the marvels of suggestion must appeal to her in some degree to enable her to drink with refreshing from Pierian springs.

We talk much and talk learnedly about "instruction" and "inspiration," and many of those who talk and most of those who listen have little or but vague conceptions of the ideas resident in these terms. If "instructing" always carried the thought that some one is building into somebody something of value then the word would contain an idea for the person who expresses it and would carry a message to the one to whom it is said. If it were a part of our common knowledge that when we speak of "inspiring" we mean that we are breathing into some one something that means life and blessing, then it would serve a purpose which it so seldom accomplishes. Teachers have *inspired* pupils to the extent of breathing into them that breath of life which has made it possible for them to become living souls, and they have been able to do this because of the quality of their personality and character of their culture.

Some words have acquired a wealth of meaning because of the associations that cluster about them. The dictionary informs us that a "home" is "a place of abode." The same definition describes the roof which shelters our *feathered* chickens. A "home" means something more than a place where people are housed. To some it is a small white cottage with green blinds, located at the western end of a small circular valley, with hills crowned with trees behind it, green fields in front of it, and a glimpse of the outside world through a notch in the mountains. It is a household presided over by a man and a woman whose portraits are painted for us by our Quaker poet in "Snow Bound." It is filled with boys who little resemble saints and as little remind one of sweet sinners. It is a place where authority is respected, obedience cheerfully and promptly rendered, simple manners cultivated, where tenderness is a ministring angel, work a saving blessing, duty an opportunity and ambition a sane and influential reality. When this word is pronounced there appears on the canvas a picture clear in outline, beautiful in suggestion, inspiring in teaching and blessed in all its molding power.

When one understands what a word originally meant, the changes through which it has passed and the significance given to it at present, then he is able to understand what others have written and to use language in such a way as to indicate he is not a novice, stumbling in the twilight of his own ignorance.

SOME OF THE MASTERS OF ENGLISH.

When one reads the addresses of Lincoln, the orations of Webster, the essays of Walter Savage Landor, the plays of Shakespeare, he discovers they bounded the words they used before they were permitted to be the servants of those princes of the realm. He soon learns that subtractions are losses, that additions do not improve, that wisdom is voiced in noble phrase and that everything has its due proportion and perspective, because these masters knew instinctively, or learned through study, the word to use and the place in which it should be found. Some of these giants may have known things they did not learn, yet they all stand as models to be studied, examples to be followed, and as springs of inspiration from which we may be filled.

The student and the teacher would do well to take note of the fact that these kings in this higher kingdom were intensive rather than extensive readers of books. Webster read his Bible, Shakespeare's dramas, Cæsar's Commentaries and Burke's speeches. Lincoln read his Bible, Bunyan's Pilgrim's Progress, Aesop's Fables and Shakespeare. Webster was the greatest orator of the last century, if not the greatest of all centuries. He had that Doric direstness which justified some one in saying he was a "steam engine in breeches' 'and that if he wanted a thunderbolt to hurl at his adversary he had only to reach out and grasp it as it went hissing by. Possibly, in his later speeches, he filed and pruned them to a point of weakening them, but in his best work his sentences are dignified, majestic, persuasive, powerful. His orations are classic and conclusive; they are the finest specimens of declamatory English extant.

The orator of the day at Gettysburg had all the advantages incident to cultured ancestors, scholarship and academic associations, and yet his oration was wanting in that quality which would have given it life and influence. Lincoln's half-score of simple sentences are familiar to every school boy and treasured in every patriotic heart. The oration of the one died an untimely death because it did not shed light or possess life. That of the other is immortal because it voices the passion of the true citizen.

It is an obvious if not a safe conclusion to deduce from these facts that he reads best who reads but few books, reads those which feed his soul and reads them until he has grown to his full stature.

THE LOCAL NEWSPAPER.

Current reading occupies a large, perhaps too large a proportion of the average reader's time. The local newspaper has a just claim to be called an educational institution. It makes a record of local and current history, fosters enterprises which seek to promote the general welfare, and renders an amount of unremunerated public service not equalled by any other agency. It has proved itself the loyal ally of the common school. For these and many other reasons the teacher should be a reader of her local paper.

THE METROPOLITAN DAILY.

In the selection of a metropolitan paper a teacher should be governed by several fundamental principles, of which the following are the most obvious. The paper selected should contain intelligent discussions of important public questions. It should fairly represent the work of persons and the policy of parties. It should be fearless, but unprejudiced and consistent, in its comments on the service and character of public officials.

Any newspaper which devotes a large proportion of its space to accounts of murders, divorces, scandals and prize fights, and which seeks to make these records of vice the most attractive features of its issues is unworthy of the age and unfit to be found in the possession of instructors of youth.

If it invades the home, or violates the privacy of individuals, or seeks to cripple, crush, or injure any person or cause, because of personal malignity or partisan motive, it should be tabooed.

No teacher can afford to read a newspaper which gives her unwholesome views of life. She is as culpable when she does this as when she assimilates any other form of moral pollution. The list is long and the worthy list is too extended for enumeration.

WEEKLY AND MONTHLY MAGAZINE.

It is necessary for the modern teacher to have a thorough knowledge of the world's work, accurate information as to the world's workers, a conception of the world's progress, an understanding of the tendencies of the times. In learning of these she will get the details of great events, the biographies of great leaders, the quality and character of the common people and a sane view of the crises of her day. *The Review of Reviews* and *The World's Work* cannot but be helpful in these studies if they are intelligently and faithfully read.

It is also important that the teacher know the spirit of her age and the life which characterizes it. She must discern the hopes, ambitions and aspirations that mold character. She must know something of the springs of action, the tendencies of the multitude, the quality of desire as well as the general trend and march of human progress in its higher aspects. What men believe, think, feel, hope, seek after and are trying to embody and live, in a word, life in all its aspects and all its possibilities, should find in her the earnest student and the candid investigator. It is conceded that *The Outlook* and *The Independent* stand pre-eminent in this field.

The progressive teacher will read at least one magazine which maintains a high literary standard. It is important that she be familiar with the thought and view of the scholar and the literary artist concerning matters of present moment and public interest. Those things which have to do with the home, the school, the church, the office, the community, should be known to her through such interpretations as are given by trained students of these subjects and skillful writers on these matters. *The Atlantic Monthly* easily stands first in the class which assumes to discuss these subjects and *The Nation* is its peer in all the fields it covers.

It goes without saying that the teacher should be in touch and in tune with young life. She should know and love the child. She should have a knowledge of his needs and information as to his surroundings and capacity. She should understand his hopes, appreciate his fears, realize his shortcomings, comprehend his ability and be able to walk with him in his mental, moral, physical, social and recreative activities. These things will come to her through contact, study, incident, story and eternal vigilance.

W. W. STETSON,
Sup't Public Instruction, Augusta, Maine.

EMERSON'S INFLUENCE IN EDUCATION.

The celebrations which have just been held in honor of Emerson have led us to think of his services to the cause of education throughout the English-speaking world. Upon educational ideals in America his influence has been penetrating and pervasive. It has been a solvent, but also an inspiration. This double quality was the secret of its power. Emerson combined with his fearless abandonment of many of the old doctrines a profound belief in the spiritual forces which manifest themselves in national and individual life. In all that he wrote there was a reality which deeply moves many readers. His work has the beauty of truthfulness. As Clarendon said of Falkland, "he was so severe an advocate of truth that he could as easily have given himself leave to steal as to dissemble." But it is not on every one that Emerson's influence gains its hold. Some words in which he described Plato's attitude towards his hearers apply to his own work:

"I have no system. I cannot be answerable for you. You will be what you must. If there is love between us, our intercourse will be profitable; if not, your time is lost and you will only annoy me. I shall seem to you stupid, and the reputation I have false. Quite above us, beyond the will of you or me, is this secret affinity or repulsion laid. All my good is magnetic, and I educate, not by lessons, but by going about my business."

Emerson, however, has had extraordinary influence on some of the men who have been leaders in the new movement in American education. The elective system of studies, which under President Eliot's authority has worked so great a change in the programs of American universities and secondary schools, is a practical outcome of Emerson's teaching. And this characteristically American theory of school curricula is beginning to prevail in Europe as well. It is a disintegrating force. It breaks up the solid masses of the traditional curricula of the Old World just as the Atlantic waves break up the rocks on the west coast of Shetland. It challenges the old conception of "general culture" which has so powerful an influence on the plan of studies in the secondary schools of Germany. It asserts the claims of new forms of culture, of hand-work as well as head-work. It assails the privilege of classical education as we know it in our English public schools, and as it has been known in the most famous secondary schools of France. It takes as the unit of organization a particular study like Latin or Algebra, instead of a traditional combination of studies. It aims at offering such a variety of possible groups of subjects of instruction as to meet the different intellectual needs of different types of ability, not less than the different practical requirements of different callings. Its strength lies in its faculty of swift readjustment to changing demands, and in its power to meet a bewildering variety of needs. Its weakness lies in its lack of the steadying force of an authoritative discipline, and in its preferring liveliness and brisk variety to steady-going thoroughness on conservative lines. But the hour has struck for change. The American influences are penetrating, every year more deeply, into the heart of European education. And, wherever they penetrate, they remind us of Emerson.

He came at a time when the Calvinism which had annealed the character of New England had lost its intellectual oppositeness. Every great system of doctrine builds up and buttresses itself with an appropriate system of education, and particularly of secondary and higher education. The Calvinism of New England had its own institutions of culture. But their ideals of learning, and consequently their methods of instruction, had begun to flag in consequence of the decay of the philosophical system which had been the cause of their existence and the real source of their power. Emerson was one of those who proclaimed America's need for a new educational ideal. Classical culture had never really flourished beyond the Atlantic. The revival of Greek ideals of life and learning, which played so great a part in the making of modern Germany, found no counterpart in the great movement for reform in American education. Emerson had "the prophesying heart," and foretold the great change which was coming over men's ideas about culture.

"We are students of words," he wrote in 1844; "we cannot use our hands or our legs or our eyes or our arms.... The lessons of science should be experimental.... Once (say two centuries ago) Latin and Greek had a strict relation to all the science and culture there was in Europe, and the Mathematics had a momentary importance at some era of activity in physical science. These things became stereotyped as education, as the manner of men is. But the Good Spirit never cared for the colleges, and, though all men and boys were now drilled in Latin, Greek, and Mathematics, it had quite left these shells high and dry on the beach.... But in a hundred high schools and colleges this warfare against common sense goes on. Four, or six, or ten years the pupil is parsing Greek and Latin, and as soon as he leaves the University he shuts those books for the last time. Some thousands of young men are graduated at our colleges in this country every year, and the persons who at forty years still read Greek can all be counted on your hand. I never met with ten. Four or five persons I have met who read Plato. Is not this absurd, that the whole of the liberal talent of this country should be directed in its best years on studies which lead to nothing?"

This appeal, against what Emerson called "the wonderful drowsiness of usage," led, in due time, to remarkable changes. He read the thoughts of his fellow-countrymen like a book, and divined their new purpose. He understood their "wish to cast aside the superfluous and to arrive at short methods." Nothing is more typical of educational effort in America today than the desire to cut away all the non-essentials and to devise a course of instruction and training which shall combine the minimum of time and effort with the maximum of intellectual efficiency and alertness.

But Calvinism comprises three elements, each of which is essential to its power. These are faith, democracy, and discipline. Emerson's extraordinary influence was due to the fact that, though he came at a time when the older form of Calvinistic discipline had become obsolete, and when his protests against it were therefore appropriate, his teaching was inspired by an intense (though, according to older standards, an unconventional) faith, and by an unflinching belief in democracy. And these are among the characteristics of American education today. Secular in form, it is inspired by religious sentiment of a sanguine and optimistic kind. From top to bottom it is heartily democratic; and it lays much more stress on interest than on discipline. From discipline, as discipline was conceived in the New England schools under the old dispensation, America has taken a long holiday. Emerson was one of those who found that the schoolmaster was dead and that the doors were open, and who proclaimed the fact that the time for the holiday had come. But the signs multiply that the fathers of New England were not wrong in their belief that self-applied discipline of a stern and searching kind is a necessary safeguard for the well-being of pure democracy. The discipline which they had set up, and which served their purpose for generations, had indeed become obsolete. It was entangled with theories and with institutions which were out of joint with the new knowledge and needs of the time. A period of liberating criticism and of destruction of old forms had to come. Emerson helped to bring it on, and to make its work thorough. But the need for discipline, as well in education as in other departments of the national life, persisted. Emerson was so far the child of his time that he did not appreciate the depth and the permanence of this need. His allusion to mathematics, which I have quoted above, shows how little, at that time, he was in the mood to appreciate the real place of mathematical discipline in a scientific education. His system, whether we apply it to education or to the other problems of civil life, fails us a little when we want a discipline which can be effectively imposed on those who are unwilling voluntarily to discipline themselves. It presupposes as normal a degree of individual energy and self-control which is really exceptional. It slurs over the difficulties caused by the fact that great numbers of people misuse freedom and need the upholding discipline of a strict public opinion and of social control. But when we have said this we have said the worst of it. Emerson is all the better when taken with a pinch of Calvin. But what in his teaching is good for all times and seasons is its brave hopefulness, its reliance on spiritual instead of material forces, its frankness and sincerity of thought, its dislike of pretension, its belief in individuality of character, its insight into the heroism which can inspire a man to accomplish a high task in obscurity, its appeal to our self-reliance, its concern for character rather than for mere agility of mind. All these things are of great moment in education, and large is our debt to Emerson for having laid such stress upon them. Much that is most vigorous in the educational life of the English-speaking peoples at the present time is Emersonian unawares.

MICHAEL E. SADLER.
The Journal of Education, London.

* * *

Department of Methodology

PHYSIOLOGY—DIGESTION.

Every teacher in dealing with the process of digestion considers at least the digestive action of the juices, and the conditions which modify their normal action. In the seventh and eighth grades I have found that simple experiments in digestion prove valuable, intelligent, and interesting to the children: and that each child can find for himself the digestive action of the juices in an elementary way. The work is simple, inexpensive and can be done by any seventh or eighth grade pupil.

Let the child collect saliva by chewing a piece of rubber or some sugarless gum, and dilute it four times with water. Then make a starch solution by boiling one half teaspoonful of starch—. corn or potato—in a pint of water. Bring from home a hard boiled egg, and a small piece of tallow. To determine the digestive action of saliva, take small vials, or bottles, or if you have them, test tubes. Put saliva in vial No. 1; in No. 2 starch solution; in No. 3 equal parts of saliva and cooked starch solution; in No. 4 equal parts of raw starch solution and saliva; in No. 5, piece of cooked white of egg and saliva; in No. 6 tallow and saliva. Now put all the vials so prepared in a warm water bath for one half hour at 99 F.

The water bath may be easily made by punching holes in the lids of small tin cracker cans or lard pails, or better by boring holes in a piece of board large enough to contain bottles, and placing it over some shallow basin, containing water at required temperature. As the temperature falls add enough hot water to keep at 99 F. Instead of bath the vials may be set aside at room temperature until next day and then examined. Test a portion of the first four vials with iodine for starch; and then the remainder of each vial for sugar. Add a little strong sodium hydrate (caustic soda) and a few drops of a 10 per cent solution of "blue stone (copper sulphate) and heat until it becomes a yellowish to brick red color.

See if the saliva dissolves the egg or tallow. You may test No. 5 by adding sodium hydrate and a drop of 1 per cent solution of "bluestone." If dissolved egg is present the solution will be a violet or rose pink color. These experiments may be extended to show the effect of extreme heat and cold: raw food: mastication: dilution with water, and strong alcohol on the digestive action of saliva. Children love to do the work and gain much from it. Far superior results are obtained than by text-book work only.

NEWELL H. BULLOCK,
San Jose State Normal School.

* * *

THANKSGIVING DAY PROGRAM.

The programs for Thanksgiving Day in Eastern journals are not always suitable to the genial climate of the Pacific Slope. The furs, snow, sleet, ice, and great log-fires do not carry with them an adequate idea of Thanksgiving. Our children are more familiar with oranges, flowers, pineapples, bananas, strawberries and out-door games. So to make a program suitable, considerable revision is necessary. It might be well to start the day with a due spirit of thankfulness for the climate of the Pacific seas, and that we are permitted to live in so glorious a country. In arranging programs, the following may be helpful:

1. Teacher read President or Governor's Thankskiving proclamation.
2. A history of Thanksgiving.
3. Recitation by pupils.
4. Songs.
5. Compositions by pupils, on "How to Eat, What to Eat, When to Eat." Teacher to give instruction on the basis of approved hygiene.

HISTORY OF THANKSGIVING.

In the United States Thanksgiving denotes an annual festival—not to celebrate a single event, but to show gratitude to God for the blessings of a closing year. It may be said to be borrowed from the Jewish feast of Tabernacles. The Hebrews, under the Mosaic law, celebrated the goodness of God under branches of trees and tents of palms. The Dutch and Germans have a festival called "Harvest Home." The custom originated in America in 1621, when Governor Branford, of New England, wrote as follows: "They began now to gather in the small harvests they had, and fitte up their houses and dwellings against winter, being well recovered in health and strength, and had all things in good plenty; for as some were thus employed in affairs abroad, others were exercised in fishing about codd and bass and other fish of which they took a good store, and of which of every family had their portion. All the somer there was no waste. And now began to come in store of foule as winter approached. And beside water foule there was a great store of wild turkies and venison." The next Thanksgiving was in 1623, when the Governor called the people together for fasting and prayer, on account of a drouth. During the celebration "soft, sweet, moderate showers" fell, and the occasion was changed to thanksgiving and rejoicing. Washington, in 1795, issued a call for a national Thanksgiving. In 1863, Lincoln issued a proclamation, making the last Thursday of November a national holiday. Every President since has followed that example.

* * *

An examiner was listening to the reading of an entrance scholarship candidate. At the phase "prosperous man" he asked for an explanation, which was promptly forthcoming in the following words:—"A man wot gives out blue light when you rub 'im.—*London Journal of Education.*

* * *

The teacher who is not a member of the reading circle, or fails to attend the teachers' meetings; is not a subscriber of a school journal, labels herself as indifferent to success. These are three of the most potent factors in determining her activity; a failure in either is a step backwards.—*School Herald.*

BOOKS AND MAGAZINES

The reviewer's table is covered with books this time. So many of them are there that most must be reviewed by title only. Though they deserve a better fate. Perhaps it will be possible in some cases to give a more extended notice later.

First we have a scholarly and interesting discussion of "The Possibility of a Science of Education',' by Samuel B. Sinclair, Vice-Principal of the Normal School, Ottawa, Canada, and student in education in the University of Chicago. The question which is asked is fundamental to an understanding of the work of teaching. The answer which is here given is the answer, not alone of the author of the book, but also of a school of educational thinkers — the school headed by the distinguished Dean of the School of Education of the University of Chicago. Can there be a science of education as there is a science of mathematics, physics, medicine ethics? And will such a science furnish the educator instruments of insight which will aid in determining the purpose and the method of education? If we mean by science a systematized body of universally valid knowledge, there is no such science of education and it may well be questioned whether there is any such science of any other phase of experience. But if by science we mean past experience forged by reflection into an instrument of insight to furnish control over future experiences, then is education such a science. The science of medicine is not and cannot be embodied in a brief volume of rules commonly called a "Family Physician" or "Every One His Own Doctor." Neither can the science of education be reduced to vest pocket form for the ready and certain guidance of the uneducated practicioner. Only patent medicine vendors proceed in that way and the onus of disgrace which is theirs belongs equally to pedagogues who apply the same methods in their calling. Just as there is no such thing as cure in general so there is no such thing as education in general. The problem is always that of the reorganization of an individual, and therefore unique, experience. The science that would help must do so through principle, not rules or guide-book directions. Where do these principles come from? Are they simply applications of biology, psychology, ethics, sociology, etc.? The view taken here is that edu-

The Possibility of a Science of Education by Samuel Bower Sinclair. The University of Chicago Press.

cation is an independent science. There is a great difference between knowing the road and directing a stranger over it in such a way that he will not miss it. There is a greater difference between knowing a subject and directing a youthful traveler through it. Only experts can write guide books, and only experts can guide to knowledge. The author believes that such expert knowledge involves a philosophical study of the general problems of education, a study of the history of education, a careful study from the standpoint of education, of the history of civilization, of ethics, sociology, political science, psychology, biology, physiology, the study of school organization, of the educational classics, of methology; of hygiene, observation and teaching in practice schools and experimentation in a laboratory school. To one who is anxious to study the principles of education, and it is believed that this is the most practical of all studies for the teacher, this book will be of very great service.

* * *

Still another volume which represents the new movement in school-keeping is Prof. William Baldwin's "Industrial-Social Education," which is largely a report of the work which is being done at the State Normal School, Hyanis, Mass. In his preface the author declares, I have become gradually but thoroughly convinced that we are working along right lines, even if our work is crude; that our faces are toward the light; that the work is very important and that our most thoughtful people of all classes are ready for something of this kind. The character of this work is indicated in the statement "the school was changed into a manufactory." The reasons for this change are indicated in the address of the principal to his teachers. I believe we are ready "to change the whole attitude of our school." When you think of a school of what do you think? Rows of desks with children in them, prisoners in their cells, not held by bars, but by the will of the teacher. When you think of the work, how much of it originates with the pupil? Is the child's standpoint receiving its due attention. Gradually but surely I have come to my present belief that much of the education of our schools is not practical because it is unnatural and artificial. We take the young child away from the fields and woods, where he longs to be, and put him into a box, which some of us have been

---

Industrial-Social Education by William A. Baldwin. Springfield: Milton Bradly Co.

trying to adorn and make into a gilded cage. Even here we are unwilling that he shall move about and exercise his young and growing muscles, but he must be trained to sit quietly in one place and in one position for the best hours of the day. Out of school he is a veritable interrogation mark; in school the tables are turned and he must answer instead of ask questions. Out of school, from morning until night, he was the personification of perpetual motion. Now modern psychology teaches what every common-sensed father knows, that activity is a necessity for the life and growth of the young child physically, mentally and morally; that the young child is continually reaching out through his special senses to lay hold upon everything about him to test it, to know about it, to see what its relation to himself may be, to see if he can use it and make something for himself with it; that he is an imitative being, delighting to say the sounds he hears, to represent the actions which he sees and hears described, and in fact, to live over and so make his own, the different experiences of the people whom he sees, and of whom he reads. Now I desire to have every teacher of the training school do something which will help to change the spirit in the school. I shall not dictate as to what you shall do, but only suggest that you do something. I shall be glad to advise as to particulars, but what I am most anxious about now is that you, in your own way, put in some kind of manual training which you can do and which will appeal to the children. Watch your children and feel your way along."

And something good and fine came of it, which is a story too long to tell here.

* * *

Another phase of the pedagogical work of the University of Chicago is represented on Dr. Dopp's volume, "The Place of Industries in Elementary Education." The author is an experienced teacher in the Normal Schools of Wisconsin and this book which has been called a noble volume is the outcome of some months of pos graduate study. Though the book is largely theoretical it has come out of years of practice and cannot be dismissed as too abstract for present educational conditions. With the revival of interest in Herbart came the announcement of the Culture-Epoch theory in education. The theory that the child in his development repeats in outline the culture history of the

The Place of Industries in Elementary Education by Katherine Elizabeth Dopp. The University of Chicago Press.

race. Not infrequently the question has arisen, of what use is this doctrine in practice? and almost invariably it has been answered that it reflects the course of life which the child must go through. Because his ancestors used the bow and arrow, lived in caves in the earth, or in trees, and fought mightily with each other, his weakness for the same activities must be indulged and tolerated. In other words, the theory was concerned to explain to adults the *raison d'etre* of certain phases of child life otherwise inexplicable. It was a theory of interpretation, not a theory of procedure. At present the tendency is to employ it as a guide in controlling the growth of the young—an indication of their mental tendencies of directive value in determining the form of doing which will be most educative to them. If this is true it becomes evident that their instructive tendencies should not merely be indulged, but should be permitted to work themselves out profitably, and it is believed that they offer the means and the only means by which the child may be introduced to a comprehension of the social life of today. The culture-epoch theory thus becomes a guide in shaping school work. First it is needful to know the stages of race history and the human motives expressed in them. The significance of hunting, fishing, pastoral life, agricultural life, the use of metals, travel, trade, transportation, the city-state, the feudal system, the handicraft system, and the factory system are briefly yet scientifically presented. This part of the work is of immense value to the study of geography and history. But it is more than that. It is an indication of the learners mastery of mental processes and a key to his growth in accomplishment. "No better means are available for assisting the child to understand the complex industrial organization of the present than to give him an experience in some of the more fundamental processes." What this means and what form elementary studies should take that they may indeed reveal the elements of social activity the teacher who is anxious to make his work as profitable as possible will not fail to find out by a study of this book.

* * *

In a recent number of the JOURNAL we called attention to the agitation for the teaching of agriculture in the public schools which is now so general and which has already resulted in making that subject a part of the regular course of instruction in

Agriculture for Beginners. Burdett, SteVens & Hill. Ginn & Co., Boston.

some parts of our country. The authors of this volume believe that agriculture is eminently a teachable subject. They see no difference between teaching the fundamental principles of farming and teaching the same child the fundamental truths of arithmetic, geography or grammar. Moreover, they hold that a youth should be trained for the farm just as he is trained for any other occupation.

There is no doubt of the force of their argument. Why should one be trained for life by being exercised in doing things he will not do rather than things he will do? Farming is an art, I had almost said a fine art. It enteres so largely into all human callings that everyone should be compelled to study it for a term of years. It is infinitely more useful and more disciplinary too, if there is any such thing, than arithmetic or grammar. And if it were not for the taint of servility in our blood which causes us still to rejoice that we are privileged to revel in "clerk's larnin," we might shape our course of study by other than traditional considerations to include it. The present volume is an excellent guide to a comprehension of this most excellent of studies. It is made in such a way as to supplement the knowledge, which a wide awake child should already have accumulated, and by its aid one may actually get somewhere in scientific farming. If the day ever comes when an elementary text is called for, this one must surely be considered. Lacking that it should be of immense service in nature study work and perhaps here and there a more than usually intelligent school board and teacher may even go so far by its aid as to establish a class in the only sort of manual training which is available for the district school. Its chapters treat of The Soil, The Soil and the Plant, The Plant, How to Raise a Fruit-tree, The Disease of Plants, Orchard, Garden and Field Insects, Farm Crops, Domestic Animals and Farm Dairying.

* * *

"The books are made up of sources, but not of sources in the garb of three centuries ago, unfamiliar to modern children. The language and spelling have been freely altered, while the thought has been preserved. Much has been omitted, but it has not been the intention to add any statement not expressed in the original.

Source Readers in American History. Four Volumes. By Albert Bushnell Hart, with collaboration of Blanche E. Hazard, Mapel Hill. Annie B. Chapman and Elizabeth SteVens. New York: The Macmillan Company.

If children are interested in this book, it will be because a modern mind has invented a story for them." These statements from the preface will indicate quite clearly the plan of this series of readers. That plan has been carried out almost to perfection. It would be difficult in all the range of children's books to find anything so nearly ideal. What may with truth be called the Iliad of our nation is here put into suitable form for use in the schools. Will children care for them? Of course they will, for they tell of the heroic age more dramatically, as the real is more dramatic than the imaginary, than any tale written for them could. Indeed, we are persuaded that no such piece of good fortune has happened to the youth of this land for a long time as the preparation of this series. Three or four worthy objects are attained in it. It places good literature in the hands of children. It lays a broad foundation for future study of history. It imparts a rich and varied knowledge of the life of the pioneers. It puts reading upon a natural basis. And the superiority of the matter offered almost guarantees successful expression. The first volume, entitled "Colonial Children," tells the story of the discovery of America, of the Indians and of the life of the colonists. The second volume is entitled "Camps and Firesides of the Revolution." The third, "How Our Grandfathers Lived." The fourth contains the "Romance of the Civil War."

* * *

This work is the first of a series designed to cover the whole field of commercial education. The Geography of Commerce treats of the relations of men to their physical surroundings. The aim has been to give an account of the physical features, the products, and the trade of the United States, and a more general view of the same aspects of the world at large. First, the physical basis is treated; second, the people; third, the products; and fourth, the trade. The work is subdivided under five headings—the first being introductory, followed by The United States, Trade of the Eastern Hemisphere, and a Review of World Commerce.

In print, maps, illustrations, style and thoroness the book is quite satisfactory. While it is intended primarily as a text-book for classes in high schools and colleges, it should be in every school library and should be freely consulted by both teacher and

The Geography of Commerce, by Spencer Trotter, M. D. New York. The Macmillan Company.

pupils in the preparation of more elementary lessons. Geography may be defined as the study of the earth, as the home of man. The geography of commerce sets forth the things that the earth does or is made to do, in supplying the material needs of men. Just as facts, the truths about the world are hardly more profitable than the truths about a sand pile. It is only when they affect human well-being that they become of value. The systematic presentation of the ways in which they affect human life cannot well be shown indirectly or in a small space. A perusal of this volume will indicate what phases of elementary geography should receive most attention and will supply much novel material for use in making its lessons definite.

* * *

The committee in charge of the Chautauqua Home Reading Course for 1903-4 have selected as the books to be read Prof. Richard T. Ely's "Evolution of Industrial Society"; Prof. A. P. Brigham's "Geographic Influences in American History"; Mr. H. S. Fiske's "Provincial Types in American Fiction," and Mr. Richard Burton's "Literary Leaders of America." These volumes, together with the "Chautauqua Magazine" for the year and a book of helps and hints, are offered when ordered together at a price or five dollars.

* * *

It is well known that the history-making of the present age is largely in the field of industrial endeavor. The changes which are going on there are more rapid and at the same time more sweeping than in any other department of human activity. Prof. Ely's volume is an effort to outline these changes. A list of chapter headings will indicate its scope. They are: The Idea of Evolution in Society, Evolution and Industrial Society, The Economic Stages, Economic Classes, Recent Tendencies of Industrial Evolution, Statistical Results, Competition, Rivalry and Success in Economic Life, Social Progress and Race Improvement, Monopolies and Trusts, Municipal Ownership, Concentration and Diffusion of Wealth, The Inheritance of Property, The Evolution of Public Expenditures, The Industrial Commissioner's Report on Labor, Industrial Peace, Industrial Liberty, Widening and Deepening Range of Ethical Obligation, Social and Ethical Interpretation, The Possibilities of Social Reform.

Clearness in statement and literary style are both sought and

The EVolution of Industrial Society, by Richard T. Ely. New York: The Chautauqua Press.

attained in it, and though the field which is traversed is immense, yet what has been done is well done and will be of very great utility.

* * *

This is a book of a new kind, for though books have been written upon man's influence upon nature, outside of incidental treatment in geographies almost nothing of a connected sort has been done to show the influence of geographical conditions upon the life of man. Geography as a why study is pretty sure to be absorbing, and the why of geography, which is at the same time the why of history, is more than doubly so. The influence of geography upon discovery and exploration, upon settlement and cultivation, upon war and peace, upon development and civilization, these are the themes which are treated here. Somebody has said recently that a railroad map is the best of all maps for school purposes, for it brings out the most important of all geographical facts—the fact of human intercourse and the means by which it is made possible. We must at least agree that the facts of human intercourse are of prime importance in understanding the growth of the nation. Waterways, roads and railroads come in for something like their fair share of attention here. The influence of natural barriers, forests, water supply, fertile soil and harbors may be said to control the distribution of men upon the surface of the earth. The character of a people is in some part determined by its dwelling place and the mental spiritual qualifications of communities are different somewhat as their habitations differ. What Hugo calls the Spirit of the Place may indeed determine whether men shall fight for liberty or for prejudice. And so it has been in our own past, and so it is in our own present. All this and much more is admirable set forth in this book. Another feature is a fairly exhaustive statement of present geographical changes and their effects upon local population. We can very easily imagine teachers reading this book and saying, " It is just the sort of book I have long been wanting. It will be a great help in giving substance and meaning to both geography and history, and should without a doubt be in the school library."

Geographic Influences in America History, by Albert P. Brigham. New York: The Chautauqua Press.

Before we had "a growing national Unity" and were consequently more removed from our present general alikeness, the land was full of "characters"—as they were called by their less interesting and racy neighbors.

Each in their own way and in their special locality reflected truly their own conditions and opinions and became a sort of social barometer of American life and activity.

They made tempting material for the writers and though no one has gathered them into that impossible whole known as the "great American novel," many have been admirably able to show them as to the manner born.

Mr. Fiske has chosen from the provincial types of the South Mississippi Valley, the Far West and New England some thirteen books from well asccredited authors, and after a brief introductory Survey of the Field leads directly into the text redolent with the spirited humor of the time and hour.

Mr. Fiske has wisely refrained from paraphrase and explanation. The text, clear and competent, speaks for itself, appealing to the sound sense and good taste which all children possess who have had the best and only the best set before them.

* * *

The intent of Dr. Burton's book is concisely stated in the preface—"a setting forth of the dozen or more great writers who have made our literature widely known."

In a book of this size no adequate quotation from even a dozen men can be given; its value then must lie in the setting forth. This seems fairly and pleasantly to prove from the contention of the introduction which defines literature as "the most beautiful way of saying something worthy," that this dozen or more writers stand really among the great. Follows, too, the how and when with some reasons for their respective flavor.

Like the rest of us Dr. Burton has his preferences but they are not permitted to become prejudices, and Longfellow is treated as well as the world compelling Poe.

* * *

Among the various studies of literature it is most agreable to come upon one which has been prepared in the manner which a sane boy of fourteen would approve. Here are lyrics, brave ballads and short stories to warm the hearts of boys and girls

---

Provincial Types in American Fiction by Horace Spencer Fiske. New York. The Chautauqua Press.
Literary Leaders of America by Richard Burton, New York. The Chautauqua Press.
An Introduction to the Study of Literature. Edwin Herbert Lewis.

just at that time when warm emotions need educating. The works are well grouped by subject and are especially adapted for reading aloud and the commitment to memory.

* * *

The Western Teacher

From a number of good things in the October issue we select a suggestion on tardiness. Why are people on time for a train? Because they fear the discipline of consequences. Arbitrary punishments for tardiness are wrong. A good rule is to make the first exercise so interesting that no one will care to miss it. Indulgences should not be granted. Under the title "Arithmetic for Children Under Twelve," objection is made to the endeavor to establish habits of accuracy at so early an age, as investigations have shown that children cannot be accurate in the earlier stages of their development. No attempt should be made to teach the *theory* of notation, in fact no general or universal truths should be formulated. On this point evey arithmetical text-book is faulty. Number work for this period should consist of (a) The solution of problems which do not require any explicit analysis of general laws; these may involve both integers and fractions. (b) Exercises in computation to form the habit of accuracy. From "Democracy in Education," an address by Miss Margaret A. Haley, we quote the following: "The educators must recognize that democracy in education, either in methods of teaching or administration, cannot be secured nor the educational system prevented from becoming an educational factory system, while the public mind is vitiated by the ideal of the industrial factory system, which makes the man at the top the only possessor of gray matter, and the thousands below the mere tools to carry out the directions of that gray matter. The educators today cannot stand alone, nor can the economists, the statesmen, the labor unions, nor any others who are trying to improve conditions. If the ideal of democracy is to be secured in one field it must be secured in all."

***

School and Home Education

The October number contains a brief discussion of Family Discipline by Dr. Wm. L. Harris. "It seems to me that one has to study his own civilization in its embyology in order to understand it. But I will readily admit that the study of Latin and Greek remains in some instances only a study of embryos without furnishing valuable concrete results, without strengthening the youth to grapple with the problems of life as they are now. It seems to me that it is a mistake to claim for the study of Latin and Greek a value simply as a mental discipline. I have always felt some impatience with my college teachers because they did not impress upon us students the true views in regard to the studies which we pursued, they did not interpret them in the light of civilization. I think that the narrow view of formal discipline was the cause of this scandalous neglect of philosophy. I have always considered it a piece of good fortune to me that I revolted against formal disciplinary studies and struck out for myself with the vague ambition to master the philosophy of the Germans. I admit there is much good in mere industry and in the discipline of exerting one's will, but there is great virtue in the selection of the regular course of study in college or university.".

The Journal of Geography for September contains articles on Geographical Societies of America, Time, Geographical Textbooks and Geographical Teaching, The Cultivation of Rice in the United States, etc.

*_**

BOOKS RECEIVED.

Elementary Geometry Plane, by James McMahon, American Book Company; Latin Prose Composition, by Henry Carr Pearson, American Book Company; Physical Labratory Manual, by E. E. Coleman, American Book Company; Elements of Arithmetic, by Hopkins and Underwood, Macmillan Company; Mental Arithmetic, by Hopkins and Underwood, Macmillan Company; Primary Arithmetic, by McLellan and Ames, Macmillan Company; The Child Life Readers, by E. A. and M. F. Blaisdell, Foundation Lessons in English, by O. I. and M. S. Woodley, Macmillan Company; Human Physiology, by John I. Jegi, Macmillan Company; Special Method in History, by Charles A. McMurry, Macmillan Company; Special Method in Primary Reading, by Charles A. McMurry, Macmillan Company; English Language and Grammar, Woodley and Carpenter, Macmillan Company; Real Things in Nature, by Edward S. Holden, Macmillan Company; How We Are Fed, by James F. Chamberlain, Macmillan Company; Applied English Grammar, by Edwin Herbert Lewis, Macmillan Company; A First Manual of Composition, by Edwin Herbert Lewis, Macmillan Company; Ways of the Six-Footed, by Anna Botsford Comstock, Ginn & Co., First Lessons in United States History, by Edward Charming, Macmillan Company; Wood Folk at School, by William J. Long, Ginn & Co.; The Spanish in the Southwest, by Rosa V. Winterburn, American Book Company; Stories of California, by Ella M. Sexton, Macmillan Company.

WESTERN SCHOOL NEWS

MEETINGS

California Teachers' Association, O. W. Erlewine, president; Mrs. M. M. FitzGerald, secretary, 1627 Folsom street, San Francisco; December 28 to 31, 1903.

Northern California Teachers' Association, Willows, Nov. 12, 13, 14.

Southern California Teachers' Association, Los Angeles, Cal., Dec. 22, 23, 24.

TEACHERS' INSTITUTES

Sacramento, B. F. Howard, Supt. Nov. 23, 24, 25.

San Joaquin, E. B. Wright, Supt. Stockton, Nov. 23, 24, 25.

Kings county, Mrs. N. E. DaVidson, supt. Hanford, Dec. 21, 22, 23.

Colusa County; Supt. Laugenour, Nov. 9, 10, 11.

Butte County, Supt. R. H. Dunn, Nov. 9, 10, 11.

Tehama county, Supt. Lynch, Nov. 9, 10, 11.

Shasta County, Supt. Mrs. Brincard, Nov. 9, 10, 11.

Yolo county, Supt. Mrs. DeVilbiss, Nov. 9, 10, 11.

CalaVeras county, Supt. Waters, Nov. 2, 3, 4, 5.

Los Angeles, Supt. Mark Keppel, Dec. 21, 22, 23, 24.

Mariposa county, Supt. Julia Jones, Nov. 16, 17, 18.

Ventura county, Geo. L. Sackett, Supt., Dec. 14-18.

Santa Clara county, D. T. Bateman, Supt. Nov. 23-25.

Tulare county, C. J. Walker, Supt. Porterville, Dec. 21-23.

NOTES

Los Angeles county now has nineteen high schools.

Haywards is to have a new school building costing $38,000.

Supt. Wilson of El Dorado county reports a scarcity of teachers.

Supt. D. H. Nelson of Utah announces a scarcity of teachers.

San Mateo high school district will vote for $23,000 school bonds November 14th.

Supt. Minnie Coulter is doing some active work in the consolidation of school districts.

J. J. Ryan has been employed at Chico State Normal School as a substitute for Prof. Miller.

The state normal school at Chico has an attendance of two hundred and forty, thirty of whom are young men.

Professor Randall, president of the University of California, has been elected superintendent of the Preston School of Industry at Ione.

Santa Clara county institute will make the "Reading Circle," under the leadership of David S. Snedden, one of the special features.

Alex. B. Coffey, A. B., Stanford, has cancelled his engagements to lecture and is now studying at the Teachers' College, New York City.

The Los Angeles City Board of Education has elected Miss Gertrude Hards special teacher in reading for the two high schools.

Calvin Esterly of the Fisk Teachers' Agency, 518 Parrott Building, San Francisco, is advertising for teachers. He has more demand than supply.

Dr. R. G. Boone, editor of "Education," and formerly superintendent of the schools of Cincinnati, has been doing institute work in the northwest.

The City Board of Education of Sacramento, at a meeting October 22, increased salaries of all the primary and grammar grade teachers. *Good.*

The receipts from the sale of school books, state series for September, amounted to $66,743. The demand for the new state history continues to be brisk.

A. E. Winship, editor of the "New England Journal of Education," will be the star attraction at the Oregon State Teachers' Association, November 23-25. Dr. Winship was recently appointed a member of the State Board of Education of Massachusetts.

Supt. James A. Barr of Stockton, Cal., has been re-elected for the fourth term as city superintendent of schools and his salary raised from $2000 to $2400. The Stockton *Record* prepared a full page of material in reference to his educational work in Stockton.

Dr. J. P. Blanton, formerly Dean of the Department of Education of the University of Missouri, recently read "Marse Chan" by Thomas Nelson Page, for the United Moderns of San Francisco. Dr. Blanton read the negro dialect in an inimitable manner.

Judge Hebbard of San Francisco has rendered an opinion that Miss Margaret McKenzie was illegally removed from the principalship of the Hancock grammar school by the San Francisco Board of Education. She will be entitled under the decision to draw over $5,000 back salary.

Kendric C. Babcock was inaugurated as president of the University of Arizona, Nov. 4th, with elaborate ceremonies. Gov. Brodie, President Benjamin Ide Wheeler and other prominent people were present. President Wheeler delivered an address at the State Normal at Tempee, and Flagstaff while on his trip.

Jenne Morrow Long, who is at the head of the Jenne Morrow Long College of Voice and Action, 2152 Sutter street, delivered a fine address before the California, Club October 22. She will lecture to the teachers of Shasta, Yolo, Sacramento and San Joaquin counties on Common Sense Methods in Reading during the month of November.

Job Wood Jr., deputy superintendent of public instruction and railroad secretary of the California Teachers' Association, has completed arrangements for one half fare from Los Angeles to San Francisco, and a rate of one and a third from other points in California to San Francisco and return for California Teachers' Association meeting, December 28-31.

Lewis B. Avery, principal of the Redlands High School, has recently compiled a course of study that has many unique features. The new High School building is shown as a frontispiece. We have also received the manual of San Bernardino County, which contains many excellent features. It has the best of the new and the best of the old in it—and is a model of its kind.

Supt. Thomas J. Kirk has paid official visits and attended institutes during the past few weeks as follows: Humboldt, Del Norte, Siskiyou, Shasta, Plumas, Mendocino, Kern and Merced Counties, and is pleased to report interest and progress in educational affairs.

Herbert Bashford, the well-known poet and literary and educational

publicist, has written a play, "The Hon. John North," which is a great
success in the East. Robert Downing takes the principal role. Mr. Bashford has also made a notable success this season as special instructor in
literature at institutes. He has attended Humboldt, Lassen, Modoc,
Plumas, San Bernardino, San Benito, Calaveras, Butte, and other counties.

The New International Encyclopaedia, edited by Dr. Daniel Coit Gilman and assisted by over 200 of the most eminent scholars, scientists and
experts in America, is the most wonderful work of the Twentieth Century.
It is complete in 17 volumes. It is the latest, best and up-to-date. G. G.
Kennedy, 561 Parrott Building, San Francisco, has the exclusive agency for
it in the schools in California. It is sold on easy installments. Write for
special introductory prices.

The Supreme Court has rendered a decision that John O. Hancock, formerly principal of the Santa Barbara high school, was entitled to his full
salary for the year for which he was engaged. Mr. Hancock was dismissed
by the board of education which succeeded the high school board. The
main point of the decision is that contracts entered into with teachers by
one school board must be carried out by succeeding boards and that salaries
must be paid during the life of the contract except in cases where service is
discontinued by mutual consent. The Hancock case has been before the
courts for the past three years.

INSTITUTES.

MENDOCINO COUNTY.

Some counties always hold the teachers' institute at the same place, the
county seat. Others pass it around to the larger towns of the county. This
plan has its advantages—instead of accepting the institute as a matter of
course, the town that gets the institute has to work for it; and consequently
appreciates its good fortune when successful.

Superintendent Barbee called the Mendocino County Institute this year
at Willitts, the terminus of the California Northern Railroad. And Willitts rose nobly to the occasion. The whole population was pleased and gratified to have the teachers come, and they showed it in many cheerful ways.
They were genial and affable on the streets; they always filled the hall with
a good audience; they furnished halls, music, decorations; banquet and
grand balls, all without cost to the institute; and they helped to make the
whole occasion a signal success. The teachers were quartered at a beautiful hotel, which gave them a generously special rate. The great hall, with
its blazing oaken logs radiating good cheer from a fire-place of magnificent
proportions, was the general meeting place at all leisure times. It was so
large that 150 teachers did not seem very many, when scattered about its
tables and arm-chairs and alcoves. The mantel piece was 12 feet high, built
of hugh beams of polished redwood. The fire was made of great tree trunks
cut into four-foot lengths, that would last all night and all day. Morning,
noon and night congenial groups would assemble for gay social talks; every

evening one would go to the piano and others dance. The banquet was a splendid one, of a dozen courses and two score toasts, lasting away into the small hours, attended by every teacher of the county. Professor Babcock, of Ukiah, was toast master, a witty and racy one, too. Mr. Patton, of Point Arena, made the funniest hit of the evening, in response to a toast of his home town. Many of the ladies made bright talks and of course all the visitors were called out, book men and all.

But it must not be supposed that nothing took place, but the gayety of the outside hours. A good solid institute filled all the working periods, one that everybody felt to be rich in practical results. Superintendent Kirk and President Dailey gave two addresses each; Miss Agnes Howe, of the San Jose Normal, gave a valuable work on teaching history, extending over two days. Dr. Fairbanks, of Berkeley, gave a three days course on geography teaching, illustrated by a fine display of lantern slides. Superintendent Barbee conducted a whole days discussion based upon Dewey's "*School and Society,*" which had been studied by all the teachers during the year. Superintendent Hyatt of Riverside filled up the vacant places for four days by a lively series of lectures touching almost all phases of the everyday work of a teacher, including a "Short Talk to Trustees," to a body of school officers who assembled Thursday afternoon. This was so pointed and practical that the trustees, the teachers and the County Board of Education united in requesting Superintendent Barbee to print it in pamphlet form for distribution to all the schools of the county.

The institute assembled on Oct. 27; and the members dispersed to their homes on the 31st.

* * *

MONTEREY COUNTY.

The Monterey County Institute was held at Salinas during the week beginning October 5. It was a five-day institute, full of solid work and some fun besides. It had a rich and varied list of outside assistants, as follows: President Dailey of the San Jose Normal School, who talked about summer sessions of the normal schools; Professor Moses of Berkeley, who gave a lecture on conditions in the Philippine Islands; Professor Cubberley of Stanford, who discussed the new law for consolidating school districts and gave two other talks on practical school topics; President Leroy Anderson of the San Luis Obispo Polytechnic School; Superintendent Edward Hyatt of Riverside County, who organized a special nature study section for a daily session, besides giving several pointed discussions of the matters that are of greatest moment to teachers; Professor Wilson of the San Jose normal, who gave several practical and jolly talks on practical pedagogy; Professor Lawrence, a local expert in music, who conducted section work on Friday; Jenne Morrow Long, of San Francisco, who gave several delightful recitations and readings.

On Thursday afternoon there was a three o'clock baseball game between the "Professionals" and the "Pedagogues," which excited the intense interest of the whole city—a great crowd was out to witness it. The Pedagogs' nine was really composed of the teachers of the county. The

County Superintendent, Mr. Sterling, played third base and played it well. The pitcher was Carmel Martin, the principal of a village school near Salinas, and he was a cracker-jack. The city superintendent played and one of the Pacific Grove high sceool teachers, Mr. James, was another good player. As a special honor to him President Dailey was invited to play—and he held down second base like a veteran. And best of all, the teachers won a hard fought game, against the best team that county seat could produce. Score, 9 to 4. How many other counties can show a team of teachers who can defeat the "professionals" at the American game?

* * *

DEL NORTE COUNTY.

The Del Norte County Institute was held September 23-26. The instructors were T. L. Heaton and State Superintendent Thomas J. Kirk. The special topics discussed were as follows: Primary reading, primary composition, oral and written geography. The evening entertainments were: Lecture, "Our Public Schools," Hon. Thomas J. Kirk; lecture, "Our Boys and Girls," Professor T. L. Heaton.

No special features. We simply had talks by the instructors, after which there were discussions, and questions by the teachers. Mr. Heaton's talk on "What and How to Spell," brought on a spirited discussion. Much interest was manifested throughout the entire session. Teachers express themselves as well pleased with the institute, and look forward to next year's institute with much pleasure. Teachers formed a reading circle which is to meet every two weeks, and are filled with a desire to improve themselves and their methods.

ALIDA M. LEISHMAN,
County Superintendent of Schools.

*

SOLANO COUNTY.

The Solano County Institute was held at Suisun, October 6-7-8-9, 1903. The instructors were President Benj. I. Wheeler, University of California; Prof. C. A. Duniway, Stanford; Dr. E. C. Moore, University of California; Miss Alma Patterson San Francisco Normal; Prof. D. S. Snedden, Stanford; D. W. Scott Thomas, University of California; Hon. W. S. Killingsworth, Vacaville. The special topics discussed were as follows: Prof. Duniway dealt with American history; Dr. E. C. Moore delivered several interesting lectures in modern theory and practice; Prof. Snedden gave some principles of general method, while Miss Patterson gave two talks on primary reading and laungage.

Two evening lectures were provided. On Tuesday Prof. Duniway gave an interesting lecture on "American Territorial Expansion," which was heartily applauded by the teachers present. On Wednesday evening, Hon. W. S. Killingsworth gave a very eloquent address on "Education, the Parent of Intelligence and Virtue." The special features of the institute were as follows: A resolution was adopted affecting the future of such bodies as this session. It is as follows: "Resolved, that notwithstanding the fact that this institute has afforded much opportunity for intellectual enjoyment yet, we believe, as many other county institutes have already resolved, that the ancient and honorable institution of County Institutes has had its day and that the $200,000 expended annually by the state of California to maintain. County Institutes might be more profitably used for the intellectual development of the teachers and the ultimate good of the growing citizen by creating a fund enabling public school teachers to attend a summer session of at least two weeks at our State University."

The above resolution must not be interpreted to mean that great good has not been accomplished by the fortieth annual session of the Solano Institutes. On the contrary, teachers have invariably expressed a sense of satisfaction with the excellent work of the instructors, which has broadened the horizon of the teachers' powers. The practical methods of Prof. Snedden and Miss Patterson; the ideal theories of President Wheeler and Prof. Moore; the searching and critical work of Prof. Duniway in American history, could not but prove an inspiration to better work. Moreover, the mingling of mind with mind—the contact of teachers with one another, has unified to a certain extent the aims in school work and accomplished what the present mode of supervision cannot furnish—a closer touch with the work of the best teachers of Solano County.

D. H. WHTIE,
Superintendent of Schools.

* * *

PLACER COUNTY.

The Placer County Institute was held October 12 to 16. The evening entertainments were re-union, lectures on Tuesday, Wednesday and Thursday nights. The special features of the institute were as follows: Particular attention given to the question of school decoration and sanitation; an exhibit of photographs of the world's greatest pictures; an especially fine lecture by Dr. Brown upon "The Greatest Man of the Nineteenth Century."

Remarks on results—We are too close to the institute to give much of an estimate of results, but judging from the comments of the teachers and visitors, several good lines of thought were started and will undoubtedly result in much good to the schools of the county. The exemplification of work in spelling and reading by classes before the institute by Deputy State Superintendent Job Wood was of practical benefit to the teachers. Dr. E. C. Moore of the State University gave us good suggestions on the subject of more systematic physical culture in the schools.

Very truly,
C. N. SHAW,
County Superintendent of Schools of Placer County.

* * *

CONTRA COSTA COUNTY.

The Contra Costa County Institue was held September 8-10-11, 1903. The instructors were Professors T. H. Kirk and Volney Rattan. The special topics discussed were as follows: Program, Promotions, Methods of Teaching the Essentials as Required by the Course of Study. The evening entertainments were, social re-union, September 8th; nature study, Prof. Rattan, September 10th.

It was a *business* institute. The program as published was strictly adhered to. The discussions were exceedingly lively and interesting. The matters discussed were practical and had direct bearing on the problems which are met every day in the schoolroom. While there was diversity of opinion, much light was thrown on the subject matter, and the best of feeling prevailed at the close. The institute was undoubtedly productive of much good. Would prefer not to enumerate the classes of bouquets received.
Very truly,
A. A. BAILEY.

* * *

LASSEN COUNTY.

At the Lassen County Institute the instructors were A. B. Coffey and Herbert Bashford. The special topics discussed were as follows: Literature of the West, and Some Mental Powers. The evening entertainments were "Fruits of the Press," A. B. Coffey; Readings from Original Poems, Herbert Bashford; reception to teachers. Refreshments were served by Eastern Star. The special features, in which every teacher took some part, were as follows: Addresses of Welcome, H. D. Burroughs, District Attorney; Rev. Theodore Taylor and J. A. McGregor. Responses by teachers, viz., R. H. Dunn, G. A. Clark, Annie H. Thompson. Hysteria in Childhood, paper, by G. P. Von Gerichten, M. D. Interest was maintained from first to last, growing, indeed, into enthusiasm and the teachers were sorry to see the end.
J. F. DIXON,
Superintendent.

* * *

SISKIYOU COUNTY.

The Siskiyou County Institute was held September 29-30 and October 1-2, 1903, at Shasta Retreat. The instructors were Profs. W. J. V. Osterhout, E. P. Cubberley and R. E. Chase. The special topics discussed were as follows: "Nature Study," "The Consolidation of Schools," "History," "Literature." The evening entertainment: Pres. B. I. Wheeler, "Characteristic Works of the Great Nationalists"; Prof. E. P. Cubberley, "Education in England"; Prof. W. J. V. Osterhout, "Scientific Inquiry into the Nature of Life." The special features of the institute were, "A Camp Life Reception," "Special Stress on Scientific Work in Schools." The interesting papers prepared by the teachers themselves.
G. A. JOHNSON,
County Superintendent of Schools.

* * *

SANTA BARBARA COUNTY.

The Santa Barbara County Institute was held October 5-8. The instructors were E. P. Cubberley, Frank Bunker, D. S. Snedden, E. McClish, and Mrs. Nico Beck-Meyer. The special topics discussed were Physical Education and Defects, Geography in Topical Study, Daily Programs in

Mixed Schools. In the evenings a reception was given by the city teachers of Santa Barbara; lecture, "The Pupil's Inheritance," E. McClish.

A hearty co-operation of teachers and superintendents in getting a satisfactory program, shorter daily sessions, a hearty social feeling on the part of all teachers, a division of the time for general culture, and detail work of the schoolroom were some of the special features.

We felt that the meetings were very practical and the talks were close to the daily work of the teachers. Afternoon sessions were short and time left for social gatherings. These regular sessions were followed by volunteer gatherings for talks not on the program.

The teachers generally felt that the institute was a very satisfactory one, and called out a good degree of enthusiasm.

W. S. EDWARDS,
Superintendent of Schools.

* * *

PLUMAS COUNTY.

The Plumas County Institute was held in Quincy, October 6-7-8-9. The instructors were Thomas J. Kirk, Prof. Alex. B. Coffey and Herbert Bashford. The special topics discussed were Course of Study. "Whats the matter with Geography" High School, Professional Ethics. The evening entertainments consisted of "Educational Problems," by Thomas J. Kirk; "Original Readings", Bashford; "Getting There," A. B. Coffey. The special features were "Teachers' Responsibilities," Judge C. E. McLaughlin; Schoolhouses, H. P. Willis.

TILLIE NAOMI KRUEGER,
Superintendent of Schools.

THE STATE SUPERINTENDENCY·

The next **State Superintendent**, the next **County Superintendents**, and the next **Governor and Legislative Officers** of California should all be pledged before election to the following platform:

1. **Free text-books** and school supplies.
2. The overthrow of the **"State Series"** system.
3. **Five-member School Boards.**
4. **The abolishment of County Boards**, and the substitution therefore of **Deputy County Superintendents** with duties wholly clerical.
5. **The County Superintendent a professional officer**, having duties and powers commensurate with the name.
6. The **election of County Superintendents** by the **School trustees** of the Counties, and of the **State Superintendent** by the **County Superintendents** of the State, by **viva voce vote in Conventions** assembled for the purpose.
7. **Eligibility** to the **higher teaching positions**, to the **County Superintendencies**, and to the **State Superintendency** to be one and the same.
8. **A Constitutional Amendment to be submitted** to remove any obstacles to the accomplishment of the above.

Respectfully submitted to the **zeal of the teachers**, and to the **intelligence of the voters** of the Commonwealth of California.

IRVIN PASSMORE, Principal of Schools, Paso Robles, Cal.

The Western Journal of Education

December, 1903

FRONTISPIECES. Educational Building, St. Louis. Speakers at the California Teachers' Association

PAGE

EDITORIAL 778
    State Teachers' Association — A State Teachers' Reading Course — Politics in Teachers' Meetings — The Institute — Physical Education — Developing the Answer — Back to the Farm — University Extension — Christmas, 1903.

LITERATURE IN THE GRADES. *D. S. Snedden* . . . 783

DEPARTMENT OF METHODOLOGY 799
    Teachers' College Notes in the Line of Art Instruction—For Teachers of Reading.

BOOKS AND MAGAZINES 804

OFFICIAL DEPARTMENT. *Thomas J. Kirk* . . . 815
    Superintendent of Public Instruction
    Certification of Special Teachers—The Examination of Pupils by County Boards of Education—Life Diplomas—Temporary Certificate—Teachers' Institutes—Non-Payment for Repairs—Non Attendance at Teachers' Institute—Quorum of County Board of Education.

CALIFORNIA TEACHERS' ASSOCIATION . . . 821

NORTHERN CALIFORNIA TEACHERS' ASSOCIATION . 821

INSTITUTES 823

WESTERN SCHOOL NEWS 831

THE WESTERN JOURNAL OF EDUCATION
723 MARKET ST., SAN FRANCISCO

Volume VIII
No. 12

$1.50 Per Year
Single Copy 15¢

NEWEST AND BEST

THE NATURAL NUMBER PRIMER

Price, 25 cents

Unlike all other books, this primer teaches the most elementary ideas and forms both of number and of language, at the same time. It may be used either with or independently of the regular reading primer. As a Language Primer it develops a practical vocabulary and the power of reading and expression. As a Number Primer it teaches in a very simple, logical way, the first steps in number. It is easy and appeals to the natural interest of the child in counting, besides being adapted to his various capacities. There are abundant illustrations and very simple drawings which serve as models for the child. Each new term is illustrated and introduced in script. In the footnotes are helpful suggestions for teachers, outlining the oral work and blackboard drill. The book will overcome many difficulties now commonly found in teaching this subject, and will supplement thoroughly and satisfactorily the work of the teacher.

THE BALDWIN SPELLER

Price, 20 cents

The words in this speller were selected by classroom teachers after observing the class vocabulary for a year. They include, therefore, those words which require special attention, and which will be of most immediate practical use to the child. They are arranged according to difficulty. The words for each year's work are divided into groups of four lessons each, each group forming a week's work, the fifth lesson of each week being an oral review. In the earlier review lessons the accentuation and pronunciation of the words are marked. Illustrative sentences show the uses and meanings of words with the same sound. Among the selections for study are such favorites as Whittier's "Barefoot Boy" and Longfellow's "Children's Hour." The book is based upon actual conditions in the school, and not upon mere theories.

MILNE'S PRIMARY ARITHMETIC

Price, 25 cents

A new arithmetic for beginners, forming with the author's Intermediate Arithmetic and Standard Arithmetic an ideal three-book series. In this book each number from 1 to 100 is developed by the spiral system through all the fundamental operations. The work in connection with each number is elaborated and carefully developed. Among the special features of the book are:
1. The illustrations are particularly well chosen and admirably adapted for their purpose. There are many devices to arouse the interest of the child.
   There is active work to sustain the interest of the child;
4. The problems are practical and deal with matters in connection with the child's experience.
5. Reviews are frequent and well planned.
6. Inductive work leads the child to discover facts for himself.
7. Fractions are developed in connection with integers.

HARMONIC SERIES—NATURAL MUSIC COURSE

Six Books and Seven Charts

This series, the newest of the well-known Natural Music Course, is unquestionably one of the most notable recent achievements in the educational world. It is a working course of power-giving quality; it affords children easy mastery over music symbols; it enables them to render appreciably and agreeably the printed page; it cultivates a love of music, rather than a mere attainment for a few songs; it develops the auditory imagination; and it makes the power to express musical thoughts a familiar possession. No other course arouses and cultivates such an aesthetic nature in the child and gives him such skill in aesthetic production. From the first lesson to the last the child is trained to enjoy pure music, and is carefully drilled in each subject as it occurs in the books and in the charts.

AMERICAN BOOK COMPANY

204 Pine Street, San Francisco.

NEW YORK   CINCINNATI   CHICAGO   BOSTON   ATLANTA   DALLAS

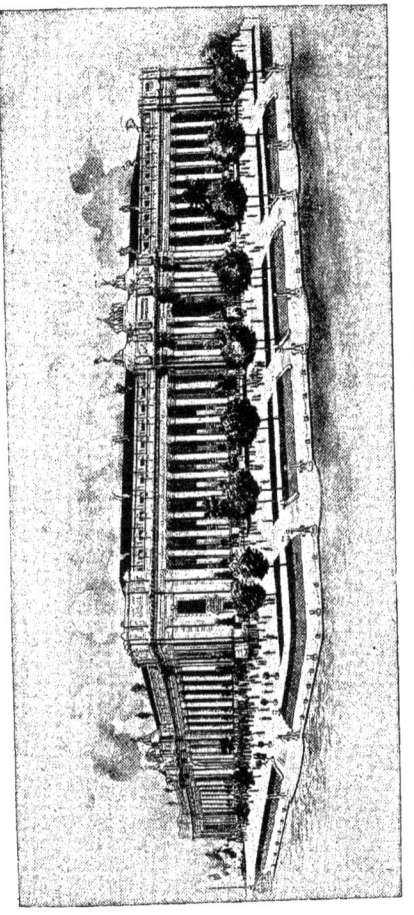

EDUCATIONAL BUILDING, ST. LOUIS

For the first time in the history of World's Fairs a separate building has been constructed exclusively for educational exhibits. On the Exposition Grounds at St. Louis a grand structure covering an area of seven acres and costing over $850,000, has been built and is now ready to receive exhibit material from the schools of the world.

This "Palace of Education," as it is appropriately called, is in the form of a key-stone, and occupies a conspicuous site, being placed in the center of an acre of magnificent buildings that adorn the Exposition grounds. The northern facade is 750 feet in length and the southern facade 450 feet. The two sides are 525 feet each. The style of architecture is modern classic. Within this palatial building will be displayed the various phases of education among different peoples and indifferent civilizations.

California has been allotted nearly 1500 square feet of floor space in which to display the work of her schools. In many localities of the state active work in selecting material has been in progress for some weeks. California will doubtless make a creditable display.

S. H. CLARK
University of Chicago
A Speaker at the California Teachers' Association
December 28–31, 1903

O. W. ERLEWINE
President of the California Teachers' Association

ARNOLD TOMPKINS
President Chicago Normal School
A Speaker at the California Teachers' Association
December 28–31, 1903

The Western Journal of Education

DECEMBER, 1903

EDITORIAL

State Teachers Association

The meeting of the State Teachers' Association is the most important educational event of the school year. What the town meeting was for developing New England, or better still, what congregation is in every religion that is the assembling together of the teachers in local or state gatherings for the cause of education. Men fight best in armies, for the spirit of the company is a very real thing, and as they rush the enemy or struggle up the hill together they catch a touch of inspiration from each other that makes them literally indomitable. Peace hath her psychology of procedure as well as war, and the spirit of the host is no less powerful a stimulus to mighty work in the one case than in the other. It means something large and fine to fellow with the army of the redeeming to which one belongs. In the first place, we come together and "together," is a very great word, as Edward Everett Hale has said. Is it any wonder that our age, among other great inventions, has discovered the power of combinations, sometimes called the greatest of all the inventions of the last century. Physical togetherness means spiritual togetherness, for it leads inevitably to it; and a unity of purposes and intention with such confidence in our fellows as always comes when we know them —these things, it may be said, are the things most needful in the educational work of our state. Irrational conservatism and distrust vanish away in such an assemblage, and one who comes to the spirit of the gathering never fails to tighten up his belt and prepare for harder and better work as he leaves it. Why? Because he has gotten an new idea of himself, of his fellows, of his profession. Less than these, but also very important, is the learning of something more about the business thru the more formal conferences of the association.

A State Teachers' Reading Course

The time has come for the organization of a state teachers' reading course. The work has already been done and well done by the teachers of several counties. It is hardly necessary to add that these counties have the best schools and the best institutes in the state. Teaching can never become a profession until the teachers become students. One cannot readily teach another to do the thing which he himself does not believe in. Teachers cannot teach pupils to study until they study themselves. Almost every week a really first class book appears written by a master, to share the well deliberated results, sometimes of years of experience, upon one phase or another of school work. Some of them at least should be read and pondered and discussed for the benefit of the schools. The work of education has never received so much or so worthy attention as at present. Mathematicians are leaving their problems, scientists their laboratories and philosophers their speculations to write books and addresses upon this or that aspect of the teaching of their subjects. For the most part these books are untechnical and could readily be comprehended by the pupils in the grades. They simply must not be allowed to pass the teacher by. It will not do to assume that the teachers are uninterested in their work. They are not, and any well organized institute will give the lie to that objection. It will not do to say that the superintendents will not co-operate, for it is to their advantage in all ways to promote the educational life of their counties. The most pathetic thing about our whole school system is the small amount of encouragement which is given to good work. Teachers want to do their best, but they are so isolated and so forgotten in their struggle for life that discouragement is apt to be their lot. The same thing is in a measure true of the frontier superintendent. What we want is some means of working together. The well organized reading course taken up by local groups of teachers under a leader who is responsible to the county superintendent for the work of his group, has been found to be an invaluable aid in the educational life of the older states. Let live and inspiring books be chosen, the co-operation of the county superintendent invited and the work is already half done. The editors of the JOURNAL believe that its pages contain material some of which at least is worth such consideration. If a state reading course were adopted, it stands prepared to print monthly discussions of the portions of the books read by the local groups of teachers.

Politics in Teachers' Meetings

The one blot upon the whole program, the one undemocratic feature of the whole gathering, is the introduction of "political methods" in the choosing of officers. It is the feature of our assembling which is opposed to the spirit of the whole undertaking, which is not open and above board, but hidden and dangerous, for it breeds rivalry and distrust, and must breed them, since it puts a premium upon qualifications which will not submit to open inspection.

Within the last two years there has been a great hue and cry raised thru the state on the subject of professional ethics. The California State Teachers' Association has adopted a resolution condemning as unprofessional conduct the submitting of any argument or plea in obtaining or retaining a position other than those constituting evidence of professional competency. The resolution has been accepted and endorsed by some local bodies of teachers. It is an excellent rule, but the body that promulgated it must practice it. The place to begin is in the State Teachers' Association itself. There, or nowhere, must the office select the man and not the man select the office. There, or nowhere, must the purging of the schools from the dangers of political methods begin. The offering of any evidence as to fitness for any of the offices in the gift of the association is unnecessary and such special pleading is bound to be regarded as "political," and quite rightly. The Teachers' Association of California will not and cannot inspire the confidence of its members, to say nothing of the people of the state; will not and cannot lead in the work of education as it should until it forever repudiates such practices. And it will not and cannot repudiate such action until each and every member of the association takes before his own conscience a Hippocratic oath to defend the honor of his profession against any and everyone who seeks self-aggrandizement at his hands. The association should choose its officers, not the officers or their too devoted friends choose themselves.

The county institute might be greatly improved. To do so it need not be abolished. To sit in a badly ventilated room for five days in order to be lectured to upon a variety of subjects which seem to bear no relation to each other and none of which appears of much importance, anyway; that surely is a depressing experience. And that is what the county institute is in some localities—a thing of deep, despair-bringing dullness. In other localities the room is well ventilated, the company keen and intelligent, the work well organized, the spirit of the meeting excellent and the results important for the future of every child in the county. The difference is largely due to the superintendent, for after all it is the superintendent and not the institute that is on trial. Superintendent A is no business man, neither is he a scholar. School problems are beyond him. He judges the teacher's work by the awe she inspires and the neatness of her official reports, or he does not judge it at all. He holds an institute because the law compels him to do so. He selects his instructors upon the basis of their reputed jocularity, or because of affiliation thru school politics. His teachers have not read anything bearing upon their work during the year. They have discussed it occasionally with people who commiserated them upon their hard lot in life. They come to the institute expecting a holiday with pay. The opening exercises drag. The chairman is listless; the room becomes "close." The teachers become apathetic. They had forgotten that they were expected to sit imprisoned for five hours a day hearing a performance in which they had no part. The instructor is introduced, but can make no headway against the prevailing dullness and discontent, and for five days this sort of thing goes on.

Superintendent B is a leader in the educational work of his county. When he visits the schools he investigates them. His presence is cheering. He takes note of good work and if all is not going as it should he helps to right the situation. His teachers know what he wants and are anxious to help in getting it. When the time for the annual institute comes around they begin to look forward to it as an intellectual treat. The best hall in the town is taken. The most zealous and skillful teachers in the state are selected as instructors. The program is made out on the basis of the needs of the schools. Local teachers whose work has been markedly successful are asked to give their fellows the benefit of their experience. The institute is divided into sections. The books which every teacher has read during the year are studied. Questions are asked, points of difficulty discussed, and the institute becomes an educational conference in which every one takes part freely. The more formal part of the program is devoted to the discussion of fundamental principles of education. For detailed statements of method the teachers are referred to books or educational periodicals. Commonplaces are out of order and talking down to the teachers is not indulged in. The program is as short as the form of instruction requires and plenty of opportunity for social intercourse is given. For an institute maintained on this level there simply is no substitute. The summer school at its best will not begin to take its place, for there are two things that it imparts which the summer school cannot supply—a sense of the solidarity of the teaching body of the community which in its effect can be compared only to the organization of an army out of a mass of scattered and straggling individuals, and abundant opportunity for the development of social and professional spirit. Indeed, if university instruction is wanted, it may be given at the county seat as well as at the university, and there these greater things may be added unto it. But university instruction is not wanted. The schools as schools are to be considered there, and the teachers as teachers meet there. The institute is a professional gathering for considering the claims of professional work. It cannot be abolished. It must be improved.

Physical Education

Of all the good gifts of the gods health of body has always been rated among the first, and like most of the characteristics of adult life, it is either gotten in childhood or not at all. It is with good reason that our age has experienced a great revival of interest in that side of education. School sanitation and physical culture of some sort are indispensable features of all school work which lays claim to any degree of acceptability. Thinking about these things makes a vast difference in the fiber of a people. No one should be compelled to enter life with defective eyesight, defective hearing, defective digestion, defective respiration and a defective heart. Yet it is the lot of many young people to emerge from the schools in this maimed and halt condition. The heart is a delicate organ. The lungs are apt to be misused or to remain in part unused. The eyes are likely to be strained, the teeth to decay and the breathing to become impeded, Sixty per cent of the children who had passed thru the schools of Breslau were found to have defective eyesight. From eighteen to thirty percent of the children tested in some half dozen cities were found to have auditory defects. Eighteen percent of the school children of Madison were found to be "mouth breathers." Ninety-five percent of the children examined in Schleswig-Holstein had defective teeth. Here is a condition that cries for attention. The school teacher cannot handle it unaided, but parents cannot be trusted to take the initiative in it. They are too much with their children to be aware of their true condition and frequently their standards are too low to be trustworthy. . The teacher is employed as an auxilliary guardian of the next generation. His work is not limited to hearing lessons but concerns the general welfare of his wards. His duty will not be fulfilled until he takes a hand in the work of making a sound body for everyone of his pupils. How may he do it? By reporting defects of the sort above noted to parents, with an urgent suggestion that they be remedied at once. His teaching of physiology ought to be practical and to claim immediate application. The rules of the State Board of Education require him to have a care for the ventilation of his schoolroom and. to set apart certain portions of each day for breathing exercises. If he will get into the habit of opening the windows at regular intervals and having all his pupils stand in the aisle and fill their lungs with air taken in in deep breaths, he will be astonished to note how much more vital they will soon become, and with how much more energy the work of each day will be performed. Too much care simply cannot be expended upon this matter of health. A gymnasium is not necessary, nor are finished drills or elaborate exercises required. Let each organ play its part and remain whole, and the thing will come of itself.

* * *

"Developing the Answer" The editor of "School and Home Education" prints some valuable observations, which apply as well to California as to Illinois, upon some school work seen in a recent tour of investigation. He finds the instruction given above the primary grades defective in knowledge, in habits of thought, and views of life. Indeed, he questions whether those who lived in past days were not better educated than are most of the students in the higher grades of our elementary schools today. One radical defect is that the pupils cannot read their text-books understandingly. In a certain high school where problems were being solved in which the specific gravity of certain substances was sought, they did not know what specific gravity was, why it was sought, or even what the word specific meant. The teacher did not seem better informed than the class. In another class the difficulty was not with the teacher, but with his method of teaching. He showed a marked inability to put himself in the place of his pupils — in other words, he was utterly unable to obey the Golden Rule: "Put yourself in the other fellow's place"—which is as strictly applicable to teaching as it is to all other human relations. Because of this inability he was teaching by the Socratic method and seeking in vain to "develop" knowledge where it was not by a continuous fire of questions. The method of developing the answer by a series of questions is not a safe method with younger pupils. The questions are too apt to bring confusion and to lead to self-distrust. Socrates used that method and used it successfully, but he used it for another purpose than imparting knowledge. He used it to break down pride and self-conceit, and to point out the need for a higher knowledge. But what is good for adults is not necessarily good for children, and questioning that does not lead to knowledge imparting is destructive to them. Questions have their place and must not be depreciated. The point is that they must not be used exclusively, as in the effort to "develop" the answer. The rule, "never tell a pupil what you can make him tell you by questioning him," is sure to work very great evil if adhered to literally and observed without intelligence.

Back to the Farm

The boy and girl have been educated away from the farm. The electric car, free rural mail delivery, the technical training in agriculture, horticulture and domestic science must bring them back. The greatest school in this state in point of future usefulness is at San Luis Obispo. It is training boys and girls, not for the city, but for the great valleys, slopes and mesa lands in California. The artist who sees the violet haze over our mountains and puts it on canvas, the poet who sings of the orange and vine, have a place—a great place in our development; but the well trained man who not only works but works with keen intelligence to make two blades of grass grow where only one grew before is a benefactor. He is a philantropist. We should have more monuments to men like Bidwell, Sutro, Joaquin Miller, Cooper, Kimball, Holt, Burbank and others who have made the world richer by the trees they have planted; by the blades of grass that have been given a chance to grow by their efforts and God's good white rain, or irrigation. Let us build fewer monuments to soldiers and celebrate the man who fights battles with the elements and wins. Not shoulder straps but shirt sleeves should be the insignia of rank.

Ex-Senator Smith of Bakersfield, who lead in the establishment of a state polytechnic school, should be given more honor than the man who raised a regiment for a commercial war. His idea was that the farmer needed trained brains as well as the lawyer, the doctor, and the engineer, and that a polytechnic school located in an agricultural community would train the boys and girls back to the farm.

The idea is right. The idea, however, of training boys and girls back to the farm should not be left exclusively to the school at San Luis Obispo. Every course of study in the state should have part of the matter that is now in cast aside, and new matter relative to the actual life of the boy and girl substituted. A good course in orchard and farm should be arranged, and a suitable text as a guide to the teacher provided. Books of country life, of ranches, fields and fireside should be prescribed as supplementary readers. A few of the old heroes should be retired, and men who were not only reared on the farm, but stayed there, should be held up as ideals. The stories, good in their place, of the barefoot country boy who went to the city and became rich and famous, has led many a country school boy away from the farm to the gutter in the city. We hear of those who succeed; what of those who fail?

Teachers who sneer at country life in the rural schools should have their certificates for good sense and good teaching revoked. The teacher and boards of education can do much in giving the right trend to courses of study and teaching along the lines of making each boy and girl believe in the opportunities right in their own dooryards. Acres of diamonds may be over the far-distant mountains, but maybe you will find them at your door. One place is just as good as another, and a little bit better if its your own.

* * *

University Extension

The series of University extension lectures inaugurated by Prof. Henry Morse Stephens will have a wide educational influence. The lectures at the Mechanics Pavilion have attracted audiences of more than two thousand people. University extension lectures are not a fad. They have become a part of our intellectual life. Entire communities are vitalized, uplifted, and pushed forward by study suggested by extension courses. The state is fortunate in having a man like Henry Morse Stephens to conduct the University extension courses. He is conservatively brilliant and stands for scholarship—new and adequate scholarship.

* * *

CHRISTMAS 1903

Christmas stands for the highest educational ideals. Its greatest lesson to humanity is love and charity. No man who gives that which he wants to another has failed to learn the lesson. We teach ethics, right conduct and morals and manners, and various general isms with the object of augumenting that which is good in the child, but no Pestalozzian lesson ever approached the one grand object lesson of Christmas giving. Selfishness, cruelty, enmity, bigotry, prejudice, all the pitiful weaknesses of humanity that we failed to unlearn in school, are forgotten on December 25th. The three wise men saw the Star of Bethelem. The wise men of today still see the star.

* * *

A state teachers' association becomes a travesty of every ideal for which the teachers' calling stands, the moment a part of its members begin to prey upon its offices. This disreputable part is usually successful because it brings the effrontery and methods of the ward boss and politician into an organization which looks for quite other motives and knows no grounds for being exploited to personal ends. These pseudo-teachers and pseudo-schoolmasters, who labor to perfect a political ring within an association of teachers, smaller part though they may be, are yet a reproach to the whole. The ultimate effect of this work will always be the disruption of the organization; for no association of teachers will long submit to blatant grafting. What possible value can accrue to the man or woman who is known to have exploited the chairmanship of a teachers' association to personal ends? Is the successful candidate not known after all either for worth in his calling, or for the lack of it? If one has but a meager professional figure to boast of, why does he set it up on a pedestal? Doesn't he know that he's known? Wherefore the emphasis? And is it, after all, worth the personal anxiety and attention of the candidate,—at least to the extent of personally providing voters with ballots and pencils, or, more thougtfully, with name-cards? Is it worth it? All in good time, the great National Educational Association fonnd itself again; for two years it has elected such men as President Eliot, and John W. Cook, to its presidency. Is there hope for the California State Teachers' Association?

* * *

President Charles W. Eliot in November "Atlantic" says: "Great improvement in rural schools has resulted from the daily bringing of the children from the farms by wagons into the central village; so that one large graded school can be carried on at the center, instead of many widely scattered small schools in which accurate grading is impossible. This improved machinery would be a doubtful blessing, if its smooth working did not require and encourage the employment of a superior class of teachers; but the evils of the machine—the lack of attention to the individual child, the waste of time for the bright children, and the tendency to work for a fair average product instead of one highly diversified—are done away with so soon as a large proportion of teachers to pupils is employed—such as one teacher for from sixteen to twenty-five pupils—while the many advantages of the good machine remain."

* * *

President Butler of Columbia proposes the following five tests of education in the broadest sense of that term:

1. Correctness and precision in the use of the mother tongue.
2. Those refined and gentle manners which are the expression of fixed habits of thought and action.
3. The power and habit of reflection.
4. The power of intellectual growth.
5. Efficiency, the power to do.

LITERATURE IN THE GRADES*

The history of educational practice shows that up to comparatively recent years literature was not taught as a subject in the ordinary schools. True to their mission as they understood it, educators undertook to prepare children for a maturity in which they should understand and appreciate literature. They did this by giving the child the ability to read, to know the meanings of words and combinations of words, and to understand the various instrumentalities by which the artist in literature accomplishes his aim. Formal reading, grammar, lexicology, rhetoric, mythology, prosody, and history of literature were the studies which prepared for the appreciation of literature. It is true that samples of literature were used in these studies, from the classical sentences and quotations used in the grammar and rhetoric, to the selected lessons and sample poems used in the formal reading and history of literature; but it is hardly likely that educators thought that thru these they were teaching literature itself, and certainly at this day we can easily say they were not. One needs not go to the histories of education to find the truth of the above; most of us can demonstrate it from experience.

During the last quarter of a century there has developed hesitatingly and uncertainly a movement in favor of the study of literature itself in the schools. The high school, as it grew out of classical traditions, gave more attention to the study of English, and the colleges, thru their admission requirements, later gave direction to this development. We find a few classics introduced to replace the readers in the upper grades. We find also that the best courses of study everywhere now urge teachers to encourage supplementary reading, this last turning towards the reading of complete, tho simple books. We find that lists of books suitable for home reading are given, and that live teachers are cooperating with the public libraries. In fact we are, educationally speaking, in the flood tide of a movement which means, not alone the throwing open to children of the world books, but which throws the best energy of the school towards encouraging the use of books. English—part formal English, part literature,—is the central subject in the curriculum today from the kindergarten at least to the college. The movement is a new one; but it has been enthusiastically, nay religiously, received.

But the new order of things is confusing. We see clearly

---
*Read before the Scholia Club, November 21.

enough that we want the children to rise to an appreciation of the best in literature; but how? Our high schools try hard enough, but the pupils leave our high schools detesting Addison and Shakespeare, at least in so many instances as to give us pause; and the pupils whom we have carefully carried thru the grades go out and create a demand for yellow journalism and the cheap novel. Furthermore, the study of literature has not made good oral readers nor good spellers, tho we were promised that it would do just this. What, in short, should be the relation of all the formal studies in the vernacular to the study of its literature? Even the doctors in literature cannot yet tell us.

But, more important still, we have with us the question of the mission of literature. Few of us who deal much with children have any patience with the cry "art for art's sake". We cannot make literature an end in itself. It must serve as a means to uplift the individual, to make him a better member of human society. It must enrich his own life, and also so mould him that he enrich the lives of others. Character, personal effectiveness, social effectiveness—these are the results that we want from education; and we require that our instruments and materials—the subjects of the curriculum—shall contribute to these ends. How, then, should we use literature? What may we expect to be its results? And how is the attainment of these results affected by this or that treatment of the subject? These are some of the questions that I shall try to answer.

I have no time to argue, either as to a definition of literature, or with reference to its mission, so shall on these points, be brief and dogmatic. Wherever ideas are conveyed thru oral or written speech, in which is involved some beauty of form, there we have literature. This definition is especially useful in dealing with the literature suitable for use in the elementary school. Good literature *is* good, because, by the standards we employ, the ideas conveyed, the feelings aroused, are good; and the form does not offend aesthetic sensibility. Furthermore, the aim of literature is to arouse and cause to grow, the higher sentiments— aesthetic and social. Literature *is* literature because the material used—the ideas—are so used by the artists as to affect certain sensibilities. And we use literature because we want these sensibilities stimulated, either for pleasure or for growth.

What is literature, so far as the elementary schools are concerned? Differentiation is more difficult here than later when appreciation becomes more delicate. Any story told to the child which arouses keen interest and enlists the imagination is certainly literature, so far as the child is concerned, just as any vivid picture is art. The child, as we all know, is interested in content rather than form, and it is difficult to make him concious of bad form. All we can say here is that that is literature to the child which read or heard makes, in some way, a strong appeal to him, and especially on the emotional side, whether owing to content or form. A great weakness in all current discussions of literature teaching is that they start with adult definitions of literature, and judge things suitable or unsuitable for children solely by these standards. Many of the stories in "Youths Companion", "St. Nicholas," etc., are literature, as are also the writings of Lear and Carrol, {and "Mother Goose", at appropriate times. Wherever the writer or story teller utilizes his materials for the purpose of kindling sentiment, arousing a play of the imagination, or otherwise affecting the sensibilities, we have literature. " Uncle Tom's Cabin", "Huckleberry Finn," "The Boys of '76", "Paul Revere's Ride"—all these are literature; as are equally the innumerable stories of travel and adventure which give vicarious experience and stimulate feelings of courage, patriotism, admiration, fear, detestation, pity, cooperation, etc. Tho literature play fast and loose with facts, it is still literature if it make an effective appeal to the emotional nature; and by this standard "Jack the Giant Killer", "Ivanhoe", "Kim", "Wolfville" and "Lobo" are all literature. If we prefer that literature sall de al with facts and truth we may reject the "Call of the Wild" and "Wild Animals I Have Known" and "Twenty Leagues Under the Sea". But, if we are aiming at something that only literature can accomplish, we must be careful to substitute that which, while resting more upon fact, shall make equal appeal to the emotional nature.

Having thus tried to make clear what we call literature when speaking of the work of the elementary school, we must next face the question of its desirability. It is evident that we may use literature here with either one of two ends in view. We may desire simply to introduce the child to literature, to form tastes and discriminations, in order that when he leaves school he may have appreciation developed. Or we may to some extent deliberately use literature in the plastic period of the child's life to bring about that development of the emotional nature which we aim at in education. The first aim all teachers have long had in view; but less often have we consciously held to the second. Education has been chiefly thought of as concerned with the intellectual; shall we also undertake the development of the higher emotional, or, as it may be called, the spiritual, nature of the child?

Is the study of literature needed in the school? The most inexpensive and most refined pleasures which come to man are those growing out of love of good literature. The man who can and does read fiction, history, science, travel and poetry has a constant source of companionship and inspiration, which is more available and less wasteful than any other sources of the more refined pleasures. Now, this taste can be cultivated. The mass of our people read, but they have not frequently formed pleasant associations with the best of reading. It is possible by having proper associations formed in youth to produce in some measure a taste for the refined and a dislike for the crude. There are few rules for accomplishing this end: contact, example, suggestion from those whose suggestions are naturally welcome, are the agencies by which taste is formed. Understanding and critical insight come later, and not with all individuals. Moreover, the educational agencies external to the school do not and cannot always form this taste. More and more is this becoming the work of the school.

The school, furthermore, is expected to contribute its share— and a share which is also increasing—to fitting the child to live an effective social life. He must acquire moral habits, must have his social tendencies developed, and his unsocial tendencies thwarted in their development. It is desirable usually to increase and widen sympathy with suffering, and to diminish the instinct to fight; it is desirable to stimulate the emotional tendencies which make for co-operation, and diminish those which make aggressive and selfish rivalry too prominent. It is desirable to promote an appreciation of the value of persistent and honest labor and to lessen the tendencies to profit at the cost of some one else. Social education of this sort is accomplished by several means. We form habits and associations as a result of contact with parents, playmates, and teachers. These people make selfishness unpleasant and usually make certain virtues pleasant in that a reward or approval follows their exercise. So social habits arise and associations are formed. Our early experience, moreover, gives us feelings of worth, appreciations, and ideals. There seems to be a disposition in the normal individual to evolve certain high standards of action and then to strive towards the attainment of these. Just why we form ideals and why we strive so hard towards their realization we do not know any more than we know the source and reason for our other instincts. But personal experience of most of us is a satisfactory demonstration of the existence of this tendency. The small child has ideals and is gratified if they are realized measurably, and wants the approval of others in reference to this realization. The youth has dreams of courageous action, a worthy life, a daring deed, the accomplishing of a work, etc., all of which become potent factors in action.

I say the basis of this ideal-forming propensity is instinctive; but the particular form taken by the ideal depends largely upon the environment. The boy reared in the seaport would emulate the life and character and deeds of sailors; the boy on our cattle ranges would exhibit the virtues of the cowboy; the college student would win a degree or write a book. Our ideals are derived largely from those about us whose lives we admire, provided, of course, there be not too great a departure from the lines of development suggested by other aspects of the instinctive nature. The boy on Nob Hill would usually rather emulate the virtues of the locomotive fireman or the sailor than those of the banker or statesman; the latter are not objective, concrete enough for his understanding and for his life of flesh and blood. Let me emphasise again that whatever contributes to the building of higher and at the same time effective ideals is of supreme importance in education. On the side of moral or social development, it becomes no less the duty of education to stimulate the building of these ideals than to form moral habits and to give knowledge of right and wrong action.

Life, itself, of course, is the most effective agency in forming ideals; but since in intellectual education, we cannot control the conditions of life itself; the school selects certain aspects of life, artificial aspects possibly, and utilizes them in education. We do this in arithmetic, in geography, and in business instruction;

and we must do it largely in moral education. We must to some extent contribute an artificial environment for the stimulation of the ideal nature. Out of life we want to select these means which most effectively claim the attention of the disposition to erect and to strive after ideals.

What are the means which can be utilized in this way? Mostly the lives and actions of other men. Since we can not present these characters in the schoolroom, we bring the best representations of them. We bring pictures of them and their actions; we bring songs and poems extolling them and holding them up to admiration; we create artificial characters who have enough reality to touch and influence us, and we follow the actions of these; and thru it all goes the work of the artist bringing into relief the things that ought to be most seen and felt, and suppressing the features that are not relevant. Out of this world of material which is produced by life, but which is also seen in artificial light, which modifies the real shades and lights of life to suit the purpose of the artist, it is possible to select that which will profoundly affect that part of our nature which is called social. Dickens can make us love and admire many of the poor and lowly of London. H. B. Stowe can awaken a great thrill of passionate indignation at slavery; a Whittier can do the same; a Longfellow can make us more appreciative of the lives of the Indians; a Kipling can make us ashamed of some of our crudities; a Scott can hold up before many a youth pictures of devotion, self-sacrifice, and valor, which leave a lasting impress.

In proper hands, then, literature may become a powerful agency in stimulating the growth and guiding the expression of all that part of our nature which is called social. In fact, aside from the personality of the exceptional teacher, I can understand no other agency within the school which can have anywhere near the same influence. The other arts may stimulate, but they cannot effectively guide. Literature may point out in great detail to the youth or man the road to be followed, and greatly affect his disposition to follow this road.

So powerful an instrument, therefore, requires careful use. It is possible and easy for tastes that are not high to be formed. It is possible to form ideals that make for social disintegration rather than for strength. The ages of strife and blood have bequeathed us a legacy of literature which, while admirable in many respects, does not tend to strengthen the ideals which fit our age. Again, one of the great uses of literature is to give a field for the vicarious satisfaction of the instincts which are an inheritance. We like to read of strife in novels or to see it in play, tho the conditions of life forbid our emulating that which we see. So the function of the teacher and guide is to point out those things which deserve emulation and those which are not contributory to our civilization.

From this point of view, then, literature has a very important function in the grades, being the chief instrument for the development of higher individual tastes and capacities for enjoyment; and for the purpose of calling into action and growth and in giving form to those emotional tendencies which largely lie at the basis of the best social life; namely, the alturistic virtues, the ideals of high action, etc. It must be remembered that in the ages when religious faith was active that faith served as an effective means for the promotion of those virtues; but we are now constrained to appeal less to religious faith as a means for the development of the moral nature.

Let us now face the practical question of where literature shall be presented, what shall be presented, and how it shall be presented.

My answer to the first is brief. Literature should be presented to the child from the opening day of school onward. In fact it may be more urgently needed in the lower grades than in the upper, tho it might be claimed that in the earlier years concrete life offers enough basis for aesthetic and social experience. But tastes and tendencies develop and form early; and while the early years may not so greatly need this subject for its social effects, they may need it in order that appreciations may not grow badly.

But the child of early years cannot easily overcome the mechanical difficulties in the way; he cannot read. I shall show in some detail later why I believe that a part of the function of the teacher is to remove the mechanical difficulties in the way of the apprehension of literature. Meantime it is sufficient to indicate that the child can be helped to much literature thru story telling, thru the reading by the teacher to him, thru the willingness of the teacher to let vague understanding be compensated for by appreciation.

What shall be used in literature? Here, as in almost any other studies, our first tendency is to judge the worth of the subject by adult standards. We think the man should know Shakespear, therefore the child is put at work on Shakespeare; the man should be able to profit by Lowell or Whittier, therefore the child is given Whittier and Lowell; adult standards pronounce the Sir Roger de Coverly papers excellent literature from the point of form—and the child is drilled on Sir Roger. Evangeline is Longfellow's choicest product, therefore we first give the children Longfellow's Evangeline. If we examine the selections of one of the older readers we shall find that they represent the things which, in the main, appeal to scholary men, to moralists, and to poets. They have been written for adults, often adults of mature appreciation.

I have no fault to find with the desire to put good things into the hands of the children; they should have the best that can be had, provided it is adapted to childish interests, powers of comprehension, and use. Some years ago a favorite debate circulated around the question as to whether the child could best have his artistic nature stimulated by a classic painting kept constantly before him, or one more simple. One would have thought the choice lay simply between poor art and good art; whereas the real choice must lie between that which is comprehensible by the child and that which is not. The Sower may have no significance to the child because he has no apperceptive basis for comprehending it, while a picture of a cat and a mouse may be very suggestive. Of course it is best for the child that the latter work should be good. The child should have the best of food, provided it is child's food; better poor child's food than excellent adult's food, if the latter be not adapted to the child's nature.

What, then, shall be used for literature? If we select literature which has stood the test of time—judged by adult standards,—if we select that which literary and scholarly men declare to be the best, then our task is simple, the only embarassment being that of choosing among our riches. But if we realize that what is best, judged by adult standards, may by no means be the best for the child, if we understand that childish powers, childish interests, childish capacities of interpretation and application be taken into account, then is our task difficult and discouraging. Pedagogy gives us few standards indeed by which to judge, and we must resort to painful experimentation. We must resort to much experimentation, for so subtle is the influence of literature, and so largely does personality enter into its interpretation, that what one teacher may make fascinating to children, another may quite fail to make attractive.

But we can find what meets this aim, if we but assume the right standards—the test of real effectiveness in accomplishing results—and the primary schools have already done much in this direction. The upper grammer grades, while not attacking the problem wholly in the right way, are, nevertheless, doing much, in the way of suggesting home reading, and in co-operating with libraries, in starting this work. It is hoped that they will soon realize the necessity of further organization.

While little can be said here on the positive side regarding the choice of literature, something can be said on the negative side. Most of the choices hitherto have been bad, as judged by results in interest and effectiveness. Out of some experience in asking persons of good education I am forced to conclude that a taste for good reading is seldom stimulated by our high school courses in English. Those who have well formed tastes, to whom literature lives, have formed their tastes independently of high school work. Moreover, very few of the pupils who leave our high schools ever manifest a preference for the English classics with which they have dealt. The fault lies partly in the method, but largely in the choice of materials. The classic literature of our high school courses has, as a rule, been written by very mature men and deliberately for very mature readers—mature, at least in experience, if not in scholarship. Take the writers who enter into our high school courses—Shakespeare, Bunyan, Dryden, Maculay, Milton, Wordsworth, Whittier, Scott, Eliot, Burke; do they not answer to this description? Moreover, when some one has understood the simple concrete mind of the child or of people in a child-like stage of development—and has written down to it, as did Bunyan, he deals with a symbolism that is so remote and unintelligible to the child of the twentieth century, that, except in the hands of the rare genius of a teacher who could make fountains gush from barren rocks, it forms little contact with the mind of the child.

But there is really much good literature that is available if we will let the children help us in the selection; literature that does not, perhaps, represent the high water mark of either content or literary form, but which is not bad and which will probably form the most natural and effective stepping stones to the higher tastes if we but have patience to wait on development instead of trying to force it. The teacher's function, it has been often said, is to guide, not to originate; and nowhere is it truer than in literature that the teacher must start with the child where she finds him, and by her tact and suggestion cause crude tastes to wear into refined ones, to cause self-centering ideals to expand into more generous ones, to widen interests and sympathies.

I cannot here go into detail as to what materials should be used. Teachers who are interested will find very many valuable suggestions in such books as "Chubb's Teaching of English," Carpenter, Scott, and Baker on the same subject, in Miss Burt's "Literary Landmarks," etc. Our current educational literature, too, will give many suggestions developed from the reading which children do in libraries. The principal pitfall in the way of the teacher is the bias in favor of the old classics which characterizes so many writers, including one even as good as Chubb. The classicists in Latin and Greek, and later those in English feel, apparently, that upon their shoulders rests the whole burden of preserving our civilization from eternal crudity. They seem to forget that each virile age developes new standards, and usually a new culture. The efforts to preserve the well of English pure and undefiled made by our college and high school teachers in these days of material development and altering standards seem about as effective as Mrs. Partington's celebrated endeavor to sweep back the rising tide; and I am not sure but the next generation will think them as ridiculous. At any rate our literature for our children should, instead of devoting itself to the fostering of classic standards, simply be dependent upon them to the extent that they aid us in selecting materials that are satisfactorily appreciated by the child. With his ready imagination and power of dramatization, the child will often revel in those things which are rather the classics of all time than of any period. Of such may be "Cinderella," "Robinson Crusoe," and "Arabian Nights." But apart from these our growing girls and boys will want the literature that is not too remote from their own age and that expresses current ideals in current symbolism. There is danger that even Hawthorne and Whittier may become somewhat foreign as we recede from the days of Puritan thought. Alcott, Kipling, Churchill, Davis, and numerous others may be writing materials which are better adapted for literary study by our twentieth century boys and girls than are the classics of Bunyan, Wordsworth, Lamb, and Bryant. The men who are editing the journals that have widest circulation among the most promising of our children are not choosing badly. We have much to learn from them in choosing literature for our schools.

Experience has, I think, satisfactorily demonstrated that successful children's literature should consist of wholes, should preserve unity, and should not, in any direct way, preach. For other characteristics I can only refer to the aids above mentioned.

How shall literature be presented? We here face the difficult question of method. It must be confessed that this subject has not been taught with very great success, even where it has been frankly recognized as literature. The first confusion arises when we attempt to teach literature as the formal studies have been taught. It is small wonder that the teacher who, having been accustomed to teach Latin, or algebra, or arithmetic, or spelling, brings to the teaching of literature his old habits and methods. Literature becomes for such a teacher simply a vehicle for the study of language; he uses it as a basis for spelling, defining, grammar, rhetoric, composition, analysis—anything in fact, but for its true end; and the child who leaves this routine with a taste for literature is to be congratulated on the happy accident.

It ought not to be necessary to point out that the conditions under which the child should approach this branch of the curriculum, if we are to attain the ends above suggested, should be quite different from those under which he approaches the other formal studies. In the first place, if literature is to produce its desired effects, it must possess largely a direct interest; it must attract of itself. One does not have the emotional or aesthetic nature agreeably stimulated where interest is weak. The interest in literature must be direct. The interest in the formal studies may be largely a borrowed interest, that is, an interest in them as means to the realization of some other end, in which interest is more direct. The atmosphere surrounding the presentation of literature should be one of ease, not work; of sympathy, not indifference or antipathy; of emotional, rather than intellectual perception. It seems to me that the more we consider this aspect of the question, the more we must feel that not only is formal work in connection with literature not helpful, but that it is actually harmful, that it destroys the effect which should be produced. We are all aware that the attempt to analyze any emotional experience is apt to result in the destruction of the emotion. Aesthetic appreciation and the higher sentiments can be made more intense by analysis and introspection only in the case of those who have had long experience in constructive work; and even here we have good authority for believing that the artist or player who analyzes, while he may derive pleasure from the analysis, fails to appreciate the beauty of the situation in the same way as do those who undertake no such analysis.

Let this presentation not be understood as in any sense justifying neglect of analytical study. Without careful study of formal language and the mechanics of expression, the child would grow very slowly in powers of comprehension. But I do emphatically believe that the two studies should be kept distinct and should not greatly deal with the same material, at least not at the same time.

It might be desirable, at this point, to make my distinction between these two aspects of the study. I know that it has long been the fashion to speak of formal and content subjects; or formal and culture aspects of the same subject; or material and expressional sides. The distinction is still a useful one, pedagogically, and no teacher of experience finds much difficulty in making it, tho of course not with clear-cut bounds. Learning to recognize and pronounce letters and words and sentences is formal work; learning to gather thought from the printed page and to express it is formal reading; studying the mechanics of expression is formal work in literature, whether it be the study of grammar, rhetoric, versification, prosody, or style. The act of memorizing is formal work. Reading for the sake of the content is not formal work, for the interest there is direct.

Let me illustrate the difference between what I conceive to be content and formal work in lower grade reading, or, as I prefer to call it, the difference between the study of formal reading and literature. At the age of seven, the average child can understand very well a story of considerable complexity if it is told or read to him. If the story be at all adapted, he gets the drift of it, interpreted, of course, by means of his own apperceptive basis; the story calls up ideas, gives information, and arouses feelings in a very real way. The child is not able to reflect upon the mechanics by which the effect is produced. He may not know how to read, knows nothing about sentence structure, and might not be able to define many of the words. For the child this corresponds to literature. In another lesson, the child drills on certain short sentences which convey no particular sense, but which he learns willingly and thru much repetition. This is formal reading. Take the same boy four years later. He finds a story or poem in his St. Nicholas or Carrol, or in some Captain Jack book. He curls himself up and reads. He cares little for the form; he is after the story, the experience, the translation of his own feelings. Here again, he might not be able to read the story well, he may not know all the words; and he certainly cares little about the sentence structure. This is, for him, literature. But in his formal reading, he goes thru some drill in expression. He must study the meanings of certain words in isolation. He must analyze structure and drill on the technique of expression in its aspects of inflection, enunciation, stress, and force. This is formal reading. There is a place and a good place for this formal read ng thruout the grades and thru the high school, rising, in the latter institution, to what we call interpretive reading and declamation. But we have pretty well learned in these days that a successful drill in reading requires that the student have a fair comprehension of meaning of that upon which he is drilling. It seems hardly probable that we shall ever go back to the stage when the pupil was drilled in reading and reciting that which it was impossible for him to sympathetically comprehend. In so far as good literature is used as material for drill work in reading it should be literature whose spirit has already been well gathered. Moreover, in this formal reading, the child should be required to rise only to those heights of expression which are justified by his comprehension of the selection read. It is possible, indeed, that there will continue to be a place in the school for the reader, strictly so called. But the reader will not be used to teach literature. It should be used only to give in compact form and serviceable gradation exercises either in gathering thought from the printed page or in giving it oral expression. This material, while it may be new to the child, must never rise above the child's literary comprehension and indeed should probably keep some distance behind it. If your pupil today can read aloud well the things that he studied as literature two years ago he is surely doing well.

And this brings me to my last point. Should the unstudied and natural approach to literature precede or follow the formal and constrained study of literature by analytical means? My answer is already obvious: The child is able to glean very much of the good from literature, if it is presented in the true way, long before he is able to approach it analytically. The curse of the ordinary teaching of literature is that the child studies it by dissection and as a basis for composition and formal reading long before he is supposed to enter into its comprehension. This is certainly the conspicuous fault of English teaching in the high school. The traditions of teaching Latin thru analysis have descended to English teaching, and English in our college and high school classes is very often a deadly bore to children and youths who are fully capable of entering into their natural heritage if they were but properly introduced. No, if we cannot feel very sure that our correlation of formal and literary English, in any grade of the school, is perfect, let us entirely separate the two kinds of work. A recent writer in the School Review, who speaks out of much experience, declares his conviction that the teaching of literature, and the teaching of spelling, grammar, and rhetoric are two distinct professions; and he declares that it is unfortunate that they should both be practiced by the same teacher. (Charlton M. Lewis, School Review for March, 1903.)

Let us separate the two studies, I say; and we shall find that literature can be presented long before the analytical studies dealing with the same material. A pupil who has had satisfactory experience with literature can appreciate Ben Hur or Kipling's poetry (some of it), or even a play of Shakespeare, in the upper grammar grades. Not its finer shades, perhaps; but who of us can? He can get vital sentiment from it however; a breath of the feelings and aspirations that are very real things to the growing boy or girl.

The time comes, of course, in the case of some people when the analytical study of literature is a source of pleasure in itself. But the average pupil of our school seldom reaches this stage; and it is one that cannot well be forced. Our schools can teach formal reading, composition, and something of rhetoric. But they ought not to do it with the materials that are, at the same time, being used to establish taste for reading and to awaken the higher sensibilities. When the pupil has once fully felt and appreciated his Evangeline, then it may be used for analytical study.

As I understand it, the Scholia Club is now to discuss the purposes and methods of the subjects of the elementary curriculum. I have endeavored to show you that literature has a place in the elementary curriculum and that it is one of the choicest of our instruments of education. So far as it disciplines or develops the intellectual nature of the child, it does so only along lines that are very easily preceived; it requires no claims of some occult capacity to develop all sides of the human being.

I raise the following questions which I do not think are yet rightly answered in general educational practice:

1. Is there enough literature used in our school courses? My answer is, No, tho we are rapidly approaching a better state, so far as mere quantity is concerned. Hitherto we have left the subject to chance influences.

2. Are we using literature with any satisfactory realization of its purpose? Answer. Only partly; we are using it to form tastes for more and better reading, which is good. But we have yet to learn how to use it as the most effective instrument at our disposal—apart from the contact of personality—to develope the higher social, moral, and aesthetic nature along the lines to which it makes appeal.

3. Are we using literature rightly? Not often, and we get, as a rule, poorest results when we teach it most strenuously. The home reading that we encourage is good; and occasionally a teacher knows how to read to her pupils, which is very good. But in the upper grammar grades and in the high school we use literary materials for purposes of dissection which is good exercise at the proper time and place, but which is, very seldom, the study of literature. College examinations and other examinations are practically never able to test the results of genuine literature teaching.

4. Can we approach the study of literature by making the same demands upon effort, application. etc., that we do in the case of the formal studies? I do not think we can. It is possible to procure intellectual results thru compulsion; but the effort to stimulate the higher emotions in the same way seems doomed to fail. In this domain, at least, we must lead; we cannot drive. Hence the teacher should feel that successful teaching demands relationships with pupils which may be very different from those which suffice in the more formal studies.

5. Can a general course of literature be prescribed which should give satisfactory results? It is doubtful; at least it cannot be done yet. So much of success in teaching literature must depend upon the teachers own choices, appreciations, etc., that one must

think it should be an individual matter. Of course teachers must be held within certain limits as to quality, quantity, etc. but in this field we must trust little to prescription.

6. Must the interests of children be consulted, even when these are largely determined by local or special conditions? Yes, in the main; for interest of a keen, direct sort is indispensable to results. It must be remembered, however, that children are very amenable to suggestion; and it is not hard, when once the teacher has found the apperceptive level (in the emotional as well as in the intellectual sense) of the children to elevate appreciation bit by bit. Owing to the great harm that follows the establishment of an adult standard of appreciation—in regard to sentiment, form, etc.—it is safer to be guided largely by the preferences of children themselves.

7. What shall the teacher do with the mechanical difficulties which interpose themselves at all stages? Remove them himself or keep them in the background, so that they may not claim the attention to the exclusion of the attention to the literature itself. It is absolutely necessary that the teacher of literature should read, sympathically and appreciativley. The teacher of younger children should also develope the capacity to tell stories brightly and effectively. This quality can be cultivated as easily as the power to sing.

8. Shall we use literature as a basis for studies and drill in composition, formal reading, etc.? Certainly; provided we do not try to merge the two essentially different kinds of studies. It is possible usually to present any given selection of literature some time before it ought to be taken up for formal analytical study. But the fact that it has formerly been presented does not make it less desirable as material for formal study; but usully more so.

Stanford University.   DAVID S. SNEDDEN.

* *

One hundred children were handed each a hot iron. Thirty-three boys and eighteen girls said "Ouch!" Twenty-five girls and ten boys said "Ooch!" Of the girls who said "Ouch!" seven had pug noses and one toed in. Thirteen boys of foreign parents said "Ooch!" The conclusions to be drawn from this interesting experiment will be embodied in a book and published in the Practical Science Series.—*Life*.

Department of Methodology

TEACHERS' COLLEGE NOTES IN THE LINE OF ART INSTRUCTION.

The work of the Applied Arts Guilds and the Arts and Crafts movement are aiming to fuse all classes together, that is, to unite the different phases of art expression and every day life.

Mr. Parsons, head of the normal art training in Teachers' College, New York, who also has charge of the art in the Horace Mann Schools, says that a living art must be a direct force in the work-a-day world. The inspiring thoughts of the Arts and Crafts movement is the same,—to touch the dullest realities with a gleam of the ideal. Just a short time ago it was manual training which received all the attention but now that is an established fact and design is coming in. We saw the exhibit of public school work shown at the Eastern Art Teacher's Association. The work had been very carefully selected from the best schools and fully nine-tenths of the work was in design.

Art in the public schools, as a thing by itself, is a sickly plant, and, on the other hand, what is handwork without art? Neither can do without the other.

The Fine Arts Department of Teachers' College includes work in theory and practice, free hand drawing, art interpretation, history of art, drawing and painting, clay-modeling, theory of design, practice of design, applied design. This last course deals with problems in various lines of work practised in the elementary schools, namely, basketry, weaving, sewing, embroidery, pottery, and construction in paper, cardboard, bent iron and wood.

The especial advantage of applied arts over the other lines of art work is that they are of every day and everywhere; for we must remember that art is truly none the less spiritual because it is applied to things of use. However, I did hear Mr. Churchill, head of the Fine Arts Department, say that his greatest fear for the future of art is that the homes of the seventy million people are to be flooded with a fearsome lot of match safes, and pen trays and baskets, and paperknives, and stamp boxes, and footstools, and pillow tops, and portieres, and photograph frames, and fiendish wriggling horrors in bent iron (the kind that fall down when you set a coffee pot on them).

There surely is great need in the homes and cities today for just this kind of work and study in Applied Arts. Go into the most inartistic house, and some of these are the homes of artists, and you will see some evidences everywhere of taste. Things have been chosen with an eye to something beyond mere utility. Stools that are of no use as seats or as rests for the feet, vases that do not hold flowers, chairs whose carvings hurt the back, and numerous other examples. Now through the present art education the hope is to develope a taste for sightly surroundings, simpler things which are more beautiful, and honest things which are true.

The Domestics Arts people are emphasizing that there must be taste in dress, that there is a place to wear everything, a fitness in the use of materials, and that otherwise sightly naturalistic effects are often used out of place in dress. Ruskin says that what we like determines what we are, and is the sign of what we are; and to teach taste is inevitably to form character.

There are two divisions of the art of design, pure and representative. The object of the poor design is to achieve beauty, the object of representative design is to achieve truth of representation. Beauty and truth are the ends to be attained. Of course what is beautiful may be true, but it is not necessarily so; and the truth is often, but not always, beautiful. It is hard to state just what we mean by beauty, but it is revealed in balance, rhythm and harmony.

The child must be taught the practical application of decorative design and composition that the full meaning of good construction be understood; then we may hope for that individuality in expression that shall give us artistic houses, institutions and surroundings, for all art must be judged in terms of its usefulness to a community. Right here I might mention the name of the ideal craftsman, William Morris, the "poet upholsterer," as he was called in derision by an English lord who probably had some admiration for poets but none for upholsterers. The significance of this man continually increases. He united capital and labor, he associated arts and crafts. He emphasized the fact that when culture and taste are observed among the buyers, they will appear among the workers. The manufacturers and tradesmen will hasten to respond to this demand; better work will be done because a more discerning generation, a generation with higher standards, has appeared.

To give our students technical training alone is doing nothing for civilization. It makes force and nothing else, ability without purpose.

Mrs. Woolman is at the head of the Decorative Art Department. She is a great worker in the trade schools and is at the head of one in New York. It is on the east side and it is here that many of the decorative art students get their teaching experience.

In decorative art they are trying to adapt the home arts to educative ends in their socializing tendencies and phases. The home needs order, managment; there is great waste of both time and money. For example, in textiles a knowledge of the structure of the fibre, tests for adulteration, durability, etc., would aid the purchaser in selection.

This department includes work in theory and practice which considers the methods of teaching and the correlation of the work with other grade work. Handwork, study of principles of plain needlework and its application; card work, raffia and weaving. Handwork has a pre-eminent place in the new education because its products may be put to immediate use. The processes involved are in themselves educative. Textiles—This course covers a study of fabrics, processes of their manufacture and development of these processes. In this work they made many excursions to factories at Newark and other places. Weaving has been a part of human life since the making of the first basket. The history of the development of textile art would be the history of man himself. One of the interesting sides of the work is the dying, involving lessons in chemistery and the effects of chemical changes upon the fibre.

There is so much being done in the lines of construction or manual training that I feel unable to add much which is not already known. Some of the lines of work in this department at at Teachers' College are: Simple knife work, turning and pattern making, moulding and foundry practice, forging and sheet metal work, machine shop work, woodcarving. Manual training is not something to be added to human possibilities or to be tacked on to the school curriculum. It is an attempt to respond to the demand of the child-nature that his entire school course be fused with the spirit of social living. It seems to me that we should have manual training in the public schools, if for no other reason than its influence upon the pupil in the lines of self-activity, independence and social power.

Dr. McMurry said: "It is not long ago that this study aimed mainly at utility by leading children to make useful objects, and at mental discipline by exercising the mind through the hand.

But now there is a marked tendency to regard handwork as a means of opening up the industrial side of life. Thru it one is not only to develop some skill in blacksmithing, masonry, basketry, bent iron work, but he is to be introduced into the constructive experiences of mankind, thus making possible many excursions to factories in order the more fully to comprehend and sympathize with this phase of human activity.

"The thought content of manual training is thereby increased far beyond the principles involved in the use of tools. The fact that we are distinguished as an industrial nation emphasizes the need of this advance on the social side while it promises an especially rich addition to the subject matter of manual training. When this is more fully realized in practice, as it can be, manual training will stand on the same educational plane as other studies.

"For one week I observed the shops of the Horace Mann Schools. They begin shop work or bench work in the seventh grade. These are a few of the steps the child must follow: He must read his drawing and carefully interpret it. He must use his imigination and actually picture his finished piece. He must analyze it and plan his method. He must lay out each piece accurately so that the whole will fit together and he must use system to get the best results. As the work progresses, each step involves some new principles which he must apply and exercise. As the models follow one another they increase in difficulty, calling for keener observation and increased determination in order to overcome difficulties.

"The spirit of self reliance and earnestness of the students from start to finish was surprising. Here children who would do absolutely nothing in other branches, were led to discover, invent, produce.

"The work in the fifth grade was whittling, making plant labels, fish line holders, key tags, calendar backs, and the like. The primary work is very simple, yet offers problems for them to solve. The stock for their work is all sawed out and finished ready to put together. On one occasion the children were told that on the next day they would be allowed to make a table and to observe all the tables that they could, so as to know how to put one together. When they came to class on the following day they were all well informed about tables, with three legs, four legs, and the like. The stock was given them and they selected the pieces intended for legs, measured them to see that they were all of the same length. Then they had to decide how and where they should be nailed together, which piece first, and so forth. This lesson showed how the children are led to use their own thought and take the initiative in these matters of instruction, which after all require only the use of the hammer and a few nails.

"One of the most interesting pieces of work was the planning and making of a doll's house. This consisted of four rooms and a garret. First came the plan of the house; the underlying thought here was to work for good proportions of spaces. Arranging these plans emphasized most forcibly the individuality of the children as to their manner of observing, and interest and choice in arranging rooms and various parts of the building. Then came the desiging of the furniture for the different rooms, each room being a problem by itself as everything had to be most carefully and consistently planned before making, with much attention spent in the selection of material for a definite use in each room.

"Wood, cardboard, bent iron and rattan were used for the furniture. Rugs and wall paper were all designed by the children, much care being given to the colors used. Then came the window curtains, pictures, mattresses for the beds. The decorative art department came in use here and all the articles were made exactly as the larger articles were made at John Wanamaker's, or any other store. Vases were modeled and decorated, pillow tops designed and made, pictures for the walls painted appropriately and consistently framed.

"In all this constructive work and its development the object was presented first as a whole, and then they worked toward detail. The building was presented first and all else clustered within or without it.

"This work seems to touch the practical side of the child's life and leads him to unite with the practical a knowledge of beauty, the power to invent and create, and through his own efforts to appreciate and love beautiful things."

ANNIE C. SWAIN,
State Normal School, Chico.

* * *

Superintendent C. S. Lyman, Amesbury, Mass.: Constructive criticism, and suggestions, given in a kindly spirit, will be gladly received, but fault finding, which is always destructive, will tend to lower the efficiency of any system.

FOR TEACHERS OF READING.

(1) Should the children tell the substance of the lesson before they begin to read in class?

(2) Should the child "keep the place with the finger"?

(3) Should the child know all the words before attempting to read?

(4) Should a child get a new word from another who already knows it?

(5) Should a child who is reading be interrupted to correct errors?

(6) Should the children watch for errors to be corrected when the reader is through reading?

(7) What kind of questions should the teacher ask concerning the reading lesson?

(8) Should the reading of one child be pitted against that of another?

(9) Should a child read until he has made a mistake?

(10) Should the children read in concert?

(11) Should the paragraph be used as the unit of class work, that is, should the change of pupils in reciting occur at the end of a paragraph?

(15) Should passages be read by the teacher as a model for the child?—*The Western Teacher.*

**

BOOKS AND MAGAZINES

A brief quotation or two will make plain the purpose of this book. "It is the office of the teacher to carry his pupils forward; his success depends on the extent to which he displays individuality; and the one all-potent means of developing a constructive and imaginative habit of mind is to engage in inquiry. The teacher who acts merely as the mouthpiece of others is only fit to train parrots; he cannot fail to exercise a narrowing influence upon his pupils. Man is by nature a reasoning being and needs to be treated as such; unfortunately in schools this fact has been more honored in the breach than in the observance."

" 'Man is a tool-using animal. Weak in himself and of small stature, he stands on a basis at most, for the flattest-soled, of

---

The Teaching of Scientific Method and other papers on education, by Henry E. Armstrong, L.L.D., Ph.D.F.R.S. New York. The Macmillan Co.

some half square foot, insecurely enough; has to straddle out his legs lest the very wind supplant him. Feeblest of bipeds! Three quintals are a crushing load for him; the steer of the meadows tosses him aloft like a waste rag. Nevertheless he can use tools, can devise tools; with these the granite mountain melts into light dust before him. He kneads glowing iron as if it were soft paste. Seas are his smooth highway, wind and fire his unwearing steeds. Nowhere do we find him without tools; without tools he is nothing, with tools he is all.'" "We sadly need a Teufelsdröck at the present day to remind us how little we do to prepare our youth for the field of action, to expose the shams of our ultra-academic system and to move the public to enforce their abandonment. How little do we bear this in mind—how little do we teach him to use tools or to understand their use."

The title of this book is "The Teaching of Scientific Method" not "The Teaching of Science." Its lesson is that the study of science can proceed only as the student is led to inquire. "We must ever seek to teach not mere facts but above all things the use of facts and how the knowledge of new facts may be gained and use made of them." Everyone who is at all conversant with the work of our schools knows that though science is taught experimentally these ends are not reached, indeed they are not even consciously sought in the majority of cases. The perusal of this book will not fail to awaken teachers of science from their dogmatic slumber.

There is hardly a phase of science teaching from nature study to the work of the university, including domestic science in elementary schools and science in rural schools, which it does not touch. Indeed more attention is given to elementary science than to advanced work. It cannot fail to be of the greatest value in helping teachers to improve their work. It is an extraordinarily good book and its use is commended without qualification.

* * *

"This book is an attempt to present in an organized form, an outline of the new science of child study for investigators, students, teachers and parents. It is the fruit of fourteen years experience in studying and teaching child study, and of seven years experience as a father." There is need of a work which should contain a digest and a summary of the real achievement of this

Fundamentals of Child Study by Edwin A. Kirkpatrick. New York. The Macmillan Co.

"science." There has been so much tumult about it that palpable results begin to be in order. While most of the so called studies which have passed the printer are of little or no value, a few are of genuine scientific worth and certain fundamental principles may be viwed as established in them. It is to the statement of such general principles that this book is devoted. Provision is made and directions given for working out each topic by further reading, observation, experiment and discussion and abundant exercises for students are appended to each chapter. Imitation, play, curiosity, expression, instinct, the development of intellect, the treatment of abnormalities, etc., enter so deeply into the work of every teacher that a sure and wise discussion of them and of their allied relations can hardly fail to be in demand. And that is what this book offers, a sane and wise discussion of the psychology of childhood based upon a careful selection of the genuine results which the extensive child study movement has produced. Reading circles and individual teachers who are students of their subject will find it a valuable addition to the practical literature of education.

Among the three or four manuals on the teaching of history which are now available, the above will probably prove most useful to the elementary school teacher. It is clearly written, replete with detailed and helpful suggestions and illustrations, and presents a consistent and practicable scheme of history teaching in the grades.

The author believes that the elementary school pupil can deal satisfactorily only with American history, which is therefore made the center of each year's work. Only minor provision is made for the introduction of that European history which closely connects with our own; and Grecian, Roman and Mediaeval history is drawn on only to the extent of an occasional story or biography for purposes of comparison. This arrangement, it is evident, is not in harmony with that advocated by some of the most influential writers on the teaching of history.

But, granting the author his position, we find that he has done his work well. In his emphasis on biography in all stages; in his suggestive setting forth of large and effective type studies in place of the condensed generalizations of the text books; in his

Special Method in History by Chas. McMurry. New York. The Macmillan Company.

arrangement of aids in the way of source materials, reference readings, etc., and, finally, in the practicable correlations suggested; the author has marked a distinct advance in the making of practicable history manuals.

* * *

This book is a companion volume to "The Authors Middle Ages" and a revision and expansion of an earlier work. It is a history of the period beginning with the New Age which discovered the New World and ending with the present time. It is a clear and orderly presentation of the most important facts in the development of the modern world and in it the author has the decided advantage of telling the story of all the nations together and thus presenting history as an intellegible interplay of human relations rather than a garbled and fragrementary part of that whole. Especially is he to be congratulated upon the excellent maps which the volume contains and the lists of references appended to each chapter.

* * *

This book has one very great advantage. It is thouroughly practical. "The central thought of the entire book is personal hygiene and public health." The various parts of the subject are presented in as close relation to each other as possible. The effects of alcohol are presented without coloring. Simple exercises and experiments are suggested which may easily be performed and reviews and summaries are appended which will be of material assistance to the learners. The careful gradation of subject matter is another matter worth mentioning. The facts treated are worth while and the method of presentation is unusually clear and interesting. In short, the author has produced an excellent text in a department where such a work is much needed.

* * *

The subtitle, "A reading book of science for American boys and girls," will indicate the author's intention in preparing this work. It is designed for young Americans of about twelve years of age and puts the elementary facts of astronomy, physics, meteorology, chemistry, geology, zoology, botany, physiology and the early history of mankind in very clear and readable form. School

The Modern Age by Philip Van Ness Myers, Boston. Ginn & Company.

Human Physiology by John I. Jegi M.S., New York. The Macmillan Company.

Real Things in Nature by Edward S. Holden, Se'D.L.L.D., New York. The Macmillan Company.

men who are clamoring for courses in general science will find in it a means to their desire. The methods of science as well as its fundamental ideas are insisted upon. If one can find any fault with so worthy an undertaking it is that it is based upon the presumption that the youth should know what his elders have accomplished in these fields and how they have set about it. Science as science in other words which is practically a pedagogical impossibility. A good teacher could do much to overcome this difficulty and make the material here presented function according to his pupils need. The reviewer can well remember the time when such a book would have been seized by him and devoured with the greatest avidity but at that time was not to be had. It may be that we have here the means for beginning the teaching of science in the grammar grades. It would be an interesting experiment to find out what could be done in this direction.

* * *

The geographical expansion of the United States begins to have an effect upon the schools of the homeland. The West beyond the West must not merely be possessed but must become known. Even the children must be made familiar with it. To this natural process of political integration we owe two new books. One on the Philippines and the other on the Hawaiian Islands. The first attempts to impart in a story-telling fashion some knowledge of the people and products and geographical features of the Philippines. The second book is a brief account of the geography, manners, customs and history of the people of Hawaii.

* * *

One of the worthiest undertakings of recent years in the book making line is the publication of the series of Philosophical Classics by The Open Court Publishing Company of Chicago. Nowhere else can one get such good books for so little money. The chief works of Descartes, Hume, Berkeley, Leibniz and Kant are offered in excellent type, on good paper and bound in

The Philippines by Samuel MacClintock, Principal of the Cebu Normal School. The American Book Co.

Alice's Visit to the Hawaiian Islands by Mary H. Krout. The American Book Co.

1. St. Anselm, Cur Deus Homo, etc. Translated by Sidney Norton Deane. Chicago. The Open Court Publishing Co.

2. The Canon of Reason and Virtue of Lao-Tze. Translated from the Chinese by Dr. Paul Carus, Chicago. The Open Court Publishing Co.

durable form at from twenty-five to fifty cents per volume, making the price of the world's best literature as low as that of the worst. The two last volumes of this series have just reached us. The first contains the chief writings of St. Anselm, including his "incontrovertible argument" in proof of the existence of God. The other, "The Cannon of Reason and Virtue," of the Chinese sage, Lao-Tze, translated by Dr. Paul Carus, expresses with all the quaint charm of antiquity the laws of life, which are the same for all peoples and all ages of men.

* * *

A striking article upon "The School" by President Eliot of Harvard University occupies the position of honor in the November number. "There is no universal type of 'The School' in the United States. Indeed, such a thing as The School no more exists in reality than The Child or The Teacher. * * The chief characteristic of the American development of schools within the last thirty years is the decided improvement of the schools as machines. The evils of the machine — the lack of attention to the individual child, the waste of time for the bright children, and the tendency to work for a fair average product instead of one highly diversified, are done away with as soon as a large proportion of teachers to pupils is employed—such as one teacher for sixteen to twenty-five pupils. The American idea that every child should go to school is not carried into effect in a single state."

The Atlantic Monthly

A few unconnected considerations apply in some measure to all schools. 1. The advocates of useful studies have gained much ground, partly because it has been perceived of late that the utilitarian and the humane are often identical, or at least harmonious. 2. "The school should provide real things for the observation and study of children; for t' _ real can be made just as fascinating and wonderful as the unreal, and it has the advantage of being true." 3. "A great object in school life is the bringing of a child into intimate contact with other children, and with other adults than its parents." 4. The reaction of the school upon the home should be one of the chief elevating influences of every school.

Under a second group of considerations applicable to all schools the following points are developed: 1. The first of the habits indispensable to that continuous growth of the soul thruout life which characterizes the finest human beings is the habit of strenuous, undivided attention. 2. Next are two habits so opposed to each other that care must be taken not to destroy the one by developing the other, namely, the habits of observation and of reading. 3. The habit of reading is the easier to implant; "the good school should guide the child's reading from its earliest years, protecting it from rubbish and leading it into real literature." 4. "The training of the reasoning faculty is the next function of the school." 5. "In all education of the young, and indeed in the whole training of life, it is a fundamental object to train the will force of the individual and his power to originate thoughts and actions." 6. The world is still governed by sentiments and every school ought to cherish and inculcate the sentiments of family love, respect for law and public order, love of freedom, and reverence for truth and righteousness. It is high time that the vigorous inculcation of the fundamental social sentiments should be made a part of every school course.

* * *

The Outlook

The issue of November 14th contains an interesting symposium upon one of the relations of the public schools and the colleges. Time and again the slumbering issue of the teaching of religion in the public schools is aroused. Quite recently several protagonists of that "reform" have been delivering themselves in regard to it. One in particular, the Rev. W. W. Geer, an Episcopalian clergyman of New York, has declared "we are bringing up all over this broad land a lusty set of young pagans, who, sooner or later, they or their children, will make havoc of our institutions." The editors of "The Outlook," fearing that such statements bode ill for the future of our public school system, have addressed inquiries to the presidents of the leading colleges of our land requesting an answer to the question, "whether in the experiences of the colleges any difference is noticeable in the moral character of young men who come from the public schools, and that of those who come from the denominational, church, or other private schools." The brief replies of nineteen college presidents are printed. Two or three are unable to answer the question because of lack of data. The others have not noticed any such difference in moral character. Not a single one of the nineteen educational leaders recognizes the needs which a certain class of churchmen are forever urging. President Wheeler points out that "our public schools are so well developed and in the main so decidedly superior to any private schools that exist among us that all classes of citizens as a rule send their children to them, except in the case of the Catholic schools few if any come to the university." President Eliot writes that 30 per cent of the young men in Harvard come from public high schools, 25 per cent from endowed schools and about 16 per cent from private schools, the rest from other colleges or scientific schools and private tutors. "We observe that the students who come from public schools cannot be distinguished from the students from other sourses on any moral grounds." President Jordan writes "As a matter of fact, with all their defects and limitations, our public schools, from the primary school to the State University are sending out a body of sturdy, self-reliant, clean young people, who have in the main the essentials of sound life. The fact that they are self-reliant and do their own thinking is one reason for the attacks made on the public schools."

In the face of such a unanimous testimony of experts it would seem that the insistent clamor for the teaching of dogmatic religion in the public schools should cease.

Apropos the teaching of religion in the schools, Augustine Birrell contributes a very interesting article upon the situation in England in a recent number of the "Independent Review." "The history of education in this England of ours is an extraordinary one, and, like 'Paradise Lost,' proves nothing, tho it illustrates admirably enough man's fallen state." A most readable and suggestive sketch of English education follows. And referring to the recent act which compels non-conformists to send their children to a church of England school, wherever there is no other, and to contribute to the support of such schools, Mr. Birrell writes: "Dogmas may be splendid things, but an ordinary British child between the ages of six and fourteen has no mind for many of them. They are an after-acquired taste. A pious teacher in love with Christianity can implant in the youthful minds the seeds of that religion without traveling outside Board-School Christianity. * * Why should we not provide a good sound secular education for the children of everybody who cares or is obliged to send his children to a public elementary school, and at the close of each day's secular work, for which alone the tax and rate-payer will be responsible, allow the children to receive in the schoolhouse the religious instruction their parents desire them to have. If no such compromise is possible, the fight must continue, with consequences to the cause of religion which will some day startle both Churchman and Dissenter."

* * *

There is a masterly article in the October number on the "Relation of the Superintendent of Schools to the Library," by F. F. Fitzgibbon, Superintendent of Schools, Columbus, Ind., which if we had space deserves to be reprinted in full. "What is the best thing that the schools can do for those under their care?" I hear the answer coming to me, "Give them a love for good books." May I ask what style of love, and for what style of good books? Is it that species of love known among school boys as "puppy love" that makes the victim don a new sentimental robe at sight of every new subject? Is it that kind of good book that leaves the reader at the end of the hour where he was at the beginning of the hour, except that he has a stronger desire to be amused again and no increased desire to free himself from the bonds of general ignorance? I know a young lady who, from childhood, has read all the "good books" usually found in the libraries, such as "Joe's Boys" and lighter ones. She has "loved good books" all her life. To be sure she has been amused, and she has been kept out of certain kinds of bad company. She is full of sentiment and sympathy of a certain species. She can shed tears in the presence of suffering and can shudder in the presence of evil, but she has not the power to think out a method of relieving the one or meeting and overcoming the other. She is a bundle of sickly sentiments without any power to plan and execute the duties of life.

The Educator-Journal

What books on the library shelf are least read? Not the sentimental, the one that amuses the reader, or lulls him to sleep. Not the one that can be interpreted without effort or needs no interpretation at all. The solid books that inspire men with those lofty sentiments that ripen into action for the public good, usually bear the dust of many days. The books that would make the life of the artist and artisan more effective are generally in the musty corner—works on ethics, economics, sociology, politics, religion, etc., those books that show the young men and women the better citizenship, are the library books that bear few finger prints. The general public are hunting something easy to read.

Many schools are surfeiting the children in every grade with numberless supplementary readers and story books, rushing them thru headlong. Quanity read, not mastery of the thing read, is the watchword. Many schools offer prizes to the pupils who read the largest number of books. That is positively vicious training. Most of the schools seem to use text-books on all subjects and their supplements, for the sake of mastering the books and not for the purpose of equiping the pupils with the power to interpret clearly the language of nature and science and history and literature. In the pupils' use of his texts and supplements he is too often lifted over the difficulties in interpretation by his teacher. Too many aids are brought to his assistance in interpreting the printed page and he is deprived of the power he might have gained because he has not been led to put time and effort enough on his lesson to master its language. Too many teachers feel that the subject must be mastered, when their possibilities should be merely opened up to the pupils, and they put in possession of a growing power and desire to master these subjects. The school that sets itself up as a finishing school has no excuse for existence. The book is looked upon too often as an end in itself, rather than a means to an end. The pupil is not well trained in the use of the book as an instrument for his development and he becomes a coward in the presence of books difficult to interpret. The best thing that the school can do for the pupil is to send him out with an ever-increasing power and determination to help himself.

This is not done in a large enough measure. In seeing that this is done the Superintendent can express his most important relationship to the library. The pupils in the public schools ought to use the public library, not so much for what is to be found in the books there, however, as for the training in the use of books. The pupils whose teacher has the privilege and inclination to gather up an armload of books from the library and take them to her school, there pointing out the page and paragraph in which the subject under treatment is discussed are unfortunate indeed. The teacher who says to the pupils, "When you have exhausted your texts on the subject in hand I will send you to the library to find what you can there," is a woman who builds much better than she knows. The school with its own reference library is usually self-satisfied and its pupils miss the opportunity for training in the use of the public library. The Superintendent can well serve the library by so conducting his schools that nothing will be done for the boys and girls that they can learn to do for themselves."

* * *

"Science" of November 6th contains the "Address of the President of the Section of Education of the British Association for the Advancement of Science"; Sir William DeW. Abney upon the subject, "State Support in the Teaching of Science."

* * *

"The Forum" for October-December contains three articles upon education, "The Educational Outlook" by Ossian Lang; "The Results of a Text in Language," by the editor, Mr. J. M. Rice, and "The Administration of Public School Systems," by C. M. Gilbert.

* * *

Dr. Rice tested over 8300 children in the reproduction of a certain story [there given] read to the pupils by the teachers. The results of the test are here tabulated and a critical interpretation of results is promised in the next number. Tho all the children were submitted to the same test it would seem certain that not all of them were tested as to their ability to use language. Perhaps not even any of them were. An illustration will indicate what is meant. A speech is made at a banquet—there are wise men and reporters there. Which of the two classes will reproduce it with most facility? The trained reproducers—the reporters. They have caught the trick—the others have learned to use language much more skilfully, however. One's power to use language simply cannot be tested by exercises in rewording the thoughts of another person. Composition used to be taught by such exercises, but it is not now, as a much better method has been devised. What the test would seem to indicate is the bookishness and artificiality of some school work which, according to the test, seems to be most effective. A psychologist would enter additional objections to such a test.

The article on administration calls attention to the enormity of school expenditures in cities, and the further fact that these vast sums are usually administered by a board of directors who are not sufficiently familiar with the business which they control. Too often the trained executives employed by them are nothing more than head clerks. How should such a system be organized for efficiency. First, by dividing into legislative and executive arms or educative and business departments. There should be a business manager and an educational manager or superintendent of schools. And both should have adequate powers. All influences should be removed from the schools except those directly connected with education. The powers of the executive officers should be statutory.

* * *

BOOKS RECEIVED.

The Negro Problem by Representative American Negroes—New York; James Potts & Co.

The People of the Abyss by Jack London—New York. The Macmillan Company.

Tennyson's Shorter Poems
Tennyson's Idylls of the King
Irving's Life of Goldsmith
Spencer's Fairie Queen
} Macmillan's Pocket American and English Classics.

Introducción Á La Lengua Castellana por H. Marion y P. J. Des Garennes—Boston: D. C. Heath & Co.

An Elementary History of the United States by A. C. Thomas—Boston: D. C. Heath & Co.

The Heath Readers—Boston: D. C. Heath & Co.

Official Department

STATE BOARD OF EDUCATION

GEORGE C. PARDEE, *President of the Board*..............Governor, Sacramento
MORRIS ELMER DAILEY............... President State Normal School, San Jose
E. T. PIERCE........................ President State Normal School, Los Angeles
C. C. VAN LIEW .... President State Normal School, Chico
BENJAMIN IDE WHEELER............President University of California, Berkeley
ELMER E. BROWN ..Prof. of Theory and Practice of Education, University of Cal.
SAMUEL T. BLACK ....President State Normal School, San Diego
FREDERIC BURK...... ....President State Normal School, San Francisco
THOMAS J. KIRK, *Sec. of Board*.. Superintendent Public Instruction, Sacramento

Recent Official Decisions.

THE CERTIFICATION OF SPECIAL TEACHERS.

Yours of the 23rd instant is before me and the question which you submit has been very thoughtfully considered. On the matter of certification of teachers there is no reference anywhere in our state law to the particular qualifications of teachers of oral instruction to the deaf; but by a liberal construction which I am disposed to give to Subdivision 2nd of Section 1772 of the Political Code, by the existence of the term "technical" my judgment is that a county board of education may lawfully grant special certificates to such persons as satisfy the board of their fitness to teach such subject. By an act of the legislature of 1903, amending Section 1618 of the Political Code, authority is given to county, city, and city and county boards of education, and boards of school trustees to maintain separate classes in the primary and grammar grades of the public schools, under certain contingencies, for instruction of deaf children. The county board in acting under the provisions of Subdivision 2nd of Section 1772 should be very careful to have the candidates satisfy the board of their proficiency in the subjects of English grammar, orthography, defining and methods of teaching.

* * *

THE EXAMINATION OF PUPILS BY COUNTY BOARD OF EDUCATION.

Replying to yours of the 11th instant, I beg to state that under the opinion rendered by the Attorney-General county boards of education are authorized to examine pupils only when they are ready for graduation from the course of study prescribed for primary and grammar schools by the county board: they are not authorized to examine pupils for promotion from grade to grade, nor from school to school, simply to provide for a "final examination."

* * *

LIFE DIPLOMAS.

In reply to your letter of the 12th instant, I beg to state that all life diplomas granted in California prior to January 1, 1880, stated upon their face in express words that the holder was entitled to teach in any public school of the state. I am therefore of the opinion that such diplomas confer license to teach in the high schools of the state. Any other construction would be ex-post facto in its character.

* * *

TEMPORARY CERTIFICATE.

Yours of the 19th instant was duly received at this office and contents noted.

The law for the granting by county superintendents of temporary certificates is found in Subdivision 7th of Section 1543 of the Political Code: "He shall have power to issue * * * temporary certificates, valid until the next semi-annual meeting of the county board of education * * * upon any certificates or diplomas upon which county boards are empowered to grant certificates without examination, etc."

A county superintendent cannot issue a temporary certificate upon any credential which cannot be recognized by the county board for a regular certificate.

* * *

TEACHERS' INSTITUTES.

Replying to yours of the 23rd instant, regarding pay of teachers for the time spent in going to and returning from the annual county institute, I have to say that in my opinion a teacher is legally entitled to claim salary only for the days actually spent in attendance at the institute; at the same time, however, it is a custom somewhat general throughout the State, where the institute is held beginning Tuesday and it takes a teacher Monday and Friday to go and return, to allow pay for a full week. But I repeat, I do not think a teacher can legally collect salary for time spent in traveling to and from the institute.

* * *

PAYMENT FOR REPAIRS.

Replying to your recent favor regarding payment of bill for $225 for repairs on school house in Blank District, I have to say that, if that district had on hand to its credit after maintaining an eight months' school last year sufficient money to pay the bill, it could and should be paid out of such balance. If, however, there was no balance carried over from last year, the bill cannot be paid from this year's school moneys until after all the expenses of an eight months' school have been met. You are right in contending that all the expenses of maintaining the school should be paid before this claim is allowed.

* * *

NON-ATTENDANCE AT TEACHERS' INSTITUTE.

Under the law I know of no authority for granting excuses to teachers for non-attendance at the regular annual institute. Subdivision 6th of Section 1543 of the Political Code stipulates that the county superintendent of schools must report to the county board of education the names of all teachers of the county who fail to attend regularly all sessions of the county institute. I think that this carries with it the right of the county board of education to determine whether or not such non-attendance is for good cause, and where cause is shown to be sufficient a teacher should be exonerated for failure to attend. This would be just in case of sickness of teacher or serious sickness or death in teacher's family.

I must also state that there is no provision in the law whereby a teacher may be paid for time of the institute when not in attendance. In certain cities of the State teachers are employed by the year, to be paid monthly, and I presume in all such cases as you instance there would be no deduction on account of non-attendance at the institute for good cause.

* * *

QUORUM OF COUNTY BOARD OF EDUCATION.

It is the general law, Subdivision 6th of Section 1768 of the Political Code, that the county superintendent of schools is at all times ex-officio secretary of the county board of education, and by Section 1671 which provides for the formation and maintenance of county high schools, such high schools are under the management and control of the county board of education. You will note by Subdivision 7th of Section 1768 the law in reference to quorum and vote required in certain specified cases. Three members constitute a quorum and by the ordinary rules that govern such boards a majority of the quorum may transact ordinary business; but, as before stated, certain acts require at least the sanction of three members. A county board of education has authority to adopt any rules or regulations not inconsistent with general law for its own government and the government of the schools of the county.

2. Your second question is not so easy to answer. The destruction of a diploma by the teacher under the circumstances which you instance would certainly be very strange, if not unprofessional conduct, and also if not a misdemeanor under law, I should say that it would be at least a subject for investigation by the county board of education, and such board has authority, under Subdivision 6th of Section 1771, to revoke or suspend certificate granted by it, and may recommend the revocation or sus-

pension of a life or educational diploma held by any teacher. The extent of guilt would, perhaps, have to be determined by considering all the circumstances connected with the act, and this on the question of misdemeanor would have to be adjudged by a court of competent jurisdiction.

* * *

THE PAYMENT OF TUITION BY HIGH SCHOOL PUPILS.

I am in receipt of yours of the 6th instant, enclosing copy of your letter to your city attorney, and his reply, in reference to the payment of tuition by pupils attending the * * * high school who are not residents of that city. I have carefully read these letters and after thoughtfully considering the case, I must state that I cannot agree with the conclusions reached * * * .

Section 6 of Article IX of the State Constitution in part reads as follows:. .

"The public school system shall include primary and grammar schools and such high schools, evening schools, normal schools and technical schools as may be established by the Legislature, or by municipal or district authority."

By the adoption of this amendment at the general election in 1902, and the passsge by the legislature of the Act creating a fund for the benefit and support of high schools, etc., approved March 2, 1903, high schools became a part of the State school system, as much as the primary and grammar schools, and are to be in part supported by State funds exactly the same as the elementary schools. It seems to me the same principle applies to both grades of schools, although it is true that the common or elementary schools will receive a much greater sum from the State than will the high schools.

Several years ago the question as to whether or not boards of school trustees could properly charge tuition for the attendance of pupils in the primary and grammar grade schools from outside districts was submitted to Attorney-General Ford and he held that the State Schools are *free* schools and therefore no tuition could be charged for attendance.

In the case of Hughes vs. Ewing, 93 Cal., 414, the Supreme Court said: "A school district is a public corporation of a *quasi* municipal character, posessing such authority as has been conferred by the legislature, to be exercised in the mode and within the limits prescribed by statute."

Nowhere in the law are trustees of a school district authorized to exact tuition fees for the attandance of outside pupils, if the opinion of Attorney-General Ford be correct, and I believe that it is; and inasmuch as a high school district is practically the same as a common school district, unless high school boards are by law specifically authorized to charge tuition fees to pupils that are not residents of the district, no such charge can legally be made. The whole matter then rests upon the construction of the last part of Section 9 of the High School Act, approved March 2, 1903, which reads as follows:

"Pupils otherwise qualified to enter a high school and residing in territory wherein no high school exists shall have the right to attend any high school that receives state aid under the provisions of this act without the payment of such tuition fee, if such schools have room or accommodations for them."

As I read these words the limitation in regard to pupils attending a high school who do not live in the district is that they may attend without payment of tuition if there be room or accommodations for them; and if there be not room or accommodations for them they cannot attend. I do not think the clause "if such schools have room or accommodations for them" refers simply to the words "without the payment of tuition fee," but that they refer to the whole of the last part of Section 9 of the Act. Therefore, I cannot agree with your city attorney that such a construction can be given to these words as to authorize the high school boards to collect tuition from such class of pupils for the purpose of providing room or accommodations for them. I know such was not the intent of the law makers at the time it was enacted nor is it the spirit of the law that provides for free public schools.

Very truly yours,
THOMAS J. KIRK,
Superintendent of Public Instruction.
Sacramento, December 4, 1903.

* * *

Sir Thomas Elyot (1531): "How many good and clear wits of children be nowadays punished by ignorant schoolmasters!"

CALIFORNIA TEACHERS' ASSOCIATION

The thirty-seventh annual session of the California Teachers' Association will convene in San Francisco, December 28, 29, 30, and 31, 1903.

The Teachers' Institute of the city and county of San Francisco will be merged into the session of the Association.

The general sessions will be held at the Alhambra Theatre, Eddy and Jones streets daily, from 2 until 4:30 o'clock.

Among the speakers on the general program are:

Arnold Tompkins, principal Chicago Normal School; S. H. Clark, dramatic reader University of Chicago; George C. Pardee, Governor of California; Eugene E. Schmitz, Mayor of San Francisco; Thomas J. Kirk, State Superintendent Public Instruction; William H. Langdon, superintendent of San Francisco schools; Thomas P. Woodward, president of the San Francisco Board of Education; James A. Foshay, superintendent of Los Angeles Schools; Morris E. Dailey, president of the San Jose Normal School; Fred T. Moore, superintendent of Alameda schools; O. W. Erlewine, superintendent of Sacramento schools and president of California Teachers' Association.

The music for the general sessions will be furnished mainly by the pupils of the San Francisco School Department.

The special sessions of the various departments of the Association will be held at the Mission High School, the Girls' High School, the Hearst Kindergarten, and Steinway Hall, daily, from 9 until 3.

The following departments will present programs:

Council of Education of California Teachers' Association.

Chemistry Room, Mission High School Building, 18th and Dolores streets, December 28th and 30th.

Chairman—Ernest C. Moore, University of California; Secretary—J. W. McClymonds, Oakland.

County Boards of Education.

Chemistry Room, Mission High School Building—December 29th and 31st.

Chairman—P. M. Fisher, Oakland; Secretary, A. A. Bailey, Martinez.

High School Teachers' Association.

Auditorium, Girl's High School Building—December 29th and 31st.

Chairman—Charles L. Biedenbach, Berkeley; Secretary, A. E. Shumate, San Jose.

Elementary School Teachers' Association.

Auditorium, Mission High School Building—December 29th and 31st.

Chairman—Charles C. Hughes, Alameda; Secretary—Rebecca M. English, San Jose.

Kindergarten Association,

Art Rooms, Mission High School Building—December 31st.

Chairman—Clara M. McQuade, Chico; Secretary—Mary T. Gamble, Oakland.

Physical Culture.

Auditorium, Mission High School Building—December 30th.

Chairman—Walter C. McGee, Berkeley; Secretary—Agnes G. Regan, San Francisco.

Industrial Arts.

Art Rooms, Mission High School Building—December 29th and 30th.

Chairman—A. B. Clark, Stanford University; Secretary, Kate E. Whitaker, San Francisco

Music.

Steinway Hall, 223 Sutter Street, near Kearny—December 30th.
Chairman—Estelle Carpenter, San Francisco; Secretary—Lida Lennon, Chico.

The Manual Training and Drawing Teachers' Association

will make a large exhibit in the Gymnasium of the Mission High School. There will be class demonstrations to illustrate the teaching of Reading, Music, Cookery, and Physical Culture.

The Department of Education of the California Club,

under the direction of Mrs. J. W. Orr, chairman, will decorate two rooms in the Mission High School Building to illustrate Schoolroom Decoration and Picture Study.

There will be no evening sessions except for the purpose of entertainment.

A grand reception will be given at the Palace Hotel by the teachers of San Francisco to the teachers of the state.

The San Francisco Teachers' Club

has placed its headquarters, room 356, City Hall, at the disposal of members of the Association and will furnish the daily papers and current magazines for their convenience.

The Mission High School is situated on the corner of Dolores and 18th streets, and may be reached by transfers from the Market, Valencia, Guerrero, Howard, Folsom, Bryant, Haight, McAllister, Ellis and Jackson Street cars.

The Girls' High School is situated on the corner of Geary and Scott street and may be reached directly by the Sutter, Geary or Ellis street cars or by transfers from any cross town line of cars.

Special transportation rates have been made as follows:

Return tickets must be bought within 48 hours after the close of the convention and are good for 24 hours thereafter. (A further extension of five days may be obtained on both the Southern Pacific and Santa Fe' lines by paying a one and two-thirds fare.)

Southern Pacific Company—Certificate receipt plan. (All certificates must be obtained from the railroad or steamship ticket agent from whom the ticket is purchased.) One and one-third regular rates. On the Coast Line, with SIXTY EACH from San Luis Obispo, Santa Barbara, or Los Angeles, one fare for the round trip. Ticket good for ten days from date of sale.

California Northwestern—Certificate receipt plan. One and one-third fare.

North Shore—Certificate receipt plan. Half rates.

Santa Fe—Certificate plan. One and one-third fare.

Pacific Coast Steamship Company—Certificate receipt plan. One and one-half fare.

MRS. M. M. FITZGERALD, 1627 Folsom Street, San Francisco.

NORTHERN CALIFORNIA TEACHERS' ASSOCIATION

The eighth annual session of the Northern California Teachers' Association was held in Willows on the 11th, 12th, 13th and 14th of November. While, owing to stormy weather the attendance was not so large as usual, the program was the best ever presented, and those in attendance entered so heartily into the spirit of the work that this session may well be regarded as one of the most profitable ever held by the Northern California Teachers' Association.

Dr. C. C. Van Liew, the recognized leader of the educational forces of northern California, was president of the Association, and this, in large measure, explains the success of the meeting, as his wide acquaintance enabled him to secure the very best talent for the program and for leaders of the several sections.

While Willows is the smallest town that has ever attempted to entertain the Northern Teachers' Association, and the numbers were far beyond the capacity of her hotels, yet double the number could easily have been comfortably housed—for which thanks are due to the hospitality of the citizens and the careful arrangement of details by the local teachers,

"The bright particular stars" of the program were Dr. Joseph Jastrow of the University of Wisconsin, Dr. Rolfe of Stanford University, and Dr. E. C. Moore of the University of California. Dr. Jastrow's lectures, "The Subconscious," "The Psychology of Belief," and "The Psychology of Speech," though masterful presentations of rather abstruse subjects, were presented in a manner that held the delighted attention of the entire audience till the close of each. Dr. Rolfe's sketch of "Charles and Mary Lamb" produced the effect of an exquisite poem, or a beautiful piece of music. Some one will have to invent a name for the high art of which Dr. Rolfe is master. Dr. Moore's address, "The Old Education and the New" was a fitting close for a superb program. He held the rapt attention of the audience, the majority of whom had been listening to addresses and lectures for six days, and at the close was compelled to bow his acknowledgment of a most hearty encore.

The president's address by Dr. C. C. Van Liew, as well as the addresses of Dr. E. E. Brown of the State University, Prof. B. M. Davis of the Los Angeles Normal, and Prof. Ray E. Chase of the Chico Normal, deserve extended remark would space permit.

The reception to members of the Association by the citizens and the teachers of Glenn county at the court house on Thursday evening was, socially, the success of the week. The building, which is always kept as clean and neat as a parlor, was prettily decorated for the occasion, and all the rooms and offices were thrown open to the visitors. Hon. B. F. Geis, on behalf of the citizens of the county, delivered a gracious and pleasing address of welcome, which was responded to in happy vein by President C. C. Van Liew. Apperson's orchestra enlivened the occasion with music, and pupils of the county high school served refreshments, while the guests were renewing old acquaintances and forming new ones.

The high school section was presided over by Dr. Geo. C. Thompson of Marysville, the grammar grades section by Principal J. D. Sweeney of Red Bluff, the primary section by Miss M. Irene Smith of Marysville, and the school of many grades section by Superietendent Ellen A. Lynch of Tehama county. The teachers eagerly took advantage of the opportunity thus offered to discuss the topics peculiar to their several lines of work and each section was voted a decided success by its attendants.

The Association voted unanimously to hold the next session in Woodland. The officers elected for the ensuing year were, Geo. C. Thompson of Marysville, president; Supt. Ellen A. Lynch of Red Bluff, secretary; E. L. Crane of Winters, corresponding secretary; J. D. Sweeney of Red Bluff, treasurer.

INSTITUTES.

CALAVERAS COUNTY.

The Calaveras Institute was called to order by Superintendent John Waters at San Andreas, Tuesday, November 3rd, and continued four days. Mr. Waters was assisted by T. H. Kirk of Santa Barbara, Herbert Bashford of San Francisco, and Edward Hyatt of Riverside. Mr. Kirk gave the teachers good professional doctrine along the line of the new education; Mr. Bashford contributed to the esthetic element by lectures on poets and literature and by recitations from his own work; Mr. Hyatt drew upon his fund of experience in California schools for the instruction and amusement of all. He also gave a simple and practical series of lessons upon the common rocks of California, eagerly taken hold of by the teachers of a mining county like Calaveras. The institute was also addressed by F. H. Day, who has a record of having taught the same school for thirty consecutive years; by James Keith, principal of schools at the county seat, and by Messrs. Floyd and Peachey, old teachers and superintendents of the county.

The school children of San Andreas presented each of the teachers with a lovely bouquet. The young men of the town prepared a complete minstrel entertainment for Tuesday evening, with fifteen burnt cork artists—songs, comedy, orchestra and all. A ball was given Friday evening, and there were two evening sessions of the institute proper, consisting of lectures by the instructors.

TRINITY COUNTY.

The Trinity County Institute was held in Weaverville, September 29-30, October 1. The instructors were Prof. A. B. Coffey and Job Wood. The special topics discussed by the teachers were many and included all the subjects in the course of study. The evening entertainments were indeed successful, being of high class order. Besides the fine musical programs rendered, Professor Coffey, in two well-delivered lectures on "Young America" and "Fruits of the Press," proved to be a great success.

The special features were as follows: The educational lectures of Professor Coffey and the very practical work shown and illustrated by Job Wood. The discussion of Discipline was indeed beautiful. One teacher brought forth the idea that the place for the constant "turners-around" was on a back seat. She found it to be very successful and advised others to use it. It is well known among teachers that this individual causes trouble and if a good remedy can be put forth it is well worth considering. In composition work the idea of the copy was discussed and met with approval by the teachers.

In general the institute was regarded as being the best ever held in Trinity county, and the able lecturers regarded the corps of teachers equal to those of any county.

Much credit is given to Miss Fox, our worthy superintendent, for the excellent success of the work, and the teachers of the county certainly appreciate her great work, and wish to thank her thru these pages for her labors, both for the educational benefit as well as the social.

J. JACKSON WASTE,
Principal Weaverville School.

* * *

EL DORADO COUNTY.

The El Dorado County Institute was held October 26-30. The instructors were T. H. Kirk, Santa Barbara, and Edwin R. Snyder, Manual Training Department, San Jose State State Normal. The special topics were: English and Composition in the Grades, Ways of Teaching Industrial and Commercial Geography, Use of Pictures in Teaching, Batavia Plan of Individual Interest, Outline of Work for New School History, Value of Maps in Teaching History, Functions of Manual Training, Heritage of the Child, Number Notion, Constructive Work in Manual Training, exemplified.

The evening entertainments were Lecture, T. H. Kirk, "The Man With the Hoe and the Man with the Brain" Wednesday 28; Lecture, "Play of the Child and its Educational Value" Thursday 29, by Edwin R. Snyder.

The special features were as follows: "Use of Pictures in Teaching," Kirk; "Value of Maps," Maggie A. Kelley; "Construction Work in Manual training" Snyder; "Outline of Work for New United States History," Superintendent Wilson. Mr. Kirk's lecture was well attended and exceedingly well rendered and received.

In the opinion of the teachers it was the most profitable institute held here for years. The attendance of town people was away beyond the ordinary. All teachers expressed a lively appreciation of the work placed before them by asking many questions of the instructors.

S. B. WILSON,
County Superintendent of El Dorado.

* * *

SAN BENITO COUNTY.

The San Benito County Institute was held October 26-29th. The instructors were Prof. David S. Snedden, of Stanford; Dr. E. C. Moore of the University of California; Herbert Bashford of San Francisco; Miss Belle Mackenzie of the San Jose Normal School; and Prof. C. A. Duniway of Stanford University. The special topics were "The Doctrine of Interest," "Physical Training" and "My Definition of a Teacher" by Dr. Moore; "The Literature of the West" and "The Lockstep in Education" by Herbert Bashford; "The Organization of the Recitation", "The Use of Literature in the Grades" and "The Significance of Some Recent Educational Experiments" by Prof. David S. Snedden; "The Function of the Story" by Belle Mackenzie.

The evening entertainments were Lecture, "American Colonial Expansion", by Prof. C. A. Duniway. A reception was tendered the teachers by the Teachers' Club.

One half day was given over to the teachers for consideration and discussion of the subjects presented and to the questions deposited in the question box during the session. It was universally pronounced one of the most interesting and profitable sessions ever held in the county.

SANTA CRUZ COUNTY.

The Santa Cruz County Institute was held October 19-23 and the instructors were Ellwood P. Cubberley, T. L. Heaton and Dr. J. C. Sundberg. The topics discussed were, Reading, Language, Arithmetic and Geography. The evening entertainments were, Monday, Social Reunion; Tuesday, lecture, "Babylonia" Dr. Sundberg; and Wednesday lecture, "Public Education in England." The special features were excellent work from instructors and intense interest on part of teachers.

JOHN LINSCOTT.

* * *

AMADOR COUNTY.

The Amador County Institute was held at Volcano November 3-4-5. The instructor was Margaret E. Schallenberger, Ph. D., acting principal of the San Jose S.N.S., training department. Evening lecturers, Miss Margaret E. Schallenberger and J. W. Phelps, D.D.

The special features were as follows: Adaptability of School Library Book to Right Education, Picture Writing and Story Telling as a Stepping Stone to Composition and Literature, The Professional Training of Teachers in Normal Schools and Universities, The Difference Between the Child Mind and that of the Adult, Nature Study in Primary Grades and The George Junior Republic, a government of and by children, by Margaret E. Schallenberger; The Parent and the Child, treated by Dr. J. W. Phelps.

The First evening's entertainment was of recitations, vocal and instrumental music and welcoming of the teachers by the townspeople, concluding with a banquet. The occasion was unique and most pleasurable. The second and third evenings there were lectures, also recitations and music.

The special features were good feeling, regular attendance, close and appreciative attention and a thorough awakening of the teacher to serious realization of her duty to herself, to her school and to the state. The value of summer schools to the teacher was made more apparent than ever before.

The resolution which follows was unanimously adopted. "Resolved, that it is the sense of this Institute that the best interests of the Schools of Amador County would be subserved by having the next Institute held at the San Jose State Normal School."

The significance of this resolution is that the teacher is fully awakened to her need of further preparation upon a strictly professional basis. The vitality within the schoolroom is commensurate with the desire upon the part of the teachers for self-improvement.

GEO. A. GORDON,
Superintendent, Jackson, Cal.

* * *

SAN MATEO COUNTY

The San Mateo County Institute was held October 27-28-29. The instructors were Messrs. Job Wood Jr., Deputy State Superintendent, Sacramento; T. L. Heaton, Deputy Superintendent Schools, San Francisco; and D. R. Augsburg, Supervisor of Drawing, Oakland.

The special topics discussed were How to Learn and Teach Drawing, by Mr. Augsburg; Arithmetic and Methods, Mr. Wood; Composition Work, Geography and Rural School Problems, Mr Heaton. The evening entertainment was "The Stratford Schoolmaster" by Hon. Frank J. Browne. A special feature of the institute was a visit to a selected number of schools on October 29th, in the school department of San Francisco.

E. M. TILTON.

* * *

YOLO COUNTY.

The Yolo County Institute was held Novemcer 10, 11, 12 and 13. The instructors were Hon. Thomas J. Kirk, State Superintendent; Miss Jenne Morrow Long, T. H. Kirk of Santa Barbara, and Job Wood Jr. of Sacramento. The special topics discussed were as follows: Choice and Handling of English Classics; Ancient Myth and Modern Story; Talk on Teaching Geography; Scope and Method of History in High Schools, by T. H. Kirk. Personal Discipline; Reading and Spelling with Classes; Essentials of Arithmetic, Job Wood Jr. Common Sense Reading; Vowel Sounds; Distinct Articulation; Illustrative Class Teaching from Fourth Grade, Jenne Morrow Long. Lecture, "The Man With the Hoe and the Man With the Brain," by T. H. Kirk. Social re-union and entertainment for teachers, trustees, and their friends.

The special features of the institute were as follows: An address of welcome by Hon. H. R. Reamer; response by Miss Lola Simpson; "Humane Education," paper by Rev. C. C. Smoot and some practical suggestions relating to school improvements and school work, by State Superintendent Kirk. Resolution passed extending an invitation to the Northern California Teachers' Association to meet in Woodland next year.

The teachers, with few exceptions, expressed themselves as well pleased with the work of this institute, which was practical and had direct bearing on the problems, which are not met every day in the schoolroom. Basing the result on the favorable comments of the teachers the institute of Yolo county for 1903 was a complete success.

The committee on the Northern California Teachers' Association were particularly active and enthusiastic. Thru its energetic chairman, Mr. T. Crane, it secured over sixty memberships for said association. The superintendent appointed a committee of five to go to Willows and invite the association to Woodland next year. The committee was successful in the effort. Much credit is due Mr. T. J. Crane for his work and enthusiasm in this matter.

The exemplification of work by classes before the institute by Mr. Wood was of much benefit and greatly pleased the teachers.

Very truly,
MINNIE DEVILBISS,
Superintendent of Yolo county.

* * *

MARIPOSA COUNTY.

One of the most successful counties in the state in the holding of institutes is Mariposa, under the enthusiastic leadership of Miss Julia Jones, the county superintendent. This year it was held at the county seat, Mariposa, November 17, 18 and 19. The teachers are peculiarly ready and happy in responding to all calls made upon them to take part in the program, and their work greatly adds to the effectiveness of the session. Among those who thus took part were Mrs. Upton, Miss Wagner, Mrs. Egenhoff, Miss Haywood, Mr. Webb, Mr. Wilkinson, Miss Jones, Miss Stern, Miss Dexter, and many others.

Mr. Wilkinson, for the committee on resolutions, reported a jocular resolution inviting Merced county to join the Mariposa institute hereafter— this in view of the fact that the Merced people had in some way expressed the opinion that institutes are a failure. The report was unanimously adopted.

On Tuesday evening the teachers were entertained at a reception, and on Thursday evening at a ball. Wednesday evening a party went down the Mariposa gold mine, 800 feet below the surface of the earth, piloted by Mr. J. E. Davis, the mine boss. Several hours were spent in the bowels of the earth, finding out all about levels and stopes and chutes and other features of underground geography.

Four periods in drawing were given by Mrs. Ada Hughes-Coldwell, supervisor of drawing in the schools of Alameda. Mrs. Coldwell is a sister of Principal Hughes of the Merced schools and also of C. C. Hughes, former superintendent of the Alameda schools. Her work was very practical and helpful, and the teachers were delighted with it.

Edward Hyatt of Riverside was present during the whole session and gave a number of his interesting talks based on every day experiences in working with the teachers of southern California.

The institute adjourned in a rainstorm; next morning the teachers filled all the outgoing stages, scattering to their mountain and valley homes—with mackintoshes, rubbers, umbrellas much in evidence.

* * *

YUBA COUNTY.

The Yuba County Institute convened at Marysville at the high school building during the week of November 10th. Supt. J. A. Scott was absent at the opening because of a death in his family. The institute was therefore opened by Dr. Thompson, principal of the high school. The Marysville teachers had decorated the rooms elegantly by masses of potted plants. Many local teachers took active part in the program, notably Principal Rich of Wheatland, Misses Ella Kelly, Emily Travis, Iznes Smith, Adah Townsend, Messrs. W. S. Bacon, E. P. Gleason, and R. R. Simonds.

Superintendent Scott arrived during the afternoon of the first day's session, and managed the rest of the meeting in his own peculiarly easy and genial way—a way so easy and genial that he had no opponent during the last campaign. Miss Kathrine Ball of San Francisco gave two half-day sessions on drawing, organizing the teachers into a great class and giving them color work; and gave an evening lecture on the Orient.

Prof. Cubberley of Stanford was peculiarly happy in translating pedagogical theories into plain terms of schoolroom work, in two of the most practical and helpful lectures.

Supt. Edward Hyatt began with some talks on the "Common Rocks of California," so simple and direct that the teachers insisted on his converting all of his periods for the three days into rock talks. Yuba, being a mining country, this kind of work struck a responsive chord.

* * *

TEHAMA COUNTY.

The thirty-second session of the Tehama County Institute convened November 9th, in the supervisors' room of the courthouse. President, Miss Ellen Lynch; vice-presidents, Members of County Board; secretaries, Principals J. D. Sweeney and A. W. Glover; music, Miss Elizabeth Herman, director; resolutions, Principal O. E. Graves, chairman. Miss Kate Ames of Napa read two interesting papers on "Why Teachers Should Read," and "Æsthetic Culture in School Training."

Miss Jenne Long of San Francisco gave two talks on "Expression and Articulation."

On Monday evening, Prof. W. D. Armes, University of California, delivered a lecture on "English Lakes and Their Literary Associations." It was illustrated by stereopticon and was well received.

Prof. Ellwood P. Cubberley, Stanford, lectured on "Public Education in England" and "Consolidation of Schools and Transportation of Pupils." F. F. Bunker, San Francisco, gave two instructive addresses on "Geography." Dr. Joseph Jastrow of University of Wisconsin lectured on Wednesday on "Seeing and Thinking."

It was voted to hold the next meeting at Corning. The institute adjourned at noon Wednesday and many of the teachers went to the Northern California Teachers' Association at Willows.

* * *

MERCED COUNTY.

The Merced County Institute was held at Los Banos November 4, 5, 6. Supt. Thomas J. Kirk; W. C. Doub, ex-superintendent of Kern county; Mrs. Ada Coldwell, supervisor of drawing, Alameda city schools; Prof. Rolfe of Stanford University, were the instructors. Some of the special topics discussed were: "Importance of Thoroness in Primary Work," "History, How It Should Be Taught in the Elementary Schools," "Geography, How It Should be Taught in the Elementary Schools," "Drawing," "The Amount and Character of Work That Should be Done in the Grammar School to Prepare Pupils to Successfully Do the Work of the High School."

Wednesday evening the teachers were entertained by the people of Los Banos at Miller Opera House; Thursday evening a lecture by Prof. Rolfe of Stanford University, "Life of Robert Louis Stevenson."

The special features of the institute discussed were lively and interesting. We found W. C. Doub to be an earnest and enthusiastic worker who is thoroly in touch with every phase of grammar school work. I think, in fact, the teachers as a whole pronounced him one of the most satisfactory instructors we have ever had.

Mrs. Ada Coldwell presented drawing in a very simple and attractive manner. No teacher could have listened to her instructions without having gained a knowledge of how to present the subject in an interesting way to her class.

Prof. Rolfe seemed particularly fitted to deliver the touching and beautiful lecture on the life and writings of Robert Louis Stevenson. I think all who heard it were enthused with a spirit to learn more of the great author whose ill-health and untimely death left his talent comparatively in its infancy.

State Superintendent Kirk was received with applause, and for an hour talked to the teachers on miscellaneous matters. Queries, which were almost as numerous as the teachers, were answered in a genial and satisfactory manner.

ANNA SILMAN,
County Superintendent.

* * *

SUTTER COUNTY.

Superintendent C. W. Ward held his first institute at Yuba City during the week beginning November 9th. The session continued three days and was conducted in the superior courtroom, a beautiful apartment finished and furnished in polished oak. The instructors were Miss Kate Ames of Napa county, H. A. Adrian of Berkeley, and Superintendent Hyatt of Riverside. These found a responsive audience in the teachers of Sutter county, and Superintendent Ward was delighted with an honest week's work on the part of everyone. An odd feature of the institute was that the county seat did not afford hotel accommodations, so that each evening all the instructors and most of the teachers would take the cars for Marysville, the county seat of a rival county, to find meals and lodgings.

* * *

BUTTE COUNTY.

Supt. R. H. Dunn held his annual institute at Oroville Oct. 9, 10, 11. Harr Wagner and Herbert Bashford were the instructors. Hon. Thomas J. Kirk gave a practical talk on school affairs, and the teachers of the county held several interesting discussions on the subject, "Discipline." Superintendent Dunn gave an informal talk at the opening of the institute, placing strong emphasis upon the necessity of training the child in accurate habits of thinking. The evening entertainments consisted of a reception of the Oroville teachers to the visiting teachers and a lecture by Harr Wagner on "Uncle Sam Jr." and original readings by Herbert Bashford. The teachers voted to lay on the table a resolution to abolish the institute and passed several strong resolutions on the subject of professional ethics.

* * *

NAPA COUNTY.

Supt. Kate Ames of Napa county held her institute at Napa, October 19, 20, 21. The instructors and lectures were Benjamin Ide Wheeler, President University of California; Prof. C. A. Duniway, Leland Stanford Jr. University; Prof. Alexis F. Lange, University of California; Dr. E. C. Moore, University of California. The topics of discussion were based on Booker T. Washington's book, "Up From Slavery," and special topics on patriotism and citizenship taken from the works of Lowell. Superintendent Ames issued a number of circulars calling special preparation on the part of the teachers for institute week.

* * *

STANISLAUS COUNTY.

The Stanislaus County Institute was held October 26-30. The instructors were H. Morse Stephens, D. S. Snedden, W. H. Langdon, Miss Alma Patterson, Frank F. Bunker, Miss Katherine Ball. The special topics discussed were as follows: The Appreciation of Literature, Report of Progress in Reading, Interests of High School Pupils, Aims and Discipline, The Course of Study, The Significance of Some Educational Experiments. The evening entertainments were: Lecture by H. Morse Stephens,"English Versus American Education"; Miss Katherine Ball, "A Trip to the Orient"; reception to teachers.

* * *

SHASTA COUNTY.

The Shasta Institute was held November 9-10-11. The instructors were Professors E. Cubberley, D. S. Snedden, W. J. V. Osterhout, E. C. Moore and Jenne Morrow Long. The evening entertainments were as follows: Lecture "What We Owe to the Arabs,"Moore;|"Dramatic Readings,"Jenne Long, Instrumental and vocal music. Dr. Osterhout's work was new in this country, also Miss Long's work. It was noted the best in years by the Press of the city.

Corning Items.

The Corning high school opened with over forty pupils. Ex-Superintendent O. E. Graves is principal, his assistants are Misses Swain and Mount. Corning has greatly improved school facilities this year. A new four-room building has been erected and the old one repaired.

Maywood district has been formed from Corning and has a neat house.

E. L. Cullen has resigned his school to become assistant county treasurer. J. M. Stark takes his school.

Red Bluff has an increased enrollment over last year.

Miss Delia Fisk has been elected president of the county board of education.

J. D. Sweeney was elected treasurer of the Teachers' Association of northern California for the third term.

WESTERN SCHOOL NEWS

MEETINGS

California Teachers' Association, O. W. Erlewine, president; Mrs. M. M. FitzGerald, secretary, 1627 Folsom street, San Francisco; December 28 to 31, 1903.

Southern California Teachers' Association, Los Angeles, Cal., Dec. 22, 23, 24.

National Educational Association, J. W. Cook, President, St. Louis, Mo., in July, 1904.

TEACHERS' INSTITUTES

Kings county, Supt. N. E. Davidson, Dec. 21-23.

Tulare county, C. J. Walker, Supt ville, Dec. 21-23.

NOTES

The teachers of New York have formed a Union thirteen thousand strong.

A change of principalship has taken place at Martinez. Mr. Fanning succeeds G. T. Boughn.

There is a strong movement to increase the pension fund for the teachers of San Francisco.

Harvard University is making a comparative study of the Cambridge and Stockton schools.

Seventy school teachers of Portland, Oregon, were fined five dollars each for not attending institute.

Supt. J. D. Graham of Pasadena, has arranged for a system of international correspondence among school children.

Supt. Coulter called a conference recently to consider the consolidation of seven school districts in the vicinity of Petaluma.

Six Fillipino pupils have entered the Redlands school. A number have entered at San Diego and other places. There are about one hundred Fillipino boys studying in the public schools in southern California.

Governor Pardee has approved the plans and specifications for the new wing to the San Diego State Normal School and has submitted the same to State Controller Colgan. The improvements call for an expenditure of nearly $50,000.

L. Dupont Syle, teacher, author, dramatist, died recently in Oakland. He is well known on the coast, having been a teacher at Grass Valley, Santa Barbara, and a professor in the department of English at the University of California for a number of years.

State School Superintendent Thomas J. Kirk, has tendered his resignation as State Director of the National Educational Association for California and upon his recommendation the N.E.A. executive committee has appointed Dr. Lyman Grègory of the Los Angeles high school in his stead.

In the case of appeal of Miss Lita Kidwell to the State Superintendent Thomas J. Kirk for salary withheld by the trustees of Cuyamaca school district, San Diego County, which appeal has been pending for several months owing to delay in securing statement of all the facts, Superintendent Kirk decides in favor of the teacher. The amount withheld was $75.

The Stockton "Record" recently published a full page testimonial from prominent educators, to the work of James A. Barr. It has taken up the question of raising the salary of teachers, and has given a number of able editorials on the subject. It secured a vigorous letter from Gov. Geo. C. Pardee advocating an increase in the wages now paid to teachers.

The State Text Book Committee, at a recent meeting in Sacramento, approved the authorization given to State Printer Shannon to print 20,000 revised grammars, 10,000 advanced geographies, 20,000 spellers, 20,000 new grammar school histories, 12,-000 third readers and 8,000 fourth readers. The State School Book Fund contains $63,064 98: the Text Appropriation Fund, $19,677.18; and the State Text Book Royalty Fund, $5966.40.

A. Megahan, at one time business manager of the OFFICIAL JOURNAL OF EDUCATION, was found dead in a vacant house in Oakland, Saturday, December 6, 1903. Mr. Megahan was a brother-in-law of Phillip M. Fisher, principal of the Polytechnic School of Oakland. He was a teacher of many years experience, and had a large number of personal friends who mourn his untimely end.

Miss Estelle Carpenter, chairman of the music section of the C. T. A., has made special preparations for the meeting in San Francisco December 28-31. The music section will be held in Steinway Hall, 223 Sutter street. There will be among other good things a quartette of strings, under direction of Alex